W9-CBY-055

A History of New England

With Particular Reference

to the Baptists

Isaac Backus

TWO VOLUMES IN ONE

ARNO PRESS & THE NEW YORK TIMES

New York 1969

Reprint edition 1969 by Arno Press, Inc.

*

Library of Congress Catalog Card No. 76-83410

*

Reprinted from a copy in
The State Historical Society of Wisconsin Library

*

Manufactured in the United States of America

A

HISTORY OF NEW ENGLAND.

WITH

Particular Reference to the Denomination of Christians

CALLED

BAPTISTS.

BY

ISAAC BACKUS.

Second Edition, with Notes.

BY

DAVID WESTON.

VOLUME I.

NEWTON, MASS.:
PUBLISHED BY THE BACKUS HISTORICAL SOCIETY.
1871.

35718

PRINTED BY THE PROVIDENCE PRESS COMPANY, PROVIDENCE, R. I.

286.109
B12

EDITOR'S PREFACE.

A historian who has been an actor in the events which he narrates, has peculiar advantages and disadvantages. He can write with more minuteness of detail, and with a fresher and more life-like coloring. He can write with more confidence, and, drawing from his own experience and observation, is in this respect more trustworthy. On the other hand, he is more liable to be warped by prejudice, to see only the excellences and none of the defects of those with whom he has been identified, and only the defects and none of the excellences of those to whom he has been opposed, to be a partizan rather than a judge, and to make his narration little more than the reflection of his personal opinions or his personal sympathy and affection, hostility and spite.

The Church History of Isaac Backus has all the above-named excellences. To a large extent he was an eye-witness of that which he describes; and where not an eye-witness, he placed himself in closest possible connection with it by personal acquaintance with the actors, and by immediate and most diligent and thorough examination of records and other evidence. While it may be too much to say that he absolutely avoided the defects above named, yet his sound judgment, his natural candor and honesty and his elevated Christian principle, have made him as nearly free from them as perhaps any author who has written in similar circumstances.

In the early history of the Baptists of New England, this work has always been justly regarded as the standard of authority. The single edition hitherto published was exhausted many years ago, and as the work became rare, the need of its republication was deeply felt. The Backus Historical Society, at a meeting in June, 1869, decided to undertake the task of republication; of which decision, the edition now presented to the public is the result.

This edition is a reproduction of the original work in full, and with only the following changes:—1. Grammatical errors and a few of the more prominent rhetorical errors have been corrected. These corrections have been made with the smallest possible variation from the text, and, for the most part, affect only some verbal form. 2. The author's errata of the first edition are corrected in the body of the work according to his direction. 3. The orthography of the work has been made to conform more nearly to the present standard. 4. The citations of the work have been collated with the originals, except in a few instances where the latter could not be found; and in many cases, more explicit references, or references to current editions, have been made in brackets. Such editorial references to Winthrop's Journal are to the New Edition by James Savage, Boston, 1853; those to Hubbard, are to Hubbard's History of New England, Massachusetts Historical Society, 1815; those to Mather's Magnalia are to the First American Edition, Hartford, 1820; those to Prince's Chronology and Prince's Annals are to the edition published in Boston, 1826; those to Morton's Memorial are to the edition of the Congregational Board of Publication, Boston, 1855. Where the author refers to Vol. I or Vol. II of "Massachusetts History," he means Hutchinson's History of Massachusetts, and the editorial references are to the edition published at Salem, 1795. By "Massachusetts History, Vol. III," the author means not the continuation of Hutchinson's work by his grandson, but the work commonly known as "Hutchinson's Collection of Original Papers." Differences between the originals and their citation by the author have been noted in brackets. In the letter of Robert Mascall, found in Vol. I, pages 311 to 313 of the present edition, Mr. Backus indicated such changes, in supplying or omitting words, &c., as he felt at liberty to make; and in the Preface to Vol. I, he said, "I have as strictly kept to the true sense in all my quotations as in that, yet I have not thought it necessary to continue such marks in all." That which is contained in brackets in the above-named letter is from the author; in all other places, from the editor. 5. Editorial foot-notes have been added, amounting in all to about a hundred pages. These are marked "ED."; and where an editorial note is appended to one by the author, they are distinguished by marking the latter "B." 6. A full Index to both volumes is appended to Vol. II, in place of the brief and very defective indices and tables of contents of the original work. 7. All the longer quotations are distinguished from the author's own words by change of type; topical headings are affixed to each alternate page, and necessary changes are made in the title pages.—Thus the only liberty taken with the original text has been to correct a few errors of language, while all other changes are so marked as to be clearly distinguished as such.

The circumstances in which the work is issued have not been favorable to typographical accuracy. The editor has been at a distance from the printers; and in order that sufficient care and labor might be expended in preparing the work for the press, and yet secure its completion without so much delay as to disappoint subscribers, it has been needful to urge it through the press with more haste than would have been otherwise desirable. It is believed however, that typographical errors will not be found to any unusual extent.

The editor would express his grateful acknowledgments to S. F. Haven, Esq., and E. M. Barton, Esq., librarians of the American Antiquarian Society, Worcester, Mass., for their kindness and courtesy in giving free access to the rare and extensive archæological library under their charge, and for the aid which they have been always ready to lend in consulting it; to his venerable relative, Rev. Silas Hall, of Raynham, Mass., who placed at his disposal a large, carefully prepared and most valuable collection of manuscripts relating to the history of New England Baptists,—a collection which has added much to the value of other historical works before this, and in which much valuable material still remains untouched;—to the Rhode Island Historical Society, for permission to use the Diary of John Comer; to Reuben A. Guild, Esq., librarian of Brown University, for permission to use the Diary of Hezekiah Smith, and for other assistance; to Rev. C. E. Barrows, of Newport, R. I., and to William E. Clarke, of Conneaut, Oo., for valuable material used in foot-notes; and to Alden A. Howe, Esq., of Worcester, Mass., for preparing the Index.

WORCESTER, MASS., December 5, 1870.

AUTHOR'S PREFACE TO VOLUME I.

History has been so often written and improved, either for party purposes, or mere amusement, that some serious persons have been ready to treat it as a thing foreign to religion, and of little service to mankind. Yet the same persons will readily own, that nothing teaches like experience ; and what is true history but the experiences of those who have gone before us? of which perhaps none have been more remarkable, since the affairs of Canaan, than those of this country. And as the present contests about liberty and government are very great, they call loudly for all the light therein that can be gained from every quarter.

Mr. Rollin, in his ancient history, says, "The powers that be are ordained of God ; but neither every use that is made of this power, nor every means for the attainment of it, are from God, though every power be of him. And when we see these governments degenerating, sometimes to violence, factions, despotic sway and tyranny, 'tis wholly to the passions of mankind that we must ascribe those irregularities which are directly opposite to the primitive institution of states ; and which a superior wisdom afterwards reduces to order, always making them contribute to the execution of his designs, full of equity and justice. This scene highly deserves our attention and admiration. It is with a view of making the reader attentive to this object, that I think it incumbent on me to add to the account of facts and events what regards the manners and customs of nations ; because these shew their genius and character, which we may call, in some measure, the soul of history."

Now it may well be supposed, that men who are striving for more power over others than belongs to them, will not nor cannot set either their own or their opponents' "genius and character" in their just light. And if it should be found, that nearly all the histories of this country which are much known, have been written by persons who thought themselves invested with power to act as lawgivers and judges for their neighbors, under the name either of orthodoxy, or of immediate power from heaven, the inference will be strong, that our affairs have never been set in so clear light as they ought to be ; and if this is not indeed the case I am greatly mistaken ; of which the following account will enable the reader to judge for himself.

The greatest objection that I have heard against this design is, that we ought not to rake up the ashes of our good fathers, nor to rehearse those old controversies, which will tend to increase our present difficulties. But what is meant by this objection? To reveal secrets, or to repeat matters that have been well settled between persons or parties, is forbidden, and its effects are very pernicious ; but what is that to a history of public facts, and an examination of the principles and conduct, both of oppressors, and of the oppressed?

Men who are still fond of arbitrary power may make the above objection ; but a learned and ingenious pædobaptist that felt the effects of such power, lately said, "The Presbyterians, I confess, formerly copied too nearly the Episcopalians. The genuine principles of universal and impartial liberty were very little understood by any ; and all parties were too much involved in the guilt of intolerance and persecution. The dissenters in our times freely acknowledge this, and condemn the narrow principles of many of their predecessors ; having no objection to transmitting down to posterity, in their true colors, the acts of oppression and intolerance of which all sects have been guilty. Not indeed, as is sometimes done, with a view of encouraging such conduct in one party by the example of others ; but of exposing it alike in all, and preventing it wholly, if possible, in time to come."[1] This is the great design of the ensuing work ; and such a work seems essentially necessary to that end. For as every one is orthodox to himself, they who have oppressed others, have always denied it. After our Baptist fathers in Boston, had been greatly injured for fifteen years, they published a vindication of their character ; but as to their sufferings, contented themselves with saying, "Some of us were oftentimes brought before councils and courts, threatened, fined, our estates taken away, imprisoned and banished." A noted minister called their vindication a fallacious narrative, and said, "Errors lie in generals, a particular account might have been more satisfying."[2] Here therefore are a great number of particulars with good vouchers to support them ; which shew that oppression on religious accounts was not of the first principles of New England, but was an intruder that came in afterward.

When I was requested by several gentlemen of note and others, to undertake this work, two great objections presented themselves to my mind against it ; namely, my great unfitness for it, and the difficulty of obtaining the necessary materials. But their importunity prevailed against the first, and divine providence has removed the other, by conveying into my hands a variety of authentic materials, much beyond what I conceived could have now been obtained in the world. Many of them I have taken

[1]Furneaux's letter to Blackstone, p. 74.   [2]Willard's *Ne sutor*, p. 10.

from the ancient records of the colonies of Plymouth, Massachusetts, Providence and Rhode Island, as well as the records of the United Colonies; though I regret the want of better acquaintance with the two latter, before the first two hundred pages of our history were printed off. Many other records have also been serviceable; and I would now return my public thanks to the several gentlemen who are keepers of them, for the candid and kind treatment they have shown on this occasion. A great variety of other manuscripts have been serviceable to me, whereof Mr. Hubbard's History, and extracts from Governor Winthrop's Journal are not the least. It is to be noted, that only the word "Hubbard" in the following quotations refers to that history, in distinction from another valuable collection, of which take the following account :—Mr. Samuel Hubbard came over to Salem in 1633, in his youth ; joined to Watertown church in 1635 ; but went the same year up to Windsor, [Conn.] where he soon married a church member that removed from Dorchester, and they settled at Weathersfield ; till in May, 1639, they removed to Springfield, and he was one of the five men who first joined in founding that church. It was constituted under Connecticut government, but falling afterward into the Massachusetts, he removed in 1647 to Fairfield. Though he says, "God having enlightened both, but mostly my wife, into his holy ordinance of baptizing only visible believers ; and being zealous for it, she was mostly struck at, and answered twice publicly, where I was also said to be as bad as she, and threatened with imprisonment to Hartford goal, if we did not renounce it or remove. That Scripture came into our minds, If they persecute you in one place, flee to another." Whereupon they removed to Newport, and joined to Elder Clarke's church there on November 3, 1648, where they lived to old age ; from whence he repeatedly visited his suffering brethren at Boston, and had an extensive correspondence both in Europe and America ; and he copied several hundred of his own and others' letters into a book, which I am now favored with ; containing a fund of intelligence, from 1641 to 1688. The writings and papers also of our elders, Holmes, Comer, Callender and others, have been useful in this design. Though, for want of room, I have been forced to leave a great many valuable articles out of this volume, and to give but a sketch of things in latter times. However I propose by divine leave to preserve and digest them in the best manner I can, for the use of those who may come after us ; and should be glad to obtain accounts of the rise, progress and present state of all our churches for the same end.

In the following work, Plymouth Register intends an account of their church from its beginning, written by our County Register, and annexed to Mr. Robbins's Ordination Sermon, 1760.[1] The History of Providence means what was published of that nature in their Gazette in 1765.[2] Perhaps the rest of my authorities are sufficiently described. So great a part

1B

of this history is given in the words of others, that continued marks of quotation would have been tedious; therefore many passages only begin and end therewith.[3] In the excellent letter you have in pages 311—313, I have marked the words which were necessarily supplied to complete the sense; but though I have as strictly kept to the true sense in all my quotations as in that, yet I have not thought it necessary to continue such marks in all. In the dates, where our fathers began the year with March, I have either plainly noted it, or else have begun the year with January, only have let the old style stand till it was altered here by law. Of the moneys, Mr. Prince says they were reckoned sterling till 1640. In 1652, when they first coined silver here, one pound of it was fifteen shillings sterling, and so it continued to 1690, when they began to make paper money, which gradually depreciated from six shillings to forty-five shillings for a Spanish milled dollar. In 1750 our currency was brought back to what it was a hundred years before, and that is our lawful money ever since. A dash [—] in a quotation signifies the omission of something there for brevity's sake;[4] betwixt figures, it is to extend the reference from one number to the other.

Whoever considers the difficulty of compiling such a work with exactness, together with the confusion of the present times, and the author's distance from the press, will not be severe upon him for every imperfection that may be discovered therein; though he has named his principal vouchers on purpose to have his performance thoroughly examined, and every material mistake corrected. Sincerity and impartiality are allowed to be the most essential rules of history; how far they appear in this the reader will judge. Only the author must say, that he has acted under a full belief, that with what measure we mete, it shall be measured to us again; so that we cannot injure others in any case, without therein wronging our own souls. And to impress this great truth upon all minds, is the aim and earnest desire of their humble servant,

ISAAC BACKUS.

MIDDLEBOROUGH, July 9, 1777.

[1]"An account of the church of Christ in Plymouth, the first church in New England, from its establishment unto the present day. By John Cotton, Esq., member of said church." This work was published in 1760. It is republished in the Massachusetts Historical Collections, Vol. IV, pp. 107—141.—ED.

[2]"This tract has been usually ascribed to the venerable Stephen Hopkins, who for eight years had been Governor of the colony, and served in that office one year after, but is better known as one of the signers of the Declaration of Independence." Introductory note to "An Account of Providence, R. I.," as republished in the Massachusetts Historical Collections, Second Series, Vol. IX.—ED.

[3]According to modern usage, this is the case with all the quotations in the present edition.—ED.

[4]In the present edition, such omissions are indicated by dots [....].—ED.

History of the Baptists in New England.

CHAPTER I.

THE SENTIMENTS AND CHARACTER OF THE FIRST PLANTERS OF THIS COUN-
TRY, WITH THEIR PROCEEDINGS DOWN TO THE YEAR 1634.

To obtain clear and just ideas of the affairs of the Baptists in New England, it seems necessary for us to look back
to its first settlement, and carefully to examine what were
the sentiments and character of the original planters. Those
that began the first colony were called Separatists, because
of their withdrawal from the national church of England;
and different parties have accused them with rigidness therein; but ingenuous minds will not choose to be turned off
with hard names, without knowing what is meant by them;
therefore let us hear those fathers tell their own story. They
separated from the national church near the beginning of
the last century, and formed societies for worship by themselves; till, after suffering much from the ruling party in
their native country, they left it, and sojourned about twelve
years in Holland, and then removed to this land.

About the time of their fleeing into Holland, Mr. Richard
Bernard, an Episcopal minister in Nottinghamshire, out of
which many of those fathers removed, published a book

against them, which he called "The Separatist's Schism," to which Mr. John Robinson, the pastor of the church which afterward began the settlement of New England, published an answer in 1610, entitled, "A Justification of Separation from the Church of England." As I am favored with this performance, containing four hundred and seventy-six pages in quarto, I shall from thence give the reader the author's own words upon the most material points of their controversy, and the rather, because the writings of that eminent father of our country are very little known at this day among us.

Mr. Bernard began his book with some things which he called "Christian Counsels of Peace," to which Mr. Robinson answers[1]:—

As God is the God of peace, so are not they God's children which desire it not; yea, even in the midst of their contentions. But as all vices use to clothe themselves with the habits of virtues, that under their [those] liveries they may get countenance, and find the more free passage in the world, so especially in the church, all tyranny and confusion do present themselves under this color, taking up the politic pretence of peace, as a weapon of more advantage, wherewith the stronger and greater party useth to beat the weaker. The papists press the protestants with the peace of the church, and, for the rent [which] they have made in it, condemn them beyond the heathenish soldiers, which forebore to divide Christ's garment ; as deeply do the bishops charge the ministers refusing conformity and subscription,[2] and both of them us. But the godly wise must not be affrighted

[1]It is perhaps unfortunate, rhetorically, that these long and, to the general reader, somewhat tedious extracts from the work of Robinson are introduced at the commencement of the History. Such a reader may need to pass lightly over these first pages, suspending his judgment of the work till he reaches the commencement of the narrative.

These extracts have been carefully collated with the work from which they were taken, as found in Vol. II of the works of John Robinson, published by the Congregational Board, London, 1851. The differences found, where there was not an obvious error, are here indicated in brackets. Many words and phrases, not strictly necessary to the sense, were found to have been omitted, some of which are here supplied in brackets. The figures in brackets refer to the pages of the above-mentioned volume.—ED.

[2]The main of those who afterward settled the Massachusetts colony were of this sort; they refused full conformity to the national church, and yet condemned an entire separation from it.

either from seeking or embracing the truth with such bugs as these are, but seeing "the wisdom which is from above, is first pure, then peaceable," he must make it a great part of his Christian wisdom to discern betwixt godly and gracious peace, and that which is either pretended for advantage, or mistaken by error, and so [to] labor to hold peace in purity. Let it then be manifested unto us, that the communion which the church of England hath with all the wicked in the land, without separation, is a pure communion ; that their service book, devised and prescribed in so many words and letters, to be read over and over with all the appurtenances, is a pure worship ; that their government by national, provincial and diocesan bishops, according to their canons, is a pure government, and then let us be blamed if we hold not peace with them in word and deed ; otherwise, though they speak [spake] unto us never so oft, both by messengers and mouth of peace, and again of peace, as Jehoram did to Jehu, yet must we answer them in effect as Jehu did Jehoram, What peace, whilst the whoredoms of the mother of fornications [fornicators], the Jezebel of Rome, do remain in so great number amongst them?   And I doubt not but Mr. Bernard, and a thousand more ministers in the land (were they secure of the magistrate's sword, and might they go on with [his] good license) would wholly shake off their canonical obedience to their ordinaries, and neglect their citations and censures, and refuse to sue in their courts, for all the peace of the church which they commend to us for so sacred a thing. Could they but obtain license from the magistrate to use the liberties [liberty] which they are persuaded Christ hath given them, they would soon shake off the prelates' yoke, and draw no longer under the same in spiritual communion with all the profane in the land, but would break those bonds of iniquity, as easily as Samson did the cords wherewith Delilah tied him, and give good reasons also from the word of God for their so doing. Pp. 13, 14. [12, 13.]

Whoever reads and well observes the history of the Massachusetts colony, I believe, will find that those remarks were neither enthusiastic nor censorious, but that they discover great knowledge, and a good judgment both in human and divine concernments.   Mr. Robinson proceeds and says:—

These things I thought good to commend to the reader, that he may be the more cautious of this and the like colorable pretences, wishing him also well to remember, that peace in disobedience is that old theme of the false prophets, whereby they flattered the mighty, and deceived the simple. Jer. vi. 14, and viii. 11. . . . . . In the church of England we do acknowledge many excellent truths of doctrine, which we also teach without commixture of error, many Christian ordinances which we also practise, being purged from the pollution of antichrist ; and, for the godly persons in it, (could we possibly separate them from the profane) we would gladly embrace them with both arms. But, being taught by the apostle, speaking but of one wicked person, and of one Jewish ordinance, that "a little leaven leaveneth the whole lump," 1 Cor. v. 6, Gal. v. 9, we cannot be ignorant how sour the English assemblies must needs be ; neither may we justly be blamed though we dare not dip in their meal, lest we be soured by their leaven. Pp. 15, 16. [14, 15.]

To Mr. B., who counsels that we should "bear with lighter faults for a time, till fit occasion be offered to have them amended," he replies : —

1. No sin is light in itself, but being continued in and countenanced, destroyeth the sinner. Matt. v. 19.   2. It is the property of a profane and hardened heart evermore to extenuate and lessen sins.   3. Though the bearing and forbearing, not only of small but even of great sins also, must be for a time, yet it must be but for a time, and that is whilst reformation be orderly sought and procured. Lev. xix. 17. But what time hath wrought in the church of England, all men see growing daily, by the just judgment of God, from evil to worse, and being never aforetime so impatient either of reformation or other good as at this day. 4. A man must so bear evil, as he be no way accessory unto it, by forbearing any means appointed by Christ for the amending it. P. 16. [15.]

I see not upon what occasion the author should shuffle into this controversy, which is merely ecclesiastical, such considerations as he doth concerning the frame and alteration of civil states, except he would either insinuate against us, that we went about to alter the civil state of the kingdom ; or, at least, that the alteration of the state ecclesiastical, must needs draw with it the alteration of the civil state ; with which mote the prelates have a long time bleared the eyes of the magistrates ; but how deceitfully, hath been sufficiently manifested, and offer made further to manifest the same by solemn disputation. And the truth is, that all states and policies which are of God, whether monarchical, aristocratical or democratical, or how mixed soever, are capable of Christ's government. Neither doth the nature of the state, but the corruption of the persons, hinder the same in one or other. . . . . . And where Mr. Bernard further adviseth, rather to offend many private persons than one lawful magistrate, I doubt not he gives no worse counsel than he himself follows, who (except I be much deceived in him) had rather offend half the private persons in the diocese, than one archbishop, though he be an unlawful magistrate. But let us remember our care be not to offend the Lord, and if with the offence of a private person, though never so base, be joined the offence of the Lord, better offend all, both lawful and unlawful magistrates, in the world, than such a little one. Matt. xviii, 6. Pp. 17, 18. [17, 18.]

Another piece of counsel given by Mr. B. is, "Use the present good which thou mayest enjoy, to the utmost; and an experienced good, before thou dost trouble thyself to seek for a supposed better good, untried, which thou enjoyest not." To this Mr. R. says: —

We may not stint or circumscribe either our knowledge, faith, or obedience, within straiter bounds than the whole revealed will of God, in the knowledge and obedience whereof we must daily increase and edify ourselves; much less must we suffer ourselves to be stripped of any liberty which Christ our Lord hath purchased for us, and given us to use for our good. Gal. v. i. And here, as I take it, comes in the case of many hundreds in the church of England, who what good they may enjoy (that is safely enjoy, or without any great bodily danger) that they use very fully. Where the ways of Christ lie open for them, by the authority of men, and where they may walk safely with good leave, there they walk very uprightly, and that a round pace; but when the commandments of Christ are, as it were, hedged up with thorns, by men's prohibitions, there they foully "step aside, and pitch their tents by the flocks of his fellows." Cant. i. 7. P. 23. [23, 24.]

Again Mr. B. says, "Never presume to reform others, before thou hast well ordered thyself." To which Mr. Robinson answers:—

True zeal, it is certain, ever begins at home, and gives more liberty unto other men than it dares assume unto itself; and there is nothing more true, and [or] necessary to be considered, than that every man ought to order himself in [and] his own steps first. That is good and the best, but not all; for if by God's commandment we ought to bring back our enemy's ox or ass that strayeth, how much more to bring into order our brother's soul and body, wandering in by-paths? P. 24. [25.]

Mr. Bernard went on to lay down a number of things, which he supposed would render it very unlikely that a separation from them could be right, before he came to the merits of the cause; as, 1. "The novelty thereof differing

from all the best reformed churches in Christendom." To
which Mr. Robinson replies:—

It is no novelty to hear men plead custom, when they want truth. So
the heathen philosophers reproached Paul as a bringer of new doctrine.
Acts xvii. 19. So do the papists discountenance the doctrine and profession of the church of England; yea, even at this day, very many of the
people in the land call popery the old law, and the profession there made
the new law. But for our parts, as we believe, by the word of God, that
the things we teach are not new, but old truths renewed; so are we no less
[fully] persuaded, that the church constitution, in which we are set, is cast
in the apostolical and primitive mould, and not one day nor hour younger,
in the nature and form of it, than the first church of the New Testament.
P. 40. [42, 43.]

2. "For that it agreeeth so much with the ancient schismatics, condemned in former ages by holy and learned men."
Answer:—

Can our way both be a novelty, and yet agree so well with ancient
schismatics? Contraries cannot be both true, but may both be false, as
these are. P. 42. [44, 45.]

Mr. Robinson tells us, that another article which Mr. B.
alleged against them is, "That we have not the approbation of
any of the reformed churches for our course." Answer:—

This is the same in substance with the first, and that which followeth in
the next place the same with them both; and Mr. B. by [his] so ordinarily pressing us with human testimonies, shews himself to be very barren
of divine authority. Nature teacheth every creature, in all danger, to fly
first and oftenest to the chief instruments either of offence or defence,
wherein it trusteth, as the bull to his horn, the boar to his tusk, and the
bird unto her wing; right so this man shews wherein his strength lies, and
wherein he trusts most, by [his] so frequent and usual shaking the horn,
and whetting the tusk, of mortal man's authority against us. But for the
reformed churches the truth is, they neither do imagine, nor will easily be
brought to believe, that the frame of the church of England stands as it
doth. The approbation which they give [of you] is in respect of such
general truths of doctrine, as wherein we also, for the most part, acknowledge you; which notwithstanding you deny in a great measure in the particulars and practice. But touching the gathering and governing of the
church, which are the main heads controverted betwixt you and us; they

give you not so much as the left hand of fellowship, but do, on the contrary, turn their backs upon you. Pp. 46, 47[1]. [49, 50.] Thus much of the learned abroad. In the next place, Mr. Bernard draws us to the learned at home, from whose dislike of us he takes his fifth likelihood, which he thus frameth : " The condemnation of this way by our divines, both living and dead, against whom, either for godliness of life or truth of doctrine, otherwise than for being their opposites, they can take no exception."

To this, Mr. Robinson answers :—

No marvel. We may not admit of parties for judges. How is it possible we should be approved of them in the things wherein we witness against them? And if this argument be good and [or] likely, then is it likely that neither the reformists have the truth in the church of England, nor the prelates; for there are many of those both godly and learned, which in their differences do oppose, and that very vehemently, the one the other. Now, as for my own part, I do willingly acknowledge the learning and godliness of most of the persons named by Mr. B. and honor the memory of some of them ; so neither do I think them so learned, but they might err, nor so godly, but in their error they might reproach the truth they saw not. I do confess to the glory of God, and mine own shame, that a long time before I entered this way, I took some taste of the truth in it by some treatises published in justification of it, which [the Lord knoweth] were sweet as honey unto my mouth ; and the principal thing which for the time quenched all further appetite in me, was the over-valuation which I made of the learning and holiness of these and the like persons, blushing in myself to have a thought of pressing one hair-breadth before them in this thing, behind whom I knew myself to come so many

[1]The ways of the church of England, wherein we forsake her, do directly and *ex diametro* cross and thwart the ways of the reformed churches, in these three main heads :—I. The reformed churches are gathered of a free people, joined together by voluntary profession, without compulsion of human laws. On the contrary, the church of England consists of a people forced together violently by the laws of men into their provincial, diocesan and parishional churches (as their houses stand) be they never so unwilling or unfit. 2. The reformed churches do renounce the ministry of the church of England, as she doth theirs; not admitting of any by virtue of it to charge of souls, as they speak, where, on the contrary, all the mass-priests made in Queen Mary's days, which would say their book-service in English, were continued ministers by the same ordination which they received from popish prelates. 3. The government by archbishops, lord bishops and their substitutes, in the church of England, is abhorred and disclaimed in the reformed churches as anti-christian; as is, on the contrary, the Presbyterian government, in use there, by the church of England refused, as anabaptistical and seditious. P. 52. [55, 56.]

Here we may see how the very name of Anabaptist was used as a weapon to fight against reformation in Mr. Robinson's day, and the practice is still followed by many.

miles in all other things; yea and even of late times, when I had entered into a more serious consideration of these things, and, according to the measure of grace received, searched the Scriptures, whether they were so or no, and by searching found much light and truth, yet was the same so dimmed and overclouded with the contradictions of these men, and others of the like note, that had not the truth been in my heart as a burning fire shut up in my bones, Jer. xx. 9, I had never broken those bonds of flesh and blood, but had suffered the light of God to have been put out in my [mine own] unthankful heart, by other men's darkness.

Every man stands bound to give this reverence to the graces of God in other men, that in his differences with [from] them he be not suddenly nor easily persuaded, but that being jealous of his own heart, he undertake the examination of things, and so proceed with fear and trembling, and having tried all things, keep that which is good; 1 Thes. v. 21 ; so shall he neither wrong the graces of God in himself, nor in others. But on the other side, for a man so far to suffer his thoughts to be conjured into the circle of any [mortal] man's or men's judgment, as either to fear to try what is offered to the contrary, in the balance of the sanctuary, or finding it to bear weight, to fear to give sentence on the Lord's side, yea though it be against the mighty, this is to honor men above God, and to advance a throne above the throne of Christ, who is Lord and King forever. And to speak that in this case, which by doleful experience I myself have found, many of the most forward professors in the kingdom are well nigh as superstitiously addicted to the determinations of their guides and teachers, as the ignorant papists unto theirs; accounting it not only needless curiosity, but even intolerable arrogancy, to call in question the things received from them by tradition. But how much better were it for all men to lay aside these and the like prejudices, that so they might understand the things which concern their peace, and seeing with their own eyes, might live by their own faith.

And, for these famous men named by Mr. B., (with whose oppositions, as with Zedekiah's horns of iron, he would push us here and everywhere) as we hear their reproofs with patience, and acknowledge their worth [worths] without envy or detraction, so do we know they were but men, and through human frailty might be abused as well, or rather as ill, to support antichrist in a measure, as others before them have been, though godly and learned as they. It will not be denied but the fathers, as they are called, Ignatius, Irenæus, Tertullian, Cyprian, Ambrose, Jerome, Austin, and the rest, were both godly and learned, yet no man, if he have but even saluted them, can be ignorant what way, though unwittingly, they made for the advancement of antichrist which followed after them ; and if they, notwithstanding their learning and godliness, thus ushered him into the world, why might not others, and that more likely, though learned and godly as the former, help to bear up his train? especially considering that as his rising was not, so neither could his fall be perfected at once. And, for us, what do we more or otherwise, for the most part, than walk in those ways into which divers of the persons by Mr. B. named have directed us by the word of God, in manifesting unto us by the light thereof what the ministry, government, worship, and fellowship of the gospel ought to be[1]? We then being taught, and believing that the word of God is a light and lantern, not only to our eyes, but to our feet and paths, as the psalmist speaketh, Psal. cxix. 105, cannot possibly conceive how we should justly be blamed by these men for observing the ordinances which themselves not only acknowledged, but contended for, as appointed by Christ, to be kept inviolable till his appearing, as some of them have expressly testified.

To conclude, let not the Christian reader cast our persons, and the persons of our opposites, whether these or others, in the balance together; but rather our cause and reasons, with their oppositions and the grounds of them, and so with [a] steady hand, and impartial eye, poise cause with cause, that so the truth of God may not be prejudiced by men's persons, nor held in respect of them. Pp. 48—53. [51—54.]

By these free and plain declarations the reader may be able to judge, whether the reproach of rigidness properly belongs to Mr. Robinson, or to his accusers and persecutors; yet because he would not stay in the church of England, when he was convinced of its being wrong so to do, Mr. Bernard accuses him and his brethren of either denying

---

[1]For proof of this, Mr. Robinson, in another place, cites a number of passages, written, he says, "by such men as I dare say Mr. B. reckons amongst the painful and conscionable ministers." Their words are these :—"The names and offices of archbishops, archdeacons. lord bishops, &c. are, together with their government, drawn out of the pope's shop, antichristian, [devilish] and contrary to the Scriptures. Parsons, vicars, parish priests, stipendiaries, &c. be birds of the same feather." 2d Admo. to the Parliament, [By Thos. Cartwright.] "There is no true visible church of Christ, but a particular congregation only." Christian Offer, prop. 4. "Every true visible church of Christ, or ordinary assembly of the faithful, hath, by Christ's ordinance, power in itself immediately under Christ to elect, to ordain, deprive and depose their ministers, and to execute all other ecclesiastical censures." Ibid., prop. 5. "The visible church of Christ, wheresoever it be, hath the power of binding and loosing annexed unto it, as our Saviour, Christ teacheth;" Matt. xviii. Discovery of Dr. Bancroft's Slanders. [Preface.] "Amongst us the holy mysteries of God are profaned, the Gentiles enter into the temple of God, the holy things are indifferently communicated with the clean and unclean." Plain Declaration. "Now," says Mr. Robinson, "let the [indifferent] reader judge whether these men in thus writing have not opened the door unto us, by which themselves enter not." Pp. 75, 76. [81, 82.]

their conversion there, or else of accounting it a false one. To which Mr. R. answers :—

For our personal conversion in the church of England, we deny it not, but do, and always have done, judge and profess it true there ; and so was Luther's conversion true in the church of Rome, else could not his separation from Rome have been of faith, or accepted of God. P. 69. [75.]

And now for particular sentiments about church affairs. Mr. Robinson's opponent had said, " The word is the constitution of the church." To which he replies :—

His meaning is or should be, that the word is the ordinary [outward] means for collecting and constituting the church of God. I grant it. But how considered? Not the word in men's Bibles alone, for then all the heretics in the world were true churches [are true Christians] ; nor yet the word preached simply, for Paul preached the word to the scoffing Athenians, and to the blasphemous Jews, yet I think he will not say that either the one or the other were churches truly constituted. How then? The word published, understood, believed and obeyed, outwardly at the least, as the spiritual sword or axe, hewing the stones in the rock, and the trees in the forest, and preparing them to be the Lord's spiritual house. And thus much the very places produced by Mr. B. [like Goliath's sword drawn out to cut off his own head,] do evidently declare.

Matt. xxviii. 19, which is the first place, shows that such as by preaching of the word were made disciples, for so much the word [Μαϑητεύσατε] importeth, were to be gathered into the church and baptized. Mark xvi. 15, shows the same, especially if you add verse 16, inferring that men by preaching must believe, and so believe as they have the promise of salvation. 2 Cor. v. 19, and xi. 2, prove that the word of reconciliation and ministry of the gospel, believed and obeyed to the forgiveness of sins, and to the preparation and sanctification of the church of [to] Christ, is the means of gathering and building up the same. Acts ii. 14, 37, 38, 41, and xvi. 32—34, are of the same nature [with the former],·and do prove that sundry of the Jews at Jerusalem, by Peter's preaching, and that the jailer's household at Philippi, by Paul's preaching, were brought to repentance, and faith in Christ, and so added to the church. But what will be the conclusion of all these premises? The proposition is this :—The true apostolic churches having a true constitution, were gathered and constituted of such men and women as by the preaching of the gospel were made disciples, had faith and repentance wrought in them, to the obtaining of the forgiveness of sins, and promise of life eternal, and to sanctification and obedience. Pp. 89, 90. [95, 96.]

Of baptism Mr. Robinson says :—

The proper ends and uses of baptism are to initiate the parties baptized into the church of Christ, and to consecrate them to his service, and so to serve for badges of Christianity, by which it is distinguished from all other professions. Matt. xxviii. 19, 1 Cor. xii. 13. P. 26. [28.] The sacrament of baptism is to be administered by Christ's appointment, and the apostles' example, only to such as are, externally, and so far as men can judge, taught and made disciples [Matt. xxviii. 19.] ; do receive the word gladly ; Acts ii. 41 ; believe and so profess ; Acts viii. [12, 13, 37] ; have received the Holy Ghost ; Acts x. 47 ; and to their seed ; Acts ii. 39, 1 Cor. vii. 14. P. 92. [99.] Baptism administered to any others is so far from investing them with any saintship in that estate, that [as] it makes guilty, both the giver and receiver, of sacrilege, and is the taking of God's name in vain. P. 110. [115.]

Of the Lord's Supper he says :—

The apostle teacheth, 1 Cor. x. 16, that the bread and wine in the supper are the communion of the body and blood of Christ, that is, effectual pledges of our conjunction and incorporation with Christ, and one with another ; and in ver. 17, that all which eat of one bread or one loaf, are one mystical body. This place alone, if Mr. B. and his fellow ministers would seriously consider, and set themselves faithfully to observe, they would rather offer their own bodies to be torn in pieces by wild beasts, than the holy mysteries of Christ's body to be profaned as they are. P. 92. [98.]

Of the keys, Matt. xvi. 18, 19, he says :—

It is granted by all sides that Christ gave unto Peter the keys of the kingdom, that is, the power to remit and retain sins declaratively, as they speak ; as also that in what respect this power was given to Peter, in the same respect it was, and is, given to such as succeed Peter ; but the question is, in what respect or consideration this power spoken of was delegated to him? The papist affirms it was given to Peter as the prince of the apostles, and so to the bishops of Rome, as Peter's successors, and thus they stablish the pope's primacy. The prelates say Nay, but unto Peter an apostle, that is, a chief officer of the church, and so to us, as chief officers succeeding him. Others affirm it to belong to Peter here as a minister of the word and sacraments, and the like, and so consequently to all other ministers of the gospel equally, which succeed Peter in those and the like administrations. But we, for our parts do believe and profess that this promise is not made to Peter in any of these respects, nor to any office, order, estate, dignity or degree in the church or world, but to the confession of faith, which Peter made by way of answer to Christ's question, [who, demanding of the disciples whom, amongst the variety of opinions that went of him, they thought him to be, was answered by Peter in the name of the rest] "Thou art Christ, the Son of the living God." To this Christ replies, " Blessed art thou ; thou art Peter, and upon this rock will I build my church ; I will give unto thee the keys," &c. So that the building of the church is upon the rock of Peter's confession, that is, Christ whom he confessed. This faith is the foundation of the church ; against this faith the gates of hell shall not prevail ; this faith hath the keys of the kingdom of heaven ; what this faith shall loose or bind on earth, is bound and loosed in heaven. Thus the Protestant divines, when they deal against the pope's supremacy, do generally expound this Scripture ; [though Mr. B. directly makes the pope and his shavelings, Peter's successors in this place, as hereafter will appear.] Now it followeth, that whatsoever person hath received the same precious faith with Peter, as all the faithful have, 2 Pet. i. 1, that person hath a part in this gift of Christ. Whosoever doth confess, publish, manifest or make known Jesus to be the Christ, the Son of the living God, and Saviour of the world, that person opens heaven's gates, looseth sin, and partakes with Peter in the use of the keys ; and hereupon it followeth necessarily, that one faithful man, yea, or woman either, may as truly and effectually loose and bind, both in heaven and earth, as all the ministers in the world. Pp. 149, 159. [157, 158.]

But here I know the lordly clergy, like the bulls of Bashan, will roar loud upon me, as speaking things intolerably derogatory to the dignity of priesthood ; and it may be some others also, either through ignorance or superstition, will take offence at this speech, as confounding all things ; but there is no such cause of exception. For howsoever the keys be one and the same in nature and efficacy, in what faithful man, or men's hands soever, as not depending either upon the number or excellency of any persons, but upon Christ alone ; yet is it ever to be remembered, that the order and manner of using them is very different.

The [These] keys in doctrine may be turned as well upon them which are without the church, as upon them which are within, and their sins either loosed or bound, Matt. xxviii. 19 ; but in discipline not so, but only upon them which are within ; 1 Cor. v. 12, 13. Again, the apostles by their office had these keys to use in all churches, yea, in all nations upon earth ; ordinary elders for their particular flocks ; Acts xiv. 23, and xx. 28. Lastly, there is a use of the keys publicly to be had, and a use privately ; a use of them by one person severally, and a use of them by the whole church jointly, and together ; a use of them ministerially, or in office, and a use of them out of office. But the power of the gospel, which is the keys, is still one and the same, notwithstanding the diverse manner of using it. P. 151. [158, 159.]

If the keys of the kingdom of heaven be appropriated unto the officers, then can there be no forgiveness of sins, nor salvation, without officers; for there is no entrance into heaven but by the door. Without the key the door cannot be opened. So then, belike, if either there be no officers in the church (as it may easily come to pass in some extreme plague or persecution, [howsoever in England a man may have a priest for the whistling,] and must needs be in the churches of Christ in our days, either in their first planting, or first calling out of Babylon; for antichrist's mass-priesthood is not essentially Christ's true ministry,) or if the officers take away the key of knowledge, as the scribes and pharisees did, and will neither enter themselves nor suffer them that would; then must the miserable multitude be content to be shut out and perish eternally, for ought is known to the contrary. To admonish the officers of their sin, [it] were "against common sense, as that the father should be subject to his children, the work domineer over the workman, the seedsman be ordered by the corn," and to excommunicate them and call new, were intolerable usurpation of the keys; "this power is given to the chief officers only;" Pp. 94, 95, and to separate from them is as intolerable. P. 88.[1] Miserable were the Lord's people, if these things were so; but the truth is, they are miserable guides who so teach.

They which may forgive sins and sinners, save souls, gain and turn men unto the Lord, to them are the keys of the kingdom given, by which they open the door unto such as they thus forgive, gain and save. But all these things, such as are not ministers may do, as these Scriptures, which I entreat the godly reader to consider, do most clearly manifest; Matt. xviii. 15; 2 Cor. ii. 5, 7;--10; Acts viii. 1, 4, with xi. 19—21; James v. 19, 20; 1 Pet. iii. 1; Jude 22, 23. Erroneous, therefore, and derogatory is it to the nature of the gospel, and free donation of Christ, thus to impropriate and engross the keys, which lie common to all Christians in their place and order. Pp. 152, 153. [160, 161.]

Concerning ordination Mr. Robinson observes :—

The officers of the church are the servants of the church; and their office a service of the Lord, and of his church. Matt. xx. 25, 26, 27. 2 Cor. iv. 5. Rom. xv. 31. Whereupon it followeth necessarily, that what power the offiers have, the body of the church hath first. P. 411. [435.] To these things I add, that what power any of the pope's clergy receive from him, the same he takes from them, and deprives them of, when they withdraw their obedience, or separate from that church. For our better proceeding, I will first consider what ordination is; and secondly how far

[1] These are quotations from Bernard.

the brethren may go by the Scriptures, and the necessary consequences drawn from them, in this and the like cases in the first planting of churches, or of reducing of them into order, in or after some general confusion. The prelates, and those which level by their line, highly advance ordination [and] far above the administration of the word, sacraments and prayer; making it, and the power of excommunication, the two incommunicable prerogatives of a bishop above an ordinary minister. But surely herein these chief ministers do not succeed the chief ministers, the apostles, except as darkness succeeds light, and antichrist's confusion Christ's order. When the apostles were sent out by Christ, there was no mention of ordination; their charge was, " Go teach all nations, and baptize them ; " and, that the apostles accounted preaching their principal work, and after it baptism and prayer, the Scriptures manifest. Acts vi. 4 ; 1 Cor. i. 17; P. 412. [436, 437.]

Ordination doth depend upon the people's lawful election, as an effect upon the cause, by virtue of which it is justly administered, and may be thus described, or considered of us, as the admission of or putting into possession a person lawfully elected into a true office of ministry. . . . . The right unto their office they have by election, the possession by ordination, with the ceremony of imposition of hands. The apostle Peter, advertising the disciples or brethren that one (fitted as there noted) was in the room of Judas to be made a witness, with the eleven apostles, of the resurrection of Christ, when two were by them presented, did with the rest present them two and none other to the Lord, that he, by the immediate direction of the lot, might show whether of them two he had chosen. Acts i. In like manner the twelve being to institute the office of deaconry in the church at Jerusalem, called the multitude of the disciples together, and informed them what manner of persons they were to choose ; which choice being made by the brethren accordingly, and they so chosen presented to the apostles, they forthwith ordained them, by virtue of the election [so] made by the brethren. To these add, that the apostles Paul and Barnabas (being thereunto called by the Holy Ghost) did pass from church to church, and from place to place, and in every church where they came did ordain them elders by the people's election, signified by their lifting up of hands, as the word[1] is, and as the use was in popular elections, throughout those countries. Act. xiii. 2, and xiv. 23. . . . . The judgment and plea (when they deal with us) of the most forward men in the land, in this case, I

---

[1] $X\epsilon\iota\rho o\tau o\nu\dot\eta\sigma a\nu\tau\epsilon\varsigma$. Mr. Robinson's argument from this word is not approved by the best criticism. " The interpretation *having appointed for them* [elders] *by their outstretched hands,* i. e., by taking their opinion or vote in that manner, is unwarranted; for it transfers the hands to the wrong persons."—Hackett; Commentary on Acts xiv : 23.—ED.

may omit; which is, that they renounce and disclaim their ordination by the prelates, and hold their ministry by the people's acceptation. Now if the acceptation of a mixed company, under the prelate's government (as is the best parish assembly in the kingdom) whereof the greatest part have by the revealed will of God no right to the covenant, ministry, or other holy things, be sufficient to make a minister, then much more the acceptation of the people with us, being all of them jointly, and every one of them severally, by the mercy of God, capable of the Lord's ordinances.[1] I acknowledge that where there are already lawful officers in a church, by and to which others are called, there the former, upon that election, are to ordain and appoint the latter. The officers, being the ministers of the church, are to execute the determinations [and judgments] of the church under the Lord. . . . . Ordination is properly the execution of election. Pp. 413—415. [437—440.]

The apostle Paul writes to the churches of Galatia to reject, as accursed, such ministers whomsoever as should preach otherwise than they had already received: and the same apostle writes to the church of [at] Colosse, to admonish Archippus to take heed to his ministry. So [did] John also, to the church of Ephesus, commendeth, [commending] it for examining, and so consequently for silencing, such as pretended themselves

[1]Mr. Robinson gives us a number of the Protestants' testimonies upon this point, of which take the following :—

"Gal. i. 8; 'If any man teach another gospel, let him be anathema.' Only the assembly where the true doctrine soundeth is the church: in it is the ministry of the gospel: in it are the keys of the kingdom of heaven. Wherefore in that very assembly [in eo ipso cœtu] there is the right of calling and ordaining the ministers of the gospel, because we must fly the enemies of the gospel, as anathema. And besides, if we should desire of them the ceremony of ordination, they would not give it, except we would bind ourselves to renounce the true doctrine; and other wicked bonds would they cast upon us. It is the confusion of order, to seek shepherds from the wolves. This hath ever been the right of the true church, to choose and call out of her own assembly fit ministers of the gospel."

Philip Melancthon.

"In the planting of churches anew, when men [want] are wanting, which should preach the gospel, a woman may perform that at the first; but so as when she hath taught any company, that some one man of the faithful be ordained, which may afterwards minister the sacraments, teach, and do the pastor's duty faithfully."

Peter Martyr.

"Tilenus being demanded of the Earl of Lavall, from whom Calvin had his calling answered, From the church of Geneva, and from Farrel, his predecessor; who also had his from the people of Geneva; who had right and authority to institute and depose ministers: which thing he also confirms by Cyprian, Epist. xiv." Pp. 421, 422. [446, 447.]

These were the sentiments of those who knew how they came out of Rome, and upon what grounds the Protestant churches were formed; but how differently are things represented by aspiring men at this day?

apostles, and were not : as also to the church of Thyatira, reproving it for
suffering unsilenced the false prophetess Jezebel. Now as these things did
first and principally concern the officers, who were in these and all other
things of the same nature to go before and govern the people ; so are
[were] the people also in their places interested in the same business and
charge. Neither could the officers' sin (if they should have been corrupt
or negligent) discharge the people of their duty in the things which concerned them ; but they were bound notwithstanding to see the commandments of the apostles, and of the Lord Jesus by them, executed accordingly. And if the people be in cases, and when their officers fail, thus solemnly to examine, admonish, silence, and suppress their teachers, being
faulty and unsound ; then are they also by proportion, where officers fail,
to elect, appoint, set up and over themselves such fit persons as the Lord
affordeth them, for their furtherance of faith and salvation. Pp. 417, 418.
[442, 443.]

Against this doctrine many objections have been raised;
the chief of which are about the people's instability, and
their tendency to confusion. In answer to which, Mr. Robinson reminds his opponent, that though his ignorant people had readily changed their religion with their prince,
even back to popery in Mary's days; yet, " The prelates
and priests were as unstable as the rest, yea their ringleaders." Says he :—

For [ourselves, Mr. B., and that whereof we take] experience in this
our popularity, as you term it, I tell you, that if ever I saw the beauty of
Sion, and the glory of the Lord filling his tabernacle, it hath been in the
manifestation of the divers graces of God in the church, in that heavenly
harmony, and comely order, wherein by the grace of God we are set and
walk ; wherein, if your eyes had but seen the brethren's sober and modest
carriage one towards another, their humble and willing submission unto
their guides in the Lord, their tender compassion towards the weak, their
fervent zeal against scandalous offenders, and their long-suffering towards
all, you would, I am persuaded, change your mind, and be compelled to
take up your parable, and bless where you purposed to curse. P. 212.
[223.] For mine own part, knowing mine own infirmities, and that I am
subject to sin, yea and to forwardness in sin, as much as the brethren are ;
if by mine office I should be deprived of the remedy which they enjoy,
that blessed ordinance of the church's censures, I should think mine office
accursed, and myself by it, as frustrating and disappointing me of that
main end for which the servants of Christ ought to join themselves unto

the church of Christ, furnished with his power for their reformation. . . . . As, on the contrary, God is my record, how, in the very writing of these things, my soul is filled with spiritual joy, that I am under this easy yoke of Christ, the censures of the church, and how much I am comforted in this [very] consideration, against my vile and corrupt nature, which, not-withstanding, I am persuaded the Lord will never so far suffer to rebel, as that it shall not be tamed and subdued by this strong hand of God, with-out which it might every day and hour so hazard my salvation. That doc-trine which advanceth an inferior and meaner state [estate] in the church, above that which is superior and the chief, that is unsound, and indeed serving in a degree for the exaltation of that man of sin above all that is called God. But the doctrine of setting the elders without and above the judgments and censures of the church, doth advance an inferior above a superior. The point I thus manifest :—

The order of kings is the highest order or estate in the church. But the order of saints is the order of kings, and we are kings as we are saints, not as we are officers. . . . . As the Lord Jesus did prove against the scribes and pharisees, that the temple was greater than the gold, because it sancti-fied the gold, and that the altar was greater than the offering, because it sanctified the offering, so by proportion the condition of a saint, which sanc-tifieth the condition of an officer, is more excellent [and greater] than it is. To our saintship, and as we have faith, is promised the forgiveness of sins, the favor of God, and life eternal, but not to our office, or in respect of it. The estate of a saint is most happy and blessed, though the person never so much as come near an office; but on the contrary, an officer, if he be not also and first a saint, is a most wretched and accursed creature. Pp. 216, 217. [227, 228.]

The reader will not wonder that those who were for na-tional churches, and unconverted ministers, discovered a strong prejudice against such writings as these; but how well do they agree with the apostles' doctrine. 1 Cor. xii. 31, and xiii. 1—3 ; Gal. i.

Of reformation, Mr. Robinson says to his opponent :—

You speak much of the reformation of your church after popery. There was indeed a great reformation of things in your church, but very little of the church, to speak truly and properly. The people are the church ; and to make a reformed church, there must be first a reformed people ; and so there should have been with you, by the preaching of repentance from dead works, and faith in Christ ; that the people, as the Lord should have vouch-safed grace, being first fitted for, and made capable of, the sacraments, and

other ordinances, might afterwards have communicated in the pure use of
them ; for want of which, instead of a pure use, there hath been, and is at
this day, a most profane abuse of them, to the great dishonor of Christ and
his gospel, and to the hardening of thousands in their impenitency.   Others
also, endeavoring yet a further reformation, have sued and do sue to kings,
and queens, and parliaments, for the rooting out of the prelacy, and with
it, of such other evil fruits as grow from that bitter root ; and on the contrary, to have the ministry, government and discipline of Christ set over
the parishes as they stand ; the first fruit of which reformation, if it were
obtained, would be the [further] profanation of the more of God's ordinances upon such, as to whom they appertained not ; and so the further
provocation of his [great] Majesty unto anger against all such as so practiced, or consented thereunto.   Is it not strange that men, in the reforming
of a church, should almost, or altogether, forget the church, which is the
people, or that they should labor to crown Christ a King over a people,
whose Prophet he hath not first been ? or to set him to rule by his laws and
officers, over the professed subjects of antichrist and the devil ? [or] is it
possible that ever they should submit to the discipline of Christ, which
have not first been prepared, in some measure, by his holy doctrine, and
taught with meekness to stoop unto his yoke ?   Pp. 300, 301.   [316, 317.]

A main plea for such confusion, both then and now, was
and is drawn from the parable of the tares.   But, says Mr.
Robinson:—

Since the Lord Jesus, who best knew his own meaning, calls the field
the world, and makes the harvest, which is the end of the field, the end of
the world, and not of the church, why should we admit of any other interpretation?   Neither is it like [likely] that Christ would in the expound-
ing of one parable speak another, as he should have done, if, in calling the
field the world, he had meant the church.   As God then in the beginning
made man good, and placed him in the field of the world, there to grow,
where by the envy of the serpent he was soon corrupted, so ever since hath
the seed of the serpent, stirred up by their father the devil, snarled at the
heel of the woman's seed, and like noisome tares vexed and pestered the
good and holy seed ; which though the children of God both see and feel
to their pain, yet must they not therefore, forgetting what spirit they are of,
presently call for fire from heaven, nor prevent the Lord's hand, but wait
his leisure, either for the converting of these tares into wheat, which in
many is daily seen,—and then how great pity had it been they should so
untimely have been plucked up—or for their final perdition in the day of
the Lord, when the church shall be no more offended by them.   And that
the Lord Jesus no way speaks of the toleration of profane persons in the
church, doth appear by these reasons :—

1. Because he doth not contradict himself, by forbidding the use of the keys in one place, which in another he hath turned upon impenitent offenders. Matt. xviii. [15—17.] 2. In the excommunication of sinners apparently obstinate, with due circumspection, and in the spirit of wisdom, meekness, and long-suffering, with such other general Christian virtues, as with which all our special sacrifices ought to be seasoned, what danger can there be of any such disorder, as the plucking up of the wheat with the tares, which the husbandman feareth? 3. The Lord Jesus speaks of the utter ruinating and destruction of the tares,—the plucking them up by the roots ;—but excommunication rightly administered, is not for the ruin and destruction of any, but for the salvation of the party thereby humbled. 1 Cor. v. 5. The Lord's field is sown only with good seed,—his church, saints [and] beloved of God, all and every one of them, though by the malice of Satan, and negligence of such as should keep this field, vineyard and house of God, adulterated seed, and abominable persons, may be foisted in, yea and suffered also. Pp. 119, 120. [125—127.] I deny not but, as it hath been said of old, there are many sheep without, and many wolves within ; many of the visible church which are not of the invisible church, and many of the invisible church which never come into the visible church. But this, say I, is not according to the revealed will of God in his word ; but by men's default and sin. It is their sin of ignorance, or infirmity, which, being of the invisible church, do not, if possibly they can, join themselves unto the visible church, there to partake in the visible ordinances. It is their sin of hypocrisy and presumption, which not being of the invisible church, do adjoin themselves to the visible church, there to profane the Lord's covenant and ordinances, to which they have no right. For how can they, being wicked and unholy, challenge the Lord to be their God, that is, all happiness and goodness unto them, which is one part of the covenant ; or profess themselves to be his people, which is another part, when the devil and their lusts is their God? Pp. 313, 314. [330.]

OF THE DIFFERENCE BETWEEN CIVIL AND ECCLESIASTICAL GOVERNMENT.

1. Civil officers [are, and] are called in the word of God, princes, heads, captains, judges, magistrates, nobles, lords, kings, them in authority, principalities and powers, yea in their respect, gods ; and according to their names so are their offices. But on the contrary, ecclesiastical officers are not capable of these, or the like titles, which can neither be given without flattery unto them, nor received by them without arrogancy. Neither is their office an office of lordship, sovereignty or authority, but of labor and service, and so they, the laborers and servants of the church, as of God. 2 Cor. iv. 5 ; 1 Tim. iii. 1.

2. Magistrates may publish and execute their own laws in their own

names. Ezra i. 1, &c. ; Esther viii. 8 ; Matt. xx. 25. But ministers are only interpreters of the laws of God, and must look for no further respect at the hands of any to the things they speak, than as they manifest the same to be the commandments of the Lord. 1 Cor. xiv. 37.

3. Civil administrations, and their forms of government, may be and ofttimes are altered, for the avoiding of inconveniences, according to the circumstances of time, place and persons. Exod. xviii. 13, &c. But the church is a kingdom which cannot be shaken, Heb. xii. 28, wherein may be no innovation in office, or form of administration, from that which Christ hath left, for any inconveniency whatsoever.

4. Civil magistrates have authority by their offices to judge offenders, upon whom also they may execute bodily vengeance, using their people as their servants and ministers for the same purpose ; but in the church the officers are the ministers of the people, whose service the people is to use for the administering of the judgments of the church, and of God first, against the obstinate, which is the utmost execution the church can perform. . . . . But here it will be demanded of me, if the elders be not set over the church for her guidance and government? Yes, certainly, as the physician is set over the body, for his skill and faithfulness, to minister unto it, to whom the patient, yea though his lord and [or] master, is to submit ; the lawyer over his cause, to attend unto it ; the steward over his family, even his wife and children, to make provision for them : yea, the watchman over the whole city, for the safe keeping thereof. Such, and none other, is the elder's or bishop's government. Pp. 135—137. [143—145.]

But, says Mr. Robinson :—

What sway authority hath in the church of England, appeareth in the laws of the land, which make the government of the church alterable at the magistrate's pleasure ; and so the clergy, in their submission to King Henry VIII, do derive, as they pretend, their ecclesiastical jurisdiction from him, and so execute [exercise] it. Indeed many of the late bishops and their proctors, seeing how monstrous the ministration is of divine things, by a human authority and calling, and growing bold upon the present disposition of the magistrate, have disclaimed that former title, and do professedly hold their ecclesiastical power and jurisdiction *de jure divino*, and so consequently by God's word unalterable : of whom I would demand this one question :—What if the king should discharge and expel the present ecclesiastical government, and plant instead of it the presbytery or eldership, would they submit unto the government of the elders? Yea or No? If Yea, then were they traitors to the Lord Jesus, submitting to a government overthrowing his government, as doth the Presbyterian government that which is Episcopal : if No, then how could they free themselves from such imputations of disloyalty to princes, and disturbance of states, as wherewith they load us and others opposing them? But to the question itself. As the kingdom of Christ is not of this world, but spirit-'ual, and he a spiritual King, John xviii. 36, so must the government of this spiritual kingdom under this spiritual King needs be spiritual, and all the laws of it. And as Christ Jesus hath, by the merits of his priesthood, redeemed as well the body as the soul, 1 Cor. vi. 20, so is he also by the sceptre of his kingdom to rule and reign over both, unto which Christian magistrates, as well as meaner persons, ought to submit themselves, and the more Christian they are, the more meekly to take the yoke of Christ upon them, and the greater authority they have, the more effectually to advance his sceptre over themselves and their people, by all good means. Neither can there be any reason given why the merits of saints may not as well be mingled with the merits of Christ, for the saving of the church, as the laws of men with his laws, for the ruling and guiding of it. He is as absolute and [as] entire a King as he is a Priest, and his people must be as careful to preserve the dignity of the one, as to enjoy the benefit of the other. P. 38. [39, 40.]

Of Ministers' Maintenance.

Mr. Bernard charged his opponents with error, in holding that ministers ought not to live of tithes, but of the people's voluntary contribution; and says, "This is against the wisdom of God, who allowed a settled maintenance under the law; and there is nothing against it in the gospel." But in reply Mr. Robinson says :—

As the Lord appointed under the law a settled maintenance by tithes and offerings, so did he a settled land of Canaan, which was holy, and a sacrament; so did he also appoint that the Levites to be maintained there, should have no part nor inheritance with the rest of the Israelites their brethren. And hath God's wisdom so appointed now? If it had, I fear many would not rest in it, so wise are they for their bellies. And where you add that there is nothing in the gospel against this ordinance in the law, the author to the Hebrews might have taught you, that the law is abolished by the gospel, in the sense we speak of; and the Old Testament by the New, in respect of ordinances, whereof this was one. If it be said that tithes were in use and given by Abraham to Melchizedec, priest of the most high God, before the law or Old Testament was given by Moses, I answer, that so was circumcision ministered and sacrifices offered before Moses; which notwithstanding were parts of the Old Testament, and assumed by Moses into the body of it, and so are abolished by the New. To conclude this point, since tithes and offerings were appurtenances unto the priesthood, and that the priesthood, both of Melchizedec and Levi, are abolished in Christ, as the shadow in the substance ; and that the "Lord hath ordained that they which preach the gospel, should live of the gospel ;" we willingly leave unto you both your priestly order and maintenance, contenting ourselves with the people's voluntary contribution, whether it be less or more, as the blessing of God upon our labor, the fruit of our ministry, and a declaration of their love and duty. Pp. 439, 440. [466, 467.]

In all these passages[1] I have recited Mr. Robinson's own expressions, without knowingly adding a single word. The spelling I have brought to the present times, but the language is entirely his ; and it may be questioned whether any talked a purer one in that day or not, if there does in this.

About the time of his publishing this book, and for some years following, "many came to his church at Leyden from divers parts of England, so that they grew a great congregation ;" "even so as to have three hundred communicants[2]." And as the Arminian controversy caused great troubles in Holland, and especially at Leyden, their two divinity professors being divided, Episcopius appearing for, and Polyander[3] against the Arminian tenets ; Mr. Robinson, though he preached thrice a week, and went through much other labor, yet went constantly to hear them both, whereby he got well grounded in the controversy ; so that when Episcopius, about the year 1613, set forth sundry Arminian theses at Leyden, which he would defend against all opposers, Polyander insisted upon Mr. Robinson's engaging against him, telling him, that "such was the ability and expertness of the adversary, that the truth is in danger to suffer, if he would not help them ; is so importunate as at length he yields ; and when the day comes, he so defends the truth, and foils the

[1]Changed from "In all these passages which begin and end with marks of quotation."—ED.

[2]Prince's Chronology, [125]; Plymouth Register.

[3]In the original edition this name stands as Polydore. Mr. Backus corrected the error in his Abridgment.—ED.

opposer, as he puts him to an apparent nonplus in this great
and public audience.   The same he does a second and a third
time, upon the like occasions, which, as it causes many to
give praise to God that the truth had so famous a victory,
so it procures Mr. Robinson much respect and honor from
those learned men and others[1]."

Several attempts were made to plant New England from
worldly motives, but they all proved abortive.   In 1607 a
hundred men were sent over to Sagadahoc[2] with furniture to
lay the foundation of a great state, and all lived through
the winter but their president; yet the next year, " the whole
colony breaks up and returns to England, and brands the
country as over cold and not habitable by our nation, and
the adventurers give over their design[3]."   Other fruitless attempts were made for a while, and then were given over.
" Sir Ferdinando Gorges and Captain Mason spent twenty
thousand pounds each, in attempts for settlement, and each
of them thought it advisable to give over their [his] designs,
and sit down with the loss.   Whether Britain would have
had any colonies in America at this day, if religion had not
been the grand inducement, is doubtful[4]."

The people whose religious sentiments are described above,
after long consideration, many earnest requests to heaven for
direction and help, and well consulting matters with English
friends, at last determined to come over to this wilderness;
and divine providence made them the honored instruments
of laying the foundation of this now flourishing country.
In December, 1617, Mr. Robinson and Elder Brewster wrote
to the Council for Virginia, who then had the management
of these affairs, wherein they say:—

[1] Prince's Chronology, pp. 36, 38.   [130, 131.]
[2] In Maine, near the mouth of the Kennebec.—ED.
[3] Prince's Chronology, pp. 21—25.   [116—119.]
[4] Massachusetts History, Vol. I, p. 3.   [11, note.]

For your encouragement we will not forbear to mention these induce-
ments. 1. We verily believe and trust the Lord is with us, to whom and
whose service we have given ourselves in many trials ; and that he will
graciously prosper our endeavors according to the simplicity of our hearts.
2. We are well weaned from the delicate milk of our mother country, and
inured to the difficulties of a strange land. 3. The people are, for the
body of them, industrious and frugal, we think we may safely say, as any
company of people in the world. 4. We are knit together as a body, in a
most strict and sacred bond and covenant of the Lord ; of the violation
whereof we make great conscience, and by virtue whereof we hold ourselves straitly tied to all care of each other's good, and of the whole.
5. It is not with us as with other men ; whom small things can discourage,
or small discouragements cause to wish ourselves at home again[1].

Herein they were not mistaken, as will soon appear ; for
though contentions among the said Council, and other things,
obstructed their proceeding till 1620, and they could not
then obtain any royal promise of liberty of conscience in
this country, only that "the king would connive at them,
and not molest them if they carried it peaceably;" "yet,
casting themselves on the care of Providence, they resolve
to venture[2]."   But as they could not obtain shipping and provision enough to carry half their company the first year, Mr.
Robinson was obliged to tarry in Holland with the larger part,
while Mr. William Brewster, their ruling elder, came over
with the other.   Most of their brethren came with them from
Leyden to Delft-Haven, where they spent the night in
friendly, entertaining and Christian converse.   And July 22,
the wind being fair, they go aboard, their friends attending
them, when "Mr. Robinson falling down on his knees, and
they all with him, he with watery cheeks commends them
with most fervent prayer to God ; and then with mutual em-
braces, and many tears, they take their leave, and with a
prosperous gale come to Southampton," in England.   July
27, 1620, Mr. Robinson wrote a letter, which was received

[1]Prince, pp. 51, 52. [143.]   [2]Prince, [148, 151.]—ED.

and read to the company at that place¹; which I think worthy of a place here. The letter is as follows²:—

LOVING CHRISTIAN FRIENDS :—I do heartily and in the Lord salute you, as being those with whom I am present in my best affections, and most earnest longing after you, though I be constrained for a while to be bodily absent from you : I say constrained ; God knowing how willingly, and much rather than otherwise, I would have borne my part with you in this first brunt, were I not by strong necessity held back for the present. Make account of me in the mean time as a man divided in myself, with great pain, and as (natural bonds set aside) having my better part with you ; and, although I doubt not but in your godly wisdoms you both foresee and resolve upon that which concerneth your present state and condition, both severally and jointly, yet have I thought it but my duty to add some further spur of provocation unto them who run [well] already, if not because you need it, yet because I owe it in love and duty.

And first, as we are daily to renew our repentance with our God, especially for our sins known, and generally for our unknown trespasses ; so doth the Lord call us in a singular manner, upon occasions of such difficulty and danger as lieth upon you, to both a narrow search and careful reformation [of your ways] in his sight, lest he, calling to remembrance our sins forgotten by us, or unrepented of, take advantage against us, and in judgment leave us [for the same] to be swallowed up in one danger or other ; whereas, on the contrary, sin being taken away by earnest repentance, and the pardon thereof from the Lord sealed up to a man's conscience by his Spirit, great shall be his security and peace in all dangers, sweet his comforts in all distresses, with happy deliverance from all evil, whether in life or death. Now next after this heavenly peace with God and our own consciences, we are carefully to provide for peace with all men, what in us lieth, especially with our associates ; and for that, watchfulness must be had, that we neither at all [in] ourselves do give, no, nor easily take offence being given by others. Wo be to the world for offences, for although it be necessary, considering the malice of Satan and man's corruption, that offences come, yet wo unto the man, or woman either, by whom the offence cometh, saith Christ. Matt. xviii. 7. And if offences in the unseasonable use of things, in themselves indifferent, be more to be feared than death itself, as the apostle teacheth ; 1 Cor. ix. 15 ; how much more in things

¹Prince, pp. 70, 71. [159, 160.]

²This letter, as given in the different editions of Morton's Memorial, and in Mourt's Relation and Neal's History of New England, is considerably varied. The words here added in brackets are from the edition of the Memorial published by the Congregational Board, Boston, 1855.—ED.

simply evil, in which neither the honor of God nor love of man is thought worthy to be regarded?   Neither yet is it sufficient that we keep ourselves, by the grace of God, from giving offences, except withal we be armed against the taking of them, when they are given by others ; for how imperfect and lame is the work of grace in that person, who wants charity to cover a multitude of offences? as the Scripture speaks.   Neither are you to be exhorted to this grace only upon the common grounds of Christianity, which are, that persons ready to take offence, either want charity to cover offences, or [wisdom] duly to weigh human frailties ; or, lastly, are gross though close hypocrites, as Christ our Lord teacheth ; Matt. vii. 1—3 ; as indeed, in my own experience, few or none have been found which sooner give offence, than such as easily take it ; neither have they ever proved sound and profitable members in societies, who have nourished this touchy humor.   But besides these, there are divers motives provoking you above others to great care and conscience this way ; as first, there are many of you strangers as to the persons, so to the infirmities one of another, and so stand in need of more watchfulness this way, lest when such things fall out in men and women as you expected not, you be inordinately affected with them, which doth require at your hands much wisdom and charity for the covering and preventing of incident offences that way.   And lastly, your intended course of civil community will minister continual occasion of offence[1], and will be as fuel for that fire, except you diligently quench it with brotherly forbearance.   And if taking offence causelessly or easily at men's doings be so carefully to be avoided ; how much more heed is to be taken that we take not offence at God himself?   Which yet we certainly do, so oft as we do murmur at his providence in our crosses, or bear impatiently such afflictions wherewith he is pleased to visit us.   Store up therefore patience against the evil day ; without which we take offence at the Lord himself in his [holy and] just works.   A fourth thing there is carefully to be provided for, viz. that with your common employments, you join common affections, truly bent upon the general good, avoiding as a deadly plague of your both common and special comforts, all retiredness of mind for proper advantage ; and all singularly affected every manner of way, let every man repress in himself, and the whole body in each person, as so many rebels against the common good, all private respects of men's selves, not sorting with the general convenience.   And as men are careful not to have a new house shaken with any violence, before it be well settled, and the parts firmly knit ; so be you, I beseech you my brethren, much more careful that the house of God, which you are and are to be, be not shaken with unnecessary novelties, or other oppositions, at the first settling thereof.

---

[1]For several years their affairs were managed in one common stock, but they afterward found the way of distinct property to be much better.

Lastly whereas you are to become a body politic, using amongst your-selves civil government, and are not furnished with persons of special emi-nency above the rest, to be chosen by you into office of government, let your wisdom and godliness appear, not only in choosing such persons as do entirely love, and will promote the common good ; but also in yielding unto them all due honor and obedience in their lawful administrations, not beholding in them the ordinariness of their persons, but God's ordinance for your good ; not being like the foolish multitude, who more honor the gay coat, than either the virtuous mind of the man, or the glorious ordi-nance of the Lord ; but you know better things, and that the image of the Lord's power and authority, which the magistrate beareth, is honorable, in how mean persons soever ; and this duty you may the more willingly, and ought the more conscionably to perform because you are, at least for the present, to have them for your ordinary governors, which yourselves shall make choice of for that work. Sundry other things of importance I could put you in mind of, and of those before mentioned, in more words ; but I will not so far wrong your godly minds, as to think you heedless of these things, there being also divers amongst you so well able both to admonish themselves and others of what concerneth them. These few things therefore, and the same in few words, I do earnestly commend to your care and conscience, joining therein with my daily incessant prayers unto the Lord, that he who has made the heavens and the earth, and sea, and all rivers of waters, and whose providence is over all his works, espec-ially over all his dear children for good, would so guide and guard you in your ways, as inwardly by his Spirit, so outwardly by the hand of his power, as that both you, and we also for and with you, may have after matter of praising his name all the days of your and our lives. Fare you well in him in whom you trust, and in whom I rest, an unfeigned well-wisher to your happy success in this hopeful voyage.

                                        JOHN ROBINSON.[1]

This excellent letter properly describes the sentiments, temper and rules of conduct of the chief founders of New England ; and may the same be duly regarded to their latest posterity!

By Dutch intrigues and others' ill conduct they were hinder-ed long, and at last forced to come with only one ship instead of two ; which sailed from Plymouth, in England, on Sep-tember 6, and arrived in Cape Cod harbor, November 11, and at the place which they named Plymouth, in December, 1620.

[1] Morton, pp. 7—10. [15—19.]

And now compare this company with that of Sagadahoc. That company, who came upon worldly designs, had a hundred men; this religious society consisted of but one hundred and one souls, men, women and children; the one arrived at the place designed for settlement in August, the other not till winter had set in ; the worldly company only buried their president, and all returned the next year to their native country again ;[1] whereas this religious people, in about five months time, buried their governor and full half their number, and yet with fortitude and patience they kept their station ; yea, though they were afterwards deserted and abused by some who had engaged to help them. We cannot now form an adequate idea of what those pious planters endured, to prepare the way for what we at this day enjoy. In the year 1623 they say, " By the time our corn is planted, our victuals are spent; not knowing at night where to have a bit in the morning, and have neither bread nor corn for three or four months together; yet bear our wants with cheerfulness, and rest on Providence."[2]

It pleased God further to try their faith, by sending a great drought and heat from the third week in May till the middle of July, which caused their corn to wither as if it were truly dead ; and a ship that they had long expected did not arrive, but they thought they saw signs of its being wrecked on the coast. " The most courageous are now discouraged. Upon this the public authority set apart a sol-

[1] This paragraph seems hardly just to the company at Sagadahoc. Doubtless their object was gain, and they lacked the fortitude and patience which religious principle inspired in the colonists of Plymouth. But they were not without trials. The Indians proved hostile; the climate is naturally much more rigorous on the Kennebec than at Plymouth, and the winter of 1607–8 was everywhere remarkably severe; in mid-winter a fire broke out in the settlement and consumed their storehouse, with most of their provisions and part of their lodgings; in addition to the loss of their president, his brother, lord-chief-justice Popham, the chief patron of the enterprise, died in England, and Sir John Gilbert, brother of their second president, died, leaving him an estate, the care of which compelled his return. Bancroft, I. 268; Prince, 117, 119; Hutchinson, I. 10.—ED.

[2] Prince, p. 135. [216.]

emn day of humiliation and prayer, to seek the Lord in this
distress, who was pleased to give speedy answer, to our
own and the Indians' admiration ; for though in the former
part of the day it was very clear and hot, without a sign of
rain, yet before the exercise is over the clouds gather, and
next morning distill such soft and gentle showers as give
cause of joy and praise to God." Their corn recovers, and
soon after arrives the ship they expected, bringing over
about sixty more of their friends, and a letter from others,
wherein they say to those here, " Let it not be grievous to
you, that you have been instruments to break the ice for
others who come after with less difficulty. The honor shall
be yours to the world's end. We bear you always in our
breasts, and our hearty affection is towards you all, as are
the hearts of hundreds more who never saw your faces, who
doubtless pray for your safety as their own."[1] Their harvest was plentiful ; and above twenty years after, Governor
Bradford says, " Nor has there been any general want of
food among us since to this day."[2]

Mr. Robinson and many of his people were detained in
Holland, till, after about a week's illness, he died there on
March 1, 1625, aged near fifty years. Governor Bradford
says, " His and our enemies had been continually plotting
how they might hinder his coming hither, but the Lord has
appointed him a better place." Mr. Prince says, " His son
Isaac came over to Plymouth colony, lived to above ninety
years of age, a venerable man, whom I have often seen,
and has left male posterity in the county of Barnstable."[3]

The cause why Mr. Robinson and the remaining part of
his church were kept back so long, was their inability to
transport themselves ; and several merchants who had engaged in the affair deserted them, pursuing separate schemes
of their own, and sent over one company of sixty stout

[1] Prince, pp. 137—140. [218—220.]   [2] Prince, p. 141. [221.]
[3] Prince, pp, 159, 160. [238.]

men, who began a plantation at Weymouth; but soon reduced themselves to such straits that several perished, and
the rest were forced to be beholden to the charity of Plymouth people, to keep them alive till they could get back
whence they came. Another worldly scheme was begun at
Braintree, which also proved abortive; while our Christian
fathers at Plymouth were enabled to keep their station.
Some of the adventurers wrote to them on December 18,
1624, and said, "We are still persuaded you are the people
that must make a plantation in those remote places, when
all others fail."[1] They were long destitute of a pastor, and
yet constantly maintained divine worship among them; of
which a noted author gives this account :—

To satisfy the reader, how a Christian church, could, in any tolerable
measure, carry on the public worship of God without suitable officers, as
was the case of those people of Plymouth, we must know that those were
a serious and religious people, that knew their own principles, knew and
were resolved on the way of their worship, but in many years could not
prevail with any to come over to them, and undertake the office of a pastor
amongst them, at least none in whom they could with full satisfaction
acquiesce, and therefore in the mean while they were peaceably and prudently managed by the wisdom of Mr. Brewster, a grave and serious person, ruling elder among them. . . . . Besides also several of his people were
well gifted, and did spend part of the Lord's day in their wonted prophesying, to which they had been accustomed by Mr. Robinson. Those gifts
while they lasted made the burthen of the other defect more easily
borne.[2]

The names of those first planters were, John Carver,
William Bradford, Edward Winslow, successive Governors;

[1] Prince p. 155. [233.]

[2] Hubbard. [p. 65.] Mr. Robinson says, "The disciples of Christ did not then first
receive power to teach when they were possessed of their apostleship, but long before
they were admitted into office, as did others also besides them, without office, as
well as they. Matt. x. 5, 6. 7, Luke x. 1—3, 9, 10." Answer to Bernard, P. 148.
[156.] "That we call prophesying, I affirm not to be so appropriated to the ministry, but that others having received a gift thereunto, may and ought to stir up the
same, and to use it in the church, for edification, exhortation and comfort, though not
yet called into the office of the ministry. Rom. xii. 6; 1 Cor. xiv. 3; 1 Pet. iv. 10,
11." Ibid, P. 235. [246. 247.]

William Brewster, elder; Captain Miles Standish,[1] John
Alden, Samuel Fuller, Richard Warren, Stephen Hopkins,
and others, each of whom have posterity remaining among
us to this day. "I am not preserving from oblivion the
names of heroes, whose chief merit is the overthrow of
cities, provinces and empires; but the names of the founders of a flourishing town and colony, if not of the whole
British empire in America."[2] Their deep poverty and the
abundance of their joy, abounded unto the riches of their
liberality, so as not only to enable them to relieve many in
distress, but also to launch out so as to help over about
thirty-five families more of their friends from Leyden, who
were transported hither in 1629, at the charge of their brethren here, which was cheerfully borne by them, though it
amounted to above five hundred and fifty pounds sterling,
besides supporting them after their arrival for sixteen or
eighteen months, till they had a harvest of their own, which
cost near as much more. "Meanwhile," says Governor
Bradford, "God gives us peace and health, with contented
minds, and so succeeds our labors that we have corn sufficient, and some to spare, with other provisions. Nor had
we ever any supply from England but what we first brought
with us."[3] The first horned cattle that they ever had here
were a bull and three heifers, which Governor Winslow
brought over to Plymouth in March, 1624.

About that time, "the fame of the plantation at New
Plymouth being spread in all the western parts of England,
the Rev. Mr. White, a famous Puritan minister of Dor-

---

[1] The original edition here gives the name of Robert Cushman. Mr. Backus evidently discovered the mistake, as he omits the name in his Abridgment. Mr.
Cushman came in the ship Fortune, in November, 1621, and returned in the same
ship after a stay of "not above fourteen days." He was the agent of the colony
until his death in 1626. Morton calls him "their ancient friend who was as their
right hand with their friends the adventurers, and for divers years had done and
agitated all their business with them, to their great advantage." Morton's Memorial,
pp. 26, 50, 83—85; Prince, pp. 172, 220, 221, 238; Hubbard, 69.—ED.

[2] Massachusetts History, Vol II. pp. 462, 463. [412, note.]

[3] Prince, pp. 156, 201. [235, 264, 265.]

chester, excites several gentlemen there to make way for another settlement in New England."[1] This was the beginning of the Massachusetts colony. In the year 1624 a few persons gathered at Cape Ann, who removed the next year, and began the town of Salem, to whom others resorted from time to time, till in the summer of 1628, Mr. John Endicott came over to govern them, and in 1629, Mr. Francis Higginson and Mr. Samuel Skelton, two Nonconformist ministers came with many others, and formed and organized a church in that place. Upon which we may see Mr. Robinson's words verified ; for these Puritans who had blamed him for an entire separation from the national church, yet were no sooner settled on this side the Atlantic, than they cast off the prelates' yoke in such a manner, that when John Brown and Samuel Brown, two of the " first patentees, men of estates, and men of parts," attempted to set up Episcopal worship at Salem, Governor Endicott convented them before him, where they "accused the ministers as departing from the orders of the church of England; that they were separatists, and would be Anabaptists, &c., but for themselves they would hold to the orders of the church of England." These speeches and practices were judged by the Governor and Council to be such as tended "to mutiny and faction, and the Governor told them that New England was no place for such as they, and therefore sent them back for England, at the return of the ships, the same year."[2]

By this and many other instances we may see, that the men who drew off from the national establishment, as soon as they were convinced that truth called them to it, were not so severe against dissenters from themselves, as they were who stayed till interest and civil power would favor the cause before they separated.

In the year 1630, Governor Winthrop with about fifteen

[1] Prince, p. 144. [224.]   [2] Morton's Memorial, pp. 84, 85. [100, 101.]

hundred people came over, and planted Charlestown, Boston, Dorchester, and Watertown, and soon formed churches in each town.   Of these people Mr. Hubbard says :—

Intending not to write an apology, but a history of their practice, nothing shall here be interposed by way of defence of their way, only to give a clear discovery of the truth, as to matter of fact, both what it was at first, and still continues to be.   Those that came over soon after Mr. Endicott, namely Mr. Higginson and Mr. Skelton, Anno 1629, walked something in an untrodden path, therefore it is the less to be wondered at, if they went but in and out ; in some things complying too much, in some things too little, with those of the separation ; and it may be in some things not sufficiently attending to the order of the gospel, as themselves thought they understood afterwards.   For in the beginning of things they only accepted of one another according to some general profession of the doctrine of the gospel, and the honest and good intentions they had one towards another, and so by some kind of covenant soon moulded themselves into a church in every plantation where they took up their abode[1] ; until Mr. Cotton and Mr. Hooker came over, which was in the year 1633, who did clear up the order and method of church government, according as they apprehended was most consonant to the word of God.   And such was the authority they, especially Mr. Cotton, had in the hearts of the people, that whatever he delivered in the pulpit was soon put into an order of court, if of a civil, or set up as a practice in the church, if of an ecclesiastical concernment.   After that time, the administration of all ecclesiastical matters was tied up more strictly than before to the rules of that which is since owned for the Congregational way.   The principal points wherein they differ from others may be reduced to these four heads :—

[1] The covenant of the first church in Boston was in these words :—
" In the name of our Lord Jesus Christ, and in obedience to his holy will and divine ordinance, we whose names are here underwritten, being by his most wise and good providence brought together into this part of America, in the Bay of Massachusetts, and desirous to unite ourselves into one congregation or church, under the Lord Jesus Christ our Head, in such sort as becometh all those whom he hath redeemed and sanctified to himself, do hereby solemnly and religiously (as in his most holy presence) promise and bind ourselves to walk in all our ways according to the rule of the gospel, and in all sincere conformity to his holy ordinances, and in mutual love and respect each to other, so near as God shall give us grace.
                                        JOHN WINTHROP.
                                        THOMAS DUDLEY.
                                        ISAAC JOHNSON.
                                        JOHN WILSON." &c.
            Mr. Foxcraft's Century Sermon at Boston.

1. The subject matter of the visible church, saints by calling; such as have not only attained the knowledge of the principles of religion, and are free from gross and open scandal, but are willing, together with the profession of their repentance and faith in Christ, to declare their subjection to him in his ordinances, which they account ought to be done publicly before the Lord and his people, by an open profession of the doctrine of the gospel, and by a personal relation of their spiritual estate, expressive of the manner how they were brought to the knowledge of God by faith in Christ Jesus; and this is done either with their *viva voce*, or by a rehearsal thereof by the elders in public before the church assembly, they having beforehand received private satisfaction, the persons openly testifying their assent thereunto, provided they do not scandalize their profession by an unchristian conversation, in which case a profession is with them of small account.

2. In the constitutive form of a particular visible church; which they account ought to be a restipulation, or mutual covenanting to walk together in their Christian communion, according to the rules of the gospel; and this they say is best to be explicit, although they do not deny but an implicit covenant may suffice to the being of a true church.

3. In the quantity or extensiveness of a particular church; concerning which they hold that no church society, of gospel institution, ought to be of larger extent, or greater number, than may ordinarily meet together in one place, for the enjoyment of all the same numerical ordinances, and celebrating of all divine worship, nor ordinarily fewer than may conveniently carry on church work.

4. That there is no jurisdiction, to which such particular churches are or ought to be subject, be it placed in classis or synod, by way of authoritative censure, nor any church power, extrinsical to the said churches which they ought to have dependence upon any other sort of men for the exercise of.

"After this manner," says Mr. Hubbard, "have their ecclesiastical affairs been carried on ever since the year 1633;" that is, down to 1680, when he wrote his history.

Here let it be well observed and ever remembered, that these were the main points wherein they differed from others; and the reader is welcome to search through all their history from that day to this, and see if he can find that these principles, in themselves considered, ever produced any evil effects. But this people brought two other principles with them from their native country, in which they did not differ from others ; which are, that natural birth, and the doings of men, can bring children into the covenant of grace ; and, that it is right to enforce and support their own sentiments about religion with the magistrate's sword. And those, let them live in England, Scotland, Rome, or elsewhere, who reproach and condemn New England for the evils which these two principles have produced, while they hold the same things, ought to consider that in so doing they will be found inexcusable before our Great Judge.

The root of a compulsive uniformity was planted at a General Court in Boston, May 18, 1631, when it was " ordered and agreed, that for the time to come, no man shall be admitted to the freedom of this body politic, but such as are members of some of the churches within the limits of the same[1]." This test in after times had such influence, that he who " did not conform, was deprived of more civil privileges than a nonconformist is deprived of by the test in England. Both the one and the other must have occasioned much formality and hypocrisy. The mysteries of our holy religion have been prostituted to mere secular views and advantages[2]."

If in any instances this people carried their zeal to a greater severity than Episcopalians have often done, let it be remembered, that the latter hold a power in their church to decree rites and ceremonies, and so consequently a power to abate or alter the same as occasion suits ; but the fathers of the Massachusetts held the Scriptures to be their unalterable rule, and having formed a plan which they thought was truly scriptural, Captain Johnson in 1651 said, " To them it seems unreasonable, and to savor too much of hypocrisy, that any people should pray unto the Lord for the speedy accomplishment of his word in the overthrow of antichrist, and in the meantime become a patron to sinful opinions and

---

[1]Prince's Annals, pp. 28, 29. [354.]
[2]Massachusetts History, Vol. I, p. 431. [380.]

damnable errors that oppose the truths of Christ, admit it be but in the bare permission of them[1]." Hence it appears, that it was this erroneous notion of using carnal weapons against what they looked upon as false opinions, that ought to bear the blame and reproach of those persecutions, and not their particular religious denomination, nor any of their zeal to promote religion by gospel means and methods.

That they were not aware how unscripturally they had confounded church and state together, appears from many facts. They were so much concerned to keep them distinct, that in 1632 the church of Boston wrote to the elders and brethren of the churches of Plymouth, Salem, &c. for their advice in three questions ; 1. Whether one person might be a civil magistrate and a ruling elder at the same time ? 2. If not, then which should he lay down ? 3. Whether there might be divers pastors in the same church ? The first was agreed by all negatively ; the other two doubtful[2]." In consequence of which, Mr. Nowell resigned his office of ruling elder, to which he had been ordained in the church, to hold those of a magistrate and secretary in the state[3]. On the other hand, Mr. John Doan, having been formerly chosen to the office of deacon in the church of Plymouth, at his and the church's request, was freed from the office of Assistant in the commonwealth[4].

Again our late Governor says, " I suppose there had been no instance of a marriage lawfully celebrated by a layman in England, when they left it. I believe there was no instance of marriage by a clergyman after they arrived, during their charter ; but it was always done by a magistrate, or by persons specially appointed for that purpose. It is difficult to assign a reason for so sudden a change[5]." I happened to observe a passage in Mr. Robinson which I suppose gives us

[1]Johnson's History, p. 206.
[2]Prince's Annals, p. 64. [398.]
[3]Hubbard, 186.—Ed.
[4]Prince's Annals, p. 92. [432.]
[5]Massachusetts History, Vol. I, p. 444. [392.]

the true reason of that great change. Mr. Bernard had charged the Separatists with an error, which he said they had given neither reason nor Scripture for, in holding that ministers may not celebrate marriage, nor bury the dead. To which Mr. Robinson answers :—

In our third petition to the king, and the fourth branch of the sixth proposition, there are almost twenty several Scriptures, and nine distinct reasons grounded upon them, to prove, that the celebration of marriage, and burial of the dead, are not ecclesiastical actions, appertaining to the ministry, but civil, and so to be performed. . . . . The apostle testifieth that the Scriptures, being divinely inspired, do make perfect, and fully furnished, the man of God, or minister, to every good work of his calling. Now I suppose Mr. B. will not be so ill advised, as to go about to prove that the celebration of marriage, and burial of the dead, are duties prescribed by the Lord Jesus to be done in the pastor's office, or that the Scriptures lay this furniture upon the man of God for the proper works of his office. They are then other spiritual lords than the Lord Christ, that prescribe these duties to be done by their men, furnished by other Scriptures than the divine Scriptures, the bishop's Scriptures, their canons and constitutions ; whereby they are furnished indeed with ring, service-book, and other priestly implements for the business[1].

This I suppose accounts for that change in our fathers' conduct then; though it is likely we are agreed in general now, that, as it was an error of popery to call marriage a sacrament, and to limit its administration to the clergy, so on the other hand that it was a mistake in those fathers to think that the civil state might not as well appoint ministers to celebrate marriages as any other persons.

These and many other things prove that those fathers were earnestly concerned to frame their constitution both in church and state by divine rule; and as all allow that nothing teaches like experience, surely they who are enabled well to improve the experience of past ages, must find it easier now to discover the mistakes of that day, than it was for them to do it then. Even in 1637, when a number of puritan ministers in England, and the famous Mr. Dod among them, wrote to

[1] Justification of Separation, p. 438. [465.]

the ministers here, that it was reported that they had embraced certain new opinions, such as "that a stinted form of
prayer and set liturgy is unlawful; that the children of godly
and approved Christians are not to be baptized, until their
parents be set members of some particular congregation;
that the parents themselves, though of approved piety, are
not to be received to the Lord's Supper until they be admitted set members," &c., Mr. Hooker expressed his fears of
troublesome work about answering of them[1], though they
may appear easy to the present generation.

[1]Massachusetts History, Vol. I, p. 81.   [80, 81.]

CHAPTER II.

Mr. Hubbard tells us, that " February 5, 1631,[1] arrived Mr. William Peirse at Nantasket ; with him came one Mr. Roger Williams,[2] of good account in England for a godly

[1]Hubbard, p. 202. Hubbard, according to the custom of his time, commences the year with March 25, and thus gives this date 1630. Winthrop (Vol. I, page 41) does the same. Backus, according to his plan, as stated in the preface to his first volume, has changed the date to conform to the present mode of reckoning. If Mr. Knowles had read and remembered this preface he would not have charged Backus with error in this date, or with neglect to observe the difference between the old and the new style. See Knowles's Memoir of Roger Williams, p. 45.—Ed.

[2]Of the life of Roger Williams, previous to his arrival in America, the accounts are meagre and often untrustworthy and contradictory. It is a tradition that he he was born in Wales, in 1599. With this agrees his own statement in a letter written in July. 1679, quoted in Chapter III, in which he speaks of himself as being " near to four score years of age." He appears to have become early a subject of experimental religion. In 1673 he wrote, " From my childhood, now about three score years, the Father of lights and mercies touched my soul with a love to himself, to his only begotten, the true Lord Jesus, to his holy Scriptures." In his youth he was taken under the patronage of the famous lawyer and statesman, Sir Edward Coke. It is said that Coke's interest in him was aroused by seeing him in church taking notes of the discourse, and upon asking to look at the notes he was so much impressed with the ability of the boy that he at once obtained permission from his parents to superintend his education, (Knowles's Memoir of Roger Williams, p. 24.) In the library of Trinity College, Cambridge, there is still preserved a letter from Roger Williams to Mrs. Sadlier, daughter of Sir Edward Coke, to which she has appended the words, " This Roger Williams, when he was a youth, would, in a short-hand, take sermons and speeches in the Star Chamber, and present them to my dear father." His patron placed him in school at Sutton's Hospital, now the Charter House, from the records of which we learn that he entered there in 1621,

and zealous preacher.   He had been some years employed in the ministry in England."[1]   Accordingly I find Mr. Williams reminding Mr. Cotton of conversation he had with him and Mr. Hooker, while they were riding together, " to and

and obtained an exhibition in 1624. (Elton, Life of Roger Williams, p. 11.) From Sutton's Hospital there is little doubt that he was sent to the University of Cambridge, where Coke himself was graduated. A Williams, whose first name is not given, entered Pembroke College, Cambridge, in 1623, and a Roger Williams, probably the same person, was matriculated a pensioner there in 1625, and took the degree of Bachelor of Arts in 1627. His signature upon the college books in subscribing to the thirty-nine articles, a prerequisite of graduation, is said to bear unmistakable resemblance to that of the founder of Providence. (Arnold's History of Rhode Island, Vol. I, p. 49.   Bancroft, Vol. I, p. 361.   Guild's Biographical Introduction to the writings of Roger Williams, Publications of the Narragansett Club, Vol. I, pp. 5-8.) It is the tradition indeed, that Roger Williams was graduated at Oxford : and Elton, (p. 10,) would identify him with Rodericus Williams who entered Jesus College, April 30, 1624, aged eighteen. But this is inconsistent with Williams's own statement of his age, already quoted, and would make him only twenty-five when he landed on the shores of the new world,—evidently allowing him too little time to have passed through the experiences which had already fitted him for the part that awaited him here.   Moreover, Wood, in his Athenae Oxonienses, in connection with another of the same name, mentions Roger Williams who wrote the key to the language of New England, with the words, " But of what university the said Williams was, if of any, I know not."

After his graduation, Williams is said to have studied law under the direction of Coke, but if so, he must have soon abandoned this pursuit for the more congenial one of theology. He received Episcopal ordination, and is said to have assumed the charge of a parish. At this time the line of separation between conformists and nonconformists was rigidly drawn. Charles I succeeded to the throne in 1625, and at once disappointed the hopes of the puritans by showing himself even less liberal than James, his father. In 1628, he placed Laud in the See of London, and in effect, entrusted to him the whole government of the English church. It was Laud's ambition to secure universal conformity. Says Macaulay, " Under his direction, every corner of the realm was subjected to a constant and minute inspection. Every little congregation of separatists was tracked out and broken up. Even the devotions of private families could not escape the vigilance of his spies." The associations of Williams's previous life were such as would incline him towards the nonconformists. Sir Edward Coke was not unfavorable to them ; they had large influence in the University of Cambridge, and Dr. Williams, bishop of Lincoln, under whom there are indications that Roger Williams held his living, was on the eve of suffering severest persecution for his leaning towards them. Moreover, Roger Williams's natural character, the Calvinism of his doctrinal views, and the fervor of his piety, all contributed to make him a puritan. He was not a man who could hide his views and principles. It was evident that persecution could not long fail to reach him, and to escape it, and to secure for himself " soul-freedom," he left his native country for the wilds of America. His subsequent history is sufficiently told in the pages that follow.—Ed.

[1]It appears by his own account that he was then in the thirty-second year of his age.

from Sempringham."[1] From whence it appears that Mr. Williams was acquainted with those two famous men, in our mother country, and the subject of that conversation shows that he could not then conform to the national church so far as they did.

Mr. Hubbard says, " Immediately after his arrival he was called by the church of Salem to join with Mr. Skelton ; but the Governor and Council being informed thereof, wrote to Mr. Endicott, to desire they would forbear any further proceeding therein, till the said council had conferred further about it. 1. Because he refused to join with the congregation [i. e. church] of Boston, because they would not make a public declaration of their repentance, for holding communion with the church of England while they lived there. 2. Because he declared it his opinion, that the civil magistrate might not punish any breach of the first table ; whereupon they for the present forbode proceeding with him, which occasioned his being called to Plymouth ;"[2] where, Governor Bradford says, " He was freely entertained, according to our poor ability, and exercised his gifts among us ; and after some time was admitted a member of the church, and his teaching well approved ; for the benefit whereof I still bless God, and am thankful to him even for his sharpest admonitions and reproofs, so far as they agreed with truth."[3]

As the two points which were so offensive to the rulers at Boston, were the foundation cause of their after proceedings against Mr. Williams, and closely affect the history of our country to this day, they demand our close attention. The Governor and Company of the Massachusetts colony held communion with the national church, and reflected upon their brethren who separated from her, while in their native island ; and on their departure from it, they from ' on

[1] Hubbard, p. 203.—Ed.   [2] Prince. p. 48. [377.]
[3] Reply to Cotton on the Bloody Tenet, p. 12.

board their chief ship wrote to those who were left behind,
April 7, 1630, in these words[1] :—

REVEREND FATHERS AND BRETHREN :— .... Howsoever your charity
may have met with some occasion of discouragement, through the misrepresentation of our intentions, ... yet we desire you would be pleased to
take notice of the principles and body of our company, as those who esteem
it our honor to call the church of England, from whence we rise, our dear
mother, and cannot part from our native country, where she specially
resideth, without much sadness of heart, and many tears in our eyes ;
ever acknowledging that such hope and part as we have obtained in the
common salvation, we have received in her bosom, and sucked it from her
breasts.   We leave it not therefore, as loathing that milk wherewith we
were nourished there, but blessing God for the parentage and education, as
members of the same body, shall always rejoice in her good. ....

JOHN WINTHROP, Governor.
CHARLES FINES.
GEORGE PHILIPS.
RICHARD SALTONSTALL.
ISAAC JOHNSON.
THOMAS DUDLEY.
WILLIAM CODDINGTON. &c.[2]

Now as Episcopalians down to this day, try to improve
this address, as an evidence that New England was first
planted by members of their church (though the foregoing
history shows that it was not so) we may safely conclude
that the ruling party of the nation did not neglect the
advantage hereby given to strengthen themselves then in their
way, which was so corrupt, that when the archbishop of
Canterbury a little after commenced a prosecution against
Mr. Cotton, the Earl of Dorset interceded for him, till he
found matters were got to such a pass that he sent Mr. Cotton word, " that if he had been guilty of drunkenness or
uncleanness, or any such lesser fault, he could have obtained
his pardon ; but inasmuch as he had been guilty of noncon-

---

[1]The letter was printed in London a few days after.   Neal's History of New England, Vol. I, p. 147.

[2]Massachusetts History, Vol. I, pp. 487—489.   [431, 432.]

formity and puritanism, the crime was unpardonable ; and therefore," said he, "you must fly for your safety[1]." Can we wonder that Mr. Williams, who came over the year after the aforesaid address was made, should not incline to join in fellowship with the authors of it, without some honest retraction ? Yet he was not so rigid but that he did hold occasional communion at the Lord's table in the church of Plymouth, with Governor Winthrop, and his minister, Mr. Wilson, of Boston, October 28, 1632[2].

Mr. Williams preached at Plymouth between two and three years, and then discerning in a leading part of the church a disagreement with some of his sentiments, and being invited to Salem, he requested a dismission there ; and though a number were unwilling for it, yet elder Brewster prevailed with the church to grant his request, fearing, he said, " that he would run the same course of rigid separation and anabaptistry, which Mr. John Smith at Amsterdam had done[3]. Such as did adhere to him were also dismissed, and removed with him, or not long after him to Salem[4]." The Court again

[1]Magnalia, B. 3, p. 19. [Vol. I. p. 241.]

[2]Prince's Annals, p. 70. [406.] —B.

See also, Winthrop, Vol. I, p. 91; Hubbard, p. 204.—Ed.

[3]Mr. Smith's church separated from the church of England with Mr. Robinson's, and removed a little before him into Holland. After Mr. Smith's death a number of his church returned and promoted the Baptist cause in London. Crosby's History, Vol. I, p. 268.—B.

Mr. John Smith began his ministry in the church of England. Early in the reign of James I, he renounced the discipline and ceremonies of that church and escaped impending persecution by flight to Holland. Here he joined the church of Brownists or Separatists, and soon became a man of note among them. Continuing to measure his belief and practice by the rule of Scripture, he was next compelled to renounce infant baptism. He was excluded by the Brownists, but his views spread so rapidly that a Baptist church was soon founded of which he became the pastor, and the other English churches in Holland were largely leavened with Baptist sentiments. Churchmen pointed to him as a warning to all separatists and nonconformists, exemplifying the legitimate end of their heresies; and the separatists themselves wrote no less than six distinct treatises against him. He was accused of having baptized himself, a charge which has since been sufficiently disproved. See Crosby, Vol. I, pp. 90—99, 265—268; Neal's History of the Puritans, Vol. II, pp. 72, 73; Cutting's Historical Vindications, pp. 57—60.—Ed.

[4]Morton, pp. 86, 87. [102.]

wrote to Salem against Mr. Williams, but could not prevent his being called to office there; and we are told that, " in one year's time he filled that place with principles of rigid separation, and tending to anabaptism[1]." For this they afterwards banished him; though as it was a confused piece of work for them thus to deal with him, so their historians have given the world a very confused account about it. Morton, Hubbard, Dr. Cotton Mather, and others, have set his banishment in 1634, yet all agree that he was not ordained till after Mr. Skelton's death, which was in August that year, and they tell us of a twelvemonth's labor with him and his church after his ordination, before his banishment; neither do they give us a better account of the true causes of that sentence, than they do of the date of it. I have taken much pains to collect as exact an account of this affair as possible, and have succeeded beyond my expectation.

The dates I find to be as follows:—Governor Winthrop and his Council first wrote to Salem against Mr. Williams, April 12, 1631[2], which occasioned his going to Plymouth. His first child was born there the first week in August, 1633[3], and Mr. Cotton, who arrived at Boston the fourth of September following, says he had removed into the Bay colony before his arrival[4]. Mr. Skelton died August 2, 1634[5], and we shall find proof enough that Mr. Williams was not banished till above a year afterward; so that instead of such hasty proceedings at Salem as his opponents would represent, he preached there more than a year before he was ordained, and as long after it.

As to the causes of his sentence, Mr. Morton has given us five articles, Mr. Hubbard six; Mr. Williams has reduced them to four, but Mr. Cotton is not willing to let them stand as he stated them, but tells us:—

[1]Morton, [103.] Hubbard, [204.]   [3]Providence Records.
[2]Prince, p. 26. [351.]   [4]Tenet washed, Part 2d, p. 4.
            [5]Magnalia, B. 3, p. 76. [Vol. I, p. 331.]

Two things there were, which (to my best observation and remembrance) caused the sentence of his banishment ; and two others fell in that hastened it.

1. His violent and tumultuous carriage against the patent.

By the patent it is, that we received allowance from the king to depart his kingdom, and to carry our goods with us, without offence to his officers, and without paying custom to himself. By the patent, certain select men, as magistrates and freemen, have power to make laws, and the magistrates to execute justice and judgment amongst the people, according to such laws. By the patent we have power to erect such a government of the church[1], as is most agreeable to the Word, to the estate of the people, and to the gaining of natives, in God's time, first to civility, and then to christianity.

This patent Mr. Williams publicly and vehemently preached against, as containing matter of falsehood, and injustice : falsehood, in making the king the first Christian prince who had discovered these parts ; and injustice, in giving the country to his English subjects which belonged to the native Indians[2].

Let it be here noted, that we have no proof that Mr. Williams ever preached or objected against the whole patent, or charter, without distinction, much less against that part of it which constituted them a civil government. His own account of this matter informs us, that the sin of the patents which lay so heavy on his mind was, that therein " Christian kings (so called) are invested with a right, by virtue of their Christianity, to take and give away the lands and countries of other men." And he tells us that this evil so deeply afflicted his soul, that, " before his troubles and banishment, he drew up a letter, not without the approbation of some of the chief of New England, then tender also upon this point before God, directed unto the king himself, humbly acknowledging the evil of that part of the patent which respects the donation of lands, &c[3].

What grounds Mr. Williams and others had for this concern will plainly appear by what follows ; for in the said patent from Charles the First, he recites that which was given by his father, King James the First, dated November 3, 1620, wherein he

---

[1]This clause is not truth.   [2]Tenet washed, p. 27.
[3]Reply to Cotton on the Bloody Tenet, pp. 276, 277.

Gave and granted unto the Council established at Plymouth, in the county of Devon, ... all that part of America lying and being in breadth from forty degrees of northerly latitude from the equinoctial line to forty-eight degrees of the said northerly latitude inclusively, and in length of and within all the breadth aforesaid throughout the main land from sea to sea, together also with all the firm lands, soils, grounds, havens, ports, rivers, waters, fishing, mines and minerals, ... jurisdictions, privileges, franchises, and pre-eminences, both within the said tract of land upon the main, and also within the islands and seas adjoining; provided always, that the said islands, or any of the premises by the said letters patent intended and meant to be granted, were not then actually possessed or inhabited by any other Christian prince or state. . . . . To have and to hold, possess and enjoy, all and singular the aforesaid continent lands, ... and every part and parcel thereof, unto the said Council, and their heirs and assigns forever. . . . . To be holden of our said most dear and royal father, his heirs and successors, as of his manor of East Greenwich in the county of Kent.

Then King Charles went on to name the Massachusetts Company, and to describe the limits of their colony through the main lands of America, and granted it to them in the same manner, "to be holden of us, our heirs and successors, as of our manor of East Greenwich[1]," &c.

Can any man claim a fuller property in any land in the world, than here was assumed over this vast tract of America? And though the men who had taken this patent banished Mr. Williams out of it, yet before we have done we may see this very principle which he abhorred turned back into their own bosoms, and made use of by a tyrannical party to give them a severe scourging, after their patent was vacated.

The other foundation cause of Mr. Williams's banishment Mr. Cotton gives in these words:—

2. The magistrates, and other members of the General Court, upon intelligence of some Episcopal and malignant practices against the country, made an order of Court to take trial of the fidelity of the people, not by imposing upon them, but by offering to them an oath of fidelity; that in case any should refuse to take it, they might not betrust them with place of public charge and command. This oath when it came abroad he vehe-

[1]Massachusetts History, Vol. 3, pp. 1—4.

mently withstood, and dissuaded sundry from it, partly because it was, as he said, Christ's prerogative to have his office established by oath ; partly because an oath was part of God's worship, and God's worship was not to be put upon carnal persons, as he conceived many of the people to be.   So the Court was forced to desist from that proceeding[1].

This case thus stated carries a sad face with it, but one acquainted with the history of the country would be ready to doubt whether it was truly stated or not; for every freeman had taken an oath of fidelity to the government before that time, and if there was no intent of imposing but only of offering this new oath, could they not find men enough for officers that would take it?   Indeed when I come to find how the truth of this matter was, by the colony records, and to think that Mr. Cotton had them at his door when he wrote, I am the most shocked about him by this publication of his against Mr. Williams, of anything I ever met with concerning him. Upon the colony records, when the General Assembly met at Boston, May 14, 1634, I find these words:—

It was agreed and ordered, that the former oath of freemen shall be revoked, so far as it is dissonant from the oath of freemen here underwritten, and that those that received the former oath shall stand bound no further thereby to any intent or purpose than this new oath ties those that take the same.

THE OATH OF A FREEMAN.

I, A. B., being by God's providence an inhabitant and freeman within the jurisdiction of this commonweal, do freely acknowledge myself to be subject to the government thereof, and therefore do here swear, by the great and dreadful name of the ever living God, that I will be true and faithful to the same, and will accordingly yield assistance and support thereunto with my person and estate as in equity I am bound, and I will also truly endeavor to maintain and preserve all the liberties and privileges thereof, submitting myself to the wholesome laws and orders made and established by the same.   And further, that I will not plot nor practise any evil against it, nor consent to any that shall so do, but will truly discover and reveal the same to lawful authority now here established, for the speedy preventing thereof.   Moreover I do solemnly bind myself in the sight of

[1] Tenet washed, pp. 28, 29.

God, that when I shall be called to give my voice, touching any such matter of this state, wherein freemen are to deal, I will give my vote and suffrage, as I shall judge in mine own conscience may best conduce and tend to the public weal of the body, without respect of persons or favor of any man ; so help me God in the Lord Jesus Christ.

This oath was framed and taken before they proceeded to election at the time above said. When the Assembly met again at Newtown, now Cambridge, March 4, 1635, they enacted as follows :—

It is ordered that every man of or above the age of sixteen years, who hath been or shall hereafter be resident within this jurisdiction, by the space of six months (as well servants as others) and not enfranchised, shall take the oath of residents, before the Governor, Deputy Governor, or two of the next Assistants, who shall have power to convent him for that purpose, and upon his refusal, to bind him over to the next Court of Assistants, and upon his refusal the second time, to be punished at the discretion of the Court.

It is ordered, that the freeman's oath shall be given to every man of or above the age of sixteen years, the clause for election of magistrates only excepted[1].

Now let the candid reader judge,

1. Who was the best friend to charter-rights ? The Massachusetts Company were limited, in three different passages of their patent, not to make any laws contrary to the laws of England ; yet one professed design of this new oath, was to guard against Episcopal practices, to effect which they left out the clause in their former oath, which bound them to submit to " all such laws, orders, sentences and decrees, as should be lawfully made and published by them ;" and instead of it obliged men to swear to submit " to the wholesome laws and orders made and established " by the government of this commonwealth. And though Mr. Cotton asserts that they did not impose but only offer this new oath, yet the colony records are express, that every man who resided within their jurisdiction six months, ser-

[1]Massachusetts Records.

vants as well as others, must swear to obey all their wholesome laws and orders, or be punished at their discretion;
yea, and also swear to reveal any plot that they should know
of against such government, "to lawful authority now here
established;"— that is, not to complain to any but themselves.

2. From whence came the power that presumed to absolve
themselves and others from their oath, to keep to acts lawfully made, and to substitute the word *wholesome* in the
room of it? Let the learned Cotton Mather answer the
question. Says he,—

The reforming churches, flying from Rome, carried some of them
more, some of them less, all of them something, of Rome with them;
especially in that spirit of imposition and persecution, which has too much
cleaved unto them all[1].

That spirit of imposition and persecution ran so high in
England at the time we are upon, that King Charles the
First gave a commission, April 28, 1634, to Archbishop
Laud, and ten courtiers more[2], some of them known paptists,
as follows :—

We do constitute you, our said Archbishop of Canterbury, &c., or any
five or more of you, our counsellors ; and to you or to any five or more of
you, do commit and give power of protection and government, as well
over the English colonies already planted, as over all such other colonies,
which by any of our people of England hereafter shall be deduced into
any other like parts whatsoever, and power to make laws, ordinances and
constitutions, concerning either the state public of the said colonies, or
utility of private persons and their lands, goods, debts and succession,
within the precincts of the same, and for ordering and directing of them,
in their demeanors towards foreign princes and their people, and likewise
towards us and our subjects, as well within any foreign parts whatsoever
beyond the seas, as during their voyages, or upon the seas to and

[1]His son Dr. Samuel Mather's Apology for the churches of New England, Appendix, p. 149.

[2]Lord Coventry, the Archbishop of York, the Earls of Portland, Manchester,
Arundel, and Dorset, Lord Cottington, Sir Thomas Edmunds, and the Secretaries
Cook and Windebank.

4

from the same; and for relief and support of the clergy, and the
rule and cure of the souls of our people living in those parts, and
for consigning of convenient maintenance unto them by tithes, obla-
tions and other profits accruing, according to your good discretion, with
the advice of two or three of our bishops, whom you shall think fit to call
unto your consultations, touching the distribution of such maintenance
unto the clergy, and all other matters ecclesiastical, and to inflict punishment on all offenders or violators of constitutions and ordinances, either by
imprisonments or other restraints, or by loss of life or members, according
as the quality of the offence shall require; with power also, our royal
assent being first had and obtained, to remove all Governors and Presi-
dents of the said colonies, upon just cause appearing, from their several
places, and to appoint others in their stead: . . . . and power also to
ordain temporal judges and civil magistrates to determine of civil causes,
with such powers, in such a form, as to you or any five or more of you
shall seem expedient; and also to ordain judges, magistrates and officers
for and concerning courts ecclesiastical, with such power and such a form,
as to you or any five or more of you, with the advice of the bishops suf-
fragan to the Archbishop of Canterbury for the time being, shall be held
meet. . . . . Giving, moreover, and granting to you, that if it shall appear,
that any officer or Governor of the said colonies shall unjustly wrong
one another, or shall not suppress all rebels to us, or such as shall not obey
our commands, that then it shall be lawful, upon advice with ourself first
had, for the causes aforesaid, or upon any other just reason, to remand and
cause the offender to return into England, or into any other place, according as in your good *discretions* you shall think just and necessary.   And
we do furthermore give unto you, or any five or more of you, letters
patent and other writings whatsoever, of us or of our royal predecessors
granted, for or concerning the planting of any colonies, in any countries,
provinces, islands or territories whatsoever beyond the seas; and if upon
view thereof, the same shall appear to you, or any five or more of you, to
have been surreptitiously and unduly obtained, or that any privileges or
liberties therein granted be hurtful to us, our crown or prerogative royal,
or to any foreign princes, to cause the same to be revoked, and to do all
other things, which shall be necessary for the *wholesome* government' and
protection of the said colonies, and our people therein abiding[1].

Thus the words "*discretion*" and "*wholesome*" were brought
in to violate charters and all public faith, and to set up
tyranny over the colonies.   But Mr. Edward Winslow being

----

[1] Massachusetts History, Vol. I. pp. 502—506. [440—443.]

sent over agent for the country, by his indefatigable endeavors, and the influence of some great men, prevented the taking place of this arbitrary commission; upon which Laud turned his resentment against him, and got him imprisoned ooventeen weeks in the Fleet prison, in London, for having sometimes taught publicly in the church of Plymouth, and for marrying people, which Laud called "assuming the Ministerial office[1]."

Had the Massachusetts fathers taken only lawful and prudent methods to guard against such Episcopal and malignant practices as these, they would have been justified, and applauded by posterity; but now we mourn to think that they brought so much of the same distemper into this country with them as they did.

The same Court that passed the act to oblige all to take the above oath, or be punished at their discretion, also passed the following, viz. :—

This Court doth entreat of the brethren and elders of every church within this jurisdiction, that they will consult and advise of one uniform order of discipline in the churches, agreeable to the Scriptures, and then to consider how far the magistrates are bound to interpose for the preservation of that uniformity and peace of the churches[2].

Upon this Mr. Williams publicly preached against the oath they had framed, of submission to such a power; for which the Governor and Assistants called him before them, March 30, 1635, when " he was heard before all the ministers, and," according to Governor Winthrop's opinion, was " clearly refuted[3]." The two things which Mr. Cotton says hastened his banishment were, Mr. Williams's stirring up his church to write to other churches to which those rulers belonged, admonishing them of injustice about some land near Salem; and his separating from his own church when

---

[1]Plymouth Register, pp. 12.–14.   [2]Massachusetts Records.
[3]Winthrop's Journal. [Vol. I, p. 158.]

they turned against him in these things[1].   Concerning the first of these articles Governor Winthrop says,—

" Salem men preferred a petition at the General Court, May, 1635, for some land in Marblehead neck, which they did challenge as belonging to their town ; but because they had chosen Mr. Williams their teacher while he stood under question of authority, and so offered contempt to the magistracy, &c. their petition was refused till, &c.   Upon this the church of Salem wrote to other churches to admonish the magistrates of this as a heinous sin, and likewise the deputies, &c.[2]

By the colony records I find that the town of Marblehead was first granted by the Assembly which met May 6, 1635, when sundry parcels of land which Salem had improved were granted to them as soon as they should want them, only with order that Marblehead should pay Salem for what they had done upon the land; among the rest, " the land betwixt the clift and the forest river, near Marblehead" was so granted, but with this proviso, " that if in the meantime the inhabitants of Salem can satisfy the Court that they have true right unto it, that then it shall belong unto the inhabitants thereof."

The generality of those inhabitants turned the next fall, and joined with the rulers in banishing Mr. Williams, and when the General Assembly met again, March 3, 1636, I find these words, viz. : " It was proved this Court that Marble Neck belongs to Salem[3]."   Now what can be more natural

---

[1] Tenet washed, pp. 29, 30.   [2] Winthrop's Journal. [Vol I. p. 164.]
[3] Massachusetts Records.

There are indications that Salem was not bribed into acquiescence with Williams's banishment as easily as these words might suggest.   Neal writes, "Sentence of banishment being read against Mr. Williams, the whole town of Salem was in an uproar ; for he was esteemed an honest, disinterested man and of popular talents in the pulpit ; and such was the compassion of the people, occasioned by his followers raising a cry of persecution against him, that he would have carried off the greater part of the inhabitants of the town if the ministers of Boston had not interposed by sending an admonition to the church of Salem, with a confutation in writing of Mr. Williams's errors, showing their tendency to disturb the public peace both in church and State, though he always opposed what he called the Bloody Tenet, that is, every kind and degree of persecution for conscience sake ; but by this means the greater part of the people were satisfied, or content at least to abandon their dear Mr. Williams, to whose opinions and doctrine they were but too much devoted."   Neal's History of New England, Vol. I, pp. 159, 160.   ED.

than to conclude from hence that the way for Salem to satisfy the Court that they had a true right to their land, was to submit their ecclesiastical as well as civil affairs to their direction?

At a General Court, July 8, 1635,—

Mr. Williams, of Salem, was summoned, and did appear. It was laid to his charge, that being under question before the magistracy and churches for divers dangerous opinions, viz. :   1. That the magistrate ought not to punish the breach of the first table, otherwise than in such case as did disturb the civil peace.   2. That he ought not to tender an oath to an unregenerate man.   3. That a man ought not to pray with such, though wife, children, &c.   4. That a man ought not to give thanks after sacrament, nor after meals [meat] ; and that the other churches were about to write to the church of Salem to admonish him of these errors, understanding [notwithstanding] the church had called him to the office of a teacher. The said opinions were adjudged by all the magistracy and ministers (who were desired to be present) to be erroneous, and very dangerous, and the calling of him to office at that time was judged a great contempt of authority.   So in fine there was given to him and the church of Salem to consider of these things till the next General Court, and then either to give satisfaction to the Court, or else to expect the sentence ; it being professedly declared by the ministers (at the request of the Court to give their advice) that they who should obstinately maintain such opinions (whereby the church might come [run] into heresy, apostacy or tyranny, and yet the civil magistrate could not intermeddle) were to be removed, and that the other churches ought to request the magistrate so to do[1].

This is the most plain and ingenuous account of the real cause of Mr. Williams's banishment that I have ever met with, from any who were opposed to him and carries the more weight with it, as it was written by one of the greatest gentlemen in the country, in the time of it, and who was personally concerned in these transactions. And by the first and last of this account it is evident, that the grand difficulty they had with Mr. Williams was, his denying the civil magtrate's right to govern in ecclesiastical affairs.

This honorable writer informs us, that on August 15, 1635,

---

[1]Governor Winthrop's Journal, Vol. I, pp. [162. 163.]

Mr. Williams, pastor of Salem, being sick, and not able to speak, wrote to his church a protestation· that he could not communicate with the churches in the Bay, neither would he communicate with them, except they would refuse communion with the rest : but the whole church was grieved thereby.

September 1.—At this General Court, Mr. Endicott made a protestation, in justification of the letters formerly sent from Salem to the other churches against the magistracy and deputies, for which he was committed ; but the same day he came and acknowledged his fault, and was discharged[1].

October.—At this General Court Mr. Williams, the teacher of Salem, was again convented, and all the ministers in the Bay being desired to be present, he was charged with his said two letters, that to the churches, complaining of the magistrates for injustice, &c. and the other to his own church. . . . . He justified both these letters, and maintained all his opinions ; and being offered further conference or disputation, and another respite, he chose to dispute presently, so Mr. Hooker was appointed to dispute with him, but could not reduce him from any of his errors, so the next morning the court sentenced him to depart out of our jurisdiction, within six weeks, all the ministers approving the sentence ; and his own church had him under question also for the same case, and he at his return home refused communion with his own church, who openly disclaimed his errors, and wrote an humble submission to the magistrates, acknowledging their fault in joining with Mr. Williams in that letter to the churches against them[2].

---

[1]Winthrop's Journal. [Vol. I, p. 166.] Mr. Endicott afterwards acted at the head of the most bloody persecutions in this country.—B.

The above sentence refers to the proceedings against Quakers, which culminated in the hanging of four persons of that sect in 1659. See Chap. v.—ED.

[2]Winthrop's Journal, [Vol. I, pp. 170, 171.] The next time the Court met they confirmed their land to them, as before observed. The province records agree with this account, only they do not set any date after the Court met in September, before Mr. Williams's sentence; but it might be October before it was passed.—B.

The exact date of Roger Williams's banishment is still undetermined. Knowles writes in his Memoir of Roger Williams, p. 73, note, " Winthrop places the banishment under date of October, but the Colonial Records, (I. 163,) state that it took place November 3, 1635." Elton, Life of Roger Williams, p. 32, gives the same date, doubtless taking it from Knowles. It were well if the matter could be thus easily settled; but the dates of the Colonial Records on this point are most uncertain. The Records give account of three sessions of the Court, dating them respectively September 1, November 3, and September 2. In the last of these, after a few items of business, there is the date September 3, in the margin; and after many other items, comes the sentence of Roger Williams. Mr. Knowles seems to have regarded the two last named sessions as belonging to the date November 3, either overlooking the dates September 2 and September 3, or rejecting them as spurious.

John Smith was banished at the same time with Mr. Williams, for his dangerous opinions, but we are not told what they were. It seems that the Court after this gave Mr. Williams liberty to stay till Spring, only enjoining it upon him not to go about to draw others to his opinions ; but in January, 1636, the Governor and Assistants were informed, that he received and preached to companies in his house, " even of such points as he had been censured for." Upon which they agreed to send him into England by a ship then ready to depart. " The reason was, because he had drawn about twenty people to his opinions, who intended to erect a plantation about the Narragansett Bay, from whence infection would easily spread into these churches, the people being many of them much taken with the apprehension of his godliness." They sent for him to come to Boston, but he sent an excuse ; upon which they sent a pinnace, with a commission to Captain Underhill, to apprehend him and carry him on board the ship then at Nantasket; but when they "came to his house, they found he had been gone three days[1]."

This I believe is the exact date of his departure, instead of being in 1634, as their historians have represented. Sixteen years after, Mr. Williams, referring to words of Mr. Cotton, says,—

" These passages occasion me to remember a serious question which many fearing God have made, to wit, whether the promise of God's Spirit blessing conferences, be so comfortably to be expected in New England

That there is an error is evident, but it cannot be remedied by rejecting entirely the dates last named, for that would assign to November 3 much more business than could possibly be transacted in one day. Probably no better explanation can be given than that of Backus. By that, we must regard the record dated November 3 as out of place, inscribed where it is by mistake ; and must suppose that the business under date of September 3 really occupied the Court till October. Unless the Court was more diligent than similar bodies in later times, a full month's work is recorded there. Thus the Colonial Records will be made to harmonize with Winthrop's Journal which is almost invariably accurate, and the probable date of Williams's banishment remains as Backus gives it, October, 1635.—ED.

[1]Winthrop's Journal. [Vol. I, pp. 175, 176.]

because of those many public sins which most of God's people in New England lie under, and one especially, to wit, the framing a Gospel- or Christ to themselves without a cross, not professing nor practicing that in Old, which they professedly came over to enjoy with peace and liberty from any cross of Christ in New. I know those thoughts have deeply possessed not a few, considering also the sin of the patents, wherein Christian kings, so called, are invested with right, by virtue of their Christianity, to take and give away the lands and countries of other men; as also considering the unchristian oaths swallowed down, at their coming forth from Old England, especially in superstitious Laud his time and domineering[1]."

It is evident by the foregoing list of errors charged upon Mr. Williams, that the Massachusetts ministers and rulers meant to carry their uniformity so far, as to oblige ministers and Christians, throughout their jurisdiction, not only to ask a blessing at the Lord's table and at common meals, but also to return thanks afterward; and it is likely that this straining of that matter beyond Scriptural example, has had not a little influence upon many since to carry them to the other extreme. Be that as it may, what human heart can be unaffected with the thought that a people who had been sorely persecuted in their own country, so as to flee three thousand miles into a wilderness for religious liberty, yet should have that imposing temper cleaving so fast to them, as not to be willing to let a godly minister, who testified against it, stay even in any neighboring part of this wilderness, but it moved them to attempt to take him by force, to send him back into the land of their persecutors! To avoid this he fled to the heathen in the depth of winter, and obtained such favor in their sight, that Osamaquin (otherwise called Massasoit) chief sachem at Mount Hope, made him a grant of part of that which is since called Rehoboth; yet the place was so far then from answering to its present name, that a letter and messenger was sent from Plymouth to let him know there was not *room* for him in

---

[1]Reply to Cotton, p. 276. Note, it was not all oaths, but those only which he esteemed unchristian ones that he objected against.

that place, because within their patent. " This is a lamentation, and shall be for a lamentation."

Mr. Williams's own testimony, upon a particular occasion at Providence, twenty-five years after, I think deserves notice here. Says he :—

I testify and declare in the holy presence of God, that when at my first coming into these parts I obtained the lands of Secunk of Osamaquin, the then chief sachem on that side, the Governor of Plymouth, Mr. Winslow, wrote to me, in the name of their government, their claim of Secunk to be in their jurisdiction, as also their advice to remove but over the river unto this side, where now by God's merciful providence we are, and then I should be out of their claim, and be as free as themselves, and loving neighbors together[1]. After I had obtained this place, now called Providence, of Canonicus and Myantinomy, the chief Nanhigganset sachems deceased, Osamaquin (the sachem aforesaid, also deceased) laid his claim to this place also. This forced me to repair to the Nanhigganset sachems aforesaid, who declared, that Osamaquin was their subject, and had solemnly, himself in person, with ten men, subjected himself and his lands unto them at the Nanhigganset, and now he seemed to revolt from his loyalty, under the shelter of the English at Plymouth[2]. This I declared from the Nanhigganset sachems to Osamaquin, who without any stick acknowledged to be true, that he had so subjected as the Nanhigganset sachems had affirmed ; but withal he affirmed that he was not subdued by war, which himself and his father had maintained against the Nanhiggansets ; but God, said he, subdued us by a plague, which swept away my people, and forced me to yield. This conviction and confession of his, together with gratuities to himself, brethren and followers, made him often profess, that he was pleased that I should here be his neighbor, and the rather because he and I had been great friends at Plymouth ; and also because his and my friends at Plymouth advised him to be at peace and friendship with me ; and he hoped that our children after us would be good friends together. And whereas there hath been often speech of Providence falling in Plymouth jurisdiction by virtue of Osamaquin's claim ; I add unto the testimonies abovesaid, that the Governor, Mr.

[1]This by the way shows a great difference between the temper of Plymouth and Massachusetts rulers of which we shall yet see more. The chief sachems' names are very differently spelt in the different writings I have met with.

[2]This perfectly agrees with the account we have of Massasoit's or Osamaquin's league he made with Plymouth people the spring after their last coming, and of the Narragansett's threatenings on that account. Prince's Chronology, pp. 102, 116, [187, 188, 199, 200.]

Bradford, deceased, and other of their Magistrates, declared unto me, both by conference and writing, that they and their government were satisfied, and resolved never to molest Providence, nor to claim beyond Secunk, but to continue loving friends and neighbors (among the barbarians) together. This is the true sum and substance of many passages between our countrymen of Plymouth and Osamaquin, and me.

ROGER WILLIAMS.[1]

The above date of Mr. Williams's removal is confirmed by Mr. Winslow's being then Governor of Plymouth; for 1636 was the only year that he sustained that office between 1633 and 1644. And as it appeared by Plymouth records that he entered on his government the first of March that year, we may conclude that Mr. Williams fled to Secunk in the depth of winter, and removed with a few friends over the river in the spring[2]. Here let us admire the wisdom

---

[1]Copied from the original, in his own hand writing, dated "Providence, 13, 10, 1661, (so called)."

[2]It is said that he, with Thomas Angell, a hired servant, and some others, went over in a canoe, and were saluted by the Indians near the lower ferry, by the word *Whatcheere?* i. e. How do you do? which gave name to a field, which Mr. Williams sold many years after, and in the deed says he satisfied the owner for it, and planted it, at his first coming, with his own hands. They went round till they got to a pleasant spring above, where is now the great bridge, where they landed; and near to which both he and Angell lived to old age.—B.

The date of Roger Williams's removal from Seekonk to Providence can be reached only approximately. In a letter to Major Mason of Connecticut, written June 22, 1770, published in the Massachusetts Historical Collections, Vol. i. p. 275, he writes that he "begun to build and plant at Seekonk," and that his removal occasioned his "loss of a harvest that year." His letter to the Massachusetts colony announcing the murder of Oldham, which Governor Winthrop states (Vol. I, p. 190) was received July 26, seems to have been written from Providence. If so, his removal must have been before this date, and after the beginning of planting time. From these dates Knowles (Memoir, p. 104) conjectures that it took place about the middle of June. Elton, (Life of Roger Williams, p. 38,) and Gamwell, (Life of Roger Williams, p. 64,) place it in the latter part of June. The words "I *begun* to build and *plant* at Seekonk" might suggest a somewhat earlier date, as the season of planting does not extend beyond the last of May. There is perhaps another clue which will fix the time more definitely. In the letter to Major Mason already quoted, Williams writes that between his "friends of the Bay and Plymouth,' he was "sorely tossed for one fourteen weeks, not knowing what bread or bed did mean." His departure from Salem was in January; at what part of the month we do not know. Elton states (p. 33) that his citation before the General Court, the immediate cause of his flight, was January 11th, but here he evidently mistakes the words of Winthrop, "11 mo. January" which mean only January the eleventh

that governs the world. " As Joseph was sold by his envious brethren, with intent to get him out of their way, yet divine providence overruled this cruel action quite otherwise than they intended, and made it the means of their future preservation ; so the harsh treatment and cruel exile of Mr. Williams seem designed by his brethren for the same evil end, but was, by the goodness of the same over-ruling hand, turned to the most beneficent purposes[1]."

Just at this juncture, the Pequods, a powerful Indian tribe, who lived upon the lands where are now the towns of Groton and Stonington, were forming plots against the English colonies, even the very year that those of Connecticut and Providence began, and when Boston was but six years old ; and as a vessel was sent by the government from thence, under the command of John Oldham, to trade with the natives at Block Island, about fourteen Indians boarded the vessel, and murdered him ; but as John Gallop happened to come upon them, in his return from Connecticut river, they leaped into the sea, where some were drowned, and others reached the shore. The first news of this sad event that they received was from Mr. Williams's pen, by two Indians who went with Oldham, and one from Canonicus, a Narragansett sachem, who arrived at Boston, July 26, 1636. Governor Vane wrote back to Mr. Williams, to let the Narragansetts know that they expected them to send home two boys who were with Oldham, and to take revenge upon the islanders. Four days after the boys came home with one of Miantinomy's men, with another letter from Mr. Williams, informing that said sachem had caused the sachem of Niantick to send to Block Island for them, and that he had near

month, according to the old style of reckoning. If we suppose Williams's escape to have taken place the latter part of January, counting fourteen weeks, we have near the middle of May, as the date of his settlement in Providence. This would be late enough for him to have "begun to plant at Seekonk," and, considering the bargains which he must make with the Indians and other delays in founding a new settlement, late enough to occasion his " loss of a harvest that year."—ED.

[1] History of Providence.

a hundred fathom of peag[1], and much other goods of Old-ham's which should be reserved for them, and that three of the seven Indians who were drowned were sachems[2]. August 26 came a third letter from Mr. Williams. Governor Winthrop says :—

> In these Indian troubles Mr. Williams was assiduous to influence the Narragansetts in favor of the English, and to keep them from joining with the Pequods[3].
>
> Sept. Canonicus sent word of some English whom the Pequods had killed at Saybrook, and Mr. Williams wrote that the Pequods and Narragansetts were at truce, and that Miantonomoh told him that the Pequods had labored to persuade them that the English were minded to destroy all the Indians. Whereupon we sent for Miantonomoh to come to us.

Accordingly he and two of Canonicus's sons and another sachem, and near twenty of their men whom they call sannups, came to Boston October 21, where the Governor called together all the magistrates and ministers, and next day a firm league was signed between them. "But because they could not make them well understand the articles, they told them they would send a copy of them to Mr. Williams, who

[1]Wampum.—ED.

[2]Hubbard, [249, 250.] Hubbard also quotes from Winthrop's Journal, Vol. I, p. 190, the statement that ten or eleven Indians were drowned.—ED.

[3]Hubbard's Journal.—B.

"The warlike tribe [the Pequods] courted the alliance of its neighbors, the Narragansetts and the Mohegans, that a union and a general rising of the natives might sweep the hated intruders from the ancient hunting grounds of the Indian race. The design could be frustrated by none but Roger Williams; and the exile, who had been the first to communicate to the Governor of Massachusetts the news of the impending conspiracy, encountered the extremity of peril with magnanimous heroism. Having received letters from Vane and the Council of Massachusetts requesting his utmost and speediest endeavors to prevent the league, neither storms of wind nor high seas could detain the adventurous envoy. Shipping himself alone in a poor canoe, every moment at the hazard of his life, he hastened to the house of the sachem of the Narragansetts. The Pequod ambassadors, reeking with blood, were already there, and for three days and nights the business compelled him to lodge and mix with them, having cause every night to expect their knives at his throat. The Narragansetts were wavering; but Roger Williams succeeded in dissolving the formidable conspiracy. It was the most intrepid and most successful achievement in the whole Pequod war;—an action as perilous in its execution as it was fortunate in its issue." Bancroft, Vol. I, p. 398.—ED.

could best interpret the same to them.   So after dinner they took leave[1]."   What would the Massachusetts have now done, if Mr. Williams had been sent to England, as they had intended, the winter before!

Let us now review their religious state.   In October, 1635, arrived Mr. Thomas Shepard and Hugh Peters, two ministers, who were much improved afterward ; also Mr. afterward Sir Henry Vane, the latter of whom was admitted a member of Boston church November 1[2].   At the General Assembly held March 3, 1636, it was

Ordered, that all persons are to take notice that this Court doth not, nor will hereafter, approve of any such companies of men, as shall henceforth join in any pretended way of church fellowship, without they shall first acquaint the magistrates and the elders of the greater part of the churches in this jurisdiction with their intentions, and have their approbation herein. And further it is ordered, that no person being a member of any church which shall hereafter be gathered without the approbation of the magistrates and the greater part of said churches, shall be admitted to the freedom of this commonwealth[3].

At the election at Boston, May 25, Mr. Vane was chosen Governor, and Mr. Winthrop Deputy Governor ; and a standing Council was formed of three men.   "The reason was, for that it was shewed from the word of God, &c., that the principal magistrates ought to be for life."   Mr. Winthrop and Mr. Dudley were chosen for life, and Governor Vane to be their President[4].   The next year Mr. Endicott

---

[1]Winthrop, [Vol. I, pp. 196, 199]; Hubbard, [253.]

[2]Winthrop, [Vol. I, p. 170.]

[3]Massachusetts Records.

[4]Winthrop's Journal, [184.]   Mr. Cotton wrote this year to Lord Say and Seal, and says, " God hath so framed the state of church government and ordinances, that they may be compatible to any commonwealth, though never so much disordered in its frame.   But yet when a commonwealth hath liberty to mould its own frame, I conceive the Scripture hath given full direction for the right ordering of the same, and that in such sort as may best maintain the *euexia* [well being] of the church.   Mr. Hooker doth often quote a saying out of Mr. Cartwright, that no man fashioneth his house to his hangings, but his hangings to his house.   It is better that the commonwealth be fashioned to the setting forth of God's house, which is his church; than to accommodate the church frame to the civil state. . . . . Nor need

was chosen for life in Vane's room. This Council soon
found work to do, one article of which here follows :—

To the Constable of Salem :

Whereas we are credibly informed that divers persons (both of men and
women) within your town, do disorderly assemble themselves both on the
Lord's days and at other times, contemptuously refusing to come to the solemn meetings of the church there (or being some of them justly cast out)
do obstinately refuse to submit themselves, that·they might be again received ; but do make conventions, and seduce diverse persons of weak capacity,·and have already withdrawn some of them from the church, and
hereby have caused much (not only disturbance in the church, but also)
disorders and damage in the civil state ; . . . . these are therefore to require you forthwith to repair unto all such disorderly persons ; and signify
to them that said course is very offensive to the government here, and may
no longer be suffered, and therefore command them from us, to refrain all
such disordered assemblies, and pretended church meetings ; and either to
conform themselves to the laws and orders of this government, being established according to the rule of God's word ; or else let them be assured
that we shall by God's assistance take some such strict and speedy course
for the reformation of these disorders, and preventing the evils which may
otherways ensue, as our duty to God and charge over his people do call for
from us. And when you have given them this admonition you shall diligently attend how it is observed, and certify us accordingly, as you will answer your neglect herein at your peril.

H. VANE, Gov.
JO. WINTHROP, Dept.
THO. DUDLEY[1].

From Boston this 30th of the 3d month, 1636.

They were somewhat too short in declaring the laws and
orders of their government already established, for that
work was yet to do; therefore this Court now passed the
following act, viz. :—

The Governor, Deputy Governor, Thomas Dudley, John Haynes, Richard Bellingham, Esquires, Mr. Cotton, Mr. Peters, and Mr. Shepard, are

we fear, that this course will, in time, cast the commonwealth into distractions, and
popular confusions. . . . . Purity preserved in the church, will preserve well ordered
liberty in the people, and both of them establish well balanced authority in the magistrates." Massachusetts History, Vol. I, pp. 497, 500. [219, 220.] His great mistake herein will soon appear.

[1]Winthrop.

entreated to make a draught of laws agreeable to the word of God, which may be the fundamentals of this commonwealth, and to present the same to the next General Court; and it is ordered that in the mean time the magistrates and their associates shall proceed in the courts to hear and determine all causes according to the laws now established, and where there is no law, then as near the laws of God as they can[1].

Soon after this came on such disputes in the country about grace and works, that " it began to be as common there to distinguish between men being under a covenant of works, and a covenant of grace, as in other countries between protestants and paptists[2]." It divided the General Court,

[1]Massachusetts Records. From the beginning, their Governor and Assistants had been their executive court, till the March preceding, when they took in associates with the magistrates, and formed inferior courts in their several towns, to try causes not exceeding ten pounds; from whence appeals might be made to the Court of Assistants.

[2]Hubbard, [294]. Captain Johnson says, " That you may understand their way of broaching their abominable errors, it was in dividing those things the Lord hath united in his work of conversion continued, carrying on a soul to heaven, in these four particulars:

" 1. In dividing between the word and the word, under pretense of a legal gospel, persuading the people their ministers were legal preachers, teaching them little better than popery, and unfit for gospel churches; denying them to be any ministers of Christ, that preach any preparation work, by shewing men what the law requires. Here's nothing, says one of them, but preaching out of the law and the prophets. Truly, says another, I have not heard a pure gospel sermon from any of them.

" 2. In separating Christ and his graces, in manifesting himself to be in the soul; and this they say makes much for the magnifying of free grace; and indeed they made it so free, that the soul that receives it shall never taste any of it by their consent, but remain still a dry branch as before. These legal Pharisees, says one of them, tell us of a thing they call inherent grace, and of a man being made a new creature; but I am sure the best of them go on in their legal duties and performances still, sorrowing for sin, hearing of sermons, observing duty morning and evening, and many such like matters. Tush man, says another, you shall hear more than this; I was discoursing with one of their scholastic preacher's disciples, a professed convert, and yet when he came to pray he begged for the forgiveness of his sins; I asked him why he used that vain repetition. since he did believe he was justified by Christ already? He made me an answer not worth repeating; but when I told him God could see no sin in his people, no more than I could see that which was covered close from my eyesight, he told me I spake little less than blasphemy. So ignorant are these men, and their learned guides also; who persuade them the more they have of the indwelling of the spirit of Christ, the better they shall be enabled to these legal duties. Nay, quoth the other, I can tell you more than all this; they make it an evidence of their good estate, even their sanctification, and yet these men would make people believe they are against popery.

and from thence it was carried into Boston church, where
it caused sharp debates on Lord's day, December 31, between the two ministers, Cotton and Wilson, and between
the Governor and Deputy Governor, who were members of
it[1]. In this controversy Mr. Cotton found what it was to
fall into the minority, for none of the ministers held fully
with him but Mr. Wheelwright, who was not a settled minister, but was preaching to a branch of Boston church, at
the place now called Braintree ; where, at a general fast on
January 19, 1637, he delivered a discourse that greatly increased the flame. Under his third use, we are told that he
said, "The second sort of people that are to be condemned,
are all such as do set themselves against the Lord Jesus
Christ, such are the greatest enemies to the State as can be ;
if they can have their wills, you see what a lamentable
state both church and commonwealth will be in ; then we
shall have need of mourning ; the Lord cannot endure those

"3. The third dividing tenet, by which these persons prosecuted their errors,
was between the word of God and the Spirit of God : And here these sectaries had
many pretty knacks to delude withal, and especially to please the female sex, they
told of rare revelations of things to come from the Spirit, as they say. . . . . Come
along with me, says one of them, I will bring you to a woman that preaches better
gospel than any of your black coats, that have been at the university* ; a woman of
another kind of spirit, who hath had many revelations of things to come ; and for
my part, saith he, I had rather hear such a one that speaks from the mere motion of
the Spirit, without any study at all than any of your learned scholars, although
they may be fuller of Scripture, and, admit they speak by the help of the Spirit,
yet the other goes beyond them.

"4. To divide between Christ and his ordinances ; and here they played their
game to purpose, even casting down all ordinances as carnal, and that because they
were polluted by the ordinance of man ; as some of these sectaries have said to the
ministers of Christ, you have cast off the cross in baptism, but you would do well
to cast off baptism itself ; as also for the sacrament of the Lord's Supper, for to
make use of bread, or the juice of a silly grape, to represent the body and blood of
Christ, they accounted it as bad as necromancy in ministers of Christ to perform
it." Johnson's History, pp. 94—97.

[1]Winthrop, [Vol. I, 210.]—Hubbard [291.]

*In Johnson's History, both the original edition and the recent excellent reprint edited by Mr.
Poole, this word is *ninneversity*. Backus seems to have taken as a mistake what was meant for a
pun.—ED.

that are enemies to himself and kingdom and people, and unto the good of his church[1]."

At the General Court, March 9, Mr. Wheelwright was called to account for the words which tended to sedition in his sermon, but the matter was deferred from Court to Court till fall, when he was banished. Contention arose to a great height. Stephen Greensmith, for saying " that all the ministers, except A. B. C[2]. did teach a covenant of works, was censured to acknowledge his fault in every church, and fined forty pounds[3]."

At the General Court, May 17, 1637, after a hot dispute they proceeded to election, when Mr. Vane and his friends were left out[4]; and a law was made, "that no town or person shall receive any stranger resorting hither with intent to reside in this jurisdiction, nor shall allow any lot or habitation to any above three weeks, except such persons shall have allowance under some one of the Council, or of two other of the magistrates their hands, upon pain that every town that shall give or sell any lot or habitation to any such not so allowed shall forfeit one hundred pounds for every offence; and every person receiving any such for longer time than is here expressed, or than shall be allowed in some special case . . . . shall forfeit for every offence forty pounds, and for every month after such person shall there continue twenty pounds[5]."

Mr. Cotton was for a while so much dissatisfied with this law, that he had thoughts of removing out of that jurisdiction[6]. Governor Winthrop wrote a defence of it, in which

---

[1]Gorton's Glass for New England, pp. 19, 20. Gorton says, in this, Wheelwright " bore testimony to the light;" and the words above he says he transcribed out of Mr. Wheelwright's manuscript.

[2]" Mr. Cotton, Mr. Wheelwright, and he thought, Mr. Hooker." Hutchinson, Vol. I, p. 62.—ED.

[3]Winthrop, [Vol. I, p. 215.]

[4]He sailed for England the 3d of August following.

[5]Massachusetts Records.

[6]Massachusetts History, Vol. I, p. 63. [64.]

he does not deny but that a principal design of that law was to keep away persons of Mr. Wheelwright's opinions, and says :—

If we find his opinions such as will cause divisions, and make people look at their magistrates, ministers, and brethren, as enemies to Christ, antichrists, &c., were it not sin and unfaithfulness in us, to receive more of their opinions, which we already find the evil fruit of?   Nay, why do not those who now complain join with us in keeping out such, as well as formerly they did in expelling Mr. Williams for the like, though less dangerous?   Where this change of their judgments should arise I leave to themselves to examine[1].

Ah! less dangerous, sure enough! for Mr. Williams was banished for holding that the magistrate's sword ought not to be brought in to decide religious controversies; but Wheelwright would have turned that sword against the rulers, ministers, and people, that he judged to be under a covenant of works, and so enemies to grace.

Mr. Wheelwright was brother-in-law to Mrs. Anne Hutchinson, who had been a principal instrument of the division in the country about grace and works.   We are told that she brought these two errors out of England with her, viz. :—
" 1. That the person of the Holy Ghost dwells in a justified person.   2. That no sanctification can help to evidence our justification[2]."   A synod of ministers and messengers from all parts of the country met at Newtown, the 30th of August, and spent three weeks in debates upon these controversies, and drew up and condemned fourscore errors. The General Court adjourned to attend on their debates, and after their result was signed by all the settled ministers except Mr. Cotton, who also appeared to incline towards the majority, they met, September 26, when it is recorded,—

Mr. Wheelwright appearing, was dismissed until he should be sent for by the Court or Courts which shall succeed. This present Court is dissolved, until a new one be called, and to be kept at Newtown.[3]

[1]Massachusetts History, Vol. 3, p. 71.   [2]Winthrop's Journal, [Vol. I, p. 200.] [3]Massachusetts Records.

Here opens something that I never heard of till I found it upon the colony records. It was customary to elect their deputies twice a year, namely, in the spring and fall; but to choose them twice in one fall was an unprecedented act, of which I believe no parallel can be found from the foundation of the country to this day. It seems that a major vote of those deputies, to execute the decrees of the late synod, could not be obtained, therefore the House was dissolved, and a new one convened on November 2, 1637 ;[1] to which a remonstrance against those former proceedings was presented, signed by above sixty men ; of whom William Aspinwall, who drew it, and John Coggshall were members of the Assembly. For this they were now excluded, and an order was sent for Boston to choose two other deputies. Also, " John Oliver, justifying the seditious libel called a remonstrance or petition, was dismissed from being a deputy in this Court."[2] The Court then proceeded to pass the following sentences, viz. :—

Mr. John Wheelwright being formerly convicted of contempt and sedi-

[1] It was enacted July 14, 1634, that there should be "four General Courts held yearly," and that Deputies should be chosen " before every General Court." March 3, 1636, it was enacted that it should " be lawful for the Governor or Deputy Governor, or any two magistrates, upon special and urgent occasions, to appoint Courts," at other than the regular times. At the same time it was ordered that thereafter there should be " only two General Courts kept in a year," one in May and one in October. In the case under consideration, probably the Governor deemed the occasion sufficiently urgent to demand a special Court, and a new election was held according to the law above cited, which required that Deputies be chosen before every Court. See Massachusetts Records.—ED.

[2] Massachusetts Records; Winthrop. The remaining members of the Assembly were Governor Winthrop, Deputy Governor Dudley, John Endicott, John Humfrey, Richard Bellingham, Roger Harlakenden, Israel Stoughton, Simon Bradstreet, and Increase Nowell, Assistants, and thirty-one Deputies. The House that was dissolved in September had twenty-six Deputies, of whom but eleven were in this new House. Mr. Atherton Hough was one who was left out, though he was a magistrate two years before. John and Isaac Heath, John Johnson, Thomas Lynde, Nicholas Danforth, William Spencer, Samuel Appleton, Joseph Metcalf, John Upham and Thomas Gardner, were also of those they left out.*

These and such like proceedings caused the removal of Mr. William Blaxton about this time, He was a minister in the church of England, but came early to this

* According to the printed records of this former Court, it had twenty-seven Deputies. The name of John Heath is not among them. It is proper to remark, however, that the printed records are not infallible.—ED.

tion, and now justifying himself and his former practice, being the disturbance of the civil peace, he is by the Court disfranchised and banished, having fourteen days to settle his affairs.

Mr. John Coggshall being convented for disturbing the public peace, was disfranchised, and enjoined not to speak anything to disturb the public peace, upon pain of banishment.

Mr. William Aspinwall being convented for having his hand to a petition or remonstrance, being a seditious libel, and justifying the same, for which and for his insolent and turbulent carriage, he is disfranchised and banished, putting in sureties for his departure before the end of the first month next ensuing.

Mrs. Hutchinson, the wife of Mr. William Hutchinson, being convented for traducing the ministers and their ministry in this country, she declared voluntarily her revelations were the ground, and that she should be delivered, and the Court ruined with their posterity, and hereupon was banished; and the meanwhile was committed to Mr. Joseph Weld, until the Court shall dispose of her.

Captain Underhill, and two sergeants, were put from office and disfranchised, one of the sergeants being fined forty pounds the other twenty pounds. Four men more were disfranchised for having their hands to said petition, one of whom was William Dyer, afterward the first Secretary of Rhode Island colony. Ten men retracted their signing that remonstrance, and were forgiven. Then upon the 20th of November the court passed the following sentence :—

Whereas the opinions and revelations of Mr. Wheelwright and Mrs.

country. It appears by Johnson's History, p. 20, that he was here in 1628, but not agreeing with Mr. Endicott and others about church affairs, he betook himself to agriculture. He had planted himself upon the neck of land where Boston stands, which from him was called Blaxton's Point, when the Massachusetts company first arrived with their charter. At a Court in Boston, April 1, 1633, they made him a grant of fifty acres of land near his house there. Massachusetts Records. Yet now he said, " I came from England because I did not like the lord bishops; but I cannot join with you, because I would not be under the lord brethren." Magnalia, [Vol. I, p. 221.] He went and settled six miles north of Mr. Williams, near what is now called Whipple's Bridge, in Cumberland, where he lived to old age, and used at times to preach at Providence, and other places adjacent, and left behind him the character of a godly and pious man. His family is extinct. He planted an orchard near where he lived, which we are told is the first that ever bore fruit in Rhode Island colony; and one hundred and forty years after, many of the trees continued to be thrifty and fruitful.

Hutchinson have seduced and led into dangerous errors many of the people of New England, insomuch as there is just cause of suspicion that they, as others in Germany in former times, may upon some revelation make sudden irruption upon those that differ from them in judgment; for prevention whereof it is ordered that all those whose names are underwritten (upon warning given at their dwelling-houses) before the 30th day of this month of November, deliver in at Mr. Keayne's house, at Boston, all such guns, pistols, swords, powder, shot and match, as they shall be owners of, or have in their custody, upon pain of ten pounds for every default to be made thereof; which arms are to be kept by Mr. Keayne till this Court shall take further order therein. Also it is ordered, upon like penalty of ten pounds that no man who is to render his arms by this order, shall buy or borrow any guns, swords, pistols, powder, shot or match, until this Court shall take further order therein.

Seventy-six men are named as being disarmed by this sentence, only if any of them would acknowledge and not justify said petition before two magistrates, they should then be free from it.[1] Of these men fifty-eight belonged to Boston, five to Roxbury, two to Charlestown, six to Salem, two to Ipswich, and three to Newbury; of whom Richard Dummer, of Newbury, had been an Assistant, and Hutchinson, Underhill, Aspinwall, Coggshall and Oliver, of Boston, Robert Moulton, of Salem, and others, had been deputies.

Directly upon the foregoing act the Assembly added the following, viz. :—

The Court being sensible of great disorders growing in this commonwealth, through the contempts which have been of late put upon the civil authority, and intending to provide remedy for the same in time, doth order and decree, that whosoever shall hereafter openly or willingly defame any court of justice, or the sentence or proceedings of the same, or any of the magistrates or other judges of any such court, in respect of any act or sentence therein passed, and being thereof lawfully convicted in any General Court or Courts of Assistants, shall be punished for the same, by fine, imprisonment, or disfranchisement or banishment, as the quality and measure of the offence shall deserve ; . . . . provided always, that seeing

[1]Massachusetts Records. It appears that the Court had much difficulty afterward with Keayne about these arms.

the best judges may err through ignorance or misinformation . . . . it is not the intent of this Court to restrain the free use of the way of God, by petition, &c.

A complaint being made at the same time that some ministers were not well maintained, the Court sent out a request, " That the several churches will speedily enquire hereinto, and if need be to confer together about it, and send some to advise with this Court at the next session thereof, that some order may be taken according to the rule of the gospel."[1] The effects of these proceedings we shall soon see ; though, by the way, it is proper to observe, that as Mr. Williams had been instrumental of procuring the Narragansetts' help against the Pequods, the several colonies sent out their forces against them, and Governor Winthrop says, May 24, " By letters from Mr. Williams we were notified, that Capt. Mason was gone to Saybrook with eighty English and one-hundred Indians,"[2] &c., so that he was constantly engaged for their good. The army was successful, the Pequods were subdued, and I find a proposal of a day of thanksgiving for the soldiers' return, at the General Court, August 1. But at the same time, they say, " Mr. John Greene, of New Providence, having spoken against the magistrates contemptuously, stands bound over in one hundred marks to appear at the next Quarter Court." At that Court he was fined twenty pounds, and committed till it was paid ; though upon a submissive petition to the General Court, September 26, he was released.[3] He with others had resorted to Mr. Williams's plantation, to which there was a great addition the next spring. A new one was begun at Rhode Island ; of which take the following account.

Mr. John Clarke, a learned physician, who I find was admitted a freeman at Boston, May 6, 1635,[4] as his brother

---

[1]Massachusetts Records.   [2]Winthrop's Journal, Vol. I. p. 223.—ED.
[3]Massachusetts Records.
[4]The John Clarke who was admitted a freeman at Boston, May 6, 1635, must have been a different person from the founder of Rhode Island plantation.   The latter

Joseph had been the March before, seeing how things were turned at the Court, in November, 1637, made a proposal to his friends, for peace sake, and to enjoy the freedom of their consciences, to remove out of that jurisdiction. The motion was accepted, and he (being then a gentleman in his 29th year) was requested with some others to look out for a place. They did so; and by reason of the heat of the preceding summer, they first went northerly into that which is now the province of New Hampshire; but the coldness of the following winter made them incline to turn the other way. " So having sought the Lord for direction, they agreed that while their vessel was passing about Cape Cod they would cross over by land, having Long Island and Delaware Bay in their eye, for the place of their residence." At Providence Mr. Williams lovingly entertained them, and being consulted about their design, readily presented two places before them; Sowams, now called Barrington, and Aquetneck, now Rhode Island. They being determined to go out of the other jurisdictions, Mr. Williams, Mr. Clarke, and two others, went to Plymouth to enquire how the case stood, who, [those at Plymouth,] lovingly entertained them, and let them know ˃that they claimed Sowams, but advised them to settle at Aquetneck, and promised that they should be looked upon as free, and to be treated and assisted as loving neighbors." Upon their return nineteen men incor-

---

writes in his " Narrative,"—" In the year '37 I left my native land, and in the ninth month of the same, I (through mercy) arrived at Boston. I was no sooner on shore but there appeared to me differences among them concerning the covenants, and, in point of evidencing a man's good estate, some pressed hard for a covenant of works and for sanctification to be the first and chief evidence; others pressed as hard for the covenant of grace that was established upon a better foundation, and for the evidence of the Spirit as that which is a more certain, constant and satisfactory witness." Mass. Historical Collections, fourth series, Vol. II. p. 22, The date thus given in the " Narrative" is verified by the fact that the difficulty on the question of covenants, which Clarke found in the colony as soon as he was on shore, does not seem to have arisen till 1636. See p. 63.—ED.

A biographical notice of John Clarke will be found in Chapter VII. —ED.

porated themselves into a body politic, and chose Mr. Coddington to be their judge or chief magistrate.[1]

Now to take things in their order, it is to be observed, that though Mr. Williams and a few of his friends had, with the consent of the Narragansett sachems, been settled at Providence near two years, yet the first deed of the place that is extant bears date the same day with that of Aquetneck ; and is as follows :—

At Nanhiggansick the 24th of the first month, commonly called March, in the 2d year of our plantation, or planting at Mooshausick, or Providence : Memorandum, that we Caunannicus and Miantinomu, the two chief sachems of Nanhiggansick, having two years since sold unto Roger Williams the lands and meadows upon the two fresh rivers called Mooshausick and Wanaskatuckett,[2] do now by these presents establish and confirm the bounds of those lands, from the rivers and fields of Pawtuckett, the great hill of Neoterconkenitt on the northwest, and the town of Mashapauge on the west. As also, in consideration of the many kindnesses and services he hath continually done for us, both for our friends of Massachusetts, as also at Quininkticutt and Apaum, or Plymouth ; we do freely give unto him all that land from those rivers reaching to Pautuxett River, as also the grass and meadows upon Pautuxett River ; in witness whereof we have hereunto set our hands.

The mark of ‡ Caunannicus,
The mark of ‖ Miantinomu.

In presence of
The mark of † Seatagh,
The mark of * Assotemewett.

1639, Memorandum, 3 month 9 day, this was all again confirmed by Miantinomu ; he acknowledged this his act and hand ; up the stream of Pautuckett and Pawtuxett without limits we might have for our use of cattle ; witness hereof.

Roger Williams,
Benedict Arnold.[3]

[1]Clarke's Narrative. [Mass. Historical Collections, fourth series, Vol. II. p. 25.]— Callender's Sermon. [R. I. Historical Collections, Vol. IV. pp. 83, 84.]

[2]The first of these rivers falls into the cove above Providence great bridge from the north, the other from the west.

[3]Literally transcribed from Providence Records. Pawtucket River riseth in or near Rutland, and runs through Leicester, Sutton, Grafton and Uxbridge, and entering Rhode Island colony, passes between Smithfield and Cumberland, and falls into Narragansett Bay, between Providence and Rehoboth. Pawtuxet River rises near the borders of Connecticut, and passing through Gloucester, Scituate and Cranston, falls into said bay, five miles south of Providence.

The deed of Rhode Island was also given the same March 24, 1638 ; and twenty years after Mr. Williams having occasion to give his testimony concerning it, says,—

I have acknowledged (and have and shall endeavor to maintain) the rights and properties of every Inhabitant of Rhode Island in peace ; yet since there is so much sound and noise of purchase and purchasers, I judge it not unseasonable to declare the rise and bottom of the planting of Rhode Island in the fountain of it.   It was not price nor money that could have purchased Rhode Island.   Rhode Island was obtained by love ; by the love and favor which that honorable gentleman Sir Henry Vane and myself had with that great sachem Miantinomu, about the league which I procured between the Massachusetts English, &c., and the Narragansetts in the Pequod war.   It is true I advised a gratuity to be presented to the sachem and the natives, and because Mr. Coddington and the rest of my loving countrymen were to inhabit the place, and to be at the charge of the gratuities, I drew up a writing in Mr. Coddington's name, and in the names of such of my loving countrymen as came up with him, and put it into as sure a form as I could at that time (amongst the Indians) for the benefit and assurance of the present and future inhabitants of the Island.   This I mention, that as that truly noble Sir Henry Vane hath been so great an instrument in the hand of God for procuring of this Island from the barbarians, as also for procuring and confirming of the charter, so it may by all due thankful acknowledgment be remembered and recorded of us and ours which reap and enjoy the sweet fruits of so great benefits, and such unheard of liberties amongst us.[1]

Mr. Williams having obtained the aforesaid grant of Providence, conveyed the same to his friends by the following instrument :—

Providence, 8th of the 8th month, 1638 (so called.)   Memorandum, that I, Roger Williams, having formerly purchased of Caunannicus and Miantinomu this our situation or plantation of New-Providence, viz., the two fresh rivers Wanasquatuckett and Mooshausick, and the ground and meadows thereupon ; in consideration of thirty pounds received from the inhabitants of said place, do freely and fully pass, grant and make over equal right and power of enjoying and disposing of the same grounds and lands unto my loving friends and neighbors, Stukely Westcoat, William

---

[1]This I copied from the original manuscript, in Mr. Williams's own hand writing, dated " Providence, 25,6, 1658 (so called)."   The affair of procuring the charter we shall hear more of anon.

Arnold, Thomas James, Robert Cole, John Greene, John Throckmorton, William Harris, William Carpenter, Thomas Olney, Francis Weston, Richard Waterman, Ezekiel Holliman, and such others as the major part of us shall admit into the same fellowship of vote with us. As also I do freely make and pass over equal right and power of enjoying and disposing of the lands and grounds reaching from the aforesaid rivers unto the great river Pautuxett, with the grass and meadows thereupon, which was so lately given and granted by the aforesaid sachems to me ; witness my hand,   ROGER WILLIAMS.[1]

Those who were thus received signed the following covenant, viz. :—

We whose names are here underwritten being desirous to inhabit in the town of Providence, do promise to submit ourselves in active or passive obedience to all such orders or agreements as shall be made for public good of the body in an orderly way, by the major consent of the present inhabitants, masters of families, incorporated together into a township, and such others whom they shall admit into the same, *only in civil things.*

By the records, compared with a more ample and full deed of Mr. Williams to the town, executed December 20, 1661, which is entered there, it appears that he generously gave the aforesaid twelve men their interest in the town freely, and the thirty pounds were paid by the next who were admitted, at the rate of thirty shillings a man, the names of whom were Chad Brown, William Field, Thomas Harris, William Wickenden, Robert Williams, Richard Scott, William Reynolds, John Field, John Warner, Thomas Angell, Benedict Arnold, Joshua Winsor, Thomas Hopkins, Francis Wccks, &c.[2] In the last mentioned deed,

[1]Providence Records. It seems the first deed of this tenure was lost, therefore this was drawn as exactly as could be remembered in 1666. Of the above men, Olney, Weston, Westcoat, Waterman and Holliman, did not depart the Massachusetts colony till April, 1638. Massachusetts Records. They, with Throckmorton, came from Salem. Massachusetts History, Vol. I, p. 421, [371], and records aforesaid. Weston had been a deputy in court.

[2]Of these I find Williams (brother to Mr. Roger) among the Massachusetts freemen, but no more of their names upon those records. Perhaps most of them might have newly arrived; for Governor Winthrop assures us that not less than three thousand arrived this year in twenty ships; and Mr. Hubbard tells us that those who inclined to Baptist principles went to Providence; others went to Newport. Seven of the first twelve, with Angell, I suppose began the settlement with Mr. Williams in 1636.

after referring to the former ones, and expressing that the sachems' deed was two years after his first purchase, he more fully explains the nature and motives of those transactions. Says he,—

Notwithstanding I had the frequent promise of Miantinomu, my kind friend, that it should not be land that I should want about those bounds mentioned, provided that I satisfied the Indians there inhabiting, I having made covenant of peaceable neighborhood with all the sachems and natives round about us, and having, in a sense of God's merciful providence unto me in my distress, called the place PROVIDENCE, I desired it might be for a shelter for persons distressed for conscience; I then considering the condition of divers of my distressed countrymen, I communicated my said purchase unto my loving friends, John Throckmorton and others, who then desired to take shelter here with me. .... And whereas by God's merciful assistance I was the procurer of the purchase, not by money nor payment, the natives being so shy and jealous that money could not do it, but by that language, acquaintance and favor with the natives, and other advantages which it pleased God to give me; and also bore the charges and venture of all the gratuities which I gave to the great sachems, and other sachems and natives round about us, and lay engaged for a loving and peaceable neighborhood with them, to my great charge and travel; it was therefore thought by some loving friends that I should receive some consideration and gratuity.

Thus, after mentioning the said thirty pounds, and saying, " This sum I received, in love to my friends, and with respect to a town and place of succor for the distressed as aforesaid, I do acknowledge the said sum and payment a full satisfaction;" he went on in full and strong terms to confirm those lands to said inhabitants; reserving no more to himself and his heirs than an equal share with the rest; his wife also signing the deed.

I trust the reader will excuse the length of this account, when he considers that these were the foundations of a now flourishing colony, which was laid upon such principles as no other civil government had ever been, as we know of, since antichrist's first appearance; " and ROGER WILLIAMS justly claims the honor of having been the first legislator in the world, in its latter ages, that fully and effectually provided for and established a free, full and absolute LIBERTY OF CONSCIENCE[1]."

[1]History of Providence. [Mass. Historical Collections, Second Series, Vol. IX, p. 190.] Massachusetts was so far from favoring this cause, that the General Court of March 12, 1638, passed this act, viz. : "Whereas a letter was sent unto this Court, subscribed by John Greene, dated from New Providence, and brought by one of that company, wherein the Court is charged with usurping the power of Christ over the churches and men's consciences, notwithstanding he had formerly acknowledged his fault in such speeches by him before used; it is now ordered, that the said John Greene shall not come into this jurisdiction, upon pain of imprisonment and further censure. And because it appears to this Court that some others of the same place are confident in the same corrupt judgment and practice, it is ordered, that if any other of the inhabitants of the said plantation of Providence shall come within this jurisdiction, they shall be apprehended, and brought before some of the magistrates, and if they will not disclaim the said corrupt opinion and censure, they shall be commanded presently to depart, and if such persons shall after be found within this jurisdiction they shall be imprisoned, and punished as the Court shall see cause."

Massachusetts Records.

Lamentable case indeed! that none of the inhabitants of that infant plantation, who were not able to send out shipping themselves, might go into the colony which was the only place where many of the necessaries as well as comforts of life were to be obtained by them; but they must either be exposed to dissemble, or to suffer imprisonment, if not worse; for how could they honestly declare that the Massachusetts did not usurp a power over men's consciences?—B.

We cannot forbear to add the oft-quoted tribute paid to Roger Williams by the historian Bancroft:—"He was the first person in modern Christendom to assert in its plenitude the doctrine of the liberty of conscience, the equality of opinions before the law; and in its defence he was the harbinger of Milton, the precurser and the superior of Jeremy Taylor. For Taylor limited his toleration to a few Christian sects; the philanthrophy of Williams compassed the earth. Taylor favored partial reform, commended lenity, argued for forbearance, and entered a special plea in behalf of each tolerable sect; Williams would permit persecution of no opinion, of no religion, leaving heresy unharmed by law, and orthodoxy unprotected by the terrors of penal statutes. . . . . We praise the man who first analyzed the air, or resolved water into its elements, or drew the lightning from the clouds, even though the discoveries may have been as much the fruits of time as of genius. A moral principle has a much wider and nearer influence on human happiness; nor can any discovery of truth be of more direct benefit to society, than that which establishes a perpetual religious peace, and spreads tranquillity through every community and every bosom. If Copernicus is held in perpetual reverence, because, on his deathbed, he published to the world that the sun is the centre of our system; if the name of Kepler is preserved in the annals of human excellence for his sagacity in detecting the laws of the planetary motion; if the genius of Newton has been almost adored for dissecting a ray of light, and weighing heavenly bodies in a balance,—let there be for the name of Roger Williams, at least some humble place among those who have advanced moral science and made themselves the benefactors of mankind." Vol. I, pp. 375—377.—ED.

None might have a voice in government in this new plantation, who would not allow this liberty. Hence about this time I find the following town act, viz.: "It was agreed that Joshua Verin, upon breach of covenant, or restraining liberty of conscience, shall be withhold from the liberty of voting till he shall declare the contrary." It appears from Mr. Hubbard, that the way in which he restrained that liberty was, in not letting his wife go to Mr. Williams's meeting so often as she was called for. Verin soon removed to Barbadoes, and left his interest in Providence in such a state as has caused much trouble since.

We will now turn to the affairs of the Rhode Island people, who, on March 7, 1638, signed the following instrument:—

We whose names are underwritten do swear solemnly, in the presence of Jehovah, to incorporate ourselves into a body politic, and as he shall help us, will submit our persons, lives and estates, unto our Lord Jesus Christ, the King of kings, and Lord of lords, and to all those most perfect and absolute laws of his, given us in his holy word of truth, to be guided and judged thereby.

THOMAS SAVAGE,	WILLIAM CODDINGTON,
WILLIAM DYRE,	JOHN CLARKE,
WILLIAM FREEBORNE,	WILLIAM HUTCHINSON,
PHILIP SHERMAN,	JOHN COGGSHALL,
JOHN WALKER,	WILLIAM ASPINWALL,
RICHARD CARDER,	SAMUEL WILBORE,
WILLIAM BAULSTONE,	JOHN PORTER,
EDWARD HUTCHINSON, Sen.,	EDWARD HUTCHINSON, Jun.,
HENRY BULL,	JOHN SANFORD[1]."
RANDAL HOLDEN.	

[1]Colony Records. Of these William Hutchinson died on the island; the other Hutchinsons, Aspinwall and Savage, went back, got reconciled. and were promoted in the Massachusetts colony afterward. Near all the others were considerably promoted afterward in Rhode Island colony, and have posterity still remaining there. All but two of the above nineteen men were disarmed by the sentence of November 20, 1637, viz.: Messrs. Coddington and Holden. Messrs. Coddington, Coggshall, Baulston, E. Hutchinson, Wilbore, Porter, Bull, Sherman, Freeborne and Carder, were all excluded or driven out of the Massachusetts colony by an act of their Assembly, on March 12, 1638, in these words, viz.:—

"Whereas you have desired and obtained license to remove yourselves and your

This was doubtless in their view a better plan than any of the others had laid, as they were to be governed by the perfect laws of Christ. But the question is, how a civil polity could be so governed, when he never erected any such state under the gospel? As much as they had been against the legal covenant, yet they now went back to the first order of government after Israel came into Canaan, and to imitate it chose Mr. Coddington their judge, and Messrs. Nicholas Easton, J. Coggshall, and William Brenton, elders to assist him. This form continued, till, on March 12, 1640, they altered it, and chose Mr. Coddington Governor, Mr. Brenton Deputy Governor, and Messrs. Easton, Coggshall, William Hutchinson, and John Porter, Assistants, Robert Jeffries Treasurer, and William Dyre Secretary, which form continued till they received a charter.

Before we proceed further upon their affairs, it may be

families out of this jurisdiction, and for that information hath been given to the Court, that your intent is only to withdraw yourselves for a season, that you may avoid the censure of the Court, for some things that may be objected against you; the Court doth therefore signify unto you that you may depart according to the license given you, so as your families be removed before the next General Court. But if your families be not so removed, then you are to appear at the next Court, to abide the further order of the Court herein." Mr. Nicholas Easton, of Newbury, who went to Newport, and Messrs. Francis Weston, Richard Waterman, Thomas Olney, and Stukely Westcoat, of Salem, who went to Providence, were also included in this sentence. Beside these there were William Lytherland, Robert Harding, John Briggs, George Barden, John Odlin, Richard Wayte, and others that were disarmed at Boston, who removed into this colony, and have left a respectful remembrance therein.—B.

Massachusetts Records, as published, give the name of but one Edward Hutchinson among those disarmed.—ED.

On page 71, the number of these signers is given, according to the above list and that in the printed Colony Records of Rhode Island, as nineteen. In the first edition it was printed eighteen, but the table of *errata* at the close of volume first directed the change. In his Abridgment, Backus gives but eighteen names, omitting from this list that of Randal Holden. In this he agrees with Callender in his Century Sermon and Hopkins in his History of Providence. Arnold, in his History of Rhode Island, (Vol. I, p. 124,) explains the discrepancy. "Holden's name is separated from the others by a line. He is believed to be one not concerned in the purchase, as his name and that of Roger Williams are signed as witnesses to the deed. There were eighteen original proprietors and nineteen signers of the compact."—ED.

proper to observe, that the Assembly, who met at Boston, September 6, 1638, made the two following laws :—

1. Whereas it is found by sad experience, that divers persons, who have been justly cast out of some of the churches, do profanely contemn the same sacred and dreadful ordinance, by presenting themselves over-boldly in other assemblies, and speaking lightly of their censures, to the great offence and grief of God's people, and encouragement of evil-minded persons to contemn the said ordinance ; it is therefore ordered, that whosoever shall stand excommunicated for the space of six months, without laboring what in him or her lieth to be restored, such person shall be presented to the Court of Assistants, and there proceeded with by fine, imprisonment, banishment, or further, for the good behavior, as their contempt and obstinacy upon full hearing shall deserve.

2. The Court taking into consideration the necessity of an equal contribution to all common charges in towns, and observing that the chief occasion of the defect herein arises hence, that many of those who are not freemen, nor members of any church, do take advantage thereby to withdraw their help, in such voluntary contributions as are in use ; it is therefore hereby declared, that every inhabitant in any town is liable to contribute to all charges both in church and commonwealth whereof he doth or may receive benefit ; and withal it is also ordered, that every such inhabitant who shall not voluntarily contribute proportionably to his ability with other freemen of the same town, to all common charges, as well for upholding the ordinances in the churches as otherwise, shall be compelled thereto by assessment and distress, to be levied by the constable or other officer of the town, as in other cases[1].

Here, my dear countrymen, let us make a little pause. Not long since, in the presence of a number of gentlemen, mention was made of the former persecutions in New England, upon which one of their legislators arose and said, " It is monstrous cruelty and injustice, thus to rake up the ashes of our good fathers, and to reproach their children therewith, when we never think of those transactions without grief and abhorrence !" If so, why are those deeds imitated by our present rulers ? And why do the people love to have it so ? Certainly the support of good order and government in the church is of greater importance than ministers' maintenance ; and to vindicate the methods then taken to

[1]Massachusetts Records.

support the former of these, Mr. Cotton brought that plain text, " Thou shalt surely kill him, because he hath sought to thrust thee away from the Lord thy God ;" and, said he, " This reason is of moral, that is, of universal and perpetual equity."[1]   But I never heard any man say so of that other text, " Thou shalt give it me now, and if not, I will take it by force," which is the most like the practice of many in this generation of anything that I could ever find in our Bible.   Governor Winthrop informs us, that the next May after the above laws were passed, Mr. Cotton, in preaching from Heb. viii. 8, taught " that when magistrates are forced to proceed for the maintenance of ministers, &c., then the churches are in a declining state.   Here he shewed that the ministers' maintenance should be by voluntary contribution." But the law to impower their executive court to punish ex-communicates, for disregarding the churches' authority, was repealed the next fall, while that to maintain ministers by assessment and distress was continued in full force.   Their practice upon it in Watertown moved Nathaniel Briscoe to write a book against it, the consequence of which was, that he was brought before the Quarter Court, at Boston, March 7, 1643, and fined ten pounds.   " John Stowers, for reading of divers offensive passages (before company) out of a book, against the officers and church of Watertown, and for mak-ing disturbance there, was fined forty shillings."   This sev-erity brought Briscoe to a public acknowledgment, and then his fine was remitted to forty shillings, " and that to be taken."[2]   The ministers thus left it to the secular arm to convince him, and said, " his arguments were not worth the answering ; for he that shall deny the exerting of the civil power, to provide for the comfortable subsistence of them that preach the gospel, *fuste potius erudiendus, quam argu-mento*, as they say of them that are wont, *negare principia*, let him that is taught communicate to him that teacheth in

---

[1]Bloody Tenet washed, p. 67.   [2]Massachusetts Records.

all good things,[1] that is, he that shall deny such an exertion of power, is rather to be taught by a cudgel than argument, as they say of them who are wont to deny first principles. But let us take heed that we are not imposed upon, by a confounding of two things together, which are as distinct in their nature as light and darkness, namely duty itself, and the right way of enforcing it. The duty of offering daily or continual thanksgivings to our great Creator, and of a liberal communication to Christ's ministers and members, are both called sacrifices to God, in Heb. xiii., and why do our rulers neglect to enforce the daily exercise of family worship, by the same sword as they do ministers' maintenance? Is not God's honor of greater concernment than men's livings! A college was founded this year in Newtown, and for that reason the place was called Cambridge; and the importance of receiving learning at that or like places, to qualify men for the ministry, has been much insisted upon ever since; and those who have not been educated at such places have commonly been called laymen. And among the many reflections that have been cast upon them, one is, that they often beg the question in argument. But who are guilty of this mean sort of conduct now? The question between us is not, whether it be the duty of those who are taught to communicate unto their teachers or not; but it is, whether that duty ought to be enforced by the sword, or only by instruction, persuasion and good example? And what have learned ministers ever done towards proving their side of the question better than begging?

The great events of this year have taken up considerable room, yet I must request a place for a few articles more, that will affect the following part of our history.[2]

---

[1] Hubbard. [412.]   Massachusetts History, Vol. I, p. 427. [377.]

[2] Mr. Hansard Knollys came over in the spring of this year, who was ordained by the Bishop of Peterborough, June 29, 1629; but he says, "About the year 1636 I was prosecuted in the High Commission Court, by virtue of a warrant, wherewith I was apprehended in Boston (in Lincolnshire) and kept a prisoner in the man's

On June 5, Uncas, the sachem of the Mohegan Indians, "having entertained some of the Pequods, came to the Governor at Boston with a present, and was much dejected because at first it was not accepted; but afterward, the

house who served the warrant upon me. But God helped me to convince him, and he was so greatly terrified in his conscience, that he set open his doors, and let me go away! but before I went, I tarried so long in London, waiting for a passage, that when I went abroad I had but just six brass farthings left, and no silver nor gold, only my wife had five pounds that I knew not of, which she gave me when we came there. By the way, my little child died with convulsion fits, our beer and water stank, our biscuit was molded and rotten, and our cheese also, so that we suffered much hardship, being twelve weeks in our passage; but God was gracious to us and led us safe through the great deeps: and ere we went on shore came one and enquired for me, and told me a friend that was gone from Boston to Rhode Island had left me his house to sojourn in, and to which we went, and two families more with us, who went suddenly to their friends and other relations in the country; and I being very poor, was necessitated to work daily with my hoe, for the space of almost three weeks. The magistrates were told by the ministers that I was an antinomian, and desired they would not suffer me to abide in their patent. But within the time limited by their law in that case, two strangers coming to Boston from Piscataqua, hearing of me by mere accident, got me to go with them to that plantation, and preach there, where I remained about four years, and then being sent for back to England, by my aged father, I returned with my wife and one child, about three years old, and she great with another. We came safe to London on the 24th of December, 1641, in which year the massacre in Ireland broke forth, and the next year wars broke forth in England, between King and Parliament." See Knollys's account of his own life. He embraced the Baptist principles, gathered a church of that persuasion in London, and used seldom to have less than a thousand auditors. He baptised Mr. Henry Jessey, an eminent minister in that city, and others; suffered much for religion, continued pastor of that church till he died in London, September 19, 1691, aged 93. Crosby, [Vol. I, pp. 226—232, 311, 334—344.] Though he was reproached as an antinomian, yet Dr. Mather says he had a "respectful character in the churches of this wilderness." Magnalia, B. 3, p. 7, [Vol. I. p. 221.] After his return to England, "he suffered deeply in the cause of nonconformity, being universally esteemed and beloved by all his brethren. Neal, Vol. 1, p. 216.—B.

To this account of Hansard Knollys it may be well to make a few additions. He was a graduate of the University of Cambridge. For two or three years after his admission to orders, he had charge of a parish in Humberstone, Lincoln. He then "began to scruple the lawfulness of several ceremonies and usages of the national church, as the surplice, the cross in baptism, the admitting wicked persons to the Lord's Supper," &c. He resigned his living, but for several years continued preaching in the established churches, refusing, however, to read the service. In 1636 he publicly joined the Dissenters. Persecuted in England he fled to America. Forbidden at once to remain in Massachusetts he went to Piscataqua, soon afterwards called Dover. Here he met with immediate opposition, but according to Winthrop, (Vol. I, p. 326,) "he gathered some of the best minded into a church

Governor and Council being satisfied about his innocency, they accepted it; whereupon he promised to submit to the orders of the English, both touching the Pequods he had received, and as concerning the differences between the

body and became their pastor." Backus says in a subsequent chapter, "Mr. Hansard Knollys was minister there from the spring of 1638 to the fall of 1641." The precise character of the church it is now impossible to determine. Benedict says, (General History of the Baptist Denomination, p. 497.) "The church at Dover to which Mr. Knollys officiated was probably on the mixed communion plan, as was very common in those days in incipient movements of this kind." The church was traduced from without and was rent with dissension within; and its pastor returned to England. He was imprisoned in London for preaching against infant baptism. In Suffolk, on one occasion he was stoned out of the pulpit, and on another, when he and the congregation who had gathered to hear him were shut out of the church and he preached to them in the church-yard, he was arrested and sent to London again as a prisoner. He afterwards established a meeting at Great St. Helen's, London, "where the people flocked to hear him, and he had commonly a thousand auditors."

Mr. Knollys was a Particular or Calvanistic Baptist, and one of the signers of the so-called Confession of 1646. He was a good scholar, especially in the ancient languages, and, besides his ministerial labors, was almost constantly engaged in teaching, and by this means, for the most part, gained his own support, He lived, says Crosby, "to a good old age, and went home as a shock of wheat that is gathered in its season," departing this life, " in a great transport of joy." 4

Winthrop calls Knollys, a "weak minister," and accuses him of slandering the government, and holding "familistical opinions." Vol. I, pp. 291, 306, 326. Winthrop's words were enough for the plagiarizing and narrow-minded Hubbard to repeat and build upon, till he represents the character of Knollys as anything but what it should be. P. 369. Savage in his edition of Winthrop, says that Knollys's history in this country was " little creditable to his morals." Vol. I, p. 292, note. There is abundant evidence, however, not only to vindicate the character of Knollys, but to prove him a man of extraordinary conscientiousness and piety. See Crosby, Vol. I, pp. 226—232, 334—344. Neal's History of the Puritans, Toulmin's edition, Vol. III, pp. 551—553.

The name of Henry Jessey, mentioned in the foregoing note of Backus, merits a more particular notice. He was born in Yorkshire in 1601. After studying six years at St. John's College, Cambridge, and being graduated Master of Arts, he received episcopal ordination in 1627, and six years later became rector of a church in his native county. The next year he was removed for nonconformity. He soon began preaching to a dissenting congregation in London, of which, in 1637, he assumed the pastoral charge. Perceiving that Baptist sentiments were making rapid progress in his congregation, Mr. Jessey was led to consider them, and after " a diligent and impartial examination of the Holy Scriptures and antiquity" "not without great deliberation, many prayers, and divers conferences with pious and learned men of different persuasions," was compelled to embrace them. He was baptized in 1644. The historian, Crosby, says, " It proved no small honor and advantage to the Baptists to have a man of such extraordinary piety and substantial.

Narragansetts and himself; and confirmed all with this compliment; laying his hand upon his heart he said " this heart is not mine, but yours; I will never believe any Indian against the English any more;" and so he continued ever after.   Uncas was alive and well in the year 1630[1]

.Mr. Cotton had entertained a favorable opinion of Mrs. Hutchinson, and when she was upon examination before the Court that banished her, he was asked what he thought of her revelation concerning her deliverance ?   He replied, " If she doth look for deliverance from the hand of God by his providence, and the revelation be in a word, or according to a word, I cannot deny it."   Upon which Mr. Endicott said, " You give me satisfaction."   " No, no," said Mr. Dudley, " he gives me none at all. . . . . You weary me, and do not satisfy me."   Mr. Nowell said, " I think it is a devilish delusion."   And Governor Winthrop said, " Of all the revelations that ever I heard of, I never heard the like ground laid as is for this.   The enthusiasts and Anabaptists had never the like."   Mr. Dudley added, " I never saw such revelations as these among Anabaptists, therefore am sorry that Mr. Cotton should stand to justify her ;" and he and others of the Court would have brought him upon trial also, but the Governor prevented it[2].

learning among them." As these words indicate, Mr. Jessey was a man of extensive cultivation. The languages of the original Scriptures, and other ancient oriental dialects were his especial pursuit. He began a new translation of the Bible, in which he was assisted by some of the most eminent scholars of the age.   For many years, Mr. Jessey escaped persecution, largely by reason of the respect which all were compelled to pay to his learning; but soon after the restoration he was imprisoned for heresy and died in confinement in 1663.   See Crosby, Vol. I, pp. 307—320.—ED.

[1]Winthrop, [Vol. I, pp. 265, 266.] Hubbard, [255] Mr. Hubbard dates his coming in July, but I follow the Governor who acted in the affair. Uncas's headquarters were about eight miles above the mouth of New London river, on the west side of it.   Though the Mohegans as well as other Indians, are greatly diminished, yet a considerable body of that tribe remain there to this day.   In 1741 a remarkable work of God was wrought among them; a church of Christian Indians was afterwards gathered, and continues there, many of whom give great evidence of true piety.   Mr. Samson Occum is of that tribe.

[2]Massachusetts History, Vol. II, pp. 514, 515. [443, 444.]—B.

It is perhaps too much to say, on the foundation of the report of the examination

After a year's consideration, at a public fast, December 13, 1638, Mr. Cotton

Did confess and bewail, as the churches' so his own security and credulity, whereupon so many and dangerous errors had gotten up, and spread in the churches, and went over all the particulars, and shewed how he came to be deceived ; the errors being formed, in words, so near the truth he had preached, and the falsehood of the maintainers of them was such, as they usually would deny to him what they had delivered to others.   He acknowledged that such as had been seducers of others (instancing in some of those of Rhode Island, though he named them not) had been justly banished ; yet he said such as only had been misled, and others who had done any thing out of misguided conscience (not being grossly evil) should be borne withal, and first referred to the church, and if that could not heal them, they should rather be imprisoned or fined than banished, it being likely that no other church would receive them. . . . . If he were not convinced, yet he was persuaded to an amicable compliance with the other ministers, by a studious abstaining on his part from all expressions that were like to be offensive ; for although it was thought he did still retain his own sense, and enjoy his own apprehension, in all or most of the things then controverted (as is manifest by some expressions of his in a treatise of the new covenant, since published by Mr. Thomas Allen, of Norwich) yet was there an healing of the breach that had been between him and the rest of the elders, and a putting a stop to the course of errors in the country for the future. . . . . By that means did that reverend and worthy minister of the gospel recover his former splendor throughout the country of New England[1].

in Hutchinson's History, that the Court would have brought Mr. Cotton upon trial but for the Governor.   That which most nearly accords with this statement is the following :—

DEPUTY GOVERNOR. " I never saw such revelations as these among the Anabaptists, therefore am sorry that Mr. Cotton should stand to justify her."

Mr. PETERS. " I can say the same, and this runs to enthusiasm, and I think that is very disputable which our brother Cotton hath spoken."

Mr. COLLICUT. " It is a great burden to us that we differ from Mr. Cotton, and that he should justify these revelations.   I would entreat him to answer concerning that about the destruction of England."

GOVERNOR. " Mr. Cotton is not called to answer to anything, but we are to deal with the party here standing before us."   Ibid.—ED.

[1]Winthrop, [Vol. I, p. 280]—Hubbard, [297, 302.]   Roger Harlakenden, one of the magistrates, died at Cambridge, November 17, this year.   Winthrop, [Vol. I, p. 277.]   Near the same time a church was gathered at Exeter, on Piscataqua river, and soon after Mr. Wheelwright, at his and their request, was dismissed with others to it, from the church of Boston, and became their minister.   Hubbard.   These facts help to discover the spirit of those times.

This year, upon an occurrence, Governor Winthrop wrote to Mr. Clarke at Aquetneck, and styled him, " A physician and a preacher to those of that island."

We are now come to an event which has made much noise in the world, I mean Mr. Williams's baptism. The reader may remember that he was charged with advancing principles at Plymouth that tended to anabaptism, and that he filled Salem therewith ; and could he have found an agreeable administrator, it is not likely that he would have neglected the putting of this principle into practice so long as he did. At length, being in such a state of exile in a heathen land, it is probable he concluded that the case about baptism, which Mr. Robinson recites, was applicable to theirs, which is in these words :—

Zanchy, upon the fifth to the Ephesians, treating of baptism, propounds a question of a Turk coming to the knowledge of Christ, and to faith, by reading the New Testament, and withal teaching his family, and converting it and others to Christ ; and being in a country whence he cannot easily come to Christian churches, whether he may baptize them, whom he had converted to Christ, he himself being unbaptized? He answers, I doubt not of it but that he may, and withal provide, that he himself be baptized of one of the three converted by him. The reason he gives is, because he is a minister of the word extraordinarily stirred up of Christ. And so as such a minister may, with the consent of that small church, appoint one of the communicants, and provide that he be baptized by him.[1]

Mr. Williams took such a method, with only this differ- ence, that one of the community was first appointed to bap- tize him, and then he baptized the rest; for Mr. Hubbard says, he " was baptized by one Holliman,[2] then Mr. Williams

---

[1]Robinson's answer to Bernard, p. 422. [447]

[2]This is the Ezekiel Holliman mentioned on page 74. We should not deem it needful to notice this, if an error in Cramp's Baptist History, pp. 461, 594, had not given the name, Thomas. As has been stated, (p. 74, note.) Holliman did not leave Massachusetts till 1638. In the Records of the General Court for that year are the words, " Ezekiel Holliman, appearing upon summons, because he did not frequent the public assemblies, and for seducing many, he was referred by the Court to the ministers for conviction." He seems to have been a leading man in Providence and afterwards in Warwick, and held various positions of trust.—ED.

rebaptized him, and some ten more." With this Governor
Winthrop agrees, and sets the date of it in March, 1639.
The Governor called Holliman a poor man, and Hubbard
styles him a mean fellow; but after the year 1650, I find
him more than once a deputy from the town of Warwick in
their General Court. The above gentlemen represent that
Mrs. Hutchinson's sister, the wife of one Scott, stirred Mr.
Williams up to this action; though afterward Mr. Hubbard
does not pretend to certainty as to that, and says it was difficult for one to give an exact account of their religious affairs
in that colony, that did not live among them. It is certain
that he and the Governor were both mistaken in calling
" those of Providence all Anabaptists ;" for it appears from
under Mr. Williams's own hand, seventeen years after, that
Arnold and Carpenter, two of the first twelve, were not
such ;[1] neither have I met with any proof that Gorton, Weston or Waterman, who went to Warwick, were ever of that
denomination.[2]

[1]Massachusetts History, Vol. 3, p. 277. [310.]—B.

The document here referred to, is a letter from Roger Williams to the colony of
Massachusetts Bay, complaining that, under the name of that colony, four persons
in Pawtuxet were obstructing all law and order in the Providence Plantations.
Massachusetts is especially appealed to in reference to two of the four. One,
Stephen Arnold, was manifesting a better spirit, and " desired to be uniform" with
those in Providence, " Zecharie Rhodes" says the letter, " being in the way of
dipping, is (potentially) banished from you. Only William Arnold and William
Carpenter, very far also in religion from you if you know all, they have some
color," that is, some pretext of protection from Massachusetts. It is a fair inference that Arnold and Carpenter were not Baptists.—Ed.

[2]This Baptist Church at Providence appears to be the second distinct society of
that denomination in all the British empire. There had been many of them intermixed with other societies from their first coming out of popery, but the first distinct church in our nation was formed out of the Independent church in London,
whereof Mr. Henry Jacob was pastor from 1616 to 1624, when he went to Virginia, and Mr. John Lothrop was chosen in his room. Prince's Chronology, [225.]
But nine years after, " several persons in the society, finding that the congregation
kept not to their first principles of separation, and being also convinced that baptism
was not to be administered to infants, but such only as professed faith in Christ,"
desired and obtained liberty, and formed themselves into a distinct church, Sept. 12,
1633, having Mr. John Spilsbury for their minister. A second Baptist church was
constituted in London this year, but I believe later in the year than ours at Providence. Crosby's History, Vol. 1, pp. 148, 149. Mr. Lothrop came over to Boston in

Before this time Mr. Peters had become minister of Salem, and he wrote to the church of Dorchester on July 1, this year, to acquaint them that their " great censure" was past upon Roger Williams and his wife, John Throgmorton and his wife, Thomas Olney and his wife, Stukely Westcoat and his wife, Mary Holliman, and the widow Reeves, and that all but two of these were rebaptized.[1]

Besides the above men, we are well informed that William Wickenden, Chad Brown, and Gregory Dexter, were of this Baptist church in Providence, and in 1765, Governor Hopkins, who is not a Baptist, said, " This first church of Baptists at Providence hath from its beginning kept itself in repute, and maintained its discipline to this day; hath always been, and still is, a numerous congregation, and in which I have with pleasure observed very lately sundry descendants from each of the above named founders, except Holliman."[2]   It seems he removed away.

I am sensible that this testimony is very different from the accounts of many New England historians, who represent that the church soon broke up, because Mr. Williams did not walk long with it.   His stop in that travel Governor

1634, was minister a while at Scituate, and then at Barnstable. Winthrop, [Vol. I, pp. 143, 144.] Prince, [225.]—B.

Crosby states that the church " commonly but most falsely called Anabaptists," which John Smith had founded in Holland, removed in 1614, with their pastor, Mr. Helwisse, to London, " where they continued their church state and assemblies for worship as publicly as the evil of the times would permit.." Vol. I, pp. 271, 272. Mr. Helwisse and his church were General Baptists, as is proved by their Confession of Faith; (Hansard Knollys Society, Confessions of Faith, &c., pp. 3—10,) though Crosby not having seen their Confession of Faith when he wrote his first volume, supposed them to be Particular Baptists. Crosby, Vol. I, pp. 270, 271. Taylor in his History of the English General Baptists, quoted by Guild, (Biographical Introduction to the writings of Roger Williams, Publications of the Narragansett Club, vol. I, p. 36, note,) " states that they formed distinct societies and had regular church officers twenty-five years prior" to the date of the founding of Mr. Spilsbury's church.   That this was the first Particular Baptist church in the British empire may be true.—ED.

[1]Massachusetts History, Vol. I, p. 421. [371.]

[2]History of Providence. Olney and Dexter were much improved in their day in public offices in the colony.

Winthrop mentions in July following; and Richard Scott, who afterward turned to the Quakers, says,—

I walked with him in the Baptists' way about three or four months, in which time he brake from the society, and declared at large the ground and reasons of it; that their baptism could not be right because it was not administered by an apostle. After that he set upon a way of seeking (with two or three of them that had dissented with him) by way of preaching and praying; and there he continued a year or two, till two of the three left him. That which took most with him was to get honor amongst men. After his society and he in a church way were parted, he then went to England, and there got a charter; and coming from Boston to Providence, at Seaconk, the neighbors of Providence met him with fourteen canoes, and carried him to Providence. And the man being hemmed in the middle of the canoes, was so elevated and transported out of himself, that I was condemned in myself, that amongst the rest I had been an instrument to set him up in his pride and folly. . . . . Though he professed liberty of consience, and was so zealous for it at the first coming home of the charter, that nothing in government must be acted till that was granted; yet he could be the forwardest in their government to prosecute against those that could not join with him in it; as witness his presenting of it to the Court at Newport.[1]

Thus Quakers, as well as pædobaptists, could cast out hard reflections against him; whether justly or not, the reader, when he has heard the whole story will judge. At present I would only remark, that this man had been Mr. Williams's neighbor thirty-eight years when he wrote this letter, and the spirit of it fully proves that he was not prejudiced at all in his or the Baptists' favor; yet the facts according to him were, that but two or three persons went off with Mr. Williams, leaving the rest in a church way still; neither does he say a word of Mr. Williams's expecting to be an apostle himself. Indeed as to that point, Mr. Hubbard goes no further than to say, " expecting (as was supposed) to become an apostle;" and Governor Winthrop has the same parenthesis; so that it was no more than a suppostion in that day; but a late historian has delivered

---

[1] Scott's letter in George Fox's answer to Williams, 1677, p. 247.

it off as fact, without the parenthesis ; and Dr. Mather from his grandfather Cotton, says, they " broke forth into anabaptism, and then to antibaptism and familism, and now finally into no church at all.[1] Such naked untruths have one generation after another told about these people !

An evident cause of Mr. Williams's refraining from a farther proceeding in church ordinances, was an apprehension of the necessity of a visible succession of regular ordinations from the apostles, to empower men to it, which succession he could not find. Yet how fond are many ministers in our day of this successive notion ? A minister's preaching upon it was vindicated in the Boston Evening Post of May 9, 1774, which informs us that the preacher said,—" God the Father sent forth the Son ; he sent forth the apostles as the Father sent him ; they sent forth others, with command to commit these things to faithful men. And the preacher said that Christ had never committed this power (to put into office) to any but such as were in office ; and consequently no other had a power to put out of office." But I am not afraid boldly to assert, that I verily believe, according to this doctrine, that there is not a minister this day under heaven but what must stop from administering baptism, as Mr. Williams did, if he is as honest as he was. A minister in Connecticut a few years ago published a pamphlet to support the above opinion ; wherein, to get over the difficulty that arises for want of any proof of such a lineal succession, he observed that none under the law were to be priests but the lawful posterity of Aaron, yet supposing a bastard son of that family should have posterity, in so long a succession that the knowledge of his illegitimacy was lost, he asserted that such priests might well be admitted into office with others. According to which doctrine, knowledge must be very detrimental to such priests, and ignorance must be the mother of such devotion. The min-

[1] Magnalia, B. 7, p. 9. [Vol. II, p. 433.]

ister who published said pamphlet is a trustee of Yale College ; and likely he is better acquainted with philosophy and school divinity than he is with his Bible, or else he would have known that Ezra the priest, a scribe of the law of the God of heaven (in distinction from earthly gods) refused to admit or suffer men upon negatives ; and such as sought but could not find " their register," were, "as polluted, put from the priesthood." Ezra ii. 62. And if we review the text[1] that is now so much harped upon, we shall find that the apostolic succession is in the line of " faithful men ;" and no others are truly in it, though false brethren have sometimes crept in unawares.

Mr. John Spilsbury, pastor of the first Baptist church in London, says,—

Because some think to shut up the ordinance of God in such a strait, that none can come by it but through the authority of the popedom of Rome ; let the reader consider who baptized John the Baptist before he baptized others, and if no man did, then whether he did not baptize others, he himself being unbaptized. We are taught by this what to do on the like occasions. I fear men put more than is of right due to it, that so prefer it above the church, and all other ordinances ; for they can assume and erect a church, take in and cast out members, elect and ordain officers, and administer the supper, and all anew, without looking after succession, any further than the Scriptures ; but as for baptism, they must have that successively from the apostles, though it comes through the hands of Pope Joan. What is the cause of this, that men can do all from the Word but only baptism ?[2]

The learned Mr. John Tombes also in that day produced the foregoing passage from Zanchy, for the same purpose that I have now done[3].

I would just add, that though the express rule to Israel was, that every male must needs be circumcised at eight days old, or be cut off from his people, yet this general rule was so far dispensed with in a particular case, that circumcision

---

[1] II Tim. ii. 2.—ED.
[2] Crosby, Vol. I, pp. 103, 104.   [3] Crosby, Vol. I, pp. 104, 105.

was omitted forty years in the wilderness ; and multitudes of them stood before God, and entered into or renewed their father Abraham's covenant in the plains of Moab, who yet were not circumcised till after they came over Jordan. Deut. xxix. ; Joshua v. 4—7. But the Christian church had been through a worse wilderness than that of Arabia, between the apostolic age and that we are now treating of ; therefore that ancient example seems to give light in the case before us.

Mr. Pelatiah Mason, who was born near Providence Ferry in 1669, told his sons (three of whom are now public preachers in Swanzey) that he heard from the fathers of that day, that in the trial they then had, they heard that the Queen of Hungary, or some in those parts, had a register of a regular succession from the apostles, and they had thoughts of sending Mr. Thomas Olney (who succeeded Mr. Williams as their pastor) into that country for it ; but at length concluded that such a course was not expedient, but believing they were now got into the right way, determined to persevere therein.

Mr. Hubbard speaking of that colony says :—

As to matters of religion, it was hard to give an exact account to the world of their proceedings therein, by any who have not been conversant with them from the beginning of their plantations ; yet this was commonly said by all that ever had any occasion to be among them, that they always agreed in this principle, that no man or company of men ought to be molested by the civil power upon the account of religion, or for any opinion received or practiced in any matter of that nature ; accounting it no small part of their happiness that they may therein be left to their own liberty ; by which means the inhabitants are of many different persuasions. But what tendency that liberty had, by so long experience, towards the promoting of the power of godliness, and purity of religion, they are best able to judge that have had occasion to be most conversant amongst them[1].

By this and many other passages, that learned writer, as well as Governor Winthrop, discovered more candor of mind

[1] Hubbard, pp. 335, 336.—Ed.

toward Mr. Williams and Rhode Island colony, than almost any other of the Massachusetts writers have ever done, first or last.   Mr. Hubbard says, that at Rhode Island "they gathered a church, but in a very disordered way; taking in some excommunicate persons, and others which were members of the church of Boston, but not dismissed; . . . . yet had they afterwards one Mr. Clarke for their minister, who had been bred to learning."

At the General Court at Boston, March 13, 1639, acts were passed as follows:—

John Smith for disturbing the public peace, by combining with others to hinder the orderly gathering of a church at Weymouth, and to set up another there, contrary to the orders here established, and the constant practice of all our churches, and for undue procuring the hands of many to a blank for that purpose, is fined twenty pounds and committed during the pleasure of the Court or the Council.

Richard Silvester, for going with Smith to get hands to a blank, was disfranchised and fined forty shillings.

Ambrose Morton, [Marten], for calling the church covenant a stinking carrion, and a human invention, and saying he wondered at God's patience, feared it would end in the sharp, and said the ministers did dethrone Christ and set up themselves; he was fined ten pounds and counselled to go to Mr. Mather to be instructed by him.[1]   Thomas Mackpeace, because of his novel disposition, was informed we were weary of him unless he reformed.[2]

The fourth of the 2d month was thought fit for a day of humiliation, to seek the face of God, and reconciliation with him by our Lord Jesus Christ in all the churches.   Novelties, oppression, atheism, excess, superfluity, idleness, contempt of authority, and troubles in other parts, to be remembered.

Mr. Robert Lenthal, upon his free acknowledgment under his hand, given into the Court, was appointed to appear at the next Court, and enjoined to acknowledge his fault and give satisfaction to the church at

[1]Mr. Richard Mather, of Dorchester.

[2]With this deserves to be quoted a record of the next Court, Dec. 1, 1640:—"Mr. Thomas Lechford, acknowledging that he had overshot himself and is sorry for it, promising to attend to his calling and not to meddle with controversies, was dismissed."—ED.

Weymouth, and to give a copy of that he gave into the Court to the church of Weymouth.[1]

John Smith and John Spur are bound in forty pounds to pay twenty pounds the first day of the next Court.[2]

Mr. Lenthal went to Rhode Island, was admitted a freeman there on August 6, 1640 ; and he kept school and preached there for a while, but before March, 1642, went back to England. The first settlement of the island began the same spring they purchased it ; the second the spring after ; the latter of which was named Newport, on May 16, 1639 ; the other was called Portsmouth, at a General Court, March 12, 1640.

At a General Court at Boston, October, 7, 1640, the following was enacted :—

It is ordered, that the letter lately sent to the Governor by Mr. Eaton, Mr. Hopkins, Mr. Haynes, Mr. Coddington, and Mr. Brenton, but coming also to the General Court,[3] shall be thus answered by the Governor, that the Court doth assent to all the propositions laid down in the aforesaid letter, but that the answer shall be directed to Mr. Eaton, Mr. Hopkins and Mr. Haynes only, excluding Mr. Coddington and Mr. Brenton, as men not to be capitulated withal by us, either for themselves or the people of the island where they inhabit, as their case standeth.[4]

[1]Mr. Lenthal was a minister whom the people of Weymouth had invited to visit them with the purpose of calling him to become their pastor. Winthrop, Vol. I, p 287.—ED.

[2]Massachusetts Records. Their crime was this, Mr. Lenthal held, " that only baptism was the door of entrance into the visible church; the common sort of people did eagerly embrace his opinion, and some labored to get such a church on foot, as all baptized ones might communicate in, without any further trial of them. For this end they procured many hands in Weymouth to a blank, intending to have Mr. Lenthal's advice to the form of the call. . . . . Mr. Lenthal, having before conferred with some of the magistrates and ministers, did openly and freely retract. . . . . So the Court forbore any further censure, though it was much urged by some." Hubbard, [275.] The next Court, Smith was fined five pounds more for contempt; but upon making his submission, and presenting his money, he got released by paying fifteen pounds. Massachusetts Records.—B.

This was not the last time that John Spur was called to suffer as a Baptist. In Chap. IV. we shall find him sentenced to pay a fine of forty shillings or to be whipped for the crime of shaking hands with Obadiah Holmes as the latter came from the whipping post.—ED.

[3]The published Records read, "but concerning also the General Court."—ED.

[4]Massachusetts Records. They at this Court granted to Mr. John Winthrop, junior, all their right to Fisher's Island, which still belongs to his posterity.

Eaton was of New Haven, the other of Connecticut, which had no more of a charter from England than Rhode Island had ; therefore it was a difference about religious affairs that caused this partiality.

Our neighbors of Plymouth had procured from hence[1] this year one Mr. Chauncy, a great scholar and a godly man, intending to call him to the office of a teacher ; but before the fit time came, he discovered his judgment about baptism, that the children ought to be dipped, and not sprinkled. .... There arose much trouble about it. The magistrates and the elders there, and the most of the people, withstood the reviving [receiving] of that practice, not for itself so much as for fear of worse consequences ; as the annihilating our baptism, &c. Whereupon the church there wrote to all the other churches, both here and at Connecticut, &c. for advice, and sent Mr. Chauncy's arguments. The churches took them into consideration, and wrote [their] several answers, wherein they shewed their dissent from him, and clearly confuted all his arguments ; .... yet he could not give over his opinion ; and the church of Plymouth, ... being much taken with his able parts, were very loth to part with him. He did maintain also that the Lord's Supper ought to be administered in the evening, and every Lord's day. And the church at Sandwich (where one Mr. Leveridge was minister) fell into the practice of it. But that being a matter of no great ill consequence, save some outward inconvenience, there was little stir about it. This Mr. Chauncy was after called to office in the church of Scituate[2].

At a Quarter Court at Boston, December 1, it is recorded :—

The jury found Hugh Buet to be guilty of heresy, and that his person and errors are dangerous for infection of others. It is ordered that the said Hugh Buet should be gone out of our jurisdiction by the 24th present, upon pain of death, and not to return upon pain of being hanged.

This is the first instance that I find upon the Massachusetts records of banishment for heresy upon this penalty. Two years before they banished three persons at once, on pain of death, for adultery. The records give no account of what Buet's heresy was, but Governor Winthrop says, it was

---

[1]England.—ED.

[2]Winthrop's Journal, [Vol. I, pp. 330, 331.]

"for holding he was free from original sin, and from actual also, for half a year before, and for holding that true Christians are enabled to live without committing actual sin[1]."

The learned and pious Mr. Henry Dunstar came over this summer, and on August 27, was chosen President of Harvard College, which flourished under his care and influence fourteen years; till having openly renounced infant baptism, such a temper was manifested against him on that account, that he resigned that office[2]. About this time it appears by Mr. Hooker's letters, that many inclined toward the Baptist way, and he expressed his apprehensions that the number would increase[3]; which it seems moved him to "resolve that he would have an argument able to remove a mountain before he would recede from" infant baptism. This resolution Mr. Mitchell, thirteen years after, adopted from him, as a shield against Mr. Dunstar's arguments[4].

The estate of Mr. Humphry, one of their magistrates, being much impaired, he sold his plantation at Lynn to the Lady Moody, and returned to England[5]. She soon embraced the Baptist principles, and suffered therefor. And divers of those at Aquidneck[6] turned professed Anabaptists[7]. Mr. Hubbard says:—

[1]Winthrop's Journal, Vol. II, p. 19. Buet removed to Providence, and for many years was well known and honored there. He was one of the Commissioners for Providence, General Sergeant of Rhode Island and Providence Plantations, Solicitor General, and held other offices. Backus has further occasion to mention him, and spells his name as he himself spelled it, Bewit.—ED.

[2]Magnalia, B. 4, pp. 127, 128. [Vol. II, p. 10.]

[3]Massachusetts History, Vol. I, p. 227. [208.]

[4]Mitchell's Life, p. 70.—B.

Magnalia, B. 4, Vol. II, p. 79. After quoting with evident approval this resolution of Hooker and Mitchell, on the next page Mather speaks of those who were troubled by the "hydrophobie of anabaptism," and who could only reply to the arguments against them, "Say what you will, we will hold our mind." For those on the one side to refuse to be convinced by reasonable argument he seems to have regarded as wisdom, for those on the other, as madness.—ED.

[5]Massachusetts History, Vol. I, p. 15. [21.]—B.

See further notice of Lady Moody near the close of this chapter.—ED.

[6]On page —, this name is spelled Aquetneck. Other writers give it in still different forms.—ED.

[7]Winthrop, [Vol. II, p. 38.]

Nicholas Easton .... used to teach at Newport. .... He maintained, that man had no power nor will in himself, but as he was acted by God; and seeing that God filled all things, nothing could be or move but by him, and so must needs be the author of sin, and that a Christian is united to the essence of God. Being shewed what blasphemous consequences would follow therefrom, they seemed to abhor the consequences, but still defended the position. .... Mr. Coddington, Mr. Coggshall, and some others, joined with Nicholas Easton in those delusions; but their minister, Mr. Clarke, and Mr. Lenthal, and Mr. Harding, with some others, dissented and publicly opposed; whereby it grew to such a heat of contention that it made a schism amongst them.[1]

Mr. Coddington and Mr. Easton afterward joined the Quakers. Mr. Clarke and his friends formed the first Baptist church on Rhode Island.

In June this year the General Assembly of the Massachusetts sent to Plymouth to know why they might not take Seekonk into their jurisdiction. They tried for it about three years, till the commissioners of the United Colonies confirmed it to Plymouth.

At a Quarter Court at Boston, September 7, Mr. William Collins, a man of learning, who had married Mrs. Hutchinson's daughter, being "found a seducer," and Francis Hutchinson, for calling the church of Boston "a whore," &c., were both fined and banished upon pain of death.[2] About two years after, they were both killed by the Indians, with their mother Hutchinson, near New York. It is evident that the planters of Rhode Island did not at first see into the true nature and grounds of liberty of conscience, but their Assembly at Portsmouth, March 16, 1641, passed an act for that purpose, which on the 17th of September following was confirmed as a perpetual law. And at an Assembly in Newport, September 19, 1642, they appointed Messrs. Coddington, Brenton, Easton, Coggshall, Baulston, Porter, Dyer,

---

[1]Hubbard, p. 343.—B.

As usual, he borrows almost word for word from Winthrop. See Vol. II, pp. 40, 41. Nicholas Easton was five years Governor at Rhode Island.—ED.

[2]Massachusetts Records.

Clarke, Harding and Jeffries, a committee to improve the first and best opportunity that presented to send home for a charter, and to write to Sir Henry Vane to solicit his assistance and influence in the design. They accordingly sent over by Mr. Williams, and obtained their request; though in the mean time a most dreadful broil broke out, and prevailed to a terrible degree among them, of which take the following account:

Samuel Gorton, a man of learning from London, arrived at Boston in 1636, and doubtless had a considerable hand in the mystical disputes that then embroiled the Massachusetts colony. From thence he went to Plymouth, where he treated their pastor Mr. Smith in such a manner, as caused the authority to take him in hand, and require bonds of him for his good behavior. This occasioned his departure to Rhode Island, where such a difficulty arose, that by Mr. Coddington's order he was imprisoned and whipped. From thence he came to Providence, where he was kindly treated by Mr. Williams and others; and he and his friends sat down at Pawtuxet, now called Cranston. I find by the records that Mr. Gorton bought half of Robert Cole's interest there on January 10, 1641. And as the Court at Newport in March following disfranchised Richard Carder, Randal Holden, Sampson Shatton, and Robert Potter, they and John Wickes, who had followed Gorton[1] from Plymouth, came and formed

---

[1] In Winthrop's Journal, Vol. II, p. 58, note, Mr. Savage quotes from an anonymous correspondent as follows :—" It does not appear that he [Samuel Gorton] was ever a freeholder or freeman of Rhode Island, though 20th, 4th, 1638, he was admitted an inhabitant. In March, 1642, Randal Holden, Richard Carder, and others, were disfranchised the Island. These, Backus says, *followed* Gorton to Newport from Plymouth, though Carder and Holden were two of the original purchasers of the Island, and both signed the original deed of incorporation. Holden, with Roger Williams, witnessed the deed to Coddington, etc., dated 24th, 1st month, 1637. I mention these facts to show how easy it is to write carelessly about men whom we hate or despise." Mr. Savage's correspondent, though described as an " inquisitive antiquary," was most unfortunate in these investigations. A glance at the words of Backus will show that they do not necessarily state that Carder, Holden, &c., but only that John Wickes followed Gorton; and this is undoubtedly their meaning. The Rhode Island Records, in a list of those admitted as inhabitants at Newport in

a considerable party at Pawtuxet. Such a contention was raised between them and the former inhabitants, that " they came armed into the field, each against the other; but Mr. Williams pacified them for the present. This caused the weaker party to write a letter to the Massachusetts rulers, complaining of the wrong they suffered, desiring aid, or if not, counsel from them. They answered them, that they could not levy war without a General Court. For counsel they told them, that except they would submit to some jurisdiction (Plymouth, or theirs) they had no calling or warrant to interpose in their contentions, but if they would submit to any, then they had a call to protect them."[1] How different was the temper here discovered, from that of the pious Mr. Williams? He was ever ready wherever he came to exert all his influence to make peace so far as he could with a good conscience, but the Court at Boston seemed willing to play one party against another, till all would submit to their power. Gorton took a like method to defend himself against them; the consequence of which was terrible indeed; the true state thereof I shall give with all the exactness I can.

William Arnold, Robert Cole, William Carpenter, and Benedict Arnold of Pawtuxet, went to the General Assembly at Boston, September 3, 1642, and submitted themselves and their lands to that government. At the same time Mr. Leveret and Edward Hutchinson were sent to Miantinomu to demand satisfaction of him, and first to tell him "of credible information received, partly by relation of the Indians

---

1638, give the name of Samuel Gorton, with the date 20th, 3d, not 20th, 4th, as stated in the above quotation; and next after him the name of John Wickes, with the date 20th, 4th, so that, as Backus states, Wickes followed Gorton. It is well nigh certain, too, that our unknown writer is in error in stating that Holden was one of the original purchasers of Rhode Island. See p. 78, note, and Arnold's History of Rhode Island, Vol. I, p. 124. Backus, in this case at least, did not write carelessly about men whom he hated or despised; and the charge comes with ill grace from one who, in the very act of making it, crowds three errors into as many brief sentences.—ED.

[1]Winthrop, [Vol. II, p. 59]; Hubbard, [343, 344.]

themselves, that they have drawn in many other sachems to
join with the Narragansetts, in making war upon the
English." Benedict Arnold and Ahauton, the Indian, were
to be their guides and interpreters.[1] Then, October 28, a
warrant was sent from Boston to cite Gorton and his friends
to come to their Court, to answer to the complaints of
Arnold's company against them, signed by the Governor
and three Assistants. To this an answer was returned on
November 20, signed by Samuel Gorton, Randal Holden,
Robert Potter, John Wickes, John Warner, Richard Waterman, William Woodale, John Greene, Francis Weston,
Richard Carder, Nicholas Power, and Sampson Shatton. It
contained a long mystical paraphrase upon their warrant
and many provoking sentences against those rulers and their
ministers, and a refusal to come to them. But in order to
get out of their reach they removed and purchased Shawomet for a hundred and forty-four fathoms of wampum, and
obtained a deed of it, signed by Miantinomu, Pumham, and
others, on January 12, 1643. John Greene had received a
deed of an island, neck of land and meadow, called Ocupas-
sutuxet Cove, dated October 1, 1642, signed by Miantinomu
and Socononco.[2]

The General Court at Boston, May 10, 1643, appointed
Messrs. Atherton and Tomlyns, with William Arnold to
speak with Messrs. Greene, Warner, and their company.
On June 22, through Benedict Arnold's influence and assistance, Pumham, sachem of Shawomet, and Socanochu, sachem
of Pawtuxet, signed at Boston a submission of their persons
and lands to that government ; and Arnold was allowed four
pounds for his pains.[3] Governor Winthrop tells us that

---

[1] Hubbard, [447.] Massachusetts Records.

[2] Gorton's Defence, [59.] Callender [89, 90.] Colony Records. The hundred and
forty-four fathoms of peag it is said was computed at forty pounds sixteen shillings
sterling. Massachusetts History, Vol. I, p. 118, [113.]

[3] Massachusetts Records. The colonies of Massachusetts, Plymouth, Connecticut and New Haven, by their commissioners, signed articles of confederation
together for mutual assistance and defence on May 19, 1643, from whence they were
called the United Colonies.

they had two or three hundred men under them. The plea
for this action was, that Gorton's company and Miantinomu
had oppressed these sachems, and wronged them of
their lands. Pumham said he was forced to sign the deed,
but would take none of the pay. The Governor, with
another magistrate, wrote to Shawomet people about it ;
and also to Miantinomu, and he came down and met said
sachems at Boston, where they were forced to confess that
they had sometimes sent him presents, and had aided him in
his wars against the Pequods ; yet they and Arnold would
have it, that they were as free sachems as he was, because
their people paid tribute to them. So the Court received
them (as is before noted) under their protection. We are
told that before this, Gorton and his company had sent a
writing of four sheets " full of reproaches against the magistrates, ministers and churches, and stuffed likewise with
absurd familistial stuff, and wherein they justified the purchase of the sachem's lands, and professed to maintain it to
the death."[1]

Miantinomu had already seen Uncas, a warlike sachem to
the west of him, putting himself and his people under the
protection of the English ; and he was accused of hiring a
young Pequod to murder Uncas, but he brought the young
man with him, who told the Court that Uncas cut his own
arm with a flint, and then charged him to report that Miantinomu had hired him to murder him. But upon private
examination, the Court were persuaded the young man was
guilty, and advised Miantinomu to send him to Uncas ; but
instead of doing it, he cut off his head by the way, as he
returned home."[2] What followed till his own death, we have
recorded by Governor Winthrop, in a more distinct and clear
light than has ever been published. I shall therefore give
it to the reader in his own words :—

August. Onkus being provoked by Sequassion, a sachem of Connecticut (who would not be persuaded by the magistrates there to a reconcilia-

[1]Hubbard, [405.]   [2]Johnson, pp. 182—184.

Lincoln Christian College

tion) made war upon him, and slew divers of his men, and burnt up his wigwams; whereupon Miantinomu, being his kinsman, took offence against Onkus, and went with near one thousand men, and set upon Onkus before he could be provided for defence; for he had not then with him above three or four hundred men.   But it pleased God to give Onkus the victory, after he had killed about thirty of the Narragansetts, and wounded many more; and among these, two of Canonicus's sons, and a brother of Miantinomu, who[1] fled, but having on a coat of mail[2] he was easily overtaken, which two of his captains perceiving, they laid hold of him and carried him to Onkus, hoping thereby to procure their own pardon.   But so soon as they came to Onkus he slew them presently; and Miantinomu standing mute, he demanded of him, why he would not speak? " If you had taken me," (saith he) " I would have besought you for my life."   The news of Miantinomu's captivity coming to Providence, Gorton and his company . . . . wrote a letter to Onkus, willing him to deliver their friend Miantinomu, and threatened him with the power of the English if he refused.   Upon this Onkus carries Miantinomu to Hartford to take advice of the magistrates there; and, at Miantinomu's earnest entreaty, he left him with them, yet as a prisoner.   They kept him under guard, but used him very courteously. So he continued till the commissioners of the United Colonies met at Boston,[3] who, taking into serious consideration what was safest and best to be done, were all of opinion that it would not be safe to set him at liberty; neither had we sufficient ground for us to put him to death.   In this difficulty we called in five of the most judicious elders (it being in the time of the general assembly of the elders) and propounding the case to them, they all agreed that he ought to be put to death.   Upon this concurrence we enjoined secresy upon ourselves and them, lest if it should come to the notice of the Narragansetts, they might attempt somewhat against Hartford for this reason, or might set upon the commissioners, &c., upon their return, to take some of them to redeem him (as Miantinomu himself had told Mr. Haynes had been in consultation amongst them) and agreed that upon the return of the commissioners to Hartford, they should send for Onkus, and tell him our determination, that Miantinomu should be delivered to him again, and he should put him to death so soon as he came within his own jurisdiction, and that the[4] English should go along with him to see the execution.   And if any Indians should invade him for it, we would send men to defend him.   If Onkus should refuse to do it, then Miantinomu should be sent in a pinnance to Boston, there to be kept until further consideration.

[1]Miantinomu.—ED.
[2]Johnson calls it a Corslet, and both he and Hubbard say he had it of Gorton.
[3]In September.
[4]Savage reads " two" in place of " the," and is probably correct.—ED.

Lincoln Christian College

" The reasons of this proceeding with him were these :—1. It was now clearly discovered to us that there was a general conspiracy among the Indians to cut off all the English, and that Miantinomu was the head and contriver of it.   2. He was of a turbulent and proud spirit, and would never be at rest.   3. Although he had promised us in the open Court to send the Pequod to Onkus, who had shot him in the arm, with intent to have killed him (which was by the procurement of Miantinomu, as did probably appear) yet in his way homeward he killed him.   4. He beat one of Pumham's men, and took away his wampum, and then bid him go and complain to the Massachusetts.   According to this agreement the commissioners, at their return to Connecticut, sent for Onkus, and acquainted him herewith, who readily undertook the execution ; and taking Miantinomu along with him, in the way between Hartford and Windsor (where Onkus hath some men dwell) Onkus's brother following after Miantinomu, clave his head with an hatchet, some English being present.   And that the Indians might know that the English did approve of it, they sent twelve or fourteen musqueteers home with Onkus to abide a time with him, for his defence, if need should be.[1]

Alas ! when good men get into an evil path, where will it carry them ?   The next news we hear is as follows.   September 12,[2] the General Court sent a warrant to require Gorton and his company to come to Boston, to answer the Indians' complaints against them.   To which they sent a verbal answer, that they were out of that jurisdiction, and would own subjection to none but the government of Old England.   Upon which the Court wrote the 19th, informing them that they intended to send commissioners to seek to right these things among them.[3]   The commissioners were, Captain George Cook, Humphrey Atherton, and Edward Johnson, who were sent, " with forty able men to attend them, which had authority and order to bring Samuel Gorton and his company, if they should not give

[1]Winthrop, [Vol. II, pp. 130—134.]
[2]In the published Records the date of this warrant is given, September 7.—ED.
[3]Gorton's Defence, [p. 97.]—B.
This reference to Gorton's Defence and those that follow are to Staples's edition, Collections of the R. I. Historical Society, Vol. II.   The exact words here referred to are these :—"This you may rest assured of; that if you will make good your own offer to us of doing us right, our people shall return and leave you in peace, otherwise we must right ourselves and our people by force of arms."—ED.

them satisfaction." A Sergeant Major-General was appointed in the colony, and the country put into a posture of war. "They of Aquidneck" were "granted to buy a barrel of powder, provided Lieutenant Morris give caution that it be employed for the defence of the island, by the advice of the Governor and Deputy." It was ordered "that the deputies should acquaint the elders, to desire them in special manner to commend this undertaking to God."

A large committee of magistrates and deputies was appointed in the recess of the General Court, "not knowing," say they, "what may fall out, concerning the expedition now on foot against Samuel Gorton, and the rest of that company.

It was ordered "that Pumham and Sochonoco should have each of them, lent them a fowling piece, and Benedict Arnold hath liberty to supply them with shot as he sees occasion."[1]

Hearing of their coming, Gorton's company sent a letter to meet them, dated September 28, to let them know, that if they came in a way of loving neighborhood, they were welcome ; but if with a band of soldiers, they charged them not to set foot on their land at their peril.[2] The commissioners wrote a reply, signifying their great desire of having conversation with them, with hope of reclaiming them from

[1]Massachusetts Records.—B.

This enactment was passed at a later session of the Court, October 17.—ED.

[2]If you come to treat with us . . . . shaking a rod over our heads, in a band of soldiers, be you assured, we have passed our childhood and nonage in that point, and are under commission of the great God not to be children in understandings, neither in courage, but quit to ourselves as men. We straitly charge you therefore, hereby, that you set not a foot upon our lands in any hostile way, but upon your peril; and that if any blood be shed, upon your own heads shall it be. . . . . If you spread a table before us as friends, we sit not as mere invective, envious or malcontent, not touching a morsel nor looking for you to point us unto our dish; but we eat with you by virtue of the unfeigned law of relations, not only to satisfy our stomachs but to increase friendship and love, the end of feasting. So also, if you visit us as combatants or warriors, by the same law of relations, we as freely and cheerfully answer you unto death." Extract from the letter of the "owners and inhabitants in Shawomet," "to certain men styled Commissioners, sent from the Massachusetts." Gorton's Defence, p. 99.—ED.

their errors; but if that could not be done, that they should then " look upon them as men prepared for slaughter, and accordingly should address themselves with all convenient speed ;"[1] which we may well suppose was very surprising to their wives and children, and it is said it scattered them and occasioned some their deaths.[2]   Some of the people of Providence went with those commissioners and soldiers, and procured a parley with Shawomet men, who demanded the reason of this proceeding ; to which the others answered, that they had done wrong to certain of their subjects, and also held blasphemous errors.   Shawomet men offered to appeal to England, but that was refused ; then they offered to leave the controversy to indifferent men in this country. This appeared so reasonable that a truce was agreed upon, till they could send to Boston to know the mind of the Court upon it.   Accordingly, Chad Brown, Thomas Olney, William Field, and William Wickenden of Providence, wrote a letter to persuade the rulers of Massachusetts to comply with this proposal.   But an answer was returned, dated October 3, refusing any such thing.[3]   After this those men were seized and forcibly carried to Boston, where the General Court by adjournment met October 17, when the accusation following was exhibited, viz. :—

The charge of the prisoners, Samuel Gorton and his company.

Upon much examination and serious considerations of your writings, with your answers about them, we do charge you to be a blasphemous

[1] " It is our great desire that we might speak with them concerning the particulars which we were sent to them about; certainly persuading ourselves that we shall be able through the Lord's help, to convince some of them at least of the evil of their way and cause them to divert their course, that so doing they may preserve their lives and liberties, which otherwise must lead to the eternal ruin of them and theirs. . . . . But if there be no way of turning them, we then shall look upon them as men prepared for slaughter, and accordingly shall address ourselves with all convenient speed, not doubting of the Lord's presence with us, being clear in the way we are in." Extract from the letter of the Commissioners to John Peise, messenger from those at Shawomet.   Gorton's Defence, p. 101.—ED.

[2] Two women are named as having died in consequence to the exposure incident to their flight; and others are said to have suffered severe physical injury.   Gorton's Defence, p. 102.—ED.

[3] Gorton's Defence, [pp. 103—111.]

enemy of the true religion of our Lord Jesus Christ, and his holy ordinances, and also of all civil authority among the people of God, and particularly in this jurisdiction.

It is ordered that Samuel Gorton shall be confined to Charlestown, there to be set on work, and to wear such bolts or irons as may hinder his escape, and to continue during the pleasure of the Court; provided that if he shall break his said confinement, or shall in the mean time, either by speech or writing, publish, declare or maintain any of the blasphemous or abominable heresies wherewith he hath been charged by the General Court, contained in either of the two books sent unto us by him or Randal Holden; or shall reproach or reprove the churches of our Lord Jesus Christ in these United Colonies, or the civil government, or the public ordinances of God therein (unless it be by answer to some question propounded to him, or conference with any elder, or with any other licensed to speak with him privately under the hand of one of the Assistants) that immediately upon accusation of any such writing or speech, he shall, by such Assistant, to whom such accusation shall be brought, be committed to prison till the next Court of Assistants, then and there to be tried by a jury, whether he hath so spoken or written, and upon conviction thereof shall be condemned to death and executed.   Dated 'the third of the ninth month, 1643.

A like sentence was passed, by which John Wickes was confined to Ipswich, Randal Holden to Salem, Robert Porter to Rowley, Richard Carder to Roxbury, Francis Weston to Dorchester, and John Warner to Boston; all on the same penalty with Gorton.   William Woodale was confined to Watertown during the pleasure of the Court, and if he escaped to be punished as they see meet.   Further:—

It is ordered, that all such cattle of Samuel Gorton, John Greene,[1] &c., as have been or shall be seized upon, for such satisfaction of charges as the country hath been put unto, by sending and fetching them in, and other charges about the trial in the Court, and expense in the prison or otherwise, shall be appraised and sold to the most advantage, and disposed of accordingly, and the overplus to be reserved, by the treasurer for their maintenance. . . . . If any of them will not do such work as they may, and as shall be appointed them, they are to be left to shift as they may.

[1] I can't find that Greene was carried now to Boston.   Hubbard says Woodale was found to be an ignorant young man.—B.

Staples says that Greene " escaped entirely," running from the house when the commissioners came to apprehend him.   Gorton's Defence, p. 137, note.—ED.

Richard Waterman is dismissed for the present, so that what is taken of his, is to go toward payment of the charge, and the rest of his estate is bound in one hundred pounds that he shall appear at the General Court the third month, and not depart without license, and to submit to the order of the Court.

Nicholas Power appearing, and denying that he set his hand to the first book, was dismissed with an admonition.

For appraising the cattle brought from Providence, the prisoners have liberty to name two, Robert Turner and the soldiers two, and the Court one. The prisoners refusing, the Court, Robert Turner, and the soldiers, chose Mr. Colbron, John Jephson and William Parks.[1]

The whole of the aforesaid charges were adjudged to amount to an hundred and sixty pounds. They were detained through the winter under the above sentence; "but finding that they could not keep them from seducing others, nor yet bring them to any sight of their folly and wickedness, the General Court (March 7, 1644,) sent them away."[2] Ah, sent them away sure enough! it was with the words following, viz. :—

It is ordered that Samuel Gorton and the rest of that company, who now stand confined, shall be set at liberty, provided that if they or any of them shall, after fourteen days after such enlargement, come within any part of our jurisdiction, either in the Massachusetts, or in or near Providence, or any of the lands of Pumham and Soconocho, or elsewhere within our jurisdiction, then such person or persons shall be apprehended, wheresoever they may be taken, and shall suffer death by course of law ; provided also, that during all their continuance in our bounds inhabiting for the said time of fourteen days, they shall be still bound to the rest of the articles of their former confinement, upon the penalty therein expressed.[3]

Such a way of treating our fellow servants as this, will doubtless appear very surprising to the present generation ;

[1] Massachusetts Records. Nicholas Power and many of his posterity have been of good note among the Baptists in Providence. Hubbard says he was released "freely, for that he was in his master's house."

[2] Hubbard, [407].—B.
Hubbard is almost the last man in whose behalf one need enter a complaint of injustice, but a wrong impression seems to be conveyed by quoting from him only the above fragment. His sentence ends with the words, "——sent them away with this caution, that they should not come into any place where the said Court had jurisdiction, upon pain of death."—ED.

[3] Massachusetts Records.

and many will be ready to say, How was it possible for any, if they had been endowed with the least spark of Christianity, or even humanity, to treat their neighbors as those rulers did? Let Captain Johnson, who was one of the three commissioners that took them, answer the question; says he :—

That holy man of God, Mr. John Cotton. among many others, hath diligently searched for the Lord's mind herein, and hath declared some sudden blow to be given to this blood-thirsty monster [the man of sin] but the Lord Jesus Christ hath inseparably joined the time, means and manner of this work together ; and therefore all men that expect the day (of his fall) must attend the means.[1]

And speaking of Gorton and his company, he says :—

To be sure there be them in New England that have Christ Jesus and his blessed ordinances in such esteem, that, the Lord assisting, they had rather lose their lives, then suffer them to be thus blasphemed, if they can help it ; and whereas some have favored them, and endeavored to bring under blame such as have been zealous against their abominable doctrines, the good God be favorable unto them, and prevent them from coming under the like blame with Ahab ; yet they remain in their old way, and there is somewhat to be considered in it to be sure, that in these days, when all look for the fall of antichrist, such detestable doctrines should be upheld, and persons suffered, that exceed the beast himself for blasphemy, and this to be done by those that would be counted reformers, and such as seek the utter subversion of antichrist.[2]

This plain account of the reasons and motives they acted upon, takes off the edge in some measure of Gorton's keen satire upon them, which he wrote from Warwick, Sept. 16, 1656, to the first Quakers that were imprisoned in Boston, saying,—

I marvel what manner of God your adversaries trust in, who is so fearful of being infected with error, or how they think they shall escape the wiles and power of the devil, when the arm of flesh fails them, whereby they seek to defend themselves for the present ; sure they think their God will be grown to more power and care over them, in and after death, or else they will be loth to pass through it.

This remark is cutting indeed, if we leave out any con-

[1]Johnson's History, p. 230.   [2]Ibid, p. 187.

sideration of duty in the case; but if that be brought in, then it is a presumption, and not faith, to expect protection and support from God in a way of disregard of the means of his appointment. Hence, the error of supposing that God has appointed the use of secular force in religious affairs, ought to bear all the blame and scandal of those cruel proceedings; and instead of venting our resentment against our dead fathers, let these things rouse the living to repentance and reformation. Those fathers could find warrant enough in the Old Testament for the use of force against idolaters and blasphemers; but the use of force to collect the priests' support was plainly censured in those times. With what face then can those who profess to be under the law of liberty, forcibly take a farthing from any to maintain professed ministers of him who has said, " Freely ye have received, freely give ;" and who commanded his disciples to shake off, and therefore not to carry away, so much as the dust of a city or house that would not receive them!

It is likely that the reader may wish to know what Gorton's sentiments really were which were so offensive. To this I answer, that he evidently was a man of smart capacity, and of considerable learning, and when he pleased could express his ideas as plainly as any man; but he used such a mystical method in handling the Scriptures, and in speaking about religion, that people are not agreed to this day what his real sentiments were. It is so common for parties to misrepresent the opinions of their opponents, that little regard is paid by many to what those in Massachusetts have said against him. I will therefore give a taste of what he published to the world, not in a way of controversy, but of friendly correspondence with the aforesaid prisoners at Boston. He first wrote a letter to them of the date I have given; to which they returned an answer; then he made a reply, October 6, 1656, wherein he gives various remarks on the sentiments expressed in their letter, and says :—

In us a child is born, in us a son is given[1], but the government is upon
his shoulder, and he is called Wonderful, Counsellor, The mighty God, The
everlasting Father, The Prince of Peace. So that wherever this lowly and
meek spirit is, there is also the spirit of the Lion of the tribe of Judah,
and the Lord thereby shall roar out of Zion, and utter his voice from Jerusalem, and the heavens and the earth shall shake ; but the Lord is the hope
of his people, and the strength of the children of Israel. True lowliness
of spirit, and the loftiest mind that ever was, are never separated ; for
these twain are made one so as never to be separated, no more than a child
(in point of all human abilities) and the Ancient of Days shall ; for as we
receive the kingdom of heaven as a little child, so we are never otherwise
in the same respect, which we know, no wisdom human, serpentine, or
upon principles proper to a creature, can ever yield unto or find out ; and
therefore we are fools unto the world, being bereaved of all their principles,
in regard of any exercise of them according to their proper intent in any
of our designs. . . . . And therefore as brute beasts are unto them, so are
they to us in the things of God.

Again he says :—

We conclude that the wisdom of God, though become foolishness unto
the world, yet doth it contain sufficiency of power in argument to overtop
any council, synod, synedrim or assembly, composed by human art or learning. . . . . For as it is in that way of the devil, to propose his temptations
from the letter of the Scriptures, to subdue Christ thereby ; so is there sufficiency of spirit and wisdom, in the true interpretation thereof, to confound
and bring them (in the party proposing them) to nought. A Christian is
still saying, Let there be light, and it is so ; he shall ever divide the light
from the darkness, and the waters that are above the firmament from the
waters that are below the outspread firmament. In a word, he is for ever
to form all things out of that ancient chaos of God and man being made
one.

Once more he says :—

If I witness to the Son, word, light, life, law, or peace of God, I must
witness unto the being of such a thing, that such a thing is, as also to the
manner of its being, how it comes to be such a thing, together with its
necessary and proper operations, which must inevitably accompany such a
manner of being, with the comprehensions and extensions of such operations and motion, or else I am not that faithful and true witness, the beginning of the creation of God, or that head and masterpiece of his work.[2]

---

[1]Observe, the word of truth says, " *Unto us*," but this perverter of Scripture says,
" *In us*."

[2]These letters are annexed to a book he published in 1636, pp. 272—294.

These extracts from his own writings, may give the reader some idea of his way of handling the Scriptures. Our Saviour vanquished the tempter by appealing to what was written, and shewing thereby that Satan perverted the text he pretended to quote ; but the *lofty mind* of this writer soared so much above that method, as to say of the world of mankind, " As brute beasts are unto them, so are they to us in the things of God." Well therefore might Mr. Williams say, " I am no more of Master Gorton's religion than of Master Cotton's ; and yet if Master Cotton complain of their obstinacy in their way, I cannot but impute it to his bloody tenet and practice, which ordinarily doth give strength, vigor, spirit and resolution to the most erroneous, when such unrighteous and most unchristian proceedings are exercised against them."[1] Besides their difference about gospel doctrines, they evidently differed in the following points of practice. 1. Mr. Williams used great plainness of speech, so that his meaning was obvious to common understandings ; but Mr. Gorton's writings are not so. 2. Mr. Williams openly stood for what he believed to be the truth, in the face of the greatest danger ; but when Mr. Gorton saw himself greatly exposed in Boston, he explained their mystical writings in such a manner, that Governor Winthrop said " he could agree with him in his answer, though not in their writings."[2] 3. Mr. Williams set a noble example of overcoming evil with good ; but Mr. Gorton was sadly ensnared in rendering evil for evil, and railing for railing. Though after he had been to England, and obtained liberty to return to and enjoy the lands they had purchased, he and sundry of his suffering companions became very useful members of civil society. But as corruption is ever the most dangerous when covered with a religious mask, it is of great importance for us all to learn to distinguish between that and true religion. Paul said to the contending Corinthians, " Are ye

[1]Reply to Cotton, p. 123.   [2]Gorton's Defence, [132.]

not carnal and walk as men?" The same query may be
made concerning those contentions betwixt Gorton and his
opponents.

Those in Massachusetts professed a high regard to their
charter, when they banished Mr. Williams; but that gave
them no right to any land or government, further than three
miles south of their bay, and of every part of Charles River.
That line crosses the great post road near landlord Maxcy's,
in Attleborough, from whence to Pawtuxet river is nineteen
miles ; and Shawomet is still further southward ; yet we are
plainly told that Arnold and his company were received
" partly to draw in the rest, either under themselves or
Plymouth.¹ And when Gorton and his friends were got out
of Arnold's reach, two petty sachems were taken in to
found a claim upon, though it was known that Miantinomu
was so much above them, that he sold Providence and Pawtuxet over their heads, some years before, in which was
contained the best title that Arnold's company had to their
lands. What work then did they make, in first enticing
subjects to revolt from their prince, and then in killing him
because he was uneasy about it ! Had they not been blinded
with such a zeal as the disciples had, when they were for
having fire to come down and consume the Samaritans, surely
they would not have violated the rules of justice and equity
as they did. They tried afterwards to vindicate their conduct by the claim of Plymouth to that land, and upon an act
of the commissioners of the United Colonies concerning it.²
But Plymouth patent extended no farther westward than
Narragansett river, and the utmost limits of Pocanokit or
Sawamset, that is Osamaquin or Massasoit's territories ;³ and
we have before heard how they fell short of the lands in
question. Further, the commissioners pleaded, that Miantinomu engaged by treaty, not to begin war with Uncas without first appealing to the English ; yet had broken that

¹Hubbard, [344.]   ²Massachusetts History, Vol. I, p. 125, [117.]
³Prince's Chronology, p. 197. [269.]

agreement.[1] But a very credible writer of their own informs us, that Miantinomu first sent his complaint to Hartford against Uncas; and when they refused to meddle in Sequastion's quarrel, he would know whether they would be offended if he should make war upon Uncas? And that they left him to take his course,[2] so that their case in truth was, like that of other invaders of their neighbor's rights; they were in danger of being awfully requited, by a man so sensible and powerful as Miantinomu, if he was not taken out of the way. This evil is greatly to be lamented, and should ever stand as a solemn warning to us all, to beware of taking one step into any course of injustice, deceit or cruelty; for it will surely prove bitterness in the latter end.

Had Gorton been duly aware of this, he would not have armed Miantinomu against Uncas, for no better reason, that we know of, than because he, being a warlike prince, stood in the way of his forming an Indian party sufficient to withstand or overcome the Massachusetts; which proceeding, together with his irritating writings against their rulers and ministers, was the evident cause of things being carried to the dreadful extremity they were. Mr. Williams ever bore as plain and full testimony against their persecuting any man for matters of conscience, as Gorton could; and had a much greater influence over the Indians than he ever had; yet he was so far from trying to raise a heathen party against Christians, to correct them for injuries done to himself, that he exerted himself with great assiduity to prevent any thing of that nature; by which he undoubtedly was the greatest instrument of saving New England of any one man that lived in that day, and for which his memory is and will be blessed.

Among the reasoners of our world, some will not allow, that men are influenced in all their voluntary actions by previous causes and motives, while others incline so much to

---

[1] Massachusetts History, Vol. III, p. 140. [2] Hubbard, [450.]

infidelity as to represent, that the very notion of religion, or of persons thinking that the Deity loves them better than others, tends to make them hate and treat those ill who, as they suppose, are not thus beloved. But as nothing teaches like experience, let the experience of those fathers be considered, and the light which facts give in the case be regarded, beyond all the suppositions or wrangles of disputants. Is it not evident, that those several contending parties were influenced in all their bad actions by the same principles of ambition, avarice, deceit, and resentment, that other men are? And is it not as evident, that those actions which were good and praiseworthy, flowed from a hearty belief of revealed religion, especially of free salvation by Christ Jesus? At present we will take a view of the head men of the three parties of Boston, Warwick and Providence.

Governor Winthrop was in such esteem in his native country, as to be made a justice of peace at the age of eighteen; had an estate of six or seven hundred pounds sterling per annum; yet sold it, and spent the main of it in promoting a religious settlement in this wilderness; where for all his vast labor and pains, in settling and managing the government, he for some years had no stated salary, and never had more than one hundred pounds a year; was several times very ungratefully treated by his own people; and what could carry him through all this with cheerfulness to the end, but the power of religion?[1]

[1]What his religious sentiments were, the reader may form some judgment by the following extracts. In the first part of his administration as Governor, he said, " In the infancy of plantations, justice should be administered with more lenity than in a settled state; because people are more apt then to transgress; partly out of ignorance of new laws and orders, partly out of oppression of business and other straits." But when some leading and learned men took offence at his conduct in this matter, and upon a conference, gave it as their opinion, that a stricter discipline was to be used in the beginning of a plantation, than after its being with more age established and confirmed, the Governor being readier to see his own errors than other men's, professed his purpose to endeavor their satisfaction with less lenity in his administrations." [Magnalia, B. 2, Vol. I, pp. 110, 111.] From this we may guess at the cause of the severities we have been treating of.

His expenses were great, and for two years he had no settled salary, yet the divine

Gorton, as we have seen, had a notion that the child was born in him and his followers, who had the government upon his shoulders, and he concurred with Wheelwright in treating those who opposed their religious sentiments as enemies to the state; which principle evidently moved him to

precept against taking bribes, had such influence upon his mind, that when he was the third time chosen Governor, May 8, 1632, he told the people publicly, "that he had received gratuities from divers towns, which he received with much comfort and content; he had also received many kindnesses from particular persons, which he could not refuse, lest he should be accounted uncourteous, &c., but he professed he received them with a trembling heart, in regard to God's rule, and the consciousness of his own infirmity, and therefore desired that hereafter they would not take it ill if he should refuse presents from particular persons, except the assistance of some special friends. To which no answer was made; but he is told after, that many good people were much grieved at it, for that he never had any allowance toward the charge of his place." [Prince's Chronology, pp. 394, 395.]

After he had acted in banishing Mr. Wheelwright and others, many of their friends in Boston church, whereof he was a member, were earnest with the elders to have the church call him forth as an offender, for passing that sentence, which he understanding, took occasion to make a public speech to them upon it, in which he said:—
"As for myself, I did nothing in the causes of any of the brethren, but by advice of the elders of the church. Moreover, in the oath which I have taken there is this clause, 'In all causes wherein you are to give your vote, you shall do as in your judgment and conscience you shall see to be just, and for the public good.' And I am satisfied it is most for the glory of God, and the public good, that there be such a sentence passed; yea, those brethren are so divided from the rest of the country in their opinions and practices that it cannot stand with the public peace for them to continue with us; Abraham saw that Hagar and Ishmael must be sent away."
[Magnalia, B. 2, Vol. I, pp. 114, 115.]

Seven years after, upon a hot debate between the magistrates and deputies about who should have the negative vote, Governor Winthrop wrote his mind upon it, some passages whereof gave offence to some noted men, which he understanding, made the following speech at the next General Court. viz.: "As for the matter of my writing, I had the concurrence of my brethren; it is a point of judgment which is not at my own disposing. I have examined it over and over again, by such light as God has given me, from the rules of religion, reason and custom; and I see no cause to retract anything of it; wherefore I must enjoy my liberty in that, as you do yourselves. But for the manner, this, and all that was blameworthy in it, was wholly my own; and whatsoever I might allege for my own justification before men, I waive it, as now setting myself before another judgment-seat. However, what I wrote was upon great provocation, and to vindicate myself and others from great aspersion; yet that was no sufficient warrant for me to allow any distemper of spirit in myself; and I doubt I have been too prodigal of my brethren's reputation. I might have maintained my cause without casting any blemish upon others. When I made that my conclusion, 'And now let religion and sound reason give judgment in the case,' it looked as if I arrogated too much unto myself, and too little to others. And when I made that profession, 'that I would maintain what I wrote before all the world,' though such words might modestly be spoken, yet I perceive an unbe-

endeavor to raise what force he could against them, even from among the barbarians ; and also to treat them with such a temper as he did from time to time.   Even so late as the year 1676, the very title of the book he then published shows the spirit of it; which is exactly in these words, viz.:—

A glass for New England, in which they may see themselves and spirits, and, if not too late, repent and turn from their abominable ways and cursed contrivances. By S. G.

seeming pride of my own heart breathing in them.   For these failings I ask pardon both of God and man.   Ibid, [p. 115.]

Once more; when a great disturbance had been made in the colony by Dr. Child and others, in 1646, Governor Winthrop was called to an account for his actings against them, before a great assembly, but he was openly acquitted; upon which he said. " Though I am justified before men, yet it may be the Lord hath seen so much amiss in my administrations, as calls me to be humbled; and indeed for me to have been thus charged by men, is itself a matter of humiliation, whereof I desire to make a right use before the Lord.   If Miriam's father spit in her face, she is to be ashamed.   But give me leave before you go to say something that may rectify the opinions of many people, from whence the distempers have risen that have lately prevailed upon the body of this people.   The questions that have troubled the country have been about the authority of the magistracy, and the liberty of the people. It is you who have called us unto this office ; but being thus called, we have our authority from God; it is the ordinance of God, and it hath the image of God stamped upon it; and the contempt of it has been vindicated by God by terrible examples of his vengeance.   I entreat you to consider, that when you choose magistrates, you take from among yourselves men subject unto like passions with yourselves.   If you see our infirmities, reflect on your own, and you will not be so severe censurers of ours.   We count him a good servant who breaks not his covenant.   The covenant between us and you is the oath you have taken of us, which is to this purpose, ' that we shall govern you, and judge your causes, according to God's laws, and our own, according to our best skill.'   As for our skill, you must run the hazard of that; and if there be an error, not in the will, but in the skill, it becomes you to bear it. Nor would I have you to mistake in the point of your own liberty.   There is a liberty of corrupt nature, which is affected both by men and beasts, to do what they list; and this liberty is inconsistent with authority, impatient of all restraint; by this liberty, *sumus omnes deteriores* : It is the grand enemy of truth and peace, and all the ordinances of God are bent against it.   But there is a civil, a moral, a federal liberty, which is the proper end and object of authority ; it is a liberty for that only which is just and good; for this liberty you are to stand with the hazard of your very lives ; and whatsoever crosses it, is not authority, but a distemper thereof.   This liberty is maintained in a way of subjection to authority ; and the authority set over you, will in all administrations for your good be quietly submitted unto, by all but such as have a disposition to shake off the yoke, and lose their true liberty, by their murmuring at the honor and power of authority."   Ibid. [pp. 116, 117.]

O, had it not been for the mistaken notion of using secular force in religious affairs, how gloriously would this and other New England fathers have shined !

And as the Quakers were about that time accused by authority of setting up their posts by God's posts, he says :—

I hope none will be so blind and ignorant as to set their posts or thresholds to the devil's post, and the professors of New England's posts, viz., their whipping post or gallows-post ; no nor yet join their threshold to their gaol-thresholds, nor their bridewell-threshold, over which and in which professors and talkers of God and Christ do and have hauled over lambs and followers of Christ, and in which they crop their ears, and out of which they bring them in their wills and madness, and banish, whip and hang them in their blind zeal. Pp. 17, 18.

And he annexes to said book a letter to Governor Bellingham, dated from Boston prison June 15, 1667, written by John Tyso, a Quaker, who speaks of it as a great error in Dr. Increase Mather to say, " there was nothing in him that he hoped to be saved by, and that there was none cleansed from all sin on this side the grave." P. 35. Gorton likewise speaking of Wheelwright's being first called before the General Court for his sermon, at their session in March, 1637, tells us that Mr. Cotton then said :—

Brother Wheelwright's doctrine was according to God, in the point controverted, and wholly and altogether ; and nothing did I hear alleged against the doctrine proved by the word of God. .... But, [says G.] that which is most to be lamented, is that those which once had a good testimony in their hearts and mouths for God, and his light and spiritual appearance ; and they not being faithful and constant to that which is made manifest and committed to them, it has even happened to them according to the saying of the Lord God, by the mouth of his prophet, that " in the day in which a righteous man turns from his righteousness, and doth wickedly, all the righteousness that he hath done shall be forgotten, and in the sin which he hath sinned he shall surely die the death." Pp. 6, 7.

Now is it not evident, that the Massachusetts were moved by the same unreasonable principle of grasping at power and gain that belonged not to them, in their dealings with Gorton, as operates in other men, though it went under a cloak of religion? And is it not as evident that he was moved with self-conceit, and carnal wit and resentment, in his carriage towards them, notwithstanding all his talk of the child's being born in him, and of a creating power " for ever to form all things out of that ancient chaos of God and man being made one!" Neither of these things can hurt the truth and excellency of the Christian religion, any more than the self confidence, rashness and dissimulation of Peter did on the one hand, or the blasphemy of Hymeneus and Alexander on the other. Though some would have it, that Mr. Williams, after his banishment, left revealed religion, and took to the exercise of reason and humanity, in distinction from it, yet his own testimony is exceeding clear to the contrary. In his address to the Quakers thirty-seven years after his banishment he says :—

> The truth is, from my childhood, now above threescore years, the Father of lights and mercies touched my soul with a love to himself, to his only begotten, the true Lord Jesus to his holy Scriptures, &c. His infinite wisdom hath given me to see the city, court and country, the schools and universities of my native country, to converse with some Turks, Jews, papists, and all sorts of protestants, and by books to know the affairs and religions of all countries. My conclusion is, that, " Be of good cheer ; thy sins are forgiven thee," Matt. ix., is one of the joyfulest sounds that ever came to poor sinful ears. How to obtain this sound from the mouth of the Mediator that spoke it, is the greatest dispute between the protestants and the bloody whore of Rome. This is also the great point between the true protestant and yourselves ; as also, in order to this, about what man is now by nature, and what the true Lord Jesus is."[1]

And upon their use of those words spoken to the saints, " The manifestation of the spirit is given to *every man* to profit withal," and other like expressions, which they would apply to mankind in general, he says :—

> The Papists catch hold upon a letter, " *This is my body* ;" you as simply as do the Generalists catch hold upon the letter : "*All*," "*Every man*," &c., whereas the scope and connection in all writings, and in all matters in the world, is rationally to be minded. The sense and meaning is, in all speech

[1]Dedication of his book against the Quakers, 1673.—B.

In a subsequent notice of this book, Backus gives its proper title,—" George Fox digged out of his Burrowes,"— but with a censure of such personalities of language on the part of both Williams and his opponents. He uniformly quotes the work as Williams's " book against the Quakers."—Ed.

and writing, the very speech and writing itself. The words *All*, and *Every one*, in our own and other tongues, are often used figuratively. It is so all the Scripture over, and thrice in one verse, Col. i, 28, where reason cannot imagine that Paul did literally and individually admonish every man, teach every man, and present every man that comes into the world perfect in Christ Jesus, which could not, cannot possibly be true, without another sense and exposition than the words literally hold out.[1]

And when they demanded the reason why he condemned them for not holding to the external use of baptism and the supper, while he did not live in the practice thereof himself, he answered :—

It is one thing to be in arms against the King of kings, and the visible administration of his kingdom, and to turn off all to notions of an invisible kingdom, officers, and worship, as the Quakers, do, and another thing, among so many pretenders to be the true church, to be in doubt unto which to associate himself. After all my search and examinations, I said, I do profess to believe, that some come nearer to the first churches and institutions of Christ than others ; as in many respects, so in that gallant, heavenly and fundamental principle, of the *true matter* of a Christian society, viz. : *actual believers, true disciples and converts*, and *living stones*, such as can give some account how the grace of God hath appeared to them, and wrought that heavenly change in them. I professed that if my soul could find rest in joining unto any of the churches professing Christ now extant, I would readily and gladly do it, yea, unto themselves whom I now opposed. But not finding rest, they knew there is a time of purity, and primitive sincerity ; there is a time of transgression and apostacy, and there is a time of the coming out of the Babylonian and wilderness apostacy[2].

These extracts may assist the reader in forming a true judgment of the motives upon which those several noted men acted in those difficult times, which also may be useful now to teach us all, what to avoid and what to pursue ; the importance of which I hope will sufficiently apologize for the length of this acconnt, and also make the reader willing to take an article or two more before we conclude this chapter.

The church at Plymouth was so unwilling to part with "a man of such eminence" as Mr. Chauncy, that they conceded

---

[1] Against the Quakers, pp. 8, 9.   [2] Against the Quakers, pp. 65, 66.

in case he would settle with them, that he should act according to his persuasion, which was that " baptism ought only to be by dipping or plunging the whole body under water," with such as desired it, either for themselves or infants, provided he could without offience suffer their other minister, Mr. Reyner, to practice in the other way, with those who desired it ; " but he did not see light to comply."[1] From thence he was called to office in the church at Scituate. Mr. Winthrop says :—

Mr. Chauncy of Scituate, persevered in his opinion of dipping in baptism, and practiced accordingly, first upon two of his own children, which being in very cold weather, one of them swooned away. Another, having a child about three years old, feared it would be frighted, (as others had been, and one caught hold of Mr. Chauncy, and had near pulled him into the water) she brought her child to Boston (with letters testimonial from Mr. Chauncy) and had it baptised here.[2]

This last action was in July, 1642 ; and not long after Mr. Winthrop writes :—

The lady Moody, a wise and amiable[3] religious woman, being taken with the error of denying baptism to infants, was dealt withal by many of the elders and others, and admonished by the church at Salem, (whereof she was) but persisting still, and to avoid further trouble, she removed to the Dutch, against the advice of her friends. Many others infested with Anabaptism, &c., removed thither also. She was after excommunicated.[4]

Here as well as elsewhere appears the honesty and ingenuousness of this great man, in stating facts plainly, when they make directly against his own persuasion. Those who deny infant baptism have been reproached from age to age with the name of Anabaptists, under which have been couched such dreadful ideas, that even to this day we see the very name used as an argument in various controversies ; so that if a

---

[1] Plymouth Register, pp. 5, 6.   [2] Winthrop, Vol. II, p. 72.—ED.
[3] Savage reads "anciently" instead of " amiable;" and adds in a note, " I fear we must infer from the text that her perversion to Anabaptism deprived her in the writer's opinion, of the ' anciently religious' character." Winthrop, Vol. II, p. 123. If this reading and inference be correct, it will detract somewhat from the praise awarded to Winthrop in the next paragraph.—ED.
[4] Winthrop, [Vol. II, pp. 123, 124.]

disputant can tell his opponent, he in that point agrees with
the Anabaptists, it is thought that therein he must be in an
error; but our honorable author gives, without a covering,
the good characters and virtues of that father and that
mother in our Israel, at the same time that he describes
plainly what he disliked in them; leaving fair grounds for
others to judge upon, without being biased with any old
stories of German madness. By this it appears that the
grand difficulty in the way of burying in baptism, is their
admitting of subjects to it who have not the faith or the
discretion which is necessary for such an action.

Though Mr. Williams had done such great services for
his English neighbors, in the late wars, yet he was not permitted to pass through their coasts, but was forced to repair
to the Dutch to get a passage to his native country. Yea,
it must needs be so, because the blessings of a peacemaker
were to come upon him, among the Dutch as well as
English.[1]

[1]As a distinct account of this affair has not been published among us, I shall give
it a place here. When the commissioners of the United Colonies met in September,
1643, they were informed of a Dutch ship that had arrived in Hudson's River, which
brought four thousand pounds of powder, and seven hundred pieces, to trade with
the natives; but the Dutch governor, having notice thereof, prudently confiscated
them to the use of the company; thereby depriving their enemies of arms, whereby
they might themselves have been destroyed, and furnishing themselves and friends
with weapons for their safety; for at this time the Indians had fierce war with the
Dutch, and if it had not been for the assistance for the English, they might have
been all cut off. The occasion of the war was this:—An Indian being drunk, had
slain an old Dutchman; the Dutch required the murderer, but he could not be had.
The people called often upon the governor to take revenge, but he still put it off,
because he thought it not just, or not safe. It fell out in that time, that the Maquas
or Mohawks, either upon their own quarrel or (as the report was) being set on by
the Dutch, came suddenly upon the Indians near the Dutch, and killed about thirty
of them; the rest fled for shelter to the Dutch. One Marine, a Dutch captain,
hearing of it, went to the governor and obtained a commission to kill as many as he
could of them, and accordingly went with a company of armed men, and set upon
them, when they feared no such thing from the Dutch, and killed seventy or eighty
men, women and children. Upon this the Indians burnt divers of their farm houses,
and their cattle in them, and slew all they could meet with, to the number of twenty
or more, of men, women and children, and pursued hard upon the Dutch, even home
to their fort Aurania (Albany) so that they were forced to call in the English to
their aid, and entertained Captain Underhill in their service. Marine was so much

When Mr. Williams arrived in England, he found the country involved in the dreadful calamities and horrors of a war between the king and parliament ; but the parliament having the command of the fleet, did by an ordinance of November 2, 1643, appoint commissioners to manage the affairs of the islands and other plantations ; from whom, by the kind assistance of Sir Henry Vane, who was one of them, Mr. Williams obtained a charter, including the lands " bordering northward and northeast on the patent of the Massachusetts, east and southeast on Plymouth patent, south on the ocean, and on the west and northwest by the Indians called Narragansetts ; the whole tract extending about twenty-five miles, unto the Pequod river and country ;" " to be known by the name of THE INCORPORATION OF PROVIDENCE PLANTATIONS, IN THE NARRAGANSETT BAY, IN NEW ENGLAND." To the English inhabitants of the tract aforesaid, the charter gives " full power and authority to rule themselves, and such others as shall hereafter inhabit within any part of the said tract of land, by such form of civil government, as by vol-

enraged to see Underhill preferred before him, that his governor was forced at last to send him home in chains. About this time Captain Patrick, who went from Boston, was shot dead by a Dutchman, upon a Lord's day, at Stamford. Though the people were all for war before, yet now they were so much offended with the governor, that he entertained a guard of fifty English about his person. And the Indians annoyed them so by sudden assaults out of swamps, &c., that he was forced to keep a running army to oppose them upon all occasions. The Indians killed and drove all before them as far as Stamford ; slew Mrs. Hutchinson and her family, all except one whom they captivated. They passed over to Long Island, and the natives there took part with them, and began to burn the Dutchmen's houses ; assaulted the house of the lady Moody, who not long before moved away from Salem upon the account of Anabaptism ; but she was defended by forty men that gathered to her house, which they assaulted divers times. But the Long Island Indians, by the mediation of Mr. Williams, (who was then there to take ship for England,) were pacified, and peace re-established between the Dutch and them. But still upon the main, they set upon the Dutch with an implacable fury, killing all they could come by, burning their houses, and destroying their cattle. without any resistance ; so as the governor and such as escaped betook themselves to their fort at Manhatoes (New York) and there lived upon their cattle. But many of the Indians being destroyed by Captain Underhill and his followers. at last they began to be weary of the sport, and condescended to terms of peace." Winthrop, [Vol. II, pp. 135, 151.] Hubbard, [440—442.]

untary consent of all, or the greater part of them, they shall find most suitable to their estate and condition," provided " the civil government of the said plantations, be conformable to the laws of England, so far as the nature and constitution of the place will admit."

This charter was signed March 14, 1644, by Robert Warwick, Philip Pembroke, Say and Seal, Philip Wharton, Arthur Haslerig, Cornelius Holland, Henry Vane, Samuel Vassel, John Rolle, Miles Corbet, and William Spurstow.[1]

[1] See said charter in the History of Providence.

CHAPTER III.

FROM 1644 TO 1651, CONTAINING THE FIRST LAW THAT WAS MADE IN NEW ENGLAND AGAINST THE BAPTISTS, AND A VARIETY OF OTHER EVENTS.

The first Baptist church in Newport, we are told, was formed and set in order about the year 1644, under the ministry of Mr. John Clarke. It is the first church of any denomination on Rhode Island that has continued by succession, and the second in the colony.[1] Also in Massachusetts

[1] The first certain date in their church records is taken from a manuscript of Mr. Samuel Hubbard in 1648, which says the church was formed about the year 1644, and by what I have quoted from Winthrop and Hubbard, it appears as likely to be earlier as later than that time.—B.

The entry in the records of the first Baptist church in Newport, here referred to, was made by John Comer as late as 1725, and is as follows :—" Having found a private record of Mr. Samuel Hubbard, who was a member of the church, by which I find that the church was in being so long back as October 12, 1648, (but how long before, justly, by any manuscript I can't find, but by private information it was constituted in the year 1644)—." Backus should therefore have given the above date on the authority of John Comer, and not of Samuel Hubbard. Comer repeated this testimony in a manuscript now in the library of the Backus Historical Society, in the words, "The church was first gathered by Mr. John Clarke about the year 1644." Callender wrote in 1738, " It is said that in 1644, Mr. John Clarke and some others formed a church on the scheme and principles of the Baptists." Century Sermon, Rhode Island Historical Collections, Vol. IV. p. 117. There is probably no evidence that Callender or any subsequent writer who has given the above date, had any authority for it beyond the tradition preserved by Comer. Backus represents that an earlier date is possible. Many regard the weight of evidence as in its favor. Some have placed it as far back as 1638, supposing that the church was founded by Clarke and his company upon their arrival on Rhode Island. See Minutes of the Warren Association, 1849, p. 14. Winthrop, indeed, mentions a church that had been gathered at Aquiday as early as 1639, but Lechford wrote in 1640, " There was a church where one Master Clark was elder; the place where the church was, is

we are told that "Anabaptists increased and spread in the
country."[1] Upon which they framed and passed the following act at their General Court, November 13, 1644:—

Forasmuch as experience hath plentifully and often proved, that since
the first rising of the Anabaptists, about one hundred years since, they have
been the incendiaries of the commonwealths, and the infectors of persons
in main matters of religion, and the troublers of churches in all places
where they have been, and that they who have held the baptizing of infants
unlawful, have usually held other errors or heresies together therewith,
though they have (as other heretics use to do) concealed the same till they
spied out a fit advantage and opportunity to vent them, by way of question
or scruple; and whereas divers of this kind have since our coming into
New England appeared amongst ourselves, some whereof (as others before them) denied the ordinance of magistracy, and the lawfulness of
making war, and others the lawfulness of magistrates, and their inspection
into any breach of the first table; which opinions, if they should be con-
nived at by us, are like to be increased amongst us, and so must necessarily bring guilt upon us, infection and trouble to the churches, and hazard
to the whole commonwealth; it is ordered and agreed, that if any person
or persons, within this jurisdiction, shall either openly condemn or oppose the
baptizing of infants, or go about secretly to seduce others from the approbation or use thereof, or shall purposely depart the congregation at the ministration of the ordinance, or shall deny the ordinance of magistracy, or
their lawful right and authority to make war, or to punish the outward
breaches of the first table, and shall appear to the Court willfully and obstinately to continue therein after due time and means of conviction, every
such person or persons shall be sentenced to banishment.[2]

called Newport; but that church, I hear, is now dissolved," Winthrop's Journal,
Vol. I, p. 297; Plain Dealing, Trumbull's edition, p. 93, Some place the date of
the present church in or about 1640, supposing that it succeeded the one which, according to Lechford, was dissolved. They reason from the improbability that the
inhabitants of Rhode Island would remain four years without an organized church,
and from the testimony of Winthrop in 1641, that "divers of them turned professed
Anabaptists," and that there arose a contention and a schism among them. See
Winthrop's Journal, Vol. II, pp. 38, 41. These indications are not without force,
still, if a church was formed in 1640 or 1641, whether fully or partially Baptist, it
may have had but a brief existence and have been succeeded by the present church
in 1644. There seems to be as yet no wiser conclusion than that of Backus, when
he gave 1644 as the only date which has any positive authority, and at the same
time allowed the possibility of a date still earlier.—Ed.

[1]Winthrop, [Vol. II, p. 174.]—Ed.

[2]Massachusetts Records. Mr. Hubbard speaking of their making this law, says,
" But with what success is hard to say; all men being naturally inclined to pity

Let it be here noted, that the evident design of this law was to guard against such as refused to countenance infant baptism, and the use of secular force in religious affairs; which the Baptists have ever done from that day to this; but the other articles inserted in this act they have not owned; and the Court then had no proof at hand, but were forced to have recourse to surmises, distant times, and foreign countries, for them. A like method of treating the Baptists, in Courts, from pulpits and from the press, has been handed down by tradition ever since. And can we believe that men so knowing and virtuous in other respects, as men on that side have been, would have introduced and continued in a way of treating their neighbors, which is so unjust and scandalous, if they could have found better arguments to support that cause upon? I have diligently searched all the books, records and papers I could come at upon all sides, and have found a great number of instances

them that suffer, how much soever they are incensed against offenders in general. Natural conscience and the reverence of a Deity, that is deeply engraven on the hearts of all, make men more apt to favor them that suffer for religion, true or false." [P. 373.] A judicious remark; yet in another instance we may see how party influence can blind great men. For this author in 1638 tells us of Arnold's opposing their censuring Verin at Providence, for refusing to let his wife go to Mr. Williams's meeting so often as she was called for, and represents that 'to censure Verin therefor, would be a breach of God's ordinance, about the "subjection of wives to their husbands." [P. 437.] But the same author informs us, that in 1644 one Painter, a poor man, was suddenly turned Anabaptist, "and having a child born, would not suffer his wife to carry it to be baptized. He was complained of for this to the Court, and enjoined by them to suffer his child to be baptized." And because he refused to obey them therein, and told them it was an antichristian ordinance, they tied him up and whipped him; which he bare without flinching, and declared he had divine help to support him; "upon which," says our author, "two or three honest men that were his neighbors affirmed that he was of very loose behavior at home," &c. [P. 342.] Be it so or not, we have no better account of Verin's character than of his, yet Verin must not be censured for withholding his wife from meeting; but if poor Painter would not give up the disposal of his children to his wife, at the Court's commandment, he must not only be censured, but also suffer corporal punishment; yea, and into the bargain, be publicly reproached for his private failings! Governor Winthrop tells us he belonged to Hingham, and says he was whipped "for reproaching the Lord's ordinance." [Vol. II, p. 175.] But did not they reproach infant sprinkling, by taking such methods to support it, much more than Painter did?

of Baptists suffering for the above points that we own; but not one instance of the conviction of any member of a Baptist church in this country, in any Court, of the errors or evils which are inserted in this law to justify their making of it, and to render our denomination odious.[1] Much has been said to exalt the characters of those good fathers; I have no desire of detracting from any of their virtues; but the better the men were, the worse must be the principle that could ensnare them in such bad actions.

The contrast betwixt their treatment of Mr. Wheelwright and Mr. Williams this year deserves notice. Upon a new running of the line, the Massachusetts had taken Exeter into their colony, which caused Mr. Wheelwright to remove to Wells, from whence he wrote to the Governor at Boston for a reconciliation, Dec. 7, 1643, and said, " It is the grief of my soul that I used such vehement censorious speeches. I repent me that I did so much adhere to persons of corrupt judgments, to the countenancing and encouraging of them in any of their errors, or evil practices, though I intended no such thing." The Court inclined to hear him of which the Governor sent him a written account, and received such a reply as would make one think of Bishop Burnet's remark. Said he, " There are none of us but what will acknowledge in general terms that our church is imperfect, though when we come to particulars, we are always in the right."[2] Yet

___

[1]There is not one instance in any government that supported Pœdobaptism by force. But Mr. Williams, when Governor of Providence colony in 1655, acted with the Court in punishing a man for opposing all government, who then was called a Baptist, but after turned to the Quakers.

[2]Said letter to the Governor is in these words :—

    R. W.*

" I have received your letters, wherein you signify to me, that you have imparted my letter to the H. C.† and that it finds good acceptance, for which I rejoice with all thankfulness; as also for liberty of safe conduct granted by the Court, and, in case I desire, letters for that end. I should very willingly (upon letters obtained) express by word of mouth, openly in Court, that which I did by writing, might I without offence express my true intent and meaning more fully to this effect; that notwithstanding my failures (for which I crave pardon) yet I cannot with a good

*Right Worshipful.—Ed.   †Honored Court.—Ed.

without waiting for his personal appearance, they at the
General Court in Boston, May 29, 1644, passed the following act, viz. :—

It is ordered that Mr. Wheelwright (upon a particular, solemn, and serious acknowledgment and confession, by letters, of his evil carriages, and
of the Court's justice upon him for them) hath his banishment taken off,
and is received as a member of this Commonwealth.[1]

Mr. Williams returned with the charter he had procured,
to Boston, the 17th of September following,[2] and brought
the ensuing letter with him :—

To the Right Worshipful the Governor and Assistants and the rest of our
worthy friends in the plantation of Massachusetts Bay, [in New England.][3]

Our Much Honored Friends :—Taking notice some of us of long
time of Mr. Roger Williams's [Williams his] good affections and conscience,
and of his sufferings by our common enemy [enemies] and oppressors of
God's people the prelates, as also of his great industry and travels [travail] in

conscience condemn myself for such capital crimes, dangerous revelations and
gross errors, as have been charged upon me. The concurrence of which, as I take
it, makes up the substance of all my sufferings. I do not see but in so mixed a
cause, I am bound to use, may it be permitted, my just defence, so far as I apprehend myself to be innocent, and to make my confession where I am convinced of
any delinquency, otherwise I shall seemingly and in appearance fall under guilt
of many heinous offences, for which my conscience doth acquit me. If I seem to
make suit to the Court for relaxation to be granted as an act of mercy upon my
sole confession, I must offend my conscience; if by an act of justice, upon my
apology and lawful defence, I fear here I shall offend your Worships. I leave all
things to your wise and holy consideration, hoping you will pardon my simplicity
and plainness, which I am forced upon by the power of an overruling conscience.
I rest your Worship's in the Lord,
                                              J. Wheelwright."
Wells, (I) I, 1643.

Winthrop, [Vol. II, p. 163.] Hubbard, [367.] Note, their way was to begin
the year with March 25, so that according to our reckoning this was March 1, 1614.

[1]At the same time they passed a sentence, that "Richard Waterman, being found
erroneous, heretical and obstinate, it was ordered that he should be detained prisoner till the Quarter Court in the seventh month, unless five of the magistrates find
cause to send him away, which if they do, it is ordered, he shall not return within
this jurisdiction upon pain of death."
                                              Massachusetts Records.
[2]Winthrop, [Vol. II, p. 193.]

[3]This letter has been often quoted and considerably changed. The form here
given is taken almost literally from Hutchinson. The words added in brackets will
indicate its form as given by Winthrop. Vol. II, p. 193.—Ed.

9

his printed Indian labors[1] in your parts (the like whereof we have not seen extant from any part of America) and in which respect it hath pleased both houses of parliament [freely] to grant unto him and friends with him a free and absolute charter of civil government for those parts of his abode, and withal sorrowfully resenting that amongst good men (our friends) driven to the ends of the world, exercised with the trials of a wilderness, and who mutually give good testimony each of the other [of other] (as we observe you do of him, and he abundantly of you[2]) there should be such a distance ; we thought it fit upon divers considerations to profess our great desires of both your utmost endeavors of nearer closing and of ready expressing those good affections (which we perceive you bear each to other) in effectual [in the actual] performance of all friendly offices. The rather because of those bad neighbors you are likely [like] to find too near you in Virginia, and the unfriendly visits from the west of England and Ireland.   That howsoever it may please the Most High to shake our foundations, yet the report of your peaceable and prosperous plantations may be some refreshings [refreshing] to your true and faithful friends.

Cor. Holland,	Robert Harley,
John Blackistow,	John Gurdon,
Isaac Pennington,	Northumberland,
Miles Corbet,	P. Wharton,
Oliver St. John,	Thomas Barrington.
Gibert Pickering,	William Masham."[3]

Hubbard says :—

Upon the receipt of this letter, the Governor and magistrates of the Massachusetts found, upon examination of their hearts, no reason to con-

[1]Mr. Williams's printed Indian labors referred to, which had considerable influence in procuring their charter, were three years before the famous Mr. Elliott began to preach to the Indians at Natic, or Mr. Thomas Mayhew at Martha's Vineyard. Magnalia, B. 3, p. 193. [Vol. 1, p. 507.] Mayhew's Indian Converts, p. 5.

[2]Mr. Williams confirmed his profession of love to them by his practice, in constantly doing them all the good in his power, both in this country and at the British court, where also his great friend, Sir Henry Vane, this year showed a truly Christian spirit of forgiveness towards Massachusetts; for when upon a certain affair "a heavy complaint was made against the government, and they were threatened with the loss of their privileges, Sir Henry Vane stood their friend, and by his great interest with the Parliament, appeased their resentment, and laid the storm which was gathering and hung over them."

Massachusetts History, Vol. I, p. 66, [67.]

[3]Massachusetts History, Vol. I, pp. 39, 40, [42.] King Charles the First's party at that time had the command of the west of England, Ireland and Virginia, and fear of visits from them is what they refer to. That party was defeated the next year and the king taken prisoner.

demn themselves for any former proceedings against Mr. Williams; but for any offices of Christian love, and duties of humanity, they were very willing to maintain a mutual correspondence with him; but as to his dangerous principles of separation, unless he can be brought to lay them down, they see no reason why to concede to him, or any so persuaded, free liberty of ingress and egress, lest any of their people should be drawn away with his erroneous opinions.[1]

The reader may remember that Wheelwright in his sentence of banishment, was charged with contempt and sedition, which he never confessed; and that Governor Winthrop declared his opinions to be worse than Mr. Williams's;[2] yet now the one is received to favor and liberty again, while the other is denied it, though he had done the colony such great and essential services as the former never did.   How can we account for this?   The best answer I can give is, that Mr. Wheelwright held to infant baptism, and to the magistrates' power to govern in religious affairs, and now yielded to their exercise of it; but Mr. Williams denied both, for which he was excommunicated by the church, after the Court had sent him away.   Wheelwright was also in such favor with Mr. Cotton, that he was dismissed from his church in fellowship, after the Court had banished him for sedition; and he now appeared very complaisant and submissive to men in power. But Williams was so "self-conceited, turbulent and uncharitable, as to give public advertisements and admonitions to all men, whether of meaner or more public note and place, of the corruptions of religion which himself observed, both in their judgments and practices; of which there needs no

---

[1] Hubbard, [348.]

[2] The Court's sentence against him was in these words:—"Whereas Mr. Roger Williams, one of the elders of the church of Salem, hath broached and divulged divers new and dangerous opinions, against the authority of magistrates, as also written [writ] letters of defamation both of the magistrates and churches here, and that before any conviction, and yet maintaineth the same without retraction: It is therefore ordered, that the said Mr. Williams shall depart out of this jurisdiction within six weeks now next ensuing, which if he neglect to perform, it shall be lawful for the Governor and two of the magistrates to send him to some place out of this jurisdiction, not to return any more without license from the Court."

Massachusetts Records, 1635.

other evidence, than what is obvious to the view of every indifferent reader, in his dealing with that famous and reverend divine, Mr. John Cotton, in his book called The Bloody Tenet."

These words Mr. Hubbard quotes from another, as the received opinion of that day. But who was this reverend divine, and how was he dealt with? Was not Mr. Williams as truly a minister of Christ as he? Does self-conceit move men to give plain warnings to great men, which have a tendency to expose self to heavy sufferings? And does it move persons to do every kind office they can from year to year, for those who will not hear reproof, but requite evil for good? This is a different sort of pride from what most men are acquainted with. However, that the reader may have a fair opportunity of judging for himself, I shall endeavor to plainly state the occasion and nature of this controversy between Cotton and Williams.

A prisoner in Newgate wrote some arguments against persecution, which were presented to Mr. Cotton, and he wrote an answer to them in a letter to one Mr. Hall, of Roxbury; who not being satisfied therewith, sent them to Mr. Williams at Providence, requesting him to write upon the subject.[1]   And as Mr. Cotton closed his letter to Mr.

[1] " Mr. Cotton says in 1647, 'Mr. Williams sent me about a dozen years ago (as I remember) a letter, penned (as he wrote) by a prisoner in Newgate, touching persecution for conscience sake; and entreated my judgment of it for the satisfaction of his friend.' This 'letter' was a part,—the sixth, seventh, eighth and ninth chapters,—of a work printed in 1620, entitled, 'A most humble supplication of the King's Majesty's loyal subjects, ready to testify all civil obedience by the oath of allegiance, or otherwise, and that of conscience; who are persecuted, (only for differing in religion) contrary to divine and human testimonies: as followeth.' It is signed by 'your Majesty's loyal subjects unjustly called Anabaptists.' It is reprinted by Crosby, History of the English Baptists, II, Appendix, pp. 10—51, and in Tracts on Liberty of Conscience, &c., Hansard Knollys Society, pp. 189—231. According to Williams 'the author of these arguments being committed by some then in power, close prisoner to Newgate, for the witness of some truths of Jesus, and having not the use of pen and ink, wrote these arguments in milk, in sheets of paper, brought to him by the woman, his keeper, from a friend in London, as the stopples of his milk bottle.' Bloody Tenet, p. 18. Dr. Underhill conjectures that it must have been written by John Murton, or as Crosby calls him, Morton, who

Hall with saying, " I forbear adding reasons to justify the truth, because you may find that done to your hand, in a treatise sent to some of the brethren, late of Salem, who doubted as you do."   Mr. Williams wrote to Mr. Sharp, elder of Salem church, for it, and obtained it.[1] He then wrote his sentiments upon the whole, under the title of " The Bloody Tenet of Persecution for Conscience Sake ;" which I suppose he now brought with him from London, though I have not been able to obtain it.[2] Mr. Cotton wrote an answer to him, which he called " The Bloody Tenet washed, and made white in the Blood of the Lamb."   It was printed in London in 1647. To this Mr. Williams pub-

was associated with Helwisse in Holland, and after his return, in England, and against whom John Robinson directed one of his controversial works. Tracts on Liberty of Conscience, &c., pp. 89, 187. Williams denies that this treatise was sent by him to Cotton, or that the reply was private, as Cotton alledged in complaint against its being printed in this work. He says, " To my knowledge there was no such letter or intercourse passed between Master Cotton and the discusser," but what I have heard is this,—One Master Hall, of Roxbury, presented the prisoner's arguments against persecution to Master Cotton, who gave this present controverted answer; with the which Master Hall not being satisfied, he sends them unto the discusser, who never saw the said Hall, nor those arguments in writing: (though he well remembers that he saw them in print some years since.)   Bloody Tenet yet more Bloody, p. 4."   S. L. Caldwell, Preface to the Bloudy Tenent, Narragansett Club. Vol. III, pp, iv., v.—ED.

[1]Williams's Reply to Cotton, pp. 290, 291.—B.

This treatise was entitled " A Model of Church and Civil Power." It probably was never printed, and its author is unknown. See Narragansett Club, Vol. III, Preface, pp. vi.—viii.—ED.

[2]The exact title of the first edition was " The Bloudy Tenet of Persecution, or the cause of Conscience, discussed, in a conference between Truth and Peace ; who, in all tender Affection, present to the High Court of Parliament, (as the result of their Discourse) these, (amongst other passages) of highest consideration." In his Bloody Tenet yet more Bloody, p. 38, Williams says of this Work :—" When these discussions were prepared for public in London, his [the author's] time was eaten up upon attendance upon the service of the parliament and city, for the supply of the poor of the city with wood (during the stop of coal at Newcastle, and the mutinies of the poor for firing. God is a most holy witness that these meditations were fitted for public view in charge of rooms and corners, yea, sometimes (upon occasion of travel in the country, concerning that business of fuel) in variety of strange houses, sometimes in the fields, in the midst of travel ; where he hath been forced to gather and scatter his loose thoughts and papers." Two editions of the work are said to have been published in London, in 1644. Backus is undoubtedly right in supposing that Roger Williams brought the book with him upon his return from England with the charter of " Providence Plantations." See Narragansett Club, Vol. III, Preface, pp. iii., iv.—ED.

lished a reply in 1652, entitled, "The Bloody Tenet yet more bloody, by Mr. Cotton's Endeavor to wash it white."[1] The last two of these performances are now before me, and from thence I shall give the reader their own words upon the most material points of their dispute.[2]

First. Mr. Cotton's Memory failed him so much as that he represented that what he wrote in answer to the prisoner's arguments, was in a private letter to Mr. Williams, and upon that said :—

I wrote my conscience, in the sight of God, and the truth of God, according to my conscience ; why should he punish me with open penance, and expose me (as much as in him lieth) before the world to open shame, as a man of blood, for the liberty of my conscience? How will it stand with his own principles, to plead for liberty of conscience and yet to punish it? Besides let him remember, if I did offend him with such an error, it was but a private offence, and the rule of the gospel required he should first have convinced and admonished me privately of it, and so have proceeded upon my contumacy, at length to have told the church, before he had published it to the world. C.,[3] p. 2.

Mr. Williams in his reply mentions Mr. Cotton's mistake about the one to whom he wrote the letter, and that he supposed his answer to the prisoner's arguments had been as public as his profession and practice was upon that tenet, and then says :—

But grant it had been a private letter, and the discourse and the opinion private ; yet why doth he charge the discusser with breach of rule, in not

---

[1] " The Bloody Tenent yet more Bloody, by Mr. Cotton's endeavor to wash it white in the Blood of the Lamb; of whose precious Blood, spilt in the Blood of his Servants, and of the Blood of millions spilt in former and later wars for Conscience sake, that most Bloody Tenent of persecution for cause of Conscience, upon a second trial, is found now more apparently and more notoriously guilty."—ED.

[2] The following quotations have been verified from the reprint of Williams's work, Narragansett Club. Vol. III, and a copy of Cotton's work in the library of the American Antiquarian Society, Worcester. Many words and phrases were found to have been omitted. As it was the object of Backus simply to give a brief abstract of the arguments of the two writers, in their own words, it has not been thought needful to notice the omissions except in the few instances in which it is required in order that the full sense of the passages may appear. There are a few unimportant instances of verbal change, probably by error of transcription, which are indicated in brackets.—ED,

[3] Note, C. and W. in this account stand respectively for Cotton's and Williams's books abovesaid; the figures for the pages therein.

using orderly ways of admonition, and telling the church, when Master Cotton in this book blames the discusser for disclaiming communion with their church, and they also (after he was driven by banishment from civil habitation amongst them) had sent forth a bull of excommunication against him in his absence! Such practice the Lord Jesus and his first apostles or messengers never taught. . . . . I never heard that disputing, discoursing and examining men's tenets or doctrines by the word of God, was, in proper English, persecution for conscience. Well had it been for New England, that no servant of God, nor witness of Christ, could justly take up complaint for other kinds of persecution. W., pp. 4, 5.

The main point of all Mr. Cotton's washings is a denial of the charge of persecuting any for cause of conscience, and he says :—

I expressly profess, 1. That no man is to be persecuted at all, much less for conscience sake. 2. I profess further, that none is to be punished for conscience sake, though erroneous, unless his errors be fundamental, or seditiously and turbulently promoted, and that after due conviction of conscience ; that it may appear, he is not punished for his conscience, but for sinning against his conscience. . . . . If this tenet have any appearance of blood in it, it is because it is washed in the blood of the Lamb, and sealed with his blood. And then though it may seem bloody to men of corrupt minds and destitute of the truth (as Paul seemed to such to be a pestilent fellow) yet to faithful and upright souls, such things as are washed in the blood of the Lamb, are wont to come forth white. C., p. 3.

In reply to this, Mr. Williams says :—

Is not this the guise and profession of all that ever persecuted or hunted men for their religion and conscience? Are not all histories and experiences full of the pathetical speeches of persecutors to this purpose? You will say you are persecuted for your conscience, you plead conscience, thou art a heretic, the devil hath deceived thee, thy conscience is deluded, &c. . . . . Time hath and will discover that such a blackamore cannot be washed in the blood of Christ himself, without repentance.

He goes on to observe, that the setting up of state religions has been the grand source of persecution in every age. W., pp. 6, 7. Against which he brought our Lord's parable of the tares of the field. Upon which Mr. Cotton said :—

It is true, Christ expoundeth the field to be the world, but he meant not the [wide] world, but (by a usual trope) the church scattered throughout the world. C., p. 41.

Mr. Williams says :—

It is no wonder to find Master Cotton so entangled, both in his answers and replies touching this parable ; for men of all sorts in former ages have been so entangled before him.   To which purpose I will relate a notable passage recorded by that excellent witness of God, Master Fox, in his book of Acts and Monuments.   It is this : In the story of Mr. George Wise-hart, in the days of King Henry VIII, there preached at the arraignment of said Wisehart one John Winryme, sub-prior of the abbey of St. Andrews ; he discoursed on the parable of the tares ; he interpreted the tares to be heretics ; and yet contrary to this very Scripture, (as Mr. Fox observeth, though elsewhere himself maintains [maintaining] it the duty of the civil magistrate to suppress heretics) I say the said Winryme concludeth that heretics ought not to be let alone until the harvest, but to be suppressed by the power of the civil magistrate.   So that both the popish prior and the [that] truly Christian Fox were entangled in contradictions to their own writings about this heavenly Scripture.   W., p. 46.

To support the notion of calling the church the world, Mr. Cotton quoted some texts wherein the redeemed are so called. C., p. 43. In reply, Mr. Williams says :—

Grant that it hath pleased the Lord in his infinite wisdom to cause the term world to be used in various significations ; yet let any instance be given of any Scripture, wherein the Lord opposing the church and world, wheat and tares, doth not distinguish between the church redeemed out of the world, and the world itself, which is said to lie in wickedness, and to be such as for which Jesus would not pray.   John xvii.   W., p. 56.

He further argued that sowing of the seed in four sorts of ground by Christ's messengers, he called the kingdom of heaven, which four sorts cannot be supposed to be of the church.   Mr. Cotton answers :—1. That Christ preached himself to those four sorts of hearers, yet he was the minister of circumcision, and seldom preached to any but members of the church of Israel. C., p. 44.   Reply :—

When they grew incurable, and received not the admonitions of the Lord, by the Lord Jesus and his servants preaching unto them, the Lord cast them out of his sight, destroyed that national church, and established the Christian church.   W., p. 57.

But Cotton says :—

It is an error to say, the church consisteth of no more sorts of hearers but one, the honest and good ground; for if the children of church members be in the church, and of the church, till they give occasion of rejection, then they growing up to years, become some of them like the highway side, others like the stony, others like the thorny, as well as others like the honest and good ground. C., p. 44.

Mr. Williams replies :—

Admit the Christian church were constituted of the natural seed and offspring, (which yet Mr. Cotton knows will never be granted to him, and I believe will never be proved by him,) yet he knows, that upon the discovery of any such portion of ground in the church, the church is bound to admonish, and upon impenitency after admonition, to cast them into the world, the proper place of such kinds of hearers and professors. W., p. 57, 58.

Mr. Cotton adds :—

Is it not a main branch of their covenant with God, that as God giveth himself to be a God to them, and to their seed, so they should give up themselves and their seed to be his people? Besides hath not God given pastors and teachers, as well for the gathering together of the saints, as for the edification of the body of Christ? And hath he not given the church, and the gospel preached in the church, to lie like leaven in three pecks of meal till all be leavened? C., p. 44.

Mr. Williams says :—

I answer, the proper work of pastors and teachers is to feed the sheep in the flock, and not the herds of wild beasts in the world. And although it is the duty of parents to bring up their children in the nurture and fear of the Lord; yet what if those children refuse to frequent the assemblies of the church, and what if those three sorts of [bad] ground or hearers will not come within the bounds of the pastors' and teachers' feeding? Hath not the Lord Jesus appointed other officers in Eph. iv. for the gathering of the saints, that is, sending out of the church of Christ apostles or messengers, to preach Christ to the three sorts of bad ground, to labor to turn them into good ground? But alas! to salve up this, the civil sword is commonly run for, to force all sorts of ground to come to church, instead of sending forth the heavenly sowers according to the ordinance of Christ. W., p. 58.

Another argument Mr. Cotton draws from the servants wondering to see the tares, which would not have been

strange in the highway. C., p. 45. In reply to which Mr.
Williams says :—

Let the highway, stony and thorny ground, be considered in their several qualities of profaneness, stoutness, stoniness and worldliness, and all
the sons of men throughout the world naturally are such ; and it is no wonder, nor would the servants of Christ be so troubled, as to desire their
plucking up out of the world. But again consider all these sorts of men
as professing the name and anointing of Christ Jesus, in a false, counter-
feit antichristian way, and then it may well be wondered whence such
monstrous Christians or anointed ones arose ; and God's people may easily be tempted rather to desire their rooting out of the world, than the rooting out of any such sorts of ground or men, professing any other religion,
Jewish, Mahometan or Pagan. A traitor is worse than a professed fox.
W., pp. 58, 59.

Again, while Mr. Cotton pleaded for the exertions of the
civil power against heretics and antichristians, he says :—

No ordinance or law of God, nor just law of man, commandeth the
rooting out of hypocrites, either by civil or church censure, though the
church be bound to endeavor as much as in them lieth to heal their hypocrisy. C., p. 47.

To this Mr. Williams answers :—

Hypocrisy discovered in the fruit of it, is not to be let alone in the
church or state ; for neither the church of Christ nor civil state can long
continue safe, if hypocrites or traitors (under what pretence soever) be
permitted to break forth in them, without due punishment and rooting out ;
this hypocrisy being especially the great sin against which Christ so frequently and so vehemently inveighed, and against which he denounced the
sorest plagues and judgments. W., p. 62.

He then proceeded to plead, that the civil state should
punish only civil offences. Upon which Mr. Cotton asks :—

What if their worship and consciences incite them to civil offences? C.,
p. 50.

Mr. Williams says:—

I answer, the conscience of the civil magistrate must incite him to civil
punishment ; as a Lord Mayor of London once answered that he was born
to be a judge, to a thief that pleaded he was born to be a thief. If the
conscience of the worshippers of the beast incite them to prejudice prince

or state, although these consciences be not as the conscience of the thief, commonly convinced of the evil of his fact, but persuaded of the lawfulness of their actions; yet so far as the civil state is endamaged or endangered, I say the sword of God in the hand of civil authority is strong enough to defend itself, either by imprisoning or disarming, or other wholesome means, while yet their consciences ought to be permitted in what is merely point of worship, as prayer and other services and administrations. Against any civil mischief the civil state is strongly guarded. Against the spiritual mischief, the church or city of Christ is guarded with heavenly armories, wherein there hang a thousand bucklers, Cant. iv. 4, and most mighty weapons. 2 Cor. x. W., pp. 66, 67.

But as he still pleaded that the civil sword was never appointed by Christ for an antidote or remedy in spiritual evils and dangers, Mr. Cotton denies it, and says :—

It is evident the civil sword was appointed for remedy in this case; Deut. xiii.[1] and appointed it was by that Angel of God's presence, whom God promised to send with his people. Exod. xxxiii., 2, 3. And that Angel was Christ, whom they tempted in the wilderness. 1 Cor. x. 9. Therefore it cannot truly be said, that the Lord Jesus never appointed the civil sword for a remedy in such a case : For he did expressly appoint it in the Old Testament; nor did he ever abrogate it in the New. The reason of the law (which is the life of the law) is of eternal force and equity in all ages. "Thou shalt surely kill him because he hath sought to thrust thee away from the Lord, thy God." This reason is moral, that is, of universal and perpetual equity to put to death any apostate, seducing idolator, or heretic.[2] C., pp. 66, 67.

In reply Mr. Williams says :—

How grievous is this language of Master Cotton! Moses in the Old Testament was Christ's servant, yet being but a servant, dispensed his power by carnal rites and ceremonies, laws, rewards and punishments, in that holy nation, and that one land of Canaan. But when Jesus the Son and Lord himself was come, to bring the truth, life and substance, of all those shadows; to break down the partition-wall between Jew and Gentile, and establish the Christian worship and kingdom in all nations of the

---

[1]This incident is older than any "Lord Mayor of London," and has suffered transformations which have little improved it. Ζήνων δοῦλον ἐπὶ κλοπῇ ἐμαστίγου. Τοῦ δὲ εἰπόντος, Εἵμαρτό μοι κλέψαι. Καὶ δαρῆναι, ἔφη. · "Zeno was scourging a slave for theft. Upon his saying 'It was fated that I should steal,' 'And that you should be skinned,' said Zeno. Diogenes Laertius.—Ed.

[2]Does not this and such like sentences make the tenet to appear *yet more bloody*.

world, Master Cotton will never prove, from any of the books and institutions of the New Testament, that unto those spiritual remedies appointed by
Christ against spiritual maladies, he added the help of the carnal sword.
If it appear, as evidently it doth, that Jesus, the antitype of the
kings of Israel, wears his sword in his mouth, being a sharp and two-
edged sword, then the answer is as clear as the sun, that scatters the clouds
and darkness of the night.   Besides, Master Cotton need not fly to the
pope's argument for children baptism, to wit, to say Christ never abrogated
Deut. xiii. therefore, &c., for Mr. Cotton knows the profession of the Lord
Jesus, John xviii. that his kingdom was not earthly, and therefore his
sword cannot be earthly.   Mr. Cotton knows that Jesus commanded a
sword to be put up, when it was drawn in the cause of Christ, and added
a dreadful threatening, that all that take the sword (that is the carnal
sword in his cause) shall perish by it.   W., pp. 95, 96.

The reader may remember, that Mr. Williams was often
blamed for holding that the civil magistrate's work was confined to the precepts of the second table.   His main argument therefor was, that Rom. xiii. speaks the most fully of
that subject of any place in the New Testament, and there
the discourse is confined to the duties included in love to
our neighbor.   Mr. Cotton grants his premises, but not his
conclusion, and says :—

Though subjection to magistrates, and love to all men, be duties which
concern the second table, yet the inference will not follow, that therefore
magistrates have nothing to do to punish any violation, no, not the weight-
iest duties of the first table.   It is a clear case, among the duties of the
second table people may be exhorted to honor their ministers, and children
may be exhorted to honor their parents ; but will it hence follow, that
therefore ministers have nothing to do with matters of religion in the
church, or parents in the family?"   C., p. 96.

Mr. Williams answers :—

If people are bound to yield obedience to civil things to civil officers of
the state, Christians are much more bound to yield obedience to the spiritual officers of Christ's kingdom ; but how weak is this argument to prove,
that therefore civil officers of the state are constituted rulers, preservers
and reformers of the Christian and spiritual state, which differs as much
from the civil, as the heavens are out of the reach of the [this] earthly
globe?   W., pp. 147, 148.

Mr. Cotton often recurs, through his book, to his notion of not punishing men for any matter of conscience, but only for sinning against their own consciences after conviction. One great article of Mr. Williams's sentence of banishment was, his writing letters against the rulers and churches before any conviction. And Mr. Cotton says of ministers and churches, " None of us had any further influence, than by private and public conviction of himself, and of the demerit of his way." C., 2d part, p.12. And when one of the magistrates was going to the Court that banished Mr. Williams, and asked Mr.Cotton what he thought of it? his answer was, " I pity the man, and have interceded for him, whilst there was any hope of doing good; but now he having refused to hear both his own church and us, and having rejected us all, as no churches of Christ, before any conviction, we have now no more to say in his behalf, nor hope to prevail for him." C., Part 2, p. 39.[1]

This notion of not punishing any in matters of religion, till they had first convinced their consciences, runs through Mr. Cotton's whole book, as those who have it may see in the quotations below;[2] and he tries to support it by Tit. iii.

[1] The charge in Roger Williams's sentence, " Whereas Mr. Roger Williams, one of the elders of the church at Salem, hath broached and divulged divers, new and dangerous opinions against the authority of magistrates, as also writ letters of defamation both of the magistrates and churches here, and that before any conviction, &c.," (see p. 131,) seems to mean that he had given public expression by word and letter to his opinions against the magistrates and churches, without affording them the opportunity of discoursing with him and convicting him of his errors. Cotton, as above represented, holds that no one should be punished for religious error, except he advance or adhere to the error *after conviction*, that is, after the error has been plainly set before him so that, in candor, he must admit it, and to cling to it longer will be a sin of obstinacy rather than of ignorance. There does not seem to be quite the inconsistency of Williams's sentence with Cotton's words, or of Cotton's words with each other in different parts of his book, that Backus represents, though it is not strange that he mistakes the ambiguous expressions. Williams is charged with expressing his opinions before any conviction, but he was not sentenced till after conviction, in their sense of the word, that is, till after the magistrates and ministers had disputed with him, and, in their view, " clearly confuted" him, and yet he persisted in adhering to his views and making them public. See pp. 51, 54. —ED.

[2] Pp. 3, 26, 189; Second Part, pp. 12, 17, 32, 37, 39.

11, which refers entirely to ecclesiastical, and not to civil government; and there not to every error, but only to gross heresy, which was to be judged of by those who were well acquainted with spiritual things.   But said Mr. Williams:—

Every lawful magistrate, whether succeeding or elected, is not only the minister of God, but the minister or servant of the people also (what people or nation soever they be, all the world over) and that minister or magistrate goes beyond his commission, who intermeddles with that which cannot be given him in commission from the people, unless Master Cotton can prove that all the people and inhabitants of all the nations in the world have spiritual power, Christ's power, naturally, fundamentally and originally residing in them, to rule Christ's spouse, the church, and to give spiritual power to their officers to exercise their spiritual laws and commands;[1] otherwise it is but profaning the holy name of the Most High.   It is but flattering of magistrates, it is but the accursed trusting to an arm of flesh, to persuade rulers of the earth that they are kings of the Israel or church of God, who were in their institutions and government immediately from God, the rulers of his holy church and people. W., p. 96.   Not a few of his opposites will say, and that aloud, that he and they were or might have been convinced, whatever he or they themselves thought.   The truth is, the carnal sword is commonly the judge of the conviction or obstinacy of all supposed heretics.[2]   Hence the faithful witnesses of Christ, Cranmer, Ridley, Latimer, had not a word to say in the disputations at Oxford.   Hence the

[1]Those who are called lords spiritual in England have no power, since the pope excommunicated them, but what they derive from the civil state.

[2]Dr. Owen wrote a piece upon toleration soon after Mr. Cotton's book was published in London, and upon this point he says, " He that holds the truth may be confuted, but a man cannot be convinced but by the truth.   That a man should be said to be convinced of a truth, and yet that truth not shine in upon his understanding, to the expelling of the contrary error, to me is strange.   To be convinced is to be overpowered by the evidence of that, which before a man knew not.   I once knew a scholar invited to a dispute with another man, about something in controversy in religion; in his own, and in the judgment of all the bystanders, the opposing person was utterly confuted.   And yet the scholar, within a few months, was taught of God, and clearly convinced, that it was an error which he had maintained, and the truth which he opposed; and then, and not till then, did he cease to wonder, that the other person was not convinced by his strong arguments, as before he had thought.   To say a man is convinced, when either for want of skill and ability, or the like, he cannot maintain his opinion against all men, is a mere conceit.   That they are obstinate and pertinacious is a cheap supposal, taken up without the price of a proof.   As the conviction is imposed, not owned, so is this obstinacy; if we may be judges of other men's obstinacy, all will be plain; but if ever they get uppermost, they will be judges of ours." Collection of Owen's Sermons and Tracts, 1721, p. 312.

nonconformists were cried out as obstinate men, abundantly convinced by
the writings of Whitgift and others ; and so in the conference before King
James at Hampton Court.   W., p. 192.

Mr. Williams in discussing his opponent's arguments observed, that his opponent had taken many charges and exhortations which Christ gave to his ministers, and directed
them to the civil magistrate.   But Mr. Cotton says, " The
falsehood of the discussor in this charge is palpable and notorious."   C., p. 88.   Yet fifty pages forward in the same
discourse Mr. Cotton says :—

> The good that is brought to princes and subjects by the due punishment
> of apostate seducers, idolaters and blasphemers, is manifold.   First, it
> putteth away evil from the people, and cutteth off a gangrene, which
> would spread to further ungodliness.   Deut. xiii. 5 ; 2 Tim. ii. 16, 17, 18.
> Secondly, it driveth away wolves from worrying and scattering the sheep
> of Christ.   False teachers be wolves.   Matt. vii. 15 ; Act. xx. 29.   C.,
> p. 137, 138.

This is a clear proof that great men cannot go straight in
a crooked path.

Mr. Williams had argued that Mr. Cotton's doctrine tended
to the setting up of a Spanish inquisition in all parts of the
world, and to frustrate the great design of our Saviour's
coming.   He denies it, and accuses Mr. Williams of rather
promoting the principal end of the Spanish inquisition, "by
proclaiming impunity to all their whorish and wolvish emissaries.   Nor is it," says he, " a frustrating of the sweet end
of Christ's coming, which was to save souls, but rather a
direct advancing of it, to destroy, if need be, the bodies of
those wolves, who seek to destroy the souls of those for
whom Christ died.   C., p. 93.

Mr. Williams replies :—

> I cannot without great horror observe, what is this but to give a woful
> occasion, at least to all civil powers in the world, to persecute Christ in
> his poor saints and servants?   Yea, if Master Cotton and his friends of his
> conscience should be cast by God's providence (whose wheels turn about in
> the depth of his councils wonderfully) I say should they be cast under the
> reach of opposite swords, will they not produce Master Cotton's own

bloody tenet and doctrine to warrant them (according to their consciences) to deal with him as a wolf, an idolater, a heretic, and as dangerous an emissary and seducer as any whom Master Cotton so accuseth [account-eth]? Master Cotton hath no reason to charge the discusser with indulgence or partiality towards Romish and wolvish emissaries; his judgment and practice is known so far different, that for departing too far from them (as is pretended) he suffers the brands and bears the marks of one of Christ's poor persecuted heretics to this day.[1] All that he pleaded for, is an impartial liberty to their consciences in worshipping God, as well as [to the] consciences and worships of other their fellow-subjects." W., pp. 141, 142.

This book Mr. Williams dedicated to the rulers of New England, wherein, after several useful remarks, he says :—

There is one commodity for the sake of which most of God's children in New England have run mighty hazards; a commodity marvellously scarce in former times, in our native country. It is the *liberty of searching after God's most holy mind and pleasure.* Of this most precious and invaluable jewel if you suffer Satan to bereave you, and that it shall be a crime humbly and peaceably to question even laws and statutes, or whatever is even publicly taught and delivered, you will find yourselves after all your long run (like that little Frenchman who killed the Duke of Guise, and was taken next morning near the place from whence he had fled upon a swift horse all night); I say you will most certainly find yourselves but where you were, enslaved and captivated in the chains of those popish darknesses, viz.: Ignorance is the mother of devotion, and, We must believe as the church believes, &c. O remember that your gifts are rare, your professions of religion rare, your persecutions and hidings from the storms abroad rare and wonderful![2] So in proportion your transgressions and public sins cannot but be of a rare and extraordinary guilt. Amongst the crying sins of our own or other sinful nations, those two are ever among the loudest, viz.: Invented devotions to the God of heaven; 2dly, Violence and oppression on the sons of men, especially of his sons, for dissenting. That the impartial and dreadful hand of the most holy and jealous God, a consuming fire, tear and burn not up at last the roots of these plantations, but graciously discerning [discovering] the plants which are not his, he may graciously sanctify and cause to flourish what his right hand will own, this is the humble and unfeigned desire and cry at the throne of grace, of you so long despised outcast; ROGER WILLIAMS." W., dedication, pp. 26, 27.

[1]One of the two points upon which the Massachusetts began their contention with him was his refusing to countenance the fellowship they had with popish corruptions in the church of England.

[2]Persecution drove them into this land, where they were hid from the bloody storm of intestine wars in England,

Thus I have laid before the reader some of the most material points of that controversy in their own words, that he may see what those principles were which New England writers have often reproached, under the name of rigid separation and anabaptism ; and also how the ruling party with all their boast of orthodoxy, could confound Jewish types with Christ's institutions, in order to keep up pædo-baptism, and the use of secular force in religious affairs; and could separate from the common rights of humanity, good Christians, and some of their own best friends, only for tes-tifying against such confusion.

Mr. Hubbard says :—

At a General Court, March,[1] 1645, two petitioners were preferred, one for suspending (if not abolishing) a law made against Anabaptists the for-mer year ; the other was for easing a law of like nature made in Mrs. Hutchinson's time, forbidding the entertaining of any strangers, without license of two magistrates : which was not easily obtained in those days. . . . . Some at this time were much afraid of the increase of anabaptism. . . . . This was the reason why the greater part prevailed for the strict observation of the aforesaid [foresaid] laws, although peradventure [on some accounts] a little moderation as to some cases might have done very well, if not [much] better. . . . . Many books coming out of England in the year 1645, some in defence of anabaptism and other errors, and for liberty of conscience, as a shelter for a general toleration of all opinions, &c., others in maintenance of Presbyterian [Presbyterial] government (agreed upon by the assembly of divines at Westminster) against the Con-gressional way which was practiced in New England ; the ministers of the churches through all the United Colonies agreed upon a meeting at Cam-bridge, where they conferred their counsels, and examined the writings which some of them had prepared, in answer to the said books ; which being agreed upon and perfected, were sent over into England to be printed,

---

[1]Hubbard evidently mistook this date. In the Massachusetts Records it is Octo-ber 18. The enactment is as follows :—" Upon a petition of divers persons for con-sideration of the law about new comers not staying above three weeks without license; and the law against Anabaptists, the Court hath voted that the laws men-tioned should not be altered at all nor explained." The attempt to secure the repeal of the latter law seems to have continued. Under date of May 6, 1646, is the record :—" The petition of divers of Dorchester, Roxbury, &c., to the number of seventy-eight, for the continuance of such orders without abrogation or weakening as are in force against Anabaptists and other erroneous persons, whereby to hinder the spreading or divulging of their errors, is granted.—ED.

viz. : Mr. Hooker's Survey, in answer to Mr. Rutherford ; Mr. Mather, Mr. Allen and Mr. Shepard, [Mr. Mather's, Mr. Allen's, and Mr. Shepard's discourses] about the same subject, &c.[1]

Our friends in London, hearing of the law made at Boston last year to banish Baptists, and the learned Mr. John Tombes having written an examination of Mr. Stephen Marshall's sermon upon infant baptism, dedicated to the Westminster Assembly, Mr. Tombes was moved to send a copy of his examination to the ministers of New England, and wrote an epistle with it to them, dated from the Temple in London, May 25, 1645 ; hoping thereby to put them upon a more exact study of that controversy, and to allay their vehemency against the Baptists.[2]   But the Westminster Assem-

---

[1]Hubbard, [413—415.]

[2]Crosby's history, Vol. I, pp. 121, 122.—B.

John Tombes was born at Bewdly, Worcestershire, in 1603. At the age of fourteen he was admitted at Magdalen Hall, Oxford, and at the age of twenty-one was made Catechetical Lecturer there. Six years later he entered the ministry, and was settled at Lemster and afterwards at Bristol. Driven from these places successively by the civil war, in 1643 he went to London. For several years he had questioned the scriptural authority of infant baptism and held that there was only one passage, I Cor. vii, 14, on which it could be defended. He had recently been led to yield this passage also, as affording it no support. Upon coming to London where he had greater advantages for investigation, he determined to examine the subject in the light of church history, and as the result of the examination, he was as fully convinced that infant baptism was without support from antiquity as from Scripture. At a meeting of ministers in London, he proposed the question, " What Scripture is there for infant baptism ?" and avowed his own renunciation of the rite. The Westminster Assembly was then in session, with the declared object of reforming religion in England and Scotland, and had appointed a committee on infant baptism. Mr. Tombes drew up in Latin his arguments against it, and sent them to the chairman of the committee, asking that they would answer his objections or reform the practice of the churches on the point in question. After a delay of months, he learned that they gave the matter no consideration save to pass a vote of censure on any who should dispute upon it.

Mr. Tombes became pastor of Fenchurch, London, agreeing with the church that he would not preach against infant baptism, and that they should admit no one to preach in their pulpit in its favor. Here he published two treatises against infant baptism, one of which was his Examen of Mr. Marshall's sermon, and, as the result, he was dismissed from his church. He next assumed charge of a parish in Bewdly, his native town. While here, he was immersed upon profession of faith, and gathered a church of those who were in agreement with him. He still continued to act as minister of the parish, and because of his acknowledged learning and ability, and of services which he had rendered to the government, he was held in repute, was entrusted with important offices in the national church and enjoyed the friendship of leading men in the country notwithstanding his religious views and practice. Several times he held public disputes upon baptism, once with Richard Baxter, when, says Anthony Wood, "all scholars there and present, who knew the way of disputing and managing arguments, did conclude that Tombes got the better of Baxter by far." Many of his most distinguished contemporaries testify to

bly were more ready to learn severity from this country, than these were
to learn lenity from any ; for the Independents on December 4, 1645, presented a request to that Presbyterian Assembly, " that they might not be
forced to communicate as members in those parishes where they dwell;
but many have liberty to have congregations of such persons who give
good testimonies of their godliness, and yet out of tenderness of conscience
cannot communicate in their parishes ;" but the Assembly returned a flat
denial, and said, " This opened a gap for all sects to challenge such a liberty as their due ; and that this liberty was denied by the churches of New
England, and we have as just ground to deny it as they."[1]

Sir Henry Vane also, when his interest in Parliament was
very great, wrote to Governor Winthrop in the following
terms :—

HONORED SIR :—I received yours by your son, and was unwilling to let
him return without telling you as much. The exercise and troubles which
God is pleased to lay upon these kingdoms, and the inhabitants in them,
teaches us patience and forbearance one with another in some measure,
though there be difference in our opinions, which makes me hope that, from
the experience here, it may also be derived to yourselves ; lest while the

his great learning and talent. A catalogue of his writings gives the titles of twenty-
six works, fourteen of which are against infant baptism.

The manuscript copy of his Examen of Mr. Marshall's sermon which was sent to
New England, is now in the library of the American Antiquarian Society, Worcester. With it is the following letter :—

" To all the elders of the churches of Christ in New England and to each in particular by name; to the pastor and teacher of the church of God at Boston,
these present:

REVEREND BRETHREN :—Understanding that there is some disquiet in your churches about pædobaptism, and being moved by some that honor you much in the
Lord, and desire your comfortable account at the day of Christ, that I would yield
that a copy of my Examen of Master Marshall his sermon of infant baptism might
be transcribed to be sent to you; I have consented thereto, and do commend it to
your examination, in like manner, as you may perceive by the reading of it, I did
to Master Marshall, not doubting but that you will, as in God's presence, and
accountable to Christ Jesus, weigh the thing; remembering that your Lord Jesus
Christ, John vii, 24, " Judge not according to appearance but judge righteous
judgment." To the blessings of him who is your God and our God, your Judge
and our Judge, I leave you and the flock of God over which the Holy Ghost hath
made you overseers, and rest.

Your brother and fellow-servant,

JOHN TOMBES.

From my study at the Temple in London, May 25th, 1645."

See Crosby, Vol. I, pp. 120—122, 278—297; Hague's Historical Discourse, pp.
152—155.—ED.

[1]Crosby's history, Vol. I, pp. 185, 186.

Congregational way amongst you is in its freedom and is backed with power, it teach its oppugners here to extirpate it and root it out, from its own principles and practice.   I shall need say no more, knowing your son can acquaint you particularly with our affairs.   Sir, I am your affectionate friend, and servant in Christ,

H. VANE.[1]

June 10, 1645.

Had not the notion of securing religion to their posterity, by infant baptism and the magistrates' power, strongly prepossessed their minds, how could they have resisted all these motives to lenity as they did?   That they were under a very strong bias may be seen in three pieces which were written this year against the Baptists.   One of them was by Mr. Cotton, who was so much afraid of having both sides of the argument examined, that he gives us neither the names of the authors he wrote against nor the titles of their works; only he owns them to be such as did not " deny magistrates, or predestination, nor original sin; nor maintain free will in conversion, nor apostacy from grace; but only deny the lawful use of baptism of children, because it wanteth a word of commandment and example from the Scripture."   And he says :—

I am bound in Christian love to believe, that they who yield so far, do it out of conscience, as following herein the example of the apostle, who professed himself, and his followers, We can do nothing against the truth, but for the truth.   But yet I believe withal, that it is not out of love to the truth that Satan yielded so much to the truth, but rather out of another ground, and for a worse end.   He knoweth the times that how, by the good and strong hand of God, they are set upon purity and reformation. And now to plead against the baptism of children upon any of those Arminian and popish grounds, which be so grossly ungracious as those above named, Satan knoweth and seeeth they would be utterly rejected.[2]   He chooseth therefore rather to play small game, as they say, than to lose all. He now pleadeth no other argument in these stirring times of reformation than may be urged from a main principle of purity and reformation, viz., That no duty of God's worship, nor any ordinance of religion, is to be ad-

[1]Massachusetts History, Vol. III, p. 137.
[2]Here is an acknowledgment, that the Baptists of that day did not hold the errors charged upon them in the aforesaid law.

ministered in the church, but such as hath *just warrant from the word of God*. And by urging this argument against the baptism of children, Satan transformeth himself into an angel of light ; and the spirit of error and profaneness into a minister of truth and righteousness. And so he hopeth to prevail, either with those men who do believe the lawful and holy use of children's baptism to renounce that principle, and so to renounce also all reformation brought in by it ; or else, if they stick to that principle, then to renounce the baptism of children ; and so the reformation begun will neither spread far, nor continue long. For if godly parents do withdraw their children from the covenant, and from the seal of the covenant, they do make void (as much as in them lieth) the covenant both to themselves, and to their children ; and then will the Lord cut off such souls from his people. Gen. xvii. 14. And so the reformation, begun with a blessing, will end in a curse, and in a cutting separation either of parents or of children, or both, from the Lord and his people.[1]

About the same time a minister at Lynn wrote a volume against various Baptist authors ; but before he came to any of their arguments he said :—

Ever since that word of old, " I will put enmity betwixt thee and the woman, and betwixt thy seed and her seed," Satan hath had a special spite at the seed of the church. Witness 'that act of Cain, who was therein of that evil one, in killing his brother Abel. Whence also that project of Satan, all the ways that may be, to lay foundations of corrupting, and in time ruining the seed of the church by unequal marriages, &c. Gen. vi. 1, 2 ; Neh. xiii. 23, 24. Whence also that act of his, in stirring up his instruments to deride little Isaac. Whence also that satanical practice of seeking to cut them off by Pharoah, Exod. i. [15—17] ; by Edomites, Psalm cxxxvii. 8, 9 ; by Babylonians, Jer. ix. [21] ; Syrians, Dan. i. 1—8 ; Herod, Matt. ii. [16—18,] &c. ; or, if they be not cut off in such sort, yet to stir up persons under pretence of religion, to devote them unto the very devil, Jer. vii. 31, &c. ; Ezek. xvi. 20, &c. ; or if they live, yet to persuade to their detainment under an Egyptian estate, and exclusion from any church care or privilege. . . . . Who seeeth not how Satan doth seek by such suggestions to undermine the succession of the true religion, and of true visible churches, which have used to be continued in and by the church seed? And what is Satan's fetch to bring this about, but the old trick, to create, (as I may say) scruples in the hearts of God's people, knowing well that it is a taking wile first to bemist through such legerdemain the eyes of the mind, and then to spoil them of truth. It took with our grandmother Eve, and was the inlet of all error and evil. " *Hath God*

[1] Cotton's Grounds and Ends of Children's Baptism, printed in 1647, pp. 3, 4.

said it ? " was the old serpentine insinuation to blind and buzzle, and so
corrupt first the judgment in point of warrant of this or that practice. . . . .
How many precious professors, to outward view at least, did at first entertain some scruples about the external interest of church members' children
in the covenant, and initiatory seal of it, which now peremptorily censure
the same as antichristian and human inventions? Let my advice be grateful to thee thus far, Christian reader, to take heed of unnecessary discourses and disputes with satanical suggestions, under what promising and
plausible pretences soever they come. . . . . It is not the first age or time,
that satanical suggestions, " *Thus it is written,*" and " *Thus saith the Lord,*"
hath been propounded.[1]

The question has often been asked in our day, what do
you think of our good fathers who held to infant baptism?
How did they get along? Here you have an answer in their
own words; and the famous Dr. Thomas Goodwin ushered
these performances into the world with a recommendatory
preface to each of them; and the sentiments and temper of
them have evidently been handed down by tradition ever
since. But I appeal to the conscience of every reader,
whether he can find three worse things on earth, in the management of controversy, than, first, to secretly take the point
disputed for truth without any proof; then, secondly, blending that error with known truths, to make artful addresses
to the affections and passions of the audience, to prejudice
their minds, before they hear a word that the respondent
has to say; and, thirdly, if the respondent refuses to yield
to such management, then to call in the secular arm to complete the argument? And were not these the methods
that were then taken to support pædobaptism? The protestants' way of defending their cause against the papists
was. " If that ye will prove that your ceremonies proceed
from faith, and do please God, ye must prove that God in
express words hath commanded them, or else shall you never
prove that they proceed from faith, nor yet that they please

---

[1] Mr. Thomas Cobbet's Vindication of the Covenant and Church Estate of Children of Church Members, printed in London, 1643, preface, pp. 7—9. Mr. Tombes
says Mr. Cotton wrote to him, that the piece he sent them was delivered to Mr. Cobbet answer.

God."[1] But when this argument was urged against infant baptism, Cotton without any proof asserts that "Satan transformeth himself into an angel of light." And the whole of the above-recited addresses to men's and women's passions, is evidently founded upon the supposition, that infant baptism is as infallibly required by God, as abstaining from the forbidden fruit was, or Abraham's circumcising his children. Having taken the very point which is disputed for truth, without any evidence, they blended that with many known facts recorded in Scripture, and thereupon rank the opposers of that point with the old serpent the devil and Satan, and with his instruments Cain, Pharoah, Herod, and other murderers ; yea, with such as sacrifice their children to devils ! This history contains abundant evidence of their adding the magistrate's sword to all these hard words, which were used in their prefaces before they came to any of the Baptists' arguments. When Mr. Cotton came to them, the first of them is, that in Christ's commission to his ministers, he ordered them first to teach or make disciples, and then to baptize them ; and he says two arguments offer themselves for his way from hence :—

" 1. Such as be disciples. they are to be baptized ; but the children of the faithful, they are disciples ; therefore children of the faithful, they are to be baptized." To support this assertion he turns to Isaiah liv. 13, " All thy children shall be taught of God ;" and says he, " If they be taught of God, then are they his disciples ; for that is the meaning of the word. Disciples are taught or learnt of God."[2] This is true, and our Lord quotes this text to shew how the father draws souls to himself, and says upon it, "Every man[3] therefore that hath heard, and hath learned of the Father, cometh unto me," John vi. 45. Can we desire

---

[1]Knox's History of the Reformation, p. 104.

[2]Cotton's Grounds and Ends, pp. 5, 6.

[3]Note. Christ shows that the word " children" in that text means posterity; men that are taught.

a more exact and certain definition of the word disciple than we have here ?   Let conscience speak before him who will judge us all.   Do you who practice in this disputed way, believe when you bring your infants to be sprinkled, that they *have heard and learned of the Father*, so as to *come unto Christ*?   And do you bring them because they *are taught of God*?   If they are not, they are *not disciples* according to the known meaning of the word.

Mr. Cotton frames his second argument from Exod. xii. 48, where God required every proselyte to have all his males circumcised, before he could come to the passover ; upon which Cotton says :—

> If then our Lord's Supper come in the room of the passover, and our baptism in the room of circumcision, like as he that hath not circumcised his males, was accounted as one uncircumcised himself, and so to be debarred from the passover, so he who hath not baptized his children, is accounted of God as not baptized himself, and so to be debarred from the Lord's Supper.   If therefore you forbid baptism to children, you evacuate the baptism of their parents, and so make the commandment, of God, and the commission to the apostles, and the baptism of believers, of none effect.[1]

These are the two main arguments for infant baptism to this day ; and they both hang upon the little word *if*, which I think is a very small pin to rest the weight of whole provinces and kingdoms upon. *If* infants are disciples by virtue of their parents' profession, then they are to be baptized ; and if our baptism comes in the place of the circumcision of Jewish proselytes, then we cannot lawfully admit bringing our infants thereto. But what if this supposition should prove to be as contrary to truth as darkness is to light, will men persist in that way still ?   Abraham had no warrant to circumcise any but such as were either born in his house or bought with his money.   The first order that was given for bringing in others by households was in the day that Israel came out of Egypt.   Now as we make no pretence of being Abraham's natural posterity, nor of being bought with Jew-

[1] Cotton's Grounds and Ends, p. 11.

ish money, the argument all turns upon a supposal that Gentile believers ought to bring their households with them to baptism, as the said proselytes did theirs to circumcision. But I know not how words can express the contrary more plainly than God himself has done in this case; for he says his new covenant is not according to that he made with Israel on said day. Heb. viii. 8—11. Upon this men often assert that the ordinances differ, while the subjects are the same. But the text assures us expressly, that the main difference is in the subjects; that the subjects of the new covenant *all know God from the least to the greatest.* When this is mentioned, they would then turn it to the difference betwixt the outward administration and inward efficacy of the covenant; but that cannot be here intended, because that distinction was as real in Abraham's time as it is now, as the apostle shows in Rom. iv. 11; which text is often brought for a proof that the covenant is the same now as with Abraham. It does prove that the internal efficacy of divine institutions was the same upon believers then as now; only their faith was fixed on a future Messiah, ours on one already come. The difference then betwixt the two covenants we are speaking of, is not internal, but external. By divine institution a whole family and a whole nation were then taken into covenant; now none are added to the church by the Lord but believers who shall be saved. Acts ii. 41, 47. Professors who had not this character were " false brethren unawares brought in." Gal. ii. 4. Their being in was owing to men's imperfection, and not to God's institution ; yet because the Baptists refused to yield to a practice they viewed to be not only without, but directly against divine institution, they were abused in the manner above described. And Mr. Cobbet concludes his discourse with a few inferences, in which he says :—

See the danger and detestableness of anabaptistical tenets, giving God and Christ (in part) the lie, vailing the glory of his preventing grace of covenant; Num. xiv. 18; .... condemning the judgment and practice of

former churches, Jews and Gentiles. .... Whence that profane trick of
some to turn their back upon the churches [when they sprinkled infants] as
if all their persons, and prayers, and fellowship, were unclean? whence the
styling of it antichristian? &c. What is this but to blaspheme the name
and tabernacle and saints of God? Rev. xiii. [6.]

Thus the Baptists were accused by those noted authors of
profaneness and blasphemy, only for their manifesting by
word and gesture their dissent from infant sprinkling.

Mr. Nathaniel Ward, of Ipswich, (the Indian name of
which was Agawam.) who, with Mr. Cotton, had often been
improved by the Court in composing their law-book, published a tract this year under a fanciful title, which contains
the following addresses to the Anabaptists:—

1. To entreat them to consider, what a high pitch of boldness it is, for
a man to cut a principal ordinance out of the kingdom of God; if it be
but to make a dislocation, which so far disgoods the ordinance, I fear it
altogether unhallows it. To transplace or transtime a stated institution of
Jesus Christ, without his direction, I think is to destroy it.[1] 2. What a
cruelty it is, to divest children of that only external privilege which their
Heavenly Father has bequeathed them, to interest them visibly in himself,
his Son, his Spirit, his covenant of peace, and the tender bosom of their
careful mother the church. 3. What an inhumanity it is, to deprive
parents of that comfort they may take from the baptism of their infants
dying in their childhood. 4. How unseasonably [unseasonable] and unkindly it is, to interturbe the state and church with their Amalakitish on-
sets, when they are in their extreme pangs of travail with their lives?
5. To take a thorough view of those who have perambled this by-path;
being sometimes in the crowds of foreign *wederdropers*, i. e. Anabaptists,
and prying into their inward frames with the best eyes I had, I could but
observe those disguised guises in the generality of them. 1. A flat for
mality of spirit, without salt or savor in the spiritualities of Christ; as if
their religion had begun and ended with their opinion. 2. A shallow
slighting of such as dissent from them, appearing too often in their faces,
speeches and carriages. 3. A feeble yet peremptory obstinacy. Seldom
are any of them reclaimed.[2]

[1] How easily may this reasoning be retorted? Christ's institution, and the apostles'
administration of baptism, were expressly to such as believed, gladly received the
word, and should be saved; and those who professed such a faith, went into the
water, and were buried in baptism; and according to this writer's doctrine, how
does it destroy the ordinance to change it into sprinkling of infants?

[2] Simple Cobbler of Agawam, pp. 16, 17; Hubbard, [155.]

By these extracts the reader may see the temper and language of Pædobaptists in that day, and how much of the same has there been in later times? of charging us with cruelty, because we hold that no acts of men can interest children in the grace of God, before they are taught and believe his truth; and because we dare not place our hopes of infants' salvation upon the doings of ministers and churches, instead of the sovereign mercy of God in Jesus Christ, unto whom we would commit them by believing prayer, and if they live, we would use all gospel methods for their conversion, and obedience to all his commands. How much also have we seen of their assuming God's prerogative, in judging the hearts of such as yield not to their arguments?

As all the foregoing means were ineffectual, some of the ministers presented a bill to the General Court this year, for the calling a synod to settle these and other ecclesiastical affairs. "The magistrates passed the bill, but some of the deputies questioned the power of the Court, to require their churches to send their messengers to such a convention, as not being satisfied that any such power was given by Christ to the civil magistrates over the churches in such cases." This caused a debate the conclusion of which was, "that the ensuing synod should be convened by way of motion only to the churches, and not in words of command."[1] The order of it began thus:—

BOSTON, 15th 3d Month, 1646.

The right form of church government and discipline being agreed, part of the kingdom of Christ upon earth, therefore the establishing and settling thereof by the joint and public agreement and consent of churches, and by the sanction of civil authority, must needs greatly conduce to the honor and glory of our Lord Jesus Christ, and to the settling and safety of church and commonwealth, where such a duty is diligently attended and performed. Upon which they sent out their motion for said synod.

[1] Hubbard, [533, 534.]

To enforce this they say :—[1]

For [Through] want of the thing here spoken of, some differences of opinion and practice of one church from another do already appear amongst us ; and others (if not timely prevented) are like speedily to ensue, and this not only in lesser things, but even in points of no small consequence and very material ; to instance in no more but those about baptism, and the persons to be received thereto, in which one particular the apprehensions of many persons in the country are known not a little to differ ; for whereas in most churches the ministers do baptize [only such children whose nearest parents, one or both of them, are settled members in full communion with one or other of these churches, there be some one who do baptize][2] the children if the grandfather or grandmother be set [such] members, though the immediate parents be not, and others, though for avoiding of difference of neighbor churches they do not [as] yet actually so practice, yet they do much incline thereto [as thinking more liberty and latitude in this point ought to be yielded than hath hitherto been done]. And many persons living in this country who have been members of the congregations in England, but are not found fit to be received at the Lord's table here, there be notwithstanding considerable persons in these churches who do think that children of these also, upon some conditions and terms, may and ought to be baptized. Likewise on the other side, there be some among us who do think that whatever be the state the parents, baptism ought not to be dispensed to any infants whatsoever ; which various apprehensions being seconded with practices according thereto, as in part they already are, and are like to be more, must needs, if not timely remedied, beget such differences as will be displeasing to the Lord, and offensive to others, and dangerous to ourselves.

These were their reasons for calling the synod. The work assigned to them was to " discuss, dispute, and clear up by the word of God, such questions of church government, and discipline, in the things aforementioned, or any other as they shall think needful and meet, and to continue so doing, till they or the major part of them shall have

---

[1]The records mention two reasons besides those here given, for calling this synod :—that it is a time of peace, and therefore convenient for settling religious questions ; and that divers friends in England have urged this good work.— ED.

[2]Backus evidently here committed an error which is one of the most frequent errors of transcription. The word "baptize" occurs twice near together, and he, misled by the recurrence, omitted the intervening words, and thus, as is shown by the words supplied, his statement in this clause is just the opposite of that of the document which he is copying.—ED.

agreed [and consented] upon one form of government and discipline, for the main and substantial parts thereof, as that which they judge agreeable to the holy Scriptures ;" which when it was finished was to be presented to the General Court, " to the end that the same being found agreeable to the word of God, it may receive from the said General Court such approbation as is meet, that the Lord being thus acknowledged by church and state, to be our Judge, our Lawgiver, and [our] King, he may be graciously pleased still to save us, as hitherto he hath done.[1]

Here we may plainly see wherein their great mistake lay. They confounded the judgment that they formed upon the Scripture with the rule itself. Also the majority assumed the power of judging for the whole, and of punishing dissenters from their judgments, as breakers of God's law ; a delusion that the world is not clear of to this day, though light and truth have gained much since that time.

We are told that opposition was made in some of the churches against sending to that synod, notwithstanding the moderate expressions in the Court's ordered for it. Mr. Hubbard says :—

The principal men who raised the objections were some who lately came from England, where such a vast liberty was pleaded for, by all that rabble of men that went under the name of Independents, whether Anabaptists, Antinomians, Familists and Seekers, far beyond the moderate limits pleaded for by [the] Congregational divines in the assembly at Westminster, such as Dr. Goodwin, Mr. Nye, Mr. Burroughs, &c., who yet [it may be intending to double the Cape of Good Hope, then in view, as was thought,] tacked about further than they need to have done. A great part of the Parliament also, then in being inclined much that way, and had by their commissioners sent word to all the English plantations in the West Indies, and Summer Islands, that all men should enjoy their liberty of conscience ; and had by their letters also intimated the same to those of New England. Some few of the church at [of] Boston adhered to these principles which made them stickle so much against the calling of the synod at that time ; against which they raised a threefold objection. 1. That by a

[1]This request was also sent to the churches of Plymouth and Connecticut colonies. Massachusetts Records.

liberty already established among the laws of New England, the elders or ministers of the churches have [allowance or] liberty to assemble upon all occasions, without the compliance of the civil authority. 2. It was observed that this motion came originally from some of the [elders or] ministers, and not from the Court. 3. In the order was expressed, that what the major part of the assembly should agree upon should be presented to the Court for their confirmation.

To the first it was answered, that [the] said liberty was granted only for help in case of extremity, if in time to come either the civil authority should grow opposite to the churches, or neglect the care of them, and not with any intent to practice the same while the civil rulers were nursing fathers to the church.[1] To the second it was answered, it was not for the churches to enquire what or who gave the occasion ; but if they thought fit to desire the churches to afford them help of council in any matter[s] which concerned religion and conscience it was the churches' duty to yield it to them ; for as [so] far as it concerns their command or request, it is an ordinance of man, which all are to submit unto for the Lord's sake, without troubling themselves about the occasion or success. . . . . For the third, where the order speaks of the major part,

---

[1] Mr. Williams in discussing Mr. Cotton's arguments observed, that the higher powers in Rom. xiii. were strangers to God and true religion, from whence he argued, that for Paul to command subjection to such in spiritual causes would have been to put out the eye of faith, reason and sense, at once. [Bloody Tenet, p. 77.] To which Mr. Cotton answers, "The cases of religion wherein we allow civil magistrates to be judges, are so fundamental and palpable, that no magistrate studious of religion in the fear of God, but if he have any spiritual discerning, he cannot but judge of such gross corruptions as unsufferable in religion.... But [as] for such magistrates as are merely natural and pagan, though Christians be bound to subject themselves to them with patience ; yet such magistrates ought to forbear the exercise of their power, either in protecting or punishing matters of religion, till they have learned so much knowledge of the truth, as may enable them to discern of things that differ." Tenet washed, pp. 101, 102. In reply to which Mr. Williams says, " O the miserable allowance which Master Cotton hath brought the kings and governors of the world unto ! We allow them to judge in such fundamental, &c." ....The magistrates must wait at their gates for their poor allowance. They shall judge, and they shall not judge ; they shall judge that which is gross and palable [and] enough to hold the people in slavery, and to force them to sacrifice to the priest's belly ; but the more sublime and nicer mysteries they must not judge or touch but attend upon the tables of the priest's infallibility." Williams's Reply, p. 152. " If Christ Jesus have left such power with the civil rulers of the world, [kingdoms and counties, of or] for the establishing, governing, and reforming his church, what is become of his care and love, wisdom and faithfulness, since in all ages since he left the earth, for the general [beyond all exception] he hath left her destitute of such qualified princes and governors, and in the course of his providence furnished her with such, whom he knew would be [and all men find] as fit as wolves to protect and feed his sheep and people !" Ibid. p. 202.

it speaks in its own language, ... but it never intended thereby to restrain [or direct] the synod in the manner of their proceeding : nor to hinder them but that they might first acquaint the churches with their conclusions, and have their assent to them, before they did present them to the Court. . . . .

This matter was two Lord's days in agitation with the church in Boston, before they could be brought to any comfortable conclusion ; but on a lecture day intervening, Mr. Norton, teacher of the church at Ipswich, was procured to supply the place at Boston, where was a great audience ; and the subject then handled was, [suitable to the occasion, viz. :] Moses and Aaron kissing each other in the mount of God. . . . . On the next Lord's day, after much debate in Boston church, it was agreed by the vote of the major part, that the elders and three of the brethren should be sent [as messengers] to the synod.[1]

This account from one of their noted ministers, may give us considerable light about the actings of that day. He informs us that the synod did not meet till near winter, when after a session of fourteen days, they adjourned to June 8,[2] 1647 ; and that summer proving sickly,[3] they were forced to adjourn again. But on August 16, 1648, they met, and completed the Cambridge platform ; the last article of which says :—

" If any church, one or more, shall grow schismatical, rending itself from the communion of other churches, or shall walk incorrigibly or obstinately in any corrupt way of their own, contrary to the rule of the word ; in such case the magistrate [Josh. 22,] is to put forth his coercive power, as the matter shall require.[4]

This principle the Baptists and others felt the cruel effects of for many years after. A clause was also inserted at the end of their tenth chapter, that no church act can be consummated without the consent of both elders and brethren ; which implicitly gives ministers a power to negative the churches' acts, and which many in later times have contended for, though that would give them such a lordly power over the church, as chief judges in the state are not allowed to

---

[1]Hubbard, [534—536.]

[2]In the original edition this date is given erroneously, June 18.—ED.

[3]The celebrated Mr. Hooker, minister of Hartford, died July 7, 1647. Hubbard, 536, 537.—ED.

[4]Magnalia, B. 5, Vol. II, p. 203.—ED.

have in the executive courts of our nation.   As to baptism,
though the order for calling the synod asserted that most
ministers do baptize the grandchildren of church members,[1]
yet that assertion was so far from truth, that those who "labored much to have this principle declared and asserted in
the platform," could not effect it because of "many worthy
men."[2]   Mr. Hooker had published his testimony, wherein
he asserted "that children as children have no right to [not
right unto] baptism, so that it belongs not to any predecessors either nearer or farther off removed from the next parents to give right of this privilege to their children."[3]   Mr.
Thomas Shepard, pastor of the church where this synod met,
had also publicly asked what members every particular visible church ought to consist of? and answered, that "Christ
being the head of every particular church, and it his body,
hence none are to be members of the church but such as are
members of Christ by faith."   And though he observes that
hypocrites do sometimes creep in, yet he says, "If they could
have been known to be such, they ought to be kept out; and
when they are known they are orderly to be cast out."[4]   And
there was still more regard paid to this first principle of the
New England churches, than could consist with the admission of persons to bring their children to baptism, who were
"not found fit" for the other ordinance.

It may be proper now to take a further view of the affairs
of Mr. Gorton and his company.   Upon their being released
and banished, as I have related, they went to Rhode Island,
and from thence over to Narragansett, where, on April 19,
1644, they procured a deed from the sachems, whereby they
resigned themselves, people, lands, rights, inheritances, and
possessions, over unto the protection and government of King
Charles; and appointed Samuel Gorton, and others their

---

[1]See p 156, note 2.—ED.   [2]Magnalia, B. IV, p. 176.
[3]Survey of Church Discipline, part 3, pp. 12, 13.
[4]First Principles of the Oracles of God, pp. 25, 26. [Works of Thomas Shepard, Doctrinal Tract and Book Society, Boston, 1853, Vol. I, p. 350.]

agents, to carry the same to him. This was signed by Passi-cus, Canaunicus and Maxan, and witnessed by two Indians and three English. The loss of their great sachem Miantinomu lay very heavy upon their spirits. Hubbard says, he " was a very goodly personage, of tall stature, subtile and cunning in his contrivements."[1] In May came a letter to the rulers at Boston, signed by Canaunicus, though written by some of Gorton's company, to this effect, that they purposed to make war upon Uncas, in revenge of the death of Miantinomu and others of their people, and marvelled that the English should be against it; and that they had put themselves under the government and protection of the king of England, and so were become their fellow subjects, and therefore if any dif-ference should fall between them, it ought to be referred to him; professing withal their willingness to continue all friendly correspondence with them. The General Court re-ceived another letter from Gorton and his company, to the like effect. " June 23, news came that the Narragansetts had killed six of Uncas's men and five women, and had sent two hands and a foot to Pumham, to engage him to join with them, but he chose to keep to Massachusetts."[2] Contentions increased so much the next year that an extraordinary meet-ing of the Commissioners of the United Colonies was called at Boston, on July 28, 1645, when they sent three messengers to the Narragansetts, who on their return brought a letter from Mr. Williams to the Commissioners, assuring them that " war would presently break forth, and that the Narra-gansett sachems had lately concluded a neutrality with Prov-idence, and the towns on Aquedneck Island." Upon which they determined to raise an army of three hundred men, in the following proportion, viz.:—One hundred and ninety out of the Massachusetts, forty out of Plymouth, forty out of Connecticut, and thirty out of New Haven colonies. Forty were raised immediately, and sent away under the

[1]Hubbard, 446.—Ed.
[2]Winthrop, [Vol. II, pp. 166, 167, 169]; Hubbard, [452, 453.]
11

command of Lieutenant Humphrey Atherton, to protect Uncas, till Captain Mason should meet him there with the western forces, who were then to proceed to meet the remainder of the forces from the eastward, in Narragansett, under the command of Edward Gibbons, Major General. After which Governor Winthrop informed the Commissioners, "that since Miantinomu's death the Narragansett sachems by messengers sent him a present, expressing their desire to keep peace with the English, but desiring to make war with Uncas for their sachem's death." The present was about the value of fifteen pounds in wampum, but he refused to receive it upon those terms. The Commissioners concluded to take the present into their hands, and thereupon sent Captain Harding and Mr. Wilbore to those sachems, who were to take Benedict Arnold with them, and inform them that their present was returned and not accepted, unless they would be at peace with Uncas as well as the English ; but if said sachems would come with them to Boston, they should have liberty safely to come and return without molestation, to treat of peace, though deputies in their stead would not now do. The messengers returning brought back the present, and informed the Commissioners that they found not Benedict Arnold at Providence, and heard that he durst not adventure himself again amongst the Narragansett Indians without a sufficient guard. They also understood that Mr. Williams, sent for by the Narragansett sachems, was going thither, wherefore they acquainted him with their message, shewed him their instructions, and made use of him as an interpreter." He prevailed with Passicas and others to go to Boston, and moved the messengers to write and acquaint Captain Mason of the prospect there was of peace ; which last article the Commissioners censured them for, as going beyond their instructions. The English demanded two thousand fathoms of wampum to pay the costs of this expedition, and for other damages ; which the Indians were compelled to yield to, and to give hostages till it was paid ; and so articles of peace were drawn up and signed between them. The Commissioners afterward drew up a formal declaration, to justify their proceedings in said war.[1]

The Indians were far from being easy under these things ; and in August, 1648, about a thousand Indians from various parts were collected in Connecticut, with three hundred guns among them ; and it was reported that they were hired by the Narragansetts to fight with Uncas. The magistrates of Hartford sent three horsemen to enquire what they designed, and to let them know that if they made war with him the English must defend him, upon which they dispersed. When the commissioners met at Plymouth the next month, they ordered four men to be sent to the Narragansetts, " with instructions how to treat with them, both concerning their hiring other Indians to war upon Uncas, and also about the tribute of wampum that was behind. Captain Atherton and Captain Prichard undertook the service, and going to Mr. Williams, they procured that the sachems should be sent for ; but they, hearing that many horsemen were come to take them, shifted for themselves ; Passicus fled to Rhode Island ; but soon after they were, by Mr. Williams's means, delivered of their fears, and came to the messengers as they were desired, and denied their hiring the Mohawks to war against Uncas, though they owned that they had sent them a present.[2]

Gorton, Holden, and Greene, went to England to carry the Narragansett's surrender of themselves and lands, as well as their own complaints, to the king ; but found him not able to help either himself or them. However, they published their case and a narrative of their sufferings, in 1645, under the title of " Simplicity's Defence against seven-headed Policy." They also applied themselves to the Commissioners whom the Parliament had appointed over the·

---

[1]Records of the United Colonies. Massachusetts History, Vol. III, pp. 138—145.
[2]Canaunicus died a very old man, on June 4, 1648. Hubbard, [464.]

affairs of the plantations, and at length obtained from them the following letter to the authority in the Massachusetts colony, viz. :—

We being especially intrusted, by both houses of parliament with ordering the affairs and government of the English plantations in America, have some months since received a complaint from Mr. Gorton and Mr. Holden, in the name of themselves and divers other English, who have transported themselves into New England, and now are or lately were inhabitants of a tract of land called the Narragansett Bay ; (a copy of which complaint the enclosed petition and narrative will represent unto your knowledge) we could not proceed [forthwith proceed] to a full hearing and determining [determination] of the matter, it not appearing unto us that you were acquainted with the particular charge, or that you had furnished any persons [person] with power to make defence in your behalf; nor could we conveniently respite some kind of resolution, without a great prejudice to the petitioners, who could have lain under much incouveniency if we had detained them from their families, till all the formalities and circumstances of proceeding (necessary at this distance) had regularly prepared the cause for a hearing.   We shall therefore let you know in the first place, that our present resolution is not grounded upon an admittance of the truth of what is charged ; we knowing well how much God hath honored your government, and believing that your spirit and affairs are acted by principles of justice, prudence and [of] zeal to God ; and therefore cannot easily receive any evil impressions concerning your proceedings.   In the next place you may take notice that we found the petitioners' aim and desire, in the result of it, was not so much a reparation of what was passed, as a settling their habitations for the future, under that government, by a charter of civil incorporation, which was heretofore granted them by ourselves.   We find withal that the tract of land called the Narragansett Bay, concerning which the question is [has] arisen, was divers years since inhabited by those of Providence, Portsmouth and Newport, who are interested in the complaint ; and that the same is wholly without the bounds of the Massachusetts patent granted by his Majesty.   We have considered that they be English, that the forcing of them to find out new places of residence will be very chargeable, difficult and uncertain, and therefore, upon the whole matter, do pray and require you to permit and suffer the petitioners, and all the late inhabitants of Narragansett Bay, with their families, and such as shall hereafter join with them, freely and quietly to live and plant upon the Shawomet, and such other part [parts] of the said tract of land, within the bounds mentioned in our said charter, on which they have formerly planted and lived, without extending your jurisdiction to any part thereof, or otherwise disquieting them in their consciences or civil peace, or interrupting them in their professions, until such time as we shall have received your answer to their claim in point of title, and you shall thereupon have received our further order therein.   And in case any others, since the petitioners' address to England, have taken possession of any part of the lands heretofore enjoyed by the petitioners, or any [of] their associates, you are to cause them that are newly possessed as aforesaid to be removed, that this order may be fully performed.   And, till our further order, neither the petitioners are to enlarge their plantations, nor are any others to be suffered to intrude upon any part of the Narragansett Bay; and if they shall be found hereafter to abuse this favor, by any act tending to disturb your rights, we shall express a due sense thereof, so as to testify our care of your honorable [honored] protection and encouragement.   In order to the effecting of this resolution we do also require, that you suffer the said Mr. Gorton, Mr. Holden, Mr. Greene, and their company, with their goods and necessaries, to pass through any part of that territory which is under your jurisdiction, toward the said tract of land, without molestation, they demeaning themselves civilly, any former sentence of expulsion [or] otherwise notwithstanding.   We shall only add, that to these orders of ours we shall expect a conformity [conforming to], not only from [for] yourselves, but from all other governments and plantations in New England whom it [which they] may concern.   And so commending you to God's gracious protection, we rest your loving friends.

From the Governor in Chief, loving Admiral, and Commissioners for foreign plantations, sitting at Westminster, 15 May, 1646.[1]

To our loving friends the Governor, Deputy Governor and Assistants of the Massachusetts plantations, in New England.

   Warwick, Governor and Admiral,
    Northumberland,   John Holland,
    Nottingham,   H. Vane,"[2] &c.

With this order and resolution Mr. Gorton and his friends returned to Boston, where they were in motion to apprehend them, till upon shewing the State's order they were permitted to return to Shawomet, which, in honor to their friend the Admiral, they called Warwick.   Sundry of them lived there to old age, and were considerably improved in the government of the colony.

[1] In the printed Rhode Island Colony Records, this clause stands as follows:—
"[Office of the] Chiefe Lo Adm'll and Comm'rs for foreign plantations, sitting at Westminster, 15 day of May, 1646.—Ed.
[2] Providence Records.

As there was no particular form of government, nor
appointment of officers in their charter, it took a length of
time to settle upon a method that was agreeable to the
majority of the inhabitants.   Their first General Assembly
met at Portsmouth on May 19, 1647, when Mr. John Coggshall was chosen President, Mr. Roger Williams Assistant
for Providence, Mr. John Sanford for Portsmouth, Mr. William Coddington for Newport, and Mr. Randal Holden for
Warwick.   Mr. William Dyre was chosen Recorder.   They
agreed upon a body of laws, chiefly taken from the laws of
England, with the addition of a few suited to their particular circumstances.   They also ordered as follows:—

> Forasmuch as Mr. Roger Williams had taken great pains, and expended
> much time, in [the] obtaining [of] the charter for this province, of our noble
> Lords and Governors, be it enacted and established, that in regard to his
> so great trouble, [travail] charges and good endeavors, we do freely give
> and grant unto the said Mr. Roger Williams an [one] hundred pounds, to be
> levied out of the three towns, viz.: fifty pounds out of Newport, thirty
> pounds out of Portsmouth, [and] twenty pounds out of Providence ; which
> rate is to be levied and paid in by the last of November.

The form of Government which they came into was thus
to elect a President and four Assistants, annually, who had
executive power, were judges in the courts of law, and kept
the peace.   An Assembly of sx Commissioners, or Representatives from each town, made laws and ordered their general affairs ; but their laws must be sent to every town, to be
deliberately considered in their town meetings, from whence
the clerk was to send an account of their votes to the General Recorder,[1] and if the majority of the towns approved
the law, it was confirmed, if not, it was disannulled.   The
Assembly chose yearly a General Recorder and General Sergeant, which are only other names for a secretary
and sheriff.   In each town six persons were yearly chosen,
who were called the Town-council, who had the powers of

---

[1] In May, 1660, they enacted that the return of their votes to the Recorder must
be made in three months.

a court of probate, of granting licenses to inn keepers and retailers, and the care of the poor.

Persons of almost all sentiments and tempers had resorted to this new colony, and various contentions and parties had appeared, which were not easily composed and reconciled ; but toward the obtaining of such a desirable end, the following covenant was drawn and signed at Providence, viz. :—

Considering the [that] great mercy afforded unto us, in this liberty thus to meet together, being denied to many of our countrymen in most parts, especially in our poor native country, now deploring their distressed condition in most sad and bloody calamities ; that ingratitude and disacknowledgments for favors received, are just causes for the deprivation of them, together with [our] home divisions and home conspiracies, the ruination of families, towns and countries ; [town and country]moreover, the many plots and present endeavors at home and abroad, not only to disturb our peace and liberties, but utterly to root up both root and branch of this our being ; that government held [holds] forth through love, union and order, although by few in number and mean in condition, yet (by experience) hath withstood and overcome mighty opposers ; and above all, the several [and] unexpected deliverances of this poor plantation, by that mighty Providence who is still able to deliver us, through love, union and order, therefore being sensible of these great and weighty premises, and now met together to consult about our peace and liberty, [liberties] whereby our families and posterity [posterities] may still enjoy these favors ; and that we may publicly declare upon all the free discharge of all our consciences and duties, whereby it may appear upon record that we are not willfully opposite, nor careless and senseless, and thereby the means of our own and others ruin and destruction ; and especially in testimony of our fidelity and cordial affection unto one another here present, that so there may be a current placable [peaceable] proceeding, we do faithfully and unanimously, by this our subscription, promise unto each other to keep unto these ensuing particulars :—
First, that the foundation in love may appear among us, what causes of difference have heretofore been given either by word [s] or misbehavior, in public or private, concerning particular or general affairs, by any of us here present, not to mention or repeat them in the assembly, but that love shall cover the multitude of them in the grave of oblivion. Secondly, that union may proceed from love, we do promise to keep constant unto those several engagements made by us, both unto our town and colony, and that to the uttermost of our powers and abilities to maintain our lawful rights and privileges, and to uphold the government of this plantation. Also that love may appear in union, we desire to abandon all causeless fears and jeal-

ousies of one another, self-seeking [s] and striving [s] one against another, only aiming at the general and particular peace and union of this town and colony. Lastly, for our more orderly proceeding in this Assembly, whereby love, [peace] and union may appear in order, if in our consultations differences in judgment shall arise, then moderately in order, through argumentation, to agitate the same ; considering the cause how far it may be hurtful, or conducing unto our union, peace and liberty, [liberties] and accordingly act, not after the will or person of any, but unto the justice and [or] righteousness of the cause.   Again, if [in case] such cause [s] shall be presented wherein such difficulties shall appear, that evident arguments cannot be given for present satisfaction, but that either town or colony or both shall suffer, then to take into our consideration a speech of a beloved friend, " Better to suffer an inconvenience than a mischief," better to suspend with a loss which may be inconvenient, than to be totally disunited and bereaved of all rights and liberties, which will be a mischief indeed.   Moreover that offences and distractions may be prevented, that so the current of business [disturbances] may peaceably proceed in this Assembly, we do faithfully promise to carry ourselves, in words and behavior, so moderately and orderly as the cause shall permit, and if [in case or] any of us shall fly out in provoking, scurrilous [or] exorbitant speeches, and [or] unsuitable behavior, that he or they so doing shall be publicly declared, branded and noted upon record to be a covenant violator, and disturber of the union, peace, and liberrty [liberties] of this plantation.   We do here subscribe without partiality. Dated December, 1647.

ROBERT WILLIAMS,   ROGER WILLIAMS,
JOHN SMITH,   HUGH BEWIT,
WILLIAM WICKENDEN,   JOHN FIELD,[1]
THOMAS HOPKINS,   WILLIAM HAWKINS.

This preferring of the public good to private interest or inclination, Mr. Williams discovered as much of, through his life, as perhaps any man has done in latter ages ; but alas ! he had to do with many who were not of this disposition.

In their General Assembly at Providence, May 16, 1648, Mr. Coddington was elected President, and Jeremiah Clarke, Roger Williams, William Baulston, and John Smith, Assistants ; Philip Sherman, Recorder, and Alexander Partridge,

[1]The original edition reads " John Tripp," instead of John Field. The error has been corrected from the Rhode Island Colonial Records. The person here referred to is undoubtedly the John Field mentioned on page 74.—ED.

General Sergeant; but Mr. Coddington absented himself, Mr. Dyre, the late recorder, having exhibited divers bills of complaint against him, and he did " not attend this Court for the clearing of the accusations charged upon him ;" upon which the Assembly passed an act that in such a case the Assistant of the town where the President lived should supply his place.[1]

Mr. Coddington wrote to Governor Winthrop the 25th of the same month :—

> Mr. Baulstone, and some others of this island, are in disgrace with the people in Providence, Warwick, and Gorton's adherents on the island, for that we will not interpose or meddle at all in their quarrels with the Massachusetts, and the rest of the colonies ; and do much fear that Gorton will be a thorn in their [and our] sides, if the Lord prevent not.[2]

And when the Commissioners of the United Colonies met in September this year, he and Captain Partridge went to them and said :—

> Our request and motion is in the behalf our island, that we the islanders of Rhode Island may be received into a combination with all the United Colonies of New England, into a firm and perpetual league of friendship and amity, for [of] offence and defence, mutual advice and succor, upon all just occasions, for our mutual safety and welfare, and for preserving of peace amongst ourselves, and preventing as much as may be, all occasions of war or [and] differences, and to this our motion we have the consent of the major part of our island.
>
> WILLIAM CODDINGTON,
> ALEXANDER PARTRIDGE.[3]

Thus, under a pretence of promoting peace, they would have separated the island from the rest of that little colony. However the Commissioners were not willing to own them as a distinct colony, but would have the island to be included in Plymouth patent, and if the majority of its inhabitants would acknowledge themselves to be under that jurisdiction,

---

[1]All the articles from Mr. Gorton's return till now are taken from the colony and Providence town records, compared with Mr. Callender and others.

[2]Hutchinson's Collection, p. 225.—ED.

[3]Ibid, p. 226.—ED.

they were willing then to afford them the same advice and help as they did to others.[1]   Mr. Edward Winslow had been sent over to England their agent, to answer the complaints of Gorton's company, and to support their claims against that little colony; but he wrote from London to the Commissioners of the United Colonies, April 17, 1651, and said :—

Since I perceived by letters from Plymouth, that after another year's warning nothing is likely to be done, in reference to the old order of Lords and Commons sent over ; I looked upon it as a vain thing to strive against the stream ; whereas [when as] indeed that was the main material objection above a twelvemonth since, which I could not answer, that we had such an order, but never looked after the performance thereof, nor made any return upon it.[2]

While various parties were exerting themselves in different ways, Mr. Williams, on August 31, 1648, made the following motion to the town of Providence, viz. :—

WORTHY FRIENDS : that ourselves and all men are apt and prone to differ, it is no new thing.   In all former ages, in all parts of the world, in these parts, and in our dear native country and mournful state of England, that either part or party is most right in his own eyes, his cause right, his carriage right, his arguments right, his answers right, is as wofully and constantly true as the former.   And experience tells us, that when the God of peace hath taken peace from the earth, one spark of action, word or carriage, is too powerful to kindle such a fire as burns up towns, cities, armies, navies, nations and kingdoms.   And since, dear friends, it is an honor for men to cease from strife ; since the life of love is sweet, and union is as strong as sweet ; and since you have been lately pleased to call me to some public service, and my soul hath been long musing how I might bring water to quench, and not oil or fuel to the flame, I am now humbly bold to beseech you, by all those comforts of earth and heaven which a placable and peaceable spirit will bring to you, and by all those dreadful alarms and warnings either amongst ourselves, in deaths and sicknesses, or abroad in the raging calamities of the sword, death and pestilence ; I say I humbly and earnestly beseech you to be willing to be pacifiable, willing to be reconcilable, willing to be sociable, and to listen to the (I hope not unreasonable) motion following :—To try out matters by disputes and writings, is sometimes endless ; to try out arguments by arms and

[1]Massachusetts History, vol. 3. pp. 225—227.   [2]Ibid, p. 229.

swords, is cruel and merciless ; to trouble the state and lords of England, is most unreasonable, most chargeable ; to trouble our neighbors of other colonies, seems neither safe nor honorable. Methinks, dear friends, the colony now looks with the torn face of two parties, and that the greater number of Portsmouth, with other loving friends adhering to them, appear as one grieved party ; the other three towns, or greater part of them, appear to be another. Let each party choose and nominate three ; Portsmouth and friends adhering three, the other party three, one out of each town. Let authority be given to them to examine every public difference, grievance and obstruction of justice, peace and common safety. Let them, by one final sentence of all or the greater part of them, end all, and set the whole into an unanimous posture and order, and let them set a censure upon any that shall oppose their sentence. One log, without your gentle help, I cannot stir. It is this. How shall the minds of the towns be known? How shall the persons chosen be called? time and place appointed in any expedition? For myself I can thankfully embrace the help of Mr. Coddington or Mr. Clarke, joined or apart, but how many are there who will attend (as our distempers are) to neither! It is, gentlemen, in the power of the body to require the help of any of her members, and both king and parliament plead, that in extraordinary cases they have been forced to extraordinary ways for common safety. Let me be friendly construed, if (for expedition,) I am bold to be too forward in this service, and to say, that if within twenty days of the date hereof, you please to send to my house, at Providence, the name of him whom you please to nominate, at your desire I will acquaint all the persons chosen with place and time, unto which in your name I shall desire their meeting within ten days, or thereabouts, after the receipt of your letter. I am your mournful and unworthy   ROGER WILLIAMS.[1]

This address had such effect, that Mr. Williams was received to act as President of the colony, till their election at Warwick, May 22, 1649, when Mr. John Smith was chosen President, and Thomas Olney, John Sanford, John Clarke, and Samuel Gorton, Assistants ; Philip Sherman, Recorder ; Richard Knight, Sergeant, and John Clarke, Treasurer. Mr. Williams was chosen " to take a view of the records delivered into the Court by Mr. William Dyre." And they made a law that if a President should be elected, and should refuse to serve, he should be fined ten pounds ; and if an Assistant refused, five pounds. Also it was " ordered that a

[1] Providence Records.

messenger be sent to Pumham and the other sachems, to require them to come to this Court; and that letters be sent to Benedict Arnold and his father, and the rest of Pawtuxet, about their subjecting to this colony." Mr. Dyre again presented his complaints against Mr. Coddington, but they were deferred.

At the Assembly at Newport, May 23, 1650, a fresh order was sent to the towns, to collect and pay what they owed to Mr. Williams for the charter, within twenty days. William Arnold and William Carpenter, instead of submitting to the government of their own colony, went again and entered complaints against some of their neighbors to the Massachusetts rulers, and they sent a citation to them to come and answer the same in their courts, dated from Boston, June 20, 1650, signed by Edward Rawson, secretary.[1] Such obstructors of good government were they who have made a great noise in the world about the disorders of Rhode Island colony! In 1651, Mr. Coddington caused a terrible difficulty among them, as will be seen in its place, though another affair must be attended to first.

[1] Providence Records.

CHAPTER IV.

It has already been seen that Mr. John Clarke was a principal instrument in procuring Rhode Island for a people who were persecuted elsewhere, and that he was the first religious minister on the island, and serviceable also in their civil government; yet all this did not prevent his being most abusively treated this year in Boston, with two other members of his church.

The best account of Mr. Obadiah Holmes that I have seen, is in a manuscript which he left to his children, that a gentleman of his posterity has favored me with, an extract of which I will give in his own words. Says he:—

First, I must remember my honored parents, who were faithful in their generation, and of good report among men, and brought up their children tenderly and honorably. Three sons they brought up at the university in Oxford; but the most of their care was to inform and instruct them in the fear of the Lord; and to that end gave them much good counsel, carrying them often before the Lord by earnest prayer; but I, the most rebellious of all, did neither hearken to counsel nor any instruction, for from a child I minded nothing but folly and vanity, and as years did grow on, and wisdom should have taken place, then the wisdom I had was wise to do evil, but to do well had no knowledge. .... As days and strength increased, even so did my transgressions, so that I became hardened in sin, not only to be drawn into it by others, but was as forward to draw others into evil as my fellows, ... being come to that height of wickedness that I did think it best when I could do the most wickedness, and began to think that

it was but a foolish thing to talk of God, that should bring man to judgment; .... continuing in such a course for four or five years, and then began to bethink what counsel my dear parents had given me, many a time
with tears and prayers; my rebellion to my honored parents then looked
me in open face, and my dear mother being sick, it struck to me my disobedient acts, which forced me to confess the same to her. After this I began to go to hear the Word preached, but every word was against me, and
left me without hope of mercy; and sometimes passing over a field called
the Twenty Acres, stood still and said, Oh! that I might lie in hell but so
many years as here are grass! It would have an end. .... That word
was ever before me, "The wicked shall be turned to hell;" "Where the
worm dieth not," &c. And yet at this time Satan tells me, It is best to
put such thoughts out of mind, and take pleasure while thou art here, and
return to thy former merry companions. and friends; which I did for a
time; but the worm in the conscience did still gnaw. I went to hear the
most noted men I could, but found it still against me; yet often heard
them say, I must repent and be humbled, and must pray, and then should
find mercy; but must confess sins and forsake them; which brought me
to a resolution, in the most public way or company I could find, ever so to
do; and had done it through ignorance, had not a friend advised me to the
contrary, and that upon good grounds. But he also put me upon prayer
and hearing. I then fell to prayer and duties, but found no rest or quiet
in my soul; for then Satan let fly at me, and told me. it was too late to return, for there was no hope for me. I answered him, and did instance
several of my wicked companions God had shown mercy unto a little before. He answered, Remember thou scorned, mocked and derided them;
yea saying the devil was in them, they were all mad, and become fools;
and withal he told me I had read and heard that there was a sin that never
could be forgiven, the which sin I had committed. With this assault he
fooled me a long time, even my life was a burden to me. Oh! the knives,
ropes, trees, coal pits, can witness the many escapes of them, as one in a
most undone, desperate condition, as one appointed to eternal destruction.
The perplexity of mind brought me to great weakness in body, and yet for
ease and comfort I turned over every stone, hearkened to all my acquaintance and friends, as to leave off my old ways, and all my old companions,
which I had done before; but all this while I never considered sin according to the true nature of it, as being loathsome to the Lord, but as it
brought judgment upon me; yet was I fearful to sin, and began to love to
read the Scriptures, and frequent prayer and other duties, and took delight
among professors that were of the strictest sort, easily seeing the gross
evil and danger of the formal ministers and professors, and so that conformity was only superstition and a name. Yet for all that I had no rest
in my soul, though I was in a manner as strict as any. As I was enlarged

in sorrow for sin, deep in humiliation, enlarged in prayer, or filled with
tears, my comfort came in and increased ; but as I failed in them, so my
sorrows renewed ; and when I looked over my best performances found
them full of sin.   Oh ! then the fears, doubts and questioning of my own
estate !   I judged it was all done in hypocrisy, which sin my soul did then
abhor.   In this sad and doubtful state I continued very long, yea many
years.   And although I could speak comfortably to others, yet had often
much disquiet within my soul ; my comforts were according to my enlargements.   Not long after this there was in me a great love to the Lord ; but
alas !   I was deceived by my own heart, and the ministers who told me
there must be such and such a love to him, as to keep to him [me] in duty,
and to part with all for him, but they left me short of understanding him
as I should, and my selfish heart was willing to love him or part with all
for him, yea my dear honored father, brethren and friends, house and lands,
and my own native country, for time, and to avoid those popish relics of
the bishops, and that filthy rabble, and to separate from them, and all those
that mention them : and was fully known in my own country, and adventured the danger of the seas to come to New England, where I tried all
things in several churches, and for a time thought I had made a good choice
or change ; but in truth it little differed from former times, and my spirit
was like a wave tossed up and down, as not yet come to dig so deep as I
should, or to consider the only ground of a well grounded hope, which God
at last brought me to consider, which is, His own love to poor lost man,
which first was in his own secret council and purpose before man was, and
revealed to man in his time ; and that there is no preparative necessary to
obtain Christ, nor any thing to deserve that love, or to merit the same.
And nothing could stay or satisfy my soul till I came to consider why,
when and upon whom he laid sin and transgression, namely, on the Lord,
and on him alone.   And looking at me when a rebel, an enemy, yea dead
in sin and trespasses, yea in my blood, he then said, Live, through the
blood of Christ be cleansed, and in him be loved, for his own love to poor
man, and that the election may obtain it, for he knows who are his ; but
good will is manifested before they have done either good or evil, so that
neither good foreseen shall prevail, nor evil original or actual shall hinder,
but that free grace may have its free course ; but manifested when he giveth
faith to believe the promise of the Father in giving a full discharge to the
soul, by taking full satisfaction from his only Son, who became sin for us,
who knew no sin, that we might be made the righteousness of God through
him ; and so remission and free pardon is granted forth, that whosoever believes in him shall not perish, but have everlasting life ; and all those that
so come to him he will no ways cast away.   And when God had given me
to see in any measure this love of his, then and not till then could I give
over working for life, and to live in working.   But at last he caused me to

say, that *from* life I must work, and then all my former turnings and re-
turnings must come to nought, yea all my righteousness as filthy rags, and
to account all as dung, so I might obtain Christ, or rather that I might be
accepted by him ; and so removed me from the covenant of works to the
covenant of grace, even that new covenant of life alone by himself, who
paid so dear a price, as to lay down his own blood to wash, cleanse and
purify the soul, and to redeem both soul and body to serve the Lord ; and
that is now the life I live by faith in the Son of God ; and this faith causes
works of faith, or rather fruits that flow from that root, so that now love
hath constrained me to yield myself to live to him, as to a King to rule me
by his holy laws and commandments, and as to an only Prophet to teach
and instruct me, both to know and to do his holy will, and as my only
Chief Priest to offer a sacrifice for me, which he did even for all, whereby
my poor imperfect prayers and all other services became accepted of the
Father ; and this love, shed abroad in my heart, wrought in me a restless
desire to know his will, that I might shew forth the praises and glory of
him, that had called me by his grace.

As the sentiments of the ancient Baptists in this country
have been grossly misrepresented, and as Mr. Holmes was
no small sufferer in that cause, I thought it expedient to let
the reader thus far hear him speak for himself, and tell his
own experience and ideas about the nature of true religion.
When he first came to this land he joined with the church
in Salem, with whom he walked six or seven years ; and
then about the year 1645 was dismissed to the Congregational church in Seaconck (Rehoboth) newly settled there,
under the ministry of Mr. Samuel Newman. He continued
in that relation about four years, till an unrighteous act, as
he judged, of the minister and part of the church, for which
they would not give satisfaction, caused Mr. Holmes and
several more to withdraw, and set up a meeting by themselves. And being convinced that the Baptists' way was
right, a number of them were baptized, I suppose by the
aforesaid Mr. Clarke, for they joined to his church. After
this Mr. Newman pronounced a sentence of ex-communica-
tion against Mr. Holmes, upon which he and two more were
presented to the General Court at Plymouth, June 4, 1650,
where they met with four petitions against them, one from

their own town with thirty-five hands to it, one from the church at Taunton, one from all the ministers but two in Plymouth colony, and a fourth from the Court at Boston, under their secretary's hand, urging Plymouth rulers to suppress them speedily.[1]

Here we may observe the great difference between our Plymouth fathers, and the Massachusetts. With all these stimulants to severity, the Court of Plymouth only charged them to desist from their practice, which others had taken such offence at, and one of them yielding thereto, the others, viz., Obadiah Holmes and Joseph Tory, were bound over to the next October Court, but were not so much as bound to their good behavior, nor any other sureties required, only they were bound " one for another in the sum of ten pounds apiece," for their appearance at said Court.

At a General Court holden at New Plymouth the second of October, 1650, before William Bradford, gentleman, Governor, Thomas Prince, William Collyare, Captain Miles Standish, Timothy Hetherly, William Thomas, John Alden, gentlemen, Assistants, [and a House of Deputies.]

PRESENTMENT BY THE GRAND INQUEST.

OCTOBER 2d, 1650.

Wee whose names are heer underwritten, being the grand inquest, doe present to this Court John Hazell, Mr. Edward Smith and his wife, Obadiah Holmes, Joseph Tory and his wife, and the wife of James Mann, William Deuell and his wife, of the towne of Rehoboth, for the continuing of a meeting uppon the Lord's-day from house to house, contrary to the order of this Court, enacted June 12, 1650.

THOMAS ROBINSON,

HENRY TOMSON, [&c., to the number of 14.[2]]

This is an exact copy of their presentment, but no sentence appears upon record against them. How different is

---

[1] Clarke's Narratives, pp. 18, 25, [46, 53, 54.] Plymouth Records.—B.

The figures in brackets appended to the references to Clarke's Narrative on this page and those that follow, refer to Massachusetts Historical Society, fourth series, Vol. II, where the Narrative is published.—ED.

[2] Plymouth Records.—B.

In the published Records the second of these names is Henry Sampson.—ED.

12

this from the actings of Boston Court the next year![1]   For on July 19, 1651, Messrs. Clarke, Holmes and Crandal, " being the representatives of the church in Newport, upon the request of William Witter, of Lynn, arrived there, he being a brother in the church, who, by reason of his advanced age, could not undertake so great a journey as to visit the church."[2]   He lived about two miles out of town, and the next being the Lord's day they concluded to spend it in religious worship at his house.   Mr. Clarke says :—

Finding by sad experience, that the hour of temptation spoken of was coming upon all the world (in a more eminent way) to try them that are upon the earth, I fell upon the consideration of that [word of] promise, made to those that keep the word of his patience, which present thoughts, while in conscience toward God, and good will unto his saints, I was imparting to my companions in the house where I lodged, and to four or five strangers that came in unexpected after I had begun, opening and proving what is meant by the hour of temptation, what by the word of his patience, and their keeping it, and how he that hath the key of David (being the promiser) will keep those that keep the word of his patience from the hour of temptation ; while, I say, I was yet speaking, there comes into the house where we were two constables, who, with their clamorous tongues, made an interruption in my discourse, and more uncivilly disturbed us than the pursuivants of the old English bishops were wont to do, telling us that they were come with authority from the magistrate to apprehend us. I then desired to see the authority by which they thus proceeded, whereupon they plucked forth their warrant, and one of them with a trembling hand (as conscious he might have been better employed) read it to us ; the substance whereof was as followeth :—

" By virtue hereof, you are required to go to the house of William Witter, and so to search from house to house, for certain erroneous persons, being strangers, and them to apprehend, and in safe custody to keep, and tomorrow morning by eight o'clock [of the clock] to bring before me,

ROBERT BRIDGES."

[1]Mr. Hazel wrote to his cousin Hubbard, of Newport, June 23, 1651, that they were then threatened with a fine of ten shillings a day for every person who set up any other meeting, and that their absence from the town meeting the day before should prove costly. Samuel Hubbard's Manuscript. Mr. Hazel died soon after, near Boston. The rest of them moved to Newport, where I find that Edward Smith, Joseph Torry, James Man and William Deuell, were admitted freemen, May 17, 1653. Smith was afterward a magistrate, and Torry many years Secretary of the colony, as well as a teacher in Mr. Clarke's church, in which Mr. Holmes also ministered for many years.
[2]Newport church papers.

When he had read the warrant, I told them, Friends, there shall not be, I trust, the least appearance of a resisting of that authority by which you come unto us; yet I tell you, that by virtue hereof you are not so strictly tied, but if you please you may suffer us to make an end of what we have begun, so may you be witnesses either to or against the faith and order which we hold. To which they answered they could not, then said we, Notwithstanding the warrant, or anything therein contained, you may. .... They apprehended us, and carried us away to the ale-house or ordinary, where at [after] dinner one of them said unto us, Gentlemen, if you be free I will carry you to the meeting; to whom it was replied, Friend, had we been free thereunto we had prevented all this, nevertheless we are in thy hand; and if thou wilt carry us to the meeting, thither will we go; to which he answered, Then will I carry you to the meeting; to this we replied, If thou forcest us unto your assembly, then shall we be constrained to declare ourselves, that we cannot hold communion with them. The constable answered, that is nothing to me; I have not power to command you to speak when you come there, or to be silent. To this I again replied, [Friend, know a little further;] since we have heard the word of salvation by Jesus Christ, we have been taught, as those that first trusted in Christ, to be obedient unto him both by word and deed; wherefore if we be forced to your meeting, we shall declare our dissent from you both by word and gesture. After all this, when he had consulted with the man of the house, he told us he would carry us to the meeting; so to their meeting we were brought, while they were at their prayers, and uncovered; and at my first stepping over the threshold I unveiled myself, civily saluted them, and turned into the seat I was appointed to, put on my hat again, and sat down, open my book, and fell to reading. [Hereupon] Mr. Bridges being troubled, commanded the constable to pluck off our hats, which he did, and where he laid mine there I let it lie, until their prayers, singing, and preaching was over; after this I stood up, and uttered myself in these words following:—I desire as a stranger [if I may] to propose a few things to this congregation, hoping in the proposal thereof I shall commend myself to your consciences, to be guided by that wisdom that is from above, which being pure, is also peaceable, gentle, and easy to be entreated; and therewith [I] made a stop, expecting if the Prince of peace had been among them, I should have had a suitable answer of peace from them. .....[1]Their

[1]Supplying the words here omitted, the Narrative reads as follows:—" But no other voice I heard but of their pastor, as he's called, and their magistrate. Their pastor answered by way of query whether I was a member of a church. Before I could give an answer, Mr. Bridges spoke, saying, 'If the congregation please to give you leave, well; if not, I shall require you silence, for,' said he, 'we will have no objections, &c.'" These last words, then, were spoken by the magistrate, and not, as represented above, by the pastor.—ED.

pastor answered, We will have no objections against what is delivered. To which I answered, I am not about at present to make objections against what is delivered, but as by my gesture at my coming into your assembly, I declared my dissent from you, so lest that should prove offensive unto some whom I would not offend, I would now by word of mouth declare the grounds, which are these :—First, from the consideration we are strangers each to other, and so strangers to each other's inward standing with respect to God, and so cannot conjoin and act in faith, and what is not of faith is sin.   And in the second place, I could not judge that you are gathered together, and walk according to the visible order of our Lord ; which when I had declared, Mr. Bridges told me, I had done, and spoke that for which I must answer, and so commanded [me] silence. When their meeting was done, the officers carried us again to the ordinary, where being watched over that night, as thieves and robbers, we were the next morning carried before Mr. Bridges, who made our mittimus, and sent us to the prison at Boston.[1]   The words of the mittimus are these :—

" To the Keeper of the Prison at Boston :

By virtue hereof, you are required to take into your custody from the constable of Lynn, or his deputy, the bodies of John Clarke, Obadiah Holmes and John Crandal, and them to keep until the next County Court to be held at Boston, that they may then and there answer to such complaints as may be alleged against them ; for being taken by a [the] constable at a private meeting at Lynn, upon the Lord's day, exercising among themselves, to whom divers of the town repaired, and joined with them, and that in the time of the public exercise of the worship of God ; as also for offensively disturbing the peace of the congregation, at their coming into the public meeting in the time of prayer in the afternoon, and for saying and manifesting that the church in [of] Lynn was not constituted according to the order of our Lord, and for such other things as shall be alleged against them, concerning their seducing and drawing [aside of] others after their erroneous judgments and practices, and for suspicion of having their hands in [the] re-baptizing of one or more among us, as also for neglecting or refusing to put [give] in sufficient security for their appearance at the said Court.   Hereof fail not at your peril.

22, 5, 51.   ROBERT BRIDGES."[2]

On July 31, Mr. Clarke was brought before the Court, and fined twenty pounds, or to be well whipped. The crimes he was charged with, beside what is above mentioned, were,

---

[1] It appears that somehow they were permitted to meet again on Monday, and were sent to prison on Tuesday.

[2] Clarke's Narrative, pp. 1—4. [27—31.]

that he met again the next day after his contempt, as they
call it, of their public worship, " at the house of Witter,
and in contempt of authority, being then in the custody of
the law, did there administer the sacrament of the Lord's
supper to one excommunicated person, to another under ad
monition, and to a third that was an inhabitant of Lynn, and
not in fellowship with any church, and yet upon answer in
open Court did affirm, that he never re-baptized any," &c.[1]
Says Mr. Clarke :—

None were able to turn to the law of God or man by which we were
condemned. At length the Governor stepped up, and told us we had denied
infants' baptism, and being somewhat transported, told me, I had deserved
death, and said he would not have such trash brought into their jurisdiction. Moreover he said, " You go up and down, and secretly insinuate
into those that are weak, but you cannot maintain it before our ministers.
You may try and dispute with them."

To this I had much to reply, but he commanded the gaol-
er to take us away. So the next morning having so fair an
opportunity, I made a motion to the Court in these words
following :—

To the honorable [honored] Court assembled at Boston :

Whereas it pleased this honored Court yesterday to condemn the faith
and order which I hold and practice ; and after you had passed your sentence upon me for it, were pleased to express, I could not maintain the
same against your ministers, and thereupon publicly proffered me a dispute
with them ; be pleased by these few lines to understand, I readily accept
it, and therefore desire you would appoint the time when, and the person
with whom, in that public place where I was condemned, I might with
freedom, and without molestation of the civil power, dispute that point
publicly, where I doubt not by the strength of Christ to make it good out
of his last Will and Testament, unto which nothing is to be added, nor
from which nothing is to be diminished. Thus desiring the Father of lights
to shine forth, and by his power to expel the darkness, I remain your well-
wisher,   JOHN CLARKE.

From the prison, this 1, 6, 51.

This motion, if granted, I desire might be subscribed by
their Secretary's hand, as an act of the same Court by which
we were condemned."[2]

[1]Neal's History of New England, Vol. I, p. 30.   [2]Clarke's Narrative, p. 7, [33, 34.]

This was presented, and after much ado, one of the magistrates informed Mr. Clarke, that a disputation was granted to be the next week ; but on Monday their ministers came together and made no small stir about the matter, and near the close of the day the magistrates sent for Mr. Clarke into their chamber, and queried with him about the matter, and demanded of him whether he would dispute upon the things contained in his sentence, and maintain his practice ; "for" said they, " the Court sentenced you not for your judgment and conscience, but for matter of fact and practice." To which, says Mr. Clarke, I replied :—

You say the Court condemned me for matter of fact and practice.   Be it so.   I say that matter of fact and practice was but the manifestation of my judgment and conscience.   And I make account, that man is void of judgment and conscience, with respect unto God, that hath not a fact and practice suitable thereunto. . . . If the faith and order which I profess do stand by the word of God, then the faith and order which you profess must needs fall to the ground ; and if the way you walk in remain, then the way that I walk in must vanish away.   They cannot both stand together.   To this they seemed to assent ; therefore I told them, that if they please to grant the motion under the Secretary's hand, I would draw up the faith and order which I hold, as the sum of that I did deliver in open Court, in [into] three or four conclusions, which conclusions I will stand by and defend, until he whom you shall appoint shall by the word of God remove me from them.   In case he shall remove me from them, then the disputation is at end ; but if not, then I desire like liberty by the word of God to oppose the faith and order which he and you profess, thereby to try whether I may be an instrument in the hand of God to remove you from the same. They told me the motion was very fair, and the way like unto a disputant, ... saying, Because the matter is weighty, and we desire that what can, may be spoken, when the disputation shall be, therefore would we take a longer time. . . . . So I returned with my keeper to prison again, drew up the conclusions, which I was resolved through the strength of Christ to stand in defence of, and through the importunity of one of the magistrates, the next morning very early I shewed them to him, having a promise I should have my motion for a dispute granted, under the Secretary's hand. The conclusions were as followeth :—

The testimony of John Clarke, a prisoner of Jesus Christ at Boston, in behalf of my Lord, and of his people, is as followeth :—

1. I testify that Jesus of Nazareth, whom God raised from the dead, is

made both Lord and Christ; this Jesus I say is the Christ, in English, the Anointed One; hath a name above every name; he is the Anointed Priest, none to or with him in point of atonement; the Anointed Prophet, none to him in point of instruction; the Anointed King, who is gone unto his Father, for his glorious kingdom, and shall ere long return again; and that this Jesus Christ is also the Lord; none to or with him by way of commanding and ordering, with respect to the worship of God, the household of faith, which being purchased with his blood as Priest, instructed and nourished by his spirit as Prophet, do wait in his appointments as the Lord, in hope of that glorious kingdom which shall ere long appear.[1]

2. I testify that baptism, or dipping in water, is one of the commandments of this Lord Jesus Christ, and that a visible believer or disciple of Christ Jesus (that is one that manifesteth repentance towards God, and faith in Jesus Christ) is the only person that is to be baptized, or dipped with that visible baptism, or dipping of Jesus Christ in water, and also that visible person that is to walk in that visible order of his house, and so to wait for his coming the second time, in the form of a Lord and King, with his glorious kingdom according to promise, and for his sending down in the time of his absence the Holy Ghost, or Holy Spirit of promise, and all this according to the last Will and Testament of that living Lord, whose will is not to be added to or taken from.[2]

[1]To confirm this article Mr. Clarke says, " If the nature of the commanding and ordering power, that suits both with the worship, and with the worshippers, which the Father of Spirits seeks for, be [also] considered, which is not a law of a carnal commandment, seconded with carnal weapons, or an arm of flesh; but a spiritual law, as the apostle calls it, Rom. viii., ' a law of the spirit of life from Christ Jesus,' spoken unto, or rather written in the heart of a Christian by the Spirit of Christ, by reason whereof he obeys from the heart readily, willingly and cheerfully, that form of doctrine which is engraven and laid up therein; Heb. viii. 10, II Cor. iii. 3, Rom. vi. 17; If this I say be considered, that the worship is spiritual, such as must begin in, spring up and rise from, the heart and spirit, and so be directed to the Father of Spirits, and so the commanding power that suits herewith must speak to the heart and spirit of the man, then there is no Lord in this matter to Christ Jesus, who speaks to the heart and spirit, and his words are as commands from the head to the members, which convey [together] spirit and life to obey them, by reason of which his commands are not grievous, for where the Spirit of the Lord is there is liberty; &c. II Cor. iii. 17, 18." pp. 48, 49, [81.]

[2]To confirm the first part of this article Mr. Clarke says, " Although there be frequent mention made of that appointment of Christ in his last Will and Testament, yet it is never expressed by the word that may be rendered *rantism*, or sprinkling, but by the word that is rendered *baptism*, or dipping;" to which he adds many proofs, pp. 50—52, [82.] The other part, which concerns the subjects of baptism, he confirms by the apostles' commission, and by their practice, and notes in particular, that on the day of Pentecost they baptized none but such as were *called, gladly received his word, were added and continued in the apostles' doctrine and fellowship, &c.* p. 54, [87.]

3. I testify or witness, that every such believer in Christ Jesus, that
waiteth for his appearing, may in point of liberty, yea ought in point of
duty, to improve that talent his Lord hath given unto him, and in the congregation may either ask for information to himself; or if he can, may
speak by way of prophecy for the edification, exhortation and comfort of
the whole ; and out of the congregation at all times, upon all occasions,
and in all places, as far as the jurisdiction of his Lord extends, may, yea
ought to walk as a child of light, justifying wisdom with his ways, and
reproving folly, with the unfruitful works thereof, provided all this be
shown out of a good conversation, as James speaks, with meekness of
wisdom.

4. I testify that no such believer or servant of Christ Jesus hath [any]
liberty, much less authority, from his Lord, to smite his fellow servant,
nor yet with outward force, or arm of flesh to constrain, or restrain his
conscience, no nor yet his outward man for conscience sake, or worship of
his God, where injury is not offered to the person, name or estate of others,
every man being such as shall appear before the judgment-seat of Christ,
and must give an account of himself to God, and therefore ought to be fully
persuaded in his own mind for what he undertakes, because he that doubteth is damned if he eat, and so also if he act, because he doth not eat or
act in faith, and what is not of faith is sin.[1]

When Mr. Clarke had thus freely given them his testimony, instead of openly and fairly meeting him as they had
talked of, to vindicate their proceedings, the next news that
he hears from them is this :—

To the Keeper of the Prison :

By virtue hereof you are to release and set at liberty the body of Mr.
John Clarke, and this shall be your discharge for so doing. Given under
my hand the 11th of the 6th month, 1651.

WILLIAM HIBBINS.[2]

Great expectations had been raised in the country of hearing these points disputed, and Mr. Clarke knowing well how
they would try to turn all the blame upon him, immediately
drew up the following address :—

Whereas through the indulgence of tender hearted friends, without my
consent, and contrary to my judgment, the sentence and condemnation of

[1] Narrative, pp. 9, 10, [34—37.]
[2] Narrative, p. 10, [37.] Four years after, Hibbins's wife was hanged for a witch.

the Court at Boston (as is reported) have been fully satisfied on my behalf, and thereupon a warrant hath been procured, by which I am secluded the place of my imprisonment, by reason whereof I see no other call for present but to my habitation, and to those near relations which God hath given me there, yet lest the cause should hereby suffer, which I profess is Christ's, I would hereby signify, that if yet it shall please the honored magistrates, or General Court of this colony, to grant my former request under their Secretary's hand, I shall cheerfully embrace it, and upon your motion shall, through the help of God, come from the island to attend it. And hereunto I have subscribed my name.

11th, 6, 51. JOHN CLARKE.

This was the next morning sent to the magistrates, who were met at the Commencement at Cambridge, upon which it was noised abroad that the motion was granted, and that Mr. Cotton was to be the man; "a man," says Mr. Clarke, " best of all approved of by myself for that same purpose, he being the inventor and supporter of that way in these parts wherein they walk." But a little before their lecture the next Thursday, he received the following paper :—

MR. JOHN CLARKE:

We conceive you have misrepresented the Governor's speech, in saying you were challenged to dispute with some of our elders, whereas it was plainly expressed, that if you would confer with any of them, they were able to satisfy you, neither were you able to maintain your practice to them by the word of God, all which we [was] intended for your information and conviction privately; neither were you enjoined to what you were then [then were] counselled unto; nevertheless if you are forward to dispute, and that you will move it yourself to the Court, or magistrates about Boston, we shall take order to appoint one who will be ready to answer your motion, you keeping close to the questions to be propounded by yourself; and a moderator shall be appointed also to attend upon that service; and whereas you desire you might be free in your dispute, keeping close to the points to be disputed on, without incurring damage by the civil justice, observing what hath been before written, it is granted; the day may be agreed, if you yield the premises.

JOHN ENDICOTT, Governor,
THOMAS DUDLEY, Dep. Governor,
RICHARD BELLINGHAM,
WILLIAM HIBBINS,
INCREASE NOWEL."

11th[1] of the 6th, 1651.

[1]It seems that this should be the 12th.

Says Mr. Clarke :—

My answer followeth superscribed,

To the honored Governor of the Massachusetts, and the rest of that honorable Society, these present :

WORTHY SENATORS :—I received a writing, subscribed with five of your hands, by way of answer to a twice repeated motion of mine before you, which was grounded as I conceive sufficiently upon the Governor's words, in open Court, which writing of yours doth no way answer my expectation, nor yet that motion which I made ; and whereas, (waiving that grounded motion) you are pleased to intimate, that if I were forward to dispute, and would move it myself to the Court, or magistrates about Boston, you would appoint one to answer my motion, &c., be pleased to understand, that although I am not backward to maintain the faith and order of my Lord, the King of saints, for which I have been sentenced yet am I not in such a way so forward to dispute, or move therein, lest inconvenience should thereby arise ; I shall rather once more repeat my former motion, which if it shall please the honored General Court to accept, and under their Secretary's hand shall grant a free dispute, without molestation or interruption, I shall be [so] well satisfied therewith ; that what is past I shall forget, and upon your motion shall attend it ; thus desiring the Father of mercies not to lay that evil to your charge, I remain your well wisher,   JOHN CLARKE.[1]

From Prison this 14, 6, 51.

I have transcribed the whole of these letters with great care, to give the reader a fair opportunity to judge for himself, whether those rulers and ministers were not afraid of the light, though they pretended the contrary. For they knew that they had then laws in force to punish any man who should dispute against infant baptism, as well as other of their ways, and what they now sent was no act of Court, but only a writing from some of their rulers met at Commencement. Mr. Clarke says, it was in Mr. Cotton's handwriting. They would thus fain have stopped Mr. Clarke's mouth, or else have drawn him again under the lash of their laws. This he says gave ground for others to conclude, "that the utmost they can say for themselves, and to stop the mouth of him that is contrary minded, lies in

[1]Narrative, pp. 11—13. [40.]

the sword and power of the magistrate, which, although it be a good ordinance of God in this present evil world to restrain the oppressor, and to let the oppressed go free, and so approved and owned by Christ and all true Christians, in case of wrong and wicked lewdness, ... yet was it never appointed by Christ (to whom all power, not only in earth, but also in heaven, is committed, and by whom all earthly powers are to be judged ; I say it was never appointed by Christ) to inform and rectify the minds and consciences of men in the worship of God, in that great mystery of godliness, and in those mystical matters concerning the kingdom of Christ, that being a matter that only belongs to the Holy Spirit of promise, and to the sword of that Spirit, which is the word (not of man, but) of God, to effect, much less to conform their outward man contrary to their minds and consciences in the worship of God ; and therefore that sword and power ought to take heed how they meddle herein, lest they attempt to take the place and enter upon the throne and kingdom of Christ."[1]

Mr. Crandal, who was fined five pounds, only for being with the others, was released upon promise of appearing at their next Court (though they did not let him know when it was, till it was over, and they exacted the fine of the keeper) and he with Mr. Clarke returned home. Mr. Holmes was kept in prison till their Court met in the beginning of September, and then, after their public lecture in Boston, the sentence of Court was executed upon him ; a particular account of which we have written with his own hand, as follows :—

Unto the well beloved brethren, John Spilsbury, William Kiffen, and the rest that in London stand fast in the faith, and continue to walk steadfastly in that order of the gospel which was once delivered unto the saints by Jesus Christ ; Obadiah Holmes, an unworthy witness that Jesus is the Lord, and of late a prisoner for Jesus' sake at Boston, sendeth greeting :

DEARLY BELOVED AND LONGED AFTER :—My heart's desire is to hear from you, and to hear that you grow in grace, and in the knowledge of our

---

[1] Narrative, pp. 13, 14. [41.]

Lord and Saviour Jesus Christ, and that your love to him, and one unto another, as he hath given commandment, aboundeth, would be the very joy and great rejoicing of my soul and spirit. Had I not been prevented by my beloved brethren of Providence, who have wrote unto you, wherein you have my mind at large; and also by our beloved brother Clarke, of Rhode Island, who may, if God permit, see you, and speak with you mouth to mouth, I had here declared myself in that matter, but now I forbear; and because I have an experimental knowledge in myself, that in members of the same body, while it stands in union with the head, there is a sympathizing spirit, which passeth through, and also remaineth in each particular, so that one member can neither mourn nor rejoice, but all the members are ready to mourn and rejoice with it; I shall the rather impart unto you some dealings which I have had therein from the sons of men, and the gracious supports which I have had from the Son of God, my Lord and yours, that so like members you might rejoice with me, and might be encouraged, by the same experiment of his tender mercies, to fear none of those things which you shall suffer for Jesus' sake. It pleased the Father of lights, after a long continuance of mine in death and dark-ness, to cause life and immortality to be brought to light in my soul, and also to cause me to see that this life was by the death of his Son, in that hour and power of darkness procured, which wrought in my heart a rest-less desire to know what the Lord, who had so dearly bought me, would have me to do, and finding that it was his last will (to which none is to add, and from which none is to detract,) that they which had faith in his death for life, should yield up themselves to hold forth a lively consimilitude or likeness unto his death, burial and resurrection, by that ordinance of bap-tism, I readily yielded thereto, being by love constrained to follow the [that] Lamb (that takes away the sins of the world) whithersoever he goes. I had no sooner separated from their assemblies, and from communion with them in their worship of God, and thus visibly put on Christ, being resolv-ed alone to attend upon him, and to submit to his will, but immediately the adversary cast out a flood against us, and stirred up the spirits of men to present myself and two more to Plymouth Court, where we met with four petitions against our whole company to take some speedy course to suppress us; one from our own plantation, with thirty-five hands to it; one from the church, as they call it, at Taunton; one from all the minis-ters in our colony, except two, if I mistake not, and one from the Court at Boston, in the Massachusetts, under their Secretary's hand; whereupon the Court straitly charged us to desist, and neither to ordain officers, nor to baptize, nor to break bread together, nor yet to meet upon the first day of the week; and having received these strait charges, one of the three discovers the sandy foundation upon which he stood, who, when the flood came and the wind blew, fell, yet it pleased the Father of mercies (to whom be the praise) to give us strength to stand, and to tell them it was better to obey God [rather] than man ; and such was the grace of our God to us-ward, that though we were had from Court to Court, yet were we firmly resolved to keep close to the rule, and to obey the voice of our Lord, come what will come.

Not long after these troubles I came upon occasion of business into the colony of Massachusetts, with two other brethren, as brother Clarke being one of the two can inform you, where we three were apprehended, carried to [the prison at] Boston, and so to the Court, and were all sentenced. What they laid to my charge, you may here read in my sentence,[1] upon the pronouncing of which, as I went from the bar, I expressed myself in these words :—I bless God, I am counted worthy to suffer for the name of Jesus. Whereupon John Wilson (their pastor, as they call him) struck me before the judgment-seat, and cursed me, saying, The curse of God or Jesus go with thee.[2] So we were carried to the prison, where not long after I was deprived of my two loving friends, at whose departure the adversary stepped in, took hold of [on] my spirit, and troubled me for the space of an hour, and then the Lord came in, and sweetly relieved me,

---

[1] The sentence of Obadiah Holmes, of Seaconk, the 31st of the 5th mouth, 1651.

Forasmuch as you Obadiah Holmes, being come into this jurisdiction about the 21 of the 5 month, did meet at one William Witter's house, at Lynn, and did here privately (and at other times, being an excommunicate person, did take upon you to preach and baptize) upon the Lord's day, or other days, and being taken then by the constable, and coming afterward to the assembly at Lynn, did, in disrespect to the ordinance of God and his worship, keep on your hat, the pastor being in prayer, insomuch that you would not give reverence in vailing your hat, till it was forced off your head, to the disturbance of the congregation, and professing against the institution of the church, as not being according to the gospel of Jesus Christ; and that you the said Obadiah Holmes did upon the day following meet again at the said William Witter's, in contempt to authority, you being then in the custody of the law, and did there receive the sacrament, being excommunicate, and that you did baptize such as were baptized before, and thereby did necessarily deny the baptism that was before administered to be baptism, the churches no churches, and also other ordinances, and ministers, as if all were a nullity ; and also did deny the lawfulness of baptizing of infants; and all this tends to the dishonor of God, the despising the ordinances of God among us, the peace of the churches, and seducing the subjects of this Commonwealth from the truth of the gospel of Jesus Christ, and perverting the strait ways of the Lord, the Court doth fine you thirty pounds, to be paid, or sufficient sureties that the said sum shall be paid by the first day of the next Court of Assistants, or else to be well whipped, and that you shall remain in prison till it be paid, or security given in for it. By the Court,

INCREASE NOWEL.

[Clarke's Narrative, p. 44.]

[2] " Mr. Wilson is represented by his cotemporaries as one of the most humble, pious and benevolent men of the age." Massachusetts History, Vol. I, p. 258. [237.] But when that darling point, infant sprinkling, was in danger, see how it makes the most benevolent act like cruel persecutors !

causing to look to himself; so was I stayed, and refreshed in the thoughts of my God.   And although during the time of my imprisonment the tempter was busy, yet it pleased God so to stand at my right hand, that the motions were but sudden, and so vanished away.   And although there were that would have paid the money if I would accept it, yet I durst not accept of deliverance in such a way, and therefore my answer to them was, that although I would acknowledge their love to a cup of cold water, yet could I not thank them for their money, if they should pay it.   So the Court drew near, and the night before I should suffer according to my sentence, it pleased God I rested and slept quietly.   In the morning my friends come [came] to visit me, desiring me to take the refreshment of wine, and other comforts; but my resolution was not to drink wine, nor strong drink that day until my punishment was over, and the reason was, lest in case I had more strength, courage and boldness than ordinarily could be expected, the world should either say, He is drunk with new wine, or else that the comfort and strength of the creature hath carried him through.   My course was this :—I desired brother John Hazel to bear my friends company, and I betook myself to my chamber, where I might communicate with my God, commit myself to him, and beg strength from him.   I had no sooner sequestered myself, and come into my chamber, but Satan lets fly at me, saying, Remember thyself, thy birth, breeding, and friends, thy wife, children, name and credit; but as this was sudden, so there came in sweetly from the Lord as sudden an answer, 'Tis for my Lord; I must not deny him before the sons of men (for that were [is] to set men above him) but rather lose all, yea wife, children, and mine own life also.   To this the tempter replies, Oh! but that is the question, is it for him? and for him alone? is it not rather for thy own, or some other's sake? thou hast so professed and practiced, and now art loth to deny it; is not pride and self in the bottom? Surely this temptation was strong, and thereupon I made diligent search after the matter, as formerly I had done, and after a while there was even as it had been a voice from heaven in my very soul, bearing witness with my conscience, that it was not for any man's case or sake in this world, that so I had professed and practiced, but for my Lord's case and sake, and for him alone; whereupon my spirit was much refreshed; as also in the consideration of these three Scriptures, which speak on this wise :— "Who shall lay any thing to the charge of God's elect?"   "Although I walk through the valley and shadow of death I will fear no evil, thy rod and thy staff they shall comfort me;" and "He that continueth to the end, the same shall be saved."

But then came in the consideration of the weakness of the flesh to bear the strokes of a whip, though the spirit was willing, and thereupon [hereupon] I was caused to pray earnestly unto the Lord, that he would be pleased to give me a spirit of courage and boldness, a tongue to speak for

him, and strength of body to suffer for his sake, and not to shrink or yield
to the strokes, or shed tears, lest the adversaries of the truth should thereupon blaspheme and be hardened, and the weak and feeble-hearted discouraged ; and for this I sought [besought] the Lord earnestly. At length
he satisfied my spirit to give up, as my soul so my body to him, and
quietly to leave the whole disposing of the matter to him ; and so I
addressed myself in as comely a manner as I could, having such a Lord and
Master to serve in this business.   And when I heard the voice of my
keeper come for me, even cheerfulness did come upon me, and taking my
Testament in my hand, I went along with him to the place of execution,
and after common salutation here stood.   There stood by also one of the
magistrates, by name Increase Nowel, who for a while kept silent, and
spoke not a word, and so did I, expecting the governor's presence, but he
came not.   But after a while Mr. Nowel bade the executioner do his office.
Then I desired to speak a few words, but Mr. Nowel answered, It is not
now a time to speak.   Whereupon I took leave, and said, Men, brethren,
fathers and countrymen, I beseech you give me leave to speak a few words,
and the rather because here are many spectators to see me punished, and I
am to seal with my blood, if God give strength, that which I hold and
practice in reference to the word of God, and the testimony of Jesus.
That which I have to say in brief is this, Although I confess I am no disputant, yet seeing I am to seal what I hold with my blood, I am ready to
defend it by the Word, and to dispute that point with any that shall come
forth to withstand it.   Mr. Nowel answered me, now was no time to dispute. Then said I, Then I desire to give an account of the faith and order
I hold, and this I desired three times, but in comes Mr. Flint, and saith to
the executioner, Fellow, do thine office, for this fellow would but make a
long speech to delude the people.[1]   So I being resolved to speak, told the
people ; That which I am to suffer for is the Word of God, and testimony
of Jesus Christ.   No, saith Mr. Nowel, it is for your error, and going
about to seduce the people.   To which I replied, Not for error, for in all
the time of my imprisonment wherein I was left alone (my brethren being
gone) which of all your ministers in all that time came to convince me of
an error ; and when upon the governor's words a motion was made for a
public dispute, and upon fair terms so often renewed, and desired by hundreds, what was the reason it was not granted. Mr. Nowel told me, it was
his fault that went away, and would not dispute , but this the writings will
clear at large.   Still Mr. Flint calls to the man to do his office ; so before
and in the time of his pulling off my clothes I continued speaking, telling
them, that I had so learned, that for all Boston I would not give my body
into their hands thus to be bruised upon another account, yet upon this I

---

[1]Thomas Flint was chosen one of their magistrates in 1642.

would not give the hundredth part of a *wampum peaque*[1] to free it out of their hands, and that I made as much conscience of unbottoning one button, as I did of paying the thirty pounds in reference thereunto.   I told them moreover, The Lord having manifested his love towards me, in giving me repentance towards God and faith in Jesus Christ, and so to be baptized in water by a messenger of Jesus into the name of the Father, Son and Holy Spirit, wherein I have fellowship with him in his death, burial and resurrection, I am now come to be baptized in afflictions by your hands, that so I may have further fellowship with my Lord, and am not ashamed of his sufferings, for by his stripes am I healed.

And as the man began to lay the strokes upon my back, I said to the people, Though my flesh should fail, and my spirit should fail, yet my God would not fail.   So it pleased the Lord to come in, and so to fill my heart and tongue as a vessel full, and with an audible voice I broke forth praying unto the Lord not to lay this sin to their charge ; and telling the people, that now I found he did not fail me, and therefore now I should trust him forever who failed me not ; for in truth, as the strokes fell upon me, I had such a spiritual manifestation of God's presence as the like thereof I never had nor felt, nor can with fleshly tongue express ; and the outward pain was so removed from me, that indeed I am not able to declare it to you, it was so easy to me, that I could well bear it, yea and in a manner felt it not although it was grievous as the spectators said, the man striking with all his strength (yea spitting in [on] his hand three times as many affirmed) with a three-corded whip, giving me therewith thirty strokes. When he had loosed me from the post, having joyfulness in my heart, and cheerfulness in my countenance, as the spectators observed, I told the magistrates, You have struck me as with roses ; and said moreover, Although the Lord hath made it easy to me, yet I pray God it may not be laid to your charge.

" After this many came to me rejoicing to see the power of the Lord manifested in weak flesh ; but sinful flesh takes occasion hereby to bring others in trouble, informs the magistrates hereof, and so two more are apprehended as for contempt of authority.   Their names were John Hazel and John Spur, who came indeed and did shake me by the hand, but did use no words of contempt or reproach unto any.   No man can prove that the first spoke any thing, and for the second, he only said thus : Blessed be the Lord ; yet these two for taking me by the hand, and thus saying after I had received my punishment, were sentenced to pay forty shillings, or to be whipped.   Both were resolved against paying their fine ; nevertheless after one or two days imprisonment, one paid John Spur's fine and he was released ; and after six or seven days imprisonment of brother Hazel, even

---

[1]A *wampum peaque* is the sixth part of a penny with us.

the day when he should have suffered, another paid his, and so he escaped ; and the next day went to visit a friend about six miles from Boston, where the same day he fell sick, and within ten days [he] ended his life. When I was come to the prison, it pleased God to stir up the heart of an old acquaintance of mine, who, with much tenderness, like the good Samaritan, poured oil into my wounds, and plastered my sores ;[1] but there was present information given what was done, and inquiry made who was the surgeon, [chirurgeon] and it was commonly reported he should be sent for, but what was done I yet know not. Now thus it hath pleased the Father of mercies so to dispose of the matter, that my bonds and imprisonments, have been no hindrance to the Gospel ; for before my return, some submitted to the Lord, and were baptized, and divers were put upon the way of inquiry. And now being advised to make my escape by night, because it was reported that there were warrants forth for me, I departed ; and the next day after, while I was on my journey, the constable came to search at the house where I lodged, so I escaped their hands, and was by the good hand of my heavenly Father brought home again to my near relations, my wife and eight children. The brethren of our town, and Providence, having taken pains to meet me four miles in the woods where we rejoiced together in the Lord. Thus have I given you as briefly as I can, a true relation of things ; wherefore, my brethren, rejoice with me in the Lord, and give all glory to him, for he is worthy, to whom be praise forevermore ; to whom I commit you, and put up my earnest prayers for you, that by my late experience who have trusted in God, and have not been deceived, you may trust in him perfectly. Wherefore, my dearly beloved brethren, trust in the Lord, and you shall not be ashamed nor confounded ; so I also rest.

Yours in the bond of charity,

OBADIAH HOLMES.[2]

Thus I have given the reader his own testimony, without adding or diminishing a single word, that all who understand may judge ; for the Scriptures assure us, that " the ear trieth words, as the mouth tasteth meat." You have heard from Mr. Holmes, that two men were put to trouble for the respect they showed to him after his sufferings. Mr. Clarke

---

[1] In a manuscript of Governor Joseph Jencks, written near fifty years ago, he says :— " Mr. Holmes was whipped thirty stripes, and in such an unmerciful manner, that in many days, if not some weeks, he could take no rest but as he lay upon his knees and elbows, not being able to suffer any part of his body to touch the bed whereon he lay. But Mr. Clarke being a scholar bred, a friend of his, paid his fine.

[2] Clarke's Narrative, pp. 16—23, [45—52.]

13

says, it was reported that warrants were sent forth to the number of thirteen, but that " some through fear were fain to hide themselves, and being strangers, to hasten away, or to change their habit." John Spur, one of their church members, who was taken, gives us the following testimony. Says he :—

Mr. Cotton in his sermon immediately before the Court gave their sentence against Mr. Clarke, Obadiah Holmes, and John Crandal, affirmed, that denying infant baptism would overthrow all, and this was a capital offence ; and therefore they were soul-murderers. When therefore the Governor, Mr. John Endicott, came into the Court to pass sentence against them, he said thus, You deserve to die, but this we agreed upon, that Mr. Clarke shall pay twenty pounds fine, and Obadiah Holmes thirty pounds fine, and John Crandal five pounds, and to remain in prison until their fines be either paid or security given for them, or else they are all of them to be well whipped. When Obadiah Holmes was brought forth to receive his sentence, he desired of the magistrates, that he might hold forth the ground of his practice ; but they refused to let him speak, and commanded the whipper to do his office ; then the whipper began to pull off his clothes, upon which Obadiah Holmes said, Lord lay not this sin unto their charge ; and so the whipper began to lay on with his whip ; upon which Obadiah Holmes said, O Lord, I beseech thee to manifest thy power in the weakness of thy creature. He neither moving nor stirring at all for their [the] strokes, breaks out in these expressions, Blessed and praised be the Lord, and thus he carried it to the end, and went away rejoicingly. I John Spur being present, it did take such an impression in my spirit to trust in God, and to walk according to the light that God had communicated to me, and not to fear what man could do unto me, that I went to the man (being inwardly affected with what I saw and heard) and with a joyful countenance took him by the hand when he was from the post and said, Praised be the Lord ; and so I went along with him to the prison ; and presently that day there was information given to the Court what I had said and done ; and also a warrant[1] [was] granted out that day to arrest both myself and John Hazel, which was executed on the morrow morning upon us, and so we were brought to the Court and examined. The Governor asked me concerning Obadiah Holmes, according as he was informed

[1] To the keeper or his deputy :

By virtue hereof you are to take into your custody and safe keeping, the body of John Spur for a heinous offence by him committed ; hereof fail not [not to fail.] Dated the 5th of the 7th month, 1651. Take also into your safe keeping John Hazel. By the Court,

INCREASE NOWEL.

by old Mr. Cole and Thomas Buttolph, of my taking of him by the hand, and smiling, and I did then freely declare what I did, and what I said, which was this:—Obadiah Holmes, said I, I do look upon as a godly man; and do affirm that he carried himself as did become a Christian, under so sad an affliction; and his affliction did so affect my soul, that I went to him being from the post, and said, Blessed be the Lord. .... But said the Governor, What do you apprehend concerning the cause for which he suffered? My answer was, That I am not able to judge of it. Then said the Governor, we will deal with you as we have dealt with him. I said unto him again, I am in the hands of God. Then Mr. Symonds, a magistrate, said, "You shall know that you are in the hands of men." The Governor then said, Keeper, take him; and so I was presently carried away to prison.

The next day about one of the clock, I was sent for again into the Court. The Governor (being then about to go out of the Court when I came in) delivered his [this] speech to me; said he, You must pay forty shillings or be whipped. I said then to those of the Court that remained, That if any man suffer as a Christian, let him glorify God in this behalf. Then I desired to know what law I had broken, and what evil I had done? but they produced no law, only they produced what the two witnesses had sworn against me.[1] My speech thereto was this:—My practice and carriage is allowed by the word of God, for it is written in Rom. 12. Be like affectioned one towards another; rejoice with them that rejoice; and it is contrary to my judgment and conscience to pay a penny. Then said Mr. Bendal, I will pay it for him, and there presented himself. I answered then and said, I thanked him for his love, but did believe it was no acceptable service for any man to pay a penny for me in this case; yet notwithstanding, the Court accepted of his proffer, and bid me begone. Then came John Hazel to be examined.   JOHN SPUR.[2]

[1] "J. Cole being in the market place, when Obadiah Holmes came from the whipping-post, John Spur came and met him presently, laughing in his face, saying, 'Blessed be God for thee brother,' and so did go with him, laughing upon him up towards the prison, which was very grievous to me to see him harden the man in his sin, and shewing much contempt of authority by that carriage, as if he had been unjustly punished, and had suffered as a righteous man under a tyrannical government. Deposed before the Court, the 5th of the 7th month.
                                                                      INCREASE NOWEL."

"I, Thomas Buttolph, did see John Spur come to Obadiah Holmes, so soon as he came from the whipping-post, laughing in his face, and going along with him towards the prison to my great grief to see him harden him in his sin, and to shew such contempt of authority. Deposed the 5th of the 7th month, 1651, before the Court.   INCREASE NOWEL."
[Narrative, p. 58.]
[2] Narrative, pp. 26—28. [56—58.]
I find that John Hazel was admitted a freeman at Boston, March 9, 1637, and John Spur, May 22, 1639. Massachusetts Records.

Mr. Hazel was one of Mr. Holmes's brethren of Rehoboth, who, though above threescore years old, and infirm in body, had traveled near fifty miles, partly indeed on other business, but chiefly to visit his beloved brother in prison; and how he was treated there, he has given us an account, written and subscribed with his own hand as follows:—

A relation of my being brought before the magistrates the 6th of the 7th month, 1651.

I, going from place to place, to buy and take up commodities for my use, was attached or arrested by the marshal, by virtue of a warrant from the Court, to appear in the Court, and there to answer for a high misdemeanor committed by me; and coming into the Court (which was then privately kept in the chamber) they asked me divers questions, among[st] which this was one, Whether I did think that Obadiah Holmes did well or not, in coming among them to baptize, and administer the sacrament? laying this to my charge, that I was one with him, and of the same judgment, and, Whether I did think he did well or no, in his so carrying himself? To which I answered, I had here nothing to do with that which another man did, but I was here to answer for what I myself had committed against their law. Then said they, You have offended our law, and have contemned authority, for you took him by the hand, and did countenance him in his sin, so soon as he was gone from the post. To which I said, If I have broken any law of the place, by what I then did, I am willing to submit unto punishment. Yea, said the Governor you took him by the hand, did you not? and spake to him; what said you? did you not say so and so? Blessed be God, &c. To which I said, I shall refer myself unto the testimonies that may or can be brought against me. Well, said the Governor, we shall find testimony enough against you. Take him to you, keeper, and we will call you forth in public, for what [that] we do with you we will proceed in public with you. And so I went to prison. This was the sum and substance of the first time I was called before them. The next day being the last day of the week, and the last day of their Court, I was in expectation all the forenoon to be called forth, but was not. So after dinner, when (as appeareth) the Court was risen, and some of the magistrates departed, I was sent for again into the chamber, where was the Governor with three others, *scil*, Mr. Bellingham, Mr. Hibbins, and Mr. Increase Nowel. As soon as I was come into the room, the Governor read my sentence, which was, that I must pay forty shillings, or be well whipped; and so immediately he departed, and when he was gone (for could not have time before) I answered, that I desired the privilege of an English subject, which was to be tried by the country, to wit, a jury, and to be made to appear (if they can) to be a transgressor by a law. To which they said, I had contemned authority, and they had a law to punish such, and said they, You did show your contempt of authority in that you did take such a person by the hand, as soon as he was from the post. To which I answered, I could not do that which I did in contempt to authority, seeing he had satisfied the law to the full, and was departed from the place of suffering; and in the next place, what I did, I did unto him as my friend; and further I said, If I had taken him by the hand so soon as he was loosed from the post, and had led him out of the town, I should not have broken any law either of God or man. To this they said, that there was a law in all Courts of justice, both in Old England and other countries, to punish contempt of authority, and so had they such a law among themselves. To which I said, that in Old England and other places, they had such a law I denied not, but that law also was both enacted and published, but what law have I broken in taking my friend by the hand, when he was free, and had satisfied the law? To this they replied, that he had not satisfied the keeper. To this I answered, that he had talked with the keeper, and there was some agreement between them, and so in that sense also not under the law, but free. Then said they, if you would have showed kindness unto your friend, you might have forborne in that place, and done it more privately. To which I answered, I knew not but that place was as free as another, he having satisfied the law. The testimony that was given by Mr. Cole, was this, "I saw John Hazel take Obadiah Holmes by the hand, but what he said I cannot tell." This is the substance of all the proceedings until the last day at night, and then they said I should be whipped; but said some of their officers, The whipper cannot be found. Then they commanded that they should be ready by the second day morning, and then I did expect to be called forth; but neither that day, nor the third, nor fourth, was I called, but am as I understand reserved unto the fifth day, to be more public in the view of the world. And when the fifth day came, as I had many before, so also then, that would have paid the fine, if I would give my consent which I denied to do, and so set myself by the power of Christ to suffer what should be inflicted upon me; but when noon came I was told I should not suffer whipping; yet not having a discharge I did not look to be freed until the keeper told me I might go about my business. Then I demanded a discharge, (meaning under the magistrates' hands) so he bade me go; he would discharge me.

The strokes I was enjoined by the Court to have, were ten with a three-corded whip; the very same number I understand, that the worst malefactors that were there punished had; of which some were guilty of common whoredom, another of forcing a little child, and one Indian for coining of money. Thus far have you a relation according to my best remembrance

from the first to the last of all the passages concerning this matter; by me
John Hazel, written with mine own hand in Boston prison, the 13th day of
the seventh month, 1651.

A postscript. Since I wrote, I understand there is report that I was
willing to pay my fine, and that the magistrates would not accept of it
without I were willing. Gentle reader, be pleased to understand that this
is false, for it was without my consent or approbation; and further
understand, that the fine was taken by them, upon the proffer of Mr.
Bendal for John Spur. It was willingly accepted by the magistrates, and
approved of, although John Spur did to their faces contradict it, and oppose
it; therefore, good reader, believe not such reports.

By me,   JOHN HAZEL."[1]

Thus far we have attended to those sufferers' own testimony, the last of whom wrote the postscript of his relation
on his death-bed; and how much the abusive treatment he
met with was the cause of his death, God only knows. Let
us now hear what others had to say about them. Mr. Clarke
went to England in November, 1651, and the next year
printed the narrative from whence we have taken these
accounts; upon which Sir Richard Saltonstall, one of the
Massachusetts' first magistrates, then in our mother country,
wrote to Messrs. Cotton and Wilson, of Boston, in this
manner:—

REVEREND AND DEAR FRIENDS, WHOM I UNFEIGNEDLY LOVE AND RESPECT :—

It doth not a little grieve my spirit to hear what sad things are reported
daily of your tyranny and persecutions in New England, as that you fine,
whip and imprison men for their consciences. First, you compel such to
come into your assemblies as you know will not join with you in your worship, and when they show their dislike thereof or witness against it, then
you stir up your magistrates to punish them for such (as you conceive)
their public affronts. Truly, friends, this your practice of compelling any
in matters of worship to do that whereof they are not fully persuaded, is
to make them sin, for so the apostle (Rom. 14 and 23) tells us, and many
are made hypocrites thereby, conforming in their outward man for fear of
punishment. We pray for you and wish you prosperity every way, hoped
the Lord would have given you so much light and love there, that you

---

[1]Narrative, pp. 29—32, [59—62.] Here note, that Mr. Neal mistakes in representing that it was the General Court that fined these men, for it was only the Court
of Assistants.

might have been eyes to God's people here, and not to practice those courses in a wilderness, which you went so far to prevent. These rigid ways have laid you very low in the hearts of the saints. I do assure you I have heard them pray in the public assemblies that the Lord would give you meek and humble spirits, not to strive so much for uniformity as to keep the unity of the spirit in the bond of peace.[1]

Mr. Cotton's answer :—

HONORED AND DEAR SIR:—My brother Wilson and self do both of us acknowledge your love, as otherwise formerly, so now in the late lines we received from you, that you grieve in spirit to hear daily complaints against us. .... Be pleased to understand we look at such complaints as altogether injurious in respect of ourselves, who had no hand or tongue at all to promote either the coming of the persons you aim at into our assemblies, or their punishment for their carriage there. Righteous judgment will not take up reports, much less reproaches against the innocent. The cry of the sins of Sodom was great and loud, and reached up to heaven ; yet the righteous God (giving us an example what to do in the like case) he would first go down to see whether their crime were altogether according to the cry, before he would proceed to judgment. And when he did find the truth of the cry, he did not wrap up all alike promiscuously in the judgment, but spared such as he found innocent.[2] We are amongst those whom (if you knew us better) you would account, [as the matron of Abel spake of herself,] peaceable in Israel. Yet neither are we so vast in our indulgence or toleration, as to think the men you speak of, suffered an unjust censure. For one of them, (Obadiah Holmes) being an excommunicate person himself, out of a church in Plymouth patent, came into this jurisdiction, and took upon him to baptize, which I think himself will not say he was compelled here to perform.[3] And he was not ignorant that the rebaptizing of an elder person, and that by a private person out of office and under excommunication, are all of them manifest contestations against the order

[1]Massachusetts History, Vol. III, pp. 401, 402.

[2]Alas ! how often do men act contrary to the good rules they prescribe for others ! How often was Mr. Cotton guilty of censuring others, without a fair and full hearing! He does it to Mr. Holmes before he has got to the end of this letter. And where there are some things wrong, yet how little care has been used by his party to distinguish the innocent from the guilty, among the Baptists! So far from such a care, that from his day to ours, it has been a common trade of that party to ransack Germany, in order to reproach the English Baptists with errors and bad actions, which we never had any more concern with, than our accusers have with the whoredom of pope Joan !

[3]What an evasion is this! Sir Richard spake of compelling persons into their worship, and Cotton here turns it as if he meant a compelling persons out of one government into another to worship in their own way.

and government of our churches, established (we know) by God's law, and he knoweth) by the laws of the country. As for his whipping, it was more voluntarily chosen by him than inflicted on him. His censure by the Court was to have paid (as I know) thirty pounds, or else be whipped; his fine was offered to be paid by friends for him freely, but he chose rather to be whipped; in which case, if his suffering of stripes was any worship of God at all, surely it could be accounted no better than will-worship.[1] The other (Mr. Clarke) was wiser in that point and his offence was less, so was his fine less, and himself (as I hear) was contented to have it paid for him, whereupon he was released.[2] The imprisonment of either of them was no detriment. I believe they fared neither of them better at home, and I am sure Holmes had not been so well clad of many years before.

But be pleased to consider this point a little further. You think to compel men in matter of worship is to make them [men] sin. If the worship be lawful in itself, the magistrate compelling him to come to it, compelleth him not to sin, but the sin is in his will that needs to be compelled to a Christian duty. If it do make men hypocrites, yet better be hypocrites than profane persons. Hypocrites give God part of his due, the outward man, but the profane person giveth God neither outward nor inward man. You know not, if you think we came into this wilderness to practice those courses here which we fled from in England. We believe there is a vast difference between men's inventions and God's institutions; we fled from men's inventions, to which we else should have been compelled; we compel none to men's inventions. If our ways (rigid ways as you call them) have laid us low in the hearts of God's people, yea, and of the saints (as you style them) we do not believe it is any part of their saintship. Nevertheless, I tell you the truth, we have tolerated in our church some Anabaptists, some Antinomians and some Seekers, and do so still at this day. We are far from arrogating infallibility of judgment to ourselves or affecting uniformity; uniformity God never required, infallibility he never granted us.[3]

Here I would remark :—

1. That they were not infallible, can easily be believed, by all who see what great absurdities and self-contradictions they were driven to, in trying to support that way. Mr.

---

[1] "Although the paying of a fine seems to be but a small thing in comparison of a man's parting with his religion, yet the paying of a fine is the acknowledgment of a transgression; and for a man to acknowledge that he has transgressed when his conscience tells him he has not, is but little, if any thing at all, short of parting with his religion; and 'tis likely that this might be the consideration of those sufferers." Governor Jencks.

[2] If the reader will look back to page 185, he may see how contrary this is to truth.

[3] Mass. History, Vol. III, pp. 403—406.

Cotton here asserts that they were far from arrogating infallibility to themselves, and yet in the same letter had said, our churches are established, " *We know* by God's law," and that in the points Mr. Holmes contested.   And the use of force in religious matters naturally carries men into this absurdity ; for it would sound very odd in any men, to compel others to their way by the magistrate's sword, and yet own at the same time that they did not know but they were compelling them into errors.   When I first came into the parish where I now dwell, as they were without a minister, their committee requested me to preach to them for some time, which I did.   But in the year following, they got a major vote to hire another sort of preaching, and taxed me with our society thereto.   This caused our society to present an address to that party, dated November 21, 1748, wherein they say, " Pray consider, would you like it if we were a few more in number than you, to be forced to help us build a meeting-house, and maintain our minister ?   We doubt it much."   To this the other party, by the help of a neighboring minister, returned a long answer, the turning point of which was in these words, viz. :—

What we demand of you is equal and right; what you demand of us is evil and sinful; and hence we have the golden rule upon our side, while you are receding and departing from it ; for if we were in an error, and out of the right way, as we see and *know* that you are in several respects, and you see and *know* it of us, as *we do* of you, we think the golden rule would oblige you to tell us of our error, and not let us alone to go on peaceably in it, that is without using proper means to recover and reclaim us ; whether by the laws of God, or the good and wholesome laws of the land, as we now treat you.

Now, only allow it to be right to join the laws of the land with the laws of God, in supporting what the majority calls the right way of worship, and then how can any one fairly withstand this reasoning ?   For we are required not to suffer sin upon our neighbor ; and if secular force be a means that Christians ought to use, to bring their neighbors from error to attend and support the truth, how can Mr. Cotton's party be condemned for seizing and punishing Mr. Clarke and his brethren for worshipping in a private house, when they had an Orthodox meeting in the town, established by public authority?   And how can the major party in any parish be blamed for imprisoning men for their minister's rates (as my neighbors did me) though they never heard him, or received the least benefit from him?   If any think these two are not parallel cases, I ask what is the difference?   Mr. Clarke and Holmes might have gone to the established worship, if they *would;* and Mr. Holmes might have had his fine paid it seems if he *would,* and so all his devotion under the whip is declared to be "no better than will worship."   According to Mr. Cotton's own words, men might then be Anabaptists, Antinomians, and what not, if they would but come to hear the right ministers, and join with the right churches; and is not the greatest complaint they have at this day against the Baptists, because they refuse to commune with Pedobaptist churches?   They professed to grant liberty of conscience then, as well as now.   Captain Johnson who wrote in the time we are upon, says of erroneous persons:—

They report in all places where they come, that New England government doth persecute the people and churches of Christ; which, to speak truth, they have hitherto been so far from, that they have endeavored to expel all such beasts of prey (who will not be reclaimed) that here might be none left to hurt or destroy in all God's holy mountain. .... Neither do they exercise civil power to bring all men under their obedience, to a uniformity in every point of religion, but to keep them in the unity of the spirit, and the bond of peace; nor yet have they ever mixed their civil powers with the authority peculiarly given by Christ to his churches and officers of them, but from time to time have labored to uphold their privileges, and only communion one with another.[1]

It is readily granted that the sentiments of Mr. Williams and Mr. Clarke, about religious liberty, have had a great spread since that day, so that men of a contrary mind can-

[1] Johnson's History, p. 107.

not carry their oppressive schemes so far now as they did then; yet as to such as still hold that they have a right to use secular force to support worship, I think the chief difference between them and their fathers in 1651, lies in these two points: Then they gave the church the whole power of electing and settling ministers; now the world is empowered to control the church in her choice; then they obliged men to hear, as well as support their good ministers; now men may hear whom they please, if they will but let the parish minister have their money; but if that is refused, men are as liable to imprisonment or confiscation of goods now as then; and whether the compelling of a man to pay for that which is no benefit to him, be not an action more void of the very appearance of justice, than the compelling of men to hear what the compellers esteemed good preaching was, is freely referred to every reader's conscience; as it also is, whether the real error in both cases does not lie in blending divine and human laws together, rather than in any mistake about applying of them then, more than now.

2. We have abundant reason to think that Mr. Clarke's narrative of their sentiments and sufferings, is a true and just one; for he published it in 1652, and it greatly concerned the Massachusetts colony to confute the same if they could, and they did not want for men of ability and inclination to vindicate themselves in that respect, if they had found matter to work upon. But Captain Johnson who published his history of that colony in 1654, is silent about this remarkable affair. Mr. John Leverett, their agent at the British Court, wrote to Governor Endicott about it; but he in a letter of June 29, 1657, says, "I cannot for the present answer your expectation touching Rhode Island, and Clarke and Holmes."[1] Mr. Morton printed his New England Memorial in 1669, in which he endeavors to vindicate the country against many other complaints, but leaves this narrative

[1] Massachusetts History, Vol. III, p. 309.

untouched.   Mr. Hubbard wrote a large history of the
country in 1680, yet touches not this affair unless in an
obscure hint which confutes nothing.   Dr. Cotton Mather
published his folio history of New England in 1702, but
passes over these sufferings in silence; yea, and so does
Governor Hutchinson, though his history is the most impartial upon religious disputes of any that has been written in
this country, yet he says, " The first persecution I find upon
record of any of the people called Anabaptists was in the
year 1665."[1]   In his third volume, which is a collection of
ancient papers, are a few references to these sufferers, which
I have now made use of, but instead of confuting, they confirm Mr. Clarke's Narrative.   Mr. Neal who wrote in London,
1720, has from that narrative given a brief account of their
sufferings, and has done them the most honor of any Pedobaptist author I ever saw; though he has made several mistakes about them.[2]

[1]Massachusetts History, Vol. I, p. 226. [208.]

[2]As in Vol. I, p. 298, he says, " Mr. Newman admonished Holmes of his offence;
but finding him obstinate, and not willing to give an account of his conduct to the
church, he excommunicated him;" for which he gives no other proof than Mr.
Clarke's Narrative, and that informs us, p. 24, [53, 54,] that the first occasion of
Mr. Holmes's separation was, " That seven of the brethren should pass an act of
admonition upon a brother, without the consent of the rest, we (says Mr. Holmes)
being twenty-three in number, who might all in one hour's space, if in health, have
come together; so when I heard of it I went to Mr. Newman, and told him of the
evil which he and the other six had done; he told me they were the church representative, and if four of them had done it, it had been a church act. When this comes
to the congregation, with much ado, he got five more to himself, and then they were
twelve and we eleven; then they owned themselves to be the church, and began to
deal with me for saying, they had abused the church, and had took from them their
power; whereupon I told them I should renounce them, till either they saw their
sin, or I further light." After which a number more drew off and set up a meeting
by themselves, and there was public notice of the day when they were to be baptized,
and many witnesses of the transaction, yet says he, " Not one man or woman of
Mr. Newman's company ever come to deal with me for evil either in judgment or
practice till a long time after." Now is it just to charge Mr. Holmes with obstinacy,
only for his refusing to submit to the other party after this? Again Mr. Neal, p. 302,
charges Mr. Clarke, with standing upon a *punctilio* against *very fair concessions* of
the Massachusetts rulers, only because he refused to dispute without an exemption
from the lash of their law.

3. By all that appears, those Baptist fathers were sound
in the faith and much acquainted with experimental and
practical religion. All that was proved against them may be
summed up in their noble testimony, that there is " none to
or with Christ the Lord, by way of commanding and ordering with respect to the worship of God; that baptism or
dipping in water is one of his commandments, and that a
visible believer or disciple of Christ is the only person that
is to be baptized; that every such believer, may in point of
liberty, yea, ought in point of duty to improve that talent
his Lord hath given him with meekness of wisdom; and
that no such believer hath any liberty, much less authority
from his Lord, to smite his fellow-servant, nor yet with outward force to restrain his conscience, nor outward man for
conscience sake, where injury is not offered to the person,
name or estate of others." This is the sum of all the principles for which they suffered such cruel things, though their
opposites have constantly accused them of others. The
assembly of Massachusetts begin their law against the Baptists in 1644, with saying, that " since the first arising of the
Anabaptists about one hundred years since, they have been
the incendiaries of the commonwealths, and the infectors
of persons in main matters of religion, and the troublers of
churches in all places where they have been ;" and great
pains have been taken by teachers and writers from that day
to this, to connect these odious ideas with the very name of
Anabaptists. But let the reader judge whether it be possible
for ministers of any denomination, to visit and worship with
any of their brethren, more peaceably than these ministers
did with their brother at Lynn; and whether he can find
one of their martyrs who showed less of a disposition for
denying the lawful authority of magistrates, or more of a
Christian temper in sufferings, under their unlawful usurpations, than these Baptists did. And whether they were
heterodox or not in main matters of religion, may be partly

gathered from the foregoing account, and still further by the confession of their faith inserted below.[1]

I shall close this chapter with an address of Mr. Roger Williams to Governor Endicott, concerning these affairs.

[1]Mr. Clarke left a confession of his faith in writing, from whence an extract was inserted in the records of his church, the main of which here follows :—

" The decree of God is that whereby God hath from eternity set down with himself whatsoever shall come to pass in time. Eph. i. 2. All things with their causes, effects, circumstances and manner of being, are decreed by God. Acts, ii. 23. 'Him, being delivered by the determinate counsel and foreknowledge of God,' &c. Acts, iv. 28. This decree is most wise; Rom. xi. 33; most just; Rom. ix. 13. 14; eternal; Eph. i. 4, 5; II Thes. ii. 13; necessary; Psa. xxxiii. 2, Prov. xix. 21; unchangeable; Heb. vi. 17; most free; Rom. ix. 13; and the cause of all good; Jam. i. 17; but not of any sin; I John, i. 5. The special decree of God concerning angels and men is called predestination. Rom. viii. 30. Of the former, viz., angels, little is spoken in the Holy Scripture; of the latter more is revealed, not unprofitable to be known. It may be defined, the wise, free, just, eternal and unchangeable sentence or decree of God, determining to create and govern man for his special glory, viz., the praise of his glorious mercy and justice; Rom. ix. 17, 18, and xi. 36. Election is the decree of God, of his free love, grace and mercy, choosing some men to faith, holiness and eternal life, for the praise of his glorious mercy; I Thes. i. 4, II Thes. ii. 13, Rom. viii. 29, 30. The cause which moved the Lord to elect them who are chosen, was none other but his mere good will and pleasure, Luke xii, 32. The end is the manifestation of the riches of his grace and mercy, Rom. ix. 23, Eph. i. 6. The sending of Christ, faith, holiness, and eternal life, are the effects of his love, by which he manifesteth the infinite riches of his grace. In the same order God doth execute this decree in time, he did decree it in his eternal counsel. I Thes. v. 9; II Thes. ii. 13. Sin is the effect of man's free will, and condemnation is an effect of justice inflicted upon man for sin and disobedience. .... A man in this life may be sure of this election, II Pet. i, 10, I Thes. i, 4; yea of his eternal happiness, ... but not of his eternal reprobation; for he that is now profane, may be called hereafter." Thus far Mr. Clarke.

Mr. Holmes says :—" Having had two or three requests from my friends and brethren, in special my brother Robert, to give some information of my present state and standing with reference to the Lord and my own soul, [I] shall as briefly as I can, give account thereof. .... But before I come to speak to the point in hand, I cannot forget the rock out of which I was hewn, and the cistern out of which I was digged; who was by nature a child of wrath as well as others, and by actual transgression added sin to sin, as my conscience and others did know. But God had mercy for me in store when I neither deserved it nor desired it, for he knows who are his; and the elect shall obtain it, forever blessed be his holy name, to whom be glory forever. Amen. Now in this faith or belief I stand, not doubting but it is the faith of God's elect.

1. " I believe there is one Essence or Being, even one God, who made heaven and earth, the waters, and all things therein contained, who governs all things by the word of his power, and hath appointed life and death to men, and bounded their habitations, whose providence extendeth to the least creature and actions. 2. I believe this God is Father to our Lord Jesus Christ; in a special understanding may be dis-

The governor having occasion (as they often had,) to write to Mr. Williams about the "peace of the English and Indians," and having at the entrance of his letter said, "Were I as free in my spirit as formerly I have been to

tinguished as Father, Son and Holy Spirit, and yet but one in Essence. 3. I believe that as God made the world, so by his word made he man in his own image without sin, and gave him a most excellent place and being, giving him commandment what he should do, and what he should forbear; but through the malice of Satan working with his wife was deceived; for she did eat, and gave her husband and he did eat, which was the first cause of the curse to him, and reached to all his posterity, by which came death natural, and death eternal. 4. I believe in this interim of time the Lord manifested his great love in that word, 'The seed of the woman shall break the head of the serpent,' but enmity was between the two seeds. 5. I believe that at that and after time the Lord was worshipped by sacrifices, though darkly held forth to us. 6. I believe after that God in his own time chose a people to himself, and gave them his laws and statutes in a special manner, though he had always his chosen ones in every generation. 7. I believe with this people he made a choice covenant to be their God, and they to be his people; which covenant they brake though he was a Father to them, and was grieved for them, and yet did not only give them his laws, but sent his prophets early and late, but they would not hear; and in fullness of time sent his only Son; but as they had abused his prophets, so they killed his only Son. 8. I believe God in his Son made a new covenant, a sure and everlasting covenant, not like that he made with Israel, of which Moses, that faithful servant, was mediator, but a covenant of grace and peace through his only Son, that whosoever believed in him should not perish, but have everlasting life. 9. I believe that all those that are in this covenant of grace, shall never fall away nor perish, but shall have life in the Prince of Life, the Lord Jesus Christ. 10. I believe no man can come to the Son but they that are drawn by the Father to the Son, and they that come, he in no wise will cast away. 11. I believe he came to call sinners to repentance, for the whole need him not, but they that are sick. 12. I believe that by the shedding of his precious blood is my redemption, and not mine only, but all that are or shall be saved. 13. I believe that as he was God so was he man, for he did not take the nature of angels, but the nature of Abraham. 14. I believe God hath laid the iniquity of all his elect and called ones, upon him. 15. I believe the Father is fully satisfied, and the debt is truly paid to the utmost farthing, and the poor sinner is quit, and set free from all sin past, present and to come. 16. I believe the Holy Scriptures which testify of Christ in dark shadows and types, and all that was written of Christ in the Prophets and Psalms; and that he was born of a virgin at Bethlehem, and come to his own and they received him not. 17. I believe he was put to death and hanged upon a tree, called the cross, and was buried, and the third day rose again according to the Scriptures, and appeared to many. 18. I believe he ascended to his Father and sitteth at his right hand, having made request for his. 19. I believe that the Father's commandment and his declaration of him is to be observed, when the Father uttered that voice saying, 'This is my beloved Son in whom I am well pleased; hear ye him.' 20. I believe there is no salvation but by him alone; no other name under heaven by which man can be saved. 21. I believe he is sent unto the world, and to be published to all men; but some, yea, many reject the counsel of God against themselves. 22. I believe

write unto you, you should have received another manner of salutation than now, with a good conscience I can express; however God knoweth who are his, and what he is pleased to hide from sinful man in this life, shall in that great day be

none have power to choose salvation, or to believe in Christ for life; it is only the gift of God. 23. I believe although God can bring men to Christ, and cause them to believe in him for life, yet he hath appointed an ordinary way to effect that great work of faith, which is by means of sending a ministry into the world, to publish repentance to the sinner, and salvation, and that by Jesus Christ; and they that are faithful shall save their own souls and some that hear them. 24. I believe that they that are sent of God are not to deliver a mission of their own brain, but as it is in the Scripture of truth, for holy men wrote as they were inspired by the Holy Spirit. 25. I believe the precious gifts of the Spirit's teaching were procured by Christ's ascension and given to men for begetting of souls to the truth, and for establishment and consolation of those that are turned to the Lord; for none shall pluck them out of his Father's hand. 26. I believe no man is to rush into the ministry without a special call from God, even as gospel ministers had of old, which was the call of the Holy Spirit, with some talent or talents to declare the counsel of God to poor sinners, declaring the grace of God through Jesus Christ, even to those that are yet in the power of Satan; yea, to bring glad tidings by and from the Lord Jesus Christ. 27. I believe this ministry is to go forth, and he that hath received grace with a talent or talents, as he hath received freely of the Lord, so he is freely to give, looking for nothing again but the promise of the Lord. 28. I believe none is to go forth but by commission, and carefully to observe the same according as Christ gave it forth without adding or diminishing; first to preach Christ, that is to make disciples, and then to baptize them, but not to baptize them before they believe; and then to teach them what Christ commanded them. For as the Father had his order in the former dispensation, so hath the Son. In former times the Lord spake in divers ways and manners, but now hath he spoken by his Son. 29. I believe that as God prepared a begetting ministry, even so doth he also prepare a feeding ministry in the church, where a called people out of the world, by the word and Spirit of the Lord, assembling of themselves together in a holy brotherhood, continuing in the apostles' doctrine, fellowship, breaking bread and prayer. 30. I believe such a church ought to wait for the Holy Spirit of promise, on whom it may fall, and to choose out among themselves either pastor, teacher, or elders ·to rule, or deacons to serve the table, that others may give themselves to the word and prayer, and to keep them close to the Lord, and their fellowship clear and distinct, not to have fellowship with the unfruitful works of darkness, but rather to reprove them. 31. I believe the church of Christ, or this company gathered, are bound to wait on the Lord for the Spirit to help them, and have liberty, and are under duty, that they may prophesy one by one. 32. I believe that the true baptism of the gospel, is a visible believer with his own consent to be baptized in common water, by dying, or as it were drowning, to hold forth death, burial and resurrection, by a messenger of Jesus, into the name of the Father, Son, and Holy Spirit. 33. I believe the promise of the Father, concerning the return of Israel and Judah, and the coming of the Lord to raise up the dead in Christ, and to change them that are alive, that they may reign with him a thousand years, according to the Scripture. 34. I believe the resurrection of the wicked to receive their just judgment, Go ye cursed to the devil and his

manifested to all." Mr. Williams referring to the sufferings of Mr. Clarke and Mr. Holmes, says :—

Sir, at the reading of this line, the speech of that wise woman of Tekoa unto David came fresh unto my thoughts : Speaks not the King this thing as one that is guilty? for will my honored and beloved friend not know me for fear of being disowned by his conscience? Shall the goodness and integrity of his conscience to God cause him to forget me? Doth he quiet his mind with this (God knoweth who are his ; God hides from sinful man ; God will reveal before all?) Oh how comes it then that I have heard so often [and] heard so lately, and heard so much, thàt he that speaks so tenderly for his own, hath yet so little respect, mercy or pity to the like conscientious persuasions of other men? are all the thousands of millions of millions of consciences at home and abroad, fuel only for a prison, for a whip, for a stake, for a gallows? are no consciences to breathe the air, but such as suit and sample his? may not the Most High be pleased to hide from his as well as from the eyes of his fellow-servants, fellow-mankind, fellow-English? . . . . Who can shut when he will open? and who can open, when he that hath the key of David will shut? . . . .

Objection. But what makes this to heretics, blasphemers, seducers, to them that sin against their conscience (as Mr. Cotton saith) after conviction? . . . . First,I answer, he was a tyrant that put an innocent man into a bear's skin, and so caused him as a wild beast to be baited to death.

angels forever. 35. I believe, as eternal judgment to the wicked, so I believe the glorious declaration of the Lord saying, Come ye blessed of my Father, enter into the joy of your Lord, which joy, eye hath not seen, ear hath not heard, neither can it enter into the heart of man to conceive the glory that God hath prepared for them that love and wait for his appearance; wherefore come Lord Jesus, come quickly!

For this faith and profession I stand, and have sealed the same with my blood in Boston, in New England, and hope through the strength of my Lord I shall be enabled to witness the same to death, although I am a poor unworthy creature, and have nothing to plead or fly unto but to grace, grace; and have nothing to rest on but only the mercy, the free mercy of God in and through Jesus Christ my Lord and Saviour; to whom be honor, glory and praise forever and ever, Amen. Thus have I given you an humble and true account of my standing, and of my dear wife's standing in our faith and order, that you may consider the same, comparing what is written by the Holy Scriptures, which are our rule towards God and man; committing this and you to the wisdom and counsel of God. Yours in all love to serve continually having you in our prayers; fare ye well.

" This for Mr. John Angher, and my brother Robert Holmes, and my brother-in-law, and sisters, with Mary Nonly, and to them that love and fear the Lord. For Robert Holmes in the parish of Manchester, Lancashire." Obadiah Holmes's Manuscript, 1675.

14

Secondly, This is the common cry of haunters [hunters] or persecutors, heretics, blasphemers, &c., and why, but for crossing the persecutors' consciences (it may be but their superstitions) whether Turkish, Popish, Protestant, &c. This is the outcry of the pope and prelates, and of the Scotch Presbyterians, who would fire all the world, to be avenged on the sectarian heretics, the blasphemous heretics, the seducing heretics, &c., had it not pleased the God of heaven who bounds the insolent rage of the furious ocean to raise up a second Cromwell to stay the fury of the oppressor, whether English, Scottish, Popish, Presbyterian, Independent, &c. . . . .

Let it not be offensive in your eyes, that I single out a point, a cause of my banishment, wherein I greatly fear one or two sad evils have [which hath] befallen your soul and conscience. The point is that of the civil magistrate's dealing in matters of conscience and religion, as also of persecuting [and hunting] any for any matter merely spiritual and religious. The two evils intimated are these : first, I fear you cannot after so much light, and so much profession to the contrary (not only to myself [and so] often in private,[1] but) before [so] many witnesses ; I say, I fear you cannot say and act so much, against so many several consciences, former and latter, but with great checks, great threatenings and inward throes [great blows and throes] of conscience. Secondly, If you shall thank God, that it is not so with you, but that you do what conscience bids you in God's presence, upon God's warrant, I must then be humbly faithful to tell you, that I fear your underprizing of holy light, hath put out the candle, and the eye of conscience in these particulars, and that delusions, strong delusions, and that from God, (by Satan's subtilty) hath seized upon your very soul's belief, because you prized not, loved not the persecuted Son of God in his despised truths and servants. . . . . I desire to say it tremblingly and mournfully, I know not which way he will please to raise his glory, only I know my duty, my conscience and my love, all which enforce me to knock, to call, to cry at the gate-of heaven, and at yours, and to present you with this loving, though loud and faithful noise, and sound of a few grounds of deeper examination of both our souls and consciences, uprightly and impartially at the holy and dreadful tribunal of him that is appointed the Judge of all the living and the dead.

Be pleased then (Honored Sir) to remember that the thing which we call conscience is of such a nature, especially in Englishmen, as once a pope of Rome, at the suffering of an Englishman in Rome himself observed that although it be groundless, false and deluded, yet it is not by any arguments of torments easily removed. I speak not of the stream of the multitude of all nations, which have their ebbings and flowings in religion (as

[1] Governor Endicott was once a member of Salem church, under Mr. Williams's ministry.

the longest sword and strongest arm of flesh carries it[1] (but I speak of conscience, a persuasion fixed in the mind and heart of a man, which enforceth him to judge (as Paul said of himself a persecutor) and to do so and so with respect to God, his worship, &c. This conscience is found in all mankind more or less. . . . . To this purpose let me freely without offence remember you (as I did Mr. Clarke, newly como up from his sufferings amongst you) I say, remember you of the story I did him of William Hartly in queen Elizabeth, her days, who receiving the sentence of hanging, ... spake confidently (as afterward he suffered) "What tell you me of hanging? if I had ten thousand millions of lives, I would spend them all for the faith of Rome !" Sir, I am far from glancing the least countenance on the consciences of papists . . . . all that I observe is, that boldness and confidence. zeal and resolution, as it is commendable in a kind when it seriously respects a Deity, so also the greatest confidence hath sometimes need of the greatest search and examination. . . . . Wise men use to enquire what motives, what occasions, what snares, what temptations were there which moved, allured, &c. . . . . Surely sir, the baits, the temptations, the snares laid to catch you were not few, nor common. . . . . It is no small offer, the choice and applause and rule over so many towns, so many holy, so many wise, in such a holy way as you believe you are in. . . . . I cannot but fear and lament, that some of these and others have been too strong and potent with [for] you. . . . . Sir, I must be humbly bold to say, it is [that 'tis] impossible for any man or men to maintain their Christ by the sword, and to worship a true Christ! to fight against all consciencies opposite to theirs, and not to fight against God in some of them, and to hunt after the precious life of the true Lord Jesus Christ. Oh remember whither your principles and consciencies, must in time and opportunity force you! . . . . Yourself and others have said it by your principles, such whom you count heretics, blasphemers, seducers, ought to be put to death. You cannot be faithful to your principles and consciences, if you satisfy them with but imprisoning, fining, whipping and banishing the heretics, and by saying that banishing is a kind of death, as some chief with you formerly said in my case.[2] I end with an humble cry to the Father of

---

[1]The following words are remarkable, viz. : " It is made by learned and judicious writers, one of the undoubted rights of sovereignty to determine what religion shall be publicly professed and exercised within their dominions. Why else do we in New England that profess the doctrines of Calvin, yet practice the discipline of them called Independent, or Congregational churches, but because the authority of the country is persuaded, that is most agreeable to the mind of God." Mr. Hubbard's Election Sermon at Boston, May 3, 1676, p. 35.

[2]Cotton, on the contrary, declared that in this country, " where a man may make his choice of a variety of more pleasant and profitable seats than he leaveth behind

mercies, that you may take David's counsel, and silently commune with your own heart upon your bed, reflect upon your own spirit, and believe him that said [it] to his over-zealous disciples, " You know not what spirit you are of ;" that no sleep may seize [upon] your eyes, nor slumber upon your eye-lids, until your serious thoughts have [seriously] calmly, and unchangeably, through help from Christ, fixed, first on a moderation towards the spirit and consciences of all mankind, merely differing from, or opposing yours with only religious and spiritual opposition ; .... secondly, a deep and cordial resolution to search, to listen, to pray, to fast, and more fearfully, more tremblingly to enquire what the holy pleasure, and the holy mysteries of the Most Holy are ; in whom I humbly desire to be, your poor fellow servant, unfeignedly, respective, and faithful.

ROGER WILLIAMS.[1]

How happy had it been for New England, and for Governor Endicott in particular, if they had then regarded this faithful admonition of their old friend ! but disregarding it, Mr. Williams's words a few years after were fully verified, when, under Governor Endicott's administration, the blood of the Quakers was shed, which has left an indelible stain upon their characters, and " sullied the glory of their former sufferings from the bishops ; for now it appeared that the New England Puritans were no better friends to liberty of conscience than their adversaries, and that the question between them was not, whether one party of Christians should have power to oppress another, but who should have that power ?"[2]

him," " banishment is not counted so much a confinement as an enlargement." Reply, &c., pp. 8, 9.—ED.

[1]Appendix of his Reply to Cotton, 1652, pp. 303—313. Mr. Cotton died the twenty-third of December, that year.

[2]Neal's History of New England, Vol. I, p. 320.

CHAPTER V.

A review of 1651, presents before us such a dark cloud and threatening gloom, upon the cause of believers' baptism, and true liberty of conscience, as must affect every heart that is not extremely obdurate. The friends of that cause had been so cruelly treated in Europe, that a number of them fled into America, where a persecuting temper followed them and expelled them out of Massachusetts colony; but God gave them favor in the eyes of the heathen, from whom they obtained a grant of lands, upon which to begin the first civil government that ever allowed equal liberty of conscience, since our Saviour died for us. With great hazard and expense Mr. Williams had procured a charter for that purpose, which they had enjoyed about seven years, when alas! Mr. Coddington, who had the deeds and records of the island in his own hands, went to England, and procured from the Council of State, a commission, dated April 3, 1651, signed by J. Bradshaw, constituting him Governor of the islands, to rule them with a council of six men, nominated by the people and approved by himself; which split this little colony into two parts, and Mr. Clarke and his brethren were to submit to a Governor that they had no hand in choosing, and their estates lay at his mercy. This melancholy news arrived just about the time that he and his brethren had been so cruelly handled in the Massachusetts, only for visiting and worshiping with an aged brother there. At the same time a party both of English and savages were supported in the heart of Mr. Williams's part of the colony, in opposition to all the good orders that he endeavored to establish among them. What could they now do? where could they go for relief? banished from their mother kingdom, and from neighboring colonies, who were exerting all their power to divide and corquer them! Indeed a man of the greatest worldly note among them, seemed as if he was like to do it effectually.[1]

[1]Near the same time the Court at Boston imposed a large fine upon the church in Malden, for calling a man to be their minister, without the approbation of the rulers and other ministers; and as they had before a law against gathering churches without their consent, their assembly now made another wherein they enacted, "that no minister should be called unto office in any of the churches, without the approbation of some of the magistrates, as well as the neighboring churches; on which ground in the year 1653, the Court would not allow the north church in Boston to call Mr. Powell, a well gifted though illiterate person to the stated office of a public teacher or minister; wherefore the people contented themselves with his being called to the place of a ruling elder. .... And whereas the plantations of New England had never as yet been acquainted, with the way of paying tithes for the support of the ministry, it was now left to the power of the county courts throughout the whole jurisdiction, to make sufficient provision for the maintenance of the ministry in the respective towns of the colony." [Hubbard, p. 551.]—B.

The Massachusetts Records give the following account of the above-mentioned dealings with the church in Malden. Under date of May 22, 1651, is the record:— "Whereas Mr. Marmaduke Matthews hath formerly and lately given offence to the magistrates, elders and many brethren, in some unsafe if not unsound expressions in his public teachings, and as it hath been manifested to this Court, and has not yet given satisfaction to those magistrates and elders that were appointed to receive satisfaction from him, since which time there hath in his public ministry been delivered other unsafe and offensive expressions by him, whereby both magistrates, ministers and churches were occasioned to write to the church of Malden to advise them not to proceed to the ordination of Mr. Matthews, which offences taken against him were also made known, yet, contrary to all advice and the rule of God's word, as also the peace of the churches, the church of Malden hath proceeded to the ordination of Mr. Matthews; this Court therefore, taking into consideration the premises and the dangerous consequences and effects that may follow such proceedings, &c." After this preamble, the act proceeds to appoint a committee of nine deputies to examine the affair, with permission to "call in the help or advice of any of the reverend elders whom they shall think meet." "The offence of the church" is then "referred to the next Court," but Mr. Matthews, for "suffering himself to be ordained contrary to the rules of God's word," is required to "give satisfaction at this session of this Court, by an humble acknowledgment of his sin for his so proceeding; which, if he refuse to do, to pay the sum of ten pounds within one month." Mr. Mathews "gave no satisfaction before the Court," and a warrant was issued to

Captain Johnson at that time said, "Familists, Seekers, Antinomians, and Anabaptists, [they] are so ill armed, that they think it best sleeping in a whole skin, fearing that if the day of battle once go on they shall fall among anti-

"levy the fine on his goods." The reverend gentleman seems not to have been encumbered with a heavy weight of worldly means, for, at the next session of the Court his fine was respited "till other goods appear besides books." He made an acknowledgment to the next General Court, and asked the remission of his fine, which was at first refused but afterwards granted.

October 14, 1651, the Court "appointed the church of Malden speedily to consider the errors Mr. Matthews stands charged with in Court," and if they refused, the Secretary was directed to give notice to the churches of Cambridge, Charlestown, Lynn and Reading, "to send their messengers in way of counsel and advice unto the church of Malden," "to debate the doctrines there delivered by Mr. Matthews." At the same session it is recorded, "The Court having perused an answer of the church of Malden touching those things wherein they have given offence, are not satisfied therewith, and do therefore judge that the members of the church of Malden shall be fined for their offences the sum of fifty pounds." This fine was levied on the estates of three members of the church, and they were empowered to apportion it upon the rest of the church except "such as consented not to Mr. Matthews's ordination." Ten pounds of the fine were afterwards remitted. May 23, 1655, certain of the church presented an acknowledgment and a petition for the repayment of the remainder of the fine, but were answered, "The Court doth not think meet to grant the petitioners' request herein."

The case of the "north church in Boston" appears from the records of the Court to have been as follows:—The church seems to have referred the question of Mr. Powell's ordination to the General Court for advice, representing themselves satisfied of his "abilities and fitness," notwithstanding his limited education; whereupon, October 19, 1652, the Court expressed themselves willing that Mr. Powell should "exercise in public" with the new church in Boston, "till it please God to provide better for them," but they advised against their proceeding to establish him as teaching elder. They gave as reasons, that Boston is "a place of such public resort," and the humor of the times to discourage learning. Four days later is the record, "The General Court having received credible information that the new church in Boston have chosen Mr. Powell to be their minister, and that he hath accepted their choice, they think it meet, in respect of the trust the country hath committed to them, lovingly to advise both the church and Mr. Powell to desist from any further proceeding." The church petitioned the next Court for liberty to call and ordain Mr. Powell, but the Court replied that they could not but judge Mr. Powell unfit for the office of pastor or teacher, nor could they consent thereto, because they could not be satisfied that Mr. Powell had such abilities, learning and qualifications as are requisite and necessary for an able ministry of the gospel. They added, "The Court conceives the church may call Mr. Powell to the office of ruling elder, and then they may enjoy all the ordinances of Christ amongst them save the sacrament, which they are supplied with in Boston; and their waiting till the Lord shall send unto them an able minister of the gospel, they hope, will not be in vain." The next year the church repeated its petition, and was curtly answered by being referred to the records of the previous Court.—ED.

christ's armies; [and] therefore they cry out like cowards, If you will let me alone, I will let you alone; but assuredly the Lord Christ hath said, 'He that is not with us, is against us;' there is no room in his army for *toleratorists*."[1] Had this been true, how could Mr. Williams and Mr. Clarke have persevered like heroes, in the cause of equity and liberty as they did? For being requested by their injured neighbors, they again crossed the boisterous ocean, and appeared as advocates for them at the British court; and also published to the world their pleas for equal liberty of conscience; and where can any writers be found of so early date, who defended that important right of mankind, so well as they did? Mr. Locke's excellent letters upon that subject were written near forty years afterward.

A little look back will give a more clear and just view of the important concerns of Mr. Williams's agency at this time.   When the Commissioners of the United Colonies met at Plymouth, September 7, 1648, Mr. Coddington and Captain Partridge tried for a confederacy with them, but were denied it, unless they would come in as part of Plymouth colony. Mr. Henry Bull then complained to them, that some Narragansett Indians had beat him, and done him other injuries; and Mr. John Smith, Assistant for Warwick, sent a writing by Messrs Holden and Warner, in the behalf of the whole town, " wherein they complain, among other things, of divers injuries, insolences and affronts offered them by the Indians that are about them, and near inhabitants to them, as, namely, killing their cattle, about a hundred hogs, abusing their servants when they take them alone, [and] sometimes making violent entrance into their houses, and striking the masters thereof, stealing and purloining their goods; and hereupon do earnestly desire to know the minds of the Commissioners herein, and to receive advice from them." Upon which the Commissioners gave them a writing to the

[1]Johnson, p. 231.

sachems and others to warn them " to prevent and abstain
from all such miscarriages for the future, and if any of them
receive any injury from the English, upon complaint in due
place and order, satisfaction shall be endeavored them according to justice, as the like will be expected from them."
When the Commissioners met at Boston, July 23, 1649,
Warwick wrote again to them ; but they refused to do any
thing for their defence, till they could find under what colony
their plantation fell; and it was then disputed whether
it belonged to the Massachusetts, or Plymouth; and they
advised the latter to take it.　When the Commissioners met
again at Hartford, September 5th, 1650, they received a letter from Mr. Easton, President, in the name of the council
of that colony, in which he declared, that " Rhode Island
and Warwick were combined and bound mutually to support one another."　Upon this the Commissioners mention
a former article of advice which they had received from the
honorable committee of parliament, " that in this and like
cases the bounds of patents should be first set out by a jury,
of uninterested persons, and that all inhabiting within the
limits so set forth, should fall under the government established by patent."　But instead of following this direction,
after mentioning that the inhabitants of Warwick claimed
an interest in Mr. Williams's patent, and refused to be
brought under the Massachusetts government, they advised
the authority of Plymouth " forthwith to resume [reässume]
the right they formerly had by patent to the place."　And
that if the inhabitants refused to submit to them, then the
advice of said committee should be taken, and if the same
was not complied with, " that real damages duly proved, be
levied by legal force, though with as much moderation and
tenderness as the case will permit."[1]　This was the treatment that was shown to Warwick; and hearing of what Mr.
Coddington had done, they joined with Providence in send-

---

[1] Records of the United Colonies.

ing Mr. Williams to England. William Arnold hired a messenger secretly to carry a letter to Boston, to apprize their rulers of it,[1] but they were notified of it in a better way ; for at a meeting of the Commissioners of the United Colonies at New Haven, September 4, 1651, they received the following letter, viz. :—

May it please this honored committee to take knowledge, that we, the inhabitants of Shawomet alias Warwick, having undergone divers oppresions and wrongs, amounting to great damage since we first possessed this place ; being forced thereby to seek to that honorable state of Old England for relief, which did inevitably draw great charge upon us, to the further impairing of our estates ; and finding favor for redress, were willing to waive for that time (in regard to the great troubles and employment that then lay on that State) all other lesser wrongs [other losses and wrongs] we then underwent, so that we might be replaced [replanted] in and upon this [that] our purchased possession, and enjoy it peaceably for time to. come, without disturbance or molestation by those from whom we had formerly suffered. But since our gracious grant from the honorable parliament, in replacing [replanting] of us in this place, we have been and daily are pressed with intolerable grievances, to the eating up of our labors, and wasting of our estates, making our lives, together with our wives and children, bitter and uncomfortable ; insomuch, that groaning under our burthens, we are constrained to make our address[es] to the honorable parliament and state, once again, to make our just complaint against our causeless molesters, who by themselves and their agents, are the only cause of this our reüttering of our distressed condition. May it please therefore this honored Assembly, to take notice of this our solemn intelligence (given unto you as the most public authorized society appertaining unto, and instituted in the United Colonies, whom our complaints do concern) that we are now preparing ourselves with all convenient speed for Old England, to make our grievances known again to the state, which fall upon us by reason that the order of parliament [of England] concerning us hath not been observed, nor the enjoyment of our granted privileges permitted to us, that we are as it were bought and sold from one patent and jurisdiction to another ; in that we have been prohibited and charged to acquit this place since the order of parliament given out and known to the contrary ; in that we have had warrants sent us, to summon us to the Massachusetts Court, and officers employed amongst us for that purpose ; in that these barbarous Indians about us, with evil minded English mixed among us, under pretence of some former personal subjection to the government of

[1]Massachusetts History, Vol. III, pp. 237—239.

the Massachusetts countenancing of them, cease not to kill our cattle, offer violence to our families, vilify authority of parliament vouchsafed to us, justifying their practices with many menances and threatenings, as being under the protection of the Massachusetts ; in that we [are and] have been restrained this seven or eight years past of common commerce in the country, and that only for matters of conscience ; in that our estates formerly taken from us remain yet unrestored, with these additions thereunto. These and the like are the grounds of our complaints, with our serious desires that you would be pleased to take notice of them, as our solemn intelligence given hereof, that as yourselves shall think meet, you may give further seasonable intelligence to your several colonies whom it may concern, so that their agent or agents may have seasonable instructions to make answer, and we hereby shall acquit ourselves, that we offer not to proceed in these our complaints, without giving due and seasonable notice thereof.   By me,

           JOHN GREENE, Jun., Clerk.

           In behalf of the town of Warwick.

Warwick, the first of September, 1651.

This brought matters to a close trial among them and the Commissioners, for those of Massachusetts (who were Mr. Simon Bradstreet, and Mr. William Hathorne, Esq'rs.) made a long declaration, how Plymouth gave up their right in that land to them in 1643 ; which was approved by all the Commissioners, who advised them to proceed against Gorton and his company, and had silently assented to what they had done from time to time since ; and that when in 1649 they were advised to return those lands back to Plymouth, their Court sent two deputies to the Assembly at Plymouth, with orders to offer, to " resign and submit the said [aforesaid] lands, and persons residing thereon to the government of Plymouth ; they only promising to do equal justice both to English and Indians there, according to our engagements ; but the government of Plymouth chose rather to ratify the aforesaid resignment of their Commissioners ;" after which they had " out of their own treasury allowed a large gratuity [quantity] of corn to the Indians under their government there, to keep them alive, the cattle of Gorton's company having destroyed most of theirs, rather than force to compel them, till all other means and ways of prudence for issuing these and the like differences were used." They closed with asking what aid the other jurisdictions would afford them, for the righting their injured and oppressed people, and bringing delinquents to condign punishment. The Connecticut aud New Haven Commissioners answered, by owning that they had their advice in 1643, to proceed against Gorton's company, and that when Plymouth Commissioners yielded up their right to the Massachusetts, the others, being neither concerned, nor understanding where the right lay, saw no cause to dissent, &c. The Commissioners for Plymouth (who were Mr. John Brown, and Mr. Timothy Hatherley (declared that what was done by the Commissioners for their colony in 1643, in resigning said lands to the Massachusetts, was not at all in their power, neither could the Massachusetts receive any such resignation without injuring the third and sixth articles of their confederation ; and that what right the authority of the Massachusetts had to send for Samuel Gorton and company, " inhabiting so far out of their jurisdiction they understand not." As to what the Governor of Plymouth and some others did in 1650, about ratifying that former resignation of Warwick to the Massachusetts, they said they had " protested against it in the Court of Plymouth, as being directly contrary to the order of the honorable committee of the parliament of England, and contrary to the articles of confederations with the rest of the colonies. " And whereas we are informed, that the Court of the Massachusetts have lately sent out several [summons or] warrants to several persons inhabiting [Shawomet, alias] Warwick and Pawtuxet, and have made seizure upon some of their estates, we do hereby protest against such proceedings if any there be."[1] Those in Massachusetts were so unwilling to have these things laid before the parliament, that they put Mr. Williams

[1] Records of the United Colonies.

to great distress only for attempting to take his passage through their colony.

The town of Newport signed an engagement and request to Mr Clarke in these words :—

We whose names are here underwritten,[1] being resolved to make our address unto the parliament of England, in point of our lands and liberties, do earnestly desire those six men that were last chosen the council of the town of Newport, and such as they shall consult with, to improve their best abilities for the managing thereof. We also do earnestly request Mr. John Clarke to do his utmost endeavors in soliciting our cause in England; and we do hereby engage ourselves to the utmost of our estates to assist them, being resolved in the mean time peaceably to yield all due subjection unto the present power set over us. Witness our hands the 15th of October, in the year of our Lord, God, 1651.

He sailed for England the next month.

Mr. Coddington having gotten the command of the islands, Providence and Warwick, each chose six deputies, who met at Providence, November 4, and unanimously concluded to stand embodied and incorporated as before, by virtue of their charter; and as president Easton had given place to Mr. Coddington, they chose another in his room, and made several laws, one of which was to prohibit any from purchasing lands of the Indians, without the Assembly's approbation, on penalty of forfeiting the same to the colony. When those two agents arrived in England, they united in a petition to the council of state, who on April 8th, 1652, referred the same to the Committee for Foreign Affairs. The Court of election at Warwick, May 18, made a law to forbid

---

[1]This was signed by John Easton, James Barker, John Cranston, Robert Carr, John Sheldon, Samuel Hubbard, John Allen, Henry Bull, Edward Thurston, Nathaniel West, William Dyre, William Lytherland, Richard Knight, Thomas Clarke, Thomas Dungan, &c., to the number of sixty-five, who with the six counsellors were almost all the free inhabitants of Newport, as Mr. Clarke said afterward to their General Assembly. Forty-one of the inhabitants of Portsmouth signed a like request. Copied from the original papers now before me.

Many of the above men were afterwards noted rulers in that colony; and Mr. Dungan was a member of Mr. Clarke's church, till about the year 1684; when he went to Pennsylvania, and became the first Baptist minister in that colony, where he left a numerous posterity. Edwards's History of the Baptists in that colony, p. 10.

the Dutch who were not inhabitants among them, from
trading with the Indians in this colony, upon penalty of forfeiting both goods and vessel to the colony if they did; and
the president was ordered to give the Governor of Manhatoes notice of it.   When their Assembly met again in the
fall at Providence, they wrote the following letter to Mr.
Williams, viz. :—

HONORED SIR :—We may not neglect any opportunity to salute you in
your absence, and have not a little cause to bless God, who hath pleased to
select you to such a purpose, as we doubt not but will conduce to the
peace and safety of us all, as to make you once more an instrument to
impart and disclose our cause unto those noble and grave senators our honorable protectors, in whose eyes God hath given you honor [favor] (as we
understand) beyond our hopes, and moved the hearts of the wise to stir on
your behalf.   We give you hearty thanks for your care and diligence, to
watch all opportunities to promote our peace, for we perceive your prudent
and comprehensive mind stirreth every stone to present it unto to the builders, to make firm the fabric unto us about which you are employed, laboring to unweave such irregular devices wrought by others amongst us, as
have formerly clothed us with so sad events, as the subjection of some
amongst us, both English and Indian to other jurisdictions; as also to prevent such near approach of our neighbors upon our borders on the
Narragansett side, which might much annoy us, with your endeavors to
furnish us with such ammunition as to look a foreign enemy in the face,
being that the cruel begin to stir in these western parts, and to unite in one
again, such as of late have had seeming separation in some respects; to
encourage and strengthen our weak and enfeebled body to perform its work
in these foreign parts, to the honor of such as take care, have been, and
are so tender of our good, though we be unworthy to be had in remembrance by persons of so noble places, indued with parts of so excellent and
honorable and abundantly beneficial use.

Sir, give us leave to intimate thus much, that we humbly conceive (so
far as we are able to understand) that if it be the pleasure of our protectors to renew our charter for the re-establishing of our government, that it
might tend much to the weighing of men's minds, and subjecting of persons who have been refractory, to yield themselves over as unto a settled
government, if it might be the pleasure of that honorable state, to invest,
appoint and empower yourself to come over as Governor of this colony for
the space of one year, and so the government to be honorably put upon
this place, which might seem to add much weight forever hereafter in the
constant and successive derivation of the same.   We only present it to

your deliberate thoughts and consideration, with our hearty desires that your time of stay there for the effectual perfecting and finishing of your so weighty affairs may not seem tedious, nor be any discouragement unto you ; and rather than you shall suffer for loss of time here, or expense there, we are resolved to stretch forth our hands at your return beyond our strength for your supply. Your loving bed-fellow is in health, and presents her endeared affection ; so are all your family. Mr. Sayles also his, with the rest of your friends throughout the colony, who wish and desire earnestly to see your face.

Sir, we are yours, leaving you unto the Lord, we heartily take leave.

From the General Assembly of this colony of Providence Plantations, assembled in the town of Providence the 28th of October, 1652.[1]

JOHN GREENE, General Recorder.

On the 2d of October, the Council of State gave an order and wrote letters to vacate Mr. Coddington's commission, and to confirm their former charter ; which were sent over by William Dyre. And about the 16th of February, 1653, he brought a letter to Providence, signed by Messrs. Sanford, Baulston, Porter and William Jefferies, requesting the two towns on the main to appoint a time to meet those on the Island, to hear and act upon the State's letters. Providence met upon the affair, and inquired why those letters were not brought to them, seeing they had continued to act upon the charter, after the Island was parted from them ? Dyre told them that the two agents had united in their petition, and that as it appeared to him that the Island was the major part of the colony, therefore they had the greatest interest in the letters, and he had left them there. President Smith, William Field, and some others, joined with Dyre, and strove to persuade them to " account themselves a disordered, confused rout, as he acknowledged the islanders were, and to account all officers' orders of court, laws and cases depending, as null, and to come to a popular meeting to lay a new foundation of government for the colony." This they could not consent to, but each town chose six commissioners who met at Pawtuxet on February 25th, and sent four messen-

[1]Providence Records.

gers to the Island for those letters or a copy of them ; and
that if the state's orders were for them all to unite again,
then to agree upon a meeting for that purpose. Dyre seeing
no other way to carry his own scheme, assumed the power
to himself to call the whole colony together by the following instrument :—

Loving friends and neighbors, these are to signify unto you, that it hath
pleased the right honorable, the Council of State, authorized by the supreme
authority of the commonwealth of England to betrust myself with letters
and orders concerning this colony, and the welfare thereof; be pleased
therefore to understand, that upon Tuesday come seven night, at Portsmouth on Rhode Island, at Mr. Baulston's house, I shall be there (God
willing) ready to attend the communication of the trust committed to my
charge, unto all such free inhabitants as shall there make their personal
appearance. Given under my hand this present 6th day of the week, being
the 18th of February, 1652.

WILLIAM DYRE.[1]

A copy of this he sent to each town, and many of the
freemen met on the said March first, but instead of throw-
ing all up, they ordered, " that all officers who were in
place when Mr. Coddington's commission obstructed, should
stand in their places, to act according to their former commissions, upon the Island ; and the rest in the colony according as they had been annually chosen, until a new election
according to former order." The Commissioners met again
at Pawtuxet on March 9th, to receive the answer of their
messengers from the Island, who reported what was done,
but that they could not obtain so much as a copy of those
letters from England. Upon which they sent again therefor, and also a proposal of joining with the towns on the
Island in the next election, if they would agree to it in their

[1] This document, together with many others relating to the early history of Rhode
Island, was copied for Backus by David Howell, then Professor in Rhode Island
College, afterwards Judge in the United States' Court. The manuscript is among
the Backus papers in the library of the Backus Historical Society. Appended to
the above document are the words, " This the town of Providence in their letter to
R. W. [Roger Williams], Agent in England, call *Dyre's Mandamus.* His conduct
herein gave great offence to Providence and Warwick."—ED.

former method, and give them ten days' notice. By some means such notice was not given, therefore the two towns on the main met at Providence, May 17th, 1653, and elected their officers. An assembly met at the same time on the Island, and chose Mr. Sanford their President, and some freemen coming from the main, they chose an Assistant for each town in the colony ; and they sent Mr. James Barker, and Mr. Richard Knight to Mr. Coddington, to demand the statute book, and book of records. And as it was then a time of war betwixt England and Holland, and mention was made of it in the letters which confirmed their charter, Dyre thought to make his advantage thereby, and procured commissions for himself, Captain Underhill, and Edward Hull to act against the Dutch in America ; and some cannon with twenty men were sent to the English[1] on the east end of Long Island, to enable them to act against the Dutch who lay to the westward of them. This alarmed Providence colony, who met again in June, and a third time at Warwick, on August 13th, when they answered a letter from the Massachusetts, and remonstrated against being drawn into a war with the Dutch ;[2] and wrote to Mr. Williams an account of Dyre's conduct, and of their being urged to give up their former actings as null ; but say they, " being still in the same order you left us, and observing two great evils that such a course would bring upon us ; first, the hazard of involving in all the disorders and bloodshed which have been committed on Rhode Island since their separation from us ; secondly, the invading and frustrating of justice in divers weighty causes then orderly depending in our courts, in some of which causes Mr. Smith, President, William Field, &c., were deeply concerned ;" therefore they could not yield to such a notion.[3]

[1] "They shall have two great guns and what *murtherers* are with us, on promise of returning them." R. I. Colonial Records.—ED.

[2] The remonstrance was made in June ; the letter to Massachusetts was written in August. R. I. Colonial Records.—ED.

[3] Callender, [p. 99.] Colony Records. To give a clear idea of their difficulties I would insert the following things :—

15

Before we proceed further upon their affairs, some transactions in the Massachusetts call for our attention. Their
ministers have often tried to persuade people, that ignorance
of the original languages in which our Bible was written, is

"The 24th of the first month called March, in the year (so commonly called)
1637-8, Memorandum, that we Canonicus and Miantinomo, the two chief sachems
of the Narragansetts, by virtue of our general command of this Bay, as also the particular subjecting of the dead sachems of Aquedneck and Kitackamuckqut, themselves and lands unto us, have sold to [unto] Mr. Coddington and his friends united
unto him, the great island of Aquedneck, laying [from]hence eastward in this Bay,
as also the marsh or grass upon Quinunnuqut, and the rest of the islands in this
bay (excepting Chibachuwesa [Prudence] formerly sold to [unto] Mr. Winthrop,
the now Governor of the Massachusetts, and Mr. Williams of Providence) also the
grass upon the rivers and bounds [coves] about Kitackamuckqut, and from
thence [these] to Paupusquatch, for the full payment of forty fathoms of white
beads, to be equally divided between us; in witness whereof we have here subscribed. Item, that by giving, by Miantonomo's hands, ten coats and twenty hoes
to the present inhabitants, they shall remove themselves from off the Island before
next winter.

In presence of,	Witness our hands,
The mark X of YOTUESH,	The mark † of CANONICUS,
ROGER WILLIAMS,	The mark ‡ of MIANTINOMO."
RANDAL HOLDEN,	
The mark ‡ of ASSOTEMUIT,	
The mark ‖ of MISHAMMOH,	
CANONICUS his son.	

"Memorandum, that I, Osamaquin freely consent that Mr. William Coddington,
and his friends united unto him, shall make use of any grass or trees on the main
land on Pawakasick side, and I do promise loving [and just] carriage of myself and
all my men to the said Mr. Coddington, and English, his friends united to him,
having received of Mr. Coddington five fathoms of wampum, as gratuity for [from]
himself and the rest.

Witness, { ROGER WILLIAMS,   The mark X of OSAMAQUIN.
         { RANDAL HOLDEN.

Dated the sixth day of the fifth month, 1638.

These deeds, with a number of receipts from the Indians, are upon the colony
records which Mr. Coddington had in his power when he obtained a commission to
be their Governor without the people's consent, and when they contended hotly
with him, it seems that he fled to Boston, where they sent after him, and prevailed
with him to sign an engagement on April 14th, 1652, in the presence of Robert
Knight and George Manning, to deliver up said deeds and records to such men as
the majority of the purchasers and freemen should appoint to receive them, and to
claim no more to himself than an equal share with the other purchasers. And the
above record shows that he had those deeds in his hands till May. 1653. The main
instance of bloodshed above referred to, was of a principal inhabitant of Newport,
who was charged with a capital crime before a town meeting, and was condemned
by them, and carried forth and shot to death in their presence. History of Providence. [Mass. Hist. Coll., Second series, Vol. IX, p. 184.]

the cause why any embrace Baptist principles. How well this agrees with their fear of a fair dispute with the learned Mr. Clarke the reader will judge, and what follows may afford further light.

Captain Johnson, speaking of the first president of Harvard College, says, that he was "fitted from the Lord for the work, and, by those that have skill that way, reported to be an able proficient both in the Hebrew, Greek and Latin languages, an orthodox preacher of the truths of Christ, and very powerful through his blessing to move the affections."[1] Mr. Hubbard speaking of Mr. Dunstar's being made president in 1640, says, " Under whom, that which was before but at best *schola illustra*, grew to the stature and perfection of a College, and flourished in the profession of all liberal sciences for many years." And Mr. Prince, upon the New England Psalm Book, says, " For a further improvement it was committed to the Rev. Mr. Henry Dunstar, president of Harvard College ; one of the greatest masters of the oriental languages, that hath been known in these ends of the earth."[2]

[1] Johnson, p. 168.

[2] Prince's preface to his own version of the psalms.—B.

"Among the early friends of the college none deserves more distinct notice than Henry Dunstar. He united in himself the character of both patron and President; for, poor as he was, he contributed, at a time of its utmost need, one hundred acres of land towards its support, besides rendering to it for a succession of years a series of official services well directed, unwearied and altogether inestimable. Under his administration the first code of laws was formed, rules of admission, and the principles on which degrees should be granted, were established. . . . . The charter of 1642, was probably, and that of 1650 was avowedly obtained on his petition. By solicitations among his personal friends, and by personal sacrifices he built the President's house. He was instant in season and out of season with the General Court for the relief of the College in its extreme wants. . . . .

" Dunstar's usefulness however was deemed to be at an end and his services no longer desirable, in consequence of his falling in 1653, as Cotton Mather expresses it, 'into the briars of anti-pædobaptism,' and of his having borne 'public testimony in the church at Cambridge against the administration of baptism to any infant whatever.' . . . . Indicted by the grand jury for disturbing the ordinance of infant baptism in the Cambridge church, sentenced to a public admonition on lecture day, and laid under bonds for good behavior, Dunstar's martyrdom was consummated by being compelled in October, 1654, to resign his office of President. . . . . He found the seminary a school, it rose under his auspices to the dignity of a college. No man ever questioned his talents, learning, exemplary fidelity, and usefulness.' Quincy's History of Harvard University, Vol. I, pp. 15—18.—Ed.

This eminent man was brought so far this year that, " he not only forbore to present an infant of his own unto baptism, but also thought himself under some obligation to bear his testimony in some sermons, against the administration of baptism to any infant whatsoever." His brethren were so vehement and violent against him therefor, as to desire him to cease preaching there, and procured his removal both from his office and from his living in the town;[1] and Mr. Jonathan Mitchell, their minister at Cambridge, wrote December 24th, 1653 :—

That day after I came from him, I had a strange experience; I found hurrying and pressing suggestions against pædobaptism, and injected scruples and thoughts whether the other way might not be right, and infant baptism an invention of men, and whether I might with good conscience baptize children, and the like. And these thoughts were darted in with some impression, and left a strange confusion and sickliness upon my spirit. Yet methought, it was not hard to discern that they were from the *evil one.* First, because they were rather injected, hurrying suggestions, than any deliberate thoughts, or bringing any light with them. Secondly, because they were unseasonable ; interrupting me in my study for the sabbath, and putting my spirit into [a] confusion, so I had much ado, to do ought in my sermon. It was not now a time to study that matter ; but when in the former part of the week, I had given myself to that study, the more I studied it, the more clear and rational light I saw for pædobaptism, but now these suggestions hurried me into scruples. .... It was a check to my former self-confidence, and it made me fearful to go needlessly to Mr. D., for methought I found a venom and poison, in his insinuations and discourses against pædobaptism. .... I resolved also on Mr. Hooker's principle, that I would have an argument, able to remove a mountain, before I would recede from, or appear against a truth or practice received among the faithful.[2]

Query. How did he know but that his hurry and darkness was caused by the opposition of his heart, and the injections of the devil against the truth ? Can anything be more unreasonable than his conclusion drawn from the time of his

---

[1]Governor Dudley died July 31, 1653, with these lines in his pocket, viz. :—

" Let men of God in courts and churches watch
O'er such as do a *toleration* hatch."

[2]Mitchell's Life, pp. 67—70. [Magnalia, Vol. II, p. 79.]

scruples? The fact was just this; in his own study he thought he saw a light for infant baptism, but when he came to converse with a gentleman who knew more than he did, it raised scruples in his mind about that practice. But where was the modesty of a youth not thirty years old, when he accused one of the most venerable fathers of that age, of having venom and poison in his discourses, only because his own self-confidence was shocked thereby? Sure I am that if any Baptist minister had told such a story, and that it made him fearful of going near a learned gentleman, whose arguments had brought him to scruple whether he had not been educated in a wrong way, but that he was resolved to have an argument able to work miracles before he would leave it, the other party would then have had such grounds, to charge the Baptist with wilfulness and obstinacy as they never yet had.

Rigidness is a word that both Episcopalians and Presbyterians have often cast upon our Plymouth fathers. Yet the Massachusetts now discovered so much more of that temper than they, that Mr. Dunstar, on October 24, 1654, resigned his office among them, and removed and spent his remaining days at Scituate, in Plymouth colony. And it seems remarkable that Mr. Charles Chauncy who, though he allowed believers to bring their infants, yet held that baptism was dipping, was, on the 27th of November following, made president of Harvard College in Mr. Dunstar's room.[1] Mr. Chauncy was born in Hartfordshire, in 1589; was educated in the university of Cambridge; " was incomparably well skilled in all the learned languages, especially in the oriental, and eminently in the Hebrew; in obtaining whereof his conversation with a Jew for the space of a year, was no little advantage.[2] He was successful in the ministry at Ware, in England, till, being persecuted, and having suffered much from Laud's party, he came to Ply-

[1]Magnalia, Book IV, p. 128. [Vol. II, p. 10.] [2]Ibid, Vol. I, p. 419.—ED.

mouth in 1638; in which place he preached about two years, and then, as has been noted, he removed and settled at Scituate, where, upon his taking the charge of that flock, he preached from that text, " Wisdom hath sent forth her maidens!" and reflecting in his discourse upon some compliances with the High Commission Court that he had been guilty of in his own country, he, with tears said, "Alas, Christians, I am no maiden! my soul hath been defiled with false worship! how wondrous is the free grace of the Lord Jesus Christ, that I should still be employed among the maidens of wisdom !"   Upon an invitation from his old people at Ware, he now came to Boston, with a design of returning to them, when the overseers of the college, " by their vehement importunity prevailed with him to accept the government of that society."[1] Here we will leave him, till we shall have further occasion to mention his testimony against degeneracy in our land.

Mr. Williams had many enemies and difficulties to encounter in pleading for the rights of his colony, but was wonderfully supported and carried through them all; of which some account is given in the following letter : —

From Sir Henry Vane's at Belleau, Lincolnshire.

April 1st, '53 (so called.)

MY DEAR AND LOVING FRIENDS AND NEIGHBORS OF PROVIDENCE AND WARWICK :—Our noble friend Sir Henry Vane, having the navy of England mostly depending on his care, and going down to the navy at Portsmouth, I was invited by them both to accompany his lady to Lincolnshire, where I shall yet stay as I fear until the ship is gone ; I must therefore pray your pardon that by the post I send this to London. I hope it may have pleased the most high Lord of sea and land to bring Capt. Ch-rst-n's ship and dear Mr. Dyre unto you, and with him the council's letters, which answer the petition Sir Henry Vane and myself drew up, and the council by Sir Henry's mediation granted us, for the confirmation of the charter, until the determination of the controversy. This determination you may please to understand is hindered by two main obstructions. The first is the mighty war with the Dutch, which makes England and Holland and the nations [to] tremble. This hath made the parliament set Sir Henry

[1]Magnalia, Book IV, pp. 134—136. [Vol. I, pp. 120—122.]

Vane and two or three more as commissioners to manage the war, which they have done with much engaging the name of God with them, who hath appeared in helping [of] sixty of ours against almost three hundred of their men-of-war, and perchance to the sinking and taking about one hundred of theirs, and but one of ours which was sunk by our own men. Our second obstruction is the opposition of our adversaries, Sir Arthur Haselrig and Colonel Fenwicke, who hath married his daughter, Mr. Winslow[1] and Mr. Hopkins, both in great place; and all the friends they can make in the parliament and council, and all the priests both Presbyterian and Independent; so that we stand as two armies ready to engage, observing the motions and postures each of other, and yet shy each of other. Under God the sheet anchor of our ship is Sir Henry, who will do as the eye of God leads him, and he faithfully promised me that he would observe the motion of our New England business, while I stayed some ten weeks with his lady in Lincolnshire. Besides here is [are] great thoughts and preparation for a new parliament; some of our friends are apt to think another parliament will more favor us and our cause than this has done. You may please to put my condition into your souls' cases; remember, I am a father and an husband; I have longed earnestly to return with the last ship, and with these, yet I have not been willing to withdraw my shoulders from the burthen lest it pinch others, and may fall heavy upon all; except you are pleased to give to me a discharge. If you conceive it necessary for me still to attend this service, pray you consider if it be not convenient that my poor wife be encouraged to come over to me, and to wait together on the good pleasure of God for the end of this matter. You know my many weights hanging on me, how my own place stands, and how many reasons I have to cause me to make haste, yet I would not lose their estates, peace and liberty [liberties] by leaving hastily. I wrote to my dear wife, my great desire of her coming while I stay; yet left it to the freedom of her spirit, because of the many dangers. Truly at present the seas are dangerous, but not comparably so much nor likely to be, because of the late great defeat of the Dutch, and their present sending to us offers of peace. My dear friends although it pleased God himself, by many favors to encourage me, yet please you to remember, that no man can stay here as I do, leaving a present employment there, without much self-denial, which I beseech God for more, and for you also, that no private respects or gains or quarrels may cause you to neglect the public and common safety, peace and liberties. I beseech the blessed God to keep fresh in your thoughts what he hath done for Providence Plantations. My dear respects to yourselves, wives and children; I beseech the eternal God to be seen amongst you. So prays your most faithful and affectionate friend and servant,

ROGER WILLIAMS.

P. S.   My love to all my Indian friends.

[1]Winslow died in the West Indies in 1655.

As men of all tempers and sentiments had resorted to that colony, and there had been from various quarters such interruptions of a regular administration of government as have been mentioned, it is not to be wondered at if many disorders appeared among them, of which enemies to their liberties did not fail to make all the advantage they could. Mr. Williams attended upon the difficult and important affairs of his agency another year, and then leaving the cause there with Mr. Clarke and other friends, he came over to take care of things here. He brought with him the following epistle, viz. :—

LOVING AND CHRISTIAN FRIENDS :—I could not refuse this bearer, Mr. Roger Williams, my kind friend and ancient acquaintance, to be accompanied with these few lines from myself to you, upon his return to Providence colony ; though perhaps my private and retired condition, which the Lord of his mercy hath brought me into, might have argued strongly enough for my silence ; but indeed something I hold myself bound to say to you, out of the Christian love I bear you, and for his sake whose name is called upon by you and engaged on your behalf. How is it that there are such divisions amongst you? Such headiness, tumults, disorders, injustice? the noise whereof echoes into the ears of all, as well friends as enemies, by every return of ships from those parts. Is not the fear and awe of God amongst you to restrain? Is not the love of Christ in you to fill you with yearning bowels one towards another, and constrain you not to live to yourselves but to him that died for you, yea, and is risen again? Are there no wise men amongst you? No public self-denying spirits, that at least upon grounds of common safety, equity and prudence can find out some way or means of union and reconciliation for you amongst yourselves, before you become a prey to common enemies? Especially since this state, by the last letter from the Council of State, gave you your freedom, as supposing a better use would have been made of it than there hath been. Surely when kind and simple remedies are applied and are ineffectual, it speaks loud and broadly, the high and dangerous distempers of such a body, as if the wounds were incurable. But I hope better things from you, though I thus speak, and should be apt to think, that by commissioners agreed on and appointed on all parts, and on behalf of all interests, in a general meeting, such a union and common satisfaction might arise, as through God's blessing might put a stop to your growing breaches and distractions, silence your enemies, encourage your friends, honor the name of God which of late hath been much blasphemed by reason of you ; and in particular refresh and revive the sad heart of him who mourns over your present evils, as being your affectionate friend, to serve you in the Lord.

H. VANE.[1]

Belleau, the 8th of February, 1653—4.

With this Mr. Williams returned to Providence ; but at first met with such treatment as caused him to address the town in the following manner :—

WELL BELOVED FRIENDS AND NEIGHBORS :—I am like a man in a great fog. I know not well how to steer. I fear to run upon the rocks at home, having had trials abroad. I fear to run quite backward (as men in a mist do) and undo all that I have been a [this late] long time undoing myself to do, viz. : to keep up the name of a people, a free people, not enslaved to the bondages and iron yokes of the great (both soul and body) oppressions the English and barbarians about us ; nor to the divisions and disorders within ourselves. Since I set the first step of any English foot into these wild parts, and have maintained a chargeable and hazardous correspondence with the barbarians, and spent almost five years time with the state of England, to keep off the rage of the English against us, what have I reaped of the root of being the stepping stone to so many families and towns about us, but grief, and sorrow, and bitterness ! I have been charged with folly for that freedom and liberty which I have always stood for ; I say liberty and equality both in land and government. I have been blamed for parting with Mooshawsick, and afterward Pawtuxet (which were mine own, as truly as man's coat upon his back) without reserving to myself a foot of land or an inch of voice in any matter, more than to my servants or strangers. It hath been told me that I labored for a licentious and contentious people ; that I have foolishly parted with town and colony advantages, by which I might have preserved both town and colony in as good order, as any [town or colony] in the country about us. This and ten times more I have been censured for, and at this present am called a traitor by [the] one party, against the state of England, for not maintaining the charter and the colony ; and it is said that I am as good as banished by yourselves, and that both sides wished that I might never have landed, that the fire of contention might have had no stop in burning. Indeed the words have been so sharp between myself and some lately, that at last I was forced to say, They might well silence all complaints if I once began to complain, who was unfortunately fetched and drawn from my employment, and sent to so vast distance from my family to do your work of a high and costly nature, for so many days, and weeks, and months together, and there left to starve, or steal, or beg, or borrow. But

---

[1] Copied from the original letter.

blessed be God who gave me favor to borrow one while, and to work another, and thereby to pay your debts there, and to come over with your credit and honor, as an agent from you, who had in your name grappled with the agents and friends of all your enemies round about you.   I am told that your opposites thought on me, and provided (as I may say) a sponge to wipe off your scores and debts in England, but that it was obstructed by yourselves, who rather meditated on means and new agents to be sent over to cross what Mr. Clarke and I had obtained.   But gentlemen, blessed be God who faileth not, and blessed be his name for his wonderful providences, by which alone this town and colony, and that grand cause of truth and [and truth of] freedom of conscience hath been upheld to this day.   And blessed be his name who hath again quenched so much of our fires hitherto, and hath brought your names and his own name thus far out of the dirt of scorn, reproach, &c.   I find among[st] yourselves and your opposites that of Solomon true, that the contentions of brethren, some that lately were so, are the bars of a castle, and not easily broken , and I have heard some of both sides zealously talking of undoing themselves by a trial in England.   Truly, friends, I cannot but fear you lost a fair wind lately, when this town was sent to for its deputies, and you were not pleased to give an overture unto the rest of the inhabitants about it ; yea, and when yourselves thought that I invited you to some conference tending to reconciliation, before the town should act in so fundamental a business, you were pleased to forestall that, so that being full of grief, shame and astonishment [amazement] ; yea, and fear that all that is now done (especially in our town of Providence) is but provoking the spirits of men to fury of desperation.   I pray your leave to pray you to remember (that which I lately told your opposites) *Only by pride cometh contention.* If there be humility on the one side, yet there is pride on the other, and .... certainly the eternal God will engage against the proud ; I therefore pray you to examine, as I have done them, your proceedings in this first particular.   Secondly, love covereth a multitude of sins. Surely your charges and complaints each against other have not hid nor covered anything, as we used to cover the nakedness of those we love. If you will now profess not to have disfranchised humanity [humility] and love, but that (as [once] David in another case) you will sacrifice to the common peace, and common safety, and common credit, that which may be said to cost you something, I pray your loving leave to tell you that if I were in your souls' case, I would send unto your opposites such a line as this :—" Neighbors, at the constant request, and upon the constant mediation which our neighbor Roger Williams, since his arrival, hath used to us, both for pacification and accommodation of our sad differences, and also upon the late endeavors in all the other towns for an union, we are persuaded to remove our obstruction, viz., that paper of contention between us, and to deliver it into the hands of our aforesaid neighbor, and to obliterate that order which that paper did occasion. This removed, you may be pleased [please] to meet with, and debate freely, and vote in all matters with us as if such grievances had not been amongst us.   Secondly, If yet ought remain grievous which we ourselves by free debate and conference cannot compose, we offer to be judged and censured by four men, which out of any part of the colony you shall choose two, and we the other.

Gentlemen, I only add, that I crave your loving pardon to your bold but true friend,   ROGER WILLIAMS.

This address had the desired effect ; and when the town came together, and Mr. Williams had a full hearing of the case, he, in the name of the town, drew an answer to Sir Henry Vane's letter, on August 27th, 1654, which now remains on record in his own hand writing as follows :—

SIR :—Although we are aggrieved at your late retirement from the helm of public affairs, yet we rejoice to reap the sweet fruits of your rest in your pious and loving lines, most seasonably sent unto us.   Thus the sun [Thus sir, your sun] when he retires his brightness from the world, yet from under the very clouds we perceive his presence, and enjoy some light and heat and sweet refreshings.   Sir, your letters were directed to all and every particular town of this Providence colony.   Surely Sir, among the many providences of the most High, toward this town of Providence, and this Providence colony, we cannot but see apparently his gracious hand, providing your honorable self for so noble and true a friend to an outcast and despised people.   From the first beginning of this Providence colony, (occasioned by the banishment of some in this place [these parts] from the Massachusetts) we say ever since, to this very day, we have reaped the sweet fruits of your constant loving-kindness and favor toward us.   Oh Sir ! whence then is it that you have bent your bow, and shot your sharp and bitter arrows now against us?   Whence is it that you charge us with divisions, disorders, &c.?   Sir, we humbly pray your gentle acceptance of our two-fold answer.

First, we have been greatly disturbed and distracted [distressed] by the ambition and covetousness of some amongst ourselves.   Sir, we were in complete order until Mr. Coddington (wanting that public self-denying spirit which you commend to us in your letter) procured, by most untrue information, a monopoly of part of the colony, viz. : Rhode Island to himself, and so occasioned our general disturbance and distractions.   Secondly, Mr. Dyre, with no less want of a public spirit, being ruined by party contentions with Mr. Coddington, and being betrusted to bring from England the letters of the Council of State for our re-unitings, he hopes for a recruit to himself by other men's goods ; and (contrary to the State's intentions and expressions) plungeth himself and some others, in most unnecessary and unrighteous plundering, both of Dutch and French, and English also, [all] to our great grief, who protested against such abuse of our power from England ; and the end of it is [even] to the shame and reproach of himself, and the very English name, [itself] as all these parts do witness."

Sir, our second answer is, (that we may not lay all the load upon other men's backs) that possibly a sweet cup hath rendered many of us wanton and too active ; for we have long drunk of the cup of as great liberties as any people that we can hear of under the whole heaven. We have not only been long free (together with all New England) from the iron yoke of wolfish bishops, and their popish ceremonies (against whose cruel oppressions God raised up your noble spirit in parliament)[1] but we have sitten quiet and dry, from the streams of blood spilt by that war in our native country. We have not felt the new chains of the presbyterian tyrants, nor in this colony, have we been consumed with the over-zealous fire of the (so called) godly Christian magistrates. Sir, we have not known what an excise means ; we have almost forgot what tythes are, yea, or taxes either, to church or commonwealth. We could name other special privileges, ingredients of our sweet cup, which your great wisdom knows to be very powerful (except more than ordinary watchfulness) to render the best of men wanton and forgetful. But blessed be your love, and your loving heart and hand, awakening any of our sleepy spirits by your sweet alarm ; and blessed be your noble family, root and branch, and all your pious and prudent engagements and retirements. We hope you shall no more complain of the saddening of your loving heart, by the men of Providence town or Providence colony, but that [Sir,] when we are gone and rotten, our posterity and children after us shall read in our town records, your pious and favorable letters and loving-kindness to us, and this our answer, and real endeavor after peace and righteousness ; and to be found Sir, your most obliged and most humble servants, the town of Providence, in Providence colony in New England.

GREGORY DEXTER, Town Clerk.

They chose commissioners who met with those from the other towns on August 31 ; when they agreed that the affairs that had been transacted by authority in each town should remain till further orders ; and that for the future their government should be managed according to their

---

[1]When those cruel oppressors had regained their power in 1662, so as to eject two thousand Protestant teachers out of their places, they wreaked their vengeance on this noble man, so as to have him publicly beheaded; but he died in an heroic manner.

charter; and that an assembly of six commissioners from each town, should transact the business of making laws, and trying their general affairs; and they ordered, "that Mr. Ezekiel Holiman, and Mr. John Greene, jun'r, are to view the general laws of the colony, and to represent [present] them to the next Court of Commissioners;" and they appointed a general election at Warwick, on Sept. 12.[1] At that election Mr. Williams was chosen president of the colony; and the assembly ordered, "that Mr. Roger Williams, and Mr. Gregory Dexter [are desired to] draw forth and send letters of humble thanksgiving, to his Highness the Lord Protector, and Sir Henry Vane, Mr. Holland, and Mr. John Clarke, in the name of the colony, and Mr. Williams is desired to subscribe them by virtue of his office." Thus far things appeared encouraging; but as tyranny and licentiousness are equally enemies, both to government and liberty, Mr. Williams often had both of them to contend with. Soon after this settlement a person sent a paper to the town of Providence. That it was blood-guiltness, and against the rule of the gospel, to execute judgment upon transgressors, against the private or public weal. But said Mr. Williams:—

That ever I should speak or write a tittle that tends to such an infinite liberty of conscience is a mistake, and which I have ever disclaimed and abhorred. To prevent such mistakes, I at present shall only propose this case. There goes many a ship to sea, with many [a] hundred souls in one ship, whose weal and woe is common; and is a true picture of a commonwealth, or an human combination, or society. It hath fallen out some-

---

[1] Providence Records. The names of the commissioners who composed and signed this amicable settlement were, Thomas Harris, Gregory Dexter, John Sayles, William Wickenden, John Brown and Henry Brown, for Providence; William Baulston, John Roome, Thomas Cornell, John Briggs and William Hall, for Portsmouth; Benedict Arnold, Richard Tew, John Coggshall, John Easton, William Lytherland and Thomas Gould, for Newport; John Greene, senior, Randal Holden, Ezekiel Holiman, John Greene, junior, John Townsend and Richard Townsend, for Warwick. Arnold left his father's party at Pawtuxet, and was received a freeman at Newport, in May, 1653; after which he was greatly promoted in the colony.—B.

The published R. I. Colonial Records give the name John Taylor, instead of John Sayles. Backus is undoubtedly correct, as it is known from other sources that

times that both Papists and Protestants, Jews and Turks, may be embarked
into one ship.   Upon which supposal, I [do] affirm that all the liberty of
conscience, that ever I pleaded for, turns upon these two hinges, that none
of the Papists, Protestants, Jews or Turks, be forced to come to the ship's
prayers or worship ; nor [secondly] compelled from their own particular
prayers or worship, if they practice any.   I further add, that I never denied
that notwithstanding this liberty, the commander of this ship ought to
command the ship's course ; yea, and also command that justice, peace and
sobriety to be kept and practiced, both among the seamen and all the pas-
sengers.   If any of the seamen refuse to perform their service, or passen-
gers to pay their freight ; if any refuse to help in person or purse towards
the common charges or defence ; if any refuse to obey the common laws
and orders of the ship, concerning their common peace or preservation ; if
any shall mutiny and rise up against their commanders and officers ; if any
should [shall] preach or write that there ought to be no commanders nor
officers, because all are equal in Christ, therefore no masters nor officers,
no laws nor orders, no corrections nor punishments ; I say, I never denied
but in such cases, whatever is pretended, the commander or commanders
may judge, resist, compel and punish such transgressors, according to their
deserts and merits.   This, if seriously and honestly minded, may if it so
please the Father of lights, let in some light to such as willingly shut not
their eyes.   I remain studious of your [our] common peace and liberty.

Roger Williams.[1]

This clear description of the difference between civil and
ecclesiastical affairs, and of the difference betwixt good
government on the one hand, and tyranny or licentiousness
on the other, confirmed by a correspondent practice through
fifty years of incessant labors, is more than a sufficient balance to all the slanders that various parties have cast upon
this ancient witness and advocate for the rights and liberties
of men, against the superstitions and enthusiasms of his day.
Having settled things as well as he could among his own
people, he, as president of his colony, addressed the general

---

there was a John Sayles in Providence at about this time, and there seems to be no
account of a John Taylor.   After the name of William Baulston, should be inserted that of Richard Barden.   It is given in the Colonial Records, and Backus by
omitting it represents Portsmouth as having only five commissioners though he has
said above that each town was to have six.   The name which stands in the first
edition as Richard Jew, we have changed to Richard Tew as it stands here and in
many other places on the Records.—Ed.

[1]History of Providence. [Mass. Hist. Coll., Second series, Vol. II. pp. 191, 192.]

assembly at Boston, in the following words, directed to their governor :—

Providence, 15, 9 month, '55 (so called.)

Much Honored Sirs :—It is my humble and earnest petition unto God and you, that you may be so pleased to exercise command over your own spirits that you may not mind myself nor the English of these parts (unworthy with myself of your eye) but only that face of equity (English and Christian) which I humbly hope may appear in these representations following :—

First, May it please you to remember, that concerning the town of Warwick, [in this colony] there lies a suit of two thousand pounds damages against you before his Highness and the Lords of the [his] Council. I doubt not, if you so please, but that (as Mr. Winslow and myself had well nigh ordered it) some gentlemen from yourselves and some from Warwick deputed, may friendly and easily determine that affair between you.[1]

Secondly, The Indians which pretend your names at Warwick and Pawtuxet (yet live as barbarously if not more than any in the whole colony) please you to know their insolences upon ourselves and cattle (unto twenty pounds damages per annum) are insufferable by English spirits; and please you to give credence that to all these they pretend your name, and affirm that they dare not (for offending you) agree with us, nor come to rules of righteous neighborhood, only they know you favor us not, and therefore send us for redress unto you.

Thirdly, Concerning four families at Pawtuxet, may it please you to remember the two controversies they have long (under your name) maintained with us, to the constant obstructing of all order and authority amongst

---

[1]Thus it appears that their invading their neighbors' rights at Warwick, caused troubles for them in England above ten years after, which Mr. Winslow, their agent, and Mr. Williams, could not quite settle; and they not complying with his reasonable proposal now, Gorton entered a complaint against them before king Charles's Commissioners in 1665, in which, besides all their other sufferings, they alleged that the Massachusetts took away and sold eighty head of their cattle. Massachusetts History, Vol. I, p. 103.

The controversy not being then settled, drew consequences after it enough to make our ears to tingle; an account of which I perceive was presented to king Charles the Second, in 1679, by Randal Holden and others, as agents from Warwick, wherein they, after describing their suffering at Boston, say, " and all this because that we (being without their jurisdiction) would not relinquish and forsake the sound doctrine and Christian principles taught us in our minority in the church of England." Upon which they go on to relate how that party disposition against them, after exasperating the Narragansetts in Philip's war, left Warwick defenceless to the fury of the savages; and that the English themselves did them other great injuries afterward. How should these things warn all to leave off contention before it is meddled with?

us. .... To obey his Highness' authority in this charter, they say they dare not for your sakes, though they live not by your laws, nor bear your common charges, nor ours, but evade both under color of your authority. .... Be pleased to consider how unsuitable it is for yourselves [if these families at Pawtuxet plead truth] to be the obstructors of all orderly proceedings amongst us; for I humbly appeal to your own wisdoms and experience, how unlikely it is for a people to be compelled to order and common charges, when others in their bosoms are by such (seeming) partiality exempted from both.

He then observes that there were in reality only W. Arnold and W. Carpenter, " very far in religion from you, if you knew all," who continued this obstruction ; and all their plea for it was a fear of offending the Massachusetts. And says he :—

I perceive your commerce with the people of this colony is as great as with any in the country, and our dangers (being a frontier people to the barbarians)[1] are greater than those of other colonies, and the ill consequences to yourselves would be not few nor small, and to the whole land, were we first massacred or mastered by them. I pray your equal and favorable reflection upon that your law, which prohibits us to buy of you all means of our necessary defence, of our lives and families ; yea, in this [most] bloody and massacring time. We are informed that tickets have rarely been denied to any English of the country ; yea, the barbarians, though notorious in lies, if they profess subjection, they are furnished ;[2] only ourselves, by former and latter denial, seem to be devoted to be the Indian shambles and massacres. The barbarians all the land over are filled with artillery and ammunition from the Dutch, openly and horridly, and from the English all over the country, by stealth, I know they abound so wonderfully, that their activity and insolence is grown so high, that they daily consult and hope and threaten to render us slaves, as they long since [and now most terribly] have made the Dutch. For myself, as through God's goodness, I have refused the gain of thousands by such a murderous trade, and think no law yet extant among yourselves or us, secure enough against such villainy ; so am I loth to see so many hundreds, if not some thousands, in this colony destroyed like fools and beasts without resistance. I grieve that so much blood should cry against yourselves ; yea, and I grieve that at this instant by these ships, this cry and the premises should now trouble his Highness and his council. For the seasonable

[1]When Mr. Williams first began among the Narragansetts, he said they had five thousand fighting men. Callendar, p. 70. [124.]
[2]See page 104.

preventing of which is this humble address presented to your wisdom, by him who desires to be your unfeigned and faithful servant,

ROGER WILLIAMS,
Of Providence Plantations, President."

He then requested them to record an order which the Lords of the Council gave him upon his last return from England, for his free taking of ship or landing at their ports, lest, says he, " forgetfulness hereafter again put me upon such distresses as, God knows, I suffered, when I last passed through your colony to our native country."[1]

The above were not all the trying things that he met with this year. No, Mr. William Harris, to whom he generously gave a share in Providence lands, and who had professed himself a Baptist, " sent his writings to the main and to the Island, against all earthly powers, parliaments, laws, charters, magistrates, prisons, punishments, rates, yea, against all kings and princes, under the notion that the people should shortly cry out, *No lords, no masters;* and in open court protested, before the whole colony assembled, that he would maintain his writings with his blood!" This was done at the election at Newport, May 22d, 1655. Upon which the Assembly appointed Messrs. Olney, Baulston and Roome to deal with him;[2] and Mr. Williams soon after received the following letter from the Lord Protector, viz. :—

GENTLEMEN :—Your agent here hath represented unto us some particulars concerning your government, which you judge necessary to be settled

---

[1]Massachusetts History, Vol. III. pp. 275—278. [R. I. Colonial Records.] This year the church of Charlestown began their dealings with Mr. Gould, which issued in his gathering the first Baptist church in Boston.

[2]In the published R. I. Colonial Records of the Court which sat at Newport, May 25, 1655, the election of which was held May 22, is the following :—" It is ordered, ... that, whereas, it hath been debated in this Court of some rising or taking up of arms to the opposing of authority by Mr. Thomas Olnie, Mr. Baulston and Mr. Roome are desired to treat with him and to declare to him the mind of this Court and the proceedings of the Colony concerning him." If this is the record to which Backus refers in the above statement,—and there appears to be no other to which he could refer,—it has been materially misread, either by him or by the copyist who prepared it for the press. It was nearly a year later, May 20, 1657, that Roger Williams impeached Harris for high treason The articles of impeachment com-

by us here, but by reason of the other great and weighty affairs of this commonwealth, we have been necessitated to defer the consideration of them to [a] further opportunity ; in the mean time we are [were] willing to let you know that you were [are] to proceed in your government according to the tenor of your charter, formerly granted on that behalf, taking care of the peace and safety of those plantations, that neither through [any] intestine commotions or foreign invasions, there do arise any detriment or dishonor to their [this] commonwealth or yourselves, as far as you by your care and diligence can prevent. And as for the things that are before us, they shall, as soon as the other occasions will permit, receive a just and sufficient [fitting] determination. And so we bid you farewell and rest,

Your very loving friend,   OLIVER, P.

March 29th, 1655.

To our trusty and well-beloved, the President, Assistants, and inhabitants of Rhode Island, together with the rest of the Providence Plantations in the Narragansett Bay, in New England.

Hereupon the Assembly met again, June 28th, and enacted as follows :—

Whereas, we have been rent and torn with divisions, and his Highness hath sent unto us an express command, under his hand and seal, to provide against intestine commotions, by which his Highness noteth, that not only ourselves are dishonored and endangered, but also dishonor and detriment redounds to the commonwealth of England ; it is ordered, that if any person or persons be found, by the examination and judgment of the General Court of Commissioners, to be a ringleader or ringleaders of factions or divisions among us, he or they shall be sent over at his or their own charges, as prisoners, to receive his or their trial or sentence at the pleasure of his Highness and the Lords of his Council.

These means had such effect, that at their Assembly at Warwick, in March following, I find it thus recorded :—

I, William Coddington, do freely submit to the authority of his Highness in the colony as it is now united, and that with all my heart.

Whereas, there have been differences depending between William Coddington, Esq. ; and Mr. William Dyre, both of Newport, we declare joy-

menced as follows :—" Whereas, William Harris, of Providence, published to all the towns in the colony dangerous writings containing his notorious defiance to the authority of his Highness the Lord Protector, &c., and the high Court of Parliament of England, as also his notorious attempts to draw all the English subjects of this colony into a traitorous renouncing of their allegiance and subjection, and whereas the said William Harris now openly in the face of the Court, declareth himself resolved to maintain the said writings with his blood," &c. Arnold's History of Rhode Island, Vol. I, p. 263.—ED.

fully for ourselves and heirs by this present record that a full agreement and conclusion is made between us, by our worthy friends, Mr. Baulston, Mr. Gorton, Mr. John Smith of Warwick, Mr. John Greene, jun. of Warwick, and Mr. John Easton ; and in witness whereof we subscribe our hands, and desire this to be recorded, this present 14th of March, 1655, –56.

In the presence of   WILLIAM CODDINGTON.
ROGER WILLIAMS, President,   WILLIAM DYRE.
JOHN ROOME,
BENEDICT ARNOLD,
JOHN GREENE, jun.[1]

Harris now turned, and cried up government and magistrates as much as he had cried them down before.[2]   Being desirous to make thorough work of it, Mr. Williams wrote again to the Massachusetts governor, and was encouraged by him to come to their Assembly at Boston, which he did, with an address, dated May 12th, wherein he says :—

HONORED SIRS :—Our first request was and is, for your favorable consideration of the long and lamentable condition of the town of Warwick, which hath been thus.   They are so dangerously and so vexatiously intermingled with the barbarians, that I have long admired the wonderful power of God in restraining and preventing very great fires, of mutual slaughters, breaking forth between them.   Your wisdoms know the inhuman insultations of these wild creatures, and you may be pleased also to imagine, that they have not been sparing of your name as the patron of all their wickedness against our English, men, women and children, and cattle, to the yearly damage of sixty, eighty and a hundred pounds.   The remedy, under God is only your pleasure that Pumham shall come to an agreement with the town or colony, and that some convenient way and time be set for their removal.   And that your wisdoms may see just grounds for such your willingness, be pleased to be informed of a reality of a solemn covenant between this town of Warwick and Pumham, unto which, notwithstanding [that] he pleads his being drawn to it by the awe of his superior sachems, yet I humbly offer that what was done was according to the law and tenor of the natives (I take it) in all New England and America, viz., that the inferior sachems and subjects shall plant and remove at the pleasure of the highest and supreme sachems, and I humbly conceive that it pleaseth the Most High and only wise to make use of such a bond of authority over

---

[1] This latter document is not in the published R. I. Colonial Records, it being regarded, perhaps, as the record of a merely private matter.—ED.

[2] Rhode Island Colony Records.   Williams against the Quakers, pp. 11—20.

them, without which they could not long subsist in human societies, in this wild condition wherein they are. Please you not to be insensible of the slippery and dangerous condition of this their intermingled cohabitation. I am humbly confident that all the English towns and plantations in all New England put together, suffer not such molestation from the natives as this one town and people. . . . . Be pleased to review this copy from the Lord Admiral[1] that this English town of Warwick should proceed, and [also] that if any of yours were there planted, they should by your authority be removed. And [we humbly conceive that] if the English, whose removes are difficult and chargeable, how much more these wild ones, who remove with little more trouble and damage than the wild beasts of the wilderness? . . . . This small neck, whereon they keep and mingle fields with the English, is a very den of wickedness, where they not only practice the horrid barbarisms of all kinds of whoredoms, idolatries and conjurations, but living without all exercise of actual authority, and getting store of liquors (to our grief) there is a confluence and rendezvous of all the wildest and most licentious natives and practices of the whole country.

He then proceeded to inculcate his other former requests, which now had their effect.[2]

The journal of governor Winthrop shows, that before they received Pumham and his fellows under their protection, the Court made them promise to keep the Sabbath, and to observe other religious rules;[3] but this account manifests the pernicious evil of invading others' rights under the mask of religion. They were awfully requited therefor. Beside the manifold troubles that it cost the Massachusetts before, in Philip's war; they not only " lost more of their substance as well as inhabitants than both Plymouth and Connecticut colonies together,"[4] but Pumham and his family had so great a hand therein, that the dispatching of a grandson of his is mentioned among the heroic exploits of Captain Denison, nine months after that war began. Pumham himself was "accounted the most warlike and best soldier of all the Narragansett sachems," and he was so bloody and barbarous through the war that when he was killed a few days before

[1]See page 165.
[2]Massachusetts History, Vol. III, pp. 278—283.
[3]Winthrop's Journal, pp. 121, 122.—Ed.
[4]Massachusetts History, Vol. III, p. 493.

Philip, within about fifteen or twenty miles of Boston, he, after he could not stand, " catching hold of an Englishman, that by accident came near him, had done him a mischief, if he had not been presently rescued."[1]

No sooner had Mr. Williams obtained such a settlement of old controversies in the country, than new ones arose in the following manner. George Fox, a very zealous teacher, had raised a new sect in England, who, from his, and his companions' quaking and trembling when they were brought before Gervase Bennett, a justice in Derby, in 1650, were called QUAKERS; though Fox says, it was because, " we bid him and his company tremble at the word of God."[2] In July (this year) a number of his followers arrived at Boston, but were soon imprisoned. Mr. Gorton wrote to them as I have related,[3] to which they gave an answer Sept. 28th, wherein they say :—

Friend, in that measure which we have received, which is eternal, we see thee, and behold thee, and have oneness with thee, in that which is meek and low, and is not of this world ;....and in that meek and low spirit we salute thee, and own that of God in thee, which is waiting for, and expecting the rising of that which is under the earth.....The ransomed of the Lord shall come to Zion with joy and gladness, being redeemed from kindreds, nations, tongues and people, by the blood of Jesus, which is spirit and life to all those that obey the light, which from the life doth come, for the life is the light of men, and whosoever believes in the light which they are enlightened with, shall not abide in darkness, which light we have obeyed in coming into these parts. The Lord is come and coming to level the mountains, and to rend the rocks of wisdom and knowledge, and to exalt that which is low and foolish to the wisdom of the world ; and blessed shall thou, and all those be, who meet him in this his work. From the servants and messengers of the Lord whom he hath sent and brought by the arm of his power into these parts of the world, for which we suffer bonds and close imprisonment.....Known in the world by these names,

CHRISTOPHER HOLDEN,   WILLIAM BREND,

JOHN COPELAND,   THOMAS THURSTON.

[1]Hubbard's History of that war, pp. 68—100.
[2]Williams's dispute with them, p. 27. Fox's answer, p. 26.—B.
[3]Page 165. See Appendix A at the close of this volume.—ED.

To this Gorton wrote a reply recited in page 110, and thereby as well as by what is in pages 116, 117, we may learn that he held with them about inward power, perfection in this life, and falling from grace received; but when he came to be acquainted with them, he did not concur with them about *Thee* and *Thou*, and the names of months and days, nor in the more important articles of refusing the oath of allegiance to civil government and a defensive war. After his return from England, his character as a member of civil society, and as a ruler, stands unimpeached in their records. And as Fox in his book in folio had said, " The Scriptures are the words of God, but Christ is the word of God in whom they end; and it is not blasphemy [as an author said it was] to say the soul is part of God, for it comes out of him, and rejoiceth in him;" which John Stubs tried to defend against Mr. Williams, from those words, God breathed into man the breath of life; Gorton, desiring liberty to speak, said, " If it be affirmed that God can be divided, and that man was a part of God, the Godhead was destroyed, and the soul of man. . . . . It is in the margin, the breath of *lives*, which Stubs acknowledged."[1]

On September 2, 1656, the Assembly at Boston wrote to the Commissioners of the United Colonies, and said :—

Having heard some time since, that our neighbor colony of Plymouth, our beloved brethren, in a great part seem to be wanting to themselves, in a due acknowledgment and encouragement to the ministry of the gospel, so as many pious ministers (how justly we know not) have deserted their stations, callings, and relations ; our desire is, that some such course may be taken, as that a pious orthodox ministry may be re-stated among them, that so the flood of errors, and principles of anarchy, [which will not long be kept out where Satan and his instruments are so prevalent as to prevail to the crying down of ministry and ministers] may be prevented. Here have [hath] arrived amongst us several persons, professing themselves Quakers, fit instruments to propagate the kingdom of Satan ; for the securing of ourselves and our neighbors from such pests, we have imprisoned them till they be despatched away to the place from whence they came.

[1]Williams, 1672, pp. 144, 145.

.... We hope that some general rules may be commended to each General Court, to prevent the coming [in] amongst us, from foreign places such notorious heretics as Quakers, Ranters, &c.

The Commissioners replied as follows :—

The Commissioners having considered the premises, cannot but acknowledge the godly care and zeal of the gentlemen of the Massachusetts to uphold and maintain those professed ends of coming into these parts, and of combination of the United Colonies, which, if not attended in the particulars aforesaid, will be rendered wholly frustrate, our profession miserably scandalized, ourselves become a reproach in the eyes of those that cannot without admiration behold our sudden defection from our first principles.

From this they went on to inculcate what Massachusetts Assembly had proposed.[1]

Though the Massachusetts rulers knew not whether those ministers had deserted their stations justly or not, yet they had approved of the settlement of Mr. John Mayo in Boston, Mr. Edward Bulkley at Concord, Mr. John Reyner at Dover (who preached in Boston, the winter after he left Plymouth,) Mr. Richard Blinman at Cape Ann, &c., all of whom were ministers in Plymouth colony, when the colonies confederated together in 1643. We learn also that Mr. John Norton arrived at Plymouth in 1635, where he preached the following winter, and Mr. Smith their pastor resigned his place to him, " and the church used him with all respect, and large offers, yet he left them, ... alleging that his spirit could not unite with them.[2] He went and settled at Ipswich, but after Mr. Cotton's death removed and took his place in Boston, where he with his colleague had not a little hand in spiriting up others to the above described measures. Another vigorous hand in the same work was Mr. Cobbet, who arrived at Boston in 1637, wrote against the Baptists in 1645, was minister at Lynn, when they suffered there in 1651, but upon the death of Mr. Nathaniel Rogers, took his place at Ipswich, where the town, on Feb. 25th, this year, voted to give him a hundred pounds to buy

[1]Massachusetts History, Vol. III, pp. 283—285.
[2]Winthrop, [Vol. I, p. 175.] Hubbard, [274.]

or build him a house, and taxed all the inhabitants to pay it. This being a new thing with them, several persons would not comply with the scheme; therefore distress was made upon them in 1657. Samuel Symonds, Esq., descended from an ancient and honorable family in Essex in England, was then one of the Massachusetts magistrates, and at last died their Deputy Governor. Before him George Giddings prosecuted Edward Brown, for seizing his pewter for said tax. The justice gave the plaintiff damage and costs, for which judgment he rendered these reasons :—

I understand this to be about a fundamental law; such a law as that God and nature has [have] given to a people; so that it is in the trust of their governors in highest place and others to preserve, but not in their power to take away from them. Of this sort are these, viz.: 1. Election of the supreme governors. 2. That every subject shall and may enjoy what he hath a civil right unto, so as it cannot be taken from him, by way of gift or loan, to the use or to be made the right or property of another man, without his own free consent. 3. That such laws, (though called liberties) yet more properly may be called rights, and in this sense this may be added, as a t[h]ird fundamental law, viz.:—That no custom or precedent ought to prevail in any moral case, that may appear to be sinful in respect of the breach of any law of piety against the first table, or of righteousness against the second. .... I shall add .... that it is against a fundamental law in nature, to be compelled to pay that which others do give; for then no man hath any certainty, or right to what he hath; if it be in the power of others by pretence of authority or without, to give it away (when in their prudence they conceive it to be for the benefit of the owner) without his own consent. .... The parliament may tax, and that justly, the whole country to give a [gift or] reward to one man for some service, for they are betrusted so to do. The reason is, it is levied upon the whole country, with their consent, and for the immediate benefit of the whole. But if they should do it between persons (though they should do it [so do] by power, and the person wronged hath no remedy in this world) yet it should be accounted tyranny. Is it not to take from Peter and give unto [it to] Paul?

Then after mentioning the law for ministers' salaries,[1] he says :—

Yet the law was framed so as such churches as chose to go in a voluntary way of weekly contribution, might so continue, as some churches in the country do to this day.

After an appeal to the County Court, the question, with the reasons each party had for and against it, was put to the General Court, whether the town vote for giving the said hundred pounds, bound the inhabitants, so that any of them who were unwilling, might be compelled to pay it, or not ? On October 20th, 1657, the deputies resolved it in the negative, which was non-concurred by the Council ; and influence enough was made the next day to bring a majority of the House round to the compelling side.[1]

Neither could they be content with using compulsion themselves, but the Commissioners of the United Colonies, wrote to that of Providence, September 25, 1656, to try to draw them into their measures towards the Quakers. To this the Assembly at Portsmouth, gave an answer, on March 13, 1657, wherein they say :—

Whereas freedom of different consciences to be protected from inforcements, was the principal ground of our charter, both with respect to our humble suit for it, as also to the true intent of the honorable and renowned parliament of England, in granting of the same to us, which freedom we still prize, as the greatest happiness that men can possess in this world, therefore we shall for the preservation of our civil peace and order, the more especially [seriously] take notice that those people, and any others that are here, or shall come among us, be impartially required, and to our utmost, constrained to perform all civil duties requisite. .... And in case they refuse it, we resolve to [take and] make use of the first opportunity to inform our agent, residing in England, &c.

They close with thankful acknowledgments of the Com-

---

[1] Massachusetts History, Vol. III, pp. 287—308. So in October, 1658, the majority of the House were against the law, to banish Quakers on pain of death; but the Council, with the help of some ministers, at last prevailed to carry it, by the majority of only one vote; which, when deacon Wozel [or Wiswal] understood, he wept, and though illness caused his absence, yet had notice been given him, he said, " If he had not been able to go, he would have crept upon his hands and knees, rather than it should have been." Thus those oppressions were carried on by a few men, against the sense of the best part of the community. Endicott, Bellingham, Bradstreet and Denison, with the ministers they sat under, were as guilty in this respect as any. Bishop's New England Judged, [Grove's Abridgment, pp. 101, 102.] Massachusetts History, Vol. I, p. 198, [182.]

missioners' care they had expressed for the peace and
welfare of the whole country, and saying :—

We rest yours, most affectionately, desirous of your honorable [honors
and] welfare.

JOHN SANFORD, Clerk of Assembly.

This did not content those Commissioners ; but they wrote
again the next fall, to which Governor Arnold and his Court
returned an answer, October 13th, which has been published.[1] And the contention growing more terrible the year
after, the Assembly at Warwick, November 5th, 1658, appointed Mr. Olney, Mr. Gorton and Mr. Crandal, who had

[1]Massachusetts History, Vol. I, pp. 526, 527. [453, 454.]—B.
The letter was as follows :—

" MUCH HONORED GENTLEMEN :—Please you to understand that there hath come
to our view a letter subscribed by the honored gentlemen, Commissioners of the
United Colonies, the contents whereof are a request concerning certain people
called Quakers, come among us lately, &c.

" Our desires are, in all things possible, to pursue after and keep fair and loving
correspondence and intercourse with all the colonies and with all our countrymen
in New England, and to that purpose we have endeavored (and shall still endeavor)
to answer the desires and requests from all parts of the country, coming unto us,
in all just and equal returns ; to which end, the colony have made suitable provision
to preserve a just and equal intercourse between the colonies and us, by giving
justice to any that demand it among us, and by returning such as make escapes
from you, or from the other colonies, being such as fly from the hands of justice,
for matters of crime done or committed amongst you, &c. And as concerning these
Quakers, (so called,) which are now among us, we have no law among us whereby
to punish any for only declaring by words, &c., their minds and understandings concerning the ways and things of God as to salvation and an eternal condition. And
moreover we find that in those places where these people aforesaid, in this colony,
are most of all suffered to declare themselves freely, and are only opposed by arguments in discourse, there they least of all desire to come, and we are informed that
they begin to loath this place, for that they are not opposed by the civil authority,
but with all patience and meekness are suffered to say over their pretended revelations and admonitions, nor are they like or able to gain many here to their way ;
and surely we find that they delight to be persecuted by civil powers, and when they
are so, they are like to gain more adherents by the conceit of their patient sufferings than by consent to their pernicious sayings. And yet we conceive that their
doctrines tend to very absolute cutting down and overturning relations and civil
government among men, if generally received. But as to the damage that may in
likelihood accrue to the neighbor colonies by their being entertained, we conceive
it will not prove so dangerous, (as else it might) in regard of the course taken by
you to send them away out of the country as they come among you. But, however,
at present we judge it requisite, and do intend to commend the consideration of
their extravagant outgoings unto the General Assembly of our colony in March

suffered from them at Boston, with Mr. Trip, to draw a letter to their agent in England,[1] which is as follows :—

WORTHY SIR, AND TRUSTY FRIEND, MR. CLARKE :—We have found, not
only your ability and diligence, but also your love and care to be such concerning the welfare and prosperity of this colony, since you have been entrusted with the more public affairs thereof, surpassing the [that] no small
benefit which [formerly] we had of your presence here at home, that we in
all straits and incumbrances, are emboldened to repair unto you, for further
and continued care, counsel and help, finding that your solid and Christian
demeanor hath gotten no small interest in the hearts of our superiors,
those noble and worthy senators, with whom you had to do in our behalf,
as it hath constantly appeared in our [your] addresses made unto them,
[which] we have by good and comfortable proofs found, having plentiful
experience thereof. The last year we had laden you with much employment, which we were then put upon by reason of some too refractory among
ourselves, wherein we appealed unto you for advice, for the more public
manifestation of it, with respect to our superiors ; but our intelligence [it
seems] fell short in that great loss of the ship, which we concluded [is con-
ceived] here to be cast away. We have now a new occasion given us by
an old spirit, with respect to the colonies round about us, who [which]
seem to be offended with us because of a sort of people, called by the name
of Quakers, who are come amongst us, who [and] have raised up divers
who at present seem to be of their spirit, whereat the colonies about us
seem to be offended with us, being the said people have their liberty with
[amongst] us, are entertained in our houses, or any of our assemblies ;
and for the present we have found no just cause to charge them with the
breach of the civil peace ; only they are constantly going forth amongst
them about us, and vex and trouble them about [in point of] their religion
and spiritual state, though they return with many a foul scar in their bodies

next, where we hope there will be such order taken, as may, in all honest and conscientious manner, prevent the bad effects of their doctrines and endeavors ; and so,
in all courteous and loving respects, and with desire of all honest and fair commerce with you, and the rest of our honored and beloved countrymen, we rest,

  Yours in all loving respects to serve you,

                              BENEDICT ARNOLD, President.
                              WILLIAM BAULSTON,
                              RANDALL HOWLDEN,
                              ARTHUR FENNER,
                              WILLIAM FIELD.

From Providence, at the Court of Trials held for the Colony, October 13, 1657.
To the much honored, the General Court, sitting at Boston, for the Colony of
Massachusetts."—ED.

[1]They were " chosen and authorized to draw up a letter to be sent to Mr. John
Clarke, in England, to be presented to his Highness and Council." Rhode Island
Records.—ED.

for the same.[1] And the offence our neighbors take against us, is because
we take not some course against the said people, either to expel them from
amongst us, or take such courses against them as themselves do, who are
in fear lest their religion should be corrupted by them. Concerning which
displeasure that they seem to take, it was expressed to us in a solemn letter, written by the Commissioners of the United Colonies at their sitting,
as though they would either bring us in to act according to their scantling,
or else take some course to do us a greater displeasure. A copy of which
letter we have herewith sent unto you, wherein you may perceive how they
express themselves; as also we have herewith sent our present answer
unto them, to give you what light we may in the matter. There is one
clause in the [their] letter which plainly implies a threat, though courtly
[covertly] expressed as their manner is; which we gather to be this, that
[as] themselves (as we construe [conceive] it) have been much awed in
point of [their] continued subjection to the state of England, lest in case
they should decline, England might prohibit all trade with them, both in
point of exportation and importation of any commodities, which were an
host sufficiently prevalent to subdue New England, not being able to subsist; even so they seem [secretly] to threaten us, by cutting us off from
all commerce and trade with them, and thereby to disable us of any comfortable subsistance, being that the concourse of shipping, and all other
sorts [so of all kinds] of commodities are universally conversant among
themselves; as also knowing that ourselves are not in a capacity to send
out shipping of ourselves, which in great measure is occasioned by their
oppressing of us, as yourself well knows; as in many other respects so in
this for one, that we cannot have anything from them, for the supply of our
necessities, but in effect they make the price, both of our commodities and
their own. Also, because we have no English coin, but only that which
passeth among these barbarians, and such commodities as are raised by the
labor of our hands, as corn, cattle, tobacco, &c., to make payment in,
which they will have at their own rates, or else not deal with us; whereby, though they gain extraordinarily by us, yet, for the safeguard of their
[own] religion, they may seem to neglect themselves in that respect; for
what will not men do for their God? Sir, this is our earnest and pressing
request unto you in this matter, that as you may perceive by our answer
unto the United Colonies [that] we fly as our refuge in all civil respects to
his Highness and Honorable Council, as not being subject to any other in
matters of our civil state, so may it please you to have an eye and ear
open in case our adversaries should speak [seek] to undermine us in our
privileges granted unto us, and plead our cause in such sort, as that we

[1]Many were whipped, some were branded, and Holder, Copeland and Rouse,
three single young men, had each his right ear cut off in the prison at Boston, the
16th of September this year. Grove's Abridgment of Bishop, pp. 64, 91, 92.

may not be compelled to exercise any civil power over men's consciences, so long as human orders in point of civility are not corrupted and violated, which our neighbors about us do frequently practice, whereof many of us have absolute [large] experience, and [do] judge it to be no less than a point of ABSOLUTE CRUELTY.

JOHN SANFORD, Clerk of Assembly.[1]

The Commissioners of the colonies who met at Boston, September 2, 1658, and continued their meeting to September 23, closed their acts with saying:—

Whereas there is an accursed and pernicious sect of heretics, lately risen up in the world, who are commonly called Quakers, who take upon them to be immediately sent of God, and infallibly assisted, who do speak and write blasphemous things, despising government, and the order of God in church and commonwealth; speaking evil of dignities, reproaching and reviling magistrates, and the ministers of the gospel, seeking to turn the people from the faith, and to gain proselytes to their pernicious ways; and whereas the several jurisdictions have made divers laws to prohibit their coming amongst them; (but they refusing to obey them, and still making disturbance) it is therefore propounded, and seriously commended to the several General Courts, ... to make a law, that all Quakers formerly convicted and punished as such, shall (if they return again) be imprisoned, and forthwith banished or expelled out of the said jurisdiction, under pain of death.

All the eight Commissioners signed this advice, only the Governor of Connecticut said, " Looking at the last as a query and not an act, I subscribe, John Winthrop."[2]   Such

---

[1]As Oliver Cromwell died Sept. 3, 1658, and his son Richard was chosen Protector in his stead, their Assembly of May 17, 1659, sent an address to the latter, wherein they say, " May it please your Highness to know, that this poor colony of Providence Plantations, mostly consists of a birth and breeding of the providence of the Most High, we being an outcast people, formerly from our mother nation in the bishops' days, and since from the New English over-zealous colonies; our whole frame being like unto the present frame and constitution of our dearest mother England; bearing with the several judgments and consciences each of other in all the towns of our colony [the] which our neighbor colonies do not, which is the only cause of their great offence against us..... Sir, we dare not interrupt your high affairs with the particulars of our wilderness condition, only [we] beg your eye of favor to be cast upon our faithful agent, Mr. John Clarke, and unto what humble addresses he shall at any time present your Highness with in our behalf."   Colony Records.

[2]Records of the United Colonies. The other Commissioners were Endicott and Bradstreet, of Massachusetts; Prince and Winslow, of Plymouth; Taliot, of Connecticut; and Newman and Leet, of New Haven.

a law was made at Boston the next month, but the like was not done in any of the other colonies. At Plymouth they had prevailed for two years past, with the majority of the Court, to imprison, fine and whip the Quakers, and to send some of them out of the colony ; and the manner of their proceedings was as follows :—

Mr. John Brown, who had long been one of their magistrates, and often a commissioner for his colony, took a voyage to England. Captain James Cudworth of Scituate, was a magistrate these two years ; and near the beginning of this year he entertained Copeland and Brend, two of the Quakers, at his house a night or two, and says:—

I thought it better so to do, than with the blind world, to censure, condemn and rail at them, when they neither saw their persons, nor knew any of their principles ; but the Quakers and myself cannot close in divers things ; and so I signified to the Court, I was no Quaker, but must bear my testimony against sundry things that they held, as I had occasion and opportunity. But withal I told them, that as I was no Quaker, so I would be no persecutor. This spirit worked in those two years that I was of the magistracy ; during which time, I was on sundry occasions forced to declare my dissent, in sundry actings of that nature ; which, although I did with all moderation of expression, together with respect unto the rest, yet it wrought great disaffection and prejudice against me.

A person took pains to go to Marshfield to procure a warrant to apprehend the Quakers he had entertained, which Mr. Hatherly understanding, said, " Mr. Envy hath procured this ;" and in lieu of it, gave them a pass under his hand, with which they travelled to Plymouth ; but were there seized and whipped by order of three other magistrates. And says Captain Cudworth :—

Truly the whipping of them with that cruelty as some have been, and their patience under it hath sometimes been the occasion of gaining more adherence to them, than if they had suffered them openly to have preached a sermon.....The Massachusetts after they have whipped them, and cut their ears, they have now gone the farthest step they can ; they banish them upon pain of death, if ever they come there again. We expect we must do the like ; we must dance after their pipe ; now Plymouth saddle is

on the *Bay* horse, we shall follow them on the career. . . . . All these carnal and antichristian ways being not of God's appointment, effect nothing
as to hindering of them in their way or course. It is only the word and
spirit of the Lord, that is able to convince gainsayers. They are the
mighty weapons of the Christian warfare, by which great and mighty
things are done and accomplished. . . . . Our civil powers are so exercised
in things appertaining to the kingdom of Christ, in matters of religion and
conscience, that we can have no time to effect any thing that tends to the
promotion of the civil weal, or prosperity of the place ; but now we must
have a state religion, such as the powers of the world will allow, and no
other ; a state ministry, and a state way of maintenance ; and we must
worship and serve the Lord Jesus, as the world shall appoint us. We must
all go to the public place of meeting, in the parish where we dwell, or be
presented. I am informed of three or fourscore last Court, presented for
not coming to public meetings ; and let me tell you how they brought this
about. You may remember a law once made, called Thomas Hinckley's
law, That if any neglected the worship of God, in the place where he lives,
and set up a worship contrary to God, and the allowance of this government, to the public profanation of God's holy day and ordinance, [he]
shall pay ten shillings. This law would not reach what then was aimed at ;
because he must do so and so ; that is, all things therein expressed, or else
break not the law. In March last, a Court of Deputies was called, and
some acts touching Quakers were made ; and then they contrived to make
this law serviceable to them ; and that was by putting out the word "And,"
and putting in the word " Or," which is a disjunctive, and makes every
branch become a law. So now, if any neglect, or will not come to the
public meetings, ten shillings for every defect. . . . . And these men altering
this law last March, yet left it dated, June 6th, 1651,[1] and so it stands as
the act of a General Court ; they to be the authors of it seven years before
it was in being ; and so yourselves have your part and share in it, if the
records lie not. But what may be the reason that they should not by
another law, made and dated by that Court, as well effect what was intended, as by altering a word, and so the whole sense of the law ; and leave
this their act, by the date of it, charged on another Court's account? Surely
the chief instruments in the business, being privy to an act of parliament
for liberty, should too openly have acted repugnant to a law of England ;
but if they can do the thing, and leave it on a Court, as making it six years

---

[1]These things Capt. Cudworth wrote to Mr. Brown, then in England, who let
Bishop publish them, pages 168--176. Morton says that Mr. Dunstar, " was useful
and helping in defending the truth against the Quakers; and that he fell asleep
in the Lord, in 1659." [186.] After Mr. Brown returned from England, he and Cudworth were called to account for this letter, but were not punished. Cudworth was
restored to the magistracy in 1674, and died their Deputy Governor, in 1681. Plymouth Records.

before the act of parliament, there can be no danger in this.....If we can but keep the people ignorant of their liberties and privileges, then we have liberty to act in our own wills what we please.....Through mercy we have yet among us worthy Mr. Dunstar, whom the Lord hath made boldly to bear testimony against the spirit of persecution.[1]

For the above things those two magistrates Hatherly and Cudworth were left out of all their offices, in June, this year. At the same time it is meet that posterity should know how those Quakers behaved under their sufferings. Humphrey Norton, one of their teachers and authors, was sent out of Plymouth colony in 1657, for being an extravagant person;[2] which charge, says Bishop, could not be proved.   On election day, June 1st, 1658, he and John Rouse came again to Plymouth, and were taken up and whipped, Norton twenty-three lashes, and Rouse fifteen, which, Bishop says, " they received for no other thing but for coming into that colony in the will of God."[3]   The records inform us, that when they were brought before the Assembly, June 3d, Norton " said unto the Governor sundry times, *Thou liest!* and said unto him, *Thomas, thou art a malicious man*, &c. For these things, and for refusing the oath of allegiance to any civil government, they were then whipped, and for officers' fees were imprisoned till the tenth, when they were released, and went to Rhode Island, where, on the 16th, Norton wrote a letter to Mr. Alden, one of their magistrates, and another to the Governor, with an answer to Christopher Winter's deposition against them, all which the Court ordered to be recorded."   The beginning and end of that to the Governor, I took from thence with my own hand, which is in the words and letters following :—

Thomas Prince, thow who hast bent thy hart to worke wickedness, and with thy tongue hast thow set forth deceite ; thou imaginest mischief upon thy

[1]See page 178, note.
[2]In the Massachusetts Records his offense is somewhat differently stated. " October 6, 1657. At this Court, Humphrey Norton, one of those commonly called Quakers, being summoned, appeared and was examined and found guilty of divers horrid errors, and was sentenced speedily to depart the government and was forthwith expelled the government by the under marshal."—ED.
[3]New England Judged, [Grove's Abridgement,] pp. 163—179.

bed, and hatcheth thy hatred in thy cecrett chamber ; the strength of dark-
nes is over thee, and a malliciouse mouth hast thow opened against God
and his anointed, and with thy tongue and lipps hast thow uttered perverse
things ; thow hast slaundered the innocent by railing, lying and false accusations, and with thy barborouse hart hast thow caused theire bloud to bee
ohod. Thow hast through all these things broke and transgresed the laws
and waies of God, and equitie is not before thy eyes. The curse causles
cannot come upon thee, nor the vengance of God unjustly cannot fetch
thee up ; thow makest thyself merry with thy cecrett mallice. .... The
day of thy wailing will bee like unto that of a woman that murthers the
fruite of her wombe ; the anguish and paine that will enter upon thy reignes
will be like knawing worms lodging betwixt thy hart and liver : When
these things come upon thee, and thy backe bowed downe with pain, in
that day and houre thow shalt know to thy griefe, that prophetts of the
Lord God wee are, and the God of vengance is our God.

HUMPHREY NORTON.

I have sent thee heer inclosed a reply to C. Winter's deposition, alsoe I
have sent already a true relation of parte of thy proceedings towards London, with a coppy of the fines laid on, and levied of the people of God,
with a coppy of thy late laws.

Superscribed, For the governor of Plymouth pattent, this with care and
speed.

After this prophecy Mr. Prince continued Governor of
that colony near fourteen years, and then died in peace, (for
ought we know). His son was a justice of peace in his day,
and his grandson was a learned and pious minister at Boston, whose writings have furnished many valuable materials
for our history. It ought also to be known, that in *rending the
rocks of wisdom and knowledge*, and *exalting that which is low*,
the Quakers meant to have civil as well as ecclesiastical
government managed by the above described power. For
in those times George Fox published a large book in folio,
in the 170th page of which he said :—

The magistrate of Christ, the help government for him, he is in the light
and power of Christ ; and he is to subject all under the power of Christ,
into his light, else he is not a faithful magistrate : and his laws here are
agreeable, and answerable according to that of God in every man ; when
men act contrary to it, they do evil ; so he is a terror to evil-doers, dis-
cerneth the precious and the just from the vile ; and this is a praise to
them that do well.

17

When Mr. Williams mentioned this passage, as one proof, that their spirit tended to arbitrary government, and fiery persecution, they said upon it :—

Is there one word of persecution here? Or can Roger Williams think himself a Christian, and look upon it to be persecution, for Christ's magistrates, by Christ's light and power, to subject all under the power of Christ, and to bring all into this light of Christ? Or can he think such an one an unfaithful magistrate? Or are those laws, and the execution of them, persecution, that are agreeable and answerable to that of God in every man? These are George Fox's words. Such magistrates, such laws, such power, and light, and subjection, is G. F. for, and no other.[1]

This opens the plain cause why they militated so hard against other magistrates and government, as in the lamentable instances following.

Our Lord directed his disciples to depart from any house or city, that they should travel into, when they refused to receive them ; and when the Gadarenes besought him to depart out of their coasts, he did so; and we have no account of his forcing himself upon them again. The Quakers took another course. Three of them who were banished, on pain of death, returned again to Boston, and were condemned to die ; and William Robinson gave in a paper to the Court, which contains the following reason for his conduct therein, viz. :—

On the eighth day of the eighth month, 1659, in the after part of the day, in traveling betwixt Newport in Rhode Island, and Daniel Gould's house, with my dear brother Christopher Holder, the word of the Lord came expressly to me, which did fill me immediately with life and power, and heavenly love by which he constrained me, and commanded me to pass to the town of Boston, my life to lay down in his will, for the accomplishing of his service, that he had there to perform at the day appointed. To which heavenly voice I presently yielded obedience, not questioning the Lord how he would bring the thing to pass. .... For the Lord had said unto me, My soul shall rest in everlasting peace, and my life shall enter into rest, *for being obedient* to the God of my life.

Marmaduke Stevenson, gave in another paper, informing the Court, how he heard a *voice* as he was plowing in York-

[1]Williams, p. 207. Fox's Answer, pp. 229, 230.

shire, saying, *I have ordained thee a prophet unto the nations;* and after he came to Rhode Island, he says :—

The word of the Lord came unto me saying, Go to Boston, with thy brother William Robinson. .... This is given forth to be upon record, that all people may know, who hear it, that we came not in our own will, but in the will of God.[1]

This was their way of following what they called the light, and the clearest account of what they meant thereby, that I have seen, is contained in the following sentences directed to Mr. Williams, viz. :—

Thou wrongest the Quakers in saying, they confess their light to be conscience. In this thou pervertest their words, and thou wouldest have it so; for George Fox's words are, The light which you call conscience, which is the light of Christ, as you may see all along in his book. .... Thou hast read our books with an evil eye, or else thou mightest see how often we mention, that Christ hath bought us with a price, which is his blood; and how that all died in Adam, and how that Christ died for all, that they that live, might live to him; and that all might believe in him, who died for them; and if they do not, they are condemned with the light, which they should believe in. .... Christ lighteth every man that cometh into the world,[2] with life in him, the word and faith. He is the light of the world, and saith, Believe in the light, that ye may become children of light, and he that believeth is saved, and he that doth not is condemned. And the condemnation is the light that is come into the world; which light is saving to them that believe in it, and condemning to them that do not believe in it, but hate it, whose deeds be evil. John 3.[3]

In all this there is a manifest confounding of grace and works, law and gospel, which the inspired writers took great pains to keep distinct. And since Christ himself says, " God sent, not his Son into the world to condemn the world; but that the world through him might be saved," " Think not that I will accuse you to the Father; there is one that accuseth you, even Moses, in whom ye trust;" John 3. 17, and 5. 45; was not the zeal of these men like that we read of Rom. 10. 2—4? Did they not trust in the law instead

[1] Bishop, [Grove's Abridgment,] pp. 127—133.
[2] Williams says, he believes Fox, in his book in folio, repeats these words, near or quite a thousand times. P. 186.
[3] Fox against Williams, Second Part, pp. 4, 6, 10.

of the gospel? As to the person of the Saviour, Mr. Williams says:—

Fox in all his book cannot endure to hear of the word *Human*, as being a new name, and never heard of in Scripture. I said in public, many words truly and properly English, are commendably used that are not in Scripture, in English. The word human comes from the Latin *humanus*, signifying pertaining, or belonging to man. So a human soul or body is such as all mankind have. Hence I told them that the word *anthropinos peirasmos*, I. Cor. 10, might have been turned *human*, but is truly turned, no temptation but such as is *common to man*. G. Fox knows, that if Christ Jesus be granted to have had such a soul and body as is human, or common to man, down falls their monstrous idol of a Christ, called light within.

To this Fox answers:—

For thee and the priests to give such names to Christ, our Lord and Saviour, which the Scriptures do not give, and yet say the Scriptures are the rule, that is abominable. And there is no such word in I. Cor. 10, that calleth Christ's body and soul *human;* and whether is Christ's body celestial or terrestial, or which glory doth he bear? I. Cor. 15, 14. G. F. doth grant, and all the Quakers, that Christ was made *like unto us*, sin excepted, and had *a body and soul*, or else how could he suffer? and is risen, the *same that descended is ascended*, as the apostle saith.[1]

And I have seen other of their writings which hold expressly, that Christ brought the same body from heaven, that he carried thither again. But they reckoned it " *abominable*" for Mr. Williams to use a word concerning our Saviour's humanity, that is not in our translation, while he at the same time approved of the reading as it is; yet when Hebrews i. 3, was brought in those times to prove the *personality* of the Trinity, the Quakers said, " That is falsely translated, for in the Greek it is not *person* but *substance*."[2] And said Mr. Samuel Hubbard, " They turn the Holy Scriptures into allegories, all unless some which they wrest to their own destruction, as the apostle Peter saith?"

They expressly held to a power of direction within them, superior to the Scriptures, which carried them into actions that light from thence, or from reason could not justify;

[1]Williams, p. 51; Fox, p. 43.   [2]Bishop, [Grove's Abridgment,] p. 360.

and their only way was to appeal to an inward motion or voice. As for instance, George Bishop speaks of Deborah Wilson, as a " modest woman, of retired life, and sober conversation ; and that bearing a great burthen for the hardness and cruelty of the people, she went through the town of Salem naked, as a sign, which she having in part performed, was laid hold of, and bound over to appear at the next Court of Salem, where the wicked rulers sentenced her to be whipped."[1]   Lydia Wardwel, a married woman of Hampton, went in the same manner into the meeting-house in Newbury, in time of public worship ; for which she met with the like treatment.[2]   Mr. Williams referred the Quakers to these instances which their own author had published ; and told them they never could persuade souls not bewitched, that the Holy Spirit would move them to do so ; to which they answer thus :—

We do believe thee, in that dark, persecuting, bloody spirit, that thou and the New England priests are bewitched in, you cannot believe that you are naked from God and his clothing, and blind ; and therefore hath the Lord in his power moved some of his sons and daughters to go naked ; yea, and they did tell them in Oliver's days, and the long parliaments, that God would strip them of their church profession, and of their power, as naked as they were.   And so they were true prophets and prophetesses to the nation, as many sober men have confessed since ; though thou and the old persecuting priests in New England remain in your blindness and nakedness. . . . . As thou didst in the dispute, so now, thou makest a great ado with our men and women going naked.   We told them then, we owned no such practice in any, unless they were called unto it by the Lord. . . . . He beginneth again to upbraid us with our men's and women's going naked, as if it were a thing commonly allowed among us in their wills, without the motion of God.[3]

As an impartial historian I thought it duty thus to state these plain facts and sentiments on both sides ; for upon Dr. Mather's saying, that some good men formerly took that wrong way of reclaiming heretics by persecution, the Quakers spent seventeen pages in the most striking recital of what they suffered in those times that their art would admit of, in

[1]Bishop, [Grove's Abridgment] p. 383.—Ed. [2]Ibid, p. 367.—Ed. [3]Fox, pp. 9, 28, 32.

order to prove, that no good man could be an actor therein.
To fix this prejudice more lastingly in the minds of all, they
turned it into verse, saying :—

> These that in conscience cannot wrong a worm,
> Are fin'd and whip'd, because they can't conform ;
> And time hath been, which ne'er shall be forgot,
> God's servants have been hanged, none knows for what,
> Except for serving of their blessed Lord,
> For quaking and for trembling at his word.
> Let these black days, like the fifth of November,
> Be writ in red, for ages to remember.[1]

And they are remembered in such a manner to this day,
that a person can hardly plead for equal liberty of conscience in Massachusetts without having the disorders of
Rhode Island colony brought up against it ; nor for the good
doctrine, and family orders of those fathers, among some in
the latter colony, without having hot irons and halters
thrown in his teeth ?   Not only so, but we have lately seen
artful men trying to prevent our union in the cause of our
civil liberties by these means.   But from the above facts the
reader may judge, whether an invasion of each other's rights,
under the name of religion, was not the real cause of those
dreadful broils ; which a true acknowledgment thereof, both
as to property and conscience, would have prevented ;
whether the grand error on both sides, was not the assuming a power to govern religion, instead of being governed
by it.

On October 20th, Robinson, Stevenson and Mary Dyre,
received the sentence of death.[2]   It was executed upon the

---

[1] Magnalia, Book 7, p. 22. [Vol. II, pp. 453, 454.] Whiting's Answer, pp. 11—29.

[2] In justice to the rulers on whom rests the responsibility of this persecution, its
whole history should be related.

September 14, 1659, William Robinson, Marmaduke Stevenson, Nicholas Davis,
and Mary Dyer, were banished on pain of death. "Nicholas Davis and Mary Dyer,"
says Bishop, addressing the rulers of Massachusetts colony, "found freedom to depart your jurisdiction, the one to Plymouth patent, the other to Rhode Island ; but
the other two, were constrained in the love and power of the Lord, not to depart
but to stay in your jurisdiction and to try your bloody law unto death."   Remaining
in Massachusetts, they were apprehended, whipped and again set free on pain of

two men, the 27th.   The woman was brought with them to
the gallows, but at the intercession of her son of Newport
and others, she was then reprieved, and sent away.[1] Returning again the next spring, she was hanged, June 1st, 1660.[2]
Twelve days after, the Court of Plymouth repealed one or
more of the sharpest laws they had made against that people.[3]   Charles the Second had been restored to the crown

death.   October 8, Mary Dyer came to Boston to visit a Quaker imprisoned there.
October 15, " W. Robinson and M. Stevenson," says Bishop, " came to Boston, and
with them Alice Cowland, who came *to bring linen to wrap the dead bodies of them
who were to suffer*."   Several other Quakers also attended them.   " These all came
together," continues Bishop, "in the moving and power of the Lord, as one, *to look
your bloody laws in the face*, and to accompany those who were to suffer by them.
Upon the trial of Robinson, Stevenson and Mrs. Dyer, the Governor said " that he
desired not their death;" and again, " We have made many laws, and endeavored by
several ways to keep ye from us, and neither whipping nor imprisonment nor cutting off ears, nor banishment upon pain of death will keep ye from us."   This conduct of the Quakers in provoking their own punishment is certainly no excuse for
the cruelty of the General Court of Massachusetts, but it is utterly inconsistent
with the example of Christ and his apostles, and, as has been observed, p. 258, with
Christ's direction.   Far different was the conduct of Clarke, Crandall and Holmes
in coming into Massachusetts, not to rush into danger, breaking no law, and, though
bold in the face of suffering, at the first honorable opportunity retiring to a place of
safety.   See p. 193.   Bishop's New England judged, Grove's Abridgment, pp. 114,
125.   Massachusetts Records.—ED.

[1]This language might be misunderstood as stating that she was brought to the gallows to be executed, and there was reprieved.   The record of the Court is as follows :—Whereas Mary Dyer is condemned by the General Court to be executed for
her offences, on the petition of William Dyer, her son, it is ordered that the said
Mary Dyer shall have liberty for forty-eight hours after this day to depart out of
this jurisdiction; after which time, being found therein she is forthwith to be executed; and in the meantime that she be kept close prisoner till her son or some
other be ready to carry her away within the aforesaid time.   And it is further ordered
that she shall be carried to the place of execution and there to stand upon the gallows with a rope about her neck till the rest be executed.—ED.

[2]Mary Dyer, like Robinson and Stevenson, came back deliberately, to challenge
her own death.   " Being asked what she had to say why sentence should not be
executed, she gave no other answer but that she denied our law, came to bear witness against it, and could not choose but come and do as formerly."   Bishop's New
England judged, Grove's Abridgment, pp. 156, 157.—ED.

[3]In 1657 it was enacted " that no Quaker or person commonly so called, shall be
entertained by any person or persons within this government, under penalty of five
pounds for every such default, or be whipped;" also, "that if any Ranter or Quaker,
or person commonly so called, shall come into any town within this government,
and by any person or persons be known, or be suspected to be such, the person knowing or suspecting him shall forthwith acquaint the constable or his deputy of them,
on pain of presentment;" and also that no meeting of Quakers or Ranters "shall be
assembled or kept by any person in any place within this government, under the

of England, on May 29th, of which Plymouth could have had no knowledge then. After the news of it arrived, Governor Endicott and his Court wrote to him, December 10th, when they said :—

Our liberty to walk in the faith of the gospel, with all good conscience, was the cause of our transporting ourselves, with our wives, little ones, and our substance, from that pleasant land over the Atlantic ocean, into this [the] vast wilderness, choosing rather the pure Scripture worship with a good conscience, in this remote wilderness, among the heathen, than the pleasures of England with submission to the [impositions of the] then so disposed and so far prevailing hierarchy, which we could not do without an evil conscience. . . . . Concerning the Quakers, open and capital blasphemers, open seducers from the glorious Trinity, our Lord Jesus Christ, the the blessed gospel, and from the Holy Scriptures as the rule of life, open enemies to the government itself as established in the hands of any but men of their own principles, [we were at last constrained, for our own safety, to pass a sentence of banishment against them upon pain of death.] . . . . The magistrate at last, in conscience, both to God and man, judged himself called for the defence of all, to keep the passage with the point of the sword held towards them ; this could do no harm to him that would be warned thereby ; their wittingly rushing themselves thereupon was their

penalty of forty shillings a time for every speaker and ten shillings a time for every hearer that are heads of families, and forty shillings a time for the owner of the place that permits them so to meet together." The same year it was enacted, "that in case any shall bring in any Quaker or other notorious heretic, by land or water, into any part of the government, [he] shall forthwith, from order from any one magistrate, return them to the place from whence they came, or clear the government of them, on the penalty of paying a fine of twenty shillings for every week that they shall stay in the government after warning."

These enactments were repealed, June 13, 1660; but, alas, they were repealed only to be reënacted on the spot, with slight modifications, or to give place to new laws quite as oppressive. The first law above mentioned, was passed again with the change of scarce a word. The second law, requiring any who might know or suspect the presence of a Quaker to give immediate notice thereof, was reënacted with a very little modification. The law prohibiting the holding of meetings by Quakers or Ranters was changed by the addition of a clause that all persons "under the government of others, as wives, children or servants," who might be present at such meetings, should be carried by the constable of the town "either into the stocks or cage," to continue there two hours, if in winter, or four, if in summer; and towns were required to provide cages for their confinement.

All these reënactments were made near the commencement of the session of the General Court which sat "at New Plymouth, June 10, 1660," probably the very day of the repeals. It was also enacted at this time that if any should furnish horses to Quakers, for travel in the colony or escape from it, such horses should be forfeited to the government. Laws of Plymouth Colony.—ED.

own act, we with [all] humility conceive, a crime bringing their blood upon their own head.[1]

In like manner they proceeded and hanged William Leddra, March 14th, 1661 ; but their friends in England procured an express from White-Hall, of Sept. 9th, which was brought over by Samuel Shattock, of Salem, requiring these rulers to forbear such things for the future, and to send such Quakers as appeared to them so obnoxious, to be tried in England. Soon after the receipt of this, Mr. Norton and Mr. Bradstreet, were sent over as agents, by whom Governor Endicott and his Court wrote to the Earl of Manchester, " to beseech his Majesty to tender them in respect of those pestilent heretics the Quakers, who have lately obtained his Majesty's letter, requiring us to forbear their punishments ; in observance whereof we have suspended execution of our laws against them respecting death or corporal punishments ; but this indulgence they [do] abuse to insolency and seduction of our people, and unless his majesty strengthen our hands in the application of some suitable remedy to suppress these and others, ill affected to our tranquility, this hopeful plantation is likely in all probability to be destroyed." They had before said, that allowing such to have liberty here, would be "so contrary to our consciences to permit, and no less oppression of us than the destroying both us and ours by the sword."[2] How justly then did Mr. Williams call the use of force in such affairs, " *The bloody tenet !*"[3]

We will now return to the affairs of baptism. Mr. Hubbard upon the year 1656, says :—

Baptism unto this time had been administered unto those children only, whose immediate parents were admitted into full communion in the churches where they lived ; but now the country came to be increased, and sundry families were found, that had children born in them, whose immediate parents had never attempted to join to any of the churches to which they belonged, and yet were very much unsatisfied that they could not ob-

[1]Hubbard, [559.] Massachusetts History, Vol. III, pp. 326, 327.
[2]Massachusetts History, Vol. III, pp. 331—360.
[3]Upon what has been said in reference to Quakers, see Appendix A, at the close of this volume.—Ed.

tain baptism for their children; the cause occasioned many debates between the ministers of the country.[1]

Connecticut took the lead therein, and sent a draught of questions about it to the rulers of the Massachusetts, requesting that the ablest ministers of both colonies might be called together, to answer the same. Such an assembly was therefore called by authority at Boston, June 4th, 1657, and sat till the 19th. Their answers to twenty-one questions were afterwards printed in London, under the title of "A disputation concerning church members, and their children." Therein they concluded, that the children of professing parents, " are by means of their parents' covenanting, in covenant also, and *members of the church*, by divine institution."

1. Because they are in that covenant for substance which was made with Abraham. Gen. 17, 7, compared with Deut. 29, 12, &c. 2. Because such children are, by Christ, affirmed to have a place and portion in the kingdom of heaven. 3. Else no children could be baptized, baptism being a church ordinance, and a seal of the covenant of grace.

And also they concluded :—

It is the duty of infants, who confederate in their parents, when grown up to years of discretion, though not yet fit for the Lord's Supper, to own the covenant they made with their parents, by entering thereinto in their own persons ; and it is the duty of the church to call upon them for the performance thereof; and if, being called upon, they shall refuse the performance of this great duty, or otherwise continue scandalous, they are liable to be censured for the same by the church. And in case they understand the grounds of religion, are not scandalous, and solemnly own the covenant in their own persons, wherein they give up both themselves and their children unto the Lord, and desire baptism for them, we (with due reverence to any godly learned that may dissent) see not sufficient cause to deny baptism unto their children.

As this disputation had its first rise in Connecticut, so was there much difference and contention raised at Hartford, ... between Mr. Samuel Stone, their teacher, and the rest of the church, occasioned at the first on some such account ; insomuch that sundry members of that church, having rent themselves off, removed to another place higher up the river, where they settled, and gathered a distinct church in that way of *schism* as the rest of the churches accounted.[2]

This unhappy difference overspread the whole colony of Connecticut, with such a monstrous enchantment upon the

[1]Hubbard, p. 562.—Ed.   [2]Hubbard, [pp. 464—570.]

minds of Christian brethren that in all the towns round about, the people generally made themselves parties to one side or the other of the quarrel. A world of sin was doubtless committed, even by pious men on this occasion. It came at last to an open breach, which could not be healed, or made up among themselves, which put them upon a necessity of calling a convention of the messengers of sundry churches in Massachusetts, who met at Boston, in 1659, and made a reconciliation between them. The practice of church-care, about the children of our churches, met with such opposition as could not be encountered with any thing less than a synod of elders and messengers from all the churches of the Massachusetts colony. Accordingly the General Court, having the necessity of the matter laid before them at their second session in the year 1661, issued out their desire and order for the convening of such a synod at Boston in the spring. After long labor the majority of them approved of the above proposition, and obtained the concurrence of the General Court thereto, on October 8th, 1662.[1] Mr. Mitchel who was the chief draughtsman, of that result, said, " We make account that if we keep baptism within the nonexcommunicable, and the Lord's Supper within the compass of those that have (unto charity) somewhat of the power of godliness, or grace in exercise, we shall be near about the right *middle-way* of church reformation."[2] And it has been called the " *Half-way* Covenant" ever since ; though this *halving* of matters in religion has done more mischief in this land as well as elsewhere, than tongue can express.

Mr. Eleazer Mather, the first minister of Northampton, wrote on July 4, this year, to Mr. Devenport, and said concerning this synod, " There was scarce any of the congregational principles, but what were layen at by some or other of the assembly ; as relations of the work of grace, power of voting of the fraternity in admission," &c.[3] President

---

[1] Hubbard, 570. Magnalia, B, 3. pp. 117, 118, [Vol. I, p. 194,] and B. 5, pp. 63, 64. [Vol. II, p. 239.]

[2] His life, pp. 76, 80. [Magnalia Book 4, Vol. II, p. 83.]

[3] Massachusetts History, Vol. I, p. 224, [206.]

Chauncey published his testimony against this new scheme ; and so did Mr. Devenport ; to the last of which Mr. Increase Mather wrote a preface, containing a distinct apology for those who dissented from it.   Mr. John Allen, of Dedham, answered Mr. Chauncey, and Mr. Richard Mather the other, while Mr. Mitchel was employed to answer his son's preface. Young Mr. Mather in that preface says, " The synod acknowledged, that there ought be to true saving faith in the parent, or else the child ought not to be baptized.   We intreated and urged again and again, that this, which them- selves acknowledged was a principle of truth, might be set down for a conclusion, and then we should all agree.   But those reverend persons would not consent to this."   No ; and Mr. Mitchel was so far from doing it in his answer, that he tells of distinguishing between faith in its hopeful begin- ning, and faith in special exercise ; initial faith and exer- cised faith, and says, " All reformed churches, unanimously grant the child's right unto baptism, by its being born within the visible church.   Besides, what have infants more than mere membership to give them right unto baptism !   We know of no stronger argument for infant baptism than this, that church members are to be baptized."[1] To which I would say, that the Jewish church indeed was first constituted of the household of Abraham, and all his offspring were born in the church, of whom the son of the bond woman was the first that was circumcised ; but the Christian church is constituted of the household of God, the children of the free woman, in distinction from those who were born after the flesh, though from Abraham's body.   Ephesians 2. Gal. 4.

Mr. Mitchell, by his reasonings drew Mr. Increase Mather over to that side ; after which he acted many cruel things against the Baptists for near twenty years, till the same measures were meeted to him again, so as very sensibly to convince him of his error therein.   Mr. Hubbard says,

[1] Magnalia, Book 5, page 77—79. [Vol. II, p. 262.]

" Some think Mr. Devenport's book hath overthrown the propositions of the synod, according to their own princi-ples."[1] Mr. Devenport was a while in Holland, before he came here, where he testified against their promiscuous bap-tism ; and he said :—

When a reformation of the church has been brought about in any part of the world, it has rarely been afterwards carried on any one step further than the first reformers did succeed in their first endeavors. He observed, that as easily might the ark have been removed from the mountains of Ararat, where it first grounded, as a people get any ground in reformation, after and beyond the first remove of the reformers. And this observation quickened him to embark in a design of reformation, wherein he might have opportunity to drive things in the first essay, as near to the precept and pattern of Scripture as they could be driven.[2]

We shall presently see other ministers promoting a sepa-ration from him for these attempts.

On the 8th of May, this year, the Assembly at Boston wrote to that of Rhode Island, and said :—

Our affection to peace and a fair correspondence, [with you] puts us upon a condescension far beneath our own reason, and the justice of our cause, once more to transmit [emit] this our last letter to you, concerning the unjust molestation and intrusion of some of your inhabitants, upon the undoubted rights of this jurisdiction, and the inhabitants thereof, in their grants and possessions in the Pequot and Narragansett country, upon pre-tence of authority from your Court, and purchase from [the] Indians, but producing no deed, record, order or commission for warranting the same ; wherein, as we conceive, they act directly against reason, righteousness, precedent, grants from England, clear conquest, purchase and possession. It is not unknown to yourselves what means have been used from time to time, both by the Commissioners of the United Colonies, and by the Gov-ernor and magistrates, General Court and Council of this jurisdiction, by their several letters, to desire you to cause your people to desist [from] such proceedings, and extend [exert] your authority for suppressing injus-tice ; but to this day [we] have received no satisfactory or particular answer in the premises ; which has given [gives] us grounds to suppose, [suspect] that at least you indulge them in their proceedings. You may hereby have [take] notice, that two of your people, namely, Tobias Sanders, and Robert Bardick, [Burditt] being long since taken on the place, and secured by us to answer their trespass, we have now called them before the Court, and find nothing from them to justify their proceedings; therefore the Court hath fined them forty pounds for their [your][1] offence, and towards satisfaction for the charges expended in carrying them before authority; and that they stand committed [to prison] till the [your] fine be satisfied, and security given to the Secretary to the value of one hundred pounds for their [your] peaceable demeanor toward all the inhabitants of this jurisdiction for the future. . . . . And we hereby signify unto you, that unless you command off your inhabitants that yet continue their possession at Sotherton and Pateskomscut, before the last of June next, you may expect we shall not continue to neglect the relief and protection of our people there [thus] molested; and shall account it our duty to secure all such persons and estates of yours as shall be found within our jurisdiction, until [all] just damages be satisfied. But this we heartily and earnestly desire may be avoided, by your prudent care and justice, and that peace and good agreement [government] may for the future be preserved between us.[2]

This reminds me of Mr. Locke's saying, "That dominion is founded in grace, is an assertion by which those who maintain it do plainly lay claim to the possession of all things; for they are not so wanting to themselves as not to believe, or at least as not to profess themselves to be the truly pious and faithful."[3] Because Mr. Williams testified against that power when he first came to Boston, the Court wrote to Salem against him; whereupon he did not stay to contend with them, but peaceably withdrew to Plymouth, where his teaching was well approved as long as Mr. Bradford was Governor. But when Mr. Winslow came into that office, who with Massachusetts was against a full toleration in religious matters,[4] Mr. Williams peaceably retired to Salem, and took the charge of that flock; but for the church's receiving him without the rulers' leave, they took away some of their possessions, till they would give up Mr. Williams; and, for his faithful admonitions to them on that account, they

[1] The original document probably had in several instances the old abbreviation, "yr," which sometimes stood for *their*, and sometimes for *your*. Backus understood it in the former sense, and the copyist of the Rhode Island Records in the latter. Backus's interpretation seems far preferable to the other.—ED.

[2] Rhode Island Records.   [3] On Toleration, p. 61.

[4] Massachusetts History, Vol. III, p. 154.

expelled him out of their jurisdiction. But who can tell how far that extends? When he came first into this country all the Indians from Boston and Plymouth bays to Paucatuck River were tributaries to the chief sachems of Narragansett; and from thence to Hudson's River, and over all Long Island, Sassicus had extended his power, even over twenty-six sachems.[1] The Pequots being thus powerful, made war upon the Narragansetts, who, in April, 1632, had a number of their tributaries out of Plymouth and Massachusetts colonies to assist them against him; yet Sassicus prevailed, and extended[2] his territories ten miles east of Paucatuck River. About the same time Natuwannute, a sachem of the country about where Hartford now stands, with a number of his men, " were driven out from thence by the potency of the Pequots," and came to our fathers at Plymouth, and requested them to go up and trade there, though " their end was to be restored to their country again." This motion was complied with, and a trading house was set up among them.[3] This was such an eyesore to the Pequots, that in 1634 they murdered Captain Stone and seven men with him, plundered his goods and sunk his vessel, because they were going up Connecticut river to trade there. Two years after they murdered Captain Oldham as I have related.[4] Upon the notice which Mr. Williams gave them of this sad event, Mr. Endicott with an armed force was sent in August 25, 1636, to try to bring the Pequots to terms; but Johnson says it proved a bootless voyage, only his leaving some men with Underhill, at Saybrook fort, prevented its being taken. Upon his return Sassicus applied to the Narragansetts for a reconciliation, that they all might join to expel these new comers; representing, " that if they should help, or suffer the English to subdue the Pequots, they would thereby make

---

[1]Connecticut Assembly's answer to the king's letter, 1773, written by Governor Trumbull.

[2]Prince's Annals, pp. 58, 59. [391, 392.]

[3]Massachusetts History, Vol. II, pp. 469, 470. [416.]

[4]Page 59.—ED.

way for their own future ruin ; and that they need not come
to open battle with the English ; for only to fire their houses ;
kill their cattle, lay in ambush and shoot them as they went
about their business, they would quickly be forced to leave
the country, and the Indians not be exposed to any great
hazard."[1]

Had two such politic and potent princes as Sassicus and
Miantinomo were, united in this scheme, when Boston was
but six years old, Providence and Hartford but a few months,
and New Haven not begun, what would have become of all
their claims they were now contending for ?   And it is most
evident that Mr. Williams was the very instrument of preventing the junction of those two great Indian powers, and
so of saving the vast interest we now have in this country.
But how was he requited for it ?   Why, after Warwick men
had obtained as fair a title to that town, as the Massachusetts ever had to Boston, yet because they were not orthodox they were fetched away by force of arms ; and the captive sachem was murdered for fear he should revenge such
doings.   And when the orthodox party afterward proclaimed
war upon his successors, because they were for revenging
his death, and Mr. Williams, to prevent the further effusion
of blood, had prevailed with them to go down and settle the
matter at Boston, how were they treated ?[2]   They were not
only compelled to sign an engagement to pay all damages
and costs, and to quit any claim to the Pequot country, but
also to say, " The Narragansett and Nyantick sagamores and
deputy, hereby agree and covenant, to and with the Commissioners of the United Colonies, that henceforward, they
will neither give, grant, sell, or in any manner alienate any
part of their country, nor any parcel of land therein, either
to any [of the] English or others, without consent or allowance of the said Commissioners."[3]   Two years after,[4] upon

[1]Major Mason's history of the Pequot war and others.   [Massachusetts Historical
Collections, second series, Vol. VIII, p. 123.]
[2]Pp. 161—163.
[3]This agreement was made August 27, 1645.—ED.   [4]July 30, 1647.—ED.

their calling for their pay, Passicus sent them word, that " when he made this covenant, he did it in fear of the army, and though the English kept their covenant with him there, and let him go from them, yet the army was to go to Narragansett immediately and kill him there; therefore said the Commissioners, *Set your hands to such and such things, or else the army shall go forth to the Narragansetts.*" In answer to which the Commissioners say, "After covenants have been solemnly made, and hostages given, and a small part of the wampum paid, and all the rest due, now to pretend fears is a vain and offensive excuse."[1] This shows that they themselves did not neglect the rule they prescribed to their General in that expedition, viz. :—

You are to use your best endeavors to gain the enemies' canoes, or utterly to destroy them, and herein you may make good use of the Indians, our confederates, as you may do upon other occasions, having due regard to the honor of God, who is both our sword and shield, and to the distance which is to be observed betwixt Christians and barbarians, as well in war as in other negotiations.[2]

Sixteen months before that covenant was made, Passicus and other heads of their tribes, had by an ample deed resigned over and submitted all those lands to the supreme authority in England, and Mr. Williams had procured a charter thereof from thence, extending unto the Pequot River and country.[3] The Massachusetts Records, upon granting Fisher's Island to Mr. Winthrop, say it lies against the mouth of Pequot River. What right of jurisdiction then had those colonies east of that river? and what right had Passicus to engage any of those lands to them, which he had submitted to another authority so long before? By re-

---

[1] Records of the United Colonies.

[2] Massachusetts History, Vol. III, p. 151.—B.

The words above quoted are from a document issued by the Commissioners of the United Colonies entitled, "Instructions for Sergeant-Major Gibbones, Commander-in-chief of our military forces, and for such as are joined with him in a council of war."—Ed.

[3] Pp. 122, 161.

18

peated endeavors the Commissioners had got all the wampum that was promised in said covenant but three hundred and eight fathoms, before they met at Hartford, on September 5, 1650; and then Captain Atherton was sent, with twenty armed men, to demand the remainder, with orders to seize their goods if the Indians refused to pay it; and if resistance should be made so as any life was lost, that a special meeting of the Commissioners should then be called to make war upon them for it. He accordingly went, and placed his men round Passicus's tent, and going into it, seized the sachem by the hair of his head, and threatened to shoot him, if any resistance was made. This terrified them so much, that the wampum was presently paid. On July 25, 1651, at the desire of the Narragansett sachems, Mr. Williams wrote to the Governor at Boston, an account of sundry complaints they had against Uncas; which letter was laid before the Commissioners when they met at New Haven, the 4th of September following; but though Uncas was present, yet they acted nothing upon it, because the Narragansetts had not sent any of their men to support the charge. At the same time a tribute of three hundred and twelve fathoms of wampum was paid by Uncas, Ninecrost and others, on account of the Pequots they had among them; and upon laying of it down they demanded:—

Why this tribute was required, how long it should continue, and whether the children to be born hereafter were to pay it? All which being considered, the Commissioners by Thomas Stanton, answered, that the tribute by agreement hath been due yearly from the Pequots since *anno* 1638, for sundry murders without provocation committed by them upon several of the English at several times, as they found opportunity; refusing either to deliver up the murderers or to do justice upon them; [and] so drawing on a war upon themselves, to the great charge and inconvenience of the English; which war, through the good hand of our God, issued first in a conquest over that treacherous and bloody people, and after by agreement, (to spare as much as might be even such guilty blood,) in a small tribute, to be paid in different proportions, by, and for their males, according to their different ages yearly; but hath not hitherto been satisfied, though demanded. Wherefore, ... though twelve years' tribute were due before the year 1650, [this last year] and though the agreement was for a yearly tribute to be paid by them and theirs, so long as they continue in this part of the country ; yet the Commissioners, something to ease their spirits [in reference to this just burthen,] and to engage them to an inoffensive and peaceable carriage, ... declared that the payment of this tribute shall be limited to ten years, [of which] this last year to be reckoned the first ; after which, [time] unless they draw trouble unto themselves, they shall be free.[1]

Such an uneasiness among the Narragansetts was discovered two years after, that another army was raised and sent against them, which compelled them into another treaty, which not being otherwise fulfilled, the sachems were brought, on October 13, 1660, to mortgage all their lands, to Major Atherton, and about twenty associates with him, for six hundred fathoms of wampum, said then to be due to the Commissioners of the United Colonies. I find also by the records, that Massachusetts and Connecticut could never agree how to divide the Pequot lands betwixt them, till the Commissioners from Plymouth and New Haven had the case referred to them ; and they on September 16, 1658, settled the line betwixt them, which was to be Mistick River (which runs in betwixt Stonington and Groton) up to the pond, by Lanthorn Hill, and thence from the middle of that pond to run a north course ; Massachusetts to have both property and jurisdiction from thence to Wecapaug Brook, which was the easterly bounds of Sassicus's conquest. Pataquamscut purchase was made partly in 1657, and partly in 1658, by some inhabitants of Rhode Island, and John Hull of Boston, (who got a great estate by coining their silver money.) This purchase was about thirteen miles in length, and seven in breadth, in the heart of the Narragansett country.[2]

[1]Records of the United Colonies.

[2]In 1668, these purchasers gave three hundred acres of their best land, for an orthodox person, to preach God's word to the inhabitants; which has cost much contention in the law. Dowglass, Vol. II. p. 104.

In 1752, Dr. Macsparran said, " I have been engaged in a law suit about Glebe land twenty-eight years, and the Independent teacher has at last obtained a decree

When their Assembly met at Newport, May 21, 1661, they appointed a committee upon the letters they had then received from the Massachusetts, " who seriously considered and debated circumstances, concerning the matter in difference, betwixt the gentlemen, and some friends with them, that are active in sharing the Narragansett lands in the colony, without the consent of the colony ; and we [do] find by their letter, that those gentlemen, Major Atherton and associates, are not so well informed of the intent of the colony as might be requisite." They concluded to write and give them better information, and to offer to leave the case to referees to settle it ; but say :—

In case a fair issue cannot be had, as is desired, then, in a speedy and convenient time and season, to forbid the said gentlemen, or any of their company, in his Majesty's name, from further proceeding in the said purchase, as to possessing or sharing of any of the said lands, and to prosecute [against] them, or any of them, in case they still proceed without consent of the colony, as concluding that such their proceedings are contrary to the crown and dignity of his Majesty, and to the peace and wellbeing of his Majesty's subjects in this colony.

The 27th of August following, an Assembly met at Portsmouth, of which Mr. Williams was a member, when they sent a commission and letters to Mr. Clarke, to solicit for a new charter.[1] April 27th, 1662, the town of Providence gave Mr. Clarke a full purchase right of land therein as a free gift. The next month came the foregoing letter[2] from Boston to their Assembly, with account of their dealings

in council in his favor; so that I am forced to sit down by the loss of at least six hundred pounds sterling." America Dissected, p. 42.

I am told that Dr. Stennett, a Baptist minister in London, had a great hand in procuring this decree for Mr. Joseph Torry.

[1]This commission was drawn up and adopted by the previous Assembly which met in Warwick, October 16, 1660, and was " drawn out," that is, copied in due form, and sealed at the session in Portsmouth. Mr. Williams was not a member of the former Assembly. The commission simply appointed Mr. Clarke the "undoubted agent and attorney" of the colony, but did not direct him " to solicit a new charter." Probably this duty was assigned him in the letters, which seem to have had their origin in the later session of the Assembly. R. I. Colonial Records.—ED.

[2]See page 269.—ED.

with men whom they called trespassers, of whom Mr. Burdick was then a member of Mr. Clarke's church. He married Mr. Samuel Hubbard's daughter, and has a large posterity remaining in and about Westerly to this day. Mr. Sanford, and Mr. Greene, were now sent to Boston to make another trial for an amicable settlement of this controversy. It is to be noted, that neither of those colonies, which had made such a noise about their rights, had ever received any charter, either from king or parliament, of any lands to the west of Providence colony, till Connecticut, by the help of Mr. Winthrop, obtained one dated April 23, 1662, which took New Haven into the same colony. When the Commissioners met at Boston the 4th of September, they wrote to Rhode Island rulers in their former strain, and informed them of a warrant they had seen, signed by Joseph Torry, their Secretary, in the name of the General Court, " warning Captain Gookin and others to desist and forbear any further or future possession of any [of the] lands at or about Paucatuck as they shall answer the contrary at their peril; yet withal expressing your submission to his Majesty's determination. Wherefore (say the Commissioners) being earnestly[jointly] desirous to prevent any further disturbance of the peace of the colonies, though we have no doubt of the present right and interests of the Massachusetts to those lands we are willing to improve the argument which [that] yourselves have owned, and therefore thought meet to certify you, that we have read and perused a charter of incorporation, under the broad seal of England, sent over in the last ship, granted to some gentlemen of Connecticut, wherein the land at Paucatuck and Narragansett are contained, which we hope will prevail with you to require and cause your people to withdraw themselves, and desist from further disturbance."

The words in said charter which they built this upon, bounded that colony east, " by the Narragansett River, commonly called Narragansett Bay, where the said river, falleth into the sea." Now it is to be remembered, that Plymouth patent was bounded westward by Narragansett River and Bay, and these colonists pretended that Warwick was included therein, which could not be, unless Paucatuck was the river meant; and if it was, where is their right now to go east of it by Connecticut charter? The truth is, names are arbitrary, and those worthy governors, Bradford and Winslow, took Patucket to be the river intended in their patent.[1] And there was now less room left for this dispute; for on July 8, 1663, his Majesty granted Rhode Island charter, which describes their west boundaries to be the middle channel of Paucatuck River up to its head, and thence a north course to the south line of Massachusetts; which river says he, " having been yielded after much debate, for the fixed and certain bounds between these our said colonies, by the agents thereof; who have also agreed, that the said Paucatuck River shall be also called, alias, Narragansett River; and to prevent future disputes that otherwise might arise thereby forever hereafter, shall be construed, deemed and taken to be the Narragansett River, in our late grant to Connecticut colony, mentioned as the eastwardly bounds of that colony." This colony of Rhode Island and Providence Plantations, was to extend three English miles east and north-east of the most eastern and north-eastern parts of the Narragansett Bay, unto the mouth of Providence River, and thence by the eastwardly bank of it up to Patucket Falls, being the most westwardly line of Plymouth colony; and thence due north to the Massachusetts line, by which it is bounded on the north, and by the ocean on the south, including Block Island, and the other islands within their bay. As the Indians had formerly sent over a submission of themselves and land, to the king's father, they had now sent another to him; whereupon he says in this charter :—

It shall not be lawful to, or for the rest of the colonies, to invade or molest the native Indians, or any other inhabitants inhabiting within the

[1] See pp. 57, 58.

bounds and limits hereafter mentioned ; they having subjected themselves
unto us, and being by us taken into our special protection, without the
knowledge and consent of the governor and company of our colony of
Rhode Island and Providence Plantations.

This charter appointed that a Governor, Deputy Governor,
and ten Assistants should be elected annually on the first
Wednesday in May, who, with deputies or representatives
from each town, were to make laws, not contrary to the
laws of England, make grants of land, constitute courts of
justice, and appoint their officers both civil and military.
Mr. Clarke sent over this charter, and Captain Gregory
Dexter[1] fetched it from Boston ; upon which a large assembly of the freemen in all the colony met at Newport, November 24th, and ordered Captain Dexter [Baxter] to take forth
the charter and read it before all the people, and hold it up
with the broad seal to their view, and then to have it safely
deposited with Governor Arnold.[2]   And they voted to pay
all Mr. Clarke's disbursements in going to England, in their
service there, and upon his intended return ; as also one
hundred pounds sterling as a free gratuity to him, besides
those expenses ; yea, and to give Captain Dexter [Baxter]
twenty-five pounds sterling for his service and faithfulness in
bringing the charter from Boston. Mr. Clarke's letters were
read, upon which letters of thanks were ordered to be sent
to the king, and to Lord Clarendon, for these great favors
they had received by their means.   The next day (after the

[1]This name should be "George Baxter."   Bancroft says, Vol. II, p. 63, note,
"Backus, almost always very accurate, here mistakes the name." He was doubtless
led into the error by the fact that Gregory Dexter is a name well known in Rhode
Island annals. Mistakes in deciphering old records are among the most excusable
of mistakes ; and the Records of Providence seem, from the wide difference between
different copyists, to be especially obscure.—ED.

[2]"Voted ; That the box in which the King's gracious letters were enclosed be
opened, and the letters, with the broad seal thereto affixed, be taken forth and read
by Captain George Baxter, in the audience and view of all the people ; which was
accordingly done, and the said letters, with his Majesty's royal stamp and the broad
seal, with much becoming gravity, held up on high, and presented to the perfect
view of the people, and then returned into the box and locked up by the Governor
in order to the safe keeping of it." R. I. Colonial Records.—ED.

Governor, Deputy Governor, and six Assistants had taken their engagements) they called the sachems of the Narragansetts and Niantics before them, and let them know what the king had done for them; upon which they said, " they return his Majesty great thanks for his gracious relief, in releasing their lands from those forced purchases and mortgages by some of the other colonies." But another thing which is by no means to be omitted is, that the king says, in their petition for the charter they declared :—

That it is much on their hearts, if they may be permitted, to hold forth a lively experiment, that a most flourishing civil state may stand and best be maintained, and that among our English subjects, with A FULL LIBERTY OF RELIGIOUS CONCERNMENTS, and that true piety rightly grounded upon gospel principles, will give the best and greatest security to sovereignty, and will lay in the hearts of men the strongest obligation to true loyalty.[1]

This petition was therefore fully granted; and above a hundred years after, a worthy gentleman well says :—

This great experiment hath been made, [and hath fully answered the expectations of the beneficent, royal mind, that proposed it,] and it hath fully appeared, that a flourishing civil state, and the most unstained loyalty, may stand without the help of any religious party tests to support them; and the Christian religion is as little indebted to human laws for its support, as it is to human inventions, for the purity of its morals, and the sublimity of its doctrines.[2]

For seven years past there had been many contentions about lands, and strivings to strain Indian purchases, beyond their just limits, in Providence, Newport, and other parts of the colony, which Mr. Williams had a great hand in composing and settling; the particulars of which would be very instructive, had we room for them. And his HOPE in

[1]It is perhaps not strange that this familiar and noble sentence has been, by implication at least, ascribed to Roger Williams. See Morgan Edwards's History of the Baptists of Rhode Island; Benedict's History of the Baptists, Vol. II, pp. 489, 490. It was the product of a spirit kindred to that of Williams, it being part of John Clarke's second address or petition to the King. R. I. Colonial Records; Arnold's History of Rhode Island, Vol. I, p. 280.—ED.

[2]History of Providence. [Massachusetts Historical Collections, Second Series, Vol. IX, p. 196.]

1647, that government, held forth through love, union and order, though by few in number, and mean in condition, yet would withstand and overcome mighty opposers,[1] was wonderfully granted and confirmed; the memory of which, in the figure of an ANCHOR with this word for its motto, in their colony seal, has been continued from that time to this.[2] Mr. Clarke returned June 7, 1664, after he had served his colony at the British Court twelve years. In October following the Assembly appointed him, Mr. Williams and others, to inspect their laws, to see if any of them were contrary to their charter, and to make a table of them.[3] A committee was also appointed to consider of their eastern and western boundaries, and to write to the other colonies concerning them. Connecticut still contended for power and jurisdiction in Narragansett and offered to leave the case to the colonies of Massachusetts and Plymouth; which Rhode Island would not do.[4] The king's Commissioners who were now sent over, heard the complaints of the sachems and others, and entered upon the Narragansett country in the king's name, and called it the king's province. But on the

[1] Page 168.

[2] In 1647, the General Assembly ordered, "The seal of the Province shall be an ANCHOR; in 1664, they ordered that the seal be changed by inscribing above the anchor the word HOPE.—ED.

[3] Two years later Mr. Clarke was again assigned a similar duty. "It is ordered that Mr. John Clarke is deputed and authorized to compare all the laws of the colony into a good method and form, leaving out what may be superfluous, and adding what may appear unto him necessary, as well for the regulation of Courts as otherwise." R. I. Colonial Records.—ED.

[4] John Leverett, afterwards Governor of Massachusetts, wrote to Sir Thomas Temple of London, as follows :--"Connecticut have offered to refer the matter [of the boundary line] to the two colonies of Massachusetts and Plymouth; to which motion, divers of Rhode Island will come, but others refuse, upon what ground is not understood, these colonies not being interested in the quarrel or reason of it; [though some of the inhabitants may be in the land, or claim an interest therein, but the government do not,] so that that course might have been neighborly, to have tried for an issue that way before there had been giving a trouble to his Majesty in so small a matter as it is supposed that will be when heard." Massachusetts History, Vol. III, [Hutchinson's Collection of Original Papers,] p. 382. Any one who knows the attitude in which the colony of Plymouth, and especially that of Massachusetts stood toward Rhode Island, will readily understand upon what grounds some in Rhode Island should refuse this proposal.—ED.

east line they allowed Plymouth colony to come to the water, till his Majesty's pleasure should be further known.[1] And so the line continued, till other Commissioners in 1741, settled the line according to Rhode Island charter, which gave them the towns of Bristol, Warren, Barrington, Tiverton and Little Compton, which Plymouth and Massachusetts had held till then.

The first Baptist church within that which is now the Massachusetts State, was constituted in Rehoboth this year; Mr. Holmes and his friends having only held a meeting there for a while, and then removed to Newport. For a more clear idea of its original we must look over into Wales, where at Ilston in Glamorganshire, a Baptist church was formed, October 1, 1649; the beginning whereof their records describe thus, viz. :—

We cannot but admire at the unsearchable wisdom, power and love of God, in bringing about his own designs, far above, and beyond the capacity and understanding of the wisest of men.   Thus, to the glory of his own great name, hath he dealt with us ; for when there had been no company or society of people, holding forth and professing the doctrine, worship, order and discipline of the gospel, according to the primitive institution, that ever we heard of in all Wales, since the apostacy, it pleased the Lord to choose this dark corner to place his name in, and honor us, undeserving creatures, with the happiness of being the first in all these parts, among whom was practiced the glorious ordinance of baptism, and here to gather the first church of baptized believers.

From thence they go on to relate, how Mr. John Miles and Mr. Thomas Proud, went up to London the next preceding spring, and, by the direction of Providence, came into the Baptist society at the Glass-house in Broad street, under the care of Mr. William Consett, and Mr. Edward Draper, " immediately after they had kept a day to seek the Lord, that he would send laborers into the dark corners of the land." These travellers were well received, and were soon sent back into their own country again, and were instrumental of gathering a Baptist church at the time above men-

[1]Massachusetts History, Vol. III, pp. 382, 414, 415.

tioned; and which, by a blessing upon their labors, increased by the close of the next year to fifty-five members. In 1651, forty more joined to it; forty-seven in 1652, and by the end of 1660, two hundred and sixty-three persons had joined to that church, whose names all now stand in a neat book of records which they kept; which contain a distinct account of the means and methods they took to promote vital and practical religion among the several branches of their society; as also letters of correspondence to and from their brethren in various parts of England and Ireland.

But here another scene opens.

The Presbyterians had been as much against equal religious liberty as the Episcopalians, and manifested as great bitterness against those who broke their power in the long parliament. These two parties joined in restoring the second Charles to the throne, who came in with plausible promises of indulgence to tender consciences; and great pains were taken to accommodate matters between them, without any good effect. The Episcopalians having got the power into their hands, determined to crush all that opposed it. Among the rest they wreaked their vengeance on Sir Henry Vane, whom they beheaded in August, 1662. "His indiscretion and insolence (says a great author) as well on his trial as his execution, have been extremely aggravated; but it is easy to see, it was only to save the king's honor, who having positively promised a pardon to all except the king's judges, could not avoid granting a pardon to Vane, without violating his promise."[1] And when Vane's friends persuaded him to make some submission in order to save his life, he said, " If the king does not think himself more concerned for his honor and word than I do for my life, I am very willing they should take it. Nay, I declare that I value my life less in a good cause, than the king can do his promise." A Presbyterian author who writes very bitterly against him,

[1]Rapin, Vol. II, p. 631. [The History of England, as well Ecclesiastical as Civil, by Mr. De Rapin Thoyras, London, 1731, Vol. XIII, p. 305.]

yet owns that, " the two things in which he had most success, and spake most plainly, were his earnest plea for universal liberty of conscience, and against the magistrates'
intermeddling with religion, and his teaching his followers
to revile the ministry, calling them ordinarily, *black coats*,
priests, and other names which savored of reproach." And
he says, " No man could die with greater appearance of a
gallant resolution, and fearlessness, than he did, though
before supposed a timorous man ; insomuch that the manner
of his death procured him more applause than all the actions
of his life."[1]   On the twenty-fourth of that month, called
St. Bartholomew's day, an act of parliament was passed,
which ejected all teachers, both of churches and schools,
out of their places, who would not declare their assent or
consent to all the forms and ceremonies of the church of
England. About two thousand were turned out by it.   The
method the church party took to procure this act, was secretly
to foment disturbances and tumults in different parts of England, and then to persuade the parliament that the Presbyterians did it, and that no peace could be had with them till
dissenters were all turned out of place.   Among those so
ejected was our Mr. Miles.[2] Upon which he and some of his
friends came over to our country, and brought their church
records with them.   And at Mr. Butterworth's house, in
Rehoboth, in 1663, John Miles, elder, James Brown, Nicholas Tanner, Joseph Carpenter, John Butterworth, Eldad
Kingsley, and Benjamin Alby, joined in a solemn covenant
together.

This church was then in Plymouth colony, concerning
whom Dr. Mather says, " there being many good men among
those—I do not know that they have been persecuted with
any harder means, than those of kind conferences to reclaim
them."[3] I suppose it was so for some years, and that because

[1]Calamy's Abridgment. Vol. I, pp. 99, 101.
[2]Calamy's Abridgment, Vol. I, pp. 178—181, and Vol. II, pp. 731.
[3]Magnalia, Book I, p. 14. [Vol. I, p. 58.]

Mr. Newman, who persecuted Mr. Holmes died this year; but four years after I find it thus recorded, viz. :—

At the Court holden [held] at Plymouth the 2d of July, 1667, before Thomas Prince, Governor, John Alden, Josiah [Josias] Winslow, Thomas Southworth, William Bradford, Thomas Hinckley, Nathaniel Bacon, and John Freeman, assistants.... Mr. Miles, and Mr. Brown, for their breach of order, in setting up of a public meeting without the knowledge and approbation of the Court to the disturbance of the peace of the place, are fined each of them five pounds, and Mr. Tanner the sum of one pound [twenty shillings] and we judge that their continuance at Rehoboth, being very prejudicial to the peace of that church and that town, may not be allowed; and do therefore order all persons concerned therein, wholly to desist from the said meeting in that place or township, within this month. Yet in case they shall remove their meeting unto some other place, where they may not prejudice any other church, and shall give us any reasonable satisfaction respecting their principles, we know not but they may be permitted by this government so to do.

And it was no longer than the 30th of October following, before the Court made them an ample grant of Wannamoiset which they called Swanzey. It then included what is now Warren and Barrington, and the district of Shawomet, as well as the present town of Swanzey.[1] There they made a regular settlement,[2] which has continued to this day. The

[1] Plymouth Records. Note. This town was named on March first, 1667-8. When by mistake the first grant is dated, in Swanzey Town Records; but the above I took from the Court Records at Plymouth.

[2] The grant of this town was made to " Capt. Thomas Willet, Mr. Paine, senior, Mr. Brown, John Allen, and John Butterworth." Of these, says John Comer, " the first two were Pædobaptists, the others Baptists." Captain Willet " made the following proposals unto those that were with him. 1. That no erroneous persons be admitted into the township either as an inhabitant or sojourner. 2. That no man of an evil behavior or contentious person, &c., be admitted. 3. That none may be admitted that may become a charge to the place.

" The church of Christ here gathered and assembling did therefore make the following address unto the said Captain Willet and his associates, the trustees, as aforesaid :—

SIRS : We being with you engaged (according to our capacities) in the carrying on a township according to the grant given us by the Honorable Court, and desiring to lay such a foundation thereof as may effectually tend to God's glory, our future peace and comfort, and the real benefit of such as shall hereafter join with us herein; as also to prevent all future jealousies and causes of dissatisfaction, or disturbances in so good a work, do, in relation to the three proposals made by our

families also of Luther, Cole, Bowen, Wheaton, Martin, Barnes, Thurber, Bosworth, Mason, Child, and others, which are numerous in those parts, sprang from the early planters of that town and church. Their first meeting-house was built a little west of Kelly's ferry, against Warren, but Mr. Miles settled the west side of the great bridge which still bears his name.

much honored Captain Willet, humbly present to your serious consideration (before we further proceed therein) that the said proposals may be consented to and subscribed by every townsman under the following explication :—

"That the first proposal relating to the non-admisson of erroneous persons may be only understood under the following explications, viz. : of such as hold damnable heresies, inconsistent with the faith of the gospel; as, to deny the Trinity, or any person therein; the deity or sinless humanity of Christ, or the union of both natures in him, or his full satisfaction to the divine justice of all his elect, by his active and passive obedience, or his resurrection, ascension into heaven, intercession, or his second coming personally to judgment; or else to deny the truth or divine authority of the Scriptures, or the resurrection of the dead, or to maintain any merit of works, consubstantiation, transubstantiation, giving divine adoration to any creature, or any other anti-christian doctrine directly opposing the priestly prophetical or kingly offices of Christ, or any part thereof; (2) or such as hold such opinions as are inconsistent with the well-being of the place, as to deny the magistrate's power to punish evil doers as well as to encourage those that do well, or to deny the first day of the week to be observed by divine institution as the Lord's day or Christian Sabbath, or to deny the giving of honor to whom honor is due, or to oppose those civil respects that are usually performed according to the laudable customs of our nation each to other, as bowing the knee or body, &c., or else to deny the office, use or authority of the ministry or a comfortable maintenance to be due to them from such as partake of their teachings, or to speak reproachfully of any of the churches of Christ in the country, or of any such other churches as are of the same common faith with us or them.

"We desire that it be also understood and declared that this is not understood of any holding any opinion different from others in any disputable point, yet in controversy among the godly learned, the belief thereof not being essentially necessary to salvation; such as pædobaptism, anti-pædobaptism, church discipline or the like; but that the minister or ministers of the said town may take their liberty to baptize infants or grown persons as the Lord shall persuade their consciences, and so also the inhabitants take their liberty to bring their children to baptism or to forbear."

This is followed by the "explication" of the other two proposals, and the document is signed by John Myles, pastor, and John Butterworth. Comer's Manuscript Diary. It is evident that this ancient Baptist church was not, at first, clear in the view that civil government has no right of interference with religious belief; and that it took upon itself the dangerous task of deciding between Christian doctrines as more or less essential.—ED.

CHAPTER VI.

Mr. Hubbard says :—

As some were studying how baptism might be enlarged and extended to the seed of the faithful in their several generations, there were others as studious to deprive all unadult children thereof, and to restrain the privilege only to adult believers.[1]

And Dr. Mather, after confessing that very odious and unjust things had been published against Anabaptists ever since Luther's time, says :—

Infant baptism hath been scrupled by multitudes in our day, who have been in other points most worthy Christians, and as holy, watchful, fruitful and heavenly people as perhaps any in the world. Some few of these people have been among the planters of New England from the beginning, and have been welcome to the communion of our churches, reserving their particular opinion unto themselves. .... At last some of our churches used, it may be, a little too much cogency towards the brethren, who would weakly turn their backs when infants were brought forth to be baptized.[2]

Twenty years before, Mr. Cobbet had called their so doing a "profane trick." What their dealings were, which are here covered under the obscure term cogency, will presently

---

[1]Hubbard, p. 590.—Ed.

[2]Magnalia, Book VII, p. 27, [Vol. II, p. 459.] Seth Sweetser, who came over to Charlestown in 1638, from Tring, in Hardfordshire, was one of those early Baptists. I find by the records that he was received a freeman that year. His son Benjamin was long a useful member of the Baptist church in Boston, and he has left a numerous posterity, one of whom has been schoolmaster and town clerk in Charlestown for sundry years past.

be seen. It was such that a number drew off and met by themselves in Charlestown, till, on May 28th, 1665, Thomas Gould, Thomas Osburne, Edward Drinker, and John George, were baptized, and joined with Richard Goodall, William Turner, Robert Lambert, Mary Goodall, and Mary Newel, " in a solemn covenant, in the name of the Lord Jesus Christ, to walk in fellowship and communion together, in the practice of all the holy appointments of Christ, which he had, or should further make known to them." Goodall came recommended from Mr. Kiffin's church in London ; Turner and Lambert from Mr. Stead's church in Dartmouth, having been regular walkers in the Baptist order before they came to this country. Gould and Osburne separated from the church in Charlestown ; Drinker and George had lived many years in this country, but had not joined to any of their churches.[1]

The king's Commissioners being here, caused the Court not to lay hold of these people so soon as otherwise they might have done. But in August a note was entered in Roxbury church records, and published in an Almanac, which has been communicated to me in these words :—

The Anabaptists gathered themselves into a church, prophesied one by one, and some one among them administered the Lord's Supper after he was regularly excommunicated by the church at Charlestown ; they also set up a lecture at Drinker's house once a fortnight.

As great noise was made about their receiving excommunicate members and officers, it is proper to give that matter a distinct consideration here. Dr. Mather says :—

Our Anabaptists formed a church .... not only with a manifest violation of the laws in the Commonwealth, relating to the orderly manner of gathering a church, but also with a manifold provocation unto the rest of our churches, by admitting into their own society such as our churches had excommunicated for moral scandals, yea, and employing such persons to be administrators of the two sacraments among them.[2]

[1]Their Church Records. Russell's Narrative, pp. 1, 2.
[2]Magnalia, Book VII, p. 27, [Vol. II, p. 459.]

They would thus represent as though that church had many such members and officers ; whereas, in fifteen years, among fourscore Baptist members, they have named but four excommunicated persons, and but one of them an officer, viz.. Thomas Gould, who, with Thomas Osburne, was of the first members ; and as the impartial reader would be willing to hear both sides upon it, I will give him their story in their own words.

Mr. Samuel Willard of Boston, who wrote against this church, says of Thomas Gould :—

Though he was first called to an account about withholding his child from baptism, yet that was not the reason of his being admonished, nor because he could not be convinced of error ; nor yet did the church proceed to admonition, till such time as he (not only spake contemptuously and irreligiously of the emptiness and nullity of that ordinance, but also) used unbecoming gestures in the time of administration. of which (being asked the reason) he (before the congregation) acknowledged they were to cast disrespect upon it ; nor then neither till after much patience. 2. At his first admonition he was not sententially suspended, but only desired, for preventing of the offence of some, to abstain from coming to the other sacrament. 3. Upon this Thomas Gould took up a trade of absenting himself from the meetings of the church to worship God on the Sabbath, which made a new offence. 4.. The church in much tenderness waited upon him, and proceeded not to excommunication, but tried with admonition upon admonition, and that by the space of seven or eight years ; nor was he excommunicated, till (having left his own) he joined to another society, without the church's leave, or once asking it ; and now also being twice sent for by the church, he disclaimed their authority over him. 5. Thomas Gould did not leave the church at Charlestown on the account of the Anabaptists' new church (as is pretended) but had many years before renounced his submission to that church. 6. He did (while under admonition) neglect public worship, and gather a private meeting on the Sabbath to his house. 7. He did wickedly slight the admonition of the church, declaring that they had by it, discharged him of all relation to them.

For Thomas Osburne ; the church's proceedings with him were with the like patience as to Thomas Gould ; only it is to be observed, that his first offence was this ; whereas it is one thing which church members engage to upon admission, to walk with the church in constant attendance upon public worship, he (without notifying any offence) did withdraw and separate, frequenting those schismatic meetings at Gould's on the Sabbath ;

19

this was the offence, nor did he when first dealt with pretend any dislike of infant baptism, but that the church gave no liberty to private brethren to prophesy, that they limited the ministry to learned men, and that he did not find his own spirit free to come ; though afterwards he spake both of that, and of their severity to the Quakers, though that church meddled not with them, but to preach against their errors. In this practice he contumaciously persisted many years, denying himself to be subject to that church, or bound to assemble with them, slighting many admonitions ; and afterwards (with Thomas Gould) went off to, and became a worthy pillar of an Anabaptist church.[1]

This is the Pædobaptist's story ; Mr. Gould has given us his in the words following :—

It having been a long time a scruple to me about infant baptism, God was pleased at last to make it clear to me by the rule of the gospel, that children were not capable nor fit subjects for such an ordinance, because Christ gave this commission to his apostles, first to preach to make them disciples, and then to baptize them, which infants were not capable of ; so that I durst not bring forth my child to be partaker of it ; so looking that my child had no right to it, which was in the year 1655, when the Lord was pleased to give me a child ; I staid some space of time and said nothing to see what the church would do with me. On a third day of the week when there was a meeting at my house, to keep a day of thanksgiving to God for his mercy shown to my wife, at that time one coming to the meeting, brought a note from the elders of the church to this effect, that they desired me to come down on the morrow to the elder's house, and to send word again what time of that day I would come, and they would stay at home for me ; and if I could not come that day to send them word. I, looking on the writing with many friends with me, I told them I had promised to go another way on the morrow. Master Dunstan[2] being present desired me to send them word, that I could not come on the morrow, but that I would come any other time that they would appoint me ; and so I sent word back by the same messenger. The fifth day, meeting with elder Green, I told him how it was ; he told me it was well, and that they would appoint another day when he had spoken with the pastor, and then they would send me word. This lay about two months, before I heard any more from them. On a First-day, in the afternoon, one told me I must stop, for the church would speak with me. They called me out, and Mas-

[1]Willard's answer to Russell, pp. 13, 14. Note, Richard Russell, one of their magistrates, was a member of Charlestown church ; and did not he act against the Quakers ?

[2]I suppose, Mr. Henry Dunstar.

ter Sims told the church, that this brother did withhold his child from baptism, and that they had sent unto him to come down on such a day to speak with them, and if he could not come on that day to set a day when he would come, and they be . at home, but he refusing to come would appoint no time, when we writ to him to take his own time and send us word.

I replied that there was no such word in the letter, for me to appoint the day ; but what time that day I should come. Mr. Sims stood up and told me, *I did lie*, for they sent to me to appoint the day. I replied again that there was no such thing in the letter. He replied again, that they did not set down a time, and not a day, therefore he told me it was a lie, and that they would leave my judgment and deal with me for a lie ; and told the church that he and the elder agreed to write, that if I could not come that day, to appoint the time when I could come, and that he read it, after the elder writ it, and the elder affirmed it was so ; but I still replied, there was no such thing in the letter, and thought that I could produce the letter. They bid me let them see the letter, or they would proceed against me for a lie. Brother Thomas Wilder, sitting before me, stood up and told them, that it was so in the letter as I said, for he read it when it came to me. But they answered, it was not so, and bid him produce the letter, or they would proceed with me. He said, I think I can produce the letter, and forthwith took it out of his pocket, which I wondered at ; and I desired him to give it to Mr. Russell to read, and so he did, and he read it very faithfully, and it was just as I had said, that I must send them word what time of that day I would come down ; so that their mouths were stopped, and Master Sims put it off, and said he was mistaken, for he thought he had read it otherwise ; but the elder said, This is nothing, let us proceed with him for his judgment. Now let any man judge what a fair beginning this was, and if you wait a while you may see as fair an ending. They called me forth to know why I would not bring my child to baptism. But before I speak to that, observe the providence of God in the carriage of this letter. Brother Wilder was with us when their letter came to my house, and after Mr. Dunstan [Dunstar] had read it, he gave it to brother Wilder and he put it into his pocket, and it lay there eight or nine weeks, till, that day I was called forth, going a good space from his house, finding it too cold to go in the clothes he had on, [he] returned again and put on another pair of breeches which were warmer, and when he had so done, put his hand into his pocket to see if he had any paper to write with, and there found that letter, and put it in again and went to meeting, yet not knowing what would be done that day concerning me. God had so appointed it, to stop their fierce proceedings against me for a lie, which they sought to take me in. Then asking me why I did not bring my child to baptism, my answer was, I did not see any rule of Christ for it, for that ordinance belongs to such as can make profession of their faith, as the Scripture doth plainly hold forth. .... They answered me, That was meant of grown persons, and not of children ; but that which was most alleged by them was, that children were capable of circumcision in the time of the law, and therefore as capable in the time of the gospel of baptism ; and asked me why children were not to be baptized in the time of the gospel, as well as children were circumcised in the time of the law? My answer was, God gave a strict command in the law for circumcision of children ; but we have no command in the gospel, nor example, for the baptizing of children.   Many other things were spoken, then a meeting was appointed by the church the next week at Mr. Russell's.

Being met at Mr. Russell's house, Mr. Sims took a writing out of his pocket wherein he had drawn up many arguments for infants' baptism, and told the church that I must answer those arguments, which I suppose he had drawn from some author ; and told me I must keep to those arguments.   My answer was, I thought the church had met together to answer my scruples, and to satisfy my conscience by a rule of God, and not for me to answer his writing.   He said he had drawn it up for the help of his memory, and desired we might go on.   Then I requested three things of them.   1st. That they should not make me offender for a word.   2d. They should not drive me faster than I was able to go.   3d. That if any present should see cause to clear up any thing that is spoken by me, they might have their liberty without offence ; because here are many of you that have their liberty to speak against me if you see cause.   But it was denied, and Mr. Sims was pleased to reply, that he was able to deal with me himself and that I know it.   So we spent four or five hours speaking to many things to and again ; but so hot, both sides, that we quickly forgot and went from the arguments that were written.   At last one of the company stood up and said, I will give you one plain place of Scripture where children were baptized.   I told him that would put an end to the controversy.   That place in the second of the Acts, 39th, 40th verses.   After he had read the Scripture, Mr. Sims told me that promise belonged to infants, for the Scripture saith, *The promise is to you and your children, and to all that are afar off ;* and he said no more, to which I replied, *Even so many as the Lord our God shall call.*   Mr. Sims replied, that I spoke blasphemously in adding to the Scriptures.   I said, pray do not condemn me, for if I am deceived, my eyes deceive me. He replied again, I added to the Scripture, which was blasphemy.   I, looking into my Bible, read the words again, and said it was so.   He replied the same words the third time before the church. Mr. Russell stood up and told him it was so as I had read it.   Ay, it may be so in your Bible, saith Mr. Sims.   Mr. Russell answered, Yea in yours too if you will look into it.   Then he said he was mistaken, for he thought on another place ; so after many other words we broke up for that time.

At another meeting the church required me to bring out my child to baptism. I told them I durst not do it, for I did not see any rule for it in the word of God. They brought many places of Scripture in the Old and New Testaments, as circumcision and the promise to Abraham, and that children were holy, and they were disciples. But I told them that all these places made nothing for infants' baptism. Then stood up W, D, in the church and said, " *Put him in the Court! Put him in the Court!*" But Mr. Sims answered, I pray forbear such words ; but it proved so, for presently after, they put me in the Court, and put me in seven or eight Courts, whilst they looked upon me to be a member of their church. The elder pressed the church to lay me under admonition, which the church was backward to do. Afterwards I went out at the sprinkling of children, which was a great trouble to some honest hearts, and they told me of it. But I told them I could not stay, for I look upon it as no ordinance of Christ. They told me that now I had made known my judgment I might stay, for they know I did not join with them. So I stayed and sat down in my seat when they were at prayer and administering that service to infants. Then they dealt with me for my unreverent carriage. ... One stood up and accused me, that I stopped my ears ; but I denied it.

At another meeting they asked me if I would suffer the church to fetch my child and baptize it? I answered, If they would fetch my child and do it as their own act they might do it ; but when they should bring my child, I would make known to the congregation that I had no hand in it ; then some in the church were against doing of it. A brother stood up and said, Brother Gould, you were once for children's baptism, why are you fallen from it? I answered, It is true, and I suppose you were once for crossing in baptism, why are you fallen from that? The man was silent. But Mr. Sims stood up in a great heat, and desired the church to take notice of it, that I compared the ordinance of Christ to the cross in baptism! This was one of the great offences they dealt with me for. After this the Deputy Governor[1] meeting me in Boston, called me to him and said, Goodman Gould, I desire you that you would let the church baptize your child. I told him that if the church would do it upon their own account they should do it, but I durst not bring out my child. So he called to Mrs. Norton of Charlestown, and prayed her to fetch Goodman Gould's child and baptize it. So she spake to them, but not rightly, informing them, she gave them to understand that I would bring out my child. They called me out again and asked me if I would bring forth my child? I told them No, I durst not do it, for I see no rule for it. One of the brethren stood up and said, If I would not let my child partake of one ordinance, it was meet I should not partake of the other ; so many of the church concluded to lay me under admonition ; but before they did it Mr. Sims told me, it

[1]Mr. Bellingham, who was chief Governor when Mr. Gould was banished in 1668.

was more according to rule for me to withdraw from the ordinance, than for them to put me by; bringing that place of Scripture, If thou bring thy gift to the altar, and there rememberest that thy brother hath ought against thee, leave there thy offering and be reconciled first to thy brother. But I told them, I did not know that my brother had any thing justly against me; for they had not shewn me any rule of Christ that I had broken, therefore I durst not withdraw from that ordinance that I had found so much of God in; but if they would put me by, I hoped God would feed my soul another way. So they proceeded to admonition. Elder Green[1] said, Brother Gould, you are to take notice that you are admonished for three things; the first is, that you refused to bring your child to be baptized; the second is, for your contentious words, and unreverent carriage in the time of that ordinance; the third is, for a late lie you told; and therefore you are to take notice, that you are not to partake any more of the ordinance of Christ with us, till you give satisfaction for these things. But when that late lie was told I know not, except it was when the letter was found in brother Wilder's pocket. This admonition was between seven and eight years before they cast me out. After this I went to Cambridge meeting, which was as near to my house as the other; upon that they put me into the Court, that I did not come to hear; but many satisfied the Court that I did come constantly to Cambridge; so they cleared me. Then the church called me to account and dealt with me for schism, that I rent from the church. I told them, I did not rend from them, for they put me away. Master Sims was very earnest for another admonition for schism, which most of the church were against; but it seems he set it down for an admonition on a bit of paper. This continued for a long time before they called me out again. In the meantime, I had some friends who came to me out of old England, who were Baptists, and desired to meet at my house of a First-day, which I granted. Of these was myself, my wife and Thomas Osburne, that were of their church. Afterward they called me forth and asked why I kept the meeting in private on the Lord's day, and did not come to the public? My answer was, I know not what reason the church had to call me forth. They asked me if I was not a member of that church? I told them they had not acted toward me as a member, who had put me by the ordinances of Christ seven years ago; .... they had denied me the privileges of a member. They asked whether I looked upon admonition as an appointment of Christ? I told them, Yes, but not to lie under it above seven years, and to be put by the ordinances of Christ in the church; for the rule of Christ is first to deal with men in the first and in the second place, and then in the third place before the church; but the first time that ever they dealt with me, they called me before the whole

---

[1] Mr. Green, as I take it, was ruling elder; Mr. Zachariah Sims, was teaching elder.

church. Many meetings we had about this thing, whether I was a member or not, but could come to no conclusion ; for I still affirmed that their actings rendered me no member.   Then Mr. Sims told the church that I was ripe for excommunication, and [he] was very earnest for it ; but the church would not consent.   Then I desired that we might send to other churches for their help to hear the thing betwixt us ; but Master Sims made me this answer : We are a church of Christ ourselves, and you shall know that we have power to deal with you ourselves.   Then said Mr. Russell, We have not gone the right way to gain this our brother, for we have dealt too harshly with him.   But still Master Sims pressed the church to excommunicate me.   Mr. Russell said, There were greater errors in the church in the apostles' time, and yet they did not so deal with them.   Mr. Sims asked him what they were ?   He said, How say some of you that there is no resurrection of the dead ?   Mr. Sims was troubled and said, I wonder you will bring this place of Scripture to encourage him in his error ?   Mr. Sims was earnest for another admonition.   Then stood up Solomon Phips and said, You may clap one admonition on him upon another, but to what end, for he was admonished about seven years ago !   Mr. Sims said, Brother ! do you make such a light matter of admonition, to say, Clap them one upon another ? Doth not the apostle say, After the first and second admonition reject an heretic ? therefore there might be a second admonition.   It was answered, it was a hard matter to prove a man an heretic, for every error doth not make a man a heretic.   Mr. Sims said, It was not seven years ago, nor above three, since I was admonished, and that was for schism.   A brother replied and said, it was seven years since I was admonished.   On that there was some difference in the church what I was admonished for.   Mr. Sims then pulled a bit of paper out of his pocket and said, This is that he was admonished for, and that was but three years since.   Brother Phips asked him when that paper was writ, for he never heard of that admonition before ?   He answered, he set it down for his own memory ; then he read it, that it was for schism, and rending from the church.   I told him I did not rend from the church, but the church put me away from them, and that was four years before this.   Then there was much agitation when the admonition was given, and what it was for ?   And this was all the church records that could be found, which was about seven years after the admonition was given ; so after many words we broke up, which was the last time we met together.   Now let any man judge of the church records that were drawn up against me, and read at the dispute in Boston, which contained three or four sheets of paper ; read by Mr. Shepard,[1] and drawn up by him, a little while before the dispute, who was not an eye nor ear witness to the church's actings not above half the time.

[1]Son to Mr. Thomas Shepard, formerly of Cambridge.

Now after this, considering with myself what the Lord would have me to do ; not likely to join with any of the churches of New England any more, and so to be without the ordinances of Christ ; in the mean time God sent out of Old England some who were Baptists ; we, consulting together what to do, sought the Lord to direct us, and taking counsel of other friends who dwelt among us, who were able and godly, they gave us counsel to congregate ourselves together ; and so we did, being nine of us, to walk in the order of the gospel according to the rule of Christ, yet knowing that it was a breach of the law of this country ; that we had not the approbation of magistrates and ministers, for that we suffered the penalty of that law, when we were called before them.   After we had been called into one or two courts, the church understanding that we were gathered into church order, they sent three messengers from the church to me, telling me the church required me to come before them the next Lord's day.   I replied, The church had nothing to do with me, for they had put me from them eight years before.   They replied, that they had nothing to do with that, but were sent by the church to tell me it was the mind of the church to speak with me.   I told them I was joined to another church, and that church was not willing I should come to them, they having nothing to do with me, therefore I would not come without the church's consent. Then they departed. The next week they sent three messengers more, who came to my house and told me that the church had sent them to require me to come to the church the next Lord's day after.   I told them that the church had nothing to do to require me to come, who had put me from them eight years, and the church I now walked with would not let me come.   They told me again that if I did not come, the church would proceed against me the next Lord's day.   I told them that I could not come for we were to break bread the next Lord's day. They told me they would return my answer to the church.   One of them asked if I would come the next Lord's day after? But another presently said, We have no such order from the church ; so they departed.   The last day of that week three loving friends coming to me of their own account, one of them was pleased to say to me, Brother Gould, though you look upon it as unjust for them to cast you out, yet there be many that are godly among them, that will act with them through ignorance, which will be a sin of them, and you are persuaded, I believe, that it is your duty to prevent any one from any sinful act ; for they will cast you out for not hearing the church ; now your coming will stop them from acting against you, and so keep many from that sin.   Upon these words I was clearly convinced that it was my duty to go, and replied, Although I could not come the next day, yet I promised them that if I was alive and well, I would come the next Lord's day if the Lord permit.   He replied, What if the church I was joined to was not willing? I told him I did not question that any one would be against it upon this ground. After I had propounded it to the church, not one was against it. I entreated these friends to make it known to the elders that I would come to them the next Lord's day after; yet, though they knew of it, they proceeded against me that day, and delivered me up to Satan for not hearing the church.

This narrative I met with among Mr. Callender's papers, and I have good reason to think it genuine, and that the manuscript now in my hands was written above a hundred years ago; which I have copied that the public may be better able to judge of what those excommunications were. It appears by Mr. Willard that the first charge they had against Mr. Osburne, was his going to meeting with that schismatical Gould; therefore, as the reader judges of the one, so likely he will of the other. Only it ought to be noted, that neither of them were excommunicated persons, when they formed that Baptist church, but had that sentence pronounced upon them afterwards, for refusing to return to those who had treated them so ill. And before that act, viz., on August 20, 1665, Richard Russell, Esq., issued a warrant to the constable of Charlestown, the original whereof is now before me, requiring him in his Majesty's name, to labor to discover where these people were assembled, and to require them to attend the established worship, which if they refused, he was to return their names and places of abode to the next magistrate. In consequence whereof they were brought before the Court of Assistants in September; to whom they exhibited a confession of their faith, which is copied into their records. The only article of which that I find objected against is in these words, viz.: "Christ's commission to his disciples is to teach and baptize, and those who gladly receive the word and are baptized, are saints by calling, and fit matter for a visible church." This was complained of as excluding all from a visible saintship but baptized persons, which we shall hereafter see they had no thought of. But their grand crime lay in not obeying the ruling party in their religious affairs.

The Court of Assistants charged them to desist from what they called their schismatical practice; and because they would not, the General Court that met October 11, convented Gould, Turner, Osburne, Drinker and George before them, to whom these Baptists exhibited the same confession as they had to the Court of Assistants, which was closed with saying, " If any take this to be heresy, then do we, with the apostle, confess, that after the way which they call heresy, we worship God the Father of our Lord Jesus Christ, believing all things that are written in the law and the prophets and apostles." This the Court called a " contemning the authority and laws here established, for the maintenance of godliness and honesty, as well as continuing in the profanation of God's holy ordinances ;" and said :—

This Court taking the premises into their serious consideration, do judge meet to declare, that the said Gould and company, are no orderly church assembly, and that they stand justly convicted of high presumption against the Lord and his holy appointments, as also the peace of this government, against which this Court doth account themselves bound to God, [to] his truth and his churches here planted, to bear their testimony, and do therefore sentence the said Thomas Gould, William Turner, Thomas Osburne, Edward Drinker and John George, such of them as are freemen, to be disfranchised, and all of them, upon conviction before any one magistrate or Court, of their further proceedings herein, to be committed to prison until the General Court shall take further order with them. Zechariah Rhodes being in Court when they were proceeding against Thomas Gould and company, and saying in Court, " The Court has not to do in [with] matters of religion ;" he was committed likewise. Being sent for he acknowledged his fault, declaring he was sorry he had given them offence. The Court judged meet to discharge him, the Governor giving him an admonition for his said offence.[1]

Can any man believe that these were measures to promote either godliness or honesty, in Rhodes, or in any one else? rather did not the Court take Jehovah's name in vain in this

[1]Massachusetts Records. Rhodes was a Baptist, but had been of Arnold's party at Pawtuxet. Massachusetts History, Vol. III, p. 277.—B.

The Massachusetts Records as published give only the surnames of the offenders and arrange them in the following order, viz.: Gould, Osburne, Drinker, Turner and George.—Ed.

act ?   The forementioned excuse, made by Dr. Mather, for
this severity, viz., their joining in church fellowship without
the approbation of other ministers and their rulers,[1] says
Mr. Neal, " condemns all the dissenting congregations that
have been gathered in England, since the act of uniformity
in the year 1662. . . . . Let the reader judge, who had most
reason to complain ; the New England churches, who would
neither suffer the Baptists to live quietly in their communion
nor separate peaceably from it ; or these unhappy persons
who were treated so unkindly for following the light of their
consciences."[2]   Yet because they still followed that light,
they were presented to the County Court at Cambridge,
April 17, 1666, " for absenting themselves from the public
worship."   And when they asserted that they did steadily
attend such worship,[3] the foregoing act of the Assembly was
produced to prove that it was not in a lawful way ; and
Gould, Osburne and George, were each of them fined four
pounds therefor, and ordered to bind themselves in a bond
of twenty pounds apiece, for their appearance at the next
Court of Assistants; and refusing so to do were committed
to prison.[4]   When the Court of Assistants came, they gave
sentence that they should pay their fines and Court charges;
and when the Assembly sat on September 11, they ordered,

[1] See page 288.—ED.

[2] Neal's History of New England, Vol. I, pp. 304, 305.

[3] "Thomas Osburne answered that the reason of his non-attendance was that the
Lord hath discovered unto him from his word and spirit of truth that the society
wherewith he is now in communion is more agreeable to the word of God, asserted
that they were a church and attended the worship of God together, and do judge
themselves bound so to do, the ground whereof he said he gave in to the General
Court.   Thomas Gould answered that as for coming to public worship, they did
meet in public worship according to the rule of Christ, the grounds whereof they
had given to the Court of Assistants, asserted that they were a public meeting
according to the order of Christ Jesus, gathered together.   John George answered
that he did attend the public meetings on the Lord's days where he was a member,
asserted that they were a church according to the order of Christ in the gospel, and
with them he walked and held communion in the public worship of God on the Lord's
days.   Massachusetts History, Vol. III, [Hutchinson's Collection of Original
Papers,] p. 400.—ED.

[4] Massachusetts History, Vol. III, pp. 400, 401.

that if they would pay the same, they should be set at liberty; but added that, " the order of Court of October, 1665, referring to the said schismatical assembly, shall be, and hereby is declared to stand in full force."[1]   Thus they went on from time to time, till the Court of Assistants at Boston, March 3, who adjourned to May 1, 1668, passed the following act, a copy of which I find among their church papers, exactly in these words, viz. :—

Thomas Gould, plaintiff, on appeal from the judgment of the last County Court at Charlestown. After the Court's judgment, reasons of appeal and evidences in the case produced were read, committed to the jury, and remain on files with the records of this Court.   The jury brought in their verdict ; they found for the plaintiff, reversion of the former judgment. The Court not accepting this verdict, commended it to the jury's further consideration, and sent them out again.   And at the adjournment, on the further consideration, they brought in a special verdict, i. e., If the intent of this law, that the appellent is accused of the breach of, be that the presentment of the Grand Jury, without their certain knowledge, or other evidence, or the person so complained of is legally convicted of the breach of the law, thereby he not making it appear he had done his duty, then they confirmed the judgment of the former Court at Charlestown, but if otherwise they acquit the appellant. The Court, on a due consideration of this special verdict, do confirm the judgment of the County Court at Charlestown. This judgment was declared, and on the plaintiff's refusal to pay the fine imposed, [he] was committed to prison.

On the 7th of this March, they also said :—

The Governor and Council, accounting themselves bound by the law of God, and of this Commonwealth, to protect the churches of Christ here planted, from the intrusion thereby made upon their peace in the ways of godliness, yet being willing by all Christian candor to endeavor the reducing of the said persons from the error of their way, and their return to the Lord and the communion of his people from whence they are fallen, do judge meet to grant unto Thomas Gould, John Farnum, Thomas Osburne and company, yet further an opportunity of a full and free debate, of their grounds for their practice ; and for that end this court doth nominate and request the Rev. Mr. John Allen, Mr. Thomas Cobbet, Mr. John Higginson, Mr. Samuel Danforth, Mr. Jonathan Mitchel, and Mr. Thomas Shepard, to assemble with the Governor and magistrates, upon the 14th day of

[1]Massachusetts Records.

the next month, in the meeting-house at Boston, at nine in the morning; before whom, or so many of them, with any other the Reverend elders or ministers, as shall then assemble, the above-said persons and their company shall have liberty, freely and fully, in open assembly, to present their grounds as above-said, in an orderly debate of this following question :— Whether it be justifiable by the word of God, for these persons and their company to depart from the communion of these churches, and to set up an assembly here in the way of Anabaptism, and whether such a practice is to be allowed by the government of this jurisdiction? To Thomas Gould :—You are hereby required in his Majesty's name, according to the order of the Council above-written, to give notice thereof to John Farnum, senior, Thomas Osburne, and the company, and you and they are alike required· to give your attendance, at the time and place above-mentioned, for the end therein expressed.

EDWARD RAWSON, Secretary.[1]

Mr. Clarke's church in Newport, hearing of this appointment, sent to the assistance of their brethren, Mr. William Hiscox, Mr. Joseph Tory, and Mr. Samuel Hubbard, who arrived at Boston, three days before the dispute. The author of Mr. Mitchel's life says :—

When the churches were troubled by a strong attempt upon them from the spirit of anabaptism, there was a public disputation appointed at Boston, two days together, for the clearing of the faith in that article ; this worthy man was he, who did most service in this disputation ; whereof the effect was, that although the erring brethren, as is usual in such cases, made this their last answer to the arguments, which had cast them into much confusion, *Say what you will, we will hold our minds!* yet others were happily established in the right ways of the Lord.

How well this corresponds with the preceding pages, the reader may judge. For therein we are informed, that Mr. Mitchel was fearful of going to a learned gentleman who had renounced infant baptism ; and that he resolved that *he would have an argument able to remove a mountain*, before he would recede from that principle.[2] And a look back to our page 185, will show what fear the ruling party had, of disputing upon their way with another learned Bap-

---

[1]Copied from the warrant now before me in Mr. Rawson's hand writing.

[2]His Life, pp. 69, 70, 72. [Magnalia, Vol. II, pp. 79, 80.] The dispute was held both the 14th and 15th of April.

tist ; but the whole power of the country now adventured to enter the lists with a few honest mechanics.

When the Assembly met at Boston in May following, they proceeded to the next argument and said :—

Whereas, the Council assembled in March last, did, for their further con-viction, appoint a meeting of divers elders, and required the said persons to attend the said meeting, which was held [here] in Boston with a great concourse of people, ... this court, being sensible of their duty to God and the country, and being desirous that their proceedings in this great cause might be clear and regular, do order that the said Gould and com-pany be required to appear before this Court, on the seventh instant, at eight in the morning, that the Court may understand from themselves, whether upon the means used, or other considerations, they have altered their former declared resolution, and are willing to desist from their for-mer offensive practice, that accordingly a meet [and] effectual remedy may be applied to so dangerous a malady.....At the time they, Thomas Gould, William Turner and John Farnum, being summoned, made their appearance, and after the Court had heard what they had to say for them-selves, proceeded. Whereas, Thomas Gould, William Turner, and John Farnum, senior, obstinate and turbulent Anabaptists, have some time since combined themselves with others in a pretended church estate, with-out the knowledge and [or] approbation of the authority here established to the great grief and offence of the godly orthodox ;....the said persons did in open Court, assert their former practice to have been according to the mind of God, and that nothing that they had heard convinced them to the contrary ; which practice, being also otherwise circumstanced with making infant baptism a nullity, and thereby making us all to be unbap-tized persons, and so consequently no regular churches, ministry, or ordi-nances ; as also renouncing all our churches, as being so bad and corrupt that they are not fit to be held communion with ; denying to submit to the government of Christ in the church, and entertaining of those who are under church censure, thereby making the discipline of Christ [in his churches] to be of none effect, and manifestly tending to the disturbance and destruction of these churches,—opening the [a] door for all sorts of abominations to come in among us, to the disturbance not only of [our] ecclesiastical enjoyments, but also contempt of our civil order, and the authority here established, ... which [our] duty to God and the country doth oblige us to prevent, by using the most compassionate effectual means to attain the same ; all of which considering, together with the danger of disseminating their errors, and encouraging presumptuous irregularities by their example, should they continue in this jurisdiction ; this Court do judge it necessary that they be removed to some other part of this country, or elsewhere, and accordingly doth order, that the said Thomas Gould, William Turner, and John Farnum, senior, do before the 20th of July next, remove themselves out of this jurisdiction, and that if after the said 20th of July [the said Thomas Gould, William Turner, and John Farnum, senior, or] either of them be found in any part of this jurisdiction, without license, [first] had [and obtained] from this Court or the Council, he or they shall be forthwith apprehended and committed to prison by warrant from any magistrate, and there remain without bail or mainprise, until he or they shall give sufficient security to the Governor or any magistrate, immediately to depart the jurisdiction, and not to return as above said. And all constables and other officers, are required to be faithful and diligent in the execution of this sentence. And it is further ordered, that the keepers of all prisons whereto the said Thomas Gould, William Turner and John Farnum, senior, or any of them shall be committed, shall not permit any resort of companies of more than two at one time to any of the said persons. And our experience of their high, obstinate and presumptuous carriage, doth engage us to prohibit them any further meeting together, on the Lord's day, or [upon any] other days, upon pretence of their church estate, or for the administration or exercise of any pretended ecclesiastical functions, or dispensation of the seals or preaching; wherein if they shall be taken offending, they shall be imprisoned until the tenth of July next, and then left at their liberty within ten days to depart the jurisdiction upon penalty as aforesaid. And, whereas, Thomas Gould is committed to prison in the county of Middlesex, by the last Court of Assistants, for non-payment of a fine imposed, this Court [having passed a censure on him and others] judgeth it meet, after the sentence of this Court is published this day after the lecture to them, that the said Gould shall be [declared to be] discharged from imprisonment in Middlesex as to his fine, that so he may have time to prepare to [and] submit to the judgment of this Court.[1]

This looked like a powerful way of arguing; but the Baptists were not convinced by it, either of its being duty to return into fellowship with those who managed the argument, or to quit their stations and enjoyments at their command. I find by the colony records, that John Farnum was admitted a freeman of that colony May 13, 1640; Thomas Gould, June 2, 1741; in which year John George bound himself to Governor Winthrop, I suppose, to pay for his

[1]Massachusetts Records.

passage over to this country.   And I have a copy before me
of a warrant for the commitment of Turner and Farnum to
Boston jail, dated July 30, this year, signed by Governor
Bellingham, Eleazer Lusher and Edward Tyng.   When the
Assembly met again in the fall, a petition was presented to
them, whereof a copy found among their church papers, is
before me, in these words :—

Whereas by the censure of this honorable Court, Thomas Gould, William Turner and John Farnum, now lie in prison deprived of their liberty,
taken off from their callings, separated from their wives and children, dis-
abled to govern or to provide for their families, to their great damage and
hastening ruin, how innocent soever ; beside the hazard of their own lives,
being aged and weakly men, and needing that succor a prison will not
afford ; the sense of this, their personal and family most deplorable and
afflicted condition, hath sadly affected the hearts of many sober and serious
Christians, and such as neither approve of their judgment or practice ; especially considering that the men are reputed godly, and of a blameless conversation ; and the things for which they seem to suffer seem not to be
moral, unquestioned, scandalous evils, but matters of religion and conscience ; not in things fundamental, plain and clear, but circumstantial,
more dark and doubtful, wherein the saints are wont to differ, and to forbear one another in love, that they be not exposed to sin, or to suffer for
conscience sake.   We therefore most humbly beseech this honored Court,
in their Christian mercy and bowels of compassion, to pity and relieve
these poor prisoners ; whose sufferings (also being doubtful to many, and
some of great worth among ourselves, and grievous to sundry of God's
people at home and abroad,) may crave a further consideration, whereby
perceiving this Court not likely to effect the end desired, but rather to
grieve the hearts of God's people ; now your wisdoms may be pleased to
think of some better expedient, and seriously consider whether an indulgence, justifiable by the word of God, pleaded for and practiced by Congregational churches, may not, in this day of suffering to the people of God,
be more effectual, safe and inoffensive than other ways, which are always
grievous, and seldom find success.   We in all humility hope, hereby occasions of difference being removed, that love and communion among all
saints, which our dying Lord so weightily charged and earnestly prayed
for, will more easily be preserved and practiced, to the glory of God, honor
of the gospel, peace and welfare of all the churches, which this honored
Court being the happy instruments of effecting, will oblige your poor petitioners, as in duty bound, to pray for your happiness both in this life and
in that to come, and that your authority may be long continued as an unparalleled blessing to this Commonwealth.

We are informed that Captain Edward Hutchinson, Captain Oliver, and many others, signed this petition; but the Court were so far from granting it, that the chief promoters of it were fined, and others compelled to an acknowledgment of their fault in reflecting upon the Court herein. We are also told, that the Honorable Francis Willoughby, who was their Deputy Governor from 1665, till he died on April 4, 1671, " was a great opposer of these persecutions against the Baptists."[1] Leverett and Symonds, his successors in that office, appear also to have been on that side of the question. The ruling party printed their sentence against those Baptists, an answer to which I find among their church papers, which is closed with these words :—

This my husband would entreat of you, to take counsel of Master Bennet, and if he and you judge it meet, to send it to England, and the printed sentence with it. It is desired that no man see it but Goodman Sweetser, and that Josiah write it fair and plain.

I conclude the person here speaking is Elder Gould's wife ; and the most material points of her answer are as follows :—

First, They call them *obstinate and turbulent Anabaptists.* 1. I desire to know wherein their obstinacy doth appear? They desired the Court to show them, from the rule of Christ, of any point that they were out of the way of God ; and if the Lord was pleased to show them wherein they were out, they would freely lay it down ; but they shewed them no other rule than their own law ; and sentenced them to be fined and imprisoned ; and this was all the rule they could give, which did not convince them. 2. They say they were *turbulent.* I desire them to prove wherein they were turbulent, when they did not disturb neither churches nor courts, neither by word nor by action , but desired to live quietly and peaceably among them, and they cannot tell of any one thing that they disturbed them in, but desired they might enjoy that liberty that Christ hath purchased for them. They know not that they spoke any word that gave offence to the Court, unless it was those few words, when Master Bradstreet pronounced that sentence against them, and charged them no more to meet together, whether on the Lord's day or on the week days, in their conventicles ; those words were returned by them, We ought to obey God rather than man ; we cannot but do the things we have heard and learned. 3. As for *Ana-*

[1]Massachusetts History, Vol. II, pp. 227, 269, [236, 246.]
20

baptists, they do not own that name, except they will be pleased to explain what they mean by it ; for they own them to be of the baptized. Again, they say, *they combined together in a pretended church estate.* They need not have said so, unless they could have proved they set up their church contrary to a rule of Christ. Beside, they gave them in a writing wherein they gave a brief account of their faith, where they declared what they owned to be a church of Christ, and the order of it according to the rule of the Scripture, which neither the Court nor the elders ever answered to this day. They say it was *without the knowledge or approbation of the authority here established as the law required.* Answer :—1. If the apostles had not set up churches in their time, without the approbation of the authority and their priests, there had been few or no churches in their time. 2. Christ is Lord and King of his church, and he will set up his government therein, and hath given them rules from himself, how to set it up and to carry it along according to his appointment, and not to ask leave of the powers of the world to set up his church ; for Christ's jurisdiction is the greatest jurisdiction in the world. 3. They had asked leave, had they found a command of Christ for it, but finding no rule of Christ they did not do it.

Again,'they say some of themselves were *excommunicated persons.* First, it is true what they say, yet that some was but two that were cast out, and that after they were gathered into this pretended church, as they call it, a good space of time. But consider for what it was, and how it was?

Here the foregoing account of Messrs. Gould and Osburne is confirmed. And of the day they were cast out she says :—

The word was carried to the elder, that if they were alive and well they would come the next day, yet they were so hot upon it that they would not stay, but Master Sims when he was laying out the sins of these men, before he had propounded it to the church, to know their mind, the church having no liberty to speak, he wound it up in his discourse, and delivered them up to Satan, to the amazement of the people, that ever such an ordinance of Christ should be so abused, that many of the people went out ; and these were the excommunicated persons. They say, *After long forbearance to use the utmost means to convince and reduce them, entreated the assistance of divers elders.* Answer :—1. It is true there were seven elders appointed to discourse with them, and there were a few plowmen and tailors to come before them ; but how they were served with a warrant to appear before these elders in his Majesty's name ! 2. When they were met, there was a long speech made by one of them, of what vile persons they were, and how they acted against the churches and government here,

and stood condemned by the Court.   The others desiring liberty to speak,
they would not suffer them, but told them they stood there as delinquents,
and ought not to have liberty to speak.   Then they desired they might
choose a moderator as well as they ; they denied them.   Two days were
spent to little purpose. .... In the close, Master Jonathan Mitchel pronounced that dreadful sentence against them in Deut. xvii. 8 to the end of
the 12th, and this was the way they took to convince them, and you may
see what a good effect it had. .... There was nothing spoken from the
rule of Christ, neither from the Court nor the elders, but such sentences as
these, fining, and whipping, and prisoning, and banishing, and Master
Mitchel's sentence, and all these are not the weapons of Christ, but carnal
weapons that never did convince any soul of the error of his ways.

Whereas, they say, *Which practice making infant baptism a nullity*, &c. ;
I answer, It is good for every one to be sure that they are upon good ground
whatsoever the practice of others may seem to condemn. .... They say,
Tending to the disturbance and destruction of these churches.   For Answer,
1. If eight or nine poor Anabaptists, as they call them, should be the destruction of their churches, then let any seeing man judge what their
churches are built upon ; then we may think they are built upon a sandy
foundation ; for the church of Christ is built upon himself, and the gates
of hell shall not prevail against it.   2. If they be the churches of Christ,
and think they shall be overthrown by them, it is from the weakness of
their faith, looking more to an arm of flesh and powers of the world to
uphold them, than to Christ and his faithful promise.   3. If they fear they
will be the destruction of their churches, now [that] all the power of the
country is for them and [they] have an arm of flesh to help them, what
will they do when all the powers of the country are against them, as are
against the other, as you say yourselves of them, that when they were in
examination before the Court, they professed themselves resolved to adhere
to the same practice ; and now suffer willingly for it.   But for the men,
what they are, I shall say nothing, for the sixty-five hands to the petition
that was put into the General Court, does [do] plainly declare to their best
discerning, that they have been honest and godly, and lived quietly and
peaceably among them a good length of time.   Again they say, *By using
the most compassionate and effectual means to attain the same.*   Answer :--1.
The Lord keep every gracious soul from such compassionate means for the
truth of the gospel !   2. For what compassionate means were used with
them, let men fearing God judge ; for one of them was called from prison
when this sentence of banishment was read against them ; and if any man
desires to inform himself wherein their compassion appears, let him read
their printed sentence against them, which was executed upon them ; for,
not moving themselves, they sent the constable, and fetched them away to
prison on a public lecture day at Boston, when the said Thomas Gould,

William Turner and John Farnum, had been all there, and newly come home to their houses, and they remain in prison to this day.

How any that feared God, could be ensnared and held in such a way of treating their fellow-servants may doubtless appear unaccountable to many ; but a careful search will help us to discover the nature of this mystery. The establishment of a Christian commonwealth, was the grand object that had been before those leaders for forty years, and it continued so to their last hours. Mr. Wilson, the first minister of Boston, had been famed for a gift of prophecy, or foretelling future events ; and as his dissolution appeared near, a large number of ministers came round him on May 16, 1667, and desired him to declare unto them, what he conceived to be the sins among them that caused the displeasure of God against the country. He told them he had long feared the following sins as chief among others, which greatly provoked God, viz. :—

1. Separation. 2. Anabaptism. 3. Corahism. [The latter he did explain thus :] when people rise up as Corah, against their ministers or elders, as if they took too much upon them, when indeed they do but rule for Christ, and according to Christ ; yet (said he) it is nothing for a brother to stand up and oppose, without Scripture or reason, the doctrine and word of the elder, saying I am not satisfied, &c., and hence, if he do not like the administration, be it baptism or the like, he will [then] turn his back upon God and his ordinances, and go away. And [saith he] for our neglect of baptizing the children of the church, those that some call grandchildren, I think God is provoked by it. 4. Another sin I take to be the making light of, [and] not subjecting to the authority of synods without which, the churches cannot long subsist. And so for the magistrates being Gallio-like, either not caring for these things, or else not using their power and authority for the maintenance of the truth, [and] gospel and ordinances of our Lord and Saviour Jesus Christ, and for bearing thorough witness against the contrary. Should the Lord leave them hereunto how miserable a people should we be !

And at night he blessed them upon their parting, with great affection, and with tears, " and all the ministers wept with him, and took their leave of him, even as children of their father, who having blessed them was about to die."

He died the 7th of August following.[1] These things affected their minds in such a manner, that upon his church's obtaining Mr. Devenport from New Haven to succeed him, who had printed his testimony against the result of the late synod about the Half-way Covenant, a minor part of the church drew off from the rest, and in May, 1669, other ministers assisted in forming them into a new church, in open separation from the first church in Boston, which schism continued about fourteen years, till an Episcopal invader of their rights drove them together again.[2] Hence see what a schismatical doctrine that is, of infant church membership, and of using secular force in religious affairs. What divisions and contentions did it produce both in Connecticut and

[1] Morton, pp. 195, 196. [211, 212.]

[2] Magnalia, B. 5., pp. 82, 83. [Vol. II, pp. 266, 267.] " There was a great difference betwixt the old church and the members of the new church, about baptism, and their members joining in full communion with either church. This was so high that there was imprisoning of parties, and great disturbances; but now hearing of my proposals for ministers to be sent over, they are joined together, about a fortnight ago, and pray to God to confound the devices of all who disturb their peace and liberties." Randolph's letter to the Bishop of London, May 9, 1682. Massachusetts History, Vol. III, pp, 531, 532. That new church is since called The Old South.—B.

The passage in the Magnalia above referred to, is as follows :—"That famous and faithful society of Christians, the first church in Boston, had, after much agitation, so far begun to attend the discipline directed in the doctrine of the synod that they proceeded ecclesiastically to censure the adult children of several communicants for scandals, whereinto they had fallen. But that church, for a supply of their vacancy upon the death of their former more synodical ministers, applying themselves unto Mr. John Devenport, the greatest of the antisynodists, all the interests of the synod came to be laid aside, therein, on that occasion. Hereupon thirty members of that eminent church offered several reasons of their dissent from their call of that worthy person. . . . . The difference produced so much division that the major part of the church, by far, proceeded to their election of that great man; this lesser part nevertheless carefully and exactly following the advice of councils fetched from other churches in the neighborhood, set up another church in the town of Boston, which hath since been one of the most considerable in the country. Very uncomfortable were the *paroxisms* which were the consequents of this ferment. *Longa est injuria, longa ambages* . . . . Indeed, for a considerable while, though the good men on both sides really loved, respected and honored one another, yet, through some unhappy misunderstandings in particular persons, the communicants of these two particular churches in Boston, like the two distinguished rivers, not mixing, though running between the same banks, held not communion with one another at the table of the Lord."—ED.

Massachusetts? Is it not evident that they proceeded from a confounding of the Jewish and Christian churches together? for a right to membership and to office, in the former, proceeded in a natural, in the latter, in a spiritual line. The gainsaying of Korah was after an infallible authority had fixed the priesthood in the line of Aaron and his seed, who were types of Christ and his saints, but officers in distinction from the rest of the lively stones whereof his house is built, are never called priests in the New Testament; yea, we have seen ministers resenting others calling of them by that name, and yet they in the above instance and down to this day, have applied the case of Korah to those who refuse practically to own them as such. And they have often told us of David's error, in carrying the ark upon a new cart, instead of the priests' shoulders; but that error is theirs, not ours; and had they been as ready to imitate David in reformation as they were in transgression what happy times might we have seen before now? The oracles of God were then carried in the ark, but now his church is the pillar and ground of the truth. I Timothy 3. 15; I Peter 2. 5. Upon Uzza's being struck dead, David was turned to search the divine rules, which taught him to rest the cause of truth upon living shoulders, instead of an earthly machine drawn by beastly force. I Chron. 15. 2. But when the rulers of the Massachusetts were moved by their ministers to exert such force against the Baptists, though they saw the chief procurers of that sentence struck dead before the time came for its execution, and many more of them about that time, yet their posterity have approved their sayings even to this day.[1] I am well sensible that the

---

[1]Mr. Henry Flint of Braintree, and Mr. Samuel Shepard of Rowley, died about the time of their dispute with the Baptists in Boston. Mr. Mitchel, who was most active in procuring the sentence against them, died July 9, aged 43, and Mr. John Eliot, junior, October 13, 1668, aged 35, both of Cambridge. Mr. John Reyner of Dover, and Mr. Richard Mather of Dorchester, both died in April, and Eleazer Mather of Northampton, on July 24, 1669, aged 32. Mr. Sims, who had treated the Baptists so ill, and Mr. John Allen of Dedham, one of the disputants against them, both died within two years after, as well as many others.

divine judgments are a great deep, and that love or hatred is not to be known merely by such outward events; yet they ought to put us all upon searching and trying our ways (as David did) by the revealed will of God; which duty was excellently inculcated upon them at that time in a letter to Captain Oliver of Boston, in the words following :—

MY DEAR BROTHER : The ardent affection and great honors that I have for New England transport me, and I hope your churches shall ever be to me as the gates of heaven. I have ever been warmed with the apprehension of the grace of God towards me in carrying me thither. I have always thought that of the Congregational churches of New England in our days. But now it is otherwise, with joy as to ourselves and grief as to you be it spoken. Now the greater my love is to New England the more am I grieved at their failings. It is frequently said here, that they are swerved aside towards presbytery; if so, the Lord restore them all. But another sad thing that much affects us is, to hear that you even in New England persecute your brethren; men sound in the faith; of holy life [and] agreeing in worship and discipline with you; only differing in the point of baptism. Dear brother, we here do love and honor them, hold familiarity with them, and take sweet council together; they lie in the bosom of Christ and therefore they ought to be laid in our bosoms. In a word, we freely admit them into churches; few of our churches but many of our members are Anabaptists; I mean baptized again. This is love, in England; this is moderation; this is a right New Testament spirit. But do you now (as is abovesaid) bear with, yea, more than bear with, the Presbyterians? yea, and that the worst sort of them, viz., those who are the corruptest, rigedest; whose principles tend to corrupt the churches; [so] turning the world into the church, and the church into the world; and which doth no less than bring a people under mere slavery. It is an iron yoke which neither we nor our Congregational brethren in Scotland were ever able to bear. I have heard them utter these words in the pulpit, that it is no wrong to make the Independents sell all they have, and depart the land; and many more things I might mention of that kind; but this I hint only, to shew what cause there is to withstand that wicked tyranny which was once set up in poor miserable Scotland, which I verily believe was a great wrong and injury to the reformation. The generality of them here, even to this day will not freely consent to our enjoyment of our liberty; though, through mercy, the best and most reformed of them do otherwise. How much more therefore would it concern dear New England to turn the edge against [those] who, if not prevented, will certainly corrupt and enslave, not only their own, but also your churches? Whereas Anabaptists are neither

spirited nor principled to injure nor hurt your government nor your liberties ; but rather these be a means to preserve your churches from apostacy,
and provoke them to their primitive purity, as they were in the first planting, in and admission of members to receive none into your churches but
visible saints, and in restoring the entire jurisdiction of every congregation
complete and undisturbed.   We are hearty and full for our Presbyterian
brethren's enjoying equal liberty with ourselves ; oh that they had the same
spirit towards us ! but oh how it grieves and affects us that New England
should persecute ! will you not give what you take ? is liberty of conscience
your due ? and is it not as due unto others that are sound in the faith ?
Read the preface to the declaration of the faith and order, owned and
practiced in the Congregational churches in England, pp. 6, 7.   Amongst
many other Scriptures, that in the 14th of Romans much confirms me in
liberty of conscience thus stated : To him that esteems any thing unclean,
to him it is unclean ; verse 13.   Therefore though we approve of the baptism of the immediate children of church members, and [of] their admission into the church when they evidence a real work of grace ; yet to
[those] that in conscience believe the said baptism to be unclean, it is unclean.   Both that and mere ruling elders, though we approve of them, yet
our grounds are mere interpretations of, and not any express Scripture.   I
cannot say so clearly of any thing else in our religion, neither as to faith
or practice.   Now must we force our interpretation, upon others, Pope-like?
In verse 5 of that chapter the Spirit of God saith, Let every one be fully
persuaded in his own mind ; therefore this being the express will of God,
who shall make a contrary law, and say, Persuaded or not persuaded, you
shall do as we say, and as we do ! and verse 23, What is not of faith is sin ;
therefore there must be a word for what we do, and we must see and
believe it, or else we sin if we do it.   And Deut. 12, and last, as we must
not add, nor may we diminish ; what is commanded we must do.   Also
28th of Matthew.   And what principles is persecution grounded upon?
Domination and infallibility.   This we teach is the truth.   But are we
infallible, and have we the government?   God made none, no not the
apostles who could not err, to be lords over [of our] faith ; therefore what
monstrous pride is this?   At this rate any persuasion getting uppermost
may command, and persecute them that obey them not ; all non-conformists
must be ill-used.   Oh wicked and monstrous principle !   Whatever you can
plead for yourselves against those that persecute you, those whom you persecute may plead for themselves against you.   Whatever you can say
against those poor men, your enemies say against you.   And what ! is that
horrid principle crept into precious New England, who have felt what persecution is, and have always pleaded for liberty of conscience ; Have not
those run equal hazards with you for the enjoyment of their liberties ; and
how do you cast a reproach upon us, that are Congregational in England,

and furnish our adversaries with weapons against us? We blush and are filled with shame and confusion of face, when we hear of these things. Dear brother, we pray that God would open your eyes and persuade the hearts of your magistrates, that they may no more smite their fellow servants, nor thus greatly injure us their brethren; and that they may not thus dishonor the name of God, and cause his people to be reproached, nor the holy way of God (the Congregational way) to be evil spoken of. My dear brother! pardon my plainness and freedom, for the zeal of God's house constrains me. What cause have we to bless God who gives us to find favor in the eyes of his Majesty, and to pray God to continue him, and to requite it graciously to him in spiritual blessings. Well, strive I beseech you with God by prayers, and use all lawful ways and means, even to your greatest hazard, that those poor men may be set free. For be assured, this liberty of conscience, as we state it, is the cause of God; and hereby you may be a means to divert the judgments of God from falling upon dear New England, for our Father in faithfulness will afflict us if we repent not. Doth not the very gospel say, What measure we mete to others shall be measured to us? God is not unrighteous. What is more provoking to him than the persecuting of his saints? Touch not mine anointed, and do my prophets no harm! Did he not reprove kings for their sake? those who have the unction the apostle John speaks of, and the spirit and gift of prophecies. With what marvellous strength did holy Mr. Burroughs urge that place against persecution? Persecution is bad in wicked men, but it is most abominable in good men, who have suffered and pleaded for liberty of conscience themselves. Discountenance men that certainly err, but persecute them not. I mean gross errors. Well, we are travelling to our place of rest; with joy we look for new heavens and new earth. We shall ere long be in the fullness of bliss, holy, harmless in the bosom of Christ. Let us pray the earth may be filled with the knowledge of the Lord, that they may not hurt nor destroy in all his holy mountain. The Lord grant we may by the next hear better things of the government of New England. My most hearty love to [you and] your brother, and to all our brethren. My respects and my service to my dear cousin Leverett, and to Mr. Francis Willoughby. The Lord make them instrumental for his glory, in helping to reform things among you. I shall be glad to hear from you. I remember our good old sweet communion together. My dear brother, once again pardon me, for I am affected! I speak for God, to whose grace I commit you all in New England; humbly craving your prayers for us here, and remain,

Your [most] affectionate brother,

ROBERT MASCALL.

Finsbury, near Morefield, the 25th of March, 1669.[1]

---

[1] Samuel Hubbard's collection.

Never did I see the true nature of these controversies better stated by any on that side. Our opponents have no better grounds for accusing us of denying Scripture consequences, than because we refuse to yield to their interpretations, which appear to us unsound. Neither are we any more rigid than themselves ; though because they hold to two or three ways of baptizing, while we believe our Lord has instituted but one baptism, they accuse us with it, if we cannot act with them as baptized persons, who appear to us not to be such. The plain question is, Whether each one shall be allowed to act the full persuasion of his own mind, according to God's law, or whether the ruling party in the State shall make the law void by their traditions ? The learned and much esteemed Dr. Goodwin, Dr. Owen, Mr. Nye, Mr. Caryl, and nine other noted dissenting ministers in London wrote to the Massachusetts Governor, upon these things at the same time, and said :—

We shall not here undertake [in the least] to make any apology for the persons, opinions and practices of those who are censured among you. You know our judgment and practice to be contrary unto theirs, even as yours ; wherein (God assisting) we shall continue to the end. Neither shall we return any answer to the reason of the reverend elders, for the justification of your proceedings, as not being willing to engage in the management of any the least difference with persons whom we so much love and honor in the Lord. But the sum of all which at present we shall offer to you is, that though the Court might apprehend, that they had grounds, in general, warranting their procedure (in such cases) in the way wherein they have proceeded ; yet that they have any rule of command rendering their so proceeding indispensably necessary, under all circumstances of fines [times?] and places, we are altogether unsatisfied ; and we need not represent unto you how the case stands with ourselves, and all your brethren and companions in the services of these latter days in these nations. We are sure you would be unwilling to put an advantage into the hands of some, who feel pretences, and occasions against our liberty, and to reinforce the former rigor. Now we cannot deny but this hath already in some measure been done, in that it hath been vogued, that persons of your [our] way, principles and spirit, cannot bear with dissenters from them. And as this greatly reflects on us, so some of us have observed how already it has turned unto your own disadvantage. We leave it to your wisdom to

determine, whether under all these circumstances, and sundry others of the
like nature that might be added, it be not advisable at present to put an
end unto the sufferings and confinements of the persons censured, and to
restore them to their former liberty.[1] You have the advantage of truth
and order; you have the gifts and learning of an able ministry to manage
and defend them; you have the care and vigilancy of a very worthy
magistracy to countenance and protect them, and to preserve the peace;
and above all, you have a blessed Lord and Master, who hath the keys of
David, who openeth and no man shutteth, living forever to take care of
his own concernments among his saints; and assuredly you need not be
disquieted, though some few persons (through their own infirmity and weakness, or through their ignorance, darkness and prejudices) should to their
disadvantage turn out of the way, in some lesser matters, into by-paths of
their own. We only make it our hearty request to you, that you would
trust God with his truths and ways so far, as to suspend all vigorous proceedings in corporal restraints or punishments, on persons that dissent from
you, and practice the principles of their dissent without danger or disturbance to the civil peace of the place.

Dated March 25, 1669.

We may reasonably conclude that this address did not
reach Boston till May or June; and Dr. Mather says, " I
cannot say that this excellent letter had immediately all the
effect it should have had."[2] So that though he allows that
some of those Baptists were " truly godly men,"[3] yet it is
likely that they were imprisoned a year or more, only for
not banishing themselves for their religion. After their release, Elder Gould went and lived upon an island in the
harbor; where they held their meeting for some years. But
this could not make the ruling party easy, as the following

---

[1] " At a Court of Assistants held at Boston, March 2, 1669, the Governor and
Magistrates being assembled in Council, and motion being made by Thomas Gould,
in behalf of himself and William Turner, now in durance by the sentence of the
General Court; the keepers of the prisons, under whose custody they now are, are
ordered to permit them liberty for three days, to visit their families, as also to apply
themselves to any that are able and orthodox, for their further convincement of their
many irregularities in those practices for which they were sentenced; the said keeper staking the engagements of the said Gould and Turner, or other sufficient caution,
for their return again to prison at the end of the said three days.

By the council,   EDWARD RAWSON, Secretary."
[2] Magnalia, B. 7, pp. 27, 28. [Vol. II, pp. 460, 461.]
[3] Ibid. [Vol. II, p. 459.]

letter to Mr. Clarke and his church at Newport plainly shews :—

BELOVED BRETHREN AND SISTERS :—I most heartily salute you all in our dear Lord, who is our alone Savior in all our troubles, that we his poor members are exercised with for his name's sake. And blessed be God our Father, that has given us such a High Priest, that was touched with the feeling of our infirmities, which is no small comfort to the souls of his poor suffering ones ; the which, through grace, the Lord hath been pleased to make us in some [small] measure partakers of. And at this present our dear brother William Turner, a prisoner for the Lord's cause in Boston, has some good experience of, both of that which Paul desired, to be comformable to our Lord in his sufferings, and also of the promises of our Lord, in the giving forth [of] the comfort of his Spirit, to uphold us all, for that he is sensible of the sufferings of his poor members, and is ready to give forth supplies as are most suitable to such a condition as he calls his to. Friends, I suppose you have heard that both he and brother Gould were to be taken up ; but only brother Turner is yet taken and has been about a month in prison. Warrants are in two marshals' hands for brother Gould also, but he is not yet taken, because he lives on Noddle's Island, and they only wait to take him at town [but he comes not over.] The cause why they are put in prison is the old sentence of the General Court in '68, because they would not remove themselves. There were six magistrates' hands to the warrant to take them up, viz., Mr. Bradstreet, Major Denison, Thomas Danforth, Captain Gookin, Major Willard and Mr. Pinchon. But all the deputies of the Court voted their liberty, except one or two at most, but the magistrates carry against all ; and because some others of the magistrates were absent, and some that were there were Gallio-like, as one Mr. R. B. G.[1] But blessed be the Lord who takes notice of what is done to his poor servants, though men little regard. The town and country is very much troubled at our troubles ; and especially the old church in Boston, and their elders, both Mr. Oxonbridge and Mr. Allen have labored abundantly, I think as if it had been for their best

---

[1] I suppose, Richard Bellingham, Governor. Thus a few men at the head of the government, by the clergy's help, carried on their oppressions against the minds of those worthy rulers, Willoughby, Symonds and Leverett, a whole House of Deputies, and the best part of the whole community. "That magistrates should thus suffer these incendiaries, and disturbers of the public peace, might justly be wondered at, if it did not appear that they have been invited by them unto a participation of the spoil, and have therefore thought fit to make use of their covetousness and pride, as a means whereby to increase their own power. For who does not see that these good men are indeed more ministers of the government, than ministers of the gospel. Locke on Toleration, pp. 71, 72.

friends in the world.[1] Many more gentlemen and solid Christians are for our brother's deliverance ; but it cannot be had ; a very great trouble [is it] to the town ; and they had gotten six magistrates' hands for his deliverance, but could not get the Governor's hand to it..... Some say one end is, that they may prevent others coming out of England ; therefore they would discourage them by dealing with us ; a sad thing if so, when God would have Moab be a refuge for his banished ones, and that Christians will not. But God will be a refuge for his, which is our comfort. We keep our meeting at Noddle's Island, every First-day, and the Lord is adding some souls to us still, and is enlightening some others ; the priests are much enraged. The Lord has given us another elder, one John Russell, senior, a gracious, wise and holy man that lives at Woburn, where we have five brethren near that can meet with him ; and they meet together First-days when they cannot come to us, and I hear there are some more there looking that way with them. Thus, dear friends, I have given you an account of our troubles, that you may be directed in your prayers to our God for us ; as also of the goodness of God to us, and the proceedings of his good work in our hands, both to our, and I doubt not, to your joy and comfort. That God may be glorified in all, is our earnest desire and prayer to God, in all his dispensations to us. Brother Turner's family is very weakly and himself to. I fear he will not trouble them long ; only this is our comfort, we hear if he dies in prison, they say they will bury him. And thus, my dear friends, I desire we may be remembered in your prayers to our Heavenly Father, who can do abundantly above what we can ask or think ; to whom I commend you all, and rest, your friend and brother,

EDWARD DRINKER.

November 30, 1670.

This occasioned the following epistle to them, viz. :—

Unto the church of Jesus Christ, meeting on Noddle's Island in New England. Grace, mercy and peace be mightily showered down upon you all, with such daily supplies to every one of you, according to your various conditions, strengthening the weak, and making you to press forward with life and courageous hearts, being valiant for the Lord and his holy truths, holding out to the end in what ye have received ; not to look back, but pressing forward to know more of his holy will, like children desiring the sincere milk of the word, to grow up therein. Samuel Hubbard, a very poor and unworthy one, yet by great grace found in my sinful estate, among the sinners in a sinful world, in a sinful age, and by free grace called by a di-

[1]Mr. Devenport died March 15, 1670, aged 72; and Mr. John Oxonbridge, who left England, after the cruel Bartholomew Act in 1662, was settled in his stead, collegue with Mr. James Allen, who came from thence about the same time.

vine call or power, being not able to resist it, but by grace shewed that it
was his will to call sinners that were weary and heavy laden to come unto
him, making a gracious promise, that they should find rest to their souls;
Matt. 11; and by his grace hath made me willing, in my very weak
measure, to be going on in what he hath shewed me; though I find a law
in my members, contrary to God's holy law, which is written in my heart,
leading me captive both in thoughts, words and deeds, which is a great
burden, and makes me go heavily. But blessed be God, my rock, who
hath shewed me that it is not by my works, but by faith in our precious
Redeemer, I am accepted with the Father. Not thereby taken off from
endeavoring to keep all his holy commandments and ordinances, but with
righteous Zacharias and Elizabeth, desirous to be found blameless, when
our Lord and King Jesus shall come, and by him enabled with joy to say,
This is my Lord, I have waited for him; when you with others shall meet
and sing the song of Moses and the Lamb, Hallelujah to God most High,
&c. Dear and precious hearts, my love is such towards you, for what of
God is in you, and what great grace hath appeared towards you, in bearing you up to stand in this hour of temptation, that your feet are not
moved, and your arms are made strong by the mighty God of Jacob; yea,
not only so, but hath crowned your endeavors with a blessing of increase of
such precious helps, as I hear you have, in which I rejoice, desiring greatly
of the Lord, that he would be still with you to the end of your race. Dear
friends, it was upon my heart to have given you a visit, whereby I might
have been refreshed by your mutual love, as I have been to see your precious order in the gospel; but it has pleased our heavenly Father to visit
me and my dear wife, by a sore stroke in taking away our only son
Samuel;[1] all we had; a man grown (whose we are also); but God of
his grace hath borne us up, blessed be his name! by which I have been
very much disappointed as in coming to you, so in many other things, and
am learning in every condition to be content; a hard lesson to learn I find.
Dear brethren and sisters, what am I, poor worm, to inform you! but to
stir up your pure minds that you would be holding fast what you have received, that you may not lose your rewards, for this is a declining day.
But know, the reward is laid up in most sure hands, for those who hold out
to the end. I beseech you, pray with all manner of prayers, and for me,
poor one, that I may have such fresh supplies of grace, that I may stand
fast in what I have received of God, and not deny his name, knowing of
whom I have received it. Pray for me that I may have more of the spirit

---

[1]He was in his 21st year, a very promising youth. Mr. Hubbard's daughter Ruth,
married to Robert Burdick, and Bethia, married to Joseph Clarke, jun'r, have left a
large posterity at Westerly; and Rachel, married to Andrew Langworthy, left a large
family in Newport; and he hoped that all his children, and some of his grandchildren were savingly converted.

of adoption, to cry in faith, Abba, Father; more of faith in those precious promises made to his in the Holy Scriptures, and more strength to run the ways of his holy commandments with more delight and largeness of heart without partiality. Oh! my dear friends, pray for Sion! they that love her shall prosper. Oh! my brethren and sisters! pardon my boldness, and accept in love my weak endeavors, and let me have from you a few lines, which would be as a dew upon my poor weak heart, which needs information, instruction and comfort. Thus, desiring your prosperity in your inward man, and outward man also, knowing that if ye seek first the kingdom of God, we have our Lord's word for it, that all other things shall be added; committing you to the Almighty to bless you with spiritual blessings, with such daily fresh supplies as you stand in need of, whereby ye may abound for his name's praise, the good of sinners, strengthening of saints, comforting one another, drawing in love in all your ways, which is as precious ointment, giving forth such a precious savor as that all Christ's virgins may love and rejoice in you, and bless God on your behalf. The God of all grace be with you all. Amen. My wife desires to have her affectionate and entire love to you all remembered. Your poor weak brother in the best relation,   SAMUEL HUBBARD.

Newport, this 4th day of the 9th Month, 1671.

Dear brother and sister, my kind love and respect with my wife's, be remembered to you with all the rest of our dear friends, hoping you welfare. These few lines are to let you understand, that your loving Christian letter you sent me I received, for which I give you hearty thanks. I delivered your letter according to your desire, and it was read in the church, wherein we understand the Lord has been pleased to take away your son, that was dear unto you. God sometimes tries his people in that which is most near and dear to them, even in their Isaacs. Jacob must part with his Benjamin, and say, All these things are against me; yet the Lord turned it about for good; and he has promised that all shall work for good unto those that love and fear him; and what he deprives us of in the creature, he is able to make up abundantly in himself. The good Lord grant that it may be so with you! Brother Turner has been near to death, but through mercy is revived, and so has our pastor, Gould. The Lord make us truly thankful, and give us hearts to improve them, and those liberties we yet enjoy that we know not how soon may be taken from us. The persecuting spirit begins to stir again. Elder Russell and his son, and brother Foster, are presented to the Court that is to be this month. We desire your prayers for us, that the Lord would keep us, that we may not dishonor that worthy name we have made profession of, and that the Lord would still stand by us, and be seen amongst us, as he has been in a wonderful manner in preserving of us until this day. We should be glad to hear how it is with you, and desire if it be the will of God, that love and peace may be continued betwixt you and the other society; although you may differ in some things, yet there may be endeavors to keep the unity of the spirit in the bond of peace, and as far as we have attained, to walk by the same rule. I shall not trouble you any further, but commit you to the guidance and protection of the Almighty, and remain your unworthy brother in the best relation,   BENJAMIN SWEETSER.

Charlestown, the first, 10th month, '71.

The next news from them is as follows :—

I perceive you have heard as if our brother Russell had died in prison. Through grace he is yet in the land of the living, and out of prison bonds ; but is in a doubtful way as to recovery of his outward health ; but we ought to be quiet in the good will and pleasure of our God, who is only wise. I remain your loving brother,   WILLIAM HAMLIT.

Boston, 14, of the 4th month, 1672.

We will now look a little back, and see how their oppressors got along. The breach in Boston church affected many ; and the Governor appeared against the new party, and in July, 1669, called his Council together, fearing, he said, " a sudden tumult, some persons attempting to set up an edifice for public worship, which was apprehended by authority to be detrimental to the public peace." But the majority of the Council were not for hindering their proceeding. On May 11, 1670, Mr. Danforth of Roxbury, who was one of those that had been called to the Baptist dispute two years before, said to the Assembly in his election sermon :—

Is not the temper, complexion and countenance of the churches strangely altered? Doth not a careless, remiss, flat, dry, cold, dead frame of spirit grow upon us secretly, strongly, prodigiously? They that have ordinances are as though they had none ; they that hear the word as though they heard it not; and they that pray as though they prayed not; and they that received sacraments as though they received them not ; and they that are exercised in holy things, use them by the by, as matters of custom and ceremony. .... Pride, contention, worldliness, covetousness, luxury, drunkenness and uncleanness break in like a flood upon us ; and good men grow cold in their love to God and one another.[1]

[1]Prince's Christian History, Vol. I, p. 97.—B.

This sermon is entitled " A brief recognition of New England's errand into the wilderness." Text, " What went ye out into the wilderness to see?" The quotations above given are from pages 12, 13.—ED.

Upon this the House of Deputies appointed a committee, to inquire into the prevailing evils that had procured the divine displeasure against the land; and they reported these among other causes, viz. :—

Declension from the primitive foundation work, innovation in doctrine and worship, opinion and practice; an invasion of the rights, liberties and privileges of churches, a usurpation of a lordly and prelatical power over God's heritage, subversion of gospel order, &c.

They then go on to speak of the late transaction of the elders, in constituting the third church in Boston, as " irregular, illegal and disorderly." But the effect was such, that among fifty deputies in their next Assembly, there were but twenty of those who were in this; and then fifteen ministers presented an address to the new-modeled house, wherein they mention their former connection with rulers, like Moses and Aaron, and then call the setting up of said church in Boston, " That weighty and worthy transaction." They prevailed with this house to correct and declare against what the preceding house had done to the contrary.[1] Such was the ministerial influence of that day. On May 15, 1672, the Assembly ordered their law-book to be revised and reprinted; and therein they say :—

Although no human power be lord over the faith and consciences of men, yet because such as bring in damnable heresies, tending to the subversion of the Christian faith, and destruction of the souls of men, ought duly to be restrained from such notorious impieties; it is therefore ordered and declared by the Court, that if any Christian within this jurisdiction, shall go about to subvert and destroy the Christian faith and religion, by broaching and maintaining any damnable heresies; as denying the immortality of the soul, or resurrection of the body, or any sin to be repented of in the regenerate, or any evil done by the outward man to be accounted sin, or denying that Christ gave himself a ransom for our sins, or shall affirm that we are not justified by his death and righteousness, but by the perfection of our own works, or shall deny the morality of the fourth commandment, or shall openly condemn or oppose the baptizing of infants, or shall purposely depart the congregation at the administration of that ordi-

[1] Massachusetts History, Vol. I, pp. 272—274. [249—251.]

nance, or shall deny the ordinance of magistracy, or their lawful authority
to make war, or to punish the outward breaches of the first table, or shall
endeavor to seduce others to any of the errors and heresies above mentioned ; every such person continuing obstinate therein, after due means of
conviction, shall be sentenced to banishment.[1]

The reader may here observe what advances they had
made since the year 1644.[2] The two articles which the
Baptists own, are now fenced with a much more formidable
catalogue of heresies and errors, than were then inserted in
their law against them. Though they still fall far behind
their mother, the church of England ; for the last man that
she burnt for religion was a Baptist, and in the warrant for
his burning, the King says :—

Whereas the reverend father in God, Kichard, bishop of Coventry and
Litchfield, having judicially proceeded in the examination, hearing and
determining of a cause of heresie against Edward Wightman, of the parish of Burton upon Trent, in the diocese of Coventry and Litchfield, concerning the wicked heresies of the Ebionites, Cerenthians, Valentinians,
Arrians, Macedonians, of Simon Magus, of Manes, Manichees, of Photi-
nus, and Anabaptists, and of other heretical, execrable and unheard of
opinions, by the instinct of Satan, by him excogitated and holden, &c.

They went on to name sixteen articles, many of them so
foolish and inconsistent, that, as the historian observes, he
must be an idiot or a madman to hold them all. Three of
them are in these words, viz. :—

13. That the baptizing of infants is an abominable custom.   14. That
there ought not, in the church, the use of the Lord's supper to be celebrated
in the elements of bread and wine, and the use of baptism to be celebrated in the element of water, as they are now practiced in the church of
England ; but the use of baptism is to be administered in water, only to
converts of sufficient age and understanding, converted from infidelity to
the faith.   16. That Christianity is not wholly professed and preached in
the church of England but only in part.

For these things Mr. Wightman was burnt at Litchfield,[3]

---

[1]Massachusetts Law-book, printed 1672. pp. 58, 59.   [2]See page 126.
[3]Descendants of this martyr to Baptist principles are said to have come early to
the country, where several of them have been well known pastors of Baptist churches.
Benedict's History of the Baptists, Vol. I, pp. 196, 501, 521.   Semi-centennial Discourse of the New London Baptist Association; Minutes, 1867, p. 40.—ED.

April 11, 1611, by a warrant from that king, who in the preface to our Bible is compared to the rising sun,[1] and whose tyranny drove our fathers into New England.

The above clearly shows that the church of England far exceeded her daughters in this land, both in the number of hard names they imposed upon the Baptists, and also in their degree of cruelty towards them; though a lamentable imitation of those evils appears in this history. And to enforce the fore-cited law among the rest, the Massachusetts placed the following motto in the title page of their law book:—" Whosoever resisteth the power, resisteth the ordinance of God, and they that resist receive to themselves damnation." But whether the assuming and exerting of such power in religious affairs, be not the way to damnation, rather than the resistance of it, deserves the serious consideration of all. Some years ago, when the Presbyterians had the upper hand in England,[2] Mr. Samuel Oates, a noted and successful Baptist minister, was imprisoned, put in irons, and tried for his life as a murderer, at Chelmsford assize, only because Ann Martin, a young woman that he had baptized, happened to die a few weeks after. But when his case came to be tried, her mother and others declared upon oath, " that she was in better health for several days after her baptism than she had been for some years before; and was seen to walk abroad very comfortably," so that he was acquitted.[3]

And now when the Episcopalians had gotten the power again into their own hands, Mr. Neal truly observes, that the enemies to the Baptists tried to ruin them, " by as unparalleled a piece of villainy as ever was heard of."

A pamphlet was published in London, in 1673, entitled, "Mr. Baxter baptized in blood; or a sad history of the unparalleled cruelty of the Anabaptists in New England; faithfully relating the cruel, barbarous and bloody

[1] Crosby's History, Vol. I, pp. 108, and Appendix, pp. 1—3.
[2] See pp. 146, 147.
[3] Crosby's history, Vol. I, pp. 237, 238.

murder of Mr. Josiah Baxter, an orthodox minister, who was killed by the Anabaptists, and his skin most cruelly flead off from his body. Published by his mournful brother, Benjamin Baxter, living in Fenchurch street, London." This pamphlet was licensed by Dr. Parker, the archbishop's chaplain, and cried about streets by the hawkers.[1] The author represents his brother as worsting the Anabaptists in a public disputation at Boston ; for which, by way of revenge, they sent four ruffians in vizors to his house a little way out of town, who, after they had bound his wife and three children, first whipped, and then flead [flayed] him alive. The author concludes, "I have published this narrative *in perpetuam rei memoriam*, that the world may see the spirit and temper of those men, and that it may stand as an eternal memorial of their hatred to all orthodox ministers."

But when search was made by authority, they could find no account of such a minister as Josiah Baxter in New England, nor of his brother Benjamin in London.   The whole story was a naked and malicious forgery,[2] and verified the words of Lactantius, in the next century after Constantine first introduced the custom of supporting such ministers by force as the court called orthodox.   Said he, "Among those who seek power and gain from their religion, there will never be wanting an inclination to forge and lie for it."[3]

As a contrast to the above, I will give a further taste of the spirit of those men who have often been accused of hatred to orthodox ministers.   In the beginning of 1665, Mr. Stephen Mumford, a Seventh Day Baptist, arrived from London at Newport, and Mr. Hiscox, Mr. Hubbard, and other members of Mr. Clarke's church, soon embraced the keeping of that day ; but in 1671, two or three men who had so done, turned back to the observance of the first day, which Mr. Hubbard and others called apostacy, though many accounted it a reformation ; and in June that year Mr. Holmes preached smartly against the others' sentiments ;

[1]Yea, it went off so current that a second edition was got into the press in a few weeks. Parker was thought to be its author. [Crosby, Vol. II, pp. 291, 292.]

[2]Neal's History of New England, Vol. I, pp. 374, 375.—B.

For a complete exposition of this forgery, see Crosby, Vol. II, pp. 278—294. —Ed.

[3]Middleton's Letter from Rome, p. 97.

and the contention increased, till in December it caused an
open separation;[1] upon hearing of which, our suffering
fathers in the Massachusetts wrote the following letter :—

To brother William Hiscox, and the rest of our beloved brethren and sisters,
  that observe the Seventh day Sabbath with him, the church of Christ in
  or near Boston sends greeting.

BRETHREN, BELOVED OF THE LORD :—We having had a view of the proceedings between yourselves and the church, cannot but be grieved to see
how busy the adversary hath been, and how easily he hath prevailed upon
the corruptions of our nature, to make breaches and divisions among those
whom [who], we dare not but judge, are united unto one Head, even Christ
Jesus. And although we dare not judge your consciences in the observation of
a day or days to the Lord, yet, brethren, your judging them that have so
done, and we hope have not unadvisedly changed their minds, to be apostates, seems to our understandings to savor too much a censorious spirit.
And we, as brethren, made partakers of the same grace of God through
the influence of his Holy Spirit, not being enlightened in the observation of
the Seventh day as a sabbath to the Lord, shall humbly beseech you all, to
put on bowels of mercy, and not to be so strait in your spirits towards
others ; but consider, the only wise God giveth to each soul what measure
of light and knowledge he pleaseth ; and it is he must give wisdom to improve that measure of knowledge so given, or else we shall make a bad improvement thereof. Now, brethren, we dare not justify your action, nor
the manner of the actions that have been between you and the church ; but
should have been glad, if it had been the good pleasure of the Lord, that
you could have borne each with other in the matter of difference, and so
have left it for the Lord to reveal more light and knowledge to those that
are yet in the dark. But may we not say, we are all in the dark, and see
and know but in part? and the little part that any one knoweth, he is ready

[1] "The covenant drawn up by the Seventh Day church when they were first
gathered, after they withdrew from the church under the pastoral care of Mr. John
Clarke.

"After serious consideration and seeking God's face among ourselves for the Lord
to direct us in a right way for us and our children, so as might be for God's glory
and our souls' good, we, viz., William Hiscox, Samuel Hubbard, Steven Mumford,
Roger Baxter, Tacy Hubbard, Rachel Langworthy, —— Mumford, entered into covenant with the Lord and with one another, and gave up ourselves to God and one to
another, to walk together in all God's holy commandments and holy ordinances according to what the Lord had discovered to us or should discover to be his mind for
us to be obedient unto; with sense upon our hearts of great need to be watchful
over one another, did promise so to do, and in edifying and building up one another
in our most holy faith; this 7th day of December, 1671." Manuscript of John
Comer ; Backus Historical Society's Library.—ED.

to conceive is the will of God, and so would have all to see with his eyes, and understand with his understanding ; and cannot patiently wait on the Lord till he shall make discoveries of it to his brethren ; so that our quick, narrow and impatient spirits are the cause of so many breaches and divisions amongst the citizens of Sion at this day. By all which we humbly desire the Lord may make you and us, and all the Lord's people, to see the corruption of our natures that is yet unsubdued, that so we may all with sincerity of soul, wait on him according to that measure of light and knowledge that each of us have [has] received from him. And now brethren, our desire is, if it may be the good pleasure of God, that this breach may be healed between you and the church. Our prayers shall be to the Lord for you, that each one of you may be truly sensible, wherein you have so far departed from the law of brotherly love, as to be an occasion of grief one to another, and to the Israel of God, and have given an occasion to the enemies to speak reproachfully of the ways of God ; not doubting but you will be willing to look back over all those actions past in these differences, and if you find anything contrary to the mind and will of God, be willing to own it both to God and his people. We shall leave you to his care and guiding, who is able to comfort you in all your tribulations, and to establish, strengthen and settle you ; to whom we leave you, and remain your poor unworthy brethren, who should rejoice in your prosperity, both in spirituals and temporals. By the appointment of the church assembled.

THOMAS GOULD,
WILLIAM TURNER,
JOHN WILLIAMS.

Noddle's Island, September 1, 1672.

This sweet letter, Mr. Hubbard has preserved, and it caused no alienation of mind, but there remained a great nearness between them as long as they lived. I find him in a letter the next year to his brother Hamlit saying, " I desire the welfare of the whole Sion, and the brethren with you ; brother Foster, brother Farlow, elder Russell and his son ; yea, to all the church, with thanks for their love to me and my wife." Mr. Hamlit wrote on June 19, 1673, that the Baptists were still persecuted for their withdrawing from the public meetings, and said, " Brother Trumbel and brother Osburne were fined last Court at Charlestown, twenty shillings apiece ; they have appealed to the Court of Assistants." But Mr. Bellingham dying, and Mr. Leverett being chosen Governor, and Mr. Symonds, Deputy Governor, things took another turn, so that Mr. Hamlit wrote to his brother Hubbard, on January 9, 1674, and said, " Brother Drinker hath been very sick near unto death, but the Lord hath restored him to health again. The church of the baptized do peaceably enjoy their liberty. Brother Russell, the elder and the younger, have good remembrance of you." And while those governors lived, that church enjoyed the greatest liberty that ever they did under their first charter. After Governor Leverett's death, I find Mr. Russell and his church, in an appointment of a day of thanksgiving, expressing their sense of " the Lord's goodness in preserving our peace and liberty beyond all expectation ; God having removed him, who was a friend to us in the authority, by reason of which our opposites have the greater advantage against us, who have not been wanting to do their endeavor to suppress us." We shall soon find how that advantage was improved. We are informed by their records, that the next members that were added, after the first constitution of the church, were Isaac Hull, John Farnum, Jacob Barney, John Russell, Jr., John Johnson, George Farlow, Benjamin Sweetser, all before Ellis Callender, who was received November 9, 1669. Mr. Hull was called also to be an elder in the church in the time of their sufferings. The next on the list are Joshua Turner, Thomas Foster, John Russell, Sr., (afterwards their pastor,) William Hamlit, James Landon, Thomas Skinner, John Williams, Philip Squire, Mary Gould, Susanna Jackson, Mary Greenleaf, &c. Elder Gould died October 27, 1675, having been a man, "in some good measure fitted and qualified (says Elder Russell) for such a work ; and proved an eminent instrument in the hand of the Lord, for the carrying on this good work of God in its low and weak beginnings." And including the other first constitutors with him, he says :—

Their trouble and temptations followed, one upon the neck of another, like the waves of the sea ; but these precious servants of the Lord, having in some good measure counted the cost beforehand, were not moved from any of these things, but were cheerfully carried on by the hand of the Lord upon them, through all the afflictions and reproaches they met with ; and are the most of them now at rest with the Lord, having served the will of God in their generation.[1]

[1]Hubbard, 624—627. Russell's Narrative, 1680, pp. 1, 2, 6.

CHAPTER VII.

The foregoing history may give the reader some idea, of the nature and causes of the contentions that long labored in the country, between the natives and the English. Mr. Samuel Hubbard in the close of Philip's war, wrote to a minister in England, and said :—

God has been long waiting with patience, by several signs and warnings, these forty years, as I can witness [to] ; but we in our turnings have not so turned to the Lord as ought to be, and his displeasure is broke forth in the country by the natives, who were forced thereto, as some of .them said (and in very deed I judge truly.)[1]

I find by their records, that the Commissioners of the United Colonies, in September, 1662, appointed Captain George Denison, Thomas Stanton, and James Averell, to manage their affairs at Paucatuck, to govern the Indians, and collect the tax imposed upon them on account of the Pequots; and then they say :—

They are also hereby authorized to act and do, or cause to be done, what, in their discretion, may best conduce, to reduce them to civility and the knowledge of God, as well by causing due punishment to be inflicted on disorderly persons according to their demerits, as by encouraging such as shall be sent to instruct them by order of the Commissioners, and by causing them to attend thereunto.

[1]Letter to Edward Stennett, 29th day 9th month, 1676. Samuel Hubbard's Manuscript.—Ed.

And nothing has been more common with their party ever since, than to represent the inhabitants of Rhode Island as an irreligious people ; but I trust the foregoing facts show that they were not all so, to which I shall add, that Mr. Samuel Hubbard's daughter Ruth was converted and joined Mr. Clarke's church in 1652, when she was not thirteen years old, and on August 4, 1666, she wrote from Westerly thus :—

MOST LOVING AND DEAR FATHER AND MOTHER : My duty with my husband and children presented unto you, with all my dear friends.....My longing desire is to hear from you, how your hearts are borne up above these troubles which are come upon us, and are coming, as we fear ; for we have the rumors of wars, and that almost every day. Even now we have heard from your island by some Indians who declared unto us, that the French have done some mischief upon the coast, and we have heard that twelve hundred Frenchmen have joined with the Mohawks, to clear the land both of English and Indians. But I trust in the Lord, if such a thing be intended, that he will not suffer such a thing to be. My desire and prayer to God is, that he will be pleased to fulfill his promise to us, that is, that as in the world we shall have troubles, so in him we shall have peace. The Lord of comfort, comfort your and our hearts, and give us peace in believing and joy in the Holy Ghost. Oh that the Lord would be pleased to fill our hearts with his good Spirit, that we may be carried above all these things ! and that we may remember his saying, When ye see these things come to pass, lift up your heads, knowing that your redemption draws nigh. Then if these things be the certain sign of our Lord's return, let us mind his command, that is, Pray always that ye may be counted worthy to escape all these things, and to stand before the Son of Man. Let us have boldness to come unto him in the new and living way, which he hath prepared for us. Through grace I find the Lord doth bear up the spirits of his in this place, in some comfortable measure, to be looking above these things. The Lord increase it more and more unto the day of his appearing, which I hope is [near] at hand. Dear father and mother, the Lord hath been pleased to give us here many sweet and comfortable days of refreshing, which is great cause of thankfulness, and my desire is, that we may highly prize it, and you with us give the Lord the praise for this benefit. I pray remember my love to all my dear friends with you in fellowship. Sister Sanders desires to be remembered to you all ; so doth sister Clarke. Your loving daughter to my power,

RUTH BURDICK.

Philip was son to Osamaquin and succeeded him as the chief sachem on the east side of Narragansett Bay. He had this name given him by Plymouth Court in 1660. Such rumors spread of his preparing for war, as brought Governor Prince, and two of his Assistants to Taunton, April 13, 1671, to meet three gentlemen from the Massachusetts, to examine into the matter. Philip kept at a distance, and sent to them to come to him at Three Mile River.[1] The Governor sent again for him to come to them, but he refused, till old Mr. Roger Williams and Mr. Brown, I suppose of Swanzey, offered to remain there as hostages; by which means he was brought forward and prevailed with to deliver up about seventy guns he had got, and to promise future fidelity, which suspended the war for four years.[2] And then it was brought on in the following manner. John Sasaman, an Indian that the English had given considerable instruction to, both as to human learning and religious affairs, being with Philip at Namasket, discovered that he was preparing for war, and informed the English of it; for which he was murdered upon a pond at Assawamset, both of which places are in Middleborough. Three Indians were apprehended for that murder, and were executed at Plymouth.

Mr. John Tracy of Norwich had married Mrs. Mary Winslow from Marshfield five years before, and returning from a visit there at this time, happened to fall in among a party of Indians in arms, waiting to hear whether their friends would be executed or not. They brought him to Philip, whom he satisfied that he was only a traveler and upon no ill design, so that he sent him away in peace.[3] But

---

[1] This river runs from Norton through the west part of Taunton, and falls into the Great River betwixt that town and Dighton.

[2] Massachusetts History, Vol. I, pp. 278, 279. [254, 255.]

[3] Callender's Century Sermon, p. 73. [127.] Mr. Tracy was my mother's grandfather.—B.

The only further information which we have of the person here mentioned is in a brief allusion to him in Mr. Backus's Gospel Comfort, a sermon on the death of his mother, in which he says, "Her father, Mr. John Tracy, was a man eminent for vital and practical religion, who died on March 27, 1726, with such comfortable

hearing soon after that those Indians were executed, they
broke out on June 24, 1675, and killed nine men in different parts of Swanzey, and fired upon one in Rehoboth;
which alarmed the country, and in four days an army was
collected there, and made Mr. Miles's house their head-quarters. Philip soon left his station at Mount Hope, now Bristol, and retired to a great swamp east of the Great River.
The Massachusetts part of the army went into the Narragansett country, and brought those Indians to promise not to
join in the war, and then returned, and, with the other forces,
attacked Philip at the swamp on July 18, but had little success therein. Soon after which, Philip and many of his
men repassed the river, and crossing Seconk plain, made
their way up to the Nepmuck Indians in Worcester county,
who had begun the war on July 14.

These alarms caused Mr. Joseph Tory and Mr. Hubbard
to send a boat which brought their friends from Westerly to
Newport this month, and they continued on the island till
the war was over. Soon after Philip had joined the Nep-
mucks, they violently assaulted a small English plantation
at Brookfield, and as Captain Hutchinson with a company
went to relieve them on August 2, they from an ambush
gave him a mortal wound. But Major Willard came two
days after with forty-eight men, and slew many of the enemy, and delivered his friends. Upon which the enemy steered
further westward, and on September 1, burnt most of the
houses in Deerfield, and killed eight men the next day at
Northfield; and Captain Beers going with thirty-six men to
fetch off the inhabitants there, had a terrible fight with the
enemy, wherein he and above half of his men fell. September 18, sundry teams went to bring off a large quantity
of grain from Deerfield, and Captain Lothrop went with
about eighty men to guard them; but not seeing any of the

views of another world, that he charged his friends to give him up, and not hold him
any longer with their prayers. He was very strict in the religious education of his
family, which this daughter of his was ever thankful for as long as she lived."—ED.

enemy, they on their return, got to picking grapes by Muddy Brook, when the enemy got a dreadful advantage of them. I have seen the stone over the place where they tell me about seventy of them were buried in one grave. Presently after, an assault was made upon Springfield, where the minister's house and library was burnt, with thirty-one houses beside. But a large body of Indians making an onset upon Hadley, October 19, and having killed one man, were so bravely repulsed by the English, that in their flight some of them were drowned in Connecticut River, and others who escaped, retired into Narragansett. In that country on a small tract of upland within a great swamp, seven miles west from the south ferry that goes over from Newport, the Indians built and stored the strongest fort they ever had in this country. Therefore the colonies gathered an army of a thousand men, under the command of Governor Winslow, and after a fierce conflict, took and destroyed it, on December 19. They supposed that a thousand of the enemy were cut off; but it cost on our side the lives of six captains, and one hundred and seventy, some said two hundred and ten men, killed or wounded. They marched sixteen or eighteen miles from Major Smith's to that fight, and returned through a terrible snow-storm the same night.[1]

[1] I have met with the original of a testimony concerning that family, and that affair, which I will give a copy of here. It is as follows:—

Narragansett, 21 July, 1679, (*ut vulgo.*)

I, ROGER WILLIAMS, of Providence, in the Narragansett Bay, in New England, being (by God's mercy) the first beginner of the mother town of Providence, and of the Colony of Rhode Island and Providence Plantations, being now near to four-score years of age, yet (by God's mercy) of sound understanding and memory, do humbly and faithfully declare, that Mr. Richard Smith, Sr., who for his conscience to God, left fair possessions in Gloucestershire, and adventured, with his relations and estate, to New England, and was a most acceptable inhabitant, and a prime leading man in Taunton, in Plymouth colony; for his conscience' sake, many differences arising, he left Taunton and came to the Narragansett country, where (by God's mercy and the favor of the Narragansett sachems) he broke the ice at his great charge and hazard, and put up in the thickest of the barbarians, the first English house amongst them. 2. I humbly testify that about forty years from this date, he kept possession, coming and going himself, children and servants and he had a quiet possession of his housing, lands and meadows; and there in his own house, with

Great stores of corn were destroyed in that fort, which reduced the Indians to terrible distress.   But a thaw in January enabled them to get some sustenance out of the earth,
upon which they burnt the deserted houses in Mendon, and
on February 10, 1676, made an onset upon Lancaster, burnt
their habitations, and killed or captivated forty persons, one
of whom was Mrs. Rowlandson, wife of the minister, who
was then gone to Boston to procure help against the enemy.
The narrative she gave of her captivity has lately been reprinted.[1]   Like mischiefs were done at Groton, Marlborough,
Sudbury and Chelmsford; and on February 21, the enemy
wheeled round and came down upon Medfield, (twenty miles
from Boston,) and burnt half their houses, and slew eighteen
men, notwithstanding two or three hundred soldiers that
they then had in town.   February 25, they did considerable
damage in Weymouth, still nearer to Boston; and the like
at Groton and Sudbury on March 10.   The 12th, they cut
off two families in Clarke's garrison at Plymouth; and the

much serenity of soul and comfort, he yielded up his spirit to God, (the Father of
Spirits,) in peace.   3. I do humbly and faithfully testify as abovesaid, that since his
departure, his honored son, Captain Richard Smith, hath kept possession (with much
acceptance with English and pagans) of his father's housing, lands, and meadows,
with great improvement, also by his great cost and industry.   And in the late bloody
pagan war, I knowingly testify and declare. that it pleased the Most High to make
use of himself in person, his housing, goods, corn, provisions and cattle, for a garrison and supply for the whole army of New England, under the command of the
ever-to-be-honored General Winslow, for the service of his Majesty's honor and
country of New England.   4. I do also humbly declare, that the said Captain Richard Smith, Jr., ought by all the rules of equity, justice and gratitude (to his honored father and himself) to be fairly treated with, considered, recruited, honored,
and by his Majesty's authority, confirmed and established in a peaceful possession
of his father's and his own possessions in this pagan wilderness, and Narragansett
country.   The premises I humbly testify, as now leaving this country and this
world.   ROGER WILLIAMS,

It appears by Governor Winthrop's journal that Taunton was first planted in 1637,
[Vol. I, pp. 252, 253,] so that Mr. Smith came there soon after.   We are told that
the mansion house of the Updike family, in North Kingstown stands where he began
among the Narragansetts.

[1] "A narrative of the captivity, sufferings and removes of Mrs. Mary Rowlandson,
who was taken prisoner by the Indians, with several others, and treated in the most
barbarous and cruel manner by the savages, with many other remarkable events
during her travels.   1773."—ED.

next day burnt almost all Groton, in Middlesex, to the ground.

Here I must open something that has been surprisingly concealed from this country. It has been the constant practice of all parties who are fond of an ecclesiastical establishment by human laws, to accuse the Baptists of disobedience to government, especially in the point of a defensive war. This the reader may see inserted in a law of the Massachusetts, but three years before this war began. Mr. Callender was then a member of the Baptist church in Boston, and was continued a great blessing to them for more than fifty years. The copy of Mr. Russell's Narrative that I am favored with, came out of his family, and in it is a manuscript note in the margin, against Mr. Russell's account of Mr. Turner, which says :—

In the beginning of the war, William Turner gathered a company of volunteers, but was denied a commission and discouraged, because the chief of the company were Anabaptists. Afterwards when the war grew more general and destructive, and the country in very great distress, having divers towns burnt, and many men slain, then he was desired to accept a commission. He complained it was too late, his men on whom he could confide being scattered ; however, was moved to accept.

They made him Captain, and his brother Drinker, Lieutenant, of a company that marched up with others in the beginning of this month, to relieve the western towns, under Major Savage as chief commander ; and by them the Indians were repulsed and driven off from Northampton on March 14. The 17th, they burnt all but one of the houses in Warwick, most of the inhabitants being gone to Rhode Island. On Lord's day, March 26, Captain Pierce being at Rehoboth, with fifty English soldiers, and twenty friendly Indians, heard of a body of the enemy up Patucket River, and wrote to Captain Andrew Edmunds, of Providence, to meet him there with his company to attack them. He sent the letter by a person who was going over to Providence meeting, but who did not deliver it till their worship was done at noon. As soon as Captain Edmunds had read the letter, he gave the bearer a sharp reprimand, for not delivering it before, and expressed his fear of the consequence as it proved ; for Captain Pierce engaging the enemy alone, who were also more numerous than he expected, he was surrounded and cut off, with all but thirteen of his men, only one of whom was of the English ; and it is said he escaped by a friendly Indian's turning and running after him with a weapon, as if he was an enemy, which others seeing did not pursue him. They tell us that another of those friends escaped in this manner: being pursued by an enemy, he took shelter behind a rock, where, as each waited for an opportunity to shoot the other, our friend gently raising his hat above the rock upon a stick, the enemy discharged his gun at it, on which the other shot him down and escaped. It is reported that Captain Pierce and his men slew one hundred of the enemy in the conflict. The people both of Marlborough and Springfield suffered considerably the same day. March 28, forty houses were burnt in Rehoboth, and twenty-nine the next day at Providence, the people retiring into garrisons.

In the Clerk's office in that town is a paper, in which Mr. Williams said :—

> I pray the town, in the sense of the late bloody practices of the natives, to give leave to so many as can agree with William Field, to bestow some charge upon fortifying his house, for security to women and children ; also to give me leave, and so many as shall agree, to put up some defence on the hill, between the mill and the highway, for the like safety of the women and children in that part of the town.

To this eleven principal inhabitants subscribed, the highest whereof was two pounds six shillings, except Mr. Williams, who subscribed ten pounds. Tradition says, that when the Indians appeared on the high lands north of their great cove, Mr. Williams took his staff and walked over towards them, hoping likely to pacify them as he had often done ; but when some of their aged men saw him, they came out and met him, and told him that though those who had long known him would not hurt him, yet their young men were so enraged that it was not safe for him to venture among them; upon which he returned to the garrison. The house where their records were kept was plundered, and they thrown into the mill pond, but were recovered, though by that means some passages are not legible, and likely many articles were lost.

In April, Captain George Denison of Stonington, with a number of English and Mohegan Indians, performed two great exploits. They penetrated into the Narragansett country, and slew forty-four of the enemy at one time, and sixty six at another, without the loss of a man. In the mean time the Massachusetts met with a dreadful blow. Captain Wadsworth and Lieutenant Bruttlebank, with above thirty men, were cut off as they were going to relieve Sudbury on April 18. Bridgewater, which was planted in 1652, was now assaulted by a great body of the enemy on May 8, when twelve deserted houses were burnt, but there was never one of their people killed in that war; neither can we learn that any English person who was born in that town, was ever slain by the sword for eighty years after.[1] Major Savage and most of his men returning, he left Captain Turner to command in that quarter. Hereupon the enemy, thinking themselves more out of danger, resorted, seven or eight hundred of them, to the great falls above Deerfield, on the fishing design. Two captive lads made their escape, and gave information of their secure state, whereupon Captain Turner and young Captain Holioke of Springfield, collected what force they could on a sudden, being not much more than a hundred and fifty men, and went up silently in the night, tied their horses at some distance, and a little before daybreak, May 18, 1676, came unawares upon the enemy, " fired amain into their very wigwams, killing many upon

---

[1] It is remarkable that the inhabitants of the said Bridgewater never yet lost one person by the sword of the enemy, though the town is situate within Plymouth colony; yet have they helped to destroy many of the enemy. Hubbard's Narrative of the Indian wars; Stockbridge, 1803, p. 171.—ED.

the place, and frighting others with the sudden alarm of their guns, made them run into the river, where the swiftness of the stream carrying them down a steep fall, they perished in the waters ; some getting into canoes, sank or overset by the shooting of our men ; others, creeping for shelter, under the banks of the great river, were espied by our men and killed by their swords. . . . . 'Some of their prisoners afterwards owned that they lost above three hundred, some whereof were principal men, sachems, and some of their best fighting men that were left. . . . . Nor did they seem ever to have recovered themselves after this defeat, but their ruin immediately followed upon it." When our people first fired upon them they cried out, *Mohawks!* but in the morning discovering their mistake, they rallied their scattered men, and Captain Turner being unwell, and so "not able for want of bodily strength (no ways defective for want of skill or courage) to assist or direct in making a retreat ; some of the enemy fell upon the guards that kept the horses, others pursued them in the rear, so as our men sustained pretty much damage as they retired, missing after their return thirty-eight of their men." One of these was Captain Turner, who was afterwards found and buried.[1] Dr. Stephen Williams says, " There were many remarkables in this affair (as related by Jonathan Wells, Esq., who was present) which are not taken notice of by Mr. Hubbard, or Dr. Mather."[2] Mr. Hubbard's account was examined and approved by three gentlemen of the Council, and so was published by authority. All the rest of the Baptists who were in that action, but their Captain, were preserved and returned. And as they again met with cruel treatment four years after, both from rulers and ministers, and the old charge of denying magistracy was revived, they said in answer thereto :—

1. It is directly against our principles, and contrary to what we asserted in a confession of our faith, that we gave into the Court, as also to that Con-

[1]Hubbard's History of that war, pp. 88, 94. [205—211.]
[2]Appendix to his father's and Deerfield's captivity, p. 66.

fession of our faith lately set forth by our brethren in old England, which Confession we own in every particular.[1] 2. Our continual prayer to God for them, according to I. Tim. ii. 1, 2, will witness against this charge. 3. Our constant subjection and obedience to their laws, both actively, as far as we can with a good conscience, and where we could not actively, there have we been passively obedient; in suffering what they inflicted on us, without seeking any revenge in the least. 4. In paying all due demands whatsoever; not being desirous to withhold from Cæsar at any time, any of his dues. In a word, both our persons and estates are always ready at command to be serviceable in the defence of the country; yea, and have been voluntarily offered on the high places of the field, in the time of the country's greatest extremity. .... Among whom was William Turner, whom they pleased to make Captain of that company, who had been one of the greatest sufferers among us, for the profession of religion. He was a very worthy man for soldiery; and Edward Drinker, who had been another sufferer, whom they pleased to make Lieutenant; and by the presence of the Lord with them, they were made instruments of the preservation of one town from the rage of the heathen, who violently broke into it, but they being there beat them out. And after that, by Captain Turner, who was then commander-in-chief, as an instrument in the hand of the Lord, was the greatest blow struck to the Indians of any they had received; for after this they were broken and scattered, so that they were overcome and subdued with ease. Here it is to be observed that those who had suffered so much from the country, and scandalized as enemies to the country, and their privileges, freely offering themselves in their service, have been (through the Lord's presence with them) some of the principal instruments

---

[1] The Confession published in London, in 1677, and revised in 1689.—B.

" God, the supreme Lord and King of all the world hath ordained civil magistrates to be under him over his people for his own glory and the public good, and to this end hath armed them with the power of the sword for defence and encouragement of them that do good, and for the punishment of evil doers. It is lawful for Christians to accept and execute the office of a magistrate when called thereunto; in the management whereof, as they ought especially to maintain justice and peace, according to the wholesome laws of each kingdom and commonwealth, so, for that end, they may lawfully now, under the New Testament, wage war upon just and necessary causes. Civil magistrates being set up by God, for the ends aforesaid, subjection in all lawful things commanded by them, ought to be yielded by us in the Lord, not only for wrath but for conscience sake; and we ought to make supplications and prayers for kings and all that are in authority, that under them we may live a quiet and peaceable life in all godliness and honesty." Confession of 1677, Chap. XXXIV. This Confession is published in Crosby, Vol. III, Appendix II; Confessions of Faith, &c., Hansard Knolly's Society, pp. 179—246; Cutting's Historical Vindications, pp. 131—188. It was highly esteemed among the early Baptists of this country. The Philadelphia Association made brief additions to it and adopted it in 1742.—ED.

to subdue the barbarous heathen, and to deliver the country from its greatest distress ; which may stand as a witness of our fidelity to the government to the world's end.   We have been vilified and greatly reproached,
and are at this day, it being without any just reason laid to us, that we are
one chief cause of all the judgments of God on the land.   We do not excuse ourselves, as not having a share or part in many of the sins that have
provoked the Lord against poor New England ; neither have we been freed
from having part with others in the general calamities that God hath
brought on this poor place.   Yet it is observable how graciously the Lord
hath dealt with us ; that in the time of great mortality by the small-pox,
when so many hundreds died, though many of us were visited with that
visitation, yet not one of our society was removed by it ; but it was not for
any thing in us, that the Lord spared us, but for his name's sake, that the
mouth of our adversaries might be silent.[1]

In answer to this, Mr. Willard said :—

The German Anabaptists were enemies to civil government ; we hope
these (though they have shown too much contempt of authority) are not
so far gone.   But for his so gloriously emblazoning their service in the
late wars, it is neither to the purpose, nor of much moment.   That they
did join against the common enemy is true.   Swanzey (a place chiefly consisting of Anabaptists, and where they had a church) was the place where
the enemy made the first onset. .... Besides, any man would fight, rather
than have his throat cut ; it was not for religion, nor civil government, but
for lives and estates. .... Nor did the Indians receive the greatest blow at
that time ; nor is it the Anabaptists' true, but vain, glory, to set such an
encomium upon their own deeds. .... We have dismissed the charge, now
comes a strong argument of their orthodoxy, a witness from Heaven, viz.,
their happy preservation in the time of the small pox.   Let it be remembered, that one of their persuasion died of it at Woburn, (where John
Russell lived, and should have observed it) and many of their children.
But be it so ; their society is small, and scattered from Dan to Beersheba.
And who knows, but God might spare them in judgment, to harden them?
These are too high things for us ; only when God comes to chasten his people,
those that are not chastened, may ask whether they are not bastards?

He had before said :—

As the honored magistrates here are Christians, so have they judged it
their duty to maintain the ways of Christ, and strengthen them by civil
laws, which hath not only been the practice of reformers of old, but the
constant judgment of the church of Christ ever since the apostles. .... On
this principle our worthy rulers have made laws against many sects and

[1]Russell's Narrative, pp. 11, 12.

intruders, and among the rest the Anabaptists.   That in quelling the Anabaptists they do not oppose the truth, but suppress error, they are fully persuaded; and although they never pretended to a lordship over men's consciences, yet they account the outward man is subject to them; and if they must tarry till all men are agreed about what is truth, before we oppose error, we shall stay till there is no need of it.[1]

According to this, we are not to imagine that those ministers ever intended to lord it over Thomas Gould's conscience, when they censured him for not standing up, and looking on when they sprinkled infants in the sacred name.   He might have thought what he pleased of it inwardly, if he would but have honored them before the people;[2] and though for refusing so to do, they excluded him from the ordinance of the Supper for seven years, and then for taking another method to enjoy it, they moved the rulers to disfranchise, fine, imprison and banish him, yet all this was for error in his outward man, not in his conscience! neither must it be supposed, that vain glory had any influence in the emblazoning of things on their side; for all these things were done by orthodox ministers, and Christian rulers.   But let the Anabaptists offer themselves ever so willingly, and at a time when the main of the enemy were remote from their churches, both of Boston and Swanzey; and let them do ever so great public service, yet it must not be thought that they were moved either by religion or loyalty.   No, all proceeded either from love to the world, or else fear of having their throats cut by the Indians in Boston, if they had not gone a hundred miles into the country to meet them!   This is spoken, not in contempt to any man's person, but to expose and detect that self-flattery which so often deceives mankind.   The above is all the mention I ever saw, in any publication from that party, that shews the chief commander in the fall fight to have been a Baptist.   Most of their histories of that war mention his name, but not a word of his being the man who had before suffered in the Baptists' cause.   And lest it should detect the slanders they still were casting upon our denomi-

[1] *Ne sutor*, &c., pp. 23, 24.   [2] 1 Sam. xv. 30.

tion, they, having gained his son to their party, entirely concealed this fact from his numerous posterity.   For though
his grandson, Captain William Turner of Swanzey, embraced
our principles, which he continued in after he removed to
Newport, where he died in 1759, bequeathing, among other
legacies in his will, his lands in Fall Town, adjoining to the
place where his grandfather was slain ; yet in June, 1774, I
was conversing with one of his daughters, together with her
son, William Turner Miller, Esq.,both members of the Baptist church in Warren, and they told me, they had often
heard of their ancestor's exploits and death in Philip's war,
but never a word before of his being a Baptist, or of his
sufferings in that cause.   Neither have any of their historians ever ventured to publish a particular account of the
Baptist sufferings, as they have of the Quakers.   For which
I can give no better reason than, because they could find
encroachments upon their rights in the latter to found a plea
upon, which they could not in the former.   And the author
of the Magnalia plainly expressed his unwillingness that
the records thereof should be kept anywhere.[1]

Captain Benjamin Church of Duxbury near Plymouth,
who had made some beginning at Sokonet, now Little Compton, east of Rhode Island, the year before the war, carried
his family on that Island after it began, as a place in his
opinion of greater safety than Duxbury or Plymouth ; and
he was an active and successful commander through the
war.   As he knew that Philip had forced the Sokonet Indians into the war, contrary to the minds of the leading part
of them, he, against his friends' advice, went over in a canoe,
and adventured himself among them in June this year, and
gained them over to our side, by whose help he took great
numbers of the enemy from day to day, who had now lost
all their courage.   At length returning to visit his wife,
whose anxious mind fainted to see him again well, he was
immediately informed by Major Sanford and Captain Gold-

[1]Magnalia, Vol. I, p. 58; Vol. II, p. 552.—ED.

ing, that one of Philip's men had fled from him (then at the foot of Mount Hope) and was come over to the Island. Hereupon they all put spurs to their horses, and having heard the Indian's account, crossed the ferry in the night with a few men, and after Captain Church had stationed his ambush, of the Rhode Island gentlemen, beat up Philip's head-quarters, upon which he set out to flee through a little swamp, but after an Englishman had snapped his gun at him without effect, Alderman, an Indian, fired a bullet through his heart, on August 12, 1676, a little before the break of day; after which the war was soon brought to a close.

This summary of that bloody war I have carefully collected from a great variety of histories and accounts. And upon the whole, it was said, that in this war were slain, twelve captains and about six hundred men; that about one thousand two hundred houses were burnt, eight thousand head of cattle, and many thousand bushels of grain destroyed; and also three thousand Indians. The loss to the English colonies was computed at one hundred and fifty thousand pounds sterling, and Captain Tom, with another chief of the Christian Indians at Natick, were taken and hanged at Boston, for being active instruments of those mischiefs.[1] Many others were faithful. Of those twelve captains, Gallop, Seily and Marshall, (who were slain at the Narragansett fort,) were of Connecticut; Hutchinson, Beers, Lothrop, Devenport, Gardner, Johnson, Wadsworth and Turner, were of the Massachusetts, and Pierce was of Scituate, in Plymouth colony. From Pierce, one Baptist elder of that name, and many members of the Baptist churches of Swanzey, Rehoboth and other places have sprung.

On November 29, this year, Mr. Samuel Hubbard wrote to Mr. Edward Stennett, in England;[2] and after what is re-

[1] Massachusetts History, Vol. III, pp. 492, 493.
[2] Mr. Stennett's son and grandson, named Joseph, and great-grandson, named Samuel, have been noted Baptist ministers in London; the two latter, Doctors of Divinity.

cited in the beginning of this chapter, he further said of the Indians :—

They have done much harm in our bordering towns, as Warwick, destroyed by fires ; only most of the people are here, and their goods, and some of their cattle ; and the like at Pawtuxet and Providence, though not altogether destroyed, for a garrison remaineth there to this day.   And for the other side over against us on the main, which once was ours, and is, I judge, by charter, many are killed by the Indians, the rest came to us with what they could bring.   Connecticut army, Plymouth and Bay armies being there, wasted very much ; when they left it, the Indians burnt near all that was left.   In Plymouth the wars began, and [they] are sore wasted [lost most men of all] ; the Bay lost very many men.   Connecticut did most service, and I have not heard of one town destroyed or fired in that colony.   In the beginning of these troubles of the wars, Lieutenant Joseph Tory, elder of Mr. Clarke's church, having but one daughter living at Squamicot, [Westerly] and his wife being there, he said unto me, Come, let us send a boat to Squamicot ; my all is there and part of yours.   We sent a boat so as his wife, his daughter, and son-in-law, and all their children, and my two daughters and their children (one had eight, the other three, with an apprentice boy) all came, and brother John Crandal and his family, with as many others as could possibly come.   My son Clarke came afterwards before winter, and my other daughter's husband came in the spring, and they all have been at my house to this day. .... Now, dear brother, although we are not destroyed by the Indians, God hath visited this land by taking away many by death, and in this place [very much, yea to this day, yea] of all sorts.   Of the old church, first Mr. Joseph Tory, then my dear brother John Crandal, then Mr. John Clarke, then William Weeden, a deacon, then John Salmon ; a sad stroke in very deed ; young men and maids ; to this day, I never knew or heard the like in New England.   Last week four or five were buried in this town. .... Brother Turner went to war, and God prospered him for a time, but he is now killed by the Indians ; the rest are well and enjoy their liberty.   Mr. Miles, that was at Swanzey, is now with them.   Brother William Gibson, who came from old England with brother Mumford, is now gone to New London to visit our brethren there.

Mr. Mumford had been over to London, and he with Mr. Gibson returned to Boston, in October 16, 1675.   Mr. Gibson afterward succeeded Elder Hiscox in the pastoral office at Newport.

The above account of the preservation of Connecticut, as well as the other articles expressed, are just, as far as I can

learn. The Mohegan Indians, under Uncas, did the English great service in that war. I have seen scarce any account of any other damages in Swanzey and Rehoboth, beside
what have been recited, except the Indians' killing Captain
Willet's son near the garrison in Swanzey this year. Mid
dleborough and Dartmouth were but just begun before the
war, and when it came on, the English and part of the Indians
therein, removed to Plymouth and other places of greater
safety ; and the large body of natives near to and upon Cape
Cod, continued in amity with the English, as those on the
islands south of it also did. Of the latter I have met with
the following entertaining account.

Thomas Mayhew, Esq., obtained a grant of Martha's Vineyard, with the islands adjacent, and began a settlement at
Edgartown, on the east part of the Vineyard, in 1642, where
he was their chief ruler, and his son their minister. In
1646, the son began to preach to the Indians with success ;
to promote which cause his father told them, " that by order
from the crown of England, he was to govern the English
who should inhabit those islands; that his royal master was
in power far above any of the Indian monarchs ; but that
as he was great and powerful, so he was a lover of justice ;
and that therefore he would in no measure invade their
jurisdictions, but on the contrary assist them if need required;
that religion and government were distinct things, and their
sachems might retain their just authority, though their subjects were Christians." And he practiced according to his
profession ; for " he would not suffer any to injure them
either in their goods, lands or persons. They always found
a father and protector in him ; and he was so far from introducing any form of government among them against their
wills, that he first convinced them of the advantage of it,
and even brought them to desire him to introduce and settle
it." This wise conduct and the gospel means that were
used with them, produced such happy effects, that a Christian church was formed and organized among them five

years before this war.   And now in the time of it, the government furnished those Christian Indians with arms and ammunition and employed them to defend the islands against the
enemy.   "And so faithful were they, that they not only resolutely rejected the strong [and repeated] solicitations of the
natives on the neighboring main, but, in observance of the general orders given them, when any landed to solicit them,
though some were nearly related by marriage, and others by
blood, yet the island Indians would immediately bring them
before the Governor to attend his pleasure."   By the divine
blessing on these means, though the Indians there were twenty
to one of the English, yet through this extensive and bloody
war, " these islands enjoyed a perfect calm of peace ; and
the people wrought and dwelt secure and quiet.[1]

[1]Prince's Appendix to Mayhew's Indian converts, pp. 293—297.   In that performance I find that Mr. Peter Foulger was early employed as a "school-master among
those Indians, and when young Mr. Mayhew went to England, in 1667, Mr. Prince
says, they had not only several Indian teachers on the island, but also 'an able,
godly Englishman named Peter Foulger, employed in teaching the youth in reading,
writing and the principles of religion by catechizing ; being well learned likewise in
the Scripture, and capable of helping them in religious matters." p. 291.   I find
by Mr. Samuel Hubbard, that Mr. Foulger became a Baptist, and joined Mr. Clarke's
church about the time of this war ; as Thomas West, an Englishman, and some Indians from thence, did to Mr. Hiscox's church in 1680.   And Mr. Foulger promoted
the Baptist principles among the Indians.   Though one of them named Japheth, who
had been his scholar, and now was got to be a noted teacher, reminded him that he
had formerly warned them against false teachers that would come, and said he,
"Now Sir, I find your prediction true, for you yourself are become one of these
teachers, you cautioned us against ; I am therefore fully resolved to take your good
counsel, and not believe you, but will continue steadfast in the truths wherein you
formerly instructed me."   Mayhew, pp. 49, 50.   However he found others not to be
so resolute, for by the time that their Governor, Mayhew, died in 1680, the Baptist
principles had prevailed considerably among them ; and by the year 1694, they had
one Baptist church on the Vineyard among the Christian Indians, and another on
Nantucket.   Magnalia, B. 6, p. 56.   [Vol. II, p. 375.]   The first Indian pastor over
those Baptists on the Vineyard, that I have seen any account of, was Stephen Tacka-
mason.   He first joined a church of the other denomination, in or about 1690.   Mr.
Mayhew informs us, that he was re-baptized some years after, and became a membe
and a teacher of that church, but says, "However, he appeared to be so serious a man,
that I cannot but judge, that he acted according to the dictates of his conscience in what
he did, and not out of any base or sordid ends."   He died in Chilmark, in 1708 ; and our
author says, "I had frequent conversation with him while he was in health, and
sometimes . . . . in the time of that long sickness whereof he died ; and never from
first to last saw anything by him, that made me any ways suspect the integrity of his

Ninegret and his Nyantick subjects, who dwelt from Point Judith up to Westerly, on the shore south of the Narragansetts, did not join in that war ; and a considerable number of their descendants now live there in Charlestown ; and in 1741 a great reformation took place among them ; a Baptist

heart, but did ever think him to be a godly and discreet man. The last time I went to see him, he professed his good opinion of those people and churches, from whom he differed in his apprehensions about the subjects and mode of baptism, and blamed some of his brethren for being too uncharitable and censorious towards them; and he on other subjects, discoursed like a good Christian. . . . . He seemed not to be at all terrified at the approaches of death towards him, of which he was very sensible, but appeared to enjoy that peace in his soul, which passeth understanding." Pp. 42—44. These are the words of Mr. Experience Mayhew, in his "Indian Converts," published in 1727. His worthy son, who succeeds him in the ministry among the Indians on the Island, treated one of my brethren in the ministry very friendly, when he was over and preached among those Baptists, near three years ago. I had requested my friend to collect some account of those Baptists, and he applied to Mr. Mayhew for that purpose; who promised he would get the best intelligence he could concerning them, from an aged aunt of his, who retained her mental powers remarkably, and from others. He sent the same in the following letter :—

" REVEREND SIR :—In compliance with your request I have got the best information I could, with respect to the origin of Anti-pædobaptists at Martha's Vineyard. My aged aunt informs me, that the first Baptist minister among the Indians on the island, that she knew or heard of, was one Isaac Decamy, who came from the mainland with his family, and preached and administered the ordinances of baptism and the Lord's Supper, a number of years. She is uncertain what year he came, but according to the best of her memory the said Decamy died near sixty years agone. She saith further, that he was a man of a sober life and conversation. The next Indian minister of this denomination, by the best intelligence I can get, was Jonas Horswet, who preached and administered the ordinances to a small society of Baptists at Gay Head. The next was Ephriam Abraham, originally of Chappaquidick, at the east end of the island, who had the charge of the society at Gay Head, as also of one, which about this time was formed at said Chappaquidick. The next ordained minister was Samuel Kakenehew, whom I had a personal acquaintance with ; he lived at Chappaquidick, was esteemed by such as knew him, to be a man of sense, and of a regular and Christian life and conversation. There were several other preachers among them, but not ordained; except Silas Paul, who is now living, and is an ordained pastor of the Baptist church at Gay Head, and who also takes upon him the care of the small society of that denomination at Chappaquidick ; preaching occasionally, and administering the ordinances to them. He is the only Indian minister of this denomination now upon this island.

This is the best information that can be obtained by your friend and fellow-laborer in the work of the ministry,

                            ZECHARIAH MAYHEW."

Chilmark, 27 August, 1774.

This was directed to Elder Hunt, who says, the said Paul informed him that he was then thirty-four years old, was baptized in 1758, ordained in 1763; that the church at Gay Head had thirteen members, and the other, sixteen.

church was formed there some years after, over whom James
Simons was ordained; and since that, Samuel Niles, both of
their own nation; and a considerable number of them have
given lasting evidence of their being pious Christians.

It may be proper to take some particular notice here of
Mr. Clarke, who left as spotless a character as any man I
know of, that ever acted in any public station in this country.[1] The Massachusetts writers have been so watchful and

---

[1]He was born October 8, 1609; married Elizabeth, daughter of John Harges, Esq.,
of Bedfordshire. In a power of attorney signed by them, May 12, 1656, he styles
himself, John Clarke, physician, of London. It was for the recovery of a legacy of
twenty pounds per annum during her life, that was given her by her father out of
the manor of Wreslingworth, Bedfordshire. Where he had his education I know
not; but the following clause in his will may give some idea of his learning, viz. :
' Item, unto my loving friend Richard Bailey, I give and bequeath, my Concordance
and Lexicon to it belonging, written by myself, being the fruit of several years'
study; my Hebrew Bibles, Buxtorff's and Passor's Lexicon, Cotton's Concordance,
and all the rest of my books." His first wife died at Newport without any issue,
and February 1, 1671, he married Mrs. Jane Fletcher, by whom, February 14, 1672,
he had a daughter born; but the mother died the 19th of April following, and the
daughter May 18, 1673. His third wife was the widow Sarah Davis, who survived
him. He gave some legacies, both to her and to the children she had by her
former husband, Mr. Bailey, who came from London with him in 1664.—B.

"It is not certainly known," says Elton, "where Mr. Clarke was born, but tradition makes him a native of Bedfordshire." Appendix to Callender's Century Sermon, Rhode Island Historical Collections, Vol. IV, p. 210. A different tradition, together with other valuable notes in connection with his history, is presented in the following extract from a letter from a descendant of the family :—" In the old family
Bible, which was Thomas Clarke's, the father of John Clarke, is this notice, viz. :
' The 2 of the 10 month, 1674, Thomas Clarke, son of Thomas Clarke, of Wastrup,
[Westthorpe, in Suffolk,] departed this life in Newport on Rod Island, in the house
of his brother [John].' I have inserted in brackets the name of the place which I
think is meant. I have many reasons for believing that the family were from Suffolk. The wife of Thomas Clarke, senior, was Rose Herrige, of an ancient Suffolk
family. There is in the Bible a family record in the hand-writing of Thomas Clarke,
commencing, ' John Clarke, my grandfather, was buried the 3d of March, A. D.
1559,' and ending with the birth and baptism of his own children, which were, ' Mar-
gret, born the 1st of February, 1600; [the dates of course are old style] Carewe,
born the 3d of February, 1602; Thomas, baptized the 31st of March, 1605; Meric,
baptized the 17th of July, 1607; John, born October 8th, 1609; William, baptized
the 11th of February, 1610; Joseph, baptized the 16th of December, born 9th,
1618.' "

The services of John Clarke can scarcely be over-estimated. In the principles
which he caused to be incorporated in the plantation of Rhode Island at its beginning, and which he diligently watched over and preserved, in the constant public
employments in which he was engaged for the united plantations of the island and

careful, to publish whatever they could find, which might seem to countenance the severities, they used towards dissenters from their way, that I expected to find something of that nature against Mr. Clarke; but have happily been disappointed. Though he was disarmed by them in 1637,[1] and imprisoned and fined at Boston, in 1651, and he exposed their injustice and cruelty, to him and his brethren, in print the next year, and continued in England, to oppose and defeat all their attempts at the Court there against his colony, till he obtained their present charter; yet among all their authors or records, that I have searched, I have not met with a single reflection cast upon him by any one ; which I think is very extraordinary. There was doubtless enough said against him, for his principles of believer's baptism and liberty of conscience, to secure him from the wo of being spoken well of by all men ; yet, like Daniel, it seems as if

the main, and especially in his work as agent for the colony in England, in securing the liberal charter under which Rhode Island as a colony and afterwards as a State was governed and prospered for nearly two centuries, he took his rank second to none, certainly, but Roger Williams, among Rhode Island's benefactors. His work has probably never been appreciated as it deserves, his fame having been unduly overshadowed by that of his contemporary, the founder of Providence.

Whether he accepted the peculiar sentiments of the Baptists among those of that faith in England, or alone in the wilds of America, we do not know; but his views on these and other points of Christian doctrine, are so clear and scriptural that they might stand as the confession of faith of Baptists today, after more than two centuries of experience and investigation.

The testimony which Backus proceeds to give to the purity of his character and to his good name, even among his enemies, has been fully corroborated by later writers. Says Allen, in his Biographical Dictionary. "His life was so pure that he was never accused of any vice which has left a blot on his memory." Bancroft says of him, "Never did a young commonwealth possess a more faithful friend," and calls him "the modest and virtuous Clarke, the persevering and disinterested envoy, who, during a twelve years' mission had sustained himself by his own exertions and a mortgage on his estate; whose whole life was a continued exercise of benevolence, and who, at his death, bequeathed all his possessions for the relief of the needy and the education of the young. Others," he adds, "have sought office to advance their fortunes; he, like Roger Williams, parted with his little means for the public good. He had powerful enemies in Massachusetts, and left a name without a spot." History of the United States, Vol. II, pp. 61, 64, 65.—ED.

[1] A "Mr. Clarke" was among those disarmed, but whether the John Clarke of this history, may be questioned. See p. 70, note.—ED.

his enemies could find no fault in him in matter of the kingdom, but only concerning the law of his God.

Few men ever merited the title of a patriot more than he
did ; for he was a principal procurer of Rhode Island, for
sufferers and exiles. And when their rights and liberties
were grossly invaded, he crossed the boisterous ocean, and
exerted all his influence, in twelve years' watchful and diligent labors for his colony, at the British Court, till he obtained a new charter for them, of great and distinguishing
privileges ; for the accomplishment of which, he mortgaged
his own estate in Newport, willing to venture his all, in so
good a cause, though he was not insensible of the covetousness and ingratitude of some great pretenders to liberty in
that colony ; whose influence had caused a great deal of
trouble and expense to Mr. Williams, without any suitable
recompence.[1] The inventions of men are scarce ever more

[1]Six years after Mr. Williams obtained their first charter, viz.: On March 22,
1650, he presented a paper to the deputies and inhabitants of Providence, which contained four requests for others, and a fifth for himself, wherein he says:—" I cannot be so unthankful to you, and so insensible of my own family's comfort, as not
to take notice of your continued and constant love and care, in your many public
and solemn orders for the payment of that money due unto me about the charter.
It is true, I have never demanded it; yea, I have been truly desirous, that it might
have been laid out for some further public benefit in each town; but observing your
loving resolution to the contrary, I have at last resolved to write unto you (as I have
also lately done to Portsmouth and Newport) about the better ordering of it to my
advantage. I have here, through God's providence, conveniency of improving some
goats; my request is therefore, that, if it may be without much trouble, you would
please to order the payment of it in cattle of that kind. I have been solicited, and
have promised my help about iron works, when the matter is ripe; earnestly desirous every way to further the good of the town of Providence, to which I am so much
engaged, and to yourselves the loving inhabitants thereof, to whom I desire to be
your truly loving and ever faithful

ROGER WILLIAMS."

Yet he never received all his pay for that first charter. And though the first Assembly that met after they received the second, voted Mr. Clarke the reward that
has been mentioned, yet they were very backward about fulfilling their promise.
Their General Assemblies from year to year, wrote to stir up the towns thereto; but
at the Assembly of April 2, 1672, an account was exhibited, examined, approved and
attested by Governor Arnold and three Assistants, which is now extant under their
own hands, wherein it appears, that when Mr. Clarke obtained said charter, he had
received but two hundred and twenty-one pounds, three shillings, though the char-

fruitful, than in finding out ways to get money, and excuses to keep it; but how few have parted with it for public good, so freely as Mr. Williams and Mr. Clarke did!

After Mr. Clarke's return, he was improved in various public offices; was elected Deputy Governor three years successively, in two of which he accepted the office; but all the concern of the State did not prevail with him, as it has done with many, to neglect the affairs of religion. His church records and other writings prove, the continuance of his pastoral relation to the first church in Newport, and his care and labors to uphold gospel worship, and discipline therein. And the instrument by which he settled his last concerns in this world, shows what his faith and hopes were, as to that which is to come; for therein he says:—

Whereas, I, John Clarke of Newport, in the colony of Rhode Island and Providence Plantations in New England, physician, am at this present, through the abundant goodness and mercy of my God, though weak in my body, yet sound in my memory and understanding, and being sensible of the inconveniencies that may ensue in case I should not set my house in order before this spirit of mine be called by the Lord to remove out of this tabernacle, do therefore make and declare this my last will and testament, in manner following; willing and readily resigning up my soul unto my merciful Redeemer, through faith in whose death I firmly hope and believe to escape from that second hurting death, and through his resurrection and life, to be glorified with him in life eternal. And my spirit being returned out of this frail body, in which it hath conversed for about sixty-six[1] years my will is, that it be decently interred, without any vain ostentation, between my loving wives Elizabeth and Jane, already deceased, in hopeful expectation, that the same Redeemer who hath laid down a price both for my soul

ter with his time and pains cost six hundred and fifty-one pounds, seventeen shillings, ten pence; one hundred pounds of which was then due to him, and was ordered to be paid in provision pay, two pounds for one; but he never received any of it in his life time. By his papers I find that he mortgaged his estate in Newport, to Captain Richard Deane, of London, the same month that he procured the charter, and that it was not taken up till September 5, 1699, when the last payment of one hundred and fifteen pounds was made to Captain Deane's heirs.

[1]The article on John Clarke in Allen's Biographical Dictionary, places his death at the age of fifty-six. It also states that Mr. Clarke paid the fine which was assessed upon him in Boston in 1651. See pp. 225, 237, 248. These things are mentioned because this article is often referred to, and, except these errors, is correct and valuable.—Ed.

and body, will raise it up at the last day a spiritual one, that they may together be singing hallelujah unto him to all eternity.[1]

Oh! what miserable things are all earthly pleasures or glories, when compared with such a life, and such a death! "Mark the perfect man, and behold the upright; for the end of that man is peace."

It has often been observed, that when one heavy affliction comes upon a person or people, others soon follow; which

[1]Copied from the original will, dated April 20, 1676. He quitted our world the same day. As he left no child, he gave many legacies to his relations and friends, both in that colony and in the Massachusetts. His brother Joseph Clarke was early a member of the church in Newport with him, and was often magistrate of the colony; whose son Joseph was also a member of that church, and then of the church n Westerly, where his posterity are numerous and respectable to this day. Elder Clarke, gave a particular lot of land in Newport, to his brother's son John, whose posterity have also been respectable among the Baptists ever since, one of whom is Mr. Edward Clarke, now a gospel preacher near Providence. Then, after giving a small lot in town to his church, and giving his wife the use of his house and farm, containing more than a hundred and fifty acres, of upland and marshes, together with ten acres in a part of Newport, called the Neck, during her life, he gave said farm and Neck to his friends, William Weeden, Philip Smith and Richard Bailey and to their assigns, "qualified and chosen in manner following forever; that is to say, that when it shall happen that either of them three decease, the two surviving shall make choice of an understanding person, fearing the Lord, to succeed in the place of him so deceased; and in case the two surviving differ in their choice of the person to succeed in the room of him so deceased, that then the choice shall be decided by lot; which person so chosen shall be the assignees of the said persons above-mentioned, and shall have equal power to act with them in all matters relating to the disposal of the profit or rent of the said land and farm, from time to time; and so all persons chosen as above said to make good the said number of three, shall be deemed and taken to be the assigns of the said William Weeden, Philip Smith and Richard Bailey, and none other; which said persons and their assigns, from time to time, chosen and succeeding as above said, shall be seized of the said farm and land called The Neck, to the use and uses following forever; that is to say, faithfully and truly to distribute and dispose of the rent and profit of my said farm and land, for the relief of the poor, or bringing up children unto learning, from time to time, forever, according to such instructions as I shall give unto them, bearing even date with these presents." Which instructions are in these words viz., "That in the disposal of that which the Lord hath bestowed on me, and I have now betrusted you with, you and your successors, shall have special regard and care, to provide for those that fear the Lord; and in all things, and at all times, so to discharge the trust which I have reposed in you, as may be most for the glory of the Most High, and the good and benefit of those for whom it is by me expressly designed.   JOHN CLARKE."

His estate was appraised at one thousand and eighty pounds, twelve shillings, by James Barker, Thomas Ward, and Philip Edes, who made oath to the inventory May

observation was remarkably verified this year. For beside those already named, Mr. Mark Luker, an ancient member, and a ruling Elder of Mr. Clarke's church, died the December after him, leaving the character of a very worthy walker.

About the beginning of 1677, came out Mr. Williams's account of his dispute with the Quakers, upon which Mr. Coddington wrote over to his friend Fox, and said :—

Here is a lying, scandalous book of Roger Williams, of Providence, printed at Cambridge, in New England. .... I have known him about fifty years ; a mere weathercock ; constant only in inconstancy ; poor man ! that doth not know what should become of his soul, if this night it should be taken from him. He was for the priests, and took up their principles to fight against the truth, and to gratify them and bad magistrates, that licked up his vomit, and wrote the said scurrilous book ; and so hath transgressed for a piece of bread. And so are all joined with the red dragon to pour out their flood against the man-child. Into their secrets let not my soul come ; my honor be not thou united. Dear G. F., I may yet more prove what I have said. One while he is a Separatist at New Plymouth, joining with them till they are weary of him (as from Morton's Memorial, in print, doth appear ;) another time you may have him placed a teacher or a member of the church at Salem. O, then a great deal of devotion is pleaded in women wearing of vails in their assemblies, as if the power of godliness was in it ; and to have the cross out of the colors ; and then to be against the king's patent and authority, and writeth a large book in quarto against it. And another time he is hired for money, and gets a patent from the Long Parliament, so that it is not long but he is off and on it again. One time for men's wearing caps, and not hats for covering their faces ; and again, hats and no caps ; one time for water baptism, men and women must be plunged into the water ; and then throw it all down again ;

17, 1666. Said farm and Neck they appraised at five hundred and thirty pounds, and its late annual income has been two hundred and twenty dollars ; as the honorable Josias Lyndon, Esq., one of the assigns, informs me ; who says, the first assigns being Mr. Clarke's intimate friends, were informed by him, that his intent was to provide for religious as well as civil instruction, though he did not insert the word *ministry*, lest the national clergy should lay claim to it. Therefore part of said profits have been improved to maintain religious teaching in that church ever since. Complaint was made in 1721, that one of these assigns was unfaithful in his trust, which caused the Assembly to take the case in hand ; who at length made a law to empower the Town Council in each town to enquire how all charitable donations therein were managed, and by a jury of twelve men, upon oath, to assess damages upon delinquents ; to whom therefore the assigns above-said have annually been accountable ever since.

so that Cotton (who in his day did know the power of God to salvation) said of him, that he was a harberdasher of small questions against the power.　So they ought to have feared God and the king, that is to punish evil doers ; and therefore not to meddle to their hurt, with him that is given to change.

He goes on to say he was credibly informed that Governor Leverett said he would give twenty pounds, and Governor Winslow five pounds, rather than that book should not be printed.　Scott's letter, which is mentioned in page 89, was also written on this occasion, wherein, after accusing Mr. Williams of acting contrary to his own principle of liberty of conscience, he says :—

Witness his presenting of it to the Court at Newport; and when this would not take effect, afterwards when the Commissioners were two of them at Providence, being in the house of Thomas Olney, senior, Roger Williams propounded this question to them :—We have a people here among us, who will not act in our government with us ; what course shall we take with them?　George Cartwright, one of the Commissioners, asked him what manner of persons they were?　Do they live quietly and peaceably amongst you?　This they could not deny.　Then he made this answer, If they can govern themselves, they have no need of your government ; at which they were silent.　This was told again by a woman of the house where the speech was spoken, to another woman, whom the complaint, with the rest, was made against, who related it to me ; but they are both dead, and cannot bear witness with me, to what was spoken there.[1]

These letters being sent over with the book to Fox, he, with John Burnyeat, published them, with an answer to Williams, in 1678, which they entitled, A New England Firebrand Quenched.　Fox's former book in folio, Williams says, was written against about six score authors and papers, to which Edward Burroughs wrote a preface ; and some things that they said in the dispute, turned his thoughts so, as from those names he called his work, George Fox digged out of his Burroughs.　Such titles were more common in that day than ours, but I have nothing to say to justify them, nor a great deal of the language that was used on both sides.　What I am concerned with is fact and not language.　As Mr. Wil-

[1] Fox, Part Second, pp. 245, 248.

liams had occasion to vindicate many things in the writings of Mr. Richard Baxter, Dr. John Owen, and others that Fox had written against, whom Williams calls pious and learned men ; he prefixed a particular address to them, in which he says :—

As to matters in difference between yourselves and me, I have willingly omitted them, as knowing that many able and honest seamen in their observations of the sun, (one picture of Christ Jesus) differ sometimes in their reckonings, though uprightly aiming at, and bound for one port and harbor. I humbly beg of you, 1. That you will more and more earnestly, candidly and Christianly study the things that differ without reflecting upon credit, maintenance, liberty, and life itself, remembering who it was that said, He that loves his life shall lose it. 2. More and more study the prophesies and the signs of the times. You know when it was that five bishops, twenty-two ministers, and almost three hundred other precious believers in the true Lord Jesus, were sacrificed in the flames, for his ever blessed sake, against that monstrous man of sin and bloody whore of Rome. These Foxians' fancy is but a feather to those high Pico's and Tenariffs, the Pope and Mahomet, whom some of you may live to see flung into the lake that burns with fire and brimstone.

To this they answer and say :—

Here you may see, though there is, and hath been, great difference betwixt R. W., R. B. and J. O.,[1] yet all these have written against God's people, that are in the truth. .... But it is well if they come to repentance for what they have done, for imprisoning and persecuting us, when they had both the sword and the bag. And so R. W. and the rest of the New England priests, have been one with them in the spirit of envy and malice against the people of God, like the wily foxes, whose blood lieth at all your doors. .... All may see what a devilish and unchristian mind is in this R. W. whose desires are to R. B. and J. O., that they may see Mahomet, and the Turk, and the whore of Rome, and us, (that he joins with them) flung into the lake of fire.[2]

And in answer to his attempt to prove that pride about spiritual matters was the root and branch of their religion they say :—

Roger, this is their condition, and the New England priests' and professors'. Oh! that your eyes were open that you might see it ! and so what thou measurest to others, it will be measured to thee again, pressed down

[1] Roger Williams, Richard Baxter and John Owen.—Ed.
[2] Fox, pp. 11, 12.

and running over ; and the god of the world will fail thee in thy proofs, and hath failed thee ; as he did thy[1] mother Eve, and thy father Adam. For this is the mouth of the pit, that thou speakest of, and Lucifer's boast in thee against the children of the Lord, that are daily in jeopardy of their lives, and some of them have lost their lives amongst you in New England, in obedience to the command of Christ their Saviour. And we know they hated Christ our Lord and Master without a cause, and so you do us. But R. W. may say, he doth not persecute with his hands ; but let him read page 200 of his book, wherein he declares himself, that a due and moderate restraint he would have inflicted upon us, yea, through pretending conscience ; and he would not have this called persecution. But would R. W. be so served himself? No, but now he lives in a peaceable government, where he cannot exercise his cruelty, and he hath not the sword in his hand, but is in a restless spirit, who grudgeth at the liberty of others, and cannot be content with his own.

Again, they mention his plea for liberty against the bloody tenet, in 1652, and say :—

But R. W. is fallen from that plea, who now desireth the magistrates to persecute us, &c., and it must not be called persecution neither, as in page 200, and many things we could bring out of his former books, which would render him very uncertain ; but we shall forbear at the present, and leave him to the Lord, for his books declare, themselves, what he said then, and what he saith now. But the reader may see how R. W. hath invented and forged many words against us, the people of God, in scorn called Quakers, which we never spoke nor wrote.[2]

They refer to that page, from one end to the other of their book, to prove him a persecutor; and when the Magnalia came out in 1702, John Whiting wrote an answer the next year, wherein he said of the author, " He compares Roger Williams to a wind-mill, that by his rapid motion was like to set the whole country on fire, ... yet commends him, though such a wind-mill, for his opposition against the Quakers ; .... but that haberdasher of small questions against the power of godliness, as their great Cotton called him, was answered by George Fox and John Burnyeat, in another book entitled, A New England Firebrand Quenched."[3] Joseph

[1] Why not *my* ?

[2] Fox, pp. 10, 11, Part Second, p. 212. In pp. 241, and 242 they repeat their reference to that page, in like manner.

[3] Whiting against Mather, pp. 55, 56.

Grove published his Abridgment of Bishop, with notes, the same year. And against where Bishop had mentioned Mr. Norton, Grove says, " This is that priest Norton, whom Cotton Mather, in his late History of New England, so much commends, and with his brother in iniquity, John Wilson, ranks with John Cotton, a man of a better spirit in his day."[1]

Thus both parties could extol Mr. Cotton, while they vented their resentment against Mr. Williams at a high rate; and by these means, and by some connection with the Coddington family, Mr. Callender, in his Century Sermon, scrupled to own him for a Baptist,[2] and in the dedication of it, set Mr. Coddington up as the main founder and supporter of that colony. Though by his papers, I find he was afterwards convinced of his error herein. And let us now examine the evidences referred to, to prove those dreadful charges against Mr. Williams.

1. Morton does not represent that the people were weary of him at Plymouth, but that they were backward to grant his request of a dismission to Salem, though their elder pre-

---

[1]Bishop, p. 124.—B.

The above sentence misplaces the names Norton and Wilson. It should read as follows :—"And against where Bishop had mentioned Mr. Wilson, Grove says, ' This is that priest Wilson, whom Cotton Mather, in his late History of New England, so much commends, and, with his brother in iniquity, John Norton,'" &c.—ED.

[2]Callender says, " Mr. Roger Williams is said, in a few years after his settling at Providence, to have embraced the opinions of the people called (by way of reproach) Anabaptists, in respect to the subject and mode of baptism; and to have formed a church there, in that way, with the help of one Mr. Ezekiel Holliman." To this he adds a note, as follows :—" Since this was transcribed for the press, I find some reasons to suspect that Mr. Williams did not form a church of the Anabaptists, and that he never joined with the Baptist church there. Only, that he allowed them to be nearest the Scripture rule, and true primitive practice, as to the mode and subject of baptism; but that he himself waited for new apostles, &c. The most ancient inhabitants now alive, some of them above eighty years old, who personally knew Mr. Williams, and were well acquainted with many of the original settlers, never heard that Mr. Williams formed a Baptist church there, but always understood that Mr. Browne, Mr. Wickenden or Wiginton, Mr. Dexter, Mr. Olney, Mr. Tillinghast, &c., were the first founders of the church." Upon these words, Elton quotes from Morgan Edwards, " I have one of the Century Sermons of Mr. Callender, with a *dele* upon this note, in his own hand-writing." Century Sermon, Rhode Island Historical Collection, Vol. IV, pp. 109, 110; Materials for a History of the Baptists, Rhode Island Historical Collections, Vol. VI, p. 303.—ED.

vailed with them to do it;[1] and Governor Bradford blessed God for the good effects of his ministry many years after he was banished.[2] 2. Like those he calls New England priests, Coddington tries to draw women's veils, and men's hats and caps over people's eyes, to prevent a just view of those affairs. Mr. Hubbard speaks of those veils, as the first article in his account of the causes of Mr. Williams's banishment, though he is so honest as to let us know, that it was Mr. Skelton who introduced the custom at Salem, which Mr. Williams only concurred with; and Governor Hutchinson shows, that Mr. Cotton had spoken in favor of that mode of dress in England; but now he went to Salem, and preached the people out of conceit of it. And among all Mr. Williams's numerous writings, I have not met with any thing about it; no, nor about his hat or cap, though in the Massachusetts Records, I find that the year before they banished him, when Coddington was both a magistrate and their Treasurer, they made a law against *superfluous and expensive fashions*, wherein they prohibited the making or wearing of *beaver hats* upon penalty of forfeiting of them if they did. 3. As to the cross in the military colors, which Hutchinson also names as a sufficient ground for the authority to take hold of Mr. Williams, it is certain from Winthrop, Hubbard, and the Colony Records, that the Assembly took hold of Endicott, and not Williams, for that act, and put him out of all office for one year therefor; and the Magnalia assures us, that the scruple about that popish sign prevailed in their colony after Mr. Williams was gone out of

---

[1] "He desired his dismission to the church of Salem; which, though some were unwilling to, yet, through the prudent counsel of Mr. Brewster, the ruling elder there, fearing that his continuance amongst them might cause divisions, and there being many abler men in the Bay, they would better deal with him than themselves could, and foreseeing what he prophesied he feared concerning Mr. Williams, which afterwards came to pass, that he would run the same course of rigid separation and anabaptistry which Mr. John Smith, the Se-Baptist at Amsterdam had done, the church of Plymouth consented to his dismission." Morton's Memorial, p. 102.—ED.

[2] See page 41.

it.[1]   4. Upon the affairs of the patent. Coddington artfully slips in the word " *authority*," willing, with his friend Cotton, to have Williams appear as a rebel against the king.   We learn from Governor Winthrop, that Mr. Williams first wrote upon that subject at Plymouth, and after he came to Salem, the Court called for a copy of it, which he granted them, and then, near the close of 1633, they had him before them; but he gave them such satisfaction about it, that they dismissed him; yet they afterward brought in and reëxamined that matter, as one cause of his banishment.[2]   5. By the foregoing history, the reader may see with what grace the Quakers could accuse Mr. Williams of being mercenary or hired for money, in procuring their first charter.   And I find that when he was setting off upon his second agency, to get Mr. Coddington's commission revoked, he, on September 3, 1651, sold his trading house and interest in Narragansett, for fifty pounds, to Mr. Richard Smith.[3]   His great crime therefore, was his advancing such questions as he did, against the power; which, in plain terms, was a power to frame to themselves a gospel and a Christ without the cross; a power to suspend obedience to what they looked upon to be truth in England, and to compel others to their judgments, when they had got out of the prelates' reach; yea, a power to confirm and support such corruptions by oaths, both there and here.[4]

Mr. Williams says:—

Cases have befallen myself in the chancery in England, &c., of the loss of great sums, which I chose to bear, through the Lord's help, rather than yield to the formality (then and still in use) in God's worship, though I offered to swear in weighty cases, by the name of God, as in the presence of God, and to attest or call God to witness; and the judges told me they would rest in my testimony and way of swearing, but they could not dispense with me without an act of parliament.[5]

[1]Book 7, p. 11. [Vol. II, pp. 433--435.]—B.
   The Magnalia also states that Mr. Williams was " but obliquely and remotely concerned " with this matter.   Ibid, p. 433.—ED.
[2]Williams's reply to Cotton, p. 277.   [3]Newport Records.
[4]See page 56.   [5]Against the Quakers, Appendix, pp. 59, 60.

And in the face of all their reproaches, I am bold in it, that I know not of one Pædobaptist or Quaker, that came to this country in that age, who acted so consistently and steadily upon right principles about government and liberty, as Mr. Williams did ; neither do I think that they had, or have, any cause to glory over him as to religion. Though Mr. Cotton represented it as a mere pretence for him to tell of church government, when he did not join fully with any church that was then extant, yet he replies and says :—

The institution of any [state] government and order is one thing, and the administration and execution, which may be interrupted and eclipsed, is another. [Indeed] Jeremiah could not rightly have been judged a pretender, when he mourned for and lamented the desolations of the temple, priests, elders, altar and sacrifices ; and neither he nor Daniel, nor any of God's [prophets or] servants, could, during the desolation and captivity, acknowledge either temple [or] altar, or sacrifice aright, extant upon the face of the earth.....Although the discusser be not satisfied in the period of the times, and the manner of Christ's [his] glorious appearing, yet his soul uprightly desires to see and adore, and to be thankful to Master Cotton, yea to the least of the disciples of Christ, for any coal or spark of true light, among so many false and pretended candles and candlesticks.[1]

Now as no man was permitted by Ezra, to officiate as a priest at God's altar, but those who could find their register of a lawful descent from Aaron, and the church had been through a more terrible captivity in mystical Babylon, between the apostolic age and that we are upon, than the Jews had in Chaldea ; how could a man, so honest as Mr. Williams was, receive any man to administer the ordinance of the Supper to him, who could not produce a register of his succession from the apostles ?[2] I know of no other consistent way, to get over this difficulty but this ; that as the lawful seed of Aaron were to govern in the Jewish church, so are the spiritual seed of Christ to govern in his church, into which none ought to be admitted, without gospel evidence of their being such ; and it seems that Mr. Williams had not attained to a clear settlement in this point. But in

[1] Reply to Cotton, pp. 106, 107.   [2] See page 91.

my opinion his greatest mistake, when he first came to this country was, his blending the duties of natural and revealed religion too much together. The light of nature teaches the importance of seeking to God for what we need, and of praising him for what we receive; which duties ought to be inculcated upon all men, as much as love to God or our neighbors; while the revealed institutions of baptism and the supper, are tokens of fellowship with Christ, and therefore cannot be our duty to perform before we are united to him. Psalms, 107; Acts 17. 27; Rom. 1. 20, 21, and 6. 3—5; I Cor. 10. 16. But for a while, Mr. Williams seemed to limit these two kinds of duties alike to the regenerate. It is also well known, that the divine rule is perfect, but that the best of men in this state are imperfect, and how far we are to exercise forbearance, and how far not, has not been an easy question to the most enlightened saints; yet Mr. Williams's grand crime in the view of both of these parties, was because he would not yield to their power in this matter. The passage the Quakers so often appealed to, as an evidence of his being a bloody persecutor, is as follows:—

An author had said, "The Quakers' spirit doth teach them to honor no man." Upon which Fox said:—

" That is a *lie*; for it teacheth them to have all men in esteem and to honor all men in the Lord; yet they are convinced by the law as transgressors if they respect men's persons as you do.

In reply to which Mr. Williams says:—

All men may see how truly they honor all in the Lord, and what Lord they mean, when his first word to his opposite is that most provoking term, *That is a lie*. It is true that Christ Jesus and his servants, used sharp reproofs, similitudes, &c., but thus suddenly, at the first dash, to give fire, *Thou liest, That is a lie*, &c., shows neither religion nor civility, but a barbarous spirit, for they that know the barbarians, know how common that word is in all their mouths.....The most Holy and only Wise knows how proudly and simply and barbarously they have run into uncivil and inhuman behavior towards all their superiors, the eldest and highest, how they have declared by principle and practice, that there are no men to be respected in the world but themselves, as being Gods and Christs. It is true our English Bibles and grammar (as Fox in his great learning often objects) makes *Thou* to a single person ; and *Thou* in Holy Scripture is used in a grave and respective way unto superiors, unto kings and parents, and God himself. But, 1. the Hebrew and Greek signify no more *Thou* than *You*, and so may be truly turned. 2, Every nation, every shire, every calling, have their particular properties or idioms of speech, which are improper and ridiculous with others. Hence these simple reformers are extremely ridiculous in giving *Thou* and *Thee* to every body, which our nation commonly gives to familiars only ; and they are insufferably proud and contemptuous unto all their superiors in using *Thou* to every body, which our English idiom or propriety of speech, useth in a way of familiarity, or anger, scorn and contempt. I have therefore publicly declared myself, that a due and moderate restraint, and punishing of these incivilities, (though pretending conscience) is so far from persecution, (properly so called) that it is a duty and command of God unto all mankind, first in families, and thence into all human societies.[1]

This is all the passage in his whole book that speaks in favor of punishing Quakers ; and compared with the instance of Norton's incivilities to Governor Prince[2] and others, and observing that the emphasis lies upon their manner of using those words, the reader will judge, whether a moderate punishing of the same, is any ways inconsistent with Mr. Williams's plea for liberty, against Mr. Cotton. As to his practice, we learn expressly that the instance Scott refers to at Newport, was that of Harris, at the election, in 1655.[3] And though he and Mr. Coddington submitted to Mr. Williams's government the next year, (a few months before the Quakers arrived) yet, after that, they and others became so

[1]Williams, pp. 199, 200.—B.

In some parts of England, the pronoun of the second person, singular, is employed, as is the case in the German language, only in addressing those with whom the speaker is most intimate and familiar; and to use it in addressing others, and especially superiors, would be, not merely eccentric but highly disrespectful. There seems to have been something of this idiom in the New England colonies.

The explanation which Backus proceeds to give of the above-cited words of Williams, is undoubtedly correct, that it was not the mere use of *Thee* and *Thou*, by Quakers, which he thought proper to restrain, but such language to Magistrates as they had been often known to employ, plainly intended to express irreverence and disrespect.—ED.

[2]See page 256.—ED.   [3]See page 241.—ED.

spiritual as to refuse to act therein. This, it seems, caused Mr. Williams to ask Mr. Cartwright what they should do with them, which, in their view, was another proof of his persecuting disposition. In 1665 their Assembly framed an engagement to the government, which they hoped those men would have taken, and so have come in to act with them again ; but in March, 1666, they pleaded that they could not in conscience do it, and prevailed with the Assembly to make a law, to allow those who pleaded that they could not in conscience take either that engagement or the oath of allegiance in England, to make their submission to the government, either before the Court or before two magistrates, in their own words, instead of any that others could frame for them. And no sooner was this point gained, than, at the election in May ensuing, they got in a Quaker Deputy Governor, and three magistrates; two of the latter being Coddington and Harris;[1] Harris was in the same office in 1667, when, on July 2, he procured an extraordinary meeting of the Assembly, to try Mr. Fenner, (another magistrate,) for a rout which Harris had charged him with making in Providence, on June 3. But the Assembly acquitted Fenner, and fined Harris fifty pounds, and put him out of office, choosing Stephen Arnold in his stead. The next fall he was fined ten shillings for breach of peace, and bound to his good behavior. Yet he had influence enough in May, 1668, to get again into the magistracy, and in the fall to have his fifty pounds remitted. He was likewise in the same office in 1669 ; and as Connecticut then revived their claim to the Narragansett country, he eagerly turned to assist them, hoping, doubtless, to share largely therein, if they prevailed.

It seems that the agents who procured their charters, agreed that some persons living near Mr. Smith's trading house in Narragansett, should have liberty to choose which

[1] Mr. Backus afterwards became convinced that Harris was not a Quaker. See Appendix A., at the close of this volume.—ED.

government they would be under; therefore from thence, and from the words of Connecticut charter, they set out afresh to grasp all that country to themselves. And for that end they would come over from Stonington and knock Westerly people down, and carry them off to jail, and persisted long in those encroachments, against the remonstrances of the authority of Rhode Island colony; one of which they sent by Mr. John Crandal to Hartford, in May, 1671. The Assembly at the same time made choice of Mr. Clarke as their agent, to go again to England upon the affair; though, after repeated applications to Connecticut Court, such a prospect appeared of having the matter settled by treaty, that they revoked that appointment the next year. But Harris, finding that the king's words in their charter had most explicitly fixed Paucatuck River as the bounds betwixt the two colonies, openly attacked the validity of the charter, because therein the king had granted full religious liberty, notwithstanding the penal laws in England. Upon which Harris declared, "that the king cannot dispense with the penal laws on the consciences of his subjects, papists or protestants, at home or abroad." Their rulers then were Benedict Arnold, Governor; John Clarke, Deputy Governor; John Cranston, John Coggshall, James Barker, William Carpenter, Thomas Harris, Roger Williams, William Baulston, John Albro, John Green, Benjamin Smith, Assistants; John Sanford, Recorder; James Rogers, General Sergeant; and Joseph Tory, Attorney General. They committed Harris to prison for denying the king's authority and prerogative. When the Assembly met at Newport, April 2, 1672, he presented a petition to them by the hand of a Quaker, but, because " not directed in those words which his Majesty, in his gracious charter, hath pleased to give the title unto the corporation, [viz., His Majesty's Colony of Rhode Island and Providence Plantations, &c.,"] the Assembly voted not to take cognizance of it.[1] At their election the next month, they chose the first

[1]Colony Records.

Quaker Governor[1] they ever had in that colony; and Mr. Williams says, " The Quakers prevailing, Harris, by their means gets loose."[2] These facts I have carefully collected from their colony records, compared with Mr. Williams's account; to which they return no better answer than to say, " It is like he doth belie W. H. as he hath done us; and, for thy story and anger against William Harris, he is of age and able enough to speak for himself."[3]

Fox and other noted teachers of theirs were now come over, and gained many proselytes; upon which Mr. Williams went to a general meeting they had at Newport, and began to present to them some considerations concerning the true Christ and the false, the true spirit and the false, but says, " I was cut off in the midst, by the sudden prayer of one, and singing of another," &c., which is afterward explained thus, viz.:—

I was stopped by the sudden praying of the Governor's wife, who also told me of her asking her husband at home, (meaning Christ, which I touched upon). I rose and said, if a man had so alleged, I would have answered him; but I would not countenance the violation of God's order so much in making a reply to a woman in public. Hereupon J. Nichols stood up and said, In Christ Jesus neither male nor female. I was replying to him and to J. Burnyeat's speech concerning their spirit, but was stopped by Burnyeat's sudden falling into prayer, and dismissing the assembly. I resolved, with God's help, to be patient and civil, and so ceased, not seeing a willingness in them for me to proceed; which experience made me not trouble G. Fox and the assembly at Providence, but rather to make a fair and solemn offer of a dispute about these matters."[4]

To this they answer and say:—

o here thou mayest see, it was thy spirit that was cut by the spirit of God, that led them to pray and sing in order, and this thou callest Confusion; and thus thou judgest of things thou knowest not, with thy doting spirit. For the true Christ we know, who is our Shepherd; and the false spirit of Christ is easily savored in thee, which was cut off by the spirit of prayer, and the spirit of singing, from the true spirit of Christ.[5]

[1] John Cranston.—Ed.   [2] Williams, pp. 14, 206, 207.
[3] Fox, pp. 21, 229.   [4] Williams, pp. 2, 12.   [5] Fox, p. 17.

Thus each party call their own way Order; but the order
and decency which the inspired apostle enjoined upon the
church of Cornith, concerned the behavior of their women.
as distinguished from men ; their women who had husbands, in the plural number, who had each a distinct
part to act in divine worship, which they ought to know
and attend unto. As all saints are one in Christ, there
is but one Husband and one bride ; and viewing things in
this distinct light, tends both to purity and peace ; but the
confounding of literal women with mystical husbands, has
often produced the grapes of Sodom and clusters of Gomorrah. And among the many instances of the Quakers assuming a power to govern the Scriptures, instead of being governed by them, take the following.

The Baptist churches in Wales, gathered by our Mr.
Miles and others, published a confession of their faith,
wherein they adopted the words of David in Psalm, 51 : 5 ;
to which Fox in page 214 of his former book said, " David
doth not say, *You* were conceived in sin, but *I.* John was
sanctified from the womb ; and the Scriptures speak of children that are clean. And so you do not speak as elders and
messengers of true churches, or men dividing the word
aright, but you are one against another, though you are all
against them you call Quakers that be in the truth." " In
which passage," says Mr. Williams, " he discovers a strong
presumption that he never felt what the woful estate of all
mankind by nature is."[1] To which they reply and say,
" Paul saith, I am crucified with Christ (mark *I am*) and
Christ liveth in me ; and the life that I live in the flesh, is
by the faith of the son of God, &c. ; is not the faith victory?
and thou fallest a railing, and speaking of our conditions,
which thou art ignorant of, and thy own, and hast abused
both the Scriptures and us."[2]

In July, 1672, Mr. Williams drew up fourteen propositions, and inclosed them in a letter to Deputy Governor

---

[1] Williams, Appendix, pp. 66. 67.   [2] Fox, Second part, p. 136.

Cranston, whom he styles, " My kind friend," for him to deliver them to Fox or his friends ; in which Mr. Williams proposed a fair dispute upon those points with any of them, seven propositions to be handled at Newport, and the others at Providence, on the days they should appoint. By some means the matter was delayed till Fox had sailed for England ; after which John Stubs, John Burnyeat and William Edmundson, engaged in the affair, and with them, Williams held the dispute at Newport, on the 9th, 10th and 12th of August, and at Providence the 17th. When they began at Newport, he publicly declared his motives to be these :—

1. The vindicating his most Holy Name, which my soul saw trodden in the dirt by Satan clothed in Samuel's mantle, and the bright garment of an angel of light, which once he was, but pride deceived him. 2. I had in my eye the vindicating this colony for receiving such persons whom others would not. We suffer for their sakes, and are accounted their abettors, that therefore, together with the improvement of our liberties which the God of Heaven, and our king's majesty have graciously given us, I might give a public testimony against their opinions in such a way and exercise, I judged it incumbent upon my spirit and conscience to do (in some regards) more than most in the colony. I may also truly say, 3. That I had it in my eye, that this exercise might occasion some soul-consideration in many.[1]

As they dwelt so much upon the word *Light*, and upon its coming into the world with all mankind, he asked them in public :—

Whether it comes into them at the conception, or at the birth, or when else? whether it was in all mankind before the coming and death of Christ, or to those since his coming, or both? whether it be in the understanding, will, memory, affections, in any of them severally, or lodged in all of them jointly?[2]

In answer to this they say :—

As to his unlearned questions, whether the light cometh into mankind at the conception, or at the birth, or when else? we leave him to what is written John 1 : 9. Christ is the true light, that lighteth every man that cometh into the world. So it is evident, all are lighted that come into the world ; and the believers witnessed it to shine in their hearts, and Abraham saw his light, or day ; and in it David saw more light, which was

[1] Williams, pp. 25, 26.   [2] Williams, p. 35.

before Christ came in the flesh ; John saith, in the Word which was in the beginning, was life, and the life was the light of men.[1]

Mr. Williams says :—

The hinge and pinch of the difference lies in the opposition which the Quakers make against the manhood of Christ Jesus to be yet extant......
Who questions but Christ Jesus, as the sun in the heavens, influenceth all parts of the world in several respects, and nothing is hid from his heat? He is felt in the bruised reed and smoking flax ; in the poor in spirit ; in the hungry and thirsty after righteousness ; sometimes in the hope of glory to come, yea, in present joy unutterable and glorious ; sometimes the Lamb's wife is visibly asleep though her heart wakes ; sometimes she is alarmed by his knocking and is sluggishly unwilling to open to him ; sometimes she rises and opens but he is gone, and she feels for him by day and night, and cannot find him.

Again he says :—

The Papists, Arminians and Quakers are one ; 1. As to the power of nature and free will in heavenly and spiritual matters ; 2. As to the losing of true saving grace ; 3. As to election and predestination in time, upon obedience, and rejection, and reprobation upon rebellion and disobedience..
.... 4. The Quakers are brethren with the Socinians, in making Christ a type and figure, a pattern and example how Christians ought to walk ; not that the blood which he shed upon the cross at Jerusalem, was a sufficient price and satisfaction unto God for the sins of the whole world.[2]

To which they say :—

This is like the rest of thy false charges and comparisons ; and what dost thou talk of election and predestination, &c., when thou callest the light of Christ an idol? for these are mysteries to thee, who art not come to take heed unto the light that shineth in a dark place.[3] [See II Cor. 10. 12.]

His last proposition was, that their spirit tended to arbitrary government and fiery persecution ; upon which he says :—

By an arbitrary government, I do not intend a ruling by force, for there could be no government in the world without the sword, but arbitrary, I said, came from *arbitrium*, which signifies will or pleasure ; and so my argument is, that, persons immediately speaking from God, it is impertinent and profane to clog and cumber them with laws, for the voice of God, the law of laws, proceeds out of their mouth, than which there could be none

[1] Fox, p. 32.   [2] Williams, p. 137 ; Appendix, p. 56.   [3] Fox, p. 154.

more just, wise or holy. . . . . I told them I must crave their patience while I must profess my fears, lest the spirit by which they were guided, might run them upon their own and others' temporal destruction. I told them I thought they had no such thing in their eye at present; but if power of the sword came into their hands, it was easy to imagine, that whom the spirit (infallible) decreed to death, peasant or prince, if it were possible, he must be executed.[1]

To this they say :—

Where there is no force there is no fear of slavery, and such an arbitrary government no body was ever afraid of. . . . . But Roger, dost thou not accuse the people called Quakers of holding, that they are acted by the Spirit of God, and not by their own spirits? If so, it is the *arbitrium* or will and pleasure of their God, and not their own wills and spirits that they are acted by; and what harm is this to just government? or how doth this set up men's will and power? O, thy blindness! thy darkness! and thy confusion![2]

He then referred them to the passage before recited about the magistrate's subjecting all into his light; and closed that head with observing, that Christ says, Out of the abundance of the heart the mouth speaketh; and asks if any professors of the Christian name except Papists, were ever so sharp and cutting with their tongue, as they, even to knowing and conscientious persons? From whence he questions, what might be expected if whips, swords and halters were permitted to fall into their hands? To which they say :—

The tongues of God's people have in all ages been as a fire and a sword to the wicked. . . . . It may be as rationally questioned of the people of God in this age, as in former ages; and God will reckon with thee, thou ungodly, unjust man, that insinuatest these wicked things against a suffering, as well as harmless people! This spirit thou art led by, in writing against us, would burn us, as it led thy forefathers to burn the martyrs in Smithfield; for ye are all of Cain's race, and are found in his steps, and shall have Cain's reward if you repent not.[3]

This was their way of *quenching a firebrand*.

The Quakers prevailed so far, that in 1675, Mr. Coddington was Governor, and Mr. John Easton[4] Deputy Gov-

---

[1]Williams, p. 204. [2]Fox, p. 226. [3]Fox, p. 231.
[4]John Easton was the son of Nicholas Easton, mentioned on pp. 78, 97.—ED.

24

ernor; when, finding that their spiritual power would not secure them against the Indians, they gave out military commissions under their hands and seals to arm both vessels and garrisons against them.[1] Harris was again chosen an Assistant in the years '73, '74 and '76, in the last of which Mr. S. Hubbard said in a letter to Boston, " The Quakers are still uppermost in government among us; I mean in outward rule, though we have put out the chief, Mr. John Easton, from being Deputy, and now Major John Cranston is Deputy Governor." Mr. Williams's book came out soon after, and at their next election, May 2, 1676, the Quakers were left out of office; and on June 28, Mr. Coddington wrote the fore-cited letter to his friend Fox; which facts may enable us to account for the spirit of it. Mr. Williams was again chosen a magistrate, but excused himself from that service; yet he wrote thus to Providence, viz. :—

I pray the town that the place of meeting be certain, and some course settled for payments, that the Clerk and Sergeant be satisfied according to moderation; that the town business may go on cheerfully; that the busi-

---

[1]Callender, p. 80, [135.] Colony Records.—B.

" It is true the Governor and the Deputy Governor, that year, were both of the people called Quakers, but there are military commissions still in being under their hands and seals, to Mr. B. Arnold, Jun., and others, to go in *an armed sloop to visit the garrisons in Providence*." Callender, R. I. Hist. Coll., Vol. IV, p. 134.

" To John Cranston, by this present Assembly appointed and chosen Major of this his Majesty's Colony of Rhode Island and Providence Plantations, for the well ordering and managing the military officers in this Colony, and for the defence of the king's subjects herein.

"You are therefore, in his Majesty's name, hereby fully and absolutely required, as Major of all, and singular, the land forces to this Colony belonging, to undertake the conduct, leading and training up of the said forces, and for the preservation of the king's subjects in this Colony, to take care that the said military be put in a suitable and absolute way of defence. You are also, by virtue hereof, to have the absolute command of all the captains and inferior officers with their respective companies within this Colony, to martial, array at your command, and to repair to such place or places as may be most for the king's interest and the safety of the inhabitants here;....and, upon assault of any enemy, with them, or either of them, to use your utmost endeavor to *kill, expulse, expel, take and destroy* all and every the enemies of this his Majesty's Colony, that shall in hostile manner be found acting against the public peace of this Colony and the inhabitants herein.....
                                                WILLIAM CODDINGTON, Governor.
April 11th, 1676."
    R. I. Colonial Records.—ED.

ness of the rate (paid by so many already) be finished; that the old custom of order be kept in our meetings, and those unruly be reproved, or
upon obstinacy, cast out from sober and freemen's company; that our
ancient use of arbitration be brought into esteem again; that (it being constantly reported that Connecticut is upon the gaining his Majesty's consent
to enslave us to their parish worship) we consider what we ought to do.

A special Court of Commissioners met at Providence,
October 3, 1676, procured by Harris; who by a jury gave
his party five verdicts for land, the first of which was against
Gregory Dexter, Arthur Fenner, and the town of Providence, wherein they gave, " two pounds in money, damage
and cost of Court; and also that the said defendants run the
line equally between Pawtuxet River and Wenasquatucket
River, till they met with a thwart line from the head of
Wenasquatucket River, directly running to Pawtuxet River."
The next two verdicts gave that party thirty pounds damages in each, with lands further southward; of which the
town of Warwick, by the hands of Mr. Holden and Mr.
Greene, gave an account two years after to the king, wherein
they mention the former ill treatment they had met with at
Boston, and represent that the late war was wholly caused
by the arbitrary conduct of the neighboring colonies. After
the Narragansett fight in December, 1675, they say :—

The neighboring colonies withdrew their forces from us, leaving our unguarded towns to the destroyer, whereby the town of Warwick was wholly
burnt, great part of our goods and cattle lost and consumed, but the lives
of most of us reserved as a prey, supported with hope that yet in time of
peace, we might be enabled to rebuild and provide for our distressed families and succeeding generations..... But William Harris of Pautuxet, came
over in 1674, and claimed land in Narragansett by Indian purchase, and
the king appointed the case to be heard by Commissioners, chosen out of
the several colonies of New England. We attended time and place according to summons, but the major part of the Commissioners, elected out of
our professed and mortal enemies, out-voted those of Rhode Island, granting and awarding to him the lands bought and improved by your petitioners, also giving him great damages, notwithstanding the testimony of one
Mr. Williams, the first Indian purchaser of those lands, and other material
witnesses in our behalf, whereby above five thousand acres of land and
meadows belonging to the poor town of Warwick, and parts adjacent are

taken away, and we prohibited to rebuild, or attempt anything for the support of our dependences.

They then went on to pray for relief.[1]

The people of Connecticut in the mean time had continued their encroachments upon the west part of that colony, till a letter was obtained from the king, dated July 9, 1679, confirming Rhode Island charter ; upon which the Assembly wrote to warn them off their lands, and to charge their own people not to obey them.   But at the same time Harris had procured an order from the king to the authority of the colony, to levy the aforesaid executions.   In consequence whereof, I have seen warrants issued to John Smith of Newport, appointing him Marshal to levy three of them, signed November 24, 1679, by John Cranston, Governor, Caleb Carr, Joseph Clarke, Arthur Fenner and John Sanford, Assistants.   But this not satisfying Harris, he soon set off again for England with new complaints.   Mr. Samuel Hubbard wrote to his children at Westerly, the 7th of February, following, informing them of a rumor he heard of turning their Governor out of his place, and of putting a Quaker into it, and of setting Narragansett, which they called the king's province, off by itself; and said he, "William Harris is gone for Old England, displeased at our Court's act, and will not accept, though offered, it is said, to be Connecticut agent's attorney.   God can have Ahithophel's counsel to fall and to hang himself."   Poor man ! he was taken and carried into Turkish slavery, from whence he never returned.   Thus ended the controversy with him, whose first title to any of those lands was a free gift from Mr. Williams.

Two considerations have moved me to be much larger and more particular upon these unhappy affairs, than I had any thoughts of at first.   One is, that harangues have often been made from pulpits, and in courts of justice, from that time to ours, upon the great disorders of Rhode Island colony, to prove that an established religion by human laws is

[1]See page 239.

exceeding necessary in every government. I thought it duty, therefore, to give the public a fair and full state of those facts, to enable them to judge righteously concerning such addresses. The other is, that I might plainly detect and expose the pernicious nature of imagining that dominion is founded in grace, or that religion endows the subjects of it with a right to act as lawgivers and judges over others. In the Assembly that banished Mrs. Hutchinson, in 1637, Mr. Coddington said, " I do not see any clear witness against her ; and you know it is a rule of the Court, that no man may be a judge and accuser too."[1] But where was that rule when he, in his letter to Fox, acted the part of an accuser, witness and judge against Mr. Williams, even as to the inward state of his soul! With all their talk about light, Mr. Cotton formerly[2] and the Quakers now, accused Mr. Williams of counteracting his own principles about liberty of conscience, only for examining and bringing to light the nature of their principles and behavior ; and the word of truth tells us what light that is. Matthew 6. 23 ; John 3. 19, 21. The Quakers have had a fame among many for honesty and liberty, and far be it from me to detract in the least from what has truly been among them of that nature ; and I readily grant that not only in those respects, but also in their moderation in dress, and solemnity in worship, (though not singularity) and hospitality to strangers, they have merited high commendation, and more so for their zeal against the slave trade. Yet what a bondage is it to be under such a power as their first leaders assumed ! What pope ever spake more haughtily than to say, " He lives in a peaceable government but is in a restless spirit, grudgeth at the liberty of others, and cannot be content with his own," only because he sought in a peaceably way to discharge his conscience, by bearing a plain testimony against what appeared to him to be very corrupt and dangerous ? And what sentence was

[1]Massachusetts History, Vol. II, p. 516, [444, 445.]
[2]See page 134.

ever more unjust than that which is delivered in their mar-
tyr-book? Grove tells us the first part of it was published
in 1661, the other in 1667, by that zealous servant of the
Lord, George Bishop. He lived in the city of Bristol, and
he entitled his work, " New England judged, not by man's,
but the Spirit of the Lord." After his account of the whipping of Humphrey Norton and Deborah Wilson, among the
rest, he reads off his sentence thus :—

Whether they will hear or forbear, they shall know that his prophets
have been amongst them.....So, see where you are, and in what case, ye
blood thirsty enemies of God ; ye men of Boston, of Plymouth patent, and
New Haven ; ye rulers of Sodom, and inhabitants of Gomorrah, who are
hardened against the hour of your visitation ; whose day is over ; who delight in blood, in the blood of the saints of the Most High God, to whom
blood will be given, for ye are worthy ; the Lord will come upon ye, you
that put his day afar off, and say, He delays his coming ; I say, He will
come upon you, in a day that ye think not of, and in an hour of which ye
are not aware ; and will cut you asunder, and appoint you your portion
with hypocrites and sinners ; and ye shall be cast into the lake that burn-
eth with fire and brimstone, there to be tormented with the devil and his
angels, which is the second death.

In 1703, in the margin against this sentence, Grove said,
" This was fulfilled in the Indian wars, wherein many of
them were cut to pieces."[1]

Now, if in Fox's view Mr. Williams discovered a devilish
spirit, in telling the ministers he wrote to, that perhaps some
of them might live to see the Pope and Mahomet cast into
that lake,[2] what a spirit did this great writer of theirs discover? What God did he worship, if this sentence came
immediately from him ? The evident reason of their favorable opinion of Mr. Cotton above his colleague, was his
countenancing the power by which Mrs. Hutchinson declared
that she should be delivered, and the Court ruined with
their posterity."[3] A gentleman of that Assembly said she
told him in London, that she had never any great thing done

[1]Bishop Grove's Abridgment, pp. 206, 207.
[2]See page 355.—Ed.   [3]See page 84.

about her, but it was revealed to her beforehand ; to which she, before the Court, replied, " I say the same thing again."[1] And how was that revelation fulfilled ? Why Bishop says, " Some of your patents endeavored to get Rhode Island under some of your governments, which occasioned some to remove under the Dutch, where Anne Hutchinson, and her son Francis, and W. Collins her son-in-law, with others, were murdered by the Indians ; the guilt and weight of whose blood lies upon you, as done by you ; who were people of an honest life, and good behavior, only differing from you."[2] The first legislator and captain that was slain in Philip's war was her son Edward, who, as Bishop tells us, entered his protest at Boston, in 1658, against their making a law to banish Quakers on pain of death. I cannot learn that any man who had ever been an Assistant in either colony was then slain by the Indians, except Mr. John Wickes, of Warwick, who had been a sufferer with Gorton. He was killed at a very advanced age.[3] Put all these things together and shall we not say with Solomon, That which is crooked cannot be made straight ?

Mr. Williams's zeal appeared to be directed, not against the person of any man, but only against men's errors. In the Preface to his Reply to Mr. Cotton, he says :—

Since it pleased God to lay a command upon [on] my conscience, to come in as his poor witness in this great cause, I rejoiced that it pleased him to appoint so able and excellent [and conscionable] an instrument to bolt out the truth to the bran ; though [so] I can humbly say in God's holy presence, it is my constant heaviness and soul's grief [as] to differ from any fearing God ; [so] much more, [ten thousand times] from Mr. Cotton, whom I have desired, and still desire, highly to esteem and dearly to respect, for so great a portion of mercy and grace vouchsafed unto him, and so many truths of Christ [Jesus] maintained by him. [And] therefore (notwithstanding some of no common judgment and respect to him, have said, he wrote his washings of the bloody tenet in blood against Christ [Jesus] and gall against me, yet) if upon so slippery and narrow a

[1] Massachusetts History, Vol. II, p. 510. [441.]
[2] Bishop, pp. 225, 226. See page 97.
[3] Callender, p. 93. [148.]

passage, I have slipped into any term or expression unbeseeming his person, or the [matter, the] cause of the Most High in hand [considered,] I humbly crave pardon of God, and Mr. Cotton also.

Although he could not say the like of the chief teachers among the Quakers, yet he said, " Many truly humble souls may be captivated among them. . . . . And many of the Quakers I love and honor." And he said, " He that shall ponder the fathers' polygamy, the best kings of Judah suffering the high places, David's slaying Uriah, Asa's imprisoning the prophet, Peter's rash using the sword, the disciples' calling for fire from heaven, shall see cause to reprove the Quakers for their rash damning of others from whom they have suffered."[1] But when they came to answer him, they were so far from regarding this admonition, that where he spake of the matter of the Christian churches, viz. : true converts,[2] and said in the margin, " This was, and I hope is, the principle of the New English churches ;" they spent three pages full of capitals about their sufferings, to prove that it could not be so, and at last said : " So it is clear, you that have destroyed men's lives, are not of God, but the devil."[3] This was the temper of their teachers ; but of others, the two Easton's, father and son, Walter Clarke, and Henry Bull, were all worthy Governors of that denomination, and I find Mr. Samuel Hubbard expressing a considerable esteem also for Mr. Coddington, after his death, in a letter to a friend. Neither have I found one reflection upon his person in all Mr. Williams's writings, unless a plain recital of facts may be so called.

A new sect came out from among the Baptists about this time, who have caused not a little trouble to themselves and others, of whom I have collected the following brief account, chiefly from the letters preserved by Mr. Samuel Hubbard. In the close of the year 1674, the family of Mr. James Rogers, of New London, called Mr. Crandal over from Wes-

---

[1]Williams, pp. 3, 25, 71, 178.   [2]See page 119.   [3]Fox, p. 63, 66.

terly, who preached among them, and baptized his sons John
and James, and an Indian named Japheth. This alarmed
the other denomination; and Mr. Bradstreet, minister at New
London, said he hoped the next Court would take a course
with them. They sent to Newport, and Elder Hiscox, Mr.
Hubbard and his son Clarke, were sent to visit them in
March, 1675, when Jonathan Rogers was also baptized, and
all four of them were received as members of their church,
by prayer and laying on of hands. Hereupon John Rogers's
father-in-law took his wife and children from him; and,
upon her complaints against him, he was carried before their
Deputy Governor, and committed to Hartford jail, from
whence he wrote to Mr. Hubbard April 6, 1675. How long
he continued there I do not find, only, he visited the church
at Newport the next September. In September 18, 1676,
those four members went with a boat, and brought Elder
Hiscox and Mr. Hubbard to New London again, when old
Mr. Rogers, his wife and daughter, were all baptized and received into that church; whereupon they were called before
the magistrate, but were soon released; though, from that
time, they began to imprison the Rogerses for working on
the first day of the week. And when Mr. Hiscox and Mr.
Hubbard visited them again, and held worship with them
two miles out of town on their Sabbath, November 23, 1677,
and Joseph Rogers's wife had next morning given them a
satisfying account of her experiences, John must needs have
them go up to town to baptize her there. Mr. Hubbard opposed it, but John carried the day ; and while Mr. Hiscox
was preaching at town, the constable came and took him, and
they all went before the magistrate ; where also was the minister, Mr. Bradstreet, who had much to say, about the good
way that their fathers had set up. Upon which Mr. Hubbard, obtaining leave to speak, said, " You are a young man,
but I am an old planter of about forty years, a beginner of
Connecticut, and have been persecuted for my conscience
from this colony, and I can assure you, that the old begin-

ners were not for persecution, but we had liberty at first."
After further discourse, the magistrate said, Could you not
do it elsewhere ?   "A good answer," says Mr. Hubbard ; and
so they were released and went to Samuel Rogers's house,
where his brother John put himself forward, prayed, and
then went out to the water and baptized his sister ; upon
which Mr. Hiscox was seized again, as supposing he had
done it, but John came before the magistrate, and was forward to make known his act therein ; so the others were released and returned home.

Jonathan Rogers had married Naomi Burdick, grand-
daughter to Mr. Hubbard ; and on March 2, 1678, Elder Hiscox baptized her at Westerly, together with James Babcock,
George Lamphere, and two others ; and on the 5th of May
following, Joseph Clarke wrote from thence to his father
Hubbard, that John and James Rogers with their father were
in prison ; having previously excommunicated Jonathan,
chiefly because he did not retain their judgment of the unlawfulness of using medicines, nor accuse himself before authority, for working on the first day of the week.   Hereupon the church at Newport sent messengers to New London about this matter, who reported on their return, that " a
practice was started up, (out of conscience) that because the
world, yea, most professors, pray in their families mornings
and nights, and before meats and after, in a customary way,
therefore to forbear prayer in their families or at meats
publicly, except some are led forth upon some special
occasion ; saying they find no command in the word of God
for it."   About this time, Elder Hiscox's church received
letters from Dr. Chamberlain, whereof one was directed to
their church, he being of the same faith and order with
them, the other was directed as follows :—

Peter Chamberlain, senior, Doctor of both universities, and first and
eldest physician in ordinary to his Majesty's person, according to the world,
but according to grace, a servant of the word of God ; to the excellent and
noble Governor of New England ; grace, mercy, peace and truth, from

God our Father, and from our Lord Jesus Christ; praying for you, that you may abound in heavenly graces and temporal comforts. I have always had a love to the intended purity, and unspotted doctrine of New England; for Mr. Cotton was of the same college and university, of Emanuel in Cambridge, as I was, and so was Mr. Hooker and others with whom we were all contemporary; and I never know them but of a holy life and conversation. I also knew Colonel Humfrey, Sir Richard Saltonstall and Mr. Peters, who were of note among you, and Sir Henry Vane, who all had some share in the foundation of your government. But certainly the first intentions were never to debar the truths of Scripture and liberty of conscience guided thereby; but to suppress sin and idolatry, and prevent all the adulteries of Rome, to whom all things are lawful, especially lies in hypocrisy, to promote their most damnable doctrines, covetous superstitions, and blasphemous supremacy. It is great wisdom to suppress sin, but not oppress the liberty of a good conscience; and whilst men grant liberty of conscience, not to admit liberty of sin. All magistrates have not attained to this wisdom, else England had been long since freed from popery and perjury. Whatsoever is against the ten commandments is sin. Rom. 3. 10; I John, 3. 4. And he that sinneth in one point is guilty of all, because he that spake one word of them spake all, and he added no more. Jam. 2. 10, 11; Exo. 20. 1. While Moses and Solomon caution men, so much against adding to, or taking from; Deut. 4. 2; Prov. 30. 5, 6; and so doth the beloved apostle; Rev. 22. 18, 19; what shall we say of those that take away of those ten words, or those that make them void, and teach men so? Nay, they dare give the lie to Jehovah, and make Jesus Christ not only a breaker of the law, but the very author of sin in others, also causing them to break them. Hath not the little horn played his part lustily in this, and worn out the saints of the Most High, so that they become little-horn men also? If you are pleased to inquire about these things, and to require any instances or informations, be pleased by your letters to command it from your humble servant in the Lord Jesus Christ,

PETER CHAMBERLAIN.

Most worthy Governor. September 1, 1677.

Copies hereof were sent to those whom it was directed to; and the church sent a letter therewith to Connecticut, from whence this answer was returned:—

HARTFORD, 8, 8, 78.

FRIENDS OF NEWPORT ON RHODE ISLAND; WILLIAM HISCOX, &c.:— Yours of 9, 4, 78, was received the 7th instant, with one enclosed from another, Peter Chamberlain, senior. The advice in both is readily complied withal and thankfully accepted. To be minded of any parts of the

Scriptures of truth is gratefully received, and were it not for a seducing devil, and a deceitful heart, they would be a rule of life unto all that have senses exercised therein, and make due application thereof. What yourselves or that worthy gentleman intend, or who or what he refers to, is not so easy to guess at. We have of late had to deal with Rogers and his of New London, towards whom the authority have shown all condescension imaginable to us; that if they would forbear to offend our consciences, we should indulge them in their persuasion, and give them no offence in the seventh day, in worshipping God by themselves. We may doubt (if they were governors in our stead) they would tell us, that their consciences would not suffer them to give us so much liberty; but that they must bear witness to the truth, and beat down idolatry, as the old kings did in Scripture; they judging so of our Lord's day worshipping. It may be that your counsel may be more taking with them, to make them forbear, than ours; which is all at present, with respects,

From your friend and servant in Christ,

WILLIAM LEETE.

The church repeatedly sent and labored with them, but to little effect. Mr. Gibson went and lived and preached a while among them at New London; but Mr. Hubbard wrote to their aged brother Thorton, (who had removed from Newport to Providence,) on November 8, 1679, informing him of his late visit to that people, when he found that "old Mr. Rogers, had the wheel of a loaded cart go over his leg a little below his knee, bruising it much, and had been so six weeks, but now could move it; their judgment is not to use any means." And, said he, " pray remember my respects to Mr. Roger Williams; I should be glad to hear of him and his wife ;" a great respect to whom was shown in all their letters as long as he lived. On June 7, 1685, Mr. Hubbard wrote to Mr. Henry Reeve of Jamaica, and informed him that messengers were then gone from their church to New London, " to declare against two or more of them that were of us, who are declined to Quakerism, I might say more; of whom be thou aware, for by their principles, they will travel by land and sea to make disciples, yea, sorry ones too. Their names are John and James Rogers, and one Donham."

From this beginning proceeded a sect which has continued to this day, who from their chief leader have been called
Rogerenes.   In their dialect and many other things, they
have been like the first Quakers in this country; though
they have retained tho external use of baptism and the supper, and have been singular in refusing the use of means
and medicines for their bodies. Their greatest zeal has been
discovered in going from meeting to meeting, and from town
to town, as far as Norwich and Lebanon, (the one fourteen,
the other twenty-four miles,) to testify against hireling teachers, and against keeping the first day of the week as a sabbath, which they call the idol-sabbath.   And when the
authorities have taken them up and fined them therefor, and
have sometimes whipped them for refusing to pay it, they
have soon published accounts of all such persecutions, which
has been the very means of keeping their sect alive. When
the small-pox was very terrible in Boston, in 1721, and great
fear of it was discovered in the country, John Rogers, their
founder, was confident he could go in where it was and not
catch it; and to prove his faith, went a hundred miles to
Boston, but caught the distemper, came home and died
with it, and scattered it in his family; yet his successors
still kept on in their way.   So late as 1763, some of them
repeatedly came and clapped shingles and pieces of boards
together around the meeting-house in Norwich town, as well
as delivered messages to the worshippers, against their keeping of the Lord's day.   But as the rulers had learned so
much wisdom as only to remove them away from disturbing
others, without inflicting either fine or corporal punishment
upon them, they have ceased from such things since in a
great measure, and as they never were a large society, there
is hope of a true reformation among them.[1] Besides these,

[1] Morgan Edwards gives the following account of this singular sect:—

" The most forward of the brothers was John; for he took upon him to form the
family, and others that he baptized, into a church, and to make a creed, and to settle rules of discipline. The first act of discipline was the excommunication of his

there have been some Sabbatarian Baptists in that place from the beginning to the present time, though not a distinct church.

We must now return to our Baptist fathers at Boston. The liberty they had enjoyed, with a blessing upon the ministry of Mr. Miles and others, had caused such an increase of members, that, in February, 1677, they agreed to divide

brother Jonathan, for using medicine and refusing to do things which would bring on him the lash of the civil magistrate. And this John Rogers was not only the founder of the sect, and the person from whom they were called Rogerenes, but the hero of the cause, in suffering and writing and defying; I say defying, for he had not been long at the head of the cause, before he printed and published the following proclamation : 'I, John Rogers, a servant of Jesus Christ, doth here make an open declaration of war against the great red dragon, and against the beast to which he gives power; and against the false church which rides upon the beast; and against the false prophets who are established by the dragon and the beast; and against the image of the beast : and also a proclamation of derision against the sword of the devil's spirit, which is prisons, stocks, whips, fines and revilings, all of which is to defend the doctrines of devils.'

"His theory relative to baptism and the Lord's supper, is scriptural, for the Rogerenes baptize by immersing professed penitents and believers; the Lord's supper they administer in the evening, with its ancient appendages. Some other articles of Rogers's creed are orthodox. The particulars of it are, 1st, All days are alike since the death of Christ. 2d. No medicines are to be used, nor doctors nor surgeons employed. 3d. No grace at meals. 4th. All prayers to be mental, and not vocal, except when the spirit of prayer compels to the use of the voice. 5th. All unscriptural parts of religious worship are idols. 6th. All good Christians should exert themselves against idols, &c. Among these idols they placed the first day of the week, infant baptism, &c. The First-day sabbath they called the New England idol. The methods they took to demolish this idol were, they would be at work near meeting-houses and in the ways to meeting-houses, and take work into meeting-houses, the women knitting and the men whittling and making splits for baskets, and every now and then contradicting the preachers. This was seeking persecution, and they had plenty of it, insomuch that the New Englanders left some of them neither liberty, nor property, nor a whole skin.

"John Rogers was an author. He published a commentary on the Revelation. He that hath patience to read it, let him read it. He also published 'A Midnight Cry;' a 'Narrative of Sufferings,' &c." Materials for a History of the Baptists in New Jersey, pp. 147, 148.

Benedict says that after the death of John Rogers, Joseph Bolles published a second edition of his book, entitled, "A Midnight Cry from the temple of God to the ten virgins slumbering and sleeping. Awake! awake! arise! and gird your loins and trim your lamps, for behold the Bridegroom cometh, go ye therefore out to meet him!"

Even as late as 1813, according to Benedict, there was a "small company of the Rogerenes in Groton, Ct., near New London." History of the Baptists, Vol. II, pp. 425, 426.—ED.

into two churches ; but in January, 1678, they revoked that act, and concluded to build them a meeting-house, in Boston, and to defer the affair of dividing, till they could obtain the settlement of an able, sufficient ministry there. They first nominated Mr. Russell for that end, and then talked of his going to Swanzey in Mr. Miles's room ; but in conclusion, Mr. Miles returned to his old flock, and Mr. Russell was ordained their pastor in Boston, July 28, 1679, and removed there. Before this time Governor Leverett had deceased, and Mr. Bradstreet had been chosen in his stead ; in consequence of which this church wrote to their brethren at Newport the 25th of January this year, that several of their brethren and sisters had been called to Court, censured, fined twenty shillings a piece and to pay Court charges, and others only admonished and to pay Court charges, which had not then been paid, and the constables were backward to make distress upon them if they could shift it off. February 9, the church met, and purchased their meeting house with the land it was built upon, of Philip Squire and Ellis Callender, for sixty pounds ; and they met in it for worship the 15th. They had built with so much caution as not openly to call it by that name till it was done. They had been often censured and reproached for meeting in private houses, but now say, " Since we have for our convenience obtained a public house on purpose for that use, we are become more offensive than before."[1] The leaders of the society were convented before the General Court of May 10,[2] who, not finding any old law to suit their term then made a new one, in these words :—

It is ordered by the Court and the authority thereof, that no persons whatever, without the consent of the freemen of the town where they live, first orderly had, and obtained, at a public meeting assembled for that end, and license of the County Court, or in defect of such consent, a license by

---

[1] Russell, p. 10.—B.

[2] In the published Massachusetts Records, the date of this transaction is May 28.
—Ed.

the special order of the General Court, shall erect or make use of any house as above said; and in case any person or persons shall be convicted of transgressing this law, every such house or houses wherein such persons shall so meet more than three times, with the land whereon such house or houses stand, and all private ways leading thereto, shall be forfeited to the use of the county, and disposed of by the County Treasurer, by sale or demolishing, as the Court that gives judgment in the case shall order.[1]

How different is this from the above language of Governor Leete! But instead of seeking for persecution as Rogers did, this peaceable people refrained from meeting in their own house for the present, waiting to see what God would do for them. And he who has the hearts of kings in his hand, moved their king to write to the Massachusetts rulers on July 24, requiring that liberty of conscience should be allowed to all Protestants, so as they might not be discountenanced from sharing in the government, much less that no such good subjects of his, for not agreeing in the congregational way, should by law, " be subjected to fines or forfeitures, or other incapacities for the same; which is a severity to be the more wondered at, whereas liberty of conscience was made a [one] principal motive for your first transportation into those parts."[2] Deplorable indeed was their case at this time. Their all was in great danger, for doing so much of that which they thought Heaven frowned upon them for not doing more of; and it was evidently the two errors I have mentioned on page 35, which brought them into this dilemna. Mr. William Hubbard, whom I have so often quoted, who was a minister at Ipswich, preached at their election in Boston, May 3, 1676; and as the permission of Quaker meetings had been declared by many ministers, to be one great cause of God's judgments upon them, which had stirred up the Court to severity against that people, he plainly gave his mind to the contrary; and that pride and worldly mindedness were the greatest evils then among them; yet lest Governor Leverett

[1]Massachusetts Records.   [2]Massachusetts History, Vol. III, p. 520.

and his Court should be too favorable to the Baptists, he, in his dedication of that sermon to them, page 6, said, " If he were not much mistaken who said it is morally impossible to rivet the Christian religion into the body of a nation without infant baptism, by proportion it will as necessarily follow, that the neglect or disuse thereof, will as directly tend to root it out." | And Dr. Increase Mather, who yielded to Mr. Mitchel's reasonings about the Half-way Covenant, and took the lead among the Massachusetts ministers after his death, in that capacity now moved the Assembly to convene what they called The Reforming Synod. First they kept a general fast in their churches, and then the Synod met at Boston, September 10, 1679, to answer these two questions: 1st. What are the evils that have provoked the Lord to bring his judgments on New England ? 2d. What is to be done that so these evils may be reformed ?

They had not gone far in their answer before they said:—

Men have set up their thresholds by God's thresholds, and their post by his post. Quakers are false worshippers ; and such Anabaptists as have risen up among us, in opposition to the churches of the Lord Jesus, receiving into their society those that have been for scandal delivered unto Satan ; yea, and improving those as administrators of holy things, who have been (as doth appear) justly under [church] censure, do no better than set up altar against the Lord's altar. Wherefore it must needs be provoking to God, if these things be not duly and fully testified against, by every one in their several capacities.

Their result was approved of by the General Court on October 15, which commended it to all their churches, " enjoining and requiring all persons in their respective capacities to a careful and diligent reformation of all those provoking evils mentioned therein, according to the true intent thereof, that so the anger and displeasure of God, many ways manifested, might be averted [from this poor people;] and his favor and blessing obtained."[1]

[1]Magnalia, B, 5, pp. 87, 89, [Vol. II, pp. 274, 275]; I. Mather's Life, p. 84. Mr. Stoddard informs us, that in this Synod " they had a dispute about persons giving, a relation of the work of God's Spirit upon their hearts, in order to coming to com-

25

This dreadful charge, coming out from the whole power
of the colony against one small society, put them upon a
critical review of their past conduct; and they found that
among about eighty members that they had received, there
were but two that had been censured in those other churches
(since Mr. Gould and Mr. Osburne, of whom we have before
spoken) one of whom was Mr. Thomas Foster, of Billerica,
who, for turning and going away when infants were sprinkled,
and for going at last and joining with the Baptists, and refusing, after they had presented him to Court, to return to
the other church, was censured and excommunicated by

munion. .... The result was, that they blotted out that clause, ... and put in the
room of it, the making a profession of their faith and repentance; and so I voted
with the rest, and am of the same judgment still." That is, a profession of a saving
change should not be required before they come to communion. Stoddard's Appeal,
p. 94. Was this reformation, or was it apostacy?—B.

Evidently the moving spirit in this Reforming Synod, was Increase Mather. His
son, Cotton Mather, in his account of his father's life, entitled, "Parentator, Remarkables of Dr. Increase Mather," pp. 84, 85, gives the following account of the
Synod :—

"Upon motion of Mr. Mather, in conjunction with others excited by him first, the
General Court called upon the churches to send their delegates for a Synod in Boston, to consider What are the evils? &c. The churches having first kept a general
fast, that a gracious direction might be obtained of God in what was now to be done,
the Synod met at Boston, September 10, 1679. The Synod also kept a day of prayer
with fasting, in which Mr. Mather was chose for one of the preachers and the venerable old Mr. Cobbett was chose for the other. Several days were then spent in
free discourses on the two questions, and at last a result, with a preface, were agreed
unto, which were of Mr. Mather's drawing up. On the day when a Committee of
the ministers presented it unto the General Court, Mr. Mather preached a very potent sermon on the danger of not being reformed by these things; and the General
Court thereupon commended it unto the serious consideration of all the churches
and people of the jurisdiction."

The Mr. Stoddard, mentioned in the above note, is Solomon Stoddard, who had
succeeded Eleazer Mather as pastor of the church in Northampton, where he was
afterwards succeeded by his grandson, Jonathan Edwards. The full title of his
work above cited, is, "Appeal to the Learned; being a vindication of the right of
visible saints to the Lord's Supper, though they be destitute of a saving work of
God's Spirit in their hearts; against the exceptions of Mr. Increase Mather." Mr.
Stoddard states in this work, page 94, that the dispute in the Synod, on the question
whether persons, in order to be received to full communion, should be required to
give a relation of the work of God's Spirit in their hearts, was chiefly between Mr.
Mather on the affirmative, and himself on the negative. A further account of the
sentiments of Solomon Stoddard on these points, and of their results, will be given
in subsequent pages.—Ed.

them.   The other was Mr. Farnum, who was the only one
the Baptists had received, after others had cast him out ;
which was from the North Church in Boston, where Mr.
Mayo and Dr. Mather were ministers.   The Baptists now
sent and obtained copies of the proceedings of that church
against him, whereby it appeared, that they were in the
height of their dealings with him, the same month that the
Assembly disfranchised Gould and Osburne for constituting
that Baptist church, viz., in October, 1665 ; and that Farnum got his temper up, and in sundry instances spake and
acted very unadvisedly ; for which the Baptists now required
him to offer satisfaction to that church, before they would
commune with him again.   This he soon after did.   Mr.
Willard owns that he offered a confession therefor both orally
and in writing ; but because he refused to return into their
communion they judged it not to be sincere.   The Baptists
say that some who had been baptized among them had afterward been refused communion by the other churches, when
they had desired it.   To which Mr. Willard says, " They
know that our churches have received some that were scrupulous about infant baptism, who were willing to carry inoffensively ; that we have refused such as were re-baptized
among those excommunicated Anabaptists, is true hypothet-
ically, viz., except they would acknowledge and repent of
that act ; because we judge it scandalous."[1]   Upon which I
would only remark, that God says, He that doubteth is
damned if he eat ; but the Massachusetts were willing to
admit persons to eat with scruples, but excommunicated such
as put their full persuasion about baptism into practice, and
judged those not to be sincere, who would not repent of that
act !   A letter at this time to their Governor deserves notice, which is as follows :—

HONORED SIR :—I have often heard of your name by Colonel Eyers,
whose first wife's name was Bradstreet ; and the character I have of you,
if you were her son, relates you a wise and understanding man.   But your

[1] Russell, p. 10 ; Willard, p. 22.

report gives you as though some Lauderdale's counsel had possessed you, which set all Scotland in an uproar. God is wiser than man, more just and righteous ; his counsel must stand. Beware of smiting your brethren, lest the ecclesiastical power of England invade you. A parliament is near at hand, when just grievances will be previously [grievously?] resented ; I hope there shall be none during your government. Samson plucked a house on his head, and fell in it. If I can serve you in any honorable way, command your humble servant,

PETER CHAMBERLAIN,

His Majesty's physician in ordinary to his Royal Person.

September 2, 1679.

Mr. Samuel Hubbard sometime after sent a letter, with a copy of this, to Governor Leete, to check their imprisoning the Rogerses at New London.   Notice being received by the Baptists in Boston, of the king's letter in their favor, they met again in their house ; but had not so done above four times before the Court met, and issued a warrant to the constable of Boston, requiring him, " in his Majesty's name, forthwith to summon Philip Squire, Thomas Skinner, and Mr. Drinker, to make their appearance before the Court of Assistants now sitting, having liberty to bring with them three or four more of their friends, to give an account of their breach of the law in erecting a meeting-house ; and that they appear at three of the clock this instant 5th March, 1680."   They appeared accordingly, and the Court required a positive answer to the question, whether they would engage, either for the whole society, or for themselves in particular, to desist from meeting in said house till the next General Court ?   They said they were not prepared to answer it, and desired time to consult their brethren. This was then denied them, but upon renewing the request next morning, they were allowed so much time as from Saturday till Monday.   The church met on Monday, and presented the following address, viz. :—

To the honorable the Governor and magistrates now assembled at Boston, at the Court of Assistants, the 8th of March, 1680, the petition and declaration of the society of the people commonly known or distinguished by the name of Baptists, residing in and about Boston, humbly showeth,

In primum, that whereas the only wise God, having by his providence led us into that order and way of the gospel of gathering into church fellowship, we do hereby confess, that what we did was not out of opposition to, or contempt of, the churches of Christ in New England, but in a holy imitation, merely for the better enjoyment of the liberty of our consciences, the great motive to this removal at first into this wilderness. 2. That the building a convenient place for our public church assembly, was not thought of affronting authority, there being no law in the country against any such practise at the erecting of this house, and we did therefore think, as the apostle saith, where there is no law, there is no transgression. The dictates of nature, or common prudence belonging to mankind, and the example or practice of the country throughout, lead to the seeking of this convenience. 3. There being a law made in May last against meeting in the place built, we submitted to the same, until we fully understood by letters from several in London, that it was his Majesty's pleasure and command (the common *supersedus* to all corporation laws in the English nation, that have not the royal assent[1]) that we should enjoy liberty of our meetings in the manner as other of his Protestant subjects; and the General Court at their last meeting not having voted a non-occurrence. 4. As therefore the two tribes and half did humbly and meekly vindicate themselves, upon the erecting of their altar, when challenged for it by Eleazer and the messengers of the ten tribes, so do we hereby confess in like manner, that we have not designed by this act any contempt of authority, nor any departing from the living God, or churches of his worship; the Lord God of gods he knows it; Joshua xxii, 22; though it be our lot, with the apostles, in the way that some call heresy so to worship the God of our fathers. Your petitioners, therefore, having no design against the peace of this place, but being still as ready as ever to hazard our lives for the defence of the people of God here, do humbly request that this our profession and declaration may find acceptance with this honorable Court, as that of the two tribes did with Eleazer; and that we may still, through your allowance and protection, enjoy the liberty of God's worship, in such places as God hath afforded us, which will greatly oblige your petitioners, as in duty bound, humbly to pray.

Signed by us in the name and with the consent of the church.

ISAAC HULL,
JOHN RUSSELL,
EDWARD DRINKER,
THOMAS SKINNER."

[1]Their charter was originally designed for a corporation in England, to be executed only by a deputation in this country, as the King observes in the letter referred to. Massachusetts History, Vol. III, p. 519.

But instead of having any ears to hear this loyal and Christian address, their marshal was sent, and finding their gate locked, forced his way through Mr. Squire's ground, and nailed up their meeting-house doors, putting a paper thereon which said :—

All persons are to take notice, that by order of the Court the doors of this house are shut up, and that they are inhibited to hold any meeting therein, or to open the doors thereof, without license from authority, till the General Court take further order, as they will answer the contrary at their peril.

Dated in Boston, 8th March, 1680.

By order of the Council,

EDWARD RAWSON, Secretary.

The Baptists required a copy of the marshal's warrant, but he refused it ; they then went to the Secretary for one, who plainly told them, " he was not to let them have any." They met the next Lord's day in their yard, and in the week ensuing prepared a shed therein for the purpose ; but when they came together the second Lord's day, they found the doors open ; and considering, say they, " that the Court had not done it legally, and that we were denied a copy of the constable's order and marshal's warrant, we concluded to go into our house, it being our own, having a civil right to it." And they met therein till the Assembly sat, before whom they were convented on May 11 ; when they gave in these pleas :—

1. The house was our own. 2. It was built before the law was made, therefore no transgression. 3. The express will and pleasure of the king, that we should enjoy our liberty. After some debate of the matter (in which we met with some hard and reviling speeches from some of them) we were dismissed for that time. Next morning we put up a humble petition, (being blamed by some in the Court that we had not done it before) that there might be a suspension of any proceedings against us.

These accounts I have taken from their church records and papers. On the colony records, under May 19, I find it thus written, viz. :—

After the Court had heard their answer and plea, perused their petition and what else was produced, the parties were [the persons being] called in, the Court's sentence in the name of the Court was published to them; that the Court, in answer to their petition, judged it meet and ordered, that the petitioners be admonished by the present honored Governor for their offence, and so granted them their petition, so far as to forgive them their offence past, but still prohibited them as a society of themselves, or joined with others, to meet in that public place they have built, or any [other] public house except such as are allowed by lawful authority; and accordingly the Governor in open Court gave them their admonition.

Dr. Mather had published a piece the preceding March, entitled, The Divine Right of Infant Baptism, containing some injurious reflections upon this people; which, with others, were briefly answered in Mr. Russell's Narrative, dated from Boston the 20th of this month, with the consent of the whole church, and sent to London, where Messrs. William Kiffen, Daniel Dyke, William Collins, Hansard Knollys, John Harris and Nehemiah Cox, noted Baptist ministers, wrote a preface to it, in which they say:—

As for our brethren of the Congregational way in old England, both their principles and practice do equally plead for our liberties as for their own; and it seems strange that such of the same way in New England, yea, even such (a generation not yet extinct, or the very next successors of them) who with liberal estates chose rather to depart from their native soil into a wilderness, than be under the imposition and lash of those, who upon religious pretences took delight to smite their fellow servants, should exercise towards others the like severity that themselves with so great hazard and hardship sought to avoid; especially considering that it is against their brethren, who avowedly profess and appeal to the same rule with themselves for their guidance in, and decision of, all matters relating to the worship of God, and the ordering of their whole conversation. . . . . For one Protestant congregation to persecute another, where there is no pretence to infallibility in the decision of all controversies, seems much more unreasonable than the cruelties of the church of Rome towards them that depart from their superstitions; and if prejudices were removed and opportunities of power not abused, but the golden rule of our Saviour were duly attended unto and rightly applied in the present case, certainly more moderation, yea, even compassion would be exercised towards these our Christian friends by such as now give them trouble.

They close with observing That Dr. Stillingstreet had already declared in his Mischief of Separation, that their rigorous course against Congregationalists in England, was justified by the process of the rulers here, against dissenters from themselves ; and pray that the governors of New England would regard their brethren there, so much as to remit these proceedings. What was said in answer thereto, we shall see presently, after I have observed, that Elder Russell was taken from his beloved flock by death, December 21, 1680 ; upon which the church met the next day, and agreed that their brother Callender, should be helpful in carrying on their worship in Boston, on Lord's days in the forenoon, and brother Drinker in the afternoon, in the absence of Elder Hull. It is evident, that the gifts and graces of Elder Russell were not small ; and his memory is precious. His grand-daughter Brooks, married in Swanzey, whose sons, Job,[1] Russell and John Mason have been, and the two latter still are, useful gospel preachers in the Second Baptist church in that town. Also Messrs. Joseph, William and Jonathan Russell, now noted traders in Providence, are of his posterity.

In 1681, a minister of the church of Boston, which was formed in a schismatical way in 1669, published an answer to the Baptist's Narrative ; and though its author was deceased, yet he entitled it, " *Ne sutor ultra crepidam :*[2] or brief animadversions upon the New England Anabaptists' late fallacious Narrative ; wherein the notorious mistakes and falsehoods by them published, are detected ; by Samuel Willard, &c." To which he adds as a motto, Romans 16. 17, 18. Dr. Increase Mather wrote a preface to this work, wherein he says :—

Many are of the mind, that it is not worth the while, to take notice of what is emitted by men so obscure and inconsiderable.....It seems to me that the reverend author of the following animadversions, hath shewed humility, in condescending to take persons in hand, between whom and himself there is such an *impar congressus*.....As for the brethren, that

[1]Elder Job Mason died since this history was in the press, aged 80.
[2]Cobbler, keep to your last.

have thought good to prefix an epistle to such a narrative, and therein declare that molestation is given and severity is exercised towards Antipædo-baptists in New England, merely for a supposed error about the subject of baptism, controverted amongst learned and holy men, they are marvelously deceived in that their supposition. Protestants ought not to persecute any, yet, that protestants may punish protestants, and as the case may be circumstanced, a congregation of such as call themselves protestants, cannot rationally be denied. Those of the Congregational way, fully concur with the old puritan nonconformists, such as Cartwright, Rainold, Whitaker, Bains, Parker, &c., in whose writings Congregational principles about church government, are to be seen.[1] Now the old nonconformists (notwithstanding their sufferings from those that took delight to smite their fellow servants) did believe that disorders in whole congregations were liable to the civil magistrate's censure. · · · ·Our famous Cotton was another Moses, in respect of meekness and Christian forbearance, as to dissenters from his judgment in matters of a lesser concernment, yet would he sometimes make a zealous protestation, that if magistrates in New England should tolerate transgressors against the rules of godliness (as well as offences contrary to what the rules of honesty require) he believed that God would not long tolerate them.....I would entreat the brethren that have subscribed the epistles seriously to consider ; 1. That the place may sometimes make a great alteration as to the indulgence to be expected. It is evident, that that toleration is in one place, not only lawful, but a necessary duty, which in another place would be destructive ; and the expectation of it irrational. That which is needful to ballast a great ship, will sink a small boat.. ....2. Let them consider, that those of their persuasion in this place have acted with so much irregularity and profaneness, that should men of any persuasion whatsoever have done the like, the same severity would have been used towards them.

This hard sentence his son has propagated to posterity.[2]

But, search through all they have said against those people, and I am confident that the greatest real disorder they

[1]These are the men referred to in page 9, who opened a door for Mr. Robinson and his brethren, by which themselves entered not. Their first Admonition to the Parliament, was presented thereto by Mr. John Field and Mr. Wilcox; for which they were committed to Newgate Prison, on October 2, 1572. This caused Mr. Thomas Cartwright to write the Second Admonition to Parliament, quoted by Mr. Robinson, and also to answer what Dr. Whitgift had written against the first. And Mr. Neal says, the reason why they could not settle the controversy, was because Cartwright was for making his Bible the only standard of doctrine, discipline and government; but Whitgift held the latter of these to be changeable, to accommodate the civil governments we live under. History of the Puritans, Vol. I, pp. 190—197. [300 —307.]

[2]Magnalia, B. 7, p. 28. [Vol. II, p. 461.]

have produced, was the church's receiving Farnum as they did ; which, when they had proper knowledge of, they rectified. But is this comparable to the disorders at Hingham, twenty years before, where Lieut. Eames was regularly chosen their Captain, and presented to the Court for a commision ; but soon upon it, a notion was started to choose another man, related to the minister, into that office, who accordingly was chosen and presented. And when the reason of it was asked for, they said Eames had resigned ; but he said he had not. Hereupon the minister censured him for lying ; and this cost three or four days' tedious labors of a council, without being able to settle it ; and occasioned the petition of Dr. Child and others, with much trouble to Governor Winthrop and the Assembly.[1] Yet the issue of all was, that the minister of Hingham excommunicated Captain Eames, contrary to the minds of other ministers, and by their advice, " those that were without just cause cast out at Hingham, were received into the church of Weymouth, the next town, and the matter so continued through the stiffness of their minds, and their self-willed resolutions."[2]

In the piece upon infant baptism, which Dr. Mather had

[1]See page 116.

[2]Winthrop, [Vol. II, pp. 261, 278, 285—295, 321.] Hubbard, [pp. 417—419.] Neal, Vol. I, p. 233. How just also was it for both ministers and courts to accuse that Baptist church, of having excommunicated officers, in the plural, when they never had but one?—B.

This difficulty with Dr. Childs was followed by another on the question of "the enlargement of privileges," which was a long and grievous trouble to Governor Winthrop and the General Court. Finally Dr. Childs and his sympathizers carried their complaint to England, where their cause was presented in a pamphlet entitled "New England's Jonas cast up at London." It is reprinted in Massachusetts Historical Collections, Second series, Vol. IV. This was answered by Mr. Winslow, in a pamphlet, entitled, "The Salamander," intimating that the opposite party were never at rest except they were in the fires of contention. It is to this latter difficulty that the above-cited passages from Winthrop and Neal refer. Savage (Winthrop, Vol. II, p. 292,) charges Hutchinson (Vol. I. p. 138,) with being misled by Mather to confound the two controversies ; and Backus, by the references he gives, might seem obnoxious to the same charge. But similar questions were agitated in both controversies, and the one was doubtless the outgrowth of the other.—ED.

published, he accused those Baptists of the sin of Jeroboam, who made priests of the lowest of the people ;[1] in which, says Mr. Russell, " we easily understand what he means ;" our evil in this respect, is our calling to office those who have not been bred up in colleges, and taught in other languages, but have been bred to other callings. It is not because we are against learning, for we esteem it, and honor it in its place ; and if we had such among us · who were together with that, otherways duly qualified for the work of the ministry, we should readily choose them. But we do not think the Spirit of God is locked up so in the narrow limits of college learning, that none are to be called to office in a church but such, nor that all such are fit for that work, be they never so great scholars ; neither do we think that all those who have not that learning, are to be accounted the lowest of the people. Indeed, the priesthood was bounded to the tribe of Levi, by divine institution, but we cannot find that the Lord hath, by divine institution, given the work of the ministry to men of such learning only. Whom he will he fits and qualifies for that work; neither are we left without a plain rule in the New Testament to direct us in this matter.[2] In these plain gospel sentiments have the Baptists, on both sides of the Atlantic, persevered to this day. But his opponent said of the text referred to :—

The Belgic and others read it, " Of both ends of the people ;" if a fit man would accept it, so ; if not, to the other end, and take one unfit. The Anabaptists would have a learned man if they could get one of their mind ; if not, John Russell the shoemaker.....Truly, if Goodman Russell was a fit man for a minister, we have but fooled ourselves in building colleges, and instructing children in learning.[3]

[1] The Divine Right of Infant Baptism asserted, and proved from Scripture and Antiquity, page 26.—Ed.

[2] Russell, p. 14.

[3] Willard, p. 26.—B.

Cotton Mather repeats the argument of his father and Mr. Willard as follows :—

" They did seem to do what Jeroboam was taxed for, in making priests of the lowest of the people ; or, as the Belgic and others do read it, Of both ends of the people ; and as the learned Zepperus lamented the wrong done to religion in it, that

Here is a plain specimen of what many call learning, though the truly learned apostle Paul, renounced it with abhorrence ; 2 Corinthians 4. 2.   Either those who have a college education, are thereby made the head of the people, and the rest are to be ranked to the other end, or else this is a handling the word of God deceitfully ; and God says, " *The prophet that teacheth lies, he is the tail.*"

Again, the Baptists had said in their confession of faith, that those who gladly receive the word and are baptized, are saints by calling, and fit matter of a visible church.[1] This Dr. Mather called a pernicious principle.[2]   But says Mr. Russell :—

Who dare deny this to be a sound truth? as for the conclusion he draws from thence, viz., that there are no visible believers but those that are baptized, [it] is his own, not ours ; the improvement he makes of it, not what we make of it. Far be it from us to judge all that are not baptized, not to be visible saints, for we judge that the Lord hath many precious people in the world that are not baptized, according to, or in the manner we baptize ; and further we judge they should be visible saints, before baptized, or else they have no right to baptism, for it is not baptism that can make saints. And as for looking upon infant baptism as nothing, or a nullity,[3] that is true ; and we can look on it no otherwise, till we see light to own it to be that which he thinks of it, viz., of divine right, which we cannot see ground from the word to do ; and as for not owning their churches, ... we never yet denied them to be churches of Christ.   It is enough for every one to prove his own work ; but we have owned them as such ; for where there is true matter

they make *ministros de extremitatibus populi, sartoribus, sutoribus, idiotis,* taylors and cobblers, and other mechanicks to be ministers, thus these people chose an honest shooemaker to be their pastor, and used other mechanicks in the constant preaching of the gospel ; which caused some other people of a more liberal education to reflect that if Goodman such an one, and Gaffer such an one, were fit for ministers, we had befool'd ourselves in building of colleges." Magnalia, Book VII ; Vol. II, p. 460.—Ed.

[1] "Christ's commission to his disciples is to teach and baptize ; and those who gladly receive the word and are baptized, are his by calling, and fit matter for a visible church ; and a competent number of such, joined together in covenant and fellowship of the gospel, are a church of Christ."   Articles of Faith of the First Baptist church, Boston ; 1665.—Ed.

[2] Divine Right of Infant Baptism ; p. 26.—Ed.

[3] In connection with what has already been quoted, Dr. Mather had said, " Now they look upon infant baptism as a mere nullity, or, as the apostle saith of an idol, that it is nothing in the world." Divine Right, &c., p. 26.—Ed.

joined together in the bond of a holy covenant they may be looked at as a true church, though not in due order.[1]

This was not enough for the other party, but their cry still was:—

They say baptized persons are true matter of a visible church, and they say those that were only sprinkled in their infancy, were never baptized; and will not this undermine the foundation of all the churches in the world but theirs? and what more pernicious! they had even as good cry with Edom's sons, Raze it, raze it to the foundation! .... Experience tells us that such a rough thing as a New England Anabaptist is not to be handled over tenderly; the spirit which they have at all times discovered under the greatest disadvantages (and God grant that they may never have more advantage over us) easily tells us what they would have been if circumstanced as those whom they accuse.[2]

Mr. Hubbard got the most out of temper upon this occasion that he ever did in a whole volume in folio, and said:—

One John Russell, a wedderdrop'd shoemaker, ... stitched up a small pamphlet, ... wherein he endeavors to clear the innocency of those commonly (though falsely he says) called Anabaptists. Surely he was not well aware of the old adage, *Ne sutor ultra crepidam*,[3] or else he would not have made such botching work.

He goes on to recite what you may see of the Simple Cobbler, in page 154, which he calls Honest stitches used to much better purpose. But having taken the old round to Germany, he recovers his senses again, and then says:—

To return to what was in hand, and give this gospel-ordered church (as John Russell terms them) what is their due, from an historian; as for the persons of those seven [first males of the church] he apologizes for, it may

---

[1] Russell, page 14.   [2] Willard, pp. 10, 27.

[3] It was truly of some age; for after James I. had preached in the Star-Chamber, "that the mystery of the king's power is not lawful to be disputed; for that is to wade into the weakness of princes, and to take away the mystical reverence that belongs to those who sit in the *throne of God*; .... it is atheism and blasphemy to dispute what God can do; .... so is it presumption and high contempt in a subject to dispute what a king can do or say;" he, the year after our fathers first came to Plymouth, reprimanded his parliament for petitioning against his taking a popish wife for his son Charles, and said, "A small mistaking of matters of this nature, may produce more effects than can be imagined; therefore, *Ne sutor ultra crepidam.*" Rapin, Vol. II, pp. 192, 211. [London, 1729, Vol. IX, pp. 393, 485.]

be more easily granted that they were good in the main, than that it was a good work for God, they were engaged in. .... Good men may be found to be ill employed ; as Peter was, whom Christ rebukes and calls Satan, and bids him get behind him. Whether any of them did absolutely deserve to be delivered to Satan, for their obstinacy in their opinions, or rather miscarriages, which either through weakness of their judgments, or strength of their passions, which in defence of their opinions or practices they run into ; or whether there were not more acrimony of the salt, than sweetness of the gospel spirit of peace, in those that managed the discipline of the church against some of them, ... must not be here discussed. .... Yet that can give no color to .... a few giddy sectaries, that fondly conceit themselves to be an orderly church, when their very constitution [coalition] is explicitly, not only without, but against, the consent of all the rest of the churches in the places, [place] as well as the order of the civil authority.[1]

I love to see honesty even if persons are erroneous ; for then we have an advantage to judge for ourselves, and to know the better how to deal with them. And I must say that Governor Winthrop, from whom Mr. Hubbard took many things, exceeded him in that noble quality ; and that Mr. Hubbard exceeded all the historians I have seen who have copied from him, except the pious Mr. Prince. Others have often given us hard names without explaining what they meant by them ; but Mr. Hubbard plainly tells us that soon after Mr. Cotton's arrival at Boston,—

The ministers [about Boston ....] did use to meet once a fortnight at one of their houses in course, where some question of moment was debated. Mr. Skelton, pastor of Salem, and Mr. Williams (as yet not ordained an [any] officer there], out of a rigid separation jealousy, took exception at it ; prognosticating that it might in time bring forth a presbytery, or superintendency, to the prejudice of the churches' liberties. (A spirit of rigid separation had, it seems, so early fly-blown their understandings) .... the venom of which spirit had soon after infected so many of that church and people at Salem, as will appear in the next chapter. But this fear was without cause ; nor did it spring from a godly jealousy, but from the bitter root of pride, that venteth itself above order, and against love and peace. No such spirit was ever observed to appear in Mr. Cotton's days, but a spirit of love and meekness, nor since his time, to the present year.[2]

[1] Hubbard, pp. 624—627.—ED.
[2] Hubbard, pp. 189, 190.—ED.

And though the author of the Massachusetts History, approves of Mr. Williams's opinion about liberty of conscience, and fixes upon his moving Mr. Endicott to cut the cross out of the training colors, as the best plea he could make for their banishing of him ;[1] yet Mr. Hubbard honostly says, " This essay did but tick at some of the upper branches, whereas Mr. Williams laid his axe at the very root of the magisterial power in matters of the first table, which he drove on at such a rate, that many agitations were occasioned thereby, that pulled down ruin upon himself, friends and his poor family."[2] Now if the reader will look back to pages 131, 148, and compare that with their actings down to this time, he will have a fair opportunity to know the meaning of the terms, Rigid separation, Turbulent Anabaptists, Giddy sectaries, &c., as they were often used by that party.

Mr. Williams closed his second plea for religious liberty, with an address to the popish, prelatical, Presbyterian and Independent clergy of the whole kingdom, wherein he makes use of the fable or similitude of a " wolf and a poor lamb coming down to drink at the same stream together."

The wolf, cruel and strong, drinks above and aloft ; the lamb, innocent and weak, drinks upon the stream below ; the wolf questions and quarrels the lamb for corrupting and defiling the waters ; the lamb (not daring to plead how easily the wolf, drinking higher, might transfer defilement downward, but) pleads improbability and impossibility, that the waters descending could convey defilement upwards ; this is the controversy, this the plea ; but who shall judge? Be the lamb never so innocent, his plea never so just, his adversary, the wolf, will be his judge, and being so cruel and so strong, soon tears the lamb in pieces. Thus the cruel beast, armed with the power of the kings, Rev. 17, sits judge in his own quarrels against the lamb, about the drinking at the waters. And thus (saith Mr. Cotton) the judgments ought to pass upon the heretic, not for matter of conscience but for sinning against his conscience.

Objection. Methinks I hear, the great charge against the Independent party to be great pleaders for liberty of conscience, &c. Answer. Oh, the horrible deceit of the hearts of the sons of men ! And what excellent physic can we prescribe to others, till, as Job said, our soul comes to be in

[1]Hutchinson, Vol. I, p. 41.—Ed.   [2]Hubbard, pp. 189, 190.—Ed.

their souls' cases?   What need have we to be more vile, with Job, before God, to walk in a holy sense of self-insufficiency, to cry for the blessed leadings of the Holy Spirit of God, to guide and lead our heads and hearts uprightly!

He then goes on to shew, that each of these denominations had been sufferers in their turns, and when so, had always complained of it, and pleaded for liberty to their own consciences ; and then says :—

New England laws, lately published in Mr. Clarke's Narrative, tell how free it shall be for people to gather themselves into church estate, how free to choose their own ministers, how free to enjoy all the ordinances of Christ ; but yet, provided (so and so) upon the point, that the civil state must judge of the spiritual, to wit, whether persons be fit for church estate, whether the gathering be right, whether the people's choice be right, doctrines right ; and what is this in truth, but to swear that blasphemous oath of supremacy again, to the kings and queens and magistrates of this and other nations, instead of the pope!   Into these prisons and cages, do those, otherwise excellent men, the Independents, put the children of God, and all the children of men, and then bid them fly and walk at liberty (to wit, within the conjured circle) so far as they please.[1]

Toward the close of this year Mr. Miles came again and ministered a while to his brethren in Boston.   And Mr. Sprague, who in those times joined the Baptist church in Providence, in writing to the Massachusetts many years after, says :—

Why do you strive to persuade the rising generation, that you never persecuted nor hurt the Baptists, which is so apparently false? .... Did you not barbarously scourge Mr. Baker in Cambridge, the chief mate of a London ship? where also you imprisoned Mr. Thomas Gould, John Russell and Benjamin Sweetser, and many others, and fined them fifty pounds a man. .... And did you not nail up the Baptist meeting-house doors, and fine Mr. John Miles, Mr. James Brown and Mr. Nicholas Tanner? &c.

I find also that a number of people from Kittery, on Piscataqua River, in the province of Maine, were baptized this year, and in the beginning of the next, sent their most gifted brother to Boston with a letter of recommendation and re-

[1] Reply to Cotton, pp. 315—318.

quest;[1] in consequence of which the church there wrote thus on January 11, 1682:—

To ALL WHOM IT MAY CONCERN :—These are to certify, that our beloved brother William Screven is a member in communion with us, and having had trial of his gifts among us, and finding him to be a man whom God hath qualified and furnished with the gifts of his Holy Spirit and grace, enabling him to open and apply the word of God, which through the blessing of the Lord Jesus may be useful in his hand, for the begetting and

---

[1] A copy of this letter is preserved in the papers of Rev. Silas Hall, of Raynham, Massachusetts. Though not faultless in rhetoric, it is of sufficient interest to justify its publication, even aside from the consideration that it is probably the oldest document in existence relating to the history of the Baptists in the State of Maine.

" Humphrey, a servant of Jesus Christ to the church which is at Boston; grace be with you, and peace, from God, even the Father of our Lord Jesus Christ, the Father of mercies and the God of all comforts, who comforteth us in all our tribulations that we may be able to comfort them that are in any trouble, as we are comforted of God. Most dearly beloved brethren and friends, as I am, through free grace, a member of the same body and joined to the same Head, Christ Jesus, I thought it my special duty to inform you that the tender mercy of God in and through Jesus Christ, hath shined upon us by giving light to them that sit in darkness, and to guide our feet in the way of peace; for a great door, and effectual, is opened in these parts, and there are many adversaries, according to the 1st of Corinthians, 16. 9. Therefore, dearly beloved, having a desire to the service of Christ, which is perfect freedom, and the propagating his glorious gospel of peace and salvation, and eyeing that precious promise in Daniel the 12th, 3d, ' They that turn many to righteousness shall shine as the stars forever;' therefore I signify unto you, that here [are] a competent number of well established people whose hearts the Lord hath opened insomuch that they have gladly received the word and do seriously profess their hearty desire to the following of Christ and to partake of all his holy ordinances, according to his blessed institution and divine appointment; therefore I present my ardent desire to your serious consideration, which is, if the Lord see it fit, to have a gospel church planted here in this place; and in order hereunto, we think it meet that our beloved brother, William Screven, who is, through free grace, gifted and endued, with the spirit of veterans to preach the gospel; who, being called by us, who are visibly joined to the church. When our beloved brother is ordained according to the sacred rule of the Lord Jesus, our humble petition is to God that he will be pleased to carry on this good work to the glory of his holy name, and to the enlarging of the kingdom of his beloved Son, our dear Redeemer, who will add daily to his church such as shall be saved; and we desire you in the name of our Lord Jesus not to be slack in this good work, believing verily that you will not, and that you are always abounding in the work of the Lord, and we humbly crave your petitions for us to the throne of grace, and we commend you to God and the good word of his grace, which is able to build you up and to give you an inheritance among them that are sanctified.

" Written by mine own hand, this 3d of January, 1681.

HUMPHREY CHURCHWOOD."

The above date is in Old Style; in modern reckoning it should be 1682.—ED.

building up of souls in the knowledge of God, do therefore appoint, approve and encourage him, to exercise his gift in the place where he lives, or elsewhere, as the providence of God may cast him; and so the Lord help him to eye his glory in all things, and to walk humbly in the fear of his name.

Signed by us in behalf of. the rest.

ISAAC HULL,
JOHN FARNUM.

But no sooner was this design heard of in their town, than Mr. Woodbridge the minister, and Hucke the magistrate, began to bestir themselves, and not only spread the slanders we have heard so much of against the Baptists at Boston, but the magistrate repeatedly summoned those people before him who had been to the Baptist meetings, and threatened them with a fine of five shillings for every such offence for the future. On January 23, he convented Humphrey Churchwood, a baptized member of Boston church, before him, where was the said minister, who, after casting those old stories upon him, said, " Behold your great doctor, Mr. Miles of Swanzey, for he now leaves his profession and is come away, and will not teach his people any more, because he is like to perish for want, and his gathered church and people will not help him." Churchwood told them it was a great untruth ; and directly wrote to Boston upon it, which letter is now before me.[1]   Several others from that place were

[1] "Humphrey, to the church of Christ at Boston : Grace be multiplied, and peace, from God our Father, and from the Lord Jesus Christ. Most dearly beloved brethren and Christian friends, I thought good to inform you that since our beloved brother Screven went from us, who, I trust is by God's mercy, now with you, by his long absence from us, has given great advantage to our adversaries to triumph and to endeavor to beat down that good beginning which God, by his poor instrument hath begun amongst us ; and our magistrate, Mr. Hucke, is almost every day summoning and threatening the people by fines and other penalties, if they ever come to our meetings any more, five shillings for every such offence.   And yesterday, being the twenty-third of this instant January, I was fetched before him by a summons, whither being come, he demanded of me how I spent my time ; being informed, as I understood, that I made it my business to go from house to house as a seducer ; but after I gave him to understand that I was joined to the baptized church of Boston, in covenant and fellowship, he told me that he was very sorry that I was deluded and misled ; and our minister, Mr. Woodbridge, being present, he began to rail upon you, and especially of being built upon excommunicate persons, naming

baptized soon after ; but to hinder their proceedings, their General Court took the matter in hand as follows, viz. :—

William Screven, appearing before this Court, and being convicted of the contempt of his Majesty's authority, and refusing to submit himself to the sentence of the Court, prohibiting his public preaching, and upon examination before the Court, declaring his resolution still to persist therein, the Court tendered him liberty to return home to his family, in case he would forbear such turbulent practices and amend for the future ; but he refusing, the Court sentenced him to give bond for his good behavior, and to forbear such contentious behavior for the future, and the delinquent to stand committed until the judgment of this Court be fulfilled.

Vera copia, transcribed, and with the records compared, this 17th of August, 1682.

per EDWARD RISHWORTH, Recorder.

one John Farnum, who, he said was a grievous, censorious man; and would not let Mr. Mader, [Mather] alone till he had cast him out of his church. Then I gave him the book set forth by Elder John Russell, and told him, if he would impartially read that book, he would not speak so evilly of them. But Woodbridge told him that he would affirm that there were many palpable untruths in that book; but I said there were many grievous, false scandals and false insinuations in their book entitled The Divine Right of Infant Baptism, falsely laid upon those who professed believers' baptism, which had been fully answered by a letter from one Kiffin, of London, and confuted by all sober men, and taken to arise from a spirit of inveteracy and animosity. And having a long dispute concerning infant baptism and ordination of ministers, and that none might preach except called by men, I affirmed that it is written God's people shall all be taught of him, and therefore, as every man has received the gift of God, so let him administer the same as good stewards of the manifold grace of God. Then Mr. Hucke answered, saying, Behold your great Doctor, Mr. Miles of Swanzey, for he now leaves his profession and is come away, and will not teach his people any more, because he is like to perish for want, and his gathered church and people will not help him. I answered, it was a great untruth, but he said he could bring two sufficient men to testify that they had it from his own mouth at Boston. Dear brethren, I cannot harbor any such thing, but it is in every one's mouth, and it is a great stumbling block to many tender consciences; therefore I request you not to fail, as soon as you can possibly, if this letter come to your hand before brother Screven cometh from thence, that you would send an answer to this thing, for the satisfaction of our friends here, and I hope you will take that into serious consideration which I sent by brother Screven. And the good will of him that dwelt in the bush, be with you to guide you in all your undertakings. And so, humbly craving your prayers for us, and that you will dispatch brother Screven as soon as he cometh back from Swanzey, for his long tarrying maketh us conclude that he is gone thither. All our friends here are well, blessed be God! and we hope the same by you, which is the tenor of our prayers.

"Written by mine own hand this 25th day of January, 1681[2].

Rev. S. Hall's Collection of papers.

The reader will observe, in this letter, a discrepancy of one day in dates. It may have been commenced on the 24th and finished on the 25th.—ED.

To this is added a copy of the same date by the same hand, of an act of their Executive Court, which says :—

This Court having considered the offensive speeches of William Screven, viz., his rash and inconsiderate words tending to blasphemy, do adjudge the delinquent, for his offence, to pay ten pounds into the treasury of the county or province. And further, the Court doth forbid and discharge the said Screven, under any pretence, to keep any private exercise at his own house or elsewhere upon the Lord's days, either in Kittery or any other place within the limits of this province, and is for the future enjoined to observe the public worship of God in our public assemblies upon the Lord's days, according to the laws here established in this province, upon such penalties as the law requires upon such neglect of the premises.

But he was so far from yielding to such sentences, that on September 13, he with the rest sent a request to Boston that Elder Hull and others might visit and form them into a church,[1] which was granted; so that a covenant was

[1]"To THOMAS SKINNER, BOSTON, FOR THE CHURCH : Dearly beloved brethren in the Lord Jesus Christ, the King of saints. I and my wife salute you with our Christian love in our Lord Jesus, hoping through grace these few lines will find you in health of body and mind. Blessed be God for Jesus Christ, in whom he is pleased to account his saints meet to be partakers of the blessed rest provided for them in his mansion-house eternally in the heavens. That will be a happy day when all the saints shall join together in sounding of his praise. The good Lord enable us to prepare for that blessed day. To that end, brethren, let us pray, every one himself, for himself, and for one another, that God would please to search our hearts and reins, so as that we may walk with God here, and hereafter dwell with him in glory.

"I had thought to have been with you last church-meeting, but my wife's condition was such I could not come, and this time by providence, I have taken some hurt, so that I cannot ride so far as yet. I hope to be with you next month, if the Lord will. And we have sent you our apprehensions about our present state. I hope we are conscientious in what we have said to you. I believe you will not judge otherwise. I am persuaded it will do much for the honor of God to have it done here. Besides, my mother-in-law hath desired to follow Christ in that ordinance. We all conceive it will be more honorable and expedient that it be done by the Elder Hull, that is so truly praised here. I pray you to consider these things. Both may be done when the messengers come up to us. My humble request to you is, that you will grant us what we have conscientiously treated you for. I conceive we are all agreed to leave our burdens, and you to agree on the time. No more at present; but rest, your unworthy brother in gospel relation.

WILLIAM SCREVEN.

"The 13th of the 7th month, [September, O. S.] 1682.
To Brother Tho. Skinner, Will. Squire, Elias Callender."
Rev. S. Hall's Collection of Papers.—ED.

solemnly signed on September 25, 1682, by William Screven, Elder, Humphrey Churchwood, Deacon, Robert Williams, John Morgandy, Richard Cutt, Timothy Davis, Leonard Drown, William Adams, Humphrey Azell, and George Litten, and a number of sisters.[1]   A Baptist church was also formed this year from that of Boston, at Newbury, by William and John Sayer, Benjamin Morse, Edward Woodman and others,[2] to whom I find Elder Hull and Elder Emblen writing as a sister church, on March 25, 1689; though how much longer they continued a distinct church I do not find.

Mr. Philip Edes, a member of the first Baptist church in Newport, died this year on March 16, of whom Mr. Samuel Hubbard says in a letter to Governor Leete, " This friend of yours and mine, one in office in Oliver's house, was for liberty of conscience ; a merchant, a precious man, of a holy life and conversation, beloved of all sorts of men, his death much bewailed by all." Mr. Thomas Olney, senior, also died this year.   He was next to Mr. Williams in the pastoral office at Providence, and continued so to his death, over that part of the church who were called Five Principle Baptists, in distinction from those who parted from their brethren about the year 1653, under the leading of Elder Wickenden, holding to the laying on of hands upon every church member. The greatest fault that I find Mr. Olney charged with is, that he was for extending the first deed of Providence up to the

---

[1] This church had but a brief existence. "As the result of a long cherished and well organized religious intolerance, venting itself in vehement and impassioned persecution, these humble Christians became disheartened and overcome. In less than one year from its recognition, the church was dissolved, and the members scattered like sheep upon the mountains." Millet's Maine Baptists, p. 27; Benedict, Vol. I, p. 309.—ED.

[2] " 1682.   Early this year, a small Baptist church was formed in Newbury, as appears from the following extract from the records of the First Baptist church in Boston:—' February 6th, 1681, [O. S.] Agreed, upon a church meeting, that we, the church at Boston, have assented unto the settling of the church at Newbury.' The persons who formed this church were probably George Little and Philip Squire, who united with the Baptist church in Boston in 1676, Nathaniel Cheney, William Sayer and wife, Mr. Edward Woodman and wife, John Sayer and Abel Merrill, all of whom became members in 1681." History of Newbury, p. 135.—ED.

head of the two great rivers it lay between, or at least as far as their charter reached, from the words *Without limits*, in page 72. In this he was opposed by our elders, Wickenden and Dexter, the latter of whom informs us that Mr. Williams said, the only intent of the expression was to prevent the Indians hurting their cattle if they wandered far into the woods. Their writings on both sides are yet extant in their town clerk's office. They tell me at Swanzey that Elder Miles permitted Mr. Brown's wife, who was not a Baptist, to commune with their church, till by Elder Olney's influence she was dismissed to Mr. Angier's church in Rehoboth. It is very evident that Mr. Olney was a capable and very useful man, both in church and state for forty-four years after he left the Massachusetts; as his son also was for many years; and his posterity are respectable in that town and State to this day. Mr. Holmes, of whom much has been said, who wrote the account of himself in 1675, that is given in pages 173—176, 206—209, and succeeded Mr. Clarke in the pastoral office at Newport, died there, October 15, 1682, aged seventy-six. He has a large posterity now remaining in New England and New Jersey.

The learned and pious Mr. Miles having returned to his flock in Swanzey, fell asleep in Jesus, on February 3, 1683; and his memory is still precious among us. We are told that being once brought before the magistrates he requested a Bible, and upon obtaining it, he turned to those words, "Ye should say, Why persecute we him, seeing the root of the matter is found in me;" Job 19. 28; which having read, he sat down; and the word had a good effect upon their minds, and moved them to treat him with moderation if not kindness. His son went back to England, and his grandson, Mr. Samuel Miles, was an Episcopal minister at Boston in 1724. Though Mr. Willard, and the Magnalia from him, accused the Baptists of Boston, of separating because they wanted to be teachers,[1] yet that was so far from truth, that

---

[1] Magnalia, Vol. II, p. 460.—Ed.

on June 27, 1681, they wrote to London for a minister, giving this as one reason for it, that, "our minister is very aged and feeble, and often incapable of his ministerial work;" and as another motive they say, "We conceive there is a prospect of good encouragement for an able man to come over, in that there seems to be an apparent and general apostacy among the churches who have professed themselves Congregational in this land; whereby many have their eyes opened, by seeing the declension and confusion that is among them." A kind answer hereto was returned by eleven Baptist ministers, which is before me.[2]

[2] "London, the 13th of the 8th [?] month, 1681.

"Beloved Brethren—For whom we pray that the Father of mercies may fill you with the knowledge of his will, in all wisdom and spiritual understanding in the knowledge of our Lord Jesus, that you may be to the praise, honor and glory of him that hath called you out of darkness into his marvelous light. We have received yours to us, wherein you acquaint us with the good hand of Providence towards you in having your liberty again to meet in your public place, and the hopes you have of a considerable increase; also the sense you have of the present want of a faithful, able man to go in and out before you in the work of the ministry, the Lord having deprived you of him that was formerly very useful to you therein, who is now fallen asleep in the Lord. We do assure you that there is nothing wanting, nor shall be, to help you herein, but at present cannot think of any, the Lord knowing the laborers are few amongst us, especially such as have the courage whereby they may have the more acceptance with you, and be able to maintain the truth against gainsayers. But you may be assured of the utmost we can do herein, and we trust and pray that the Lord will be pleased to spirit such amongst yourselves as may be a means to build you up in the ways of holiness. We have had experience that when such help hath been wanting amongst us as you desire, the Lord hath made it up with his special presence, and the assistance he hath given to poor, despised, unlearned men hath been so blessed that greater addition hath been to the churches than now; and we hope what may be wanting in the gifts you wait for, the Lord will help you to make up by that humble and gracious frame of spirit, shining in your love to Christ and to each other, as may put to silence those that may take an occasion to reproach you for want of having those abilities amongst you as they have amongst them. He that hath the abundance of the Spirit, is able to make supply to all your wants, according to the riches of his glory by Jesus Christ.

"And since the Lord hath abated the heats of some men's spirits amongst you, and you have now liberty to move more freer than formerly, you have need be very watchful over your own hearts and the great enemy of our peace, Satan, lest any occasion be given for any to stumble, that are now making inquiry after the farther manifestations of the mind and will of God amongst you; and we are persuaded that, as he hath opened a door amongst you, so he will furnish you with abilities and strength from himself, for your farther edification and comfort. We kindly thank you that you have the remembrance of us to God, in your prayers, and we desire

And now, as some singular and curious things are generally expected from a new country, I shall relate the closing part of one of the greatest curiosities I have met with in modern history ; the sum whereof is this. A large number of people fled out of the old world into this wilderness for religious liberty ; but had not been here long before some put in high claims for power, under the name of orthodoxy ; to whom others made fierce opposition professedly from the light within ; and their clashings were so great that several lives were lost in the fray. This made a terrible noise on the other side of the water. But as self-defence is a natural principle, each party wrote volume after volume to clear themselves from blame; and they both conspired to cast a great part of it upon one singular man, whom they called a weathercock and a windmill.[1] Now let the curious find out

the continuance thereof, not knowing what, nor how soon, troubles and sorrows may befall us. The cloud has been black a great while over us, and it is marvelous in our eyes that our peace hath been and is lengthened out as it is; but surely a very great storm is a-coming, and who shall be able to stand in that day, the Lord only knoweth. That indeed is our comfort, that we are under the promise of a faithful God, that as the day is, so our strength shall be. We are very glad to have some lines from you, and desire it may be continued as often as you have any opportunity; and we trust we shall not be wanting to return answers to them. With our prayers to the Lord to keep you faithful to the end, and our real love to you all, remain,

WM. KIFFEN,	WILLIAM DIX,
HAN. KNOLLYS,	ROBERT SCELLING,
DANIEL DYKE,	TOBIAS RUSSELL,
WM. COLLINS,	MAURICE KING,
NEH. COXE,	JNO. SKINER."
EDW. WILLIAMS,	

The original of this letter, with the autograph signatures, is preserved among the Backus papers in the library of the Backus Historical Society.—ED.

[1]"Here is a lying, scandalous book of Roger Williams of Providence..... I have known him about fifty years, a mere *weathercock*, constant only in inconstancy..... They ought to have feared God and the king, that is to punish evil doers, and therefore not to meddle to their hurt with him that is given to change." Coddington's Letter. See pp. 353, 354.

"In the year 1654, a certain windmill in the Low Countries, whirling round with extraordinary violence, by reason of a violent storm then blowing; the stone, at length, by its rapid motion, became so intensely hot as to fire the mill, from whence the flames, being dispersed by the high winds, did set a whole town on fire. But I can tell my reader, that about twenty years before this, there was a whole country in America like to be set on fire by the rapid motion of a *windmill* in the head of one particular man. Know then that about the year 1630, arrived here, one Mr. Roger Williams," &c. Magnalia, Vol. II, p. 430.—ED.

if they can, first, how men of university learning, or of divine inspiration, came to write great volumes against a windmill and a weathercock? secondly, how such a strange creature came to be an overmatch for them all, and to carry his point against the arts of priestcraft, the intrigues of court, the flights of enthusiasm and the power of factions, so as after he had pulled down ruin upon himself and his friends, yet to be able, in the midst of heathen savages, to erect the best form of civil government that the world had seen in sixteen hundred years? thirdly, how he and his ruined friends came to lie under those reproaches for a hundred years, and yet that their plan should then be adopted by thirteen colonies, to whom these despised people could afford senators of principal note, as well as commanders by sea and land? The excellency of this scene above those which many are bewitched with, consists in its being founded upon facts and not fictions; being not the creature of distempered brains, but of an unerring Providence.

According to Mr. Williams's own testimony, his soul was renewed by divine grace when he was not more than ten or twelve years old.[1] And the mystery of his being rigidly set in his way, and yet " given to change," is to be explained thus. Neither frowns nor flatteries could move him to part with what he judged to be truth, or to assent to anything contrary thereto. As he scrupled the exactness of the calendar then in use, so he discovered it in all his dates. Even when dedicating his Quaker dispute to the king, he dated it March 10, 1672, 3, (*ut vulgo.*) On the other hand he was ever ready to change, when he could obtain light for it from any quarter. While he ministered to his brethren at Plymouth, he objected against their custom of giving their neighbors the title of *Goodman*, if they were not judged to be godly persons. When Governor Winthrop paid them a visit in 1632,[2] and his advice was asked upon it, he showed them that they ought to distinguish betwixt theological and

[1] See p. 118. [2] See p. 43.

moral goodness, and observed that when trials by jury were first introduced in England, after the names of fit persons for the purpose were called over, the crier called them to attend, *Good men and true*, from whence proceeded the custom then in question ; and he thought it a pity to make a stir about a custom so innocently introduced.[1]   Mr. Williams readily embraced this advice, and made a very good use of it afterward, in exposing the mischiefs that arose from a confounding of those two sorts of goodness together, as Mr. Cotton and many others had done.   And because he was earnestly looking for a better church establishment than he had then seen, they imposed the name of Seeker upon him.   The great Mr. Baxter calls him The father of the Seekers in London.[2]   When he went there in 1643, and published his testimony against the Bloody Tenet, Mr. Cotton, among other reflections, said, " Thus men that have time and leisure at will, will set up images of clouts, and then shoot at them."[3]   In answer to which Mr. Williams appealed to the people of Plymouth, Salem and Providence, that he had not led such a life in this country ; and as to the other, he says :—

I can tell that when these discussions were prepared for the public in London, his time was eaten up in attendance upon the service of the parliament and city for the supply of the poor of the city with wood, during the stop of coal from Newcastle, and the mutinies of the poor for fireing. ....These meditations were fitted for public view in change of rooms and corners, yea, ... in a variety of strange houses, sometimes in the fields in the midst of travel.

For this service, through the hurry of the times, and the necessity of his departure, he lost his recompence to this day.   He continues :—

Well, notwithstanding Master Cotton's bitter censure, some persons of no contemptible note nor intelligence, have by letters from England, informed the discusser, that by these " images of clouts" it hath pleased God to stop no small leaks of persecution, that lately began to flow in

[1]Magnalia, B. 2, p. 14. [Vol. I, p. 117.]   [2]Crosby, Vol. I, p. 118.
[3]Tenet washed, p. 31.

upon dissenting consciences, and among others, to Master Cotton's own, and to the peace and quietness of the Independents, which they have so long, and so wonderfully enjoyed.[1]

As to his later services, he was so far from being meanly hired, as they said, for a piece of bread,[2] to write against the Quakers, that after he had done it, he wrote thus to Newport :—

MY DEAR FRIEND, SAMUEL HUBBARD : To yourself and aged companion, my loving respects in the Lord Jesus, who ought to be our hope of [and] glory, begun in this life and enjoyed to all eternity. I have herein returned your little, yet great, remembrance of the hand of the Lord to yourself and your son late departed. I praise the Lord for your humble kissing of the holy rod, and acknowledging his just and righteous, together with his gracious and merciful, dispensation to you. I rejoice also to read your heavenly desires and endeavors, that your trials may be gain to your own souls, and the souls of the youth of the place, and all of us. You are not unwilling, I judge, that I deal plainly and friendly with you. .... After all that I have seen and read and compared about the seventh day (and I have earnestly and carefully read and weighed all I could come at in God's holy presence,) I cannot be removed from Calvin's mind, and indeed Paul's mind, Col. 2, that all those sabbaths of seven days were figures, types and shadows, and forerunners of the Son of God, and that the change is made from the remembrance of the first creation, and that (figurative) rest on the seventh day, to the remembrance of the second creation on the first, on which our Lord arose conqueror from the dead. Accordingly I have read many, but see no satisfying answer to those three Scriptures chiefly, Acts. 20, I Corinthians 16, Revelation 1, in conscience to which I make some poor conscience to God as to the rest day..... As for thoughts for England, I humbly hope the Lord hath hewed [shewed] me to write a large narrative of all those four days agitation between the Quakers and myself; if it please God I cannot get it printed in New England, I [yet] have great thoughts and purposes for Old..... Mine age, lameness, and many other weaknesses, and the dreadful hand of God at sea, calls for deep consideration. What God may please to bring forth in the spring his holy wisdom knows. If he please to bring to an absolute purpose I will send you word, and my dear friend Obediah Holmes, who sent me a message to the same purpose. At present I pray salute respectively Mr. John Clarke and his brothers, Mr. Tory, Mr. Edes, Edward Smith, William Hiscox, Stephen Mumford and other friends,

[1] Reply to Cotton. p. 38. See pp. 130, 146, 147, 157, &c.
[2] See p. 353.—ED.

whose preservation, [and] of the Island, and this country, I humbly beg
of the Father of mercies, in whom I am yours, unworthy.

R. W.

If the reader reviews Dr. Chamberlain's first letter,[1] and is
informed that he with the brethren he wrote to, took the
whole of the ten commandments to be moral and immutable,
and held that it was the little horn that changed the time
from the seventh to the first day ; but that Mr. Olney and
his church observed to their brethren, that Paul speaks of a
glory which was done away, that was written and engraven
in stones ; II Corinthians 3. 7 ; compared with this letter,
he will then have a plain idea of the nature of that controversy on both sides, as it was managed in that day.   And,
to go on, it is to be remembered,   that some persons in different parts of the colony had such a conceit of liberty, as
that officers should manage the government without any
reward from them ; by which means Mr. Clarke received
but part of his pay for procuring their charter as long as he
lived ; and this occasioned a remonstrance from his executors to the Assembly upon it soon after his death.   A clause
from Mr. Williams upon it, I have already recited ;[2] to which
I now add the following. In August, 1678, he was appointed to assist Mr. Daniel Abbot in setting their town records
in order, the latter being then chosen their clerk. Three years
after, Mr. Williams wrote to him thus :—

MY GOOD FRIEND : Loving remembrance to you.   It hath pleased the
Most High and Only Wise, to stir up your spirit to be one of the chiefest
stakes in our poor hedge.   I therefore, not being well able to come to you,
present you with a few thoughts about the great stumbling block, to them
that are willing to stumble and trouble themselves,—our rates.   James
Matison had one copy of me, and Thomas Arnold another.   This I send
to yourself and the town (for it may be I shall not be able to be at meeting.)   I am grieved that you do so much service for so bad recompence ;
but I am persuaded you shall find cause to say, The Most High God of
recompence, who was Abraham's great reward, hath paid me.

[1]See pages 378, 379.   [2]See page 371.

CONSIDERATIONS PRESENTED, TOUCHING RATES.

1. Government and order in families, towns, &c., is the ordinance of the Most High, Romans 13, for the peace and good of mankind. 2. Six things are written in the hearts of all mankind, yea, even in Pagans, 1st. That there is a Deity; 2d. That some actions are naught; 3d. That the Deity will punish; 4th. That there is another life; 5th. That marriage is honorable; 6th. That mankind cannot keep together without some government. 3. There is no Englishman in his Majesty's dominions, or elsewhere, who is not forced to submit to government. 4. There is not a man in the world except robbers, pirates and rebels, but doth submit to government. 5. Even robbers, pirates and rebels themselves, cannot hold together but by some law among themselves, and government. 6. One of these two great laws in the world, must prevail; either that of judges and justices of peace in courts of peace, or the law of arms, the sword and blood. 7. If it comes from the courts of trials in peace, to the trial of the sword and blood, the conquered is forced to seek law and government. 8. Till matters come to a settled government no man is ordinarily sure of his house, goods, lands, cattle, wife, children, or life. 9. Hence is that ancient maxim, It is better to live under a tyrant in peace, than under the sword, or where every man is a tyrant. 10. His Majesty sends governors to Barbados, Virginia, &c., but to us he shows greater favor in our charter, to choose whom we please. 11. No charters are obtained without great suit, favor or charges. Our first cost an hundred pounds, (though I never received it all,) our second about a thousand, Connecticut about six thousand, &c. 12. No government is maintained without tribute, customs, rates, taxes, &c. 13. Our charter excels all in New England, or in the world, as to the souls of men. 14. It pleaseth God, Romans 13, to command tribute, custom and consequently rates, [&c.,] not only for fear, but for conscience sake. 15. Our rates are the least by far of any colony in New England. 16. There is no man that hath a vote in town or colony, but he hath a hand in making the rates by himself or his deputies. 17. In our colony the General Assembly, Governors, magistrates, deputies, towns, town clerks, raters, constables, &c., have done their duties; the failing lies upon particular persons. 18. It is but folly to resist, (one or more, and if one why not more?) God hath stirred up the spirit of the Governor, magistrates and officers, driven to it by necessity, to be unanimously resolved to see the matter finished; and it is the duty of every man to maintain, encourage and strengthen the hand of authority. 19. Black clouds (some years) have hung over Old and New England heads. God hath been wonderfully patient and long suffering to us; but who sees not changes and calamities hanging over us? 20. All men fear that this blazing herald from heaven denounceth from the Most High, wars, pesti-

lence, famines; is it not then our wisdom to make and keep peace with God and man?

Your old, unworthy servant,

ROGER WILLIAMS.[1]

Providence, 15th January, 1680,[1] (so called.)

The last act that I have found upon record, performed by this eminent peacemaker, was on January 16, 1683, when he, with Mr. Carpenter, and the heirs or assigns of the other eleven original proprietors, signed a full settlement of the long continued controversy about Pawtuxet lands. On the 10th of May following, Mr. John Thornton wrote to Mr. Hubbard and said:—

Dear brother, you gave me an account of the death of divers of our ancient friends; since that time the Lord hath arrested by death our ancient and approved friend Mr. ROGER WILLIAMS, with divers others here. The good Lord grant that we may be stirred up, with the wise virgins, to be trimming our lamps, and getting them full of the spiritual oil, and standing with wise Habakkuk upon our watch towers till our appointed change.

Thus lived and thus died the first Baptist minister in New England, and the first founder and supporter of any truly free civil government upon earth, since the rise of antichrist; "and he was buried with all the solemnity the colony was able to show."[2] This was in the eighty-fourth year

[1] These excellent observations are still extant in his own hand writing. The last article refers to a remarkable blazing star that appeared in those times.—B.

Professor Howell, who copied the above document for Backus, appended to the last sentence the following note: "Alluding to the very remarkable appearance of the comet of 1680, the tail of which was said to be eighty-two millions of miles long, its period five hundred and seventy-five years, and that it came so near the sun as to be heated two thousand times hotter than red hot iron." Many testimonies remain of the terror with which this comet was then regarded. Professor Howell had doubtless seen it at its reäppearance in 1758, after a period of a little more than seventy-five years, instead of five hundred and seventy-five; and its appearance in 1835, is still well remembered. It is the same comet which, in 1456, evoked the famous order of Pope Calixtus III, that all church bells should be rung each noon, an extra Ave Maria be repeated and the prayer added, "Lord, save us from the devil, the Turk, and the comet!"—the same which, according to the speculations of Whiston, successor of Newton in the professorship of mathematics at Cambridge, swept its tail over the earth in the days of Noah and produced the deluge!—ED.

[2] Callender, p. 93, [147]. In 1686 Mr. S. Hubbard wrote that Mr. Thornton, and Mr. Joseph Clarke, were all that were then living who were baptized in New England before him.

of his age, being fifty-two years after his arrival in this country.

His wife, whose name was Mary, came with him from England ; their children were, 1. Mary, born at Plymouth the first week in August, 1633. 2. Freeborn, at Salem in October, 1635. 3. Providence, born at the place he so called, in September, 1638, said to be the first English male born there. 4. Marcy, born July 15, 1640. 5. Daniel, born February 13, 1642. 6. Joseph, born in December, 1643. The last of these, and a grandson of the same name, were magistrates in that colony, and some of great knowledge, compute his present posterity at near two thousand. Thomas Ward, Esq., who was a Baptist before he came out of Cromwell's army, and was a very useful man in this colony, was ancestor to two late governors, and to the present secretary of it, in the male line, as Mr. Williams was in the female ; one of them was the Honorable Samuel Ward, Esq., who died a member of the Continental Congress at Philadelphia, on March 26, 1776, aged 52. The family of Hopkins in Providence, which has afforded an honorable member of that Assembly, and two commanders for the continental fleet, descended in the male line from Mr. Thomas Hopkins, who followed Mr. Williams from Plymouth, and in the female from Mr. Wickenden, an early member, and long a teacher of the Baptist church there. The noted family of Brown, in Providence, sprung from Mr. Chad Brown on the one side, and from Mr. Williams on the other. And our Generals, Greene and Arnold, sprung from two of the first twelve proprietors of those lands, which were given for a place of refuge for such as were distressed for conscience sake elsewhere. May that great design never be forgotten by us or ours ? Some have been ready to make those religious contentions and oppressions an argument against all revealed religion, but if they duly consider the following things, compared with the foregoing, perhaps it may alter their minds. To guard against evil biases in our dealings,

the great Author of our religion said, With what judgment
ye judge, ye shall be judged ; and with what measure ye
mete, it shall be measured to you again.   Was not his word
verified in the following instances ?

1. The ruling party in the Massachusetts, had not only
raked up the real faults of the Baptists, and exposed them
in their worst colors, but also slandered them in many particulars.   And now Edward Randolph went eight voyages
to England in nine years, and treated them in the same manner at the British Court, on purpose to get away their charter.[1]   2. By a plea from the king's grant in that charter,
they had cruelly oppressed their brethren and neighbors in
many instances ; now in 1684 the charter was vacated by a
decree in chancery, without giving them opportunity to
answer for themselves ; and " those who were in confederacy with Sir Edmund Andros, for the enriching themselves
on the spoils [ruins] of New England, did invade the property as well as liberty of the subject; . . . . and gave out,
that now their charter was gone all their lands were the
king's ; that themselves did represent the king, and therefore men that would have any legal title to their lands must
take patents of them, on such terms as they should see meet
to impose.   What people that had the spirits of Englishmen could endure this ?"[2]   3. Their charter never gave
them any right to establish their mode of worship by force;
but in order to do it they presumed to leave the word *lawful* out of their oaths ;[3] and Ipswich gave an early example
of seizing their neighbors' property in that illegal way,
against the weighty arguments of Judge Symonds.[4]   Now
the scale was turned, so that an arbitrary Governor and Council made laws and imposed taxes upon all, without any
House of Representatives ; and for refusing to carry an
order for such a tax into execution in Ipswich, Mr. John

[1]Massachusetts History, Vol.I, pp. 329, 335, [297, 301.] Vol. III, pp. 480, 490, &c.
[2]Revolution in New England Justified, printed 1691, and reprinted 1773, p. 17.
[3]See pp. 47, 49.   [4]See pp. 248, 249.—Ed.

Wise, a minister, who spake upon it in their town meeting, was imprisoned, and denied the benefit of the Habeas Corpus Act; and when he upon his trial pleaded the Magna Charta, and laws of England, he was told by one of the judges, that " he must not think the laws of England followed them to the ends of the earth." " Mr. Wise," said he, " you have no more privilege left you, than not to be sold for slaves." The honorable John Appleton, Esq., was treated in the same manner; and both were put from office, fined fifty pounds apiece, and ordered to give bonds of one thousand pounds each, for their good behavior for one year. Four other men of that town received like sentences, only in less sums.[1] Was not this a teaching by cudgel instead of argument?[2] To justify or excuse their making the law against the Baptists in 1644, Mr. Hubbard said :—

It were well if [all] those who cannot comply with the religion of the state or place where they live, yet had so much manners as not to jostle against nor openly practise that that is inconsistent therewith, as if they would bid a kind of defiance thereunto. Moses would not do that in Egypt, upon [the] account of religious worship, that might seem a matter of abomination to them who were lords of the place.[3]

And Dr. Mather had lately said :—

If a considerable number of Antipædobaptists should (as our fathers here did) obtain liberty from the state, to transport themselves and families, into a waste American wilderness, that so they might be a peculiar people by themselves; practising all, and only the institutions of Christ; if now Pædobaptists should come after them, and intrude themselves upon them,....surely they would desire such persons either to walk orderly with them, or return to the place from whence they came. Let them then do as they would be done by.[4]

Now John Palmer, one of Andros's council, to vindicate their conduct, said, " It is a fundamental point, consented to by all Christian nations, that the first discoverer of a country inhabited by infidels, gives [a] right and dominion of that country to the prince in whose service [and employ-

---

[1]Revolution in New England, Justified, p. 16. [2]See page 80.
[3]Hubbard, pp. 373, 374.—ED. [4]Preface to *Ne Sutor*, p. 5.
27

ment] the discoverers were sent." But they of Massachusetts say, " We affirm that this fundamental point, as he calls
it, is not a Christian, but an unchristian principle."[1] Yes,
and it was as much so when they banished Mr. Williams,
as it is now. 4. We have seen how Dr. Mather treated the
characters of the Baptists ; now, a letter is forged in his
name, full of ridiculous and treasonable expressions, which
being pretendedly detected in its way to Holland, was laid
before the British ministry, and then was printed and spread
through the nation to expose him. When he came to know
it he said, " That which troubled me was, that I was like to
suffer as an evil doer, through the malice and falsehood of
wicked men. Might I have suffered for any truth which I
had borne witness to, I could have rejoiced in it."[2] Yes ;
but his persecutors were as little inclined to give him that
honor, as he was the Baptists. 5. Governor Bradstreet who
helped to banish Mr. Williams, for opposing an oath that
was contrary to his conscience, lived to feel and see what
such impositions meant upon themselves. For refusing to
swear on the book, many were not only put by from serving
on juries, but were fined and imprisoned ; and, says the historian, " the faithful of New England chose rather to suffer affliction, than to use a rite in the worship of God,
which they suspected sinful."[3] And Dr. Increase Mather
took pains to publish a discourse upon " The unlawfulness
of using common prayer ; and of swearing on the book."
6. Andros carried his Episcopal worship into Mr. Willard's
meeting-house, after their exercise was over, and threatened
" to shut up their doors if he was refused, and to punish
any man who gave two pence towards the support of Nonconformist ministers ; and that public worship in the Congregational way, should not be tolerated." This felt so to
them, that when King James sent over his proclamation, of
indulgence and liberty of conscience, " the ministers of Bos-

---

[1]Revolution justified, p. 44.   [2]His Life, pp. 93, 94.
[3]Magnalia B. 7, pp. 3, 12, 13, [Vol. II, pp. 434, 438, 439.]

ton proposed unto their congregations to keep a day of thanksgiving, to bless God for what they enjoyed ; [but the Governor assured them] " that if they did, he would clap a guard on their persons and their churches too," and so prevented it. Hereupon they thought proper to send Dr. Mather as their agent to England. He had accused Randolph or his brother, of forging the aforesaid letter to expose him ; upon which Randolph prosecuted him for defamaation ; and though he was acquitted upon trial, yet, to prevent his going to England, Randolph designed by another writ to seize, and clap him up in prison ; to avoid which, Dr. Mather escaped out of town in disguise, and was carried on board a ship in the night, April 7, 1688 ; and upon his arrival at London, he with others petitioned the king, " that there might be liberty of conscience in matters of religion, ... and that all their meeting-houses may be left free to them, according to the intention of the builders thereof ; but this application met with no success."[1]

Do not these things verify the truth of the Christian revelation ? They brought Dr. Mather over to acknowledge, that the parable of the tares was a declaration of our Saviour's will for a toleration ; and " that a good neighbor and a good subject has a claim to all his temporal enjoyments before he is a Christian ; and he thought it very odd, that the man should lose his claim, from his embracing of Christianity, because he does not happen to be a Christian of the uppermost party among the subdivisions. For an uppermost party of Christians to punish men, in their temporal enjoyments, because in some religious opinions they dissent from them, or with an exclusion from the temporal enjoyments which would justly belong unto them, is a robbery."[2] And how were the Baptists treated after this ?

Their church at Boston had received Elder John Emblen .from England, July 20, 1684. Mr. Richard Dingley was

---

[1] His Life, pp. 103—111. Massachusetts History, Vol. I, p. 368, [327.]
[2] His Life, pp. 58, 59. See Isaiah, 61. 8.

received a member there the same year, and soon after succeeded Mr. Holmes in the pastoral office at Newport, where he continued about ten years, and then went to Carolina. Mr. Samuel Luther succeeded Mr. Miles at Swanzey, where he was ordained by our elders, Hull and Emblen, on July 22, 1685, and he was continued a great blessing to them thirty-two years. But Elder Emblen dying about 1699, that church remained in destitute circumstances for some years, and then chose Mr. Callender in his room; to whom the following letter was directed, the original of which is now before me.

16d. 1m. 1714.

SIRS :—As in the distresses of the winter, we did, with the solemnities of humiliation, call upon our gracious God, so, since he has graciously recovered so many of our people, and sent in such seasonable provisions for our necessities, it has been proposed among the ministers of the [this][1] town, that our good people may acknowledge these favors of our prayer-hearing Lord, with the solemnity [solemnities] of a thanksgiving, in our several congregations; for which, also, we have had the encouragement of the government. The time we would propose for such a service is Thursday, the first of April, if the churches have no objection against it. And it was desired that you might be seasonably apprised of this proposal, because we are well assured of the welcome, which a motion of such a nature will find with you, and the people of God unto whom you stand nearly related. Having thus discharged the duty in this matter incumbent on me, I take leave to [and] subscribe,

Sir, your brother and servant,

COTTON MATHER.

To my worthy friend, Mr. Ellis Callender, elder of a church of Christ in Boston.

His son Elisha had joined that church the tenth of August preceding, and he gave him an education at Cambridge; and Dr. Increase Mather having signified his willingness for such a thing, the church called him, his son, and Mr. John Webb, to assist in ordaining the said Mr. Elisha Callender,

---

[1]The words in brackets, indicate the form of this letter according to the copy in Rev. S. Hall's Collection of papers.—ED.

their pastor[1] on May 21, 1718 ; and in the preface to that Ordination Sermon, the old gentleman says :—

It was a grateful surprise to me, when several of the brethren of the Antipædobaptist persuasion came to me, desiring that I would give them the Right Hand of Fellowship in ordaining one whom they had chosen to be their pastor. I did (as I believe it was my duty) readily consent to what they proposed ; considering the young man to be ordained is serious and pious, and of a candid spirit, and has been educated in the college at Cambridge ; and that all of the brethren of that church with whom I have any acquaintance, (I hope the like concerning others of them) are, in the judgment of rational charity, godly persons.

Two of them were old Elder Callender and Deacon Sweetser, who were principal members when their meeting-house was formerly nailed up. Dr. Cotton Mather preached the Sermon, which he entitled Good Men United. After opening the nature and importance of such a union, he says :—

It is very sadly true, that many ecclesiastical communities, wherein piety has its votaries, yet are guilty of this evil, that they impose terms of communion which many that have the fear of God, are by just exceptions kept from complying withal. Now in this unhappy case what is to be done? Do this ; let good men go as far as they can without sin in holding communion with one another. But where sinful terms are imposed, there let them make their stops ; there a separation becomes a duty ; there the injunction of heaven upon them is, Be ye separate, saith the Lord, and touch not the unclean thing, and I will receive you. The imposers are

---

[1] "The following is the copy of the letter sent to the church under the care of Dr. Mather and Rev. Mr. Webb, on Mr. Callender's ordination:

"HONORED AND BELOVED IN THE LORD : Considering that there ought to be a holy fellowship maintained among godly Christians, and that it is a duty for us to receive one another as Christ also received us, to the glory of God, notwithstanding some differing persuasions in matters of doubtful disputation; and although we have not so great latitude as to the subject of baptism as the churches of New England generally have; notwithstanding, as to the fundamental principles in your doctrine of Christ, both as to faith and order of the gospel, we concur with them; being also satisfied that particular churches have power from Christ to choose their own pastors, and that elders ought to be ordained in every church; and having chosen our well beloved brother, Elisha Callender, to be our pastor, we entreat you to send your elders and messengers to give the Right Hand of Fellowship in his ordination."
Notes to Memoir of John Callender, R. I. Historical Collections, Vol. IV, p. 27.
—ED.

the schismatics. .... The unity which beautifies the true people of God, is called The unity of the Spirit. Eph. 4. 3. The right basis for a union among us, is, the Holy Spirit inclining us to glorify God, with an obedience to his will revealed in his word ; and to glorify our Saviour with a dependence on him for all the blessings of goodness ; and to love our neighbor as ourselves. There have been many attempts to unite people in forms and terms, that are not the pure maxims of living unto God ; and so to build the tower of Zion, on a foundation which is not the tried stone and the precious, and so not the sure foundation. There has hitherto been a blast from heaven upon all those attempts ; they have miscarried, as being rather calculated for the tower of Babel. .... We are sometimes fearful of paying the respects which we really owe to a people of true piety, (such a people as we this day meet withal) forsooth, lest we confirm them in what we take to be an error, or mislead others into it. I hope it is needless fear. .... O, you who cannot but own yourselves brethren to one another, and bound up in one bundle of life ; how is it possible for you to require of one another, submission to terms which, you cannot but think that men may be good men, and have the evident tokens of salvation upon them, without submitting to? And the terms which you have so pitched upon, how can you proceed so far, as not only to withdraw your fellowship from the good men to whom they do not appear so necessary, but also inflict uneasy circumstances upon them, under the wretched notion of *wholesome severities !* *Cursed the anger, for it is fierce ; and the wrath, for it is cruel !* good for nothing but only to make divisions in Jacob, and dispersions in Israel. Good men, alas ! good men have done such ill things as these ; yea, few churches of the reformation have been wholly clear of these iniquities. New England also has, in some former times, done something of this aspect, which would not now be so well approved of ; in which, if the brethren in whose house we are now convened, met with any thing too unbrotherly, they now with satisfaction hear us expressing our dislike of every thing that has looked like persecution in the days that have passed over us.[1]

I thought it best thus to collect these passages into one view, which may remind us of the apostle's words, "Happy is he that condemneth not himself in that thing which he alloweth." After the vacation of the Massachusetts charter, Mr. Joseph Dudley was appointed President of the colony, till Governor Andros arrived in December, 1686, who had all New England and New York included in his commission.

[1]Mather's Sermon at Callender's Ordination, pp. 18, 25, 34, 38, 39.

Randolph brought a *quo warranto* against Rhode Island charter, June 22, 1686, upon which the freemen met, and gave
their opinion to the General Assembly, and then left the affair with them, who, on June 29, concluded not to stand
suit with his Majesty, but sent a humble address to him,
" to continue their privileges according to charter."   Andros's commission was published among them the 12th of
January following, and he, with a few mandamus counsellors, tyrannized over all these colonies, till John Winslow
brought a copy of King William's proclamation to Boston,
and Andros imprisoned him therefor ; upon which the people arose, April 13, 1689, and seized him and his council,
and resumed their former order of government ; which being heard of in Rhode Island colony, their freemen met at
Newport, May 1, and voted to resume their charter, and to
have their former rulers take their places again.   They met
again February 20, 1690, and elected new rulers in the
place of some who declined serving, and they, with Connecticut, have enjoyed their privileges to the present times.

I shall close this chapter with a list of New England
rulers, and a few remarks thereon.   Plymouth never had
any charter but only from the Council for New England that
was established at Plymouth in Devonshire.   Their form of
government was settled by voluntary agreement among themselves.   At first they only chose a Governor ; the next year,
one Assistant with him ; in 1624, they chose five, and in
1633, seven Assistants, and kept to that number to the end
of their colony.   Mr. Bradford was always an Assistant
when he was not Governor, as long as he lived ; his son was
Assistant and then Deputy Governor till the revolution ; and
he and several of his posterity have been Counsellors in this
province ; and one of his descendants[1] is now Deputy Governor of the State of Rhode Island.   In 1639, they began
to have a House of Deputies in their General Court ; and
about 1662, they agreed that their eldest Assistant should

[1] William Bradford.—ED.

have the power of a Deputy Governor, to act in the Governor's place when he was absent. This continued till 1680, when, by reason of Mr. Alden's age, though they continued him an Assistant, they began to choose other Deputy Governors.

A LIST OF PLYMOUTH GOVERNORS, THE YEARS THEY RULED, AND THE TIME OF THEIR DEATHS.

1. John Carver, 1620; died, April, 1621.
2. William Bradford, 1621—33,[1] 35, 37, 39—44, 45—57; died May 9, 1657, æt. 69.[2]
3. Edward Winslow, 1633, 36, 44; died May 8, 1655, æt. 61.
4. Thomas Prince, 1634, 38, 57—73; died March 29, 1673, æt. 73.
5. Josiah Winslow, 1673—80;[3] died December 18, 1685, æt. 52.
6. Thomas Hinckley, 1681—86, 89—92; died 1705, æt. 74.[4]

DEPUTY GOVERNORS.

1. William Colliar, 1662—66.
2. John Alden, 1666—80.
3. Thomas Hinckley, 1680.
4. James Cudworth, 1681. He went their agent to England, and died there the same year.
5. William Bradford, 1682—86, 89—92.

ASSISTANTS; THE YEARS WHEN FIRST CHOSEN, AS FAR AS I CAN FIND FROM THEIR RECORDS.

Isaac Allerton,	1621	William Colliar,	1634
Edward Winslow,		Thomas Prince,	1635
Miles Standish,		Timothy Hatherly,	1636
John Howland,		John Brown,	1636
John Alden,		John Jenny,	1637
John Doane,		John Atwood,	1638
Stephen Hopkins,		Edmund Freeman,	1640
William Gilson,[5]	1633	William Thomas,	1642

[1]From the election in 1621 to the election of his successor in 1633. This explanation applies to the other terms of office, similarly indicated, in these tables.—ED.

[2]He was in his sixty-ninth year. Generally, in these tables, Backus seems to have given the ages in this manner.—ED.

[3]He was reëlected in 1680, and died in office.—ED.

[4]Allen's Biographical Dictionary gives his age, seventy-five.—ED.

[5]Here should be inserted the name of William Bradford. In 1633 he declined reëlection as Governor, and was made an Assistant. See Morton's Memorial, p. 115.—ED.

Thomas Willet,	1651	Nathaniel Bacon,	1667
Thomas Southworth,	1652	Const. Southworth,	1670
James Cudworth,	1656	Daniel Smith,	1679
Josiah Winslow,	1657	Barnabas Lothrop,	1681
William Bradford,	1658	John Thatcher,	1682
Thomas Hinckley,	1658	John Walley,	1684
James Brown,[1]	1665	John Cushing.	1690
John Freeman,	1666		

NOTE.—The Appendix to Morton, mistakes in placing the first choice of Cudworth and Brown after 1670 ; and the Magnalia sets Smith too early.

MASSACHUSETTS GOVERNORS.

1. Matthew Cradock, 1628.
2. John Winthrop, 1629—34, 37—40, 42—44, 46—49 ; died March 26, 1649, æt. 62.
3. Thomas Dudley, 1634, 40, 45, 50 ; died July 31, 1653,[2] æt. 77.
4. John Haines, 1635.
5. Henry Vane, 1636 ; died 1662, æt. 50.
6. Richard Bellingham, 1641, 54, 65—72 ;[3] died 1672, æt. 81.
7. John Endicott, 1644, 49, 51—53, 55—65 ; died March 23, 1665.
8. John Leverett, 1673—78 ; died March 16, 1678.
9. Simon Bradstreet, 1678—86, 89—92 ; died March 27, 1697, æt. 94.

DEPUTY GOVERNORS.

1. Thomas Goff, 1628.
2. John Humphrey, 1629.
3. John Endicott, 1629, 41—44, 50, 54.
4. Thomas Dudley, 1630—34, 37—40, 46—50, 51, 52.
5. Roger Ludlow, 1634.
6. Richard Bellingham, 1635, 40, 53, 55—65.
7. John Winthrop, 1636, 44, 45.
8. Francis Willoughby, 1665—71.
9. John Leverett, 1671—73.
10. Samuel Symonds, 1673—77.
11. Simon Bradstreet, 1677, 78.
12. Thomas Danforth, 1678—86, 89—92.

[1]In the first edition, this name is given, James Bawn. It is a typographical error, as the name is afterwards correctly given.—ED.

[2]Allen's Biographical Dictionary, usually the best authority in early New England biography, gives this date erroneously, 1652. The American Cyclopædia copies the error. See p. 228; Morton's Memorial, p. 166.--ED.

[3]He was reëlected in 1672, and died in office.—ED.

ASSISTANTS.

Sir Richard Saltonstall,	H. Atherton,	1654
Isaac Johnson,	Richard Russell,	1659
John Endicott,	Thomas Danforth,	1659
Increase Nowel,	William Hawthorn,	1662
William Vassel,	Eleazer Lusher,	1662
William Pinchon,	John Leverett,	1665
Edward Rossiter,	John Pinchon,	1665
Roger Ludlow,	Edward Tyng,	1668
Thomas Sharp,	William Stoughton,	1671
John Revel,	Thomas Clarke,	1673
William Coddington,	Joseph Dudley,	1676
Simon Bradstreet,[1]	Peter Bulkley,	1677
John Humphrey,	1632	N. Saltonstall,	1679
John Winthrop, jun.,	1632	Humphrey Davy,	1679
John Haines,	1634	James Russell,	1680
Atherton Hough,	1635	Samuel Nowel,	1680
Richard Dummer,	1635	Peter Tilton,	1680
Richard Bellingham,	1636	John Richards,	1680
Roger Harlakenden,	1636	John Hull,	1680
Israel Stoughton,	1637	B. Gidney,	1680
Richard Saltonstall,	1637	Thomas Savage,	1680
Thomas Flint,	1642	William Brown,	1680
Samuel Symonds,	1643	Samuel Appleton,	1681
Will. Hibbens,	1643	Robert Pike,	1682
Herbert Pelham,	1645	Daniel Fisher,	1683
Robert Bridges,	1647	John Woodbridge,	1683
Francis Willoughby,	1650	Elisha Cooke,	1684
Thomas Wiggan,	1650	William Johnson,	1684
Edward Gibbons,	1651	John Hawthorn,	1684
John Glover,	1652	Elisha Hutchinson,	1684
Daniel Gookin,	1652	Isaac Addington,	1686
Daniel Denison,	1653	John Smith.	1686
Simon Willard,	1654		

Their charter appointed eighteen Assistants, but they had scarce ever chosen above half so many, till by the King's order they chose the full number in 1680.

[1]These twelve were here in 1630, but Johnson and Rossiter died before the year was out. Saltonstall, Vassel, Sharp and Revel soon went back.—B.

Eighteen Assistants were chosen in 1628, only five of whom are here named. Others, not mentioned here, were chosen between 1629 and 1632.—ED.

RHODE ISLAND RULERS.

Roger Williams, was truly the founder of that Colony, and a principal ruler among them, as we have seen from the beginning. Those who began upon the Island had a different notion about government from him at first, and as their covenant on page 74, was printed from an imperfect copy, I shall here insert it exactly from their records as follows :—

We whose names are under-written do here solemnly, in the presence of Jehovah, incorporate ourselves into a body politic, and as he shall help, Exod. 34, 3, 4.¹ ⎫ will submit our persons, lives and estates, unto our Lord 2 Chron. 11, 3. ⎬ Jesus Christ, the King of kings and Lord of lords, and to 2 Kings 11, 17. ⎭ all those perfect and most absolute laws of his, given us in his Holy Word of truth, to be guided and judged thereby.

They then appointed Mr. Coddington as Judge, and Mr. Aspinwall Secretary, to rule them according to this covenant, till on January 2, 1639, an assembly of the freemen said :—

By the consent of the body it is agreed that such who shall be chosen to the place of Eldership, they are to assist the Judge in the execution of justice and judgment, for the regulating and ordering of all offences and offenders, and for the drawing up and determining of all such rules and laws as shall be according to God, which may conduce to the good and welfare of the commonweal; and to them is committed by the body the whole care and charge of all the affairs thereof; and that the Judge together with the Elders, shall rule and govern according to the general rules [rule] of the word of God, when they have no particular rule from God's word, by the body prescribed as a direction unto them in the case. And further, it is agreed and consented unto, that the Judge and [with the] Elders shall be accountable unto the body once every quarter of the year, (when as the body shall be assembled) of all such cases, actions or [and] rules which have passed through their hands, by them to be scanned and

¹This reference is retained, as printed in the former edition, and as Backus gave it twenty-seven years later in his Abridgment, page 43. We are informed of a recent "letter from Hon. John R. Bartlett, Secretary of Rhode Island," which states "that the original manuscript of the covenant of the early settlers of Rhode Island has the marginal notes precisely as published by Mr. Backus." The published R. I. Colonial Records give the reference, Exodus 24. 3, 4; and Professor Elton, in an Appendix to Callender's Century Sermon, R. I. Historical Collections, Vol. IV, p. 213, gives it in the same form. This passage seems to have a plain significance and the one given above scarce any significance in connection with the covenant.—ED.

weighed by the word of Christ; and if by the body or any of them, the
Lord shall be pleased to dispense light to the contrary of what by the
Judge or [and] Elders hath been determined formerly, that then and there
it shall be repealed as the act of the body; and if it be otherwise, that
then it shall stand, (till further light concerning it) for the present, to be
according to God, and the tender care of indulging [indulgent] fathers.

WILLIAM DYRE, Clerk."

They then chose the elders named in page 78, and went
on as is there mentioned, till March 16, 1641, when they disfranchised Carder, Holden, Shatton and Potter, and suspended
from voting George Parks,[1] John Briggs, and Mr. Lenthal,
who was gone for England; and then said, " It is ordered
by the authority of this present Court, that none be accounted
a delinquent for doctrine, provided it be not directly repugnant to the government and laws established."   In September following they said, " The law concerning liberty of conscience in point of doctrine is perpetuated."   After they received their charter, their rulers were as follows:—

PRESIDENTS OR GOVERNORS.

John Coggshall, 1647.
Roger Williams, 1648[2], 54—57; died 1683, æt. 84.
John Smith, 1649, 52.
Nicholas Easton, 1650, 51, 72, 73; died 1675.
Gregory Dexter, 1653.
Benedict Arnold, 1657,—60, 62—66, 69—72, 77, 78; died June 19,
1678.
William Brenton, 1660—62, 66—69, died 1674.
William Coddington, 1774, 75, 78; died November 1, 1678, æt. 78.
Walter Clarke, 1676, 86, 96, 97; died June, 1714.
John Cranston, 1678—80; died March 12, 1680.
Peleg Sanford, 1680—83.
William Coddington, 1683—85; died 1688.

---

[1]This name should probably be *Parker*. It is several times given thus in the
Rhode Island Colonial Records.—ED.

[2]William Coddington was elected President this year. As he did not appear at
the Assembly, and charges arose against him, Jeremy Clarke was appointed to fill
his place, with the title of President Regent. At a special Assembly in Warwick,
in March, 1649, before the close of this legislative year, Roger Williams was chosen
to act as President. See pp. 168—171; Rhode Island Colonial Records; Arnold's
History of Rhode Island, Vol. I, pp. 219—225.—ED.

Henry Bull, 1685, 89.

John Easton, 1690—95 ; died 1705, æt. 85.

Caleb Carr, 1695.

Samuel Cranston, 1698—1727 ; died April 26, 1727.

Joseph Jencks, 1727—32 ; died June 15, 1740, aged 84.

William Wanton, 1732—34.

John Wanton, 1734—41.

Richard Ward, 1741—43.

William Greene, 1743—45, 46, 48—55, 57.

Gideon Wanton, 1745, 47.

Stephen Hopkins, 1755—57, 58—62, 64, 67—69.

Samuel Ward, 1762—64, 65—67.

Josias Lyndon, 1769.

Joseph Wanton, 1770—75.

Nich. Cooke, 1775—77.

DEPUTY GOVERNORS.

William Brenton, 1663—66.

Nicholas Easton, 1666—69, 70.

John Clarke, 1669, 71.

John Cranston, 1672, 76—78.

John Easton, 1674, 75.[1]

James Barker, 1678, 79.

Walter Clarke, 1679—85, 1701—14.

John Coggshall, 1690.

John Greene, 1690--1701.

Henry Tew, 1714.

Joseph Jencks, 1715—21, 23—27.

John Wanton, 1721—23, 29—34.

Jonathan Nichols, 1727.

Thomas Fry, 1727—29.

George Hazard, 1734—38.

Daniel Abbott, 1738—40.

Richard Ward, 1740.

William Greene, 1741—43.

Joseph Whipple, 1743—45, 46, 52 —54.

William Robinson, 1745, 47.

William Ellery, 1748—50.

Robert Hazard, 1750—52.

J. Gardner, 1754, 56—64.

Jonathan Nichols, 1755.

Joseph Wanton, jun., 1764, 67—69.

Elisha Brown, 1765—67.

Nicholas Cooke, 1769, 75.

Darius Session, 1770—75.

William Bradford, 1775—77.

ASSISTANTS.

Roger Williams,	1647	Samuel Gorton,	1649
John Sanford,	1647	William Field,	1650
W. Coddington,	1647	John Porter,	1650
Randal Holden,	1647	John Wickes,	1650
Jeremiah Clarke,	1648	John Sayles,	1653
John Smith,	1648	Stukely Westcoat,	1653
Thomas Olney,	1649	Thomas Harris,	1654
John Clarke,	1649	John Roome,	1654

[1]The name of William Coddington should here be inserted, as Deputy Governor in 1678.—ED.

Benedict Arnold,	1654	John Albro,	1671
William Baulston,	1656	Richard Smith,	1672
John Coggshall,	1656	Francis Brinley,	1672
Arthur Venner,	1657	Henry Brown,	1672.
Richard Tew,	1657	Walter Clarke,	1673
Joseph Clarke,	1658	Daniel Gould,	1673
John Greene,	1660	Job Almy,	1673
James Barker,[1]	1663	Henry Bull,	1674
Walter Todd,	1664	Benjamin Barton,	1674
John Gardner,	1665	Edward Thurston,	1675
Edward Smith,	1665	Thomas Barden,	1675
William Carpenter,	1665	William Codman,	1676
John Brown,	1665	Samuel Gorton, jun.,	1676
Samuel Wilbore,	1665	John Whipple,	1677
John Easton,	1666	Thomas Greene,	1678
William Harris,	1666	Caleb Carr,	1679
Richard Carder,	1666	Thomas Ward,	1679
Benjamin Smith,	1666	William Coddington,	1680
Peleg Sanford,	1667	Joseph Jenckes,	1680
William Reape,	1667	George Lawton,	1680
Stephen Arnold,	1667	Richard Arnold,	1681
John Cranston,	1668	John Potter,	1685
Thomas Olney, jun.,	1669	Walter Newbury,	1686
Joshua Coggshall,	1669	Benedict Arnold,	1990
John Tripp,	1670	Christopher Almy,	1690
James Greene,	1670		

CONNECTICUT GOVERNORS.

Edward Hopkins, 1636; died in England, 1657.

John Haines,

George Wyllys.

Thomas Wells.

John Webster.

J. Winthrop,[2] 1662—76; died April 5, 1676, æt. 71.

William Leete.

Robert Treat.

J. Winthrop,[3] died 1707.

G. Saltonstall, 1707—24.

J. Talcot, 1724—41; died October, 1741.

Jona. Law, 1741—50; died 1750.

R. Woolcot, 1750—54.

Thomas Fitch, 1754—66.

Wm. Pitkin, 1766—69; died 1769.

Jona. Trumbull, 1769—77.

---

[1]The above-named Messrs. Baulston, Porter, Williams, Olney, Smith, Greene, Coggshall, Barker, Field and Joseph Clarke, were the ten Assistants appointed in their last charter.

[2]John Winthrop son of John Winthrop of Massachusetts.—ED.

[3]John, otherwise called Fitz John, Winthrop, son of a previous Connecticut Governor.—ED.

NEW HAVEN GOVERNORS.

Theo. Eaton, 1637—57 ; died 1657.   Wm. Leete, 1660—62.
F. Newman, 1657—60 ; died 1660.

BRIEF REMARKS.

1. These facts may teach us what to think of the excla-
mations that have often been made against a free government, where each freeman may have a voice in choosing
their chief rulers.   Plymouth had this liberty in its full
extent ; having full power to lay the plan of their government as they pleased, and to elect whom they would into
office.   Each freeman in that colony had his equal vote in
the annual choice of their Governor ; and had not Governor
Bradford requested them sometimes to elect others into that
office, it is probable that in the whole seventy-three years
of their continuance as a distinct colony, they would never
have changed it into any more hands than death obliged
them to ; and, in fact, they never did but five times in all
those years ; and New Haven made no such change while
they remained a distinct government.   And we have a good
evidence that even a sergeant in Plymouth militia was treated with more honorable regards than captains have now
been for these many years past.   In Connecticut where
their Governors have always been elected annually, by votes
of the freemen sent in from every town in the colony, they
have chosen but sixteen men in a hundred and forty years,
and but ten in a hundred years, only two or three of whom
were left out of office till they died.   And the Massachusetts chose but eight Governors in sixty-three years.   But
since this fickle popularity (as some call such government)
was taken away, and the power was vested in a crowned
head, to fix Governors over us by a steady commission, in
which the people had no voice, the province in eighty-two
years has had a Phips, Stoughton, Bellamont, Dudley, Tai-
lor, Shute, Dummer, Burnet, Belcher, Shirley, Phips, Pownal, Bernard, Hutchinson, and Gage, for commanders-in-

chief, who have each in their turns been invested with
power, to negative our councillors when elected, and to negative any and every act that our Assembly could pass, and
to dissolve them when they pleased. All these in a space
when Connecticut had but about half so many governors,
and in thirty-four years of the time Rhode Island had but
two. And the evil effects afterward of a depreciating currency, and of party influence in elections, all need to beware
of at this day. Hence, 2. Learn the importance of viewing
persons and actions in their distinct light, so as not to confound good and evil, truth and falsehood, together. God
says, Only by pride cometh contention ; but with the well-
advised is wisdom. Pride caused a contention about who
should be greatest, even among the apostles, and made them
think of calling for fire from heaven to consume such as
would not receive them. And Dr. Owen well says, " Gospel constitutions, in the case of heresy or error, seem not to
favor any course of violence, I mean of civil penalties.
Foretold it is, that heresies must be ; I Cor. 11. 19 ; but
this for the manifesting of those who are approved, not the
destroying of those that are not. . . . . Perhaps those who
call for the sword on earth, are as unacquainted with their
own spirits, as those that called for fire from heaven. Luke
11. And perhaps the parable of the tares gives in a positive rule as to this whole business."[1] These sentiments were
inculcated upon our Plymouth fathers before they came to
this country.[2] Governor Bradford was the owner of the
book which contained them, that I am now favored with;
and while he continued Governor, Mr. Williams could be
comfortable at Plymouth ; but when Mr. Winslow came
into that office in 1633, he requested a dismission to Salem.
And the second time Mr. Winslow was Governor, he wrote
to Mr. Williams to remove out of that jurisdiction,[3] and a
law was made that year to forbid the gathering of any

---

[1]See pp. 18, 22.   [2]Collection of his Tracts, 1721, p. 314.   [3]See p. 57.

church therein without the rulers' leave.   He and Mr. Colliar were the Commissioners for Plymouth, who, on September 7, 1643, signed the articles of confederation that the other three colonies had entered into the May before ; and who then concurred in the delivery of Miantinomo to Uncas to be slain, (though without torture,) and in advising the Massachusetts to send an armed force to Warwick. He was again a Commissioner in their meeting at Hartford, September 1, 1644, when they wrote to each colony, to enter upon a method of rating all persons by authority, that refused or neglected to give what the rulers judged to be their meet proportion toward ministers' maintenance ; against which Mr. John Brown, the other Plymouth Commissioner, entered his dissent.   In October, 1645, in a thin Assembly at Plymouth, Mr. Winslow propounded, " and after a whole day's agitation" got something of this nature allowed and entered upon their waste book ; but when a full Assembly met the next week, Mr. Brown and other magistrates, " excepted the entry of that order, as pernicious and destructive to the weal of the government, and tendered a proposition, to allow and maintain full and free tolerance of religion, to all men that would preserve the civil peace, and submit to government."[1]   But Mr. Winslow had influence enough to prevent the putting of that matter to vote.   When the Commissioners met at New Haven, September 9, 1646, they said :—

Upon information of what petitions have been lately put up in some of the colonies against the good and straight ways of Christ, both in the churches and in the Commonwealth, the Commissioners, remembering that these colonies, for themselves and their posterity, did unite [enter] into this form of [firm and] perpetual league, as for other respects, so for mutual advice, that the truth and liberties of the gospel might be preserved and perpetuated, [propagated] thought it their duty seriously to commend it to the care and jurisdiction [consideration] of each General Court within these United Colonies, that, as they have laid their foundations and measured the house [temple] of God, the worship and worshippers, by the rod [that straight reed] God hath put into their hands, so they would

[1] Massachusetts History, Vol. III, pp. 153, 154.

28

walk on, and build up (all discouragements and difficulties notwithstanding) with an undaunted heart and unwearied hand, according to the sure
rules and patterns;....that anabaptism, familism, antinomianism, and
generally all errors of like nature, which oppose, undermine and slight
either the Scriptures, the Sabbath or other ordinances of God, and bring in.
and cry up unwarrantable revelations, inventions of men, or any carnal
liberty, under a deceitful color of liberty of conscience, may be seasonably and duly suppressed; though they wish as much forbearance and
respect may be had of tender consciences, seeking light, as may stand with
the purity of religion and peace of the churches.

The commissioners for Plymouth, Brown and Hatherly,
did not concur with this.[1]

Mr. Winslow was then gone to England, from whence he
never returned; and not having his influence, all the ministers in Plymouth colony, and the Massachusetts Court to
help them, could not prevail in 1650, with Governor Bradford and his Court, to inflict so much as a fine upon Mr.
Holmes; who was most cruelly whipped at Boston, the next
year.[2] Said ministers were not of the original planters of
Plymouth colony, and because their Court would not be
governed by them, the most of them left it, and carried
their complaints to Boston, from whence fresh exertions
were made, which then in a measure introduced a State-
worship, and State-way of maintenance into Plymouth colony. Though the bloody work that followed at Boston,
gave such a shock to it as turned them back again in a
great measure. Mr. John Brown had been a magistrate
seventeen years, and a Commissioner for his colony eleven
years, even down to 1656. And we are told that he was,
"well accomplished with abilities [in] both civil and religious
[concernments] and attained, through [God's] grace, unto a
comfortable persuasion of the love and favor of God to
him; he, falling sick of a fever, with much serenity and
spiritual comfort fell asleep in the Lord, at Wannamoiset
near Rehoboth, in the spring of the year 1662."[3] His son
James joined the next year in forming a Baptist church

<hr>

[1]Records of the United Colonies. [2]See page 177, &c. [3]Morton, pp. 175, 176.

there, and both in 1665 and 1666, the freemen through the
colony elected him for one of their magistrates, at the same
time that the Massachusetts Court disfranchised two of their
ancient freemen, for no worse crime than Mr. Brown then
lived in.[1] Though he did not see cause then to accept of
that office, yet being chosen again in 1673, he accepted it,
and served his colony therein eleven years; in the midst of
which time persecution was again revived at Boston, and
Mr. Brown and his minister were fined for visiting their
afflicted brethren there. With what face then can any man
reproach New England in general, with the persecutions
which its first founders, and many of its best members afterward abhorred? And of all men how inexcusable are
Episcopalians in so doing, when it was the errors which
Massachusetts brought out of their church that produced
all those mischiefs, of which they were then, and have been
ever since, much more guilty than those they complain of
here! In England and Scotland they, in that day, destroyed
more hundreds of lives, in trying to establish their supremacy over the consciences of men, than the Massachusetts
hanged persons. And they have not only always taxed dissenters to their ministers wherever they could get power to
do it, but also in Virginia, they have fined and imprisoned
our ministers only for preaching without their license; and
continued this cruel trade till the present rupture put a stop
to it. 3. Hence, see the pernicious evil of using carnal
weapons in religious affairs. Papists, Episcopalians, Presbyterians and Congregationalists, have all tried it in their
turns; but, instead of giving up the root of this mischief,
they have each of them tried to cast all the reproach of it,
upon the bad dispositions of their neighbors; and so it has
been a constant source of raillery and slander. But where
can a better set of men be found upon earth, since Constantine first brought the carnal weapon into the church, who
concurred in using of it there, than the fathers of the Mas-

[1]See pages 298, 303.—ED.

sachusetts ? Look back to pages 114—116, and then tell
me where you can find a more excellent ruler than Governor Winthrop, that ever traveled in that path ?   And Mr.
Shepard of Cambridge, who died five months after him,
said :—

Surely all the persons, whose hearts the Lord stirred up in this business,
were not rash, weak-spirited, inconsiderate of what they left behind, or
what it was to go into a wilderness. But if we were able to recount the
singular workings of Divine Providence, for the bringing on this work to
what it is come unto, it would stop the mouths of all. Whatever many
may say or think, we believe after times will admire and adore the Lord
herein, when all his holy ends, and the ways he has used to bring them
about shall appear. .... What shall we say of the singular providence of
God, in bringing so many ship-loads of his people through so many dangers, [as on eagles' wings] with so much safety from year to year?[1] the
fatherly care of our God, in feeding and clothing so many in a wilderness,
giving such healthiness and great increase of posterity? .... But above all,
we must acknowledge the singular pity and mercies of our God, that hath
done all this, and much more, for a people so unworthy, so sinful, that by
murmurings of many, unfaithfulness in promises, oppressions, and other
evils that are found among us, have so dishonored his Majesty, exposed his
work here to much scandal and obloquy, for which we have cause forever
to be ashamed ; that the Lord should yet own us, and rather correct us in
measure, [mercy] than cast us off in displeasure, and scatter us in this
wilderness.[2]

We are informed that when Governor Winthrop lay on
his death bed, Mr. Dudley requested him to sign a warrant
to banish Mr. Mathews, a Welsh minister, but that he refused, saying, " I have had my hand too much in such things
already."[3]

[1] It was computed that from 1628 to 1643, (when the times turned in England, and
some went back,) the number of ships which brought them over were two hundred
and ninety-eight; the men, women and children who came in them, twenty-one
thousand two hundred, or thereabout. That the passage of the persons cost ninety-
five thousand pounds, the live stock, twelve thousand pounds, beside the price of
them in England; procuring food till they could raise it here, forty-five thousand;
nails, glass and other material for building, eighteen thousand; arms and ammunition, twenty-two thousand; in all, one hundred and ninety-two thousand pounds, beside much more which the adventures laid out in England for their use. Johnson,
pp. 28—31.

[2] Magnalia, B. 3, p. 89. [Vol. II, pp. 350, 351.]   [3] Bishop, p. 226.

Captain Roger Clap, one of the first planters of Dorchester, the commander of Castle William for twenty years, and who bore several other offices in the State with honor, and died in Boston in 1691, in such esteem that the whole General Assembly attended his funeral, wrote some memorials of those early times, with his fatherly advice to his children. And, observing that their straits were sometimes so great that the very crusts of his father's table in England would have been as a dainty in this wilderness, he says :—

I took notice of it, as a great favor of God unto me, not only to preserve my life, but to give me contentedness in all these straits ; insomuch that I do not remember that I ever wished in my heart that I had not come into this country, nor wished myself back again [to my father's house.] Yea, I was so far from that, that I wished and advised some of my dear brethren to come hither also ; which accordingly one of my brothers, and those who married my two sisters, sold their means, and came hither. The Lord Jesus Christ was so plainly held out in the preaching of the gospel unto poor lost sinners, and the absolute necessity of the new birth, and God's Holy Spirit, in those days, accompanied [was pleased to accompany] the word with such efficacy upon the hearts of many, that our hearts were taken off from old England, and set upon heaven. .... Many were converted, and others established in believing. Many joined unto the several churches where they lived, confessing their faith publicly, and showing before all the assembly, their experiences of the workings of God's spirit in their hearts, to bring them to Christ ; which many hearers found very much good by, to help them to try their own hearts, and to consider how it was with them. .... Oh, the many tears that have been shed in Dorchester meeting-house at such times, both by those that have declared God's work on their souls, and also by those who heard them ! In those days God, even our own God, did bless New England.[1]

Another of their captains who came over in 1630, says:—

Those honored persons who were now in place of government, having the propagation of the churches of Christ in their eye, labored by all means to make room for inhabitants, knowing well that where the carcass is, thither will the eagles resort. But herein they were opposed by certain persons, whose greedy desire for land, much hindered the work for a time ; as indeed such persons do to this day ; and let such take notice how these were cured of this distemper. Some were taken away by death, and then, be

[1]Prince's Christian History, Vol. I, pp. 70—72.

sure, they had land enough. Others, fearing poverty and banishment, supposing the present scarcity would never be turned into plenty, removed themselves away, and so never beheld the great good the Lord hath done for his
people. But the valiant of the Lord waited with patience, and in the miss
of beer, supplied themselves with water ; even the most honored as well as
others, contentedly rejoicing in a cup of cold water ; blessing the Lord that
had given them to taste of that living water, and that they had not the water
that slakes the thirst of their natural bodies given them by measure, but
might drink to the full ; as also in the absence of bread, they pleased
[feasted] themselves with fish. The women once a day, as the tide served,
resorted to the muscles and clam-banks, where they daily gathered their
families' food, with much heavenly discourse of the provisions Christ formerly made for many thousands of his followers in the wilderness. Quoth
one, My husband hath travelled as far as Plymouth, [about forty miles]
and hath with great toil brought a little corn home, and before that is spent
the Lord will assuredly provide ; quoth the other, Our last peck of meal is
in the oven at home a-baking, and many of our godly neighbors have quite
spent all, and we owe one loaf of that little we have. Then spake a third,
My husband hath ventured himself among the Indians for corn, and can
get none, as also our honored Governor hath distributed his so far, that a
day or two more will put an end to his store and all the rest ; and yet, methinks our children are as cheerful, fat and lusty, with feeding upon these
muscles, clams [clam-banks] and other fish, as they were in England with
their fill of bread, which makes me cheerful in the Lord's providing for us ;
being further confirmed by the exhortation of our pastor to trust in the
Lord, whose is the earth, and the fullness thereof. As they were encouraging one another in Christ's careful providing for them, they lift up their
eyes and saw two ships coming in, and presently this news comes to their
ears, that they were come from Ireland full of victuals.[1]

Oh! how gloriously do they shine, and how manfully do
they talk, when exercising themselves in the gospel armor,
to what they do when they come down to the use of earthly
weapons in heavenly concernments! In 1645 they compared the Baptists' opposition to such conduct, to what
Amalek did to Israel when they were weak. And the
erecting of a small Baptist church in 1665, was called a

---

[1] In one of those ships came Mr. Roger Williams. Johnson, pp. 48, 49 ; Prince's
Annals, pp. 18, 47. [344, 377.] We are told that one of the fathers of that day,
having dined with his friends on clams without bread, devoutly returned thanks, that
God had caused them to *suck of the abundance of the sea, and of treasures hid in
the sand.* Magnalia, B. 1, p. 22. [Vol. I, p. 72.]

strong attempt against them from the spirit of Anabaptism ; the permission of which among them they said, manifestly tended to the destruction of their churches, though they had above forty of them then in their colony, in joint communion with about as many more in neighboring colonies.[1] And in 1781 they compared their ecclesiastical establishment to a small boat, and those few illiterate Baptists to the ballast of a great ship, which was like to sink it. Hence it was their weakness, and not their strength, that caused them to treat the Baptists so cruelly. The extending of the gospel ordinance of baptism to subjects who are in a state of nature ; limiting the church of Christ to human schools for ministers, and compelling all to support such and only such, are points which had but a weak bottom to stand upon in that day, when the power of godliness was so well known in the country.[2]

[1] Christian History, Vol. I, p. 64.

[2] The seven foregoing chapters, with an Appendix which will be found at the close of this volume, constitute Volume I of the original edition. This will explain the character of the last few pages ; and also, as Volume II was not published or written till several years later, will explain certain differences of style and method which the reader will notice in the chapters that follow, as compared with those that have preceded.--ED.

CHAPTER VIII.

A FIRST PRINCIPLE OF THESE CHURCHES.—OF WITCHCRAFT.—UNJUST ATTEMPTS TO TURN IT AGAINST THE BAPTISTS.—OPPRESSIVE LAWS. —EFFECTS THEREOF.—PLYMOUTH PROCLAMATION.—THEIR CHURCH ORDER.—EVILS OF DENYING IT.—FIRST MINISTERS OF MIDDLEBOROUGH AND DARTMOUTH—OF PLYMPTON.

The fathers of New England came much nearer to the apostolic order of the church, than most other reformers had done. Dr. Cotton Mather published a specimen thereof in the year 1690. Says he, " A church (as the Greek name for it allows us to think) is to consist of a people called out from the ways of sin, by the powerful and effectual work of God upon their souls. Regeneration is the thing without which a title unto sacraments is not to be pretended. Real regeneration is the thing which, before God, renders men capable of claiming sacraments ; and visible and expressed regeneration is that which, before men, enables us to make such a claim."[1] From the first planting of the country to 1662, none were allowed to come to the ordinance of the supper, nor to bring their infants to baptism, without such a profession. The synod of that year opened a door for the children of church members to bring their infants upon a lower profession ;[2] though in the Massachusetts a profession of regeneration was still held to be necessary, in order for coming to full communion, or having a vote in the government, either of church or State. This was essential to

[1]Companion for Communicants, pp. 29, 30, 37.   [2]See page 267.—ED.

the nature of their plan of a holy government, in imitation of the church of Israel.   And for the church to govern the world, for good men to govern bad ones, seemed much more rational and scriptural, than for the world to govern the church about soul-guides, as they have done since.   Previous to this, the country was involved in most deplorable circumstances ; their charter lost ; their sea coasts infested with privateers and pirates, and their frontiers with savage enemies.   An attempt to take Quebec in 1690, was defeated, which enraged the enemy the more against them, and also involved the country in a heavy debt; to discharge which, paper money was first made here, the effects whereof were very pernicious.   Officers and people were greatly divided in their minds about the causes of these calamities, and about what was the best way to remove them.   And in this juncture they were alarmed with an apprehension that the powers of hell were let loose upon them, which amazed and confounded them inexpressibly.   The scene was introduced in the following manner :—

A variety of books concerning witchcraft, had been published in London and Boston, which were dispersed in New England.   And near the close of 1691, a young daughter and a neice of Mr. Samuel Parris, minister of Salem Village, (now Danvers,) with two other girls in the neighborhood, made such complaints of distress and injuries upon their bodies, that a physician pronounced them bewitched. Hereupon an Indian woman from New Spain, that lived at the minister's house, tried some experiments to find out the witch, which she pretended to have been used in her own country.   This coming to the knowledge of those children, they accused her of being the witch ; of appearing to them and pinching, pricking and tormenting them.   Teachers, rulers and people, were so much affected with this calamity, as to keep days of fasting and prayer for its removal ; first at said minister's house, next in the village, and then through the colony.   Such notice being taken of, and pity shown to, those children, they increased their complaints ; and others advanced like accusations, not only against the Indian woman, but also against two other old women in the place, so that all the three were committed to prison on March 1, 1692. And this noise increased, and such accusations spread, till about an hundred persons were imprisoned on that account. In the midst of which distress, on May 14, Sir William Phips, the Governor, arrived at Boston with their new charter, in company with Dr. Increase Mather, who procured it. The Governor and Council were so much concerned to purge this growing evil from the land, that they did not wait for the meeting of the Legislature, to whom the constituting of Courts of Justice belonged, but constituted one themselves, whereof Lieutenant Governor Stoughton was President, and by their sentence one woman was hanged on June 10 ; and by September 22, they executed seven men and thirteen women ; after which that Court was dissolved. And by the time that a Court of Oyer and Terminer was constituted according to charter, rulers and ministers were so far convinced that they had acted upon wrong principles, and had also admitted the testimony of accusers without sufficient care and caution, that all the rest of the accused were either acquitted upon trial, or pardoned by authority. A first principle that they acted upon in those condemnations was, that God, in his providence, would not suffer the devil to appear to and afflict any in the shape of an innocent person. And they admitted one accuser to one instance, and another to another, of those spectral appearances, to make up two witnesses. They also who would confess themselves to be witches, were admitted as witnesses against others. And, says a gentlemen who was a careful observer of those transactions, " These confessors, by their plausible confession and accusations of others, begetting credit, have been a great, if not the greatest engine of Satan to carry on the accusing and apprehending of others, until this matter came to such a height, that, if it had not been stopped, might have brought the best Christians in the country under the imputation of that abomination, and have involved all in confusion and blood.[1]" Deplorable indeed was the case of New England at that time; though we are assured, by men who have searched fully into the matter, that a greater number of persons were executed for witch-craft in only one county in England, even in the loose reign of Charles the Second, than all that were put to death here; and also that these executions were under the influence of laws and precedents from thence.[2] But this being a new country, it was more taken notice of, and was more severely felt than there.

We cannot find that the Baptists had any hand in those confused and bloody proceedings; yet much pains have been taken to turn the same against them. A late minister of Danvers, the place where those delusions began, says, " It is reported of witches, and those that hold unlawful com-merce with evil spirits, that in order to their entering into confederacy with them, they are solicited to renounce their baptism, even though received in infancy; which shews that such a renunciation of baptism, which Dr. Gill pleads for and commends, is a matter of great impiety."[3] What Dr. Gill pleaded for, was the renouncing of infant sprink-ling, and the practicing of believer's baptism, according to primitive institution. But how far was that from the witch-craft àt Danvers or Salem! The plainest instances of any mention of baptism therein were as follows. In the exami-nation of a woman before authority, July 21, 1692, were these questions and answers, viz. :—

Question. Goody Lacey, how many years ago since they were baptized? Answer. Three or four years ago, I suppose. Q. Who baptized them? A. The old serpent. Q. How did he do it? A. He dipped their heads in

---

[1] A Modest Inquiry into the Nature of Witchcraft; by John Hale, Minister of Bev-erly, 1697, p. 88.

[2] Hale, pp. 25, 26, 69. Hutchinson, Vol. II, pp. 22, 69. [22, 60.]

[3] Clark against Gill, 1752, p. 33.

the water, saying they were his, and that he had power over them. Q. Where was this? A. At Falls River. Q. How many were baptized that day? Some of the chief, I think there were six baptized. Q. Name them. A. I think they were of the higher powers.

Also Captain Osgood's wife, of Andover, was made to confess, that she with others, had been carried through the air to a certain pond, where the devil dipped her face in the water, and made her renounce her former baptism. But she with five others, in prison, gave in a retraction of their confessions to the Court, wherein they declared that they were amazed and affrighted out of their reason, by some gentlemen who told them they knew they were witches, and therefore they assented to what was suggested to them, as the only way they had left to save their lives; but when they came to be better composed, they professed that they were innocent and ignorant of such things. And fifty-three of their neighbors gave in a written testimony to the Court, that they believed this to be an honest retraction; one of whom was Dudley Bradstreet, Esq. Mr. Parris and other ministers were very officious in those examinations of persons accused of witchcraft;[1] and sixty years after, Mr. Clark must bring up the same, to prove that " renouncing of his early dedication must appear such an instance of impiety, as to a considerate person were enough to put a stop to his proceedings, how inclinable soever he might be to those principles on other accounts."[2] Such methods have they taken to frighten people from seeing with their own eyes, and from acting according to their own judgments, in the great concerns of the soul and eternity.

The second Massachusetts charter, which was dated October 7, 1691, allowed equal liberty of conscience to all Christians, except Papists. The first General Court under it met at Boston, June 9, 1692, to which Dr. Cotton Mather delivered a sermon, wherein he said, " The civil Magistrate

[1] Hutchinson's History, Vol. II, pp. 31, 36, 40—44. [31, 35, 39, 43, 44.]
[2] Against Gill, p. 33.

is most properly the officer of human society, and a Christian, by non-conformity to this or that imposed way of worship, does not break the terms on which he is to enjoy the benefits of human society." And ten years after, he published this and other passages, in his history of New England, and said he would thereby stop the noise about persecution therein. [1]But how could that be done? for he said, " The General Assembly may, by their acts, give a distinguishing encouragement unto the religion which is the general profession of the inhabitants;"[2] that is, may empower some to judge for others about worship, and to enforce their judgments with the sword; which is the root of the worst persecutions in the world. He knew that such acts as he spoke of could not take place here without the royal assent; yet said he, " I am verily persuaded, that the nearness of our dependence on the crown will be found one of our most glorious advantages." His reason therefor is, its giving them a greater security in future shaking times. But experience has now demonstrated, that it is better to trust in the Lord than to put confidence in princes. He, in that sermon, called Cambridge College "A river, the streams whereof made glad the city of God;"[3] which method of applying those words of divine revelation to human schools, is doubtless a perverting of them; and is a way which has done much hurt to mankind. Christians are required to withdraw from such as suppose that gain is godliness; yet now a freehold worth forty shillings a year, or other estate worth fifty pounds (which was soon after reduced to forty) gave every inhabitant a right to vote for legislators; and an Assembly so elected, in their session at Boston, October 12, 1692, enacted :—

That the inhabitants of each town within this Province shall take due care, from time to time, to be constantly provided of an able, learned and orthodox minister or ministers, of good conversation, to dispense the word

[1]Magnalia, B. 7, p. 28, 29. [Vol. II, p. 462.]
[2]Account of his father's life, p. 141.   [3]Sermon, pp. 57, 66, 87.

of God to them ; which minister or ministers shall be suitably encouraged, and sufficiently supported and maintained by the inhabitants of such town. And all contracts, agreements and orders, heretofore made, or that shall hereafter be made, by the inhabitants of any town within this Province, respecting their ministers or school-masters as to their settlement or maintenance, shall remain good and valid, according to the true intent thereof, the whole time for which they were or shall be made, in all the particulars thereof, and shall accordingly be pursued, put in execution, and fulfilled. And where there is no contract and agreement made in any town, respecting the support and maintenance of the ministry, or when the same happens to be expired, and the inhabitants of such town shall neglect to make suitable provision therein, upon complaint thereof made unto the Quarter Sessions of the Peace for the county where such town lies, the said Court shall, and hereby are empowered to, order a competent allowance unto such minister, according to the estate and ability of the town, the same to be assessed upon the inhabitants, by warrant from the Court, directed to the Select Men, who are thereupon to proceed to make and apportion said assessment, in manner as is directed for other public charges, and to cause the same to be levied by the constables of such town, by warrant under the hands of the Select Men or of the town clerk by their order.

Be it further enacted, that where any town shall be destitute of a minister qualified as aforesaid, and shall so continue by the space of six months, not having taken due care for the procuring, settling and encouragement of such a minister, the same being made to appear upon complaint unto their Majesty's Justices of the General Sessions of the Peace of the county, the said Court shall, and hereby are empowered to, make an order upon every such defective town, speedily to provide themselves of such a minister as aforesaid, by the next sessions at the furthest ; and in case such order be not complied with, then the said Court shall take effectual care to procure and settle a minister qualified as aforesaid, and order the charge thereof, and of such minister's maintenance, to be levied on the inhabitants of such town.

And it is further enacted, that the respective churches, in the several towns within this Province, shall at all times hereafter use, exercise and enjoy, all their privileges and freedoms respecting divine worship, church order and discipline ; and shall be encouraged in the peaceable and regular profession and practice thereof.

And further it is enacted, that every minister, being a person of good conversation, able, learned and orthodox, that shall be chosen by the major part of the inhabitants of any town, at a town-meeting duly warned for that purpose, (notice being given to the inhabitants fifteen days before the time of such meeting) shall be the minister of such town ; and the whole town shall be obliged to pay towards his settlement and maintenance, each man his several proportion thereof.

They had here entered upon a new and untried scene; and the glaring contradiction betwixt the last two paragraphs of this law, with their finding that some towns had more than one church therein, as also that Boston would not submit to it, caused the Assembly, in their next session of February 3, 1693, to repeal those two paragraphs, and in addition to the rest of that law to enact, "that each respective gathered church, in any town or place within this Province, that at any time shall be in want of a minister, such church shall have power, according to the directions given in the word of God, to choose their own minister;" yet not to settle him without the concurrence of the majority of voters in town affairs, who usually meet therewith for worship; but that being obtained, then "all the inhabitants and ratable estates lying within such town, or part of a town, or place limited by law for upholding the public worship of God, shall be obliged to pay in proportion towards the minister's settlement and support; provided, that nothing herein contained is intended, or shall be construed to extend, to abridge the inhabitants of Boston of their accustomed way and practice, as to the choice and maintenance of their ministers."

Here it is to be noted, that like causes may ever be expected to produce like effects. One of our most essential rights is that we shall not be taxed where we are not represented. And it is most certain, that a civil legislature are not our religious representatives; and in order then to tax the country to religious teachers, they were *abridged* of the rights which Boston would not part with. So when Governor Hutchinson was pursuing the scheme, in 1769, of having America taxed by Britain, he said, "there must be an abridgment of what are called English liberties." But the bloody effects of that attempt, are a loud warning to all after ages. The Assembly went on, in said law, to empower the ratable inhabitants of any town where no church was gathered, to call and settle a minister, by the advice and direction of three neighboring ordained ministers, who should be supported as others were; and also to enact, that if any town or place neglected to obey these laws, their Select-men, or other officers, should be convented before their county Court, and, upon conviction of such neglect, be fined forty shillings for the first offence, and four pounds for every after conviction. As a fruit of which, a warrant was sent from Bristol Court, "requiring the town of Swanzey to choose a minister according to law." The town met upon it August 28, and adjourned to October 17, 1693, when they concluded to report to the Court, that Elder Samuel Luther was their minister.[1] He was ordained pastor of the first church there, July 22, 1685, by the assistance of the Elders Hull and Emblen, of Boston. And the rulers of Plymouth Colony had publicly owned him in that office; one instance whereof take as follows:—

At a Court of Assistants held at Plymouth, the first Tuesday of August, 1690, it being manifest that the Lord our God calls his poor people in this wilderness to great humiliation and mourning, for those awful tokens of his displeasure that are upon us, and our manifold sins, the procuring cause thereof, the Governor and Council do therefore commend it to all the churches of God and people in this Colony, to set apart and observe the last day of this instant as a day of solemn fasting and prayer, wherein to deprecate those heavy judgments impending, and to entreat the Lord to take away all our iniquities, and receive us graciously: particularly that God would prosper the Agents of the country in their weighty negotiation in the other England; that our address may be accepted with our lord the king, and we may have a settled establishment of our ancient liberties and privileges, sacred and civil; that God would call back the commission he hath given to the sword of the enemy to be drawn among us, and direct and manage all the counsels of his servants in this dark and difficult day of war, and give success in the destruction of our adversaries, and restore peace to us; that contagious and afflictive distresses may be removed; that the necessities of the poor may be supplied, and the judgment of scarcity and famine prevented; and that God would bless the labors of our hands, and give both seed-time and harvest; and that, in a way of humiliation and reformation, we may be prepared to meet God, and wait for him in the way of his judgments, and that mercy may be the latter end of all his dispensations to us.

Per order of the above-said Court,   SAMUEL SPRAGUE, Recorder.
To Samuel Luther, Elder of the church of Swanzey, for him to communicate to the church and congregation there.

[1] Swanzey Town Records.
29

This I carefully copied from the original preserved in Elder Luther's family; and Bristol Court could not be ignorant of his being thus owned as the settled minister of Swanzey; yet this attempt must be made for the other denomination, though they have never been able to set up their worship in that town to this day. A second Baptist church was formed therein, and Mr. Thomas Barnes was ordained pastor of it in '1693. It may be serviceable to enquire into the reason of their being so much better treated when under Plymouth government, than they were after they were incorporated with the Massachusetts.

Plymouth people were taught in Holland, that the church was the school wherein Christ trained up his ministers; though they were far from despising human learning in its place. One of their proofs was the 14th chapter of the First Epistle to the Corinthians; upon which their learned pastor, Mr. Robinson, made the following remarks. Says he :—

That the apostle in this chapter directs the church in the use of extraordinary gifts, is most evident. Neither will I deny but that the officers are to guide and order this action of prophesying, as all other public business, [businesses] yea, even these wherein the brethren have greatest liberty : But that he intends the establishing of, and so takes order, and gives direction for an ordinary, constant exercise in the church, even by men out of office, I do manifest by these reasons. (1.) Because the apostle speaks of the ministration of a gift or grace, common to all persons, as well brethren as ministers, ordinary as extraordinary, and that at all times, which is love; as also of such fruits and effects of that grace, as are no less common to all than the grace itself, nor of less continuance in the churches of Christ, to wit, of edification, exhortation and comfort; verse 3, compared with I Thes. v. 11, 14. (2.) In verse 24 he permits all to prophesy, and speaks as largely of prophesying as of learning, and receiving comfort. But lest any should object, May women also prophesy? the apostle prevents that objection, and it may be reproves that disorder amongst the Corinthians, ver. 34, by a flat inhibition, enjoining them expressly to keep silence in the church, in the presence of men, to whom they ought to be subject, and to learn at home of their husbands, [ver. 35,] and not, by teaching [the] men, to usurp authority over them; I Tim. ii. 11, 12; which men in prophesying, do lawfully use. (3.) Now .... in that Paul forbids women, he gives liberty to all men, gifted accordingly, opposing women to men, sex to sex, and not women to officers, which were frivolous. And again, in restraining women, he shews his meaning to be of ordinary, not extraordinary prophesying; for women immediately and extraordinarily [and miraculously] inspired might speak without restraint; Exod. xv. 20; Judg. iv. 4; Luke ii. 36; [Acts xxi. 9]. (4.) The prophets here spoken of were not extraordinary, because their doctrines were to be judged by other prophets, and their spirits to be subject unto the spirits of others; ver. 29, 32; whereas the doctrines of the extraordinary prophets were neither subject to nor to be judged by any; but they, as the apostles, being immediately [and infallibly] inspired, were the foundation upon which the church was built, Jesus Christ himself, being the chief corner stone; Eph. ii. 20, and iii. 5. (5.) The apostle [ver. 37] makes a prophet and a man spiritual all one, whom he further describes, not by any extraordinary gift, but by that common Christian grace of submission unto the things he writes, as the commandments of the Lord: unto whom he opposeth a man wilfully ignorant, ver. 37, 38, teaching us, that he doth not measure a prophet, in this place, either by the office of ministry, or by any extraordinary prophetical gift, but by the common Christian gift of spiritual discerning. (6.) It is the commandment of the Lord by the apostle, that a bishop must be apt to teach, and that such elders or bishops be called as are able to exhort with sound doctrine, and to convince the gainsayers. Now, except men, before they be in office, may be permitted to manifest their gifts, in doctrine and prayer, [Tit. i. 9; Acts vi. 4,] which are the two main works requiring special qualification in the teaching elders, how shall the church (which is to choose them) take knowledge of their sufficiency, that with faith and good conscience they may call them, and submit unto them for their guides?[1]

Now, as the church of Plymouth had always acted upon these principles, it was easy for them to look upon Elder Luther as a minister of Christ, whose church was of the same mind about that point of gospel order. But a minister of chief note among the Massachusetts says:—

That custom, of the prophesying of private brethren, was not observed in any of the churches of New England besides themselves; the ministers of the respective churches there not being so well satisfied in the way thereof as Mr. Robinson was. The most judicious and leading elders among said churches, as Mr. Cotton, &c., that were not absolutely against the thing, were yet afraid that the wantonness of the present age would not

----

[1] Robinson against Bernard, pp. 236, 237. [Works of John Robinson, Congregational Board, London, 1851; Vol. II, pp. 247—249.]

well bear such a liberty as that great light of these churches expressed, to a person of great quality, to whom he bore no small respect, a few hours before he departed this life.[1]

Mr. Robinson says :—

It is apparent, both in the Scriptures and ecclesiastical writers, that not only pride and contention, but heresy, and almost all other evils, have sprung from the officers and governors of the church. And surely nothing hath more in former days advanced, nor doth it this day more uphold the throne of antichrist, than the people's discharging themselves of the care of public affairs in the church, on the one side, and the priests and prelates arrogating all to themselves on the other.[2]

Two brethren of Plymouth church were ordained pastors of other churches in 1694. One of them was Mr. Jonathan Donham, who was ordained at Edgarton, on Martha's Vineyard. The other was at Middleborough, fourteen miles west of Plymouth. About sixteen families began to plant here a little before Philip's war; who moved away when the war broke out, and returned again after it was over; and Mr. Samuel Fuller preached to them till a church was constituted among them this year, and he was ordained their pastor. The settlement of Dartmouth began about the same time with Middleborough, and their first teacher was also from Plymouth, but not in the same way. His name was John Cooke. He was a deacon in Plymouth church for some years; but was cast out of it in the latter part of Mr. Reyner's ministry there, who left them in November, 1654. It is said that Cooke was excommunicated for having been the author of much dissension and division, and for afterwards running into sectarian and anabaptistical principles; and also that Reyner's removal was partly occasioned by the unsettledness of the church, too many of the members being leavened with prejudices against a learned ministry, by means of sectaries then spreading through the land.[3] Some light

[1]Hubbard, [pp. 65, 66.]

[2]Robinson, p. 204. [Works of John Robinson, Vol. II, p. 213.]

[3]Plymouth Register, pp. 4, 12. [Massachusetts Historical Collections, Vol. IV, pp. 111, 118.]

concerning them may be gathered from the following facts. Plymouth church took much pains to obtain learned pastors, if they were otherwise well qualified; but they refused to be confined to human schools for ministers, or to compel the world to support them. They labored hard to get the learned Mr. Charles Chauncy to settle as a colleague with Mr. Reyner; but Mr. Chauncy could not consent to it, because gospel baptism appeared to him to be dipping, and that sprinkling for baptism was unlawful, as their church records witness. In 1650 a separation commenced at Rehoboth, because Mr. Newman, their minister, with six others, assumed all the power of church government to themselves, under the name of " The church representative."[1] For this usurpation a number of the church withdrew, and set up worship by themselves; and the ministers tried hard to move Plymouth Court to suppress them by force, but could not prevail therein. These people soon after became Baptists; and one of them was most shamefully and cruelly persecuted the next year at Boston.[2] By searching into these matters, Mr. Dunstar, President of Harvard College, was brought openly to renounce infant baptism; and seeing the temper which was discovered in the Massachusetts, he removed into Plymouth Colony, the very year that Reyner moved out of it; as several other ministers also did about that time, because they could not bring Plymouth rulers into the use of tax and compulsion for their support.[3] And though Reyner excommunicated Cooke, yet, not being able to bring the church into all his measures, he left them, and robbed them of their church records, which they never recovered; so that what records Plymouth church now has, were afterwards collected from memory and private writings. These facts may help the reader in forming a judgment of what Cooke's sectarian

[1] Clarke's Narrative, p. 24. [Massachusetts Historical Collection, Fourth Series, Vol. II, p. 54.]—B.
See also pages 176, 177, 204.—ED.   [2] See page 192.—ED.
[3] See pages 227—229, 256.

principles were, and also how he came by them. His posterity inform me, that he was a Baptist, and that he preached
the doctrine of election, with the other doctrines of sovereign grace, in Dartmouth for a number of years. And it
appears by Mr. Samuel Hubbard's letters, that a Baptist
church was formed upon the west borders of Dartmouth, in
the year 1685, wherein Hugh Mosier and Aaron Davis were
principal leaders ; which church is continued by succession
to this day ; though the Quakers are the most numerous of
any one sect in that town.[1]

On August 24, 1695, the church of Middleborough was
bereaved of their beloved pastor, aged 66 ; " a great loss to
the place," said Mr. Cotton, " he being a sincere, godly man,
and useful preacher." Mr. Isaac Cushman, another member of Plymouth church, was invited to succeed him ; but
having a call at Plympton (betwixt here and Plymouth) at
the same time, he accepted it ; and was ordained there in
1698 ;[2] and was continued a great blessing to them for about

[1] " Next to the Friends in numbers and influence, stood the Baptists. John Cooke,
whose name we meet with on the first and on nearly every page of the early records
of the town, as a deputy and a select-man, filling various offices of trust and honor,
was a Baptist minister for many years. But this same town official, October 29,
1670, was fined ten shillings ' for breaking the Sabbath by unnecessary travel thereon.' If the record of the case had been preserved, it would have appeared, we
think, that Elder John Cooke was not a Sabbath-breaker, but travelling upon his
circuit as a Baptist preacher." Old Dartmouth Centennial, p. 86. Backus says in
his Abridgment, page 135, " Cooke was a Baptist minister in Dartmouth many years,
from whence sprung the Baptist church in the east borders of Tiverton." Benedict
says of this church in Tiverton, that it " was formed in the adjoining town of Dartmouth about 1685 ; the members at first lived in Dartmouth, Tiverton and Little
Compton. Their first minister was Hugh Mosier, and next to him Aaron Davis.
This was the seventh Baptist church formed on the American continent. In process
of time, its seat was removed from Dartmouth to Tiverton, where it continues to
the present day." History of the Baptists, Vol. I, p. 503. The church will be sub-
sequently noticed in this work, as the First Baptist church in Tiverton, R. I.—Ed.

[2] Mr. John Cotton, above referred to, was son to the famous minister of that name
in Boston. He was minister at Plymouth about thirty years, till contentions about
the above points of church order occasioned his dismission, by advice of a council
in 1697 ; and the next year he went and gathered a Congregational church in
Charleston, South Carolina, where he died, much lamented, September 18, 1699.
Plymouth Register, pp. 21. 22. [Massachusetts Historical Collections, Vol. IV, pp.
127, 128.]

forty years.   But thirteen ministers, in and near Boston, published a letter of advice to the churches, dated December 28, 1699, in the eighth page of which they represent it to be a *jesuitical principle* for any to hold, "that *illiterate* men may be serviceable and admirable preachers."   This with other things moved their churches to look only to colleges for ministers for a long time after.   In the meanwhile, as the empowering the world to control the church in the choice of pastors was an untried path to them, it took them three years to find out what to do, when a parish did not concur with the church therein.   But when the Assembly met at Boston, May 29, 1695, they enacted, that in such a case the church should call a council of three or five neighboring churches, who should decide the controversy thus.: If the council approved of the person elected, the parish must submit and support him, if not, then the church must give up their choice, and call another minister ; and in this method they have proceeded ever since.   And it may be serviceable to hear the judgment of a number of their most eminent men, about the state of religion in New England in those times.

CHAPTER IX.

The learned and pious Mr. Thomas Prince, says :—

The second generation rising and growing thick on the stage, a little
after 1660 there began to appear a decay, and this increased to 1670, when
it grew [very] visible and threatening, and was generally complained of and
bewailed bitterly by the pious among them ; and yet much more to 1680,
when but few of the first generation remained.

One of his proofs hereof is what Mr. William Stoughton
delivered in an Election Sermon at Boston, April 29, 1668 ;
when he said:—

The death and removal of the Lord's eminent servants in one rank and
in another, hath manifested the *lie* in many of us. Whilst they lived, their
piety and zeal, their light and life, their counsels and authority, their examples and awe, kept us right, and drew us on in the ways of God, to profess
and practice the best things. But now [that] they are [dead and] gone,
ah ! how doth the unsoundness, the rottenness and hypocrisy of too many
among us make itself known, as it was with Joash after the death of
Jehoiada. ![1]

Other of his proofs are in pages 320, 321.

[1]Christian History, Vol. I, pp. 94, 95. In 1671, Mr. Stoughton **was** elected into
the Council, and he died there, Lieutenant Governor in 1702.

In 1680, Mr. Willard said :—

Be sure, when the glory of God and the spiritual good of your brother requires it, that you carry on your reproofs to conviction. There are some things that arise only from sudden passion, and there a transient rebuke may be enough; other things may be [more] deliberate, and men are led into them more gradually; they may also be eminently reproachful to religion, and a dangerous snare to the souls of them that are [so] tempted; our connivance in such cases may not only blemish our profession, but be a great hazard to it also. At such times, and in such [a] case, you break your covenant if you suffer sin in your brother, without using all the means which Christ hath prescribed, and in the order he hath prescribed them, till the end be obtained. If private admonition, followed with gentleness and patience will not gain, but they still persist in evil courses, or are not humbled for such faults, you must proceed by steps as far as Christ hath bid you. And I believe there is no one thing wherein the covenant is more universally broken, than in the neglect of this duty; and if the use of these ordinances shall once come to cease among the churches, and the sins of church members be not regularly suppressed, by reason of the unfaithfulness of brethren, religion will languish, and the power of godliness fail. It is not the extending of the covenant to Christians, (as some dream) but [it is] the neglect of covenant duties towards them, that is like to be the bane of our profession, if any thing. Eli indulged his sons, and one professor indulgeth another; and it is to be feared, that if this were searched to the [root and] bottom [of it,] it would be found that the original of it is self-indulgence, and that when men wink at scandals in their brethren, it is because they expect the like in way of retaliation. And if things once come to this pass, let any sober and prudent man conjecture whether this be not the way to cherish apostasy.[1]

Dr. Increase Mather, in the Preface, gave a special recommendation of this passage. Three years after, another of their fathers, who was minister at Weymouth, delivered a sermon before their Legislature, which he called " A plea for the life of dying religion ;" wherein he said :—

There is already a great death upon religion, little more left than a name to live..... Consider we then how much it is dying respecting the [very] being of it, by the general failure of the work of conversion, whereby only it is that religion is propagated, continued and upheld in being, among any people. As converting work doth cease, so doth religion die away; though more insensibly, yet most irrecoverably.....How much is it dying,

---

[1] Willard on Covenant-keeping, pp. 110, 111.

respecting the visible profession and practice of it, partly by the formality of churches, but more by the hypocrisy and apostacy of formal hypocritical professors.[1]

The life of Mr. Jonathan Mitchel was published in 1697; and Dr. Increase Mather dedicated this work, which his son had compiled, to the church and college at Cambridge; to whom he said:—

A learned and renowned author, [Dr. Owen,] has evinced, that the letting go this principle, that particular churches ought to consist of regenerate persons, brought in the great apostasy of the Christian church. The way to prevent the like apostasy in these churches, is to require an account of those that offer themselves to communion therein, concerning the work of God on their souls, as well as concerning their knowledge and belief. .... Mr. Mitchell says, [in a manuscript of his which I have seen, has these weighty words:] The over-enlarging of full communion, or admission of persons thereto, upon slight qualifications, without insisting upon the practical and spiritual part of religion, will not only lose the power of godliness, but in a little time bring in profaneness, and ruin the churches, these two ways. 1. Election of ministers will soon be carried by a formal, looser sort. 2. The exercise of discipline will by this means be rendered impossible. Discipline failing, profaneness riseth like a flood; for the major part wanting zeal against sin, will foster licentiousness. It is not setting down good rules and directions, that will save it; for the specification of government is from men, not from laws. Let never so good a form of government be agreed upon, it will soon degenerate, if the instruments that manage it be not good.[2]

When Mr. Mitchel wrote this, about 1664, he had no idea of pastors being elected in New England by any others but communicants; and he gives these weighty reasons against admitting such upon slight qualifications, which Dr. Mather, then President of the College, endeavored to enforce.

In the year 1700, Mather published another book, which he dedicated to the churches of Christ in New England, to whom he said:—

The Congregational church discipline is not suited for a worldly interest, or a formal generation of professors. It will stand or fall as godliness, in

[1]Torrey's Election Sermon at Boston, May 16, 1683, p. 11.
[2]Dedication of the Life of Jonathan Mitchel, pp. 16, 17. [Magnalia, Vol. II, p. 59.]

the power of it, does prevail, or otherwise. That there is a great decay of
the power of religion throughout all New England, is lamentably true ; if
that revive, there will be no fear of departing from the holy discipline of
the churches of Christ. .... If the begun apostasy should proceed as fast,
the next thirty years, as it has done these last, surely it will come to that
in New England, (except the gospel itself depart with the order of it) that
the most conscientious people therein will think themselves concerned to
gather churches out of churches.

He goes on to caution and warn them against many evils;
one of which is a dull formality in relations of experiences,
in order for admission to communion.   And he then says :—

There are reports, as if in some churches persons have brought *written*
relations, first to the minister and then to the church, which were not of
their own dictating, but devised by others for them.   I hope these reports
have nothing of truth in them ; but if they have, I am sure that such *liars
to the Holy Ghost* have exceedingly provoked the Lord.

Another evil which he warns the churches against, is
admitting any but communicants to vote for pastors ; and he
cites Acts i. 26 ; vi. 2—5 ; xiv. 23, to prove that God has
plainly given this privilege " to the brethren of particular
churches ;" and declares it to be " simonical to affirm, that
this sacred privilege may be purchased with money.[1]   This
testimony was then given by one of the most eminent ministers in the land, who had been President of Harvard College
about twenty years; but by unfair means he was removed
from that office the next year.[2]

[1]Vindication of the Order of the Gospel in New England, pp. 11, 12, 38, 67, 68.
[2]His life, p. 173.—B.

"There were some disaffected men who, for some reasons, (God knows what they
were,) were willing to have the College taken out of Dr. Mather's hands.   To
accomplish it, they obtained a vote of the General Assembly which appeared of a
plausible aspect, that no man should act as President of the College who did not
reside at Cambridge.   The leaders in this vote knew very well that the Doctor
would not remove his habitation from a loving people at Boston to reside at Cambridge, while the College was as it then was.   But yet his abdication was after all
brought about, I will but softly say, not so fairly as it should have been.   I think
there are thanks due to me for my forbearing to tell the story.   This was in 1701,
twenty years after his beginning to serve that society in quality of a President.   And
I think it will do no hurt for me to mention a passage which he wrote on this occasion.   'I have received more discouragement in the work of God, from those whom I
have laid under the greatest obligations, than by all the world besides.   Let not my

Mr. Willard also published a discourse in the year 1700, entitled, " The Perils of the Times Displayed;" in which he said :—

That there is a form of godliness among us is manifest ; but the great inquiry is, whether there be not too much of a general denying of the power of it. Whence else is it, that there be such things as these that follow, to be observed? that there is such a prevalency of so many immoralities among professors? that there is so little success of the gospel? How few thorough conversions [are] to be observed, how scarce and seldom. ... It hath been a frequent observation, that if one generation begins to decline, the next that follows usually grows worse, and so on, until God pours out his Spirit again upon them. The decays which we do already languish under are sad ; and what tokens are on our children, that it is like to be better hereafter? God be thanked that there are some among them that promise well ; but alas, how doth vanity [and a fondness after new things] abound among them ! How do young professors grow weary of the strict profession of their fathers, and become strong disputants for the [those] things which their progenitors forsook a pleasant land for the avoidance of.[1]

And forty years after, Mr. Prince said, " We have been generally growing worse and worse ever since."[2]

The greatest evils that our fathers came here to avoid, were the mixture of worthy and unworthy communicants in the churches, and the tyranny of secular and ministerial Courts over them ; but these evils were now coming in like a flood upon New England. A church was formed in Brattle Street, Boston, in 1699, with a professed design of not requiring such a strict profession of communicants as their fathers did.[3] And Dr. Colman, their minister, was judged

children put too much confidence in men. It may be, such as they have laid under the greatest obligations of gratitude, will prove the most unkind unto them. I have often had experience of it.' " Parentator ; Remarkables in the Life of Dr. Increase Mather, pp. 473, 174.—ED.

[1] Christian History, Vol. I, pp. 100, 101.   [2] Ibid, p. 108.

[3] "We only propose that the Holy Scriptures may be publicly read every Sabbath in the worship of God, which is not practised in other churches of New England at this time ; and that we may lay aside the relation of experiences which are imposed in other churches, in order to the admission of persons to the Lord's table." Extract from the Letter of Invitation to Mr. Colman ; Drake's History of Boston, p. 519. It is not surprising that this church in later years drifted still farther from orthodoxy. It is now the well known Brattle Street Unitarian Church.—ED.

to have the chief hand in publishing an anonymous answer to President Mather's vindication of their former order. And a discourse was printed in London, in 1700, written by Mr. Solomon Stoddard, of Northampton, wherein he blends the Jewish and Christian dispensations together, in such a manner as to hold, that as all who were circumcised were obliged to keep the passover, so all who have been baptized ought to come to the Lord's Supper, yea, "*though they know themselves to be in a natural condition.*" And by confounding the work of Jewish and Christian officers together, he asserted that the power of admitting, censuring, and restoring members, is wholly invested in the elders, so that, "the brethren of the church are not to intermeddle with it." When any of them were unjustly dealt with, they might appeal to a classical, provincial and national judicature. And says he, " A national synod is the highest ecclesiastical authority upon earth. . . . . Every man must stand to the judgment of the national synod ; Deut. xvii. 12."[1]

These are the words of a minister of great note in New England, whose doctrine has had an extensive spread therein ever since. Yet these are some of the main principles that formerly brought on the antichristian apostasy ; and no text in the bible could be more aptly turned to favor their bloody persecutions than the one here brought to prove his last point. For it says, " The man that will do presumptuously, and will not hearken unto the priest, or unto the judge, even that man shall die." The priest was to explain God's law, and the judge was to carry the same into execution. This is the very passage that the ministers brought in 1668, to prove that the Baptists in Boston ought to be banished.[2] But Dr. Owen, in his piece upon toleration in 1648, truly observed, that, as God was the head and lawgiver of that nation, idolatry, blasphemy, or seducing of others from his worship, were capital crimes ; and that applying of those

[1] Stoddard on Instituted Churches, pp. 12, 21, 29, 33.   [2] See p. 307.

laws to cases of worship or discipline in other nations, with
the infliction of any other punishment than death, was
nothing but arbitrary proceedings. To which I may add,
that Jesus Christ, and souls who are born again, are all the
priests that are named in the New Testament; 1 Pet. i. 23;
ii. 5; and the name is never applied therein to officers, in
distinction from other saints. Men who have tried to take
the power of church government out of the hands of the
saints, in particular churches, have never been able to fix
any rational bounds to it elsewhere. A synod of each nation is the bounds that Mr. Stoddard proposed in this piece,
but would exclude the English bishops therefrom, because
they are not chosen by the church, but the State;[1] but they
were for other measures.

When his book was published in London, a small Episcopal society in Boston was the only one of that denomination
in all New England. But on June 16, 1701, a charter was
procured, to incorporate a society to propagate (what they
called) the gospel in foreign parts. And they sent over missionaries, and got their matters in such forwardness, in about
twelve years, as to obtain an order from the Crown to bring
a bill into Parliament, to establish Episcopacy in America;
and its speedy accomplishment was expected, when Divine
Providence prevented it by the sudden death of Queen Anne,
August 1, 1714. And the two succeeding princes did not
see cause to revive that scheme.[2] In 1701, the two eldest
ministers in this province published their testimony for the
ancient order of these churches, and against growing declen-
sions and corruptions; namely, Mr. John Higginson, of Salem, aged 85; and Mr. William Hubbard,[3] of Ipswich, aged
80; wherein they give their particular approbation of President Mather's vindication of that order.[4] In 1702, Mather

[1]Stoddard on Instituted Churches, p. 30.
[2]Chandler's Appeal, 1767, pp. 50—54. [3]The historian so often quoted.
[4]See Wise's works, [A vindication of the Government of New England Churches.
By John Wise, A. M., Pastor of a church in Ipswich.] pp. 68—74.

published another book, entitled, "The Glory Departing from New England;" wherein he says :—

Alas ! what a change is there in that which hath been our glory ! ....
What a glorious presence of Christ was there in all his ordinances ! Many were converted, and willingly declared what God had done for their souls ; and there were added to the churches daily such as should be saved. ....
There is sad cause to fear, that greater departures of the glory are hastening upon us.   Neither our civil or ecclesiastical state is ever like to be what it once was.[1]

The Massachusetts Legislature, which met October 15, 1702, made a long preamble about some irreligious towns, that refused or neglected to receive and support orthodox ministers ; upon which they added another law to empower the County Courts, after fining such assessors as did not fulfill their orders, to appoint others to do it, and then to procure a warrant from two Justices of the Quorum, requiring the constables of delinquent towns or districts to collect such taxes, upon the same penalty as for other taxes ; and the fines imposed upon delinquent officers were to go to pay these new assessors for their service ; and the ministers, who were thus supported, were then contriving to get a classical judicature established over the churches. They drew up proposals for associations to be formed in each county, who should have the power of licensing candidates for the ministry, and of directing particular societies, in the call and settlement of ministers ; to which was to be added a Standing Council, whose sentence should be final and decisive, but not without the concurrence of the majority of the pastors present. A number of ministers signed these proposals November 5, 1705, a hundred years to a day after the gunpowder plot was to have blown up the Parliament in Westminster. They were sent round for others to sign, in order to their being presented to the Legislature. But Mr. John Wise had been so well taught, by the briers and thorns of tyranny,[2] that, instead of signing them, he wrote a sharp

---

[1]Christian History, Vol. I, pp. 102, 103.   [2]See page 417.

answer to them ;[1] and though he was forced to send into another colony to get it printed, yet their design was defeated thereby. The ancient church of Plymouth changed their way of receiving members, from verbal to written relations, in this month of November, 1705.[2]

Dartmouth and Tiverton, where the Quakers were the majority, were put to trouble, from time to time, because they did not receive and support such ministers as others called orthodox ; and they also met with ill treatment elsewhere. An old law was in force in Connecticut, entitled, Heretics, which forbade any town or person to entertain any Quaker, upon penalty of five pounds a week, and required that they should be imprisoned and sent out of the Colony ; that none should hold unnecessary discourse with them, upon penalty of twenty shillings ; that none, except rulers and ministers, should keep any Quaker books, upon penalty of ten shillings, and that all such books should be suppressed ; and that no master of any vessel should land any Quakers, without carrying them away again, under the penalty of twenty pounds. And though this law was not rigorously executed, yet it was not repealed ; therefore their friends in London made application, in 1704, to the Presbyterian, Congregational, and Baptist ministers there, desiring that, as they would shew themselves friends to equal liberty, they would use their influence in their favor, and apply to the queen for a repeal of said law. This was thought not to be so agreeable, as to try for a reformation in New England ; and therefore said ministers in London wrote, to some ministers of

---

[1]This treatise bore the following title :—" The Churches' Quarrel Espoused, or a Reply, in Satyr, to certain Proposals made in answer to this Question : What further steps are to be taken that the Councils may have due constitution and efficacy in supporting, preserving and well-ordering the interest of the Churches in the country? By John Wise, A. M., Pastor of a Church in Ipswich,

' Wherefore rebuke them sharply, that they may be sound in the faith.'

Abjiciendus pudor quoties urget necessitas?"—ED.

[2]Plymouth Register, p. 31. [Massachusetts Historical Collections, Vol. IV. p. 138.]

influence here, a letter to be communicated to others, where-in they said :—

> We cannot but judge it disagreeable with the spirit and principles of the gospel, and an encroachment upon the divine prerogative and the undoubted rights of mankind, to punish any for their conscientious and peaceable dissent from the established way of religion, while they are not justly chargeable with any immorality, or what is plainly destructive of civil society.[1]

But as that law was not repealed here, the queen and Council repealed it, October 11, 1705 ; a copy of which act was published by John Rogers, of New London, soon after; and the same is in a late history.[2]

In the beginning of the year 1705, such a revival of religion was granted in Taunton, in the county of Bristol, as turned the minds of the people there in general from vain companies, and many immoralities, to an earnest attention to religious worship and conversation.[3] Some things of like nature appeared in Boston, and in several other places. About the same time, Elder Valentine Wightman,[4] from North Kingstown, went and settled at Groton, seven miles north of New London, where he became pastor of the first Baptist church in Connecticut. For some years they were oppressed by the ruling party; but in his latter days they enjoyed liberty, and also much of a divine blessing. He ministered there to good purpose for more than forty years, and died June 9, 1747, as his son who succeeds him informs me. Their brethren at Boston, being destitute of a pastor, wrote again to England for help, from whence a number of ministers sent them the following answer :—

> To the church of Christ, baptized on profession of their faith, in Boston, New England :
>
> London, March 17, 1706–7.
>
> DEAR BRETHREN :—We are heartily concerned for you, since we have heard of your being destitute of a pastor ; and are so much the more troubled, because we cannot think of a minister, who is at liberty, proper for you. We are glad to hear that you find so much kindness among the

[1]Calamy's Abridgment, p. 671.   [2]Douglas, Vol. II, pp. 389, 340.
[3]Christian History, Vol. II, pp. 108—112.   [4]See page 322, note.—ED.

ministers of another denomination, that they are willing to assist you, and should more rejoice to hear you had a minister well qualified of your own persuasion ; but at present we can serve you no otherwise than to pray for you that you may have an agreeable settlement ; that you may increase both in knowledge and grace, and may adorn the doctrine of our God and Saviour, by a holy conversation. So pray, dear brethren, your brethren and servants in the gospel of Jesus Christ,

NATHANIEL WYLES,	RICHARD ADAMS,
RICHARD PARKES,	JOHN PIGGOT,
JOSEPH STENNETT,	BENJAMIN STINTON,
NATHANIEL HODGES,	RICHARD ALLEN.
JOSEPH MASTERS,	

The Baptist church which was formed at Kittery, in 1682,[1] returned again to their connection with the church at Boston, and Mr. Drown moved there, whose son Shem was long serviceable in the office of deacon among them. Elder Screven went to South Carolina, to whom the church at Boston now wrote ; and on June 2, 1707, he returned an answer, wherein he said :—

Dearly beloved, this may inform you, that I have many thoughts of heart about you, and am much concerned for you ; and hope I may say, my prayers are to God for you, though I am not with you ; nor can I come as I was inclined to do, our help being taken from us ; for our minister who came from England is dead, and I can by no means be spared. I must say it is a great loss, and to me a great disappointment, but the will of the Lord is done. I have longed to hear that you was supplied with an able minister, who might break the bread of life among you ; but if the Lord do not please to supply you in the way you expected, your way will be to improve the gifts you have in the church. Brother Callender and Joseph Russell, I know, have gifts that may tend to edification, if improved. I think you should call one or both of them to it.

They did so to Mr. Callender, as appears by a letter from Charleston, South Carolina, to him, of August 6, 1708, which mentions it ;[2] and the letter closes thus :—

I have been brought very low by sickness ; but I bless God I was helped to preach and administer the communion last Lord's day, but am still weak.

[1] See page 405.
[2] "I rejoice that you are inclined to, and employed in, the blessed work of the Lord for the support of his cause, and the comfort of his saints left of a poor, languish

Our society are for the most part in health, and I hope thriving in grace. We are about ninety in all. I rest your affectionate brother and fellow-laborer, in the best of services, for the best reward,

WILLIAM SCREVEN.

We must now consider how error had a further spread in this country. Mr. Stoddard published a sermon from Exod. xii. 47, 48, wherein he says, "A minister who knows him-self unregenerate, may nevertheless lawfully administer bap-tism and the Lord's Supper. Men who are destitute of saving grace may preach the gospel, and therefore adminis-ter and so partake of the Lord's Supper." President Mather answered him in 1708, when he said of this passage, " I am mistaken if in this logic there is not sophistry." But the misery of both of them was, an entanglement in an incon-sistent scheme. The advocates for the Half-way Covenant in 1662, said, we know of no stronger argument for infant baptism than this, that church members are to be baptized ;[1] and now Stoddard says, "This sacrament is a converting ordi-nance to church members only, and not for other men. The children of God's people should be baptized, which are gen-erally at that time in a natural condition." Upon which his opponent says, " We are to judge as charitably of the child as we do of the parent. We baptize them as being disci-ples and believers, and visibly belonging to the kingdom of heaven ; Dr. Goodwin says, the infants of believers are the purest part of the church."[2]

How imperfect is human knowledge! Stoddard pub-lished a reply in 1709, wherein all his arguments turn upon these points, viz., that " if unsanctified persons might law-fully come to the passover, then such [they] may lawfully

ing church with you; as it must and will, with the blessing of God, be, if you have the blessed ordinances of the holy Jesus among you again. . . . . I pray God to be with your spirit and strengthen you to the great work to which you are called; and that the little vine may be flourishing under your hand." Extract from Screven's letter to Callender; Rev. S. Hall's Collection of Papers.—ED.

[1] See page 268.

[2] Stoddard's Sermon, pp. 13, 27; Mather's answer, pp. 67, 68.

come to the Lord's Supper; and they who [do] convey to their children a right to [the sacrament of] baptism, have a right themselves to the Lord's Supper, provided they carry inoffensively."[1] He could plainly see that there was no half-way in the Jewish church; and his opponent could see as plainly, that fruits meet for repentance were required in order for baptism, even of such as were in the covenant of circumcision. But as tradition had taught them both to build the Christian church upon that covenant, neither of them could act consistently thereon; though they were two of the most eminent ministers then in New England. Most of their successors have held fast their errors, but not their virtues. And as these things shew how the churches were corrupted, so what follows discovers how they were enslaved.

The third Governor Winthrop[2] died November 27, 1707, upon which a special meeting of the Assembly of Connecticut was called on December 17, to choose them another Governor. By a law then in force, he was to be elected out of a certain number of men in previous nomination; but they broke over those limits, and elected an ordained minister of New London for their Governor; who, when they sent an account of it to him, readily quitted the solemn charge of souls, for worldly promotion, and was sworn into his new office, January 1, 1708; after which they repealed the law that they had before broken, and enacted that for the future, the Governor might be chosen out of any of the freemen.[3] Mr. Gurdon Saltonstall, son to a Massachusetts magistrate, and a graduate of Harvard College, was the Governor thus chosen, and by annual elections he was continued in that office for sixteen years. He was a great politician, and he exerted all his influence to raise ministerial power as high as possible. He took the proposals of 1705, and pre-

[1] Appeal to the Learned, pp. 50, 89.
[2] Fitz John Winthrop. See p. 430.—ED.
[3] Trumbull's History of Connecticut, Vol. I, Chapter XVIII, pp. 431, 432.—ED.

sented them to their Legislature, where their unscriptural form was soon taken notice of ; for there was not a text of Scripture in the whole scheme.   Perceiving that it could not be received so, it was withdrawn without much noise, and the following method was taken to carry his point.   An act was passed by the Assembly that met at Hartford, May 13, 1708, which says :—

This Assembly, from their own observation, and from the complaint of [many] others, being made sensible of the defects of the discipline of the churches of this government, arising from the want of a more explicit asserting the rules given for that end in the holy Scriptures, from which would arise a firm [permanent] establishment amongst ourselves, a good and regular issue in cases subject to ecclesiastical discipline, glory to Christ our Head, and edification to his members ;[1] hath seen fit to ordain and require, and it is by authority of the same ordained and required, that the ministers of the churches, in the several counties of this government, shall meet together at their respective county towns, with such messengers as the churches to which they belong shall see cause to send with them, on the last Monday in June next, there to consider and agree upon those methods and rules for the management of ecclesiastical discipline, which by them shall be judged agreeable and conformable to the word of God ; and shall at the same meeting appoint two or more of their number to be their delegates, who shall all meet together at Saybrook at the next Commencement to be held there,[2] where they shall compare the results of the ministers of the several counties, and out of and from them to draw a form of ecclesiastical discipline.

This was to be presented to the Assembly for their acceptance, and the expense of those meetings was to be borne out of the Colony treasury.   This order was obeyed ; and the ministers who met at Saybrook, September 9, 1708, adopted the Confession of Faith that was composed at the Savoy in London, 1658,[3] and the heads of agreement en-

[1]Church and State are here confounded together; as if a being members of the civil community, made men members of Christ, and him their Head.

[2]This was the Commencement of the "Collegiate School of the Colony of Connecticut," afterwards Yale College, which was founded at Saybrook and continued there till 1716.—Ed.

[3]The Savoy Confession of Faith was drawn up and adopted by an assembly of the ministers and messengers of Independent churches. It is a modification of the Westminster Confession, omitting from that the articles relating to church discipline, and adding instead a few articles affirming and explaining Independency. Neal's History of the Puritans, Toulmin's edition, Vol. IV, pp. 213—218.—Ed.

tered into between Presbyterians and Independents in London, 1690, and then added fifteen articles concerning church discipline, which were the proposals of 1705 new modeled, with Scripture references annexed to each article ; though a gentleman of that day observed, that the text which speaks of Balaam's saddling his ass would have been as much to the purpose as many they brought. Their second article, which contains a summary of the whole scheme, is in these words, viz. :—

That the churches, which are neighboring each to other, shall consociate for mutual affording to each other such assistance as may be requisite, upon all occasions ecclesiastical ; and that the particular pastors and churches, within the respective counties in this government, shall be one Consociation (or more if they shall judge meet) for the end aforesaid. Psalm cxxii. 3—5 ; cxxxiii. 1 ; Eccl. iv. 9—12 ; Acts xv. 2, 6, 22, 23 ; I Tim. iv. 14 ; I Cor. xvi. 1.[1]

The first of these texts speaks of princes on their thrones, and not of church officers. And when we come to the antetype of Aaron's and David's line, we find none therein but Jesus Christ, and regenerate souls. Officers, as distinguished from other saints in the Christian church, are never called priests nor kings in the New Testament. And, said an eminent father of New England, " The order of officers in the church is an order of servants, and the order of saints an order of kings (which is the highest order in the church) sitting upon the thrones of David for judgment, whom the ministers are to serve, in guiding and going before them in, and ministering of, their judgments."[2] Their second proof refers to the unity of brethren under our great High Priest, who most explicitly excludes all striving about who shall be the greatest from his kingdom. Neither is the third text any more to their purpose. The fourth gives an account of the meeting of one church, at the request of another two hundred miles off, upon a special occasion, and not of the

[1]Trumbull's History of Connecticut, Vol. I, Chapter XIX, pp. 481—483.—Ed.
[2]Robinson against Bernard, p. 227. [Works of John Robinson, Vol. II, p. 238.]

meeting of neighboring churches upon all occasions ecclesiastical.   The last two treat of gifts received by prophecy,
and of orders given to the churches by apostolic authority ;
and until ordinary ministers can prove that they, as such,
are princes on their thrones, and are endowed with apostolic
authority over the churches, we may safely conclude that
the above application of Scriptures was a perverting of them
from their genuine meaning and design.   Yet thereby two
kinds of judicatures were set up over the churches.   The
one called Consociations, consisting of ministers meeting in
their own persons, and churches by their messengers, whereof each church may send one or two, though the want of
them is not to invalidate the acts of any council ; but none
of their acts are esteemed valid without the concurrence of
the majority of the pastors present.   They are the Standing
Council within each circuit upon all occasions ecclesiastical,
though in cases of special difficulty they may call the next
Consociation to sit and act with them.   They are to have a
new choice of messengers and moderators once a year, if
not oftener, and the last moderator is to call a new meeting
when it is judged proper.   Their sentence is to be final and
decisive.   Their other judicatures are called Associations,
which are meetings of ministers by themselves in each circuit, as often as they think proper, to hear and answer questions of importance, to examine and license candidates for
the ministry, to receive complaints from individuals or societies, and to direct to the calling of the Council to try the
same, when they judge proper; to direct destitute churches
in calling and settling of pastors, and to make complaint
to their Legislature against such as they judge to be negligent of their duty in that respect.   And each Association
sends a delegate or two to a General Association once a year,
from all parts of that government.

    This scheme was not introduced without glaring deceit ;
for their Fourth Article says, "that according to the common
practice of our churches, nothing shall be deemed an act or

judgment of any council, which hath not the major part of the elders present, concurring. and such a number of the messengers present, as makes the majority of the council,"[1] whereas this practice was so far from being common, that it was an innovation then made, directly subversive of the fundamental principles of the New England churches ;[2] as we are assured by Mr. Wise, Dr. Mather, and others. No man knew better what those principles were than Mr. Thomas Hooker, the first minister of Hartford ; and he is full in it, that, though it is expedient on special occasions to call councils or synods, yet elders act therein as commissioners sent, and not as pastors ; and that other messengers sent have equal power with them.[3]   Says he, " God hath set officers in the church ; I Cor. xii. 28 ; therefore the church is before officers."   And from Matt. xviii. 15—18, and I Cor. v. 12, he concludes, " that each man and member of the society, in a just way, may be directed, censured, reformed or removed, by the power of the whole, and each may and should judge with the consent of the whole.   This belongs to all the members, and therefore to any that shall be in office, if they be members.   They are superior as officers, when they keep the rule ; but inferior as members, and in subjection to any when they break the rule. . . . . Christ gave some to be pastors, some to be teachers.   He alone, out of his supreme and regal power. doth furnish them with graces and abilities, appoints the work, lays out the compass thereof, the manner of dispensing, and the order and bounds of their dispensation."   And he observes, that to remove the power of censure from a particular church, leads into endless disputes ; because no General Council was called in the

[1]Trumbull's History of Connecticut, Vol. I, Chapter XIX, p. 483.—Ed.

[2]Mr. Backus seems to have misapprehended the force of the above Article. It does not state that it had been the common practice of the churches, to hold ecclesiastical councils, or to allow them the authority which they afterwards exercised, but only that it had been the common practice of the churches to require a majority vote of both the elders and messengers in order to the validity of any act.—Ed.

[3]Survey of Church Discipline, Part I, p. 119.

first three centuries, and no man can tell as there will ever be another.[1] Says he, " The truth is, a particular congregation is the highest tribunal, unto which the grieved party may appeal in the third place, if private council, or the witnesses of two, have seemed to proceed too [much] sharply. If difficulties arise in proceeding, the council of other churches should be sought to clearthe truth ; but the power of censure rests in the congregation, where Christ placed it. . . . . The churches sent them, and therefore are above them."[2] Yet now the churches were not allowed the power to say whether their ministers should meet at Saybrook, or not; and the result of their meeting being laid before the Legislature of October 14, 1708, they said :—

This Assembly do [doth] declare their great approbation of such a happy agreement, and do ordain that all the churches within this government, that are or shall be thus united, in doctrine, worship and discipline, be, and for the future shall be owned and acknowledged, established by law, provided always, that nothing herein shall be intended and construed to hinder or prevent any society or church, that is or shall be allowed by the laws of this government, who soberly differ or dissent from the united churches hereby established, from exercising worship and discipline in their own way, according to their consciences.[3]

Thus artfully was this new scheme established, and all others declared to be no more than allowed or tolerated.

Mr. John Woodward, another Cambridge scholar, was then minister of Norwich ; and he soon got and read off to his congregation the first part of this act, but without the proviso. Richard Bushnel and Joseph Backus,[4] Esquires, who had opposed that scheme in the Assembly, informed their church of the liberty that they had to dissent from it ; but the minister carried a major vote against them ; therefore those representatives, and other fathers of the town, withdrew from that tyranny, and held worship by themselves

[1]Survey of Church Discipline, Part I, pp. 119, 188, 190, 232, 238.
[2]Ibid, Part IV, pp. 19, 47.
[3]Trumbull's History of Connecticut, Vol. I, Chapter XIX, p. 487.—ED.
[4]Joseph Backus was the author's grandfather.—ED.

for three months. For this, the minister and his party censured them ; an account of which being sent to the next
meeting of the Assembly, they were expelled therefrom.
Hereby we may see how far corruption had prevailed in our
land. For in 1641, three years after the first taxing law for
ministers was made in New England, a law was made at
Boston, which said, "·No church censure shall degrade or
depose any man from any civil dignity, office or authority,
he shall have in the Commonwealth."[1] How much more
equitable was this, than another law in Connecticut, which
said :—

Whatsoever persons shall on the Lord's day, under any pretence whatsoever, assemble themselves together in any of the public meeting-houses,
provided in any town, parish or society, for the public worship of God,
without leave or allowance of the minister and congregation for whose use
it was provided, and be thereof convict, every such person shall incur the
penalty of ten shillings for every such offence. Nor shall any persons
neglect the public worship of God in some lawful congregation, and form
themselves into separate companies in private houses, on penalty of ten shillings for every such offence.

This part concerning separate meetings caused sore exercises to many serious minds, and great difficulties in procuring civil officers ; yet it was never repealed until October,
1770. But not long after the Norwich minister had censured their representatives, he consented to refer the matter
to a council ; and they followed it, with council after council, for about six years. Governor Saltonstall came there
himself upon one of those occasions ; and Mr. Stoddard of
Northampton was Moderator of the last but one of those
councils. My grandfather went a journey as far as Boston
and Ipswich, a hundred and thirty miles, to consult with Mr.
Wise and the two Mathers upon these affairs. At last, by
advice of a council that met August 31, 1716, said minister
was dismissed, and the church in Norwich determined to
abide upon their ancient foundation. And it was known
that when the church was constituted at Saybrook, in 1660,

[1] Massachusetts Law-book, printed 1672, p. 44.

with the approbation of other ministers, Mr. James Fitch
was ordained their pastor, by the laying on of the hands
only of their two deacons, as a token that the power of
ordination is in the church as a body. They came and
planted Norwich the same year; and Mr. Fitch was continued one of the most useful ministers in Connecticut for
near fifty years. The church in East Windsor, under the
care of Mr. Timothy Edwards, father of Mr. Jonathan, also
refused to receive the Saybrook Platform. And the temper
of those who introduced it farther appears by the incorporating act of the town of Killingly, passed in May, 1708;
which says, " No person now inhabiting on said lands, or
any other persons dwelling without this colony, who have
purchased any lands within the said township, that shall not
give due obedience to all the laws of this colony for the upholding the worship of God, and paying all public charges,
shall have any benefit by this act." At the same time they
gave their Governor two hundred acres of land therein.
This account is carefully taken from the public records and
laws, and other authentic vouchers.

A few things concerning baptism shall close this chapter.
An aged and honorable gentleman near Piscataqua River
informed me, that about the year 1710, a number of people
in Dover[1] were so fully persuaded that they ought, in a literal sense, to be buried in baptism, that on a Lord's day
and the day after, Mr. Pike, their minister, baptized nine
persons in that way, in a branch of that river. But such a
noise was made, and opposition raised against it, as prevented any further proceedings therein. About the same time
a Baptist meeting was set up at Scituate, in the county of
Plymouth, where President Dunstar spent his latter days to
good purpose.[2] Mr. John Peirce preached to them for some
time, until he and others removed to Swanzey, in or about
1711, and on October 19, 1715, he was ordained a pastor of

---

[1] Mr. Hansard Knollys was minister there, from the spring of 1638 to the fall of
1641. See pp. 81, 82.

[2] See pp. 255, 256.

the second church there, colleague with Elder Joseph Mason, who was ordained in July, 1709. And they continued in good esteem in their offices, until Elder Mason died, May 19, 1748, and Elder Peirce, September 8, 1750, being each of them near ninety years old. On March 16, 1714, Dr. Cotton Mather wrote the letter to the Baptist church in Boston, which is in page 420; subscribed thus, viz., "To my worthy friend, Mr. Ellis Callender, elder of a church of Christ in Boston." He joined it in 1669; was a leading member of it when the Court nailed up their meeting-house in 1680; and he was continued a great blessing to them until he died in a good old age, after the year 1726.

CHAPTER X.

Governor Lyndon informed me, that when the Quakers were hanged at Boston, a view of the cruelty then exercised towards them, and of their behavior under their sufferings, moved Peter Wanton to join with that people. And his son Joseph was a teacher among them in Tiverton for many years; whose daughter Richardson told me, that, during Governor Dudley's administration, her father was frequently sent to Boston, to defend his town against the arbitrary claims of other ministers; and that the Governor privately favored him therein. Some extracts from the records of the Quaker society show, that in 1707, a cow worth three pounds, was taken from John Packom, of Little Compton, for a ministerial tax of six shillings and twopence; and that their monthly meeting on Rhode Island, in the seventh month, 1708, sent Joseph Wanton with an address to Governor Dudley, " desiring relief from sufferings for priests' rates, by a repeal of those laws; " informing him that if it was not done here, they thought it their duty to address the British Court upon it. A like application was afterwards made by the hand of Ebenezer Slocum, who reported to a meeting in 1709, that the Governor appeared kind and friendly; but as no relief was granted, they then sent to England upon those matters.   By the same records we are informed, that in 1716, five cows and calves, worth twenty-five pounds, were taken from Peleg Slocum, and twenty-four sheep worth eight pounds, eight shillings, from John and Abraham Tucker, all upon Slocum's Island, and near all for " a demand of Priest Holmes, of· Chilmark," to which town said island belonged, although the great channel betwixt the main and Martha's Vineyard must be crossed to get to it. However, ministers were far from being content with all the power they had yet obtained, and therefore presented a petition to their Legislature, that they would call a General Synod; doubtless to revise and carry into effect the proposals of 1705.   The Council voted to grant their petition, but it was not concurred with by the other branches of the Legislature.[1]   And two excellent ministers had such a sight of their danger, as to write the following letter to Mr. Wise.

Gloucester, March 25, 1715.

REVEREND SIR :—We have had the favor and satisfaction of reading, and, according to our measure, considering, the transcendent logic, as well as grammar and rhetoric, of your Reply to the Proposals, by which our eyes are open to see much more than ever before we saw of the value and glory of our invaded privileges; and are of opinion, that if your consent may be obtained to a new edition, it may be of wonderful service to our churches, if God shall please to go forth with it.   However, it will be a testimony that all our watchmen were not asleep, nor the camp of Christ surprised and taken before they had warning.   We are, Reverend Sir, full of dutiful respect and gratitude, your sons and servants,

SAMUEL MOODY,
JOHN WHITE.

It was reprinted accordingly; and, with Mr. Wise's other works, it had two editions more in 1773, upon an occasion which will then be mentioned.   These two ministers lived to see and rejoice in the glorious work of divine grace,

[1] Douglas, Vol. II, p. 378.

which was granted in New England, in and after the year
1740.   Mr. Moody was minister at York, beyond Piscataqua
River.   He preached without notes, and refused to be supported by tax and compulsion ; and was the most powerful
and successful preacher of almost any in the land in those
days.

Such opposition was raised against Governor Dudley, that
he was removed, and never acted with our Legislature after
August, 1715 ; and when they met again November 23, with
the pliant Lieutenant Governor Taylor in the chair, the following act was added to their other taxing laws, viz.:—

AN ACT FOR MAINTAINING AND PROPAGATING OF RELIGION.

Whereas the laws of this province have made good and wholesome provision, that every town within the same be continually supplied with an able,
learned, orthodox minister or ministers, of good conversation, to dispense
the word of God unto them ; and that such minister or ministers be suitably encouraged, and sufficiently supported and maintained, by the inhabitants of such towns ; for the rendering the said laws more effectual, and to
prevent the growth of atheism, irreligion and profaneness : Be it enacted
and ordained by the Lieutenant Governor, Council, and Representatives,
in General Court assembled, and by the authority of the same, that the
Justices of the Court of General Sessions of the Peace, within the several
counties, at the opening of their Courts from time to time, do give in special
charge to the Grand Jury, to make diligent inquiry and presentment of all
towns and districts within such county, that are destitute of a minister, as
by law is directed ; and of such towns and districts that neglect to fulfill
their contracts and agreements, and do not make suitable provision for the
support and maintenance of their minister or ministers accordingly.   And
upon such presentment, complaint, or information in any other manner,
the Court are directed and required vigorously to put the laws in execution,
for the redressing of all defects and neglects of that kind,[1] and forthwith
to make the necessary orders to that end, as by law they are empowered.
And in case their orders, so made, be not duly observed, or by the contriv-
ance and practice of ill men be eluded and rendered ineffectual ; for the
speedy remedying and reforming of so great an evil, the Justices of such
Court are to represent and make report of their proceedings unto the next
session of the General Court or Assembly.

[1]From Scripture and all experience it plainly appears, that ministers have been
as often guilty of defects and neglects as the people ; but they made no law to punish ministers therefor ; which partiality promoted atheism and irreligion, instead of
preventing it.

31

Upon this the Assembly were to send a minister, recommended by three others, to every such town or district, and to provide for his "honorable maintenance," by adding a sufficient sum for the purpose to the province tax upon such places; and were to do the like to each place that neglected to fulfill former contracts with ministers; as also to "supply and support a minister in places that are destitute, where the Justices neglect their duty." All which sums their ministers were to draw out of the province treasury. This act was made for seven years, and then was revived and continued till 1730; and that method of charging the Grand Jury has been continued ever since.

Rhode Island Colony was now ruled by Governor Cranston, and Deputy Governor Jencks, in conjunction with other worthy men, under whose administration they enjoyed the greatest peace, for above thirty years, that they ever did since they were a distinct government. And for the continuance of the same, and to prevent any society or sect from trying for any preëminence in the government, their Assembly of May 2, 1716, enacted, "that what maintenance or salary may be thought necessary by any of the churches, congregations, or societies of people, now inhabiting, or that hereafter shall or may inhabit, within the same, for the support of their respective minister or ministers, shall be raised by free contribution, and no otherways." This law is still in force; and we shall presently hear a number of ministers commending the good fruits of these measures, which yet they were very unwilling to come into.

President Mather published another piece in 1716, wherein he says:—

For ministers to pretend to a negative voice in synods, or for councils to take upon them to determine what elders or messengers a church shall submit unto, without the choice of the church concerned, or for ministers to pretend to be members of a council without any mission from their churches, nay, although the church declares that they will not send them, is prelatical, and essentially differing not only from Congregational, but from Presbyterian principles.   And now that I am going out of the world, I could not die in peace, if I did not discharge my conscience, in bearing witness against such innovations and invasions on the rights and privileges belonging to particular congregations of Christ.[1]

Yet all these innovations and invasions were made in the Saybrook scheme.   And to shew that brethren, when chosen by the church, have a right to equal votes in Councils with elders, he says :—

There are mechanics, who although they do not excel in that which is called human learning, are well versed and learned in the Scriptures, spending much time in consulting those oracles of God, and being men of great piety, and excellent natural accomplishments, they may be very useful in synods.   Ecclesiastical historians give a remarkable account of what happened in the Nicene Synod.   A pious old man, who was no clergyman, nor exercised philosophical notions, by his plain discourse did more towards the conviction of an heretical philosopher, than all the learned bishops in the Council could do.[2]

These things naturally led him and his brethren into another sort of behavior towards the Baptists, than when he was Scribe of the Synod of 1769, who declared that they were setting up their posts by God's posts; which moved the Court to nail up the doors of the Baptist meeting-house. For Elder Callender's son Elisha was added to the church under his father's care, August 10, 1713; after which[3] he was educated at Harvard College, and called into the gospel ministry; and, as President Mather had expressed his willingness for such a thing to Elder Callender, his church called the President, his son, and Mr. John Webb, to assist in ordaining Mr. Elisha Callender, as pastor of the Baptist

---

[1] Disquisition concerning Ecclesiastical Councils, Preface, p. 13.

[2] Ibid., p. 19.

[3] "His son, Elisha Callender, became his successor in the pastoral office. He had received a liberal education at Harvard College, and was one of the fourteen students who were graduated in the year 1710. He was baptized and received into the church August 10, 1713..... Mr. Backus observes, ... that Mr. Callender received his education at Harvard College *after* he had joined the church; but in this he must be mistaken.   Historical Sketch of the First Baptist church in Boston; James M. Winchell; p. 21.—ED.

church in Boston, May 21, 1718.   And Dr. Cotton Mather, in the Ordination Sermon, said :—

It is very sadly true, that many ecclesiastical communities, wherein piety has its votaries, yet are guilty of this evil, that they impose terms of communion which many that have the fear of God, are, by just exceptions, kept from complying withal.   Now in this unhappy case what is to be done?   Do this ; let good men go as far as they can without sin, in holding communion with one another.   But where sinful terms are imposed, there let them make their stops ; there a separation becomes a duty ; there the injunction of heaven upon them is, " Be ye separate saith the Lord, and touch not the unclean thing, and I will receive you."   The imposers are the schismatics.   There have been many attempts to unite people in forms and terms, that are not the pure maxims of living unto God ; and so to build the tower of Zion on a foundation which is not the tried stone and the precious, and so not the sure foundation.   There has hitherto been a blast from heaven upon all these attempts ; they have miscarried, as being rather calculated for the tower of Babel.   New England also has, in some former times, done something of this aspect, which would not now be so well approved of ; in which, if the brethren, in whose house we are now convened, met with any thing too unbrotherly, they now with satisfaction hear us expressing our dislike of every thing that looked like persecution in the days that have passed over us.[1]

The case of a member who soon after joined that church, I think proper here to mention.   Samuel Jennings, Esq., was born in Sandwich, in the county of Barnstable, February 19, 1685, where he lived till he was above eighteen years old, and then went a voyage to sea, where he was pressed on board a man-of-war.   But meeting with very ill treatment there for five months, he, in the evening of March 26, 1704, the ship being in a bay at Barbados, attempted to make his escape therefrom by swimming ; but by the way he was seized and hauled under water by a shark.   A terrible case indeed !   Yet, as he cried to God for help, the venomous creature let him go, and his life was preserved, with the loss only of a part of a foot and an arm.[2]   He returned, married,

---

[1] See pp. 420, 422.

[2] " I had not swum far before I saw a shark, just as he took hold of my left hand. He pulled me under water in a moment. .... I thought of a knife I used to carry in my pocket, but remembered I left it on board.   Then I kicked him several times

and lived in good repute in his native town, which he represented several times in our Legislature. After he had served them two years in that office, he wrote as follows concerning his soul affairs.   Says he :—

Though I had heard much preaching, and read many books, to support the baptizing of infants, and had never read any books, or discoursed on that head with any that were against it, yet I found so much in the Scripture to the contrary, that I could not believe it to be right.   Notwithstanding I went to several ministers, and discoursed [with] them on that point to get light, and also prayed to God to direct me in the right way ; yet still it appeared to me unscriptural and erroneous.   Then I went to Mr. Callender, the Baptist minister at Boston, who not only discoursed with me, but lent me books set out by those of his persuasion, to support the truth thereof; which when I had read, I found so agreeable with the Scriptures, and with the apprehensions I before had from them, that I quickly sought to be admitted into the communion of that church at Boston.   And having made a verbal profession, before the church and congregation, I was baptized (that is, dipped in the water) by Mr. Elisha Callender, minister of the gospel, on the 9th day of June, 1718, in the thirty-fourth year of my age.   And truly I may say, as is said of the Ethiopian eunuch, that I came away rejoicing.   In a short time after, I arrived to a considerable degree of bodily health, which I had lacked for eight years before.

He served his town afterwards as their Representative, and in other offices ; and, without his seeking, a commission of Justice of the Peace was sent him, which, for some reasons, he chose not to accept.   He continued a member of said church in Boston till his death in 1764.

Soon after Mr. Callender was ordained, he opened a correspondence with friends in London, which, with other means, had very great and extensive effects.   Thomas Hollis,

with my right foot, but that proving ineffectual, I set my foot against his mouth, intending to haul my hand away or to haul it off.   Then he opened his mouth a little and took part of my foot into his mouth with my hand and held them both.   Then I cried to God mentally that he would have mercy on my soul, which I thought would soon be separated from my body, but still did not cease striving, but punched him with my right hand, though to little purpose.   At last, being almost drowned, for I was all this while under water, I had almost left off striving, and, expecting nothing but present death, all at once my hand and foot came loose, and I got up to the top of the water, and, having cleared my stomach of water, I called out for help, and swam towards the nearest ship."   Extract from "A Narrative of the Wonderful Escape of Samuel Jennings;" Rev. S. Hall's Collection of Papers.—ED.

Esq., one of the most liberal men upon earth, had some acquaintance with President Mather, when he was agent for this province in England;[1] and now, receiving accounts of the transactions and catholic sentiments that were delivered at the ordination of a Baptist minister in Boston, who was educated at Harvard College, he became the greatest benefactor thereto that they have ever had to this day.

> " Nor yet to Harvard all his views confin'd ;
> His active soul still nobler work designed.
> A kingdom's welfare dwelt on ev'ry thought ;
> For gen'ral good his heav'nly candor wrought ;
> To public peace his prudent schemes invite,
> Faction to quell, and clashing sects unite."[2]

With or near his first donation to the College, came the following letter from a minister of his acquaintance to his friend in Boston :—

London, March 9, 1720.

MUCH ESTEEMED BROTHER CALLENDER :—I thank you kindly for the particular account you gave me in your last ; and I cannot but lament the sad consequences of sin, and the great degrees of it which remain, even in God's own people ; for surely the greatest part, if not all those who suffered so much for their religion at home, and at last left their native country, and run such great hazards as they did for the sake of their consciences, must, in the judgment of charity, be esteemed the faithful servants of Christ.   But when I consider the methods which these took, or encouraged others to take, with those who differed from them in matters not fundamental, I cannot but wonder at the depth of folly which remains with us, that any body of men should so soon and so zealously pursue those very methods which they had so justly condemned, and so greatly suffered by ! It is a consideration enough to check the towering thoughts of vain man, and to shew the reasonableness of the apostolical advice, " Let him that

[1]Increase Mather's Life, p. 170.—B.

The words here referred to in the Life of Mather, (Parentator, &c.,) are as follows :—" When he went over to England he carried his care of his beloved College with him.   Among other expressions of it, he procured some valuable donations to it.   Yea, it was his acquaintance with, and his proposal to, that good-spirited man and lover of all good men, Mr. Thomas Hollis, that introduced his benefactions unto that College, to which his incomparable bounty has anon flowed unto such a degree as to render him the greatest benefactor it ever had in the world."--ED.

[2]Rudd's Poem on Hollis's Death, p. 29.

thinketh he standeth take heed lest he fall ;" for I think we are but too subject to the lesser degrees of this temper and carriage, in almost every station of life. For though there is so good an understanding among the three denominations of dissenters, viz., Presbyterians, Independents and Baptists ; yet we have too many who are whisperers and backbiters, who, by magnifying the weaknesses, or diminishing the real worth and usefulness of those who differ from them, shew that this spirit, as much as it is destroyed, is yet too much alive, and, were it clothed with power, would soon be formidable. But our wise and gracious Governor makes the weaknesses and wrath of men to praise him, and the remainder thereof he doth restrain.

As I heartily rejoice that the Lord hath preserved the baptized church, at Boston, through so many difficulties, so I am glad he hath raised up to them one so able and willing to promote the public good among them. May the Lord succeed you, my dear brother, that so peace and truth may spread and flourish in your days ! I am indeed troubled at the paucity[1] of those of our denomination, in New England ; though I cannot wonder at it, considering the treatment they have generally met with. I am grieved that any who profess the plain Scripture baptism should bring it into contempt, by holding with it such wild and unscriptural opinions ; but so it hath been with us, and yet remains ; though I think the number of such is diminished, within a few years last past. But although we have but few Soul-sleepers or Sabbatarians, &c., yet the number of those that plead for general redemption, and some other of the distinctive notions of Arminius, seem to increase among us. However, they seem not quite so rigid and uncharitable as formerly, and there is, I hope, the greatest number of our denomination free from these things. As to the method of educating youth among you, it must be allowed, that the design seemed to be well laid for promoting useful knowledge ; and I hope your college will be improved to a very great advantage ; but I find you have to lament, what we are not strangers to, viz., that those things which in themselves are good, and tend to fit persons for more extensive usefulness, are made necessary for a person in order to the ministry, or should be thought, at any time, to be a sufficient qualification for so great a work. Surely a man blessed with a good natural genius, who has been brought to a true sense of sin, and the saving knowledge of Jesus Christ, though he should want the advantage of human literature, must be better capable than one that has it, and is destitute of the other, to guide souls into the ways of salvation ; because, as he knows something of the deceitfulness of sin, and the wiles of Satan, so he is more capable to comfort poor souls in distress, with the comforts wherewith he himself has been comforted of God. Therefore, though I have a high esteem for human learning, and wish every minister had the advan-

[1] Fewness in number.

tage of a good degree of it, yet I conceive it is far from being necessary to a man's being employed in the public ministry, and much less do I think it, in itself, a qualification sufficient for so weighty an undertaking. You will excuse me for so freely declaring my mind upon this head.

Before this comes to hand, I hope you will have received a letter, subscribed, Thomas Hollis. This worthy gentleman is my very good friend, and one who, with his plentiful estate, has done much good among poor ministers and churches here ; and I hope New England will find yet more happy effects of his liberality, and that, with your kind assistance in finding and procuring proper objects, something may be done by him for the particular encouragement of our denomination. For, in conversing with him upon this head, he desired me to intimate to you, that he shall be well pleased, if you can find a proper person of the Baptist persuasion, for him to recommend to the governors of the college ; and I doubt not but he will give some further encouragement to such an one, who is desirous to be qualified for public usefulness. I entreat you therefore to turn your thoughts to this subject, and give me a line, so soon as you have found a fit person, that so good a work as this may be begun. I am ready to believe, that, besides Mr. Hollis's interest with the governors, in behalf of a hopeful young man, who is of our persuasion, he may be prevailed upon to allow ten pounds per annum, of your money,[1] towards defraying the charges of the college ; which will be some encouragement for one, who, with promising natural parts, is desirous to devote himself to study, in order to fit himself for public usefulness, but is not well able to go through the charge. I leave this with you, and pray God to direct you. You will find a copy of Mr. Hollis's to you ; to which I have added a catalogue of the chest of books therein mentioned ; and if any are not disposed of to the college library, yourself, &c., that then you would use your interest to obtain some of them for Mr. Daniel White.[2] When you have read Mr. Neal's History of New England, I desire you to give me your thoughts of it in general ; and if you find anything in it which deserves to be taken notice of, in order to be altered in a second edition, pray freely communicate it to me, and I will do the same to the author, who is a very honest gentleman, and will be glad to be set right, in any thing wherein he may have been mistaken. Just now a gentleman has been with me, whose name is Spurier, who hath brought some hundred tons of silver ore from New England, and desires me to assist him in presenting a petition to the government, for encouragement.[3] If you have heard any thing of any late dis-

---

[1] Mexican silver was then about thirteen shillings per ounce, in our money. Douglas, Vol. I, p. 494.

[2] Mr. White came over from Mr. Wallin's church two years before, and was then preaching at Newport. Mr. Neal's history first came over this year.

[3] Great fraud and iniquity was practised in the nation, about such things, in the year 1720.

coveries made of silver mines with you, or any thing of the character of the man, or what notion the people have of it, and will please to give me a line, it may be of use to me; for, as I would willingly serve any honest man, according to my ability, so I would gladly know the persons I move for. I am now obliged to conclude at present, and with all my heart commend you to God and the word of his grace, which is able and I hope will build you up in all things. May the Lord be with you, and the church of Christ under your care, causing all blessings to abound towards you in all things. So rests your cordial friend, and unworthy brother in the Lord's vineyard,

EDWARD WALLIN.

Before this came to hand, our friends here had sent a letter directed thus: "The church of Christ at Boston, in New England, of the faith and order of the gospel, baptizing visible believers upon the profession of their faith, and believing the principles of a particular election of a certain number, who shall continue in the perseverance in grace; unto the several churches of Christ that are in the same faith and order of the gospel, in London, do heartily desire your increase and growth in the knowledge of our Lord Jesus, and in all the graces of his Holy Spirit." They go on to give an account of the first rise of their church, which say they, "Several wise and learned men endeavored, but could not accomplish it; however, God was pleased to succeed the endeavors of our brethren, who were not so accomplished with acquired parts and abilities, by enduring, and to appear for them under all their troubles, so that we continue, through rich grace, a church unto this day."[1]   By

---

[1] This letter is preserved, and, we judge, is of sufficient interest to warrant its publication.

"The church of Christ at Boston in New England, of the faith and order of the gospel, baptizing visible believers upon the profession of their faith, and believing the principles of a particular election of a certain number, who shall likewise continue in their perseverance in grace; unto the several churches of Christ that are in the same faith and order of the gospel in London, do heartily desire your increase and growth in the knowledge of our Lord Jesus, and in all the graces of his Holy Spirit.

"Honored and dearly beloved friends and brethren; we take this freedom of writing these few lines to acquaint you with the circumstances of our condition, whereby there may be a sympathy which the Holy Spirit of God promotes in Christians at a

those wise and learned men, I suppose they intended President Dunstar and some with him, who did not accomplish what Elder Gould and his brethren did.　One design of this letter was to request some assistance in enlarging and repairing their meeting-house; and it occasioned the following answer :—

London, August 3, 1720.

DEAR AND HONORED BROTHER CALLENDER: I received the honor of the church's and your letter together, by Captain Lawrence.　After I had a little considered the contents of both, I waited upon our honored friend, Mr. Thomas Hollis, with the case, with whom I left it ; and some little time after, he told me, that himself and brother, Mr. John Hollis, would advance some money to repair your meeting-house, upon condition I would prevail with my brethren, concerned in our little fund, to make a present

distance.　It pleased the Lord, by his divine and wise disposing providence, to spirit a small number of men who were very gracious and enlightened in the knowledge of his truth as it is in Jesus, and to appear for the vindication thereof, and to encourage them for their gathering into a church in the way and order of the gospel as above mentioned, which several wise and learned men endeavored but could not accomplish it.　However, God was pleased to succeed the endeavors of our brethren who were not so accomplished with acquired parts and abilities by learning, and to appear for them under all the troubles and difficulties they were exposed unto; And when we were favored with our liberty by virtue of the King's letter to the government, it pleased the Lord to put it into our hearts and to encourage us to build a meeting-house for the worship of our God; which is now about forty years since. And when we lost our elders, such as were accomplished for the work of the ministry in so public a place, we made our application to the churches in London, and unto Mr. Gifford, in that, if it were possible, we might have had a man suitable for the work of the ministry sent over to us, but could never obtain any; so that we were forced or necessitated to make use of our brethren for the upholding of our church and meeting.　And now, God hath been graciously pleased to raise up one amongst ourselves, viz., a son of one of our brethren whom he hath brought up to learning, and whom God hath been pleased so to succeed with his blessing, as to spirit him with grace and principles and also to accomplish him with not only acquired parts and abilities but, we hope we may truly say, also with gracious qualifications for the work and service of the Lord among us.　And this is our present concernment, that, having, by the blessing of our God upon us, obtained this blessing of a minister to break the bread of life to us, our meeting-house which, by reason of so long standing, has gone much to decay, requires repairing, and, being but a small company here in this town, and some of our small number, by reason of age, requiring relief, and those few of our brethren that live in this town being such as God is pleased to make his choice amongst, as mentioned in the 2d of James, 5th verse, we take this boldness of acquainting you therewith, that if the Lord may be pleased to incline the hearts of our dear and well beloved brethren with you, in the several churches, to afford us a small matter of your assistance towards the repair-to Mr. Callender, as a token of our Christian respects to him. The motion pleased me well; I willingly undertook my part, and happily accomplished it, though it were out of the common way of our exhibitions; and by the time this comes to hand, I hope you will find remitted by Mr. Hollis what I hope will fully answer the church's request, together with a small present, which I hope will not be unacceptable, to my brother Callender himself, and show at least our concern for the good of the baptized interest in Boston, though we may not be capable to promote it in that measure we heartily desire.

Concerning the state of the Arian controversy with us, and our ministers' concern therein, I shall briefly relate the whole, as follows. Some few years ago one Dr. Clarke,[1] of the established church, a gentleman of deserved reputation, wrote a book, entitled, The Scripture doctrine of the Trinity; in which he endeavors (after very high expressions of the dignity of the Redeemer's person and nature) to deny him to be a necessary, self-existent being; which is construed by his adversaries as a consequential denying his proper divinity, and a degrading our Saviour into a subordinate God, notwithstanding all he hath offered in honor to this hope of a true Christian. This made a great stir, and set many pens to work; some for and some against the Doctor's notions, among several of note in the church of England, and others; some of whom I think carried the point much further than the Doctor appears to have designed. I wish the contest had always continued in the established church; but a little time carried it among the dissenters, and one Mr. Pierce, a Presbyterian minister, of ingenuity, and considerable note, among others, espoused Dr. Clarke's notions openly (if he went no further.) The debates, *pro* and *con*, began to be managed with warmth, not only in the city, but in divers parts of the country. But Mr. Pierce being a man of so much note, and a minister in the city of Exeter, where the Presbyterian interest is in much credit, he was the first person who was very publicly noted among the dissenters. His people (after some considerable time, and several methods used to accommodate matters) proposed parting with him, as a man not sound in the faith. This occasioned each party to advise with their friends in the ministry, and others, what to do in the case. Some of the persons

ing of our meeting-house, we conclude it would be a good work of charity and redound to your honor here and to your good account in the day of retribution. If amongst the several churches, it might be but to the value of twenty pounds and laid out there with what may be suitable for this place, it would be treble that money here, and would find a welcome and a thankful acceptance with us. This, with our prayers that God would direct and bless you in all your concerns, and multiply your numbers, and increase in you all the graces of his Holy Spirit; and desiring likewise your prayers, for the like mercies for us, we remain your brethren in gospel bonds." Rev. S. Hall's Collection of papers.—ED.

[1] Samuel Clarke, D. D.

wrote to upon this account, (which were not a few) thought that **Mr.** Pierce had given too much cause for his people to believe that he had departed from the orthodox faith, in relation to the doctrine of the Trinity. Others, though they did not deny this, yet apprehended his people had not dealt so kindly by him in this matter as they ought to have done, by a man of his character and usefulness.

The case was some time before a committee of ministers and gentlemen of the three denominations in London, to see if they could find a way to accommodate matters at Exeter, and prevent divisions upon the same account in other places ; but they were not all of one mind. Then the whole body of ministers in and about London was called together, and a paper of advices, proposed to be considered of in order to sign, for accommodating matters at Exeter. Some of the ministers, who were zealously concerned for the doctrine of the Trinity, at the same time proposed, that a declaration of our faith, with respect to that important doctrine of the Christian religion, should be signed, and sent down with the advices ; but, upon a division of the ministers, it was rejected by a majority of about five persons. It was then agreed at the next meeting to consider the paper of advices, paragraph by paragraph ; at which meeting were about one hundred and thirty ministers of three denominations, who placed your poor friend in the chair. That part who were against signing a declaration of faith, as above, earnestly insisted upon proceeding directly to read the paper of advices, as supposing it to be the immediate work of the meeting ; the other side proposed that article in the church of England which relates to the doctrine of the Trinity, and those answers in the Assembly's Catechism to the same purpose, to be subscribed by the London ministers, before they proceeded to consider the paper of advices. Warm debates there were indeed for two or three hours, when on a sudden those brethren who resolved to subscribe those articles withdrew into the gallery ; which, however just their zeal might be for the truth contended for, was not looked upon as a sufficient reason for the breaking up the meeting at that time. So, after some messages sent from the one part to the other, those above proceeded to subscribe those articles, as containing their sentiments of the doctrine of the ever-blessed Trinity ; and the other proceeded to consider the paper of advices, and drew up a general article of their faith as to that doctrine, which was signed by their moderator by appointment. This they sent to Exeter ; while the others drew up another set of advices, and sent down with the articles they had subscribed, and henceforward we came under the distinguishing characters of subscribers and non-subscribers, which distinction I fear will be too long remembered by us, for the common benefit of true religion.

Some of the too warm among the non-subscribers would fain fix the odious charge of persecution on the other, while they again, with full as much warmth, would fix the charge of Arianism upon them. But this severity is not allowed by the greatest part of either side of the question; and I hope time will produce a better temper in both parties; but at present the matter is not accommodated, nor so good a harmony among the ministers as could be heartily wished. As I am satisfied that some among the non-subscribers are gone too far into some of the distinctive notions of Arius, so I think some of the subscribers have given too much ground of jealousy, that they intended to set up those forms as a test of orthodoxy, and the signing of them as necessary to persons being acceptable and useful in the ministry. But I dare say for the much greater part of both sides, that they intended no evil to their differing brethren; and that it was a zeal for the doctrine of the Trinity, and the real divinity of our Saviour, which made some subscribe the articles, and not any desire to impose upon others; and that those who refused the subscription, did it with a design to maintain Christian liberty, rather than any design to encourage or promote Arianism. There is no great difference in the number of either side; but I think there are not so many of our denomination among the non-subscribers as are on the other side; and though I cannot say that there are none of our ministers who too much favor the new scheme, yet I may venture to say in general, that our ministers, especially those of the Particular denomination,[1] are sound in the faith, as to the real divinity of Christ, and the true doctrine of the blessed Trinity. Therefore those who upbraid you with their being contrary, act either from prejudice or misinformation. But such have been the visible consequences of this difference, that brotherly love and charity, that indispensible ornament of the Christian religion, have been greatly lost in the debates. May the Lord increase light and love, as well as zeal and faithfulness, among all the disciples of our blessed Redeemer. So I must have done. The Lord be with you and yours.

EDWARD WALLIN.

Mr. James Peirce, above referred to, was ejected from his church, in March, 1719; but a party followed him, and built another meeting-house for him, in the city of Exeter; to encourage whom, he declared his expectation, that by what they suffered, " the spirit of imposition and persecution would be rendered more odious." And he accused that church of attempting to set up an Inquisition, only because they brought on such a trial as constrained him to own his new opinions, which caused his removal from a profitable

---

[1] Those who hold to particular election.

living.[1]   Mr. Benjamin Wallin, son and successor in office
to Mr. Edward, published an excellent little volume upon
the Sonship of Christ, in 1771, wherein he informs us, that
ever since the above-mentioned time, creeds and catechisms
have been cried down, and a regular Christian education
much neglected, under a pretence of reason and liberty.
And America has been much infected with the same distemper.   But it is not all traditions and human creeds that such
men reject, as the following extract from Peirce plainly
shews.   Under an appearance of a great regard to the
Scriptures, he published a catechism, wherein the answers
were in Scripture words ; part of which say :—

> Question. How many Gods are there?   Answer. There is one God.
> Q. Who is this God?   A. Though there be that are called Gods, whether
> in heaven or in earth, (as there be gods many and lords many,) yet to us
> there is but one God, the Father, of whom are all things, and we for him.
> One God and Father of all, who is above all, and through all, and in you
> all. I Cor. viii. 5, 6 ; Eph. iv. 6.

This creed is so far from delivering any from the tyranny
of human inventions, that where the Scripture puts no more
than a semicolon between the mention of the Father and the
Son, Peirce puts a period and three pages in his book.   And
when he comes to speak of the Son, he picks out words that
speak of his subjection and obedience to the Father, excluding those which assert his equality with him, which are
many.[2]   Whereas, if we leave out the succession of time,
and the mode or manner wherein earthly relations commence,
which have no place in the Deity, it is easy to conceive of a
Father and Son of equal capacity and excellency ; with such
a oneness in nature, and peculiarity of relation, as no others
have ; and also that one may, by voluntary contract, subject
himself to another for wise purposes, and take upon him the
form of a servant, and yet remain perfectly equal in nature.
How unreasonable then are those great pretenders to reason,
who profess to take the Scriptures as their rule, and yet re-

[1]Pierce's Works, printed 1728, pp. 115, 136.   [2]Ibid, pp. 352, 418—422.

ject all those truths therein, which cross their darling notions! Those who are convinced of the infinite evil of sin,
see the necessity of infinite merit to remove their guilt, and
infinite power to change their hearts and lives, and to guide
them to glory. We are told, that by openly owning these
doctrines, Mr. Hollis gave a check to some who had no great
opinion of them.[1]

The Baptists in Boston received from him and his brother,
one hundred and thirty-five pounds two shillings, for repairing their meeting-house, for which a letter of thanks was
returned. And in Harvard College Mr. Thomas Hollis
founded a professorship of theology, with a salary of eighty
pounds per annum to the professor, and an exhibition of ten
pounds apiece per annum to ten scholars of good character,
four of whom should be Baptists, if any such were there;
as also ten pounds a year to the college treasurer, for his
trouble, and ten pounds more to supply accidental losses, or
to increase the number of students.[2] And as by charter the
ministers of Boston, for the time being, were constituted a
part of the overseers of the college, Mr. Hollis moved that
Mr. Callender might have a seat among them. And in a
letter to Mr. Callender, of February 8, 1721–2, Mr. Wallin
said, " I congratulate my friend upon his admitment to the
honor of an overseer of the college. I pray God that truth
and Christian love may more and more abound." But we
are informed by the late Mr. Condy, that Dr. Sewall, at the
head of other ministers, positively denied him a seat there.
Yet how often have such men accused the Baptists of being
much more rigid than themselves? and there was not a word
in their charter to exclude him.

Declension and stupidity had long prevailed in the land,
till a revival in several places was granted in 1721. Windham had so large a share of it, under the ministry of Mr.
Samuel Whiting, as to add eighty communicants to their

[1]Rudd's Poem, p. 23.
[2]Neal's History of New England, Vol. II, pp. 220, 221.

church this year ; for which they kept a special day of thanksgiving to God. One curious event then happened there which I shall mention. The word preached was such a looking-glass to one man, that he seriously went to Mr. Whiting, and told him he was very sorry that so good a minister as he was should so grossly transgress the divine rule, as to tell him his faults before all the congregation, instead of coming to labor with him in private. The minister smiled, and said he was glad that truth had found him out, for he had no particular thought of him in his sermon. Norwich, ten miles from thence, enjoyed a considerable measure of this blessing the same year, from whence my pious mother dated her conversion.[1] Many young people in Boston were turned to a serious regard for religion in 1721. The small-pox coming there in April, and prevailing most terribly through the year, had a deep effect upon many souls. It was thought that not more than a quarter of the inhabitants had passed through that distemper before, and none of them who were under eighteen years.[2] One of them deserves particular notice here.

John Comer was born in Boston, August 1, 1704, and sat under the ministry of the two Mathers. Having a great inclination for learning, he, by President Mather's influence, was taken from an apprenticeship to a trade, and put to

[1] Mrs. Elizabeth Backus, the mother of the author of this history, has already been incidentally noticed in connection with John Tracy, her father. See p. 331. In his sermon on her death, Mr. Backus says, " She has often mentioned to her children a work of conviction and conversion which she experienced about the year 1721." Gospel Comfort for Mourners, p. 19. Before her conversion she had united with the regular church in Norwich, and she remained a member there until 1745, when, together with her son, she joined the Separatists. Denison's Historical Notes, p. 44 ; Life and Times of Backus, pp. 27, 42. Her fidelity and her sufferings in the cause of religion will be noticed hereafter. Says the biographer of Mr. Backus, " The mother of Isaac Backus was, in the truest and highest sense of the expression, an excellent woman. Often does he speak of her in terms of deep respect and love. With special satisfaction does he dwell upon the fruits of genuine piety which appeared in her life. In a sermon occasioned by her death, he calls her ' My dear, godly mother,' and there is ample reason for the belief that she was worthy of such a designation." Life and Times of Backus, pp. 26, 27.—ED.

[2] Christian History, Vol. I, p. 130. Vol. II. p. 375.

school, in December, 1720. Serious turns of concern about his soul had been frequent with him for several years ; which greatly increased for seventeen days after he had taken that infection. " Nothing," says he, " but the ghostly countenance of death unprepared for, was before me, and no sight of a reconciled God, nor any sense of the application of the soul-cleansing blood of Christ to my distressed soul. I remained in extreme terror until November 22. All the interval of time I spent in looking over the affairs of my soul; and on that day I was taken sick. As soon as it was told me that the distemper appeared, all my fears entirely vanished, and a beam of comfort darted into my soul, and with it satisfaction from those words, 'Thou shalt not die but live, and declare the works of the Lord.' Yea, so great was my satisfaction, that immediately I replied to my aunt who informed me, 'Then I know I shall not die now;' but gave no reason why I said so." He recovered, and afterwards became a Baptist minister ; and his ingenious diary and papers have furnished many valuable materials for our history. Ephraim Crafts, one of his young brethren, was baptized and added to that church in Boston, January 27, 1723. John Dabney, from London, had been received by them December 4, 1720, and Richard Bevens, from Wales, the next August, who were members of Baptist churches before they came here. Other members from Europe were added to them, both before and since.

32

CHAPTER XI.

Ill Treatment about Worship at Swanzey.—At Freetown.—Tiverton and Dartmouth.—Some Relief from England.—Ministers' Attempts for more Power defeated.—Hollis's and Wallin's Letters.—Further Donations, and Springfield Affairs.—First exempting laws from ministerial Taxes.—Sufferings at Rehoboth.—The Lyme Dispute.—Connecticut Laws, and Yale College.

Equal religious liberty, by virtue of a special act, was enjoyed in Boston; but was so much denied in the country, that most of the Baptists had no heart to send their sons to Harvard College; though a few of them did so, whereby they made some use of Mr. Hollis's donations there. Great pains were taken to compel every town to receive and support such ministers as the Court called orthodox. A law was also made at Boston, in the May session of 1718, to tax all to the building and repairing of parish meeting-houses. In 1717 the pious and judicious Elder Luther fell asleep, leaving the care of the first church in Swanzey to Elder Ephraim Wheaton, who had been a colleague with him about thirteen years. The second church in Swanzey had then two ordained pastors; yet in April, 1719, their Selectmen were convented before Bristol Court, "for not having a minister according to the law of the province." But upon proving that Elder Wheaton was their lawful minister, they were dismissed, "paying costs."[1] His meeting-house stood

[1]Bristol Court Records.—B.
A similar experience of this church is recorded on page449.—Ed.

near the borders of Rehoboth; and he and many of his people who lived therein were taxed to Pædobaptist ministers of that town, of which we shall hear more presently.

Freetown, which lies on the east side of Great River against Swanzey, met with worse treatment than they did. For on September 9, 1717, they made choice of Thomas Craghead, a minister from Ireland, for their pastor; and he accepted of their call. But instead of an amicable agreement with them about his support, he went in January, 1718, and procured an act of Bristol Court, to compel Freetown to pay him a salary of sixty-five pounds a year, to begin from the day he was chosen their minister. And for refusing to pay it, about fourteen of the inhabitants were seized and imprisoned at Bristol; one of whom was Benjamin Chase, a member of a Baptist church in Newport. In April, 1719, each party carried witnesses about these matters to Bristol Court; but the Court dismissed them all, and required the town to obey their former order. In 1720, Thomas Gage and George Winslow, their Select-men, were fined forty shillings apiece for not assessing Craghead's salary. At last he was defeated in a trial at law, and was forced to quit the town; but these broils produced great and lasting evils therein. Little Compton had settled a legal minister; and as Elder Tabor owned some land in that town, he was taxed to him; for which a riding-saddle was taken from Tabor, as a person informed me who saw it.

Tiverton and Dartmouth were the only remaining towns in the province[1] which had not yielded to the ruling party about worship. When orders for that purpose had come from their Courts, they had reported, that Joseph Wanton was the minister of Tiverton, and Elder Tabor the minister of the west part of Dartmouth, and another man for the east part. But as the Court did not esteem them to be orthodox, a complaint against those towns was presented to

[1]Tiverton was at that time included in the colony of Massachusetts Bay, but was afterwards set off to Rhode Island. See page 282.— ED.

their Legislature in 1722; which annexed such sums as they thought proper for the purpose to their province tax. This being heard of, their Selectmen refused to assess it; for which two of them out of each town were seized on May 25, 1723, and were imprisoned at Bristol. Hereupon Thomas Richardson, who married friend Wanton's daughter, was sent over to London; and with Richard Partridge, agent for Rhode Island Colony, presented a memorial to the king in Council; wherein they observed, that our charter allows equal liberty of conscience to all Christians except Papists; and that neither the charter nor any law had established any test of orthodoxy in this province, only as Presbyterians and Independents had set up their major votes as such; whereby dissenters from them were frequently brought under great sufferings; from which no redress could be obtained here, " the Assembly always opposing whatever the Governor and Council were at any time disposed to do on that behalf." And as the king, at his accession to the throne, promised protection and liberty of conscience to all his dissenting subjects without exception, they prayed that he would denounce his negative upon those laws or parts of laws among us, that interfered therewith, and also order those prisoners to be released.[1] A committee was appointed upon the case; whose report, with the act of Council thereon, is as follows:—

To the King's most excellent Majesty: May it please your Majesty, in obedience to an order in Council, from the late Lord's Justices, during your Majesty's absence abroad, bearing date the 24th day of October last, we did make a representation upon an act passed in the

_____

[1]This Memorial shows the affairs of Baptists and other dissenters from the Standing Order at that time, in so clear and just a light, that, notwithstanding its length, we insert it in full.

"To George, King of Great Britain, &c.: The humble petition of Thomas Richardson and Richard Partridge, in behalf of Joseph Anthony, John Sisson, John Akin and Philip Tabor, prisoners in the common jail at New Bristol, in the king's province of the Massachusetts Bay, in New England, as also their friends (called Quakers) in general, who are frequently under great sufferings for conscience sake in that government; Showeth:

"That William and Mary, late King and Queen of England, &c., by their royal

province of the Massachusetts Bay, in New England, in 1722, intituled, An
act for apportioning and assessing a tax of £6,232, 13, 11 ; since which
time another act, mentioned in the said order of reference, passed the 29th
day of May, 1723, intituled, "An act for apportioning and assessing a tax of

charter, bearing date the seventh day of October, in the third year of their reign,
did (for the greater ease and encouragement of their loving subjects inhabiting the
said province, and of such as should come to inhabit there) grant, establish and
ordain, that forever thereafter, there should be a liberty of conscience allowed, in
the worship of God, to all Christians except papists, inhabiting or which should
inhabit or be resident within the said province, 'with power also to make laws for
the government of the said province, and support of the same ; and to impose taxes
for the king's service, in the necessary defence and support of the said government,
and protection and preservation of the inhabitants ; and to dispose of matters and
things whereby the king's subjects might be there, religiously, peaceably and civilly
governed, protected and defended ;' and, for the better securing and maintaining
liberty of conscience, thereby granted,—commanded that all such laws, made and
published by virtue of said charter, should be made and published under the seal of
the said province, and should be carefully and duly observed, kept and performed ;
and put in execution, according to the true intent and meaning of the said charter :

"That those sorts of Protestants called Presbyterians and Independents, being
more numerous in the said country than others, (to whom the said charter gives
equal rights) they become makers of the laws by their superior numbers and votes,
and ministers of the privileges of the said charter, so as, in great measure, to elude
the same, and disappoint all others of the king's protestant subjects, of the good
and just ends of transporting themselves and families at so great hazard and charges,
our great encouragement and inducement thereto being liberty of conscience and
ease from priestly impositions and burdens :   That in the year 1692, they made a
law in the said province, entitled, 'An Act for the settlement and support of Ministers and Schoolmasters,' wherein it is ordained 'that the inhabitants of each town
within the said province, shall take due care, from time to time, to be constantly
provided of an able, and learned orthodox minister or ministers, of a good conversation to dispense the word of God to them ; which minister or ministers shall be
suitably encouraged and sufficiently supported and maintained by the inhabitants of
such towns ;' That the said law was further enforced by another made in the year
1695, reciting its title aforesaid ; as also by another made in the year 1715, entitled
'An Act for maintaining and propagating religion,' in which said last Act, the prevention of the growth of atheism, irreligion and profaneness, is suggested as one
great reason of its being ; and the power of determining who shall be ministers
under the qualifications, is, by the said laws, assumed by the General Court or
Assembly, with the recommendation of any three of the ministers of the said same
sects, already in their orders, and settled and supported by virtue of the said laws ;
though it is not determined, (as the petitioners humbly presume) either by the said
charter or by any act of parliament in Great Britain, or by any express law of the
said province, who are orthodox and who are not, or who shall judge of such qualifications in such ministers :   And in all which said several laws, no other care is
had or taken of religion (even in their own sense) than only to appoint ministers of
their own way, and impose their maintenance upon all the king's subjects conscientiously dissenting from them.   By force of which said laws, or some of them,

£6,205, 15, 7½," is come to our hands ; by which act a tax is laid in express terms upon the inhabitants of Dartmouth and Tiverton for the support of a Presbyterian, whom they call an orthodox minister, which falls almost entirely upon the Quakers, there being very few inhabitants of any other

several townships within the said province, have had Presbyterian or Independent preachers obtruded and imposed upon them for maintenance without their consent, and which they have not deemed able, learned or orthodox, and which, as such, they could not hear or receive : That by another law, made in the years 1722 and 1723, it is ordained that the town of Dartmouth and the town of Tiverton, in the said province, be assessed for the said years, the respective sums of one hundred pounds, and seventy-two pounds and eleven shillings over and beside the common taxes for support of government, which sums are for the maintenance of such ministers : That the said Joseph Anthony and John Sisson were appointed assessors of the taxes for the said town of Tiverton, and the said John Aikin and Philip Tabor for the town of Dartmouth ; but some of the said assessors being of the people called Quakers. and others of them also dissenting from the Presbyterians and Independents and greatest part of the inhabitants of said towns being also Quakers or Anabaptists or of differing sentiments in religion from Independents, though the said assessors duly assessed the other taxes upon the people there, relating to the support of government, to the best of their knowledge, yet they could not in conscience assess any of the inhabitants of these towns anything for or towards the maintenance of any ministers ;   That they, the said Joseph Anthony, John Sisson, John Aikin and Philip Tabor, on pretence of their non-compliance with the said law, were, on the 25th of the month called May, 1723, committed to the jail aforesaid, where they still continue prisoners, under great sufferings and hardships, both to themselves and families, and where they must remain and die, if not relieved by the king's royal clemency and favor :   That the people called Quakers in the said province, are, and generally have been, great sufferers by the said laws, in their cattle, horses, sheep, corn and household goods, which from time to time have been taken from them by violence of the said laws for the maintenance of ministers who call themselves able, learned and orthodox ; which said laws, and the execution and consequences thereof, are not only, (as the petitioners humbly conceive) contrary to the liberty of conscience and the security of religion, civil liberty, and the rights and privileges granted in the said charter, to all the king's protestant subjects, there eluded and made null and precarious, but opposite also to the king's royal and gracious declaration at thy happy accession to the throne, promising protection and liberty of conscience to all thy dissenting subjects without exception to those of the said plantations :   That after repeated application made to the said government there for redress in the premises, and no relief hitherto obtained, (the Assembly always opposing whatever the Governor and Council were at any time disposed to do on that behalf,) the king's loyal, suffering and distressed subjects, do now prostrate themselves at the steps of the throne, humbly imploring thy royal consideration, that it may please the king to denounce his negative upon the said laws or such part or parts of them or any of them as directly or consequently effect the lives, liberty, property, religion or conscience of thy protestant subjects in the said province, and their families and privileges granted and intended in the said royal charter, or such other relief as thy royal wisdom and goodness may please to provide."

Rev. S. Hall's Collection of papers.—ED.

persuasion in those two towns.[1] But as by the charter granted to this Province, a free and absolute liberty of conscience to all Christians (except papists) was intended to have been their foundation and support, and as by several laws passed there, it seems to have been laid down as a just and equitable rule, that the majority of each town congregation should have the choice of their own teachers, we cannot see why the Quakers should be refused this liberty, in the towns where they are so great a majority, and be obliged to maintain a teacher of a different persuasion. Wherefore we humbly propose to your Majesty, that this act may be repealed ; which is most humbly submitted.

WESTMORELAND,
T. PELHAM,
M. BLADEN,
EDW. ASHE.

Whitehall, May 6, 1724.

At the Court at St. James's, 2d day of June, 1724.

Present, the King's most excellent Majesty, his Royal Highness the Prince of Wales, A. B. of Canterbury, Lord Chancellor, Lord President, Lord Privy-Seal, Lord Chamberlain, Duke of Roxburg, Duke of New Castle, Earl of Westmoreland, Lord Viscount Townsend, Lord Viscount Torrington, Mr. Speaker of the House of Commons, Mr. Vice-Chamberlain, William Pultney, Esq.

Upon reading this day at the Board a report from the Right Honorable the Lords of the Committee of Council, upon the petition of Thomas Richardson and Richard Partridge, on behalf of Joseph Anthony, John Sisson, John Akin and Philip Tabor, prisoners at the common goal at New Bristol, in his Majesty's Province of the Massachusetts Bay, in New England, for not assessing the inhabitants of the towns of Dartmouth and Tiverton the additional taxes of £172, 11, imposed upon them by an act passed there in the year 1722, which appears to be for the maintenance of Presbyterian ministers, who are not of their persuasion ; and also in behalf of their friends called Quakers in general, who are frequently under great sufferings for conscience sake in that government : by which report it appears that their Lordships are of opinion, that it may be advisable for his Majesty to remit the said additional taxes, so imposed on the said two towns, and to discharge the said persons from goal :   His Majesty in Council taking the said report into consideration, is graciously pleased to approve thereof, and hereby to remit the said additional taxes of one hundred pounds, and seventy-two pounds, eleven shillings, which were by the said act to be assessed on the said towns of Dartmouth and Tiverton. And

[1]The Memorial says, "The greatest part of the inhabitants of the said towns being Quakers, or Anabaptists, or of differing sentiments in religion from Independents and Presbyterians. Quaker Records.

his Majesty is hereby further pleased to order, that the said Joseph Anthony, John Sisson, John Akin and Philip Tabor, be immediately released from their imprisonment on account thereof. And the Governor, Lieutenant Governor, and Commander in Chief, for the time being, of his Majesty's said Province of Massachusetts Bay, and all others whom it may concern, are to take notice, and yield due obedience hereunto.

TEMPLE STANYAN.

Before this, I find Mr. Wallin, in one of his letters, saying of king George the First, " Without any partiality to him as our reigning prince, I believe he is the greatest man, and the most fit for government, of any prince in the Christian world." And his son and successor, then Prince of Wales, was not inferior to him. By the above act our friends were released from a thirteen months' imprisonment. And as Jacob Tabor and Beriah Goddard, of Dartmouth, were imprisoned for not assessing said tax of 1723, Henry Howland, their other assessor, laid their case before the Assembly at Boston, who, on November 26, 1724, passed an act to release them, " to signify their ready and dutiful compliance with his Majesty's declared will and pleasure." Anthony and Sisson were of Tiverton, the rest were of Dartmouth, and Philip Tabor was a Baptist minister therein. These things were far from affording any satisfaction to the ministerial party here, as the following facts will shew. For at the annual convention of their ministers at Boston, May 26, 1725, they drew up an address to their Legislature, which says :—

Considering the great and visible decay of piety in the country, and the growth of many miscarriages, which we fear may have provoked the glorious Lord, in a series of various judgments, wonderfully to distress us; considering also the laudable example of our predecessors to recover and establish the faith and order of the gospel in the churches, and provide against what immoralities may threaten to impair them, in the way of General Synods convened for that purpose; and considering that about forty-five years have now rolled away since these churches have seen any such conventions; it is humbly desired, that the honorable General Court would express their concern for the interests of religion in the country, by calling the several churches in the province to meet by their pastors and messen-

gers in a Synod, and from thence offer their advice upon that weighty case
which the circumstances of the day do loudly call to be considered :[1] What
are the miscarriages whereof we have reason to think the judgments of
heaven upon us call us to be more generally sensible, and what may be the
most evangelical and effectual expedients to put a stop unto those or the
like miscarriages? This proposal we humbly make, in hopes that, if it be
prosecuted, it may be followed with many desirable consequences, worthy
the study of those whom God has made, and we are so happy to enjoy, as
the nursing fathers of our churches.

COTTON MATHER.

In the name of the ministers assembled in their General Convention.[2]

On June 3, the Council voted to grant their petition ; but
the Representatives voted to defer the matter till their next
session, which the Council concurred with, and Lieutenant
Governor Dummer consented thereto. June 11th, a committee of the General Court, whereof Samuel Sewall, Esq.,
was chairman, appointed upon the affair of ministers' salaries, brought in a report, to have a law made to compel every
parish to make up to their ministers their several salaries,
equal to what they were when their contracts were made ;
and for the Judges of their County Courts to determine how
much their currency had depreciated. This report was not
accepted ; but instead of it a resolve was passed, recommending it to every town, precinct and parish in the province, to
make up to their respective ministers their salaries equal to
what money was when their contracts were made ; which resolve they ordered to be read to each congregation the next
Lord's day after it was received, and also in their parish
meetings the March after.[3] Episcopalians sent an account
to the Bishop of London of the said petition for a synod,
who laid the same before the Lords Justices of the Regency ;
from whom a sharp reprimand was written to Mr. Dummer,
October 7, 1725, for giving any countenance to said petition,

[1] What they wanted was to *recover and establish* the power which ministers claimed;
and, like the Synod of 1679, which they refer to, to represent to rulers and and people that the judgments of heaven would follow them, if that was not granted.   See
page 385.

[2] Hutchinson, Vol. II, p. 322. [292.]   [3] Massachusetts Records.

and for not sending over an account thereof immediately after it was presented and acted upon. They declared that inquiry had been made by proper authority, and they could not find that there was any regular establishment of a national or provincial church here, so as to warrant the holding synods of the clergy ; but that if there were, it was the king's prerogative to call them, which therefore was invaded by the General Court when they intermeddled therewith. And if such a synod was called, and should be sitting when their letter arrived, they wrote to Dummer :—

Cause such their meeting to cease, acquainting them that their assembly is against law, and a contempt of his Majesty's prerogative, and that they are forbid to meet any more. But if, notwithstanding such signification, they shall continue to hold such an assembly, you are then to take care that the principal actors therein be prosecuted for a misdemeanor ; but you are to avoid doing any formal act to dissolve them, lest it be construed to imply that they had a right to assemble.

CHARLES DELAFAYE.

Mr. Dummer, in a letter to the Board of Trade, endeavored to excuse himself, by observing, that a like vote of the Council upon a like petition was passed in 1715, which was never censured from home as he knew of.[1] But then it was not countenanced by the other branches of the Legislature, as this was. The minister who, in behalf of the rest, signed the above petition for a synod, published a book in 1726, wherein he promises a faithful account of the discipline of the New England churches. Much of it was written many years before, and an attestation was prefixed to it by Dr. Increase Mather, dated December 10, 1719. After sixty-six years' labor in the great work of the ministry, he fell asleep, August 23, 1723, aged eighty-five. Though he was a friend to councils and synods, yet he testified against giving them such power as his son and many more wanted. But he and others being removed, their children renewed their attempts for that power. His son had a strong affec-

[1]Douglas, Vol. II, pp. 337, 378.

tion for the proposals of 1705, and for Governor Saltonstall, who procured the establishment of that scheme in Connecticut; even so that when Saltonstall died in 1724, Mather preached a funeral sermon for him at Boston, a hundred miles off, and got it printed at New London. He also now discovered his resentment against Mr. Wise, for writing against said proposals.[1] And having declared that four synods had been called by authority in the Massachusetts, he says, " The synods of New England know no weapons, but what are purely spiritual. . . . . They have no secular arm to enforce any canons ; they ask none ; they want none. And they cannot believe, that any Protestant secular arm would, upon [a] due information, any more forbid their meetings, than they would any of the religious assemblies upheld in the country."[2]   Had this been true, we have no reason to think that their meetings would have been forbidden.   But plain facts shew, that the immediate effect of the first of those synods was the dissolving of a House of Representatives (who would not punish such as the synod had condemned) and the calling of another ; who disfranchised, disarmed and banished a considerable number of persons. And their second synod declared it to be the duty of the magistrate to put forth his coercive power against schismatics, the effects whereof were the fining, imprisoning, scourging, banishing and hanging of those whom they so called.   And the result of the fourth synod caused the nailing up of the Baptist meeting-house in Boston.[3]   Are all these weapons *purely spiritual?*   His meaning no doubt was, that their synods only informed rulers of what was their duty, which they were to do out of regard to God, and not to them. But the most horrid persecutions that ever were practiced were done under such pretences.   And this author was in earnest to have their order of ministers supported by taxes,

[1]Ratio Disciplinæ Fratrum Nov. Anglorum, p. 184.
[2]Ibid, pp. 172, 173.
[3]See pages 66—69, 159, 180, 192, 262, 393, 328, 385.

imposed and collected " in the king's name." To justify which, he says, " If the most of the inhabitants in a plantation are Episcopalians, they will have a minister of their own persuasion ; and the dissenters, if there be any in the place, must pay their proportion of the tax, for the support of this legal minister."[1] He knew that such an instance had not then taken place in New England ; and we know that every thing of that nature has been earnestly opposed therein ever since. And he then commended some of his party, for involving a salary for their ministers in a general rate for all town charges, " where Quakerism was troublesome,"[2] which he might have said was likewise done to the Baptists in Rehoboth, if he had been willing the whole truth should be known.

Mr. Hollis's ideas of the nature of religion, and of the state of this country, appear in the following letter to Elder Wheaton :—

London, March 13, 1723.

DEAR SIR :—I have newly received, under covert of Mr. Elisha Callender, your long looked-for letter, dated the 25th of December, and give you thanks for the account you give me of the affairs of your church, your circumstances, and your neighbors'. I am glad the books sent you are of use unto you ; by the same hand you will have another forwarded, which I value, and suppose you will. I rejoice in the success of your ministry, and increase of your church, which will naturally increase your cares with your joy. I mourn because of the ignorance of your sleeping Sabbatarians ; let us be thankful for our light, pity them and pray for them, and endeavor in love to lead them into the light also. God, that hath shined into our hearts by his gospel, can lead them from the Sinai covenant and the law of ceremonies, into the light of the new covenant and the grace thereof. I pity to see professors drawing back to the law, and desire to remember that our standing is by grace ; and therefore not to be high-minded over them, but fear, remembering our Lord's words, Watch and pray, lest ye enter into temptation. Every word of God is precious ; the saints love it ; and they that honor him he will honor ; and in keeping of

---

[1] Ratio Disciplinæ, &c., p. 21.
[2] Ibid, p. 22.—B.

" Where Quakerism is troublesome, some towns are so wise to involve the salary of the ministry in the general rate for all town charges, and so the cavils of those who would else refuse to pay the rate for the ministry, are obviated."—ED.

it there is present peace, and a promise of future reward. We now live by faith and not by sight. He that endureth to the end shall be saved. Go on, sir, sowing the seed, looking up to him whose work alone it is to give the increase, whoever be the planter or waterer ; and as you do abound in your labors, and do find him multiplying seed unto you, may you yet abound more and more to the end, which is my sincere wish. Let no man rob us of our comfortable hope, that when we cease to be here we shall be present with the Lord, in whose presence the saints believe is fullness of joy in a separate state, and expectation of greater in the resurrection, when it shall be fully manifested how he loved them. Let none jeer us out of our duty now to lisp forth his praises with our tongues, since we expect hereafter to sing in a better manner the song of the Lamb, with a much more noble chorus.

In reference to your poll-tax and other taxes, which are necessary for support of the government and society, [they] are not to be esteemed a burthen ; it is giving tribute or tithes to whom tribute is due, unless the taxes do oppress you unequally, because you are Baptists and Separatists ; if so, then let me know, (who profess myself a Baptist) and I will endeavor to have a word spoken for you to the Governor, that you may be eased. You know that our profession is not mody in your country nor ours ; few if any of the great men submitting to plain institution ; and as we profess ourselves disciples of Christ, it is our duty to take up our cross with patience, and pay parochial duties where we live, and voluntarily maintain our own charge, and be thankful for our liberty, as men and Christians, to our good God, who in his providence has inspired many magistrates and ministers in your province with a truer spirit of catholic charity than formerly. You have heard, or may be informed by Mr. Callender, of my foundation in Harvard College, and the provision I have made for Baptist youth to be educated for the ministry, and equally regarded with Pædo-baptists. If you know any as may be duly qualified, inform me, and I shall be glad to recommend them for the first vacancy. And to close ; while we profess to worship God nearer to the rule of primitive institution and practice of our great Prophet and Teacher, the Lord Jesus Christ, and his apostles, let our light so shine before men in all holy conversation, that such whose inclinations may be ready to speak evil of our way, may be ashamed. May serious religion and godliness in the power of it flourish among us ; every thing that goes in to make up the true Christian. Where the image of Christ is formed in any, I call them the excellent of the earth ; with such I delight to associate and worship, whatever particular denomination they may go by among men ; and this I would do till we all come into the unity of the faith, &c. Acts xx. 32.

Your loving friend,

THOMAS HOLLIS.

This I copied from the original letter; and would just observe upon it, that the generality of parish rates here were only for the support of one way of worship, and not for the government, as he supposed. And further light about the conduct of that day may be gained from the following letter:—

London, February, 18, 1724–5.

DEAR BROTHER CALLENDER: I had the pleasure of yours by Captain Lawrence, and am glad to hear of your welfare. May the Lord preserve your health and usefulness. I rejoice at the increase of your members, and the good prospect you have of more being added to your church, even of such who shall be saved. It is sweet encouragement to a poor laborer in Christ's vineyard, to find the Lord works with him; and some visible instances of sovereign grace and love among his people make his drooping spirit revive and sing. May you have more of these, especially among the rising generation; for it is a particular pleasure to see young ones look Zionward, and truly remember their Creator in the days of their youth; though in this case we have always reason to rejoice with trembling, because so many who seemed to run well for a time, have been turned aside by youthful lusts, (which war against the soul) to the wounding the hearts of their ministers, and the dishonor of Christ. I am sorry you have so much cause to complain, with us, of the great decay of the power and purity of religion. I am afraid this inquisitive age of professors spend too much time, and almost all their zeal, about matters of speculation, and neglect the closet and inward experimental religion too much. I observe by some letters and papers, by Captain Lawrence, that there is a number of young men formed into a society at Boston, who have taken upon them the name of the Berean Society. It is a noble design to be wholly governed by Scripture, and [I] wish every professor had such a resolution. They seem to be in earnest about what they propose, and if any of their zeal, for any particular point in dispute among Christians, should flame too high, I am glad they are under your conduct, by which I hope they will be well directed for their mutual edification, and the honor of truth. They will have some books, contained in the catalogue, sent soon, when I hope to write more particularly on this head. I met Captain Lawrence at our honored friend Mr. Thomas Hollis's, where we had some particular discourse about your place and people, and how his bounty to your church was laid out. From the whole, I apprehend Mr. Hollis was not displeased, but approved of what you had done, and hath been so good as to order the remaining part of the money for your own use; besides which, he hath been pleased to send you a present of books. I have often, my dear friend, adored the divine goodness, in disposing this gentleman's

mind to so much service for the interest of Christ in general, in New England as well as Old; but especially for the providence by which such a
gentleman came to the knowledge of our small interest in those Colonies,
who had such a love to despised truth, as to own and encourage it in the
face of so many and powerful opposers.   It is this good providence, I
apprehend, hath occasioned some persons to look favorably towards the
baptized interest in Boston, and gives an encouraging view of greater advantage in years to come.   His favors to you and yours hath doubtless
been ungrateful to some of your neighbors, and perhaps some have been
unkind and weak enough to design you a prejudice by some accounts
given; but be in no pain for that, for Mr. Hollis is no stranger to the
weakness which good men are liable to; nor will he be easily persuaded
into hard thoughts of any, notwithstanding their many weaknesses, who in
their general conduct have acquitted themselves like Christians and honest
men; nor do any who attempt to draw his displeasure upon another person
without good reason, do himself the least service thereby with Mr. Hollis.
That the good will of him that dwelt in the bush may be with you and
yours, is the hearty desire of your sincere friend and unworthy brother,

EDWARD WALLIN.

In addition to his other donations, Mr. Hollis founded a
professorship of the mathematics and experimental philos-
phy in Harvard College in 1726, with a salary of eighty
pounds a year to the professor; and he sent over an apparatus for the purpose, which cost about one hundred and fifty
pounds sterling, besides large additions to the college library.[1] And by a letter to Mr. Callender, from Gay Head, on
Martha's Vineyard, of September 11, 1727, I find Jonas
Horswet, an Indian minister, sending for some of the books
he had received, and also mentioning Thomas Sekins,
another Indian preacher at Nantucket.[2] About this time
four Baptists were seized for ministerial taxes in the country, and were cast into prison at Boston; but were soon
released again by the special order of Lieutenant Governor
Dummer.[3] Near the same time there came a letter from
Springfield, signed by thirty men, directed to the Baptist
church in Boston, requesting that their pastor might be sent
up to labor among them.   He went accordingly, and on

[1]Neal, Vol. II, pp. 220, 221.   [2]See page 347.
[3]Proctor's Remonstrance, in 1754.

July 23, 1727, baptized John Leonard, Ebenezer Leonard, William Scott, Abel Leonard, and Thomas Lamb, of Springfield, and Victory Skyes and Marcy Lawton,[1] of Suffield. A letter to him dated July 19, signed Daniel Brewer, Ebenezer Devotion, Stephen Williams, Samuel Hopkins, Nehemiah Bull, blames him for not first coming to them, and says, " We cannot think that preaching to or treating with particular persons in a private manner, to instil into them doctrines that we think are not according to truth and godliness, to be so Christian-like; and we assure you is not what we expected from Mr. Callender, whatever we might have feared from some others." Mr. Devotion was minister in Suffield, and Bull in Westfield; the other three were of Springfield. When Mr. Callender went there again the next year, the three Springfield ministers wrote to inquire whether he came prepared for and expecting a public dispute about baptism.[2] His answer was in these words:—

Springfield, September 17, 1728.

REVEREND SIR: It is not my custom and manner to go about the country to dispute and debate and wrangle with those that differ from me in opinion. It is well known that I am for peace with all men, and for

[1] In addition to these names, a manuscript of John Comer gives the names of Jonathan Worthington, John Pullin, Richard Gardner, and Mary Worthington. Also in his Diary, Comer wrote under date of October, 1727, that on the 23d of the previous July, Elisha Callender had baptized eleven persons in Springfield; and a letter from Springfield, given in the succeeding note, states that eleven persons had been baptized there.—ED.

[2] The correspondence in connection with this important movement in Springfield, this spontaneous springing up of Baptist principles in a new field, seems to be of sufficient interest and value to justify giving it in full.

To the Church of Christ in Boston under the care of Elder Elisha Callender, the subscribers hereunto send greeting:

BELOVED: Although we are no church nor members of any church, yet we have formerly looked upon ourselves, at least some of us, to have been members of such church or churches whose faith and practice is to baptize, or rather sprinkle, infants; but through God's goodness, by searching the Scriptures, and such other helps as we have received from some of your church, have been made sensible that our former practise with relation to baptism, has been grounded too much upon the traditions of men. And as, through grace, we hope we have in some measure been made sensible of the error that the churches in this land in general are in, with respect to baptism, both as to manner and subject, the which, in times past, we have

33

Christians to live in love and charity, and for every man to act as he is fully persuaded in his own mind. But if you will not be quiet and easy, and will insist upon it that your people must hear what is to be said in opposition to what I think contrary to truth and godliness, you may inform, Sir, your humble servant,   ELISHA CALLENDER.

    To the Reverend Mr. Daniel Brewer.

too fondly imbibed and embraced, so we desire to renounce and forsake the same, as not in the least corresponding with the word of God. And understanding that the church at Boston practises and allows of no other but believers' baptism; we, the subscribers, do therefore spread our case before the church, humbly entreating your advice under our present circumstances; and if it agree with the pleasure and advice of the church, (in order for the attaining further knowledge in the ways of God) to grant that Elder Elisha Callender may give us a visit and preach some sermons among us, who as yet, the most of us, never heard a sermon preached by a Baptist. And if it may stand with the pleasure of the church to grant this the request of our souls, we entreat the favor of a line to inform us when it may be. And now, leaving our concern with God, desiring the prayers of the church to the throne of grace that God would carry on the work which we hope through grace he has begun, and that he would perfect it to the end, we desire to subscribe, though unworthy, your brethren in the bonds of the gospel,

                  JONATHAN WORTHINGTON,"

                     [and fifteen others.]

"We, the subscribers, are hesitating in the doctrine of infant sprinkling, and desire further instruction to understand the true institution of baptism according to the word of God, and to be in the use of all proper means to attain the same.

                  JOS. BEDURTHA, jr.,"

                    [and twelve others.]

REVEREND SIR: We had a desire to have seen you and discoursed with you in a Christian, moderate, and calm manner, respecting your visiting the people of our parts and charge, and to have known from you whether it can be that the kingdom and interest of our glorious Lord Jesus is likely to be advanced and the welfare of precious souls furthered, by the measures you are now pursuing; or whether the interest of pure and undefiled religion is not like to suffer. We are not fond of men's being called the followers of Paul or Apollos, but if the good of men's souls be furthered, we shall rejoice. But, Sir, if heats, debates and divisions do follow, (as we fear they will) to the wounding of religion and the danger of vital piety, we ask whether blame must not be at your door? If you esteem of us as ministers of Jesus Christ, and would have been pleased to have conferred with us, we would, any of us, have endeavored to have given you as true account as we were capable, of the circumstances of these people; and should be glad to join with you, or any good man, in doing anything for the revival of decayed piety, &c. But we cannot think that preaching to or treating with particular persons, in a private manner, to instil into them, doctrines which, we think, are not according to truth and godliness, to be so Christian-like, and we assure you, is not what we expected from Mr. Callender, whatever we might have feared from others; and we should have thought it more fair if you had desired to have preached in one of our pulpits where we might have heard you and have had an opportunity to have made our remarks and replies [if we thought it not according to truth.) See Matthew 10. 26, 27. As to the book you were pleased to send to Mr. Brewer and Mr. Williams, just now we shall make no remarks upon it.   EBENEZER DEVOTION, &c.

    Springfield, July 19, 1727."

I find no answer to this.

Upon the receipt of their second charter, Dr. Cotton Mather said, " Religion is forever secured ; a righteous and generous liberty of conscience established. And the General Assembly may, by their acts, give a distinguishing encouragement unto that religion which is the general profes-

A few weeks later, those who had been baptized in Springfield, still seeking for light and guidance, wrote as follows :—

Springfield, September 6, 1727.

"To the church of Christ in Newport, under the care of Elder Peckom and Elder Comer; we, the subscribers hereunto, in the name and in behalf of eleven persons lately baptized hereabouts, we being of the number also, all baptized upon the profession of faith; send greeting."

DEARLY BELOVED IN OUR LORD JESUS, THOUGH UNKNOWN TO US: Whereas it pleased God, in infinite mercy to discover to us his will in his holy word, and our indispensable duty to submit to him in his ordinances; the which (we hope in obedience) we have so far done as to submit to his holy ordinance of baptism; and now are like sheep without a shepherd: do therefore write to entreat and beseech your prayers at the throne of grace that God would please send a laborer into his harvest here, and add daily unto us, such as shall be saved. We are not only as sheep without a shepherd, and few in number, but we are environed round about with enemies, and such as sometimes prove potent. Indeed, we are not without fear that the clergy which we are surrounded with, are enemies to our cause. Do therefore crave your advice and assistance at this difficult juncture especially. The same we have requested of the church at Boston, and have had Elder Callender with us, and being now wholly destitute of such help, desire also that your Elder Comer might give us a visit, preach amongst us and administer the ordinance of baptism, if any should present to the same: and that God would enable and assist us to persevere to the end, and build us up into a church, that so we may live in the enjóyment of all his holy ordinances, the which our souls long for and thirst after. Thus hoping and entreating that both the church and Elder Comer will grant these our desires, which are not the desires of the persons above mentioned only, but of divers others also; we subscribe, though unworthy, with our Christian love presented, your loving brethren in the bonds of the gospel,

WILLIAM SCOTT, &c.

Mr. Comer relates in his Diary that he set out for Springfield with two brethren, "arrived safe at the house of Mr. Jno. Devotion at Southfield," Thursday, September 19, and the next day "went over to Springfield and found all things agreeable." The following Lord's day he preached to about "seventy auditors." Two ministers of the Standing Order came to see him, one of whom, he says, "seemed much troubled about the affair I came upon."

In his visit to Springfield the next year, Mr. Callender baptized Thomas Durkee of Windham, and Daniel Blodget of Stafford. The letter above mentioned, which he received at this time from ministers of the Standing Order, is as follows:

REVEREND SIR: Our laboring to wait upon you together on last year, not being well received by some, we shall not now take pains after any such thing; but take this method to ask you whether you came prepared for and expecting of a

sion of the inhabitants."[1]   And for thirty-six years they made
no act to exempt either Baptists or Quakers from taxes to
his party of ministers.   The great earthquake was in the
evening of October 29, 1727 ; and the Assembly that met
the 22d of the next month passed the first act of exemption
therefrom, that they ever did for any denomination.   It was
to empower every settled Episcopal minister to draw all the
money which was assessed upon any of his society, who
lived within five miles of his meeting, if they usually attended
worship there ; who were also to be exempted from taxes
for building or repairing of meeting-houses for the established way.   But it required each parish to make up to
their ministers, within two months, all the money that might
by their means be taken from them.   The five-mile limitation was dropped afterwards ; and by an act in 1742, the
minister and church wardens were required to give certificates to each parish treasurer, where any of their society
lived, in order for their drawing said money.

Nothing is more amazing among men, than the influence
which the love of power and gain has to blind their minds.
The admission of the houses both of Orange and Hanover
to the British throne, was upon the principle that government is founded in compact.   And the most essential article
of the national compact was, that none should be taxed but
by their own representatives.   Yet because the representatives in this government refused to put it out of their power

public dispute concerning the subjects and modes of baptism. We ask your answer
by the bearer. From, Sir, your humble servants,

DANIEL BREWER,
STEPHEN WILLIAMS,
Springfield, September 16, 1728.   SAM'L HOPKINS.

"Please, Sir, by a line or two, to favor us with a reply to this as soon as possible,
directing it immediately to me, D. B., or, (if an opportunity offers convenient,)
immediately to Mr. Williams at the Meadows."

The answer to this, Backus gives in full.

Ten years later the Baptists in Springfield secured stated preaching, and after
two years more a Baptist church was formed there.—ED.

[1]Account of his father's life, p. 141. He himself died February 13, 1728, aged
sixty-five.

to give or withhold the salary demanded by the Crown for
governors that they could have no choice in appointing or
removing, an attempt was made in England to bring the case
before the Parliament, and to take away our second charter.
But Mr. Jeremiah Dummer, brother to the Lieutenant Governor, published in London such a defence of our charter
rights in 1721, as, with other things, prevented it. Though
in 1725 an explanatory charter was added, which deprived
the representatives of power to put their own Speaker into
office, without the consent of the Governor. These things
were justly complained of, by those who daily practised a
like iniquity themselves. For it is not more certain that
America is not represented in the British Parliament, than
it is that a quantity of *money* does not give any men a right
to judge for their neighbors about soul-guides, and to enforce
their judgments with the sword. Yet this was daily practised, to support teachers, that many who were taxed to
them had no more voice in choosing, than said representatives had in their governors. But as hot contentions still
continued about the Governor's salary, and other dangers
hung over them, when their Assembly met at Boston, in
May, 1728, they made a law, as follows :—

That from and after the publication of this act, none of the persons commonly called Anabaptists, nor any of those called Quakers, that are or
shall be enrolled or entered in their several societies as members thereof,
and who allege a scruple of conscience as the reason of their refusal to pay
any part or proportion of such taxes, as are from time to time assessed for
the support of the minister or ministers of the churches established by the
laws of this province, in the town or place where they dwell, shall have
their polls taxed towards the support of such minister or ministers, nor
shall their bodies be at any time taken in execution, to satisfy any such
ministerial rate or tax, assessed upon their estates or faculty ; provided,
that such persons do usually attend the meetings of their respective societies, assembling upon the Lord's day for the worship of God, and that they
live within five miles of the place of such meeting.

The way prescribed for their being known, was for each
County Court, at their next session after the first of June

annually, to appoint meet persons of those societies, "to bring in a list, upon oath or solemn affirmation, of all persons within their respective towns or precincts, that profess themselves to be Anabaptists or Quakers, and usually attend their meetings as aforesaid, after which the clerk of the peace of the county shall give in to the assessors of each town or precinct a list of their names."

Here we may see that arbitrary power is always the same in nature, in every age, and every country. " Go ye, serve the Lord ; only let your flocks and your herds be stayed," said Pharaoh. Let their polls be exempted, but their estates and faculties be taxed, said the Massachusetts. Herein they imitated him ; but in two other points they went beyond him. " Go not very far away," said Pharaoh ; " Go but five miles," said the Massachusetts ; though many of their own parishioners, from that day to this, must go much further than that to meeting. Neither did Pharaoh require a list of the people upon oath, as these did. Little did Mr. Hollis know how his brethren here were treated. His friend Wheaton, who, as was before observed, with many of his society, lived within the bounds of Rehoboth, now hoped for some relief; and for that end applied to their next County Court; but they were told by the judges that said law did not take place that year. And for refusing to pay that year's tax to John Greenwood and David Turner, ministers of that town, twenty-eight Baptists, two Quakers, and two Episcopalians,[1] were seized and imprisoned at Bristol, by Jonathan Bosworth and Jacob Ormsbee, constables of Rehoboth ; the main of them on March 3, 1729. Hereupon

[1]Obadiah Bowen, Azriakim Peirce, Jonathan Thurber, Jeremiah Ormsbee, Squire Wheeler, Daniel Bullock, Samuel Goff, Joseph Bowen, James Hicks, Seth Guernsey, Edmund Ingalls, Benjamin Ingalls, Ephraim Martin, Miel Peirce, Samuel Thurber, William Wheeler, Philip Wheeler, Gideon Hammond, Jeremiah Ormsbee, jun., Ephraim Martin, jun., John Jones, James Lewis, Thomas Horton, Richard Round, Jotham Carpenter, Samuel Bullock, Richard Bullock, Ephraim Wheaton, jun., Baptists; Henry Finch and John Hicks, Quakers; Samuel Carpenter and John Bowen, Episcopalians. Philip Wheeler was Colonel of the militia in that county afterwards. Wheaton was son to their minister.

they sent a petition to Governor Burnet in Council; wherein they claimed charter rights, and mentioned the late declaration from England, that there was no national or provincial
church established here, and the release of prisoners upon
that footing; and that if relief was not granted to them,
they soon expected the imprisonment of several Baptists and
Quakers of Taunton and Norton, on the same score. The
Governor and Council, on March 8, gave their opinion, that
said law did take place the preceding year; and ordered
Seth Williams, Esq., Chief Judge of that county, to convene
a number of Justices at Bristol, and to do all they lawfully
could for the release of those prisoners. He convened some
of them, but gave no relief to those men. Mr. Comer came
and preached to them March 11. And as no other way appeared of deliverance from a nauseous place which had injured their health, but paying said taxes and costs. this was
soon after done by their friends. However, lest further
complaints should be carried to England, the Assembly at
Boston. November 19, 1729, added an act to exempt their
estates and faculties also; but " under the same conditions
and limitations that their polls were before." And it was
not to exempt from any tax that was made, and then in collectors' hands, nor to continue in force any longer than their
May session, 1733.

After the death of Governor Saltonstall, the Connecticut
Assembly of October 8, 1724, elected Joseph Talcott, Esq.,
in his stead; under whose administration they enjoyed more
liberty for seventeen years, than they had under his predecessor. Stephen Gorton was ordained, at New London, pastor of the second Baptist church in Connecticut, November
28, 1726, by the assistance of their elders, Wightman, of
Groton, and Comer, of Newport. And as Wightman was
called to preach in Lyme, Mr. John Bulkly, a learned minister of Colchester, came and held a public dispute with
him at Lyme, June 7, 1727, upon baptism and ministers'
support. The question concerning the latter point Wight-

man stated thus :—" Whether ministers of the gospel ought
to be maintained, in the least, by goods taken away by force
from men of contrary persuasions ?"   And he gave these
reasons against that practice :—" 1. Because there is no precept nor precedent for so doing in the New Testament.
2. Because so to do is what we would not be done unto ourselves.   3. Because the Lord requires only volunteers, and
not forced men in his service."   But Bulkly refused to dispute upon this footing, and shifted the question, to whether
their way was lawful or not ?   And, after going far about,
he said, " Lawful authority have a right to determine the
undetermined modes of moral duties."   To which Wightman said, " 1. But they must always determine the mode in
the order of morality, and so they may do to others, as they
would they should do to them in like case.   Now would you
have the superior powers of England so to determine for
you, that you may have liberty and only bear your own
charges in this affair ?   2. This point, I think, is not undetermined in Scripture, which shows us no other way for the
support of the gospel ministry, but what is from the free-
will offerings of the people."   And as Bulkly raked together
many scandalous things that had been published against the
Baptists, and then said, " They are but of yesterday, and so
consequently the truth cannot be with them, as being not
known in the world till about two hundred years past;"
Wightman replied and said, " I never read of a Presbyterian
longer than the said term ; how then can the way of truth
be with them ?   If you say there were men of your principles many years before, I answer, that there were men professing the doctrines maintained by us long before that time."[1]

The May session of Connecticut Legislature, in 1729,
passed an act in favor of Quakers, to exempt all from ministerial taxes, " who do attend the worship of God in such
way as is allowed, and shall produce a certificate from such
society, of their having joined themselves to them, and that

[1] Bulkly, pp. 132, 176; Wightman, pp. 25, 28, 41.

they do belong unto their society." At an association of Baptist churches at North Kingstown, September 6, 1729, they drew a petition to the General Assembly of Connecticut, that their brethren who were scattered up and down in that Colony, might be exempted from taxes to ministers and meeting-houses that they dissented from; which was signed by Richard Sweet, Valentine Wightman, Samuel Fisk, John Comer, elders; Timothy Peckom, Joseph Holmes, Ebenezer Cook, Benjamin Herenden, and other brethren, to the number of eighteen, one of whom was Thomas Durkee of Windham; to which was afterward added these lines, viz.:—

We, the subscribers, do heartily concur with the memorial of our brethren on the other side, and do humbly request the same may be granted, which we think will much tend to Christian unity, and be serviceable to true religion, and will very much rejoice your honors' friends, and very humble servants,

JOSEPH JENCKS, Governor,
JAMES CLARK,
DANIEL WIGHTMAN, Elders.

Newport, September 10, 1729.

Hereupon the Assembly, who met at New Haven, October 9, 1729, passed an act to allow the Baptists the same privileges as were granted to the Quakers the May before; both of them being perpetual laws, and not such temporary acts as the Massachusetts have perplexed themselves and others with. President Stiles informs me, that the Baptists in Saybrook were the first who took the benefit of this act.

A concise account of the affairs of the college over which he presides shall close this chapter. Connecticut Legislature first granted a charter for it in 1701. It was then intended to be at Saybrook; but after hot contentions, wherein a large and valuable part of their library was lost, it was settled at New Haven in 1718. Elihu Yale, Esq., Governor of the East India Company in London, made large donations to it, upon which it was called Yale College. In 1719, Mr. Timothy Cutler, minister at Stratford, was chosen Rector of it. But in September, 1722, he resigned that office, and went to England for Episcopal ordination, from whence he also received the title of D. D., and was a missionary many years in Boston.   After his departure, Mr. Samuel Andrew, minister at Milford, presided at their Commencements, until Mr. Elisha Williams, of Wethersfield, was chosen their Rector in 1725 ; which office he sustained with honor to himself, and advantage to others, till he resigned it on October 31, 1739, and removed back to Wethersfield. He often represented this town in their Assembly, and was serviceable in other offices, one of which was to go over as a special agent for his colony to England.   Mr. Thomas Clap, of Windham, succeeded him in the college ; the government of which, by their first charter, was in the Trustees, who chose the Rector and tutors.   But by a more ample charter from their Legislature, dated May 9, 1745, their order was changed to that of, " The President and Fellows of Yale College, in New Haven," whose number is twelve. The eleven Fellows are all settled ministers, who elect the President, and also their own members, when any of them resign, die, or are displaced ; seven of the Corporation being a quorum.[1]

[1]Douglas, Vol. II, pp. 183—188.

APPENDIX A.[1]

Having had several interviews with divers of the people called Quakers, on the subject of the first volume of my History, and finding I have not clearly expressed their sentiments and practices, and some facts appearing to me different from what they did when I wrote, I am desirous, with them, to have the History corrected, and matters put in such a light, that posterity may not misapprehend them. Let the reader therefore receive the following correction, as what appears to me most consistent with the truth, and in justice to that people ought to be transmitted to posterity.

In page 117, the following extract from John Tyso's letter, "There was nothing *in* him (i. e. Dr. Increase Mather, as he said) that he hoped to be saved by," having been made by me to manifest an error in Friends respecting Christ within ; I would observe, that I do not look upon it as an error, provided Christ without be also acknowledged, and it be held agreeably to the true sense of John vi. 56, xvii. 26 ; I John iii. 24 ; in which sense I am informed it is held by Friends.

In pages 118, 119, I have quoted some of Roger Williams's arguments against Friends' sentiments of the grace of God having appeared, or being manifested to all mankind universally ; for their answer to which arguments, I would refer to Fox, &c., Answer, pages 17—20, Second part.

In page 245, I mentioned that Quakers were so called from Fox and his companions trembling and quaking before Gervase Bennet, a Justice in Derby. I meant not to insinuate, that their trembling on that occasion, or others, was occasioned by the fear of man ; neither do I on a review of proofs find sufficient grounds to reject Fox's account of their receiving said name, which follows in the same page ; though it is allowed by Barclay, as well as Mosheim, that their quaking and trembling in other places occasioned their being commonly called by that name.

[1] In the former edition, this Appendix is at the close of Volume II. As the arrangement of volumes is changed in the present edition, and the Appendix refers entirely to Volume I, it is inserted here.—ED.

In page 256, I undertake to inform posterity how those Quakers behaved under their sufferings ; upon a review of which it appears just to add, that I find, and that by other parts of Cudworth's uncontroverted letter, not quoted by me, that he was turned out of office, as he expressly says, "Because I had entertained some of the Quakers at my house, that thereby I might be the better acquainted with their principles ; the Court professing they had nothing at all against me, only in that thing, of giving entertainment to the Quakers." And he informs us, "that when the Quakers were committed to prison, they must be kept on coarse bread and water ; no Friend may bring them any thing, none permitted to speak with them, nay, if they have money of their own, they may not make use of that to relieve themselves ; they have many adherents ; and, a little to acquaint you with their sufferings, which is grievous unto and saddens the hearts of most of the precious saints of God, it lies down and rises up with them, and they cannot put it out of their minds, to see and hear of poor families deprived of their comforts, and brought into penury and want. As far as I am able to judge of the end, it is to force them from their homes and lawful habitations, and to drive them out of their coasts. As for the means by which they are impoverished, these in the first place were scrupulous of an oath." This does not appear to be confined to allegiance or fidelity to government, but oaths at large, which principle, I understand, they maintain from our Saviour's command ; Matt. v. 34 ; I say unto you swear not all, &c. "Why then we must put in force an old law, that all may take the oath of fidelity ; —they cannot—then a fine of five pounds. On this account thirty-five head of cattle, as I am credibly informed, hath been by the authority of the Court taken from them the latter part of this summer. A poor weaver that has seven or eight small children, himself lame in his body, had but two cows, and both taken from him. The marshal asked him what he would do? The man said, that God, who gave him them, he doubted not, would still provide for him. To fill up the measure yet more full, though to the further emptying of Sandwich men, the Court of Assistants, the first Tuesday of this instant, was pleased to determine fines upon them for meetings, one hundred and fifty pounds, and among others the poor weaver spoken of, twenty pounds, &c." And after his mentioning their not suffering their friends of Rhode Island to come and trade with them, proceeds, " So that unless the Lord steps in to their help and assistance, in some way beyond men's conceiving, their case is sad and to be pitied, and truly it moves bowels of compassion in all sorts except those in place, who carry it with a high hand towards them. Our bench now is Thomas Prince, Governor, &c." See the letter in Bishop's History, pages 168—177, or more at large in the second volume, folio, of the book of sufferings of the Quakers, pages 191—195, which last I did not see till since the publication of the first volume of my History.

From the foregoing account, and what Bishop charges upon Governor Prince, viz., " That in thy conscience they were such a people as deserved to be destroyed, they, their wives, their children, their houses and lands, without pity or mercy ;" which sentiment of his against the Quakers, I am told, is remembered in the family, being handed down to those of his posterity now living, it must therefore be acknowledged, he must have had too great a share in the persecutions mentioned ; and as the persecuted Norton said, the strength of darkness must then have been too unhappily over him.   And in justice to Humphry Norton's character (which is understood to be lessened by my manner of inserting his letter, and treating this subject, in pages 247, 257, of my History) I think further to manifest his and J. Rouse's behavior under their sufferings, by inserting a paragraph in Bishop's History, page 179, which would render my account more intelligible and full.   Speaking of the number of lashes, which I mentioned, he adds, " Which as it drew store of blood, so it took much with the spectators, who beheld them in the stocks first praying, then saluting each other, and bidding the executioner have patience a little (when he came to take off their clothes) and he should see they could give their backs to the smiters."   And Bishop adds, that "They gave in a paper assigning the grounds and reasons of their returning, when they were demanded wherefore they came in, which the magistrates would not suffer to be read ; and so envious were they, that for taking John Rouse by the hand they put three of the inhabitants of Sandwich in the stocks."   And it appears by the said Bishop's History, and the book of Friends' sufferings, that other whippings and persecutions followed in Plymouth Colony, and the said Humphry Norton, under whippings and other persecutions at New Haven, appears to have behaved in a Christian temper, when being loosed from the stocks after being whipped, having a great iron key tied athwart his mouth, and burnt deep in his hand with a red hot iron, " He kneeled down and prayed to the Lord, uttering his voice towards heaven, to the astonishment of them all."   The reader is referred thereto for a more particular account.

In page 257, I intrepreted the figurative expressions of " Rending the rocks of wisdom and knowledge, and exalting that which is low," as directed against civil and ecclesiastical government, which I supposed they meant to subject to a supposed spiritual power in Christians without outward laws and rules : but on further inquiry and conversation with Friends, I am convinced that they thereby referred to the coming of the Lord, by his spiritual work, to level the wise and great, compared to mountains ; and the literal knowledge and mere scholastic divinity, compared to rocks, as being hard to penetrate and break ; for that which is meek and low to be exalted, even Christ within, the hope of glory. In which sense I perceive that passage is now understood by Friends.

In the same page I observed, on some preceding extracts from Fox's and

Williams's writings, " This opens the plain cause, why they (the Quakers) militated so hard against other magistrates and government." And in the form of an allegory, in page 408, it is said, " To whom others made fierce opposition professedly from the light within ; and their clashings were so great that several lives were lost in the fray." The terms " militate," " fierce opposition," and " clashing" to the loss of lives, used to represent the conduct of Friends in those days, in respect to civil government, are too harsh to be justified by any authenticated facts. I conceive it to be essential to civil government, that the magistrate have a power to inflict corporal punishments, and also to arm his subjects to war against invaders of their rights, and therefore that the teaching of a contrary doctrine in either of these points, so far as it has influence, tends to obstruct or pull down government ; and in no other sense did I ever mean to charge the Quakers with militating against or obstructing government.

I find they allow magistrates to inflict corporal punishments upon their subjects, who transgress the rules of equity ;[1] but do not approve of arming their subjects to war against others. And in all States where they have been, I know nothing but that, as a society, they have been either actively obedient thereto, or have passively suffered what they were pleased to inflict upon them, without plotting against the government thereof, or using any forcible resistance against it. And I desire the reader to remember that I mean to correct every thing in my History that seemingly or really contradicts these ideas, and this character of the society.

In page 258, I speak of our Lord's direction to his disciples, Mat. x. 23, and of his own conduct towards the Gergesenes, Mat. viii. 34, as forming a general rule for us, thence charging some blame upon those Quakers who returned into the Massachusetts ; whereas they now both appear to me to refer to special and peculiar cases.

As to the writings I referred to on page 260, I rather think my memory failed me in that respect ; and as to not having light from Scripture, for actions, in the same page, I find that they suppose that Isaiah xx. 2, and Micah, i. 8, prove, that the women there mentioned might be moved by the divine Spirit to do those actions ; of which the reader is left to judge for himself.

Upon a review of pages 259 and 367, compared with their own writings, I find that I had some mistaken ideas of what they held concerning the light within, and therefore freely refer the reader to their own authors for information in that respect.

I did not mean, in page 367, to charge them with calling darkness light, any further than wherein they appeared to be against allowing others the

---

[1]See Fox's Epistle to Friends at Nevis, in 1675. Also, Isaac Pennington's Works, folio, First part, p. 323.

free liberty of examining, and by arguments opposing sentiments which they judged to be erroneous ; which, whether they were against or not, I freely submit to the reader's judgment.

William Harris is referred to in page 128, note 1, and in page 363, is named as a Quaker ; I am now convinced that he was not one then, if he ever was ; and the word *only*, as I twice used it in page 373, and once in page 375, in a way that seems to acquit Mr. Williams from any blame in his dispute with the Quakers, was more than I intended ; for I really think there was a great deal of imperfection discovered by him, as well as his opponents, in the management of that dispute ; and if he meant to punish any merely for their plain use of Thee and Thou (which I think he did not) I do not concur with any such thing.

In page 368, I have not so fully quoted Friends' answer to Roger Williams's objections as might be necessary to give an adequate view of both sides of the dispute ; therefore I refer my reader to their writings on that subject, particularly George Fox's Answer to said objections, page 155, and Appendix, pages 117, 118.

Page 374, line 22, after the word " sentence" insert, " viz., blood will be given," which words are particularly marked, as referred to by Grove.

As by the "grapes of Sodom and clusters of Gommorah," in page 366, some might suppose I meant to charge the vices, that are couched under those expressions, upon the Quakers ; I here declare that I meant no such thing.

Perhaps the partiality, in favor of Mr. Cotton, which I mention in page 374, was owing to Mr. Coddington's particular affection for him, rather than to the cause there assigned.

APPENDIX B.

CONTAINING A BRIEF SUMMARY OF THE ECCLESIASTICAL AFFAIRS OF THIS COUNTRY DOWN TO THE PRESENT TIME. [1777.][1]

Four principles have, in different ages and countries, been proposed to found government upon, viz., nature, grace, power and compact. James the First took much pains to persuade his people, that he was born to rule them; even so that the privileges he was pleased to allow them, were rather favors from him, than original rights in them. And his flattering courtiers, perceiving his humor, gave him the title of "Sacred Majesty," which the kingdom was very little acquainted with before. His high claims occasioned perpetual troubles to himself, and cost his son his crown and the head that wore it. And when facts are examined it appears, that Henry VII, from whom came their hereditary title, had as little right by birth to the crown of England, as any man that had worn it in five hundred years; and he made his way to it through blood and slaughter.[2] The pope has been the most notable advocate for founding dominion in grace; and by deceitful reasonings from the Jewish hand-writing, he has usurped the seat of him who is head of all principality and power. Henry VIII took offence at the pope's conduct, and rejecting his power assumed it to himself; and many others, not holding the Head have subjected souls to slavish ordinances, after the doctrines and commandments of men. Col. 2. Cromwell was a notable actor upon the third principle, who, having gotten the power into his hands, pleaded that he ought to use it for the good of the nation; and his enemies acknowledge the excellency of his talents for government, if he had but obtained his power in a righteous way. But

[1]This Appendix closed Volume I of the former edition. Being the summary of the history of a period that is treated in full in the succeeding volumes, it is largely repeated in them. Parts of it will be recognized in the last four chapters, which were in Volume II of the former edition, and parts in Volume II of the present edition.—ED.

[2]Rapin, Vol. II, pp. 160, 161.

he, dying, left the nation in great confusion ; to get relief from which they
restored the second Charles, with good words and fair speeches, without
settling any fixed and certain conditions with him.   Soon after this, priestcraft was used to stir up tumults in different parts of the country, and then
to cry, The church is in danger ! which moved the parliament to make
laws to exclude all persons from teaching either in churches or schools,
who refused an assent and consent to their ordinances of men, and also
to declare it to be unlawful to take up arms against the king, upon any
pretence whatsoever.   And, as Dr. Calamy observes, passive obedience
and non-resistance, was the doctrine that for twenty-five years made their
pulpits ring and presses groan.   Yet, no sooner was this doctrine turned
against the Episcopalians than, behold ! they called in the prince of Orange
with an armed force, to drive their king from his throne !   And now the
fourth principle is preferred, and a compact, containing a large Bill of
Rights, is made with William before his coronation ; and he and his queen
were brought, " solemnly to promise and swear to govern the people of the
kingdom of England, and the dominions thereto belonging, according to
the statutes in parliament agreed on, and the laws and customs of the
same ; and, to their power, to cause law and justice to be executed in
mercy, in all their judgments."   They enacted that this oath should be
taken by all their successors in that office.

Now the word of God plainly shows, that this way of mutual compact
or covenant, is the only righteous foundation for civil government.   For
when Israel must needs have a king like the rest of the nations, and he
indulged them in that request, yet neither Saul nor David, who were
anointed by his immediate direction, ever assumed the regal power over
the people, but by their free consent.   And though the family of David
had the clearest claim to hereditary succession that any family on earth
ever had, yet, when ten of the twelve tribes revolted from his grandson,
because he refused to comply with what they esteemed a reasonable proposal, and he had collected an army to bring them back by force, God
warned him not to do it, and he obeyed him therein.   Had these plain
precedents been regarded in later times, what woes and miseries would
they have prevented !   But the history of all ages and nations shows, that
when men have got the power into their hands, they often use it to gratify
their own lusts, and recur to nature, religion or the constitution (as they
think it will best serve) to carry, and yet cover, their wretched designs.
A lamentable proof of this is now before us.

Dr. Mather, as a capable and faithful friend to his country, labored un-
weariedly to have the rights and privileges of it restored and enlarged ; in
order to which he prevailed with Archbishop Tillotson to tell the king that,
" it would by no means do well for him to take any of those privileges
from the people of New England, which king Charles the First had granted

them." He likewise obtained a promise from Bishop Burnet that, "on the first opportunity he would declare openly in the House of Lords, that there was a greater sacredness in the charter of New England, than in those of the corporations in England; because those were only acts of grace, whereas the charter of New England was a contract between the king and the first patentees. They promised the king to enlarge his dominions on their own charges, provided they and their posterity might enjoy such and such privileges; they had performed their part; now for the king to deprive their posterity of the privileges therein granted unto them, would carry a face of injustice in it." This had some effect upon the king's mind, and caused a scruple whether he might lawfully take from us the privilege of choosing our chief rulers or not. To this some of his arbitrary councillors said, "Whatever might be the merit of the cause, inasmuch as the charter of the Massachusetts stood vacated by a judgment against it, it was in his power to put them under what form of government he should think best for them."[1] This was so flattering and plausible that it took with William, who had often heard of their persecutions here, and thought that by reserving to himself a power to negative all their acts, he should prevent the like for the future.

Accordingly a new charter was drawn, dated October 7, 1691, which included Plymouth colony, consisting of the counties of Plymouth, Barnstable and Bristol; the Massachusetts colony, which contained the counties of Suffolk, Middlesex, Essex, Worcester, Hampshire and Berkshire; the Province of Maine, viz., the counties of York and Cumberland; and Sagadahoc, which, with lands annexed in the county of Lincoln, extends to Nova Scotia. The islands south of Cape Cod were included in this charter of The Province of the Massachusetts Bay in New England, which reserved an arbitrary power in the crown, to appoint our Governor, Lieutenant Governor and Secretary; but that the people might choose a House of Representatives annually, to meet upon the last Wednesday in May; when they were to elect twenty-eight Councillors, which was to be their Legislature; the Council and House to have a negative on each other's acts, and after both were agreed therein, yet the Governor, or in his absence the Lieutenant Governor, might negative any act they could pass, and also negative the election of as many Councillors as he pleased. Upon all times, except election day, he could call, adjourn, prorogue or dissolve the Assembly at pleasure. He had the sole power of appointing military officers; and was to appoint all officers of the courts of justice with the consent of the Council; other civil officers were elected by the two houses, where he had his negative; and no money could issue out of the treasury but by his warrant, by the advice and consent of the Council. And after

[1]Mather's Life, pp. 126, 127, 132.

all, the king in council could, at any time within three years, disannul any act or law that all three branches here could make. Now from whence came this arbitrary power in the crown of England over this country? Their plea founded upon the vacation of the former contract, would disannul any contract that could possibly be made with any distant people in the world ; for a complaint against us was entered and judgment was passed, before we could possibly have opportunity to answer for ourselves. The charter of the city of London was vacated by the same court, where they had opportunity to answer ; but they would not crown William and Mary till that judgment was reversed, and all the charters in England restored, and their privileges enlarged much beyond what they were when the contract was made with New England. And in that, the king engaged for himself, his heirs and successors, that we should hold our lands, " in free and common socage, and not *in capite*, nor by knights' service, we yielding and paying to him, his heirs and successors the fifth part only of all ore of gold and silver, which from time to time and at all times hereafter shall be gotten, had or obtained, for all services, exactions and demands whatsoever."[1] And let our oppressors show if they can that we ever violated this contract.

As to affairs here, the charter declared " liberty of conscience in the worship of God to all Christians, except Papists, inhabiting or which shall inhabit or be resident within our said province or territory." But this most important article was construed by the ministers, as meaning, " that the General Court might, by laws, encourage and protect that religion which is the general profession of the inhabitants."[2]

Accordingly they in October of this year began the practice, which a noted author described thirty-four years after, in the following manner. After reciting an old saying, that ministers of the gospel would have a poor time of it, if they must rely on a free contribution of the people for their maintenance, he says, " The laws of the province having had the royal approbation to ratify them, they are the king's laws. By these laws it is enacted, that there shall be a public worship of God in every plantation ; that the person elected by the majority of the inhabitants to be so, shall be looked upon as the minister of the place ; that the salary for him which they shall agree upon, shall be levied by a rate upon all the inhabitants. In consequence of this, the minister thus chosen by the people, is (not only Christ's, but also) in reality the king's minister ; and the salary for him is raised in the king's name, and is the king's allowance unto him. If the most of the inhabitants in a plantation are Episcopalians, they will have a minister of their own persuasion ; and the dissenters, if there be any in the place, must pay their proportion of the tax for the support of this legal

[1] Massachusetts History, Vol. III, pp. 8, 9.
[2] Massachusetts History, Vol. II, p. 10. [17.]

minister. In a few of the towns, a few of the people, in hope of being released from the tax for the legal minister, sometimes profess themselves Episcopalians ; but when they plead this for their exemption, their neighbors tell them, they know in their consciences, they do not as they would be done unto. And if a Governor go by his arbitrary power to supersede the execution of the law, and require the justices and constables to leave the Episcopalians out of the tax, the people wonder he is not aware that he is all this while forbidding that the king should have his dues paid unto him ; and forbidding the king's minister to receive what the king has given him. .... Sometimes the Quakers also have given some occasion for uneasiness ; but where Quakerism is troublesome, some towns are so wise as to involve the salary for the ministry in a general rate for all town charges, and so the cavils of those, who would else refuse to pay the rate for the ministry, are obviated."[1]

A few facts may help to explain this, and to show how much greater liberty of conscience we have enjoyed since the Revolution[2] than before. Before that memorable event, no man in the Massachusetts colony was allowed a vote, in choosing either minister or ruler, but members in full communion in their churches. And the skill of knowing that those who dissented from their judgments, sinned against their own consciences, was then limited to such good men ; but now, having forty pounds worth of personal estate, or a freehold worth forty shillings a year, entitles every inhabitant to a vote in all such affairs, and to a power of judging that their neighbors sin against the golden rule, if they will not put into the mouths of him whom the majority has declared to be the legal minister. From that day to this, it is made a doubt among our lawyers and judges, whether a church of Christ be a society known in law, so as to be capable of holding a meeting-house or other estates, without having other persons to be trustees or guardians for them. The honorable Edward Goddard, Esq., of Framingham, who had been a member both of the Lower and Upper House, in our Legislature, described this matter to the life, in a piece he published in 1753, wherein he says :

> "Good conscience men allow, (they say)
> But must be understood,
> To say as they say themselves do say,
> Or else it can't be good."

For thirty-six years after the Massachusetts received their last charter, they exerted all their power, both in their legislative and executive courts, with every art that ministers could help them to, in attempts to compel every town to receive and support such ministers as they called orthodox.

[1] Mather's Ratio Disciplinæ, pp. 20--22.
[2] The abdication of James II, and the accession of William and Mary.—ED.

They made two attempts of this nature upon Swanzey; and in 1722, they added the sum of one hundred and seventy-two pounds eleven shillings, to the province taxes upon Dartmouth and Tiverton, for such ministers, intending that they should draw it out of the province treasury. For refusing to assess the same, Joseph Anthony, John Sisson, John Akin, Quakers, and Philip Tabor, a Baptist minister, Select-men of those towns, were seized and confined in Bristol jail, till the case was carried to England, and those taxes were disannulled by the king in council, and an express order was sent over to release them.

The first act that was made in our province, to exempt either Baptists or Quakers from taxes to Pædobaptist ministers was in 1728; which says, "that from and after the publication of this act, none of the persons commonly called Anabaptists, nor any of those called Quakers, that are or shall be enrolled or entered in their several societies as members thereof, and who allege a scruple of conscience as the reason of their refusal to pay any part or proportion of such taxes as are from time to time assessed for the support of the minister or ministers of the churches established by the laws of this province, in the town or place where they dwell, shall have their polls taxed toward the support of such minister or ministers, nor shall their bodies be at any time taken in execution, to satisfy any such ministerial rate or tax, assessed upon their estates or faculties; provided, that such persons do usually attend the meetings of their respective societies, assembling upon the Lord's day for the worship of God, and that they live within five miles of the place of such meeting." Here we may see that tyranny is always the same. "*Go ye serve the Lord ; only let your flocks and your herds be stayed,*" said Pharaoh. Let their bodies be exempted, but their estates and faculties be taxed, said the Massachusetts. "*I will let you go, that ye may sacrifice to the Lord your God in the wilderness ; only you shall not go very far away,*" said Pharaoh. Go but five miles, said the Massachusetts. Mr. Thomas Hollis, of London, had received such accounts of their catholic temper at Harvard College, confirmed by the ordination of a pious youth in Boston who was educated there,[1] that he became the greatest benefactor to that college that they ever had. I have a letter which he wrote to Mr. Ephriam Wheaton, pastor of the first church in Swanzey, dated March 23, 1723, wherein he says, "You have heard, or may be informed by Mr. Callender, of my foundation in Harvard College, and the provision I have made for Baptist youth to be educated for the ministry, and equally regarded with Pædobaptists. If you know any as may be duly qualified, inform me, and I shall be glad to recommend them for first vacancy." But what heart could he have to send any youths there, while a large number of his brethren, who, with himself, lived within the bounds of Rehoboth, were taxed from year to year to

[1]See pp. 420, 421.

Presbyterian ministers! After the above exempting act was made, they were told by their County Court, that it did not take place that year. For refusing to pay such taxes any longer, Elder Wheaton's son, and twenty-seven more of his people were seized on March 3, 1729, and confined in Bristol jail. More or less of such things, which by their eminent fathers are called tyranny and robbery,[1] have been practised to this day, under the mask of religion.

My dear countrymen, I must here solemnly call you to review the text which has often been cast upon us, viz., " Mark them who cause divisions and offences, contrary to the doctrine which ye have learned, and avoid them : for they that are such, serve not our Lord Jesus Christ, but their own belly ; and by good words and fair speeches deceive the hearts of the simple." The uppermost party in every state has always been ready to apply this word to those who refuse a submission and conformity to them in religious matters. But the mark is set upon them who *cause* divisions, not merely upon such as are divided. Joseph was separated from his brethren, without his being the faulty cause of it. Again the mark is put upon such as cause divisions, *contrary to Christ's doctrine;* otherwise he declares himself, that he came to send divisions upon earth, and even betwixt near relations. This matter is justly stated in pages 421, 422. The inspired apostle commands us in the name of Christ to withdraw from every brother that walketh disorderly :—for we behaved not ourselves disorderly among you, neither did we *eat any man's bread for naught;* yet this great disorder has long been practised under good words and fair speeches. A pagan minister who loved the wages of unrighteousness once cudgelled his beast most cruelly for not carrying him forward against a drawn sword, whereby he would have been slain : and though the dumb ass, speaking with man's voice, forbade the madness of the prophet, yet the above practice which never had any better support than the cudgel,[2] is madly pursued by many who call themselves Christians to this day.

A convention of ministers published a discourse among us five years ago, entitled Catholicism, or Christian Charity ; wherein, after saying many excellent things about charity, they, in page 38, accuse those who separated from their constitution in 1744, of zeal, yea rather fury against " giving and receiving ministerial support ;" and with a want of " consistency and honesty," for now coming into that practice themselves. It is well known that this censure is leveled against many of my brethren and myself with them. I readily confess that I separated from their constitution about the close of that year ; but positively deny that ever I appeared against giving and receiving ministerial support, and know not that any of my brethren in the ministry who separated from them ever did so. Had they said that we were zealous against assessing and forcing in such cases, they would not have wronged the truth and their neighbors, as they have now done.   The constitution that we separated from, was formed in Saybrook in 1708, which says, "that the churches which are neighboring to each other, shall consociate for mutual affording to each other such assistance as may be requisite, *upon all occasions ecclesiastical.*"   Their first proof to support this article is Psalm 122. 3—5, which speaks of the thrones of judgment that were set in Jerusalem for the house of David.   A crafty ministerial Governor,[1] son to a Massachusetts magistrate, prevailed with the Connecticut legislature to approbate this platform the next year.   Another Cambridge scholar[2] was then minister of Norwich, and was resolute to introduce the scheme there.   The law whereby it was approbated said, "Provided, that nothing herein shall be intended or construed to hinder any society or church that is, or shall be, allowed by the laws of this government, from exercising worship and discipline in their own way, according to their consciences."   Yet, because Richard Bushnel and Joseph Backus, Esquires, representatives for Norwich, (with other fathers of the town,) withdrew from the minister's party, rather than come under that yoke, they laid them under church censure, and by that means procured their expulsion out of the next Assembly when they met.   About the same time, Mr. Stoddard publicly advanced his scheme of the Lord's Supper being a converting ordinance.[3]   And though with much labor Norwich got rid of said minister, and settled another upon their former principles, yet, before I left this latter minister, he not only plainly discovered his fondness for Saybrook Platform, but actually procured a vote of the church to receive members without so much as a written account of any inward change ; and they practise so to this day.   A few months before I separated, Mr. Elisha Williams, a former President of Yale College, published A Seasonable Plea for the Rights of Conscience, wherein he says, " The fountain and original of all civil power is from the people, and is certainly instituted for their sakes ; the great end of civil government, is the preservation of their persons, their liberties, and their property.   A Christian is to receive his Christianity from Christ alone ; for what is it which is necessarily implied and supposed in the very notion of a Christian but this, that he is a follower and disciple of Christ !   As Christ's officers have authority to teach men his mind in things pertaining to his kingdom ; so they have no authority to teach men anything but the mind and will of Christ.   It is a truth that shines with a meridian brightness, that whatever is not contained in a commission, is out of it, and excluded by it ; and the teaching his laws only being contained in the commission, what is not his

---

[1] Gurdon Saltonstall, minister in New London, before his election as Governor. See p. 469.—ED.

[2] John Woodward.   See p. 474.—ED.

[3] See p. 385, note.—B.   See also pp. 462, 468.—ED.

law is out of it, and by that commission they are excluded from teaching it, or forbid by it."

But what can be more contrary hereto than for a civil legislature to form every town and parish into religious societies, and to force every inhabitant therein either to support the minister which the majority have chosen, or else to pay a yearly acknowledgment to that usurped power over their consciences? And this is as real a breach of public faith in our charter, as ever it was for the British Court to take from us the right of choosing our own Governors, and then to burn our towns and cut our throats for not paying them as much money as they demanded. I have the express testimony of the elders and brethren of seventeen of our Baptist churches, who met last year at Grafton, that they entirely agree with the sentiments and principles recited in our history, pages 10—22,[1] excepting that of infant baptism; yet great numbers of them have been taxed to Pædobaptist ministers since that time, only because we refuse to pay any further acknowledgment to the above-said usurped power over our consciences. And, since it is abundantly evident that our former sufferings would have been greater from the ruling party here than they were, if it had not been for restraints from the British Court; and as it is also certain that attempts have been made from thence to prevent our uniting now with our country against their invasions, how can those who still incline to oppress us ever expect to prosper, if they view the matter either in a natural, or a judicial light? Considered in a natural light; when we know and can prove that several thousand dollars' worth of estates have been wrested from us on religious accounts, since the present contest for civil liberty commenced, with what heart can we obey or support the power which still denies us equal liberty of conscience with themselves? And considering things judicially, let such read the warnings their fathers had, with their effects, on pages 209—212, 311—313, 416—418, and then venture on further in that way if they dare.

It is to be noted, that a very large number of our countrymen of various denominations are for the equal liberty we speak of; and I desire all to act in the case by the rule Mr. Robinson prescribes, pages 8, 9. I shall close with the words of the aforesaid Mr. Goddard, viz. :—

> "In ancient ages, when the English realm
> And popish zealots, placed at the helm
> To 'stablish that religion; tithes were fix'd

[1] "Our Agent having given an account of his and the Committee's proceedings in the year past, in presenting our memorial to the Assembly, &c., and having read a state of the difference betwixt our churches and those who oppress us, to be inserted in our history, it was voted, unanimously, That the account Elder Backus has drawn up, of the sentiments and practices of the Baptist societies, is entirely agreeable to the minds of this Association.

JAMES MANNING, Moderator."

Minutes of the Warren Association, Grafton, September 1⁰, 11, 1776, p. 6.—ED.

35

By canon laws; with civil intermix'd,
Which form'd the English constitution so,
That after ages can't the tithes forego;
And hence dissenters are obliged there,
To pay incumbents, whom they never hear,
Which some condemn, as a prelatic game,
Who yet, by MAJOR VOTE would play the same;
And LORD MAJORITY would claim the purse
For his incumbents; than which nothing worse,
LORDLY diocesan, himself, can claim;
So these two LORDS do differ, but in name,
One pleading English laws, for his support;
The other feigning acts of our own Court;
Alleging law, in a perverted sense,
To render CHARTER grant, a mere pretence;
And as if law and charter both intend
To crush one church, another to befriend;
They'd make them mean, the same that Pharaoh said,
' *Go serve the Lord, but let your flocks be stay'd.*'
But if one church be tax'd, to serve another,
No matter whether, done by this or t'other."

END OF VOLUME I.

A

HISTORY OF NEW ENGLAND.

WITH

Particular Reference to the Denomination of Christians

CALLED

BAPTISTS.

BY

ISAAC BACKUS.

———

Second Edition, with Notes.

BY

DAVID WESTON.

———

VOLUME II.

NEWTON, MASS.:
PUBLISHED BY THE BACKUS HISTORICAL SOCIETY.
1871.

PRINTED BY THE PROVIDENCE PRESS COMPANY, PROVIDENCE, R. I.

AUTHOR'S PREFACE TO VOLUME II.

The powers of thinking and choice are so essential to all rational spirits, that without them no idea can be formed of their existence. A desire of the knowledge and enjoyment of the best good, also appears essential to their nature. Therefore, as finite knowledge is limited, finite spirits would ever be liable to err, if they had not some sufficient guard against it. And the best guard we can conceive of, is a clear, fixed persuasion in the heart, that God is the only fountain of all good ; and that every desirable good is to be obtained and enjoyed in the way of obedience to his revealed will, and nowhere else.

That he is the absolute Proprietor, and the sovereign Ruler of the worlds he has made, is a truth too evident for any but madmen to deny. All nations have been forced to appeal to him, to avenge injustice and perjury, in order to establish any government among themselves. Yet how far have they been from a willingness to be governed entirely by him ! He made man upright ; but they have sought out many inventions. Objects of worship and forms of worship, even without number, have been invented by mankind ; the folly whereof God has exposed in all his dispensations : Yet self-conceit, self-seeking, and self-dependence, are still the ruining errors of the world.

His design in all his dispensations, in every age, and every country, is undoubtedly the same in nature with that declared to Israel, in the passage which adorns our title page.[1] Three things deserve particular notice therein. 1. That it is the Lord who leads his people through all the changing scenes of life, in this wilderness world. At different times and places their circumstances vary exceedingly ; yet he orders or overrules in all, so that a sparrow cannot fall to the ground, nor a hair from their head, without him. 2. All his dealings are calculated in infinite wisdom, for their trial and humiliation ; to discover what is in their hearts, whether they will keep

[1]Deut. viii. 2. Title page, Vol. II, old edition.—Ed.

his commandments, or not. Therefore, 3. He requires them to remember all the way wherein he leads them, for this end.

Christianity, the only true religion, has its name from Christ, the Foundation, Lawgiver, and only Head of his church. And one of the greatest historians of our age gives us the following account of its primitive order and government. Says he, "The rites instituted by Christ [himself], were only two in number, and these designed to continue to the end of the church here below, without any variation. These were Baptism and the Holy Supper; which were not to be considered as mere ceremonies, nor yet as symbolical representations only, but also as ordinances, accompanied with sanctifying influence upon the heart and affections of true Christians." Of those who heard and believed the preaching of John the Baptist, he says, "They were initiated into the kingdom of the Redeemer, by the ceremony of *immersion* or *baptism*." And during the first century, he says, " The sacrament of baptism was administered [in this century] without the public assemblies, in places appointed and prepared for that purpose, and was performed by *immersion* of the whole body."[1] This was the primitive way of admission into the Christian church; and of its government our author says, " The people were, undoubtedly, the first in authority; for the apostles shewed by their example, that nothing of moment was to be carried on or determined without the consent of the assembly. Acts i. 15; vi. 3; xv. 4; xxi. 22. .... A bishop, during the first and second century, was the person who had the care of one Christian assembly, which, at that time, was, generally speaking, small enough to be contained in a private house. In this assembly he acted not so much with the authority of a master, as with the zeal and diligence of a faithful servant." And he assures us, that until about the middle of the second century, " the churches were entirely independent; none of them subject to any foreign jurisdiction, but each one governed by its own rulers, and its own laws;" and that an alteration was then made, by industriously propagating the opinion, that Christian ministers succeeded to the rights and privileges of the Jewish priesthood.[2] Heathen philosophy was also called in to interpret the Scriptures by; from whence teachers adopted this maxim, viz., "That it was an act of virtue to deceive and lie, when by that means the interests of the church might be promoted." To which they added, in the fourth century, under Constantine, the use of temporal penalties, and corporal tortures, for the same end.[3]

In the mean time a controversy arose about bringing infants to baptism. In the beginning of the third century, Tertullian, who is the first writer that mentions it, opposed it, saying, " What need is there that the godfathers should be brought into danger? because they may either fail of their

[1]Mosheim's Eccl. Hist., Vol. I, pp. 32, 91, 96. Dublin edition.
[2]Ibid, pp. 70, 76, 77, 139. [3]Ibid, pp. 155, 314.

promises by death, or they may be mistaken by a child's proving of a wicked disposition." But not long after, Origen appeared for the practice, and said, "Let it be considered what is the reason, that whereas the baptism of the church is given for the forgiveness of sins, infants also are, by the usage of the church, baptized. It is for that reason, because by the sacrament of baptism the pollution of our birth is taken away, that infants are baptized."[1] Origen is the first man that any have produced, who pleaded for infant baptism : and he also held that the torments of the damned will have an end ; and that Christ will be crucified in the next world to save the devils.[2] Now when heathen philosophy was set up as a rule to interpret Scripture by ; when the shadows of the Old Testament were taken to draw a veil over the truth and church order described in the gospel, and teachers pretended to confer renewing grace by their administrations, before the subjects were taught or believed ; and also called in the secular arm to enforce their measures by temporal penalties and corporal tortures, what could be expected but the antichristian apostasy? Oh, how dark was the night that followed !

Yet God did not leave himself without witnesses in the darkest times ; some of whom I will name. Peter de Bruys, during a ministry of twenty years, made the most laudable attempts to reform abuses, and to remove the superstitions that disfigured the beautiful simplicity of the gospel, and had a great number of followers, in Languedoc and Provence, in France ; and he was burnt therefor at St. Giles, in the year 1130. His disciples were called Petrobrussians ; and a leading article of their faith was, " That no persons whatever were to be baptized before they came to the full use of their reason." Soon after, another minister, whose name was Henry, travelled from Switzerland through various parts of France, preaching the gospel with great success, until he came to the city of Thoulouse, where the Pope and his creatures raised great opposition against him, and cast him into prison in 1148 ; and he ended his days there not long after. He was thus dealt with because " He rejected the baptism of infants ; censured with severity the corrupt and licentious manner of the clergy, and treated the festivals and ceremonies of the church with the utmost contempt."[3]

This account is given by a very learned Lutheran author, who was strongly prejudiced against the modern Baptists, because he held that the Christian church was in its minority, when it was governed in the manner above described ; and that in its mature age, " the regulation of it was, in some measure, to be accommodated to the time, and left to the wisdom and prudence of the chief rulers, both of the State and of the church ;"[4] which opinion the Baptists have ever opposed. He freely owns, that the peculiarities of their churches in Germany and Holland are derived from a maxim

[1]Clark against Gill upon Baptism, pp. 105, 111.   [2]Mosheim, Vol. I, p. 476.
[3]Mosheim, Vol. II, pp. 437—439.   [4]Ibid, Vol. I, pp. 68—70.

of reformation, which was held by the Waldenses, Petrobrussians, Wickliff-
ites, and Hussites, long before Luther's day; which is, "That the kingdom of Christ, or the visible church he had established upon earth, was an
assembly of real and true saints, and ought therefore to be inaccessible to
the wicked and unrighteous, and also exempt from all those institutions,
which human prudence suggests to oppose the progress of iniquity, or to
correct and reform transgressors." This maxim he declares to be the
source of all their peculiarities. In 1525, and in 1533, a few men who
were called Anabaptists, took the lead among mixed multitudes, that had
taken up arms against cruel tyrants, in hopes of recovering both civil and
religious liberty thereby; but they perished in the attempt: A sight of
which carried the Baptist churches in that country so far into the other extreme, as not to allow their members to be magistrates, to use the sword,
or to take an oath ;[1] which are now the sentiments of the German Baptists
in Pennsylvania. But the English Baptists, both in Europe and America,
have carefully avoided each of these extremes, for these hundred and fifty
years; yet those scandals in Germany have been constantly cast upon them,
even down to this day; not because they ever had the least concern therewith, but because this has been found to be a powerful engine to prejudice
the populace against allowing equal religious liberty, and for forcing people
into religious covenants, before they can choose for themselves.

All the reformation that ever took place, in any age or country, was produced by the word of truth, enforced by the spirit of truth, upon each
heart and conscience. And the admission of unsanctified communicants
into the Christian church, and of the inventions of men to govern it, has
caused endless confusions; as thereby three opposite interests have been set
up. The interest of religious teachers, of civil officers, and of the people.
The two former have conspired together, to enslave the latter; and yet
have been far from an entire harmony betwixt themselves. Their contests
for preëminence have been long and tedious in this country; but a great
and effectual door is now opened for terminating these disputes, and for a
return to the primitive purity and liberty of the Christian church. To
trace out the evil effects of the apostasy, and to promote, as much as may
be, such a return, is the great design both of this and the former volume.
In compiling them a large number of records, books and papers, have been
searched, and much pains taken to set principles and actions in as clear
light as possible. And the author is so far from desiring indulgence in any
mistakes, that he earnestly requests the help of all to correct them.

MIDDLEBOROUGH, August 2, 1784.

[1] Mosheim, Vol. III, pp. 524, 525, 549.

AUTHOR'S PREFACE TO VOLUME III.

The former volumes of our history were published under great disadvantages. The first of them came out in the height of our war, when all the power of Britain was exerted to compel America to give up her most essential rights; while one sect here were as earnest to compel all others to submit to their power in religious matters. How difficult then was it for a very imperfect man to give a just view of these affairs! And the many mistakes of the printers rendered the work still more obscure. And though the second volume was better composed, and more correctly printed, yet the last part of it was hurried through the press, so as to prevent its being finished as I intended. Yet I know not of any public dispute about the truth of facts in the history. Many have privately discovered their dislike of the publication of them, because their own schemes of power and gain were exposed thereby.

For the capital scheme of policy, for two centuries past, both in Europe and America, has been to maintain a balance of power among the nations, and among religious sects, so as to compel all to submit to government. And a man of great knowledge in Pennsylvania, when he read my first volume, in 1779, said in a letter to me, "I think it needs not a spirit of prophecy to predict, that America is to be stained with the blood of the saints. I am afraid there is a foundation laid for it already. I wish it may not be with particular design. Formerly there was a proper balance of power between Episcopalians and Dissenters, taken in England and America together; but now that balance is lost. Formerly there was a check on the licentiousness of power in America, by an appeal to the crown; but where shall the persecuted Americans appeal now? Not to Congress, not to the united force of America; they disclaim any such right; they will be judges of no such matters. They can then only appeal to their oppressors and accusers." And he had the following reasons for his fears:—The American war begun between Episcopalians and Congre-

2B

gationalists, and the Presbyterians joined with the latter, and they were the uppermost party in Pennsylvania through the war. And when the Warren Association sent an agent to Philadelphia, while the first Congress was sitting there, in 1774, the members of it from the Massachusetts plainly manifested that they would sooner yield to the power of Britain, than they would give up their power of supporting Congregational ministers by tax and compulsion. And Boston, where the war began, was the only place in America where they had hanged men for religion. And an eminent man in Virginia says, "Several acts of the Virginia Assembly, of 1659, 1662 and 1693, had made it penal in parents to refuse to have their children baptized; had prohibited the unlawful assembling of Quakers; had made it penal for any master of a vessel to bring a Quaker into the State; had ordered those already here, and such as should come thereafter, to be imprisoned until they should abjure the country; provided a milder punishment for the first and second return, but death for their third. .... If no capital executions took place here, as did in New England, it was not owing to the moderation of the church, or spirit of the legislature, as may be inferred from the law itself; but to historical circumstances which have not been handed down to us."[1] Though the following things may alter his mind :—

1. The light of revelation hath ever enlarged the capacities of men beyond any other means in the world, so that wars among such have been the most destructive of any upon earth. Half a million of men were slain in one day, in a battle between Judah and Israel. II Chron. xiii. 17. And we have no record of such a slaughter in any other day since Adam fell. And the Quakers were so fierce against the teachers and rulers of the Massachusetts, that they did not see how they could possibly keep up their religious government without hanging some of them. But the government of Virginia was in no such danger from them.

2. The first of those laws in Virginia was made but just before Charles the Second came to the throne, who put a stop to those bloody executions here; and no man has been hanged since for religion, in England or America.

3. The Quakers hold that their children are born in their church, which, by a secret policy, has been upheld as one great body in Europe and America; and they held so much with Britain in the late war, that two of them were hanged, and others were banished, by the government of Pennsylvania, as enemies to their country. But as the Baptists hold all religion to be personal, between God and individuals, and that all church power is in each particular church, it is impossible for them ever to form any great body, that can be dangerous to any civil government.

[1]Jefferson's Notes on Virginia, p. 167.

The Baptists and Quakers have therefore been unjustly ranked together, when their principles are opposite to each other. And when the church of Christ shall come to be governed wholly by his laws, independent of all the inventions of men, all sectarian distinctions will cease, and wars will come to an end. Though Europe and America are now so far from this, that sectarian distinctions are often begun with capitals, while those important names, Christian and Christianity, are begun with small letters.

And as I have met with some high claims of sectarian power in 1783, that I had not seen when our Second Volume was published, I begin this in that year; and through the whole have compared actions and events with the word of God, according to the best light I could gain from every quarter. For as the Massachusetts have now determined not to revise their constitution of government, and they, with three other States, are constantly oppressing the Baptists, while they are using all their arts to entice all into the use of force to support religious ministers, there appears to be great need of holding up light against these evils.

The list of Baptist churches in our southern States, and of some in New England, I have taken from Mr. John Asplund's Register, for 1794; but the most of them in New England are taken from later accounts. As he was at Boston when my list was printed, he prevailed with my friends there to insert some names that I did not intend to have mentioned.

This Volume was written with an expectation of closing it with 1795, but as it was not finished till June, 1796, some things are added in this year. All the dates are set in old style, until the new took place, in 1752.

History of the Baptists in New England.

CHAPTER XII.

A GENERAL VIEW OF THE AFFAIRS OF RHODE ISLAND COLONY.—OF PAR-
TICULAR ERRORS THEREIN.—THEIR CIVIL STATE CONCISELY DESCRIBED.—
THEIR ORDER COMMENDED BY MASSACHUSETTS MINISTERS.—REMARKS
THEREON.—ACCOUNT OF THE ROGERENES.—THE SAME INSTRUCTIVE TO
OTHERS.

Since the disorders in Rhode Island Colony have often
been recurred to, as a prevailing argument for supporting
worship by tax and compulsion, the evil effects of which
have had a great influence in continuing some of those
disorders, a humble attempt shall here be made to search
this matter to the bottom. And in the first place we are to
remember, that the existence of that colony, as a distinct
government, was long an eyesore to many of their neighbors;
who tried a variety of mean and cruel methods to divide and
conquer it. Solomon says, Surely oppression maketh a wise
man mad; and none will pretend that all the inhabitants of
that colony were wise men. Yet all the madness of their
wise men, and all the ignorance and folly of others, have
been industriously held up to the world, as a convincing
proof of the necessity of an established religion by human
laws. And as the terms *learned* and *orthodox* have been con-

1

nected in this argument, colleges and persecution have grown up together in the ideas of multitudes ; and in not a few, Calvinism, family worship, and a religious regard to the Christian Sabbath, have gone into the same connection. Notwithstanding, it is most certain that Mr. Williams, the founder of said colony, and Mr. Clarke, who procured their second charter, were men of superior learning, and held strictly to the doctrines of sovereign grace, and to the duties of private and public worship ; as many other fathers of the colony also did. But their children, as well as others, have been more ready to retain their errors than their virtues ; some of which I will name.

Daily prayer to God for what we need, and praises for what we receive, are duties taught by reason as well as revelation ; and every person is inexcusable that neglects the immediate practise of those duties. Psalm cvii. 8, 15, 28, 43 ; Acts xvii. 27 ; Rom. i. 20, 21. But the ordinances of special communion in the Christian church, are only known by pure revelation, which requires previous personal qualifications before any may partake therein. But Mr. Williams, about the time of his banishment from the Massachusetts, blended these two kinds of duties so much together, as to oppose the inculcating of prayer upon the unregenerate,[1] as well as the immediate practise of church communion ; as if a criminal might not petition for help and mercy, nor give thanks for what he received, any more than to act in fellowship with his prince before he was pardoned and reconciled. And casting off fear, and restraining prayer before God, is so exceeding natural to fallen men, that great numbers have held fast this error. Above three years after Mr. Williams was banished, he also stumbled upon another error, which many who reproach him are still tenacious of ; namely, the opinion that ministerial authority must be derived by an external succession from inspired men. The con-

[1]See Vol. I, p. 68,—ED.

founding of the Jewish priesthood with the gospel ministry, is the source of this error. Upon their return from Babylon, those priests who could not produce a register of their succession from Aaron, were not suffered to officiate as such, until a new mission should be given from above. Ezra ii. 62, 63. And not finding a like register from the apostles, caused Mr. Williams to refrain from church communion in his latter days,[1] though not from public worship. And how ready have many been from hence to excuse themselves in a careless neglect of all religion! To this Gorton's teaching and influence added great force. He had a singular knack of turning the Scriptures in mist and allegory,[2] under a pretence of great spirituality; and also at running down his opponents with satire and ridicule; arts that have been very bewitching in latter ages. The coming and sufferings of Christ he held to be mystical, and not literal; and he treated the doctrine of visible, instituted churches with the utmost contempt. Says he, " Such pharisaical interpreters, who erect churches as true churches of God, that admit of decay and falling from God, in whole or any members thereof, are they who have deceived and undone the world, from the foundation thereof unto this day, and are the proper *witches* of the world which the Scripture intends." And he construed the mint, anise and cummin of the Pharisees, as applicable to all who practice the external administration of baptism, breaking of bread, and church censures.[3] He was a leader in public worship at Warwick for sixty years, by way of teaching, prayer and singing; but having no successor furnished with his art, a neglect if not a contempt of public worship and of other religious duties has greatly prevailed in those parts, enforced with the remembrance of former cruelties shown to their fathers under religious pretences. And as Calvinism was the general plan of orthodoxy among their oppressors, the opposite sentiments more

[1]See Vol. I, p. 360.—ED.   [2]See Vol. I, pp. 132, 133.—ED.
[3]Gordon's Antidote against Pharisaical Teachers, pp. 42, 52.

easily prevailed in most of the Baptist churches, though it
was an apostasy from the doctrines they were founded upon.
And running into extremes, on other accounts, increased
their unhappiness. Being hardly accused with the want of
valid administrators, moved seven Baptist churches, who met
in London in 1643, to declare it as their faith, that by
Christ's commission, every disciple who had a gift to preach
the gospel, had a right to administer baptism, even before
he was ordained in any church.[1]   But it is to be observed,
that Philip was an ordained officer in the church before he
baptized the young believers at Samaria; while none but
apostles laid on hands after baptism, both there and at
Ephesus; acts which were attended with extraordinary
effects in each place. Acts viii. 14, 17; xix. 6. Yet Mr.
Samuel Hubbard informs us, that in 1652 the practice was
adopted, first at Providence, and then at Newport, of gifted
disciples administering both baptism and laying on of hands,
who were not ordained officers in any church; which practise was continued by some for many years after.   In 1725,
the second church in Swanzey voted to make laying on of
hands a term of their communion. Perhaps others had
done so before.[2] Many contentions and divisions were
caused by these things, which greatly obstructed gospel
order in their churches.   But as the Christian church is the
pillar and ground of the truth, and baptism is the initiating
ordinance thereof, it surely must belong to her, especially at
ordinary times, to set men apart to administer it.

   Internal right, and an external warrant to exercise it, are
distinct things. Every renewed soul has an internal right
to the special privileges of the church of Christ; and those

---

[1]Crosby, Vol. I, Appendix p. 21.—B.

   " The person designed by Christ to dispense baptism, the Scripture holds forth to
be a disciple; it being no where tied to a particular church officer, or person extraordinarily sent, the commission enjoining the administration being given to them as
considered disciples, being men able to preach the gospel."   A Confession of Faith
of seven Congregations or Churches of Christ in London, which are commonly but
unjustly called Anabaptists.   Article XLI.—Ed.

   [2]See Vol. I. p. 405.—Ed.

to whom he has given special gifts for the ministry, have an internal right to improve them ; but a person must be received as an orderly member of a particular church in order to his acting as such ; and those who are qualified for officers ought to be set apart as such before they baptize others. This is now generally allowed. Both Scripture and reason plainly shew, that actions may be done in extraordinary cases, which ought not to be done in ordinary times.

As to their civil affairs, the first charter of Providence Colony extended to the Pequot River and country, that is, into the heart of New London County ; and it was given eighteen years before Connecticut charter. And the second charter to Rhode Island Colony was given by the same authority which gave that of Connecticut ; and this authority fixed the line betwixt them in a most explicit manner. Yet Connecticut made a practice of violently crowding over that line for above sixty years after they received their charter. In 1720 Governor Jencks was sent over as agent to England for help against them. At length, on September 27, 1728, Roger Wolcott, James Wadsworth, and Daniel Palmer, Commissioners for Connecticut, and William Wanton, Benjamin Ellery, and William Jencks, for Rhode Island, signed a settlement of that line. The south part is exactly according to Rhode Island charter ; the north part bears a little east thereof. Plymouth Colony was only a voluntary combination among themselves, as to government ; though they were allowed to continue so till the revolution. And Rhode Island charter was given twenty-eight years before Plymouth was incorporated with the Massachusetts ; yet the line on that side was never established, until it was done by a special commission in 1741, according to the oldest charter ;[1] which gave Rhode Island the towns of Little Compton, Tiverton, Bristol, Warren, Barrington, and Cumberland, that they had not enjoyed before.[2] The history of their

[1]Douglas, Vol. I, p. 400; Vol. II, p. 94.
[2]See Vol. I, pp. 278, 282.

2

civil government may properly be divided into four periods. Before the revolution of 1688, parties both on secular and religious accounts caused much unhappiness. From thence to 1732 their government was in wise and steady hands; so that they had but two Governors in thirty-four years. Afterwards a depreciating paper currency, with bribery in elections, produced many and great evils; a sight of which moved the two competitors for the office of Governor amicably to give up their pretensions, and to prevail with a very peaceable gentleman[1] to accept the chair in 1769. Since then, bribery and party influence have been better guarded against. And can any or all of these things afford the least reason against equal liberty, or for the use of compulsion in the support of worship? Yea, have not our opponents given evidence to the contrary in that Colony? The first Congregational church therein was formed at Newport, and Mr. Nathanael Clap, from Dorchester, was ordained their pastor, November 3, 1720. He was a man of eminent piety, who began to preach there in 1695, and was a great blessing among them till his death, on October 30, 1745, aged 78; for whom Mr. John Callender preached and printed a Funeral Sermon. Mr. Clap was a hearty friend to the primitive order of their churches; but Mr. John Adams, a young teacher of the modern stamp, gained the affections of a large part of his church; and because Mr. Clap could not consent to his settling as colleague with him, nor break bread to a number of the members, a party council divided the church, and the young minister was ordained over a majority, April 11, 1728; so that Mr. Clap was shut out of his meeting-house, and his people built another for him. The third Congregational church in that Colony was constituted at Providence, over which Mr. Josiah Cotton was ordained, October 23, 1728.[2] Some things previous to

[1] John Cranston.—ED.

[2] Comer's Diary and papers. In less than two years Adams was dismissed by his church, and not recommended.

this last event call for a place in our history.   After considerable labors in Providence for it, the Massachusetts ministers sent them the following letter :—

To the Honorable Joseph Jencks, Esq., late Deputy Governor, William
Hopkins, Esq., Major Joseph Williams, Joseph Whipple, Esq., Colonel
Richard Waterman, Arthur Venner, Esq., —— Wilkinson, Esq., Philip
Tillinghast, Esq., Captain Nicholas Power, Captain Thomas Harris, Cap-
tain William Harris, Andrew Harris, Esq., —— Brown, Esq., John
Burton, Esq., Jonathan Sprague, jun., Esq., and to the other eminent
men in the town of Providence.[1] Pardon our ignorance, if any of your
honorable Christian names, or if your proper order be mistaken.

HONORABLE GENTLEMEN :   We wish you grace, mercy and peace, and
all blessings for time and eternity, through our Lord and Saviour Jesus
Christ.   How pleasing to Almighty God and our glorious Redeemer, and
how conducible to the public tranquility and safety, an hearty union and
good affection of all pious protestants, of whatsoever particular denomination on account of some differences in opinion, would be, by the divine
blessing, yourselves as well as we, are not insensible.   And with what
peace and love, societies of different modes of worship have generally entertained one another in your government, we cannot think of it without
admiration ; and we suppose, under God, it is owing to the choice liberty
granted to protestants of all persuasions, in the royal charter graciously
given you ; and to the wise and prudent conduct of the gentlemen that
have been improved as Governors and Justices in your Colony.   And the
Rev. Mr. Greenwood, before his decease at Rehoboth, was much affected
with the wisdom and excellent temper, and great candor of such of yourselves as he had the honor to wait upon, and with those worthy and
obliging expressions of kind respect he met with, when he discoursed
about his desires to make an experiment, whether the preaching of our
ministers in Providence might not be acceptable, and whether some who
do not greatly incline to frequent any pious meeting in the place, on the
first day of the week, might not be drawn to give their presence to hear
our ministers, and so might be won over (by the influence of heaven) into
serious godliness.   And although God has taken that dear brother of ours
from his work in this world, yet it has pleased the Lord to incline some
reverend ministers of Connecticut, and some of ours, to preach among
you ;[2] and we are beholden to the mercy of heaven for the freedom and

[1] I am well informed, that Jencks, (newly returned from his agency in England)
Hopkins, Williams, Venner, Tillinghast, Power, Richard, Brown and Sprague,
were all Baptists; Whipple, an Episcopalian Waterman, Samuel Wilkinson, Burton, and the Harrises, were Friends.

[2] Mr. Moody, of York, with as much power as any.

safety they have enjoyed, under the wise and good government of the place, and that they met with kind respect, and with numbers that gave a kind reception to their ministrations among them.   These things we acknowledge with all thankfulness; and if such preaching should be continued among your people, (designed only for the glory of God and Christ Jesus in chief, and nextly for the promoting of the spiritual and eternal happiness of immortal souls, and the furtherance of a joyful account in the great day of judgment,) we earnestly request, as the Rev. Mr. Greenwood, in his lifetime, did before us, that yourselves, according to your power, and the interest and influence that God has blessed you with, will continue your just protections; and that you add such further countenance and encouragement thereunto, as may be pleasing to the eternal God, and may, through Christ Jesus, obtain for you the greater reward in heaven.   And if ever it should come to pass, that a small meeting-house should be built in your town, to entertain such as are willing to hear our ministers, we should count it a great favor, if you all, gentlemen, or any of yours, would please to build pews therein, in which you and they (as often as you see fit) may give your and their presence and holy attention.   And we hope and pray, that ancient matters (that had acrimony unhappily in them) may be buried in oblivion; and that grace and peace, and holiness and glory, may dwell in every part of New England; and that the several provinces and colonies in it may love one another with pure hearts fervently.   So, recommending you all, and your ladies, and children, and neighbors, and people, to the blessing of heaven, and humbly asking your prayers to the divine throne for us, we take leave to subscribe ourselves, your friends and servants.

PETER THATCHER, ⎫ Committee
JOHN DANFORTH, ⎬ of the
JOSEPH BELCHER, ⎭ Association.[1]

Dated October 27, 1721.

The town of Providence sent them an answer, dated February 23, 1722, signed in their name by Jonathan Sprague; wherein they say:—

We take notice how you praise the love and peace that dissenters of all ranks entertain one another with, in this government.....We answer, This happiness principally consists in their not allowing societies any superiority over one another; but each society supports their own ministry, of their own free will, and not by constraint or force, upon any man's person or estate; and this greatly adds to our peace and tranquility.   But the contrary, that takes any man's estate by force, to maintain their own or any

---

[1] Ministers in Boston, Dorchester and Dedham.

other ministry, it serves for nothing but to provoke to wrath, envy and strife. And since you wrote this letter, the constable of Attleborough has been taking away the estates of our dear friends and pious dissenters, to maintain their minister; the like hath been done in Mendon. Is this the way of peace? Is this the fruit of your love? Why do you hug the iniquity of Eli's sons, and walk in the steps of the false prophets, to bite with your teeth, and cry Peace, but no longer than men put into your mouths but you prepare war against them? . . . . You desire that all former injury, done by you to us, may be buried in oblivion. We say, far be it from us to revenge ourselves, or to deal to you as you have dealt to us, but rather say, Father forgive them, they know not what they do. But if you mean, that we should not speak of former actions, done hurtfully to any man's person, we say, God never called for that, nor suffered it to be hid, as witness Cain, Joab and Judas are kept on record to deter other men from doing the like.

A reply hereto was printed at Boston, dated September 7, 1722, which did not pretend to deny the facts here mentioned; but made a great flourish upon a *word*, which was not in their first printed letter, but was the error of the press in a second edition; and then took occasion, from what they said about recording hurtful actions, to publish a copy of a sentence of Court against Sprague in Boston, April 28, 1674, "for reproaching and scandalizing the magistrates, and for lascivious carriage." And it insinuated that their complaints about persecution were because of such sufferings as this.

Sensible how the populace had been deceived by such arts, Sprague wrote a rejoinder, dated January 24. 1723, in which he makes some apology for taking notice of such an anonymous, reviling piece, which profanely sets the Court Records of Boston upon a level with God's infallible record concerning Cain and Judas; and informs us that one of the two witnesses against him, in that case at Boston, was afterwards brought to repentance, and joined the Baptist church he belonged to in Providence; when she asked and received his forgiveness, for wronging him in her testimony in that case. He also observes, that the affair was in his early days, before he made a profession of religion, when he really was

a vile sinner.   And for the satisfaction of serious people, he
says :—

> My youthful walk I'll not commend,
> Nor go about it to defend ;
> But to God's glory do confess,
> I liv'd in sin and wickedness.
> Until God's love to me appear'd,
> His dreadful wrath I greatly fear'd ;
> But when I hear'd Christ's lovely voice,
> My heart within me did rejoice,
> That he for sinners freely dy'd,
> That sinners might be justify'd ;
> That all such sinners he would save,
> As mercy of him humbly crave ;
> And do obey his holy will,
> As 'tis declar'd in his gospel ;
> So on his grace do I now rest,
> And so must all that shall be blest.

But lastly, why do you strive to persuade the rising generation, that you
never persecuted nor hurt the Baptists?   Did you not barbarously scourge
Mr. Obadiah Holmes, and imprison John Hazel, of Rehoboth, who
died and came not home?   And did you not barbarously scourge Mr. Baker,
in Cambridge, the chief mate of a London ship? where also you imprisoned Mr. Thomas Gould, John Russell, Benjamin Sweetser, and many
others, and fined them fifty pounds a man.   And did you not take away a
part of the said Sweetser's land, to pay his fine, and conveyed it to Solomon Phips, the Deputy Governor Danforth's son-in-law, who after, by the
hand of God ran distracted, dying suddenly, saying he was bewitched?
And did you not nail up the Baptist meeting-house doors, and fine Mr. John
Miles, Mr. James Brown, and Mr. Nicholas Tanner? .... Surely I can
fill sheets of paper with the sufferings of the Baptists, as well as others,
within your precincts ; but what I have mentioned shall suffice for the
present.

Mr. Sprague preached for many years to a small society
of Baptists in that which is now the east part of Smithfield;
and died in January, 1741, aged ninety-three.   Mr. Comer
knew him, and speaks of him as a very judicious and pious
man.

As a further proof of the evil effects of coercive measures
about religious worship, I shall here add some account of

John Rogers, of New London, and his followers, who are briefly described in Vol. I, pages 376—382. He intermixed a number of precious truths, with many things of a contrary nature. Governor Leete well observed, in a letter there published, that if Rogers and his party had been Governors in Connecticut, it might be doubted whether they would have allowed people so much liberty in keeping the first day of the week as a Sabbath, as the government there allowed to him and his followers in the opposite way. For Rogers, imagining that the law which required the keeping of that day established idolatry, was as zealous to pull it down, as the Jews were against idols in old times. And the sufferings which he met with, for his zeal about this and other religious matters, seemed to be his life ; until, to shew how strong his faith was, he went to Boston, and among the infection of the small-pox there ; but caught it, and came home and died with it, and caused the death of some others thereby. This, many might think was quite enough to open the eyes of his followers ; but it was far from doing it. Perhaps they might think he was taken away in judgment to them, for their coldness and negligence. Certain it is that Joseph Bolles now published a second edition of Rogers's book, entitled, "A Midnight Cry from the Temple of God to the Ten Virgins Slumbering and Sleeping ; Awake ! awake ! arise ! and gird your loins, and trim your lamps, for behold the Bridegroom cometh, go ye therefore out to meet him !" Bolles wrote a preface to it, in which he says of the author, " For his religion he lost his wife and children, and suffered continual persecution, being near one third of his lifetime, after his conversion, in prisons. And in the seventy-third year of his age, he died in his own house, at New London, 1721." Hereupon his son, and others of that sect, set out afresh in zealous attempts to pull down the idol Sabbath; and as a number of them came into Norwich, in their way to Lebanon, on a first day, having things with them to discover that they were upon worldly business, and meant to appear against having that day kept as a Sabbath, they were seized by authority ; and on July 26, 1725, they were brought before Joseph Backus,[1] Justice of the Peace, who fined them according to law ; and refusing to pay it, they were whipped.[2]

Governor Jencks being informed of their sufferings, and that it was because they were going to Lebanon to worship, and to administer baptism, wrote a paper, giving some account thereof, as a warning to people against the Presbyterian sect, and set it up in a public place in Providence. The Justice having obtained a copy of that paper, published an answer to it ; a manuscript reply to which, in the Governor's own hand-writing, is before. me. He does not pretend to reply to it all ; for says he :—

Such unchristian-like behavior, in giving them disturbance when at their public worship, if true, may justly be condemned by all sober people, and is that which never entered into my thoughts to justify, in John Rogers or any other man.

But says the Governor :—

It is very well known, to all the elderly inhabitants of Providence, that the Presbyterian governments in New England in general, and Connecticut in particular, have for a long time been using their utmost skill and endeavors to bring the greatest part if not all this little Colony under their rule and government. But finding themselves disappointed in the several measures they have hitherto taken, they are now (as is supposed by many others as well as myself) about to try one artifice more in order to obtain their desire ; and that is by sending in their ministers among us, under a pretence of doing good to souls ; whereas the design chiefly is, to gain such a party as may be sufficient to over-vote us in our elections, and so to gain the rule over us.

Experience has since given much greater light about these things than was then enjoyed in the country. In 1758, the

---

[1]Grandfather of the author.—ED.

[2]" Some of the sect had previously been taken up in other parts of the county and fined five shillings per head for breaking the Sabbath; and they now travelled in defiance of the law and its penalty, boasting that they could buy the idolaters' Sabbaths for five shillings apiece. But, on arriving at Norwich, they found, as Mr. Justice Backus observed, that they had *risen in price*, for, being taken before the said Justice, they were sentenced to pay a fine of twenty shillings per head, or to be whipped ten or fifteen lashes each. Not being able to pay, they were obliged to submit to the latter punishment." Caulkins's History of Norwich, p. 271.—ED.

Rogerenes published an abstract of the history of ancient persecutions in New England, with high encomiums upon those Quakers who returned and were hanged at Boston, after they had been banished on pain of death; and a reproof to their own society and others for their declension from that temper and spirit. Many were hereby stirred up to travel from town to town, and to interrupt others in their worship, especially in the year 1763. But when they did so, at Norwich and other places, the authority removed them away until their worship was ended, and then released them, without fine or correction; which had a much better effect than their former punishments. Indeed in New London, where most of them lived, Mr. Mather Byles was so uneasy at their surrounding his gate, and calling him a hireling, that in 1768 he made a bitter complaint that their laws were not put in full execution against said people; and for this and other reasons he resigned his pastoral charge there, and went off to Episcopacy. About which time, a number of the Rogerenes were seized in a clandestine way, and were scourged in a most barbarous manner; for which may all the actors or abettors thereof be brought to true repentance! An instance or two of late suicide among the members of the Rogerene church, gave a great shock to the rest; and a number of their children are now become agreeable members of other communities. And if all persons and societies were impartially protected by authority, and none but spiritual weapons were made use of, and they with due faithfulness, to propagate and support the Christian religion, who can tell how happy the effects would soon be?

CHAPTER XIII.

Some revival of religion among the Baptists, as well as opposition thereto, is now to be described. Mr. John Clarke was a chief leader in forming the first Baptist church in Newport, in 1644; and he continued their pastor until his decease, April 20, 1676. Mr. Obadiah Holmes succeeded him in that office, and died October 15, 1682. Near three years after, Mr. Richard Dingley, from Britain, by the way of Boston, became their pastor. An address of his to the church is before me, wherein he describes the duty of a pastor to his people, and of a people to their pastor, in a clear, scriptural light. About 1694, he left that church and went to Boston, and from thence to South Carolina. After his departure they had only occasional supplies till 1710, when they elected Mr. William Packom for their pastor, in whose ordination Elder Luther of Swanzey assisted. In 1718, Mr. Daniel White, from Mr. Wallin's church in London, was chosen for colleague with Elder Packom; but as he was a strict Calvinist, disputes soon arose about doctrines, which were greatly increased by a leader in the church, who was an assign of Mr. Clarke's estate, and unfaithful in his trust.   Councils were called from Boston and Swanzey upon it; and the Legislature of the colony were moved to put him out of that office, and to put another man into it; though upon further search they saw that this was not in their power.   Therefore in 1721 they made a law, which requires all men who are entrusted with charitable donations annually to give an account of their proceedings therein to their Town Council, which is still in force.   But a separation took place in that church, and White administered to one party for several years, till it dissolved, and he went to Philadelphia in 1728.   A difference in sentiments about laying on of hands, and some other things, caused the rise of the second church in Newport, about the year 1656; and Mr. William Vaughan was their first minister, who died in 1677, and was succeeded by Thomas Baker, and he by John Harden, who died in 1700.   In 1701 James Clarke was ordained their pastor, by the assistance of the Elders Pardon Tillinghast and John Brown of Providence.   In 1704 Daniel Wightman was ordained a colleague with him; and they were successful, and much esteemed in their places to old age.

Mr. Comer, before mentioned, being at school at Cambridge, joined to the first church there in February, 1723. Ephraim Crafts, his intimate friend, had joined to the Baptist church in Boston just before.   This, Comer thought was a very wrong action, and took the first opportunity he had to try to convince him of it; but after a considerable debate, Comer was prevailed with to take and read Stennet upon baptism, which gave him quite other views of the subject than he had ever had before.   However he concluded to be silent about it; and as education was the cheapest at New Haven, he went and entered the college there in September, 1723, and continued a member of it until October, 1724; when infirmity of body caused his return by water to Boston; and a terrible storm at sea, with the death of a peculiar friend just as he arrived, brought eternity so directly before him, as to spoil all his plausible excuses for the neglect of baptism. He informs us that those words of Christ, "Whosoever shall be ashamed of me, and of my words, in this adulterous and sinful generation, of him also shall the Son of Man be ashamed when he cometh in the glory of his Father, with the holy angels," had such influence upon him, that after proper labors with those he was previously connected with, he was baptized and joined to the Baptist church in Boston, January 31, 1725 ;[1] and concluded to pursue his studies in a private way. Four months after, he was called to preach the gospel,[2] and on May 19, 1726, he was ordained a pastor of the first church in Newport, colleague with Elder Packom,[3] and a great blessing was granted

---

[1] "January 31, 1725. This day I was baptized by the Rev. Mr. Elisha Callender, and was admitted into full communion with the Baptist church in Boston, having before waited on the Rev. Mr. Appleton of Cambridge, and discoursed with him on the point of baptism, together with my resolution ; upon which he signified I might, notwithstanding, maintain my communion in his church : by which I discovered the candor and catholic temper of his spirit." Comer's Manuscript Diary.—ED.

[2] Mr. Comer was at this time teaching school in Swanzey. In his manuscript Diary he writes as follows : "Thursday, May 6, 1725. I set out from Boston to Swanzey to visit the church and to keep school if nothing hindered. Saturday, 8. I visited the minister, Mr. Ephraim Wheaton, and was invited by him to preach the next day ; which I accepted, having been earnest with the Lord for the bestowment of suitable gifts and graces for so sacred a service. Lord's day, May 9. I began my public ministry in the town of Swanzey, in the congregation and by the request of the pastor of the church of Swanzey ; from those words, I Peter, i. 16, 'Be ye holy for I am holy.' Thus, I hope in the sincerity of my soul, with a hearty and sincere aim to God's glory and the advantage of precious souls, I entered into the work of the sacred ministry. 'Who is sufficient for these things.' 'My grace is sufficient.'"—ED.

[3] While resident in Swanzey, Mr. Comer continued to share the labors of the pastor of the church there, preaching for him once each Lord's day. August 5, 1725, the church voted to invite him to remain with them and continue this service one year. At about the same time, he was invited to preach temporarily at Newport. A lack of unanimity in the action of the Swanzey church, together with the advice of his pastor, Mr. Callender, led him to accept the latter invitation. The following extract from Mr. Callender's letter of advice is quoted, both because of its bearing on the present matter, and as a valuable indication of the character and views of Mr. Callender himself.

"The first thing you have to do is to consider which congregation doth most want help, i. e., Swanzey or Newport ; and then, where you may have the fairest prospect of doing good. These two things, I think, would determine me to go to Newport. And then, besides, some other considerations fall in, which should have their

upon his ministry in that town. Their first church had but
seventeen members when he came there; to whom thirty-
four were added in less than three years. And says Comer,
" There was no public singing until I came, and by the
blessing of heaven introduced it." Neither had they any
church records, before he got a book, and collected into it

force; and they are these :—your own comfort in the benefit of conversation, of
which, to be sure, there is greater choice at Newport; and then, again, as to your
subsistence, which, as far as I can learn, is as like to be as comfortable at Newport
as elsewhere. What other considerations you may have, I know not : but, upon the
whole, I pray God to direct you. But if you incline to go to Newport, I must
advise you to these things : 1. To study well all your public discourses and look
upon it your business to compose sermons in a handsome style and good method. 2.
Carefully avoid all controversy in the pulpit. 3. Be sure that you never enter into
the contention that has been at Newport.

Elisha Callender."

Mr. Comer went to Newport November 1, and was called to the pastoral office
there, November 15. After three months' consideration, he accepted the call, in
these words :

" Newport, February 6, 1726.

"Brethren and beloved in the Lord Jesus Christ : You have, some time
since, solemnly called upon the Lord of the harvest, by humble and earnest prayer,
that he would send forth a laborer into this part of his harvest,—such a one as might
break the bread of life to you, and dispense the living oracles of the Holy One of
Israel in this place. Hereupon you were directed to make choice of the unworthy
instrument who now reminds you hereof.

" I trust, beloved, you have duly considered the awfulness of the call of a laborer
to be improved in God's harvest; with the difficulties, discouragements and temptations such are exposed to. I have, also, seriously weighed, and humbly spread the
case before the Lord, earnestly beseeching him to guide and direct me in so important and momentous an affair, in being an ambassador for Christ, to beseech sinners,
in his name and stead, to be reconciled unto God. Hereupon, I have considered :

I. What the Lord Jesus Christ expects of such as preach the gospel.

II. What men expect from them.

I. What the Lord Jesus Christ expects; and here, 1. Christ expects they should
be faithful in it. I Tim. 1. 11, 12. 2. Christ expects they should keep close to,
and not vary from, his commands to them. I Thes. 2. 2—5. 3. They are accountable for all the acts of their office. Heb. 13. 17. 4. All such as are called are
under obligation to preach the gospel. I Cor. 9. 16. 5. Christ expects his word
should not be corrupted to please men. II Cor. 2. 17. They should keep close to,
and not vary from, his institutions, in both the matter and manner and end of their
ministry; that so they may say as Christ did when sent. John 7. 16. So Paul
could say of what he delivered. I Cor. 11. 22, 23. So Timothy must keep what
was committed to him. II Tim. 1. 14.

II. What men expect; and here, men expect that such should be examples to
others, 1. In doctrine; 2. In conversation; 3. In faith; 4. In purity.

" I have also considered my own inability to perform these ministerial acts which

the best accounts that he could obtain of their former affairs.[1] Out of a manuscript written by their first pastor, he transcribed the Confession of Faith, mentioned in our Vol. I, pages 206—209. For his support he received eighty-five pounds in 1726, ninety-three pounds, twelve shillings, four pence, in

are incumbent on those who are thereunto called; of being the mouth of God's people to him and his mouth unto them; of admitting into, and ejecting out of, his visible kingdom, and of administering the seals of the covenant to his people. But while I was musing and ruminating hereupon, that precious promise took deep impression upon me, II Cor. 12. 9, 'My grace is sufficient for thee;' and that, Matt. 28. 20, 'Lo I am with you alway.' When I considered my small standing in the school of Christ, the tenderness of my years, the smallness of my experiences, the various temptations I am exposed to, and the greatness of the work I am to engage in, I was almost discouraged; but considering the necessity of this flock of Christ, I was moved to a compliance with your invitation.

" Therefore, beloved in our Lord Jesus Christ, I now, by the grace of God assisting me, resolve to improve my utmost strength that God may afford me in this place, by a compliance with your call to the work of the ministry among you. This I do in the name of the great God and the Lord Jesus Christ, in the presence of the elect angels, and of this assembly; promising by the help of the Holy Ghost, to perform the ministry you have called me to, agreeable to God's word, and your expectation, viz., to declare the whole counsel of God, and to keep back nothing, that I either do or shall know to be agreeable to God's will, from you; and to administer the ordinances of the gospel, baptism and the Lord's Supper, as God has prescribed in his holy word, without human alteration or unwarrantable tradition. So, brethren and beloved in the Lord Christ, I humbly beg your prayers to God for me, to help and assist me in a work of so great importance, which I should have laid before you, but the service of this afternoon [a sermon from II Cor. 2. 16] hath made it sufficiently manifest. So, devoting myself to the service of your souls and the souls of yours, in the gospel of Christ, whom I entreat, through the blood of the everlasting covenant, to make you all perfect, stablish, strengthen and settle you, working in each of you that which is well pleasing in his sight through Jesus Christ, to whom be glory in all the church, world without end. Amen.

JOHN COMER."

At his ordination, Mr. Comer presented a confession of his faith, which he afterwards transcribed into his Diary. It is noteworthy that he followed the advice of Callender to keep clear of the former contentions of the church, by making no mention of those points known as the distinctive doctrines of Calvinism, the church having been divided on those matters. In one article of his confession, the result of which was soon seen, he declared his belief "that singing the high praises of God in the assembly of his people, is a divine ordinance, grounded in the New Testament, which the church of God should be in the due and diligent practice of." The Seventh-Day church in Newport was invited to assist in Mr. Comer's ordination, but, he writes, "A letter of denial was sent, because of our non-observance of the seventh day."—ED.

[1]He was very curious and exact also in recording other events. He observes that the year 1727 was a year of many remarkable occurrences. It was so for the death

1727; but not a third part of this last sum in 1728, because two leading members of the church, who disliked his close and searching ministrations, had influence enough to turn a great part of the society against him. At length Comer gave them an occasion, which they eagerly made use of, to crowd him out of his office in that church; for, without giving them any previous notice, he, on November 17, 1728, preached up the laying on of hands upon every member as a Christian duty, though not as a term of communion.[1] Upon the close of that year he says :—

This has been a year of great exercise to me. I have been as it were in the furnace of affliction. The difficulty in my flock has been heart-wounding, and sometimes almost confounding. But I see God's grace is

of rulers. King George I, died June 11; and in Rhode Island Colony the Hon. Edward Thurston, one of their Council [father of the present pastor of the second church in Newport] died in April; Governor Cranston, April 26; Deputy Governor Nichols, who was elected in May, died in July. From July 28 to August 7, the heat was so intense as to cause the death of many. Through the three first nights in August, the lightnings were constant and amazing. On September 26, was a terrible hurricane; and a more terrible earthquake October 29, which was followed with a smaller one in the morning of January 28, 1728. He first mentions the northern lights, in the evening of July 16, 1728, which were much greater on October 2, following. Dean Berkley arrived at Newport January 23, with whom Comer had an interview July 14, 1729. Governor Burnet came to Newport, in his way to Boston, July 12, 1728, and died at Boston, September 7, 1729. Several persons were baptized by way of immersion by Episcopalian ministers, as Mr. Carpenter, by Mr. Usher, of Bristol, January, 1725; Nathaniel Brown, and four others, at Rehoboth, by Mr. Piggot, of Providence, in July, 1726; A woman at Newport, by Dr. M'Sparran, of Narragansett, in November, 1728.—B.

"Mr. Comer's manuscript journal, two volumes, folio, is now deposited in the cabinet of the Rhode Island Historical Society. It is a curious production, giving an account of all the remarkable events with which he became acquainted, interspersed with prayers, religious reflections, &c. Mr. Comer had formed the design of writing the history of the American Baptists, and had collected many useful materials for this purpose, which were of great advantage to Edwards, Backus, and Benedict in their Histories." Rhode Island Historical Collections, Vol. IV, p. 38. —Ed.

[1]The records of the church state that the above-mentioned sermon was "full of reviling and hard censures upon the church, and was looked upon by them that were not of the church, as well as those that were, to be so in a great degree." The following minutes are also taken from the church records :—"The church in their trouble sent a letter to the church in Boston, for their Christian advice, and when the letter was read before the church, and the advice of the church asked thereupon, their advice was this, That, inasmuch as we were all of one mind, and continued

sufficient for me. I am fully and clearly convinced that I should have fallen into many hurtful evils, if sovereign grace had not wonderfully prevented. Bless the Lord, O my soul! .... About this time I found my people so uncomfortable that we must divide from each other, which was exceeding grievous to me.

January 8, 1729, Mr. Comer was dismissed from his church; and the next day, he says, "I passed under hands by Mr. Daniel Wightman, and offered for transient communion until spring, or till I saw how God in his holy providence might dispose of me." A revival of religion in that second church in Newport began the fall before; and as Elder Clarke was above eighty, and unable to preach, Mr. Comer was received to preach one half of the Lord's days with Elder Wightman for two years. And above forty members were added to that church before he left it, which was the greatest increase they had ever received in such a length of time; at the close whereof they had one hundred and fifty communicants, being the largest church in the colony. For Comer's support the society gave him one hundred and twenty-nine pounds in 1729, and one hundred and forty-four pounds, twelve shillings, ten-pence in 1730. As Newport was the head town of the government, Governor Jencks went and lived there, in order more conveniently to attend upon the duties of his

fixed in our principles, so they advised us we would maintain our principles, though our minister should part from us, and advised us to continue in love and of one accord, and not give way to any unwritten tradition." "June 28, 1731. At a meeting gathered at the request of Mr. Comer, and by consent of our elder, William Packom, after some discourse with Mr. Comer concerning the difference that has been a long time between him and the church, Mr. Comer being sensible of his mistakes, desired forgiveness, and in particular his timing that discourse concerning laying on of hands, and in a sermon which he afterwards preached, which was very offensive to the church, charging them with such crimes as they were no ways sensible they were ever guilty of; which he desired might be overlooked. And it was agreed that all papers written on both sides, relating to the difference, might be produced and burned, which was accordingly done; and the meeting finished in love and peace, with prayer by Mr. Comer."

These extracts may indicate that the blame did not so exclusively belong to the church, as the words of Mr. Backus might imply. It is evident, however, from the papers of Mr. Comer, that he never ceased to regard the action of the church as unjust.—ED.

3

office ; where he joined in worship and communion with said church, wherein Mr. Comer also now introduced regular records, which they lacked before.   And as Mr. John Walton, a young gentleman of a liberal education, was invited to preach at Providence, where a like reformation might be hoped for, in the church whereof the Governor was a principal member, and opposition was raised against it, he wrote the following letter to Mr. James Brown, their pastor :—

Newport, March 19, 1730.

BELOVED BROTHER :—I am heartily sorry to hear of the difference in our church at Providence, about Mr. Walton's coming to settle there; as also for the unkind treatment he there met with from some, especially considering he came not there with a design to impose himself upon the church, but at the request of several of the brethren.   And why his coming there should be so strenuously opposed, as I understand it is, I cannot conceive. As to his singing of psalms, I have heard him say, he would not urge that as a duty upon the church.   And if it were for that he might expect some allowance, by way of contribution for his support, it most certainly is an error in those who oppose that as a thing unlawful.   For I think the Scriptures are very clear in that point, that it is not only lawful for a minister or elder that preaches the gospel to receive (by way of contribution) a competent maintenance, but also the duty of the church, according to their ability, to afford it to him ; and this I doubt not but I can fully prove by Scripture against all contradiction.   And I believe there are several of my brethren who can remember, that Elder Tillinghast, (in his life-time) who was a man exemplary for his doctrine, as well as of an unblemished character, did several times in his teaching declare, that it was the duty of a church to contribute towards the maintenance of their elders, who labored in the word and doctrine of Christ ; and although for his own part he would take nothing, yet it remained the church's duty to be performed to such as might succeed him.   And as to what Mr. Walton holds with respect to laying on of hands upon believers as such, I do not understand by him that he opposes it any other ways, than if it be performed for the obtaining the extraordinary gifts of the Holy Ghost ; but he thinks it ought not to be any bar to communion with those who have been rightly baptized.   And as I have been informed, by one or more of the ancient members of our church at Providence, that such was the opinion of the Baptists, in the first constitution of their churches throughout the colony ; and that such as were under laying on of hands continued their fellowship with those that were not, until one who was in great repute for wisdom amongst them did, in his teaching, declare, that the doctrine of laying on of hands was a doctrine of devils, upon which a separation was made. And, as I was informed when in England, the separation there was upon some such like occasion. But further, as to Mr. Walton's receiving, by way of contribution, if the church in Providence can freely hold fellowship with him, and do account he may be serviceable to them in preaching, as well as instrumental of doing good to others, I cannot imagine why any one should oppose his receiving some allowance for his labor, from such as are free to give it, none being under any compulsion ; for I think it is highly rational, if he leaves his own home, where he can, by overseeing the management of his farm, live honorably, and removes to Providence purely to serve his brethren, that they should consider him accordingly.

I am, with due regard, sir, your affectionate Christian brother,

JOSEPH JENCKS.

Elder Brown was of his mind ; but Deacon Samuel Winsor took the lead of a party, who were resolutely set against what the Governor had proposed. A Council was called there, September 3, 1731, who advised them not to divide upon it ; but at a meeting in October, Winsor and his party were for censuring Walton as a transgressor, for joining in prayer with Baptists who were not under hands. Elder Brown reasoned with them upon it, and said, "If we admonish brother Walton and set him apart, what will you do with others who hold that point as he does, as Elder Clarke, Elder Wightman, the Governor, and some others ?" Their answer was, "We must go through with it." And Elder Peter Place of Smithfield, came and assisted in making an open separation in Providence church upon these points. And Winsor taught publicly, "That all those who took any thing for preaching were like Simon Magus." This account is taken from original writings of Elder Brown and others, now before me. And as he died October 28, 1732, aged sixty-six,[1] Winsor's party prevailed, and ordained him as the

[1] He was grandson to Chad Brown, one of the first planters of Providence; and son to John Brown, who was elected into their Council in 1665, and was afterwards an elder in Providence church. From Elder James Brown's son James, sprang the four brothers who are now very noted traders in Providence, and great promoters of learning, and of the Baptist cause there. Said elder's son Elisha was Deputy Governor of the colony in 1765, and his son Andrew was Justice of Peace in the State, and long an exemplary Christian in the Baptist church in Gloucester, until he died in peace, 1782.

minister of that church. Walton quitted the ministry, and
followed other employments, whereby many were confirmed
in their prejudices against him and his sentiments.

Perhaps a concise account of a piece of villainy, which
was now detected at Swanzey, may be of service, to warn
all others against doing the like. That town was first
granted to five men, three of whom were Baptists ; and they
laid out sundry parcels of land, which they called pastors'
and teachers' lots. They had a large and curious book of
church records, which was brought from Wales ; and the
surveys of those lots were recorded therein. Barrington
was originally included in Swanzey, and when it became a
distinct town, they had their share of those lots for Pædobaptist ministers. In 1718 Richard Harden became both a
deacon and the clerk of the first church in Swanzey ; and
was encouraged to build and make improvements upon one
of those lots, near their meeting-house ; and he was also a
leading man in town affairs. Having such advantages, he
was tempted with a notion, that by destroying the records of
those lots, he could obtain that whereon he lived as common
land. And, behold ! all the records of Swanzey church, betwixt 1663 and 1718, were taken out of the book, and have
never been recovered since ! When the church came to
know it, as the government was in the hands of Pædobaptists, they invited Barrington to join with them in suing for
their rights, with an offer, that if they would be at propor-
tionable expense, they should have two-fifths of what they
recovered. The offer was accepted, and Harden was sued
by a writ of ejectment, at the County Court, in July, 1730,
and was cast. He appealed to the Superior Court in September ; but was also cast there. By a reference the next
year, he obtained one hundred and twenty-five pounds for
what he had done upon the land, and was obliged to quit it;
and he took to keeping loose company, and drinking to excess. Elder Wheaton, and a large part of his church, had
been desirous of settling Mr. Comer with him, before Comer

went to Newport, but Harden's influence prevented it.   O
what is man when left to himself!

The pious and liberal Mr. Hollis died in 1731.   When
the news of it arrived, Dr. Colman preached a funeral sermon for him, before the General Court at Boston, April 1 ;
which was published by their order.   The two professors
upon his foundations in the college each published a discourse upon the occasion, and President Wadsworth wrote
a preface thereto.   Professor Wigglesworth says:—

> By his frequent and ample benefactions, for the encouragement of theo-
> logical as well as human knowledge among us, who are Christians of a
> different denomination from himself, he hath set such an example of gener-
> ous, catholic and Christian spirit, as hath never before fallen within my
> observation, nor, so far as I now remember, within my reading.

Dr. Colman says :—

> That which is singular in the piety and benefits of Mr. Hollis, unto these
> churches, was, that though he was not strictly of our way, nor in judgment
> with us in the point of infant baptism, yet his heart and hand was the same
> to us, as if we had been one in opinion and practice with him.   And in
> this let him stand a teaching pattern and example to us, of a noble, Chris-
> tian, apostolic spirit of love ; which makes those that differ in lesser mat-
> ters to receive one another to the glory of God, and a shining testimony
> against a narrow party spirit, which is so much the disgrace and detriment
> of the protestant interest, and which so early began among the apostles of
> Jesus, and was rebuked by him, even in John himself,. that apostle of love
> and charity afterwards, who once said to Christ in a fret of zeal, Master,
> we saw one casting out devils in thy name, and he followeth not us, and
> we forbade him, because he followeth not us ; but Jesus said, Forbid him
> not.[1]

We shall have occasion to remember this hereafter.   In the
mean time, the last letter that I have seen from Mr. Hollis's

[1]Crosby, Vol. IV, pp. 213—229.—B.

Thomas Hollis was born in 1659.   At the age of twenty he made a public profession of religion.   He was an enterprising and wealthy London merchant.   His character for integrity and virtue was above reproach, and the testimonies to his simple
and earnest piety are many and undoubted.   Says Dr. Colman in his Funeral Sermon, " Mr. Hollis merits to be named among great men, and to stand before kings.
He was one of those righteous men that should be had in everlasting remembrance.
Like Araunah, he gave as a prince for the house of his God.   And like David, the
king, he set his affection, and prepared with all his might, of his own proper goods,

intimate friend discovers so much of the views and comforts of Christianity, in a near sight of mortality, that I shall annex it to the foregoing account. It was directed to Mr. Elisha Callender :—

London, November 10, 1732.

DEAR SIR :—I readily own that it was my turn to have wrote to you long before now ; but the long and threatening illness under which I have labored, for more than twelve months past, have so reduced me, both in flesh and spirit, that I have been incapable, great part of the time, of writing ; which will, I hope, plead my excuse with you. I am, through divine goodness, able to preach once a day on Lord's days, but hardly ever expect to get over my indisposition. It is a wonder to the doctors, and all others who saw my case, that I am alive. I could not for several months but expect to be removed ; but blessed be the Lord, I had a comfortable prospect of another world, and was rather grieved than pleased at the view of a return into this. Here methinks is nothing pleasant to the mind, but rather everything sullying and discomposing. Why then should not those who have tasted divine grace, long to stretch and swim in the immense ocean ? How sweet is a drop here, therefore how ravishing must the full enjoyment be ! But, Lord, grant faith and patience, to wait thy time, even thy time, O Lord. I am glad to hear the baptized interest thrives, and wish that the power of religion were in a more flourishing condition with you than it is with us ; for surely Jacob is small and low. We have many controversies agitated, which seem to put a stop to the growth of pure religion and the power of godliness among us. National vice gains strength, but vital

of silver and gold. And this he did, not to us, no, be it known to us, nor for our sakes, but unto Christ, whose he accounted us to be."

The following quotation will show that Mr. Hollis was one of a family whose spirit and works were kindred to his own :—" Concerning the Hollis family, who, for nearly a century, continued their benefactions to Harvard College, we may here state in brief what Pierce and Quincy have given at length in their histories of the University. Thomas Hollis, the father of the ' benefactor,' was born in 1634, and died in 1718. His son, called, by reason of his donations to Harvard, Thomas Hollis, 1st, died in 1731. A second son, Nathaniel, died in 1738. A third son, John, was a partner in business with his brother Thomas. Thomas Hollis, 2d, son of Nathaniel, died in 1735. The total amount of the benefactions of this family up to this date, ' exceeded,' says Quincy, ' six thousand pounds currency of Massachusetts, which, considering the value of money at that period, and the disinterested spirit by which their charities were prompted, constitutes one of the most remarkable instances of continued benevolence on record.' Thomas Hollis, 3d, was born in 1720, and died in 1774. His donations to Harvard College during his lifetime exceeded fourteen hundred pounds sterling. Timothy Hollis died in 1791, at an advanced age. He gave twenty pounds sterling for the library. Thomas Brand Hollis, the last of the benefactors, was born 1719, and died in 1804." Manning and Brown University, pp. 121, 122.—ED.

religion is declined to a mere skeleton ; yet the Lord's arm is not shortened. Humble service attends you, from your affectionate, though at present afflicted, friend and servant,

EDWARD WALLIN.

All the letters of Mr. Wallin that I publish are carefully copied from the originals now in my hands. He finished his course with joy, in his fifty-fifth year, June 12, 1733.[1]

To return to our own history, I would observe, that Rhode Island Colony was first divided into three counties, in June, 1729 ; and in February, 1730, Providence was divided into the towns of Providence, Smithfield, Glocester, and Scituate. There were thirteen Baptist churches, most of them small, who now held annual associations[2] to promote discipline and communion among them, upon the six principles

---

[1] Crosby, Vol. IV, p. 394.—B.

Edward Wallin, whose name has often occurred in this history, held an honored rank among English Baptists of the last century. He was converted early in life. The fortune of his parents was too narrow to keep him at school, and he was hurried into business; yet he found opportunity to acquire a considerable knowledge of Greek, Hebrew, and Oriental dialects. He had expressed no purpose of entering the ministry, but two churches at the same time invited him to the pastorate. He accepted the call of the poorer and less promising church, and earnestly devoted himself to the work of the ministry, bearing a large part of the burden of his own support by teaching school. His church was largely prospered under his ministry, and his influence outside his own immediate field of labor, was extensive and valuable. Rev. John Gill, in preaching his funeral sermon, spoke of him as follows :— " He had a large experience of the grace of God, and a considerable share of light and knowledge in the great truths of the gospel. He had a heavenly skill to lay open the wretched and miserable state and condition of sinners by nature, and to set forth the glory of Christ in his person, blood, righteousness, and sacrifice. His language was plain and easy, though strong and masculine; far above contempt, and yet free from the swelling words of vain rhetoricians. His reasoning was clear and nervous, his mien and deportment was grave, his address was with majesty, which at once had a tendency to command awe, engage attention, and strike the affection." See Crosby, Vol. IV, pp. 390—392.—ED.

[2] These annual associations were commonly known as " yearly meetings." Knight, in his History of the Six-Principle Baptists, states that the Baptist churches in Rhode Island began to hold yearly meetings about the close of the seventeenth century. Comer's Diary mentions the yearly meeting of 1732, and gives the names of ten ministers who were present. The churches were represented as in modern Associations, by their elders and delegates, and reported their condition by letters. Copies of several of these letters are preserved in Rev. S. Hall's Collection of Papers. One of these yearly meetings is referred to in Vol. I, page 521. See Manning and Brown University, p. 73.—ED.

in Hebrews vi., viz., one in Providence, the Second in Newport, two in Smithfield, the Second in Swanzey, and one in
each of the towns of Dartmouth, Warwick, North Kingstown, South Kingstown, Scituate, Groton, New London, and
New York. The two in Connecticut had introduced singing in public worship, to promote which their Elder Wightman published a little pamphlet; but it was opposed by
many among other churches. One church in Newport held
the keeping of the seventh day Sabbath as a bar of communion, and refused to assist in ordaining Mr. Comer, in
1726, on that account. Mr. Mumford, who first led them
into that principle, introduced singing among them in 1677.
In that, and in their sister church at Westerly, Comer says,
were now about one hundred and forty communicants; and
also, that general redemption was held by the majority of all
those fifteen churches. The first church in Newport had
now about fifty members, the first in Swanzey, two hundred,
and their sister church in Boston, eighty. These held to
particular election, and did not make laying on of hands a
bar to communion, and sang in public worship; and the
above named were all the Baptist churches then extant, north
of New Jersey.

Mr. Comer had held a correspondence by letter with ministers in New Jersey for several years; and in March, 1731,
he went there by water, and visited their churches in Middletown, Piscataqua, Cohansey, &c. He went as far as
Philadelphia; and upon his return declared great satisfaction, in the sight he had of the faith and order of those
churches. On July 2, he said:—

I desired and obtained a dismission from the church where I had preached
more than two years, because I was never settled there, and found that
some could not bear my preaching the doctrines of grace.

In August he removed to Rehoboth, where, on January 1,
1732, he said:—

I begin a new year, in a new place, but not in a new employment; for
my delight of soul is in serving my dear Redeemer in the sacred work of

the ministry ; which I prefer and esteem above and beyond every thing else ; though I acknowledge, unfit and unworthy in myself.   Lord, who is sufficient for these things?   My sufficiency is alone of God, in whom I rest and rely continually.   January 20, a Baptist church was gathered in Rehoboth ; and January 26, I was publicly installed pastor of it.   Elder Ephraim Wheaton of Swanzey preached from I Thess. v. 12, 13, and gave me the right hand of fellowship.

A precious number of souls were hopefully converted under his ministry there.   In June he visited Sutton and Leicester, and baptized Thomas Richardson, Daniel Denny, Esq., brother to Mr. Prince's wife of Boston, and six more. In July he preached and baptized a man in Middleborough.[1] November 30, he baptized fifteen persons at home, who were chiefly seals of his ministry.

Two learned ministers were now settled in Newport. Mr. John Callender, nephew to their minister in Boston, who had enjoyed the benefits of Mr. Hollis's donations in Harvard College, was ordained a pastor of the first church in Newport, October 13, 1731, colleague with Elder Packom, who died three years after.   Mr. Nicholas Eyres, who was born in Wiltshire, August 22, 1691, and educated in the city of Bristol, became a Baptist after he came over to New York ; and he was ordained pastor of a small Baptist church there in 1724, by the two Elders Wightman.   A collection was made in Newport, Providence, &c., to help them in building a meeting-house in that city.   But in 1730, the church became much broken ; Eyres says, " Some of them deserted under a pretence of love to the principles of absolute election and predestination."   Therefore he came and settled at Newport, October, 1731, colleague with Elder Wightman.   Elder James Clarke, of that church, died December 1, 1736, aged 88, much esteemed by those who knew him.

[1] "An account of such persons that have been baptized by me, John Comer, in remote places from my habitation, from the year 1732.   Sutton, June 18, 1732; Thomas Richardson, Daniel Dennie, Elisha Nevers, Martha Green.   Leicester, June 20, 1732; Joshua Nichols, Abiathar Vinton, Bathsheba Nevers, Lydia Vinton. Middleborough, July 17; Benjamin Booth."   Comer's Manuscript Diary.—ED.

Mr. James Bound, a sensible Baptist, came over from England, and dwelt a while in Salem village, now Danvers, where Mr. Peter Clark was minister; who could not be content with personal disputes, but also frequently preached against the Baptist principles, when there were no others in the place that held them. Bound told him that it was an unfair way of treating mankind; but he persisted in it, until he turned a number of his people from his own way; who removed, and began a Baptist society in Sutton. Mr. Bound's son John married a member of Mr. Clark's church, and removed to that town, where the preaching of the Sutton minister for infant baptism turned her from it; and when Clark heard thereof, he wrote her a long letter upon the subject. This she communicated to Mr. Walton, and he wrote an answer thereto, and sent it in a sealed letter to Mrs. Bound. But by some means Clark got it into his hands, and published both letters, with animadversions thereon, in 1732. She told me that she never saw Walton's letter to her, till she saw it in print. How well this agrees with the gentleman, or the Christian, the reader will judge.

In December, 1731, an act was passed in Boston, for the Quakers only; which left out the affirmation, and five-mile limitation, and required the assessors in each parish, where any Quakers lived, to make an annual list of them, and to deliver it to their parish clerk by the 20th of July; and if any of them should happen to be omitted therein, two principal members of the Quaker society might certify the same to the assessors by the 10th of August; and they should also be exempted from taxes to the established worship. As the exempting laws for Baptists expired in 1733, Mr. Comer's people were immediately taxed to other teachers; and some of them were imprisoned therefor. But upon application to their Legislature they were released in 1734; and a like law was made for the Baptists as had lately been for the Quakers; though no penalty was laid upon their assessors, for breaking those laws, which they frequently did.

The Baptist churches in Swanzey and Rehoboth met with sore bereavements in 1734; when Elder Wheaton died, April 26, aged 75; and Mr. Comer, the 23d of May following, before he had completed his 30th year. But how much did he do in a little time! A decline immediately followed, from which neither of those churches have fully returned to this day; though the first of them has lately done so in a great measure. On September 16, 1735, a Baptist church was constituted at Sutton; and September 28, 1737, Benjamin Marsh and Thomas Green were ordained joint pastors of it. The former was from Salem, and the latter from Malden; being an early planter in Leicester. And September 28, 1738, by mutual agreement, the brethren at Leicester, became a church by themselves, and Green their pastor. May 16, 1736, Elder Wightman, of Newport, baptized the wife of Mr. Nathaniel Mather, a Presbyterian minister of Long Island.[1] November 4, 1736, a Baptist church was formed in Brimfield;[2] and on November 4, 1741, Ebenezer Moulton was ordained their pastor;[3] who descended from a member of the first House of Representatives at Boston, in 1634, but who was a sufferer from the ruling party there three years after.[4]

March 24, 1738, a century after the deed of Rhode Island was given by the Narragansett Indians, Mr. John Callender delivered a sermon at Newport, which he published, with enlargements; containing the best history of that colony then extant.[5] His uncle at Boston was taken from his beloved flock the last day of that month; and he finished

[1]Eyres's Register.

[2]This church is now the Baptist church in Wales.—Ed.

[3]He married the above named John Bound's widow.

[4]Robert Moulton, of Salem, who was one of those who were disarmed in 1637. See Vol. I, p. 69.—Ed.

[5]An Historical Discourse on the Civil and Religious affairs of the Colony of Rhode Island. By John Callender, M. A. Reprinted in R. I. Historical Collections, Vol. IV.—Ed.

his course in the following happy manner. March 21, he said, "When I look on one hand, I see nothing but sin, guilt and discouragement; but when I look on the other, I see my glorious Saviour, and the merits of his precious blood, which cleanseth from all sin. I cannot say I have such transports of joy as some have had, but through grace I can say I have gotten the victory over death and the grave." Being asked what word of advice he had for his church, he earnestly replied, " Away with lukewarmness! Away with such remissness in attending the house of prayer, which has been a discouragement to me: and I have been faulty myself!" The Boston Evening Post of April 3, says :—

Friday morning last, after a lingering sickness, deceased the Rev. Mr. Elisha Callender, minister of the Baptist church in this town ; a gentleman universally beloved by people of all persuasions, for his charitable and catholic way of thinking. His life was unspotted, and his conversation always affable, religious, and truly manly. During his long illness he was remarkably patient, and in his last hours (like the blessed above) pacific and entirely serene ; his senses good to the last. "I shall," said he, "sleep in Jesus," and that moment expired.

Mr. Jeremiah Condy, who took his first degree at Harvard College in 1726, after preaching a while in this country, went over to England ; but he was now sent for from thence, and was ordained pastor of the Baptist church in Boston, February 14, 1739.[1] The third Baptist church in Connecticut was constituted and organized the same year in Wallingford. By reading Delaune's plea for the noncon-

[1]As in the ordination of Elisha Callender, so now in that of Mr. Condy, the Baptist church in Boston invited aid from the Congregationalists. The following letter was sent to the church in Cambridge :

" To the church of Christ in Cambridge under the pastoral care of the Rev. Mr. Nathaniel Appleton :

" HONORED AND BELOVED IN THE LORD : This is to request you to send your Reverend Elders and Messengers to assist in the ordination of our elected pastor, on the second Wednesday in February next. A request of the like tenor with this, we have made to the churches in Boston under the care of the Rev. Messrs. Webster and Gray, and Mr. William Hooper.

"Honored and beloved, we heartily wish you all spiritual blessings in Christ

formists and other means, a number of people were brought to embrace their sentiments, and joined to the Baptist church in New London; but ordinarily met for worship at Wallingford, from 1731 till they had a regular dismission on August 20, 1739; and after being formed into a distinct church, ordained Mr. John Merriam for their pastor. Mr. Edward Upham, of Malden, son to a member of the Baptist church in Boston, took his first degree at Harvard College in 1734; and after preaching at Springfield about two years,

Jesus, the glorious Head of the Church. We are, in behalf and by order of the Church, your affectionate brethren in the gospel.

SHEM DROWNE, Deacon,
JOHN CALLENDER,
JAMES BOUND,
BENJ. LANDON,
JOHN PROCTOR."

R. I. Historical Collections, Vol. IV, p. 37.

The following letter shows that this course of the Boston church did not meet with universal approbation:

"We, the subscribers, of the Baptist Church of Christ in Swanzey, under the pastoral care of Elder Samuel Maxwell: to the Baptist Church of Christ in Boston, sendeth greeting, wishing grace, peace and mercy, in our Lord Jesus Christ, may be multiplied.

"BELOVED BRETHREN: We rejoice to hear that the loss of your minister is so likely to be made up in the settlement of another whom we hear you have chosen to supply the place of your deceased pastor. But we shall be sorry to hear that you make use of, or improve, other ministers of other persuasions in the ordination of him whom you have chosen for that work; for we believe it to be not agreeable to your own principles; for we suppose you do not look upon them as persons regularly baptized, and, for that reason, not qualified to ordain your minister; for we do not find by the rules of the gospel of our Lord Jesus Christ that any were received into the Christian church before baptism, much less to ordain others to the work of the ministry. Therefore we pray you to take it into your serious consideration, before you proceed; for if you proceed in that way, it will be matter of grief to us, and we believe to the whole church, and particularly to our brothers and sisters at Providence. Therefore, brethren, we leave these things to the blessing of Almighty God, praying that he would give you grace and wisdom in all things to do his will. So, not having opportunity to call the church together, we thought it our duty to send these lines, in love and good will towards you. So we take leave to subscribe ourselves, your beloved brethren in the bonds of the gospel,

JONATHAN KINGSLEY, &c.

Swanzey, February 8, 1738-9.

"Beloved Brethren, we desire that this letter may be communicated to the church before they proceed to the ordination of their pastor."

John Callender, of Newport, preached the Ordination Sermon, which, by request of the church, was published. R. I. Historical Collections, Vol. IV. pp. 19, 20. —ED.

a church was constituted there, October 14, 1740, and the next day he was ordained their pastor, by·the assistance of Mr. Condy and Mr. John Callender.[1]

The exempting law for Baptists had again expired, and their church in Rehoboth, being afraid of further trouble, requested the town to vote them clear. This was considered of at a town meeting, January 24, 1740, when it was declared that they could not lawfully do it; yet at another meeting, February 13, they voted, "that they were willing to grant or agree upon a salary for the minister of the Baptist church the present year, in case the said Elder will accept thereof." For this they had no more law than the other, and it was evidently done to ensnare them if possible. In May following, said exempting law was revived, to continue seven years.

[1] "He was ordained by Elders John Callender, Jeremiah Condy, and Samuel Maxwell." Paper in Rev. S. Hall's Collection.—ED.

CHAPTER XIV.

A REVIEW OF PAST DARKNESS.—OF LIGHT AT NORTHAMPTON.—AND EX-
TENSIVELY THROUGH THE LAND.—THE NATURE OF THE WORK DESCRIBED.
—HOW FAR IT PREVAILED.—WRITINGS FOR AND AGAINST IT.—CLASSES
AGAINST IT.—AND COURTS ALSO.—WHERE THE REAL BLAME LIES.

A very great change is before us, which some have called
the Great Reformation, and others great confusion; which
diversity of opinion is no new thing. Concerning the
founder of Christianity, some said, He is a good man; others
said, Nay, but he deceiveth the people. In 1680 a sermon
was delivered before the corporation of the city of London,
wherein the dissenters were accused of obstructing the cause
of reformation, because they would not conform to the national worship; and recourse was had to the severities of
Congregationalists in New England, against the Baptists and
others, to justify the severities that were exercised towards
dissenters in England. Therefore, Dr. Owen published a
book in 1681, wherein he observes, that all the reformation
that has taken place since the rise of Antichrist, was produced entirely by these three principles, viz., taking the
Holy Scriptures as their only perfect rule in all religious
matters; allowing each rational person to judge of their
meaning for himself; and holding that all the power of
office and government in the church of Christ is derived
from him, by his word and Spirit, to each particular church,
and not by a local succession from any other power in the

world.   And so far as any have declined from this last principle, he assures us that therein they have rejected a main
reason of separation from the church of Rome.[1]   If so, then
New England was involved at this time in darkness that
might be felt.   Very few of the common people had any
idea, that a person could have a right to the gospel ministry
without a degree from college, any more than the Israelites
could to the priesthood, who were not of the seed of Aaron.
And so great and good a man as Mr. Jonathan Edwards
warned ministers against breaking over this line,[2] even in
the same book wherein he says, " It has certainly sometimes
been so with our colleges, that instead of being places of
the greatest advantage for true piety, one cannot send a child
thither, without great danger of his being infected as to his
morals."[3]   A professor and a tutor of Harvard College, a
little before this time, were convicted of gross immoralities.[4]
And in 1738, a minister at Eastham, on Cape Cod, was deposed from his office for heterodoxy in principles; which
affected others who were of his sentiments so much, that Dr.
Charles Chauncy published a sermon upon liberty of conscience in 1739.   And on June 9, 1740, he met with ten
other ministers at Salem, and signed a paper in favor of that
deposed minister; who owned to the world, that his belief
was, " that men can do that, upon the doing of which they

[1]Original of Evangelical Churches, pp. 291—297.

[2]It has been thought by some that . . . . the gospel ministry need not be limited,
as it used to be, to persons of a liberal education; but some, of late, have been for
having others, that they have supposed to be persons of eminent experience, publicly licensed to preach, yea, and ordained to the work of the ministry; and some
ministers have seemed to favor such a thing. But how little do they seem to look
forward and see the unavoidable consequences of opening such a door! . . . . Not
but that there may probably be some persons in the land that have had no education at
college, that are, in themselves, better qualified for the work of the ministry than
some others that have taken their degrees, and are now ordained. But yet I believe the breaking over those bounds that have hitherto been set, in ordaining such
persons, would, in its consequences, be a greater calamity than the missing such persons in the work of the ministry." Edwards's Thoughts on the Revival of Religion
in New England; Works, Vol. III, p. 380.—Ed.

[3]Edwards's Thoughts, 1742, pp. 266, 350. [Works, Vol. III, pp. 380, 414.]

[4]Hobby's Defence of Whitefield, p. 20.

shall certainly be saved; and that men's obedience is a cause of their justification.[1] A minister of the capital town in New Hampshire, says of the state of the churches at this time :—

No serious Christian could behold it without a heavy heart, and scarce without a weeping eye; to see the solid, substantial piety, for which our ancestors were justly renowned, having long languished under sore decays, brought so low, and seemingly just ready to expire and give up the ghost. How did not only Pelagianism, but Arianism, Socinianism, and even Deism, and what is falsely called Free-thinking, here and there prevail! The instituted means of salvation, in many places, were but lightly esteemed, and a horrid contempt was put upon the ministry of the word.[2]

And in England Bishop Butler said in 1736 :—

It is come, I know not how, to be taken for granted, by many persons, that Christianity is not so much as a subject of inquiry; but that it is now at length discovered to be fictitious; and accordingly they treat it as if in the present age this were an agreed point among all people of discernment, and nothing remained but to set it up as a principal subject of mirth and ridicule, as it were by way of reprisals, for its having so long interrupted the pleasures of the world.[3]

But God ever works like himself, even so as to demonstrate to all, that our help is in him, and not in any arm of flesh. Mr. Stoddard's doctrine had greatly prevailed in this country before his decease, February 11, 1729. His grandson, Jonathan Edwards, was settled a colleague with him two years before; who has since been a chief instrument of reformation in our times. A revival of religion began under his ministry, near the close of 1733, which arose to such a height in the spring of 1735, that he entertained hopes of about thirty conversions among his people in a week, for six weeks together;[4] so that scarce a grown person in the place remained unaffected, and many children were effectually

[1]Osborn's Letter to the Convention at Boston, July 7, 1743, pp. 6, 23.
[2]Shurtleff's Defence of Whitefield, p. 4.
[3]Whitefield's Life, Chap. II. ["Advertisement" to the first edition of Butler's Analogy.]
[4]See Edwards's Narrative of Surprising Conversions; Works, Vol. III, p. 240. —ED.

4

called.   Our Elder Clark, of Wilbraham, dates his conversion there, at that time, when about twelve years old.   This work was powerful in several adjacent towns ; and they had a less degree of it in a number of towns in Connecticut. Edwards's Narrative of that work was much esteemed in London, where a preface was written to it, by Dr. Watts and Dr. Guyse.   In the mean time two scholars were converted in the University of Oxford, in 1733, who were furnished with such gifts, that one of them with his tongue, the other by his pen, were greatly instrumental of reviving doctrinal and experimental Christianity, through the whole British empire.   Mr. George Whitefield, the first of them,[1] was ordained by the Bishop of Gloucester, June 20, 1736; embarked for Georgia in December, 1737 ; returned through Ireland to England a year after ; embarked again for America in August, 1739; and travelled and labored with great success, as far northward as New York.

These things being heard of at Boston, where religion was at a very low ebb, earnest invitations were sent him to come over and help them.   He therefore sailed from South Carolina, and landed at Newport, September 14, 1740, where he labored three days to good purpose ; and then travelled to Boston, and as far eastward as York, to see the aged and pious Moody, who received him joyfully.   After his return to Boston, he went up a hundred miles westward to Northampton, to visit our excellent Edwards, and from thence down by Hartford to New Haven, and away through the southern colonies, until he embarked from Delaware Bay, December 1, when he said :—

O my soul, look back with gratitude on what the Lord hath done for thee in this excursion.   I think it is the seventy-fifth day since I arrived at Rhode Island.   My body was then weak, but the Lord has much renewed its strength.   I have been enabled to preach, I think, one hundred and

---

[1] The other was Mr. James Hervey, who was born near Northampton, in England, February 26, 1714.   And after a very pious and useful life in the ministry, and many excellent publications in the cause of true religion, he died near the place of his birth, December 25, 1758.

seventy-five times in public, besides exhorting frequently in private. I have travelled upwards of eight hundred miles, and gotten upwards of seven hundred pounds sterling, in goods, provisions and money, for the Georgia orphans. Never did God vouchsafe me greater comforts. Never did I see such a continuance of the divine presence in the congregations to whom I have preached.[1]

As he went through New Jersey he prevailed with Mr. Gilbert Tennent to take a tour into this field, which was then white unto the harvest; who came to Boston in December, and labored in these parts through the winter. In their preaching, both of them laid open the dreadful evil and danger of hypocrisy as well as profaneness, and spake as plainly against unconverted teachers and professors as any other sort of sinners, and the effects were exceeding great and happy.

Some indeed tried to persuade the world, that the great change then made in the land was chiefly owing to the mechanical influence of their terrible words, gestures, and moving ways of address. Dr. Chauncy took much pains to put this color upon things. But Mr. Thomas Prince says:—

As to Mr. Whitefield's preaching, it was, in the manner, moving, earnest, winning and melting; but the mechanical influence of this, according to the usual operation of mechanical powers, in two or three days expired, with many in two or three hours; and I believe with most as soon as the sound was over, or they got out of the house, or in the first conversation they fell into. But with the manner of his preaching, wherein he appeared to be in earnest, he delivered those vital truths which animated all our martyrs, made them triumph in flames, and led his hearers into the view of that vital, inward, active piety, which is the mere effect of that mighty supernatural operation of a divine power on the souls of men; which only will support and carry through the sharpest trials, and make meet for the inheritance of the saints in light.

[1] Collection of his Journals, p. 437. He was born in the city of Gloucester, December 16, 1714; and after a life of incessant labors, in Europe and America, he died at Newburyport, in New England, September 30, 1770. Mr. Tennent was born in Ireland, February 5, 1703. His father came over with his family, and was a Presbyterian minister at Neshaminy, in Pennsylvania; where he kept an academy, wherein a number of excellent ministers were educated. Gilbert was ordained in 1726, and after a very useful life he died at Philadelphia, July 23, 1764. President Finley published some account of him.

Of Mr. Tennent, Mr. Prince says :—

In private converse with him, I found him to be a man of considerable parts and learning; free, gentle and condescending; and from his own various experience, reading the most noted writers on experimental divinity, as well as the Scriptures, and conversing with many who had been awakened by his ministry in New Jersey, where he then lived, he seemed to have as deep an acquaintance with the experimental part of religion as any I have conversed with ; and his preaching was as searching and rousing as ever I heard.   He seemed to have no regard to please the eyes of his hearers with agreeable gestures, nor their ears with delivery, nor their fancy with language ; but to aim directly at their hearts and consciences, to lay open their ruinous delusions, show them their numerous, secret, hypocritical shifts in religion, and drive them out of every deceitful refuge wherein they made themselves easy, with a form of godliness without the power.[1]

March 2, 1741, Mr. Tennent preached his farewell sermon at Boston, and came round by Plymouth, Middleborough, Bridgewater, Taunton, Newport, and Providence, and so returned home through Connecticut ; in all which places his labors had some good effect.   Religion was much revived in Boston, Northampton, and places adjacent, in the fall and winter.   In February and March, it was so in New Haven, Hebron, and Lebanon Crank.   At their general election in May, Mr. Jedidiah Mills preached in a powerful manner at Hartford, from whence his fame spread extensively.   Proceeding eastward in his labors, Dr. Benjamin Lord, of Norwich, hearing when he was to preach at Lebanon, ventured to appoint a lecture for him in his own pulpit on Tuesday, June 2 ; but Mr. Mills was otherways engaged, and Mr. Wheelock came and preached it ; and Mr. Mills came and preached there twice the Friday following.   These were the first that I heard of those itinerant ministers.   Such darkness had prevailed before, and many spake so freely of the light they now received, that the name of Newlights was soon cast upon them.   But an old saint, who was converted under Mr. Flavel's ministry in England, but now lived at our Norwich, being asked what she thought of them, readily re-

[1]Christian History, Vol. II, pp. 384—387.

plied, " Newlights ! It is new to such as never saw it before; but it is what I knew above fifty years ago." The work prevailed very powerfully in Norwich through the summer. In August, Mr. James Davenport, from Long Island, came there, where Mr. Eleazer Wheelock and Mr. Benjamin Pomeroy met him, and they labored incessantly for three days, and a great reformation was wrought in the town ; and in this and the following year, that glorious work of divine grace prevailed, in a greater or less degree, in most parts of New England, New York, New Jersey, Pennsylvania, and many other places. A measure of it was granted to the Baptists in Boston, Leicester, Brimfield, Newport,[1] Groton, and Wallingford ; but as the work was begun and carried on almost wholly by Pædobaptists, from which denomination their fathers had suffered much, most of the Baptists were prejudiced against the work, and against the Calvinian doctrine by which it was promoted. Though I find that Elder Robert Feke, of Oyster Bay, on Long Island, wrote to his brethren in Newport, November 29, 1741, and said, " God has begun a glorious work among us, and I hope he will carry it on. There have been seventeen added to our little band in about three months." And the work was powerful among the Baptists in New Jersey and Pennsylvania.

All allow that many imperfections attended this revival of religion ; but the great difficulty has been to determine what they were, so as to encourage what was right, and to guard against all that was not so. Mr. Edwards delivered a sermon upon this subject at New Haven, in September, 1741, which he enlarged and published,[2] with a preface by Mr. William Cooper, of Boston ; and it circulated through the nation, and was much esteemed. But an anonymous answer to it was published at Boston,[3] which condemned Mr. Coop-

---

[1] Betwixt March and August, 1741, forty-eight persons were baptized, and joined to the Second church in Newport.

[2] The marks of a Work of the True Spirit. Edwards's Works, Vol. I, p. 525.—ED.

[3] This answer was commended, if not written, by Dr. Chauncy. See Chauncy's Thoughts, p. 332.

er's saying " Some of the *learned* and *knowing* among men
have had those things revealed to them of the Father in
heaven, which flesh and blood doth not teach." This writer
said he could not guess who they should be. To which it
may be replied, that Mr. William Hobby, of Reading, one
of the eleven signers to the paper in favor of Osborn's
Arminianism, Mr. Daniel Rogers, a tutor at Harvard College, and a number more of their teachers, freely confessed
that they were blind guides, until they were savingly enlightened under Mr. Whitefield's preaching. Said writer discovered a great dislike of Cooper's saying " These fruits do
not grow on *Arminian* ground ;" and also of what Edwards
wrote against unregenerate ministers. As no law could take
place in the Massachusetts, without the consent of Episcopalians, Presbyterian ministers could not carry their power
so far there as in Connecticut, where the whole power of
making laws was in one denomination, who therefore improved their power in the following manner.

Governor Talcot died in October while their Assembly
was sitting. They then elected a Cambridge scholar in his
stead, who was strongly attached to their Saybrook establishment. By an order from their Legislature, a General
Consociation from all the counties of that colony met at
Guilford, November 24, and drew up sundry resolves ; in
one of which they say, " that for a minister to enter into
another minister's parish, and preach or administer the seals
of the covenant, without the consent of or in opposition to
the settled minister of the parish, is disorderly." Mr. Robbins, of Branford, had done so at New Haven before, for
which other ministers had reproved him, and he had made
some concessions to them therefor. In December he received
a written request[1] from the Baptist minister in Wallingford,
informing him, that Dr. Bellamy had preached in their soci-

[1]Sir: After suitable respects to yourself, this note is to inform you that Mr.
Bellamy has been with us at Wallingford and preached in our Baptist Society, to
very good satisfaction and success on several persons, both of our people, and those

ety to mutual satisfaction, and desiring that he would come and do the like. This request appeared agreeable, and he appointed a meeting for the purpose, January 6. 1742. But, two days before the time, a deacon from Wallingford brought him two letters, the one signed by forty-two men of that town, the other signed by Jacob Hemenway and Isaac Stiles, ministers who lived by 'the way, requesting him not to go and preach to those Baptists, without giving any reason against it, but only their desire. This did not appear to him a sufficient reason for him to violate his promise, and to disappoint a people who were desirous of hearing the gospel. He therefore went and preached two sermons there, with an evident good effect. Yet for so doing he was complained of as a *disorderly* person, to the Consociation of New Haven county, in their meeting of February 9. He inquired wherein the disorder lay, seeing he preached in a particular society, at the written request of their pastor? It was answered that said society was not a lawful society, but a disorderly company. He replied, that Governor Talcot had advised Wallingford collectors not to distrain ministerial taxes from them; and the authority sent them annual proclamations for fasts and thanksgivings, as to other societies. But as the Consociation thought themselves better judges of those matters than civil rulers were, they expelled Robbins from their Classical Court for preaching to those Baptists.[2] A son of the Wallingford minister was then a

of your denomination, with whom we desire to join heartily in the interests of religion, though we cannot in the form; so that it seems to be the desire of both denominations here, that yourself would oblige us with a sermon or two, as soon as you can after next week; and please to send me when. This is also my desire for the good of souls and the glory of God. Sir, yours in good affections,

JOHN MERRIAM, Elder.

Wallingford, Dec. 23, 1741.

A Plain Narrative of the proceedings of the Reverend Association and Consociation of New Haven County, against the Rev. Mr. Philemon Robbins, p. 4.—ED.

[2]His Narrative, pp. 1—6.—B.

"Resolved: That the Rev. Mr. Robbins's so preaching was disorderly.

"Resolved: That the Rev. Mr Philemon Robbins should not sit as a member of this Council for his disorderly preaching." A Plain Narrative, &c., p. 6.—ED.

tutor in Yale College, of which David Brainard was a member ; and the tutor having prayed more pathetically than usual with the scholars, one of Brainard's intimates asked him what he then thought of the tutor ?   " He has no more grace than this chair," said Brainard.   The sentence was overheard, and carried to the rulers of the College ; though the accuser could not tell who it was against.   However they extorted this from his friends, and expelled Brainard out of the College just about the time that Robbins was expelled from their Consociation.[1]   And more effectually to guard against such disorders for the future, a draught of a law was made, and ministers conveyed it into the Legislature at Hartford, in their session of May 13 ; who were not only prevailed with to pass it, but also to direct the heads of their College not to suffer any scholars therein who refused to obey it.[2]

AN ACT FOR REGULATING ABUSES, AND CORRECTING DISORDERS IN ECCLE-
SIASTICAL AFFAIRS.

Whereas, this Assembly did by their act, made in the seventh year of the reign of her late Majesty Queen Anne, establish and confirm a confession of faith, and an agreement for ecclesiastical discipline, made at Saybrook, Anno Domini 1708, by the Reverend Elders and [the] Messengers delegated by the churches in this Colony for that purpose ; under which establishment his Majesty's subjects, inhabiting in this Colony, have enjoyed, great peace and quietness, until [till] of late sundry persons have been guilty of disorderly and irregular practices ; whereupon this Assembly, in October last, did direct to the calling of a General Consociation, to sit at Guilford in November last, which said Consociation was convened accordingly ; at which Convention it was endeavored to prevent the growing disorders amongst ministers that have been ordained or licensed by the Associations in this government to preach ; and likewise to prevent divisions and disorders among the churches and ecclesiastical societies, settled by order of this Assembly ; notwithstanding which, divers of the ministers, ordained as aforesaid, and others licensed to preach by some of the Associations allowed by law, have taken upon them, without any lawful call,

[1] Brainard's Life, p. 20.
[2] See their reasons for expelling the Cleavelands, in 1744.   Col. Hezekiah Huntington told me, that this law was prepared and sent in by ministers

to go into parishes immediately under the care of other ministers, and there to preach to and teach the people ;[1] and also sundry persons, some of whom are very illiterate, and have no ecclesiastical character or any authority whatsoever to preach or teach, have taken upon them publicly to teach and exhort the people in matters of religion, both as to doctrine and practice ; which practices have a tendency to make divisions and contentions among the people in this Colony, and to destroy the ecclesiastical constitution established by the laws of this government, and likewise to hinder the growth and increase of vital piety and godliness in these churches, and also to introduce unqualified persons into the ministry : and more especially where one Association doth intermeddle with [the] affairs that by the platform and agreement abovesaid, made at Saybrook aforesaid, are properly within the province and jurisdiction of another Association ; as by licensing persons to preach and ordaining ministers : Therefore,

Be it enacted by the Governor, Council, and Representatives in General Court assembled, and by the authority of the same, that if any ordained minister, or other person licensed as aforesaid to preach, shall enter into any parish not immediately under his charge, and shall there preach or exhort the people, shall be denied and secluded the benefit of any law of this Colony, made for the support and encouragement of the gospel ministry, except such ordained minister or licensed person shall be expressly invited and desired so to enter into such other parish, and there to preach and exhort the people, either by the settled minister and major part of the church in [of] said parish, or, in case there be no settled minister, then by the church or society within such parish.

And it is further enacted by the authority aforesaid, that if any Association of ministers shall undertake to examine or license any candidate for the gospel ministry, or assume to themselves the decision of any controversy, or as an Association to counsel or [and] advise in any affair that by the platform or agreement above mentioned [made at Saybrook aforesaid,] is properly within the province and jurisdiction of any other Association, then and in such case every member that shall be present in such Association, so licensing, deciding or counselling, shall be each and every of them denied and secluded the benefit of any law in this Colony, made for the support and encouragement of the gospel ministry.

And it is further enacted, [by the authority aforesaid,] that if any minister or ministers, contrary to the force, intent and meaning of this act, shall presume to preach in any parish not under his immediate care and

[1]Besides those before named, Mr. Samuel Buell travelled and labored successfully through the country, who has since enjoyed great blessings in his pastoral labors at East Hampton, on Long Island. Mr. James Sprout, born in Middleborough, since minister in Philadelphia, was another of those itinerant preachers.

charge, the minister of the parish where he shall so offend, or the civil authority, or any two of the committee of such parish, shall give information thereof in writing, under their hands, to the clerk of the parish, or society where such offending minister doth belong, which clerk shall receive such information, and lodge and keep the same on file in his office ; and no Assistant or Justice of the Peace in this Colony shall sign any warrant for the collecting any minister's rate, without first receiving a certificate from the clerk of the society or parish where such rate is to be collected, that no such information as is above mentioned hath been received by him, or lodged in his office.

And it is further enacted, [by the authority aforesaid,] that if any person whatsoever, that is not a settled and ordained minister, shall go into any parish, and without the express desire and invitation of the settled minister of such parish, if any there be, and the major part of the church, or if there be no such settled minister, without the express desire of the church or congregation within such parish, publicly preach and exhort the people, shall for every such offence, upon complaint made thereof to any Assistant or Justice of the Peace, be bound to his peaceable and good behavior until the next County Court, in that county where the offence shall be committed, by said Assistant or Justice of the Peace, in the penal sum of one hundred pounds lawful money, that he or they will not again offend in like kind ; and the said County Court may, if they see meet, further bind the person or persons offending as aforesaid to their peaceable and good behavior, during the pleasure of said Court.

And it is further enacted, [by the authority aforesaid,] that if any foreigner or stranger, that is not an inhabitant within this Colony, including as well such persons that have no ecclesiastical character or license to preach, as such as have received ordination or license to preach by any Association or Presbytery, shall presume to preach, teach or publicly [to] exhort, in any town or society within this Colony, without the desire and license of the settled minister and the major part of the church of said town or society, or at the call and desire of the church and inhabitants of such town or society, provided that it so happen that there is no settled minister there, that every such preacher, teacher or exhorter, shall be sent as a vagrant person, by warrant from any one Assistant or Justice of the Peace, from constable to constable, out of the bounds of this Colony.

The reader may here see how catholic those ministers were, and how concerned to preserve union and order in every part of that colony, and it doubtless would have extended much further, had their power been equal to their inclinations. But there were three things which lay much in their way.   They could not command the thoughts of the people, nor the pens of ministers in other governments, and were unable to move their own rulers to carry violence so far as they did their censures.   The second itinerant minister whom they accused of making divisions and disturbances, published a sermon this year, which had an extensive circulation ; wherein he says :—

The proper cause of sinful divisions, is the [that] enmity against God and holiness, which is in the hearts of natural men, of every order ; being stirred up by the devil, and their own proud and selfish lusts.   And very often natural men, who are the proper cause of such divisions, [are wont to] deal with God's servants as Potiphar's wife did by Joseph ; they lay [all] the blame of their own wickedness at their doors, and make a loud cry.

And as their common talk was, that to go over parish lines to meeting was going out of God's way, so that if any thought they got good thereby, they were deceived, Mr. Tennent says, " There are three monstrous ingredients in this [the] objection, namely, a begging [of] the question in debate, rash judging, and limiting of God."   For they who would confine religious worship to lines which men have drawn, assume a power which is justly questioned, and thereby attempt to limit God ; and how rash is it to judge all those to be deceived who refuse a tame submission to such usurpations !¹   Mr. Edwards also now observed :—

If ministers preach never so good doctrine, and are never so laborious in their work, yet if at such a day as this they shew to their people that they are not well affected to this work, they will be very likely to do their people a great deal more hurt than good ; for the very fame of such a great and extraordinary work of God, if their people were suffered to believe it to be his, and the example of other towns, together with the preaching they might hear occasionally, would be likely to have a much greater influence upon the minds of their people, to awaken and animate them in religion, than all their labors with them.   And we that are ministers, by looking on this work, from year to year, with a displeased countenance, shall effectually keep the sheep from their pasture, instead of doing the part of shep-

¹Tennent's sermon on The great Danger of an Unconverted Ministry, pp. 16, 18.

herds, by feeding them ; and our people had a great deal better be without any settled minister at all, at such a day as this. .... Those awful words of Christ to the Jewish fathers should be considered by us ; Matt. xxiii. 13 ; Wo unto you, for you shut up the kingdom of heaven ; ye neither go in yourselves, neither suffer ye them that are entering to go in. The times of Christ's remarkably appearing in behalf of his church, to revive religion, and advance his kingdom in the world, are often spoken of in the prophecies of Scripture, as times wherein he will remarkably execute judgment on such ministers or shepherds as do not feed the flock but hinder their being fed, and so deliver his flock from them ; as Jer. xxiii ; Ezek. xxxiv : Zech. xi ; Isai. lvi., &c.[1]

How weighty and solemn are these considerations ! yet the imperfections and mistakes of the real servants of Christ, and the hypocrisy and apostasy of others, have often been caught at as a shield against the authority of truth in these respects ; as the following facts will further shew.

[1] Edwards's Thoughts, 1742, pp. 133—135.

CHAPTER XV.

Mr. Davenport derived his descent from the first minister of New Haven, and was son of a minister of Stamford in Fairfield county. He and Mr. Daniel Bliss, a lively minister at Concord, took their first degrees at Yale College in 1732, as Mr. Wheelock and Mr. Pomeroy did theirs in 1733, and Timothy Allen his in 1736; who all dated their conversion before these times. Allen was ordained at West Haven; but upon uttering some unguarded expressions, about how unprofitable the Scriptures were to the unregenerate, their Consociation deposed him from his office. Davenport was an instrument of great awakenings in many places; and no man before him ever labored to so good purpose as he did, among the Mohegan and Nyantic Indians; from whence also sprang a great work among the Narragansetts.[1] But having always lived among ministers who

[1] The Commissioners at Boston, for sending out and supporting missionaries among the Indians, sent Mr. Joseph Park to Westerly, upon that business, in 1733. In 1738 the east part of that town, where the Narragansetts chiefly resided, was set off by the name of Charlestown. But in nine years, he was not able to bring one English family, in those two towns, to set up family worship; nor above a dozen Indians to attend on his ministry. Until, being greatly enlightened himself, by means of those itinerant ministers, a revival began among his people, and a church of four-

claimed a like power in the Christian church, as the seed of
Aaron had in that of the Jews; and being deeply sensible
of the mischiefs which unconverted teachers do to precious
souls, he imbibed a strong persuasion, that it was his duty to
examine the ministers wherever he came, and to warn the
people against hearing such as he judged to be blind guides.
For these things he was taken up and brought before Connecticut Legislature, who sent him out of their Colony.
Separations were hereby caused at New London, New Haven
and Milford. And it was impressed upon sundry minds,
that they must go their way forth, and erect a *shepherd's
tent* at New London, to educate persons in for the ministry.
Such a school was therefore opened, to which a number
resorted, wherein Allen presided. And though he was
once imprisoned for preaching, and others suffered much, it
did but animate them the more. And Davenport must
needs go and preach to the great metropolis of New England. Upon his arrival he had long conferences with the
ministers of Boston and Charlestown; until on July 1, 1742,
most of them signed a declaration, wherein they said :—

He appears to us to be truly pious, and we hope God has used him as
an instrument of good to many souls; yet we judge it our duty to bear
testimony against the following particulars. 1. His being acted much by
sudden impulses. 2. His judging some ministers in Long Island and New
England to be unconverted; and thinking himself called of God to demand
of his brethren, from place to place, an account of their regenerate state,
when or in what manner the Holy Spirit wrought upon and renewed them.
3. His going with his friends, singing through the streets and highways,
to and from the houses of worship, on Lord's days and other days.[1] 4. His
encouraging private brethren to pray and exhort in assemblies gathered
for that purpose. We judge it therefore our present duty not to invite him

teen English members was formed in May, 1742: which was succeeded with so
great a work among the Indians the next year, as brought many of them into that
church, and a hundred of them usually to attend on his ministry. Christian History, Vol. I, pp. 202—210. Mr. Park died there March 1, 1777.

Stephen Babcock, a member of that church, became the pastor of a Baptist
church in 1750, and continued so until his death in 1775.

[1]In this way of singing he was almost entirely singular, even from those who
were otherwise engaged with him in the general cause.

into our places of public worship, as otherwise we might have readily done.

But this did not prevent his going to examine each of them, and then declaring publicly against them; naming some as unconverted, and comparing others to Jehosaphat in Ahab's army, and calling the people to separate from them.[1] He proceeded farther eastward in this way, and upon his return to Boston in August he was imprisoned and brought upon trial in Court, for slandering their ministers, but the jury judged him to be *non compos mentis*, and so acquitted him.[2] Separations hereupon took place in Boston, Ipswich and Newbury. After his return to Long Island, he was brought over to New London; where he and others were carried so far, under a notion of purging away all error, as to burn a considerable pile of books, that in their view were erroneous, near the town wharf, on Lord's day, March 6, 1743, just as people were returning from public worship. Norcott upon Baptism was cast into the pile, but was caught out by another hand. The next day, under a conceit of destroying idolatry, they collected a large heap of fine clothes and ornaments, but were hindered from burning them, partly by a gentleman's coming to Davenport, and assuring him, that if all he had idolized must be burnt, he must burn him first. Great confusion was caused by these things, and the "shepherd's tent" broke up soon after.[3]

Those who teach God's fear by the precepts of men, "watch for iniquity." Isaiah, xxix. 13, 20. And they had now got so much of it, as emboldened them to appear very openly against the work in this land. The annual convention of ministers at Boston, May 25, published their testimony upon this subject; and especially against " The spirit and practice of separation, from the particular flocks to

[1] Christian History, Vol. II, pp. 406—408.
[2] Chauncy's Thoughts, pp. 164—165.
[3] March 5, 1743, Mr. Prince and his son began a weekly publication, and continued it for two years, under the name of The Christian History; which is very serviceable in ours.

which persons belong, to join [themselves] with and support lay exhorters or itinerants.[1] This moved some friends to the late revival to publish an invitation, in the Boston papers, to all ministers who had favorable thoughts of that work, to meet there the day after the ensuing Commencement at Cambridge, to give their minds concerning it ; and such as could not well come, were desired to send in their thoughts in writing. In answer to this request, about ninety ministers met at Boston, July 7, and elected a committee, to draw up a testimony and letter of advice to the churches, to be laid before them next morning. But twenty of them went off, and did not stay to hear it. Of those who stayed, forty-four signed it without reserve ; wherein they testify, that a glorious work of divine grace had been wrought in this land, in the three preceding years ; but advise :—

That *laymen* do not invade the ministerial office, and, under a pretence of exhorting, set up preaching; which, (say they) is very contrary to gospel order, and tends to introduce errors and confusion into the churches : that ministers do not invade the province of others, and, in ordinary cases, preach in another's parish without his knowledge, and against his consent.

Fifteen more signed it, with an exception in these words, viz. :—

We concur with the testimony, for the substance of it, excepting that article of itinerancy, or ministers and others intruding into other ministers parishes without their consent, which great disorder we apprehend not sufficiently testified against therein.

At the head of these was Dr. Colman ; who twelve years before called it a fret of zeal, and a narrow party spirit, in the apostle John, to desire our Saviour himself to forbid others, because, said John, *they follow not us.*[2] The other signers to this exception were Checkley and Eliot of Boston, Fowle of Hingham, Baxter of Medfield, Carpenter of Hull, Bradstreet of Marblehead, Abbot and Prentice of Charlestown, Turrell of Medford, Dorr of Mendon, Park-

---

[1]Chauncy's Thoughts, p. 299.
[2]Colman's Sermon on the death of Thomas Hollis. See p. 25.—ED.

man of Westborough, Eells of Scituate, Bass of Hanover, and Maccarty of Kingston. On the other hand, nine ministers were sensible that in many cases ministers might preach in the parishes of others without their consent, and that, " this liberty cannot be invaded or denied, without inhumanly invading the *essential rights of conscience.*" These were Sewall and Prince of Boston, Diman of Salem, Chipman of Beverly, Emerson of Topsfield, Emerson of Malden, Goddard of Spencer, Weld of Attleborough, and Cotton of Providence.[1] Others were so much set against that liberty, as to procure the publication of the before-cited Connecticut law in a Boston newspaper.[2] And it was evidently the want of power, that prevented the enacting of such laws in the Massachusetts; notwithstanding all the obligations they were under to the Hollis family. Mr. Isaac Hollis, a pious Baptist minister near London, was now sending over liberal communications, towards christianizing the Stockbridge Indians, as Dr. Colman himself informs us.[3] Yet how were the Baptists treated here!

Mr. James Bound, John Dabny, and Thomas Boucher, from Britain, with John Proctor, a town schoolmaster in Boston, members of the Baptist church there, withdrew from it, and began another church in July; and Mr. Ephraim Bound (son to James) was ordained their pastor, September 7, 1743. The reasons of their withdrawal were because Mr. Condy taught Arminian doctrine, contrary to the original principles of the church, and also opposed the late work of God in the land.[4] Philip Freeman, member of a Baptist church in London, came over to Boston, and joined that new church; who sent an account of their principles and conduct to Dr. John Gill, which obtained his approbation, and a considerable present was sent them from Lon-

---

[1] Christian History, Vol. I, pp. 155–166, 198.
[2] Chauncy's Thoughts, p. 41.
[3] Christian History, Vol. I, p. 150.
[4] A fuller account of these matters will be given in a subsequent chapter.—Ed.

don.   The increase of the Baptists in New Jersey soon after moved Mr. Jonathan Dickinson, the first president of their college, to write a dialogue upon infant baptism.   It was printed both at New York and Boston, in 1746, but without any name to it.   Mr. Freeman sent one of them to Dr. Gill, with a request that he would answer it.   He did so in 1749, and began with these words, viz. :—

Many being converted under the ministry of the word in New England, and enlightened into the ordinance of believers' baptism, whereby the churches of the Baptist persuasion at Boston and in the country have been increased, has alarmed the Pædobaptist ministers of that Colony; who have applied to one Mr. Dickinson, a country minister, who, as my correspondent informs me, has wrote with some success against the Arminians, to write in favor of infant sprinkling.

In 1752, Mr. Clark, (who wrote against Walton twenty years before) published a reply to Gill, wherein he said, "In this introductory passage, there are several gross mistakes in fact, or manifest untruths."   And he takes up above five pages, in trying to prove this charge; thinking, undoubtedly, that if he could prove him to be a false man in his introduction, his book might more easily be answered, in the opinion of most; who generally have men's persons in admiration because of advantage.   He allows that Dickinson wrote against the *Sectaries*, and names as such the Quakers, Anabaptists, Arminians and Antinomians; not mentioning that himself was one of the eleven signers of the paper in favor of Osborn's Arminianism in 1740.   The proofs for his charge against Gill consist in limiting his words to the Massachusetts, instead of all New England, and denying any great increase of the Baptists, so as to alarm the ministers; or that any in or near Boston sent to Dickinson to write upon that subject, (which was not affirmed.)   But what shall we think of Clark?   Gill was never here, and therefore might easily mistake the geography of the country; but his accuser was born and educated in it; and he says of that new church :—

They have set up an illiterate teacher. To this Separate society there have been, indeed, some few enthusiasts and Separatists from some churches in Boston, and from the adjacent parts of the country, who have joined themselves. .... Besides, ... I know of no other Baptist church, except at the outskirts of the province towards Rhode Island and Providence, where I am informed there are two or three societies that call themselves Baptist churches.[1]

Whereas, at the time when he wrote thus, there were two Baptist churches in Boston, two in Swanzey, two in Rehoboth, and one in each of the towns of Bellingham, Sutton, Leicester, Sturbridge, Brimfield and Springfield. And how guilty must a man be, thus to misrepresent the state of his own province, in order to fix an odium upon a gentleman who never was in it! He unjustly accused him of holding conversion to be to a particular sect; but how many reproachful names does he himself cast upon dissenters from his own sect! "Arminians" is one of those names; whereas the largest addition to said church in Boston, that they had received from any one town in the country, was of a number of judicious Christians in Medfield, who refused to join in the settlement of an Arminian minister there, who has since been forced to resign his office, because of his having a child by his maid.

After the great earthquake November 18, 1755, Mr. Bound's lectures were flocked to from all parts of the town; and such a blessing was granted upon his ministry, that they had a hundred communicants in that church. His life was unblemished and exemplary, and he died with great peace in his own soul, and much lamented by others, June 18, 1765.

In 1742, Mr. Edwards published his Thoughts, in five parts; shewing that the work going on in the land was a glorious work of God; the duty of all to acknowledge and promote it, and the great danger of the contrary; wherein its friends had been injuriously blamed; what ought to be corrected among them, and what positively ought to be done

[1] Clark against Gill, pp. 1—6.

to promote the work.[1]   Upon a view of which, Dr. Chauncy set off and travelled through New England, New York and New Jersey, to collect matter for an answer to him, which was published this year, with the names of three Governors, two Lieutenant Governors, many Counsellors, and in all above seven hundred men, as subscribers for it.   Above three hundred pages in the book are taken up upon things that he said were of a bad and dangerous tendency in the land.[2] He ranks them under seven heads, namely, Itinerant preaching, Great terrors, Sudden light and joy, Censuring of others, Impulses, Confounding of many exercises together, and A spirit of error.   Under this last head, seven particulars are named, viz., Holding that unconverted ministers could not convert others, Separations, Presumptuous depending upon the assistance of the Spirit, Assurance of Conversion, and of the time of it, Vilifying good works, and Not allowing sanctification to be an evidence of justification. And, lest all the bad stories he had raked together from every part of America, should fail of clothing these points with a garb sufficiently odious, a number are added thereto from Europe, and some from the dregs of popery.   A touch upon what he says, about itinerant preaching, and rash judging, may give some idea how strong his arguments were. Against the former he brings 2 Thes. iii. 10—15 ; 1 Pet. iv. 15, and 2 Cor. x. 12—17; which condemn the eating of other men's bread for naught, acting as busy-bodies in other men's matters, and the commending of themselves, and going into another man's line, of things made ready to our hands.   But by whom is this line drawn? by God or man? Teachers who are fond of support by tax and compulsion, and promote the use of violence towards such as follow not them, most evidently fall under the lash of these Scriptures.

[1]Thoughts on the Revival of Religion in New England; Edwards's Works, Vol. III.—Ed.

[2]To be strictly accurate, only two hundred and ninety-eight pages of the work are on this head.   Part I, which discusses it, reaches to page 332, but of these pages, the Introduction fills thirty-four.—Ed.

According to Chauncy, rash and uncharitable judging was begun in these parts by Mr. Whitefield, "who," he says, " seldom preached, but he had something or other in his sermon against unconverted ministers." And why was this uncharitable? Because Dr. Cotton Mather said, " No man becomes a minister or a communicant in our churches until he hath[1] been severely examined about his *regeneration*, as well as conversation."[2] When was it so? This testimony was given in 1696; and how clearly does it prove that their practice remained the same in 1740! His other arguments are alike conclusive.

Connecticut had a more powerful way of reasoning. In October, 1742, they forbade the erection of any public place of education, without license from authority; and also debarred all teachers from any benefit of their laws for their support, who had not been graduated by some protestant college.[3] And on February 16, they issued a proclamation for a general fast, to be on April 13, 1743, to deprecate the judgments of heaven, for their iniquities,—

Particularly the great neglect and contempt of the gospel and the ministry thereof, and the prevailing of a spirit of error, disorder, unpeaceableness, pride, bitterness, uncharitableness, censoriousness, disobedience, calumniating, and reviling of authority; divisions, contentions, separations and confusions in churches; injustice, idleness, evil speaking, lasciviousness, and all other vices and impieties which abound among us.[4]

[1] " No man becomes a minister in our churches till he be first a communicant, and no man becomes a communicant until he hath, &c."—ED.

[2] Chauncy's Thoughts, pp. 42, 140, 142.

[3] These were separate enactments, and the latter refers to religious, and not secular teachers. The language is as follows :—

" Be it enacted, ... that no particular persons whatsoever shall presume, of themselves, to erect, establish, set up, keep, or maintain any college, seminary of learning, or any public school whatsoever, for the instruction of young persons, other than such as are erected and established by law, without special leave from the Assembly.

"And be it further enacted, that no person that has not been educated or graduated in Yale College, or Harvard College in Cambridge, or some other allowed Protestant college or university, shall take the benefit of the laws of this government respecting the settlement and support of ministers."—ED.

[4] Chauncy's Thoughts, pp. 295, 296.

This was issued early enough to have influence in the choice of their Legislature. Colonel Hezekiah Huntington had been a member of their Council for three years; but at their election at Hartford, May 12, he was left out of it; and John Bulkley, Esq., was chosen in his stead; who sent Zebulon Waterman and others, of Colchester, to Hartford jail the summer before, for teaching and exhorting at a religious meeting. Waterman was soon after ordained the pastor of a Baptist church in Colchester. It was well known that Huntington was much engaged in the late revival of religion in the land, and that he openly testified against the persecutions therein. King William's Act of Toleration was adopted in Connecticut, in May, 1708, just before their Saybrook scheme was formed. But because it had been extended, by their County Court, to the dissenters in New Haven and Milford, it was now repealed, with a declaration, " that those commonly called Presbyterians or Congregationalists shall not take benefit of said law." And it was enacted, that none of other denominations should, for the future, be allowed the privileges of dissenters, but such as should, " before the Assembly, take the oaths and subscribe the declaration provided in the act of Parliament, in cases of like nature." And as Mr. John Owen, of Groton, was complained of, for having, in April before, preached against such proceedings, an order was given out to bring him before the Assembly, to answer therefor, at their next session. In the mean time a Presbyterian minister came from New Jersey, and preached at Milford; for which he was taken up on a Saturday. And as they spake of confining him until Monday, he said, " Sir, I hope you will not confine me from preaching Christ." " *That is what we took you up for*," said the Judge. He was carried, as a *vagrant* person, out of that Colony; but then he returned and preached at New Haven. And as the people there had got into the way of concealing their ministers on week days, an officer came and seized this minister, at their meeting-house

door, on a Lord's day morning, and carried him off. Yet
when he was let go, he returned again and preached to the
people; an account of which being laid before the Assembly at New Haven, of October 13, they added another act,
which required ministers who should so return, to pay the
cost of their transportation, and to be committed until they
should give a hundred pounds' bond, not to offend again in
like kind. Such were their proceedings against a precious
minister of Christ; whose name and subsequent title are,
SAMUEL FINLEY, D. D., President of New Jersey College.

As Mr. Owen avoided being taken, and like complaints
were exhibited against Mr. Pomeroy, orders were given to
arrest them both, and to bring them to the next session of
their Assembly. Accordingly, at their meeting at Hartford,
May 10, 1744, Owen came with a humble confession, and
they forgave him, he paying costs. Pomeroy was brought
and stood trial for some hours; but was condemned and
ordered to be committed till he would pay the costs, and
bind himself for one year, in a recognizance of fifty pounds,
not to offend again in like manner. He then yielded to
their requirements. On July 28, Mr. Davenport signed a
retraction of the four articles which were condemned at
Boston, and of his enthusiasms at New London; which
was sent to Mr. Prince to publish with all speed. He did
so, but prefixed thereto an extract from an ancient author,
who says :—

It is no uncommon thing for those who love God in sincerity, through an
impatience with the bold impieties of wicked men, to transgress the limits
of a regular zeal. And when this impatience betrays them into mistakes,
for which they meet with too severe treatment, either from friends, or from
men in power ; instead of correcting only the irregular sallies of their zeal,
they are apt to suppress the most regular and laudable expressions of it,
and become lukewarm and indifferent.[1]

The sequel will demonstrate the propriety of this remark.
In January, Elder Timothy Packom and Daniel Greene

[1]Christian History, Vol. II, pp. 234—240.

visited their Baptist brethren at New London and Saybrook, and baptized some persons at each place.   At Saybrook the people laid some things across a stream on a Lord's day, to raise the water to baptize in.   False charges were added to what was fact in the case ; and said two teachers, and several other persons, were seized and imprisoned at New London ; one of whom was a woman with a child at her breast. But the above evils were well exposed in a piece, entitled, " The essential rights of Protestants ;" dated March 30, 1744.   Col. Elisha Williams, the best President they ever had at Yale College, was the undoubted author of it ; though, being printed at Boston, it was sent as a letter from thence to a friend in Connecticut.   Having described the origin, design and limits of civil government, he says :—

Man by his constitution, as he is a reasonable being, capable of the knowledge of his Maker, is a moral and an accountable being ; and therefore, as every one is accountable for himself, he must reason, judge and determine for himself.   That faith and practice which depend on the judgment and choice of any other person, and not on the person's own [understanding,] judgment and choice, may pass for religion in the synagogue of Satan, whose tenet is that ignorance is the mother of devotion ; but with no understanding Protestant will it pass for any religion at all. . . . . Ecclesiastical officers, ... as they are Christ's officers, they have authority to teach men his mind in things pertaining to his kingdom ; so they have no authority to teach men any thing but the mind and will of Christ.   It is a truth that shines with a meridian brightness, that whatever is not contained in a commission, is out of it and excluded by it ; and the teaching his laws only being contained in the commission, what is not his law is out of it, and by that commission they are excluded from teaching it, or forbid by it.[1]

And from hence he plainly exposed their persecuting laws and measures.   But though this was printed at Boston, and dispersed in Connecticut, yet the ruling party had no eyes to see it, nor ears to hear it.   We must maintain the good old way, was their cry, although what they so called was diametrically opposite to the first principles of New England.   And though, for reasons before given, the Massachu-

[1] Essential Rights, pp. 8, 17.

setts could not go so far as Connecticut did, yet their disposition is conspicuous in what follows.

Mr. Peter Thatcher was the third minister of Middleborough, where he began to preach in September, 1707, and he continued their pastor until his joyful exit, April 22, 1744. He was much affected with Mr. Tennent's preaching in these parts, and labored earnestly for a reformation among his people, but with much sorrow of heart, until such a blessing was granted at a meeting, November 23, 1741, that about a hundred persons, professors and others, were greatly awakened; and the ensuing harvest was so great, that when he died they had three hundred and forty-three communicants, above half of whom were males.[1] The church met soon after, and elected a committee to manage their affairs, and in particular to provide preaching for them; but the parish committee, who were men of influence in the town,[2] were very opposite to the late work among them, and they counteracted the church in that matter. And when the church had voted to hear Mr. Silvanus Conant four sab-

[1]Christian History, Vol. II, pp. 77—96.—B.

Mr. Tennent preached in Middleborough in March, 1741. "Some half a dozen," says Mr. Thatcher, "were roused." "In the beginning of October following," he continues, "I proposed a day of prayer, and spake to my brother Shaw for his assistance. This was our errand to the throne of grace, to ask the outpouring of the Spirit on this dry fleece. That week, some of my lately awakened brethren obtained a visit from the Rev. Mr. Crocker. .... The 23d day of November, Mr. Crocker came [again]. We began about one. He preached from Romans, 8. 1. This he opened largely; giving the characters of them that were in Christ; and inferred the misery of those who found not the characters in themselves of their being in Christ; there was nothing but condemnation for them; showing what that damnation was, &c. After sermon there, was an exhortation delivered. Many now melted down. After the blessing, the people generally stayed, till some cried with terror, which flew like lightning into every breast; I suppose, none excepted. I have written accounts of seventy-six, that day struck, and brought first to inquire what they should do to escape condemnation. There were a number of professors of religion that day, whose lamps went out. They discovered there was no true oil of grace in them. .... In a few days from that 23d of November, so greatly to be remembered, there appeared to be above two hundred awakened. .... The work grew daily; the numbers were increased; near one hundred and seventy, the following year, joined to the church." Account of the Work of Grace in Middleborough; Rev. Peter Thatcher in the Christian History. See also Great Awakening, pp. 171—176.—ED.

[2]Mr. Jacob Thompson, Benjamin White, Esq., and Captain Ebenezer Morton.

baths upon probation, they went and got another man to supply the pulpit the same days, the first of which was September 9 ; when Conant was permitted to preach in the afternoon. But on September 13 they received the following advice from a Council at Duxbury, viz., " that though it belongs to the church to lead the congregation in the choice and call of a minister to office, that it is the right, as it has been the custom of the several parishes (when destitute of a minister) to apply, by a committee chosen by the whole parish, to such person or persons as shall be recommended to them for that purpose ; and we advise the gentlemen, and all concerned, to follow this laudable custom." The ministers who gave this advice were Eells of Scituate, Gay of Hingham, Lewis of Pembroke, Bass of Hanover, Perkins and Angier of Bridgewater.[1]   And by these means, the body of the church were shut out of their meeting-house, with the minister they chose ; and had no better place than a barn to meet in, until they built another house. And less than a quarter of the church called themselves the standing part, held the old house, and went on and settled another minister. Mr. Conant was ordained, according to their laws, by the advice of a council of five churches, March 28, 1745 ; and ministered there to good purpose, until his decease, December 7, 1777. Mr. John Cotton, then of Halifax, now of Plymouth, published a narrative of these transactions ; to which a virulent answer was returned ; both in 1746. Judge Oliver was of that opposing party ; and he and others had such influence at Boston, that the church could not have any proper hearing there for about four years. But when that was once granted, and every man in the parish had liberty to choose for himself, and each to support the minister he chose, the opposers were soon sick of their minister, and in less than ten years he was dismissed, and their society soon after dissolved ; leaving a loud warning to all against empowering the world to control the church about soul-guides.

[1]Morton against Cotton pp. 14, 15.

CHAPTER XVI.

A DELIVERER RAISED UP IN AN UNLIKELY WAY.—HIS PREACHING AND
SUCCESS.—THE DIVISION AT CANTERBURY.—SUFFERINGS FOR PREACH-
ING THE GOSPEL.—EXPULSIONS FROM COLLEGE.—THE TRUE STATE OF
THE CONTROVERSY.—OPPOSITION TO WHITEFIELD.—NEW CHURCHES
FORMED.—CLASSES AND COURTS AGAINST THEM.—BUT WERE DE-
FEATED.—ESPECIALLY IN THE BRANFORD CASE.

By whom shall Jacob arise, for he is small? saith one
prophet.   Jerusalem hath none of her sons to guide her,
saith another.   And how much was this the case with New
England in 1744?   Although some of their ministers had
been alive in religion, and had done a great deal to promote
the power of it; yet they were agreed with formalists in
confining the ministry to a college education, and in having
it supported by tax and compulsion; therefore, none of them
could now lead the church out of her Egyptian bondage.
And where could such a leader be found?   Could any man
think of looking to the barren shores of Cape Cod for his
birth, to the obscure village of Canterbury for his education,
or to a bench of lawyers for his integrity and faithfulness?
Of all things this seemed most unlikely!   Yet such was the
event.   Mr. Elisha Paine, of Eastham, upon said Cape, removed with his family to Canterbury, and was one of the
seven men who formed a church there, June 13, 1711.
His wife was of the family of Deacon John Doane,[1] one of
the early magistrates of Plymouth Colony.   Mr. Paine had

---

[1] His daughter Abigail married a Lothrop in Norwich, where she was much esteemed, both for her capacity and her piety, until her death in 1735, aged 104.

four sons, whom he brought up in the nurture and admonition of the Lord.[1] The second of them dated his conversion about the time of the revival of religion at Windham, in 1721, and before the general revival, twenty years after, he was become one of the greatest lawyers in Connecticut, and was in very prosperous circumstances in the world. In one of his private papers he says :—

God hath so ordered it in his providence, that ever since I was a child I have had an inquiring mind after knowledge, of almost all sorts ; but religion bore the sway. I seemed to have a regard for good men, and therefore took great care to watch persons, especially to see how they kept the Sabbath. Before my conversion I had the curiosity to hear all the different worships in New England, and inquired into their principles, and observed their behavior, both in and out of their worship. And I saw so little, or rather nothing, of the power of godliness in any of them, that I was then, even in my carnal estate, afraid that the true religion was not in

[1]Three of the brothers, Solomon, Elisha and John, were well known New Light, or Separate preachers. Solomon Paine, pastor of a Separate church in Canterbury, Connecticut, from 1748 to his death in 1755, was one of the chief leaders in the cause. He seems to have been especially esteemed as a counsellor, and was often sent for from a distance to advise in the perplexities and practical difficulties of the new movement. He also defended the Separatists vigorously and efficiently with his pen, in a work several times quoted in this history, entitled, A Short View of the Difference between the Church of Christ and the Established Churches in the Colony of Connecticut, in their Foundation and Practice, with their Ends. John Paine, pastor of a Separatist church in Rehoboth, was evidently a man of ability and influence. But foremost of the brothers, and in many respects, of all who were engaged in the new movement, the first declared Separatist, the first man ordained as a Separatist preacher, and the first sufferer in the cause, was Elisha Paine. Earnest and devoted in piety, bold and determined in measures, zealous and impassioned in address, he was the herald who summoned to the new standard those who had already revolted from, or were disaffected in, the ranks of the Standing Order. In what Mr. Backus says of him, there may seem to be too much prominence given to one whose name is now so little known. But Mr. Backus, himself an early and ardent Separatist, would naturally cherish a high regard for the man in connection with whom, and largely through whose means, the cause first took form and became established. Moreover, at this day, the Separatist movement is not appreciated as it deserves. We have too nearly forgotten our obligations to those men who dared to break away from the corrupt and worldly churches of the Standing Order, though they were armed with all the power of the State, of which they were a part, and to establish other churches in which vital godliness was the condition of membership. It was a transition movement, it is true, and of necessity only temporary, but its results were enduring. Many of the Baptist churches in New England sprung from it directly, and through them, indirectly, almost all the rest; and other evangelical churches are largely indebted to it for their vitality and efficiency.—ED.

this land. Yet worldly pleasure, and the form which was most acknowledged, would soon make me easy again. But when conviction came to lay hold of me, let who would be of the true religion, I saw mine was of no value.

In July, 1742, he received an internal call to preach the gospel, and in December following he offered himself for examination before some pious ministers ; and they gave him encouragement about entering into that work, but were for his doing it upon the Saybrook plan, which he never liked. The church he belonged to had been destitute of a pastor near two years, when they met on January 27, 1743, and declared by vote, " that the platform of church discipline agreed upon by the Synod at Cambridge, in 1648, is most agreeable to the former designed practice of this church, excepting their having ruling elders as distinct officers, and most agreeable to the Scriptures ;" though they did not withdraw their fellowship from the consociated churches. Soon after this Mr. Paine set out upon a journey ; but for preaching the gospel in Woodstock, which then belonged to the Massachusetts, he was seized on February 19, by virtue of a warrant from John Chandler, Esq., of that town, and was imprisoned at Worcester.[1]

But his bonds proved to be for the furtherance of the gos-

---

[1] " Feb. 19. I was seized at the house of Mr. John Morse. Had liberty to sing the 23d Psalm. From thence I was carried (by Mr. Right [Wright] the officer) to the house of Colonel Chandler, of said town, [Woodstock,] who granted the warrant; who supposed that I designed to give bond as the warrant required. But before he sat down he put the question to me whether that was my design. I replied, I had not determined to do it. .... Monday, the 21st. Went to Worcester. Lodged at Captain Howard's. Saw Colonel Chandler, of that town, who offered to take bond according to the warrant; but it not being clear to me to give such bond, I desired until morning to consider of the proposal. But soon after I laid my head on my pillow, I had such a sense of the contempt that was cast upon the truths of God's word by the warrant, that I could not give bond. .... Invited to Colonel Chandler's, and breakfasted there the 22d, and then was committed into the dirtiest prison I ever saw. I begged a broom and swept a place to walk in. I had a sweet contentment in and resignation to the will of God, and have had ever since first taken. Blessed be God for it. After about an hour I was permitted to come and sit by the fire. Many persons visited, persuaded hard to give bail according to the warrant; Colonel Ward and many others offered to be my bail, but conscience forbade a compliance." Elisha Paine's Journal.—ED.

pel, and he preached it to good purpose in prison.   And on March 10, four ministers met at Lebanon, and signed a testimony in his favor; wherein, after mentioning the cause why he was not approbated in the preceding December, they say:—

From the knowledge we then had of him, we were of the opinion that he was qualified, and that it was his duty to preach the gospel.   And we think it our duty to give our testimony for him, that he is, so far as we know or have ever heard, of a regular Christian life and conversation; and we esteem him sound in the faith, and of good understanding in the doctrines of the gospel of Christ.

> Eleazar Wheelock,
> Benjamin Pomeroy,
> Joseph Meacham,
> Samuel Mosely.

This, Mr. Mosely sent to him, in a letter, wherein he said:—

Dear Sir, stand fast in the faith; be strong.   They that be with you are more than they that be with our adversaries.   Never think it hard to suffer for Christ.   It is enough for the servant that he be as his Lord.

Yet the next year all these men were overpowered by the enemy, so as to turn and act against him, in the great cause of reformation.   On May 13, Worcester Court was constrained to give him a discharge, as having been imprisoned without law; and he went round and preached the gospel in the adjacent towns for a fortnight, and then returned home.   July 8, he set off again and travelled to Providence, Bristol, Boston, Cambridge, and as far northward as Dunstable and Lancaster, preaching the gospel with great power; and returned home December 3, having, according to a journal he kept, preached two hundred and forty-four sermons in that journey.   And hearing of the measures many were then pursuing, under a pretence of promoting peace and good order, he said:—

Let me speak freely of the peace that Connecticut was in.   For these forty years we have had the name of a contentious people in the law. This was so customary, that to sue a man for debt was become not much more than a compliment. And scarce a meeting-house has been set up for many years, without sundry petitions to the Assembly; with great heats [of] animosity, party against party, not in love, as is too well known to be denied.

And yet by their laws it was forty pounds fine for any people to set up a meeting-house without leave from Court. And, referring to what Daniel says of those who shall be corrupted by flatteries, he said of this time :—

I verily believe they know not what they are doing; for they seem to be zealous to maintain peace, but take the direct way to break it. Christ is a peaceable Prince, and Prince of peace; and if there was nothing in the way of his kingdom, it would be as peaceable here as it is in heaven. The Spirit is compared to water; water maketh no noise unless it is interrupted; so is the Spirit of Christ.

In June, 1744, he went and labored with success in his native country of Cape Cod, from whence sprang the Baptist church in Harwich.[1]

[1]The following letter will indicate the character and success of Mr. Paine's labors on Cape Cod.

"Chatham, July 3, 1744.

DEAR WIFE AND CHILDREN: I long to see you; and would write oftener but opportunity fails. I am purposing every day to come home, but dare not leave the Lord's harvest lest the wild beasts should devour and the wild boars should root up what the Lord seems to be doing here, with the greatest power that ever I saw here, or, I think, anywhere. The Lord is doing wonders in this sandy land; but as Christ triumphs, Satan rages. The Lord hath hitherto sustained me and delivered me from the rage of the adversary. O pray for me and the cause of dear Jesus. The pine woods in Harwich ring hallelujahs and hosannas, even from babes; I never heard the like before; from little ones from six years old and upwards, saying, "Holy, &c.," "Hallelujah, &c.," God is bringing of them in from the hedges. Our relations, the most of them, stand at a distance. Cousin Ebenezer Paine and his family seem exceeding opposite, except one daughter and her husband, I hope, are made to know Christ. Uncle Doane and his family seem to be created anew, except his wife. The world is full of lies, and falsehood is the covering wherewith the opposers cover themselves. The devil hath some very faithful servants in the country, that went from this place, that write the most awful letters that were ever writ; and as false as strange. But the Lord reigns, and the saints shout aloud for joy. The Christians, what few were alive, are much quickened and many added to their number since I came down. But the most wonderful shower began on the 28th of June,—a colony fast. I preached from Ez. 14. 3. and from Rev. 2. 21. After service we sang a hymn. I felt the Spirit of the Lord come upon me. I rose up and exhorted and persuaded them to come to Christ; and immediately there was a screeching and groaning all over the multitude, and hath ever since been very powerful. Some whole families, I hope, have received Christ, and others continually

Upon his return a division took place in Canterbury in the following manner. The parish had called a candidate there to preach, whom most of the church were not edified by. In August a committee of their Association met there, at the call of the parish, to give advice in the case. Mr. Paine was requested to give them his objections against said candidate, but he refused, because they were not called there by the church. Another member gave them a copy of their church vote against him ; which the ministers in their result said " was signed in behalf of the *aggrieved part* of the church ;" and advised the parish to go on and settle their candidate. For this, Paine, on September 12, wrote a smart reproof to one of those ministers, for wronging the truth, in calling that an aggrieved part, which was the church ; and for encouraging the world to usurp such a power over the church of Christ. Hereupon he was disciplined by the secular arm. Their charge, his plea, and their judgment thereon, were as follows. Their charge was :—

That Elisha Paine, of Canterbury, in the county of Windham, who is not a settled and ordained minister, did, on the 10th day of April, A. D. 1744, go into the third parish in Windham, in the county aforesaid, and in said parish, in the house of Mr. Benjamin Cleaveland, there the said Paine did publicly preach and exhort in matters of religion, both as to doctrine and practice, to a great number of people then present, that were notified many days before.

Windham, ss.   September 22, 1744.
At a Justice's Court.   Present, Nathaniel Huntington, Justice of Peace.

And now the prisoner at the bar being brought before this Court, for preaching the gospel of Jesus Christ, and exhorting a number of people, (as presentment) pleads, that this Court hath not jurisdiction of this case ; for [that] the facts complained of are warranted by the law of God and the king, and therefore not triable by any Court or law inferior thereto ; and this he is ready to verify judgment.   ELISHA PAINE.

crying out against their own hearts. I hope the Lord will carry on his work in his way, and by his own means. If it be his will to keep me here longer, let it not grieve your heart nor alienate your affection from me, for it doth not mine from you nor the children. The Lord keeps you all near my heart. And I hope you will not cease to pray for me, for I am in the midst of wolves and dragons; but God is above them all. So let us rest. Amen.
                                              ELISHA PAINE."

This Court having considered the plea of the prisoner, do judge it insufficient; and say, that this Court hath jurisdiction of this case; and the said Paine refused to make any other plea; whereupon it is considered by this Court, that the said Elisha Paine shall become bound to the Treasurer of the County of Windham, in the recognizance of one hundred pounds, lawful money, to his peaceable and good behavior, that he, the said Paine, will not again offend in the like kind, between this time and the setting of the County Court, to be holden at Windham, in and for the County of Windham, on the second Tuesday of December next, and then appear at said Court on said day, and take up his bond, unless the Court shall see cause to continue the same; and pay cost of this prosecution, and stand committed until bond is given. Cost allowed, two pounds, thirteen shillings, old tenor bills. The said Paine refused to give bond as above mentioned, or any ways to comply with the judgment, and was committed the day and year above written.

NATHANIEL HUNTINGTON, Justice of Peace.[1]

By giving security to the keeper, he got liberty to preach in the jail-yard, which he frequently did to very good purpose. The day after one of those seasons, he wrote to his beloved wife and said :—

Take no thought for the morrow; the Lord will take care of all his. Be not at all concerned about what the world can do to me; for they are all chained fast, and cannot touch me but by leave of the blessed Jesus, and if you are not afraid of his hurting of me, then be not afraid of the worms of the dust. I trust the Lord is about to do some great thing. It was a day of conviction yesterday, especially among the little ones. I never had so great a sense of the Lord's being angry with the wicked, as yesterday morning. O may he pity you and all Zion! I pray God to keep you and me, and all his, from a wicked and perverse generation, among whom we dwell, and cause us to shine as burning lights. O may he cheer up our souls, humble our natures, by giving the victory to the spirit over the flesh! I know not when I shall be delivered from this pleasant house; I seem to be willing to tarry here just as long as my Father and your Father shall see cause to use me here; though I seem to have a strong persuasion that I shall not tarry here long; but how the Lord will bring it about I know not. Let us leave it to him, and wait with patience until the appointed time shall come. And if I go from prison to Paradise, it will be as sweet as if I went from a throne. I desire to commit you, myself, and all ours and his, to the wise disposal of a holy God. So farewell in the Lord Jesus. Amen. ELISHA PAINE.

Windham Prison, October 8, 1744.

[1] Paine's View of the churches, pp. 20—22.

6

His persecutors soon found that their cause was weakened more by his preaching and conduct in prison, than out of it, and therefore released him about October 19.   In the mean time, as their church at Canterbury had no way to avoid hearing a man they were not edified by, but by leaving the meeting-house, they withdrew and held their worship at another house.   And two members of it, who had one of them been at Yale College three years, and the other newly entered, when at home in vacation time, met for worship with their church on Lord's days.   For this they were convented before the rulers of the college in November ; who, after hearing and considering of their pleas, said :—

Since the principal [end and] design of erecting this college, (as declared in charter) was to train up a succession of learned and orthodox ministers, by whose instruction and example people might be directed in the ways of religion and good order ; therefore, to educate persons whose principles and practices are directly subversive of the visible church of Christ, would be contrary to the original design of erecting this society ; and we perceive that it would be a contradiction of [to] the civil government, to support a college to educate students to trample upon their own laws, and break up the churches which they establish and protect, especially since the General Assembly, in May, 1742, thought proper to give the governors of the college some special advice and direction upon that account, which was to this effect, that all proper care should be taken to prevent the scholars' imbibing those or such like errors ; and that those who would not be orderly and submissive, should not be allowed the privileges of the college. Neither can we conceive that it makes any odds, whether such pernicious errors are imbibed and practiced, and the laws of God and the civil government are broken, in or out of the vacancy of the town of New Haven ; or with or without the concurrence of their parents, since the pernicious consequences thereof to the college and religion will be just the same.

THOMAS CLAP, Rector.
CHAUNCY WHITTLESEY,
JOHN WHITING,
THOMAS DARLING, Tutors.[1]

---

[1] Paine's View, pp. 15, 16.—B.

The two Cleavelands were expelled according to the following law of the college :—

"No scholar, upon the Lord's or another day, under pretence of religion, shall go to any public or private meeting, not established or allowed by public authority,

For these reasons Mr. Paine's two nephews, John and
Ebenezer Cleaveland, were expelled from college ; and three
years after, the eldest of them was settled at Ipswich, and
the other afterwards at Cape Ann. Paine was repeatedly
cited to appear before the ministers of that county, to an-

or approved by the President, under penalty of a fine, confession, admonition, or
otherwise, according to the state and demerit of the offence."

The college record of the transaction is as follows :—

"Yale College, November 19, 1744.
" Present, the Rector and Tutors.

" Upon information that John Cleaveland and Ebenezer Cleaveland, members of
this College, withdrew from the public worship of God in the meeting-house in Canterbury, carried on by Mr. Cogswell, a licensed and approved candidate for the
ministry, preaching there at the desire of the first parish or society in Canterbury,
with the special direction of the Association of the county of Windham, and that
they, the said Cleavelands, did go and attend upon a private Separate meeting, in a
private house, for divine worship, carried on principally by one Solomon Paine, a
lay exhorter, on several Sabbaths in September or October last; the said Cleavelands, being several times sent for, acknowledged the facts as above related, and
justified what they had done, and gave in the reasons given in writing by the said
Separatists for their separation aforesaid, the most material of which are these, viz. :
' That the first society in Canterbury keep up only the form of godliness, and deny
the life, power, and spirituality of it, and had given Mr. Cogswell a call in order for
settlement, whom they, the said Separatists, had declared to be destitute of those
essential qualifications that ought to be in a minister of Jesus Christ, and therefore
cannot join with the society in their choice, but look upon it to be their indispensable duty to choose one after God's own heart, one that will be able to comfort the
wounded with the same comfort wherewith he himself is comforted of God, and not
a blind guide; for then the blind will lead the blind into the ditch of God's eternal
wrath ; and many of the said society spoke evil of those things which the said Separatists received and held to be the effects of the Holy Ghost.' And the said Cleavelands say that this, being the act of the major part of the members, in full communion with the said society, is a sufficient warrant for them to join with them.
They also say that the said Solomon Paine has sufficient knowledge and ability to
expound the Scripture and to preach the gospel, and therefore has a right to do it.
And therefore, say they, that in withdrawing from the public worship and attending
upon the preaching of the said Solomon Paine, they have not acted contrary to any
divine or human law.

" Whereupon it is considered by the Rector and Tutors—1. That we (depending
in this matter upon the unanimous judgment of the Association in the county of
Windham,) do judge that the said Mr. Cogswell is sufficiently qualified to be a
preacher of the gospel, and therefore that the reflections cast upon him, as aforesaid,
are groundless. 2. That if there were any reasons why the said Separatists should
not choose to receive Mr. Cogswell as minister, or if it should be doubtful whether
it is convenient that Mr. Cogswell should be ordained, where so great a number are
against him, (which things properly belong to the hearing and judging of a council,)
yet we can't see that this could be any justification of their setting up a Separation

swer to complaints they received against him; but he knew
their way too well to be drawn into their trap.   Twelve of
them met November 13, and drew up a paper against him
and his brethren,[1] and published it in a newspaper.   December 11, a larger number met, and published a pamphlet, as

in the mean time. 3. That neither the major part of the members in full communion, nor any other persons in any parish or society, have any right or warrant to appoint any house or place for worship on the Sabbath, distinct and separate from, and
in opposition to the meeting-house, the public place of worship appointed by the
General Assembly and the parish; but, on the contrary, all such places and separate
meetings are prohibited by the ancient laws of this government.

" Whereupon, it is considered and adjudged by the Rector and Tutors, that the
said John and Ebenezer Cleaveland, in withdrawing and separating from the public
worship of God, and attending upon the preaching of lay exhorters, as aforesaid,
have acted contrary to the rules of the gospel, the laws of this Colony and of the
College; and that the said Cleavelands shall be publicly admonished for their faults
aforesaid; and if they shall continue to justify themselves, and refuse to make an
acknowledgment, they shall be expelled.
                                             " Thomas Clap, Rector.

"About a week after this, John Cleaveland gave in a paper, wherein he says, ' I
did not know that it was a transgression either of the laws of God or of the Colony,
or of this College, for me, as a member of and in covenant with a particular church,
as is generally owned to be a Church of Jesus Christ, to meet together with the major part of the said church for social worship; and therefore beg and entreat that my
ignorance may be suffered to apologise for me in that respect.'

" Upon which it was considered, that whatever might be in his former ignorance
and mistake, yet, after all means of light and conviction, he still persisted in justifying what he had done, and would acknowledge no error in it, though sometimes he
seemed to be brought to such a doubt and stand in his own mind as that it seemed
probable that he would have made some acknowledgment if he had not been prevented by ill advice.   And since the principal, &c.," as quoted above.   Paine's View,
pp. 12—15.--Ed.

[1]This paper commenced as follows :—
"At an Association of ministers of Windham County, convened November 13,
1744.   This Association having taken into serious consideration the sad and deplorable state of the churches in several parts of the country, by reason of the woful
degeneracy and corruption of the experiences of Christians, and the delusions which
prevail over many poor souls, to that degree as to bring them to neglect, and, in a
great measure, to set aside the ordinance of preaching the gospel, and forsake the
public instituted worship of God, and cast contempt upon it; and having humbly
sought to God for light and direction as to our duty in this matter, and, as carefully as we could at present, inquired into the causes of it; we are fully satisfied
that, among other things, some of the chief apparent causes of the sins and distractions above referred to, have been the late unwarrantable attempts of Mr. Elisha
Paine, Solomon Paine, Thomas Marsh, and others, who have, for some time past,
and in divers places in this county, gone about pretending publicly to preach the
gospel, to expound the doctrines of the Bible, and make public exhortations to the

a letter from them to their several societies, which at the
foot of page 52 is signed by Joseph Coite, Ebenezer Williams, Joseph Meacham, Samuel Dorrance, Solomon Williams, Jacob Eliot, Marston Cabot, Samuel Mosely, Ephraim
Avery, Ebenezer Devotion, Eleazer Wheelock, Abel Stiles,
Stephen White, John Bass, Richard Salter, William Throope.
A single passage therein will give a plain idea of the nature
of their controversy. Having quoted Deut. xiii. 1—3, as a
warning to the people against hearing Mr. Paine and his
brethren, they say :—

> The case here supposed is an attempt to draw the people to idolatry ;
> and this you will say is not your case ; these prophets and dreamers en-
> deavor to draw you to Christ, and not from him. But then they endea-
> vor to draw you from his institutions, to a way of worship which he
> has not instituted. Though the case is not so strong, yet the argument
> against your compliance is the same ; for whatsoever worship God has not
> instituted and directed in his word, is false worship, and therefore if there
> seem to be never so many appearances of God's power attending it, you
> may not go after, any more than after a false god.[1]

Now observe, Christ says concerning the field, which is
the world, Let both grow together until the harvest. While
he says to the church, Put away from among yourselves that
wicked person. In agreement herewith Mr. Paine applied
the first of these precepts to the State, and said, "The

> people ; and, as far as we can find, having no better warrant than a persuasion of an
> inward call and motion of the Holy Ghost ; acting upon that principle that every
> Christian who has, i. e., who is persuaded that he has, an inward call, is sufficiently
> authorized for such an undertaking."
> The paper proceeded to declare that this principle is " wrong and unwarrantable,"
> and that no man is fitted to preach or make public religious exhortations "who is
> not qualified with a good doctrinal knowledge of the Scriptures, sound in the faith,
> of a good and blameless character, holy, and moved to the work of the ministry by
> the Spirit of God, by the voice of the church, and laying on of the hands of the
> presbytery :" and that the forementioned practice must " end in Quakerism, open in-
> fidelity, and the destruction of all Christian religion, and make endless division in
> the Christian church till nothing but the name of it would be left in the world." It
> also mentions divers testimonies that Elisha Paine and the others before mentioned,
> besides lacking knowledge and gifts for the work of exhorting, "hold, or have
> vented some dangerous doctrines of fatal tendency to religion." The paper was
> signed by those whose names are given as subscribing to the pamphlet next men-
> tioned, except Joseph Coite, Ebenezer Williams, Marston Cabot, and John Bass.—ED.

[1] Association Letter, p. 43.

church is to cast her tares out when they appear, or the whole church is leavened."[1] But they contradicted him; and calling the field the visible church, asserted that Christ would not let the servants " go and root up the tares, even when they appeared."[2] Thus those who use secular force in religious affairs, violate the divine command both ways; they obstruct discipline in the church, and invade the rights of conscience and humanity in the State. This was remarkably verified in Canterbury; for November 27, their church met, and sixteen males against twenty-three joined with the parish in sending for their Consociation to ordain Mr. James Cogswell there; and the Consociation met for that purpose December 26, but not having the majority of the church for him, they could not get along according to their own laws. At length they called the parish together, and got them to declare, by vote, their willingness that the Assembly should set off those who did not choose him from supporting him; " and that they may have all legal privileges of a distinct religious society;" and so went on and ordained him. Which proceeding, an advocate for them in 1771 called judicious, cautious, and gentle.[3] Yet thereby the first church in Canterbury was stripped of all legal privileges of a distinct religious society; and because they desired no new incorporation from the Assembly, but only petitioned to be exempted from supporting a teacher they never chose, their petition was disregarded, their goods were torn away, or their persons imprisoned therefor, for fifteen years; and the ministers who ordained him discovered no more compassion towards them than the priest and Levite did to the man that fell among thieves. This is the plain truth without any exaggeration.

New England now received a second visit from Mr. Whitefield, who came over in a mast-ship, and landed at York, November 2. But how were ministers alarmed at the news!

---

[1]Association Letter, p. 10.   [2]Ibid, p. 21.   [3]Fish's Examiner Examined, p. 76.

His first coming caused a great shaking among the dry bones; what then could they look for in the present state of the churches? An opposing party in Plymouth, disliking the preaching of the pious Mr. Leonard, had formed a new church there, and Dr. Chauncy preached at the instalment of their minister, five days after Whitefield landed; when Chauncy said:—

I beseech my fathers and brethren in the ministry to mark this man who has caused divisions and offences, contrary to the doctrine which ye have learned, and avoid him. Turn your view, my brethren, into all corners of the land. Behold the confusion in towns; the contentions in churches! .... Perhaps it will be said, these mischievous things are only accidental effects, and not to be charged upon him. So far from it, that they are the unavoidable consequence of that spirit in which he appeared.[1]

This is undoubted truth; and the reader may judge of the nature of that spirit, by the foregoing and following facts. For the heads of Harvard College soon published a testimony against Whitefield, which was followed by another by an Association of ministers at Weymouth, January 15, 1745, and a third by an Association at Marlborough, the 22d. The like was done by many other collective bodies, and by individuals. And much pains were taken to persuade the world, that he was a dishonest man, especially because of his saying so much as he had done against unconverted ministers, while himself was a minister of the church of England. A number of answers were returned, by himself and others; some of which we have mentioned under the year 1740. On May 28, 1741, the President of Harvard College[2] delivered a sermon before the annual Convention of ministers at Boston; when, referring to Mr. Whitefield and Mr. Tennent, he said, "Those two pious and valuable men of God, who have been lately laboring more abundantly among us, have been greatly instrumental in the hand of God to revive this blessed work; and many, no doubt, have been savingly converted from the error of their ways, and many more have

[1] Sermon at Frink's Instalment, p. 38. [2] Rev. Edward Holyoke.—ED.

been in some measure roused from their lethargy." But
being now reminded of this,[1] his reply was, " Alas, how was
I deluded with show and appearance!" And had he and
the college now got free from delusion? In the eighth page
of their testimony against Whitefield they say, " The believer
may have satisfaction, that he hath the assistance of the
Spirit of God with him, in so continual and regular a manner, that he may be said to dwell in him, and yet he have
no feeling of it." But observe, to be *past feeling* is the depth
of Pagan darkness; Eph. iv. 19. And one of the worst
things that was now alleged against Mr. Whitefield, was his
saying their colleges were in 'darkness that might be felt.
Therefore it was ingeniously asked upon this occasion, why
they need to produce the evidence of their own condemnation?[2] The heads of Yale College wrote a private letter to
him, and he returned an answer, with several pamphlets
upon the subject; but they were not satisfied therewith, and
therefore published a declaration against him, dated February 25, 1745, wherein they say, " From these two principles
which you have laid down, viz., that the generality of ministers are unconverted, and that all unconverted ministers
are such baneful and pernicious men, it naturally and necessarily follows, that the people ought to discard them, or
separate from them. If these two principles are right and
true, we are satisfied your design is good, and we would
readily join with you." But being of a contrary mind, they
accused him of a design of rooting out the standing ministers of the country, in order to introduce foreigners in their
stead, and asserted that he told Mr. Edwards a story of that
nature,[3] This, Edwards publicly contradicted; neither is

---

[1] Whitefield's letter to that college, pp. 20, 21.

[2] Hobby's Defence of Whitefield, p. 23.

[3] Said declaration, pp. 6—10. The taking of Cape Breton this year was a very
remarkable event. Governor Shirley first proposed the attempt to the Assembly at
Boston. By a very small majority they voted to undertake it, and to request assistance therein from other Colonies, January 25; but the vote was no sooner passed
than a general union appeared in carrying it into effect. And such dispatch was

there the least evidence since, of Whitefield's having any
such intent.   In August, 1745, I heard him preach at Lebanon, Windham, Norwich, Mohegan and New London;
before which I had never seen him.   He then spoke against
separations; and his plan evidently was, to labor for the conversion and edification of souls, and to leave the building
and government of churches to others. In 1768, the Corporation of Harvard College, with the same President at their
head, gave him a letter of thanks for his benefactions thereto.

A year having rolled away, since Canterbury church was
robbed of her rights, only for refusing to give up their judgment about soul-guides, to men who ruled with force and
cruelty, without the least appearance of any design in them
of relinquishing their claims, a number of teachers and
brethren met at Mansfield, and having prepared a confession
of faith and covenant, and given a verbal account of their
experiences to mutual satisfaction, they signed covenant
together, October 9, 1745.   And they elected Mr. Thomas
Marsh for their pastor, who had, for many years, been a deacon in good esteem in the second church in Windham; and
his ordination was appointed to be on January 6, 1746.
But he was seized the day before, and imprisoned at Windham, for preaching the gospel without license from the
parish ministers.   On the day he was to have been ordained,
Mr. Elisha Paine preached a suitable sermon, to a great
concourse of people, at the close of which about fourteen
learned ministers came up, and tried to scatter that flock,
after their shepherd was smitten; but they got no advantage
against them.   In February they chose and ordained Mr.
John Hovey for their pastor, who ministered to them for

made, that an army consisting of four thousand and sixty men, under General Pepperell, rendezvoused at Canso, in April, where a small fleet met them, under the
command of Sir Peter Warren.   The army landed on Cape Breton April 30, to the
great surprise of the enemy; and the strong fortress of Louisburg was given up to
them on June 17, 1745.   Old Mr. Moody, who went their chaplain, publicly declared
a full belief that they should take it, before the army left Boston.   Others went
away saying, Pray for us, while we fight for you.   That event was a great means of
restoring peace to Europe, as well as America.

many years.[1] Mr. Thomas Denison was baptized in July, 1743, and was ordained pastor of a small church at Ashford the November after ; but they dissolving, he retracted what is called re-baptizing, and had a chief hand in forming this new church at Mansfield ; and he laid on hands and gave the charge, in this and several succeeding ordinations. They held the power of ordination to be in the church ; but as others have made a great noise about a successive power in ministers, it is to be observed, that Elder Denison was ordained by Elder Moulton, and he by Elder John Callender, who was ordained by Elder Elisha Callender, in whose ordination three of the most noted Congregational ministers in Boston assisted in 1718. And this line was never broken, by any act of censuring or deposing, as was the case with dissenters from episcopacy, and also from popery. With my beloved mother, I visited Mr. Marsh in the spring, and found him comfortable in mind ; but his body was closely locked up in prison ; while a physician, who was put into a room over his head, for giving a single woman a potion to destroy the fruit of her womb, which destroyed her own life, was allowed, with an officer to attend him, to visit the sick in various parts of the town. How much was this like Barabbas and Jesus! In June Mr. Marsh was released, and in July he was ordained a colleague with Hovey ; and many such churches were soon after formed and organized.[2]

[1]The first leader in these separations, and the first pastor they ordained, after much public service and conflict, fell asleep in the beginning of the late war. Mr. Paine was ordained at Bridge Hampton, on Long Island, in May, 1752, and preached to his beloved flock, until within fifteen days of his decease, August 26, 1775, aged 84. Mr. Hovey died, October 28 following.

[2]Solomon Paine was ordained at Canterbury, September 10, 1746; Thomas Stephens at Plainfield, September 11; Thomas Denison at Norwich-Farms, October 29; Jedidiah Hide at Norwich-Town, October 30; *Matthew Smith* at Stonington, December 10; John Fuller at Lyme, December 25; Joseph Snow at Providence, February 12, 1747; Samuel Wadsworth at Killingly, June 3; Paul Park at Preston, July 15; *Elihu Marsh* at Windham, October 7; Ebenezer Frothingham, at Wethersfield, October 28; Nathaniel Shepherd in Attleborough, January 20, 1748; *Isaac Backus* at Bridgewater, April 13; John Paine at Rehoboth, August 3; *William Car-*

The Consociation of Windham County had an account of many of these things laid before them, January 13, 1747 ; upon which they adjourned to February 11, and sent citations to the Elders Marsh, the Paines and Stevens, to return answers to accusations, then received against them. In the mean time the Consociation requested their own churches to keep a day of fasting and prayer, for divine direction. When they met again, they inserted a copy of the Mansfield articles and covenant in their result, with objections against many parts of it; one of which is in these words, viz., " Though most of us agree in the article of infant baptism, yet a difference in that particular doth not break the spiritual communion of saints ; therefore it is no just bar to our covenanting and partaking of the ordinances together, wherein we are agreed." This the ministers objected against, as it tended " to let in Anabaptists, and seems (say they) more agreeable to the inclinations of parties than the word of God." And having inserted many reports and reflections against said people, the same were published at Boston, under the title of " The result of a Council of the consociated churches in the county of Windham, relating to the principles and practices of the several bodies of people in said county, who have separated from the communion of the churches in this land, and set up an uninstituted worship among themselves ;" containing twenty-two pages in octavo. All their arguments proceed upon the supposition, without

penter at Norton, September 7; _John Blunt_ at Sturbridge, September 28; _Ebenezer Mack_ at Lyme, January 12, 1749; Joshua Nickerson at Harwich, February 23; Samuel Hide at Bridgewater, May 11; John Palmer at Windham, May 17; _Samuel Hovey_ at Mendon, May 31; Samuel Drown at Coventry, October 11; Stephen Babcock at Westerly, April 4, 1750; _Joseph Hastings_ at Suffield, April 17; Nathaniel Ewer at Barnstable, May 10; Joshua Morse at New London, May 17; Jonathan Hide at Brookline, January 17, 1751; Ezekiel Cole at Sutton, January 31; Ebenezer Wadsworth at Grafton, March 20; Nathaniel Draper at Cambridge, April 24; Peter Werden at Warwick, May 17, &c.

  Those in _Italics_ became Baptists afterwards; Drown, Babcock, Morse, Draper and Werden, were so before they were ordained. Draper was a graduate at Yale College, and the only person among them who had such a degree; and he deserted that cause two or three years after.

proof, that theirs were the instituted churches; and, therefore that to separate from them was a revolt from God, and a rebellion against his government in the church. And for teaching and exhorting the people without their leave, the before-named Elder Frothingham was imprisoned five months, John Paine eleven months, and John Palmer from September, 1747, to January, 1748; all at Hartford. Solomon Paine was imprisoned a fortnight for that cause at Windham; besides much more of like nature done to others. And only for being members and deacons in those Separate churches, three gentlemen, at different times, were expelled out of their Legislature; namely, Captain Obadiah Johnson of Canterbury, Captain Thomas Stevens of Plainfield, (father to their minister) and Captain Nathan Jewett of Lyme. But overstraining their power weakened it; and it now began to decline.

At the election at Hartford, May 12, 1748, Colonel Huntington was again chosen into their Council, out of which he had been excluded five years.[1] Solomon Paine came to this Assembly, with a memorial, signed by three hundred and thirty men; praying for a repeal of all their laws, which debarred any inhabitants in the Colony from the liberty granted by God and tolerated by the king, or that the execution thereof might be forbidden. After long waiting, he had liberty to read, and speak to, the memorial in the Assembly; and though it was then dismissed, yet some light was communicated thereby. In December, 1748, he was prosecuted at Windham Court, for marrying a couple of his own people. His brother came and pleaded his cause. The king's attorney, in pleading against Solomon, allowed that

[1] He was the fifth son of Deacon Christopher Huntington, the first English male that was born in Norwich, after it was planted in 1660. This son experienced an early conversion, succeeded his father in the deacon's office, and did much to promote a reformation in the town, in and after 1741. Henceforward, by annual and full elections, he was continued a Counsellor, and for a number of years the first man therein; was Chief Judge of their County Court for twenty years, and a Judge of Probate, until he died in peace, February 10, 1773, aged 76.

he was ordained the pastor of a church of Christ in Canterbury, in as solemn a manner as could be ; but then pleaded that he was not a civil officer, because not chosen by the majority of the parish, which was the thing which made their ministers civil officers ; and he said it was in that capacity that they were supported by tax, and had power to marry persons. And upon this plea the case was turned against him ; and also another case at the same time against one of his society, about a tax to a legal minister. Hereupon Mr. Elisha Paine wrote an account of these proceedings to other ministers, to show the absurdity of their way of professing to be ministers of Christ, and to be supported in the name of the king of England, while their constitution differed essentially from the churches under either of those heads. At the same time they met with a great shock from another quarter.

As long as Mr. Robbins continued a regular minister, and yet was excluded out of their Consociation,[1] it served to weaken their power. A complaint was therefore received against him May 31, 1743, signed by six of his hearers, before he had any notice of who the complainants were, or what they complained of; and a committee of ministers were appointed to go to him upon it. As soon as he discovered who the complainants were, he went and gave them satisfaction, and they wrote an account of it to said committee ; yet they came to him, and insisted upon his being reconciled to their Consociation. This he tried for, without success. However, perceiving what a storm was gathering, he drew three confessions, which he carried to another of their meetings ; wherein he went as far as he could towards giving them satisfaction, short of confessing that he broke the law of God in preaching to those Baptists, contrary to the desire of Presbyterians. But as he could not in conscience confess that, he returned home, without being reconciled to them. On May 29, 1745, a second complaint was

----

[1] See page 43.—Ed.

received against him, without his having previous notice of it, and another committee was sent, who prevailed with him to go and offer them a fourth confession; wherein he pleaded that his ignorance of its being a crime to preach to the Baptists as he did, might apologize for him, so that a reconciliation might be effected.[1] But they inform us, that instead of accepting what he had drawn, they drew a confession for him to this purpose, viz., " I, the subscriber, acknowledge, that I am sorry I preached *disorderly* at Wallingford, and prayed at the separation at New Haven, and promise not to do so again." And only because he refused to sign this, without explaining the word disorderly, they say, " The man appeared *stiff* and *self-willed* to the last degree."[2] Be that as it may, he then went home, and laid the confession they had rejected before his parish, who voted it to be sufficient, and desired him to continue in the ministry with them, and also that no councils nor committees might be sent there again, without their request. His church met November 4, 1745, and renounced the Saybrook Platform, and said, "We receive the Scriptures of the Old and New Testament, as the only perfect rule and platform of church government and discipline;" but did not renounce fellowship with the consociated churches.[3] This in their view was worse than all he had done before; and a third and much larger complaint was received against him, and the Consociation was called to try the same at Branford, September 30, 1746. Their moderator sent a copy of the complaint to him, and said upon it :—

You, the said Philemon Robbins, are hereby, *in the name of Christ*, cited and required to appear before the said Consociation, at the time and place aforesaid, then and there to answer the several articles of the said complaint, and thereof you may not fail.

By NATHANIEL CHAUNCY, Moderator.

Durham, August 28, 1746.

[1] Robbins's Narrative, pp. 13, 14.   [2] Their Answer. p. 10.
[3] Robbins's Narrative, p. 15.

Robbins drew answers to each article, and laid them before his people, who declared their satisfaction therewith; and his church appointed a committee to lay a copy of their votes. before the council, and earnestly to declare against their jurisdiction over them. This was accordingly done; yet they resolved that they had jurisdiction over Mr. Robbins, and went on to hear accusations against him in his absence, and to condemn him in ten articles of his public teaching, without naming any witnesses, or any time or place when or where either of them was delivered. And concerning his conduct they say:—

He hath led off a party with him, to rise up against and separate from the ecclesiastical constitution of this colony, under which this church was peaceably established; reproachfully insinuating, in a church meeting, that under the Saybrook Platform it is King Association, in opposition to Jesus Christ, the only King of the church. .... In which articles, upon mature deliberation, we judge said Mr. Robbins is criminally guilty of the breach of the third, fifth and ninth commands, and many gospel rules, for which he ought to give Christian satisfaction, by making a confession to the acceptance of this Consociation.[1]

This he was so far from doing, that he published a Narrative of the whole affair at Boston. They waited a year, and then met again September 29, 1747, and after telling of their lenity, and his obstinacy, they say:—

The Consociation do, *in the name of the Lord Jesus Christ*, according to the word of God, and the powers invested in this Consociation, by the ecclesiastical constitution of this government, depose the said Mr. Philemon Robbins from his ministerial office, and ministerial and pastoral relation to the first church in said Branford, and debar and suspend him from communion in any of the churches. And this Consociation do hereby forbid the said Mr. Philemon Robbins to preach the gospel, or administer the holy sacraments, and suspend him from communion, in any and all the churches of our Lord Jesus Christ, until he shall have, in a public and Christian manner, reflected on himself for the crimes and faults above mentioned, to the satisfaction of the Consociation of this county of New Haven.

The above voted:

Test,   SAMUEL WHITTLESEY, Jr.,
                                     ROBERT TREAT, Scribes.[2]

[1] Narrative, pp. 18—29.   [2] Their Answer, p. 117.

This is in an Answer to Robbins, said in the title page to be
" printed for the Consociation and Association of New Haven County, 1748 ;" without any author's or printer's name.
It represents, that when the Presbyterian and Congregational
churches formed the Saybrook Platform, it became their own
voluntary contract ; and that, being established by their Legislature, it became the ecclesiastical constitution of the whole
colony, as much as their charter, which united the colonies
of Hartford and New Haven in one, was their civil constitution; and that Mr. Robbins and his church had no more
right to renounce their jurisdiction, than his parish had to
renounce the authority of the civil government of Connecticut ;[1] that a toleration was never intended to destroy an establishment; and that as the Baptists he preached to had
not fully complied with the Act of Toleration, they were not
an orderly society, " but only a number of men that in a *disorderly* manner refused submission to their pastor." And
they accuse Robbins of intruding himself into the *bishoprics*
of Mr. Whittlesey, at Wallingford, and of Mr. Noyes, at
New Haven.[2] To prove which they quote the same Scriptures that Dr. Chauncy, their champion, had cited before ;
one of which, they say, means " in plain English, his doing
the office of a bishop in another's diocese ; and this the
apostle ranks with some of the greatest crimes ; I Pet. iv.
15."[3] But who formed those dioceses! Because Robbins
laid his fourth confession, which they rejected, before his
parish, who voted that it was sufficient, the Consociation observed, that a freehold rated at fifty shillings, or forty pounds,
in the common lists, made every inhabitant a voter in such
meetings, and from thence they exclaimed against him for
that procedure, saying, " What if half the society were
scandalous persons !"[4] Ay, what indeed ! how dreadful must
the consequence be ! just such as Connecticut had felt for
forty years ! For their laws made such votes equal to the

[1]Their Answer, pp. 86, 94, 112.   [2]Ibid, pp. 6, 8, 106.
[3]Ibid, p. 43.   [4]Ibid, p. 101.

votes of the best saints among them, in the choice of their Legislature.   And an Assembly thus chosen broke over their own law, and elected an ordained minister for their Governor ;[1] by whose influence the Saybrook scheme was formed and established, without allowing the churches liberty to say whether their ministers should meet to form it or not.   And now, because Mr. Robbins continued to preach the gospel to his people, a complaint was carried to their Legislature against him, with a prayer that he might be turned out of his pulpit, so that a regular man might be introduced in his stead.   This was so far from being granted, that a council was appointed out of other counties, who prevailed with said Consociation to restore Mr. Robbins to a seat with them, which he held until his death in 1781 ; but his church sent no messengers with him.   In October, 1749, their Assembly revived their act concerning the Saybrook establishment in 1706 and their acts in 1729, to exempt Quakers and Baptists from it ; and ordered a new edition of their laws, which was printed in 1750 ; out of which were excluded all their persecuting acts since the late revival of religion, without a formal repeal of any of them.   Governor Wolcot published a pamphlet against the Saybrook scheme.   Governor Fitch published another to explain away its power ; and it has been upon the decline ever since.

[1]See Vol. I. p. 469.—ED.

7

CHAPTER XVII.

Reformation has ever been attended with great difficulties. Declension is natural to fallen men, but a return to the right way is not so. When Israel came out of Egypt, a mixed multitude went up. And when David withdrew from Saul's tyranny, many resorted to him, not only of his kindred, but also "every one that was in distress, and every one that was in debt, and every one that was discontented.;" yet when it was said of his cause in general, "There be many servants nowadays that break away, every man from his master," the Scripture calls it *railing*, and gives the person who uttered it the character of a fool or madman. But how full is our world of such folly and madness! David became the captain of those who resorted to him; but the people, who now came out from the above described tyranny over the churches, had no such commander. Even the father who led them out had too much knowledge, and cautious deliberation, to be long followed as their chief guide; and he retired to a distant island, and settled there. Such evils had been practiced under the name of learning, orthodoxy and regularity, that many were prejudiced against the truth of what others falsely called by those names. Christian liberty had been so much invaded, that many ran into licentiousness to avoid tyranny. The right which the gospel gives to all saints, freely to improve their several gifts, for mutual edification, had been so much denied, that frequent instances were now seen, of persons putting themselves forward in exercises which they had not a gift for; being so earnest to maintain the liberty of speaking, as not duly to regard others' right of judging. And as some precious ministers had evidently lost much of their former life and freedom, by their attempts to correct errors, disorders and imprudences, a number of pious souls were afraid of appearing against almost any thing that wore the garb of power and life in religion. The example of the Erskines in Scotland, who came out of their national church for reformation, and yet rejected Mr. White- field, because he would not come into all their measures, was held up as a warning here, against stopping in what any had already attained to. And just in this juncture a man came from Windham to Norwich, in the summer of 1746, with a proclamation of liberty, and an opening of the latter day glory; exclaiming against the legal bondage of praying every night and morning in families, whether persons felt a spirit of prayer or not; declaring that if they had not a spirit of prayer, God did not then call them to pray; and so of other duties. In this way sundry persons, chiefly at Windham, proceeded, until they asserted that they had passed the first resurrection, and were perfect and immortal; and one of them declared that he was Christ. But this spirit soon carried them into knavery in temporal dealings, intemperance, and what not? About the beginning of 1748, some people in Cumberland advanced the opinion, that if a saint found that he or she had not been married to the per- son that was made for them, they were not held by legal bonds from a right now to take their true mate, if they saw who it was. Hereupon an only child of a rich father, not living comfortably with her husband, ventured to reject him, and to lodge with another man. Some brethren of Attle- borough hearing of it, went to labor with her father, and others, to turn them from this delusion; but he said he did not believe there was any harm in it, for they lay with the Bible between them. But to his sorrow and shame his daughter proved to be with child by her new companion, and her husband obtained a legal divorce from her. About the same time, a member of the first church in Canterbury declared that it was revealed to him, that a certain single woman would become his wife, though he then had a wife and children. For such conversation the church called him to an account; and, after seven months' labor, they excommunicated him on September 27, 1749. In the winter following he purchased some mercury at Norwich, and it was judged that the woman he had a fancy for poisoned two children, they giving out that a new and strange distemper was come among them, and then he poisoned his wife, so that all the three died. This was not doubted to be the fact, though she was acquitted upon trial in Court, and he married her, and afterwards went into the war, and died in Canada. Some of her relations were called to an account, and were cast out of the church in Canterbury, for perjury, when acting as witnesses in Court upon that case.

Now though no actors in the first two of these scenes of iniquity were ever members of any of those Separate churches, and said church had so clearly acquitted themselves of the third, yet ministers, even from their pulpits, through the whole country, cast these scandals upon the Separate cause in general, to prove the dreadful danger and effects of separating from them; and the populace were very ready to follow their guides, in this way of slander and railing. Such glaring injustice to their character, added to much violence upon their persons and estates, served greatly to confirm them in their way, and to guard their minds against receiving any instruction or correction from men who treated them so abusively. A first principle of their separation was, that the leadings of the divine Spirit are ever to be followed, and not fleshly wisdom, nor man's inventions; but how little was the meaning and right application of this principle understood? When it was asserted, that none but the regenerate ought to be admitted to full communion, ministers would answer, You cannot know who they are. And when it was mentioned, that our Lord says, Ye shall know them by their fruits; the question was shifted, whether they held to a satisfactory or an infallible knowledge? which dispute was often carried to extremes on both sides. And while many would confine the word *fruits* to dry morality, others ran to the opposite extreme, and formed their judgments of persons by their inward feelings towards them, rather than upon an intelligent view of what came from them by words and actions. The evils also which many had suffered from an overbearing majority, turned some to plead against receiving any members till every individual had fellowship with them, and the like in other church acts. At length they found that hereby the least member might tyrannize over the whole church. Again, though the undue power of councils had been much complained of, yet the Separates run into that evil in a new way. When councils were called, they were received into fellowship with the church that wanted advice; and when they had heard the case, and given their advice, in many instances the council acted with the church in censuring delinquents; though sometimes there were more of the council than of the acting members of the church.[1] After some years this practice was dropped. Other mistakes will appear in the course of this history.

[1] "Wednesday, May 8, [1751.] We met together, and there came brother S. Paine, T. Stevens, S. Wadsworth, Drown, Shepherd, Carpenter and some others; and, after prayer, brother John Paine said that our work he viewed to be this: that because they were so broken that they were not capable of acting as a church in dealing with some that had sinned, therefore we should embody together there as a church to hear and try those cases."

"Wednesday, January 15, [1752.] I went, being sent for, to Bridgewater Town, to a church meeting, and brother Carpenter was there; and we were taken into their fellowship to act with them upon the case of some that have transgressed in this church." Mr. Backus's Manuscript Diary.—ED.

Having good men against them in the cause of reformation was matter of peculiar trial.   It was as much so with
regard to Mr. Edwards, as any one man.   His success was
very great, and by acting upon Mr. Stoddard's doctrine, the
church in Northampton had become very numerous; into
which he essayed to bring gospel discipline, in 1744.   But
when some of their chief families perceived that it would
expose their own conduct, they were inflamed against Mr.
Edwards.   And though it could not be honorable to reject
such an eminent minister on that account; yet finding that
he had turned from good old Mr. Stoddard's doctrine, that
change was eagerly taken hold of, as a cover for their resentment.   And all his prudent endeavors could never bring
that church, as a body, to give him a fair hearing of his
reasons for altering his sentiments upon that point; they
were therefore published at Boston this year.[1]   Some of his
clearest proofs against admitting unsanctified persons to the
ordinance of the Supper, are Rom. ii. 29, vi. 1—4.   Phil.
iii. 3.   Col. ii. 11, 12.   From whence he says, " that baptism, by which the primitive converts were admitted into
the church, was used as an exhibition and token of their
being visibly regenerated, dead to sin, and alive to God. . . . .
The saintship, godliness and holiness, of which, according to
Scripture, professing Christians and visible saints do make
a profession and have a visibility, is not any religion and
virtue that is the result of common grace, or moral sincerity
(as it is called) but saving grace."[2]   Which point was the
capital article that the Separate churches were built upon;
but for fear it should be improved in their favor, he reminded
the reader of what he had said against them, in his Treatise
on the Affections, and in Brainard's Life; and then said, " I
am still of the same mind concerning their lay-ordinations,
their lay-preachings, and public exhortings, and administer-

[1]Qualifications for Full Communion.   Edwards's Works, Vol. I.—ED.
[2]On a Right to Sacraments, pp, 20—23. [Qualifications, &c., Works, Vol. I. pp.
103, 105.]

ing sacraments; their assuming, self-confident, contentious, uncharitable, separating spirit."[1] And yet he lived remote from almost all the numerous communities whom he thus censured, and knew but very little of the real state of their controversy.   The excellent rules which he had published seven years before, were then out of his mind; namely, to judge of a work by the real nature of it, and not by the circumstances and means of its introduction; to make the Scriptures the whole rule to judge by; and well to distinguish between the good and the bad among the subjects of the work.[2]   A due regard to these rules of his own would have prevented the above reflections, as well as many things in the two other books named.   A Separate minister, in the east part of Connecticut, wrote to Mr. Edwards upon this subject, and in particular desired him to answer two questions.   1. As he had described an excellent new house, how we could get into it without going out of the old one, which was in a ruined condition?   2. What he meant by the word *Lay*, which he so often used; whether the same as the Latin church did?   He returned an answer, wherein he allowed the old house to be in a ruinous condition; but thought we were not yet called to leave it.   And to explain what he meant by laymen, he had recourse to the old opinion about a successive power in ministers; but he soon after felt such effects of that power, as he hardly could have believed before.

For his people were so uneasy, that he agreed to call a mutual council of ten churches, to settle the controversy betwixt them.   But in the large county of Hampshire, which then included Berkshire also, he could find but three ministers of his judgment, upon the point in dispute; and the church was strenuous against allowing him liberty to go out of that county for the other two whom he was to choose. At length they yielded so far; but when the council met,

[1]Preface, p. 5. [Works, Vol. I, p. 87.]
[2]Thoughts on the work, 1742, pp. 1—40. [Works, Vol. III, pp. 267—310.]

one of the churches had refused to send to it ; so that though their minister was received to act in the council, yet he had no delegate with him ; therefore Mr. Edwards was *separated* from his dear flock, by the major vote of only one delegate in that council. And the only charge that they had against him they stated in these words, viz. :—" The pastor insisting upon it as necessary to the admission of members to full communion, that they should make a profession of *sanctifying grace ;* whereas the brethren are of the opinion, that the Lord's Supper is a converting ordinance, and consequently that persons, if they have a competency of knowledge, and are of a blameless life, may be admitted to the Lord's table, although they make *no such profession.*"[1] And Dr. Solomon Williams, who wrote against him, says, "Nothing should be expressed in the words of the profession, but what some unsanctified men may say and speak true."[2] And he was a chief actor in all that the ministers of Windham county had done against the Separates. And Mr. Edwards, who had been moved to censure them so hardly, yet was now *separated* from the people he dearly loved, upon the same point ; and he removed and settled at Stockbridge, where he became more extensively serviceable to mankind ; especially by his incomparable treatise upon the Freedom of the Will, and his answer to Taylor on Original Sin ; both of which have been reprinted in London. At last he was chosen President of New Jersey College ; but soon died there of the small-pox, March 22, 1758, aged fifty-six.

The fundamental principle above described, naturally leads to the exclusion of infant sprinkling ; but the generality of those who came out in separation had no such idea. The Mansfield articles held up internal union as the rule of church communion, although persons were of different sentiments about baptism ; but there were very few Baptists in

---

[1] Result of the council at Northampton, June 22, 1750, pp. 3, 4. [Works, Vol. I, p. 82.] Also, Edwards's Life.
[2] Answer to Edwards, p. 47.

any of their churches before 1749.   In June, that year, Elder Moulton baptized thirteen members of the Separate
church in Sturbridge, one of whom was Deacon Daniel Fisk;
and in a little time after, all their officers, and the main body
of the church, were baptized, even above threescore persons.[1]
The exempting law for Baptists had again expired in 1747,
when it was revived and continued for ten years.   In order
that the benefit of it might be extended to that society, two
principal members of the second Baptist church in Boston
wrote a certificate in their favor to Sturbridge assessors, January 23, 1750.   In May following, two principal members
of the Baptist church in Sturbridge gave in a list of their
society according to law ; yet they were all again taxed to
Mr. Caleb Rice, a minister in that town.   And, only for this
and the following year, five men were imprisoned at Worcester, three oxen and eight cows were taken away, and a great
deal of other property, for such taxes.   Aaron Allen was
the collector who did it for 1750, and Jonathan Mason for
1751.   The first took a good cow from David Morse, a ruling
elder in said Baptist church, for a tax of one pound, one
shilling and four-pence ; and the other took a pair of oxen
from him, valued at eleven pounds, for a tax of less than
five dollars.   Such havoc did they make of their neighbors'
goods, under religious pretences![2]   Sundry prosecutions

---

[1]The Separate church in Sturbridge was formed in 1748. The present Baptist
church was formed from it in 1749. In Rev. S. Hall's Collection of Papers is an
account of early ecclesiastical affairs in Sturbridge, written by Henry Fisk, an elder in the Baptist church, entitled, "The Testimony of a People inhabiting the
Wilderness." Under date of May 16, 1749, he writes :—"About this time the trial
concerning baptism came up. Now the voice is, ' *Take heed how ye build ;* for every
man's work shall be tried, of what sort it is; for the day shall try it.' The day is
come that shall burn as an oven. Now the daughter of Zion is called to arise and
thresh. The Lord made her horn iron and her hoof brass. Infant sprinkling,
which we called baptism, went away like the chaff of the summer threshing-floor."—
ED.

[2]From Henry Fisk's "Testimony" we extract the following record of oppressions
of Baptists in Sturbridge :—" They stripped the shelves of pewter, of such as had
it; and of others that had not they took away skillets, kettles, pots and warming-
pans. Others they deprived of the means they got their bread with, viz., workmen's
tools, and spinning-wheels. They drove away geese and swine from the doors of

were commenced against those collectors; and when one of the cases came to the Superior Court, both parties agreed to refer it to the judges; and they gave judgment in favor of the Baptists. This gave a shock to their oppressors; but a scheme was soon contrived to nonsuit the other actions commenced; and that was by pleading, that the suit should have been against the assessors, and not the collectors. By this trick Mr. Morse was injured to the value of above twenty pounds; and the whole society estimated their damages at more than a hundred pounds. And in a warrant for their town meeting of March 2, 1752, an article was inserted, to see if the town would indemnify their collector for his expenses, in the action which was turned against him. Moses Marcy, Esq., was Moderator, and as this article was objected to, it was proposed to raise the money by subscription, and they inquired how much it was. Upon which the Moderator drew out and read a paper, containing an account of " so much for going to a lawyer, and so many dollars given to Colonel Brattle at one time, and so many to another man, &c.," and he said the whole, with the execution, amounted to above twenty pounds. This moved the people so, that it did not seem likely that they would vote it by it-

some others; from some that had cows; from some that had but one they took that away. They took a yoke of oxen from one. Some they thrust into prison, where they had a long and tedious imprisonment. One brother was called from us and ordained a pastor of a Baptist church, and came for his family; at which time they seized him and drew him away, and thrust him into prison, where he was kept in the cold winter till somebody paid the money and let him out. A. Bloice had a spinning-wheel taken away in 1750, and was imprisoned in 1751. D. Fisk had five pewter plates taken from him in 1750, aud a cow in 1751. John Cory imprisoned, 1750. J. Barstow imprisoned, 1750. J. Pike, a cow taken, 1750. A cradle in 1750, and a steer in 1751, were taken from J. Perry. Trammel, andirons, shovel and tongs were taken from J. Blunt in 1750, and he was imprisoned the next year. John Streeter had goods taken in 1750 and 1751; Benjamin Robbins, household goods and carpenters' tools. Household goods and a cow were taken from H. Fisk in 1750 and 1751. Josiah Perry was imprisoned in 1750, and a cow taken from him in 1751. Nathaniel Smith was imprisoned in 1750. David Morse was imprisoned and a cow taken away in 1750, and a yoke of oxen in 1751. Goods were taken from Phinehas Collier in 1750 and 1751. John Newel, goods taken 1750 and 1751. John Draper imprisoned, 1751."—ED.

self; therefore, contrary to law, (which was insisted upon by the Baptists present) that article was blended with another, about school money, and the vote was carried, whereby the Baptists were again taxed to pay the expenses of an illegal law-suit against themselves.[1]   And this was not enough; but said Moderator, who was a member of the Legislature, moved them so with these things, that when they met, November 22, 1752, they broke in upon their own law, and enacted, that the minister, with two principal members of the Baptist church, should sign their certificates for the future; and also that no minister or church should have any power to give lawful certificates, until they should have obtained " from three other churches, commonly called Anabaptists, in this or the neighboring provinces, a certificate from each respectively, that they esteem such church to be of their denomination, and that they conscientiously believe them to be Anabaptists." All such certificates were to be lodged with the town clerk where the Baptists lived, before their several assessments were made. This act was to continue in force five years.   And said Moderator presented a petition to the Assembly in June following, that all the unimproved lands in Sturbridge might be taxed to his minister; but did not obtain it,   It is to be observed, that those who lately became Baptists were not in fellowship with most of the old Baptist churches; therefore this act was passed to prevent their being exempted from taxes to State worship, It also required them to certify a conscientious belief of a point which they never did believe, viz., that they were Anabaptists, (*rebaptizers*,) a name of reproach cast upon them by their persecutors.

Among the many instances that discovered how tenacious our oppressors were of their taxing power to support worship, take the following.   Esther White, of Raynham, had

---

[1]These facts about said meeting were sworn to by three men at Worcester, August 31, 1753, one of whom was Deacon Daniel Fisk, who died a member of our Legislature in 1778.

a small interest left her, for which she was taxed *eight-pence* to the parish minister, from whom she had withdrawn four years; and she seriously declared that it was against her conscience to pay it. Therefore, for no more than that sum, she was seized on February 28, 1752, and was imprisoned at Taunton until March, 1753, when said minister's own people were constrained to go and release her, without her paying any acknowledgment to that taxing power.[1] She soon after became a Baptist, and continued to give abiding evidence of true piety, until she died in peace in 1774. The case of Framingham, twenty-five miles westward of Boston, affords a further demonstration of the iniquity of supporting ministers by tax and compulsion. The Honorable Edward Goddard, Esq., formerly one of the Council in this Province, with other fathers of that town, could not concur with the majority in the settlement of a minister; and by the advice of other ministers they became an organized church by themselves in 1747, and wanted nothing but the sanction of the civil power, to make them as regular and orthodox a society in law as any others were. But as they were zealous friends to the late revival of religion, such an incorporation was denied them. And they had been all taxed to a minister they never chose, for six years before the publication upon the subject, which is quoted in Vol. I, Appendix B, pages 533, 537, 538. Three years after, their

[1] Wednesday, March 11, [1752.] Went to Taunton to visit sister Esther White and David White, that were put into prison from Raynham, on the 28th of February, for refusing to pay the minister's rate, and I found them something comfortable; especially sister Esther appeared to be in a sweet frame. She told me that the first night she was in there she lay upon the naked floor, and she said that she never imagined that the floor was so easy to lie upon before; she rested much more comfortably than she'd done many nights this winter on her bed: and she said that she was easy to stay there as long as God saw best she should." "Wednesday, May 20. Went to Taunton. Visited sister White in prison; found her composed and comfortable." "Thursday, June 19. Went to Taunton, and I had a season with sister White in prison, and the Lord granted divine refreshments both in conversation and prayer together." "Wednesday, October 14. I went with my wife to Taunton to visit the prisoners. Sister White is here in prison for the minister's rate, and she is wonderfully upheld by divine power in her sufferings. I preached a short sermon in the prison." Backus's Manuscript Diary.—ED.

minister left them, and a Baptist society is now formed among them.[1] And Connecticut still kept pace with the Massachusetts in oppression, of which the place of the author's nativity now exhibited a striking example. A widow who had withdrawn from their worship seven years, and steadily attended and supported worship in another church, gives so clear an account of it, that her letter is here presented to the reader, without adding or diminishing a word:—

Norwich, November 4, 1752.[2]

MY DEAR SON : I have heard something of the trials amongst you of late, and I was grieved, till I had strength to give up the case to God, and leave my burthen there. And now I would tell you something of our trials. Your brother Samuel lay in prison twenty days.[3] October 15, the collectors came to our house, and took me away to prison about nine o'clock, in a dark rainy night.[4] Brothers Hill[5] and Sabin were brought

---

[1] In Vol. III, of the old edition, written twelve years later than the above, Backus says, "A Baptist meeting has been upheld for many years in Framingham, where no church is yet formed." In the History of Framingham, under the head of "The Baptist Church," are the words, " The first recorded notice of this society is contained in the town records, March, 1763; when an article was presented in the town warrant to see if the town will abate the ministerial rates to a number of persons of this town who pretend to be of the persuasion of Anabaptists, and have sent in their names to the Select-men. . . . . In 1811, the society took the name of the Baptist Church of Weston and Framingham." At what date the church was actually constituted, we are not informed. In 1826, it was dissolved, and from it, in a new location, the present Baptist church in Framingham was formed.—ED.

[2] By act of parliament eleven days were taken out between the 2d and 14th of September this year; but as it was not done in our almanac, this date was in Old Style.

[3] "July 9, [1752.] I received a letter from my brother Samuel at Norwich, that informed me that he was in prison for rates, but yet appeared comfortable in soul." Backus's Manuscript Diary.—ED.

[4] "She was sick, and, thickly wrapped in clothes to produce perspiration, sat near the fire by her stand, reading the family Bible. The officer thought that, under the circumstances, she would yield and pay the rates. But Mrs. Backus was not the woman to abandon her religious principles." Denison's Historical Notes, p. 28. —ED.

[5] The following letter, published first in Denison's Historical Notes, p. 29, and afterwards in the Life and Times of Backus, p. 53, is of too much interest to be omitted here.

"Norwich Goal, November the 1st day, 1752.

"MR. LORD; SIR : I take this opportunity to present you with these few lines, which I should have thought you would have prevented by visiting us. Pray, Sir, consider whether or no you do not neglect to minister to Christ, for, "Inasmuch as

there the next night. We lay in prison thirteen days, and then set at liberty, by what means I know not. Whilst I was there a great many people came to see me ; and some said one thing and some another. O the
innumerable snares and temptations that beset me, more than I ever thought
on before ! But, O the condescension of heaven ! though I was bound
when I was cast into this furnace, yet was I loosed, and found Jesus in tho
midst of the furnace with me. O then I could give up my name, estate,
family, life and breath, freely to God. Now the prison looked like a palace
to me. I could bless God for all the laughs and scoffs made at me. O
the love that flowed out to all mankind ! Then I could forgive as I would
desire to be forgiven, and love my neighbor as myself. Deacon Griswold
was put into prison the 8th of October, and yesterday old brother Grover,
and [they] are in pursuit of others ; all which calls for humiliation. This
church hath appointed the 13th of November to be spent in prayer and
fasting on that account. I do remember my love to you and your wife,
and the dear children of God with you, begging your prayers for us in such
a day of trial. We are all in tolerable health, expecting to see you.
These from your loving mother,

ELIZABETH BACKUS.

Some time after, her brother, Mr. Isaac Tracy, was imprisoned for the same cause, while he was a member of their
Legislature ; and they furiously went on, in imprisoning of
persons[1] and spoiling of goods, to support State worship,

ye did it not to them, &c. And further, if you come not to see us, there are other
prisoners here, and, as you sustain the character of a minister, see to it you neglect
them not; and I should be glad of opportunity to see you. Ye lay heavy burdens,
and refuse to touch them with one of your fingers. You say it is the authority.
Simeon and Levi are brethren; instruments of cruelty are in their habitations.
Genesis xlix. 5—7. Pray, Sir, read the third chapter of Micah's prophecy, and
may the Lord make the application. Consider also that our Lord Jesus hath told
us that his kingdom is not of this world; also that he that taketh the sword shall
perish by the sword. I could wish you a deliverance from mystical Babylon and
from her merchandize. My soul looks to and longs to see her receive the cup of
the Lord's vengeance and that all his plagues may come upon her in one day, and
that God's children may come out of her, and that the kingdom may be given to the
saints of the Most High. These lines, with our cause, I leave with God, who will,
I trust, defend it; and so subscribe myself a prisoner of hope.

CHARLES HILL."

[1] " Wednesday, January 17. Here I would a little review what I have seen at
Norwich. Last year, the enemies have done more at haling the saints to prison,
than they have done ever before since our separation. But it is remarkably evident that, as it was with Israel, so it has been here; the more they oppressed them,
the more they grew. This congregation, I think, is near as large again as it was
the last time that I was here before. The Lord has indeed wrought wonders among
them." Backus's Manuscript Accounts of Journeys.—ED.

for eight years, till the spiritual weapons of truth and love vanquished those carnal weapons; and they have not been so used in Norwich for these many years past. As great a victory was also gained in Canterbury. The fall after Mr. Elisha Paine was settled on Long Island, he came over to Canterbury for some necessaries for his family, when Samuel Adams, a collector, seized and imprisoned him at Windham, on November 21, 1752; where he wrote thus :—

I cannot but marvel to see how soon the children will forget the sword that drove their fathers into this land, and take hold of it as a jewel, and kill their grandchildren therewith. O that men could see how far this is from Christ's rule ; that all things that we would have others do unto us, that we should do even so unto them ! I believe the same people that put this authority into the hands of Mr. Cogswell, their minister, to put me into prison for not paying him for preaching, would think it very hard for the church I belong to, and am pastor of, if they should get the upper hand, and tax and imprison him, for not paying what he should be so un-justly taxed at ; and yet I can see no other difference, only because the power is in his hands ; for I suppose he has heard me as often as I ever have him. Yet he hath taken by force from me two cows and one steer, and now my body held in prison, only because the power is in his hands.

And on December 11, he wrote to Canterbury assessors, and said :—

To you, gentlemen, practitioners of the law, from your prisoner in Wind-ham gaol, because his conscience will not let him pay a minister that is set up by the law of Connecticut, contrary to his conscience and consent. The Roman Emperor was called Pontifex Maximus, because he presided over civil and ecclesiastical affairs ; which is the first beast who persecuted the Christians that separated from their established religion, which they called the holy religion of their forefathers ; and by their law fined, whipped, imprisoned, and killed, such as refused obedience thereto. We all own that the pope or papal throne is the second beast, because he is head of the ecclesiastical, and meddles with civil affairs ; and for which he is also styled Pontifex Maximus, or High Priest. He also compels all under him to submit to his worship, decrees and laws, by whips, fines, prisons, fire and faggots. Now what your prisoner requests of you, is a clear distinc-tion between the ecclesiastical constitution of Connecticut, by which I am now held here in prison, and the aforesaid two thrones or beasts, in the foundation, constitution and support thereof. For if by Scripture and rea-son you can shew they do not all stand on the throne mentioned in Psalm xciv. 20, but that the latter is founded on the Rock Christ Jesus, I will confess my fault, and soon clear myself of the prison. But if this constitution hath its rise from that throne, then come forth to the help of the Lord against the mighty ; for better is it to die for Christ, than to live against him. From an old friend to this civil constitution, and long your prisoner, ELISHA PAINE.

Five days after, he was released ; but the extremity of the winter hindered him a great while from getting over to his family, who suffered much in an unfinished house, for want of his help. Mr. Solomon Paine published this year a view of the difference between the church of Christ, and the churches established by law in Connecticut. And though the contest was hot for eight years longer, yet it then abated, and in 1771 Mr. Cogswell was dismissed ; and such taxes were entirely dropped in the place, and a number of actors therein were brought to confess their faults for the same. In the mean time, another unsuccessful address to their Assembly, signed by a large number of men, was presented in 1753. After which, twenty churches joined in a memorial to the King in Council, supported by authentic records and testimonies, to which Governor Fitch affixed the seal of the Colony ; and Mr. Bliss Willoughby, and Mr. Moses Morse, carried it to London in 1756. But, having laid it before the deputation and committee for the Dissenters, whereof Dr. Avery was Chairman, they judged that if those plain violations of charter rights were presented to the King in Council it would endanger the taking away of Connecticut charter; which the petitioners were by no means willing for. Therefore said agents returned in 1757 ; and said committee wrote to Connecticut rulers against those oppressions. And by their advice a process in executive courts was commenced, with a design of carrying it to England by way of appeal; but having proceeded some ways therein, they dropped it.

8

CHAPTER XVIII.

A CHANGE AMONG THE BAPTIST CHURCHES.—ESPECIALLY IN NARRAGAN-
SETT.—THEIR MISTAKES DID NOT HINDER THE PREVAILING OF THEIR
SENTIMENTS.—THE AUTHOR'S CASE.—HIS SETTLEMENT IN THE MINIS-
TRY.—HOW HE BECAME A BAPTIST.—TWO GENERAL MEETINGS ABOUT
IT.—THE TRUE STATE OF THE CONTROVERSY.—A NEW BAPTIST
CHURCH FORMED.

Timothy Packom was an aged and pious member of the
second church in Newport, before a division took place
therein, in the following manner:—Daniel Greene, a gifted
member of it, experienced a sudden turn in his mind, from
general to particular redemption; and in the fall of 1739,
James Brown joined with him, and brought a charge, in
general terms, into their church against Elder Eyres, of his
wanting the gospel qualifications of an elder; and then
named some instances of apparent anger and severity against
members who did not concur with his measures, to prove it.
This caused much unhappiness. At length, on January 10,
1740, he read to the church a general confession of his imperfections in those respects; and they voted the same to be
satisfactory. Said brethren inquired whether he meant to
confess the particulars they had mentioned, but could obtain
no answer from him, nor a copy of his confession. This appeared so grievous that they went and complained of it to
their brethren of North Kingstown, who sent to inquire into
the matter. For these things Greene and Brown were censured; and Packom and others joined with them, and car-

ried their complaints to one general meeting of their churches at Swanzey, and to another at Providence ; and not obtaining satisfaction, they formed a new church, and got some of their elders to ordain Mr. Packom as pastor of it.   And in 1742 they published a vindication of themselves in these proceedings.   But private letters afterwards from each of those men, to Elder Eyres and his church, express deep sorrow for those hasty proceedings, and their want of a fruitful understanding, humility and candor, with their zeal therein ; for which they earnestly desired forgiveness.   But not seeing their way clear to return into full fellowship with that church, a removal of their censure was denied them. Greene, in a letter July 2, 1745, gives the following as the chief reason why he could not commune with said elder, viz. :—

So far as I can gather, thou believest, that man's salvation, conditionally bestowable, is the free purchase of Jesus Christ, and so the free gift of God ; but then that the security of the bestowment, or obtaining this salvation, doth turn and depend upon a condition, which is so left to man to perform, that it may or may not be performed, not as God himself shall be pleased absolutely, to cause, but as man, supposed to be a self-inclining agent, shall of himself be disposed, in the improvement or misimprovement of divine assistance.   Whereas I believe, I think with all my heart, that man is in no respect an independent agent ; and that if he obtains salvation, it is not owing to himself at all ; but that his salvation, and its whole security to him, depend altogether upon the free pleasure and causation of Almighty God, who worketh all things according to the council of his own will, working in his children both to will and to do of his good pleasure.

Such ideas, but not so clear, were impressed upon David Sprague's mind, before he began to preach, in the Baptist church in Scituate ; where he was told, that if he went on in that way he would become as bad an *electioner* as any of the Presbyterians.   This, as he informed me, turned him in a great measure into their general way of preaching ; and he was settled in that way, at North Kingstown, about the time of the abovesaid division at Newport.

By the labors of Separate ministers many were converted,

and a Baptist church was formed in Coventry, and a pastor
was ordained in it, October 11, 1749. Elder Sprague went
there, and was prevailed with to assist, with other Baptists,
in that ordination. And he there got such an acquaintance
with some Separate elders, as to invite them to come and
preach in the Narragansett country. This was done with
very extensive effects; and Sprague was drawn so far as to
act with Solomon Paine in Elder Babcock's ordination the
next spring; which was then the first instance of the union
of the two denominations in such acts. The majority of
the church at North Kingstown grew so uneasy, that above
seventy of them, male and female, signed a paper May 20,
1750, which divided the church. They therein represent,
that their church was of about forty years' standing, and that
good order had generally been kept up in it, until within the
last seven years.

Since that, [say they,] our elder and some of the brethren have imbibed
doctrines which neither we nor our general community ever did choose
should be brought into the church. The doctrines crowded upon us were :
1. That Adam, by his eating the forbidden fruit, did bring mankind under
condemnation in respect to the life which is to come at the day of judgment. 2. That every person who is truly converted, cannot, in the course
of his life, sin himself out of God's blessings at the day of judgment.
3. That it was a duty for Christians to sing, with loud and joined voices,
with rhyme and tunes of man's composure, in public assemblies.

These doctrines and their effects were then shut out of
their meeting-house; though they proposed to leave it to
others to settle the matter with their dissenting brethren
about their interest therein. Upon which Elder Sprague,
and those who were of his sentiments, constituted a church
in Exeter, and several other churches were soon after formed
in those parts, in fellowship with them.

Some among them, who had been baptized in the time of
their former darkness, were now baptized again; which
moved Elder Eyres to write to Elder Sprague about it, De-

cember 1, 1750.[1] and a stop was put thereto.   Also a sight
of former divisions, upon circumstantials, carried a few so
far into the opposite extreme, as to admit some to table
communion without any water baptism at all.   There were
at least two instances of this, the one at Exeter, the other
at Warwick ; but that practice was soon over.   And these
and other mistakes could not hinder an extensive spread of
believers' baptism among the Separate churches ; whose
elders, Mack of Lyme, Stearns of Tolland,[2] Hastings of
Suffield, Meacham of Enfield, Marshal of Somers, and
others, were baptized.   But fierce opposition being raised
against what was called rebaptizing, which was represented
to be a most wicked and pernicious thing, several teachers
and others retracted their acting therein.   And as the
author's refusing to follow their example brought him to be
a public object of resentment, and succeeding events have
made him more extensively so, a clear idea of this part of
our history cannot be given, without a more distinct account
of his personal conduct, and the motives thereof, than otherwise would have been expedient and becoming.   This he
thinks is confirmed by ancient examples.   Acts xi. 2—18 ;
xxii. 3—21.

His being born of religious parents, and having a religious (though not what is called a liberal) education, he has
ever esteemed an unspeakable favor.   Yet he neglected the
great salvation for more than seventeen years, because he
secretly imagined that it would abridge his present liberty
and comfort ; and also, that when he got ready to set about

---

[1] A copy of this letter is preserved in the collection of Rev. S. Hall.   It is a full,
clear and spirited discussion of the point in question.   We would gladly insert it,
but its length forbids.—ED.

[2] Elder Shubael Stearns (having baptized Noah Alden, in July, 1754, and left him
to preach to the part of his society who remained there) set off with others for North
Carolina ; and he, Jonathan Polk, Daniel Marshal, and others, were instrumental of
a great work in those parts.   I am well informed that from thence have sprung a
large number of Baptist churches ; which, by a blessing upon the succeeding labors
of many, now extend through various parts of Virginia, North and South Carolina,
and into Georgia.

the work in good earnest, God would be moved to help, pardon and save him. But in May, 1741, his eyes were opened to see, that time was not at his command, and that eternity was directly before him, into which he might justly be called the next moment. Then he knew what it was to work for his life for three months ; until on August 24, as he was alone in the field, it was demonstrated to his mind and conscience, that he had done his utmost to make himself better, without obtaining any such thing ; but that he was a guilty sinner in the hands of a holy God, who had a right to do with him as seemed good in God's sight ; which he then yielded to, and all his objections against it were silenced. And soon upon this a way of relief was opened to his soul, which he never had any true idea of before, wherein truth and justice shine with lustre, in the bestowment of free mercy and salvation upon objects who have nothing in them- selves but badness. And while this divine glory engaged all his attention, his burthen of guilt and evil dispositions was gone, and such ideas and inclinations were implanted in his heart as were never there before, but which have never been rooted out since, though often overclouded. Hereupon he was led to make a profession of religion, in the church where he had always attended worship, and to walk therein for about two years. But then their minister obtained a vote in the church, to empower him to admit communicants by a major vote, without giving the church so much as a written relation of any inward change. It also appeared that the minister inclined to think that the ordinance of the Supper was a converting ordinance ; and he discovered a strong affection for the Saybrook scheme, which the church had rejected just before they settled him. The author therefore withdrew from that church, about the time that Canterbury church was robbed of their rights, in the manner before described. He had no expectation of entering into the work of the ministry, until September, 1746 ; and the grounds he acted upon then are described in his discourse, published eight years after, entitled, The Nature and Necessity of an Internal Call to preach the Gospel. The manner of his settling among the people he still ministers to, here follows.

In a place called Titicut, upon the river between Bridgewater and Middleborough, a powerful work was wrought, in and after the year 1741, chiefly by means of the preaching of Mr. Eliab Byram; which moved the people to petition for a new precinct, in order to settle him as their minister; but the matter was delayed until he was gone and settled in New Jersey. And after Titicut precinct was constituted, in February, 1743, ministers refused to dismiss the communicants therein, so as to form a new church, lest they should call a minister whom they did not approve of. They were thus denied the rights which both the laws of God and man allowed them, until the brethren determined not to be restrained by such tyranny any longer; but came out and began to worship by themselves on December 13. 1747. The author was then unknown to them, and they to him; but by the disposal of Providence he was brought among them the next Saturday, in company with Mr. Snow, of Providence, who staid and labored ten days with remarkable effects; and the author was prevailed with to tarry and preach among them. And the precinct committee, perceiving that open opposition would then be in vain, came and requested him to preach to them, and to take regular steps for settlement. He informed them, that he was willing to act regularly according to the gospel, but could not submit to the power that ministers and parishes had assumed over the churches, which was contrary thereto. Yet they requested him, and he consented, to preach to them for a while. Such a revival took place as produced the hopeful conversion of about twenty souls, and the quickening of many others. A church was formed February 16, 1748, which increased to threescore members in ten months. But the opposite party met in March, and voted a large sum of money to finish their meeting-house, and to hire other sort of preaching, and assessed it upon all the inhabitants. Therefore our society, on November 21, drew an address to them, to remind them of past transactions, and to invite them into a reconciliation ; or, if not, yet to entreat them not to violate the golden rule in their dealings towards us. They returned an answer which says, " What we demand of you is equal and right ; what you demand of us is evil and sinful ; and hence we have the golden rule upon our side, while you are receding and departing from it." And they went so far as to call it " gross ignorance and enthusiasm for any to deny that Christian rulers have a right to compel their subjects to receive and support orthodox ministers. And February 6, 1749, the author was seized as a prisoner, for thirteen shillings and fourpence assessed upon him in said tax. But as he refused to pay it, they after about three hours confinement settled it among themselves.[1] This was the best reward they ever offered him for preaching two months at their request. One of his brethren was imprisoned at Plymouth for said tax.[2] But when distress was made upon another of his hearers, they were prosecuted therefor, and it was found upon trial that said money was voted at an illegal meeting. They therefore appealed to the Superior Court ; and in the mean time, on December 14, 1749, procured an act of the Legislature which says, " That the proceedings of the meeting mentioned in the petition be, and they hereby are, held and deemed good and

---

[1] " February 6. This morning I was seized by the officer, and he threatened to carry me to prison for the precinct rate, but, glory to God! he gave me a sweet calmness and serenity of soul, not to fear him nor to treat him with any bitterness. I told him that they were going on in an unscriptural way to support the gospel, and therefore I could not do anything to countenance them in such a way. He told me that if I would not pay him he would immediately carry me to jail; but just as he was going to drag me away, there came in a man [Captain Abiezer Edson] and called him out and paid him the money; so that he was forced to let me go." Backus's Manuscript Diary.—Ed.

[2] April 4, [1749.] Yesterday I went to Plymouth to see Brother W. Hooper that is put in prison there for the precinct rate. I found him very comfortable. Ibid. —Ed.

valid law, the defect of the notification for calling said meeting notwithstanding." And by virtue of this act the case
was turned against the appellee in the next trial; which
shews that a worship supported by tax, is partiality established by law. In June preceding, a memorial against it was
carried to the Assembly at Boston, by Mr. John Paine, and
Mr. Samuel Peck, signed by a large number of men ; but it
was rejected,[1] as a like memorial also was in 1754.

As to baptism, disputes about it were first brought into
the church in Titicut in August, 1749; and a disagreeable
temper was soon discovered, and much heat in debates, for
three weeks. And as the author was essaying, in his secret
approaches to the throne of grace, to give up this case to
God, a sudden conclusion came in, that the Baptist way is
certainly right, because nature fights so against it. And he
was hurried on to preach it up the next day; which caused
confusion among the hearers, and returned with a horrible
gloom over his own mind; and he was turned back to his
former practice. Hereupon a number of the church drew
off, and ten persons were baptized in September by Elder
Moulton.[2] About three months after, when the heat of con-

---

[1] "May 24, 1749. Many of the saints met together in Attleborough, to seek the
Lord's direction and to confer about petitioning the Court to set us free from the
oppression of being forced to pay to the support of a worship that we can't in conscience join with ; and we had considerable clearness in sending, and drew a petition and sent copies around to the saints in various parts of the governments ; and
it fell to my lot to carry a copy down to the Cape. Accordingly, on May 19, I set
out, and got that day to Barnstable. The next day I visited three Harwich brethren
in Barnstable prison for rates." Backus's Manuscripts. A hundred and eighty-
three persons signed this petition, and contributed twenty-seven pounds for the cost
of its presentation. The House voted to refer it to a joint committee, but the Council refused.— Ed.

[2] "September 23. I came home ; and I found that Ebenezer Moulton, of Brimfield, had been here among my people preaching, and had *plunged* some of them
last Lord's day. . . . . Next day he *dipped* William Hooper, &c." Backus's Manuscripts. All but one of those baptized by Elder Moulton, were members of Mr.
Backus's church. Difficulties on the subject of baptism soon produced an open
rupture. Mr. Backus writes :—" February 3, 1749-50. This day Elder Moulton
came here again, and Lord's day, February 4, he preached at Abiezer Edson's, and
most of our people went to hear him. And in the evening the Baptist brethren met
at Brother Wood's, and there embodied into a church and signed a copy of Brother
Moulton's Articles of Faith and Covenant." This church soon dissolved. May 27,

troversy was abated, the question was put to his conscience, in his retired hours, Where is it, and in what relation to the church do those stand, who are baptized, but not converted? He could see that all the circumcised were obliged to keep the passover; and, had seen that there was no half way in the Christian church, nor any warrant to admit any to communion therein without a credible profession of saving faith. No tongue can tell the distress he now felt. The neglect of gospel discipline a little before, lay heavy upon his mind; and the disputes and divisions in the church greatly added to his burthen. And near the close of 1749, a number of people in Easton and Norton made so high a profession of being led into believers' baptism, that no ordained minister in the land would do to administer it to them. But they met by a place of water, and one would baptize another, and then he the next; so that about twenty persons were dipped, by four or five administrators among themselves. Parting from their lawful wives and husbands, and taking of others, immediately followed; until some bastard children were born among them, with many other abominations. Could the author therefore have discovered any foundation for his former practice, he would most certainly have continued therein. But all his efforts failing, he was at last brought to the old standard; so as to leave good men and bad men out of the question, and inquire, *What saith the Scripture?* Hereby a settlement was granted, and he was baptized August 22, 1751.[1]

three of its members, and July 21, three more joined the First Baptist church in Swanzey.—ED.

[1] "Thursday, August 22. Brother Benjamin Pierce, pastor of a church in a part of Warwick, preached among us at Brother Hinds's, this day, with considerable power, and then, in the evening, concluded to baptize some persons. .... When I came to see him baptize sundry persons, I having been convinced before that the way that I used to go on in, in baptizing infants, and by sprinkling, was not according to Scripture, and having this opportunity to practice, as I now believed was right, I dared not put it off. Therefore I told some account of my conversion, and then, of my experiences as to these things, which gave satisfaction; then I went down into the water with him and was baptized. And then, and afterwards in the evening, I felt a sweet calmness of mind, and some things opened with special clearness to my soul. Blessed be God." Backus's Manuscript Diary.—ED.

The difficulties were become so great in the church, that a mutual council of five churches was called, October 2; which, after long labor, brought sixteen members to renew their covenant to go on together, and the council declared fellowship with them, and censured all the rest, and solemnly charged those sixteen to follow all the other members with labor, until they were recovered to fellowship, or cut off by discipline. Three of the sixteen were Baptists, and no hint was given of breaking communion between the two denominations. The author had no objection then against their advice, but was held back about a month by inward discouragements. But getting relief therefrom, he came forward, and was freely received in his office by all but two of those brethren; and they refused to receive him, unless he would baptize infants. A close labor was hereby brought on, and it was most fully declared, that we meant to give free liberty to every one to act according to his conscience in that respect; but to require a man to administer an ordinance in the name of God which he saw no command for, was requiring him to wrong his own conscience, to satisfy others. Yet those two brethren, who had lately renewed their covenant, refused to walk with their elder, or with those who received him, unless he would sprinkle infants. For this schism in the body they were censured; and, after ten months' labors, were excommunicated. In the midst of which time five Baptists were censured for refusing to commune with this body. Those two were no sooner cast out than they sent for three of the churches who were of the former council, who met here November 1, 1752, and fully justified them, and censured all who had acted against them, and declared that unless they manifested repentance therefor, they must mark and avoid them. Strangers cannot conceive how unaccountable it appeared, for eminent fathers thus to treat their children this year, for acting according to their own solemn charge the year before. It alarmed the Baptists in general, and our elders, Sprague, Babcock, and

Worden, being sent for, met here in council January 31, 1753; and, in conjunction with many of both denominations that came, they appointed a general meeting of these churches, and sent out citations therefor. In answer to which, twenty-seven churches met at Exeter, May 23, and unanimously agreed, that a turning to or from infant baptism was not a censurable evil; but that each should leave the other with God, according to Phil. iii. 15. And by their advice a council met at Middleborough July 11; under whose influence those censures, both of the two and of the five members, were revoked, and fellowship was again declared with this church. But the elders at Canterbury and Plainfield refused to come to the Exeter meeting, or to concur with these subsequent acts. For this, Elder Babcock refused to act with Elder Paine in an ordination at Stonington, May 29, 1753, though he did not then give his reasons therefor. And because he afterwards gave them to that church, and they sent to Canterbury to inquire into the matter, a process was commenced against Babcock as a transgressor, for laying in complaints against his brethren to another church than their own. This charge was carried to his church, but not succeeding there, Paine joined with Babcock, in calling a general meeting at Stonington May 29, 1754, to search into these matters, that the churches might come into a gospel settlement. Elders and brethren from forty churches then met, viz., from twenty-four in Connecticut, eight in the Massachusetts, seven in Rhode Island, and one on Long Island. After long and tedious debates, the question was put to every member of the conference, whether any just cause of offence was given to the Baptists in the result at Middleborough, of November 1, 1752? Thirty-seven said Nay; thirty-five said Yea, and seven chose to be silent about it. And after hard attempts to cast the blame of the breach upon the Baptists, and manifesting a willingness to commune with Christians who wanted light for infant baptism, Mr. Paine and sundry others declared non-communion with such as professed to have light against it. I now find, that on the back of the paper which called his brother over from Long Island to this meeting at Stonington, Elisha has stated the question in these words, viz.:—

A holds out his principles. 1. He declares he will administer baptism to none but adult believers. 2. That he will go to any church, and baptize all persons that were baptized in infancy, if they will declare they were dissatisfied with their infant baptism. B holds out his principles, and declares that he will administer baptism to all adult believers and their infant seed, and that he doth it in the name of the Trinity, in obedience of a divine precept. Now the question is, Be these two persons agreed in their principles? or will there be any essential difference between their practice, if they practice according to their professed principles? Is it a matter of indifference for a pastor of a church to say, he baptizes an infant in the name of the Father, Son, and Holy Ghost, in the fulfillment of a divine precept? My dear brother, if you can reconcile the above principles, in the essential parts thereof, you will remove all the grounds of bars and disputes; but if there be an essential difference in the above articles, and consequently in the practice on them, then there is an Achan in the camp; and no marvel that Israel hath, in all reformations, been troubled therewith. Either B sins in making infants the subjects of baptism, or A in cutting them off. Now it is clear to me, that infants were once the subjects to be sealed with the seal of Abraham's faith; therefore, if I allow a person to have Abraham's faith, I must shew that God hath forbid the seal to be put to their seed, or else forbid it in my own name; for there is but one covenant of grace, and that had Abraham's seed in it. Now if we allow a person to have Abraham's faith, why not his privilege? I pray God to pinch up our minds, until the troubler be found; for it is not a division between Pædo and Antipædobaptists, but promiscuously runs through the body of Christians, and will rend all cords of union between the dear lambs of God but what are made by human and party bands. Oh! my dear brethren! if God hath cut off infants, by forbidding water to be put on them, let us never tolerate the practice of putting it on; but if not, let none dare to forbid it, but do it in proper office and time.

Thus spake that eminent father of these churches; though the author then knew nothing of it, and never saw him nor his brother after that meeting.[1] A strong persuasion was still held by many, that if a right temper was in

[1] Mr. Solomon Paine died, after a short illness, October 25, 1754. Mr. Stevens died November 13, 1755. They were principal leaders among those churches.

exercise, Christians might, and ought to, commune together, although of different judgments about baptism. The author and his church labored earnestly to go on in that way ; but when some pious members manifested a belief of duty to be buried in baptism, others refused to go to the water to see it done, because, in their view, they were already baptized, and to repeat it would be taking the sacred name in vain. And when an elder came and sprinkled some infants, the Baptists felt a like difficulty, though they did not leave the meeting where it was done. Being unwilling to part, attempts were made to convince each other, which led into warm debates ; to avoid which, at the next meeting, each one was afraid to mention the subject, lest it should cause disputes. Thus edification, the great end of Christian society, was marred instead of being promoted, by that which is called large communion.[1] It was so far from answering to that name, that, with their utmost endeavors, the author and his brethren could never arrive at communion in the ordinance of the Supper, from September, 1754, to the end of 1755. To be unsettled in religious matters was very disagreeable to the author ; but he could not avoid a fresh search into the cause of these difficulties.

[1]The Baptist churches of this period gave full trial to the experiment of " mixed communion." Many circumstances were most favorable to its success. The Baptist and the Separate Congregational churches were bound together by the closest ties. The former left the latter from no ill feeling but with heartiest love, and this love continued, on both sides, after their separation. Their members had been converted together in the Great Awakening; together they had come out from the Standing Order; together they had suffered and were still suffering for the truth; they had the same enemies and oppressors; they felt the force of the same unjust and cruel laws; their plundered goods were sold at the same auctions, and their bodies confined in the same prisons; they had many kindred views and feelings, by which they sympathized most closely, and in which there were no others to sympathize with them. Moreover, they mutually desired inter-communion. Council after council and conference after conference recommended it, and there seemed to be no voice against it. And yet it failed. Practical difficulties arose, such as are described above. The truth could not be escaped that Baptist churches, by renouncing infant baptism and sprinkling, and then practically recognizing them again as a proper declaration of discipleship and initiation to membership in the visible church, placed themselves in a position of direct inconsistency. One by one, reluctantly, but at last universally, they abandoned the untenable ground.—ED.

The arguments of the beloved Bunyan, for a free communion with all saints, had before appeared conclusive to
him and others ; but a review of them discovered his mistakes.   One argument is, that plain laws, of old, were sometimes dispensed with ; as circumcision was omitted in the
wilderness ; David, ate of the shew-bread that was not lawful for him, and the people in Hezekiah's time ate of the
passover, otherwise than it was written.   But it was found
upon search, that all of these were extraordinary cases,
which were not repeated ; and therefore could afford no plea
for dispensing with rule at ordinary times.   And as to Bunyan's capital argument, which is, *God hath received them,
therefore we ought to ;* it was observed, that his example is
often inimitable by us ; but as far as it is imitable, it is always
in the truth.   Hence truth is never to be violated for any
one, no, not to save natural life, which all lawful means
should be used to preserve.   And truth so clearly requires
baptism before the Supper, that Pædobaptists do never come
to the table with any but such as are baptized in their esteem.
Neither could we understandingly act in being buried in
baptism, until we were convinced that what was done to us
in infancy was not gospel baptism ; therefore to commune
at the Lord's table with any who were only sprinkled in
infancy, is parting with truth, by practically saying they are
baptized when we do not believe they are.   I since find that
the learned and pious Dr. Watts allows this argument to be
just,[1] though many still wrangle against it.

A number of brethren being convinced that though freedom towards all men ought to be shown, as far as it can be
in the truth, yet that truth limits church communion to
believers, baptized upon a profession of their own faith,
constituted a church at Middleborough, in this way, on January 16, 1756 ;[2] and, by assistance from Boston and Reho-

---

[1] Rational Foundation of the Christian Church, pp. 189, 260.
[2] "July 3, [1755.]   This was kept as a day of public fasting. .... I read a new
draft of Articles that I've drawn up, in which is expressed my faith about the sub-

both, the author was installed their pastor the 23d of July following.[1] He had in the mean time published a discourse from Gal. iv. 31, to shew that Abraham's first son that was circumcised was the son of the bond-woman, an emblem of the national church of the Jews; in distinction from regen-

jects of baptism; and the brethren all concurred with the rest of the Articles, but upon that we had some discourse, and all present that are of the Baptist principle thought it duty to proceed anew to gather a church agreeable to our faith; and the other brethren said they would not stand in the way."

"January 2, 1756. We had a conference meeting at my house, and brother Hinds was with us. .... I now declared that I firmly believed that, as none are the proper subjects of baptism but real saints, so every such soul ought to be baptized by immersion before they come to the Lord's Supper. .... And I did solemnly entreat and invite my brethren to arise and build the old wastes; and the most who were present discovered a willingness so to do. So we appointed another meeting next week to labor on these affairs."

"January 16. Our people met according to appointment, and Brother Hinds came and preached a sermon from I Cor. 5. 7, 8; and he laid open in many things, clearly, how we ought to purge out the old leaven in order to be a new lump. And my soul had a very weighty sense of the greatness of the affairs before us and of the infinite importance of carefully keeping to the rules of Christ's house both in admitting members, and also in after dealings with them. And had not my soul believed that Christ would go before me, I should not have dared to step forward, but being satisfied of that (after some free discourse with our brethren who do not see with us,) I read the Articles and Covenant which I had drawn, and then proceeded, solemnly, in the presence of God and his people, to sign them; and the following brothers and sisters signed with me, viz., Timothy Briant and John Hayward, Mary Caswell, Esther Fobes and my dear consort. And there appeared a good degree of solemnity and sense of divine things in acting therein." Backus's Manuscript Diary.—ED.

[1] "June 23. I went early to pour out my soul to God, and was enabled to rest all my affairs with him, and especially the work of this day, (for none of the elders that were sent to were yet come,) and I found a measure of willingness to leave the case with the Lord to send whom he pleased. Not long after came Elder Bound and Deacon Collins from the Baptist church in Boston, and Elder Round and Esquire Bullock and Joshua Briggs, brethren from the second Baptist church in Rehoboth. And they proceeded to read the letters from us and their churches' answer thereto, and embodied into a council and chose Elder Round, Moderator, and Elder Bound, Clerk; and after inquiring into the principles and standing both of the church and myself, and of our coming together in this relation, they declared themselves satisfied therewith. Then we went out in public before a great congregation of people, and Mr. Bound preached from Dan. 12. 3. .... Then these two elders laid on hands, and Elder Round made the first prayer and gave the charge, and Elder Bound gave the Right Hand of Fellowship, and made the last prayer. And through the whole exercise, my soul felt a great solemnity. We concluded with singing the first part of the 132d Psalm. O that that Psalm may ever be fulfilled among us. Backus's Manuscript Diary."—ED.

9

erate souls, the spiritual seed of Abraham, of whom the Christian church was constituted ; into which neither natural birth, nor the doings of others, can rightly bring any one soul, without its own consent.[1]   Upon these principles was the first Baptist church in Plymouth county then founded ; it being the first of this persuasion, in an extent of country above a hundred miles long, from Bellingham to the end of Cape Cod, and near fifty miles wide, betwixt Boston and Rehoboth, wherein are now seventeen churches.

Men who regard carnal ease, or temporal honor and interest, more than truth, cannot be pleased with the foregoing account of things ; but their scorn or rage is contemptible, when compared with the divine favor or displeasure. Young Christians who highly regard God's favor and fear his frowns, yet are far from being aware of how nearly truth and error may be blended in honest minds; and nothing can teach them the nature and effects thereof like experience.   The Spirit of truth taught Peter that Jesus was the Christ the Son of the living God ; but Peter was greatly mistaken, in concluding from thence that he had inherent strength enough to die for his Saviour.   On the day of Pentecost he and others received vastly greater light and strength ; yet how much were they still mistaken in supposing that all who were converted to Christianity must be circumcised! And though a new vision from heaven taught Peter to go freely to the Gentiles, yet what dissimulation was he and Barnabas afterwards insnared in about those matters ! Gal. ii. 11—14. Great care is ever to be taken, not to condemn any thing but what is really evil, nor to expose what is so unecessarily. If the author has done either in the preceding narrative, he desires to lie open to conviction.   It is drawn from a large number of original papers and records, which any

---

[1] "January 20. This evening I finished writing a discourse concerning the bond-woman and the free, which is designed for the press, wherein I have shown the grounds upon which I have changed my principles concerning baptism. May heaven's blessing follow it for the good of the people of God!" Backus's Manuscript Diary.—ED.

who desire it are welcome to see. His experience in these affairs has very sensibly taught him, that mistaken conclusions are often drawn from good premises ; and also, that wrong judgments are the natural effects of erroneous principles. In particular that truth is not to be embraced only because nature fights against it, nor rejected because bad men have professed it, or good men have fought against it. Also that the holding of internal union as the rule of church communion, naturally leads to the censuring of brethren of both denominations, if they refuse to act according to that rule, which is making our affection to creatures the standard instead of the revealed will of God. Likewise to censure serious Christians, because of difference in opinion about worship, in the same manner as if they were guilty of a plain breach of moral precept, is doubtless erroneous. In a word, truth is to be received and held for its own sake, and not upon any exterior motives ; and it is never to be violated or forsaken for any consideration whatsoever.

CHAPTER XIX.

Little do men know of themselves, until they are tried; and as little do they know of the designs of the Most High, when he is trying them. When Mr. Davenport judged Mr. Noyes to be unconverted, an ample testimony was published in his favor, by President Clap, and others.[1] But the same man was judged to be heterodox, by the same President, eight or nine years after; and then himself went to the same Separate meeting that he had censured others for going to. And at a meeting of the corporation of Yale College, November 21, 1753, it was resolved that no member of the corporation, nor officer of instruction therein, should hereafter be admitted, until he had given his explicit consent to their ancient forms of orthodoxy, and renounced all opposite principles; and that, as this was a known condition of their admission, if any of them should afterwards embrace a contrary system, common honesty would oblige them to own it, and to resign their places. It was likewise resolved, that if any of their members or officers should be suspected of heterodoxy, he should be brought upon examination before said corporation.[2] In October, 1753, an act of their Legis-

[1] Chauncy's Thoughts, pp. 158—161.
[2] Clap's History of Yale College. pp. 63, 64.

lature was procured, to establish a professorship of divinity
in the college; which terminated in setting up worship on
the Lord's days, and the gathering of a church therein. A
great noise, in print and otherwise, was made about these
proceedings; which had so much influence about this time,
as to cut off an annual grant of a hundred pounds from
the government to the president, which has not been restored since. Much pains were taken, by him and others,
to prove that none but orthodox ministers ought ever to be
elected as members of the college corporation.

In the mean time, contentions about bishoprics, among
Presbyterian ministers, turned many over to Episcopacy;
and very tedious controversies were carried on, about the
validity of Presbyterian ordination, and other points connected therewith. So much smoke and dust was raised hereby, as opened a pleasing prospect to a number, of expelling
the ancient plan of orthodoxy, under the name of bigotry
and tyranny; which, said they, " degrades men from their
just rank, into the class of brutes. It damps their spirits;
it suppresses arts; it extinguishes every spark of noble ardor and generosity in the breasts of those who are enslaved
by it. . . . . 'There are virtuous and candid men in all sects;
all such are to be esteemed. There are also vicious men
and bigots in all sects; all such ought to be despised."[1]
And the writer of this, became, for sixteen years, the most
popular author in New England. He got so far in five
years, as to insinuate that the doctrine of three eternal persons in the Godhead came from the pope or a general council, and that it ought to be treated with contempt. And he
asserted, "that the Scripture teaches no such doctrine as
that of God's *imputing* the perfect righteousness of Christ to
sinners for justification."[2] Four senior ministers of Boston
joined upon this occasion in publishing a testimony for the
essential and eternal deity of our Saviour, and in expressing

[1] Preface to Mayhew's Mystery of Charles's Martyrdom, 1750.
[2] Mayhew's Sermons, 1755, pp. 157, 417, 418.

their grief at what had lately been published against it; but
as they did not mention his name, he let it pass with contempt. But his party in Connecticut soon after could not
help discovering themselves very plainly.

The Baptist meeting at Wallingford was removed twenty
miles, to Southington, four years before Mr. Whittlesey died,
in 1756. Yet in two years, among twenty candidates whom
they tried, they could not agree in the settlement of a minister in that parish. Therefore on April 26, 1758, four ministers advised them to send to Cambridge for a candidate; in
compliance wherewith a man came, highly recommended,
from thence. And in June they gave him a call to settle,
with an offer of two hundred pounds settlement, and a salary
of eighty pounds the first year, ninety the second, and a hundred a year ever after, as long as he continued their minister. This call he carried to Cambridge, where he was advised to accept it; and he returned and published his acceptance thereof, and his ordination was appointed to be on
October 11. And now we are to see more of what their
Saybrook Platform is. Like civil courts, it does not hinder
persons and societies from voluntary agreements among themselves, where there is no opposition; but when contentions
break out, it was designed as a known and fixed tribunal,
within each circuit, so that no party might have "liberty to
choose their own council where they pleased;" as Dr. Cotton
Mather declares, who well understood it.[1] Yet in this case,
though much opposition arose against said candidate, before
his ordination was appointed, his party sent for several ministers out of the Massachusetts, for one out of the county of
Hartford, as well as for such as suited them in their own
county, to be the ordaining council.[2] Before their call was
given, a justice of the peace, who was a father in that
church, went to talk with their candidate about his doctrine;
but was answered in a short and angry manner; and the
candidate said, "he was too young to be examined; and if

[1]Ratio Disciplinæ, p. 183.   [2]Todd, p. 11.

there were any objections against what he had delivered in preaching, he would answer them before the ordaining council." To this testimony the justice has signed his name. Two others of the society also certify, that they waited upon him some time before his settlement and salary were voted, to obtain satisfaction about his principles; "and particularly desired him to let them know his sentiments with regard to original sin, and the saints' perseverance, the power of free will, and falling from grace;" but he refused to tell them.[1] Therefore the Consociation was convened at Wallingford, the day before the time appointed for his ordination, to hear and act upon a complaint exhibited against said candidate; but he and his party protested against their meeting at that time, and refused to be tried by them. And a minister from Hingham, in the Massachusetts, and six more of those who were sent for, formed themselves into a council, and went into their meeting-house, and heard the candidate for ordination vindicate himself before judges that his accusers refused to be tried by. Though while they were there, they received a paper, signed by ninety-five inhabitants of that parish, who were in possession of about half the freehold estate therein, desiring them not to proceed in the ordination. With this paper came a message from their Consociation, warning and beseeching them not then to proceed. Yet in the face of all this, those ministers went on and ordained the candidate, as the pastor of that parish. Such an instance was never before known in this land; therefore their Consociation adjourned, and called in the Southern Consociation of Hartford county to act with them in the affair. But all their united efforts could not bring said party to submit to a trial before them; therefore, at their meeting of April 3, 1759, the sentence of non-communion was passed against the minister so ordained in the first society in Wallingford, and against the members who should continue with him. And the ministers of that county who acted in that ordination

[1]Eells, pp. 9, 10.

were declared to be disorderly persons, unworthy to sit in any of their councils, until they gave satisfaction for that offence ; and these were Joseph Noyes, Isaac Stiles, and Chauncy Whittlesey, of New Haven, Samuel Whittlesey, of Milford, Theophilus Hall, of Meriden, and Jonathan Todd, of East Guilford.[1] The last of these, with Mr. William Hart, of Saybrook, (who collected many stories against the New Lights,[2]) wrote in favor of that ordination; and Mr. Eells and Mr. Noah Hobart wrote against it. Two of these "*disorderly*" ministers were sons to the former minister of Wallingford ; the second of them was the tutor for whose sake David Brainard was expelled the college; and his father was Moderator of the Consociation that deposed Mr. Timothy Allen from his pastoral office, at a meeting which was not called for that end.[3] Mr. Robbins was now one of their judges, in an affair which affords many useful lessons.

Here we may see how self can blind the children of men. The scene of these actions was in the same town, from whence all their actings against him originated. He only preached there occasionally ; they settled a minister in the parish. He acted against the request of two ministers, and forty-two inhabitants ; they against the Consociation of the county, and ninety-five inhabitants. In the first case the Saybrook Platform was fairly renounced, and the oracles of God received in its stead ; in the other, those ministers only protested against the meeting upon it, at that time ;[4] but intended to act upon it themselves afterwards, when a "smart young gentleman from Cambridge" should have effected an agreeable change among them.[5] Robbins's plea for liberty of conscience was rejected, and his confessions also ; because, they say :—

The Council at Guilford did not sit to make a number of new laws, by virtue of some legislative power in themselves, but sat to inquire what were the laws of Christ. He omits to tell the world, that the Association inquired of him, whether, in his third confession, he acknowledged the

[1]Eells, pp. 32—48.   [2]Chauncy's Thoughts, pp. 183—195.   [3]Ibid, p. 215.
    [4]Todd, p. 25.   [5]Todd, p. 4. Eells, p. 10.

transgression of any law of God, in any respect, and that he declared to them he did not. Would any one expect that the Association would sit to hear one *flam* after another.[1]

But now what terrible invasions are made upon their rights and liberties ! First it is said :—

The complainants were their own members, and have no right by the constitution to call a Consociation to sit in judgment upon them and exercise jurisdiction over them.   They are a Congregational church, having power of church discipline within themselves ; and the constitution secures them in the peaceable enjoyment of the Congregational privileges, and did not subject them to the prosecution of their own members.

And says their advocate :—

It always appeared to me a thing not only unprecedented and unconstitutional, but cruel,[2] to advise the Moderator to call the Consociation upon a complaint against the church, without letting the church know that any complaint was exhibited against them, or giving them opportunity to shew, if they were able, that there was no occasion therefor.

And he insinuates that the love of money had some influence in raising opposition against that ordination.[3]   At the same time Mr. Hart (his second in this affair) has recourse to the laws of England, about the induction of ministers into profitable livings, to vindicate their ordination of said teacher at Wallingford ; which word *Induction* has been made use of by Episcopalians, in the Colony of New York, to rob Presbyterians of their rights ;[4] because it was said in the Consociation, " The constitution is in danger of being overset, but it is better that the Arminians do it than we ;" they said, " It certainly must be a very wicked thing, to dub men heretics, brand them with ill names, and ascribe to them principles that they disclaim, only to compass some particular designs.[5]   But one of their most knowing and candid ministers assures us, that he never heard any of them so spoken of since, who had not the same character before.[6]

[1]Their Answer to Robbins, pp. 8, 9.

[2]How cruel then were they, in all their proceedings, against the minister of Branford !

[3]Todd, pp. 9, 14, 26.   [4]Hobart, p. 31.   [5]Todd, p. 72.   [6]Hobart, p. 36.

And it is certain, that all their proceedings against Mr. Robbins were upon the complaints of a small party, contrary to the minds of a large majority, both of his church and congregation. And those attempts were to root out a minister who was well settled ; these were to settle one who had preached in the place but a few weeks before he received his call, when the opposition openly appeared. From all this we learn, that what they call *free-will power*, is a power to conform to or dispense with rule, divine or human, as they judge best, and to plead liberty of conscience for so doing ; yea, a liberty to brand dissenters from their judgments with as many ill names as they please, but to deny that liberty to others concerning themselves. From hence we also learn, that their Consociation power over the churches, instead of preventing, causes divisions and offences, contrary to the doctrine of Christ. It now caused a division in Wallingford, and those who adhered to the ancient faith of their churches were forced to draw off, and form another church, and settle another minister ; and the secular arm, from whence their Consociation power was derived and is supported, upholds said minister in that place, and has called him to preach an Election Sermon at Hartford. His name and present title are James Dana, D. D.

These remarks are greatly confirmed by succeeding events. Sandeman's letters on Theron and Aspasio came out in 1758, which give those teachers a most severe lashing who point their hearers to something good in themselves, for encouragement, instead of Christ's finished atonement. Mr. Ebenezer White, of Danbury, readily adopted these sentiments, and most of his hearers also ; but a minor part of them were so much displeased therewith, as to enter a complaint against him to the Eastern Association of Fairfield county. Upon hearing of which, he and a large majority of his church met June 28, 1763, and renounced the Saybrook Platform ; though they did not withdraw their fellowship from the churches that were under it. In August the Consociation in that circuit met at Danbury, and, viewing the case to be difficult, they adjourned, and called in the Western Consociation of that county, to act with them. After much labor, at their meeting of March 27, 1764, they rejected Mr. White and the majority of his church, as men who had separated from their constitution; and owned the minority who adhered to it as the first church and society in Danbury, declaring that they were released from all obligations to Mr. White as their minister, and that the Consociation could not recommend him as such to any other people, until he gave them satisfaction. But this last clause was protested against as unreasonably severe, by five ministers of their number.[1] Mr. Izrahiah Wetmore was one of them, who in an Election Sermon at Hartford nine years after, gave an explicit testimony against any attempts to establish the church of Christ by human laws. Another of them was Mr. David Judson, of Newtown, who in 1770 renounced the Saybrook scheme, as his church also did in 1773; and several meetings of the Consociation were called upon it, and pamphlets were published against them by Mr. Judson, and for them by Mr. Robert Ross.[2]

If we again turn our eyes to Boston; the same temper presents itself to view. The Separate society that began there in 1742, growing small, dismissed their minister, and dissolved their society; and a parish upon Casco Bay called and settled him as their pastor. This displeased a few of the inhabitants so much, that they brought their complaints to Boston, in 1760; and were not only set off themselves to

---

[1] White's Narrative, pp. 22, 23.

[2] In 1762, Mr. Ross published a labored piece at New Haven, against the Baptists and others, who had separated from his party; wherein he advanced facts and arguments to prove them to be deluded enthusiasts. One of his plainest facts is, that a few foolish people at Wrentham, a hundred and sixty miles from him, once ventured to appoint a time to ordain a minister over them, who had not consented thereto; and they were confounded in it. His plainest argument, to prove that the Baptists and others are a deluded people, is in these words, viz. : "If you had not embraced some errors about experimental religion, why do you separate *from us!*" Ross's Address, pp. 45, 105.

another parish, but procured a general law of the province to prohibit the settling of any minister for the future, in their way, who had not an academical degree, or an approbation from the majority of the settled ministers of the county where the parish lies. At the same time their Grand Jury, in their several County Courts, were charged by the Judges from year to year to enter complaints upon oath against every parish that neglected to settle and support an orthodox minister. But about this time an Episcopal church was erected near the College in Cambridge, whose minister, at the opening of it, exclaimed most bitterly against the fathers of New England and their doctrines, and published some high commendations of the Episcopal way. This moved the popular author before named, at Boston, to appear against that party. And having quoted the 9th, 11th, 13th and 17th articles of the church of England, which speak of Original Sin, Justification by faith in Christ's imputed righteousness, Works done before justification, and of Predestination and Election, he says :—

To speak sincerely, I own it is my private opinion, that it has been too common a thing for people in New England to express themselves in a manner justly exceptionable upon these points, however agreeably both to the letter and spirit of the articles aforesaid; but yet, I believe, not more exceptionably than many eminent divines of the church of England did in the last century.[1]

This last remark is undoubtedly just; but can any say so of what follows?

The eldest of the two brothers who were expelled out of Yale College[2] published an essay at Boston, to prove that two of this author's sermons were erroneous, about the person and atonement of Christ. Directly upon which it was declared in some of the Boston papers, "that it was as much out of character for a gentleman of the Doctor's reputation to enter into a controversy with Mr. Cleaveland, as it would

[1]Mayhew's Observations upon the Episcopal Society, 1763, pp. 91, 92.
[2]See p. 71.—ED.

for a general of an army to accept of a challenge from a subaltern." To which was soon added, "A Letter of Reproof to Mr. John Cleaveland, of Ipswich, by Jonathan Mayhew, D. D." Therein the author of the essay was considered "as a person unworthy to be reasoned with." Says Mr. Mayhew:—

It was my determination from the first, not to enter into a dispute with such a *wrong headed and worse hearted wretch !* .... Had I not a right to speak my sentiments upon these points? If you disliked them, could you not content yourself with preaching your own? Or, if you must needs publish them, would it not have been more *decent* and *expedient* for you to do it, without engaging in a personal controversy with me? Would not any end [which] you could propose to yourself have been answered as well, though you had never mentioned my name?[1]

Upon which it was observed, that the eternal Jehovah says to wrong headed and worse hearted sinners, "Come now and let us reason together;" which this great pretender to virtue and liberty was unwilling to do with a fellow-minister! but would have it esteemed an *indecent* as well as an *inexpedient* attempt, for such as did not stand in so high a class as himself to expose his inconsistencies and errors.[2] A sight of these things moved President Clap, and the corporation of Yale College, to send to Mr. Cleaveland a degree of Master of Arts, in 1764, as they afterwards did to his brother. Yet when Mayhew died June 9, 1766, Chauncy gave him a high character, in a funeral sermon, and reflected upon his answerer, calling him "An obscure person, without reputation;" but he could not at the same time conceal his own corruption.

For Robert Sandeman, whose writings had made a great stir in this country, came over from Scotland, and landed at Boston in October, 1764, and gathered a church in Boston, another in Providence, and a third in Danbury. Therefore, to guard against his influence, Chauncy published a volume

[1]Letter of Reproof, pp. 4, 20, 39.
[2]Cleaveland's Reply, 1765, pp. 3, 14.

of sermons in 1765, wherein he gives his ideas concerning fundamental points in the following words. Says he :—

The original promise of life was not suspended upon *perfect obedience* to what is commonly called *the natural or moral law of God.* In contradiction hereto, I know it is said, by *most* Christian writers, that the first man was so placed under this law, that he must work his way to life by perfectly doing all things commanded by it; insomuch that he could not have obtained it but by a persevering obedience in every point of duty, without the least failure. But this is said entirely without book. The Scripture nowhere insinuates, that he was under *such a covenant of works.* It suggests, on the contrary, that God, in favor to him, did not put him upon so *severe* a trial for life. His trial, if we may believe the sacred record of it, was in a *single instance,* and this not of doing, but of forbearing to do. .... That which was made the test of Adam's subjection to God, was a command not of the moral but positive kind; a command, not deducible from reason, but known only by revelation. .... It would be the exact truth, should I say, that the first parents of men, while innocent, in common with their posterity since the elapse, could have obtained life in no way but that of *grace through faith.*

And after a labored criticism upon Rom. v. 12, he says :—

The judicial sentence of God, occasioned by the offence of one man, is that which fastens *death*, with all its natural causes and appendages, upon the human kind; and 'tis IN CONSEQUENCE of this sentence, UPON men's coming into existence under the disadvantages arising from it, that they *sin* themselves.[1]

This is his account, accented in this manner. From whence we may see, that his principles were contrary to most Christian writers about original righteousness, original sin, the nature of grace, and the justice of God in his government of the world. For the moral law is to love God with all our powers, and to love our neighbors as ourselves; which can never be called severe, without implicitly denying his infinite excellency and righteousness. And though the precept concerning the forbidden fruit could only be known by pure revelation, yet by violating it man revolted from heaven, and seized upon the earth as his own; and we are all born in that state of revolt, which is original sin.

[1] Chauncy's Twelve Sermons, pp. 18—20, 23.

And grace and works are as distinct as wages and gifts. Rom. vi. 23; xi. 6. Wages cannot be justly claimed but upon doing the work ; while the most proper subjects of gifts are such as are sensibly guilty and helpless.   Neither can the justice of God, in sending death upon infants, be clearly vindicated in any other way, than by viewing them as sinners in our first public head.   And to deny God's right to constitute him as such, implicitly militates against his justifying souls by the imputed righteousness of the second Adam.

CHAPTER XX.

Divisions and perverse disputings, in all parts of the
land, brought the churches into terrible circumstances; and
each party was ready to cast the blame of it upon others.
And a national war began in 1755, which ever tends to corrupt the morals, as well as to destroy the property and lives
of men. Its influence was very extensive; and it issued in
February, 1763, in the cession of the whole continent of
America north of the Mississippi to the Crown of Great
Britain; a vast territory indeed. Many rejoiced greatly
upon this occasion, imagining that our wars, which for near
a century had been frequent and very distressing, were now
come to an end. But, alas! to the whole British empire,
these were but the beginning of sorrows. Upon the conquest of Quebec, Governor Wentworth, of New Hampshire, appointed a public thanksgiving upon Saturday,
November 10, 1759, because it was the birth day of an aged
and good king; and he said in his proclamation, "The ministers of the gospel are hereby directed to perform divine
service, in their respective congregations, in the morning
only, the afternoon being devoted to public rejoicings, and
lawful diversions." But when the day came, instead of

10

rejoicings, the Governor had to mourn over the dead corpse of his only son.[1]   And on October 25, 1760, that aged and good king was taken from the nation.   When the news of it arrived, the pastor of the Second Baptist church in Boston preached from those words of Solomon, " Wo to thee, O land, when thy king is a child;" which is a truth that others have had occasion to remember since.   And because the great reformation, in and after the year 1740, was begun and mainly carried on among Pædobaptists, many had asserted that the Baptist principles always came in at the tail of a reformation, when the life of religion was gone, and people were for settling down upon the bare letter of Scripture.   For a dozen years, this argument was much harped upon, until it was silenced in these parts by clear evidence to the contrary.

The Second Baptist church in Middleborough ordained their pastor on January 26, 1758.[2]   And our Third church in the town was formed and organized in 1761.   And though we have three meeting-houses of our denomination in this town, yet the nearest are nine miles apart, and the farthest above eleven.   On April 1, 1761, Mr. William Carpenter, and his church at Norton, were established in the Baptist order, and he enjoyed a considerable blessing upon his labors both there and in Attleborough ; and some revivings were granted in several other parts of the land.   But a much greater work came on in June, 1762, in the Third Baptist church in Middleborough, and prevailed through the year, and extended its blessings into other societies and denominations.   The subjects of this work discovered much more of fruitfulness in their understandings, and good government of their passions, than appeared in the revival twenty years before.   And it was very evident, that the labors of Baptist ministers were the chief means of beginning and carrying on this work; which was powerful, undoubtedly, to the

[1]Langdon's sermon on said day, pp. 45, 46.
[2]This church was formed November 16, 1757—ED.

saving benefit of many souls.   And though the world said, they spent so much time in religious exercises, that they would all starve, or come to want and misery, yet the contrary was remarkably demonstrated, by the dispensations of Providence.   For in many places almost the whole staff of bread was cut off, by a severe drought; while a few seasonable showers, in the parts where people were so much engaged in religion, caused not only a good supply for themselves, but also a large quantity to impart to others the next spring.   This was very convincing to many.   Divine influences upon the souls of men were more extensively granted afterwards.   Near the close of 1763, such a work began under Mr. Cleaveland's ministry in Ipswich, as caused the addition of ninety communicants to his church, in less than a year.   A like blessing was granted in Providence and in Norwich, and a greater one on the east end of Long Island, of which Mr. Buell published a narrative.   The work extended to New York, New Jersey, and elsewhere.   The beginning and progress of a revival at Woodstock was also very remarkable.   As Mr. Noah Alden passed through the town in December, 1763, he preached a sermon to a few people, one of whom[1] had been a chief leader in mirth and frolicking among young people there.   But God was pleased to direct an arrow of conviction to his heart, which ended in conversion in March, 1764.   No sooner did this news come abroad, than four of his former companions went one evening to try if they could not draw him back to his former ways again.   He willingly retired with them to an adjacent school-house, where they spent the evening together.   But, instead of turning him back to vanity, he prevailed with them to appoint a religious meeting the next week, which led on to others of that kind, until a large harvest of souls was granted there.   And who could help rejoicing, to see a large number of young people turned from lying vanities, to an earnest engagement in religion, and the great affairs of

[1]Biel Ledoyt.—ED.

the soul and eternity! Yet the minister and professors with whom they met for worship, finding that a cold formality could not give them satisfaction, appointed a fast, and called in the neighboring ministers to assist therein; who fell to exclaiming against false teachers, Satan's turning himself into an angel of light, separations, Anabaptism, &c.; which plainly taught those young believers, that edification, the great end of Christian society, was not to be enjoyed in that way. And they being convinced of the truth of believers' baptism, a church was constituted in that order in February, 1766; and on May 29, 1768, the man who had been their chief leader from vanity to real religion was ordained their pastor; under whose ministrations great blessings have been granted since. And such a door is now opening for the removal of ancient prejudices, as had not been before in many ages.

The covenant of circumcision gave those who were born in it a right to treat all others, both as to worship and commerce, as no others had any right to treat them. A right to office also in that church was hereditary. When our Saviour came, he fulfilled the law, both moral and ceremonial, and abolished those hereditary distinctions among mankind. But in the centuries following, deceitful philosophy took away the name which God has given to that covenant, (Acts vii. 8) and added the name *Grace* to it; from whence came the doctrine, that *dominion is founded in grace*. And although this latter name has been exploded by many, yet the root of it has been tenaciously held fast and taught in all colleges and superior places of learning, as far as Christianity has extended, until the present time; whereby natural affection, education, temporal interest, and self-righteousness, the strongest prejudices in the world, have all conspired to bind people in that way, and to bar their minds against equal liberty and believers' baptism. But the writings of our learned ministers in England have communicated much light in this country; to which more was added by the travails and labors of our southern fathers and brethren.   And hereby the Philadelphia Association[1] obtained such an acquaintance with our affairs, as to bring them to an apprehension that it was practicable and expedient to erect a college in the colony of Rhode Island, under the chief direction of the Baptists; wherein education might be promoted, and superior learning obtained, free of any sectarian religious tests. Mr. James Manning, who took his first degree in New Jersey College in September, 1762, was esteemed a suitable leader in this important work.   Therefore on a voyage to Halifax, in July, 1763, he called in at Newport, and proposed the affair to the Honorable Samuel Ward, John Gardner, Josias Lyndon, and other Baptist gentlemen and friends; who readily concurred therewith, and entered upon the use of means to accomplish it.   And notwithstanding secret contrivances, and some open attempts against it,[2] an ample charter for the purpose was granted by their Legislature, in February, 1764.   In the summer following, Mr. Manning removed to Warren, to preach to a society newly formed there, and to begin the school.   In September, 1765, he was chosen President of the college, and on September 7, 1769, seven young gentlemen took their first degrees therein, and it was removed to Providence the next Spring, where a further account of it may be given hereafter.   Mr. Hezekiah Smith, a classmate with Mr. Manning, having travelled and labored in the gospel as far southward as Georgia, returned and came into New England in the spring of 1764, and was received to preach in the pulpits of Pædobaptists, in Providence, Rehoboth, Attleborough, Ipswich, Newbury, and other places, with an evident blessing upon his labors.   He expected to return to New Jersey in the fall; but a vacant parish in Haverhill prevailed with him to alter his purpose, so as to stay and preach with them.   Hereupon some ministers, who

[1] A yearly meeting of the Baptist churches in those parts, which began in 1707.
[2] These matters are more fully treated in a subsequent chapter.   Their whole history is given in Manning and Brown University. pp. 46—62, 465—482.—ED.

had freely received him as an itinerant minister, turned and
exerted all their influence against him.[1] Yet many seals
were granted to his ministry, and a Baptist church was
formed in Haverhill, on May 9, 1765, and he became their
pastor ; before which there was but one small Baptist church
in any part of our country northward of Boston.   Their increase also elsewhere made others very uneasy.

   Dr. Benjamin Lord published a discourse in 1763, wherein he says :—

Some few, I perceive, begin to hearken to corrupt doctrines, which tend
to their renouncing of their infant baptism, and their interest in the very
ancient covenant with Abraham and his seed ; which you may be assured
is a dangerous road, and often issueth very fatally ; .... witness the Anabaptists in Germany, two hundred and forty years ago, and others since.[2]

   Directly upon this, he, with six other ministers, made
some additions to Dickinson's Dialogue, and got it reprinted
at Providence.   In a preface to it, they say :—

It seems people do not think in season what a sinful, God-provoking and
soul-destroying evil it is, to break over God's institutions.   First be wavering, unsettled, not steadfast in any right principles, nor in the covenant in
which their infant baptism declares them to be ; and then break covenant,
and separate themselves, as being in their own esteem holier and better
than others.   It is hid from them, that evil men and seducers wax worse
and worse.   It is hid from them, or rather they will not see, that they have
fell into the way of Cain, and are in danger of perishing in the gainsaying
of Core.

   [1]"On the 13th of June, 1765, Mr. Smith writes :—' I went to the Fast kept at
Bradford, and heard Mr. Flagg and Mr. Tucker preach, and in my opinion souls
are to be pitied who sit under such preaching.   Then went home, and something
expected to have more stones thrown into my chamber that night, after the ministers had reflected so much upon myself and the people who had separated from
them.' And this was in the very place where, eight months before, three or four
hundred people had assembled to hear the prayer and exhortation offered by Mr.
Smith at the evening worship of the family.   On the 10th of July he writes :—
' Went to Newbury to Mr. Ward's ordination.   Mr. Cleaveland and Mr. Lasley ordained him in the alley of Mr. Parsons's meeting-house.   I was not invited to dine
with the ministers, neither did I speak with one of them.'   Yet this was Mr. Cleaveland who had given Mr. Smith such a cordial welcome at Chebacco, and for whom
he had preached with such evident tokens of divine favor ; and this was Mr. Parsons's meeting-house, in which Mr. Smith had preached to about four thousand people, as it was supposed, less than a twelvemonth before."   Centennial Discourse of
the First Baptist Church, Haverhill ; Rev. A. S. Train, D. D. ; p. 20.—ED.
   [2]Discourse on Sober Mindedness, pp. 16, 17.

A sight of this discourse from the minister where the author was born, and from whom he separated, moved him to send the Doctor a printed letter in 1764, to open the injustice and abusive nature of such treatment of mankind;[1] to which he returned no answer, but has since been more friendly to the Baptists than before. As Dr. Gill had answered said dialogue, a copy of this new edition was sent to him. An addition to it was made in these words, viz. :—

St. Irenæus, who lived about a hundred and fourteen years after the death of Christ, being the disciple of St. Polycarp, who was the disciple of St. John the Evangelist, says, in his epistle, *Ad. Rom. lib.* 5, " The church received a tradition from the apostles, to administer baptism to little children, or infants." By *tradition*, [say these ministers,] the ancients meant the word of God, agreeable to that of the apostle, 2 Thess. ii. 15 ; iii. 6.[2]

Upon a sight of this, Dr. Gill published an advertisement, in the end of the London edition of his reply to Clarke, wherein he charges this passage as a forgery, and challenges the whole literary world to produce or point out any such passage in the writings of Irenæus, if they can ; and says, " What a wretched cause must infant baptism be, to require such management as this!" Various methods have been taken to wipe off this reproach, if possible. The first I heard of was, that those ministers sent to Yale College, and there found a Latin translation of Irenæus, which had that passage in it. I was afterwards told, by one of their most learned ministers, that the controversy turned upon men's

---

[1]"A Letter to the Rev. Mr. Benjamin Lord, of Norwich; occasioned by some harsh things which he has lately published against those who have dissented from his sentiments about the Ministry, the Church, and Baptism. By Isaac Backus, pastor of a church of Christ in Middleborough. ' Great men are not always wise. .... I said, I will also answer my part, I also will show mine opinion.' Job xxxii. 9, 17."

"April 9, 1764. Mr. Lord, the minister where I was born, has treated us, and the truths which we hold about the ministry, the church, and baptism, in so abusive a manner, in three pieces which he has published within this twelvemonth, that I have thought it to be real duty to write some things to him thereupon; and finished the same to-day." Backus's Manuscript Diary.—Ed.

[2]Dialogue, p. 5.

different opinions about the meaning of a Greek word or two ; which therefore could not properly be called a forgery. But in 1781, Mr. Moses Hemmingway, of Wells, published a piece upon infant baptism, wherein he would persuade us, that it was only a slip of memory in those ministers to write Irenæus, when Origen was the person intended ; and therefore that Dr. Gill discovered a very bad temper, in making such a noise about so harmless a mistake. To which I reply, that those ministers name Origen in their next paragraph, and say he lived about a hundred and ninety years after Christ. And how came a minister a hundred and eighty miles from them to know that they meant Origen, in the disputed passage, when it does not appear that they ever knew it themselves ? However, the use of the secular arm has ever been their worst argument.

When the Legislature at Boston broke in upon their own exempting law, in 1752, the Baptists were so much alarmed as to call several meetings,[1] and to elect Mr. John Proctor their agent, to carry their case to England ; and they subscribed above a hundred pounds therefor ; and he drew a remonstrance upon the subject, which was presented to the Assembly at Boston, in May, 1754. It stated matters so plainly, that a motion was made by some to take the signers of it into custody ;[2] but Governor Shirley, newly returned from Europe, convinced them of the impolicy of such a step ; and then they appointed a committee to confer in a friendly way with the Baptists ; and matters were shifted along, until the war came on, and their design for England was dropped. At length all their exempting laws for Baptists and Quakers expired, and the Assembly of November 23, 1757, made a new one, wherein both denominations were again included

[1] A meeting was held in Medfield, March 15, 1753, one in Bellingham, May 23, and one in Boston, February 6, 1754.—ED.

[2] A copy of this Remonstrance is preserved in the Backus Manuscripts. It is a paper of much merit and historic value. We hope the time is not far distant when this, and other papers of kindred interest relating to our early history in New England, will be published.—ED.

in one act.   By it no Baptists were to be exempted from
ministerial taxes, in the places where they lived, "but such
whose names shall be contained in a list or lists, to be taken
and exhibited on or before the 20th of July annually, to the
assessors of such town, district, precinct, or parish, and
signed by three principal members of the Anabaptist church
to which he or they belong, and the minister thereof, if any
there be ; who shall therein certify, that the persons whose
names are inserted in the said list or lists are really belonging thereto, that they verily believe them to be conscientiously of their persuasion, and that they frequently and
usually attend public worship in said church on the Lord's
days."   And the like was required of the Quakers.   It was
continued in force thirteen years ; and no tongue nor pen
can fully describe all the evils that were practiced under it.
Only because a difficulty arose, in 1763, between the Third
Baptist church in Middleborough and their minister, so as
to prevent his signing a new certificate for them, they were
all taxed to the parish worship.   And though, after distress
was made upon some, they were advised to apply to Plymouth Court for help ; yet, instead of affording any, they
took twenty dollars more from them.   And this was but a
trifle, compared with what was done at Haverhill.   For on
May 23, 1765, a paper was given to their parish assessors,
which said :—

This may inform you, that we who have formed ourselves into a Baptist
church, according to the laws of this government respecting Baptists,
called by some Anabaptists, do hereby certify, that we verily believe that
Major Edmond Moors, and Mr. John White, merchant, are conscientiously
of our persuasion, and that they do frequently and usually attend public
worship with us on the Lord's days.

This was signed by the minister and three principal members.   Yet after this was given, the first parish in said town
met, and voted a large sum of money to build them a new
meeting-house ; and taxed the Baptists with the rest, to pay
both that and the parish minister's salary.   And on Septem-

ber 15, 1766, they seized a large quantity of Mr. White's goods for that tax. For this he sued the assessors, at their County Court in December; but the action was continued till March, and then was carried up to their Superior Court by way of demur. It was to have been tried at Ipswich, in June, 1767; but it was then put off, because two Baptist gentlemen, a major and a captain, were not allowed to be witnesses of plain facts, concerning the seizure of said goods; neither could a few hours be obtained, though requested, to fetch other witnesses from Haverhill. Their adversaries then moved for an agreement, to have the case tried the next term, and that the same should be a final trial. This was concurred with, and the agreement was entered by the Clerk of the Court. The next term was at Salem, in November, when, after a fair and full hearing, the jury found for the Baptists thirty pounds damages and costs. This was immediately complained of as excessively high; therefore, rather than not have the matter settled, Mr. White consented to remit twelve pounds of it; and the Court gave judgment to have the rest paid. Yet the lawyers prevailed to have it referred to a future Court, whether they should not have another trial. And finally, in June, 1769, another trial was brought on, and the case was turned against the Baptists; which in all cost them about eighty pounds. The reason given for violating an agreement in Court, about a final trial, was that it was a matter of great consequence. And the plea which finally prevailed was built upon the ambiguous clause, belonging thereto, in their certificate law. It might mean a baptized church member, or only a steady worshipper therewith. The Court owned that the latter was the intent of the law; yet, because those words were not in their certificate, though that meaning was full in it, the case was turned against the Baptists. And the reason given against admitting any of them as witness of plain facts, was because they were parties concerned; that is, because the Congregationalists are the majority, they may violate their promises to the minority, in matters of great importance; and may construe words as they please, and refuse to allow the minority to be so much as witnesses, of plain facts, because, forsooth, the majority are not parties concerned!

The noise about this case reached as far as Philadelphia, and inquiry was made from thence, what it meant? We were told that a noted minister in New England, wrote for answer, that where the Baptists could get the power, they were as bad oppressors as those they complained so much of; which story was framed from the following actions:—On September 11, 1765, a Baptist minister[1] was ordained in South Brimfield, whose preaching was agreeable to some Pædobaptists near him, who disliked a minister then ordained in the east part of that district, of their denomination. They therefore got some of the Baptists to join with them in a petition for a new parish there. Upon which the Assembly at Boston, January 15, 1766, incorporated the west part of said district into a new parish, invested with all the powers and privileges, and subjected to all the duties of other parishes, without any mention of the Baptists in the whole act. Hereupon the majority of this parish made a tax for the Baptist minister, the most of whose church lived without those bounds; and some within never concurred therewith. When the year came round, those Pædobaptists moved to have the Baptist meeting-house voted to be the parish meeting-house; and because they would not thus give away a valuable house, built for a Baptist church, and chiefly by men who did not live in that parish, the first movers in said taxing scheme refused to pay their own tax. A gentleman from Boston was then their collector; and, seeing the matter must be tried, he told me that he resolved to act impartially; and therefore made distress upon one Baptist, who had ever opposed that scheme, and upon one of the other party. The case was then carried to Springfield Court, where it was soon turned against the Baptist minister;

[1]James Mellen.—ED.

and why ? he had studied both Greek and Latin, but he had neither an academical degree, nor an approbation from the majority of the ministers in that county, which was their legal test of orthodoxy.   He continued the beloved pastor of that church, until he finished his course with joy, August 5, 1769 ; after which that church sent a confession abroad, among their brethren, of their fault in not opposing said taxing scheme as they ought to have done, a copy whereof is before me.   How mean then was the pretence, that the Baptists hereby discovered as bad an inclination as their opponents did!

As great meanness was discovered at Haverhill.   The want of learned ministers had often been cast as a reproach upon the Baptist churches ; but when such a one was obtained there, all manner of evil reports concerning him could not suffice, without many instances of personal abuse.   A beetle was cast at him as he was walking the street one evening, which he took up and carried to his lodgings.   Also a stone, large enough to kill him, was cast through a window near his head, where he was in bed.   And his enemies went so far as to cut off his horse's mane and tail in the night, and to set up a paper upon the door where he quartered, threatening worse treatment to him if he did not depart ; and as he went to preach at Solomon Kimball's in Bradford, Amos Milliken, a Sheriff, came at the head of a mob to prevent it.   And as Mr. Smith was going to begin the worship of God, the chair he stood behind was snatched away ; and the man of the house tried in vain to quell the tumult, and to command peace in his own house.   At length Mr. Smith, with undaunted resolution, engaged in his public work, and the rioters withdrew, and gave no further disturbance to the exercise.   And though some of them laid wait for him in the evening, yet it was so ordered that he did not return home, until the coldness of the air forced them to quit their cruel design.   After Mr. Kimball's decease, his widow, who also was of the Baptist society in Haverhill, and had the same certified to Bradford assessors, yet was taxed to their parish worship. And late in a winter evening she was seized for it, and carried some miles; and then, calling at an inn, she was prevailed upon to pay the tax; after which she was left to return home, in the dead of the night, through frost and snow, to her three small, fatherless children.[1] Also the widow Mary Corliss, of Haverhill, a mem-

---

[1] Of the following letters the former is published in Life and Times of Backus, p. 184, and in Cramp's Baptist History, p. 530; the latter, we think, was never before published:—

"MR. BACKUS:—I understand that you are collecting materials for a Baptist History, in which you propose to let the public know how the Baptists have been oppressed in Massachusetts Bay. This is to let you know, that in the year 1768, in a very cold night in the winter, about nine or ten o'clock in the evening, I was taken prisoner and carried by the collector in the town where I live, from my family, consisting of three small children, in order to be put into jail. It being a severe cold night, I concluded, by advice, while I was detained at a tavern in the way to jail some hours, to pay the sum of about 4–8 L. M., [Legal Money] for which I was made a prisoner, it being for the ministerial rate. The reason why I refused paying it before, was because I was a Baptist, and belonged to the Baptist society in Haverhill, and had carried in a certificate to the assessors, as I suppose, according to law. Thus they dealt with a poor widow woman in Bradford, the relict of Solomon Kimball, late of said town, at whose house the Rev. Hezekiah Smith was shamefully treated by many of the people in Bradford; who came, headed by the Sheriff, Amos Milliken, at a time when Mr. Smith was to preach a sermon in our house at the request of my husband, and warmly contended with him, and threatened him if he did proceed. However, Mr. Smith went to begin service by singing, notwithstanding the noise, clamor, and threats of the people. But one of their number snatched the chair, behind which Mr. Smith stood, from before him; upon which my husband desired Mr. Smith to tarry a little till he had quelled the tumult; but all his endeavors to silence them were in vain. Upon which my husband desired Mr. Smith to begin public service; which accordingly he did, and went through then without further molestation.   "MARTHA KIMBALL.

"Bradford, September 2, 1774.

"N. B.—The above I can attest to. It may be observed that the tavern whither they took me, is about two miles from my house. After I had paid what they demanded, then I had to return to my poor fatherless children through the snow, on foot, in the dead of the night, exposed to the severity of the cold."

"MR. BACKUS:—I understand that you are preparing materials for a Baptist History of New England, in which you design to give an account of their sufferings in these parts. This is to inform you that amongst many others, I am a sufferer. For since I was baptized and belonged to the Baptist church in Haverhill, through mistake I was omitted in the list which was carried in to the assessors one year, which the West Parish of Haverhill, where I live, took the advantage of, and rated me in the ministerial rate; which I refused paying, because I was a Baptist, had a regular standing in the Baptist church, constantly met with them for public worship on the

ber of the Baptist church there, had one of her cattle taken away for a ministerial tax. "Thus," says she, "I was oppressed in a province where there is a universal cry for LIB-ERTY! the cry of the widow and fatherless they regard not!" So far from it, that further attempts were now made to inflame the resentment of the ruling party against all dissenters from their worship.

A book was published in 1767, and dispersed through New England, wherein it was said of the Baptist churches in general, "They little think, as I charitably believe, how far they join with the gates of hell, in opposing the church of Christ, by laying waste the nursery, out of which his vineyard is supplied."[1] As if natural growth could fit children for Christian communion; or, that a requiring fruits meet for repentance, in order for admission thereto, were a destroying of them. In the same book were many odious reports concerning the separations in and after 1744; several of which were not true in fact; and having introduced a plea in favor of those people, that they are not such now, the writer says, " It is readily granted, that they are now much more moderate and civil than they were in that day, are very peaceable, kind, obliging, good neighbors. . . . . But what does this reasoning argue? Why it only shows that they have lost a degree of their own original spirits, as Separates."[2] And yet he began his preface with saying, " The special occasion of the following discourses was, the revival of the spirit and principles of Separation and Anabaptism." Accord-

---

Lord's days, helped support the ministry in said Baptist church, and never went to hear the Congregational ministers in the West Parish, where I live. However, they took one of my cattle out of my yard, by distress, and sold it at a public outcry for said rate. Thus I was oppressed, a few years past, in the province where there is such a universal cry for liberty. The cry of the fatherless and the widow they regarded not.

" Haverhill, September, 1774.

"P. S.—The above distress was made in the year 1770. This I can attest to.
" MARY CORLISS.—ED.

[1]Fish's Nine Sermons, p. 95.   [2]Ibid. p. 158.

ing, therefore, to his own testimony, they were peaceable, kind, obliging, good neighbors, after that spirit was revived. Neither were his party any more consistent with themselves in a following publication. For upon the British claims of taxing America, an evident design was forming to establish Episcopacy therein; to guard against which, it was said, in 1768:—

We are, in principle, against all civil establishments in religion. .... It does not [indeed] appear to us, that God has entrusted the State with a right to make religious establishments. If the State in England has this delegated authority, must it not be owned, that the State in China, in Turkey, in Spain, has this authority also? .... And as they must severally be supposed to exert this authority in establishments conformable to their own sentiments in religion, what can the consequence be but infinite damage to the cause of God and true religion? And such in fact has been the consequence of these establishments *in all ages, and all places*.[1]

And this publication appeared of such importance, to the annual Association of ministers from all parts of Connecticut, in June, 1768, that they published a letter of thanks to Dr. Chauncy therefor, in a Boston newspaper. Yet, for these forty years, he has written the most to uphold their religious establishments in New England, of any man upon earth. And a still greater demonstration of the pernicious effects thereof is before us.

[1]Chauncy against Chandler, pp. 152, 153.

CHAPTER XXI.

Ashfield planted.—Lawful rights denied to the Baptists therein.—To which new acts were added.—And slanderous publications.—Likewise a spiteful prosecution.—Relief from England.—Remarks thereon.—Oppression at Montague.—And at
Berwick.

A grant was made in 1735, to Ebenezer Hunt and others,
of a township six miles square. westward of Deerfield. A
plan of it was to be drawn in sixty-three equal shares ; one
of which was to be for their first minister, one for the ministry, and one for the school ; and certain improvements were
to be made upon each of the other shares, within three years
after the confirmation of the plan. They were also to settle
a learned, orthodox minister, and to build and finish a convenient meeting-house for public worship. By reason of
succeeding wars, the planting of that place was delayed until 1751. In the mean time a complaint was entered to the
church in South Hadley, that one of their members had
propagated a reproachful lie concerning Chileab Smith, a
father therein. But the complaint was disregarded, which
moved him to inquire into the constitution of the church ;
and, to his surprise, though the words of their covenant implied a profession of saving faith, yet he found that such a
profession was not held to be necessary in order for their
communion. He then labored to convince the church that
this was a dangerous error ; and, being invited, he went to
a meeting of ministers at Hatfield, August 6, 1750, and laid

11

before them many scriptural reasons against it. But they gave him no satisfaction, only referred him to Mr. Edwards, who was dismissed from Northampton two months before, for rejecting that principle. Edwards approved of Smith's reasons against it, but not of a separation therefor. But as Smith judged otherwise, he openly withdrew from the church ; and in 1751 he removed to Huntstown, with eight children, when there were but two or three families therein. Others came in soon after, and lived without public worship for some time ; and then eternal concernments were so clearly opened to his mind, that he called the inhabitants together, and prayed with them, and expounded the Scriptures to them, to such good purpose that his children and many others were hopefully converted. In November, 1753, his eldest son was called to preach the gospel ; and, with great hazard and expense, they kept their station, and maintained public worship, through a bloody Indian war of seven years' continuance ; near the close whereof they were led into believers' baptism, and became an organized church on August 20, 1761 ; by assistance from Killingly, Sturbridge, and Stafford, and by the close of that year the church increased to twenty-four members, half of whom were males.

In 1762, a State tax was imposed upon that plantation ; and as the law exempts all settled ministers therefrom, two of their assessors allowed their minister that privilege. But, for this, the other assessor entered a complaint against them to Springfield Court. The Baptists desired time to prove that their minister was regularly ordained ; but the Court refused it, or to allow of any appeal from their judgment ; and extorted a large fine and costs from them, for not taxing their minister contrary to law. When he was ordained, there were but five families, out of nineteen in the place, against him ; but, the danger of the war being over, others moved in, and in February, 1763, they ordained Mr. Jacob Sherwin over that party ; and not only gave him all the privileges of the first minister of the town, but also a hundred pounds settlement and sixty-four pounds a year salary, to which they added a large sum to build them a meeting-house, and taxed the Baptist minister and his people with others to pay it. The plantation being only a proprietyship, it was said the exempting law for Baptists did not extend there ; and when it was incorporated in 1765, by the name of Ashfield, the word *Support* was artfully inserted, which had no place in their original grant, nor in the incorporating acts of the towns of Charlemont and Lanesborough, passed at the same session. New taxes were hereupon imposed upon the Baptists in Ashfield, to support a minister whom they never chose ; but their oppressors at length found them-selves ensnared in the work of their own hands. For pro-prietors and inhabitants are two distinct bodies of men in law, governed by different rules ; the votes of the latter be-ing equal, but of the former according to their interest ; so that the vote of a proprietor, who owns five hundred acres, is equal to ten inhabitants who own but fifty acres apiece ; and by their act of incorporation, the power of taxation in Ashfield was put into the hands of the inhabitants and pro-prietors, both of whom could not do it together, nor either of them apart, according to that act.

This confusion afforded some respite to the Baptists ; but hearing of further designs against them, they came to the Assembly at Boston, of May 25, 1768, with a memorial of their services and sufferings in promoting that plantation, and a prayer for a full exemption from taxes to a worship that they did not join with.[1] A committee of three was appointed upon it ; two of whom brought in a report to grant the petition ; but Edson, their chairman, was for giv-ing time to their opposites to bring in objections; and to him the Assembly hearkened, and on May 31 ordered that the clerks of the inhabitants and proprietors of Ashfield should be notified of this memorial, that they might bring in objec-tions against it, on the second Tuesday of the next session

[1] This petition is in the Life and Times of Backus, pp. 346, 347.—Ed.

of the Assembly, and that the further collection of taxes
from the petitioners should be suspended in the mean time.
Colonel Israel Williams was received a representative from
Hatfield the next day, who was the most resolute judge in
fining the Ashfield assessors in 1762; and before the close
of this session a new act was passed which took the power
of taxation out of the hands of the inhabitants of Ashfield,
three years after the town was incorporated, and empowered
the proprietors to impose what taxes they judged proper
for the support of their minister, as well as other uses, and
to lay the same wholly upon the lands, in whose hands
soever they might be, which were to be sold, if the owners
refused to pay the tax. This was done under the same
influence which has since involved the nation in blood and
confusion. For in the preceding winter our Assembly came
into a resolution to write letters to sister colonies, to request
them to unite in the use of prudent means against the
attempts that were making, to bring America to be taxed
where they were not represented. On June 30, our House
of Representatives were required to rescind that resolution;
which Edson, Williams, and fifteen more, voted to do; but
ninety-two members rejected that arbitrary mandate, one of
whom was Captain Benjamin White, a Baptist, representative from Middleborough. For this noble stand against tyranny, that House was dissolved, and no other called through
the year; so that the Baptists could have no hearing, while
power was on the side of their oppressors. The latter
advertised their lands to be sold on May 3, 1769. But when
they met, such defects were pointed out in their proceedings,
that the sale was omitted; and each party came with memorials to the Assembly of May 31.[1] Contention betwixt the
House and the Governor served as an excuse for not hearing the Baptists, but their oppressors were heard; and on
July 5, it was resolved, "That all the votes and transactions

---

[1] See extracts from the memorial of the Baptists, Life and Times of Backus, pp.
347, 348.—ED.

of the said town of Ashfield, in their several town-meetings, since their incorporation to this time, be and are hereby ratified and confirmed ; any omissions or neglect of making due and proper returns on the several warrants for calling the same meetings, or any of them, notwithstanding." Williams and Leonard (two of the Mandamus Counsellors in 1774) were of the committee who framed this resolve, though it was not passed into a law. July 15, the Assembly was prorogued to January, and in the meantime a new tax was imposed in Ashfield, and the Baptist lands were advertised to be sold April 4, 1770. In January they sent to Boston, but the Assembly was prorogued to March 15, when they sat at Cambridge, but did not receive the Baptists' petition until the 27th, and it was dismissed April 4, the day their lands were to be sold. Some friends in Boston laid the cruelty hereof before some of the members so plainly, that their petition was resumed on April 10 ; but instead of their granting any relief, they were only put to more costs, to notify their oppressors to bring in objections. On April 4, the assessors of Ashfield met, and sold three hundred and ninety-eight acres of the Baptists' lands to support the worship of the opposite party. For a demand upon the Baptist minister of one pound, two shillings, they sold ten acres of his home lot. His father had one of the best orchards in the town, which is of special service in a new place ; yet twenty acres of improved land, containing the main of his orchard, with a burying-yard, and a small dwelling-house, were struck off to Elijah Wells, for thirty-five shillings ; who, on May 4, came and forcibly entered upon it, and measured it off ; and the next day came and pulled up a number of the smaller apple trees, and carried them away, and offered to sell the house. These facts were proved by a number of witnesses before authority, though, to shift off the odium they were exposed to, by a new survey, they left out the house and burying-yard, and then accused the Baptists of falsehood in the first account. But nothing better could be expected, from men who could deal so unjustly, and could laugh at a mock sermon, delivered by Wells upon that occasion, which breathed as great cruelty as words could express. Repeated applications were made to the Legislature for help, but in vain ; and the Baptist agent was at last told plainly, that it was not worth while to wait any longer, for they would keep them under the law by which those lands were sold, as long as they saw fit. Receiving such a plain declaration from a member of the Assembly, in the presence of others, he went and acquainted the Baptist ministers of Boston therewith, who thought proper to publish an advertisement to all the Baptists in this province, dated July 31, requesting them to bring in exact accounts of their cases and sufferings to their ensuing Association,[1] " When meas-

---

[1] A yearly meeting of their churches, begun at Warren, September 8, 1767, called The Warren Association.—B.

This important movement in the history of New England Baptists, the founding of the Warren Association, merits a more extended notice. The leader in the movement was James Manning, pastor of the church in Warren and President of Rhode Island College. Wishing "to unite all the churches of his faith and order in New England in an association similar to the one formed in Philadelphia," " he submitted his plan to the members of his own church, who cordially seconded his views, as appears from a formal vote on the subject, which we find recorded under date of August 28, 1766." See Manning and Brown University, p. 74. Other pastors entered into the project, and a conference was called, in which eleven churches were represented. The pastors and delegates of only four churches, Warren, Bellingham, Haverhill and Second Middleborough, were ready for organization, the rest fearing lest the new body would conflict with church independence. Isaac Backus, the first Clerk, commenced his Minutes as follows :—

"Whereas there hath of late been a great increase of Baptists in New England, which yet have not such an acquaintance with each other and orderly union together as ought to be, it has been thought by many that a general meeting or association might be a likely means to remove this evil, and to promote the general good of the churches. Therefore, a number of elders, being occasionally together last year, did appoint a meeting at Warren, in Rhode Island Colony, on September 8, 1767, and sent an invitation to others of their brethren to meet them there, to confer upon these affairs. Accordingly a considerable number of elders and brethren met at the time and place appointed; and Elder John Gano, from New York, opened the meeting with a suitable sermon from Acts, xv. 9."

The Association soon proved an important agency in the struggle for religious freedom. In 1769 it adopted the following "plan to collect grievances."

"Whereas complaints of oppressions, occasioned by a non-conformity to the religious establishment in New England, have been brought to this Association, and whereas the laws obtained for preventing and redressing such oppressions have,

ures will be resolutely adopted, for obtaining redress from
another quarter than that to which repeated application hath
been made unsuccessfully. Nay, complaints, however just
and grievous, have been treated with indifference, and
scarcely, if at all, credited." Accounts were accordingly
brought to a meeting of fifteen churches at Bellingham,
September 11, which unanimously resolved to apply to the
King in Council for relief, if it could not be obtained here ;
and they made choice of agents and a committee for the purpose ; and wrote to their southern brethren for assistance in

upon trial, been found insufficient (either through defect in the laws themselves, or
iniquity in the execution thereof) ; and whereas humble remonstrances and petitions have not been duly regarded, but the same oppressive measures continued:
This is to inform all the oppressed Baptists in New England that the Association of
Warren, (in conjunction with the Western or Philadelphia Association) is determined to seek remedy for their brethren where a speedy and effectual one may be
had. In order to pursue this resolution by petition and memorial, the following
gentlemen are appointed to receive well attested grievances, to be by them transmitted to the Rev. Samuel Stillman of Boston; namely, Rev. Hezekiah Smith of
Haverhill, Rev. Isaac Backus of Middleborough, Mr. Richard Montague of Sunderland, Rev. Joseph Meacham of Enfield, and Rev. Thomas Whitman of Groton in
Connecticut." Backus's Manuscript Minutes, copied and preserved by Rev. S.
Hall.

In pursuance of this plan, the committee published the advertisement above
referred to. It appeared in the Boston Evening Post of August 20, 1770, and was
as follows :—

"To the Baptists in the Province of the Massachusetts Bay, who are, or have
been, oppressed in any way on a religious account. It would be needless to tell you
that you have long felt the effects of the laws by which the religion of the government in which you live is established. Your purses have felt the burden of ministerial rates ; and when these would not satisfy your enemies, your property hath
been taken from you and sold for less than half its value. These things you cannot forget. You will therefore readily hear and attend, when you are desired to
collect your cases of suffering, and have them well attested ; such as, the taxes you
have paid to build meeting-houses, to settle ministers and support them, with all the
time, money and labor you have lost in waiting on courts, feeing lawyers, &c. ; and
bring or send such cases to the Baptist Association to be held at Bellingham ; when
measures will be resolutely adopted for obtaining redress from another quarter than
that to which repeated application hath been made unsuccessfully. Nay, complaints,
however just and grievous, have been treated with indifference, and scarcely, if at
all, credited. We deem this our conduct perfectly justifiable ; and hope you will
pay a particular regard to this desire, and be exact in your accounts of your sufferings, and punctual in your attendance at the time and place above mentioned.

"Boston, July 31st, 1770."

—Ed.

the design.[1]   This alarmed some politicians at Boston, who
urged the Baptists to present an address to our Legislature,
and they promised to exert their influence in their favor.   A
memorial was therefore drawn, and was signed in behalf of
the Baptist churches, by their ministers at Boston and Haverhill ;[2] wherein the late testimony of our Assembly, against
the taxing of people where they are not represented, was
commended, and this liberty was pleaded for in the church,
and in particular that the said Ashfield law might be repealed,
and their property be restored ; that others who had suffered in such ways might recover damages, and equal religious liberty be allowed to all.   Soon after this was received
by the Assembly at Cambridge, a piece was published from
thence, dated October 22, 1770, representing that the Baptists had complained without any just reason at all, and that
it would be serviceable to have an authentic account of the
Ashfield affair published.   And, after many great, swelling
words about the charity and lenity of these times, the writer
said, " It was astonishing to most people among us, to hear
the newspaper complaints exhibited by the Baptists ; they
could not so much as guess from whence they could arise."
This was inserted in three or four Boston papers.[3]   And
then, on November 15, the Assembly gave orders that Ashfield proprietors should be notified to bring in objections
against the first prayer of the Baptists' memorial, to their
next session.   And their old certificate law being out of date,
a new one was framed, which changed their title to Antipædobaptists, and changed the time of giving in certificates to
the first of September ; which were to be signed by three or
more principal members, and the minister, if there be any.
The word Congregation was to be used instead of the word
Church ; and the parishes were empowered to vote the Bap-

---

[1] A Circular Letter, written by President Manning, was sent to the churches, requesting them to collect money to defray the expense of this appeal to the king.   It
is given in full in Manning and Brown University, pp. 185, 186.—ED.

[2] It is published in The Life and Times of Backus, pp. 177—180.--ED.

[3] It is in the Boston Evening Post of October 29.—ED.

tists clear, if they pleased, without certificates. But the word *Conscientiously* was still retained, and the certificates were required to be given in annually to parish assessors.

Mr. Davis, clerk of their committee, now called them together ; and, upon examination, they declared themselves not satisfied with this law, and they advised Davis to answer the Cambridge piece. He did so, in the Massachusetts Gazette of December 27, by giving a plain and concise view of the Ashfield affair, and asserting that it was the sole cause of their complaining publicly at this time ; and signed himself A Baptist. But instead of any fair reply, a writer appeared in the Boston Evening Post of January 7, 1771, saying:—

> There is a little upstart gentleman, lately settled in [this] town, who calls himself A Baptist ; and the youth discovers a most insufferable arrogance and self-sufficiency. .... I very much suspect, that he is one of those deluded young men, who are employed [by the enemies of America] to defame and blacken the colonies, and this town and province in particular. .... I am of the same persuasion in religion with this young hero, ... and I cannot say what the General Assembly could do for the Baptists in general, or the Ashfield brethren in particular, that they have not done. .... And I believe this is the opinion of the Baptists in general, and of all others but enthusiastical bigots.

And he had the impudence to annex to this, and much more of the same kind, the signature of A Catholic Baptist. When Mr. Davis came to see it, he said he would never put pen to paper to answer such mean and dirty stuff. In the Gazette of February 7, came out another piece, from a minister near Ashfield, supposed to be of Deerfield, who said, " It is a very common observation among us, that the people called Separate Baptists in these parts will not stick at any false representations to serve their purpose ;" which he attempted to prove by facts. But Elder Smith, of Ashfield, came down and answered him in the same paper, of March 21, when, from public records, he fairly turned that charge back upon the minister who advanced it.

The Assembly met at Cambridge six days after, to whom
was exhibited so large a bundle of reasons against their
granting the first prayer of the Baptists' memorial, as cost
them twenty shillings to get a copy of it from the Secretary,
it being twelve pages in folio.   And yet there was no attempt
in it to prove that the word *Support* was in the original grant
of Ashfield, nor other points that were truly to the purpose.
Two passages in it may give a proper idea of the whole performance.   They say, "Natural rights are in this province
wholly superceded in this case by civil obligation, and in
matters of taxation, individuals cannot with the least propriety plead them."   Exactly the doctrine of the British
Court at this time ; but which never could be carried into
effect at any time without covering it with religious pretences;
therefore, they went on to flatter our rulers in that respect,
and to say of the Baptists, "Some have had the effrontery
to say, that the standing ministry is corrupt, ministers themselves unconverted, the churches impure and unholy, admitting unconverted and unsanctified persons into their communion."   As if it were a very uncharitable and daring
thing, for any not to look upon them to be a sanctified people, when they absolutely refused to profess themselves to
be such !   For our excellent Edwards was rejected by that
county with much heat and bitterness, only for his insisting
upon such a profession from communicants.   We had direct
intelligence that this piece was drawn in Judge Williams's
family, and it was signed in the name of the proprietors of
Ashfield, by Jonathan Taylor, Timothy Lewis, Samuel Beld-
ing, Benjamin Phillips, Philip Phillips.   The three latter were
the assessors who sold the lands before mentioned, and the
last of them was the man who got his brother assessors fined
in 1762, for not taxing their minister contrary to law.   The
Council and House joined in a committee upon said memorial ; and they say in their report :—

There is an essential difference between persons being taxed where they
are not represented, therefore against their wills, and being taxed when

represented, and when what is taxed is only in consequence of what was the very condition of their grant. .... What other method can be devised, but to sell the lands of those who *conscientiously say that they will not be as good as their word, or keep their covenant*, though it be so greatly to the prejudice of the public! .... Your committee find, that in the sale of those lands there was no unfairness, but every thing was quite fair, quite neighborly, and quite legal. .... It is our opinion that said petition be dismissed.

W. BRATTLE, by order.

Accordingly, on April 24, the Council voted to dismiss it. And though the House was alarmed, and did not concur with this, but proposed to have a bill brought in to repeal the Ashfield law, yet their proposal was rejected, and the petition with it. And what a cloud was hereby brought over an oppressed people! On the side of the oppressors was power, but they seemed to have no helper. But, behold! in a Boston paper of October 21, it was declared that the King in Council had disannulled that law. What a surprise did this occasion! How could so despicable a people get access to the throne, and obtain such an act, especially in so short a time! However it was soon said, that there was a man in Hatfield that would hinder the Baptists from reaping any advantage thereby. This was a mystery, till it was explained on November 8, when two officers, with a numerous aid, came to old Mr. Smith's house before he was up in the morning, with a warrant from Judge Williams to seize his person, and to search his house and shop for bad money. Smith readily promised the use of his keys, and desired that no lock might be broken, and also that he might have liberty to pray with his family before he was carried off. Liberty for prayer was granted by one officer, but in the mean time the other broke the lock of his shop, and damaged his goods there, and afterwards in his house ; and then he was carried before a Court at Judge Williams's, where he was compelled to stand till ten witnesses were examined ; from whom no evidence could be obtained against him, " nor any circumstance tending to prove the indictment," as seven of them gave from under their hands a few days after. Yet Mr.

Smith was held a prisoner through the night, in a cold room, and denied either bed or fire, to the great injury of his body, he being above sixty years old, and infirm before. In the morning Judge Williams insinuated several things against him, without suffering him to make any answer, and bound him over to their next Superior Court, in large bonds with sureties. Like warrants were issued, it was said, against their pastor, who then happened to be absent on a journey. Reports were therefore industriously spread in the country, that notwithstanding all their talk, those Baptists were a parcel of money makers, and their minister was gone to scatter it, and would never dare to return. But herein they were soon found liars; and though the country was ransacked in the spring for witnesses against his father, yet they all failed them. At last a man was brought near thirty miles for the purpose, who testified to the Court at Northampton that he should not know the man if he met him in the room. So he was discharged, and the law was open for him to sue for damages for this malicious prosecution. But, lo! a bankrupt, son to the minister of Sunderland, had been brought over the river to enter the complaint against him, so that he might never obtain any recompense in this world. Yet God often takes the wise in their own craftiness.

When such noise was made at Boston about the Ashfield affair, Governor Hutchinson happened to look and find that the word *Support* was not in the original grant of those lands; and perhaps he might hope, that by relieving the Baptists, he should draw them to his side of the controversy betwixt America and Britain. Be that as it may, he privately sent for one of their committee, and advised him to send the Ashfield law to a friend in London, who might present it to the King in Council; and he promised to write to Governor Bernard, who passed it, to use his influence to have it repealed. This was done, and its repeal was effected, and then their oppressors had their turn at waiting upon one Assembly after another unsuccessfully; for though several acts were framed for them, yet the consent of the Governor could not be obtained, till they found out what his mind was, and conformed to it.   In January, 1773, the Assembly appointed a committee out of their members, to go up to Ashfield, and to hear both parties, and then to make a tax to pay all that they judged to be behind concerning Mr. Sherwin's settlement and meeting-house, and the charges which had arisen about the same ; and what they judged any of the Baptists had paid more than this, should be refunded to them, and for the future they should stand upon the same footing with their brethren elsewhere.   The doings of that committee were confirmed by a subsequent act in February, 1774, and the small tax which was laid upon some of the Baptists they paid, and by this time their oppressors were sick of their own minister, and he was dismissed from his office, so that they lost the right in the town which they took so much pains to wrest from Elder Smith, besides the other unspeakable evils and scandals which sprang from thence.

This account is carefully taken from our printed laws, journals of the House of Representatives, and other writings and testimonies; and our opponents are welcome to point out any mistakes therein, if they can.   A gentleman of great influence in our Legislature informed me, that it was asserted in the Assembly, that those petitioners acted with the rest in settling Mr. Sherwin, but now wanted to slip out their necks, and leave an intolerable burthen upon their neighbors, which story had great influence to hinder the granting of any relief to the Baptists.   Whereas, if they had been informed of it, they would have demonstrated that this story was a glaring falsehood, as also was the report of the committee whereof Brattle was chairman; for Wells, who bought Smith's lot, sued him for cutting the grass upon it in August, 1770, and upon trial in the winter, the Court turned the case against Wells, because the sale was *not legal*, two months before Brattle reported that it was *quite legal*.

The law being repealed, all those sales of land fell, of course. And who can describe all their guilt in those transactions! If it had been right to tax the Baptists to Sherwin's settlement and meeting-house, taxes of six times the value of his settlement had been laid upon them, before the law was made to sell their lands for his support; yet, for three years after, their oppressors asserted with brazen impudence, that those taxes were only to fulfil the original condition of their grant. But according to what our delegates to Congress asserted in Philadelphia, October 14, 1774, before many witnesses, the settling of Elder Smith in Ashfield in 1761 fulfilled that condition, and the denying of him the privileges of the first minister of the town was a violation of the faith of government; for which, as well as for their great trouble and expenses, caused by subsequent acts, they have received no recompense.

Because Governor Hutchinson procured relief to that society, some have blamed the Baptists for not adhering to him and his party in the general contest betwixt Britain and America; but they had good reasons against it then, and have greater since. For many copies of his letters have been found among us, one of which is dated from Boston, January 23, 1771, directed to Governor Bernard, wherein Hutchinson expressed his earnest desire that Castle William might not again be put under the pay of this Province,[1] and that the power of choosing the Council might be taken from our representatives; and, said he, "Something. I repeat it, must be done this session, to shew the sense parliament has of our past conduct." And after further urging to inflammatory measures, he says:—

The Baptists have made a little stir, and complain of being oppressed; but in general they have all the liberty which can consist with a legal establishment for maintaining public worship, without which we should be worse than we are. No Baptist in principle is obliged to pay to ministers

[1] In a clandestine way he had given it up to the British troops, September 10, 1770.

upon the establishment. All who attend a Baptist minister are not exempt; if they should be, the congregations would be broke to pieces in all parts of the province.

He then gave reasons why the Ashfield law ought to be repealed, and said to Bernard : —

I suppose you would not have passed it, if you had considered the force of the word *Support*, and that it militated with the general law in favor of Baptists. I have no doubt it was artfully slipt in by one of the Hampshire representatives.

Equal religious liberty, therefore, was far from his design, though he appeared for their help in that case. And the artful representative referred to was, for being one of the seventeen *rescinders*,[1] set up as Chief Judge of their County Court; in which office he oppressed other Baptists in the following manner.

They formed a regular church in Montague, July 1, 1765; and gave certificates to parish assessors according to law ; yet they were taxed to other worship, and distress was made therefor. Several attempts were made in parish meetings to have this disorder rectified, but in vain, therefore Samuel Harvey sued the Montague assessors for a cow and a calf, that had been taken from him for a tax to their minister. After the writ was served, a parish meeting was called, which voted to stand by their assessors, and said they meant to try the merits of the cause, whether these were the Baptists whom the law exempted or not. When Judge Williams came to deliver the case to the jury, he did not call that point in question, yet he said, " The law says, the certificate shall be signed by three principal members of the Baptist church, and the plaintiff is one of the signers, and he can- not certify for himself, therefore there are but two, and the law says there shall be three." To him the jury hearkened, and turned the case against the Baptists, in August, 1769.

---

[1] In the General Assembly of Massachusetts, June, 1768, a vote was taken upon the question of rescinding the measures of the previous Assembly in opposition to British oppression. Seventeen voted in favor of rescinding and ninety-two in oppo- sition. See p. 152; Bancroft, Vol. VI. p. 165.—ED.

They appealed to the Superior Court the next month; but the action was continued till September, 1770, when the case was called, and the witnesses appeared; but because they were Baptists, they were not admitted, and the case was again put off, and the Baptists were required to pay half the jury's fees.   At last, on May 1, 1771, a trial was brought on, when Judge Oliver and others turned the case against the Baptists, upon the same point as Williams had before done. Upon which it is to be remarked, that before 1752, their laws required but two signers to a certificate; and the law they now acted upon allowed of no more than three, where there was not a minister, as was the case at Montague; and the signers could not have been exempted, if their names had not been in the list.   Yet because they were strained upon, and not others, the case was turned against them, without trying the merits of the cause, as was promised; and after the expense of above a hundred dollars, the Baptists were left without any hope of remedy from our Courts. To worry them out, distress was again made upon their committee, and not others.   A yoke of oxen was taken from Harvey, a cow from Sawyer, and Major Richard Montague was seized and carried six miles toward the prison, kept all night, and then released, and the officer went back and took a swine that he was fatting for his family,   O how dark was this cloud over that little flock!   Yet one of them said to his brethren, " Who knows but that God will bring good out of this evil? though we are stripped of our substance, yet unborn ages may praise him for this."   Yea, they themselves have lived to see some happy fruits of their sufferings.   One thing which gave a check to oppression, was a determination of authority, that the ministers of Baptist churches were lawful ministers, so as to have a right to marry people, and to be exempted from civil taxes.   This was determined by the Superior Court, in one trial at Worcester, and another in Hampshire; the last of which was this year.

None of their opponents appeared willing to release them, till they had tried the matter, and were taught the folly of oppression by experience. If we turn our eyes from the west to the east, we shall see further evidence of this. By assistance from Haverhill, a Baptist church was regularly constituted at Berwick, in the county of York, June 28, 1768. Mr. Joshua Emery was their teacher, though not ordained. They gave certificates according to law, yet were all taxed to other ministers; and John Gowen was imprisoned therefor in December, 1769. The like was done to Mr. Emery the next month; and he sued for recompense in both cases, but they were delayed till July, 1770, when Emery asked for a summons to bring the collector with his warrant. The judge ordered the clerk to give one, to bring the collector with his original list. He came with it, but not the warrant, and the counsel for the defendant said there could be no trial without the warrant; and the case was turned against Emery. He appealed to the Superior Court, where the collector was brought with his warrant; but then he swore that he did not take Emery as a prisoner. Emery told the Court that he did take him and carry him to York, and held him as a prisoner thirty hours, and requested time to prove it, either now or at the next term. This was denied him, and judgment was given against him. With difficulty he obtained a continuance of his friend's case; and the parish committee promised to let the Baptists alone till that case was tried. Yet in a few days another tax was imposed and demanded. Upon this a complaint was entered to authority against the former collector for false swearing, and he was bound over to Court upon it; but he repeatedly said, he hoped the day of death would come before that day of trial. And behold! he died suddenly just before the Court! Yet this did not hinder the next collector from coming and seizing Mr. Emery's horse, while he was visiting a sick person. The parish assessors were sued therefor

12

in January, 1771, and though they tried a number of crooked ways to delay the matter, and to defeat the design, yet both this and his friend's case, that was continued, were finally turned against the assessors.   John Emery, of York, joined to said society, and got the same certified to the assessors of the parish where he lived ; yet he was taxed to their worship, and when he was from home, a collector came and seized his pewter therefor.   But experience has since taught their oppressors to cease from such violence.   This account is carefully taken from authentic vouchers now in my hands.

CHAPTER XXII.

A small Baptist church at Newton, in the south borders of New Hampshire, formed out of a Separate society there in 1755, was the only church of that denomination in that province, before 1770. In and after the year 1764, many were hopefully converted in several parts of it; where believers' baptism has since been introduced in the following manner:—About the year 1720, one Scammon, of Stratham, on Piscataqua River, married Rachel Thurber, from Rehoboth, who was a firm believer in the Baptist principles; but the country round her was so full of prejudices against them, that in forty years she could gain no more than one person to join with her therein; and that was a pious woman in the neighborhood, who travelled fifty-five miles to Boston, and was baptized by Elder Bound. But Mrs. Scammon had such a desire to have others enlightened, that having obtained Norcott's Plain Discourse upon Baptism, she carried it to Boston, with a design to get it reprinted upon her own cost; though when she came to speak to a printer about it, he informed her that he had then one hundred and ten copies of that book on hand; whereupon she purchased them all, and came home and gave them away to her acquaintance, and to any people who would accept of them; by which means they were scattered through the country, and among poor people in new plantations. And she would often say to her pious neighbors, that she was fully persuaded, that a church of Christian Baptists would be formed in Stratham, though she might not live to see it. This came to pass soon after her death, and the like in other places, by the following means:—One Samuel Shepard, born at Salisbury, near Newbury, in 1739, was brought to the knowledge of internal religion when very young; and he learned the art of physic, and settled in the practice of it in Nottingham, near Piscataqua River. He had no knowledge of Mrs. Scammon, nor of any other Baptists, till he happened to see, in a house that he visited, one of Norcott's books; and upon reading it, there appeared such a fair examination of the Scriptures therein, as struck his mind with conviction that believers' baptism was the truth. But it being a principle hardly named among his acquaintance, the conviction went off for some years. In the mean time, as Mr. Ebenezer Jones, a Baptist minister, travelled through Stratham, he preached a lecture, which was the means of the conversion of a young man named Eliphaleth Smith, who was afterwards called to preach the gospel; and in January, 1770, was ordained the pastor of a Congregational church in a part of Nottingham called Deerfield. In May following, as he was preaching to his people upon the obligation that all who love Christ are under to keep his commandments, the command to believe and be baptized was opened with peculiar clearness to the preacher's mind; upon which he immediately found such a want of any warrant for bringing their infants, as caused him to pass it over in his sermon. and put him and most of his church upon such an examination of that matter, as convinced them that they had not been rightly baptized.

Before this, Mr. Shepard, by hearing about Elder Smith, of Haverhill, was brought again to think of what he had read in Norcott's book, and to search the Scriptures concerning baptism, and was thereby convinced that the arguments for infant baptism were groundless, and was made willing to become a Baptist. Hereupon he improved opportunities of discoursing upon the subject with Christians of his acquaintance, which was large ; inquiring whether he and they might not have been heretofore mistaken about the subjects and manner of baptism? Many were hereby put upon searching into the matter, which issued in a turn of mind to believers' baptism. And Mr. Hezekiah Smith was sent for to Deerfield, where, on June 14, 1770, he baptized their minister and thirteen others ;[1] and within seven days he baptized twenty-four more, who belonged chiefly to Nottingham, Brentwood, and Stratham ; and among those thirty-eight persons were a Congregational minister and two deacons, with Mr. Shepard ; who, by special teaching, was brought freely to begin the great work of preaching the gospel on July 8, 1770, and he soon had some evident seals of his ministry. Mr. Smith, of Deerfield, with the most of his church, were united and established as pastor and flock in the Baptist order. Churches in that order were also formed in Stratham, Brentwood, and Nottingham ; who all united in calling Mr. Shepard to receive ordination, and for the present to take the pastoral care of them. He was accordingly ordained at Stratham, September 25, 1771 ; and the ordination sermon, preached by Mr. Stillman, of Boston, was printed, together with the charge, by Mr. Smith, of Haverhill, and the right hand of fellowship by President Manning, of Providence ;

---

[1] They first sent for President Manning, but, on account of the distance, he excused himself, and Mr. Smith went in his stead. Mr. Smith wrote in his diary as follows :—" Wednesday, June 13th. Went to Deerfield, and preached from Acts xi. 23, 'Who, when he came, and had seen the grace of God, was glad, and exhorted them all, that with purpose of heart they would cleave unto the Lord.' After sermon, I examined the Rev. Eliphalet Smith and a number of his hearers for baptism. Thursday, 14th. I preached in Mr. Smith's meeting-house from Col. ii. 11, 12. After sermon I baptized fourteen persons." See Manning and Brown University, p. 122.—ED.

and their principles have now had a very extensive spread in those parts. Thus Mrs. Scammon's bread, cast upon the water, seems to have been found after many days ; the books that she freely dispersed being picked up, and made useful to many. Neither did the writings of learned ministers against the Baptists, weaken their cause, but strengthen it, as what follows will shew.

Mr. Moses Mather, of Stamford, in his first piece upon the covenant, published in 1769, owns ingenuously, that the covenant of circumcision, in Gen. xvii. was not, strictly speaking, the covenant of grace, but a divine institution whereby that nation was taken into visible covenant with God ; and that the ordinances of that church were appointed as means for the regeneration as well as comfort and strengthening of its members. And he labors hard to prove that the covenant is the same with the Christian church ; and that the Lord's Supper is " a converting ordinance." And to those who hold that persons ought to profess saving faith, in order to come to full communion, he says, " This scheme makes infant baptism a mere nullity, or thing of naught. To me this conclusion appears just and unavoidable."[1] Mr. Ebenezer Farris, of Stamford, was roused hereby to such an examination of the subject, as not only brought him to embrace believers' baptism, but also to publish a defence of that doctrine at New York. And he and others called Elder Gano from thence to baptize them in 1770 ; and in 1773 a Baptist church was constituted at Stamford, and another at Greenwich, ten miles nearer to New York. At the same time, the increase of the Baptists in Boston (above sixty members being added to the First Baptist church there) caused a great uneasiness among other ministers, and Dr. Chauncy published five sermons in 1772, to persuade people that it was their indispensable duty to come up to full communion in their churches. And after laboring hard to

[1]Discourse, pp. 17, 54, 57.

remove their objections against coming, especially because of fears that they were not born again, he says :—

The divinely appointed way, in which persons become members of the visible church of Christ, is utterly inconsistent with the supposition, that, in order to their being so, they must bo tho subjects of saving faith, or judged to be so. .... The children of those who are members of Christ's visible church arc, by the constitution of God, from their first coming into existence, members of his kingdom in common with their parents. So it was under the Jewish dispensation ; and so it is now, [under the Christian] if there is any validity in one of the principal arguments, by which we vindicate our practice, in baptizing the infants of those who are members of Christ's church.[1]

The consequence indeed appears clear, that if there is any validity in their main argument for infant baptism, their want of regeneration ought not to keep them back from the other ordinance. But then this is directly against the testimony for the purity of their churches, which this author produced in 1743, cited on page 57.

The disposition of that party is further discovered by another publication at this time. A Convention of their ministers at Bristol, May 20, 1772, agreed to publish a discourse, entitled, Catholicism ; or, Christian Charity; and it was printed this year at Providence. Many excellent things are inserted therein, about charity and a catholic disposition and behavior, and false pretences thereto are well exposed, especially in the following passage. Say they :—

Liberty and candor are the great basis of human happiness. We often hear persons extolling the advantages of both, who yet seem to be really acquainted with neither. For if they have any design on foot, any end to answer, or purpose to carry into execution, if you entertain different views, and with freedom speak your mind, you are instantly deemed an enemy, and you must be treated as such ; so that if you escape without the sword, it is not so much owing to a generous spirit of liberty, as a want of power. To supply the defect of their power, your reputation must be blasted, your influence weakened, and your interest injured. Such liberty deserves no better name than tyranny, and such freedom the basest slavery.[2]

[1] His sermons on Breaking of Bread, pp. 106, 107.
[2] Catholicism, p. 65.

The truth of this sentence is readily allowed ; but to whom is it applicable ? Those ministers evidently intended it against such as refused communion with their churches. They name the people who began to separate therefrom about the year 1744, and represent them as being furious then against giving and receiving ministerial support, but as now being so inconsistent and dishonest as to come into the same practice themselves.[1] Had they said assessing and forcing, instead of giving and receiving, they would have discovered a regard to truth and consistency that is now wanting in their performance. At this time they censure those as very unreasonable men, who hold immersion to be essential to baptism.[2] And, speaking of asking ministers to preach occasionally, the writer says :—

> I cannot see the propriety nor expediency of inviting the assistance of any man, be his profession what it may, that denies me the rights and privileges of the church of Christ. .... If we cannot eat and drink of one bread and one cup, in token of mutual fellowship, I see no reason why I should encourage such persons in their uncharitableness.

Is not this the charity they had before condemned, which begins and ends in self?[3]

In October, 1770, an act of their Legislature was obtained, to incorporate a number of men in Providence into a society, by the name of " The Benevolent Congregational Society in the town of Providence," for the purpose of raising and managing a fund, to support public worship in the first church of that denomination there. This was the first act of that nature ever passed in that Colony; and it was published in a pamphlet the next year; in the introduction to which they recite their law against the use of force to support ministers,[4] and say upon it, " Although this act was wisely intended, yet it was followed with great inconvenience in those societies where the support of the minister was thought to be a duty incumbent on the people, as thereby the burthen of the expense thereof was borne by very few

---

[1]Catholicism, pp. 37, 38.   [2]Ibid, p. 64.   [3]Ibid, pp. 25, 66.   [4]See Vol. I, p. 482.

persons. The Congregational society aforesaid has had a large share of this difficulty." And could they have had their desire, they would, undoubtedly, have introduced tax and compulsion for their support. But as the college in that town was formed upon another plan, the ministers refused to encourage it.[1] And though its charter, granted by their Legislature, explicitly exempts the persons and estates of the President and Professors of the college " from all taxes," yet the vote of a town-meeting in Providence was procured in August, 1772, to limit the meaning of those words to colony taxes only. And because the Baptist assessors in 1773, left said officers out of their town tax, a town-meeting was called February 7, 1774, which censured those assessors therefor, and published their resolves in the Gazette against extending that law to town taxes. It is hoped that many who were active in that affair are now convinced of their error, and are sensible that they did not then show the regard they ought to have done both to liberty and to learning. Their honorable exertions in this cause since are freely acknowledged; and these facts are only mentioned to remove the ill effects of those publications, and to guard against such evils for the future.

For the same end I shall give a concise view of another controversy at this time. A minister[2] at Bolton, in Worcester county, after being intemperate at other times, drank to excess on a sacramental season, so as to shock the whole congregation. But when his church called him to account therefor, he at first denied the crime, and then confessed it; yet he violated his promise about offering satisfaction to the

---

[1] One of the first class of graduates in that college [Charles Thompson] was ordained at Warren, July 3, 1771, who has since been a great blessing in those parts. Others also were very successful, so that in the years 1771 and 1772, about two hundred and thirty persons were baptized, in the adjoining towns of Warren, Swanzey, Rehoboth and Dighton. And President Manning being called to preach and administer ordinances to the Baptist church in Providence, caused a great turn in their affairs; and ill treatment from others was made to work for their good.

[2] Thomas Goss.—ED.

congregation.   Three councils were called, who were all for
continuing him in office there.   But as he had assumed the
power to negative the acts of the church, even when dealing with him, and to dissolve their meeting without their
consent, they called a meeting themselves, and chose a
Moderator and Clerk, and made some proposals to their
minister, and adjourned.   But as he gave them no satisfaction, they, at their second adjournment, August 8, 1771,
dismissed him from his office, and from their communion;
and the town concurred therewith.   This alarmed many
others, who exerted all their influence to prevent the settlement of another minister there in those circumstances.   Mr.
Zabdiel Adams published a sermon against it in 1772, which
was answered by one who styles himself A Neighbor; and
each wrote again upon the subject in 1773.   Two editions
of Mr. Wise's works were also now published; on the other
hand a pamphlet came out, said in the title page to be published " by the Convention of the ministers of the Province
of the Massachusetts Bay, at their annual meeting in Boston,
May 26, 1773;" the whole labor of which is to prove, that a
church has not a right to dismiss their minister contrary to
his consent, or to the direction of others, where a Council
of them can be had.   For this end, they insert a passage
from the Cambridge Platform, which says, " In case an elder
offend incorrigibly, the matter so requiring, as the church
had power to call to office, so they have power, according to
order, (the council of other churches, where it may be had,
directing thereto) to remove him from office."   Now it is a
known rule in grammar, that though a parenthesis is useful
in its place, yet the sense is good without it.   So are councils useful in difficult cases, if they hold up true light, but it
is a violation of said rule, to make the direction of a council essential to the church's act in dismissing their minister.
Another authority produced by this convention is a passage
from Mr. Hooker, which declares for the use of councils,
and for the right of churches to withdraw their communion

from an erroneous church, that will not be reclaimed. This will not be denied ; but the question in hand was, Where the power of doing it lies? Whether in the body of each church, or in a collection of officers above them? To confute the latter, and to establish the former of those points, was the main design of Hooker in that book ; of which I have given plain proofs,[1] and am ready to advance more if necessary. Directly after their pamphlet came out, a Council of seven churches, viz., four from Boston, one from Cambridge, one from Roxbury, and one from Dedham, met at Bolton, August 3, at the call of said deposed minister and his party. And, in their printed result, they have given it as their opinion, that the act of the church in deposing him ought to be looked upon as a nullity, because it had neither his consent. nor the direction of a Council of others, where it might have been had. They also deny its being the act of the majority of all the male members of Bolton church ; which last assertion was soon after proved not to be true in fact. In another publication he is introduced, saying, " I have three times been tried by my peers, and so far acquitted, that but little blame hath been cast upon me." And his advocate says of him, " Having never been condemned by the lawful judgment of his peers, and being still their minister in the eye of the constitution, he is justly entitled to the support they at first contracted to give him ; neither is it in the power of his people to withhold it."[2] Which is making them lords over God's heritage, instead of being examples to the flock. Yea, it is claiming such a power in the church, as the British Court, even at this time, denied in the State. For the Governor and Council of the Massachusetts were, in some cases, a Court of Appeal, finally to decide executive matters ; and Governor Hutchinson claimed a negative power in this, as well as in his legislative capacity. But as the question concerning it was referred to the King

[1] See Vol. I, p. 474.   [2] Adams's Reply to the Neighbor, pp. 13, 52.

in Council, it was determined against the Governor, that he should not have a negative power in that Executive Court; which determination he was obliged to publish in Boston in January, 1774. And it is most certain, that the Christian church is only an executive judicature; yet those ministers were now contending for a negative power therein.

And though the Baptists had no hand in the Bolton controversy, yet it serves more clearly to justify their opposition to such claims of power at this time. A leader in this opposition was Mr. John Davis, son to a Baptist minister in the State of Delaware, and educated at the college in Philadelphia. He came to Boston in May, 1770, and was ordained pastor of the Second Baptist church there, the 9th of September following. He was one of the committee who signed the address of the Baptist churches to our Legislature the next month; but perceiving soon after that our charter gave them no right to support any religious worship by tax and compulsion, he plainly declared it to men of note; which was the chief cause of the mean and scurrilous treatment from the press, that he met with the next winter. General Brattle, when acting as chairman of the committee of the Legislature in the spring, treated him in like manner; but when he had done, Davis arose, and distinctly answered his arguments, without taking any notice of the personal abuse that was offered him. A gentleman present said, the worth of the man never appeared so great before. September 10, 1771, the Warren Association made choice of him as their agent, to use his best endeavors, by the advice of their committee, in concert with their agents in London, to obtain the establishment of equal religious liberty in this land. And the compiler of this history was then requested by a number of ministers to undertake the work; and Mr. Davis promised his assistance therein. But, alas! he had done but little towards it before his health failed, and his life followed after. In August, 1772, he took a voyage to Philadelphia, hoping to receive benefit from his native air. And obtaining some relief, and meeting with one of his brethren in the ministry, who was going to preach to the western Indians, he set out with him, in company with friends who were going to settle upon the Ohio. But on February 1, 1773, the following account was published in Philadelphia, viz.: " By advices from the Ohio we learn, that upon the 13th of December the Reverend John Davis, A. M., Fellow of Rhode Island College, and one of the members of the American Philosophical Society, died there, after an illness of three weeks, in the 36th year of his age." The minister he was with informs us, that some of his last words were these: " In a little time I expect to be with Christ, to see and know him as he is now known, and as he is not known. My faith in my Saviour is unshaken.[1]

In September, 1772, the author was chosen an agent of the Baptist churches in Mr. Davis's room ; and the follow- ing events took place among them. Though their church in Chelmsford had given in certificates according to law, yet they were all taxed to parish teachers ; and in a cold sea- son, January 26, 1773, three of their society were impris- oned therefor at Concord, one of whom was eighty-two years old ; and they commenced a suit in law for recom- pense ; but their cases were long delayed. In Bellingham equal liberty was enjoyed, because there was none but a Bap- tist minister in the town ; but a number of his hearers who lived in Mendon were so much oppressed with taxes to other ministers, that in the three preceding years they esti- mated their damages on that account at near fifty pounds. And these and other things being laid before the Baptist committee, May 5, they advised their agent to write to all their churches, to consider whether it was not their duty to refuse to give any more certificates to the power that op- pressed them ; and to bring in their conclusions upon it to their next Association.[2] And further light was held up by

---

[1] Jones's Journal, p. 24.

[2] This Circular to the Churches is published in the Life and Times of Backus, pp. 188—190.—Ed.

their enemies a few days after.   For, to vindicate their practice, they published an account of all their exempting laws in the Boston Evening Post, of May 17, and as the first of them ordered Episcopalians in each parish to be taxed with the rest, and then that their ministers should draw the money out of the parish treasury, it was now said :—

Had the same prudent precaution been taken with respect to the Anabaptists, when they were exempted from being taxed towards the maintenance of the ministers of the churches by law established, those avaricious and dissolute persons, who get under water to wash away their minister's rates, without any expectation or desire of washing away their sins, would have had little or no temptation to declare themselves Anabaptists.

When the Warren Association met at Medfield, September 7, 1773, they concluded to refrain from giving any more certificates to that power[1], for these reasons :—

1. Because it implies an acknowledgment, that civil rulers have a right to set up one religious sect above another, which they have not.   2. Because they are not representatives in religious matters, and therefore have no right to impose religious taxes.   3. Because such a practice emboldens the actors therein to assume God's prerogative, and to judge the hearts of those who put not into their mouths.   4. Because the church is presented as a chaste virgin to Christ; and to place her trust and love upon any others for temporal support, is playing the harlot, and so the way to destroy all religion.   Hos. ii. 5.   5. Because the practice above-said tends to envy, hypocrisy and confusion, and so to the ruin of civil society.[2]

When the author came to Boston to complete the publication of his Appeal to the Public, he met with two printed letters against the design ; to which he returned the following reply, on October 14 :—

MR. DRAPER :—As you have allowed a pretended Baptist room for two long letters in your paper of the 2d and 30th of September, I hope you will give a real Baptist room for a short answer to him in your next.   I call

[1]See account of the discussion upon this matter in Life and Times of Backus, pp. 191—193.—ED.
[2]Appeal to the Public, pp. 43—47.—B.
The above arguments are substantially, but not literally, quoted from the "Appeal to the Public." The Appeal, a pamphlet of sixty-two pages, is an earnest and vigorous plea for religious freedom.   Mr. Backus submitted it to the Warren Association at the meeting in Medfield, and the Association requested its publication.—ED.

him a pretended Baptist, and think I have reason so to do ; for though he gives his word for it that he is of our denomination, yet the whole tenor of his letters is, to persuade us to be easy under the taxing laws of the other party ; and towards the close of his first letter, he says, " Had we for a little while borne only the little finger of the Episcopalian hierarchy, we should think the burthen comparatively light, though we were called to bear the weight of the loins of the Presbyterians of New England." And is not the hand of Joab in all this ? For my part, I am not able to get a pair of scales sufficient to weigh those two great bodies in, the Episcopal hierarchy and the New England Presbyterians, so as to find out exactly which is heaviest. But if this pretended brother had felt what father Obadiah Holmes once felt in Boston from our opponents, he would not have been so easy as he now seems to be.

Hereby a stop was put to that mean and scandalous practice, of assuming the Baptist name in writings against their welfare. Neither did any answer ever appear to the above reasons for equal liberty, though oppression was still carried on under religious pretences.

By assistance from Haverhill, a Baptist church was regularly formed at Gorham, near Casco Bay, June 20, 1768. And Joseph Moody, a member of it, who lived in Scarborough, had the same certified annually to their parish assessors according to law ; yet distress was still made upon him for taxes to parish worship. For such a tax of about six dollars, a good riding beast was taken from him in 1771; he therefore presented proper vouchers of these facts to the Assembly at Boston, January 26, 1774, with a petition, that like the good Samaritan, they would again set him upon his own beast.[1] A committee was sent out upon it, whose report was to dismiss the petition, which was done. About this time eighteen men, of the Baptist society in Warwick, in a very cold season, were seized for a parish tax, and carried forty miles, and cast into Northampton jail. On Febru-

[1] "As the case of your petitioner somewhat resembles the case of the poor man, who, travelling from Jerusalem to Jericho, fell among evil men, your petitioner, from principles of charity and equity, doth believe that you will not pass by him on the other side of the way, but, with the good Samaritan, show pity, bind up his wounds, and set him on his own beast, which has been violently taken away." Extract from the petition of Joseph Moody.—ED.

ary 15, an account thereof was brought to the agent of the
Baptist churches, who directly laid their case before the Legislature at Boston, praying that they might be released, that
recompense might be made them, and effectual measures
taken to prevent such things for the future.[1]   But, though a
committee was sent out upon it, no help was granted.   This
moved one of the Baptist committee to express his astonishment thereat, in the Gazette of March 3, and to ask how
this news would be received in sister colonies, or at the British Court, from whence late help had been afforded to our
Ashfield brethren?   A reply hereto came out March 14,
which said, " No one can deny that they have been in great
trouble of late ; and whoever considers how dangerous the
occupation of counterfeiting an established currency is, they
cannot greatly admire at it."[2]   Which inuendo was caught
at and enlarged upon in the Providence Gazette.   Though
in fact a Pædobaptist church member in Ashfield had, before

[1] " I have direct information that eighteen men of the inhabitants of Warwick,
who belong to the Baptist church in Royalston, and had the same certified to the
assessors of Warwick, last June, yet were seized last week, for the minister's rate
of that town, and carried prisoners to Northampton jail ; by which they are deprived of their precious rights, and their dear families, in a new country, are exposed to suffering greatly for want of their help.   This is therefore to beseech your
Excellency and Honors, as guardians of the rights of your people, immediately to
order these men to be set at liberty, and that reparation be made of the damages
they have sustained ; and also to take some effectual methods, as in your wisdom
you shall see fit, that, for the future, all persons within this province who shall demean themselves as good members of civil society, may not be despoiled of the
aforesaid rights, under a pretence of supporting religious worship, but that all persons who shall presume thus to encroach upon the rights of their neighbors may be
punished according to the demerit of their crimes."   Extract from the above-named
petition: The whole petition is published in the Life and Times of Backus, pp. 198,
199.—ED.

[2] The article in the Massachusetts Gazette of March 3, was signed "A Friend to
Liberty, Civil and Religious ;" that of March 14, appeared in the Boston Evening
Post, and was signed "Veritas."   It was well answered in the Gazette of April 7,
over the signature of " Catholic."   " Veritas " replied in two long articles in the
Post of April 11, and April 18 ; the latter of which was accompanied by an article
in the Baptist interest, signed "A Real Friend to his Country."   Another article
from " Catholic " was in the Post of May 2.   This whole controversy is spirited and
interesting, and well worth perusal.   Of the authorship of the articles we are ignorant, except one dated April 18, of which Backus writes in his Diary, "April 19.
My piece against Veritas was printed in the Evening Post of yesterday."—ED.

this, been convicted of harboring a counterfeiting club at
his house, for which the Court gave judgment that he should
be fined, set in the pillory, and have his ears cropped ; while
a Baptist member, whom they had ensnared, was only fined.
Thus do men expose themselves, when they drag into religious controversy things which have no relation to it. In
a Boston paper of April 7, the assessors of Warwick published a vindication of themselves in taxing those Baptists,
in which they said :—

> We apprehend that every body politic have a right to choose their relig-
> ion, and to enact laws for its support, and that they ought so to do ; and
> since Congregationalism is the choice of the people of this province, the re-
> ligion which our forefathers had in view to establish in coming over to this
> country, we think there is good reason why dissenters from us should pay
> to the support of it ; especially since it is one condition upon which they
> receive and hold their lands.

This last article is flatly denied, and let any of that party
prove it if they can. And will any still plead for a practice
that cannot be upheld without lying ! Another evil effect of
it is before us.

One of the Chelmsford cases was now tried at Charlestown. Jonathan Sewall, the lawyer who was most active
against the Baptists of Haverhill, undertook for them ; and
he must needs put the collector as well as the assessors into
the writ. The effect of which was, that the jury judged
the assessors to be guilty, and the collector not guilty; and
that the Baptist should recover of the assessors three pounds
damages and costs, while the collector should recover costs
of the Baptist for carrying him to prison, where he was confined above three days. The guilty assessors soon had their
expenses paid by the town ; but as the judges and the lawyer went off directly, the other Chelmsford cases were never
tried, nor the small sum now adjudged to one of them received. No exempting law for the Baptists in this province
was now in force. These things being heard of at Philadelphia, caused an uneasiness among the Presbyterians there,

13

and a man was sent from thence to Boston, and a new exempting act was passed at Salem in June ; after which it was declared in a Philadelphia paper, that relief was granted to the Baptists in the Massachusetts. Such pains have that sect taken to keep up their credit and influence in this country. But that act was so far from affording us any relief, that it required annual certificates to be recorded in each parish where the Baptists lived, a copy of which could not be had without fourpence of our money, which is threepence sterling ; the very tax upon a pound of tea that brought on the American war.

CHAPTER XXIII.

Disputes about power and gain, under a religious mask, could no longer be restrained to words, but must come to dreadful blows. To this those claims have always tended. When Henry VIII revolted from the church of Rome, and set himself up as head of the church of England, he ruled as tyrannically as the pope did; though his allowing the common people to have the Bible in their own tongue, gave much light to the nation. And a greater reformation was produced thereby, in the short reign of his son Edward, than the church of England has ever attained to since. Neither do their ideas differ so much from ours about facts, as about the names they ought to be called by. An Episcopal minister of considerable note, after thirty years' labor to promote their way in New England, gave the following account of the cause of its first plantation. Says he :—

While the virgin queen, of immortal memory, sat at the helm, she steered so steady a course, and rode with so tight a rein, that Calvin's English disciples, impregnated with the leaven of Geneva, could do little more upon their return, after the Maria persecution, than fret in their fetters, murmur, and mutter their discontents in secret. .... To Elizabeth succeeded James, father of the martyr. He, imagining it more for his ease, threw away the queen's curb, and rode with a snaffle. Under this soft sovereign the *non-cons* seem, by the Galiotism of the State, and Grindalizing of the church, to have grown into great numbers. But Charles resumed, in some sort, the heroine's bridle, and gave leave to Laud to make use of whip and spur; so the sturdy Puritan, unused to restraint, and growing restive, finding that flouncing and plunging would not throw down, ran away from his riders, and took sanctuary in New England. But, good God! how dearly did that most pious prince and holy prelate pay for this! and how fatal and lasting have been the consequences of that grand rebellion, that brought both of those great personages to the block![1]

That is, Charles claimed a right to impose laws and taxes upon the people without their consent, and Laud endeavored to cover and enforce the same with religious pretences; and because they drove on furiously in that way, until both of their necks were broken, arbitrary teachers have canonized them for saints and martyrs, and have stigmatized resistance to such power with the odious name of *Rebellion*. After the flames of war which they kindled had raged through three bloody campaigns, between the king and parliament, their commissioners met at Uxbridge, January 30, 1645, to treat about reconciliation. But it could not be obtained, because a secret instruction from Charles to his commissioners said:—

As the king's duty is to protect the church, so it is the church's to assist the king in the maintenance of his just authority. Wherefore my predecessors have been always careful (especially since the reformation) to keep the dependency of the clergy entirely upon the crown, without which it will scarcely sit fast upon the king's head; therefore you must do nothing to change or lessen this necessary dependency.[2]

Before the reformation the pope rode foremost, and sometimes compelled princes to walk on foot, yea, to hold his stirrup; but since, as is here observed, they have been always careful to keep the reins in their own hands. And this contest has caused infinite mischiefs in New England.

The first planters of New England, requested no more

---

[1]Letters from Narragansett, 1752, by James M'Sparran, D. D., printed at Dublin, 1753, under the title of America Dissected, pp. 23, 24.

[2]Rapin, Vol. II, p. 510.

than equal liberty of conscience ; and though the crown
would only give a conditional, and not an absolute promise
thereof, " yet, casting themselves on the care of Providence,
they resolved to venture."[1]   On this foundation was New
England planted in 1620 ; and this has been its only support
ever since.   For though the Massachusetts company came
over ten years after, with an ample charter from Charles ;
yet he and Laud soon attempted to vacate it, and at length
positively required the company to send it back again.[2]   And
the loss of their heads, and the overthrow of Episcopacy,
was the cause why these plantations were not then entirely
ruined.   In the mean time, an imagination of great purity
at Boston emboldened the church to assume the whole government in this wilderness, with an expectation of exhibit-
ing to the world such a view of the glory of Christianity, as
had never before been seen.   And the leaders here were en-
chanted with this bright image, until their charter was
wrested from them in 1684 ; upon which the world resolutely
took the bridle again into their own hands.   And how flattering was their late prospect of riding where they pleased
without control ?   Methinks I hear the British ministry saying, " Our fleets and armies have triumphed over all our enemies, and we are revered to the remotest regions.   The
wealth of both the Indies is ours, and our resources are
boundless.   The vast continent of North America is wholly
at our command, and who can hinder our doing as we please?
Arts and sciences are already carried very high, and who
knows how much greater improvements may be made ?   As
to religion, fanaticism and bigotry are quite out of fashion,
and reason and liberty are the darling topics of the age.
Episcopacy prevails in almost all our colonies, and soon will
in the remainder.   Parliaments have formerly made dreadful work ; cut off the head of one king, and driven another
from his throne ; but those days of superstition and cruelty

[1] Prince's Chronology, pp. 57, 60. [147, 148, 151.]
[2] Hutchinson, Vol. III, pp. 105, 106.

are at an end.   The Parliament is now entirely at our command ; and the establishment of its supremacy over the colonies is all that is wanting to complete the happiness of the empire ; and who can prevent so great a good ?   Can a few factious fellows at Boston do it ?   The thought is contemptible !   And we are assured, by the most respectable gentlemen upon the continent, that as soon as it is seen that government is determined to maintain its authority, opposition will cease, and the land will be at rest.   At their head is a man,[1] who, by the best history of his country that was ever published, has discovered a perfect knowledge of their affairs, civil and religious.   And his influence is so great, that after he was made Lieutenant Governor of the province, he was freely elected into their Council.   At the same time he had the command of their castle, the key of their chief harbor, was Judge of Probate in their head county, and Chief Judge of their Supreme Executive Court through the colony ; until his Majesty has been pleased to raise him to the highest seat in their government.   Who then can scruple the truth of his testimony, or the sufficiency of his influence to accomplish our desires ?"

I am sensible that these ideas will not please some men ; therefore the following facts are adduced to support them. The most plausible plea for the claim of Britain to tax America was, that we were indebted to her for protection. If so, why did she pay us large sums, for assisting her in her wars ?   Our conquest of Cape Breton, in 1745, brought her into debt to us, for which she sent us over a good quantity of cash, whereby we were enabled to call in our paper money.   Yet, through jealousy of our power, acts of parliament were passed in 1749 to prohibit, under great penalties, the erection of any tilt-hammers here to plate iron, furnaces to make steel, or slitting-mills to cut nail-rods ; although no country abounds more than ours with iron.   All this and much more was patiently borne, and requisitions from the

[1]Thomas Hutchinson.—Ed,

crown, of assistance in the succeeding wars, were obeyed beyond our proportion; for which large sums were repaid by parliament. Did this look as if they thought we were in debt to thom? By no means. But soon after the peace of 1763, they passed an act to compel the colonies to furnish certain articles for a standing army therein in the time of peace;—the great engine of despotism. And as this act was but partly obeyed in New York, their legislative power was suspended, until they should do it fully. To this the stamp-act was added, to deprive America of any legal deeds of our lands, or securities for our money, without paying a tax therefor to Britain. And when they were forced to repeal that act in March, 1766, it was resolved, " that his Majesty in parliament, of right, had power to bind the people of the colonies by statutes *in all cases whatsoever*." William Warburton, Bishop of Gloucester, had delivered a sermon, the preceding month, before the society which supported their missionaries in America, wherein he called the inhabitants of it factious people, ready to laugh at the Bible ; and said, " The spreading of *Gentilism* in the colonies calls for our rejected charity." And to render them as odious as possible, he accused them of annually stealing slaves from the opposite continent, and sacrificing them to their great idol, the god of gain. " Nothing," says he, " is more certain, than that the infamous traffic for slaves directly infringes both divine and human law. Nature created man free, and grace invites him to assert his freedom."[1] Yet it is most certain that his party, in the southern colonies, and in the West India Islands, have had the chief hand in that infamous traffic. February 20, 1767, John Ewer, Bishop of Landaff, before the same society, said of the first planters of New England:—

What reproach could be cast heavier than they deserve? who, with their native soil, abandoned their native manners and religion; and ere long were found in many parts living without remembrance or knowledge of

[1]Gloucester's Sermon, February 21, 1766, pp. 11, 13, 25, 26.

God, without any divine worship, in dissolute wickedness, and the most brutal proflicacy of manners. Instead of converting barbarous infidels, as they undertook to do, they became themselves infidels and barbarians. And is it not some aggravation of their shame, that this their neglect of religion was contrary to the pretences and conditions under which they obtained royal grants and public authority?

And having expressed his earnest desire and hopes of the speedy establishment of bishops in America, he says :—

This point obtained, the American church will soon go out of its infant state ; be able to stand upon its own legs, and without foreign help, support and spread itself. Then the business of this society will have been brought to the happy issue intended.[1]

Dr. Thomas Bradbury Chandler, of New Jersey, now published a book upon the same subject; wherein he owns it as the opinion of many, that the circumstances of the nation now afforded the most favorable prospect of the speedy establishment of bishops here, that had ever appeared since Queen Anne's death. Yet he had the face to declare that such a plan was agreed upon, " that bishops shall not interfere with the property or privileges, whether civil or religious, of churchmen or dissenters . . . . but shall only ordain and govern the clergy, and administer confirmation to those who shall desire it.[2] The Tea-and-glass-act was passed this year; which moved the Pennsylvania Farmer[3] to write his elegant letters upon our public danger; the first of which was dated November 5, 1767. As those letters were greatly esteemed, and had very extensive effects, ten letters by way of answer to them were published at Boston, in 1769. Much pains were taken therein to persuade us that the Farmer had given false alarms, and that our liberties were in no real danger; and yet in the ninth letter it was said, " The question whether the parliament can lay internal taxes could be determined best by considering the power of that body to alter or vacate charters. The parliament can annul our

[1]Landaff's Sermon, pp. 6, 7, 25, 26.   See also Vol. I, pp. 462, 463.
[2]Chandler's Appeal to the public, pp. 50—54, 79.
[3]John Dickinson.—ED.

charters at will,[1] without alleging *pro causa misuser or abuser*, because the king is joined by the whole Council of the nation." And in January, 1773, Governor Hutchinson purposely drew our Assembly into a debate upon this subject; and when he closed it the 6th of March, he said, " It is essential to the being of government that power should always exist which no other power within such government can have right to withstand or control ; therefore when the word *power* relates to the supreme authority of government, it must be understood *absolute* and *unlimited*." And he refused his consent to an act passed in that session, to grant the salaries of the Judges of our Superior Executive Court, because he expected that the king would pay them out of the American revenue then collecting. In June following, his letter to a member of parliament, of January 20, 1769, was published by the Assembly at Boston, wherein he said, "I never think of the measures necessary for the peace and good order of the colonies, without pain. There must be an *abridgment* of what are called English liberties." This, and other original letters, were procured and sent back by the amiable and judicious Franklin, our agent at the British Court ; who, as soon as this was known there, was spurned from thence with much scorn and bitterness ; an infallible evidence that what they were in pursuit of were the works of darkness ; for he that doth truth cometh to the light, that his deeds may be made manifest. John iii. 20, 21.

In November following, arrived large cargoes of tea, which were sent over to establish a precedent of the power of the British parliament to tax this country internally. From Philadelphia and New York it was sent back, and not suffered to be landed ; and the same was earnestly tried for at Boston ; but Governor Hutchinson reduced his native town

---

[1]Here is a power claimed by man, which, with reverence be it spoken, is what the eternal Jehovah never assumed! His infinite perfections render it impossible for him to lie, to act inconsistently, or to entice any into sin; all which have been frequently done, by men who have assumed the power to support religious teachers by tax and compulsion.

to the cruel necessity of either suffering it to be landed, and the tax thereon paid, or else of casting it into the sea ; and the latter was chosen.   Now the character of those who teach God's fear by the precepts of men, is to " watch for iniquity."[1]   And when accounts of this and other transactions arrived in March, 1774, the British ministry imagined that they had got enough of it to cover and carry their arbitrary designs.   And such use was made thereof, as to procure one act of parliament to shut up the port of Boston, until their power was obeyed there ; a second to rob the people of this province of their right to choose their own Council ; a third to screen the executors of their orders from punishment, even if they committed murder in doing it ; and a fourth greatly to enlarge the province of Quebec, to establish popery therein, and to deprive its inhabitants of their right of trials by jury, and other English liberties. As these were hostile measures, Thomas Gage, the chief commander of all the British forces in America, was appointed Governor of the Massachusetts, in order to carry them into effect.   He arrived at Boston May 13, where he met the Assembly the 25th, but soon prorogued them to Salem, where a few acts were passed, and then they were dissolved, never to meet again upon their former constitution.   The port of Boston was shut up in June, and in August, twenty-four of the thirty-six Counsellors, appointed for us by the crown, were sworn into office ; and writs were issued for a new choice of representatives, to meet them at Salem the 5th of October.   But a week before that time the Governor, by proclamation, forbade their meeting, because the people had compelled some of those Counsellors to resign their commissions, and the rest were afraid to venture out of Boston.   Yet most of the representatives met, resolved themselves into a Provincial Congress, and sat at several times and places, until they dissolved on December 10 ; having taken various steps towards the internal regulation and

[1] Is. 29. 13, 20.—ED.

defence of the country, and proposed a new choice of delegates from the towns, to meet in February. In the mean
time all these colonies considered the case of Boston as their
own, and sent large contributions to its suffering inhabitants. Delegates from twelve Colonies met at Philadelphia,
September 5, and sat until October 26, stated the unalienable rights of mankind, and the nature, limits and end of
civil government, in a clear manner; and sent addresses to
the throne, and to various parts of the empire, well calculated to expose, and, if possible, to remove the dangers that
hung over our liberties. They also recommended wise
measures for our internal regulation; and, in the name of
their constituents, solemnly covenanted to refrain from im-
porting any British goods, or exporting any of ours to them,
after certain times set, if said oppressive acts should not
then be repealed, until their repeal was effected.

In the night preceding September 1, a party of soldiers
went and seized a large quantity of powder, in a public store
in Cambridge, which, with some field pieces, they brought off
to Boston; upon which a report flew like the wind, that
Gage had sent out his troops, who were killing the people.
Multitudes were alarmed hereby, and were marching in arms
to relieve their friends, until this report was contradicted.
And on Lord's day, February 26, 1775, a field officer, with
about a hundred men, sailed from the Castle to Marblehead,
and then marched nimbly to Salem, to fetch some pieces of
artillery from thence; but they were defeated in their design
by the vigilance of the people. After this, Colonel Gilbert collected a quantity of arms and ammunition at Freetown, and
sent to the Governor for protection; who thereupon wrote
to the authority of Bristol county, to make provision for two
hundred soldiers there. But, before they marched, some
thousands of the inhabitants assembled on April 10, seized
those war stores, and dispersed that nest of enemies at Freetown. Yet after all this, and much more of like nature, we
are informed, that the Mandamus Counsellors at Boston were

under such an infatuation, as to give it as their opinion, that their countrymen would not venture to fight against the king's troops; and to advise their Governor to try the experiment, by sending a body of them to destroy or bring away the stores that were collected at Concord.   But though this advice was followed with great secresy, by crossing the water from Boston Common in the dead of the night, so as to get twelve miles in their way before sunrise, yet they then saw a company of the militia collected to oppose them; of whom they killed eight[1] men on the spot, and then marched six miles further to Concord; where they shot down two men more, before our people fired upon them.[2]   And they not only used their endeavors to destroy some cannon and carriages, but also cast a considerable quantity of flour into the river. Hereupon the cowardly Americans drove the heroic Britons back to their ships the same day, with much terror and slaughter, although near two thousand of their best troops were employed in the affair; which will transmit the remembrance of Lexington, and the 19th of April, down to the latest posterity.

But how the inhabitants of a country of fifteen hundred miles extent, divided into thirteen colonies, very differently constituted, wherein were persons of almost all nations, sects and opinions, could unite against the arbitrary claims of the most powerful kingdom upon earth, and could persevere therein for eight tedious years, in defiance of the utmost exertions both of craft and violence, until those claims are fully given up, is matter of universal astonishment, and will be the subject of curious inquiry to future ages.   To me it is past all doubt, that no other sufficient reason can be given for this unparalleled event, than the design which God has declared to us, in the passage that adorns our title page. Pride and disobedience to him had arrived to such height in

[1] "Seven of the men of Lexington were killed; nine wounded; a quarter part of all who stood in arms on the green."   Bancroft, Vol. VII, p. 294.—Ed.

[2] This is a most certain fact, though it was contradicted by our enemies in London.

both countries, that we must become dreadful scourges to each other, to discover what was in our hearts, whether we would keep his commandments or not.

A second Provincial Congress met at Concord, February 1, and proceeded to further measures for the defence of our liberties; and other colonies did the like. The Assembly at Providence, in December, had ordered the cannon to be brought up there from their fort near Newport, which were now conveyed to the camp before Boston, formed by the militia, who assembled by thousands, and filled the towns and villages, from the bay south of Boston to Mystic River on the north; being a circle of twenty miles. On the other hand, the British Generals, Howe, Burgoyne, and Clinton, arrived with large reinforcements to their army at Boston. Charlestown, to the north of it, lies, as Boston does, upon a peninsula, the latter betwixt Charles and Mystic rivers. It contained above four hundred houses, many of them very elegant. June 17, the British commanders perceived that the Americans had begun to fortify a hill on the north side of Charlestown; upon which the town was surrounded with their ships and floating batteries, and then their army landed to attack our entrenchment. Burgoyne was upon a hill in the northeast part of Boston; and eight days after, he wrote the following account of the action to England. Says he:—

If we look to the height, Howe's corps ascending the hill in the face of entrenchments, and in a very disadvantageous ground, was much engaged; to the left, the enemy pouring fresh troops, by thousands, over the land, and in the arm of the sea our ships and floating batteries cannonading them; straight before us a large and noble town in one great blaze; the church steeples, being of timber, were great pyramids of fire above the rest; behind us, the church steeples and heights of our own camp covered with spectators of the rest of our army which was engaged; the hills round the country covered with spectators, the enemy all in anxious suspense; the roar of cannon, mortars and musketry, the crush of churches, ships upon the stocks, and whole streets falling together in ruins, to fill the ear; the storm of redoubts, with the objects above described, to fill the eye, and the reflection that perhaps a defeat was a final loss of the British empire in

America, to fill the mind, ... made the whole a picture and complication of horror and importance, beyond any thing that ever came to my lot to be witness to. .... Yet the day ended with glory, and the success was most important, considering the ascendancy it gave the regular troops; but the loss was uncommon in officers, for the number engaged.

Can this be believed by posterity? Major Pitcairn, who was most forward in firing upon our people at Lexington, was now slain, with two other field officers, two of Howe's aids, seven captains, and about eight hundred men, besides near as many more who died of their wounds, while our loss was but about half that number. All this in driving the despised Americans from a redoubt they had raised in one night, under the direction of a physician[1] as their chief commander; and after he fell, the British veterans did not venture to pursue our people, though it might have been done for half a mile, under the protection of their own ships and batteries. Is this their glory? it was glorying in their shame! And a plain account of their motives here follows. Charles Lee had been an officer under Burgoyne in the last war, and had contracted a near friendship with him, and hearing of his arrival at Boston, he sent him a letter, which Burgoyne answered from thence, July 8, and said, " The vital principle of the constitution, in which it moves and has its being, is the supremacy of the king in parliament; a compound, indefinite, indefeasible power, coëval with the origin of the empire, and coëxtensive over all its parts." And having laid this as his foundation, he, in an artful manner, went on to compare our conduct with theirs who beheaded Charles and set up Cromwell, and that of his party, to those who expelled James and crowned William; and then says, " These principles, depend upon it, actuate the army and fleet throughout; and let me at the same time add, that there are few if any gentlemen among us who would have drawn their swords in the cause of slavery. .... I know

---

[1]The Honorable Joseph Warren, of Boston, who had just before been appointed a Major General by our Provincial Congress.

Great Britain is ready to open her arms upon the first overture of accommodation. I know she is equally resolute to
maintain her original rights; and if the war proceeds, your
one hundred and fifty thousand men will not be a match for
her power." This was their capital argument; which, however, failed him and his army at Saratoga two years after.
Our second Continental Congress met at Philadelphia, May
10, and sent a petition to the king, wherein they assured
him, that their ardent desire was, for the restoration of the
former harmony between the two countries, and for its establishment upon a permanent and lasting basis ; and said,
" Our breasts retain too tender a regard for the kingdom
from which we derive our origin, to request such a reconciliation as might in any manner be inconsistent with her
dignity and welfare." And they prayed him to direct to
some mode wherein such a reconciliation might be accomplished. On September 1, this petition was delivered to
Lord Dartmouth, by Governor Penn, and Mr. Arthur Lee ;
to whom the minister said, " no answer would be given."
Now compare this with Burgoyne's declaration. He called
their claims over the colonies original rights, and the vital
principle of the constitution ; which was so opposite to truth,
that it is impossible for any men ever to have such a right to
power over others. And instead of a readiness for accommodation, they were earnestly barring the door against it.
General Gage covenanted with our friends in Boston, that if
they would deliver up their arms and ammunition, they
should have liberty to go out with their other effects. But
when he had thus disarmed them, he violated his promise in
a shameful manner ; which raised both the resentment and
the contempt of the country against his party. It taught
the people not to confide in their promises, and also to despise them ; as being afraid, that if our women and children
were not kept there as hostages, the people would rush in
and destroy or captivate their boasting army.
    On the other hand, because Cromwell, with the wisdom

of the serpent, but not the innocency of the dove, made
a great overturn in the nation, which yet ended in confusion
and slavery, our enemies imagined that nothing better could
take place here, if we revolted from their king.   But how
far are God's thoughts above theirs ?   He raised up a man
in Virginia, the oldest of our colonies, who, by the Congress, was unanimously appointed the chief commander of
our armies ; and as such arrived at the camp at Cambridge,
July 2.   And through eight perilous campaigns he was preserved in safety and health, was enabled to unite reason and
resolution, authority and mildness, until his country was delivered from the most imminent dangers, and peace restored
to the nations ; and then he as readily resigned his command as he received it, and joyfully retired into a private
station, followed with the universal esteem and blessings of
his country ; while a demonstration is hereby held up to all
the world, that prudence, uprightness, and benevolence,
will procure and preserve that honor, authority and happiness, which are in vain sought for in any other way.

CHAPTER XXIV.

REASONS WHY THE BAPTISTS JOINED IN THIS WAR.—GRACIOUS VISI-
TATIONS IN OUR LAND.—LABORS FOR EQUAL LIBERTY.—NEW AT-
TEMPTS TO DIVIDE AND ENSLAVE AMERICA.—THE FOLLY THEREOF
EXPOSED.—GREAT EXPLOITS PERFORMED.—TO WHICH SUCCEEDED
TERRIBLE INROADS OF THE ENEMY.—YET WONDERFUL RELIEF WAS
GRANTED AGAINST THEM.—THEIR AMAZING CRUELTY.—VAST UNCER-
TAINTY OF OUR AFFAIRS.—THE CLOSING SCENES OF THE WAR.

Since the Baptists have often been oppressed in this land,
and would have suffered more than they did, had it not been
for restraints from Great Britain, how came they to join in
a war against her? Many have wondered at it, and some
have censured them severely therefor. But they had the
following reasons for their conduct. 1. Where Episcopalians have had all the power of government, they have never
allowed others so much liberty as we here enjoyed. In
England all are taxed to their worship, while none are admitted into civil offices but communicants in their church. In
Virginia they cruelly imprisoned Baptist ministers, only for
preaching the gospel to perishing souls without license from
their courts, until this war compelled them to desist therefrom. Of this we had incontestible evidence. Therefore
we could have no rational hopes of any real advantage in
joining with them. 2. The worst treatment we here met
with came from the same principles, and much of it from
the same persons, as the American war did. Many proofs
of this have already been given, and more are at hand if

14

called for.   3. The first Baptist minister in America publicly held forth, that all righteous government is founded in compact, expressed or implied; which is equally binding upon rulers and ruled; so that every officer, whether succeeding or elected, who intermeddles in any matter not fairly derived from thence, goes beyond his .commission.[1] When therefore our countrymen adopted these principles, and founded their opposition to arbitrary claims wholly thereon, how could we avoid joining with them? For, 4. those claims appeared to us absolutely unjust, and a direct violation of the immutable rules of truth and equity; so that a concurrence with them would have brought such guilt upon our consciences, as is infinitely worse than all the frowns of men.   5. Though heavy corrections were to be expected, yet a strong hope was begotten of final deliverance to this land; the good effects whereof might hereafter return to the people who now invaded our rights.   It is not pretended that our denomination were all agreed, or had equal clearness in these points; but a majority of them were, more or less, influenced thereby.[2]

A main ground of the hope now mentioned, was the gracious visitations granted from time to time, in various parts of this country, which bespoke a design of final deliverance, and not of destruction or slavery.   Within seven years past several thousands had been hopefully converted from the errors of their ways, in Virginia, the Carolinas, and Georgia. In and after the year 1773, a powerful work prevailed in Pittsfield, Adams, Lanesborough, Hancock, and other towns

---

[1] See Vol. I, pp. 141, 142.

[2] The following extract from a letter of Dr. Rippon of London, to President Manning, written in 1784, shows that Baptists in England as well as America, favored the cause of the colonies:—

"I believe all our Baptist ministers in town except two, and most of our brethren in the country, were on the side of the Americans in the late dispute. .... We wept when the thirsty plains drank the blood of your departed heroes, and the shout of a king was amongst us when your well fought battles were crowned with victory.   And to this hour we believe that the independence of America will for a while secure the liberty of this country; but if that continent had been reduced, Britain would not long have been free."   Manning and Brown University, p. 314.—ED.

in Berkshire county; and the like in the adjacent parts of
the county of Albany, and into the State of Vermont; which
raised and increased many Baptist churches there. And, to
come nearer home, the second Baptist church in Middleborough was reduced very low, until a revival began in the
spring of 1773, which by the fall of 1775, caused the addition of ninety members to that church, and thirty to our
third church in this town. The work extended into the
eastern and most uncultivated part of Freetown, where it
raised a new church, and another in Dartmouth. In November, 1744, a like blessing was granted in Attleborough, which
in ten months added thirty members to the First Baptist
church there, and a number more to other societies. In
December this revival extended into Providence, where it
prevailed gloriously through the winter. Their college enjoyed a precious share of it, the good effects whereof are
still experienced in distant churches. In ten months, more
than a hundred persons were added to the Baptist church
there, beside large additions to other churches in the town.
And, though the alarms of war in the spring caused a great
interruption of spiritual exercises and enjoyments, in places
near the scene of action, yet the same were promoted thereby in distant places. At the time of the Bunker Hill battle,
a young physician[1] was converted at Harvard, thirty-five miles
off, who was called the next year to preach the gospel; and
he is now pastor of a large Baptist church there, the members of which are chiefly the seals of his ministry. Royalston and Richmond to the northward, and Suffield to the
westward, were favored with a considerable revival of religion at this time, as Pomfert, Killingly, and other towns in
Connecticut, were in 1776. And while the defence of the
civil rights of America appeared a matter of great importance, our religious liberties were by no means to be neglected; and the contest concerning each kept a pretty even pace
through the war.

[1] Isaiah Parker.—ED.

Viewing the Continental Congress as our highest civil resort, the Warren Association, at their meeting at Medfield, September 13, 1774, agreed to send their agent to Philadelphia, there to follow the best advice he could obtain, to procure some influence from thence in their favor.[1]   A Convention of the county of Suffolk, at this time the head county of our province, gave countenance to this procedure; for their seventeenth resolve says, " This county, confiding in the wisdom and integrity of the Continental Congress, now sitting at Philadelphia, will pay all due respect and submission to such measures as may be recommended by them to the colonies, for the restoration and establishment of our just rights, civil and religious."[2]   These resolves were carried by said agent to that city ; where he met with an Association of

[1]"September 7,[1774.] Went over to Providence to Commencement. Met with Mr. Gano of New York, and Mr. Wm. Van Horne of South Hampton, in Pennsylvania. They with Messrs. Manning and Hezekiah Smith all were in earnest for me to go to the Association and also to the Congress at Philadelphia, and represented that now was the most likely time to obtain our religious liberty that we had ever known. I had many objections against it, but when I awoke next morning, the religious liberties of three colonies or more, appeared so weighty to my mind that, if I might do anything for their relief, I was made willing to do it, and leave my private concerns to him that orders all things."

"September 14. The Association were all unanimous that I should go to Philadelphia, and contributed £6, 10, 1¾ towards it." Backus's Manuscript Diary.

The Association gave to Mr. Backus the following certificate :

"To the Honorable Delegates of the several colonies in North America, met in a general Congress in Philadelphia :

"HONORABLE GENTLEMEN : As the Antipædobaptist churches in New England are most heartily concerned for the preservation and defence of the rights and privileges of this country, and are deeply affected by the encroachments upon the same, which have lately been made by the British parliament, and are willing to unite with our dear countrymen, vigorously to pursue every prudent measure for relief, so we would beg leave to say that, as a distinct denomination of Protestants, we conceive that we have an equal claim to charter-rights with the rest of our fellow-subjects; and yet have long been denied the free and full enjoyment of those rights, as to the support of religious worship. Therefore we, the elders and brethren of twenty Baptist churches met in Association at Medfield, twenty miles from Boston, September 14, 1744, have unanimously chosen and sent unto you the reverend and beloved Mr. Isaac Backus as our agent, to lay our case, in these respects, before you, or otherwise to use all the prudent means he can for our relief.

JOHN GANO, Moderator,
HEZEKIAH SMITH, Clerk.—ED.

[2]The Congress gave their special approbation of these resolves.

Baptist churches, from several adjacent colonies who elected a large Committee to assist in the affair, and by their request a conference was procured in the evening of October 14, with the Honorable Delegates from our Province to Congress, in the presence of several more of their members, and other gentlemen. It was opened by reading a brief memorial of our chief grievances in the Massachusetts, on religious accounts,[1] which our Delegates endeavored to answer; first by denying that we had any cause for such complaints, and then by attempting to cast all the blame thereof upon the executive department, and asserting that our Legislature were entirely clear of it; but plain facts, especially in the Ashfield affair, confuted both of these pleas; and the conference was closed with a promise from said Delegates of the exertion of their influence in our favor.[2] But as some in

[1]This memorial was read by President Manning. It claimed liberty of conscience for the Baptists in Massachusetts Bay, both as a natural and as a charter right, and showed how this right had been violated by various enactments of the General Assembly, and especially in the cases of Sturbridge and Ashfield. It closed as follows :—

"It may now be asked, *What is the liberty desired?* The answer is : As the kingdom of Christ is not of this world, and religion is a concern between God and the soul, with which no human authority can intermeddle, consistently with the principles of Christianity, and according to the dictates of Protestantism, we claim and expect the liberty of worshipping God according to our consciences, not being obliged to support a ministry we cannot attend, whilst we demean ourselves as faithful subjects. These we have an undoubted right to, as men, as Christians, and by charter as inhabitants of Massachusetts Bay."

This memorial, in full, is in the Life and Times of Backus, pp. 204—210.—ED.

[2] "The delegates from Massachusetts used all their arts to represent that we complained without reason. John Adams made a long speech and Samuel Adams another; both of whom said, 'There is, indeed, an ecclesiastical establishment in our province; but a very slender one, hardly to be called an establishment.' When they would permit, we brought up facts, which they tried to explain away, but could not. Then they shifted their plea, and asserted that our General Court was clear of blame, and had always been ready to hear our complaints, and to grant all reasonable help, whatever might have been done by executive officers; and S. Adams and R. T. Paine spent near an hour more on this plea. When they stopped, I told them I was very sorry to have any accusations to bring against the government which I belonged to, and which I would gladly serve to the utmost of my power, but I must say that facts proved the contrary to their plea; and gave a short account of our Legislature's treatment of Ashfield, which was very puzzling to them. In their plea, S. Adams tried to represent that *regular* Baptists were quite easy among us; and

Philadelphia made an attempt to turn these things against the general union of the colonies, in the defence of our civil rights, a report was industriously spread in New England, before the Baptist agent got home, that he had been to Philadelphia on purpose to break that union.[1] And while he was gone, the first parish in his town voted to tax all the Baptists therein to their minister, because they refused to give them any more certificates. He therefore soon met the Baptist committee at Boston, by whose advice a plain memorial of their grievances and desires was laid before our Provincial Congress;[2] to which the following answer was returned.

In Provincial Congress, Cambridge, December 9, 1774.

On reading the memorial of the Reverend Isaac Backus, agent to the Baptist churches in this government:

Resolved, That the establishment of civil and religious liberty, to each denomination in the province, is the sincere wish of this Congress. But being by no means vested with powers of civil government, whereby they

more than once insinuated that these complaints came from enthusiasts who made it a merit to suffer persecution ; and also that enemies had a hand therein. Paine said, there was nothing of conscience in the matter ; it was only a contending about paying a little money ; and also that we would not be neighborly and let them know who we were, which was all they wanted, and they would readily exempt us.

" In answer, I told them they might call it enthusiasm or what they pleased ; but I freely own, before all these gentlemen, that it is absolutely a point of conscience with me ; for I cannot give in the certificates they require without implicitly acknowledging that power in man which I believe belongs only to God. This shocked them ; and Cushing said : '*It quite altered the case;* for if it were a point of conscience, he had nothing to say to that.' And the conference of about four hours continuance, closed with their promising to do what they could for our relief ; though to deter us from thinking of their coming upon equal footing with us as to religion, John Adams at one time said, we might as well expect a change in the solar system, as to expect they would give up their establishment." Backus's Manuscripts. See a more extended sketch of this controversy, with accounts of it by Dr. Stiles and John Adams, in the Life and Times of Backus, pp. 203—215, 349—351. See also Works of John Adams, Vol. II, pp. 397—399 ; Manning and Brown University, pp. 237—239:—ED.

[1] See Life and Times of Backus, pp. 214, 215.—ED.

[2] This memorial pleaded the cause of the Baptists by the arguments that were used at that time against British oppression ; showed that to support the ministry by taxes collected by force was unscriptural ; explained the reasons of the appeal to the Continental Congress, and recited the oppressions in Ashfield, Montague, Haverhill, Gorham, Warwick and Chelmsford. It is given entire in the Life and Times of Backus, pp. 215—221.—ED.

can redress the grievances of any person whatever, they therefore recommend to the Baptist churches, that when a General Assembly shall be convened in this colony, they lay the real grievances of said churches before the same, when and where their petition will most certainly meet with all that attention due to the memorial of a denomination of Christians so well disposed to the public weal of their country.

By order of the Congress,

JOHN HANCOCK, President.

A true extract from the minutes.

BENJAMIN LINCOLN, Secretary.

Our former charter provided, that when the province should happen to be destitute of any Governor or Lieutenant Governor, the Council and Representatives should have the whole legislative power therein. Therefore, by the advice of the Continental Congress, such an Assembly was convened at Watertown, July 19, 1775; to whom, in September, the Warren Association presented a memorial, wherein, after mentioning the above advice, they say :—

Our real grievances are, that we, as well as our fathers, have, from time to time, been taxed on religious accounts where we were not represented ; and when we have sued for our rights, our causes have been tried by interested judges. That the Representatives in former Assemblies, as well as the present, were elected by virtue only of civil and worldly qualifications, is a truth so evident, that we presume it need not be proved to this Assembly ; and for a civil Legislature to impose religious taxes, is, we conceive, a power which their constituents never had to give ; and is therefore going entirely out of their jurisdiction. .... Under the legal dispensation, where God himself prescribed the exact proportion of what the people were to give, yet none but persons of the worst characters ever attempted to *take it by force.* I Sam. ii. 12, 16 ; Mic. iii. 5—9. How daring then, must it be for any to do it for Christ's ministers, who says, *My kingdom is not of this world !* .... We beseech this honorable Assembly to take these matters into their wise and serious consideration, before him who has said, With what measure ye mete it shall be measured to you again. Is not all America now appealing to heaven against the injustice of being taxed where we are not represented, and against being judged by men who are interested in getting away our money? And will heaven approve of your *doing the same thing* to your fellow servants? No, surely. .... We have no desire of representing this government as the worst of any who have imposed religious taxes ; we fully believe the contrary. Yet, as we are persuaded that an entire freedom from being taxed by civil rulers to religious worship, is not a mere favor, from any man or men in the world, but a right and property granted us by God, who commands us to stand fast in it, we have not only the same reason to refuse an acknowledgment of such a taxing power here, as America has the above-said power, but also, according to our present light, we should wrong our consciences in allowing that power to men, which we believe belongs only to God.

This memorial was read in the Assembly, and was ordered to lie a week on the table, and was then read again, and debated upon, and was referred to a committee, upon the receipt of whose report it was read a third time, and liberty granted to bring in a bill in our favor ; and such a bill was received and read once, and a time set for a second reading. But then other business was crowded in, and nothing·more done upon it.[1]   Such is the disposition of mankind.

As the British ministry were deceived, and entirely disappointed in their first scheme, a new one was invented, in the close of 1775 ; which was, by acts of parliament, to declare all these colonies to be in a state of rebellion, and out of the king's protection ; to hire a large army from Germany, to add terror to the roarings of the British lion ; and then to appoint commissioners to proclaim pardon and peace to any colony or place that should submit to their power, and promise to raise as much money among themselves as the Court of Britain should judge to be their proportion, towards the support and defence of government ; their peace to last as long as this was done.   And in order to man the British ships, and to make all afraid of their power, their commanders were ordered to enter the names of as many of the captives whom they should take as they thought proper, among the list of their hands on board, so as to compel them to fight against their own country, and to be punished as deserters, if they should attempt to make their escape.   And had not

---

[1]A full account of the action of the Assembly upon this memorial, is given in the Life and Times of Backus, pp. 226—228.   See also in the same work, pp. 229—231, a letter sent by the Warren Association to all the Baptist churches on the continent, " stating the true nature and importance of religious liberty," and proposing a general meeting of delegates from all the societies to consult upon the means by which this liberty might be secured.—Ed.

the Lord been on our side, when men thus rose up against
us, how soon would they have swallowed us up ! But when,
in his wise dispensations, he had given them all the advantages that could well be conceived of, how easily did he turn
their counsels into foolishness ? For when the British party
in Boston came to look out in the morning of March 13,
1776, behold ! two stately forts appeared on the top of two
hills in Dorchester, capable of commanding both the town
and the ships in the harbor. Burgoyne's letter to England
the June before informs us, that his party had laid a plan
to take possession of those hills, which was to have been
executed the 18th of that month ; but was prevented by the
Bunker Hill battle the preceding day. And as the only land
passage on to those heights was across an open marsh, within half a mile of their guards on Boston Neck, and as they
had a multitude of their friends scattered through the country, was it possible for several hundred tons weight of materials to be prepared before, and then to be carted some
miles on to those hills, and two forts to be erected there in
one night, by the undisciplined Americans, and the sagacious
Britons know nothing about it ? Yet such was the event ;
and let them deny it if they can. Not only so, but while
they were preparing to go over and attack those forts, the
winds and waves were put into such a commotion, as finally
prevented the attempt. And on March 17, the British army,
with a large number of our inimical countrymen, fled from
Boston ; and soon sailed to Nova Scotia or to Britain. Indeed, some of their men-of-war were left in Nantasket Road,
out of the reach of our cannon ; yet on May 17, a small
armed vessel took a large store-ship of theirs in the bay,
which was conveyed into Boston in their sight, and they had
not power to prevent it, having on board a thousand stands
of arms, fifteen hundred whole barrels of powder, and a
large quantity of other necessary supplies for our army.
And on June 14, their ships were compelled to quit the lower
harbor, by the firing of some cannon which our people had

conveyed down the night before; whereby that port was again opened, which was cruelly shut up two years before. And about four hundred and fifty of their troops were captivated by our cruisers about this time; and a vast quantity of their goods of all kinds were taken and brought into our country.

Not aware of such events, the next object of British policy was, to appoint such men to execute their new plan as should be able to divide the colonies, by drawing some part of them to accept of their pardons. And as Lord George Howe, who was slain near Ticonderoga, July 6, 1758, was so much beloved here, that the Massachusetts were at the expense of erecting a monument for him in Westminster Abbey, who could be so likely to gain upon our people as his two brothers? William was already appointed Governor of this province and Chief General of their armies; and Richard, successor in title to George, and an intimate friend to Dr. Franklin, was now made Chief Admiral of their fleet; and they were made joint commissioners to proclaim pardon to all who would accept of it on the above terms. And as an army of thirty-five thousand men was to be at their command, who would not be glad to receive their pardon and protection, rather than to be a mark for their resentment? But alas! the winds and waves were so contrary, that the two brothers could not meet to send out their proclamations, until July 12, eight days after the Congress, by the consent of the people in the thirteen colonies, had declared them to be FREE AND INDEPENDENT STATES. However, from on board their ships near New York, they sent forth their proclamations, which our people readily propagated through all these States. And, with a packet to Congress, Lord Howe sent a letter to his friend Franklin, a member of it, wherein he says:—

Retaining all the earnestness I ever expressed to see our differences accommodated, I shall conceive, if I meet with the dispositions in the colonies which I was once taught to expect, the most flattering hopes of proving serviceable, in the objects of the king's paternal solicitude, by promoting the establishment of lasting peace and union with the colonies. But if the deep-rooted prejudices of America, and the necessity of preventing her trade from passing into foreign channels, must keep us still a divided people, I shall, from every private as well as public motive, most heartily lament that it is not the moment wherein those great objects of my ambition are to be attained.

Franklin returned an answer from Philadelphia, July 30, wherein he says :—

The official dispatches to which you refer me, contain nothing more than we had seen in the act of parliament, viz., offers of pardon upon submission ; which I am sorry to find, as it must give your Lordship pain to be sent so far on so hopeless a business. Directing pardons to be offered to the colonies, who are the very parties injured, expresses indeed that opinion of our ignorance, baseness and insensibility, which your uninformed and proud nation has long been pleased to entertain of us ; but it can have no other effect than that of increasing our resentment. It is impossible we should think of submission to a government that has, with the most wanton barbarity and cruelty, burnt our defenceless towns, in the midst of winter ; excited the savages to massacre peaceful farmers, and our slaves to murder their masters ; and is even now bringing foreign mercenaries to deluge our settlements with blood.[1] .... Long did I endeavor, with unfeigned and unwearied zeal, to preserve from breaking that fine and noble china vase, the British empire ; for I knew, that being once broken, the separate parts could not retain even their shares of the strength and value that existed in the whole ; and that a perfect reunion of these parts could scarce ever be hoped for. .... The well founded esteem, and, permit me to say, affection, which I shall always have for your Lordship, make it painful for me to see you engaged in conducting a war, the great ground of which, as described in your letter, is the necessity of preventing the American trade from passing into foreign channels. To me it seems that neither the obtaining or retaining any trade, how valuable soever, is an object for which men may

---

[1] October 17, 1775, the enemy burnt four hundred and seventeen buildings in the town of Falmouth in Casco Bay. In the evening of the 7th of that month, their ships fired upon the town of Bristol, near Swanzey ; which caused the death of Mr. John Burt, their minister, and some others. Lord Dunmore, Governor of Virginia, retired on board an armed ship, and drew off all the slaves and others that he could ; and, after much other mischief, they burnt the town of Norfolk on January 1, 1776 ; in which cruel action, besides the unnatural nature of it, the whole loss to the inhabitants was computed at above three hundred thousand pounds. And a man was taken up, upon his way to the Ohio Indians, with a Colonel's commission from General Gage, to command all the savages and others that he could raise in the wilderness against us.

justly spill each other's blood ; that the true and sure means of extending and securing commerce, are the goodness and cheapness of commodities ; and that the profits of no trade can ever be equal to the expense of compelling it, and holding it by fleets and armies.

The real nature of the controversy is here stated in a fair and elegant manner ; and its whole progress verifies the truth of the word which says, Only by pride cometh contention ; and the love of money is the root of all evil. And can a clearer demonstration thereof be given, than for the inhabitants of one country to claim a right to be lawgivers and judges for others three thousand miles off, so as to dispose of their persons and property without their consent? A darling practice of our age, especially among high politicians, is to set up reason above divine revelation ; but how will their rules suit in this case ? One of their noted authors expressly denies that God had a right to command Abraham to sacrifice his son, with an intent to have it obeyed, and says, " The command might be given in order to convince Abraham, that even his honesty and integrity, when not under the direction of his understanding, might mislead him in the conducting of his actions." The reason given for thus setting up an inward rule above the written word, is this : says he, " It was right and fit, in the nature of the thing, that Abraham should guard and protect the life of Isaac ; which obligation, as it is founded in nature, so it is independent of, and antecedent to, any divine command ; yea, it is antecedent to the consideration of a deity, because it must and would be the same, if there were no such thing as a deity.[1] Yet when he comes to the question, " From whence does evil proceed ?" he says, " The difficulty in this case may not arise from the state of things, but from the weakness of our understandings, and the shortness of our knowledge, which render us incapable of seeing through and to the end of them."[2] Very true ; why then do these

[1] Chubb's Tracts, printed in London, 1754, Vol. II, pp. 3, 12. [Chubb's Treatises, XIX, pp. 240—246.]
[2] Ibid, p. 22. [Chubb's Treatises, XX, p. 254.]

weak and dark minds refuse entire submission and ready obedience to him whose understanding is infinite ? Had any due regard been paid to his authority in our mother island, we should never have heard of paternal solicitude, in invading the unalienable rights of her children ; nor of pardons brought upon the points of bayonets ! At the same time we have just cause to confess, that all our sufferings were less than our iniquities deserved, and that we were far from giving God all the glory of our support and deliverance, as we ought to have done. To give a particular history of this war is out of my province, though a concise view of the chief events of it comes into my plan. Yet, wanting time and means for it, my narrative must necessarily be incomplete.

As Canada had long been a dreadful scourge to New England, and the repeating of those bloody tragedies was intended by our enemies, amazing exertions were made to prevent it, and to unite that country with ours. Most of its inhabitants desired it, which was a great inducement to this attempt. Therefore the Colonels Ethan Allen and Seth Warner, encouraged thereto by the authority of Connecticut, surprized and took the strong fortresses of Ticonderoga and Crown Point, May 10, 1775, without the loss of a man on either side ; whereby above two hundred pieces of cannon, two vessels on Lake Champlain, and a large quantity of other stores fell into our hands. All this was done by three hundred and thirty men, chiefly from the State of Vermont. An army followed under General Montgomery, and after a close siege took St. Johns, at the farther end of said lake, and obtained the city of Montreal, November 13 ; previous whereto, Allen was taken and carried to Europe. In September Colonel Arnold set off from Cambridge with eleven hundred men, and marched to Newburyport, from whence they sailed into Kennebeck River, and went up to its head. And though near a third part of them then turned back, yet the remainder went forward, through a great and terrible

wilderness, over rivers, hills and mountains, where they saw
not the habitation of any human person for thirty-one days,
until they arrived among the Canadians on November 3, by
whom they were kindly treated, And the falling snows,
severe coldness of the air, and other unspeakable difficulties
in that northern region, did not hinder their march forward,
nor the junction of Montgomery's forces with them in December before Quebec, the capital of Canada.   These were
some of the doings of a people, whom British policy, or rather
folly, had declared to be cowards and paltroons.   Allen and
Arnold sprung from the despised Rhode Islanders.   On the
other hand, as General Clinton had sailed from Boston with
some forces, General Lee set off by land, and headed him at
New York, in Virginia, and in North and South Carolina.
At length, being reïnforced from Britain in June, by Admiral
Parker and Lord Cornwallis, a furious attack was made
upon the fort on Sullivan's Island, near Charleston ; but they
were defeated, with great damages in their shipping, as well
as loss of their men; and the remainder returned and joined
their main body near New York.   General Washington with
our main army was there, and had erected various fortifica-
tions in that city, and upon Long Island.   And through the
land many gloried in what the Americans had done, and
evidently treated their enemies with contempt.   But how
vain did their glorying soon appear ?

Our army met with a terrible defeat on Long Island,
August 28; were forced to evacuate the city of New York,
September 13 ; fought on a retreat at the White Plains;
Fort Washington was given up November 16 ; General Lee
was taken December 13 ; and General Washington with the
small remnant of our army retreated beyond the Delaware.
Ravishing of women and plundering of houses, by an enraged enemy, was seen through all the beautiful country of
New Jersey, and their cantonments were extended into the
towns of Trenton, Bordentown and Burlington, on the Delaware ; the latter within twenty miles of Philadelphia, over

to which a few freezing nights might give them an easy passage. If we turn our eyes to the north, we behold General Montgomery slain, December 31, in attempting to storm Quebec. In the spring our army was forced to make a hasty retreat from thence, being most cruelly harassed by the enemy, and greatly distressed at the same time with the small pox. And though a costly fleet to oppose them was formed on Lake Champlain, yet it was lost on October 12. And on December 8, the enemy, with a powerful force, took possession of Rhode Island, near the heart of New England. Our first army enlisted for eight months, the second for a year, which was now expiring, and the soldiers were daily returning home. Our paper money had been kept in good credit, until large additional sums were made in September, which lessened its value; and such vast quantities of goods were taken by our cruisers, and sold at public auction, that sugars rose from five dollars and a third per hundred to ten dollars in three months, and the like in other goods. Thus our prosperity seemed likely to destroy us, for if our public credit failed, confusion and slavery appeared the unavoidable consequence. And, to accomplish this, if possible, the enemy counterfeited our paper currency at New York, and in a clandestine manner dispersed large quantities of it through the country. Every earthly help failed us; but as our appeal had been to heaven against oppressors, many cries now undoubtedly ascended there, saying Give us help from trouble, for vain is the help of man. And what an answer thereto was returned!

While the enemy were expecting in a few days to march in triumph to Philadelphia, on December 26, General Washington takes near a thousand of them, and carries them there as captives. And though a large reïnforcement of the enemy marched up to Trenton, and expected to have our General and his forces in the morning, yet the next news they hear of him is at Princeton, a dozen miles off, where he captivates another party of their troops, and is soon gone out of their way, January 2, 1777. These things terrified the enemy in such a manner as to call in and confine them at Brunswick, within sight of their shipping, until spring, when they returned to New York. Hard attempts indeed were made by some, to persuade the world that bribery moved the British General thus to act. As if men who could scarcely reward their friends for necessary services, could outbid their enemies, who had the wealth of both the Indies at command! Such violence will courtiers offer to reason, rather than to confess that, wherein they deal proudly, God is above them, and easily turns their counsels into foolishness. For though their main army sailed into Chesapeake Bay, and marched from thence to Philadelphia in September, and kept it one winter, yet they got no real advantage thereby. Rather, by dividing their forces, they prepared the way for their own confusion. Burgoyne had acquired a large share of military skill and fame, in former wars in Europe and in the East Indies ; and thirteen thousand troops were assigned him, besides savage auxiliaries, to invade our country from Canada. Ticonderoga was thought by many to be almost impregnable, and yet it was deserted by our army, July 5, before it was fully invested by the enemy, who pursued and harassed our people most terribly. And if the strongest fortress in the land was thus given up, only upon seeing the manner of the enemy's approach, how easily might they subdue an open country, and march where they pleased ! Where is the power now that can defend us ! A great consternation spread through the country ; and to pursue this advantage with the utmost speed, moved Burgoyne to take such methods as effectually defeated his designs. Had he returned a little, and taken the advantage of a water passage over Lake George, he might have reached Fort Edward much sooner than he did. But fearing an abatement of the ardor of his troops, and of the consternation of the Americans, he pursued them in a way attended with great natural impediments, which were much augmented by fallen trees and other obstacles then thrown in their way. So that by the time he sent out a party towards Bennington, with a haughty proclamation to intimidate our countrymen, their spirits were revived, and on August 16, they faced the enemy's encampment, and forced their lines with undaunted resolution. His western detachment, under St. Leger, was also defeated. And the chief commanders in that department being removed, and others appointed, in whom our people had confidence, they were all alive in the defence of our country. Ticonderoga was recovered, and every resource and way of escape was cut off; so that the haughty General and his army had no way left but to surrender themselves and their weapons into the hands of the people they had greatly abused and despised. This was on October 17. All Europe was astonished at this event; and one of their most powerful princes soon made the proposal, which was accomplished on February 6, 1778, of coming into an alliance with the United States of America. Hereby a great turn was made in our affairs, and a door was opened for our deliverance, though not without many other trying scenes.

As the invaders of our rights called us rebels, it was very difficult settling a cartel for the exchange of prisoners; and when that was agreed upon, new difficulties about it soon arose. When they had taken General Lee, who had been one of their officers, he was not dealt with as our country officers in their hands were; which moved the Congress to order some retaliation upon their officers in our hands, which caused reciprocal complaints, and many terrible actions on both sides. On January 1, 1777, two hundred of our countrymen, who had been prisoners at New York, were brought to Milford to be exchanged; but they had been so cruelly used, that a very large part of them died before their friends could have notice of it, so as to afford them any relief. Two young men from Middleborough, and a pious member of a Baptist church in Attleborough, died there in that manner. And during the war their prison-ships at New York destroyed

15

many thousands of our people, in a much more cruel manner than common murder.   Therefore when there was a
want of union and vigor in the defence of our country at
any time, new attempts of the enemy against us never failed
of supplying that want.   They plainly acted like thieves and
robbers in all parts of the land.   In the morning of May
25, 1778, a party of them came up to Warren, and burned
their meeting-house and minister's house, with some others;
plundered their goods, and carried off several of the inhabitants that were not in arms, one of whom was the pastor of
the Baptist church there, who was confined for some time in
a prison-ship at Newport.   On their return they burned a
number of houses in Bristol, among which was their Episcopal church.   But I must not enlarge upon this subject.
Other commissioners were now sent over, with new offers of
pardon, and also of an enlargement of our privileges, if we
would submit to the British government.   Copies thereof
were sent to the Congress, and to the Governors of the several States.   In answer to those sent to Governor Trumbull,
he well said :—

There was a day when even this step, from our then acknowledged parent
State, might have been accepted with joy and gratitude ; but that day, Sir,
is past irrecoverably.   The repeated rejection of our sincere and sufficiently
humble petitions ; the commencement of hostilities ; the inhumanity which
has marked the prosecution of the war on your part in its several stages ;
the insolence which displays itself on every petty advantage ; the cruelties
which have been exercised on those unhappy men, whom the fortune of
war has thrown into your hands ; all these are insuperable bars to the very
idea of concluding a peace with Great Britain, on any other conditions than
the most absolute, perfect independence.

However, the vast uncertainty of human affairs must yet
be largely experienced, before such a peace could be obtained.

General Howe was recalled, and Clinton took his place as
chief commander ; and he evacuated Philadelphia, after they
had possessed it near nine months, and marched his army
across the lower part of New Jersey, where General Wash-

ington gave them battle, near Monmouth Court House, June 28 ; when many were slain on both sides, and the excessive heat of the air cut off many more. No sooner had the British troops arrived at New York, than a powerful French fleet appeared upon the coasts, and came before that place. British fears and American hopes were raised hereby ; which alternately were as changeable as the winds. The French made no attempt upon New York ; but their speedy arrival at Rhode Island caused considerable destruction of the British shipping, and raised the hopes of our people of seeing that place delivered. Many thousands were collected for that purpose, who, under the command of General Sullivan, landed upon the island, August, 9. But the appearance of the British fleet drew that of France out of the harbor the same day; and a terrible storm soon dispersed and shattered both fleets, so as to prevent any general engagement, or a deliverance to Rhode Island. In December, the capital of Georgia was taken by a party of the British troops. In 1779, various attempts were made to open a passage up the North River; but finding it impracticable, a strong party was sent to New Haven, who slew a number of the inhabitants, and plundered the town ; and then went and burned the beautiful towns of Fairfield and Norwalk. Their malignity was hereby further discovered; but it could not draw the sagacious Washington from the mountains, while he saw a powerful fleet and army below him. From Georgia a party of their troops marched to the gates of Charleston; but the arrival of a French fleet on the coasts turned them back to Savannah; which place our friends attempted to take by storm on October 9, but without success. Thus the hopes of help from our allies were a second time disappointed. The produce of the field was also so much cut short last year, that bread was the scarcest the beginning of this that we had ever known. And to have the judgment of famine added to that of the sword, would be terrible indeed. But infinite goodness now gave us an earlier harvest than we had ever seen, and in a few months our scarcity was turned into plenty. And on October 24, the enemy went off from Rhode Island, which was a great relief to this part of the country.

Having made sufficient trial of these northern hills, they flattered themselves with much greater advantages in the southern plains of America. And for a while it seemed as if in that way they would have carried all before them. A large force sailed from New York in December, and though they had a tempestuous passage, yet after some repairs at Georgia, they came and besieged the capital of South Carolina; which was compelled to yield to them May 12, 1780. The country then lay open to their ravages; and on August 16, General Gates, who had gained great fame in the north, was entirely defeated in those southern regions. And though a French fleet and army arrived at Rhode Island July 10, yet none could then tell whether we should obtain any solid benefit thereby. Our public credit was sinking daily, even so that scarce any recruits for our army could be obtained, but upon private, personal security. And in November the officers constrained the Congress to promise them half-pay during life, to prevent their deserting the public service of their country. In June our currency had depreciated so far, that seventy-five paper dollars were readily given for one of silver. By orders from Congress, the New England States then came into such measures as kept it at a stay until February, 1781; when the pouring in vast quantities of it from the southward gave it such a rapid turn, that it ran entirely down in May, so as to stop passing. Before this, General Greene, on March 14, lost a large number of men in the battle of Guilford Court House, in North Carolina; from whence Lord Cornwallis marched with a powerful army into Virginia, where he spread much terror, and laid waste the country; while the credit of Congress was sunk so low, that they were scarcely able to send the least supply to General Greene. Yet, to the astonishment of our enemies, he was made instrumental of an entire recovery of South Carolina and Georgia. A loan of money from France revived our public credit; their troops marched through the land, from Rhode Island to Virginia; the winds and seas, with the hearts of the people, all concurred together to compel another experienced British General, with a large and powerful army, to yield themselves as ·prisoners to the despised and much injured Americans, October 19, 1781. The effect of which was, that on November 30, 1782, the British Court fully gave up their claims to these thirteen United States; which treaty was to take place as soon as peace was settled with France and the other powers concerned. Preliminaries for it were signed January 20, and the peace was settled in September, 1783. Though before we say more upon it, we must take a further look at things among ourselves.

CHAPTER XXV.

A NEW CONSTITUTION FRAMED, BUT NOT ACCEPTED.—PEPPERELL RIOT.
—GOVERNMENT AND LIBERTY DESCRIBED.—BUT MUCH OPPOSED.—OUR
PRESENT CONSTITUTION BROUGHT IN.—BAPTIST TESTIMONIES REJECTED.
—WHAT THEIR FAITH AND ORDER IS.—A CHARGE TO EMBRACE FUR-
THER LIGHT AS IT OPENS.

Our Assembly for 1777 were empowered to frame a new
constitution of government, which was to be established or
rejected by the next Assembly. This was done in the winter after, but without any Bill of Rights ; and an article was
inserted therein to adopt their old ecclesiastical laws ; which
caused the Baptist agent and committee to meet at Boston,
February 21, 1778, and to draw up an address[1] to our next
Assembly against those laws, with a prayer that it might be
fixed as a fundamental principle of our government, " that
ministers shall be supported only by Christ's authority, and
not at all by assessment and secular force ; which impartial
liberty has long been claimed and enjoyed by the town of
Boston." A hundred copies of it were printed and dispersed, and a large number from various denominations subscribed it. This gave such an alarm, that an earnest warn-

[1]We learn from his Diary that this address was written by Mr. Backus himself.
Another paper from the same pen, in the same cause, had just preceded it. In several towns in the State, particularly in Medfield, ministerial rates had been recently
collected by distraint from Baptists. This led Mr. Backus to prepare an " Address
to the people of New England," rehearsing the pleas for liberty of conscience. It
was read at the meeting of the Warren Association in 1777, and published with their
Minutes as a circular to the churches.—ED.

ing was given to our rulers, in the Election Sermon at Boston, May 27, against making any alteration in their established modes and usages in religion ; when it was said, "Let the restraints of religion once be broken down, as they infallibly would be by leaving the subject of public worship to the humors of the multitude, and we might well defy all human wisdom and power to support and preserve order and government in the State."[1]   However, that constitution was set aside ; and his party in the country, soon after, gave a remarkable discovery of what their ideas were about religion and good order.

For two young Baptist ministers were called to preach in Pepperell, near forty miles north-westward of Boston, to whom six persons offered themselves as candidates for baptism.   Therefore, on June 26, they met in a field by a river side, where prayers were made, and a sermon begun, when the chief officers of the town, with many followers, came and interrupted their worship.   The owner of the field warned them to depart out of it, if they would not be peaceable ; but they refused to go.   One of the Baptist ministers desired them to act like men, if they would not like Christians ; and reminded them of the liberty of conscience which is generally allowed, and even by the powers we were at war with ; and began to open the divine warrant therefor ; upon which an officer said, "Don't quote Scripture here !" Another of them, who was a communicant in their church, cast the odious name, *Tory*, upon one of those candidates for baptism.   And he no sooner attempted to discover the injustice thereof, than the officer said, " Hold your tongue, or I'll beat your teeth down your throat !"   And a dog was carried into the river and plunged, in evident contempt of our sentiments.   A gentleman of the town then invited the Baptists to go and hold their meeting at his house, which was near another river.   They accepted of it, and so went through with their worship.   At the close of which a man

[1]Payson's Sermon, p. 20.

was hired with a bowl of liquor to go into the river, and dip another two or three times over; where also two or three dogs more were plunged.   After which three officers of the town came into the house where the Baptist ministers were, and advised them immediately to depart out of that town for their own safety.   Being asked whether their lives would be in danger if they did not depart, no answer was returned. But seeing their temper, the Baptists agreed to disperse, and to meet at a distant place of water; which was done, and those six persons were decently baptized, though further abuse was offered at the close of it.   By direction of the Warren Association, an account of these things was published in the Independent Chronicle of October 15;[1] which others laid before the Grand Jury of the county of Middlesex.   But they were prevailed with to suspend the matter, until the town should vindicate themselves.   This they attempted in the Chronicle of November 12.   It mainly turned upon disputing the names of actions, and about the persons who performed them.   The Baptist account charged the hiring of a person to go into the water upon an officer, which was said to be by way of mockery.   But say the town :—

The misrepresentation of this affair, and indeed a most unpardonable one it is, appears from considering, that the conduct of said Bynton and Lawrence was altogether from the instigation of a youngster, who promised Bynton a bowl of liquor on complying with his proposal ; and this was done inconsiderately, and not meant as a piece of religious mockery.   The officers of the town had no concern in that affair. .... They were quite opposite, and particular care was taken by the officers of the town to prevent riotous behavior, and to maintain peace and good order.   That we did, as a town, pay particular attention to the conduct of those dangerous persons, is a fact we do not wish to conceal.[2]

[1]This account was written by Mr. Backus, and published over his signature, as agent of the Baptist churches.   It is a detailed account of the disgraceful transactions, giving the names of many concerned in them.   By advice of the Warren Association, Mr. Backus had visited the town and obtained exact information of the facts. —Ed.

[2]This vindication of the town of Pepperell was " signed by order of said town; Nehemiah Hobart, Town Clerk."   While it charged the article of Mr. Backus with

Now the dangerous person, who then carried into Pepperell the dangerous practice of quoting Scripture to defend
liberty of conscience, and of burying in baptism, was Isaiah
Parker, pastor of the Baptist church in Harvard, who from
that day to this is allowed by authority to be a regular minister of Jesus Christ, though he is not a State minister.
Another event, still more dangerous to their way, was as
follows :—

By the unanimous voice of the Warren Association of
September 8, a pamphlet was published, which says :—

As the affairs of government and liberty are the greatest points of controversy now in the world, it certainly is of great importance that our ideas
be clear and just concerning them. Permit us [me] therefore to offer a
few thoughts upon a familiar metaphor, which the Holy Ghost has used to
illustrate their true nature. In Amos v. 24, he says, Let judgment run
down as waters, and righteousness as a mighty stream. From whence we
may observe; 1. That judgment and righteousness are essential to freedom. When we would represent any thing as quite free, we say it is as
free as water. And not only the flow of mercy and grace from God to
men, but also its effects in them, in producing obedience unto him, are often
compared thereto in the word of truth. John iv. 14, [and] vii. 38 ; Titus
ii. 11, 12, [and] iii. 5—8. This is most certain, because, 2. Freedom is
not acting at random, but by reason and rule. Those who walk after their
own lusts, are clouds without water, carried about by [of] winds ; or raging
waves of the sea, foaming out their own shame ; while the true sons of lib-

falsehood in general, it attempted to deny scarce any one of its statements in particular. Its main object was to claim that neither the officers nor the people of the
town were responsible for the treatment of the Baptists, but only a few thoughtless
persons.

This was not the end of this newspaper controversy. In the Independent Chronicle of December 3, was a piece from Mr. Backus, reässerting the statements of his
former article, and containing a certificate from six men of Pepperell, describing
the indecencies of the town meeting that was called in consequence of Mr. Backus's
former article, and showing that the piece published in vindication of the town was
so prepared as to be untrustworthy in itself, and not a true expression of the sense
of the town. In the Boston Gazette, February 1, 1779, was a scurrilous piece, signed
" Swift," which stated that Mr. Backus himself wrote the above named certificate,
and induced the signers to subscribe it, promising that he would not publish it. The
signers were defamed as tories, cheats and thieves, and it was more than intimated
that Mr. Backus was no better. In the Gazette of February 22, Mr. Backus denied
the statements with regard to the procuring of the certificate ; and in the same paper
of March 8, was a second article from " Swift," in the same tone as the former.
—Ed.

erty are like streams which run down in a clear and steady channel. David says, I will run the way of thy commandments, when thou shalt enlarge my heart. I will walk at liberty, for I seek thy precepts. Streams and rivers must have steady channels to run in ; but they that promise liberty while they despise government, are wells without water, clouds that are carried with a tempest. II Peter ii. 10—19. 3. Though tyranny and licentiousness often make a great noise, yet government and liberty are much stronger than they are. The former, like raging waves, dash themselves against the rocks, and die upon the shore ; or like a tempest, after making sad waste and devastation, their strength is gone, and their force is over. While the latter, like a mighty stream, carry all before them, and never rest till they can get through or over all obstacles [which are] put in their way. 4. Streams and rivers are of great use, and cause a constant flow of refreshment and blessings wherever they come ; so does the exercise and administration of judgment and righteousness, among all people that enjoy them. Hence, 5. The command of heaven is, Let them run down ; put no obstruction in their way. No, rather be in earnest to remove every thing that hinders their free course. 6. The context plainly shews, that a main obstruction to these great blessings among the people then spoken to, was their assuming a power to govern religion, instead of being governed by it. True religion is a voluntary obedience unto God. And the great design of all ordinances and acts of worship towards him, is that thereby we may obtain pardon and cleansing, with direction and assistance to behave as we ought towards our fellow men. But instead of this, those people added their own inventions to divine institutions, and substituted their acts of devotion towards God, in the place of a righteous practice towards men ; or for a cover to their contrary conduct. And they would fain have been thought very religious, although they turned judgment into wormwood, hated him that rebuked in the gate, and abhorred him who spake uprightly.[1]

Infinite wisdom disposed things in such a manner, as to give a keener edge to this remonstrance than could be foreseen by man. For an extract from the last Election Sermon, and also from Chauncy against Chandler, was added to the above observations, with some remarks thereon.[2] At

[1] "Government and Liberty described, and Ecclesiastical Tyranny Exposed. By Isaac Backus, Pastor of a Church in Middleborough. 'Stand fast therefore in the liberty wherewith Christ hath made us free, and be not entangled again with the yoke of bondage.' Gal. v. 1." Pp. 1, 2.—Ed.

[2] A part of the extract from the Election Sermon is on page 220 ; and a part of that from Dr. Chauncy, on page 147. The treatise shows the inconsistency of these authors with each other, and Dr. Chauncy's inconsistency with himself.—Ed.

the same time our army on Rhode Island saw such danger of being surrounded by the British fleet, that they wisely came off with all their stores, in the night after August 30. Chauncy imagined that this defeat might be turned to ministerial advantage; and therefore at his next lecture, when many of our rulers were present, he delivered a discourse from the seventh of Joshua, wherein he represented that one of the accursed things which caused that defeat, was their neglect of making a new law to help ministers about their salaries, which the depreciation of our currency had greatly lessened. This sermon was soon printed and dispersed in the country. And in the Continental Journal of October 8, it was highly commended, and its author also; and then it was said, "Although the General Assembly has now been sitting for some time, no motion (as I can learn) has as yet been made, or is likely to be made, for this purpose. . . . . Are the clergy then to submit to this treatment? Are they as an order, and [as] the only order of men in the community, to remain subjected to injustice and fraud!" Now it was so ordered, that the above passages in the Baptist pamphlet were inserted in the Independent Chronicle the same day, in the same street, in Boston. By which means the same author was declaring to the world in one paper, that all religious establishments were of infinite damage to the cause of God and true religion; and in another, that the want of further exertions in that way was an accursed thing, which caused the defeat of our army. And what could be done in such a case? In the Boston Gazette of November 2, it was declared, that said Baptist pamphlet "exhibited only a compound of ignorance, impudence and abuse."[1]

---

[1] This was the commencement of another protracted newspaper controversy. The article of November 2, was largely a personal attack upon Mr. Backus. It was signed "Hieronymus." Similar articles with the same signature appeared in the Gazette December 28, January 18, 1779, February 1, and March 8. Mr. Backus replied to the first in the Gazette of December 14, 1778; and a Baptist writer, signing himself "Milton," vindicated Mr. Backus against "Hieronymus" in the Independent Chronicle, November 19, 1778, December 17, and February 25, 1779.—ED.

And their refusal to comply with ministerial demands, was declared to be a using force against them; upon which it was said, "I cannot conceive that it is more proper to use force against ministers than for them; yet this is the subject from which a set of men, who have occasioned more disturbance and damage to this State than would be repaired by all the money which selling them all for slaves would produce, derive [all] their importance." And the secular arm was called for to punish them. This was so far from being obtained, that the pastor of the First Baptist church in Boston was called to preach the Election Sermon there, May 26, 1779, in which the difference between church and State was well described, with the importance of keeping them entirely distinct; and it was printed and sent through the State by order of authority.[1] However our opponents were far from yielding this point.

Delegates from the several towns, elected entirely for the purpose of framing a new constitution of government, met on September 1, and chose a large committee to make a draft for their consideration, and adjourned. When they met again they took in hand a Bill of Rights which was laid before them. The Third Article therein was to give civil rulers power in religious matters, which occasioned much debate; until a Baptist member moved to have that article recommitted. The motion was concurred with, and he was elected the Chairman of a committee of seven upon that article. Five of them were great politicians, and they brought in a new draft, which, after warm debates, was passed by a majority, November 10, as it now stands in our constitution. In order to obtain this vote, it was asserted that there never was any persecution in this land; but that what had been so called were only just punishments upon

---

[1] "A Sermon to the Honorable Council, &c., May 26, 1779. By Samuel Stillman, A. M. Render to Cæsar the things that are Cæsar's, and to God the things that are God's. Mark 12. 17." Backus says in his Diary, that seventy-eight out of eighty-six voted for Mr. Stillman as preacher.—Ed.

disorderly persons, and disturbers of the public peace.   And
the Baptists were accused of sending their agent to Philadelphia in 1774, with a false memorial of grievances, in order to break the union of the colonies.   Sharp debates were
caused hereby for some time ; but the first volume of our
history·was brought in and laid upon the table, which silenced the first part of those declamations, and their agent,
being informed of the latter part; published said Third Article in the Chronicle of December 2, with reasons against
the power claimed in the middle part of it ;[1] and then named
his accusers concerning the Philadelphia affair, and charged
them with a violation of their promise made there ; and
challenged them to a fair hearing before any proper judges.
This was so far from being granted, that a long, reviling
piece, full of glaring deceit, came out in the Chronicle of
February 10, 1780 ;[2] which was soon after reprinted in the
Providence Gazette, where the appeal it pretended to answer was not known.   It accused the Baptist members of

[1] The objectionable part of the Third Article of the proposed constitution, was as
follows :—

   " The people of this Commonwealth have a right to invest their Legislature with
power to authorize and require the several towns, parishes, precincts, and other
bodies politic, or religious societies, to make suitable provision, at their expense, for
the institution of the public worship of God, and for the support and maintenance
of public protestant teachers of piety, religion, and morality, in all cases where such
provision shall not be made voluntarily.   And the people of this Commonwealth
have also a right to, and do invest their Legislature with authority to enjoin upon all
the subjects an attendance upon the instructions of the public teachers aforesaid, at
stated times and seasons, if there be any one whose instructions they can conveniently and conscientiously attend ; provided, notwithstanding, that the several towns,
parishes, precincts, or other bodies politic, and religious societies, shall at all times
have the exclusive right of electing their public teachers, and of contracting with
them for their support and maintenance.   And all monies raised by the subjects to
the support of the public worship, and of the public teachers aforesaid, shall, if he
request it, be uniformly applied to the support of the public teacher or teachers of
his own religious sect or denomination, provided there be any on whose instructions
he attends ; otherwise it may be paid to the teacher or teachers of the parish or
precinct where the money is raised."—ED.

[2] This article claimed to be written "by a member of the Convention."   Mr.
Backus writes in his Diary, "An answer to my publication of December 2, was in
the same paper of February 10 ; said to be written by Mr. S. West, of Dartmouth."
—ED.

the Convention of bitterness and rage against their ministers, especially for comparing them to the sons of Eli; and
to prove that they were not worthy of that charge, the writer says, "Eli's sons were not to blame for taking that part
of the offerings which the law allowed them, but for the illegal manner in which they took it." Very true; and the
only cause of the bitterness and rage now discovered against
the Baptists, was their refusal to countenance such an illegal
and wicked manner of proceeding. An anonymous Baptist
writer began some publications in the Chronicle, against the
power of taxation claimed in the above-said Third Article,
about the time that the constitution was finished. In answer
to whom, a writer appeared in the Continental Journal of
March 9, saying :—

> The wicked enemies of our civil and sacred rights, are like the troubled
> sea, whose waters cannot rest, but being driven by furious winds are con-
> tinually casting up mire and dirt. .... There is a certain junto composed
> of disguised tories, British emissaries, profane and licentious deists, avari-
> cious worldlings, disaffected sectaries, and furious, blind bigots, who had
> much rather overturn and destroy the Commonwealth, than not have the
> gratification of their own humor.

And he subscribed himself "Irenæus, a member of the Convention."[1] The Baptist agent and committee met, April 6,
and published an appeal to the people of this State, against
the taxing power for religious teachers claimed in the new
constitution, then sent out for their acceptance or rejection.
But their opponents were so much concerned about it, that
no less than three different pieces against the Baptist agent
were published in the Boston papers in the month of May,
to two of which the writers subscribed their names,[2] which had
not been done before. One of them was as follows : The first

---

[1] Five articles from the Baptist writer above referred to were in the Independent
Chronicle from March 2 to April 13. They were signed "Philanthropos." He also
answered "Irenæus" in two articles in the Continental Journal, March 23 and April
6. The controversy between them was then transferred to the Boston Gazette, and
afterwards to the Independent Ledger. It continued for several months.—ED.

[2] Independent Ledger, May 22; Independent Chronicle, May 18, an article signed
William Gordon; May 25, an article signed Francis Faulkner.—ED.

part of the Third Article in our Bill of Rights says, " The
happiness of a people, and the good order and preservation
of civil government, essentially depend upon piety, religion
and morality, and these cannot be generally diffused through
a community but by the institution of the public worship of
God, and of public instructions in piety, religion and morality;" which part, said agent, in his publication of December 2, declared a full concurrence with.   Upon which a
minister of Roxbury, in the Chronicle of May 18,[1] said,
" Mr. Backus, by inadvertently concurring fully with this
part, gave up the whole cause for which he was agent."
This he endeavored to prove, by fixing an emphasis upon
the word *Essentially*, and then observing that government
can exist without Christianity.   And his evident design was
to sink the credit of the agent among his brethren, in order
to terminate this controversy.   But the agent answered all
those three publications in one paper,[2] June 26, when he
observed, that " no government could ever be established
without appeals to the Deity ; the knowledge of whom is as
much greater under the gospel than it is in pagan countries
as seeing in day-light is above feeling in the night.   Matt. v.
14; Acts xvii. 27.   And men can have no more right to add
to God's laws about his worship, and to judge the consciences
of such as refuse to submit to their additions, than they
have power to cause the day-spring to know his place. Job
xxxviii. 12; Luke i. 78.   And is not gospel light essentially
necessary for the good order of government, although government can exist without it !"   And notwithstanding their
Third Article expressly excludes all subordination of one
religious sect to another, yet he observed that since it was
passed, four Baptist brethren had been imprisoned, and a
fifth had a cow taken from him, for no other cause than a
refusal to acknowledge such subordination.   Two of them

[1]This was one of a series of articles by Dr. Gordon, in defence of the Third Article of the proposed constitution.—ED.
[2]The Independent Ledger.—ED.

were of Bridgewater, the others were of Lancaster.[1] Those of Bridgewater were threatened this month with imprisonment for another ministerial tax ; but it was prevented in the following manner.   One of them was lieutenant of a company of militia ; and, as the public credit was sunk so low as to render it exceedingly difficult to raise recruits for our army ; news came to him that the town had chosen him a member of a special committee to procure a number of men that were wanted, which news came just after the collector had threatened to carry him to jail for said tax, and prevented it.   But a third Baptist from Lancaster was imprisoned at Worcester, June 26, where two of his brethren had been from April 12, and they were confined there until fall.

Yet when the new constitution took place, October 25, 1780,[2] it was said :—

We may rely that the present government will do all it fairly can, by authority and example, to answer the end of its institution, that the members of this Commonwealth may *lead a quiet and peaceable life in all* GOD-

---

[1] "Two members of the Convention, who resided in the south parish of Bridgewater, were led by these false accusations [against Mr. Backus] to move the collector of their minister's salary to go with a constable and seize Lieutenant Elijah Ames and his brother Joseph Ames, Jr., members of the First Baptist church in Middleborough, for said minister's tax, which they declined paying.   These officers commanded two regular hearers of Mr. Backus to assist in carrying the recusant brothers to Plymouth jail, but they were promptly disobeyed. 'Then,' says Mr. Backus, 'they went and took to themselves some lewd fellows of the baser sort, and came again with ropes to bind our brethren.   And they did bind one of them, and carried them both a mile or two to a tavern, when one of that party paid the money and released the prisoners. . . . . Before our said brethren were seized they mildly labored to convince these officers that they had no right to do it.   But the constable said, Our churches are built upon the law.   Lieutenant Ames replied, I knew that before; but I thought you would be ashamed to own it.'"   Life and Times of Backus, p. 240.

"The second Tuesday of March, 1779, the First Precinct in Lancaster voted a salary to their minister, Mr. Timothy Harrington, wherein John Hawks was taxed £6, 16, Nathan Willard, £14, 8, 6; for which they were seized . . . . April 11, and were both committed to Worcester jail on April 12."   Backus's Manuscripts.—ED.

[2] By vote of the Warren Association, at their meeting at Royalston, September 13, 1780. the following protest was circulated and presented to the General Court which was to decide the question of the ratification of the Constitution :—

We, whose names are hereunto subscribed, inhabitants of this State, who are

LINESS as well as *honesty*, and our liberty never be justly reproached as licentiousness. I know there is diversity of sentiment respecting the extent of civil power in religious matters. Instead of entering into the dispute, may I be allowed from the warmth of my heart to recommend, where conscience is pleaded on both sides, mutual candor and love.[1]

And in the Boston Gazette of February 5, 1781, it was said :—

Last summer, a certain rich man in the county of Plymouth, altered his principles with regard to baptism, was rebaptized, and admitted into Mr. Backus's church in Middleborough. Some neighbors were so uncharitable and censorious as to imagine that this person changed his religion in order to be freed from ministerial taxes. .... However, it remained a question in the minds of many people, by what means his estate could be exempted legally, inasmuch as they verily supposed that Mr. Backus had declared he would give no more certificates to any body whatsoever, always pleading,

twenty-one years of age and above, of various religious denominations, enter our PROTEST against the power claimed in the Third Article of the declaration of rights in the new plan of government introduced among us; for the reasons following, viz. :—

" 1. Because it asserts a right in a people to give away a power they never had themselves; for no man has a right to judge for others in religious matters; yet this Article would give the majority of each town and parish the exclusive right of covenanting for the rest with religious teachers, and so, of excluding the minority from the liberty of choosing for themselves in that respect. 2. Because this power is given entirely into the hands of men who vote only by virtue of *money* qualifications, without any regard to the church of Christ. 3. Because said Article, contradicts itself; for it promises *equal* protection of all sects, with an exemption from any subordination of one religious denomination to another; when it is impossible for the majority of any community to govern in any affair, unless the minority are subject to them in that affair. 4. Because by this Article the civil power is called to judge whether persons can conveniently and conscientiously attend upon any teacher within their reach, and oblige each one to support such teachers as may be contrary to his conscience; which is subversive of the unalienable rights of conscience. 5. Because, as the Convention say, ' power without any restraint, is tyranny;' which they explain as meaning the union of the legislative, executive and judicial powers of government in the same hands; and it is evident that these powers are all united in the Legislature, who, by this Article, are empowered to compel both civil and religious societies to make what they shall judge to be *suitable provision* for religious teachers ' in all cases where such provision shall not be made voluntarily."— ED.

[1] Cooper's Sermon, pp. 37, 38.—B.

" A Sermon preached before his Excellency, John Hancock, Esq., Governor, the Honorable the Senate and House of Representatives of the Commonwealth of Massachusetts, October 25, 1780; being the day of the commencement of the Constitution and inauguration of the new government. By Samuel Cooper, D. D."—ED.

as they received it, that the practice was contrary to the dictates of his conscience.   Nevertheless, contrary to the expectation of every one, our assessors have been furnished with a certificate. .... I hope the public will put
the most favorable construction upon the late remarkable conduct of our
agent for a thousand souls ; that his laudable example will be punctually
imitated by all others of the same profession, and thereby finish one part of
the tedious dispute which has long subsisted.

This paper was left for him three days after, by a noted
lawyer, at a house he was to preach at in Bridgewater.
From thence he went into Boston, and demanded the name
of the writer of that libel.   This was refused by the printer, though he was ready to publish an answer to it.   An
answer was therefore left, upon an express promise from
the printer, that he would not publish a reply without the
writer's name.   Yet this promise was violated on March 5,
without so much as sending the reply to the agent.   He was
however so unwise as to send another piece, which was published May 7, wherein some expressions were so turned,
as to cast the printer's faults upon the public.   From hence
three or four reviling pieces were published in the Boston
papers against him ;[1] in one of which he was threatened
with a halter and the gallows.   Yet for all this noise, they
had no other foundation than a line that was given July 12,
1780, which certified that a man in Pembroke was a baptized member of the First Baptist church in Middleborough,
signed only by their pastor, at a time when no certificate law
had been in force for some months, and none ever could be
again, according to said Third Article, which excludes all subordination of any one sect to another.   And the line given did
not answer to any law ever made in this government, from
its foundation to this day.   It may therefore be proper in
this place to give a distinct account of what the faith and
order of these Baptist churches are, against which such opposition has been made.

In general, their faith and practice come the nearest to

[1] See Boston Gazette, May 21, two articles ; May 28, June 4.—Ed.

that of the first planters of New England, of any churches now in the land, excepting in the single article of sprinkling infants. In particular, they believe ; 1. That God set Adam as the public head of all mankind ; so that when he revolted from heaven, and seized upon the earth as his own, all the human race fell in him, and all bear his earthly image, until they are born again. 2. That in infinite mercy the eternal Father gave a certain number of the children of men to his beloved Son, before the world was, to redeem and save ; and that he, by his obedience and sufferings, has procured eternal redemption for them. 3. That by the influence of the Holy Spirit, these persons individually,[1] as they come into existence, are effectually called in time, and savingly renewed in the spirit of their . minds. 4. That their justification before God, is wholly by the perfect righteousness of Jesus Christ, received by faith. 5. That every such soul will be kept by the power of God, through faith, unto eternal salvation. 6. That, according to God's institution, regenerate souls are the only materials for particular Christian churches. 7. That the right way of building such churches is by giving a personal, verbal account to the church of what God has done for their souls, to the satisfaction of the church. 8. That the whole power of calling, ordaining, and deposing officers, is in each particular church ; although it is ordinarily proper and expedient to call in the advise and assistance of sister churches upon many such occasions. 9. That the whole power of governing and disciplining their members is in each particular church ; though advice and counsel from others, in some cases, is becoming and even necessary. 10. That the government of the church should be wholly by the laws of Christ, enforced in his name, and not at all by the secular arm. 11. That gospel ministers ought to be supported by his laws and influence, and not by tax and compulsion enforced by the civil power. 12. That ministers ought to preach, and not read

[1]Substituted for " each of these persons."—ED.

their sermons, at least in ordinary times, that being evidently the apostolic practice; and the contrary enables men to impose upon people, by reading the works of others, and is attended with other evils.   13.   That free liberty ought to be allowed for every saint to improve his gifts according to the gospel; and that the church should encourage and recommend such as are qualified for the gospel ministry. 14.   That officers, when chosen and ordained, have no arbitrary, lordly, or imposing power; but are to rule and minister with the consent of the brethren, who ought not to be called *The laity*, but to be treated as men and brethren in Christ.   These are the chief points of faith and order, wherein we differ from others, and for which such resentment has been shewn against us.   And in this and the former volume of our history, we have clearly proved that all these points were held by the fathers of Plymouth Colony.   And Governor Winslow, one of their first planters, informs us that when they parted with Mr. Robinson, their dear pastor, in Holland, in 1620, he gave them the following advice and solemn charge, viz.:—

"We are now to part asunder, and the Lord knoweth whether ever I shall live to see your faces again.   But whether he has appointed it or not, I charge you, before God and his blessed angels, to follow me no further than I follow Christ.   And if God shall reveal any thing to you by any other instrument of his, be as ready to receive it as ever you were to receive any truth by my ministry; for I am very confident that he has more truth and light yet to break forth out of his holy word."   He took occasion also miserably to bewail the state and condition of the reformed churches, who were come to a period in religion, and would go no further than the instruments of their reformation.   As for example, the Lutherans could not be drawn to go beyond what Luther saw; for whatever part of God's will he has further imparted and revealed to Calvin, they will rather die than embrace it.   "And so you see the Calvinists; they stick where he left them; a misery much to be lamented, for though they were precious shining lights in their times, yet God had not revealed his whole will to them; and were they now living, they would be as ready to embrace further light as what they had received."   Here (says Winslow) he put us in mind of our church covenant, whereby we promise and covenant with God, and one another, to receive whatsoever light and truth shall be made known to us from his written word; but withal exhorted us to take heed what we receive for truth, and well to examine and compare it with other Scriptures before we received it; for, said he, "it is not possible the Christian world should come so lately out of such thick anti-christian darkness, and that full perfection of knowledge should break forth at once."[1]

Such were the noble sentiments and solemn charge of Mr. Robinson, that eminent father of the planters in New England, to which I shall annex a caution he gave, in his preface to a defence of their cause ten years before. Says he :—

I desire the Christian reader to take knowledge of this one thing, that as the pretence of zeal in [the] forward ministers against all corruptions is a thick mist, holding the eyes of many well-minded people from seeing the truth, so the person with whom I now particularly deal, trusts to this insinuation above all others, conveying himself under this color into the hearts of the simple, and hereby making way most effectually not only for his [sage-seeming] counsels and advertisements, for the quenching of their affections towards the truth, but also for his idle guesses and likelihoods,[2] with such personal comparisons and imputations as his book is stored with, to alienate men's hearts from it. But the godly reader is to consider that to accept persons [the person] in judgment is not good, especially in the Lord's cause [cause of the Lord]; and that his faith, [the faith of our glorious Lord Jesus], is not to be held in respect of persons. James ii. 1.[3]

Let this be remembered in our next chapter.

[1] Winslow's Answer to Gorton, pp. 97, 98.
[2] See Vol. I, pp. 5, 6.
[3] Preface to his Answer to Bernard, pp. 5, 6. [Works of John Robinson, Vol. II, p. 3.]

CHAPTER XXVI.

Dr. Mayhew published two sermons, in the beginning of 1763, from those words, The Lord is good to all, and his tender mercies are over all his works. From whence, after laying down many just observations, he endeavors to prove, that the Lord is good to all the different ranks, orders or species of his intelligent and sensitive creatures; and good and kind to all the individuals of which these species consist. He allows that the terms *all, every,* and the like, are sometimes used in a limited sense in Scripture, and that there are many places which must necessarily be so understood; but denies any limitation here, because God's goodness is perfect and infinite, as well as his other perfections. And, beginning with a greater number and coming down to a less, he at last comes to the lowest individual; and if any hold that he is not good to that individual, Mayhew says :—

I think you should paraphrase the text thus : The Lord is good to all *but one,* and his tender mercies are over all his works, *excepting a single* insignificant creature, which either escapes his notice, or at which he is angry, and so makes it miserable, though it neither has nor is capable of offending him.

And he goes on to observe, that John says, God is love; and then says :—

It is worthy of particular remark, that though God is infinitely wise and powerful, &c., as well as good, yet he is never styled in Scripture, Wisdom or Power in the abstract, as he is here styled Love.   Perfect goodness, love itself, is his very essence, in a peculiar sense ; immeasurable, immutable, universal and everlasting love.[1]

Again says he :—

Nothing was prior, not even the existence of God, to his will to be good. .... God is then not only eternally, necessarily and essentially, but infinitely or perfectly good.   And if so, then equally, universally, and immutably good in all times and places.

Necessity therefore he ascribes to the will of God, though his party strenuously deny that it can be consistent with the liberty of our wills.   And he had before asserted, that " there is no medium betwixt God's being actually kind and merciful to all, and his being positively cruel and unmerciful to some."[2]   And to give his ideas of the atonement, he says :—

Infinite goodness itself, considered in connection with infinite wisdom, requires that order, and the highest veneration for the majesty of God, his laws and government, should be preserved amongst all his reasonable creatures.   Their own good essentially depends upon it.   And this important end is most effectually attained by the sacrifice of Christ, by whom we have received the atonement. We are assured in the Holy Scriptures, that God forgives the sins of men through this great sacrifice intervening, rather than without any, not because he is in his own nature deficient in goodness, or not perfectly merciful, but because he is infinitely wise as well as merciful. .... There was a fitness and congruity in it, as the wisest and best method for saving sinful men, without any kind of reference to that common but yet strange supposition, of divine justice being entirely distinct from divine goodness.[3]

It is to be noted, that here he owns that he rejects the common sentiments of our fathers ; and, says he :—

I seriously declare, that if I were to form my conceptions of God's moral character, by such discourses as I have sometimes heard and read, and such as were, by many, thought to be truly evangelical, instead of thinking him really good to all, and his tender mercies over all his works, essentially good, and infinitely the best of beings, I could not but conclude him to be infinitely more unjust and cruel than any other being in the universe !

[1]Mayhew's Thanksgiving Sermons, pp. 39, 44.   [2]Ibid, pp. 35, 46.   [3]Ibid, p. 64.

And he at length ventures to say of infants, " To suppose that . . . . the sin of Adam and Eve is or can be so imputed to them, as to render them justly liable to eternal misery, without any offence of their own, is one of the grossest of all absurdities." And to hold that any of the human race are not chosen in Christ to eternal life, is a doctrine which he rejects in the same manner ; after which, he says :—

If, therefore, my brethren, you know of any particular scheme or system of Christianity (so called) two or three of the most distinguishing and leading principles of which, and the basis on which the whole rests, are plainly and certainly repugnant to the doctrine of God's universal goodness, and his tender mercies over all his works ; you may be certain that such scheme or system is false ; absolutely and wholly false, so far as it has any connection with or dependence upon those [leading, fundamental and most distinguishing] principles.[1]

He allows that there will be a future punishment to the wicked, but leaves the words concerning it undefined ; and concludes with mentioning, that in the other world the meaning of that passage in the Revelation will be more clearly opened than we can conceive of it here, " Every creature which is in heaven, and on the earth, and under the earth, and such as are in the sea, and all that are in them, heard I saying, Blessing, and honor, and glory, and power be unto him that sitteth upon the throne, and unto the Lamb forever and ever."

The reader may now judge whether this author had not a design against some of the most important principles of the protestant reformed system of Christianity, as it had long been professed in this and other countries. Yet because Mr. Cleaveland represented his sermons in that light, in his essay to defend that system, Dr. Mayhew called it "A defamatory libel ;" and said to Cleaveland :—

Can you possibly think it became you, an obscure person from another province, and one so unlettered as you are, an outcast from the college to which you was a disgrace? . . . . Did [Do] you not show the utmost assurance, in thus setting up your little self ? . . . . Poor, unhappy man ! You

[1]Mayhew's Thanksgiving Sermons, pp. 50, 62, 63, 83, 85.

doubtless thought to emerge from your obscurity, and to appear as a person of some consequence, by this vain attempt. .... It is as much beneath me to play the critic on such a performance as yours, as it would be particularly to expose the vanity of your criticisms on my sermons. .... But I will proceed to the main business of this letter, which is to set your falsehood and iniquitous proceedings, with reference to my sermons, in some order before your eyes ; and to administer the reproof and correction which you deserve, or rather a part thereof. For it is only they that hold the *sword of public justice*, that can legally punish such wickedness to the extent of its demerits. Your villainy in this affair appears written, as one may say, even upon your forehead.[1]

And his whole letter of forty-nine pages is in this strain ; which, instead of universal goodness, discovers how such men would treat their opponents, if their power was equal to their wills. A sight of these things moved the President and Corporation of the college, which expelled Cleaveland, to give him the title of A. M. the same year. Yet when Mayhew died two years after, Chauncy reflected upon Cleaveland (as before observed, page 130) and called him an obscure person without reputation. And to this day the persons of those two men are held in such admiration by multitudes, that they are much sooner disturbed at hearing their errors exposed, than at hearing their Maker blasphemed, while they are highly pleased at seeing eminent ministers of opposite principles treated with a high degree of abuse and contempt as appears in what follows.

All establishments of worship by human laws, that ever were erected under the Christian name, were built upon calling the covenant in Gen. xvii. the covenant of grace. Yet our excellent Edwards was separated from his dear flock at Northampton, only for insisting upon a personal profession of sanctifying grace in order for full communion.[2] From thence he went and settled at Stockbridge, on the west borders of our State ; where his successors have endeavored to pursue his plan of reformation. A considerable number of ministers, in various parts of the land, have also labored

---

[1]Mayhew's Letter of Reproof, 1764, pp. 4—6.   [2]See page 93.

in the same cause. About the close of 1768, Dr. Joseph Bellamy published a small piece upon the Half-Way Covenant; which was soon answered, and he wrote not less than six pamphlets upon the covenant, to prove that a profession of saving faith was a necessary term of communion in the church, and of being active in baptism. The piece on the opposite side, mentioned in page 170, was occasioned hereby. And within six years, above twenty pamphlets were written by different parties upon this subject, through the country from New Jersey to Boston. The name of a Half-Way Covenant was disowned by all these writers, and their controversy turned entirely upon the question, whether a profession of saving faith ought to be required of communicants, or not? For both parties agreed that none should be active themselves in baptism, but such as had a right to come to the other ordinance ; and they were as unable to settle this matter as Stoddard and Mather were seventy years before.[1] How to reconcile divine sovereignty with human liberty, and efficacious grace with the use of means for conversion, were also questions that they had long and tedious debates upon. At length a singular act of discipline at Stockbridge seemed to give the other party an occasion, and it was eagerly improved, to give them as bad a thrust with their horns, as ever was given by any bulls in Bashan. It was as follows :—Those who have seen the nature of original sin, cannot tell how to keep up the idea of children's being born in the covenant of grace, without some regard to grace in their parents. And in the same chapter where the unbelieving consort is said to be sanctified by the believer, a widow is required to marry only in the Lord. Therefore, because a young widow in Stockbridge church married an immoral, profane man, in the beginning of 1777, she was censured and excluded from their communion. This occasioned the calling of a council in January, 1779, which was adjourned to May, and from thence to October, when they

---

[1]See Vol. I, pp. 468, 469.

justified the church in that act. The man who married said widow was from Connecticut; and he got a learned minister from thence to plead his cause in the last of those Councils, who was son to the ruler that sent a man to prison forty years ago, for preaching the gospel.[1] As his client was not relieved by that Council, he published his plea for him, which has passed through three or four editions. It was answered from Stockbridge, upon which he published a larger piece in 1780, entitled, Letters of Friendship; which being replied to, he, in 1781, gave what he called a Gentle Reprimand. And in 1782 these three pieces were printed in one at Boston. Their evident design was to relieve that woman, to prevent division among their ministers, and to keep up the use of force for their support; all which it is said are accomplished thereby. Be that as it may, it is certain that much deceit and cruelty have been used in this affair. Many would limit the word *Persecution* to corporal punishments; which is so opposite to truth, that reviling and mockery contain a great and cruel part of it. Matt. v. 11; Heb. xi. 36. Colonel Gardiner, who was converted sixty-five years ago, declared that " he would much rather have marched up to a battery of the enemy's cannon, than have been obliged so continually as he was to face such artillery as this."[2] Yet in order to carry his point, this advocate advanced a parable of a church who refused to allow a brother therein to marry a woman he dearly loved, because not a gracious person; and advised him to marry a member of theirs that was sound in the faith, which is most shockingly described; and then saying of her person :—

As to some trifles, which a carnal man would object to, it becomes you, as a spiritual man, to make no objection. It is true, she is of a mean family, and a very weak understanding; she is peevish and fretful to the highest degree; her shape is semicircular; she is what the world calls monstrous ugly; every feature is adapted to mortify carnal desires, which is much better than to have them gratified; she is the queen of sluts, and

[1]See page 69.   [2]Gardiner's Life, p. 35.

without any polite education. But she has grace, saving grace ; she is regenerated ; let your grace wed with hers, and a sweet bride she will be. Moreover, she is past the flower of her age, and we suppose need so requires.[1]

Now is it possible to dress up a church and Scripture phrases in a more odious and scandalous manner than is here done? Yet in his Reprimand, which he calls *gentle*, he insinuates that for any to be offended at it argues guilt; because, says he, " It was expressly declared that it is to be applied only as truth applies it." But when we look into his Plea, we find him saying, " Let the following parable apply where it *will* apply.[2] Truth cannot apply it to any church upon earth ; but his *will* has published the names of thirteen ministers in that plea, more worthy than himself, for the world to laugh at as much as they *will*. And this is doubtless the chief reason of its circulating so extensively. But how mean and spiteful is it to treat the word *Grace* in this manner! Affixing the word to the covenant of circumcision, where God never put it, is the source of that difficulty at Stockbridge. The words *Sanctified* and *Holy*, in I Cor. vii. 14, are both of a kind, and the latter the effect of the former; and their meaning may be ascertained by I Tim. iv. 5. But if we must go to the law for the meaning of the word *Holy* there, the same word in the law is given as the reason why they should not marry with unholy persons. Deut. vii. 36. Every soul therefore will be self-condemned that affixes the name *Grace* to the covenant of circumcision, and at the same time censures the church at Stockbridge for attempting to act consistently upon it.

His second pamphlet is directed to ministers who had essayed to withdraw from the major party in the country; to whom he applies the apostolic warning, Beware of dogs, beware of the concision ; which warning was levelled against those who held to the covenant of circumcision after it was out of date, and could not bear to quit all confidence in the

[1]Plea, p. 29.   [2]Plea, p. 27; Reprimand, p. 15.

flesh. Phil. iii. 2, 3. The General Association of ministers in Connecticut, June 3, 1780, stated the nature of those ministers' crime in these words, viz. : " Refusing intercourse of ministerial labors, and to receive our members, on recommendation from the pastors and churches to which they belonged, to their communion, without a particular and personal examination.[1] But in the Boston edition this passage is left out; and some ministers are accused of renouncing communion with others, in consequence of that affair at Stockbridge. Such deceit are men guilty of! And it is asserted, that " the churches in New England are generally full as strict in their practice, as the church at Stockbridge, and require full as much religion in the profession, life, and conversation of the candidate." And the minister of Lebanon (mentioned in page 93[2]) is referred to as an example thereof.[3] Yet he was a man who held tenaciously that the field where saints and the visible children of the wicked one are ordered to grow together, intends the visible church; which an excellent writer says gave others occasion to reflect, " that those churches whose practice is agreeable to his loose principles, do that at noon-day, in the presence of God, angels and men, which the devil did in the night, while men slept!"[4] It is also to be observed, that a member of the church in Stockbridge detected said advocate in several violations of truth, as to matters of fact there. But instead of any honest retraction, he said of that member, " Where he is known, he can perhaps hurt no man's character, either with his tongue or pen; and it is a question whether, at this period of time, he can hurt his own." And again, "He has exerted himself with all his might, to suppress the gospel ministry in this land, laboring among other efforts to remove the only probable means for the support of it."[5] That is,

[1]Letters of Friendship, p. 133.   [2]Solomon Williams.—ED.
[3]Letters of Friendship, pp. 62, 115.
[4]Edwards's reply to Williams, p. 103. [Works, Vol. I, p. 256.]
[5]Letters of Friendship, p. 138. Reprimand, p. 13.

the man he points to, being of the Convention who formed our new constitution, labored to exclude the use of violence from it in supporting religious teachers. And his character was such as to be freely chosen one of the Massachusetts senators, in May, 1781. How then did his opponent despise government!

Mr. Locke long since observed, that learned disputants often act as deceitfully about the main words of their controversy as a trader would do if he took the figure 8, and called it sometimes seven and sometimes nine, as would suit his advantage. And how much was that the case in this dispute? The most puzzling argument of the advocate for the profane man, was declaring that by baptism he was in the church, and ought to have been disciplined, rather than his wife for marrying him. And in 1773, the same author published an address to the Baptists, wherein he represents the covenant of circumcision to be such an ample charter of church privileges, that it would even have been an impeachment of the sacred character, or reflection upon the perfections of God, to expect an express description of who were the subjects of baptism in the New Testament. Now it is certain that every man in Israel who should forbear to keep the passover as it was instituted, must be cut off from his people. Numb. ix. 13. And if the covenant is the same now, every person among their churches who has been sprinkled in infancy must come to the ordinance of the supper, or be excommunicated, be he converted or unconverted, moral or profane. Yet the abovesaid pleader has the effrontery to say to his opponents, " You tell us, gentlemen, that some of us do not agree with you, in our notions of the terms of church communion, or admission of church members. . . . . But . . . . no mortal knows, or can know, who has grace or who has not. . . . . Let us speculate and dispute as long as we please, we must practice alike, or we cannot practice at all."[1] But if many are in darkness, and

¹Letters of Friendship, p. 20.

know not where they are going, does that prove that others have no true light? And if they love darkness rather than light, can their evils make void the word of Christ? who says, He that doth truth, cometh to the light, that his deeds may be made manifest, that they are wrought in God: and also says, Every tree is known by his own fruit; A good man out of the good treasure of his heart, bringeth forth that which is good; and an evil man out of the evil treasure of his heart, bringeth forth that which is evil, for of the abundance of the heart the mouth speaketh. And the way wherein greedy dogs are to be known, who can never have enough, is that they all look to their own way, every one for his gain, from his quarter. They bite with their teeth, and cry, Peace; and he that putteth not into their mouths, they even prepare war against him. . . . . Yet will they lean upon the Lord, and say, Is not the Lord among us? none evil can come upon us. This is their learning, their logic; from a negative proposition they form a positive conclusion. They are in covenant with death, and agreement with hell, and from thence think to secure themselves; and they scornfully slight all warnings of future danger. But the time is hastening when their bed will be too short for them, and their covering too narrow; and it will be a vexation only to understand the report of the gospel. Is. xxviii. 14—20; Rom. x. 16. Union and communion with God, who is Light and Love, was the life of man at first; and a revolt from him, into darkness and disorder, was death, the penalty of the law. And the character of hell is lying and murder. John viii. 44. Therefore I conclude, that the known use of deceit and cruelty is the covenant with death and agreement with hell, wherewith scornful officers have often thought to secure themselves against present and future dangers. This I take to be a scriptural glass, and return our opponent's compliment upon it. Says he, "Why do the Letters of Friendship offend them, since it is so expressly premised that no person is pointed at in them unless justly characterized? If my face is dirty, and not fit to be seen, I wash it, and never quarrel with my glass about it."[1] And since his zeal has been so great for the relief of one censured woman, let him appear for another nearer home. For a woman of good character, in the head county of his own State, was censured in 1781, and excommunicated in 1783, by a minister who is a Fellow of Yale College, for no other crime than refraining from coming to the Lord's table with such as hold the Lord's Supper to be a converting ordinance.

This may lead us to take a further view of their claims of power over the churches. About twenty years ago, a minister, who was a Fellow of Yale College, published a pamphlet to prove that the power of ordination is inherent in ministers, and that Christ never gave that power to the church as a body. This he dedicated to their Governor; and he therein allowed that the people have a right to choose their ministers, but not to ordain them, any more than the freemen of Connecticut have to swear their magistrates into office. An answer was written to him, and he made a reply in 1766. But then both his patron and his comparison failed him, because his Governor and several magistrates were left out of office by the people, for favoring the stamp-act. And what could he then do? He slipped over the line, and said:—

The Governor of a province is, by the king's commission, invested with power and authority as such an officer, distinct from the rights, powers and privileges, belonging to the government, by the constitution, charter, and laws of the land. And though the magistracy and other officers, and the House of Representatives, have a legislative and executive authority with him, under his precedency, and act with him in judgment, in many cases; yet are these distinct branches of authority, originating from different fountains of power; the former from special commission from the king, the other from the constitution and laws of the government. I take the case to be much parallel in ecclesiastical government.[2]

[1] Reprimand, p. 15.
[2] Beckwith's second letter against Lay Ordinations, pp. 42, 43.

17

And we have shewn (in page 175,) that the Massachusetts ministers claimed a higher power than the king allowed to his Governor; and he was the head of their establishments for worship, both there and in Connecticut.[1]   Therefore they are now in a deplorable case; for an ocean three thousand miles wide rolls betwixt the head and the body of that constitution, so that they have only a dead, polluted carcass left in their high places.   Ezek. xliii. 7.   And those who have so often rejected the reasonable testimonies and petitions of the Baptists, are forced now to become suppliants to them, in order to save their polluted scheme.   In a Boston paper,[2] before mentioned, of February 5, 1781, they tell a story of a gentleman's babe, that was taken by an ape and carried to the roof of the house, while he and his family were at church, and a careless maid got to sleep; and yet that the babe was saved by their prayers.   Upon which they name the Baptist agent,[3] whom they accuse of doing the like with their religion; but expressed their hopes of having it now returned into its former condition.   But herein they appear more contemptible than the priests of Baal did in Elijah's time; for they came out like men, and performed their devotion in the sight of the people, while these only published their prayers in newspapers, and were afraid that their names should be known.   And the babe they pray for is not a human creature, but a monster, begotten upon a whore; and great happiness is promised to those who shall dash such little ones against the stones.   Psalm cxxxvii. 8, 9.   And the Baptists not only covet such happiness, but obedience to government requires it of them.   For all protestant kingdoms have set up their king as head of the church; but that name is now excluded from our Legislature.   And to move the people to receive this constitution, the compilers of it said to them, " Your delegates did not conceive themselves

---

[1] See p. 81, Vol. I, p. 509.   [2] The Boston Gazette.—ED.
[3] The Baptist agent is not directly named in the article referred to, but some expressions in it were probably intended to designate him.—ED.

vested with power to set up one denomination of Christians above another; for religion must at all times be a matter between God and individuals."[1]   And no man can take a seat in our Legislature until he solemnly declares, "I believe the Christian religion, and have a firm persuasion of its truth."[2] And as surely as it is true, Christ is Head of all principality and power, and the church is complete in him, and required to do all her acts in his name.   Therefore all worship that is supported in any other name is only will-worship.   Col. ii. 9, 10, 23 ; iii. 17.   And though recourse has often been had to Germany, for matter to prejudice people against equal liberty and believers' baptism, yet twenty thousand mercenaries have lately been brought from thence to fight against such principles, and to deluge our land with blood ; against whom no denomination in America have acted with more prudence and vigor than the Baptists.   In the fall of 1778, our Legislature passed an act to debar inimical persons from returning into this State, wherein three hundred and eleven men were named as such ; and our enemies are welcome to point out one Baptist among them if they can.   Yet our opponents are still so unwilling to allow equal liberty, and that the power of church government should be in the body of each community, that a pamphlet was published at Boston against it, near the close of 1783, wherein it is said, "If the power of dismissing its pastors is determined to be lodged in the church, without the intervention of any indifferent persons, the clergy of New England are of all men the most miserable."[3]   This author was an active member of the Convention which formed our new constitution; but they are now ensnared in the work of their own hands ; and to move others to relieve them, he says :—

The world produces not a set of ministers more holy in their lives, more free from immorality of every kind, more pure in their doctrines, or more ingenious, animated and pathetic in their addresses, than the clergy of New

[1]Address before the Constitution, March 2, 1780, p. 17.
[2]Constitution, Chap. VI.   [3]Thatcher's Observations, p. 11.

England. .... The observation hath often been made, that it is natural to
the clergy to be fond of power. Without dispute they are so, for they are
men, and subject to the same feelings and inclinations with others. But in
New England, let them have felt ever so much of this inclination, they
have not discovered it. Where is the man who can point out the instance,
where the ministry have attempted to encroach upon the rights of the
churches ?[1]

Such attempts have been so openly discovered, that at
present I shall only point the reader to his now doing of it,
in the name *Clergy* he so often assumes. It is derived from
the word [Κλῆρος] that is translated *heritage*, in I Pet. v. 3 ;
which name has long been usurped by ministers, in order to
avoid the scandal of lording it over the church. And the
following facts may discover his vanity in boasting of their
general purity as to doctrine.

All Mayhew's arguments against the doctrines of sovereign grace, pointed directly to universal salvation, though the
minds of the people were not then prepared to receive it.
But an artful teacher from Britain, who by the way of New
York came into New England in 1772, by deceitful addresses
to the passions of its inhabitants, and procuring an edition
of Relly upon Union at Boston in 1779, and another at
Providence in 1782, prepared the way for the ministers of
the country to discover themselves. And in August, 1782,
a pamphlet was published in Boston, which soon passed a
second edition, entitled, Salvation for all men. Dr.
Chauncy, undoubtedly, had a chief hand therein, and most
of the ministers in Boston seemed to favor the scheme, and
others continued in fellowship with those who have openly
owned it. Their main arguments turn upon extending the
divine goodness to every individual, and Christ's merits also ;
although they do not attempt to tell how long it will be
before all come to enjoy the same. They say, " There will
be a great deal to be done, after the second coming of Christ.
.... Indeed (say they) the doctrine of purgatory, as now

---

[1] Thatcher's Observations, p. 5.

taught by the Papists, seems to be a corruption of a genuine doctrine held by the ancient fathers, concerning the fire of hell, which will burn up sin and lust."[1] But we do not hear of any yet who have ventured to assert with Origen, that Christ will be crucified in the next world to save devils. Several valuable pamphlets have been written against these delusions. but those ministers are still held in fellowship. Though Dr. Chauncy himself, says, " I am clearly of the mind, that a visibly wicked minister is the greatest scandal to religion, and plague to the church of God ; nor is it a hurt but a real service to the cause of Christ, to expose the characters of such, and lessen their power to do mischief."[2] And again he says, " The religion of Jesus has suffered more from the exercise of this pretended right [to make religious establishments] than from all other causes put together ; and it is with me past all doubt, that it will never be restored to its primitive purity, simplicity and glory, until religious establishments are so brought down as to be no more.[3]

[1]Salvation for all Men, pp. 14, 21.   [2]Chauncy's Thoughts, 1743, p. 141.
[3]Reply to Chandler, 1770, p. 144.

CHAPTER XXVII.

When we have conceived an ill opinion of any denomination, it is exceedingly difficult to treat them fairly. An
instance hereof is before me, that may be proper to mention.
Edwards's treatise on The Will has passed through one edition at Boston, and two or more in London, without ever
being answered, although it is levelled directly against the
turning point of Arminianism, to which the opinion of universal salvation naturally succeeds. Many who do not own
either of those names, yet have conceived a strong prejudice against Calvinism, which Edwards professed to own,
though not every opinion that Calvin advanced. A late
learned performance from London, reprinted at Philadelphia
in 1783, contains the following things. The author, when
giving his own deliberate ideas, says :—

The visible world demonstrates, it was made by an omnipotent power,
and is preserved by the same power. .... What doth not necessarily exist,
must be originally created, and continually upheld by the power that made
it. .... There is no medium betwixt [between] self-existence and dependence on its cause ; therefore a cessation from it of the power that made it
is annihilation to it. Thus, as all created things were made, and still subsist
solely by the energy of the Creator's will and power, he must necessa-

rily, whilst they exist, be omnipresent with them, in them, and through them ; therefore cannot be ignorant of anything relating to them, nor unconcerned about them, or any part of them.[1]

If so, then the creature can do no act but what his Creator sees cause either to order or permit, which is the essence of Calvinism. No, says this author, " We attribute the whole of man's salvation to the light or grace within, first and last, without at all placing man's destruction to the account of his Maker, which John Calvin directly doth."[2] And after attempts to prove this charge from ancient writings, he tries to confirm it from Edwards on the Will. And in reference to his main point, he says :—

We are told, The will is always determined by the strongest motive. Has the will no liberty then at any time? Is it always so forcibly determined, in all its motions, by circumstances and motives successively arising upon it, from the original constitution of things, that every man is necessarily obliged to think, speak and act, just as he doth? .... Was this really the case, our inevitable acts would certainly render us no proper subjects of reward and punishment ; of Come, ye blessed, or Go, ye cursed. We must be equally unentitled to approbation and censure.[3]

But I must tell him and all his friends, that I am much better acquainted with Edwards's writings than they are, and I absolutely know that the ideas naturally arising from the words *Forcibly* and *Inevitable*, as here used, when charged upon Edwards, are entirely unjust and abusive. And it tends to raise an evil temper in those who read the same, against all the friends of Edwards's writings, of whom I am heartily one. I am certain that the author who has thus censured him, is not a greater friend to the full liberty of the human will, and against every idea of positive influence from God to restrain men from good, or to impel them to evil, than Edwards was. And I know that from my inmost thoughts I abhor and detest every thing of that nature, and challenge

---

[1] Phipps against Newton, pp. 37, 38. [The original and present state of man briefly considered. .... To which are added some remarks on the arguments of Samuel Newton of Norwich. By Joseph Phipps. New York, 1788, pp. 40, 41.]
[2] Ibid, p. 86. [96.]   [3] Ibid, pp. 97, 98. [109.]

all the sons of men to prove the contrary if they can. Whether said author will like the following description of liberty is uncertain. In a Boston paper of June 21, 1784, we are informed, that a new book of Dr. Chauncy's is now in the press, which gives a view of man, "As an *intelligent moral agent;* having within himself an *ability* and *freedom* to *will*, as well as to *do*, in opposition to *necessity* from any extraneous cause whatever."

This perfectly agrees with that disregard to God, and to equal liberty among the common people, which has lately been so conspicuous in that metropolis. Perhaps a text could not be found more suitable to preach upon, at the commencement of our new constitution, than the following: "Their children also shall be as aforetime, and *their congregation shall be established before me*, and I will punish all that oppress them. *And their nobles shall be of themselves, and their Governor shall proceed from the midst of them,* and I will cause him to draw near, and he shall approach unto me; for who is this that engaged his heart to approach unto me? saith the Lord." Jer. xxx. 20, 21. But a noted minister of Boston[1] took out the words here printed in italics and not the rest for the subject of his sermon at that time; in which he told of conscience being pleaded on both sides of the question about religious liberty. And the two sides are exactly these. The Baptists pleaded that Christ's ministers might be supported only by his laws and influence; their opponents pleaded still to be called by his name, but that they could not in conscience give up the use of secular force to support them. The Baptists never asked for any greater liberty in this respect in the country than Boston has long enjoyed; Their opponents plead conscience for denying it to them, which doubtless is supposing that gain is godliness, and from such we are commanded to withdraw. The minister of Chelsea, who in 1778 defied our Legislature to preserve order in the State, if they allowed equal liberty in the

[1] Samuel Cooper, D. D.   See p. 230.—ED.

church,[1] was received a member of that Assembly in 1783, to tax others, while he pays none himself. But who can wonder at their treating the people thus, since their treatment of their Maker is so flagrant! claiming his promises without regarding his precepts, which is the practice the tempter would have drawn our Saviour into. Matt. iv. 6, 7. But greater absurdity and blasphemy can scarcely be conceived of, than to claim God's promises to support us in disobedience to his precepts, and to deny his right to govern our wills, further than we please. His authority and commands are certainly a cause without us; but we have already seen that the above writer thought them too severe even for Adam in innocency, and that grace gives an exemption from that severity.[2] But I have seen a record concerning one, who was as zealous for confidence in the flesh as these late disputants are, and had as fair a claim to it as any of them, who at length was made to know that the law was holy, just, and good; that it was spiritual, but he a carnal slave to sin, instead of having such high dignity and liberty as he before imagined he had. And *necessity* brought him most *freely* to preach the faith that he before endeavored to destroy. I Cor. ix. 16; Gal. i. 16, 23. And any person in the world can as soon cease to exist, as cease to desire happiness, and to escape misery. A false imagination of *good* in the forbidden fruit, drew our first parents into rebellion against God; and such imaginations are the only source of sin in all their children. James i. 14, 15. *Good* is still their pursuit, but they have lost the knowledge of who can give it, or of what it is; but the regenerate soul knows both, and this is the precise difference between them. Psalm iv. 6, 7. Who does not know that debtors and criminals are not fit judges in their own causes? yet that is the case with all reasoners against the truth and perfection of God's written word. How would wrong judgment proceed in civil courts, if the judges or jurors were allowed to construe laws according to

[1]Philips Payson. See p. 220.—ED.   [2]See p. 131.

a rule within them, instead of a fixed known standard ! If we believe the word of truth, a most obstinate tyrant, a most hardened wretch, yet *gladly* sent Israel away with rich treasures, the same night which God had told Abraham of four hundred and thirty years before. Exod. xii. 31—33, 39, Psalm cv. 37, 38. Which turn of his will and choice was by a cause without him, which brought him to act voluntarily and exactly according to a previous, immutable decree, and without giving any renewing grace to his soul. But as soon as death was out of view, he eagerly pursued Israel into the Red Sea, where he and his army perished. And none but infidels will pretend to deny the justice of God in that destruction, although it was he that exactly disposed all the circumstances which moved Pharoah voluntarily to act as he did. And the gospel refers to this instance, to show how, by much long-suffering, vessels of wrath are fitted to destruction, according to the sovereign will of God. Rom. ix. 17, 18, 22. And those who will not believe him here, will in vain cry for mercy hereafter. Those who are effectually drawn to Christ by divine teaching, know that they could not have come without it, nor avoid coming most freely with it. John vi. 44, 45. And to hear many speaking evil of things which they know not, but what they know naturally as brute beasts, and in those things to corrupt themselves ; to see them tread down the good pastures, and foul the deep waters, and thrust others with side and shoulder, serves to confirm believers in the truth of revelation, and in the hope of a speedy deliverance from such evil beasts. Jude 10. Ezek. xxxiv. 18, 25. As the wages of sin is death, God cannot be just in paying the same to infants, but upon his right to constitute Adam as their head to act for them, and dealing with them as sinners in him; for justice cannot pay wages where they are not due. And as Christ came into the world purely to save sinners, infants could have no part in his salvation, if they were not sinners. That infants may partake of that salvation, even in their mother's womb, is certain. Luke i. 44.[1] And it is as certain, that though the first Adam was a figure of the second in some things, yet he was not so in others; and in none more plainly than these three, viz.: The one brought death, the other life; The one by a judicial sentence of law, the other by a free gift of grace; The one by a single offence ruined the world, the other atoned for many offences, and will finally bring forth a much more glorious world than that which Adam destroyed. I conceive that these ideas, both of the resemblance and the difference betwixt the two public heads of mankind, are plainly contained in the fifth of the Romans, and fifteenth of the first to the Corinthians. Yet how many are there who will have it, that Christ died equally for all the human race, and yet that he saves but a part of them, because their wills defeat his good desires and intentions? To these, others have succeeded, who assert that he died for every one of them, and will finally bring them all to happiness, though not until many of them have been in hell-flames for thousands of years, to burn up their corruptions. But I boldly declare I would as soon worship the pagan god of flies, as any imaginary saviour that could possibly be mistaken or disappointed in any of his designs. I fully believe that God's plan of government was and is infinitely perfect; that it is calculated so in infinite wisdom, that all his dispensations shall demonstrate to all intelligent creatures, that all desirable good is to be enjoyed in obedience to his revealed will, and nowhere else; but that disobedience thereto is infinitely hateful and dreadful, how pleasing soever it may appear at first; that he gives sinners opportunity to try their inventions to the utmost extent of them, most plainly warning them of their danger in the mean time; and that examples of their defeat, and of just

---

[1] Probably most of his readers will question the author's inference from this passage. The author himself might have considered it more carefully if the inference had been used in his day, as it has in later times, as an argument for infant baptism. —ED.

punishments inflicted upon the impenitent, will be visible to the blessed, and cause high praises to him forever and ever; which words are equally made use of to describe the continuance of his glories, the happiness of the saints, and the misery of the wicked. Rev. v. 13; xiv. 9—11; xix. 3; xx. 10; xxii. 5. As it was the old serpent that poisoned our first parents, by setting up reason against revelation, especially in calling in question the truth of the penalty of the law, so the same poison is exceedingly visible and pernicious among their children at this day.

It is most certain that the reformation in the church of England, which took place in the days of Edward the Sixth, was produced by preaching the doctrines of original sin, justification by faith in Christ's imputed righteousness, and his sovereign and efficacious grace upon the souls of men, to their eternal salvation. And it is as certain that a departure from these doctrines has been growing upon that church ever since. Taylor's work against Original Sin, though he was a dissenter, yet was brought into the east part of Connecticut by an itinerant missionary of the church of England above forty years ago; and it has had an extensive circulation through this country. Many of other denominations were pleased with it, while they tried hard to persuade the world that Whitefield was a dishonest man, and upon evil designs against this country, when he preached the gospel according to the doctrines established by law, both in Old England and New.[1] Ten years after, a professor of Harvard College tried to fix that odium upon his character in the minds of his pupils; and at the same time denied the liberty of gospel ministers to preach in any parish where another was settled, without his license.[2] And if facts are fairly examined, will it not be found, that those in our day, who have been most fierce for taxing others where they are not represented, yet are not willing to own that their Maker had a right to constitute Adam as their representative?

[1] See p. 75. [2] Wigglesworth's Lectures concerning Ministers' Power, 1754, pp. 14—16.

In 1628 a charter was granted to the Massachusetts from the British Court, which exempted this colony from all taxes thereto, but only the fifth part of the gold and silver ore that should be found in it; and it gave the colony the exclusive right to choose their own Governors. But in 1684 these privileges were wrested from them, and their lands were all claimed by the crown, and great tyranny was here exercised for some years, until the king was driven from his throne, and another was placed thereon by compact. He gave us a new charter of many privileges, but reserved a power to tax our trade, and an arbitrary power in the crown to appoint our Governors, and to demand our property for their support. And, as those who turn every one to his own way can never have enough, the remainder of our charter privileges were taken away in 1774, and fleets and armies were sent to compel this country into an unlimited submission to the wills of the British parliament. And after many terrible frowns of Providence upon their unmerciful proceedings, a speech from the British throne of November 2, 1780, said:—

The present arduous situation of public affairs is well known; the whole force and faculties of the monarchies of France and Spain are drawn forth, and exerted to the utmost, to support the rebellion of my colonies in North America, and, without the least provocation or cause of complaint, to attack my dominions; and the undisguised object of this confederacy manifestly is to gratify boundless ambition, by destroying the commerce, and giving a fatal blow to the power of great Britain. By the force which the late parliament put into my hands, and by the blessing of Providence on the bravery of my fleets and armies, I have been enabled to withstand the formidable attempts of my enemies, and to frustrate the great expectations they had formed; and the signal successes which have attended the progress of my arms in the provinces of Georgia and Carolina, gained with so much honor to the conduct and courage of my officers, and to the valor and intrepidity of my troops, which have equalled their highest character in any age, will, I trust, have important consequences in bringing the war to a happy conclusion. It is my most earnest desire to see this great end acccomplished; but I am confident you will agree with me in opinion, that we can only secure safe and honorable terms of peace by such powerful and respectable preparations, as shall convince our enemies, that we will not submit to receive the law from any power whatsoever.

Lord Cornwallis was one of his most successful officers in Carolina, who there gave orders, on August 30, 1780, "that every militia man who had borne arms with us, and afterwards joined the enemy, shall be immediately hanged." Yet on December 30, General Clinton and Admiral Arbuthnot, as Commissioners from the king for restoring peace to the colonies, gave out a declaration from New York, " That Great Britain had manifested the sincerity of her affectionate and conciliatory intentions, in removing forever your pretended grounds of discontent, by repealing among other statutes those relating to the duty on tea, and the alterations in the government of Massachusetts Bay, and exempting forever not only the continental, but the insular colonies from parliamentary taxations ;" and so invited all or any of " the colonies in rebellion" to come in and receive pardon and peace. And before they had got through they said, " The loyal are exhorted to persevere in their integrity for the preservation of their country, its religion and liberties." And this declaration arrived and was published in Boston just before the king's speech, which expressed a resolution not to receive law from any power whatsoever, not even excepting the power of heaven. And how much better were the wills of men in this land.

For six months after the war began, the general welfare of the country was kept so much in view, that men enough were easily obtained to fill up our army, which was also plentifully supplied with provisions. But a committee from the southward met at the camp in or near Cambridge, in October, 1775, to settle the affairs of the next campaign, who raised the wages of officers, and lowered those of the private soldiers, which directly caused an uneasiness ; and a looking to private interest, both in and out of the army, gradually prevailed from that time, until in the fall of 1780, it procured a promise of half-pay to officers during life. And just before the news of peace arrived, this selfishness arose so high in the officers, as to lead them to appoint a public meeting in the camp at West Point in the beginning of March, 1783 (without leave from General Washington, who was there) to consult about either marching in arms to Philadelphia, and compelling the Congress to grant their desires, or else drawing off into the wilderness, and leaving the country defenceless to the ravages of the enemy. And though, with a wise and masterly address, General Washington prevented their taking either of those horrid steps, yet none can tell how much influence these contrivances had, to produce a vote in Congress for five years whole pay in lieu of the half-pay during life. And though the war was levelled against hereditary claims of power over others, and to secure equity among all the inhabitants, and the articles of union and confederation between these States expressly forbade their granting any titles of nobility, yet in May following, those officers presumed to incorporate a society among themselves, to have a hereditary succession, and each a golden medal and blue ribbon, with a large fund of money at command, and power to elect our chief rulers into their society. This discovered their dispositions, whatever alterations may have been made in their society since.

The above proceedings have caused unspeakable difficulties through these States, which have been loudly complained of by multitudes, who still are bewitched with the opinion, that they are born in a like covenant as the seed of Abraham were, which gave them a right to make servants of others who were not in that covenant. Yea, and also with the opinion that civil Legislatures have a right to empower some men to covenant for others with religious teachers, and to compel them to fulfil it. And this practice (which is directly against the law of God even as it was given to the Jews) was at the commencement of our new constitution called GODLINESS, in capitals, while *honesty* was put in small letters.[1] Which things are not mentioned because I think myself better by nature than others, for I know the contrary.

[1] See pp. 229, 230.—ED.

And after renewing grace was granted, I was such a dull scholar in Christ's school, that I was thirty-two years in learning a lesson of only six words, viz.: *One Lord, one faith, one baptism.* It took ten years to get clear of the custom of putting baptism before faith, and near five more to learn not to contradict the same in practice ; after which above seventeen trying years rolled over us, before we could refrain from an implicit acknowledgment of more than one Lord in religious affairs. And what noise has been made in the world since, only because we will not give up this lesson, and obey man rather than God! And the chief movers therein, undoubtedly, are men who deny his right to impute Adam's sin to them, or to damn them for not receiving Christ's imputed righteousness for their justification. Neither can any own these doctrines, and be self-consistent, in holding that natural birth or human doings can bring infants into the covenant of grace. If it be of grace, then it cannot be of the birth or works of nature. That which is born of the flesh is flesh, says our blessed Lord. Circumcision was a type of his death, and of our being cut off from confidence in the flesh, and ingrafted into him by regeneration. Before his personal coming, this sign was, by divine institution, put upon many who had not the thing signified within them ; but as Abraham had it, it was a *seal* to him, while it was only a sign or type to many others. Rom. iv. 11 ; Col. ii. 11, 12. By the covenant with Abraham, none were to be circumcised but such as were born in his house, or bought with his money : in which capacity he was an eminent type of Christ, whose church is constituted of persons purchased with his blood, and regenerated by his spirit. Aaron was also a noted type of him, and his lawful seed a type of regenerate souls, who are the spiritual house which is built upon the foundation that is disallowed of men. And in vain do any of them try to prove the covenant to be the same now that it was with Abraham, until they can prove that Christ is hereafter to come and endure another crucifix-

18

ion. *Mystery, Babylon,* which means the mystery of confusion, was erected by *confounding* type and anti-type, church and state, together. For a woman after marriage to refuse to be governed by her husband, and to say, I will go after my lovers, that gave me my bread and my water, my wool and my flax, mine oil and my drink, proves her to be a harlot. And by this practice the church of Rome became the mother of harlots, and abomination of the earth. Kings have committed fornication with her; and by her sorceries were all nations deceived. How much have protestants been deceived with these abominations! To set up any mere man as head of the church, is an imitation of those who crucified our blessed Lord, by holding to an earthly kingdom of the Messiah. The taking away of the property of the people by force, for the priests in the church of Israel, brought amazing vengeance upon those who gave countenance to that practice; yet the like iniquity has been tenaciously held fast, by men who call themselves ministers of the gospel; and forcing away the property of the Baptists for such, has been done in various parts of this country, even down into this year 1784; and much clamor is made against them, only for refusing to give any countenance to such wickedness. But the call from heaven to all the saints is, Come out of her, my people, that ye be not partakers of her sins, and that ye receive not of her plagues; for her sins have reached unto heaven, and God hath remembered her iniquities. Rev. xvii. 5; xviii. 3, 4, 5, 23.

Late reasonings have set the creature man so high, as to deny that a cause without him can determine his choice; while they hold that God's choice must be determined by what he sees in the creature, and not in himself. But the only seed that can produce the new birth gives such a turn to the mind, as to view all flesh but as fading grass, and the inhabitants of the world but as grasshoppers before God; yea, as a drop of the bucket, and small dust of the balance. And to set the contrast in its full light, it is declared that all nations before him are as nothing, and they are counted to him less than nothing and vanity. This is the incorruptible seed, of which souls are born again. Isai. xl. 6—17 ; I Pet. i. 23, 24. In our natural darkness we imagine that our obligation to serve God and to come to Christ depends upon our will and pleasure ; and that when we get ready to set about the work in earnest, his goodness and mercy will necessarily bring him to appear for our help, and to pardon and save us. Whereas, in truth, it is as much impossible for any rational person ever to be exempt, for one moment, from obligation to love God with all his powers, and to love his neighbors as himself, as it is for him to escape out of God's presence, or to put an end to his own existence. When Christ came and laid down his life for us, he gave the fullest demonstration of the truth and love of God, (as it was previously revealed in predictions and figures) and greatly enhanced our obligation to love and obey him ; and also clearly opened the way for our doing it, in newness of the spirit, and not in the oldness of the letter. The oldness of the letter lays every sin and defect as a bar in the way of approach to a holy God ; but the newness of the spirit, while it cuts us off from any confidence in the flesh, makes all our sins and wants powerful arguments for our daily coming to the throne of grace for supplies. Though Adam in innocency could have no idea of a mediator, or of pardon and cleansing from sin ; yet his obligation to the God of truth made it his indispensable duty to believe and obey him, in all his revealed will, and highly criminal to call the same in question. And unbelief still remains unspeakably criminal in his posterity ; for their natural powers of thinking and choice are not lost. Therefore the more unable we are to love God with all our powers, and to believe and obey his revealed will, the more guilty, and inexcusable ; because we love the creature instead of the Creator, and regard lying vanities in opposition to eternal truth ; which is confirmed by every event that ever happened. Good men and bad, angels and devils, all act according to the characters given of them, in the Holy Scriptures. No soil can bear good wheat until the roots naturally in it are broken up, and the wheat sown therein ; so the new birth cannot be wrought in any but by divine revelation. It is not a creation of new faculties, but the giving new ideas and dispositions, which were our indispensable duty before, but our evil hearts were contrary thereto. Breaking up of the thorns and briers in a field, is removing things which ought not to be there ; and the good seed being sown, and a union formed between the seed and the soil, the birth, the growth is produced. By such means as these, great relief was granted to our country, when its ruin seemed inevitable. For at the close of 1779, public credit was sunk so low, that forty paper dollars would not buy more of the produce of our own country, than one would in 1775 ; and from hence to the end of the war very few soldiers were raised in New England, but upon private, personal securities ; and large quantities both of clothing and provisions, that were raised for them, never reached their camps, by reason of the unfaithfulness and treachery in those who should have conveyed the same to them. But in the year 1779 a fresh revival of religion was granted, which increased in the year 1780, and spread the most extensively and powerfully through New England, that any revival had done for near forty years. Besides considerable additions that were made to some of the Congregational churches, it greatly increased the Baptist churches that were formed before, and raised about twenty new ones. According to the best accounts yet obtained, there were not less than two thousand persons baptized upon a profession of saving faith, in New England, only in the year 1780 ; and chiefly in the States of New Hampshire and the Massachusetts. And though true religion is directly opposite to wars and fightings among men, yet it teaches an inviolable regard to truth and equity ; and no small part of the duty of love is a defence of the innocent, when their rights are invaded, and their lives are in danger. The gospel shews that the only lawful use of the sword, is to punish such as work ill to their neighbor; and subjection to the powers that do it is a matter of conscience with believers. Rom. xiii. 1—10. And this revival of religion was undoubtedly a great means of saving this land from foreign invasion, and from ruin by internal corruption; though the latter is still so great, that there has been but little rejoicing, and less thankfulness, for the deliverance and peace which are wonderfully granted to us. The Warren Association, at their meeting, September 9, 1783, gave their views of these times, in the following address to their countrymen, viz. :—

DEARLY BELOVED : After a long and very distressing war, we rejoice at this opportunity of congratulating you, upon the return of peace to the nations, and to our land in particular, with a prospect of unspeakable advantages to the present and future generations. Indeed we are not insensible that many are sorrowful and complaining, instead of rejoicing at these times; several causes whereof are obvious. For ever since our first parents revolted from heaven, in order to please their eyes and their taste, their children have been chiefly influenced by carnal sense, instead of reason and truth. And the burthen of taxes, the great scarcity of cash, with the pressing calls for money from every quarter, have drawn a terrible gloom over many minds; which is greatly increased by a view of the untried scene of political existence into which we have entered, where none can tell what is before us; and we have no such arm of flesh to trust to as formerly. Added to which, are a great variety of disappointments and losses, with the use of corrupt schemes to repair them, and to get more power and gain, among all orders of men in the land, which make a number think our case almost desperate. But the gospel gives light, and opens the most glorious prospects, where nature can see nothing but darkness. It assures us that sufficient unto the day is the evil thereof, and forbids anxiety about to-morrow, because a sparrow cannot fall to the ground, nor an hair from your heads, without the providence of our heavenly Father. And what confirmations of this truth have we had! yea, and which now surround us! A main hope of our enemies was built upon the prospect of starving us into submission; but, behold! the showers and shines of heaven were not at their command; no, nor the hearts of the people neither. The events of this war are unparalleled. .... Deceitful reasonings from the power given to the members and rulers of the Jewish church, have persuaded people for many ages, that some men are born with a right to govern others, and that they are accountable to the people for what they receive and do; which has been the grand source

of oppression and tyranny through the world.   But how has God rent away
this veil of darkness !   The American Revolution is wholly built upon the
doctrine, that all men are born with an equal right to what Providence
gives them, and that all righteous government is founded in compact or
covenant, which is equally binding upon the officers and members of each
community. .... And as surely as Christianity is true, Christ is the only
lawgiver and head of his church ; whom he will save from the power both
of gallies and gallant ships, those modern engines of tyranny.   Is. xxxiii.
16—24.   And his laws determine that his ministers shall neither be tyrants
nor slaves ; shall neither be supported by forcing away any man's property
without his personal consent, nor go a warfare of their own charges.   Matt.
x. 7—10, Luke x. 3—12 ; I Cor. ix. 7—14.   Opposite extremes about
these matters have long served to uphold each other.   The terms *Hire* and
Reward, on one hand, have been taken to drag this affair into secular courts ;
and the word *Freely*, on the other, to excuse people from doing anything to
support their ministers ; as if freedom belonged only to ministers, while the
people were slaves to their lusts.   Whereas it is as clear as the daylight,
that the obligations between pastors and people are mutual ; and that their
union and welfare greatly depend upon a free and faithful discharge thereof,
out of supreme love to God ; viewing themselves to be but stewards of all
their gifts and treasures, who must soon give account unto him of their
stewardship : yea, and that he only can give them success or enjoyment
in any undertaking whatever.   These laws naturally tend to keep his flock
from being devoured by such as feed themselves and not the flock, as well
as to exclude all members therefrom who refuse to be governed by him ;
and likewise to guard against all sinful divisions.   Corrupt men will not
have such advantage as they formerly had, to deceive the simple with artful addresses to their passions, either about the licentiousness or tyranny of
others.   The cry of persecution will be stopped, while those who love the
truth will endeavor to unite with societies who walk most clearly therein,
and be in earnest to fill their places with duty and usefulness ; knowing that
mutual esteem and confidence are most surely promoted thereby, without
which societies are unhappy, if not broken and dissolved.

CHAPTER XXVIII.

The Rise of a church on Martha's Vineyard.—The State of the Baptists in the County of Barnstable.—Also in the County of Plymouth.—Of a Riot at Hingham.—Of the Baptists in Bristol County.—Likewise in Suffolk, Essex, and Middlesex.—In the Counties of Worcester and Hampshire.—Of a Revival of Religion to the Westward.—Also to the Northward.—And on our Eastern Shores.

The next thing before us, is to give a distinct though brief account of the late revival of religion, and of the state of the Baptist churches.[1] And we may begin with the affairs of Martha's Vineyard, an island about twenty miles long, and ten broad, whereon are the towns of Edgarton, Tisbury, and Chilmark. They are a county by themselves, for holding of inferior courts, from whence they may appeal to superior courts in other counties. From Falmouth, in Barnstable county, to the entrance of the harbor of Holmes's Hole, on said island, is nine miles ; which harbor is much frequented by those who sail upon these coasts, and piloting of vessels round Cape Cod and elsewhere is no small part of the business of its inhabitants. The line betwixt Edgarton and Tisbury comes down upon the head of said harbor, so that the inhabitants round it are upon the corners of two towns, seven or eight miles from the meeting-houses in either of them ; which I am told some of their children of fifteen

---

[1] A more detailed account of particular churches is in a latter part of the book. Whatever notes we shall add in relation to them are therefore, for the most part, deferred.—Ed.

or sixteen years old never saw. For the soil is generally thin and barren, so that but very few horses can be kept there, and the men are much employed upon the sea, or in getting sustenance out of it. Yet they have been all taxed to a worship that they or their families could but rarely attend, and from which they seemed to get no good; so that at length very few of them went to any public worship at all. It is said, however, that but few intemperate persons were found among them. The war added greatly to their calamities, as our State could not protect them, and they lay at the mercy of our enemies; who came there with a powerful force in the fall of the year 1778, and took from the island all their arms and ammunition, besides three hundred head of cattle and a thousand sheep, and most of the produce of the land near said harbor. Dark indeed did their case appear; and on December 26, was such a cold snow storm as caused the death of seventeen men in a privateer sloop at the east end of the island, and seventy-five more in a brig near Plymouth. Yet this terrible storm drove into a creek, at the head of Holmes's Hole, such a vast quantity of bass as supplied the inhabitants of the whole island with as many of them as they were pleased to take, and more than they could make use of. And not long after, a British vessel was cast away upon the west part of the island, which gave the inhabitants a good supply of rice. And greater favors of another kind were before them. By afflictive providences, and private means of grace, four persons near Holmes's Hole were awakened to a sense of their sin and danger, and in the spring of 1780, they experienced a happy deliverance of soul. And no sooner was light granted to them than they endeavored to hold the same forth to others, which brought them to set up religious meetings, and a number were hopefully converted by these means. And about the last of June they sent for Elder Lewis, of Freetown, who went over in July, and preached and baptized a number of them. He did the like again in August and October, as

Elder Hunt also did in November; and, by particular request, I met them there in December, when a careful inquiry was made into their sentiments and views, and the order of the gospel, with the solemn nature of the Christian profession, was publicly laid open and inculcated. After which, on December 21, 1780, we saw fifty persons solemnly sign covenant together, to whom six more were added on the 24th, and all then sweetly communed together at the Lord's table. The high sheriff of the county was a leading member of this church, which contained some persons of every rank among them. The husband of one of them was born among the Portuguese, and now was newly returned from a distressing captivity in England. By seeing and hearing of these wonders of divine grace, his vows in trouble were brought with authority upon his mind; and though the tempter set in violently with his suggestions, that there was no mercy for him, and that he had better go and drown himself, in the evening after this communion, yet sovereign grace prevented it, and set his soul at liberty, so that he was soon after baptized and joined to that church, as a considerable number more also did. I have received no late accounts of the Indian Baptist church on that island.[1]

Our next view is of the county of Barnstable. The Separate minister at Harwich, named in page 79, has removed to Tamworth, in New Hampshire, and the other of Barnstable is now a pastor of a Congregational church at Newmarket, in that State; and Baptist churches are raised out of each of those Separate societies. A Baptist church was formed and organized at Harwich in 1757; but by advice of a council, their minister was deposed from his office in 1777, for immoral conduct, and they are now destitute of a pastor, though they have an agreeable teacher with them. They have some members from Wellfleet, where our ministers have frequently preached to attentive audiences. A small parish in the south part of Harwich got a Baptist minister

[1] See Vol. I, p. 347.

from the west part of our country to preach in their parish meeting-house; and in 1781 they formed a Baptist church there, and he was ordained their minister; but he is upon the Arminian plan, and not in fellowship with our churches. The Baptist church in Barnstable was constituted June 20, 1771; but they were very small for seven years, and then a revival was granted, and another in 1781; and things at present appear encouraging among them, though they have not been able as yet to get a settled pastor. There is the beginning of a Baptist society in Sandwich, in that county; but we may truly say of our times, The harvest is great, and the laborers are few.

The rise of the First Baptist church in Middleborough has been described; but coldness and stupidity had greatly prevailed therein for five years before the late revival of religion, which began in the latter part of 1778, and was at its height in July, 1780. The first person added to the church in this revival was on February 28, 1779, and eighty-five have been received since, above two-thirds of whom belong to Bridgewater, in the west part of which town a large Baptist meeting-house was built last year, eight miles from ours, and they have now got a minister to preach to them, though as yet they remain a branch of our church. The rise of the second Baptist church in Middleborough was as follows: Mr. Thomas Nelson, who was born in the town, June 6, 1676, just before Philip's war broke out, removed into that part of it called Assawamset, in 1717; about which time he joined the First Baptist church in Swanzey, as his wife also did August 5, 1723. In 1753 he and his sons, with a few more, set up a meeting at his house, and obtained Mr. Ebenezer Hinds to preach to them. Four miles southwestward from thence, Mr. James Mead was ordained pastor of a Separate church in 1751; but he died in 1756, after which the body of his church became Baptists, and Mr. Hinds's hearers joined with them, and ordained him their pastor, January 26, 1758, in which office he still continues. Mr. Nelson died before this church was formed, in his eightieth year; but his wife, Mrs. Hope Nelson, lived to be a member of it and communed with them at the Lord's table after she was a hundred years old. She died December 7, 1782, aged a hundred and five years and seven months. Her living posterity, besides all that had deceased, were two hundred and fifty-seven in the year 1774. But as some of them are removed to Nova Scotia, and to other distant places, their number when she died has not since been obtained. Many of them are members of Baptist churches, and three of them are public teachers therein. Mr. Ebenezer Jones was ordained the pastor of the Third Baptist church in Middleborough, October 28, 1761; but whisperers, who separate very friends, caused such a division there two years after, as not only removed him from being their pastor, but also broke up their meeting for a time. He has been preaching for some years past at Steventown, in the county of Albany. Mr. Hunt was ordained the pastor of said church, October 30, 1771; in which year they had a considerable revival, and another much greater in 1780. Their letter to the Warren Association, in September that year, gives the following account of it. Say they: —

In our letters for several years past, we had to lament the sad decay of religion among us, and the abounding of iniquity, which in the last year increased to the greatest degree ever known in this place. Men were bold in wicked ways, and all the endeavors of a few faithful ones among us could not prevent it. But blessed be God, things have taken another turn this year; for when sin, the great enemy of mankind, was coming in like a flood, the Spirit of the Lord has lifted up a standard against him. About the middle of March, on a Lord's day in the afternoon, there appeared a very visible alteration in the face of the whole assembly; they were all attention to the word, and concern was discovered in their countenances, which increased so that by the beginning of April several scores of persons appeared under deep concern about their souls and eternal salvation. And since the work began we have reason to hope that about one hundred souls have been turned from darkness to light, and eighty-three have been baptized....It is very remarkable in our view to see so many suddenly turned from darkness to light, and have such a clear understanding of the nature of religion, and so ready to practise what they know. . . . . We have been remarkably free from disorders, by means of which those who appeared to oppose this work, (who are chiefly of another denomination) and were waiting to see how things turned out, have seen such things as have greatly stilled and convinced them. Thus has it pleased our gracious God to visit a most unworthy people, and, after a dark night of sorrow and mourning, to make us glad with his salvation.[1]

From the beginning of the revival to September, 1781, more than a hundred persons were added to that church, above half of whom were males.

A branch of this church is at Marshfield, where a steady society for worship has been kept up for some years; and in the late revival a number of persons were hopefully converted in Scituate, on the north borders of our county; and frequent religious meetings were held there. This caused a

---

[1] From letters of Mr. Hunt to Mr. Backus we quote the following :—

" God is doing wonders amongst us. We have baptized eleven, and there are not far from thirty more hopefully brought into liberty. . . . . The work has increased from the beginning; this week has brought forth more than any time before, and yesterday was such a time as I never saw. After the worship was over at the meeting-house, a body of the people repaired to my house, and we began to sing and pray. The divine power was like Pentecost; and by sunset, six persons obtained liberty, and such rejoicing of saints and such cries of sinners I never heard." Dated May 31, 1780.

" We thought, about ten or twelve days ago, that the work was abated, but since then it has revived. Numbers are newly struck under convictions, and seem as powerfully impressed as any that we have seen; and some brought out; and others who have received comfort, understandingly led into baptism and have cheerfully gone forward in that ordinance. The number is as follows; viz : Baptized on May 12th, five; 13th, two; 14th, one; 23d, three; June 14th, seventeen; 27th, six; July 5th, eleven; 11th, nine; total, fifty-four. This number have been hopefully converted since the middle of March, except four or five. In the number are four boys about twelve years old, three of whom were awakened on the fast day when you were with us. I suppose the whole that have been brought in are just about seventy, in our society only." Dated July 12, 1780.

" When I returned from the Association, I found about half a dozen young converts brought out clear while I was gone. Six were baptized last week; and last Lord's day another, a young man who had been very careless, appeared to give as clear, convincing declaration of a work of grace in his soul, as any one out of ninety which we have heard among us since the work began. . . . . When I think of these things, together with the favor of God to my own soul, I sometimes conclude myself the happiest man in the world. O for humility and gratitude! I have preached three sermons lately at Rochester, and our gracious Lord was with me. Some were pricked in the heart. I believe the Lord has begun there. The work goes on gloriously at the Vineyard." Dated October 14, 1780.—ED.

great uneasiness in the adjacent town of Hingham, where their ministers had long taught the world to tyrannize over the church.[1]　And as an exhorter from Rhode Island government had attended several meetings in Scituate, the people of Hingham could not be content without shewing their particular resentment against him.　Therefore one of them followed him into Abington, as he was upon his return home, and importuned him to go and hold a meeting at his house. This he at last consented to; and a number of people met there for religious worship in the evening of May 28, 1782. But just as they were going to begin their exercise, a large mob came up, whose leader was a communicant in one of the churches in Hingham, and, by leave of the man who had invited said exhorter to his house, they went in and seized him, and carried him away with the Bible in his hand; but upon his telling them that it was the best law he ever heard of, they knocked it out of his hand, and stamped it under foot, with oaths and execrations too horrid to be repeated!　And they bruised and injured his body, as well as tore his clothes; and forcibly carried him and two other baptized brethren out of Hingham; and afterwards threatened his life, if he ever came there again.　By good advice, a a complaint was exhibited to the Grand Jury of that county against the chief of those rioters, and a bill was found against five of them, supported by eight witnesses; and four of the rioters were arraigned before the Court at Boston, October 10, and pleaded Not guilty; upon which their trial was appointed to be on January 14, 1783; and they were laid under bonds then to appear; and the Court bound the witnesses also to appear at that time, four of whom were men, and the others women.　The season proved to be exceeding difficult, by reason of snow, ice and a severe air, yet the four male witnesses appeared at the time appointed, but none of the rioters, neither was any forfeiture of their bonds exacted; but their trial was put off for two days, and

[1]See p. 62.

all the witnesses were required then to appear.   A sleigh was therefore procured to carry two of the female witnesses; but as they called at a friend's house in Hingham in the evening, to refresh themselves, it was conveyed away and cut to pieces, and they could not find their horse till next day.   Yet all the eight witnesses appeared in Boston at the time last appointed; but then the lawyers prevailed to have the trial put off until April; one of whom was the man that pleaded conscience for supporting worship by tax, in our conference at Philadelphia, mentioned in page 200.   But the world may now see what consciences such men have. In the spring those rioters found that they could no longer put the case off, and then they were in earnest to settle it without a public hearing, which was finally done, by their engaging to pay all costs.   But let the politicians of Boston remember, that it is but a few years since they declared to the world, that a delay of justice is a denial of justice; and therefore that wherein they judged others they are self-condemned.   And they appear more openly so from the following instance.   The burthen of our civil taxes being exceeding heavy, and a pair of oxen being exposed to sale therefor in Taunton, opposition was made against the sale; until a gentleman offered a generous price for them, and then the matter was settled.   Yet to deter persons from any such thing for the future, two men of Taunton were seized in the night and carried off to Boston by armed men, the August after said riot at Hingham.   What right they had thus to bring men out of another county, belongs not to me to determine; but if an impartial regard to the public peace, as well as to the rights of Christianity, had prevailed in the breasts of some men in Boston, could those rioters in their own county have possibly been indulged as they were, and those sufferers have been so cruelly treated?

Officers in the church as well as the State often do much mischief if unfaithful, and much good if faithful, in their several stations.   Our churches in Swanzey and Rehoboth have had large experience of this. The blessings which the first church of Swanzey enjoyed under the successive minis-trations of their elders, Miles, Luther and Wheaton, are touched upon in Volume I, pages 284, 406, 499; Volume II, pages 29, 31. Mr. Samuel Maxwell was ordained a col-league with the last of them the year before his death. Mr. Maxwell lived to a great age, and was esteemed a pious man; but he was so unsteady in his principles and conduct, as to cause much unhappiness in the churches. On this account he was, by his own request, dismissed from Swanzey in 1739, and though he took the charge of the Baptist church in Rehoboth six years after, yet he did not continue four years with them. In 1742 said church in Swanzey settled a gifted minister from Narragansett, who had a thronged audience for a few years, yet then he was accused of the sin of un-cleanness, which charge he never cleared up, but went off and left the church. Their next minister was accused of taking unjust methods to get into that place; and he was much influenced by a few men in the church who were attached to Arminianism; and by these means, the church that had two hundred members in pious Elder Wheaton's days, was reduced to a very small number, and the congre-gation also. After about thirty years he was dismissed at his own request, and removed away. And as the meeting-house and minister's house in Warren were burnt by the enemy, and the place was still exposed to their rage, they agreed at present to unite with Swanzey church, three miles off; and their pastor was called and settled there. And such a divine blessing was granted, that when I was there in October 1781, I was informed that within two years about two hundred persons had been added to the two churches in Swanzey. The former elders of the Second church in Swan-zey are before mentioned.[1] Their next elder, Job Mason, was ordained May 22, 1738, and was well esteemed in his office until his decease in August, 1775, aged eighty. His

[1] See Vol. I, pp. 449, 450, 476.

brother, Russel Mason, their present pastor, was ordained November 2, 1752. General redemption had been so much held there, that they admitted members upon a general declaration of their faith, until a powerful work among them, in the beginning of 1772, introduced particular relations of the work of divine grace upon their souls ; and light has greatly increased among them since. And in this late revival singing has been introduced in their public worship. The town of Rehoboth calls for our next attention. The Baptist church formed there under Mr. Comer's ministry[1] increased to ninety-five members in less than two years. But in 1736 a minister was ordained in his stead, whose principles were unsound ; and six years after he took a whore instead of his wife, and went off with her. Since which, diversity of sentiments about doctrines, terms of communion, &c., have produced many small societies in that town, which I shall not attempt particularly to describe here, as a list of them may hereafter be given. The two Baptist churches in Attleborough were formed out of Separate churches there. The pastor of the church in Norton (mentioned in page 134) after a pious and useful life, fell asleep on August 23, 1768 ; after which the church united with a small society in the north borders of Taunton, where they are become a large society ; and their present pastor was ordained November 12, 1772. In the year 1780 there was a most precious harvest of souls among them. No other Baptist churches in that county have had more than one pastor ; and their names may hereafter be given.

The three counties last mentioned contain the whole of the ancient colony of Plymouth (the first in New England) excepting the few towns since set off to Rhode Island. The Colony of Massachusetts is the next before us, the head county whereof is Suffolk. The affairs of the two Baptist churches in Boston, their capital, have been described.[2] To which I shall add, that Mr. Condy was a gentleman of su-

[1]See p. 29.   [2]See Vol. I. pp. 285, 467, 483; Vol. II. pp. 32, 53, 170, 176.

perior powers and learning, and of a very respectable character; but the sentiments he had imbibed about the doctrines of sovereign grace, impeded his public usefulness in the ministry; and upon the instalment of their present pastor, January 9, 1765, he freely resigned his office in that church. The present pastor of their second church succeeded Mr. Davis in 1774. The next Baptist church in that county is in Bellingham, which was constituted October 15, 1750. Their first pastor was Mr. Elnathan Wight, a pious and useful man, who died in November, 1761. To him succeeded their present pastor, who was installed there, November 12, 1766. He was first ordained at Stafford, June 5, 1755; but was dismissed from thence by the advice of a Council, August 28, 1765, because the majority of the church appeared to be so much out of a gospel line of travel, that other churches withdrew their fellowship from them. The rest of the Baptist churches in that county have had no more than one minister. In Essex, beside the church of Haverhill, of which we have spoken,[1] Baptist meetings are held at Danvers, Rowley, and Methuen. In Middlesex, the church whereof Mr. Draper was pastor in Cambridge[2] dissolved after he left them, and the time of the constitution of our present church there may be hereafter seen. Mr. Elisha Rich was the first pastor of our Chelmsford church, who was ordained there October 5, 1774, but he removed into the State of Vermont near four years after. Their present pastor was ordained September 24, 1783. Baptist meetings are steadily held at Framingham and Weston, but churches are not formed there.[3]

In Worcester county, the church at Sutton, mentioned in page 31, was become small when their aged pastor died, January 4, 1775, and they are since dissolved. The second Baptist church there settled a minister in 1768, who was dismissed four years after for not being sound in the faith. Elder Green, of Leicester, after a very laborious and use-

[1]See p. 138.   [2]See p. 79.   [3]See p. 98, note.—ED.

ful life, was taken to his rest August 20, 1773, aged seventy-three. Benjamin Foster, A. M., educated at Yale College, was ordained there October 23, 1776, and an evident blessing attended his labors for a considerable time. But differences about some points of practice arising among them, he was dismissed by mutual consent, about six years after, and removed, and preaches to a new society in Danvers, his native place. The first pastor of the Baptist church in Sturbridge died in 1755, and they have gone through many trying scenes since, but have at present a prospect of settling an agreeable pastor soon. Mr. Samuel Dennis was ordained at Petersham in October, 1778, but he was taken from his beloved flock by death in April, 1783. The first pastor of South Brimfield church, in the county of Hampshire,[1] removed from thence to Nova Scotia, (though he came back afterward) and Mr. James Mellen was their second pastor, who is mentioned in pages 143, 144. Their present pastor was ordained November 11, 1773, when the church was very small and feeble, but a great blessing has been since granted there. They had but twenty-three members in the church before a revival began among them in 1779, which in their letter to our Association, in September that year, was thus described; viz: —

Dear brethren, we have to inform you, that by the grace of God we are at peace among ourselves, and enjoy much of that love which passeth knowledge. The Lord, of his mercy, is come down among us, by his great and mighty power. Such solemn meetings we never had before; it comes like the showers of rain upon the mown grass. O the agonies of soul that some feel, and the joys that some are full and more than full of! It seems as if heaven was come down here. Numbers are born of the Spirit, and feel the sweet liberty of the gospel. O the solemn cries for the salvation of sinners! O the amazing joys we feel! Never, never did we before see such a happy day! May the Lord have all the glory. O that it may spread through all the earth! Through divine goodness it does spread more and more. Brethren, pray for us. Some who a few weeks ago seemed the most stupid, are now speaking freely of their amazing joys, and beholding their bleeding and very precious Redeemer. The work is so

[1]See p. 31.

great that we cannot consent to our elder's meeting you in Association this year. We have this year thirty-four added by baptism; our whole number is fifty-seven.

From our sister church in Wilbraham, adjacent to them, they wrote at the same time and said: —

We pray God to direct you in conferring upon matters that concern the visible kingdom of Christ, and do that which may be for his glory, and the lasting peace and benefit of his churches. Beloved, the love of Christ, that bond of peace, still unites our hearts. God, of his infinite grace and goodness, is carrying on a glorious work by his Spirit. Saints are quickened thereby, and sinners are converted to him. It is wonderful to behold the change that has been in the space of one year with us. The hearts of fathers are turned to the children, and the children to the fathers. God is to us a place of broad rivers; we desire to exalt him, and give him all the glory. .... Added to the church this year fifty-one; died, none. Our present number is one hundred and thirty-three.

An elder from Berkshire county wrote August 29, 1779, and said:—

I snatch a moment to acknowledge the debt of love. I read the refreshing lines from you, and rejoice in your prosperity. May Zion's King enlarge her borders. It is a most remarkable time of the work of our God in New Providence,[1] Lanesborough, Hancock, New Lebanon, Little Hoosac, and some other places. In the fore part of June, at Shaftsbury, I baptized twenty-nine in one day. At Wallomstock[2] I attended the ordination of Elder Wait, and had a charming interview with Elder Gano. In a few weeks past I have baptized thirty-two, who have joined to our church. Elder Mason has baptized perhaps near thirty more, and a number have declared what God has done for them, that are not yet baptized. O brethren help us to praise the God of love!

From Ashfield they wrote in September, 1780, and said:—

The Lord has been pleased to pour out of his Spirit abundantly in this place, to the quickening of his children, and the conviction and conversion of many souls, as we, in a judgment of charity, have reason to believe. O help us to praise the Lord for his goodness, and his wonderful works to the children of men, and to us in particular! .... We have had the addition of nine members by letters, and thirty-six by baptism; have dismissed two to the church in Coleraine, and excluded one. Our present number is ninety-four.

[1] Now part of the town of Adams. [2] Near where the Bennington battle was.

And in all the churches and members that were added to the Warren Association in 1780, there was an increase of seven hundred and ninety-six members. Ninety were added to the church in South Brimfield alone, which formerly had passed through many and sore trials. And from a minister in the State of New Hampshire, to whom I wrote, I received the following remarkable account, dated March 15, 1781. Says he :—

I rejoice, Sir, to hear that in the midst of judgment, God is remembering mercy, and calling in his elect, from east to west. You have refreshed my mind with good news from the west and south, and in return I will inform you of good news from the north and east. Some hundreds of souls are hopefully converted in the counties of Rockingham, Stafford and Grafton, in New Hampshire, within about a year past. In the last journey I went, before my beloved wife was taken from me, I baptized seventy-two, men, women, and some that may properly be called children, who confessed with their mouths the salvation God had wrought in their hearts, to good satisfaction. Meredith, in Stafford [county], has a church gathered the year past, consisting of between sixty and seventy members. I baptized forty-three in that town in one day, and such a solemn weeping of the multitude on the shore I never before saw. The ordinance of baptism appeared to carry universal conviction through them, even to a man. The wife, when she saw her husband going forward, began to weep to think she was not worthy to go with him : in like manner the husband the wife, the parent the child, the children the parent ; that the lamentation and weeping methinks may be compared to the inhabitants of Hadadrimmon, in the valley of Magiddon..... Canterbury, in Rockingham county, has two Baptist churches gathered in the year past, one in the parish of Northfield ; the number I cannot tell, but it is considerably large : I baptized thirty-one there, and a number have been baptized since by others : the other is in the parish of Loudon, in said Canterbury, containing above a hundred members. .... Another church of about fifty members is gathered in Chichester ; another in Barrington, consisting of a goodly number, and one in Hubbardston, all three in Stafford county. Two churches in Grafton county, one in Holderness, the other in Rumney. The church in Rumney had one Hains ordained last August, much to the satisfaction of the people. All these seven churches have been gathered in about a year past. .... One church was gathered last fall in Wells, over which brother Nathaniel Lord, late of Berwick, is ordained. .... There appears to be a general increase of the Baptist principles through all the eastern parts of New England.

A large part of those plantations, for a hundred and fifty miles upon our eastern shores, have no Congregational ministers. Near thirty incorporated towns in the county of Lincoln have scarce five such ministers settled in them. But I have received the following entertaining account of the revival of religion in those parts.

A man who was born there, and was about ten years old when such a noise was made against Mr. Whitefield, as we have described in page 75, says :—

I was then convinced that neither myself, nor those men who spake with so much spite and malice, were the children of God ; and I was rationally convinced that those they spake against were his children, although they called them deluded, possessed with the devil, Highflyers and Newlights ; and though they spake it as a scandal, yet I believed I must know that light or perish in darkness ; and I still retained a selfish or legal love to those people, though never so much despised. And from that time until I was twenty-six years old, the Spirit of God was striving with me, by awakening my conscience, convincing me of sin, and that I must be born again. And so I went on sinning and repenting, reforming and forgetting, looking upon God to be such a God as I would have him to be ; in hopes, that for what good there was in me, he would shew mercy to me. But when about twenty-six years of age, and my affections much set upon the things of the world, just about the time I was married, I was suddenly taken down with sickness, and part of the time deprived of reason ; and those who saw me despaired of my recovery. But, glory be to God, he dealt not with me according to my deserts, but according to his rich love and free grace in Jesus Christ ; for he enlightened my understanding, and awakened my conscience, and set my sins in order before me, and that which I had forgotten came all to memory, with the breach of many vows and promises, which grieved me to the heart as I thought. O, I cried to God to forgive my sins, and to shew mercy for Christ's sake ; for I saw myself a condemned sinner, and told those who came to discourse with me about religious matters, that I saw myself to be the greatest sinner of all men ; and had I owned all this globe, I would have given it all for an interest in Christ. Yea, all the men upon earth could not have persuaded me out of the opinion that I was more willing to receive Christ than he was to receive me. But it pleased the Lord, in about a month, to raise me up to a considerable state of bodily health, with a great earnestness, as I thought, to seek and serve him ; reading the Scriptures often, praying in secret and in my family, exhorting many others to seek and serve God, and warning them against evil practices. Yet in all this I did not think I was born again, neither did

I think I could do anything of myself to forward the work of regeneration; and here I got clear of one false hope, and began to build upon
another; now I put great dependence in my non-dependence, and so went
on with my reformation, thinking all the good I did that it was God who
wrought it in me, and the evil came from the devil and my own corrupt
nature; and this hope gave me great joy in my good performances, but
great grief, guilt and repentance, for the commission of any known sin, or
the omission of any known duty; and so I went on for ten or twelve
years, and after that I grew more engaged after the treasures of the world,
and then my delight in religion died away. . . . . At length I began to think
I was blind, and ignorant both of my own miserable estate, and of the
remedy God had provided. I prayed that God would enlighten my understanding; but still I grew more blind, ignorant and wicked, as I thought,
but kept it to myself, till at last I got hedged up so that I could neither
read nor pray, which lasted but a short time. This was a Sabbath morning, September 30, 1781. . . . . Now I began to see the base views I formerly had of the Lord Jesus Christ, and of the plan of salvation; for when
I had a discovery of actual sins, and the danger I was exposed to thereby,
I would repent and reform, and think what a glorious Saviour Christ was,
and that some time or other he would save me from hell, and take me to
glory, with a desire to be happy, but no desire to be holy. But, glory be
to God, he now gave me another view of salvation; now I saw his law to
be holy, and loved it, though I and all my conduct was condemned by it.
Now I saw that God's justice did not strike against me as his creature, but
as a sinner, and that Christ died not only to save from punishment, but
from sin itself. I saw that Christ's office was not only to make men happy,
but to make them holy, and the plan now looked beautiful to me; I had no
desire to have the least tittle of it altered, but all my cry was to be conformed to it. . . . . On October 3, the load of guilt and condemnation was
instantly removed, and my soul was filled with joy and peace. Then it was
asked me, could I desire anything more? And at first I saw no want, till
I found a want of love and gratitude in me to return thanks to God for
this great deliverance, which I began to cry and plead for; and those words
were spoken to me, Greater love hath no man than this, that a man lay
down his life for his friend; which came with such light, life, love and
power, that I knew it to be the voice of my blessed Jesus, who by his Holy
Spirit set that glorious seal to my soul that God is true; and now, by his
grace, I could speak forth redeeming love and free grace without dread or
fear. At this time there was no work or moving of religion among us, or
round about us.

But he was constrained to go and visit his neighbors from
house to house, and to lay open to them the vast concerns of

the soul and eternity, whereby many were awakened, and a large number have been hopefully converted since. Two new Baptist churches have been formed in this year, and there is a prospect of greater and more extensive blessings in those new plantations.

CHAPTER XXIX.

Of the Baptist Churches in the County of Providence.—In Newport County.—And Westward from thence.—The Folly of Man
exposed.—Even among all Sects.—How Truth is held in Unrighteousness.—By the Shakers as well as others.—The only
Remedy against Delusions, and Measure of our real Happiness,
is a hearty Obedience to God's revealed Will.

When we turn our eyes westward, and take a view of the
first Baptist church in America, the folly of man and the
goodness of God appear very conspicuous therein. The
learned Mr. Callender, in his Century Sermon, expressed
some scruple whether Mr. Roger Williams, the founder of
that town and colony, was ever a member of that church,
or not. But he was convinced of this mistake afterwards.[1]
Governor Winthrop, the most ingenuous and upright writer
of any at Boston in that day, whose writings have come
down to us, dates the beginning of the Baptist church in
in Providence in March, 1639, and says it began by Ezekiel
Holliman's baptizing Mr. Williams, and then he baptizing the rest. But that in July after, the opinion mentioned in page 3 put a stop to his further travel with them.
And Richard Scott, who was one of them, says two or three
of the church withdrew with Williams.[2] Thomas Olney
was their next minister. But the diversity of sentiments
mentioned in this volume, pages 1—4, brought such darkness over their affairs, that no regular records before 1770

[1] See Vol. I. p. 357.—Ed.   [2] See Vol. I. pp. 86-89.

are now found therein.   Their ancient fathers, Olney, Dexter, Wickenden, Tillinghast and others, could write well, as their civil records and some private papers witness; and I cannot but hope that more distinct accounts of their religious affairs will hereafter be discovered.   Elder Tillinghast, whose memory is precious,[1] plainly told his people their duty to future ministers; but himself was so far from being chargeable to them, that he gave the lot upon which their first meeting-house was built.   He died in a good old age, in 1718, and his posterity are now numerous and respectable.   Mr. Ebenezer Jencks, brother to the Governor, was a pastor of that church from 1719, to his decease in 1726, colleague with Elder James Brown.[2]   And their two families have, in late years, done the most of any families upon earth for the promotion of learning and the Baptist cause in Providence.   Elder Winsor, there mentioned, continued in that office until his death in 1758, aged eighty-one.   Elder Thomas Burlingham was a colleague with him, and died in 1770, aged eighty-two.   Elder Winsor's son Samuel succeeded him in the care of the church in Providence, from 1759 until 1771, when he and a minor part of the church drew off, on account of differing sentiments concerning the doctrines of grace, and singing in public worship, then introduced, (which was a return to the first principles of the church) and he and his followers formed another church in Johnston.   One of the two churches in Smithfield (mentioned in page 28) is dissolved: Elder John Winsor officiates in the other, where Elder Place did; but I have not been favored with any distinct account of their affairs, nor of those of the church in Scituate, where Elder Hopkins succeeds Elder Fisk.   The like is to be said of the church in Cumberland, where Elder Ballou succeeds Elder Cooke.   These three churches hold to general redemption, and make laying on of hands a term of their communion. But Elder Joseph Winsor, son to the first Elder Winsor in

[1]See pp. 16, 22.   [2]See p. 23.

Providence, who succeeds Elder Thomas Knowlton in Glou-
cester, is in full fellowship with our churches. And so is
Elder Rufus Tift, who was ordained in North Providence
June 16, 1784, successor to Elder Ezekiel Angell, who died
September 27, 1780.

Of the ministers of the First and Second churches in
Newport, we have before spoken.[1] The learned Mr. Callender died there January 26, 1748 ; and Mr. Upham's society at Springfield being small, he was prevailed with to
remove to Newport the next year, where he ministered the
chief of his time until 1771, when he returned to his flock
at Springfield, whom he had often visited in the mean time.
And Mr. Kelly, from Philadelphia, was ordained pastor of
the first church in Newport, October 9, 1771 ; and though
the war caused his removal from them, yet he has since returned to them again. Elder Wightman, of the Second
church there, died August 31, 1750, aged eighty-two. Elder Eyres was taken from them February 13, 1759, aged
sixty-eight; and their present pastor, who had often preached
to them before, was ordained the twenty-ninth of April following. He was almost the only dissenting minister who
continued to preach on the island through all the distressing
season of its being possessed by the enemy ; and he has
had a precious harvest of souls there since. The Third
church in Newport, which keeps the seventh day, began under
the ministry of Mr. William Hiscox in 1671, who continued
their pastor until his death, May 24, 1704, aged sixty-six.
Elder William Gibson from London was his successor, and
died March 12, 1717, aged seventy-nine. Elder Joseph
Crandall had been a colleague with him for two years, and
continued their minister until he died, September 13, 1737.
Elder John Maxson was their next minister, from 1754 until
his decease, March 2, 1778. Mr. Ebenezer David (who was
converted in Providence College, and took his first degree
there in 1772) belonged to this church ; and having been a

[1]See pp. 15, 16, 29.

chaplain much esteemed in our army, died therein not far from Philadelphia, a few days after Mr. Maxson. Their present pastor was ordained a colleague with him.

The church in Dartmouth (mentioned in Vol. I. pages 454, 505) now have their meeting-house and the majority of their members within the bounds of Tiverton. Elder Tabor died in 1752; after which they had Elder David Round for their minister a number of years, and some others; but it was a dark, trying time with them, until a late remarkable revival was granted. Their present pastor is from Newport. He removed there in the spring of 1775, but labored under many discouragements for five years; and then heavy afflictions were made to work for good to him and his people. He was ordained April 13, 1780, and much of a spirit of prayer was granted for the revival of religion; which prayers were answered in such a manner, that betwixt the first of June that year, and June 27, 1781, ninety members were added to that church. In which time say they, " We have seen as it were many Pentecost days, and enjoyed heaven upon earth. All glory to God forever and ever. The subjects of the work seem to be of all ages, from fifteen to sixty, and all circumstances of life. They tell clear experiences of a work of grace; and some who have been professors several years can now tell something like a new conversion."

When we pass over the Narragansett Bay, I perceive that the church in South Kingstown (mentioned in page 28) has long been dissolved; those in North Kingstown and Warwick continue, but my intelligence concerning them is too imperfect to be of any service to the public. The like may be said concerning the Seventy-day church at Westerly and Hopkinton which continued to act as one church with their brethren of Newport, until they were regularly dismissed therefrom in 1708. The church in the west part of Warwick, where Elder Worden was ordained,[1] is dissolved; and

'See p. 79.

after he had preached for some time to the church in Coventry (mentioned in page 105) many of them removed to the place where he is now settled in Berkshire county. The west part of Coventry, with the adjacent borders of Scituate and Foster, had scarcely the appearance of religion among them, until Elder Nichols was raised up, and made instrumental of a very considerable reformation in those parts. Elder David Sprague died in Exeter, in 1777, and his son before and since has been made a very useful man there. Oliver Babcock, succeeded his father in office at Westerly. Elder Wightman's son is his successor in Groton. The church at New London[1] is dissolved, by means of the ill-conduct of their minister. The pious Elder Merriman died at Southington, last winter, aged eighty-eight. Such a revival of religion was granted in Woodstock, in 1780, as added ninety members to the Baptist church there, in less than two years. To the honor of Governor Trumbull it is to be remembered, that he has repeatedly interposed his influence in favor of that society, to relieve them when taxed to the worship of their opponents. The present Baptist minister of Suffield was ordained in 1775; and such a blessing was granted upon his labors, that their church increased in about a year from sixty to two hundred members. And our principles prevail more and more in all parts of the country; so that we may truly adopt the language of Moses's prophetical song, For their rock is not our rock, even our enemies themselves being judges. They have often declared that their ministers and churches would come down, if they were not supported by compulsion. They have now tried that power against us, and to support themselves, until it plainly fails them, while our rock stands firm. Let all the glory be given to God therefor. We are so far from deserving any part of it, that like babes we have need again to be taught which are the first principles of the oracles of God.

[1]See Vol. I, p. 519.

Let us take a brief view. of those principles, and of the folly of man in departing from them. If we pay any regard to the word of Christ, we must know, that no man can see his kingdom, nor have right to any power therein, without regeneration; and also that all striving about who shall be the greatest is excluded therefrom. John i. 12, 13; iii. 3; Matt. xviii. 1—4; xx. 25—28. Agreeably to this, the fathers of New England were taught as follows :—

As the kingdom of Christ is not of this world (John xviii. 36) but spiritual, and he a spiritual king; so must the government of this spiritual kingdom, under this spiritual king, needs be spiritual, and all the laws of it. And as Christ Jesus hath, by the merits of his priesthood, redeemed as well the body as the soul, (I Cor. vi. 20), so is he also, by the sceptre of his kingdom, to rule and reign over both. Unto which Christian magistrates, as well as meaner persons, ought to submit themselves; and the more Christian they are, the more meekly to take the yoke of Christ upon them; and the greater authority they have, the more effectually to advance his sceptre over themselves and their people by all good means. Neither can there be any reason given, why the merits of saints may not as well be mingled with the merits of Christ for the saving of his church, as the laws of men with his laws for the ruling and guiding of it. He is as absolute and [as] entire a king as he is a priest, and his people must be as careful to preserve the dignity of the one, as to enjoy the benefit of the other.[1]

And as the teachers in the church of England continued to call baptism regeneration, as Origen did, and yet the author against whom Mr. Robinson wrote, told of his begetting many of his hearers in Christ by his preaching, Robinson said to him :—

Their baptism was true baptism, and so the true seal of their forgiveness of sins, and new birth, as you affirm, p. 119, and this their seal of the new birth hath stood good upon them all this while, visibly and externally; and yet, after all this, you preach unto them and beget them anew, visibly and externally (for only God knoweth that which is true within.) You have begotten [begot] them through the gospel. Behold a monstrous generation! a man begetting children twenty, thirty or forty years after they be born! If Nicodemus had heard of this, he might well have said, How can these things be.[2]

[1] Robinson against Bernard, p. 38. [Works of John Robinson, Vol. II, p. 40.]
[2] Robinson against Bernard, preface, pp. 11, 12. [Works of John Robinson, Vol. II, p. 11.]

And how is the folly of others also now exposed in our land? In 1638, the year Harvard College was founded, a law was made at Boston, to empower the voters in each town (which then were only the communicants in their churches) to compel every inhabitant therein to contribute proportionally with others, "for upholding the ordinances in the churches, whereof he doth or may receive benefit." And because a man wrote some arguments against this practice, he was fined ten pounds; and another was fined forty shillings, only for reading the same before company; and the ministers said such men were "rather to be taught by cudgel than argument."[1] But how is their folly now made manifest unto all men, according to God's promise? II Tim. iii. 5—9. Corrupt ministers have done the most to promote infidelity and a contempt of revealed religion of any men upon earth. After these things had broken forth in the nation most terribly, in and after the reign of Charles the Second, bishop Burnet said:—

I am forced to declare, that having had much free conversation with many that have been fatally corrupted that way, they have very often owned to me, that nothing promoted this so much in them, as the very bad opinion which they took up of all clergymen of all sides. They did not see in them that strictness of life, that contempt of the world, that zeal, that meekness, humility and charity, that diligence and earnestness, with relation to the truths of the Christian religion, which they reckoned they would most certainly have, if they themselves firmly believed it. Therefore they concluded, that those whose business it was more strictly to enquire into the truth of their religion, knew that it was not so certain as they themselves, for other ends, endeavored to make the world believe it was. And that, though for carrying on of their own authority or fortunes, which in one word they call their *trade*, they seemed to be very positive in affirming the truth of their doctrines; yet they in their own hearts did not believe it, since they lived so little answerable to it, and were so much set on raising themselves by it; and so little on advancing the honor of their profession, by an exemplary piety and shining conversation. This (says Burnet) is a thing not to be answered by being angry at them for saying it, or by reproaching such as repeat it, as if they were enemies to the

[1] See Vol. I, pp. 79, 81.

church; these words of heat and faction signify nothing to work upon or convince any.[1]

And he well observes, that a real reformation is the only effectual remedy. And such a door is now opened for an extensive reformation, as never has been before among any people since the rise of antichrist. He rose and has prevailed by the connection of the officers of church and State together, so as to level the terrors both of this and the future world against all that attempted to resist their power. But how is that connection now broken! A learned gentleman in the law, published an answer last January, to the minister mentioned in page 248, who tells him plainly:—

A church hath a right, beyond all obligation that human laws can lay upon them, to dismiss their pastor when they please. Churches may advise churches, and members may reason with members; but to advise will always suppose, that the advice may be accepted or rejected; and should it be rejected, I know not to what earthly tribunal the pastor, as pastor, could repair with his complaint against his church.....The first principle in a religious body is, that they will act according to the dictates of a good conscience, advising, not controling one another. There is nothing more plain than that when they consent to do that which their consciences disapprove, they do not act as a religious society.[2]

This is a most important truth, but how little is it regarded.

Can the conscience of any man approve of his taking away the property of another for nothing? or requiring him to do much service for a community, without any support or reward? Christ says, The laborer is worthy of his reward; and his command is, Let him that is taught in the word communicate unto him that teacheth, in all good things. Be not deceived; God is not mocked. Yet how many are there at this day that make high pretences of regard to a free gospel, and at the same time treat those whom they applaud as true teachers of it worse than they do their oxen? not only neglect to communicate good things to them

[1]Preface to his Pastoral Care, 1692, pp. 12, 13.
[2]Strictures upon Thatcher, by J. S., pp. 19, 22.

themselves, but hinder others from doing of it. Such an instance has been described in page 23. And there are persons now in all parts of the land, who are ready to spit their venom, and if possible to ruin the characters of all teachers who will not either be tyrants or slaves; either be confederate in forcing away the property of people for nothing, and worse than nothing, or else spend their lives and strength for the good of souls, and receive nothing from them but empty words. The great design of religion is to make men just and merciful; but how opposite thereto is it, to set a man up in a public and expensive office, exposed to the resentment of earth and hell, and require him to go this warfare of his own charges! I Cor. ix. 7—14. Can any wonder if a curse is sent upon the blessings of men who refuse to lay these things to heart? Mal. ii. 2; iii. 9, 10. Truth and love bring teachers and members to act in union, and to regard each other's case as their own, which a precious number do in our day; but pride and covetousness cause divisions and offences, contrary thereto; and all such are to be marked and avoided. Those in general who have made use of secular force in religious matters have been such schismatics,[1] neither can others be free of that guilt, who lay heavy service and burthens upon their officers, and will not touch them with one of their fingers. The time is coming when the vile person shall no more be called liberal, nor the churl bountiful; but the liberal deviseth liberal things, and by liberal things shall he stand. Is. xxxii. 5—8. Nearly or quite half of the expense of the sitting of the Legislatures, both of Massachusetts and Connecticut, ever since they have supported ministers by tax, (except in the late time of war) has been to contrive how to take and give property that they had no more right to meddle with, than they had to appoint some men to make a weekly feast in each town, and compel all to pay for it, whether they liked it or not;

[1]See Vol. I, p. 484.

20

yea, although they discovered poison therein. For worse poison for bodies was never found upon earth, than a great deal of the teaching thus paid for in our land is to the souls of men. The apostle speaks of oppositions of science falsely so called, and of those who hold the truth in unrighteousness; and perhaps the following are instances of it.

That Christianity is essentially necessary to the good order of civil society, is a certain truth;[1] but men hold it in unrighteousness, when they assume a power to add to Christ's laws about his worship. Pretenders to new, immediate revelations do this as really as State politicians. Special teachings of the Holy Spirit we all need continually, to give us a right understanding of the Holy Scriptures, so as to apply and obey them in a right manner; but they are perfect in themselves, and sufficient to furnish the man of God for every good work, when he takes the apostles as the true expounders of the prophets. On this foundation the Christian church was built. Eph. ii. 19, 20. And though confounding them together produced Mystery, Babylon, yet, when she shall be destroyed that order will be again observed. Rev. xviii. 20. Their writings, with the united church of believing Jews and Gentiles built thereon, appear to be the two witnesses mentioned in Rev. xi. 3—15. Directly after their resurrection, the kingdoms of this world will become the kingdom of Christ; which undoubtedly intends an entire submission to his laws and government. Reference is there had to Zech. iv. 11—14, which speaks of one candlestick, of two olive trees, and of golden oil communicated into it through them. There was then but one church; but after the partition wall betwixt Jews and Gentiles was broken down, both have access by one spirit unto the Father; which spirit is plainly the golden oil communicated to souls through the word of truth. This united church is the light of the world, and the pillar and ground of the truth. Matt. v. 14;

[1] See p. 228.

I Tim. iii. 15.   The chief disputes in the world have been whether God's revealed mind is strictly true? or if true, how it can be equal?   The apostles and prophets, and all hearty believers of their writings, have ever witnessed for both of these points; but it has long been in sackcloth or mourning.   And perhaps when they are killed, and yet the people will not permit them to be buried, means, when officers become so corrupt that truth falls in the street, and equity cannot enter, though the people will not entirely part therewith.   Hereupon Jehovah will arise and render vengeance to his enemies according to their deeds, yea, recompense to the islands.   After which the Redeemer shall come to Zion, and to them that turn from transgression in Jacob; who will be established in a way of covenant obedience to the words of his mouth, by the influence of his Spirit. This prophecy the apostle applies to future times, which will be as life from the dead.   Is. lix. 14—21; Rom. xi. 15, 26.   Again, because it is a most important truth that God is no respecter of persons, many deny his right to do what he will with his own grace, though in a way of perfect justice. He is perfectly just in all his dispensations, while he shews mercy to whom he will shew mercy.   To deny this is to deny him the right which every freeman has with his own property.   Oh, madness!   It is also an essential truth, that God is *love* in the abstract; but it is a fatal delusion to imagine that he loves every individual sinner, so as not to inflict endless punishment upon such as die in impenitency.   The devils are his creatures, and were a higher order of them then men; yet their endless punishment is declared as one evidence against those who turn grace into lasciviousness. Jude 6.   Again, Christ's finished atonement is the object of faith, and all our encouragement to come to God by him, is ever to be derived from the record thereof given in the gospel, which is as true before we believe it as afterwards; but it is a most deceitful trick to argue from thence, that the true believer is not conscious of an inward change in his soul, so as to be enabled to do such acts as are well pleasing to God. Heb. xiii. 16. When any in Israel were bitten with the fiery serpents, all hope of life was cut off, save only from an object without and above them, to which each of them must look, or death was his portion; yet when he looked, a change was wrought within him; the poison was expelled, and health recovered; and it would have been a wicked thing in any of them not to rejoice and be thankful therefor. Now Christ himself explains faith and regeneration hereby. John iii. 14, 15. Yet Robert Sandeman, and James Relly after him, have poisoned the souls of many with artful representations that it is pharisaical pride for any to tell of inward experiences, and to rejoice in what God has done within them. And the latter of them, by deceitfully representing that our own interest is part of the first object of faith, has carried his argument in many minds, that every individual will finally be saved, because if it were not so, it could not be a crime not to believe a point which was not true in fact. Whereas in the passage that he builds most upon, a not believing the record as it stands in the book is the crime charged; and life is there declared to be in the Son, and given to us, and also that none have life but those who have that gift. I John v. 10—12. Now compare this with Christ's own words concerning the brazen serpent, and Relly's argument appears as false as it would to have argued that it could not have been a crime for a poisoned person to refuse a look to it, unless healing was as certainly his before as afterwards: no crime to make light of the gospel call, unless the feast they are called to is certainly theirs, and they may come to it when they please; and that God's infinite love obliges him to receive them whenever they shall cry for it in good earnest. Matt. xxii. 1—4. The devil himself never preached worse doctrine than this, yet how many are strongly attached thereto!

Another essential truth of the gospel is, that we must daily deny ourselves and take up our cross, or we cannot be

Christ's disciples, But this truth has often been held in unrighteousness in every age. The people, mentioned in page
111, ran to a great length in that way. A man from Charlestown, near Boston, was their head, who, about 1758, assumed
God's essential prerogatives in such a blasphemous manner,
that he was complained of to authority, upon which he fled,
and his followers concealed him for many years, and a house
was built for that purpose in Harvard, where they privately
resorted to him; and he declared himself to be perfect and
immortal, until death arrested him, and he was buried with
great secresy. Since which the same house in Harvard has
been made the headquarters of a small company from
Britain, who have a woman for their head. They privately
got together in the county of Albany, and formed their
scheme; and then in April, 1780, it was suddenly proclaimed, that a new dispensation was begun, greater than
had ever been known in the world before, which all were
called to enter into, or they could not be saved. A Pædobaptist minister in New Lebanon, New York, and a Baptist
minister in Pittsfield, fell into the snare; and many hundreds were drawn into it, in various parts of Massachusetts,
New Hampshire and Connecticut. The said Baptist minister in Pittsfield, after being a few months with them, was
delivered from that delusion, and published an account of
their scheme, which was printed at Hartford, Norwich,
Providence and Boston. I was at his house in June, 1782,
and went with him to visit a considerable number of them.
They earnestly inculcate that doctrine of devils of forbidding
to marry, and require so much bodily exercise, in singing
and dancing, &c., as has destroyed the health and even the
lives of some; a cruel cross indeed! while their chief leaders delight themselves much in feasting and drinking spirit-
uous liquor. I would by no means misrepresent any of their
sentiments or conduct; but I have obtained most certain
evidence that these seven abominations constitute the essence of their scheme. 1. They hold an earthly head to

their church. 2. That out of it is no salvation. 3. That the only way into it is by confessing even secret sins to them. 4. That when any have so done, they must believe as the church believes, and do as they say. 5. They teach *Do and live.* 6. Their doings are unnatural and violent. 7. They endeavor to enforce and propagate their scheme with a strange power, signs and lying wonders. Some of them at Norton and elsewhere have carried matters so far this year, as for men and women to dance together entirely naked, to imitate the primitive state of perfection. And their forcibly stripping a woman of one of their families, who testified against their wickedness, has moved the authority of Bristol county lately to take them in hand therefor. Forbidding men and their wives to lodge together is a point they are strenuous upon. But a number who were with them have renounced their delusions, and their party is evidently on the decline. And so is that of another company, of whom take the following concise account. Jemima Wilkinson, born among the Quakers in Cumberland, in the county of Providence, being a young woman of a retentive memory, and an eloquent tongue, declares that in October, 1776, she was not only taken sick but actually died, and her soul went to heaven; soon after which, she says, her body was reäni-mated by the spirit and power of Christ; upon which she set out as a public teacher, and for a while had large assem-blies to hear her in various parts of the county of Bristol, and from thence westward to New London. Indeed she has travelled as far as Boston on one hand, and Philadelphia on the other; but her chief followers were within the above limits. A young man, who was an intimate counsellor of hers for some years, gives the following account of her, and of how he and other people were ensnared by her. He first heard her at Tiverton, in 1778, and says he : —

The first appearance seemed to be something singular and extraordinary, in a habit different from what is common amongst women, wearing her hair curled in her neck, without any other covering on her head, except when she travelled out she put on a hat much like a man's, only with the brim down. Her visage a good deal bright, with a very agreeable countenance; her voice very grum and shrill for a woman, and seemed pathetical and engaging in her discourse, in which were abundance of Scripture expressions, though not much explained, or light held up from them; neither did I ever hear her advance much Scripture doctrine of the principles of religion; but her exhortation seemed to be very affecting, shewing a very sedate countenance with seriousness and solemnity, admonishing all to repent and forsake evil, and learn to do well, and live as they would wish to die....And as the state of mankind at this day is much like the Athenians, that spent their time in nothing else but either to hear or tell some new thing, her coming forth as a preacher different from all other sects or denominations of people, being a woman of extraordinary natural abilities, speaking as an orator, of a great memory in the Scriptures, and having abundance of strange reports spread abroad concerning her, some false and some true, produce abundance of spectators and enquirers. And she appears zealously engaged, and says she devotes herself and service wholly to the glory of God, and the good of souls. She exhorts people in a pathetical manner, with great confidence and boldness; and says she has an immediate revelation for all she delivers; that she is the greatest minister that God has sent to the people these seventeen hundred and odd years; and advancing herself to live as she exhorts others to, fully in a state of perfection, with no liability of error or defect in any respect, seems to have great influence upon many serious people; for no one would rationally think that a person in their right senses would dare to hold forth and affirm such great and exalted things concerning themselves, unless it were so in reality.[1]

This is a brief view of the substance of his account of her way of proceeding, which brought a number of ignorant people, and some who have been officers in the State, to follow and cleave to her affectionately, as a person invested with immediate and great power from above, even power to work miracles. But her influence has not been half so great and extensive as that of the other woman mentioned; both of whose schemes are now dying away.

And thus I have pointed out some of the ways wherein men have gone a whoring with their own inventions. (Psal. cvi. 39) which is fixing their affections and dependence thereon, instead of the God of truth. And though it is

[1] Brownell upon Enthusiastical Errors, 1783, pp. 5—7.

a maxim with earthly politicians, that their king can do no wrong, thereby imputing all that is wrong to others, yet they have long taken the opposite course concerning the kingdom of Christ. All the frauds, oppressions and licentiousness, that have been practised under his name, have been cast upon Christianity itself; as if because men are false, therefore God is not true. Instead of owning his just authority, they have exalted themselves above him, and have arraigned his sayings at their bar. Rom. iii. 4. What he says concerning the entire depravity of man, and their enmity of heart against God, they make a chief argument against the truth of his sayings in his written word; and thus they plainly confirm the truth of it, by their arguments against it. And because errors and heresies more openly break out, where he has poured out his Spirit, than where people like Moab are settled upon their lees, many conclude that it was not his Spirit that moved upon the minds of the people; which argument is about as conclusive as it would be to say, that the influences of the sun are not really good in the spring and summer, because they cause a very disagreeable stench to arise from dunghills and dead carcasses, which we do not smell when the sun is at a great distance, and these things are hard frozen in the winter; or to say that the showers of heaven are not good, because they make the thorns to grow as well as the wheat. These reasoners often declare, that if we are entirely dependent upon the sovereign will of God, for renewing and saving grace, then all our use of means to attain salvation is in vain; but why do they use means for their bodies? If the Lord will, we shall live, and do this or that. Who were they that said a few years ago, " *We will* bring America to our feet! We *will* not receive law from any power whatever!" Where is their Governor who required us to submit to an *absolute* and *unlimited power* in man?[1] God's plan of government is absolutely perfect and immutable; and he has appointed the means and

[1] See pp. 189, 258.

the end, and the means in order to the end, in the moral
as well as natural world. The means of grace are calculated in infinite wisdom to open the eyes of men, and to turn
them from darkness to light, and from the power of Satan
unto God. Precepts and promises, rewards and punishments, calls and warnings, are all motives to influence the
choice of man. And the strongest hold that the devil has
in this world is to persuade man, that a being governed in
his choice by motives without himself, is inconsistent with
the liberty of moral agents; and to persuade him at the
same time that necessity obliges God to pardon and save
them, whenever they shall become sincere penitents.
Thus they assume a sovereignty to themselves, which they
deny to their Maker; and treat him as a servant, to whom
they may say, Go thy way for this time, and when I have a
convenient season I will call for thee; making his choice
dependent upon theirs. If motives without us do not determine our choice, it would be impossible for God to govern
us; and, as the excellent Edwards observes, Arminian principles truly involve in their nature the horrid blasphemy
which they falsely cast upon the Calvinists, of charging God
with acting a deceitful part towards men, in appointing the
means of grace; for these are motives to determine their
choice on the side of virtue, which he could not be sincere
in appointing, if their choice is not determined by motives
without themselves.[1] His immutable designs are so far from
interfering with the liberty of moral agents, that where they
are known, the believer dares not make them the rule of his
conduct; and hereby subjects and rebels are distinguished.
An express precept required Saul to destroy Agag, as well
as the rest of the Amalekites; and by disobedience thereto
he lost his kingdom and his soul. On the other hand, David
knew that God designed to remove Saul, yet having no precept to kill him, he refused to do it, though much provoked
thereto, when he had very convenient opportunities to cut

---

[1] Edwards on the Will, p. 266, third edition. [Edwards's Works, Vol. II, p. 117.]

him off. And though the prophet Samuel, by immediate direction from above, anointed David to be king over Israel, yet he never assumed that power but by their free choice and covenant; and when this was done by part of them, he made no use of their arms to compel others to receive him. And when ten tribes revolted from his grandson, who collected an army to bring them under him again, God warned him not to do it, and was obeyed therein. And if a power of will opposite to the Bible had not been dreadfully set up in latter ages, Mystery Babylon would not have been drunken with blood as she now is. A revelation to the Jews of God's design, that Jesus should die for that nation, did not at all lessen the guilt of those who thereupon took counsel together for to put him to death. John xi. 51—53. Obedience to what he requires of us, is the measure of our duty and felicity, without attempting to get into the place of the universal Ruler. At the same time no honest soul could be happy under his government, if he thought it possible for men or devils to deceive him, and to defeat his designs. And whether the whole history of this country, as well as others, does not demonstrate, that a hearty and unfeigned obedience to his revealed will is our wisdom as well as duty, and that all disobedience thereto is infinitely hateful and dreadful, is now freely referred to the reader's conscience.

CHAPTER XXX.

The Nature of Covenants explained.—The Sentiments of the Baptist Churches about Terms of Communion, the Power of Councils, and the Nature and Place of Human Learning.—A List of their Churches in New England.

The word *Covenant*, when used concerning contracts between man and man, includes many ideas that can have no place in the affairs betwixt the creature and his Creator; and so much darkness has appeared in controversies upon this subject, that some worthy men have thought it best to adopt the word *Testament* instead of *Covenant* in the latter case. But a review must convince us that we cannot get free of difficulties by this change of words; because *Testament*, when used about a father's will who is absent from us, is essentially different from the will of God, who is ever present, and sees our inmost thoughts. Yet *Testament* ever means the will of the testator expressed, and also a free disposal of his property as he pleaseth; which, when well ratified, is as good a title as any in the world, although it would spoil it for the legatees to have any hand in forming it. And mutual consent, with mutual obligations and privileges, are essential ideas in all covenants. *This do, and thou shalt live*, was the language of God to Adam in innocency, with which his heart concurred; and this obligation to love is immutably binding upon all his children. Luke x. 27, 28. To withhold this obedience is to rob both God and man of their right; and God justly requires every sinner to give again that he had robbed, and to walk in the statutes of life without committing iniquity. And the new covenant is the writing the law of love in the believer's heart, which yields a free consent to it, in the tenor of *I will, and They shall.* Ezek. xxxiii. 15; Rom. viii. 3, 4; Heb. viii. 10, 11. All who have this work wrought within them ought to confess the same with their mouths, and to receive each other as Christ received them, to the glory of God. Says the apostle, They first gave their own selves to the Lord, and unto us by the will of God. Rom. x. 10; xv. 7; II Cor. viii. 5. This is the exact nature of a church covenant; which shews that no person can be brought into it without his own consent, that the covenant cannot bind any person or community to act any thing contrary to the revealed will of God, nor ever exempt any from their obligation to act agreeably thereto with all their hearts.

Great imperfections still remain among us in these respects; yet it is thought best to exhibit to the world a list of the churches in New England who profess these principles, at least so far as not to allow that persons can be forced into religious covenants. A few of them admit some Pædobaptists to their communion, and it is but a few; neither can that practice last long, as our opponents know that practice speaks louder than words; and a noted minister and church in the county of Plymouth openly debarred one of their pious members from their communion last year, for no other crime than a being buried in baptism; by which act say they, "She has practically declared infant baptism a nullity, and this church to be a company of unbaptized persons." And the Separate churches in Connecticut published their terms of communion three years ago, which were these, viz.:— "As to our Baptist brethren, we are free to hold occasional communion with such as are regular churches, and make the Christian profession as above said, and acknowledge us to be baptized churches," &c.[1] Hereby they confirm our terms of communion, as described on page 116. Our sentiments concerning the use and power of Councils are the same as those described by our fathers, in Volume I, pages 473, 474, and we refuse to hear any complaints of censured persons in our annual Associations, because that would imply jurisdiction over the churches, which we disclaim; and we hold that a Council freely chosen, and meeting near the place of difficulty or grievance, where a fair hearing of the parties concerned may be had, is the most rational and scriptural method of proceeding in such cases. Our sentiments about the nature and proper place of human learning are well expressed in Volume I, pages 487, 488. Confining the ministry to an education at college, as well as compelling people to support such, has produced infinite mischiefs in all ages, which could never have prevailed as they have, if cruel arts had not been made use of to keep the people in ignorance, and to prejudice their minds against true knowledge, both sacred and civil. The foundation for learning laid at Providence, (mentioned in page 137,) has suffered much in the late war, but the school appears now again in a promising way. All other colleges have been very expensive to governments, but this has never received any thing in that way, (no, not to repair damages which government has occasioned therein,) but personal generosity laid its foundation, and has been its support hitherto. Gentlemen of various denominations, chiefly in the town of Providence, subscribed above four thousand pounds therefor before the college edifice was erected in that town; and considerable sums have been given since, especially in the year past, to augment their library. And as liberal sentiments are taught therein, and persons of all denominations, whose civil and moral conduct is agreeable, have equal privileges for learning in it, liberal communications are earnestly solicited for the necessary support of this institution.

[1]Declaration of said churches, met at Killingly, September 19, 1781, p. 21.

A brief View of the present State of the Baptist Churches in New England, according to the latest and best Accounts that have been received.

The first column contains the Year when each church was constituted, the second the Name of the Town, the third their Minister's Name, if they have any, and the fourth the Number of their Members, if that is known.

MASSACHUSETTS.—COUNTY OF SUFFOLK.

Year.	Town.	Ministers.	No.
1665	Boston,	Samuel Stillman, A. M.	158
1743		Isaac Skillman, A. M.	43
1750	Bellingham,	Noah Alden,	56
1769	Wrentham,	William Williams, A. M.	39
1776	Medfield,	Thomas Gair, A. M.	72
1780	Needham,	Noah Baker.	
1780	Stoughton,	Vacant.	

COUNTY OF BRISTOL.

Year.	Town.	Ministers.	No.
1663	Swanzey,	Charles Thompson, A M.	
1693		Russel Mason.	
1753	Rehoboth,	Nathan Peirce,	
1762		John Hicks,	100
1772		Jacob Hicks.	
1777		James Sheldon,	48
1780		Vacant.	
1761	Taunton,	William Nelson, A. M.	79
1769	Attleborough,	Job Seamans,	80
1781		Elisha Carpenter,	59
1772	Dighton,	Enoch Goff,	120
1774	Freetown,	Abner Lewis,	95
1781		David Seamans,	50
		Vacant.	
1774	Dartmouth,	Vacant,	19
1781		Daniel Hicks,	
1780	Raynham,	Vacant,	35

COUNTY OF PLYMOUTH.

Year.	Town.	Ministers.	No.
1756	Middleborough,	Isaac Backus,	137
1757		Ebenezer Hinds,	70
1761		Asa Hunt,	194

COUNTY OF BARNSTABLE.[1]

Year.	Town.	Ministers.	No.
1757	Harwich,	Vacant,	43
1781		Samuel Nickerson.	
1771	Barnstable,	Vacant,	41

COUNTY OF ESSEX.

1765	Haverhill,	Hezekiah Smith, A. M.,	190

COUNTY OF MIDDLESEX.

1771	Chelmsford,	Abishai Crossman,	87
1780	Newton,	Caleb Blood,	79
1781	Cambridge,	Thomas Green,	27

DUKES COUNTY.

	Chilmark,	Silas Paul.	
1780	Tisbury,	Vacant,	79

COUNTY OF WORCESTER.

1738	Leicester,	Vacant,	70
1749	Sturbridge,	Jordan Dodge,	53
1762	Charlton,	Nathaniel Green,	155
1765	Sutton,	Ebenezer Lamson,	78
1767	Grafton,	Elkanah Ingalls,	38
1768	Petersham,	Vacant.	
1770	Royalston,	Whitman Jacobs,	89
1774	Douglass,	Vacant.	
1775	Dudley,	Vacant,	33
1776	Harvard,	Isaiah Parker,	110
1779	Ashburnham,	Vacant,	37
1780	Northbridge,	Vacant,	25
1782	Templeton,	John Sellon,	23

COUNTY OF HAMPSHIRE.

1736	South Brimfield,	Elijah Codding,	236
1740	West Springfield,	Edward Upham, A. M.	
1761	Ashfield,	Ebenezer Smith,	90
1762	Granby,	James Smith.	
1765	Montague,	Vacant,	32
1768	Wilbraham,	Seth Clark,	159
1772	New Salem,	Samuel Bigelow,	35
1780	Shutesbury,	William Ewing.	
1780	Colerain,	Vacant,	26
1780	Bernardston,	Joseph Green,	50
1780	Chesterfield,	Vacant.	

[1] The churches in Barnstable county, and the third in Freetown, were omitted by Mr. Backus in his list, but given in a note at its close.—ED.

COUNTY OF BERKSHIRE.

Year.	Town.	Ministers.	No.
1769	Adams,	Peter Worden,	133
1771	Lanesborough,	Nathan Mason,	150
1772	Pittsfield,	Valentine Rathbun,	15
1772	Hancock,	Clark Rogers,	85
1777	Washington,	Vacant.	
1779	Sandisfield,	Joshua Morse,	30
	Alford,	Jacob Drake.	
1781	West Stockbridge,	Elnathan Wilcox,	15

COUNTY OF YORK.

1768	Berwick,	William Hooper,	53
1772	Sanford,	Vacant.	
	Wells,	Nathaniel Lord,	56
1782	Coxhall,	Simon Lock,	32

COUNTY OF CUMBERLAND.

1768	Gorham,	Vacant.
1782	New Gloucester,	Vacant.

COUNTY OF LINCOLN.

1784	Bowdoinham,	Job Macomber,	27
1784	Thomaston,	Isaac Case,	50

NEW HAMPSHIRE.

1755	Newton,	Vacant.	
1770	Richmond,	Matturean Ballou,	122
1771	Lebanon,	Vacant,	12
1771	Westmoreland,	Ebenezer Baily.	
1771	Brentwood,	Samuel Shepard,	156
1771	Deerfield,	Elipheleth Smith.	
1772	Gilmanton,	Vacant,	30
1777	Marlow,	Eleazer Beckwith.	
1778	Croydon,	Vacant,	22
1779	Canterbury,	Vacant.	
1780		Vacant.	
1780	Northwood,	Edmund Pillsbury,	44
1780	Salem,	Samuel Fletcher,	60
1780	Rumney,	[Cotton] Hains.	
1780	Holderness,	Vacant.	
1780	Meredith,	Nicholas Folsom.	
1780	Chichester,	Vacant.	
1780	Barrington,	Vacant.	
1780	Hubbardston,	Vacant.	
1782	New Hampton,	Jeremiah Ward.	

Year.	Town.	Ministers.	No.
1782	Perryston,	Samuel Ambrose.	
1782	Temple,	Vacant.	
1782	Savil,	Vacant,	12
1783	Weare,	Vacant.	
1783	Canaan,	Thomas Baldwin,	18

CONNECTICUT.—COUNTY OF HARTFORD.

1739	Southington,	Vacant,	18
1743	Colchester,	Vacant.	
1755	Stafford,	Vacant.	
1760	Enfield,	Vacant.	
1775	Suffield,	John Hastings.	
1780	Coventry,	Vacant.	
	Farmington,	John Davis.	
1783	Chatham,	Solomon Wheat.	

COUNTY OF FAIRFIELD.

1751	Stratfield,	Seth Higby.	
1773	Stamford,	Elkanah Holmes.	
1773	Greenwich,	Vacant.	

COUNTY OF NEW LONDON.

1705	Groton,	Timothy Wightman.	
		Silas Burris.	
1775		Rufus Allen.	
	Stonington,	Eleazer Brown.	
1765		Simeon Brown.	
1775	Stonington Point,	Vacant.	
	New London,	Zadoc Darrow.	
	Saybrook,	Elipheleth Lester.	
	Lyme,	Jason Lee.	
1782	Norwich,	Christopher Palmer.	

COUNTY OF WINDHAM.

1750	Killingly,	John Martin.	
1776		Vacant,	59
1766	Woodstock,	Biel Ledoyt,	143
1776	Pomfret,	Vacant.	
1774	Ashford,	Vacant.	
1779		John Rathbun.	
1780	Willington,	David Lillebridge.	
1780	Mansfield,	Vacant.	

21

RHODE ISLAND.—COUNTY OF NEWPORT.

Year.	Town.	Ministers.	No.
1644	Newport,	Erasmus Kelly, A. M.,	25
1656		Gardner Thurston,	230
1671		William Bliss,	39
1685	Tiverton,	Peleg Burroughs,	134

COUNTY OF PROVIDENCE.

1639	Providence,	James Manning, A. M.,	127
	Scituate,	Reuben Hopkins.	
	Smithfield,	John Winsor.	
	Cumberland,	Abner Ballou.	
	Glocester,	Joseph Winsor,	79
	North Providence,	Rufus Tift.	
1771	Johnston,	Samuel Winsor.	
	Foster,	Nathan Young.	

COUNTY OF WASHINGTON.

1708	Hopkinton,	Joshua Clarke.
1750	Westerly,	Vacant.
		Josiah Wilcox.
	Charlestown,	Samuel Niles.
	South Kingstown,	Benjamin Waite.
		Vacant.
1710	North Kingstown,	Nathan Hill.
		Philip Jenkins.
		William Northup.
1750	Exeter,	Solomon Sprague.
1772	Richmond,	Thomas West.
		Vacant.

COUNTY OF KENT.

	Warwick,	Abraham Lippitt.	
1743	East Greenwich,	John Gorton.	
	Coventry,	Thomas Manchester.	
		Caleb Nichols,	300
	West Greenwich,	Elisha Greene.	

COUNTY OF BRISTOL.

1764	Warren,	Vacant.

Total number, 4,783.[1]

---

[1] In the first edition, this chapter was followed by the Appendix given in Volume I as Appendix A, which was the close of Volume II.—ED.

CHAPTER XXXI.

Introduction,—An Election Sermon.—Remarks thereon.—The true
Way of Dignity and Holiness.—A false Charge.—An unjust Law.
—Remarks upon it.—How Ministers came by their Power in New
England.—The bad Use they made of it.—How a Bishop came
here.—And two to the southward.—Methodism described.—
And the Doctrine of Universalism.—Cruel Oppression—An In-
surrection followed.

When peace was restored to America, she entered upon
such a new state of political existence as no people were
ever in before. All the governments among men that ever
were before formed, were forced upon the people by a few
powerful leaders, or else were given by immediate inspiration from God. But the people in this land have framed
their own governments, and elected their own rulers, without
inspiration from Heaven, or violence from men. Though in
doing these things, they have gone through great changes,
which have discovered many of the corruptions of men, and
of the infinite perfections of God. And a plain record
thereof in New England, especially as to religious affairs,
may be very serviceable to mankind. Instructive and useful
histories of our military, civil and political concerns, have
been already published; but the state of our churches since
the war, has been but slightly touched. Therefore, an account of the state of religion, and of the government of our
churches, is here attempted. And as Connecticut has ever
elected her own rulers, and made her own laws, they have

framed no new constitution of government since the Revolution, but only altered their laws as they thought proper.

And to prepare the way for a new system of laws, the president of their university said to their legislature, " Dominion is founded in property ; and resides where that is, whether in the hands of the few or many." And he held that the power of religious ministers is derived by an external succession from the apostles, through the churches of Rome and England ; and said of New England, " The induction of the ministers of the first churches, was performed by lay brethren, and this was called ordination, but should be considered what in reality it was, only induction or instalment of those who were vested with official power. These were all ordained before by the bishops in England." And he encouraged them to go on in supporting such ministers by force, by saying :—

God be thanked, the senatorial Assembly of this happiest of all the United States, still embosoms so many Phinehases and Zerubbabels, so many religious patriots, the friends of Jesus and his holy religion ; and that the Messiah's cause is here accompanied with civil government and the priesthood ; allusively, the two olive trees upon the right of the candlestick (the churches) and upon the left ; the two golden branches, which, through the two golden pipes, Moses and Aaron, empty the golden oil out of themselves, and diffuse their salutary influence of order and happiness through the community. Zech. iv. 11. As to nominal Christianity, I have no doubt but that it will be upheld for ages in these States. Through the liberty enjoyed here, all religious sects will grow up into large and respectable bodies. But the Congregational and Presbyterian denomination, however hitherto despised, will, by the blessing of Heaven, continue to hold the greatest figure in America, and, notwithstanding all the fruitless labors and exertions to proselyte us to other communions, become more numerous than the whole collective body of our fellow protestants in Europe. The whole proselytism of New England in particular for sixty or seventy years past, has not exceeded eight or ten thousand, while our augment in that term, by natural increase, has been half a million.[1]

These things were published by the highest authority in Connecticut, just after the news of peace arrived, and many

[1] Election Sermon at Hartford, May 8, 1783. By Ezra Stiles, D. D., President of Yale College, pp. 8, 61, 73.

were pleased therewith. But we would now desire to ask a few questions. And first, As it is easier for a camel to go through the eye of a needle, than it is for any who trust in riches to enter into the kingdom of God, how can dominion be founded in property? Mark x. 24, 25. Yea, as all our American governments are founded in covenants, and not in riches, how dangerous is the above teaching? And as our rulers have solemnly sworn to renounce all foreign jurisdiction over us, how can they compel any to support teachers who hold their power of office by succession from Europe? And as persons who are born again, are the only holy priesthood that God hath under heaven, how can the priesthood be conveyed by an external laying on of hands? I Peter i. 23; ii. 5, 9. And as the golden oil is the Spirit and grace of God, how can it be diffused through a community by the laws of men enforced by the sword? Zech. iv. 6—12. For our Lord warns us to beware of the leaven of hypocrisy, which is caused by covetousness; to avoid which he refused to be concerned in dividing of estates. Luke xii. 1—15. Neither could Peter give any countenance to the distinction between Jews by nature, and sinners of the Gentiles, without dissimulation; and a little leaven leaveneth the whole lump. Gal. ii. 12—15; v. 9. The covenant of circumcision made natural birth the first door into the church of Israel; and how can natural increase make any better churches now, than it did of the seed of Abraham, who were a generation of vipers, and had no right to baptism without personal repentance? Matt. iii. 6—10. And God says, If any man have not the Spirit of Christ, he is none of his. Rom. viii. 9. How then can any man be a minister of Christ without his Spirit, let him be ordained by whom he may? God was the only lawgiver to the church of Israel; and Phinehas and Zerubbabel were no more than executors of the laws of God in that church. And he never allowed any to use force in the collection of the support of his ministers therein; but every man was to bring in the tithes and offerings which he

required of them, as they would desire his blessing, and to
escape his awful curse. Mal. iii. 7—12. Even so hath the
Lord ordained, that they who preach the gospel should live
of the gospel. I Cor. ix. 14. And how great is the difference between the gospel of Christ, and the laws of men enforced by the sword? Each man in Israel was to bring in
all the offerings which God required, so as to be able to say
to him, I have not transgressed thy commandments, neither
have I forgotten them. And upon this Moses said, Thou
hast avouched the Lord this day to be thy God, and to walk
in his ways, and to keep his statutes, and his commandments,
and his judgments, and to hearken unto his voice. And the
Lord hath avouched thee this day to be his peculiar people
as he hath promised thee and that thou shouldest keep all
his commandments : and to make thee high above all nations
which he hath made, in praise, and in name, and in honor,
and that thou mayest be an holy people unto the Lord thy
God, as he hath spoken. Deut. xxvi. 13, 17—19.

A willing obedience to all the revealed will of God, and
about his house and worship in particular, was the way in
which he made them high above all other nations, especially
in the days of David and Solomon ; and they were no otherwise a holy people, than as they obeyed all his commandments, and as the visible presence of God was among them,
in his tabernacle and temple. Yet the above president of
the second university in America, took the last of these
verses for his text, and applied that promise of God to
Israel which they could only enjoy in obedience to his laws,
unto the people of America, and especially to those of the
Congregational and Presbyterian denomination, who support
their ministers by the laws of men, enforced by the sword.
Yea, and the rulers who make and enforce those laws, received their power from the people, who can take it away
again at the next election, while said ministers hold their
power by succession from Europe, and hold that no men can
ordain ministers but ministers who hold to such a power; and

when they have ordained them over a particular society, that society must be forced to support them, until ministers will release them therefrom. But if the people have given never so much for the settlement of a minister, he can leave them when he pleaseth, if other ministers will approve of it, and the people can have no recompense. Thus partiality is established by law ; and the root of it is the yoke which ministers have laid upon children in their infancy. And to those who loose themselves from that yoke, a noted minister in Connecticut said, " When you re-baptize those in adult years, which we have baptized in their infancy, you and they jointly renounce that Father, Son and Holy Ghost, whom we adore and worship as the only living and true God, and on whom we depend for all our salvation."[1] And what greater evil can any men be accused of in this world? For they who secretly enticed any away from the service of the true God, were to die without mercy. Deut. xiii. 6—11. But they who were sprinkled in infancy answered no conscience towards God at all, neither did it produce any change in them, as all experience who have any right to baptism. For all who have a right to that ordinance, are first made dead to sin, and alive unto God through Jesus Christ our Lord. Therefore we are *buried* with him by baptism into death ; that like as Christ was raised up from the dead by the glory of the Father, even so we also should walk in newness of life. Rom. vi. 2—11. For as many of you as have been baptized into Christ, have put on Christ. Gal. iii. 27. And this is done by the obedience of faith, and in no other way ; and in vain do any accuse such of renouncing the only living and true God. But having such teaching from their ministers, a new law-book was published in Connecticut, in 1784, wherein, by one law, they gave all the societies that were before constituted, all their meeting-houses and ministerial lands, with power to support their ministers by tax

---

[1] An Address to his Anabaptist brethren. By Joseph Huntington, DD. 1783, p. 23.

and compulsion.   And then they made another law, as follows :—

An act for securing the rights of conscience in matters of religion, to Christians of every denomination in this State.

As the happiness of a people, and the good order of civil society, essentially depend upon piety, religion and morality, it is the duty of the civil authority to provide for the support and encouragement thereof ; so as that Christians of every denomination, demeaning themselves peaceably, and as good subjects of the State, may be equally under the protection of the law : and as the people of this State have in general been of one profession in matters of faith, religious worship, and the mode of settling and supporting the ministry of the gospel, they have by law been formed into ecclesiastical societies, for the more convenient support of their worship and ministry : and to the end that other denominations of Christians who dissent from the worship and ministry so established and supported, may enjoy free liberty of conscience in the matters aforesaid :

Be it enacted by the Governor, Council, and Representatives, in General Court assembled, and by the authority of the same, That no persons in this State, professing the Christian religion, who soberly and conscientiously dissent from the worship and ministry by law established in the society wherein they dwell, and attend public worship by themselves, shall incur any penalty for not attending the worship and ministry so established, on the Lord's days, or on account of their meeting together by themselves on said day, for public worship agreeable to their consciences.

And be it further enacted by the authority aforesaid, That all denominations of Christians differing in their religious sentiments from the people of the established societies in this State, whether of the Episcopal church, or those Congregationalists called Separates, or the people called Baptists, or Quakers, or any other denomination who shall have formed themselves into distinct churches or congregations, and attend public worship, and support the gospel ministry in a way agreeable to their consciences and respective professions ; and all persons who adhere to any of them, and dwell so near to any place of their worship that they can and do ordinarily attend the same on the Sabbath, and contribute their due proportion to the support of the worship and ministry where they so attend, whether such place of worship be within this, or any adjoining State, and produce a certificate thereof from such church or congregation, signed by their order, by the minister or other officer thereof, and lodge the same with the clerk of the society wherein such person or persons dwell, every such person shall be exempted from being taxed for the support of the worship and ministry of said society, so long as he or they shall continue so to attend and support public worship with a different church or congregation as aforesaid.

And be it further enacted by the authority aforesaid, That all such protestant churches and congregations as dissent from the worship and ministry established as aforesaid, and who maintain and attend public worship by themselves, shall have liberty and authority to use and exercise the same powers and privileges for maintaining and supporting their respective ministers, and building and repairing their meeting-houses for the public worship of God, as the ecclesiastical societies constituted by act of the General Assembly of this State by law have and do exercise and enjoy ; and in the same manner may commence and hold their meetings, and transact their affairs, as occasion may require for the purpose aforesaid.

And all persons shall be taxed for the support of the ministry and other charges of the society wherein they dwell, who do not attend and help support any other public worship ; any thing in this act notwithstanding.

And every person claiming the benefit of this act, shall be disqualified to vote in any society meeting, save only for granting taxes for the support of schools, and for the establishment of rules and regulations for schools, and the education of children in them.

The wisdom of this world is here remarkably discovered. And a minister who was born in Connecticut, has lately said of their religion, " The best in the world, perhaps, for a republican government. As to the mode of exercising church government and discipline, it might not improperly be called a republican religion."[1] Yet it may be serviceable to review the way by which it was introduced, and by which it grew up to its present height. Our fathers who planted Plymouth Colony, held that the church of Christ was to be governed by his laws, independent of all the laws of men ; and they never would support religious ministers by force so long as Governor Bradford lived, which was thirty-seven years after they came to Plymouth. But the next year after they came into the use of force for that purpose, two Quakers were hanged at Boston. The congregational name was invented by the Massachusetts, who held that the church ought to govern the world, and to force all to submit to their power. And when that power was in great danger, partly by the increase of the Baptists among them, one of their greatest ministers said, " It is made by learned and judicious writers,

---

[1]Morse's Geography, third edition, 1791, p. 109.

one of the undoubted rights of sovereignty to determine what religion shall be publicly professed and exercised within their dominions.   Why else do we in New England that profess the doctrine of Calvin, yet practice the discipline of them called Independent, or Congregational churches, but because the authority of the country is persuaded that it is most agreeable to the mind of God?"[1]   But their charter was taken away eight years after, and in 1692 their second charter took place, which gave the world a power above the church about religious ministers ; though this was so odious in the eyes of many fathers in Boston, that they procured a special act, the next winter, to exempt Boston from the cruel yoke that hath been laid upon the country ever since.

The Presbyterian and Congregational ministers in England had formed a connection together a little before, and the like was tried for in the Massachusetts soon after ; but the writings of Mr. John Wise prevented it.   But in the close of 1707, a minister who came from the Massachusetts, was elected Governor of Connecticut,[2] and he prevailed to carry that scheme.   And it was done by bringing a bill into their Legislature, which met May 13, 1708, which said :—

This Assembly, from their own observation, and from the complaint of others, being sensible of the defects of the discipline of the churches of this government, arising from the want of a more explicit asserting the rules given for that end in the Holy Scriptures, from which would arise a firm establishment amongst ourselves, a good and regular issue in cases subject to ecclesiastical discipline, glory to Christ, our Head, and edification to his members, hath seen fit to ordain and require, and it is by the authority of the same ordained and required, that the ministers of the churches in the several counties of this government, shall meet together at their respective county-towns, with such messengers as the churches to which they belong shall see cause to send with them, on the last Monday in June next, there to consider and agree upon those methods and rules for the management of ecclesiastical discipline which by them shall be judged agreeable and conformable to the word of God ; and shall at the same meeting appoint two or more of their number to be their delegates, who

[1]Hubbard's Election Sermon at Boston, May 3, 1676, p. 35.
[2]Gordon Saltonstall. See Vol. I, pp. 469, 536.—ED.

shall all meet together at Saybrook at the next Commencement to be held there, where they shall compare the results of the ministers of the several counties, and out of, and from them, draw a form of ecclesiastical discipline.

Their College was then at Saybrook, which afterwards was removed to New Haven. The ministers met according to appointment, and drew up their scheme of discipline, which the legislature, which met October 14, 1708, established by law. It allows each church to elect her own officers, and to discipline her members ; but if any person thinks that he is unjustly censured, he may appeal from the sentence of the church to a Consociation in each county, whose sentence is to be final and decisive, if the majority of the ministers pre sent are in the vote, and not without. Neither can any man obtain a meeting of the Consociation to hear his case, unless an Association of ministers advise them to meet. At the same time the ministers in each county meet in Association when they please, without any act of their churches, and claim the whole power of licensing candidates for the ministry, and of advising churches whom to call to preach to them. And the ministers in each county choose delegates out of their number, to meet once a year in a General Association from each county in their government, to consult about their affairs, and to complain to their legislature against any society or person as they think proper.

When the Lord poured out his Spirit in a most glorious manner in 1741, under the ministry of travelling preachers, they complained of it to their legislature in October, which ordered a special Consociation to meet upon it in November, and they declared it to be very disorderly for any minister to preach in a parish where another was settled, without his consent. And in May, 1742, an act was passed by their legislature, to exclude all their settled ministers from any benefit of the laws for their support, who should preach in any other parish without the consent of the parish minister. And if any man who was not a settled minister, should

preach or exhort in matters of religion, in any parish, against
the consent of the parish minister, he should be imprisoned
until he would give a bond of one hundred pounds not to do
so any more ; and if any minister from other colonies should
come and preach without such consent, he was to be carried
by authority out of Connecticut government. And because one
of their settled ministers preached two sermons in a Baptist
church, against the consent of a Presbyterian minister in the
town, other ministers persecuted him for five years, until they
declared him to be deposed from his office, and excluded
from the communion of their churches, and said they did it
" in the name of the Lord Jesus Christ, according to the
word of God, and the powers invested in this Consociation,
by the ecclesiastical constitution of this government."[1]   Thus
they held that the Lord Jesus Christ was the head of the
government of Connecticut, and that his laws and theirs
were blended together ; and is not this a part of Mystery
Babylon ? And they now say, "All persons shall be taxed
for the support of the ministry and other charges of the society wherein they dwell, who do not attend and help support any other worship."   And is not this a mark of the
beast ? for he is of a scarlet color, and is very changeable.
He was, and is not, and yet is.   Rev. xiii. 17 ; xvii. 3, 5, 8.
Blood hath ever followed the support of worship by the
sword of the magistrate.   But where the children of God
and the children of the devil dwell in the field of the world,
and appear to be such by their fruits, our Lord says, Let
both grow together until the harvest. Mat. xiii. 30, 38.
But in the church we are commanded to turn away from all
men who have *a form* of godliness, but deny the power
thereof, while we are required to hold fast *the form* of sound
words, in faith and love which is in Christ Jesus.   And this
he explains by saying, All Scripture is given by inspiration
of God, and is profitable for doctrine, for reproof, for correction, for instruction in righteousness ; that the man of

[1]See pp. 42—46, 83; Vol. I, pp. 469, 470.

God may be perfect, thoroughly furnished unto all good works." II Tim. i. 13 ; iii. 5, 16, 17. The only reason why he allows the men of the world to make laws, and to enforce them with the sword, is because they will not obey the laws of God, nor refrain from injuring their neighbors, without such forcible restraints. And it is readily granted, that piety, religion, and morality, are essentially necessary for the good order of civil society, and so are the showers and shines of heaven. But what a figure would any body of men make, if they should enact laws to determine when the sun should shine, and how often the showers should fall! For the Lord God is a *sun* and shield ; the Lord will give grace and glory ; no good thing will he withhold from them that walk uprightly. Psalm lxxxiv. 11. For it is time to seek the Lord, till he come and *rain* righteousness upon us. Hosea x. 12. Every good gift, and every perfect gift, is from above, and cometh down from the Father of *lights*, with whom is no variableness, neither shadow of turning. Of his own will begat he us with the word of truth. . . . . Pure religion and undefiled, before God and the Father, is this, To visit the fatherless and widows in their affliction, and to keep himself *unspotted* from the world. James i. 17 —27. The beast is as *spotted* as a leopard, as cruel as a bear, and as terrible as a lion. Rev. xiii. 2. And how can any man keep himself unspotted from the world, if he forces the world to support his worship ?

As Congregational and Presbyterian ministers have done this, and hold to a successive power to do it, which came through the church of Rome, a minister who was born in Connecticut, obtained the title of Bishop of Connecticut, in a more direct line than our ministers have done. For he was ordained Bishop of Connecticut, by three bishops in Scotland, November 14, 1784, who derived their succession from three bishops in England, who refused to swear allegiance to King William, after he had driven the popish King James from the throne. So that his line came directly from the church of Rome, without any connection with the government in Great Britain for a hundred years past. And this bishop holds that his authority came from Christ, as much as any can, and says, "A church in which Christ has no authority, cannot be his church ; it may be the Pope's church, or Luther's church, or Calvin's church, or Wesley's church, ... but Christ's church it cannot be, unless it be founded on his authority and governed by his commission. .... The apostles being divinely inspired, and acting under the immediate direction of the Holy Ghost, in all things necessary to the establishment of the church according to the will of Christ, none of their successors could have authority to change the government they had established, unless they could plead the authority of Christ for the change, with as much certainty as the first apostles could for the original establishment, and could give the same proof of divine inspiration as those apostles had given."[1]

This is a most important truth ; and where can we find that the apostles called any ministers *Priests*, in distinction from other brethren of the church ?   Until such a word can be found in their writings, we may boldly reject all pretences to the Christian priesthood, in all men who give no evidence of their being born again of the Spirit of God.   And as soon as this man assumed the character of Bishop of Connecticut, it caused great concern in the church of England ; and a gentleman of great note therein,[2] wrote a letter to a Baptist minister in New England, to inform him that those bishops in Scotland had not good authority to consecrate others, and also that the people of Connecticut ought to elect their bishop, before he could lawfully act as such ; and he desired that some proper men might be sent over to be ordained by bishops in England.   This letter was shown to

[1]Bishop Seabury's Ordination Sermon at Portsmouth, New Hampshire, 1791, pp. 14, 15.
[2]Granville Sharpe.—ED.

many Episcopalians, and one of them in New York took a copy of it, to lay before a convention of their ministers, who were to meet at Philadelphia in September. But this affair lay so heavy upon the mind of the said gentleman in England, that he wrote to Dr. Franklin upon it, October 29, 1785, and informed him that those bishops in Scotland had admitted " prayers for the dead, and extreme unction among them."[1] And one minister from New York, and another from Philadelphia,[2] were sent over, and were consecrated by bishops in England ; and each of them have been chaplains to our senators in Congress, with a salary of five hundred dollars a year. But as our rulers have solemnly sworn to renounce all foreign jurisdiction over America, how can they have a right to give public money to any who hold a commission from Europe? Can any man wonder at the confusion which is now in our country, while promises and oaths are so little regarded ?

And as little of it appears among a new sect which is now formed in America. Mr. John Wesley was ordained a presbyter of the church of England, with a solemn oath to obey and teach her articles of faith, and forms of worship ; and yet he published a sermon in 1739, against several of those articles, and he preached against them in England, Scotland and Ireland, for above forty years, and then he and his followers, seeing how the American war ended, reduced their thirty-nine articles to twenty-four, with new forms of worship and order, and published them in London in 1784, and called them The Sunday Service in North America. Three orders of ordained officers are prescribed therein, besides

---

[1] Historical Collections at Boston, Vol. III, p. 164. In February, 1795, Bishop Seabury published a letter to his brethren, in the Connecticut papers, in which he styles himself " Samuel, by divine permission, Bishop of Connecticut and Rhode Island;" though he has but about thirty societies in Connecticut, and four in the State of Rhode Island, and there are between three and four hundred religious societies in those two States, of other denominations. What then could be expected from such men, if their power was equal to their inclinations?—B.

[2] Samuel Prevoost, D. D., and William White, D. D.—Ed.

preachers who are not ordained. And when they ordain
the lowest of the three, they say :—

Will you reverently obey them to whom the charge and government
over you is committed, following with a glad mind and will their godly admonitions? Answer. I will endeavor so to do, the Lord being my helper.[1]

And many of his followers met at Baltimore, in Maryland, December 27, 1784, and drew up a pamphlet, entitled,
"A Form of Discipline for the Ministers, Preachers, and
Members of the Methodist Episcopal Church in America."
They allow no man to be a preacher in their church, but
such as profess a belief that perfection is attainable in this
life. They date the beginning of their societies in America,
from the labors of some preachers who came over from Ireland about the year 1764 ; and they say :—

What may we reasonably believe to be God's design in raising up the
preachers called Methodists? Answer. To reform the continent, and spread
Scripture holiness over these lands. As a proof hereof, we have seen in
the course of fifteen years a great work of God, from New York through
the Jerseys, Pennsylvania, Maryland, Virginia, North and South Carolina,
even to Georgia.

And they say :—

We are thoroughly convinced, that the church of England, to which we
have been united, is deficient in several of the most important parts of
Christian discipline ; and that (a few ministers and members excepted) it
has lost the life and power of religion. We are not ignorant of the spirit
and designs it has ever discovered in Europe, of rising to preëminence and
worldly dignities by virtue of a national establishment, and by the most
servile devotion to the will of temporal governors ; and we fear the same
spirit will lead the same church in these United States (though altered in
name) to similar designs and attempts, if the number and strength of its
members will ever afford a probability of success ; and particularly to obtain a national establishment, which we cordially abhor as the bane of
truth and holiness, the greatest impediment in the world to the progress of
vital Christianity. For these reasons, we have thought it our duty to form
ourselves into an independent church. And as the most excellent mode of
church government, according to our maturest judgment, is that of a moderate episcopacy ; and as we are persuaded, that the uninterrupted succes-

[1] Sunday Service, p. 283.

sion of bishops from the apostles, can be proved neither from Scripture nor antiquity ; we therefore have constituted ourselves into an Episcopal church, under the direction of bishops, elders, deacons, and preachers, according to the forms of ordination annexed to our prayer book, and the regulations laid down in this form of discipline.[1]

Thus they undertook to be lawgivers for all North America, and to form a church therein that never had any existence until the year 1784. And their teachers have taken great pains to draw off people from all other religious communities in our land, by confounding works and grace together. Mr. Wesley held that Christ died equally for all mankind, but that men are saved by their own faith and obedience, which yet they may fall from, and perish forever. And he says :—

Unconditional election cannot appear, without the cloven foot of reprobation. I believe *election* means, a divine appointment of some men to eternal happiness. But I believe this election to be conditional, as well as the reprobation opposite thereto. I believe the eternal decree concerning both, is expressed in those words, He that believeth shall be saved ; he that believeth not shall be damned. And this decree, without doubt, God will not change, and man cannot resist. According to this, all true believers are in Scripture termed *elect ;* as all who continue in unbelief are so long properly reprobates, that is, unapproved of God, and without discernment touching the things of the Spirit.[2]

But all men may know that there is no such decree in the word of God, and also that he never set reprobation in opposition to election. For he says, The election hath obtained it, and the rest were blinded. Rom. xi. 7. In whom the god of this world hath blinded the minds of them who believe not, lest the light of the glorious gospel of Christ, who is the image of God, should shine unto them. II Cor. iv. 4. As Jannes and Jambres withstood Moses, so do these also resist the truth ; men of corrupt minds, reprobate concerning the faith. II Tim. iii. 8. Jesus Christ is in you, except ye be reprobates. II Cor. xiii. 5. And is it not blas-

[1]Methodist Form of Discipline, printed at New York, 1787, pp. 1—6, 13, 30.
[2]Wesley on Predestination, fifth edition, pp. 9, 10.

22

phemy, for any to say, that God cannot elect, sanctify and save a part of mankind, without putting unbelief, blindness and corruption into all the rest? Yet Wesley and his followers insist upon this with daring boldness. And he also says, "One who is a true believer, or, in other words, one who is holy or righteous in the judgment of God himself, may nevertheless finally fall from grace."[1] But the Son of God says, All that the Father giveth me, shall, come to me; and him that cometh to me, I will in no wise cast out. John vi. 37. He that believeth not God, hath made him a liar. I John v. 10. And how awful is their case!

Yet a minister in Boston, who had published the most, for forty years, of any man in America, to keep up the Congregational establishment, published a book in 1784, to prove that Christ not only died for all men, but also that he will finally save them all from hell. And he denied that there was any word in the Bible, that we could know by it that it meant without end, without other considerations than the word itself. And he says, "In what point of light soever we take a view of sin, it is certainly in its nature, a finite evil. . . . . And the consideration of hell as a purging fire, is that only which can make the matter sit easy upon one's mind."[2] But if the Holy Scriptures have no word in them to distinguish certainly between a limited time, and endless continuance, it is the most imperfect book upon earth. And the fire of God's wrath in a future state, is so far from being a purging fire, that he says, Behold the day cometh that shall burn as an oven; and all the proud, yea, and all that do wickedly, shall be stubble: and the day that cometh shall burn them up, saith the Lord of hosts, that it shall leave them neither root nor branch. But unto you that fear my name shall the Sun of righteousness arise with healing in his wings; and ye shall go forth, and grow up as calves of

[1]Wesley on Predestination, p. 49.

[2]Chauncy on Salvation for all Men, pp. 319, 324. Dr. Jonathan Edwards published a full answer to him in 1790.

the stall. And ye shall tread down the wicked; for they shall be ashes under the soles of your feet, in the day that I shall do this, saith the Lord of Hosts. Mal. iv. 1—3. Again he says, The hand of the Lord shall be known toward his servants, and his indignation toward his enemies. For, behold, the Lord will come with fire, and with his chariots like a whirlwind, to render his anger with fury, and his rebuke with flames of fire. For by fire and by his sword will the Lord plead with all flesh : and the slain of the Lord shall be many. Is. lxvi. 14—16. And afterwards great numbers shall be converted, from all nations; and God says, As the new heavens, and the new earth, which I will make, shall remain before me, saith the Lord, so shall your seed and your name remain. Is. lxiv. 22. And if we compare these prophecies with the last four chapters in the Revelation, have we not reason to conclude, that the awful destructions among the nations, which God is now making by fire and sword, are to usher in the latter day glory ? Yea, are not these the burnings which shall introduce the new heavens and new earth, wherein dwelleth righteousness? II Pet. iii. 12, 13. For the scoffers, walking after their own lusts, were never so open and daring against all religion before, in any age or country, as they are now in Europe and America. But the unlearned and unstable, wrest the Scriptures unto their own destruction. II Pet. iii. 3, 4, 16. And one way in which this is done, is by putting earthly universities in the place of the teaching of the Spirit of God, calling them *Rivers*, the streams whereof shall make glad the city of God.[1] For he says, Blessed is the man that walketh not in the counsel of the ungodly, nor standeth in the way of sinners, nor sitteth in the seat of the scornful ; but his delight is in the law of the Lord, and in his law doth he meditate day and night. And he shall be like a tree planted by the *rivers* of water, that bringeth forth his fruit in his season ; and his leaf also shall not wither, and whatsoever he doeth shall pros-

[1] See Vol. I, p. 446.—Ed.

per. Psalm i. 1—3; xlvi. 4. And Jesus said, If any man thirst, let him come unto me and drink. He that believeth on me, as the Scripture hath said, out of his belly shall flow *rivers* of living water. John vii. 37, 38. But how often have men put human learning in the place of saving faith in the Son of God!

The first university in America is in Cambridge, where an early example of oppression appeared after the war. A Baptist church was constituted in that town in 1781, and they had a pastor ordained in 1783 ; yet they were all taxed for the support of Congregational ministers, and three men were imprisoned therefor in 1784. Therefore they sued the assessors who taxed them, and their case was carried through their inferior and superior courts in 1785, and was turned against the Baptists, which cost them more than a hundred dollars. The constitution of our government restrained our rulers from making any certificate law, as they did in Connecticut, whereby dissenters from the ruling party might be exempted from taxes to their worship ; and if any persons might draw off from them without acknowledging that they had power to bind and loose in such affairs, the use of force to support religious ministers would come to an end. Therefore a great lawyer informed those oppressed people, that if they would give in certificates to the ruling sect, that they belonged to said Baptist society, and would have their money go to the minister thereof, he might sue the money out of the hands of those who took it. This advice he founded upon the words in our constitution which say :—

All moneys paid by the subject to the support of public worship, and of the public teachers aforesaid, shall, if *he* require it, be uniformly applied to the support of the public teacher or teachers of his own religious sect or denomination, provided there be any on whose instructions he attends ; otherwise it may be paid towards the support of the teacher or teachers of the parish or precinct in which said moneys are raised.

This article was drawn by another great lawyer ; and men of that profession are interested in supporting religious teachers by force as really as any men in the world; for a great part of their gains come by controversies about religion; and when teachers and lawyers are in confederacy together, they will make words to mean any thing which they please. And in the above article, they construed the word *He* to mean the teacher who was to receive the money, and not the man who paid it. And rather than to suffer continually, those Baptists in Cambridge complied with the advice of the lawyers, and their minister sued the money out of the hands of their oppressors from time to time, until they left off collecting such money; and the like was done in various parts of the country.[1] Our constitution says, " All men are born free and equal, and have certain natural, essential, and unalienable rights." And the right to receive and support faithful teachers, and to refuse to support those who are unfaithful, is one of the most essential rights of conscience that can be named; yet this right is daily violated by all men who support their teachers by tax and compulsion. Again, the Massachusetts constitution says, " No subordination of any one sect or denomination to another, shall ever be established by law." Yet the Congregational denomination have constantly violated this article also. Though to hide it they made a law in March, 1786, which confounded ministerial and civil taxes together, and empowered every man in each town who pays two-thirds more in one

[1] " October 31, [1785.]   Met with all our Committee upon the following affair, viz.:   In Menatomy parish in Cambridge, Greshom Cutler, and two more of the Baptist society there were strained upon last fall for taxes to parish worship, and they sued for recompense, and after long delays the case was turned in their favor at the County Court at Concord, in September; but at the Superior Court in Cambridge, on October 26, Judge Sargeant declared their old laws to be in force, and that they knew no society in this Commonwealth but corporate bodies; with whom Judge Sewall concurred, and the jury turned the case against the Baptists the next day.   The other judges said little upon the case.   Our committee, when now met, concluded that if they would go on and take away our people's money, that our ministers should demand it again, according to the judges' interpretation of the Third Article in our Bill of Rights; all but myself, who could not concur therewith.   Our elders Stillman, Skillman, Smith and Blood, all thus differed from me."   Backus's Diary.—ED.

tax than a poll tax, to vote in such affairs. And the act says :—

The freeholders, and other inhabitants of each respective town, qualified as aforesaid, at the annual meeting, for the choice of town officers, or at any other town meeting regularly warned, may grant and vote such sums of money as they shall judge necessary, for the settlement, maintenance and support of the ministry, schools, the poor, and other necessary charges arising within the same town ; to be assessed upon the polls and property within the same, as by law provided.

Here is not the least regard paid to the church of Christ ; but fornicators, drunkards, railers and extortioners, have equal votes with all the best men in the land, to determine who shall be guides for their souls, and how they shall be supported. And God says of antichristian teachers, They are of the world, therefore speak they of the world, and the world heareth them. I John iv. 5. But how terrible were the effects of such things ? For the love of the world had induced many to run into debt, and it made others now fierce for calling in their debts, and collectors to get their taxes, which caused much business in courts, and a great increase of lawyers ; therefore a man in Boston began to publish essays in their papers against lawyers, the same month in which the above law was made, which essays were collected into a pamphlet in July. And the people felt themselves so much distressed, that, in August and September, they arose in arms against their courts, in the counties of Hampshire, Berkshire, Worcester, Middlesex, and Bristol.[1] Hereupon the town of Boston wrote to all the towns in the Massachusetts, requesting them to bring in accounts of their grievances, and promising to use their influence in their favor. And the legislature was called together, and heard many complaints, and they published an address to the people, November 14, 1786, in which they said :—

We feel in common with our neighbors the scarcity of money ; but is not this scarcity owing to our own folly ? At the close of the war, there

---

[1] The well known Shays's Rebellion.—ED.

was no complaint of it; since that time, our fields have yielded their increase, and Heaven has showered its blessings on us, in uncommon abundance. But are we not constrained to allow that immense sums have been expended for what is of no value, for the gewgaws imported from Europe, and the more pernicious produce of the West Indies; and the dread of a paper currency impedes the circulation of what remains? .... As the difficulty in paying debts increased, a disregard to honesty, justice, and good faith,[1] in public and private transactions, became more manifest. Some persons have artfully affected to make a distinction between the government and the people, as though their interests were different and even opposite; but we presume, the good sense of our constituents will discern the deceit and falsity of these insinuations. Within a few months the authority delegated to us will cease, and all citizens will be equally candidates in a future election.

But all their reasoning could not quiet those people; therefore an army was sent up and subdued them by force. Though in the next election, the Governor and above half the Legislature were left out of office, and fourteen men, who had been condemned to be hanged for rebellion, were all pardoned. And how came religious ministers to have a higher power over the people, to force away money from them, than our governors or legislators have? yea, higher than the kings of Great Britain? For the ministers who were formerly supported in the name of those kings, and since in the name of this State, still hold a power above them all. And are they not ministers of the great city which reigneth over the kings of the earth? And the voice from heaven says, Come out of her, my people, that ye be not partakers of her sins, and that ye receive not of their plagues. Rev. xvii. 18; xviii. 4.

[1] See Matt. xxiii. 23.

CHAPTER XXXII.

A new Plan of Government.—No religious Tests therein.—Bribery exposed.—A concise view of the Warren Association.—Southern Labors for religious Liberty.—Opposition to Christian Baptism. —Another Connecticut Law.—A View of the College at Providence.—Dr. Manning faithful therein.—Public Faith universally violated.—Oppression at Barnstable and elsewhere.—Evils at Rehoboth described.—And at Taunton and Pomfret.—Also among the Ministers in general.—The Doctrine of Laying on of Hands opened.—And the first Principles of Congregational Churches.

As long as the fear of foreign dangers prevailed, our Congress was wonderfully obeyed ; but as that fear abated, the love of the honors, riches and pleasures of this world weakened their authority, until they could not govern this great country. For while some States made laws to regulate trade, and to guard against foreign encroachments, other States took advantage to enrich themselves. These things were very distressing in these northern parts, while the people to the southward were not benefited thereby. For Virginia had long received their religious teachers from Europe, as well as many civil merchants ; and Baptist ministers had often been imprisoned for preaching the gospel without license from Episcopalians, until the war put a stop to it. And after the war they tried hard to revive that power again. But the Baptists and others prevailed, in the beginning of 1786, to have a law made, which says :—

That no man shall be compelled to frequent or support any religious worship, place or ministry whatsoever, nor shall be enforced, restrained, molested, or burthened in his body or goods, nor shall otherwise suffer on account of his religious opinions or belief; but that all men shall be free to profess, and by argument to maintain, their opinions in matters of religion, and that the same shall in no wise diminish, enlarge, or affect their civil capacities.[1]

Yet their houses for worship, and their large tracts of ministerial lands, were still held by Episcopalians; and the frequent addresses of the Baptists to their legislature, to have those lands sold for public uses, or that they and their houses for worship might be free for all such ministers as the people chose, were disregarded. So hard is it for men to give up any worldly advantage which they have obtained under the mask of religion. The beast had feet like a bear. Rev. xiii. 2. And no bear ever grasped harder to hold his prey, than men now do to hold the power and gain which religious pretences have given them. Yet, by a motion from Virginia, the Congress recommended it to all these States, to elect delegates to meet at Philadelphia, in order to form a better plan of government than they then enjoyed. Accordingly twelve States met there by delegation, and labored upon it for about four months, until they finished a new constitution of government on September 17, 1787, and sent it out to all these States, and some of them adopted it soon, while others did not receive it in two years. And if men find it to be so hard a matter to agree about the affairs of time, why should they pretend to force all to unite in the great concerns of eternity? If they differ so much about perishing things which are visible, how can they unite in the service of the invisible Jehovah, who is beloved by his children, and is hated by the world? For every one that doeth evil, *hateth the light;* and Jesus says, *I am the light of the world; but they hated me without a cause.* John iii. 20; viii. 12; xv. 25. And though this hatred hath been covered, in every age, under the name of religion or government, yet the feast of the gospel, in the church of Christ, will destroy the face of the

[1]Jefferson's Notes on Virginia, p. 243

covering cast over all people, and the vail that is spread over all nations. Is. xxv. 6, 7. The Christian nations have laid *bands* upon children, before they could choose for themselves, and have forced them to support the national worship all their days. But God says to his people, Loose thyself from the *bands* of thy neck, O captive daughter of Zion. For thus saith the Lord, Ye have sold yourselves for nought, and ye shall be redeemed *without money*. .... Thy God reigneth. Is. lii. 2, 3, 7. This is the *gospel of peace.* Rom. x. 15. And as surely as he reigneth above, no men below can have any right to make laws to bind any in religious affairs. But how hardly are men brought to give up this power over the consciences of others ! For on January 9, 1788, a convention of delegates from all parts of the Massachusetts met at Boston. and debated long upon the new constitution of government which was formed in Philadelphia, until they, with great difficulty, adopted it on February 6, by a majority of nineteen votes, there being a hundred and eighty-seven against a hundred and sixty-eight[1].

[1] "A new Constitution for the United States of America was finished at Philadelphia, September 17, 1787; and our town met on December 17, and chose four delegates to meet in Boston, January 9, 1788, with others in Convention, to establish or reject it; of which delegates I was the first, without the least motion of mine that way. When I was first informed of it, on December 20, I thought I should not go, but as religious liberty is concerned in the affair, and many were earnest for my going, I consented, and went as far as Elder Briggs's January 14, and went into Boston January 15, and met with the Convention that day and the next in the State House, but as we had not room enough there, we removed, the 17th, to Mr. Belknap's meeting-house, in Long Lane, where we continued our meetings from day to day, until the Constitution was ratified on February 6, by a hundred and eighty-seven yeas against a hundred and sixty-eight nays, being a majority of nineteen. Each delegate had full liberty, in his turn, to say all he pleased, by means of which I obtained much more light about the extensive affairs of our country, the nature of the proposed Constitution, and the security of the rights of the people therein, than I had when I went from home, and therefore voted for it. And yet Elder Alden of Bellingham, Elder Rathbun of Pittsfield, Elder Tingley of Waterbury, County of York, all voted against it, and so did two-thirds of the Baptist members of the Convention, of which there were above twenty. Elder Stillman and I, with twelve Congregational ministers, voted for it, though, doubtless, with very different views. The exclusion of any hereditary, lordly power, and of any religious test, I view as our greatest securities in this constitution; but perhaps many mean no more thereby than the exclusion of such lordship as they have in England, and of requiring any assent to any prescribed forms of faith or worship." Backus's Diary.—ED.

One of the greatest objections that was made against it, was, that no religious test was required therein, of any of the officers of government. But after much had been said upon it, a Congregational minister[1] arose and said :—

The great object of religion being God supreme, and the seat of religion in man being the heart or conscience, that is, the reason God has given us, employed on our moral actions, in their most important consequences, as related to the tribunal of God, hence I infer, that God alone is the God of the conscience, and consequently, attempts to erect human tribunals for the consciences of men, are impious encroachments upon the prerogatives of God.

But as this did not silence their objections on that head, a Baptist minister arose five days after, and said :—

Nothing is more evident, both in reason, and in the Holy Scriptures, than that religion is ever a matter between God and individuals ; and therefore no man or men can impose any religious test, without invading the essential prerogatives of our Lord Jesus Christ. Ministers first assumed this power under the Christian name ; and then Constantine approved of the practice, when he adopted the profession of Christianity as an engine of State policy. And let the history of all nations be searched, from that day to this, and it will appear that the imposing of religious tests hath been the greatest engine of tyranny in the world. .... The covenant of circumcision gave the seed of Abraham a right to destroy the inhabitants of Canaan, and to take their houses, vineyards, and all their estates as their own ; and also to buy and hold others as servants. And as Christian privileges are much greater than those of the Hebrews were, many have imagined that they had a right to seize upon the lands of the heathen, and to destroy or enslave them as far as they could extend their power. And from thence the mystery of iniquity carried many into the practice of making merchandise of slaves and souls of men.[2]

But this was not suffered to be printed in the same paper in Boston, in which the speech of the Congregational minister was printed. Though the wisdom which is from above, is without *partiality* and without *hypocrisy*.[3]

[1]Rev. Philips Payson, of Chelsea. See "Debates, Resolutions, &c., of the Convention," pp. 151, 152.—Ed.

[2]This Address was by Mr. Backus himself. See "Debates, Resolutions, &c., of the Convention, p. 182.—Ed.

[3]The address of Mr. Payson appeared in the Massachusetts Gazette of February

But men often carry these evils farther under the name of religion and government, than they can do in any other way. For if any are dishonest in their private dealings, and refuse to perform their promises, others can avoid having any further trading with them; but promises and oaths are frequently violated in public affairs, when the most upright cannot bring the guilty to justice, nor escape from being injured by such men. A notable instance hereof now appeared in the State of Rhode Island. A number of men therein artfully represented to the people, that if a large bank of paper money was made, they might easily pay off their public and private debts; and they were accordingly elected into their legislature in 1786, and made such a bank. Some religious teachers were active in this scheme, by which the widow and the fatherless, with many others, were amazingly defrauded and oppressed. And in March, 1787, the men who were guilty of these evils, passed an act to cut off every man in the State from voting in their next election of rulers, until they had taken a new oath against bribery. By such means they were elected again into office, and they would never allow a convention to be called in that State, to consider of the new constitution of government for these United States, until the year 1790;[1] since which those deceitful men have been left out of office, and as great harmony is restored there as in other places. But in all parts of America the public promises of government are still violated, beyond what men in private stations can possibly do to each other, and yet continue in power and credit. And no men have suffered more in these times, than religious ministers who have conscientiously refused the use of force for their support. And as our Lord says, My kingdom is not of this world, how can his ministers have a right to force the world to support them? How can they exhort rulers and people

22, and in the Boston Gazette of February 25, neither of which papers, though in general they gave full reports of the Convention, noticed the speech of Mr. Backus. —ED.

[1] It was adopted there May 29, 1790.

to venture their eternal all upon the truth of Christianity, if themselves refuse to trust it for their temporal living? Can any wonder that carelessness and infidelity prevail under such conduct? But as long as rulers can force away money from the people, for the support of religious teachers, it bribes them to exert all their influence in their favor; and this bribes rulers to continue in that practice; and God says, A gift doth blind the eyes of the wise, and pervert the words of the righteous. Deut. xvi. 19. From whence we may learn the cause, why so many wise and righteous men are ensnared in these ways. At the same time, if men can save their money by renouncing the use of force to support religious ministers, many will use their liberty for an occasion to the flesh, and as a cloak of maliciousness, which serves to prejudice others against the liberty of the gospel.

The churches which formed the Warren Association, presented many addresses to our rulers, and publications to the world, against oppression, and for religious liberty, from their first formation in 1767, to the close of the war in 1783 ; and as long as the fear of suffering from others was powerful, it moved them to unite against their oppressors ; but as that fear abated, the love of self and of earthly things, has in some instances prevailed against solemn promises and obligations. So our Lord says, Woe unto the world because of offences ; for it must needs be that offences come, but woe to that man by whom the offence cometh. And he requires us to give each brother two opportunities to speak for himself, before the offence is told to the church, whose sentence is to decide the case. Matt. xviii. 7—18. But where teachers are supported by force, all are accounted offenders who refuse to have fellowship with that way. And many offences will arise among churches who have no such exercise of power, which require more discretion and patience in dealing with offenders according to the laws of Christ, than most Christians have attained unto. And when they have crowded matters into the church, without a due regard to his laws, they want a higher power to appeal to, than a particular church of Christ. To call in advice, where the accuser and accused may be heard face to face, and suitable counsel be given for the church to act upon, is a practice which is warranted by Scripture and reason ; but a power in councils above particular churches, has no foundation in Scripture, and is an endless source of confusion among Christians. Of this we have had much experience. When the Warren Association met at Middleborough, September 7, 1784, a minister who had censured some of his brethren, and refused to let them call in advice from other churches, came with a complaint against some who had gone to hear them without his consent; but he was reproved therefor. Yet when the Association met at Wrentham, September 13, 1785, he came with some queries which pointed to the same thing. And a man who had been excluded from another church, then came with an earnest request that the Association would interpose their influence in his favor; and because they refused to do it, he published a bitter complaint in a Boston newspaper. When they met at Newton, September 12, 1786, a complaint of a division in another church caused a considerable labor, and then a vote to leave them out of the Association, which is the farthest that they have a right to go in such cases. Their meeting at Chelmsford, September 11, 1787, was not interrupted with such things. Yet when they met at Sturbridge, September 9, 1788, a complaint was brought against the majority of another church, who had withdrawn from their minister and a part of their brethren, and the majority were left out of the Association, and the minister with the minority were recommended as the church. But as this was going too far, so the effects have been very unhappy ever since. And when the Association met again at Sturbridge, September 8, 1789, another minister made hard attempts to crowd a complaint against a church into it; but it was kept out, though with difficulty, and he has been since disowned by all our churches. And all experience hath shown, that a particular church of Christ is the highest judicature that he hath established upon earth to carry his laws into execution in his name. And he says, Where two or three are gathered together in my name, there am I in the midst of them. Matt. xviii. 20. In all earthly governments, the laws are executed in the name of the supreme authority of it, which can see but a little of what is done in its name. But the Son of God is present in every church, as well as through the world, by his universal knowledge and power; and if any of his churches leave their first love, and will not repent, he removes the candlestick out of his place. Rev. ii. 1—5.

Wise measures were now taken to the southward, to secure religious liberty. A general committee of the Baptist churches in Virginia, presented an address to the excellent Washington, upon his being chosen President to these United States, dated August 8, 1789, in which they said :—

When the constitution first made its appearance in Virginia, we, as a society, had unusual struggles of mind, fearing that the liberty of conscience (dearer to us than property or life) was not sufficiently secured. Perhaps our jealousies were heightened, on account of the usage we received in Virginia, under the regal government, when mobs, bonds, fines and prisons, were our frequent repast.

President Washington returned them an answer, wherein he said :—

If I could have entertained the slightest apprehension that the constitution framed in the convention where I had the honor to preside, might possibly endanger the religious rights of any ecclesiastical society, certainly I would never have placed my signature to it.

And he said to those Baptists:—

While I recollect with satisfaction, that the religious society of which you are members, have been, throughout America, uniformly and almost unanimously the firm friends of civil liberty, and the persevering promoters of our glorious revolution, I cannot hesitate to believe, that they will be the faithful supporters of a free, yet efficient general government.[1]

[1]Leland's Virginia Chronicle, pp. 47, 48.

And the next month the Congress proposed a number of amendments to our federal constitution, one of which says : —

Congress shall make no law, establishing articles of faith, or a mode of worship, or prohibiting the free exercise of religion, or abridging the freedom of speech, or of the press, or the right of the people peaceably to assemble, and to petition to the government for a redress of grievances.

This was dated September 23, 1789 ; but the Massachusetts legislature were so far from adopting of it, that we cannot find any record of any debates upon it. When this State was since sued, before the federal court at Philadelphia, our legislature was called together upon it, who instructed our members in Congress to use all their influence to procure an amendment of the constitution in that respect, and it was effected, and the amendment was readily adopted by the Massachusetts Legislature ; but the amendment about liberty of conscience is kept out of sight. But in vain do they think to hide their iniquity from the eternal God, who is no respecter of persons, but will reward every man according to his works. And the above testimony in favor of the Baptists in general, is confirmed by experience, and by the nature of things. For where no person can be made a member of the church, without his own consent, and each one can withdraw from it when he will, all cruel oppression is excluded. And such churches are not accountable for any over whom they have no power. Yet all the Baptists in Europe and America, have often been reproached with the madness of Munster, in 1533, where they tried to support their religion with the sword. Though the parliament of England revolted from the pope the same year, and set up their king as the head of the church. And all men who love the wages of unrighteousness, are guilty of madness. II Pet. ii. 15, 16. But they who are guilty of it, are commonly false accusers of all who soberly refuse to have fellowship with them therein. And the prophecy is fulfilled, which says, I beheld another beast coming up out of the

23

earth, and he had two horns like a lamb, and he spake as a dragon, and he exerciseth all the power of the first beast before him, and causeth the earth, and them which dwell therein, to worship the first beast, whose deadly wound was healed. Rev. xiii. 11, 12. The two horns are, undoubtedly, the officers of church and State, uniting their influence in schemes of power and gain, under the name of religion and government. The sword of the Spirit, which is the word of God, gave the first beast a deadly wound, when the pure doctrine of salvation by grace was proclaimed in the reformation. But that doctrine, and the government of the church of Christ by his holy laws, are as much opposed now by Protestants, as ever they were by the church of Rome. And how little do the people of New England now act according to the high opinion that others have entertained of them? For an excellent author in South Carolina, speaking of the beginning of the war in 1775, says:—

It was a fortunate circumstance for the colonies that the royal army was posted in New England. The people of that northern country have their passions more under the command of reason and interest than in the southern latitudes, where a warmer sun excites a greater degree of irascibility. One rash, offensive action against the royal forces at that early period, though successful, might have done great mischief to the cause of America. It would have lost them European friends, and weakened the disposition of the other colonies to assist them. The patient and the politic New England men, fully sensible of their situation, submitted to many insults, and bridled their resentment.

And he also says :—

It was one of the peculiarities of these new forms of government, that all religious establishments were abolished.[1]

They were so in the southern States, but this is obstinately refused in New England, to their unspeakable shame in foreign parts. Yea, the example of our Lord and Saviour is here openly rejected, lest their darling traditions should come down.

[1] Ramsay's History of the American Revolution, Vol. I, pp. 186, 355.

For in January, 1790, a book was published in Boston, entitled, " The Baptism of Jesus Christ not to be imitated by Christians." It was written by two ministers in the county of Worcester. Their argument is, that John was a priest in the church of Israel, and that when he baptized Jesus, he initiated him into the office of the priesthood, to make atonement for sin, which none can do but the Son of God. And they say, " It will not be denied by any, that the words *washing* and *baptism* are of like import. .... The baptism of Christ then must be considered as the fulfilment of the law of priestly consecration." Yet as Aaron and his sons were to wash their hands and feet, these men say, " Is it not almost certain that Christ was not plunged all over in water ?"[1] Answer. Moses was to bring Aaron and his sons unto the door of the tabernacle, and to wash them with water. This was done once by Moses, at their consecration. But Aaron and his sons were to wash their own hands and feet, from time to time. Exod. xxix. 4 ; xxx. 19, 21; Lev. viii. 6. In the first case there is no mention of hands and feet. Moses washed them all over. But if washing their hands and feet was baptism, then Aaron and his sons were *Anabaptists.* Yea, and they baptized themselves too, which is opposite to all ideas of gospel baptism. Neither had John any right by the law of Moses to consecrate Jesus as a priest in the Hebrew church. For it is evident that our Lord sprang out of Judah, of which tribe Moses spake nothing concerning priesthood. And it is yet far more evi-dent ; for that after the similitude of Melchizedec there ariseth another priest, who is made, not after the law of a carnal commandment, but after the power of an endless life. Yea, he is of an order above Abraham ; and the priesthood of Aaron is disannulled. Heb. vii. 5—19. And his chil-dren say joyfully to him, Thou art worthy to take the book, and to open the seals thereof ; for thou wast slain, and hast

[1]Essay of Fish and Crane, [Rev. Elisha Fish, of Upton, and Rev. John Crane, of Northbridge,] pp. 8, 20.

redeemed us to God by thy blood, out of every kindred, and tongue, and people, and nation ; and hast made us unto our God *kings* and *priests*, and we shall reign on the earth. Rev. v. 9, 10.   So Peter says to all who are born again, Ye are a chosen generation, a *royal priesthood*, a holy nation, a peculiar people.   I Pet. ii. 9.   By the death of Christ he disannulled all claims to power by natural birth, and united the great offices of priests and kings in his church, in those who are born of the Spirit.   Jesus is the only lawgiver for his church, and his children are the only executors thereof in his name.   And God says, Beware lest any man spoil you through philosophy and vain deceit, after the tradition of men, after the rudiments of the world, and not after Christ. For in him dwelleth all the fulness of the Godhead bodily ; and ye are complete in him, who is the *Head* of all principality and power.   In whom also ye are circumcised with the circumcision made without hands, in putting off the body of the sins of the flesh, by the circumcision of Christ ; *buried with him in baptism*, wherein also ye are risen with him through the faith of the operation of God, who hath raised him from the dead.   Col. ii. 8—12.   Yet philosophy and vain deceit have prevailed so long, that it is now denied that Christians should imitate the baptism of Christ, because the ceremonial law was not abolished until his death.   But the same men hold infant baptism from the covenant of circumcision, which was the foundation of the national church of Israel.   Yea, Mr. Fish, one of the authors of this book, published one before, in 1772, which he called Japheth dwelling in the tents of Shem, from Gen. ix. 27; in which he went back ten generations before Abraham, for a warrant for infant baptism.   And their essay now, to prove that the baptism of Christ is not to be imitated by Christians, hath been so pleasing to the world, that it hath passed three editions.

And the folly of men in other respects is daily exposed. For the law in Connecticut, called, " An act for securing the

rights of conscience in matters of religion, to Christians of
every denomination in this State," proved to be so ineffectual
to their purpose, that they made an addition thereto in May,
1791.   By this addition no certificate could be legal, until it
was approbated by two justices of the peace, or only by one
if there was no more in the town where the dissenter lived.
Thus the civil authority in the uppermost religious party in
their State, was to judge the consciences of all men who dissented from their worship.   And when they had done it, the
act says :—

Which certificate, upon being lodged with the clerk of the ecclesiastical
society in which such dissenter dwells, shall thereafter, so long as he shall
attend the public worship of the church or congregation to which he has
joined himself, and shall continue to pay such his proportion towards the
support of the public worship and ministry thereof, exempt him from all
civil obligation to the society from which he dissents, excepting taxes
granted before the time such certificate is lodged with the clerk of said
society as aforesaid.

And this is a plain imitation of the British parliament,
who resolved in 1775, that they would not tax any colony in
America, who should raise as much money among themselves for the support of government, as the parliament
judged that they ought to, as long as they did so, and no
longer.   But as God hath delivered us from that tyranny,
how can any submit to a like tyranny over the consciences
of men ?   For a freehold rated at fifty shillings, or forty
pounds in the common list, gives every inhabitant in Connecticut the power of voting for their legislature, and makes
him eligible to it.   And all the privilege that their churches
have, in the choice and support of their ministers, is, that
communicants may vote with the rest of the congregation in
these affairs, if they have not so much estate as is required
of voters for rulers, and are twenty-one years of age.   But
a great part of their ministers and churches readily receive
persons into their communion, without any evidence of their
being born again.   And for one party of such men to assume

the power of judging the consciences of all who dissented
from their worship, alarmed many in all parts of the government, and they drew up a remonstrance and petition, in
which they said :—

> We cannot find that Jesus Christ or his apostles ever gave orders to civil
> rulers to establish the Christian religion at large, much less one distin-
> guished denomination, who profess it, and use the civil law to support its
> doctrines, forms or preachers ; or that the subjects of Christ's kingdom
> (which is not of this world) should acknowledge any ruler but Christ alone,
> in religious concerns. And we long to see religion left entirely in the hands
> of Christ, to be governed alone by his laws ; that the grand controversy
> may be decided, whether religion is such an adjective that it cannot stand
> of itself, or so important that it will support itself upon its own merits, and
> all who trust in it.

This produced a repeal of said law, in October, 1791 ;
though they then made another, to allow every man to give
in his own certificate, if he dissented from the ruling sect.

The uppermost party among Christians have ever had
the command of all colleges, to educate religious teachers,
as well as other men of superior learning, until very lately.
Even in 1780, no ministers but Congregational ministers
were allowed to be overseers of the university at Cambridge,
by the Massachusetts constitution of government. And
great sums have been given to that university by the government, from time to time, ever since it began in 1638.
But as Providence and Rhode Island colony was planted by
men who were banished from the Massachusetts, because
they conscientiously dissented from the use of force in religious affairs, and that colony suffered amazingly from neighboring colonies for more than a hundred years, the people
therein have grown up with great prejudices against colleges, and against obeying the laws of Christ for the support
of his ministers. But as a minister died this year,[1] who
has done much towards removing those prejudices, I shall
give a concise account of the affair. Mr. Isaac Eaton, who

---

[1] Rev. James Manning, D. D. See notice of him in a later chapter.—Ed.

was pastor of the Baptist church in Hopewell in New Jersey, from 1748 to 1772, set up a school for the education of youth for the ministry, as well as for other callings, in 1756, and kept it for eleven years.[1] One of his scholars was Mr. James Manning, who went from his school to the college at Princeton, where he took his first degree in September, 1762. And as the Philadelphia Association were for erecting a college in Rhode Island government, they fixed their eyes upon him as a proper leader in the affair. He therefore called in at Newport, on his voyage to Halifax, in July, 1763, and proposed the matter to a number of Baptist gentlemen, who readily concurred therewith; and as they had a high opinion of a learned Congregational minister among them,[2] they desired him to make a draft of a charter for a college in that government. It was proposed to take in some members of the several denominations among them, but that the Baptists should always be the majority of the corporation. He drew a charter which appeared to be upon this plan, and it was introduced into their legislature; but a Baptist gentleman discerned that there was a door left open for the Congregational denomination to become the majority hereafter. Therefore the charter was not then passed into a law; and when their legislature met again, the charter was not to be found. When this was heard of at Philadelphia, two gentlemen were sent from thence, who assisted in drawing a new charter, which was established by the legislature of Rhode Island in February, 1764;[3] and Mr. Manning re-

---

[1] See account of Mr. Eaton and of his school, in Manning and Brown University, pp. 25, 26.—ED.

[2] Rev. Ezra Stiles, D. D., afterwards President of Yale College.—ED.

[3] Hon. Daniel Jenckes.

For a full confirmation of the above account, and for farther developments in the strange history of the chartering of Rhode Island College, see the testimony of President Manning and of Hon. Daniel Jenckes, the copy of the charter drafted by Rev. Dr. Stiles, and other evidence, in Manning and Brown University, pp. 46—62, 465—482. The author of that work, Mr. R. A. Guild, Librarian of Brown University, after giving the various testimonies, carefully sums them up as follows:—

"From the foregoing accounts or narratives, it appears, (1.) That President Manning drew up a plan of the college, and presented it to a company of Baptist

moved to Warren in the summer following, to preach to a
Baptist church newly formed there, and to begin the school.

In September, 1765, he was chosen president of the college, and diligently attended to the duties thereof, and seven
young gentlemen took their first degree there, September 7,
1769. One of them[1] was afterwards a member of Congress,
and then a general in the American army, and lastly a judge
of the courts in our western territory, where he died. Three
of them are now useful Baptist ministers.[2] In February,

gentlemen at Newport, in the month of July, 1763. (2.) That the Hon. Josias Lyndon and Colonel Job Bennet were appointed to draw a charter, in accordance with
said plan, to be laid before the next General Assembly, with a petition that it might
be made a law. (3.) That the assistance of Rev. Dr. Stiles, afterwards President of
Yale College, was solicited and obtained. (4.) That the drafting of the charter was
left entirely to Dr. Stiles; and that he, in turn, was assisted by the Hon. William
Ellery. (5.) That the charter was accordingly drawn, and a time and place were
appointed for the parties concerned to meet and hear it read. (6.) That Manning
being obliged to leave on that day for Halifax, was unable to be with the committee
long enough to see whether the original design was secured, and that the Baptists,
being satisfied, without sufficient examination into the authority vested in the Fellowship, and reposing entire confidence in Dr. Stiles, agreed to join in a petition to the
General Assembly, to have the charter confirmed by authority. (7.) That the petition and charter were accordingly presented to the General Assembly in August,
1663, but that action thereon was postponed until the next session, through the influence of the Hon. Daniel Jenckes, the attempts of Mr. Ellery and others, of the
Presbyterians to the contrary notwithstanding. (8.) That the charter was found, on
inspection, to be so drawn as to vest the main power and direction of the institution
in a board of twelve Fellows, eight of whom were to be Presbyterians, and the other
four of the same denomination, for aught that appeared to the contrary: and that,
in general, it did not answer to the original design. (9.) That, in this emergency,
application was made to the Philadelphia Association, 'where the thing took its rise,'
to have their mind on the subject. (10.) That they immediately sent to Newport
the Rev. Samuel Jones, who was accompanied by Robert Strettle Jones, and that,
when they arrived, Dr. Eyres, of Newport, was added to the Committee. (11.)
That, meanwhile, the original copy of the charter, presented to the General Assembly in August, which had been intrusted by that body to Mr. Jenckes, had been lost.
(12.) That the Committee found at Newport a rough draft of a charter, which they
happily remodelled, and that the most material alterations were, appointing the same
number of Baptists in the Fellowship that had been appointed of the Presbyterians
by Dr. Stiles; settling the presidency in the Baptist society? adding five Baptists
to the Trustees; putting more Episcopalians than Presbyterians in the corporation;
and extending the membership of the corporation to persons residing out of the colony or State."—Ed.

[1]Hon. James Mitchell Varnum.—Ed.

[2]Rev. William Rogers, D. D., Rev. Charles Thompson, and Rev. William Williams.—Ed.

1770, the corporation concluded to remove the college to Providence, where a large brick house was erected for the purpose, entirely by personal generosity ; and education was well carried on there, until the British troops came to Newport in December, 1776, and our army came to Providence to oppose them, and used the college edifice as a barrack. After these obstructions were removed, President Manning engaged again in the work of education for a little while, and then said edifice was seized, by the order of a council of war, for a French hospital, on Lord's day, June 25, 1780, while Dr. Manning was gone to preach in town, and they held it till May 27, 1782. And although no government upon earth ever gave any thing towards that building, yet no recompense has ever been obtained for the great damages which were done to it by government.[1] However, President Manning, being encouraged by the friends of the college, heartily engaged again in his public work, and learning flourished under his administrations, and the Baptist church in Providence enjoyed many blessings under his ministry, until he was suddenly called out of our world, July 29, 1791, in the fifty-third year of his age. He was so well esteemed in the government, that he was elected a delegate to Congress in the spring of 1786, which office he accepted for six months, in hopes of obtaining a grant from thence to indemnify the college at Providence. But though he was highly esteemed in that honorable body, yet it was then out of their power to do justice in this case, as well as many others. Neither could President Manning obtain the whole of his salary for many years, which was to be paid out of the interest of money that was collected elsewhere, and was lent to Rhode Island government. His perseverance, therefore, in the midst of so many difficulties, and his rising above them all in faithfulness and kindness, will endear his memory

[1]There is some hope of it soon from Congress.—B.

Remuneration to the extent, according to Benedict, of two thousand dollars, was made by act of Congress, April 16, 1800. Benedict's History of the Baptists, Vol. II, p. 447 ; Manning and Brown University, p. 388.—ED.

to the latest posterity. And these things demonstrate to all men, that the principles of believers' baptism, and of equal liberty of conscience, are more friendly to true learning and knowledge, than any party schemes of religion ever were, or ever can be. For all loving of self above God and our neighbors, though covered with a mask of religion or government, can never make the subjects of it willing to have their real character seen.

And how is this love of self now exposed in our country? For the first Congress upon our new constitution met in March, 1789, and made laws to regulate the trade of America, which revived public credit, and the merchandise of this country was carried round the world. Also the creditors of government were encouraged to bring in their notes to the loan offices that were appointed in each State, where the interest of said notes was cast up to the close of 1791; after which new notes were given out, of three denominations. The first were to carry the interest which was formerly promised, the second but half so much, and the third were to pay no interest at all for ten years. But who would trust any single man in the world, if he should act in this manner? Surely no man upon earth could obtain credit and esteem in such a way. And our Lord Jesus Christ, who requires the gospel ministry to be committed to faithful men, says, If we be dead with him, we shall also live with him; if we suffer, we shall also reign with him; if we deny him, he also will deny us; if we believe not, yet he abideth faithful; he cannot deny himself. II Tim. ii. 2—13. This is the only line of succession for his ministers. But deceitful men in every station imagine that the security of a whole government is so much stronger than the promises of individuals, that they say, Cast in thy lot among us, let us all have one purse. .... Their feet run to evil, and make haste to shed blood. This God says of all the world. Prov. i. 14, 16 ; Rom. iii. 15, 19. How vain then are all the arguments which are advanced against the universal depravity of mankind! Yea, or against the power of God in changing the heart, who says, Turn ye at my reproof; behold I will pour out my Spirit unto you, and will make known my words unto you. But all men who hate knowledge, and will not choose the fear of the Lord in this life, will cry in vain for mercy, when destruction cometh as a whirlwind. Prov. i. 23—29. The several funding systems established by government, as well as supporting religious teachers by compulsion, have been productive of oppression and injustice ; and Jehovah says, Hear, ye that are far off, what I have done ; and ye that are near, acknowledge my might. The sinners in Zion are afraid, fearfulness hath surprised the hypocrites; who among us shall dwell with the devouring fire? who among us shall dwell with everlasting burnings? He that walketh righteously, and speaketh uprightly, he that despiseth the gain of oppressions, that shaketh his hands from holding of bribes, that stoppeth his ears from hearing of blood, and shutteth his eyes from seeing evil. Isa. xxxiii. 13—15. This is the only way of safety and happiness. But how opposite hereto were the following actions?

A Baptist church was formed in Barnstable in June, 1771, and when they had given in certificates to the ruling sect, they were generally exempted from taxes to their ministers for ten years. But a fresh revival of religion came on among them in the beginning of 1781, and increased their church and society, until they built a convenient meeting-house, and then ordained a pastor, December 4, 1788. He had preached to them for four years before he was ordained, yet in that time, with three years after, above a hundred and fifty dollars were extorted from that society, for the Congregational ministers of the first parishes in Barnstable and Yarmouth. In January, 1790, a collector in Barnstable took away a good horse from one of the committee of that Baptist society, for a ministerial tax of less than two dollars ; and though he offered to return a small part of the value of the horse, yet the Baptist gentleman refused to receive it, and so to have fellowship with their works of darkness.   But those cruel oppressions were pursued, until the committee of the Warren Association met at Boston, January 24, 1791, and wrote to the officers of those two parishes in such a manner, that they have generally refrained from taxing the Baptists to Congregational ministers since,[1] though they have not returned the money which they had before unjustly taken from them.   The west parish in Barnstable, and many others through the country, have not made distress upon the Baptists for the support of parish ministers, as these have done. And our rulers give Baptist ministers the same power to

[1] This letter is a good illustration of the boldness and vigor with which Baptists of that day were accustomed to assert their rights.   It is as follows :—

" GENTLEMEN :—The Baptist church in Barnstable belongs to the Association of regular churches, and as such, claims the advice and protection of the whole body, so far as their case requires it and they have power to afford it.   By the Warren Association at their meeting in September last, we were appointed a Standing Committee, to which all churches of our denomination in this Commonwealth are to apply for advice and assistance when oppressed on a religious account.   Having therefore received a well attested account from Barnstable, that some of the members of our society have been repeatedly taxed and their property taken from them to support the Congregational minister of that place, from whom they conscientiously dissent, and though they have a minister of their own to maintain, we, the committee of the Baptist churches, think it our duty to say, that in an age and country as much enlightened as this is, such acts of injustice were not to be expected; and in all companies in which the affair has been mentioned, it has been a matter of astonishment.   As a denomination of Christians we stand on an equal footing with any in the Commonwealth, and this equality we mean to maintain, by every proper method in our power.   If the parish refuse to return the moneys taken from our society, and continue to tax them to the support of the Congregational minister of Barnstable, we shall be reduced to the disagreeable necessity of publishing the whole to the world, and of taking such other steps as shall appear to us necessary.

" It is our most earnest wish that the different denominations of Christians throughout the Commonwealth may live together in love and friendship, agreeable to the spirit of the gospel.

We are, with sentiments of respect, yours, &c.,

> SAMUEL STILLMAN,
> ISAAC BACKUS,
> THOMAS BALDWIN, } *Committee.*
> THOMAS GREEN,
> JOSEPH GRAFTON,

" Boston, January 24, 1791.

" To the Gentlemen, the Committee of the First Parish in Barnstable."

" The like," adds Mr. Backus, " was sent to the Committee of the First Parish in Yarmouth."   Backus's Manuscripts.—ED.

marry people, and to be exempted from civil taxes, that they do to other ministers. But they have not yet gone so far as a king of Persia did, who gave liberally for the house of God out of his own treasures, and exempted the ministers of the sanctuary from civil taxes, without imposing any ministerial tax upon the people. Ezra vii. 11—24. And we have no evidence that God ever allowed any rulers in Israel to use any secular force for the support of his priests in their church; but when two priests sent their servants to the people with this language, Thou shalt give it now; and if not, I will take it by *force*, they were both slain in one day, and their father's neck was broken. For God had said, Them that honor me, I will honor, and they that despise me shall be lightly esteemed. I Sam. ii. 16, 30; iv. 11, 18. And how far are teachers from honoring our Lord Jesus Christ, if they refuse to be content with all the good things that his laws and influence will give them!

Imprisonments and spoiling of goods, for the support of Congregational ministers in Rehoboth, for thirty years, had brought that sect to be the minor part of the inhabitants of the town; therefore they obtained liberty to sell their ministerial lands, and an act of our legislature in 1762, to incorporate the committee who should be annually elected in each parish, to manage that fund of money, and what should be added to it by subscription, so that the interest thereof might support their ministers And it was supposed that as long as this act continued in force, they had no right to tax all the inhabitants to them, as they had before done. And this appeared the more necessary, because Mr. Samuel Peck was ordained the pastor of a Congregational church in Rehoboth, October 8, 1751, who refused to have any fellowship with those who used tax and compulsion in that affair; and he ministered to them until he died November 26, 1788, aged eighty-two. But the sinking of our public credit, and other means, brought their fund of money in the first parish in Rehoboth down to less than six hundred pounds; and as

Mr. John Ellis was installed their minister in March, 1785, with a promise of a salary of a hundred pounds a year, they ventured to tax all the inhabitants to pay it, though he was not elected by a third part of them. And as they paid but little more than the salary of one year in five, he sued the parish for the rest, and recovered judgment against them in March, 1791. But they appealed to the superior court in October following; and they called a parish meeting in September, and offered the use of their meeting-house, and of their fund of money to Mr. Ellis's party, as long as he continued their minister, if they would pay off that debt, and support him, without taxing any who did not choose him; and adjourned for three weeks. But as this offer was not accepted, at their next meeting, fifty voters against fourteen voted to shut him out of their meeting-house, and chose a special committee to get Baptist ministers to preach therein. And as they had not got any Baptist minister to preach in it the first Lord's day after he was shut out, he came and demanded it to be opened, before two justices of the peace; and because it was not opened they published an account of it in the Providence newspapers, and called the men *insurgents*[1] who shut him out. The next Lord's day, while a Baptist minister was in the pulpit, he came and interrupted the public worship of God; but he was brought before a justice of peace therefor, and bound to his good behavior till the next March court, and Baptist ministers preached in the house all that time. In March, he, with difficulty, obtained a release from those bonds, though he could not recover his former place of worship. Therefore his party applied to our legislature in June, 1792, and obtained a repeal of the act of 1762, which invested their parish committee with power to manage their fund of money, and an act to incorporate his party as the Congregational society in the first precinct in Rehoboth. But as they did not obtain the meeting-house nor fund of money thereby, they called a special court for

---

[1] A name given to those who resisted our courts in 1786.

that purpose, August 30, 1792 ; yet judgment was then given against them, which they were so far from yielding to, that they rushed into the meeting house the next Lord's day, and some of them continued in it night and day for a fortnight ; though others also stayed there and prevented their getting possession of the house. Afterwards Ellis's party called another special court, who gave them possession of said house.

Now can any man believe, that such proceedings as these have any tendency to promote piety, religion or morality? Yea, are they not as contrary thereto as darkness is to light? And these are the natural effects of supporting religious ministers by force. Neither would that little party at Rehoboth have been able to go so far as they have done, if rulers and ministers in general had not viewed it as their own cause. For if one congregation can shut their minister out of their meeting-house when they think proper, another may also, and supporting worship by force will be excluded from our land. And though many have reflected on the Baptists, because that society in Rehoboth called them in to assist in their worship, and to exclude oppressors ; yet the first parishes in Rochester and Wrentham have shut their ministers also out of their meeting-houses, without any concern with the Baptists therein. And it daily appears, that the ruling party in our land, as well as through the world, are trying to grasp the honors and profits of religion to themselves, while they deny the power of godliness. And the doctrines of grace, and the order of the first churches in New England, are trampled upon through the country. Of this we have a notable instance in the town of Taunton, the shire-town of Bristol county. As a number of leading men in that town disliked the preaching of their minister, they informed the parish that they had no right to vote him any salary, because they were the minor part of the inhabitants of the town ; and, after several meetings, a council was called, and he was dismissed, near the close of 1790. After which they obtained an incorporation as the Congregational society in Taunton, with power to settle and support ministers by tax and compulsion ; only if any man therein desired to withdraw from them, he might go to their clerk at the end of the year, and get his name out of the list, and be free from them for the future.   But any number of men can form a stronger society than this, without putting our government to such vast costs as have been laid upon us in such affairs.   And it soon appeared, that said society and the first Congregational church in Taunton could not agree in calling another minister ; therefore another church was formed, in open separation from the first church in Taunton, and they called a minister who was so disagreeable to the first church, that they went and built another meeting-house, and called another minister to preach to them.   But the new party sent for two ministers out of Boston, and obtained ten more from various parts of the country, to give a sanction to their proceedings.   And in a Boston paper of May 25, 1792, it was said, " Wednesday, the 16th instant, the Rev. John Foster was installed to the pastoral care of the first Congregational church and society in Taunton."   And the same was declared in a Providence paper ; though the church in which he was installed was constituted that year, and the society the year before.   And was not this lying in religious affairs ? and in the winter following a church was formed in Pomfret in Connecticut, and a minister was ordained therein, in open separation from the first church in that town.

Yet in the Election Sermon at Boston, May 30, 1792, the ministers in general, who are supported by law in our country, are called, " The Christian priesthood."[1]   And a book was published there this year, the whole labor whereof was to prove that all the children of professors of Christianity are born in the church, and ought to come to the Lord's Supper, if they are not openly scandalous, whether they are satis-

[1]Tappan's Sermon, p. 9.

fied that they are born again, or not. And the author says, "It is the will of God that many be admitted into the church who are *not in heart* friends to him. And if the greater part be of this character, can we imagine that the true interests of Christ's kingdom are in any danger, while Christ has his *enemies* as much in his power as any, and can use them as his instruments, or restrain them, or make them his willing people, or cut them off, whenever he pleases ?[1] It is readily granted that Christ has all the world under his power, but his revealed will requires a profession of saving faith of all who are received into his church ; and they who imagine that he allows his *enemies* to come into it, implicitly put him beneath all rational men. For all such men, be they never so deceitful themselves, yet endeavor to guard against enemies in their own families and societies. And Jesus says, I am the *door :* by me if any man enter in, he shall be *saved.* But he assures us, that they who climb up some other way are *thieves* and *robbers.* John x. 1—9. And he requires us to contend earnestly for the faith, against men who *creep* in unawares, and turn the grace of our God into lasciviousness. Jude 3, 4. Yet another book, which had six editions in about two years, received the sixth edition at Boston, in the beginning of 1793, which represents all ministers among us who were not ordained by ministers who received their office power by succession from Europe, as wolves in sheep's clothing. And the author says, "It is by no means necessary, that, by historical deduction, we should prove an uninterrupted succession ; we have a right to presume it until evidence appears to the contrary. If any say, the succession has failed, the burthen of proof must lie wholly on them. . . . . It is well known that the first ministers in the country were ordained in England by men whose authority is not controverted."[2] Thus he builds his scheme upon negatives ; but God says, Who hath required this at your hand to tread

---

[1]Hemmenway's Discourse, concerning the church, p. 50.

[2]Lathrop's Discourses on Matt. vii. 15, 16, pp. 56, 63.

24

my courts? . . . . Your hands are full of *blood*. Is. i. 12,
15. And how much hath this been the character of all
national churches? And can *bloody* hands convey the Holy
Ghost to others ?[1]

After the Babylonian captivity, the priests who could not
shew a register of their lawful descent from Aaron, were, as
polluted, put from the priesthood, until a priest stood up
with Urim and Thummim. Ezra ii. 62, 63. The words
signify *light* and *perfection*, which is found only in the Son of
God, who is the author of eternal salvation unto all them
who obey him. And to such it is said, Therefore leaving
the principles of the doctrine of Christ, let us go on unto
perfection; not laying again the *foundation* of repentance
from dead works, and of faith towards God, of the doctrine
of baptisms, and of laying on of hands, and of resurrection
of the dead, and of eternal judgment. Heb. v. 5—9; vi.
1, 2. Now the principles of repentance from dead works,
of faith in the Son of God, of resurrection of the dead, and
of eternal judgment, were never known by men but by pure
revelation from God ; and the same is true of regeneration,
and of justification by our sins being laid upon Christ our
sacrifice. For God saves us by the *washing* of regeneration,
and renewing of the Holy Ghost, which he shed on us
abundantly through Jesus Christ our Saviour. Titus iii. 5,
6. And the word *Baptisms*, here in the sixth chapter, is rendered *Washings* in the ninth, which speaks of a more *perfect*
tabernacle, in which Christ, through the eternal Spirit,
offered himself without spot to God, to purge the conscience

---

[1] An eminent author who lately lived in Italy, the head of the church of Rome,
says : "To the art of printing it is owing, that the atrocious crimes of our ancestors,
who were alternately slaves and tyrants, are become less frequent. .... They may
contemplate the effects of what was so improperly called ancient simplicity and good
faith; humanity groaning under implacable superstition, the avarice and ambition
of a few staining with human blood the thrones and palaces of kings, secret treasons,
and public massacres, every noble a tyrant over the people, and the ministers of
[the gospel of] Christ bathing their hands in blood, in the name of the God of all
mercy." The Marquis Beccaria on Crimes and Punishments, pp. 25, 26. Yet an
external succession of ministerial power, through all that blood and wickedness, is
still held fast by many in Europe and America.

from dead works to serve the living God. For by one offering he hath *perfected* forever them that are sanctified. Heb. ix. 10—14 ; x. 14. God required the *laying on of hands* upon offerings for sin, not less than nine times in the law of Moses. Levit. i. 4; iii 2, 8, 13; iv. 4, 15, 29; xvi. 21; Numb. viii. 12. And an inspired prophet says, All we like sheep have gone astray ; we have turned every one to his own way, and the Lord *laid on him* the iniquity of us all. Is. liii. 6. And Jesus said, I lay down my life for the sheep. John x. 15. And Peter says, His own self *bare our sins* in his own body on the tree. I Peter ii. 24. And this *foundation* is never to be *laid again.* The gospel ordinance of baptism is always in the singular number, but the washings under the law were many. And God says to his children, There is one body, and one Spirit, even as ye are called in one hope of your calling; one Lord, one faith, one baptism, one God and Father of all, who is above all, and through all, and in you all. Eph. iv. 4—6. But the holding to an external laying on of hands upon officers, as a foundation point in ministerial authority, hath made them lords over God's heritage, in every age, and in every country where the Christian name hath been known. And holding to the laying on of hands upon every member, after baptism, has caused great divisions among the Baptists, which should put all upon examination of this point. Laying on of hands upon officers in ordination, is no more than a solemn swearing of them to be faithful in their work, and civil rulers are also inducted into their offices by an oath, after the people have given them their power, which they can take away again at appointed times. And this was the original plan of the Congregational churches in New England; only none were allowed to give ministers their power, but those who were judged to be real Christians.

The first church in Dorchester, with Mr. Wareham, their minister, removed up to Windsor, and began the colony of Connecticut, in 1635, in which year Mr. Richard Mather came over to Dorchester. And on April 11, 1636, a meeting was held there for the purpose of gathering a new church; but it was not then done, because the rulers and ministers present were not satisfied with the experiences of the most of the persons who were to be of the church. Says Winthrop :—

Most of them had burdened their comfort of salvation upon unsound grounds, viz., some upon dreams and ravishes of spirit by fits; others upon the reformation of their lives; others upon duties and performances, &c.; wherein they discovered three special errors. 1. That they had not come to hate sin because it was filthy, but only left it because it was hurtful. 2. That by reason of this they had never truly closed with Christ (or rather Christ with them) but had made use of him only to help the imperfection of their sanctification and duties, and not made him their sanctification, wisdom, &c. 3. They expected to believe by some power of their own, and not only and wholly from Christ.[1]

And in 1639, their legislature punished a minister and some people at Weymouth severely, for attempting to gather a church there, in which " all baptized ones might communicate without any farther trial of them."[2] This account was given by Governor Winthrop, one of the greatest and best men then in New England. And as no men had a vote in the choice of ministers but communicants in their churches, so they held the power of ordination to be in each church. Mr. Cotton said :—

The power of the ministerial calling is derived chiefly from Christ, furnishing his servants with gifts fit for the calling; and nextly from the church (or congregation) who, observing such whom the Lord hath gifted, do elect and call them forth to come and help them.

Again he says :—

Though it be our manner (and as we believe according to the word) that every church chooseth and calleth their own ministers, and ordaineth them by the presbytery of the same church; yet if the presbytery of other churches commend a minister to a vacant church, and upon the acceptance of the church, if the presbyters of those churches do ordain him, with the consent of the church, we do not profess that this is no calling of Christ, or that these are no ministers of Christ.[3]

[1] Winthrop's Journal, p. 98. [Vol. I, p. 184.]
[2] Ibid, p. 171. [Vol. I, pp. 387, 388.]—B.   See also, Vol. I, p. 94.—ED.
[3] Answer to Williams, Part Second, 1647, pp. 82, 131.

And the next year they said in the Cambridge Platform:—

In such churches where there are elders, imposition of hands in ordination is to be performed by those elders.   In such churches where there are
no elders, imposition of hands may be performed by some of the brethren
orderly chosen by the church thereunto. .... Nevertheless, in such churches
where there are no elders, and the church so desire, we see not why imposition of hands may not be performed by the elders of other churches.

They also say :—

In case an elder offend incorrigibly, the matter so requiring, as the
church had power to call him to office, so they have power according to
order (the council of other churches, where it may be had, directing thereto) to remove him from his office.[1]

Now it is a known rule in grammar, that though a parenthesis is useful in its place, yet the sense is complete without
it.   But in our day, most of those who are called Congregational ministers, deny the church's power to ordain or dismiss them, unless a mutual council direct thereto.   Thus
they have gone off from the first principles of Congregational churches, while they hold the name for worldly ends.
But Mr. William Hubbard, in his manuscript history, written
in 1680, says :—

There is no jurisdiction, to which, as such, particular churches are or
ought to be subject (be it placed in classis or synod) by way of authoritative censure, nor any church power, extrinsical to the said churches, which
they ought to have dependence upon any other sort of men for the exercise of.[2]

And Mr. Jonathan Mitchel of Cambridge, had before
said :—

The over-enlarging of full communion, or admission of persons thereto,
upon slight qualifications, without insisting upon the practical and spiritual
part of religion, will not only lose the power of godliness, but in a little
time bring in profaneness, and ruin the churches, these two ways : 1.
Election of ministers, will soon be carried by a formal looser sort. 2. The
exercise of discipline will by this means be rendered impossible. Discipline failing, profaneness riseth like a flood. For the major part, wanting
zeal against sin, will foster licentiousness. It is not setting down good rules

[1]Platform, Chapters, IX, X. [Magnalia, Vol. II, pp. 191, 192.]
[2]Hubbard, p. 184.—Ed.

and directions, that will salve it; for the specification of government is from men, not from laws. Let never so good a form of government be agreed upon, it will soon degenerate, if the instruments who manage it be not good.[1]

Mr. Mitchel died in 1668, when he had no idea of their admitting any men to a governing vote for pastors of churches, but communicants therein; and he gave these weighty reasons against receiving any to communion without good evidence of their being godly persons; and Dr. Increase Mather dedicated these things to the college at Cambridge in 1697, of which he was then president. And how can any men reasonably complain of the Baptists for their holding fast the good principles of our fathers, and renouncing their mistakes? Especially the laying of bands upon children before they could choose for themselves, and forcing all to support such worship? Had it not been for these two evils, the characters of the fathers of New England would outshine almost any men who have lived in latter ages. Indeed the fathers of Plymouth colony renounced all the use of force to support their ministers.

[1]Dedication of Mitchel's Life, pp. 17, 18. [Magnalia, Vol. II, p. 59.]

CHAPTER XXXIII.

THEY WHO DENY INFANT BAPTISM ARE COMPARED TO BALAAM.—EVI-
DENCE THAT THE COVENANT OF CIRCUMCISION IS REPEALED.—THE
ERROR OF BALAAM DESCRIBED. — MISTAKES OF GOOD MEN COR-
RECTED.—THE COVENANT WITH ABRAHAM OPENED.—CORRUPTIONS AT
PROVIDENCE EXPOSED.—AND ALSO AT ROCHESTER.—THE IMPORTANCE
OF HAVING THE GOVERNMENTS OF CHURCH AND STATE DISTINCT.—
TYRANNICAL POWER GROWS WEAKER IN OUR LAND.—MARKS OF FALSE
TEACHERS CONSIDERED.—EXTRACTS FROM WILLIAMS AND COTTON.—
AND FROM MATHER, ABOUT CONGREGATIONAL CHURCHES.—A CONCISE
VIEW OF THE PRESENT STATE OF GOVERNMENT AND RELIGION.—
MANY PRACTICALLY DENY THAT CHRIST IS COME.

Having described the first principles of Congregational
churches, let us see how they are now held by eminent men.
A book was published in Boston in the beginning of 1793,
which has had a most rapid sale, wherein are the following
things. The author says :—

The apostles, when they first began to administer Christian baptism, and
form a church, baptized none but such who gladly received the word.
Acts ii. 41. When the eunuch desired to be baptized, Philip said, If thou
believest with all thine heart, thou mayest. Acts viii. 37. This implies
that he was not qualified for baptism, or a fit subject of that ordinance,
unless he were a true believer in Christ ; and that he could not baptize him,
unless he professed and appeared to be such a believer.[1]

But in order to find a warrant for infant baptism, he goes
back to the covenant of circumcision which God made with

---

[1]The System of Doctrines, contained in divine revelation, explained and defended.
By Samuel Hopkins, D. D., pastor of the First Congregational church in Newport,
Vol. II, p. 306. [The Works of Samuel Hopkins, D. D., Boston; Doctrinal Tract
and Book Society, 1854; Vol. II, p. 101.]

Abraham, and holds that it never was repealed.   And, after much labor to prove this point, he says :—

They who are expecting and demanding, that Christ or his apostles should expressly renew and enjoin on Christians, the appointment and command of God, to apply to the infants of believers the initiating seal of the covenant, in order to warrant men to do it ; refusing to acquiesce in the decision of this point, which God had already made ; *if the argument above be conclusive*, are imitating Balaam, who did not rest satisfied with the decision which God had once made, respecting his going to curse Israel, but expected and required that God should speak again, if he did really forbid his doing it.[1]

These are the words of a minister who hath made such additions to Calvinism that his plan is called Hopkintonianism through America.   And *if his argument is conclusive*, the Baptists are some of the worst men upon earth, as Balaam was such a one.   But if he is entirely mistaken, and God has disannulled the national covenant which he made with Abraham, it is very hurtful for any to hold the contrary.   It is therefore of great importance for all to have right ideas of this subject.   And the following considerations are offered for that end :—

First, Abraham had no right to circumcise any stranger, until he had bought him as a servant for money.   Gen. xvii. 12, 13.   But God says to his children, Ye are bought with a price, be not ye the servants of men.   I Cor. vii. 23. And he says to his ministers, Feed the church of God, which he hath purchased with his own blood.   Acts xx. 28. He also says, Ye have sold yourselves for nought, and ye shall be redeemed without money.   And this is the gospel of peace.   Is. lii. 3, 7 ; Rom. x. 15.   Thus do the apostles explain the prophets.   Secondly, The children of Israel had no right to receive strangers into the church by households, until the day in which they came out of Egypt, when the passover was instituted.   And then God said, Every man's servant that is bought for money, when thou hast circum-

---

[1] Hopkins's System, Vol. I, p. 318, margin. [Works of Samuel Hopkins, D. D., Vol. II, p. 109.]

cised him, then shall he eat thereof. Exod. xii. 44—48.
Circumcision and the passover were as binding upon servants
as children ; and both ordinances pointed to the blood of
Christ, which he was to shed for his people. And in refer-
ence to that, God said, Behold, the days come, saith the
Lord, that I will make a new covenant with the house of
Israel, and with the house of Judah ; not according to the
covenant that I made with their fathers, in the day that I
took them by the hand, to bring them out of the land of
Egypt. Jer. xxxi. 31, 32. And an inspired apostle says,
In that he saith, A new covenant, he hath made the first old.
Now that which decayeth and waxeth old is ready to vanish
away. He taketh away the first, that he may establish the
second. Heb. viii. 7—13 ; x. 9. And can *old* and *new*,
first and *second*, mean but one covenant? Surely no.
Thirdly, *Circumcision* is the name which God gave to his
covenant with Abraham. Acts vii. 8. And though Jews
and Mahometans are still zealous for it, yet all Christians
allow that circumcision is repealed. But after the apostolic
age, men took away the name which God gave to that covenant, and added the name *Grace* to it ; and they held that
dominion is founded in grace. And from thence the nations
have made merchandise of all the vanities of time, and of
slaves and souls of men. But the plagues of Babylon will
come upon all men who add to the word of God, and take
away from the words of his book, if they refuse to come out
of that practice. Rev. xviii. 4—13 ; xxii. 18, 19. And
there is not a word in all the Bible for bringing any child to
baptism without his own profession of faith in Christ, nor
for forcing any man to support any religious minister ; and all
national churches are built upon these two superstitions.
Fourthly, Circumcision was the shedding of human blood ;
and when Abraham received it, it was a seal of the righteousness of the faith which he before had in Christ, in whom
believers are justified by his blood. Rom. iv. 11, 23 ; v. 9 ;
Gal. iii. 16 ; Gen. xv. 6 ; xvii. 24. It was a seal to him ;

but neither circumcision nor baptism are ever called seals to any other person in all the Bible. But God says to true believers in Christ, In whom also after that ye believed, ye were sealed with that Holy Spirit of promise. And he also says, Grieve not the Holy Spirit of God, whereby ye are sealed unto the day of redemption. Eph. i. 13 ; iv. 30. After believing in Christ, the Holy Spirit seals the merits of his death, and the promises of his grace to the soul. And all believers from the beginning, looked through the bloody ordinances which God appointed, to the blood of Christ for justification. And after the beast arose out of the bottomless pit, God said, All that dwell upon the earth shall worship him, whose names are not written in the book of life of the Lamb slain from the foundation of the world. Rev. xiii. 8. Force and cruelty is the general character of the beast; but Jesus, who is the root and offspring of David, will cause all evil beasts to cease out of the land. Ezek. xxxiv. 4, 25 ; Rev. xxii. 16. Fifthly, The believing Jews were suffered to go on in circumcision for a number of years after the death of Christ, and then God said to them, If ye be circumcised, Christ shall profit you nothing. .... Whosoever of you are justified by the law, ye are fallen from grace. Gal. v. 2—4. So far was the covenant of circumcision from being the covenant of grace. That bloody sign not only pointed to the death of Christ, but also to the death of all true believers in him. Therefore Paul says, I through the law am dead to the law, that I might live unto God. I am crucified with Christ, nevertheless I live ; yet not I, but Christ liveth in me ; and the life which I now live in the flesh, I live by the faith of the Son of God, who loved me, and gave himself for me. .... The fruit of the Spirit is love, joy, peace, long-suffering, gentleness, goodness, faith, meekness, temperance ; against such there is no law. And they that are Christ's, have crucified the flesh, with the affections and lusts. Gal. ii. 19, 20 ; v. 22—24. Adam and Christ are the only two public heads of mankind, as to the great affairs of the soul and eternity. For as by one man's disobedience, many were made sinners ; so by the obedience of one, shall many be made righteous. Rom. v. 19. For parents to bring up their children in the nurture and admonition of the Lord, is of infinite importance ; but we can find no warrant for any to bring them to baptism without a personal profession of faith in Christ.

Let us now inquire what was the error of Balaam ? When God took the nation of Israel to be his church, he was an husband unto them. Jer. xxxi. 32. And Moses said unto him, If thy presence go not with us, carry us not up hence. For wherein shall it be known here, that I and thy people have found grace in thy sight ? is it not in that thou goest with us ? So shall we be separated, I and thy people, from all the people that are upon the face of the earth. Exod. xxxiii. 15, 16. But Balaam, for an earthly reward, taught Balak how to destroy that separation. And it was done by the Midianites, among whom Balaam dwelt, who enticed Israel into adultery and idolatry ; and those Midianites were of the posterity of Abraham. Numb. xxv. 6 ; xxxi. 8, 16 ; Gen. xxv. 4. And how many children of believers are now guilty of this iniquity ! for covetousness is idolatry. Col. iii. 5. And many make a god of their belly. Phil. iii. 19. And idolatry is also adultery in the sight of God, who said of the church of Israel, Their mother hath played the harlot ; she that conceived them hath done shamefully ; for she said, I will go after my lovers, that give me my bread and my water, my wool and my flax, mine oil and my drink. Hosea ii. 5. All lawful things, but they were sought in an unlawful way. So one apostle says of many teachers and professors, An heart they have exercised with covetous practices ; cursed children ; who have forsaken the right way, and are gone astray, following the way of Balaam the son of Bosor, who loved the wages of unrighteousness ; but was rebuked for his iniquity ; the dumb ass, speaking with man's voice, forbade the madness of the prophet. II Peter ii. 14,

15, 16.   Another says, Woe unto them ; for they have gone
in the way of Cain, and ran greedily after the error of Balaam for reward, and perished in the gainsaying of Core.
Jude 11.   And Christ says by a third, I have a few things
against thee, because thou. hast there them that hold the
doctrine of Balaam, who taught Balak to cast a stumbling-
block before the children of Israel, to eat things sacrificed
unto idols, and to commit fornication.   Rev. ii. 14.   Now,
since covetousness and luxury are idolatry in the sight of
God, and idolatry is also adultery, how many are there in
the world who entice Christians into these evils, in order to
grasp the honors and profits of religion to themselves ! Yea,
and who go out from the ways of God to gratify their love
of the world !   I John ii. 15, 19.   These be they who separate themselves, sensual, having not the Spirit.   Jude 19.
Mystery Babylon is the mother of harlots, and abominations
of the earth.   Rev. xvii. 5.   And it is generally held that
these things were spoken. against heathen idolatry, and
against the abominations of the church of Rome.   But have
ministers in our land come out of those abominations ?   For
we have before proved that Dr. Stiles and Dr. Lathrop hold
to a successive power of office through the church of Rome,
and Dr. Hopkins does the same, notwithstanding his great
difference from many about the doctrines of grace, and the
power of godliness.   For he says :—

A visible church may be very corrupt, and yet be a visible church of
Christ, and the public administrations and acts of the officers of it, authentic and valid.   And who can prove, that the pope, and his adherents,
were visibly antichrist, and that the church of Rome was visibly not the
church of Christ, but a false church, and was really and properly renounced
and excommunicated, by. the true church of Christ, before the time of the
reformation from popery ?[1]

Thus he allows that the church of Rome was a visible
church of Christ, until the Protestants renounced her power,
and set up national churches, who have now carried blood

---

[1]Hopkins's System, Vol. II, p. 273. [Hopkins's Works, Vol. II, p. 78.]

and slavery round the world, in galleys and gallant ships, as far as the Papists ever did. So God says'of the second beast, He causeth all, both small and great, rich and poor, free and bond, to receive a mark in their right hand, or in their foreheads; and that no man might buy or sell save he that had the mark, or the name of the beast, or the number of his name. Here is wisdom. Let him that hath understanding count the number of the beast, for it is the number of a man; and his number is six hundred, three-score and six. Rev. xiii. 16—18. God gave his people rest, on the seventh day, in the seventh month, and the seventh year. But the inventions of men give no rest, in hundreds, in tens, nor in units. The wicked are like the troubled sea, when it cannot rest. Is. lvii. 20. Raging waves of the sea, foaming out their own shame. Jude 13. They have no rest day nor night, who worship the beast and his image, and whosoever receiveth the mark of his name. Rev. xiv. 11. But our Lord says, Come unto me, all ye that labor and are heavy laden, and I will give you rest. Matt. xi. 28. For we which have believed do enter into rest. Heb. iv. 3. And how clearly do these things discover the difference between all the believers in Christ, and all other men in the world! For their rock is not as our Rock, even our enemies themselves being judges. For they who think to purchase the gift of God with money, are in the gall of bitterness, and in the bond of iniquity. Deut. xxxii. 31—33; Acts viii. 20 —23. All the governments of this world are supported by force and money, but the church of Christ is purchased with his own blood, and is governed by his word and Spirit; and believing in him, and obeying the revealed will of God by the assistance of his Spirit, is the only way of ministerial succession that he has appointed.

Our author says :—

The church is not a worldly society; and is not ruled or regulated by civil laws, or rulers of political, worldly societies; such rulers have no more authority in the church than any other members of it. The visible church is called in Scripture, The kingdom of heaven; the kingdom of God, and of Christ, who says, My kingdom is not of this world.[1]

How then can any national churches be churches of Christ? For he says, Whosoever shall not receive the kingdom of God as a little child, he shall not enter therein. Mark x. 15. Except ye be converted, and become as this little child, ye shall not enter into the kingdom of heaven. Matt. xviii. 3. And the Father says to the Redeemer, This is my covenant with them, saith the Lord. My Spirit that is upon thee, and my words which I have put in thy mouth, shall not depart out of thy mouth, nor out of the mouth of thy seed, nor out of the mouth of thy seed's seed, saith the Lord, from henceforth and forever. Is. lix. 20, 21. Which prophecy is applied to future times, when there shall be life from the dead. Rom. xi. 15, 27. But our author applies it to each believing head of a family.[2] And in the same place he recites part of another prophecy, which might rectify his mistake in this, even the place where God says, I will pour water upon him that is thirsty, and floods upon the dry ground; I will pour my Spirit upon thy seed, and my blessing upon thine offspring; and they shall spring up as among the grass, as willows by the water-courses. One shall say, I am the Lord's; and another shall call himself by the name of Jacob; and another shall subscribe with his hand unto the Lord, and surname himself by the name of Israel. Is. xliv. 3—5. So when God poured out his Spirit, after the ascension of Christ, they who gladly received his word, were baptized. And again he says, Believers were the more added to the Lord, multitudes both men and women. Acts ii. 41; v. 14. Circumcision was only for the males, but females are equally the subjects of baptism, which proves an essential change of the covenant. And our Lord gave the gospel commission to the eleven, who were all born again; and he said to them, Go teach all

[1] Hopkins's System. Vol. II, p. 262. [Hopkins's Works, Vol. II, p. 71.]
[2] Ibid, pp. 336, 337. [Hopkins's Works, Vol. II, p. 122.]

nations, baptizing them in the name of the Father, and of the Son, and of the Holy Ghost; teaching them to observe all things, whatsoever I have commanded you; and lo, I am with you alway, even unto the end of the world. Amen. Matt. xxviii. 16—20. This promise is only to his children, in the way of obedience to all his commandments. And as the covenant of circumcision gave Israel a right to buy the heathen for servants, and circumcision was only for the males, the gospel says to believers, Ye are all the *children of God* by faith in Christ Jesus. For as many of you as have been baptized into Christ, have put on Christ. There is neither Jew nor Greek, there is neither bond nor free, there is neither male nor female; for ye are all one in Christ Jesus. And if ye be Christ's, then are ye Abraham's seed, and heirs according to the promise. Gal. iii. 26—29. Abraham was an eminent type of Christ, and none are his spiritual seed but believers in Christ. How great then is the mistake of all who put themselves in the place of Abraham! Our author was so far from believing that the Baptists sinned against the light of their consciences, as Balaam did, that he says, "There is reason to believe, that most, if not all, who believe in the baptism of children, and practice it, are more guilty and offensive to Christ, in their treatment of this institution, than the Antipædobaptists are."[1]

And another minister of his sentiments has given further light in this matter, in an answer to Dr. Hemmenway. He observes that the covenant of grace is always the same, under every dispensation thereof, and that a peculiar design of God's promise to Abraham was, "to keep up the visible church, and maintain a constant succession of pious men, in his family, until the appearance of the promised Messiah.[2] This is undoubtedly true, and a most important truth; for God said of Abraham, I know him, that he will command his children and his household after him, and they shall keep

[1] Hopkins's System, Vol. II, p. 398. [Hopkins's Works, Vol. II, p. 165.]
[2] Emmons against Hemmenway, 1793, p. 27.

the way of the Lord, to do justice and judgment; that the
Lord may bring upon Abraham that which he háth spoken
of him. Gen. xviii. 19. *He will*, and *They shall*, was the
language of God's covenant with Abraham; but *I will*, and
They shall, is the language of the new covenant, since the
death of Christ. Heb. viii. 10; x. 9. It was the will of
God that the visible church should continue in the line of
Abraham's posterity, until Christ came and died for his people, and then the Holy Spirit was given, and believing Jews
and Gentiles were united in his church. And they never
were called Christians, until believing Gentiles were received
into the church without circumcision. Acts xi. 26. Yet,
as our author says :—

Dr. Hemmenway has followed other writers in arguing from the former
dispensations of the covenant of grace to the present, and endeavored to
prove what the peculiar duties of believers are, under the present dispensation of the covenant of grace, from what they were under its former dispensations. But this mode of reasoning is by no means conclusive. It
was the duty of believers under former dispensations of the covenant of
grace to offer sacrifices; but can we hence infer, that it is their duty now?
It was the duty of believers under former dispensations of the covenant of
grace, to circumcise their children and attend the passover; but does it
hence follow, that those duties are still binding? or can we justly conclude
that it is the duty of believers now to circumcise their children, or even to
baptize them, because it was once their duty to circumcise them?
The truth is, we must learn the peculiar duties of believers under
the present dispensation of the covenant of grace, from the dispensation itself, which enjoins all the peculiar duties which belong to it. ....
The Christian dispensation, which is allowed to be the freest from types
and figures, plainly speaks for itself. And we ought to look into the clear
dispensation of the gospel, in order to discover the peculiar duties of believers at this day.[1]

Yea, and how happy should we soon be, if the gospel
light was followed by all, without trying to draw the vail of
the law over it? As long as the death of Christ was a
future event, the bloody ordinances of the law, and circumcision in particular, were given to many who did not know
him; but since his death he says, All shall know me, from

[1]Emmons against Hemmenway, pp. 43, 44.

the least to the greatest. Heb. viii. 11. And in baptism
and the holy supper, all the lawful subjects thereof openly
manifest their faith in the death of Christ as a past event,
and their engagement to love and live to him all their days.
And if it were fully allowed that God hath disannulled the
covenant of circumcision which he made with Abraham, as
well as the rest of the law of typical ceremonies, and hath
built his church upon a better covenant, established upon
better promises, the effects would be very glorious, and
silence many controversies. But the holding that the children of believers are born in the covenant of grace, or that
baptism can bring them into it, without their own knowledge
or choice, is such a confounding of grace and works together
as holds multitudes in blindness and bondage. And this
appears in the following instance.

Mr. Joseph Snow, of Providence, met with a happy change,
in the glorious revival of religion in 1741 ; and he was soon
called to preach the gospel, and a Congregational church
was formed under his ministry, and he was ordained their
pastor, February 12, 1747. A meeting-house was built for
them, which was afterwards enlarged, and they became a
numerous and honorable society,[1] and collected a fund of
money for the support of their ministers. And as Mr.
Snow was advanced in years, and a young minister arrived
there from Ireland, in the spring of 1791, he was called to
assist him in preaching for two years. But in that time he
drew off the majority of the church and congregation from
the doctrine of sovereign grace, to the way of confounding
works and grace together. And as Mr. Snow tried to get
him dismissed from them, a majority of the church drew up
a number of accusations against Mr. Snow, and attempted
to silence him from preaching. But he and his brethren
called a council, who fully cleared him from those accusa-

---

[1] His Excellency, Nicholas Cooke, a member of that church, was chosen Governor
of the State of Rhode Island, in 1775, and was continued in that office to 1779. He
died September 14, 1782. He was a Baptist himself, though in communion with a
Congregational church.

tions. And as said teacher was of the Methodist denomination, he could not have a legal right to the property of that
Congregational society; therefore he changed his name to
that of Congregational; and a majority of the church sent
to four churches in the Massachusetts, and to two in the
State of Rhode Island, for assistance in ordaining said minister in their church. Upon which Mr. Snow, and many of
his brethren, sent for another council, to meet at the same
time; and they advised Mr. Snow, and those who held with
him, to persevere in their former faith and conduct, and to
withdraw their hand of fellowship from all their brethren
who had gone off from the same, and refused to return.
And this advice was taken, and Mr. Snow and those who
held with him, warned the other council not to ordain the
young minister in their meeting-house. Yet in the face of
all this, they went into said house, on October 17, 1793, and
ordained him as a colleague pastor in that church. A number of that part of the church who were so resolute for the
young minister, were Baptists, who had communed with
others who were only sprinkled in infancy. But as they
could then dispense with one plain law of Christ, so they
now could with another, in the manner above described.
And in the summer of 1794, Mr. Snow and his brethren
were entirely shut out of their meeting-house, because they
would not join with a minister whom they viewed as one
who perverted the gospel of Christ. Gal. i. 7.[1] At the
same time, the ministers in the Massachusetts were for holding fast their power to the last extremity.

The first parish in Rochester settled a minister in 1768,
with a promise of two hundred pounds settlement, and
eighty pounds a year salary, as long as his pastoral relation
to them continued. But his loose principles carried him
into such evils, that a mutual council was called there in
September, 1791, who judged him to be guilty of gross im-

---

[1] In 1795, a new meeting-house was built for Mr. Snow, by the help of generous
persons of various denominations.

moralities ; and another council was called by the church in December following, who advised them to dismiss him, which they did, and the parish shut him out of their meeting-house. Yet he held worship with a minor part of the people elsewhere, for two years and a half, and then sued the whole parish for his salary all that time. But as he was cast at the inferior court, he appealed to the supreme judicial court, which met at Plymouth, May 20, 1794; and after the hearing of a whole day, the judges gave their opinion in his favor, but the jury turned the case against him. The judges allowed several Rochester men to be witnesses for said minister, but refused to admit any man from that town as a witness against him, because they said they were interested persons. So in two former cases, when the Baptists sued for their rights, noted men of their denomination were not admitted as witnesses of plain facts.[1] But God says, With what judgment ye judge, ye shall be judged; and with what measure ye mete, it shall be measured to you again. Matt. vii. 2. And how is he fulfilling his word! For taxes to support religious ministers, is taxing men where they are not represented, as no man can answer for another to God in such cases. Yet America has been full of this wickedness ; and all the blood that was shed in the American war turned upon this point. And how full is our land now of complaints against our chief rulers, because their property has been taken away by the British powers, and they must sue for it again in British courts? Though those powers are no more interested against America, than every hireling teacher is, against all who refuse to support him. For they bite with their teeth, and cry, Peace ; and he that putteth not into their mouths, they even prepare war against him. Micah iii. 5. And how much is this cry now heard in Europe and America! And one of the principles of Congregational churches is, that no church act can be consum-

[1]See pp. 142, 163, 164.

mated without the consent of both elders and brethren.[1] Which is giving ministers such a power over the church, as our supreme judges have not over the jury.   And said minister in Rochester was settled in the name of the king of Great Britain, and he has been supported lately by the carcass of that authority.   But God says, Let them put away their whoredom, and the carcasses of their kings far from me, and I will dwell in the midst of them forever. . . . . This is the law of the house ; upon the top of the mountain, the whole limit thereof round about shall be most holy ; behold, this is the law of the house.   Ezek. xliii. 9, 12.   But false men say, Stand by thyself, come not near to me, for I am holier than thou.   Is. lxv. 5.   Teachers claim a holy power of office, above the church of God ; and in every nation, the ruling sect imagine themselves to be holier than those who have not the power of the magistrate to support their worship.   Though God says to his children, This ye know, that no whoremonger, nor unclean person, nor covetous man, who is an idolater, hath any inheritance in the kingdom of Christ, and of God.   Let no man deceive you with vain words ; for because of these things cometh the wrath of God upon the children of disobedience.   Be not ye therefore partakers with them.   Eph. v. 5—7.   But how can any church avoid partaking with whoremongers, unclean persons, and covetous men who are idolaters, if they have any fellowship with worship and ministers that are supported by force ?   For such men have equal votes in government with the most pious men in the land.

Our Lord and his apostles were very careful to keep the church from interfering with civil government.   For when a man desired Jesus to interpose his influence in dividing of an inheritance, he said unto him, Man, who made me a judge, or a divider over you ?   And he plainly holds forth, that the leaven of hypocrisy is promoted by confounding the governments of church and state together.   Luke xii. 1, 14, 15.

[1]Cambridge Platform, Chap. X, Sec. II. [Magnalia, Vol. II, p. 193.]

And in order to purge the old leaven from the church, Paul says, I have written unto you, not to keep company, if any man that is called a·brother be a fornicator, or covetous, or an idolater, or a railer, or a drunkard, or an extortioner, with such an one, no not to eat. For what have I to do to judge them also that are without? Do not ye judge them that are within? But them that are without, God judgeth. Therefore put away from among yourselves that wicked person. I Cor. v. 7—13. Covetousness is here put before idolatry, for it is the root of all evil. I Tim. vi. 10. And it is easier for a camel to go through the eye of a needle, than for a rich man to enter into the kingdom of God. But blind guides strain at a gnat and swallow a camel. Matt. xix. 24; xxiii. 24. And who can tell how many blind guides there are in our day? And the confounding the constitutions of the Hebrew and the Christian churches together, is the way in which they yoke Christians with the world. But God says to his church, Be ye not unequally yoked together with unbelievers; for what fellowship hath righteousness with unrighteousness? and what communion hath light with darkness? and what concord hath Christ with Belial? or what part hath he that believeth with an infidel? and what agreement hath the temple of God with idols? For ye are the temple of the living God; as God hath said, I will dwell in them, and walk in them; and I will be their God, and they shall be my people. Wherefore come out from among them, and be ye separate, saith the Lord, and touch not the unclean thing; and I will receive you, and will be a Father unto you, and ye shall be my sons and daughters, saith the Lord Almighty. II Cor. vi. 14—18. And this call is not of a local, but of a spiritual nature. It is not from civil commerce with unbelievers, but from being yoked with them in communion in the·church, which is the temple of the living God, and is to be governed wholly by his revealed will, under the influence of his Spirit. But where worldly force is used to support religious ministers, it will be conscientiously opposed by the faithful, and villains will hide behind such opposition, and so the government both of church and state are injured.   Whereas, if all were protected impartially, they who act from heavenly motives would strengthen the hands of civil rulers, and hold up light to draw others out of evil ways, and to guard against all iniquity.   And it will yet be said, Look upon Zion, the city of our solemnities : thine eyes shall see Jerusalem a quiet habitation, a tabernacle that shall not be taken down ; not one of the stakes thereof shall ever be removed, neither shall any of the cords thereof be broken.   But there the glorious Lord will be unto us a place of broad rivers and streams, wherein shall go no galley with oars, neither shall gallant ships pass thereby.   For the Lord is our judge, the Lord is our lawgiver, the Lord is our king; he will save us.   Is. xxxiii. 20—22.   Now if we consider, that galleys and gallant ships are the greatest engines of war and slavery in all the world, and that they are upheld by national churches, how loud is the call from Heaven to come out and be separate from all such churches !

Indeed Dr. Lathrop, in order to keep up the power of ministers, which he pleads for, says :—

A Christian church is compared to a household, and to a city, in respect of the order and government, the peace and unity, that ought to be preserved in it.   But if every man might assume the office of a teacher at pleasure, where would be the order and unity?   There would be the same confusion and distraction, as in a State where every one claimed a right to exercise the powers of magistracy.[1]

But in all the States of New England, the people can leave their governors, and all their legislators out of office every year, if they please, while all the ministers, who are supported by tax and compulsion, deny the people any such liberty concerning themselves.   When the people have elected their rulers, some men are appointed to give them an oath, to be faithful in their offices ; and when the church

[1]Discourses on Matthew vii. 15, 16, pp. 10, 11.

of Christ has chosen her ministers, she has a right to call
other ministers to ordain them, and to give them a solemn
charge to be faithful to God and to his people. But ever
since ministers have claimed a power of office above all
other men in the world, the government of the churches,
the cities of God, has lain waste, to the grief of all pious
people. Though the time is coming when our Lord will
give such comfort and strength to them who mourn in Zion,
that he says, They shall build the old wastes, they shall raise
up the former desolations, they shall repair the waste cities,
the desolations of many generations. Is. lxi. 1—4. This
our Lord applies to the blessings of his Spirit under the
gospel. Luke iv. 18, 19. Every church of Christ is a holy
city, which has a right to censure and exclude all members
and officers who break his laws, and refuse to manifest repentance therefor. And when they shall come to exercise
this power faithfully, independently of all the powers of the
world, such peace will be enjoyed as never has yet been
upon earth. And the power of one sect in our land to
compel all others to bow to them in religious affairs, is daily
consuming, by the light and power of the gospel. One evidence of this lately appeared in Medfield. A Baptist church
was constituted there in 1776; and they built them a convenient house for worship, and another for the ministry, and
they have maintained regular worship among them ever since.
Yet all the Baptists in Medfield were lately taxed to the
Congregational minister of that town; and one of their committee was seized for that tax, and was imprisoned at Boston, July 2, 1794. But it caused such an alarm in Boston,
and the news from thence which reached Medfield the next
Saturday, caused such an alarm there, that two men were
sent twenty miles on the Lord's day, who released the prisoner, without his paying the tax, or any costs about it. And
very few now in our country will dare to make distress upon
any for ministerial taxes.

If the marks of false teachers, which the above author

has published, were rightly applied, the church of Christ
would soon have such deliverance from their power as she
has not yet enjoyed. For he says, " Another mark of false
teachers, is an implacable malignity against the standing,
regular ministers of the gospel'" And again he says, This
sort of teachers are guided by no line, and confined to no
measure ; but run from place to place, enter into other men's
labors and build on on other men's foundations.[1] Very
true ; and the word of Christ is daily fulfilled, who said to
false teachers among the Jews, Ye compass sea and land to
make one proselyte, and when be is made, ye make him two-
fold more the child of hell than yourselves. Matt. xxiii.
15. And we may see at this day, that the Jews have a fixed
regard for the laws of Moses, and for the land of Canaan ;
but proselytes to revealed religion, who are not born again,
have no fixed rule of conduct, nor any country that can set
any bounds to their love of riches, honors or pleasures.
Some deceitful men in the church of Corinth, accused Paul
of going beyond his authority in what he had written to that
church. Therefore he said, The weapons of our warfare
are not carnal, but mighty through God to the pulling down
of strong holds, casting down imaginations, and every high
thing that exalteth itself against the knowledge of God, and
bringing into captivity every thought to the obedience of
Christ ; and having in a readiness to revenge all disobedience, when your obedience is fulfilled. For we stretch not
ourselves beyond our measure, as though we reached not
unto you ; for we are come as far as to you also, in preaching
the gospel of Christ : not boasting of things without our
measure, that is, of other men's labors ; but having hope,
when your faith is increased, that we shall be enlarged by
you according to our rule abundantly, to preach the gospel
in the regions beyond you, and not to boast in another man's
line, of things made ready to our hand. But he that glori-

---

[1] Discourses on Matthew, vii. 15, 16, pp. 29, 31.

eth, let him glory in the Lord. For not he that commendeth himself is approved, but whom the Lord commendeth.
II Cor. x. 4, 5, 14—18. The line and measure which he
spake of was drawn by God himself, and not by any worldly
powers. So the same apostle said to another church, I will
not dare to speak of any of those things, which Christ hath
not wrought by me, to make the Gentiles obedient, by word
or deed, through mighty signs and wonders, by the power of
the Spirit of God; so that from Jerusalem and round about
unto Illyricum, I have fully preached the gospel of Christ.
Yea, so have I strived to preach the gospel, not where
Christ was named, lest I should build upon another man's
foundation. Rom. xv. 18—20. And can any man believe
that the words, *Measure*, *Line*, and *Foundation*, as Paul used
them, can justify the use of carnal weapons in forcing all
people within lines which men have drawn, to support
teachers who stand upon worldly establishments? For other
foundation can no man lay than that which is laid, which is
Jesus Christ. Now if any man build upon this foundation,
gold, silver, precious stones, wood, hay, stubble : every man's
work, shall be made manifest. For the day shall declare it,
because it shall be revealed by fire ; and the fire shall try
every man's work, of what sort it is. I Cor. iii. 11—13.

And the fiery trials of the present day may afford much
clearer light than our fathers enjoyed. For they banished
Mr. Roger Williams, because he testified against any use of
the sword in religious affairs, and against their receiving the
grant of American lands from the kings of England. One
of his reasons against such things, was what our Lord says
of the tares of the field, which Williams held to be the
world, and not the church.[1] But Mr. Cotton said :—

It is not the will of Christ, that [antichrist, and antichristians, and] anti-
christianity should be tolerated in the world, until the end of the world.
For God will put it into the hearts of faithful princes (as they have given
their kingdoms to the beast, so) in fulness of time to hate the whore, and

[1] Williams on the Bloody Tenet, 1644, p. 44.

to leave her desolate and naked, and to burn her flesh with fire.   Rev. xvii. 16, 17.[1]

Williams had before said :—

This hating, and desolating, and making naked, and burning, shall not arise by way of an ordinance warranted by the institution of Christ Jesus ; but by way of providence, when (as it useth to be with whores and their lovers) the church of Rome and her great lovers shall fall out ; and, by the righteous vengeance of God upon her, drunk with the blood of the saints [or holy ones,] these mighty fornicators shall turn their love into hatred, which shall make her a poor, [desolate,] naked whore, torn and consumed.[2]

But Cotton made no reply to this ; and how have the nations of Europe now fallen out, and have taken the riches of the national churches, to support war and vengeance against their cruel oppressors !   And is not this eating her flesh, and burning her with fire?   But the fathers of that day were so much afraid of the tyranny of European powers, that Cotton said, " The Lord keep us from being bewitched with the whore's cup, lest while we seem to detest and reject her with open face of profession, we do not bring her in by a back door of toleration."[3]   And Dr. Increase Mather quoted this passage thirty years afterwards, and then said, " I believe that antichrist hath not at this day a more probable way to advance his kingdom of darkness, than by a toleration of all religions and persuasions."[4]   This was reprinted in Boston the year after their charter was taken away.   But Mather and his brethren were so cruelly persecuted by the ruling powers here, that he went over to England three years after, and thanked the popish King James, for his declaration for liberty of conscience.   After which he believed that our Lord meant the world, when he said, Let both grow together until the harvest.[5]   Let all men be equally protected, and no worship be established by human

[1]Cotton on the Bloody Tenet Washed, 1647, pp. 42, 43.
[2]Williams, p. 246.   [3]Bloody Tenet Washed, p. 192.
[4]Election Sermon at Boston, May 23, 1677 ; reprinted 1685: p. 106.
[5]Increase Mather's Life, pp. 58, 110.—B.   See Vol. I, p. 419.—ED.

laws, nor ministers supported thereby, and the danger they feared is at an end. Naked popery is weak in our land. For Mr. John Thayer, who was born in Boston, went to Rome, and joined their church in May, 1783, from whence he returned through Maryland, and arrived at Boston in January, 1790 ; and he hath preached up the infallibility of the church of Rome, prayers for the dead, and other opinions of theirs, with very little success. But our greatest danger is from the power of the world over the church of Christ.

Dr. Increase Mather said to the churches of New England :—

If we espouse such principles as these, namely, That churches are not to inquire into the regeneration of those whom they admit unto their communion ; that admission to sacraments is to be left wholly to the prudence and conscience of the minister ; that explicit covenanting with God and with the church is needless ; that persons not qualified for communion in special ordinances shall elect pastors of churches ; that all professed Christians have a right to baptism ; that brethren are to have no voice in ecclesiastical councils ; that the essence of a minister's call, is not in the election of the people but in the ceremony of imposing hands ; that persons may be established in the pastoral office without the approbation of neighboring churches or elders ; we then give away the whole Congregational cause at once, and a great part of the Presbyterian discipline also.[1]

But declension prevailed for forty years longer, until the churches and the world were much alike ; and then God poured out his Holy Spirit, in the most extensive manner that was ever known in America ; and great numbers flocked into the churches, where ministers favored the work. Though, as a new piece of cloth when put into an old garment will make the rent worse, and new wine will burst old bottles, even so was it with old churches, in which the doings of men were blended with the perfect righteousness of Christ for justification, and the inventions of men with his laws for their government. For by the year 1744, all the ministers in New England who were supported by the laws of men, were afraid to preach in any parish where another

[1] Vindication of Gospel Order, 1700, p. 8.

minister was settled against his consent; which was making ministers lords over God's heritage, to gratify their love of filthy lucre. I Peter v. 2, 3. And separations from such ministers and churches took place from that time, until many embraced believers' baptism, in and after 1749. And a great change has also taken place in many old Baptist churches. And now loud complaints are made against the Baptists, because they dare not commune in the ordinance of the Supper, with those who were only sprinkled in their infancy. But how unreasonable are these complaints! For our apostle says, We, brethren, as Isaac was, are the children of promise. But as then, he that was born after the flesh persecuted him that was born after the Spirit, even so it is now. Nevertheless, what saith the Scripture? Cast out the bond woman and her son; for the son of the bond woman shall not be heir with the son of the free woman. So then, brethren, we are not the children of the bond woman, but of the free. Stand fast, therefore, in the liberty wherewith Christ hath made us free, and be not entangled again with the yoke of bondage. Gal. iv. 28—31; v. 1. And how can we obey this law of Christ, if we commune with any in the Holy Supper who were only sprinkled in their infancy? And a late instance may help to shew the evil of such covenants. A man in one of the Congregational churches was convinced that he was not born again, and therefore refrained from coming to the ordinance of the Supper. And after he obtained relief in his own mind, he viewed such evils in the church, and his wife also, that they thought they could not in conscience come to communion therein, and refrained from it. The church sent a committee to labor with them, and they requested a dismission from the church; but instead of it, a censure was sent to them, which said, " With grief of heart we inform you, that we are greatly stumbled at your conduct, in breaking a solemn and sacred covenant with us, in which you bound yourselves in the presence of the great God, to walk in communion with us. By thus breaking communion with us, you are guilty of the worst kind of perjury. By refusing to attend communion, or even public worship with us, you have unchristianized the whole church, and have really excommunicated us." And after trying to prove this from Scripture, and reciting the law of Christ about the power of binding and loosing, they say, "We accordingly have met in the name of Jesus, and in his name we bind you under the censure of its first admonition." This was dated November 28, 1794. The minister who sent them this censure has been a noted advocate for supporting their way by law in our country. But how great must be the bondage of any people, who must come to communion in any society where church and world are bound together, or be accused of the worst kind of perjury? However, the said man and his wife renounced those ways, and were baptized this year, and joined a Baptist church. And how great is the privilege which we enjoy, to answer a good conscience towards God, in the midst of all the confusions of the world!

Europe is full of confusion and blood; and America is become so wanton and extravagant, that it cost above a million of dollars, and required an army of fifteen thousand men last year, to compel a few counties in Pennsylvania to submit to the taxing power of our government. And the victory over them was accounted so great a favor, that a day of thanksgiving therefor was kept through all these United States, February 19, 1795. But the whole country has been full of controversy about our public affairs ever since. And are not these the shakings among the nations which God will pursue, until the Desire of all Nations shall come? Hag. ii. 7. All men desire safety and happiness; and this can only be enjoyed under the government of the Son of God, of whom it is said, In his days Judah shall be saved, and Israel shall dwell safely; and this is his name whereby he shall be called, the Lord our Righteousness. I am against the prophets, saith the Lord, that steal my words every one from his neighbor. Behold, I am against the prophets, saith the Lord, that use their tongues, and say, He saith. Behold, I am against them that prophesy false dreams, saith the Lord, and do tell them, and cause my people to err by their lies, and by their lightness ; yet I sent them not, nor commanded them ; therefore they shall not profit this people at all, saith the Lord. Jer. xxiii. 6, 30—32. The precepts and promises of God are ever connected together ; and no man hath any more right to any promise which Christ hath made to his ministers, who doth not love and obey him with all his heart, than thieves and robbers have to the property of honest men. John x. 1—9. And how much stealing of his words is there in our land ? The Congregational scheme of church government, came as near the gospel plan, as any plan ever did which was upheld by the sword. But a zealous advocate for it lately said, " It is difficult to say what is the present ecclesiastical constitution of the Congregational churches." And as to their faith, he says, " The body of them are Calvinists ; a respectable proportion are what may be denominated Hopkinsian Calvinists ; besides these, some are Arminians, some Arians, a few Socinians, and a number who have adopted Dr. Chauncy's scheme of the final salvation of all men."[1] This account is doubtless true in general, though it is questionable whether there are not more Arminians in the churches who are supported by law in this country, than there are of Calvinists. And vast pains have been taken, both in Europe and America, to persuade the people, that all the wars and tyranny that have ever taken place under the Christian name, have proceeded from the doctrines of Calvinism. For it is well known that Augustine, and other fathers of the church in the third and fourth century, held to the same doctrines which Calvin embraced in the time of the reformation from popery. But God says, Woe be to the shepherds of Israel, that feed themselves ; should not the shepherds feed the flocks ? Ye

[1] Morse's Geography, 1793, first part, pp. 252, 253.

eat the fat, and ye clothe you with the wool, ye kill them that are fed, but ye feed not the flock. The diseased have ye not strengthened, neither have ye healed that which was sick, neither have ye bound up that which was broken, neither have ye brought again that which was driven away, neither have ye sought that which was lost; but with force and with cruelty have ye ruled them. .... And as for you, O my flock, thus saith the Lord God, Behold, I judge between cattle and cattle, between the rams and the he-goats. Seemeth it a small thing unto you, to have eaten up the good pasture, but ye must tread down with your feet the residue of your pastures? and to have drunk of the deep waters, but ye must foul the residue with your feet? Ezek. xxxiv. 2—18. This is an exact description of the behavior of false teachers and professors, in every age and country, where revelation hath been known. The love of self, and of earthly power and gain, with ignorance of the infinite perfections of God, and a going about to establish a righteousness of their own, hath caused all the oppressions and cruel persecutions that ever were upon earth. And men have trampled upon the precious doctrines of the gospel, and have defiled the deep waters of revelation, as wantonly and as cruelly as wanton cattle ever did, against the weak or the diseased. But if men in general were willing to be taught of God, and to obey the pure voice of his holy word, such peace and happiness would soon be enjoyed, as they will not now believe to be possible in this world.

Arians and Socinians, both deny that Jesus Christ is God by nature, and the latter hold him to be no more than a man. But there is no such faith as theirs in heaven, nor in hell, nor in heathen darkness. For all the angels of heaven worship Jesus as the Son of God. Heb. i. 6; Luke ii. 9—14. And the devils said, What have we to do with thee, Jesus thou Son of God? art thou come hither to torment us before the time? Matt. viii. 29. And the great philosophers at Athens, the greatest seat of learning in the heathen world, got no further than to erect an altar to the unknown God, in the midst of many idols. Acts xvii. 23. So that all men who profess to worship but one God, and yet deny that Jesus Christ is truly God, have corrupted their minds more than the devils ever could do, and have carried philosophy and vain deceit beyond what the old heathens ever did. And God says, These speak evil of those things which they know not ; but what they know naturally, as brute beasts, in those things they corrupt themselves. Jude 10. It is impossible to harden brute beasts against fear of danger, to the degree that many men harden themselves against the fear of God's wrath in a future world. The cause why earthly governments have no right to admit sureties in capital cases, is because the children of men cannot justly lay crimes upon any innocent person, nor raise a dead one to life, nor change the heart of a criminal. But it is as certain as any truth in the Bible, that the Son of God freely gave himself to die for our sins, and that he arose again for our justification, and that he gives the Holy Spirit to change the heart of the chief of sinners, and to guide them in the way of holiness to eternal happiness. And it is not more certain from the word of God, that the righteous will have everlasting life, than it is that all men who die in their sins will have everlasting misery in hell. And all men who hold the contrary, destroy the influence of promises and oaths, more than they do in the church of Rome, where they hold that some men will have their sins purged away after death, by the help of the prayers of the living. Therefore the Congregational churches in New England, have more pernicious errors held up among them, than there are in the church of Rome. And the apostle John says, Beloved, believe not every spirit, but try the spirits whether they be of God ; because many false prophets are gone out into the world. Hereby know ye the Spirit of God : Every spirit that confesseth that Jesus Christ is come in the flesh, is of God. And every spirit that confesseth not that Jesus Christ is come in the flesh, is not of

God: and this is that spirit of antichrist, whereof ye have
heard that it should come, and even now is it already in the
world. Ye are of God, little children, and have overcome
them; because greater is he that is in you, than he that is
in the world. They are of the world, therefore speak they
of the world, and the world heareth them. I John iv. 1—5.
Worldly property is the only qualification for voters in our
governments, for rulers and ministers; and yet each parish
in Connecticut, is called an ecclesiastical society in the laws
by which they support their ministers. That is, they are
worldly churches. And though the Massachusetts do not
call each parish a church, yet they put the whole power of
taxation for religious teachers into the hands of the world,
without the least regard to the church of Christ in that
respect. In another law, which was made in 1786, the deacons of each church are empowered to receive donations for
religious purposes, which they are to manage according to
the design of the donors, for the good of the church. And
this opens a door for leading a quiet and peaceable life in all
godliness and honesty. But the compelling of any man to
support any religious teacher whom he doth not choose, is a
denial of the authority of Christ. For he says, As ye would
that men should do to you, do ye also to them likewise. For
every tree is known by his own fruit; for of thorns men do
not gather figs, nor of a bramble-bush gather they grapes.
A good man out of the good treasure of his heart bringeth
forth that which is good; and an evil man out of the evil
treasure of his heart bringeth forth that which is evil; for
of the abundance of the heart his mouth speaketh. And
why call ye my Lord, Lord, and do not the things which I
say? Luke vi. 31, 44—46. How do all men practically
deny Jesus Christ to be Lord, who refuse to believe and
obey him? For unto the pure all things are pure; but unto
them that are defiled and unbelieving, is nothing pure; but
even their mind and conscience is defiled. They profess
that they know God, but in works they deny him, being

26

abominable, and disobedient, and unto every good work reprobate. Titus i. 15, 16. And all men allow that actions
speak louder than words, and also that injuries from professed friends, are more grievous than from open enemies.
How full then is the world of the iniquity of denying that
Jesus Christ is come in the flesh? And this is according to
the prophesy which says, There are certain men crept in
unawares, who were before of old ordained to this condemnation, ungodly men, turning the grace of our God into lasciviousness, and denying the only Lord God, and our Lord
Jesus Christ. Jude 4. All men who indulge themselves in
sin because God is infinitely gracious, are more or less guilty
of these evils. And though the national church of Israel
was constituted by God himself, yet all orders among them
became so corrupt that he said, The best of them is a brier,
the most upright is sharper than a thorn-hedge. Micah vii.
4. And if it was so with a church which God formed, how
much more destructive are churches that are formed by the
laws of men, enforced by the sword? How do all men
practically deny Jesus Christ to be Lord, who refuse to obey
his laws for the government of his church? But how have
the churches increased in our land, who hold him to be their
only lawgiver?

CHAPTER XXXIV.

A LIST OF THE BAPTIST CHURCHES IN THE FIVE STATES OF NEW ENGLAND, FOR THE YEAR 1795.

The first column contains the year in which the church was constituted, as far as it is known ; the second the name of the town ; the third its distance from Boston ; the fourth, the name of their minister, if they have any ; the fifth the number of members in each church where it could be obtained.

MASSACHUSETTS.—COUNTY OF SUFFOLK.

Year.	Town.	Miles.	Ministers.	No.
1665	Boston,		Samuel Stillman, D. D.,	267
1743			Thomas Baldwin, A. M.,	158

COUNTY OF NORFOLK.

1750	Bellingham,	34	Noah Alden,	51
1769	Wrentham,	30	William Williams, A. M.,	40
1776	Medfield,	20	*Edward Clarke,*[1]	42
1780	Randolph,	16	Joel Briggs, A. M.,	58

COUNTY OF PLYMOUTH.

1756	Middleborough,	33	Isaac Backus,	91
1757		42	Ebenezer Hinds,	29
1761		43	Samuel Nelson,	107
1785	Bridgewater,	25	George Robinson,	53
1788	Marshfield,	33		26
1791	Carver,	50	John Tripp,	52

[1]Those in *Italics* are not ordained ministers.

COUNTY OF BRISTOL.

Year.	Town.	Miles.	Ministers.	No.
1663	Swanzey,	52	Charles Thompson, A. M.,	150
1693		55	Russel Mason,	346
1753	Rehoboth,	51	Thomas Seamans,	45
1762		48	John Hicks,	40
1772		48	Jacob Hicks,	130
1777		40	Jeremiah Irons,	56
1780		45		15
1789		42	Aaron Wheeler,	36
1794		44	John Peirce Jones,	31
1761	Taunton,	37	Ebenezer Nelson,	55
1769	Attleborough,	32	*Laban Thurber*,	68
1781		38	Elisha Carpenter,	49
1772	Dighton,	50	Enoch Goff,	250
1774	Freetown,	48	John Lawrence,	20
1781		50	Philip Hathaway,	50
1774	New Bedford,	53	*Zaccheus Tobey*,	18
1781	Dartmouth,	58	Daniel Hicks,	347
1780	Raynham,	37		14

COUNTY OF BARNSTABLE.

Year	Town	Miles	Ministers	No.
1757	Harwich,	84	Abner Lewis,	72
1771	Barnstable,	74	Enoch Eldridge,	58

DUKES COUNTY.

Year	Town	Miles	Ministers	No.
1693	Chilmark,	99		16
1780	Tisbury,	97	David Leonard, A. B.,	45

COUNTY OF ESSEX.

Year	Town	Miles	Ministers	No.
1765	Haverhill,	33	Hezekiah Smith, A. M.,	176
	Amesbury,	50	Moses Chace.	
1785	Rowley,	26		50
1793	Danvers,	18	Thomas Green,	30

COUNTY OF MIDDLESEX.

Year	Town	Miles	Ministers	No.
1771	Chelmsford,	25	John Peckens,	95
1780	Newton,	9	Joseph Grafton,	94
1781	Cambridge, } Woburn, }	7 10	Shubael Lovell,	84
1789	Weston,	14		18

COUNTY OF WORCESTER.

Year	Town	Miles	Ministers	No.
1738	Leicester,	58	Nathan Dana,	45
1749	Sturbridge,	65	*Zenas L. Leonard*, A. B.,	96

Year.	Town.	Miles.	Ministers.	No.
1762	Charlton,	60	David Rathbun,	113
1765	Sutton,	47	*Samuel Waters*,	52
1786		46		37
1792		41	William Batcheller,	57
1768	Hardwick,	70		40
1770	Royalstone,	80	Moses Kenney,	155
1776	Harvard,	35	Isaiah Parker,	129
1779	Ashburnham,	60		57
1780	Northbridge,	40	John Cooper,	47
1782	Templeton,	60		97
1791	Upton,	45	Simeon Snow.	

COUNTY OF HAMPSHIRE.

Year.	Town.	Miles.	Ministers.	No.
1736	South Brimfield,	80	Elijah Codding,	155
1789	West Springfield,	100	Jesse Wightman,[1]	30
			Edward Upham, **A. M.**	
1761	Ashfield,	117	Ebenezer Smith,	26
1788		117	Enos Smith,	92
1765	Leverett,	95		59
1768	Wilbraham,	83	Seth Clark,	228
1793		85		34
1772	New Salem,	85	Josiah Orcott,	45
1780	Shutesbury,	88	Joseph Smellage,	57
1780	Leyden,	112	Joseph Greene,	64
1780	Chesterfield,	106	Ebenezer Vining,	45
1780	Coleraine,	116		52
1789		116	Edmund Littlefield,	19
1784	Westfield,	105		85
1785	Russell,	111	Ebenezer Stow,	45
1786	Shelburne,	112	David Long.	
1788	Conway,	110		82
1789	Whateley,	107	Asa Todd,	45
1789	Buckland,	120		26
1789	Bernardstown,	112	Levi Hodge,	50
1789	Granville,	120		28
1790	Charlemont,	123		31
1793	Monson,	80	Samuel Webster.	
1795	Belchertown,	85	Samuel Bigelow,	18
1795	Granby,	85	*Silas Palk*,	15

COUNTY OF BERKSHIRE.

Year.	Town.	Miles.	Ministers.	No.
1769	Cheshire,	140	Peter Worden,	155
1771		142		35

[1] Mr. Wightman is the present pastor of this church.

Year.	Town.	Miles.	Ministers.	No.
1791		144	John Lelaud,	173
1772	Pittsfield,	140	Valentine Rathbun,	31
1772	Hancock,	150	Clark Rogers,	54
1777	Washington,	135	John Nichols,	68
1779	Sandisfield,	126		88
1788			Benjamin Baldwin,	60
1788	Bullocksgrant,	135	Nathan Haskins,	55
1789	Great Barrington,	140	Jeduthan Grey,	76
1790	Stockbridge and West			
	Stockbridge,	150	Samuel Whelpley, A. M.	86
1791	Middlefield,			20
1794	Williamstown,	135		16

COUNTY OF YORK.

Year.	Town.	Miles.	Ministers.	No.
1768	Berwick,	86	William Hooper,	93
1772	Sanford,	98		34
1780	Wells,	88	Nathaniel Lord,	63
1781	Shapleigh,	108	Tozer Lord,	40
1785			Nehemiah Davis,	55
1782	Coxhall,	108	Simon Lock,	57
1795	Limerick,		Levi Chadbourn,	50
1782	Parsonsfield,		Samuel Weeks,	13
1791	Waterborough,	110	Pelatiah Tingley, A. M.,	30
1791		110	Henry Smith,	28
1791	Fryeburg,	160	Zebadiah Richardson,	25
1792	Cornish,			47

COUNTY OF CUMBERLAND.

Year.	Town.	Miles.	Ministers.	No.
1768	Gorham,	130	James M'Corson,	28
1785	Harpswell,	162	Samuel Woodward,	53
1791	Hebron,	162	*Samuel Flagg,*	39
1791	Buckfield,	165		32
1791	Paris,	170	James Hooper,	34
1793	Livermore,		*Elisha Williams, A. M.*	60
1782	New Gloucester,	146		10
1794			Nathan Merrill,	16
1794	Raymondstown,		Zechariah Leach,	40

COUNTY OF LINCOLN.

Year.	Town.	Miles.	Ministers.	No.
1784	Bowdoinham,	172	Job Macomber,	40
1784	Thomaston,	215	Elisha Snow,	90
1784	Edgecomb,		Daniel Hebbard,	100
1788	Bowdoin,	166	James Potter,	37

Year.	Town.	Miles.	Ministers.	No.
1791			William Stinson,	54
1794				24
1788	Vassalborough,	203	Nehemiah Gould,	39
1789	Ballston,	195	Joshua Young,	23
1791	Sidney,		Asa Wilbur,	53
1791	Cushing,	216	Ephraim Hall,	49
1792	Sterling,		Eliphalet Smith,	51
1792	Readfield,	190	Isaac Case,	80
1792	Lewiston,			58
1793	Muscongus,	205	Andrew Fuller,	31
1793	Greene,			51
1793	Nobleborough,	192		15
1794	North Sandwich,		Lemuel Jackson,	18
1795	Clinton,		Mephibosheth Cain,	30
1795	Barrettstown,			18
1794	North Vineyard,			20
1790	Sandy River,		Edward Lock,	100

COUNTY OF HANCOCK.

Year	Town	Miles	Ministers	No.
1791	Islesborough,	260	Thomas Eames,	30

8,463

Churches, 136 ; ministers, 105.

RHODE ISLAND.—COUNTY OF PROVIDENCE.

Year	Town	Miles	Ministers	No.
1639	Providence,	45	Stephen Gano,	210
1706	Smithfield,	55	John Winsor,	150
1625	Scituate,	56		62
1766			John Westcoat.	
1732	Cumberland,	34	Abner Ballou,	48
1762		36		36
1649	Gloster,	60	Joseph Winsor.	
1778			William Bowen,	58
1790			Stephen Place,	60
1771	Johnston,	48	Samuel Winsor,	50
1766	Foster,	63	John Williams,	107
1789			John Hammond,	91
1765	North Providence,	48	Rufus Tefft,	170

COUNTY OF NEWPORT.

Year	Town	Miles	Ministers	No.
1644	Newport,	72	Michael Eddy,	90
1656			Gardner Thurston,	225
1671			William Bliss,	54
1788			*Caleb Greene,*	30

Year.	Town.	Miles.	Ministers.	No.
1685	Tiverton,	70	Peleg Burroughs,	122
1781		62	James Boomer,	24
1772	New Shoreham,	85	Thomas Dodge,	45

COUNTY OF BRISTOL.

1764	Warren,	53	Luther Baker,	52

COUNTY OF WASHINGTON.

1708	Hopkinton,	90	John Burdick,	462
			Asa Cooh.	
1770			John Gardner,	52
1710	North Kingstown,	67	Nathan Hill,	70
1767		66	Philip Jenkins,	77
1788		70	William Northup,	127
1750	Exeter,	70	*John Tillinghast,*	249
1750	Westerly,	95		123
1770				301
1778	South Kingstown,	75	Benjamin Weight,	36
1794				51
1772	Richmond,	75	Henry Joslin,	116
1774			Benjamin Barber,	66
1774				37

COUNTY OF KENT.

1725	Warwick,	58	Samuel Littlefield,	40
1791		54		35
1743	East Greenwich,	60	Thomas Manchester,	50
1752	Coventry,	58	Thomas Manchester,	124
1774		66	*John Benson,*	100
1780	West Greenwich,	67	Elisha Greene,	50
				3,850

Churches, 40; ministers, 34.

CONNECTICUT.—COUNTY OF NEW LONDON.

1705	Groton,	113	Timothy Wightman,	182
1765		117	Silas Burris,	81
1743	Stonington,	100	Peleg Randal,	145
1765		104	Simeon Brown,	194
1775		110	Valentine W. Rathbun,	46
1793			Samuel Northup,	46
1767	New London,	115	Zadoc Darrow,	268
1786		118	Davis Rogers,	24

Year.	Town.	Miles.	Ministers.	NO.
1743	Colchester,	105	Abel Palmer,	90
1784		100	Christopher Palmer,	58
1752	Lyme,	120	Jason Lee,	264
1786	Montville,	110	Reuben Palmer,	52
1786	Preston,	85		60

COUNTY OF WINDHAM.

Year.	Town.	Miles.	Ministers.	NO.
1750	Thompson,	57	John Martin,	100
1766	Woodstock,	66		73
1792		68	Amos Wells,	76
1774	Ashford,	74	Dyer Stark,	90
1776		72	John Rathbun,	54
1792		69		38
1794		67	Daniel Bolton.	
1776	Killingly,	65		
1776	Hampton,	70	Peter Rogers,	63
1792	Plainfield,	72	Nathaniel Cole,	87

COUNTY OF HARTFORD.

Year.	Town.	Miles.	Ministers.	NO.
1739	Farmington,	127	Calvin Hulbert,	40
1775	Suffield,	107	John Hastings,	103
1780	Bristol,	115		70
1786	Wintonbury,	112	Ashbel Gillet,	50
1789	Hartford,	106		50
	Windsor,	110		
1789	East Hartford,	101	Stephen Shepard,	47
1790	Somers,	104	Seth Parsons,	20
1792	Enfield,	100	Christopher Minor,	15
1793	Symsbury,			7

COUNTY OF NEW HAVEN.

Year.	Town.	Miles.	Ministers.	NO.
1787	Wallingford,	130		33
1792				29

COUNTY OF FAIRFIELD.

Year.	Town.	Miles.	Ministers.	NO.
1751	Stratfield,	166	Stephen Royce,	119
1773	Stamford,	194	Ebenezer Ferris,	25
1773	Greenwich,	204	Nathaniel Finch,	45
1785	Danbury,		Elijah Wheeler,	40
1790				48
1789	Ridgefield,		Elias Lee,	27
1794	Newtown,		John Sherman,	21

COUNTY OF LITCHFIELD.

Year.	Town.	Miles.	Ministers.	No.
1786	Warren,			30
1788	Torrington,			50
1789	Canaan,			27
1789	Litchfield,		Amos Tuttle,	23
1790	New Hartford,		Epaphras Thompson,	75
1790	Roxbury,			31
1791	Watertown,		Daniel Wildman,	25
1791	New Milford,			38
1793	Colebrook,		Rufus Babcock,	31
1793	Sharon,			44

COUNTY OF MIDDLESEX.

Year	Town	Miles	Ministers	No.
1760	Saybrook,	136	Eliphalet Lester,	30
1788			William Hill,	
1778	Chatham,	127	Solomon Wheat,	63
1783				72
1790	East Haddam,	118	Simeon Dickinson,	47

COUNTY OF TOLLAND.

Year	Town	Miles	Ministers	No.
1780	Willington,	81	David Lillebridge,	48
1780	Coventry,	92		10
1786	Stafford,	87		24

                                                          3,547

Churches, 60 ; ministers, 40.

STATE OF NEW HAMPSHIRE.—COUNTY OF ROCKINGHAM.

Year	Town	Miles	Ministers	No.
1771	Brentwood,	53	Samuel Shepard,	456
1780	Northwood,		Edward Pilsbury,	104
1780	Salem,	46		57
1796	Newton,	40	John Peak.	

COUNTY OF STRATFORD.

Year	Town	Miles	Ministers	No.
1772	Gilmanton,		Walter Powers,	67
1780	Meredith,		Nicholas Folsom,	64
1780	Sanbornton,		John Crocket,	61
1793	Sandwich,		Jacob Jewel,	112

COUNTY OF HILLSBOROUGH.

Year	Town	Miles	Ministers	No.
1782	Sutton,		Samuel Ambrose,	87
1782	Temple,			43
1783	Weare,		Amos Wood, A. B.,	40
1786	Mason,		William Elliot,	36

Year.	Town.	Miles.	Ministers.	No.
1787	Hopkinton,		Elisha Andrews,	75
1787	Amherst,			30
1788	New London,		Job Seamans,	118
1791	Hollis,			31
1793	Salisbury,		Elias Smith,	134

COUNTY OF CHESHIRE.

Year.	Town.	Miles.	Ministers.	No.
1770	Richmond,		Isaac Kenney,	145
1771	Westmoreland,		Ebenezer Bailey,	39
1791			*Nathaniel Wilbore,*	18
1777	Marlow,		Eleazer Beckwith,	131
1778	Newport,		Biel Ledoyt,	89
1781	Wendal,		Nehemiah Woodward,	25
1785	Dublin,		Elijah Willard,	33
1787	Cornish,		Jedidiah Hebbard,	28
1790	Fitzwilliam,			
1791	Alstead,		Jeremiah Higbie,	54
1792	Swansea,			18
1792	Hanover,	130	Abel Bridgman.	
1792	Plainfield,	126	Jonathan Cram,	36

COUNTY OF GRAFTON.

Year.	Town.	Miles.	Ministers.	No.
1780	New Holderness,		Jeremiah Ward,	32
1780	Rumney,		Cotton Hains,	78
1783	Canaan,	120	*Uriah Smith,*	34
1785	Grafton,	110		16
1788	Landaff,		Isaiah Stone,	101
1790	Dartmouth,		Daniel Brainard,	20
1792	Cockermouth,			32
1793	Dorchester,			50
1793	Wentworth,		Samuel Currier,	38
1794	Lyme,	135		15
1794	Alexandria,			15
				2,562

Churches, 41 ; ministers, 30.

STATE OF VERMONT.[1]—COUNTY OF BENNINGTON.

Year.	Town.	Miles.	Ministers.	No.
1768	Shaftsbury,			24
				30
1780				30

[1]The distances of the towns in Vermont from Boston, are so little known that they are omitted.

Year.	Town.	Miles.	Ministers.	No.
1788			Caleb Blood,	160
1773	Pownal,		Caleb Nichols,	165
1781	Manchester,		Joseph Cornel,	39
1784	Halifax,		Abner Bemis,	14
1791	Somerset,			27

COUNTY OF ADDISON.

Year	Town	Miles	Ministers	No.
1786	Leicester,			
1787	Orwell,			108
1788	Brandon,		Calvin Chamberlain,	65
1793	Georgia,			20
1794	Shoreham,			30

COUNTY OF RUTLAND.

Year	Town	Miles	Ministers	No.
1780	Wallingford,		Henry Green,	88
1782	Middletown,		Silvanus Hains,	43
1782	Ira,			49
1783	Pittsford,		Elisha Rich,	45
1684	Clarendon,		Isaac Beals,	46
1785	Pultney,			
1787	Hubbardston,			23
1790	Pawlet,			24

COUNTY OF WINDHAM.

Year	Town	Miles	Ministers	No.
1780	Guilford,			102
1782			Peleg Hicks,	
1791			Whitman Jacobs,	53
1782	Westminster,			32
1783	Dummerston,		Rufus Freeman,	171
1783	Athens,			25
1786	Putney,			63
1789	Rockingham,			40
1790	Jamaica,			26
1792	Wardsboro',		Simeon Coombs,	29

COUNTY OF CHITTENDEN.

Year	Town	Miles	Ministers	No.
1793	Fairfax,		Roswell Meers,	22
1793	Cambridge,		Joseph Call.	
1794	Alburgh,			13
1793	Monktown,			20
1794	Bolton,			15
1794	Richmond,			25

COUNTY OF WINDSOR.

Year.	Town.	Miles.	Ministers.	No.
1780	Woodstock,		Elisha Ransom,	144
1782	Bridgewater,			101
1784	Windsor,		Roswel Smith,	57
1784	Royalton,		John Hebbard,	51
1788	Reading,			31
1789	Chester,		Aaron Leland,	67
1789	Hartford,		John Drew,	45
1789	Thetford,			13
1789	Sharon,			16
1792	Norwich,		Robert Low,	43
1794	Hartland,			30

COUNTY OF ORANGE.

1783	Corinth,		Thomas West,	88
1788	Danville,		Isaac Roots,	28
				2,480

Churches, 48 ; ministers, 23.

The whole number of Baptist churches, ministers and members, in these States, is as follows :—

	Churches.	Ministers.	Members.
Massachusetts,	136	105	8,463
Rhode Island,	40	34	3,850
Connecticut,	60	40	3,547
New Hampshire,	41	30	2,562
Vermont,	48	23	2,480
In all New England,	325	232	20,902
New York,	84	111	5,263
New Jersey,	30	30	2,177
Pennsylvania,	31	35	1,368
Delaware,	8	10	390
Maryland,	17		920
Virginia,	227	272	22,793
Kentuckey,	57	67	3,483
North Carolina,	112	172	8,017
South Carolina,	76	98	4,554
Georgia,	61	79	3,227
North West Territory,	18	25	1,336
	1,152	1,125	73,767

The account of the churches, ministers and members south of New England is taken from Asplund's Register for 1794, as some are in New England; though the most of these are from later accounts.   He has numbered all licensed preachers, but I reckon only those who are ordained.

CHAPTER XXXV.

A CONCISE VIEW OF THE SECTS IN AMERICA, AND OF THEIR DIF-
FERENT ASSOCIATIONS.

Religious Liberty is not the Cause of Sects and Parties among
Christians.—A View of our Southern States.—Each Church of
Christ should act as one united Body.—An Account of the
Warren Association.—And of those of Stonington, New Hamp-
shire, Shaftsbury, Woodstock, Bowdoinham, Vermont, Meredith,
Danbury and Leyden.—The Nature of these Associations de-
scribed.—And of three others ; with general Observations upon
the universal Rule of Equity.

What shall we think of the prophecy in the beginning of
this volume ?[1]   For it says :—

Through the liberty enjoyed here, all religious sects will grow up into
large and respectable bodies.   But the Congregational and Presbyterian
denomination, however hitherto despised, will, by the blessing of Heaven,
continue to hold the greatest figure in America ; and, notwithstanding all
the fruitless labors and exertions to proselyte us to other communions, become more numerous than the whole collective body of our fellow Protestants in Europe.   The whole proselytism of New England in particular,
for sixty or seventy years past, has not exceeded eight or ten thousand,
while our augment in that term, by natural increase, has been half a
million.

In the first place there was a great mistake, in supposing
that religious liberty would favor the growth of religious sects.
For cruel oppression was the cause of the increase of sects in
England, as it was the flight of our fathers into America.   And

[1]Vol. III, old edition.   See p. 312.—Ed.

the hanging of four Quakers in Boston, greatly promoted their sect in this country; and the light and liberty which has been enjoyed in latter years has been far from increasing their number. The sect which John Rogers began at New London in 1677, owed its increase to the severity of Connecticut government against them; and since that has ceased, their society has nearly dissolved.[1] And although the Sandemanians made a great noise in New England, from 1764 to 1775, yet, having no oppression to complain of, they have hardly a name now left amongst us. The followers of Jemima Wilkinson, also, who made their appearance, October, 1776, and continued for some years after, are now all gone from among us. And though the Shakers were a large body when the above prophecy was published, yet we seldom hear of them now, unless it be by way of observing that the power which then actuated them is gone; and their attention is much fixed upon worldly schemes of gain. Episcopalians received vast sums of money from England to support their ministers, from 1701 to 1775, and those who turned to them were exempted from taxes to Congregational ministers; and as oppression was greater in Connecticut, than in other governments in New England, they increased the most there; but since the independence of America, they do not increase in most parts of the country; and in the whole of the old colony of Plymouth they have but one minister, and he has but a few hearers. And if the Congregational and Presbyterian ministers in the Massachusetts, Connecticut, New Hampshire and Vermont, had not the sword of the magistrate to support them, no one can tell how small their number would soon be.

And as the above prophecy refers to all America, we are called to look into our southern States. After our independence was established, the Presbyterians in those parts entered upon measures to unite all their societies under one head; to promote which, a book was published in North

[1]See pp. 10—13, Vol. I, pp. 337, 388.

Carolina in 1788, wherein the author says, "I have often thought. that the popular Congregational government of the Independents, joined to the Presbyterial judicatures, as a final resort, would form the most perfect model of church government that the state of things on earth will admit of." But this model has been tried in Connecticut, with the sword of the magistrate to help it, ever since 1708, and how far is it now from perfection? In the same page, the author says of the Baptists in those parts :—

Considering that they have no written standard of orthodoxy, and that their preachers are men without a liberal education, I have often sat with wonder and pleasure to hear them so sound in doctrine as they really are. In church government, the Baptists have adopted the independent plan ; the inconveniency of which they often experience, as it provides no final and decisive judge of controversy, nor tribunal to pronounce on heresy or false doctrine. But the distinguishing characteristic of the Baptist profession is their excluding infant and practicing only adult baptism, and making it their great term of communion, excluding all other Christians from the Lord's table among them, and not suffering their members to communicate with other churches. How they can acknowledge any other people to be a church of Christ, and yet continue this bar of separation, is not to be accounted for.[1]

But if the Holy Scriptures are not a perfect standard of orthodoxy, and if each particular church of Christ has not power from him to receive all members and officers who are described therein, and also to exclude all officers and members who break his laws and refuse to manifest repentance therefor, we know not where to go for any rule of faith and conduct; nor for power to govern us in religious affairs. And as to his last difficulty, it may be observed, that circumcision was as necessary in a member of the church of Israel, as baptism can be in the church of Christ; yet Moses, that eminent servant of God, did not circumcise his children while he was in Midian ; but when he was going to lead Israel out of their bondage in Egypt, he was constrained to have them circumcised, even at the peril of his own life.

[1]Pattillo's Sermons, pp. 48, 49.

27

Exod. iv. 24, 25. And the nation of Israel were the church of God in the wilderness, and yet they did not circumcise their children for forty years ; though they were not suffered to neglect it in the promised land. Joshua v. 2—5. And the church of Christ has been in Egyptian bondage, and in a great and terrible wilderness, ever since the beast arose out of the bottomless pit. Rev. xi. 2, 8 ; xii. 14 ; xiii. 5. The cause why many Christians were for continuing circumcision, after it was out of date, was the fear of persecution for the cross of Christ. But Paul said, God forbid that I should glory, save in the cross of our Lord Jesus Christ, by whom the world is crucified unto me, and I unto the world. For in Christ Jesus neither circumcision availeth anything, nor uncircumcision, but a new creature. Gal. vi. 12—15. But infant baptism binds the church and world together, instead of crucifying any one to the world, and the world to him.   Yet our author says of the Baptists, " They made their appearance in Germany soon after the reformation began. But the present race of Baptists are happily very unlike the furious and bloodthirsty bigots who wore the name at that time."[1]   As if Christ and his disciples had not been Baptists near fifteen hundred years before the reformation in Germany.   And has any man ever been able to produce a mention of infant baptism before the third century ? And in the next century, Constantine brought the sword into the church to punish heretics, and to support religious ministers ; and blood and slavery, deceit and cruelty, have followed those superstitions ever since, though many good men have been ensnared in those ways. In the year 1789, many Presbyterians met at Philadelphia, and formed a tribunal which they called, "The General Assembly of the Presbyterian Church, in the United States of America." And they opened a correspondence with the General Association in Connecticut ; and a delegate from thence to the Presbyterian Assembly at Philadelphia in May, 1793, said in a letter to England the fall after,

[1]Pattillo's Sermons, p. 47.

"There are nearly as many ministers of our order in Connecticut, as there are Presbyterians in all the States to the southward of Connecticut."[1] That is, in ten States, in which are nearly three millions of people, they have but about two hundred Presbyterian ministers. How far then is the Congregational and Presbyterian denomination in America from rising above all other Protestants, both here and in Europe.

And if we search the Scriptures, we shall find, that a being born again by the power of the Spirit of God, and a receiving special gifts from him for the ministry, is the only way that he has revealed, for any to come into the church, and into the work of preaching the gospel as they ought, let their education be what it may. Hence the first apostle says, As every man hath received the gift, even so minister the same one to another, as good stewards of the manifold grace of God. If any man speak, let him speak as the oracles of God; if any man minister, let him do it as of the ability which God giveth; that God in all things may be glorified through Jesus Christ. .... The elders which are among you I exhort, who am also an elder, and a witness of the sufferings of Christ, and also a partaker of the glory that shall be revealed; Feed the flock of God which is among you, taking the oversight thereof, not by constraint, but willingly; not for filthy lucre, but of a ready mind; neither as being lords over God's heritage, but being ensamples to the flock. And when the chief Shepherd shall appear, ye shall receive a crown of glory that fadeth not away. Likewise, ye younger, submit yourselves unto the elder; yea, all of you be subject one to another, and be clothed with humility; for God resisteth the proud, and giveth grace to the humble. I Pet. iv. 10, 11; v. 1—5. Lordship is of the Gentiles, and they tread the holy city under foot forty and two months, or for a time, and times, and half a time, while the church is in the wilderness. Mark x. 42; Rev. xi. 2; xii. 14. Men trample upon the holy gov-

[1]Rippon's Register, Vol. II, p. 131.

ernment, which Christ hath appointed in his church, as long as the power of the beast continues. And they say, Who is like unto the beast? who is able to make war with him? .... They that dwell on the earth shall wonder (whose names are not written in the book of life from the foundation of the world) when they behold the beast that was, and is not, and yet is. Rev. xiii. 4 ; xvii. 8. Deceit and cruelty under a mask of religion and government, have changed into all shapes that can be conceived of ; and Who hath been like the present scheme? or Who is able to war with the governing powers? are the great reasons for complying with the established worship, or at least for not boldly appearing to renounce all the laws and inventions of men in the worship of God, and in the government of his church.

The Congregational ministers in the Massachusetts meet in associations when they please, without any act of their churches; and they act many things in private, and claim the whole power of licensing candidates for the ministry; and in Connecticut they also advise the calling a consóciation in each county, when they think proper, to revoke acts of particular churches, or to censure such ministers or churches as they judge to be guilty. They likewise choose delegates in each county, to meet once a year in a general association of ministers by themselves, from all parts of that State. But the Baptists had suffered so much from these measures, that they could not be persuaded to meet in associations for many years, though upon quite a different plan. Yet in September, 1766, a number of elders and brethren agreed to send an invitation to their churches, to appoint a meeting the next year, to confer upon these things. And on September 8, 1767, ten churches met by delegation at Warren, with three ministers from the Philadelphia Association, and a letter from thence on the subject. Most of those who met, thought they were not prepared to proceed then, but four churches were ready, and they formed an association, and named it from the town where they met;

namely, the churches of Warren, Haverhill, Bellingham, and the Second in Middleborough.[1] And as the annual Commencement at our college is on the first Wednesday in September, and some who come to it from a distance would desire to attend the Association also, it was appointed to be on the Tuesday after the Commencement. They accordingly met at Warren, September 13, 1768, when four churches joined this Association, as four more did at Warren, September 12, 1769. Their next meeting was at Bellingham, September 11, 1770, and they met again at Sutton, September 10, 1771, when they had increased to twenty churches, and eight hundred and thirty-seven members ; and they then began to print minutes of their proceedings, which they have done ever since. And the churches in the foregoing list who are now in the Warren Association, are the two in Boston, those in Bellingham, Haverhill, Warren, Middleborough,

[1]See pp. 154, 155.

Mr. Backus's Diary contains the following account of this meeting :—

"Tuesday, September 8, [1767.] We went to Warren, where a general conference was appointed; and it was opened in the afternoon by a sermon from Acts 15. 9, by Mr. Gano, after which the following elders and brethren met in conference, viz. :—Of Warren, Elder James Manning, and brethren Benjamin Cole and Daniel Brown; Rehoboth, Elder Richard Round, brethren Samuel Bullock and Daniel Bullock; Haverhill, Elder Hezekiah Smith, brethren Jacob Whittier and Jonathan Shepherd; Norton, William Carpenter; Bellingham, Elder Noah Alden; Middleborough, Elder Ebenezer Hinds, Elder Isaac Backus; Cumberland, Elder Daniel Miller; Boston, Deacon Joseph Collins, brother Philip Freeman; Attleborough, brethren Abraham Bloss and Joseph Guild. Elder Abel Griffith, of Pennsylvania, and Elder Noah Hammond, of Long Island, were also present. Elder Gano was chosen Moderator, and Elder Backus, Clerk. The design of this meeting was to inquire into the state of the churches, and to see if they would come into the method of annual associations as they do in the western churches; and the elders and brethren from four churches now came into such an agreement, namely, those of Warren, Haverhill, Bellingham, and Elder Hinds, of Middleborough; but I did not see my way clear to join now, if ever I do."

Mr. Backus's church joined the Association in 1770. "They waited until they could be satisfied that this Association did not assume any jurisdiction over the churches, before they joined. And they now joined upon the express condition that no complaint should ever be received by the Association against any particular church that was not of the Association, nor from any censured member of any of our churches." Backus's Manuscripts. See Life and Times of Backus, pp. 155, 156; also Manning and Brown University, pp. 72—82, where may be found the above-mentioned letter from the Philadelphia Association, and the " Sentiments and Plan of the Warren Association," drawn up by President Manning.—ED.

Charlton, Royalstone, Wrentham, South Brimfield, the First in Attleborough, Wilbraham, Woodstock, and Freetown, those in Chelmsford, Harwich, Barnstable, New Salem, Leicester, Medfield, Harvard, Newton, Salem in New Hampshire, Cambridge, Northbridge, Providence, Gloucester, Sturbridge, Ashburnham, Templeton, Rowley, Weston, Bridgewater, Randolph, Marshfield, Carver, Hollis, Hardwick, and Belchertown; extending over all the old colonies of Plymouth and the Massachusetts, excepting what is west of Connecticut River, and into three adjoining States. This Association has begun to collect a fund for the purpose of assisting pious young men in obtaining human learning, with a view to the gospel ministry. Thirteen men were chosen by this Association, and were incorporated by the Legislature of the Massachusetts in February, 1794, to manage a fund for this purpose. This Association is to fill up vacancies, when any happen, as long as the Association continues; and if it should ever be dissolved, the corporation are then to elect their own members, in perpetual succession. They are invested with all necessary powers for receiving estates, real or personal, until the income thereof shall amount to a thousand pounds; and to use and improve the income of the fund for the assistance of such young persons in their education for the Baptist ministry, as the majority of the Trustees shall determine to be subjects thereof. A small fund for this purpose is already collected, and all their generous friends are solicited to increase it, to promote such a useful institution.

The benefits of the Warren Association soon became so evident, that others were formed in many parts of the country. The Stonington Association began in 1772, which now includes three Baptist churches in Stonington, the first in Groton, New London, and Saybrook, those in Colchester, Montville, Chatham, East Haddam, second and third in Ashford, the second in Woodstock, those of Hampton, Plainfield, Exeter, West Greenwich, and two in Richmond, in the

States of Connecticut and Rhode Island. Their annual meeting is on the third Tuesday of October. The New Hampshire Association began in 1776, and now includes the Baptist churches of Brentwood, Northwood, Gilmantown, Salisbury, Madbury, Berwick, Sauford, Wells, Coxall, one in Shapleigh, and Waterborough, Cornish, and Frye-burg, extending across the east part of New Hampshire, and over the county of York in the Massachusetts. Their annual meeting is on the second Wednesday in June. The Shaftsbury Association began in 1781, in which are now three churches in Shaftsbury, two in Cheshire, those of Pow-nal, Pittsfield, Chesterfield, Hancock, Bullocksgrant, Stock-bridge, Washington, first in Sandisfield and Great Barring-ton, with Williamstown, in Vermont and the Massachusetts, and twenty-five churches in the State of New York. Their yearly meeting is on the first Wednesday in June. The Woodstock Association began in 1783, in which are now the churches of Woodstock, Canaan, Bridgewater, Windsor, Hartford, Royalton, Sharon, Thetford, Norwich, Cambridge, Alburgh, Chester, Rockingham, Westminster, Wardsburgh, Westmoreland, Marlow, Mason, Temple, Dublin, Newport, Alstead, Cornish, Wendal, Plainfield, Sutton, New London, Hopkinton and Grafton, in New Hampshire and Vermont, and one in Canada. Another connection of churches was formed in those parts in 1795, called The Richmond Con-vention, of which I have not obtained a particular account. The annual meeting of the Woodstock Association is on the last Wednesday of September. The Bowdoinham Associa-tion began in 1787, and it now contains the Baptist churches of Bowdoinham, Harpswell, Bowdoin, Hebron, Buckfield, Paris, Thomaston, Vassalborough, Ballston, Sidney, Read-field, Sterling, Muscongus, Cushing, Lewiston, Nobleborough, Greene and New Sandwich, in the counties of Cum-berland and Lincoln, in the District of Maine. Their annual meeting is on the third Wednesday in August. The Ver-mont Association began also in 1787, and it contains the

churches of Clarendon, Manchester, Middletown, Hubbardston, Ira, Wallingford, Orwell, Pittsford, Brandon, Pawlet,
Shoreham and Georgia, in Vermont, with three in the State
of New York. Their annual meeting is on the first Wednesday of October. The Meredith Association began in
1789, and it includes the churches of Meredith, Sandwich,
Holderness, Rumney, Landaff and Bradford, Dartmouth,
Wentworth, Cockermouth, Sanbornton, Corinth and Ver-
shire, and Danville, in New Hampshire and Vermont. Their
annual meeting is on the second Wednesday in September.
The Danbury Association began in 1790, and it includes the
churches of Danbury, Suffield, Westfield, Canaan, Wallingford, Farmington, Roxbury, Warren, Watertown, New Hartford, New Milford, Sharon, one in Sandisfield, Colebrook,
East Hartford, Newtown, Litchfield, Stratfield, and three in
the State of New York. It extends from the south borders
of the Massachusetts west of the great river across Connecticut to the sea. The churches of Ridgefield, Stamford
and Greenwich, belong to Warwick Association in the State
of New York. The annual meeting of the Danbury Association is on the third Wednesday of September. The Leyden Association began in 1793, in which are the churches of
Leyden, Bernardston, Richmond, Leverett, two in Guilford,
Coleraine, Putney, Somerset, Dummerston, Halifax, Buck-
land and Ashfield, on the north side of the Massachusetts,
and on the corners of Vermont and New Hampshire. Their
annual meeting is on the second Wednesday of October.
As I failed of obtaining the last minutes of the Vermont,
Meredith, and Leyden Associations, their numbers stand as
they were in 1794, the others as they were in 1795. If any
mistakes are discovered, and any man will point them out,
the author would account it a favor, and take the best way
he can to correct them.

These associations refuse to hear and judge of any personal controversy in any church, or to intermeddle with the
affairs of any church which has not joined with them.

When any church would join any association, they send a letter and messengers thereto, informing when their church was constituted, the faith and order of it, and their number of members. If satisfaction is obtained, they are received by a vote of the association, and the moderator gives the messengers the right hand of fellowship. And each church sends a letter and messengers, or a letter at least, to the association every year, to give an account of the state of the church, and how many have been added, dismissed, have died, or have been excluded in the year past. If these things are neglected for a number of years, or if the church departs from her former faith or order, she is left out of the association. By these means, mutual acquaintance and communion has been begotten and promoted; the weak and oppressed have been relieved; errors in doctrine and practice have been exposed and guarded against; false teachers have been exposed, and warnings against them have been published; destitute flocks have been occasionally supplied; many have been animated and encouraged in preaching the gospel through the land, and in our new plantations in the wilderness. And it is hoped that these duties will yet be more attended to, and that greater blessings will hereafter be granted. For our Lord said to his disciples, I have yet many things to say unto you, but ye cannot bear them now. Howbeit, when he, the Spirit of truth, is come he shall guide you into all truth. He had just before said, The time cometh, that whosoever killeth you, will think that he doeth God service. John xvi. 2, 12, 13. And what is there that is harder to bear than to hear of being killed for Christ's sake? Reviling and lying on the one hand, and worldly enticements and flatteries on the other, are much harder to stand boldly against than open violence, torture and death. For the earth helped the woman, when she was enduring bloody persecution, and the people forced her persecutors to desist from their cruel measures. But it is very hard to make the people believe, that we are suffering for the cause of Christ, when we refuse to call in the power of the magistrate to support religious ministers, or to punish any who injure us on religious accounts.   Yet God says, Avenge not yourselves, but rather give place unto wrath; for it is written, 'Vengeance is mine ; I will repay, saith the Lord.   Rom. xii. 19.   Deceit and cruelty have ever prevailed more in the world, under the mask of religion and government, than they possibly could in any other way.   Therefore our Lord requires his ministers to depart out of every city or house where they refuse to receive his gospel, and he says, Freely ye have received,. freely give.   Matt. x. 8, 15.   But this command has ever been violated, where teachers have been supported by the sword of the magistrate.   And the combination of teachers and rulers, in schemes of power and gain, under the name of Christianity, has filled the world with blood and slavery.   And I believe that this combination is the beast and the false prophet, who will be cast into the burning lake.   Rev. xix. 11—21.   For where ministers are supported by the sword, deceitful men are armed against the children of God.   And where that power is renounced, many will require the ministers of Christ to go a warfare at their own charges, because he says, Freely ye have received, freely give.   As if freedom belonged only to ministers, while the people are slaves to their lusts.   For God says, To whom ye yield yourselves servants to obey, his servants ye are to whom ye obey ; whether of sin unto death, or of obedience unto righteousness.   Rom. vi. 16.

But our associations appeared to be so helpful to guard against these evils, and to promote real religion, that the churches which held to mixed communion began a yearly meeting in 1785, under the name of, The Groton Conference. And it now includes the Baptist churches of Dartmouth, New Bedford, two in Rehoboth, two in North Kingstown, one in South Kingstown, New Shoreham, two in Westerly, and one in each of the towns of Groton, Stonington, Lyme, Saybrook, Sutton, Preston and Canterbury, extending over part of three States. The church in Dighton, the second in Attleborough, and some others, have given up communion in the ordinance of the Supper with any who were only sprinkled in infancy, and the rest of those churches appear inclined to do the same, and to come into fellowship with our associated churches. The old Baptist churches have revived their associations, since the year 1774, though the second churches in Swanzea and Newport do not attend them, nor the first in Cumberland. But the churches of Johnston, Smithfield, two in Rehoboth, two in Scituate, two in Gloster, two in Warwick, the first in the towns of Foster, Coventry, North Kingstown, and Richmond, one in East Greenwich, the second in Cheshire, and the third in Shaftsbury, are in that connection. The Baptist churches who hold the seventh day of the week as the Sabbath, have also their annual meetings. Of these are the third church in Newport, the first in Hopkinton, the second in New London, and the church in Bristol in Connecticut. There are a number more of Baptist churches in various parts of our land which have not joined to any association, but they are coming into them from year to year, while many others are formed. I have also heard of a few Baptist churches upon our eastern coasts, who do not hold with other churches there about the doctrines of grace; but I have not obtained so distinct account of their affairs and connections as may be serviceable to the public. The world is so full of controversy, that all our powers ought to be engaged to promote truth and peace among all men. And for this end God says, Charge them that are rich in this world, that they be not high-minded, nor trust in uncertain riches, but in the living God, who giveth us richly all things to enjoy; that they do good, that they be rich in good works, ready to distribute, willing to communicate; laying up in store for themselves a good foundation against the time to come, that they may lay hold on eternal life. For perverse disputings, profane and vain babblings, and oppositions of science, falsely so called, all proceed from the love of money, which is the root of all evil. I Tim. vi. 5, 10, 17—20. The knowledge of the truth is ever the same, in every age, and every country; but the opposition of false notions of knowledge, has filled the world with controversy and confusion. Further evidence of this will appear in the following history of particular churches, and of the oppressions which many have endured.

CHAPTER XXXVI.

THE FIRST PRINCIPLES OF NEW ENGLAND ABOUT BAPTISM.—THE HISTORY OF THE FIRST BAPTIST CHURCH IN BOSTON FOR FIFTY YEARS.—AND TO THIS TIME.—OF MR. ROOTS.—THE BEGINNING OF THEIR SECOND CHURCH.—THEIR HISTORY FOR TWENTY YEARS.—AND TO THE PRESENT TIME.—OF THE PUBLICATIONS OF THEIR MINISTERS.—OF THE BAPTIST CHURCHES IN THE COUNTY OF NORFOLK.—OF THE FIRST IN MIDDLEBOROUGH.—OF THEIR HISTORY TO THIS TIME.—OF THE SECOND IN MIDDLEBOROUGH. — OF THE THIRD. — OF BRIDGEWATER.—OF MARSHFIELD.—AND CARVER.[1]

Our fathers fled to America for religious purity and liberty, with a persuasion that each believer stands in the same relation to his children, as Abraham did to his, in the covenant of circumcision. But soon after they came to Boston, a difficulty arose about their children who were grown up so as to have families and yet were not true believers themselves, so as to bring their children upon their own faith to baptism. The church in Dorchester wrote to the church in Boston, to inquire whether a grandfather might not bring such infants? Mr. Cotton and his church concluded that he might, only with two cautions. " 1. That the grandchild, baptized by the right of the grandfather's covenant, be committed to the grandfather's education. 2. That the parents of the child, do not thereby take occasion to neglect the due and seasonable preparation of themselves for entrance into covenant with God and his church." This was dated December 16, 1634, about four years after Boston was planted. And on October 11, 1648, Mr. Cotton wrote to a friend in England, and said, " Though they be not fit to make such a profession of visible faith as to admit them to the Lord's table, yet they may make profession full enough to receive them to

---

[1]This chapter and those which succeed it, are a review, with many enlargements, of the history of particular churches, already given. As being not a continuation of the history, but virtually an appendix, though for many reasons the most valuable part of the work, they are put in smaller type.—ED.

baptism, or to the same state Ishmael stood in after the circumcision."[1] But Ishmael and Esau were both excluded from the covenant of circumcision long before the passover was instituted, of which servants were obliged to partake, as well as all the children of Israel. And Mr. Henry Dunstar, the first president of Cambridge college, saw their mistake in these things so clearly, that he boldly preached against infant baptism, and for believers' baptism, in the pulpit at Cambridge in 1653, the year after Messrs. Clarke, Holmes and Crandal were imprisoned at Boston, only for worshipping God by themselves, without leave from the ruling powers in the Massachusetts. But those powers compelled Mr. Dunstar to resign his office in the college ; and he removed out of their jurisdiction, and spent the rest of his days, even five years, at Scituate in Plymouth colony.

In the year 1655, Thomas Gould, of Charlestown, was so fully convinced that infants had no right to baptism, that he refused to bring his child thereto ; but for this he was censured in the church and prosecuted in their courts, until some Baptists came to him out of England, and they formed a Baptist church there, May 28, 1665, and Gould became their pastor. But the leaders of this church were fined and imprisoned, from time to time, until a sentence of banishment was passed against Thomas Gould, William Turner and John Farnum ; and because they would not banish themselves, they were imprisoned at Boston, in July, 1668, where they were confined about a year. But in the Indian war, seven years after, a company of those Baptists were sent out against the enemy, and Turner was their captain, and sacrificed his life for the government by which he had been persecuted. And in January, 1678, this church had increased so much, that they concluded to build them a meeting-house in Boston, though with so much caution as not to let the ruling powers know what it was designed for, until they met in it, February 15, 1679. But in May following a law was made, to forbid all persons to erect or make use of any house for public worship, without license from the ruling powers, upon penalty of forfeiting the house and land, and all private ways leading to it. And a synod was called in September, who gave it as their opinion, that suffering those Baptists to meet for worship by themselves, was a cause of the judgments of God upon the land ; therefore their meeting-house was nailed up by order of court in March, 1680, and Dr. Increase Mather published a book against them the same month, in which he said, " Antipædobaptism is a blasted error."[2] But he and his brethren met with such cruel oppression soon after, as moved them to procure a special act, to exempt Boston from any compulsive power for the support of any religious ministers. And he and his son Cotton Mather, with Mr. John Webb, went into the

[1]Increase Mather on the first principles of New England about baptism, 1675, pp. 2, 3, 6.
[2]Divine Right of Infant Baptism, p. 20.

house which their party had nailed up, and assisted in ordaining a Baptist minister, as a pastor of that Baptist church. Mr. Gould was a pastor of that church, from its beginning until his death about 1676 ; and he was such an example of meekness, faith and patience as is seldom found. Mr. Isaac Hull was called to the pastoral office in that church in the time of their sufferings, and continued therein till 1689, and how much longer, their records do not discover. Mr. John Russell, who suffered imprisonment for the cause of conscience, was ordained a pastor of that church, July 28, 1679, and he wrote a defence of their cause in 1680, which was printed in London, with a preface by six noted ministers there. But he was taken away by death, December 21, 1680, much lamented by his people ; and his posterity are numerous and respectable in these parts to this day. Their next minister was Mr. John Emblen, from England, who ministered to them from 1684, to 1699, or thereabouts. He appears to have been well esteemed among them, as far as I could obtain any information. After his death the church wrote again to England for a minister, but obtained only a respectful letter from thence. They wrote also to Mr. William Screven in South Carolina, who had been of this church, but he could not leave his flock there. Therefore in 1708, they called Mr. Ellis Callender to be their minister, who had been a member of their church ever since 1699, and he continued in high esteem among them until 1726.

His son, Mr. Elisha Callender, was wrought upon by divine grace very early, and joined that church on August 10, 1713 ; and he was educated in the university at Cambridge, and was ordained a pastor of that church May 21, 1718, by the help of three Congregational ministers in Boston, before named. And this transaction, with his correspondence with friends in England, and other information, moved Thomas Hollis, Esq., of London, to become the greatest benefactor to the university at Cambridge of any one man in the world. Mr. Elisha Callender was a very faithful and successful minister of the gospel, until he fell asleep in Jesus, March 31, 1738. Mr. Jeremy Condy was educated in the college at Cambridge, where he took his first degree in 1726 ; after which he went over to England, from whence he was called by this church, and was ordained their pastor February 14, 1739. But he had quite other sentiments, concerning the nature and power of the gospel, than those of his predecessors ; and he opposed the powerful work which came on in Boston the year after he was ordained, and another church was formed in a way of separation from him ; and the First Baptist church in Boston was in a declining condition, until they called and settled Mr. Samuel Stillman as their pastor, January 9, 1765, when Mr. Condy resigned his office, and lived a retired life, well esteemed among his acquaintance, until he died, August 9, 1768, aged fifty-nine. A revival of religion began in that church in 1769, which caused the addition of eighty members in three years, to a church which had not seventy members before. The Congregational ministers of Boston were much alarmed at this increase of the Baptists, and published several things to guard against them, and to draw young people into their own communion. One of them had published a book against the work of God in 1743, when many were drawing off from unconverted ministers, and then he said, "No man becomes a minister, or a communicant in our churches, until he hath been severely examined about his *regeneration*, as well as conversation." But he published another book in 1772, to guard against the Baptists, in which he said, "The divinely appointed way, in which persons become members of the visible church of Christ, is utterly inconsistent with the supposition, that, in order to their being so, they must be the subjects of *saving faith*, or judged to be so."[1] Thus do men condemn themselves. When the American war began in Boston, this church was much scattered, and their pastor removed to Philadelphia ; and after his return and his brethren, earthly-mindedness greatly prevailed, until the year 1785, when religion was again revived, which added fifty members more in three years. In 1790, a happy work of the Spirit of God was again granted in Boston, and above seventy members were received into the First Baptist church there in about two years, and their present number is two hundred and sixty-seven, besides all that have died, have been dismissed or excluded.

Another minister, who is a member of this church, is not to be forgotten. Mr. Peter Philanthropos Roots, A. M., was born at Symsbury, in Connecticut, where his father was minister,[2] March 27, 1765. But as many of the people disliked his father's searching preaching, he requested a dismission, which was granted, and he went and settled at Rutland, in Vermont, where a happy work of grace was granted in 1783, when his son experienced a change of heart ; and he was educated in Dartmouth College, after which he was licensed to preach in the Congregational way, in March, 1790. He had many scruples about infant baptism while he was at college, and they followed him afterwards, until he made them known to the most able ministers of his own denomination, desiring them to shew him a divine warrant for that practice, if they could, as he had no desire to become a Baptist, if he could avoid it with a clear conscience. But as they could not satisfy him, and he obtained full conviction that a credible profession of saving faith was a necessary qualification for baptism, he came to Boston, and was baptized and joined the First Baptist church there, June 3, 1792. And the church being satisfied with his qualifications for an itinerant minister, called others to assist in his ordination at Providence, September 4, 1792, the day before the Commencement at the university there ; and in the winter following he travelled and preached the gospel through all the States as far as Georgia. And Mr. Roots has devoted himself to the work ever since, often preaching to destitute churches in various parts of our country, and he has been received to preach in the pulpits of many Con-

[1] See pp. 57, 171.   [2] Mr. Benaiah Roots.

gregational ministers, as well as in places where no steady worship had been maintained; and as inquiry was often made, why he embraced the Baptist principles, he published a book to give the reasons thereof near the close of 1794.

As the Second Baptist church in Boston began in a way of separation from the First, they gave them the following reasons for it :—

1. We have for a considerable time been dissatisfied with Mr. Condy's doctrine, being of opinion, from many discourses which we have heard him deliver from the pulpit, and from conversation with him at several times, that he is what we call an Arminian, in that we apprehend he holds general redemption, is a free-willer, holds to falling from grace, and denies original sin. We mean by his denying original sin, that he softens, moderates and explains away the guilt, malignity, corruption and depravity of human nature exactly as the high Arminian clergy forever do. 2. We conceive that he denies the doctrines of election and predestination. If Mr. Condy does not deny these doctrines, we freely confess that we do not understand the scope or design of his sermons, nor of his conversation when we have heard him discourse on these points of our faith. He publicly owned at a church meeting, that he never had preached election, and believed he never should; alleging as a reason for it, that if he should preach up election, he should offend the greater part of his church. This excuse we look upon to be no sufficient reason for his declining to instruct his people in this important doctrine, but it rather ought to have animated him, if he believed this doctrine himself, to set his church right in an article of such importance. We hope we need not take up your time nor our own in proving that it is the indispensable duty of a faithful minister of Christ, to declare to his church the whole counsel of God, let who will be offended thereat; so that we conclude that Mr. Condy does not believe the doctrine of election himself. 3. We are enough dissatisfied with his way of thinking on that great, that most solemn doctrine of regeneration. Whenever we have heard him discourse on the new birth, his sermons were so illgrounded, so intermixed with man's free-will agency, and so widely different from what our Lord taught and intended thereby, that we cannot avoid questioning whether he ever experienced the saving operation of that most important doctrine in his own soul. 4. We were sufficiently affrighted at a declaration in one of his sermons, that Christians cannot know or distinguish the operation of the Spirit of God upon their souls, from the operations of their own minds. This assertion we look upon to be of the most dangerous tendency; a striking at the root and main evidence of the Christian consolation and hope. . . . . We are now willing to return to our former places with you, if we can find that your principles and practices are the same with those on which, by the grace of God, our church was first founded. But if your articles of faith are, in fact, contrary to those on which this church was first established, you cannot, we think, justly blame us for separating from you, and uniting with others who are like minded with ourselves. The Lord give you understanding in all things, and may your hearts be directed into the love of God, and to be ready always to give an account of the hope that is in you, with meekness and fear. The grace of our Lord Jesus Christ be with you all.

JAMES BOUND,	THOMAS BOUCHER,
JOHN DABNEY,	JOHN PROCTOR.

Boston, September 29, 1742.

28

The first two of these men came formerly from England, the third from Wales, and the fourth was a schoolmaster in Boston. Mr. Ephraim Bound, son to James, met with a happy change in those times, and was baptized by Elder Moulton, of Brimfield, and he began to preach the gospel in this new society. And as they obtained no satisfaction from the old church, James Bound, John Procter, Ephraim Bosworth, John Dabney, Thomas Boucher, Ephraim Bound and Thomas Lewis formed a new church in Boston, July 27, 1743, and elected Ephraim Bound as their pastor. ·His human learning was not great, but his powers of mind, and his spiritual teaching, made him an excellent teacher and minister of the gospel. But as most of the old Baptist ministers and churches in our country were prejudiced against the late revival of religion therein, these people found it difficult to obtain help in the ordination of their minister. Elder Wightman, of Groton, in Connecticut, was clear in that work, but he was advanced in years, and could not well travel so far as Boston; therefore this church sent some of their members to meet him in Warwick, where Mr. Bound was ordained, September 7, 1743, by the help of Elder Wightman, and Elder Greene, of Leicester. And many subjects of the late work of grace in the land joined this church in Boston, from Newton, Needham, Medfield, and other places. Deacon Ephraim Bosworth, of the town of Hull, having no children, gave this church a good estate, which they still enjoy. Also in the month of February, 1749, this church received the following generous donation from England, viz. :—From the Rev. John Gill, D. D., for the communion table, one large cup, four smaller ones, two dishes and two plates, also one large, rich damask table cloth; also seven complete sets of baptismal garments, namely, one for the minister, and three for men and three for women; also books to the amount of about fifty dollars. At the same time they received a further gift of forty-eight volumes of the late Rev. Mr. Hill's Sermons; (an Independent minister in London, successor to Dr. Ridgely.) Mr. Hill's sermons were sent by his father, the editor, to be given away at the discretion of the church. And after the great earthquake in 1755, Mr. Bound set up a weekly lecture, which was attended by many from all parts of the town; " and many owned him to be the instrument of their conversion, who yet joined to Pædobaptist churches; and he was greatly respected by people of various denominations, and especially by his own society. But in the midst of his usefulness, it pleased God to seize him with a paralytic disorder, in the morning of December 17, 1762, from which he never recovered, though he revived so as to preach a few sermons." Mr. Bound died, much lamented, though with great comfort in his own soul, June 18, 1765. This church had increased under his ministry to about a hundred and twenty members; and as soon as he was taken ill, they not only obtained occasional supplies from sister churches, but also sent for Mr. (now Dr.) Samuel Stillman,

from New Jersey. He was born in Pennsylvania, and educated in South
Carolina, where he was ordained ; but the climate not suiting his constitution, he came and preached for some time at Bordentown, in the Jersey,
from whence he came to Boston, and ministered a year to this church, and
then, in September, 1764, he went to the First Baptist church in Boston, in
which he has been a successful minister to this day.

The Second Baptist church in Boston being again left destitute, sought
and obtained some help from sister churches, and looked out for another
pastor, but could not obtain one in many years. Many of their old brethren were dead, and others were scattered into different parts of the land,
so that they feared a dissolution of their church. Such is the changing
state of things in this world, both as to our temporal and spiritual concerns ;
and happy are they who humble themselves under the mighty hand of God,
that he may exalt them in due time. Mr. John Davis paid this church a
visit in the fall of 1769, and at their request, he removed there from the
State of Delaware in May, and was ordained their pastor, September 9,
1770. He was educated in the college at Philadelphia, and was a man of
great powers of mind, which he exerted in a noble manner in the cause of
religious liberty, and for the welfare of our churches, until his health failed,
which led him to ask a dismission, which was granted, July 19, 1772, and
he sailed from Boston in August, and died near the Ohio, December 13,
1772, greatly lamented. Mr. Isaac Skillman, who was born in New Jersey, and educated at Princeton college, was the third pastor of this church,
from September, 1773, to October, 1787, when he went back to New Jersey, and is now the pastor of the Baptist church at Salem in that State.
Directly after his departure, this church called Mr. Thomas Gair to be their
pastor, who was born in Boston, educated in the college at Providence, and
ordained at Medfield, September 18, 1776, where he ministered to good
purpose for ten years. But then, as some of their ablest brethren were
dead, and peculiar difficulties arose in the church, they dismissed and recommended him ; and his labors were much blessed in Boston, until he was
suddenly called away by death, April 27, 1790. And it is very remarkable that two pastors of this church, Davis and Gair, each died in his 36th
year, and were the only ministers who had died out of the Warren Association since it was formed in 1767. In July after the decease of the latter, the church obtained a visit from Mr. Thomas Baldwin, who was born
at Norwich, in Connecticut, December 23, 1753, and ordained at Canaan
in New Hampshire, June 11, 1783, and preached with success in those
parts until he was now called to Boston, where he was installed the pastor
of this church, November 11, 1790. They had but forty-two members when
Mr. Skillman came there in 1773, and when he left them they had increased
to sixty-six, and when Mr. Gair died they had eighty-nine, and now have
one hundred and fifty-eight.

These churches in Boston have equal liberties with other denominations, and no man in that town has been compelled to support any minister that he did not personally choose, since the year 1693 ; but this liberty is wickedly denied to the generality of our towns in the country, contrary to the promise of our delegates at Congress in 1774.   Dr. Stillman preached the Election Sermon at Boston, May 26, 1779, when he clearly described the difference between civil States, and the government of the church of Christ, shewing that they ought to be entirely distinct.   Yet in the constitution of our government, which was formed the winter following, church and State are confounded together.   He had published four sermons in 1769, upon original sin, the efficacy of divine grace in conversion, justification alone by faith in the perfect righteousness of Christ, and the infinite importance of holy obedience to all the laws of Christ.   This was in the beginning of a happy revival of religion in Boston.   He has also published several other sermons and tracts since.   Mr. Gair published an Ordination Sermon, which he delivered at Cambridge in 1783 ; and also a circular letter in the minutes of the Warren Association.   Mr. Baldwin published a discourse in 1789, at the request of the Woodstock Association, to shew the reasons why the Baptist churches refuse to commune in the ordinance of the Supper with any who were only sprinkled in infancy.   Upwards of two years after, the Rev. Noah Worcester, of Thornton, (N. H.) published an answer to him, wherein he set up godly sincerity as the rule of communion, and not any external mode of baptism.   To this Mr. Baldwin replied, in March, 1794, which reply was so much esteemed, that it passed a second edition in about two months.   He proved plainly, that this controversy all turns upon these two questions. 1. Who are the subjects of baptism according to the law or Christ?   2. What is the mode or manner of the baptism which he hath instituted?   Mr. Worcester published another piece last winter, in which he refused to meet him upon this ground, saying, " The attempt would be to dissolve the distinction between the two denominations, rather than to open the way for a free communion between us, as two denominations. For I presume, that, were we agreed upon these two questions, we should not be two denominations."[1]   Very true ; and why should any be unwilling to have but one Lord, one faith, and one baptism?   Yet this author has now published above a hundred pages upon other things, while he refused to come to the point in hand.

Bellingham, in the county of Norfolk, was so abusively treated by Congregational ministers, that they have never settled one of them in that town in above forty years past.   The Baptist church there, was constituted October 15, 1750 ;[2] and Mr. Elnathan Wight was their first pastor, who was

---

[1] Worcester's Discussion, p. 8.

[2] A Baptist church of fifteen members was formed in Bellingham, November 23, 1737.   In 1742 and 1743 twelve were added to them, and in the latter year they built

ordained January 14, 1775, and was a faithful and useful minister there, until he was taken away by death, November 6, 1761, aged forty-six. Mr. Noah Alden was born in Middleborough, May 31, 1725, converted there in 1741, and was ordained at Stafford in Connecticut, June 5, 1755. But he was dismissed from thence, by the advice of a council, August 28, 1765, and he was installed at Bellingham, November 12, 1766, and continues their pastor to this day. Mr. Aaron Leland was raised up in this church, who is pastor of the Baptist church at Chester, in Vermont. Peace has generally been enjoyed in Bellingham, and they have been favored with several revivals of religion, though their church has never been very large. And the like may be said of the Baptist church in Wrentham, which was constituted in 1769.[1] William Williams, A. M., was ordained their pastor July 3, 1776. He was born in Pennsylvania, and was educated in Rhode Island College, being one of the first class therein, and he is now a Fellow of that corporation. He also keeps a Latin school, in which many young gentlemen have been fitted for the college. The Baptist church in Medfield was formed August 18, 1776, and Mr. Gair was ordained their pastor the next month, as was before observed. In 1787 their church had increased to eighty-one members; but in 1789 they dismissed fourteen members to form a church in Weston. Mr. Edward Clarke removed to Medfield soon after, and has preached there ever since, though he is not ordained. He sprang from the family who were fathers of the first Baptist church in Newport, which was formed in 1644; and he has published a reply to Messrs. Fish and Crane upon baptism, and some other things. The last Baptist church in the county of Norfolk was formed August 24, 1780, upon the borders of Stoughton and Braintree, where now is the town of Randolph. Former revivals of religion had been granted there, but the work was more powerful in that glorious year 1780. Joel Briggs, A. M., was born in Norton, April 15, 1757, educated in the college at Providence, and preached to this church about three years, before he was ordained their pastor, December 5, 1787. A powerful work was again wrought among them in 1790, which caused the addition of above twenty members to this church: and it extended its happy influence into Bridgewater and Abington.

The county of Plymouth, where our fathers began the settlement of New England, calls for our next attention. The first principles and measures of

a meeting-house. There is no record of the dissolution of this church; and it was held by Abial Fisher, D. D., for many years pastor in Bellingham, that the original church still continues. "Century Sermons, delivered in Bellingham in the year 1822," p. 6. Between 1743 and 1750 the church must have reached a low condition, if it did not lose its existence altogether. It is often impossible to decide whether a church became extinct, and another was afterwards formed in its stead, or whether it ceased active operations and was afterwards revived.—ED.

[1]September 29.—ED.

the first planters of the country, are as much retained here as in any part of the land.   And this may be a cause why no person has been hanged in the county of Plymouth for sixty years past.   The inhabitants are as much upon a level, and there are as few foreigners among them, as in any part of America.   The people are generally supported by their own labors, and not by the labor of others.   A powerful work of the Spirit of God in Middleborough, in and after 1741, prepared the way for the gathering of the first Baptist church in the county, in this town.   After the death of their minister in April, 1744, Judge Oliver, who came from Boston, with a few more leading men in Middleborough, shut the next minister whom the church chose, and two-thirds of the people, out of their meeting-house, and from the use of their ministerial lands.   And when a new precinct was constituted in February, 1743, consisting of part of Middleborough, and part of Bridgewater, the communicants therein were denied a dismission from the old churches for five years, lest if a church were formed in this precinct, they should call a minister whom the world did not like.   The communicants therefore set up a meeting without license from arbitrary ministers, in December, 1747, and formed a church here February 16, 1748, and ordained a pastor therein the 13th of April following.   But in the month between, their opponents held a parish meeting, and voted a large sum of money, to finish their meeting-house, and to hire other sort of preaching, and taxed the church and their minister, with the rest of the inhabitants, to pay it.   But after distress had been made upon several of them, it appeared in a trial at Plymouth court, that said money was voted at an illegal meeting, and the case was turned against their collector.   But they appealed to their Superior Court, and in the mean time sent an agent to Boston, and obtained an act of the legislature to establish said meeting as legal, and the Superior Court gave judgment against the defendant upon this act, which was passed after the suit was commenced in the first executive court.   And this shews that the temporal interest of no people can be secure, where one party of ministers are supported by tax and compulsion.

In August, 1749, a dispute about baptism was brought into this church, which was managed with an unhappy temper by many, and caused great difficulties among the people.   Nine members of this church, and one who was not a member, were baptized in September, and they set up a meeting from the church in October, because their minister and church did not immediately become Baptists, so as to obtain an exemption from taxes to Congregational ministers.   They went the next year and joined to old Baptist churches, and obtained such an exemption.   These things, with the unhappy temper which many discovered, caused a great fear in others that there was some secret iniquity in the Baptist principles, as tradition had long said there was.   But they were led by degrees, to distinguish between the truth of God, and the corruptions of men who profess a zeal for it;

and their minister was baptized in August, 1751, and others afterwards, who yet held communion with those who were only sprinkled in infancy, until they were convinced that this was a practical saying that they were baptized when they believed in their consciences they were not. Therefore they formed a Baptist church here, January 16, 1756, and their former minister was installed their pastor the 23d of June following, in which office he is still continued. He was born at Norwich, in Connecticut, January 9, 1724, converted in 1741, and began to preach in September, 1746. This was then the only Baptist church in an extent of country of above a hundred miles long, from Bellingham to the end of Cape Cod, and near fifty miles wide, between Boston and Rehoboth. Their number was small for many years, though they had some revivings from time to time, until such a work came on in 1779, as increased their number in three years, from fifty-nine to one hundred and thirty-eight. And in forty years they have buried thirty-four, dismissed sixty-one, and excluded twelve, while ninety-one remain. Seven members of this church have been ordained to the work of the gospel ministry, namely, James Mellen, Abner Lewis, Asa Hunt, Elijah Codding, Job Macomber, Samuel Nelson and David Leonard; the last of whom was ordained as an itinerant, December 17, 1794. He was born in Bridgewater, and educated at the college in Providence, where he took his first degree in 1792. His brother, Zenas Lockwood Leonard, graduated at that college in 1794, and was soon approbated by this church to preach the gospel, and has been accepted in that work in various parts of the country. Stephen Smith Nelson was a class-mate with him, and he was approbated as a gospel minister by this church last May. He is great-grandson to the first Baptist in Middleborough, of whom we shall say more presently. The pastor of this church published a discourse upon an internal call to preach the gospel, in 1754; and he has published the most since of any Baptist in America; but their value is left entirely to the judgment of the public.

The Second Baptist church in Middleborough was formed in the following manner:—Thomas Nelson, who was born here in June, 1675, discovered such evils in the second minister of the town, as caused him to examine the Scriptures concerning their principles; and finding nothing therein for infant baptism, he went and joined the First Baptist church in Swansea. In the year 1717 he removed into the south part of Middleborough, called Assawamset, his being the first English family who settled there. Baptist ministers frequently preached at his house, until he got one to preach there steadily, in the spring of 1753. This was Mr. Ebenezer Hinds, who was born in Bridgewater, July 29, 1719, and began to preach in 1749. About four miles southwestward from this meeting, in a place called Beech-woods, Mr. James Mead was ordained the pastor of a Separate church, October 3, 1751, and continued in that office until he died, October 2, 1756.

The majority of that church became Baptists soon after, and joined with Mr. Hinds's hearers in forming a Baptist church, November 16, 1757, and he was ordained their pastor, January 26, 1758.[1] They purchased a house and farm for the ministry, and built a convenient meeting-house forty-two miles from Boston. Mr. Nelson died before this church was constituted, aged eighty, but his widow lived to commune with them in the ordinance of the Supper, after she was a hundred years old. She died December 7, 1782, being a hundred and five years and seven months old ; and she had then living of her posterity three hundred and thirty-seven, as near as the account could be collected ; for some of them were in Nova Scotia. William, Samuel and Ebenezer Nelson, three of her grandsons, are now ordained Baptist ministers. Mr. Hathaway, a minister in Freetown, also sprang from this church. Such a revival of religion was granted among them in 1773, as increased the church to a hundred and four members the next year. But a number of them were dismissed to form a church in Freetown soon after, and they never have been so large since. Mr. Hinds has had two wives, and fifteen children, of whom he has buried eight ; and the great expenses in his family, with different sentiments about the support of ministers and the government of the church, have caused many contentions among them, which have reduced the church to a much smaller number than they once had ; yet he is still continued in his office there.

The Third Baptist church in Middleborough sprang chiefly from the First. The lands near the corners of Middleborough, Rochester, Wareham and Carver, were but little cultivated until 1754 ; and Baptist ministers were called to preach there from time to time afterwards, and persons from thence joined our church, until they obtained a dismission, and ten persons were formed into a church there, August 4, 1761.[2] Mr. Ebenezer Jones had preached to them for a while before, and he was ordained their pastor the 28th of October following. A revival of religion came on among them the next spring, which prevailed through the year, and spread its happy influence into many other societies, the good fruits whereof are visible to this day. Yet some evil behavior in Mr. Jones's wife, which drew him into a snare, caused a great division in the church and society in 1763, which terminated in his removal from them ;[3] and he travelled and preached in

[1]Mr. Hinds was baptized by Mr. E. Moulton, and joined himself to the Second Baptist church in Boston, March 3, 1751.

[2]Six were from the First church, one from the Second, the other three had probably not been previously connected with any Baptist church.—ED.

[3]The chief offence of Mrs. Jones seems to have been the spreading of evil reports against the deacon of the church. These coming to the light, involved the whole church in dissension. On page 271, the blame in connection with this difficulty is charged to other parties than the pastor and his family. A letter of Mr. Backus to a son of Mr. Jones, written in 1805, shows that both that representation and the one above given were correct. He writes :—" Gospel rule was greatly disregarded on

various parts of our land, until he died in the county of Albany, in September, 1791. This church was in a furnace of affliction for several years; but in the spring of 1770, they obtained Mr. Asa Hunt to preach to them, and he was ordained their pastor, October 30, 1771.[1] He was born in Braintree, in July, 1744, and preached in Raynham for a year before he went to them, when he joined the First Baptist church in Middleborough. His preaching was very acceptable, and they gave him a good place for a settlement, beside the use of the ministerial lot; and they built a convenient meeting-house, above eleven miles from the First Baptist meeting-house in this town. And such a work of the Spirit of God began among them in March, 1780, as caused the addition of a hundred and thirteen members to their church by September, 1782, when they had a hundred and ninety-four in all.[2] But in the time of great changes in our country about money and worldly property, Mr. Hunt entangled himself so much in the affairs of this life, as caused much unhappiness, and he insisted upon a dismission from his church, which they granted, though with reluctance, in December, 1789. He had been a journey into Virginia, where he preached to good purpose the year before, and he travelled into New Jersey and Pennsylvania after his dismission; but he never removed his family. He was called to visit his eldest son, who was sick with the dysentery in the college at Providence, where the father was seized with the same distemper, and died there, September 20, 1791. His son recovered, while he was taken away; and his memory is precious to many, notwithstanding his imperfections. The church was in low circumstances for some time, and young people got to be so extravagant in vanity, that they could hardly be kept civil in times of public worship. But the church prevailed with Mr. Samuel Nelson to remove there to preach to them, in May, 1793. And in the beginning of the next month, such a divine influence was granted, that old Christians became all alive in religion, and such a concern for the soul and eternity appeared among old and young through all the busiest time in the summer, that they had frequent and crowded meetings, in season and out of season, without the least disturbance from vain persons, which before were so troublesome. Mr. Nelson was ordained their pastor January 16, 1794; and above thirty were added to their church in about a year. He was born in this town April 6, 1745, and is still useful in this church. Mr.

both sides. .... Your father often confessed his faults. .... His wife also appeared to repent of her faults, and had hope in her death. I preached at her funeral, August 13, 1766. Both of them were of good moral character and of Christian behavior, only in the things which I have mentioned."—Ed.

[1] Mr. Backus preached at Mr. Hunt's ordination, from II Cor. iii. 6. The sermon was published with the title, " Evangelical Ministers described, and distinguished from Legalists."—Ed.

[2] See pp. 271, 272.—Ed.

John Tripp and Mr. Simeon Coombs have been of this church, who are now ordained ministers in other places.

A few persons in the west part of Bridgewater had been members of the First Baptist church in Middleborcugh near thirty years, before a happy revival of religion began there in 1779, when their number increased so much that they were encouraged to hold meetings among themselves, from time to time, until sixteen members were dismissed, and a church was formed there, June 7, 1785. Mr. George Robinson had preached to them for a year before, and he became their pastor. He was born in Attleborough in November, 1754, and was ordained at Killingly, in Connecticut, November 13, 1776, where he ministered for more than seven years. But such difficulties then arose in their church, partly occasioned by the public disorders in our country, that they called a council, and, by their advice, dismissed and recommended him, and he removed to Bridgewater, where many blessings have been granted under his ministry. Mr. Seth Howard was baptized there, March 10, 1779, and was one of the first members of this church, and he continued in their communion, until he died in a joyful manner, October 11, 1794, aged nearly ninety-two. Mr. Eleazar Snow, who was born in Bridgewater, July 25, 1701, also joined the First Baptist church in Middleborough, and was then one of the first members of this church, and is now the oldest man in Bridgewater.[1]

Some persons of Marshfield joined the First Baptist church in Boston, before Elder Callender died in 1738, and others joined their Second church in Elder Bound's time; but their number was small, until Deacon Josiah Eames invited Baptist ministers to preach there in 1773,[2] and a meeting was set up, in which Thomas Eames began to preach. But these

---

[1] Mr. Snow, full of divine consolation, died February 18, 1796.

[2] Mr. Backus visited Marshfield, December 24, 1773, and labored there a week. He writes in his Diary: "I learn that Mr. Callender of Boston baptized some persons of this town at Boston, near forty years ago, and that two men named Macomber, and one Mrs. Briant joined Mr. Bound's church, above twenty years ago. Deacon Josiah Eames and his wife, Thomas Eames and his wife, David Thomas Junior and his wife, Thomas Joyce and his wife, and some others, seem not only to be convinced that the parish worship is very corrupt, but also that the Baptist principles are right; were very thankful for my coming, and there is a hopeful prospect of an agreeable society being formed here." June 5, 1774, Elder Hunt of Middleborough, baptized in Marshfield. Thomas Eames, Grace, his wife, and Rebecca, his mother; Thomas Joyce and Lucy, his wife; Hannah Williamson, and Mary Thomas. March 5, 1781, Elder Hunt wrote:—"At Marshfield, last week, I preached five sermons, and baptized six persons. The work increases. I left a number under powerful convictions. The handful of brethren are joyful and lively, and much encouraged. There is considerable opposition; but some persons of note are brought to favor the work." Mr. Hunt labored again in Marshfield in the revival in 1786. Eleven of the constituent members of the church in Marshfield were dismissed from his church in Middleborough.—ED.

men removed away, and the last of them is now a pastor of a church in Islesborough in the county of Hancock ; and the Baptists in Marshfield were in low circumstances, until a revival was granted in 1786, and they built them a meeting-house the next year, and a church was formed among them, June 11, 1788. They received assistance from neighboring ministers, from time to time, until Mr. Joseph Butterfield came to preach there steadily in the fall of 1791, and he was ordained their pastor, May 16, 1792. His gifts were promising, and his hearers increased for some time ; but from imprudent conduct, he proceeded to the use of deceitful means to obtain a temporal living. Therefore a mutual council was called May 8, 1793, which advised the church to depose him from his office, which they did, and he confessed it to be just. He was then forgiven and restored as a brother, and recommended to another church, and he removed to Weston, and lately into the District of Maine. They have experienced many trying things since at Marshfield, but it is hoped that all will work for their spiritual good.

The town of Carver was formerly the south parish in Plympton, between Middleborough and Plymouth. Their first meeting-house was built near the north end of the parish, because most of the people lived there. But when the south end was also planted and cultivated, the inhabitants claimed a right of having it removed into the centre ; and because this was denied them, they built another meeting house towards the south end and obtained occasional preaching in it for some years. At length they got Baptist ministers to preach there, and their principles prevailed, until a Baptist church was formed there, July 13, 1791,[1] and Mr. John Tripp[2] was ordained their pastor the 28th of September following. Most of the first members were dismissed from the Third Baptist church in Middleborough, as others have been since. And a happy revival of religion in both churches in 1793, caused a large increase of this church. Mr. Tripp preached an Ordination Sermon at Barnstable, April 29, 1795, which was printed soon after at Boston.

In January, 1793, a great revival of religion began in Plymouth, the first town that was planted in New England ; and it prevailed to a greater degree than any work of the Spirit of God has done there since the year 1742. Their minister, the Rev. Dr. Robbins, was much engaged in it, and in the summer of 1794, he baptized one woman by immersion, which was a new thing in that town.

[1]This church was formed of nine men and three women.—ED.

[2]John Tripp was licensed by the Third Baptist church in Middleborough, September 18, 1787. Elder Backus preached his Ordination Sermon.—ED.

CHAPTER XXXVII.

An Account of the First Church in Swansea.—Of the Second Church there.—Of two in Rehoboth that are dissolved.—Of Six Churches now there.—Of Mr. Winchester.—Of Mr. Ellis. —Of the last Baptist Church in Rehoboth.—Of Taunton—Of Attleborough.—Of Dighton.—Freetown. — New Bedford and Dartmouth. — Raynham. — Harwich. — Barnstable. — Martha's Vineyard.

The first Baptist church in the Massachusetts is in Swansea, which was originally in Plymouth colony, the first in New England. Mr. John Miles was a father of the Baptist churches in Wales, which began in 1649 ; and he was pastor of the Baptist church in Swansea in that country, until he was ejected from thence by a cruel act of parliament, which turned about two thousand teachers out of their places in 1662. He then came over to our country, and brought their book of records with him, which is in Swansea to this day, containing many things concerning the first Baptist churches in Wales, that are nowhere else to be found, and which have been lately transcribed and sent over to them. Nicholas Tanner, Obadiah Bowen, John Thomas, and others, also came over to this country ; and one of Bowen's posterity is now Chancellor of the university at Providence.[1] A Baptist church was formed in Rehoboth in 1663, and Mr. Miles was their pastor ; and four years after, they obtained a grant of the town of Swansea, from the legislature at Plymouth ; and there have been none but Baptist churches in that town to this day. Mr. Miles often visited and labored with his brethren at Boston, in the time of their sufferings ; and he continued the faithful pastor of the church in Swansea, until he fell asleep there, in a good old age, February 3, 1683. Mr. Samuel Luther, who had been a representative for Swansea in their legislature, and was otherwise useful in the town, was ordained a pastor of this church, July 22, 1685, by the

---

[1] Hon. Jabez Bowen.—Ed.

assistance of the elders Hull and Emblen of Boston; and he was much esteemed at home and abroad, until he died in 1717; and his posterity are numerous to this day.   Mr. Ephraim Wheaton, who lived within the bounds of Rehoboth, had been a colleague with him about thirteen years, and he was a faithful and successful minister until he died, April 26, 1734, aged seventy-five.   He baptized and received fifty members into his church in five years after a revival began in 1718, of which he wrote an account to Mr. Hollis in London.[1]   Mr. Samuel Maxwell was ordained a colleague with him, April 18, 1733; but he was unsteady in his sentiments, and in 1738, he embraced the opinion of keeping the seventh day of the week as the Sabbath, which caused his dismission from this church, April 15, 1739.[2] Elder Benjamin Herrington, formerly of Narragansett, was their next pastor, and was installed in this church, August 18, 1742, and he had a crowded audience for several years; but then he was accused of the sin of uncleanness, and he went off to Canterbury in Connecticut, where he preached to a few people, and lived in obscurity to old age.   In March, 1748, Mr. Jabez Wood, of Middleborough, was called to preach to this church, and he was ordained their pastor, September 5, 1751.   He was grandson to Mr. Thomas Nelson; but as the old gentleman judged that Wood had made use of unjust and deceitful measures to obtain that place, where was a good farm for the ministry, he removed his membership to the First Baptist church in Rehoboth, and others went to other churches; and the first church in Swansea was in a declining condition, until Elder Wood asked and received a dismission in 1779, and he removed into Vermont, where he died in 1794.   But as the enemy had burnt their meeting-house, and house for the ministry at Warren, three miles off, in May, 1778, the two churches agreed for the present to meet at Swansea, and Elder Thompson was received into this church, October 7, 1779, and has been their pastor ever since.   And such a rain of righteousness was granted there in 1780, as caused the addition of above ninety members to that church in two years, and they have had other revivals since.

The Second church in Swansea was formed upon different principles from the First, and they held the laying on of hands upon every member as a term of communion, and did not sing in their public worship.   Men who removed from Providence, and from other places, set up worship by themselves there about 1680, and continued it until they formed a church, and Mr. Thomas Barnes was ordained their pastor in 1693; and he was

[1]See Vol. I, p. 510.
[2]See p. 275. A letter from Mr. Maxwell to Elisha Callender shows that at one time he was greatly troubled, and greatly troubled his church, upon the question of infant baptism, he having publicly declared that he had been " much exercised with doubting whether or no infants, though not particularly expressed, might not be baptized in some of those households."—Ed.

well esteemed in his place, until he died, June 8, 1706. Samson Mason was a soldier in Cromwell's army, and he came over to America upon the turn of times in England, and settled in Rehoboth, and his posterity are now as numerous as, perhaps, those of any man who came to our country in his day, and they have had the chief lead in this church. His sons were Noah, Samson, James, John, Samuel, Joseph, Isaac, Pelatiah and Benjamin. James and John went to Boston, but six of the others lived in Rehoboth and Swansea, until the youngest of the six was seventy years old. Isaac Mason was ordained a deacon in this church, at the same time that Barnes was ordained their pastor, and he lived to January 25, 1742. His brother Joseph was ordained their pastor in July, 1709, and continued so till he died, May 19, 1748. Mr. John Peirce was ordained a colleague with him, October 19, 1715, and died September 8, 1750, being each of them near ninety, and their memory is precious to their posterity. Mr. Pelatiah Mason was born in March, 1669, and died in March, 1763, and three of his sons have been pastors of this church. Elder Job Mason was born February 28, 1695, ordained May 22, 1738, and died July 17, 1775. His character as a judicious man, a good preacher, and an exemplary walker, was high among his acquaintance. Elder Russel Mason was born April 22, 1714, ordained November 2, 1752, and is now able to preach frequently, and to discharge other duties of his office to the acceptance of his brethren. Elder John Mason was born in October, 1716, ordained March 26, 1788, and is well esteemed in his office. In the mean time, as their church has greatly increased in latter years, and they had many who joined it from distant places, and gifted men were raised up among them, they ordained many elders. Elder Benjamin Mason was ordained September 15, 1784, Elder Nathaniel Cole, December 12, 1787, and Elder Philip Slade, October 15, 1788. Elder Cole is now settled in Connecticut, while the others remain in this church in Swansea. It is also to be observed, that a church in Rehoboth sprang from this church in 1753, and a large part of another church ten years after to go to Nova Scotia. When all North America was ceded to Great Britain, Nathan Mason and his wife, Thomas Lewis and his wife, Oliver Mason and his wife, with Experience Baker, of this church, and Benjamin Mason and his wife, Charles Seamans and his wife, Gilbert Seamans and his wife, from other churches, were formed into a church, and Nathan Mason was ordained their pastor, April 21, 1763, and they went and settled at the head of the Bay of Fundy. But after some years they removed back to New England, and most of them went and settled in Berkshire, in the Massachusetts. It is also to be observed, that the powerful work of grace which was wrought in this country, under the ministry of men who held to infant baptism, and who had oppressed the Baptists, was attended with such evil reports as prejudiced the Baptists against the work for many years. But some ministers from

New Jersey came and preached among the Baptists in these parts, in and after 1754, which served to remove those prejudices, in some measure. And in 1756, Colonel Andrew Cole, of Swansea, invited some of our new ministers to preach at his house, and from time to time afterwards. And though these Baptist churches had received members by a general confession of their faith, yet in a great revival which began in the fall of 1771, a particular relation of experiences of an inward change of heart was introduced, which produced powerful effects upon many. Several hundred persons were added to the Baptist churches in Swansea and Rehoboth within two years after. The work was still greater in and after 1780, and singing in public worship was soon after introduced into the Second church in Swansea. But as they still held laying on of hands as a term of communion, a number drew off, and formed another church, and ordained Mr. Michael Eddy as their pastor, in August, 1785 ; though it is since dissolved, and he removed to Newport in 1790, where he is still useful.

Rehoboth is a large town, extending from Taunton and Dighton to Providence, about twelve miles ; and in 1791, there were four thousand, seven hundred and ten persons therein, and ten religious societies, which is more than we have in any other town of their numbers in these parts. Cruel oppression, on the one hand, and an abuse of liberty, on the other, have been the cause of it. Many had joined with the Baptists in Swansea, from time to time, until Mr. John Comer came and assisted in forming a church in Rehoboth. Some account of him is in Volume I, pages 496, 497 ; Volume II, pages 16—22, 28—31. He was an excellent preacher of the gospel, and an eminent instrument of reviving doctrinal and practical religion in Newport, for six years before he removed to Rehoboth in August, 1731 ; and a Baptist church was formed there, January 20, 1732, and he became their pastor, and it increased to ninety-five members in less than two years. And in that time he went and labored in Sutton, Leicester, Middleborough and other places. But he exerted his powers so much in this noble cause, that he fell into a consumption, and died joyfully, May 23, 1734, before he was thirty years old. His son is now a member of the Baptist church in Warren, and he lent me his father's diary, and other writings, which have been very serviceable in our history. Nathaniel Millard was ordained the next minister of this church, June 24, 1736. But his principles and conduct were corrupt, and he was dismissed in 1742, after which he went off with another woman instead of his wife. And as Mr. Maxwell had retracted his opinion concerning the Sabbath, this church called him to be their pastor, in October, 1745. But in about three years, Congregational ministers, who had oppressed the Baptists, had invited him to preach for them, and he yielded so much to them that this church dismissed him, and he published a complaint about it in 1749.[1] He often

---

[1] See pp. 275, 434.—Ed.

preached in other places, and was esteemed as a pious man, and lived to a great age, but never had the charge of any other church.[1] In the mean time, a Second Baptist church was formed in the northeast part of Rehoboth,[2] and Mr. Richard Round was ordained their pastor, July 13, 1743; and in nine years it increased to forty members. He was one of the seals of Mr. Comer's ministry, and preached the gospel faithfully, until his health failed, and he removed to the south part of the town, for the benefit of the sea air. And about that time a division took place in both churches, and a part of both joined together at their first place of worship, and Elder Round was their pastor until he died, May 18, 1768, aged sixty-two. His character as a minister of the gospel, and as a pious man, was very good. Those churches are since dissolved.

Mr. John Hicks was born in Rehoboth, May 10, 1712, and became a member of the First Baptist church there, and then a preacher therein, until they gave him a call to be their pastor; but he did not accept it, because many of the church appeared to him to be unsound in principle, and to oppose the power of godliness. But after much labor, a new church was formed, and Mr. Hicks was ordained their pastor, November 10, 1762; and in the glorious year 1780, they had a hundred and six members.[3] Mr. Nathaniel Round, brother to Richard, was a member of this church, and called to preach the gospel therein; and on May 11, 1768, he was ordained as a minister of the gospel, to go and labor in Nova Scotia, with a people who went from these parts. He went accordingly, and was a successful laborer there for several years, and then he removed back, and settled in the east part of Attleborough, and preached occasionally round the country, until he died at home, July 18, 1781, in the sixty-fourth year of his age. Another church was raised out of this, in the following manner. A powerful work began among them in the fall of 1771, and Elder Hicks baptized forty persons, and then was taken sick in the winter, and Mr. Winchester came and baptized twenty more; and such power appeared to attend his

---

[1]This First Baptist church in Rehoboth was known as the Oak Swamp church. It had thirty constituent members, thirteen men and seventeen women, all dismissed from the church in Swansea. John Comer was publicly installed as their pastor, January 26, 1732. A revival commenced immediately. Converts were baptized in March, and every subsequent month of the year,—forty in all.

Mr. Millard had been a deacon in this church before he was ordained its pastor. —Ed.

[2]This church was organized April 14, 1743. It consisted of nine men and nine women.—Ed.

[3]This church was organized with fifteen male members. They joined the Warren Association in 1780. In their letter to that body, they say:—"It was a low time with us before the reformation; but the Lord was remarkably good to appear once more for our relief in that he hath poured out his Holy Spirit to the comforting and quickening of the saints, and the conviction of sinners; there being forty-one added since the fall past."—Ed.

29

ministry, that many were taken with the opinion, that baptism by immersion ought not to be held as a term of communion in the church. A council was called upon it, in September, 1772, and they who were not convinced by them, formed another church, and ordained Mr. Jacob Hicks as their pastor, January 20, 1773. He is the eldest son of their old pastor, and was born January 1, 1740. This division caused much unhappiness for many years; but both societies have usually held their worship together in late times, and they now meet in the same house that was first built for Mr. Comer's church. Elder John Hicks is now so old and infirm as not to be able to preach, but he appears still steadfast in the faith and hope of the gospel. His son has none in his church at home but those who have been buried in baptism, and seems to have almost given up occasional communion with others; and so have other churches, with which he is connected. For as they communed with those who were only sprinkled in infancy, because they loved them as Christians, and not because they viewed them as baptized persons according to the written word, they have found this to be an impediment in the way of enforcing the written word as a rule in other cases. And to receive any member, to the grief of any already in the church, they also find to be unwarrantable. Another such church was formed on the north borders of Rehoboth, after a happy revival of religion there October 2, 1777; and Mr. James Sheldon of Providence, was ordained their pastor, September 6, 1780. And he purchased a good farm for sixteen hundred dollars; but after he had paid a thousand of it, he was pressed upon for the rest, in the trying year 1786, in such a manner as to compel him to sell it again, with the loss of about seven hundred dollars. And there was reason to conclude, that a hope of his removal from that people, and of breaking up that meeting, caused the Congregational party to press harder in this case, than they otherwise would have done. But be that as it may, Elder Sheldon removed his family back to where he had formerly lived, though he often came and ministered to this people for several years, and then he obtained a dismission, and removed into the State of New York in 1792. This church have obtained occasional supplies since, from time to time, until Mr. Jeremiah Irons was ordained their pastor, September 24, 1795. He was born in Gloster, above Providence, October 14, 1765. In the east part of Rehoboth, a Baptist church was formed, January 17, 1780, in which were a number of very respectable members; but as they never obtained a pastor, they now often go to other meetings. Two Baptist churches have also been formed in Rehoboth, which refused to commune with any baptized persons but those who had laying on of hands and prayer after baptism. They likewise excluded singing in their public worship, as most of the old Baptists in New England did, before our great reformation. In order to form the first of these churches, above thirty persons were dismissed from the Second church in

Swansea, and formed a church in Rehoboth, and ordained Mr. Daniel Martin as their pastor, February 8, 1753 ; and Mr. Nathan Pierce was soon ordained a colleague with him. Mr. Martin published a discourse in 1770 against particular election and efficacious grace in conversion. But an answer to him was published the next year, which was convincing to many minds.[1] Elder Martin died in an advanced age, November 17, 1781, and Elder Pierce died in 1794. Elder Thomas Seamans had been a colleague with him for a number of years, and he still ministers to that people ; but their number is small. Another church sprang from them, in the northeast corner of Rehoboth, and was formed on April 4, and two elders were ordained therein, April 20, 1789, viz., the elders Aaron Wheeler and Sylvester Round. The doctrines of grace, and the power of godliness, have lately gained ground among them.

Mr. Elhanan Winchester was born in Brookline, near Boston, September 19, 1751, and was very studious from a child ; and he obtained a considerable measure of human learning, before he made a profession of religion, was baptized, and began to preach with much zeal. And his preaching in Rehoboth caused a separation in Mr. Peck's church,[2] and another church was formed, and he was ordained their pastor, September 4, 1771, before he was twenty years old. And though he was baptized himself, yet he was exceeding zealous for the communion of all Christians together, let them be sprinkled in infancy or baptized by immersion ; and as his preaching appeared to be very powerful and successful, it caused a division in Elder Hicks's church before mentioned. But soon after Mr. Winchester was ordained, a Baptist minister pointed out to him the inconsistency of his conduct in such a manner, that, after eight month's consideration, he declared to his church, that he could no more administer the ordinance of the Supper to any who were only sprinkled in infancy, though he was still willing to discharge all the duties of his office to them that he could do with a good conscience. But upon this the majority of his church refused to let him preach another sermon among them ; and they soon after censured him for not fulfilling his first covenant with them. Yet they called their way *large communion*, and the Baptist way *close communion*. This church ordained Mr. Jonathan Chaffee as their pastor, in May, 1778, but their church has decreased until it is now nearly dissolved. Mr. Winchester called a council of Baptist churches in December, 1772, which advised him to confess his imprudent conduct to that church, and then to offer himself as a member to some Baptist church. He did so, and was received into the church in Bellingham ; after which he travelled and labored abundantly, through all

[1] The Doctrine of Sovereign Grace, opened and vindicated. By Isaac Backus ; Providence, 1771.—ED.

[2] A Separate church in Rehoboth.—ED.

the country as far as South Carolina. But in the beginning of 1781, he was rejected by the Baptist church in Philadelphia, because the fathers of it discovered that he had fallen into the doctrine of universal salvation. He had preached there but a few months, but in that time he had admitted many members, by which means his party became the majority ; therefore they sued for the meeting-house and the house for the ministry, with other property which belonged to that church. Though after much cost in courts, for several years, they were defeated, and the property secured to the original church. After this, he came and spent a year in New England, without visiting many of his old friends, and then returned to Philadelphia, from whence he sailed for England, in July, 1787. In London he published a book, in which he said :—" I have, at the expense of character and popularity with the religious world, at the hazard of temporal interest and emolument, and refusing no other sacrifice, in what I apprehended to be the cause of God and truth, come forth as a writing witness on this subject ; and a defender of the faith which once I destroyed."[1] Though it is well known, that he concealed his opinion upon that subject as long as he could, and that he grasped at the temporal property of said church as long as he could hope for it. And what is the faith which he would now defend ? Why he says :—" Punishment, without having the reformation and subjection of rebels for its end, is unworthy of the Being we adore." Again he says :—" Since goodness is the perfection of God, and evil the imperfection of the creature, there can be no doubt, that as good existed before evil, so it shall exist to all eternity, when evil shall be no more."[2] But how can any man believe, that the punishment which God has inflicted upon the fallen angels, for near six thousand years, is designed for their final salvation ? Yea, or that the destruction of unbelievers in the wilderness, or of the Sodomites by fire from heaven, was designed for their endless happiness ? How can any government or dominion be supported upon these principles ? And as God was infinitely good before he created angels or men, how do we know that he will not reduce them all back again to nothing ? For he created all things good, and the serpent persuaded our first mother, that death and ruin could not come from eating the forbidden fruit. And one apostle says to Christians, I fear lest by any means, as the serpent beguiled Eve through his subtility, so your minds should be corrupted from the simplicity that is in Christ. II Cor. xi. 3. And another says, I will therefore put you in remembrance, though ye once knew this, how that the Lord, having saved the people out of the land of Egypt, afterwards destroyed them that believed not. And the angels which kept not their first estate, but left their own habitation, he hath reserved in everlasting chains under darkness, unto the judgment of the great day. Even as

---

[1] Preface to Winchester's Dialogues, 1788, pp. 6, 7.
[2] Winchester's Dialogues, pp. 23, 32, 33.

Sodom and Gomorrah, and the cities about them in like manner, giving themselves over to fornication, and going after strange flesh, are set forth for an example, suffering the vengeance of eternal fire. Likewise also these filthy dreamers defile the flesh, despise dominion, and speak evil of dignities. Jude 5—8. Here our times are exactly described by God, who saw them perfectly seventeen hundred years ago. Yet Winchester has followed others in denying that the words *everlasting* and *eternal*, when applied to future misery, mean without end. And he says :—"The foundation of endless misery, came from the pagan theology." Though in the same book he says :—" The great number of heathens, that die without ever being favored with the light of the gospel, and certainly without ever hearing of endless misery, convinces me, more than any logical arguments, that God has many ways of instructing and reclaiming his creatures, in another state, that we are at present unacquainted with."[1] And he has published this glaring contradiction now in Boston, seven years after he first published it in London. So God says, Their folly shall be manifest unto all men. II Tim. iii. 9. Mr. Winchester returned to America, and landed at Boston in July, 1794, and is spreading his opinions in this country ; which makes it needful to hold up light against them.[2]

[1]Winchester's Dialogues, pp. 30, 151; Boston edition, 1795, pp. 68, 158.

[2]The manuscripts of Mr. Backus furnish some additional facts which are worthy of notice in the history of Mr. Winchester, who, after his brilliant, but brief and erratic course as a Baptist, became a leader in American Universalism. One of Mr. Backus's papers is as follows :—

" Original Minutes about Elhanan Winchester, who hath been *given to change.*

"Elder Samuel Peck, of Rehoboth, having treated the Baptists with roughness, Elhanan Winchester from Brookline has taken advantage thereof, and gathered a society out of his, in a confused manner. The best account I have gained of it is this.

" He professed to have been converted last year, and began to preach at Brookline ; but his father's maid soon appeared to be with child by him ; yet he refused to make a confession of it, alleging that by covenant they were one before, though they had not the ceremony of external marriage. For this, Elder Hide's church barred his improvements there. But he went up to Canterbury and was baptized by Ebenezer Lyon, and joined with his church ; and after gathering a number at Rehoboth, he, with two of Mr. Peck's members, viz., John Allyn and Simeon Bowen, went up to Canterbury, and at sacrament there, got so high in their views as to appoint his ordination, without any such thing being agreed upon when they went up, yea, he told Deacon Everett that he had not then concluded upon it in his own mind. And though Bowen now opposed it, yet they determined upon Lyon's coming for that purpose, the fourth of September. And the week before, he went to Brookline, and complied so far as to confess that he was wanting in not complying with the ordinance of man in marriage, for the Lord's sake, sooner than he did; upon which that church wrote a letter in his favor, with which his father, who is a deacon at Brookline, came and met Lyon and one of his members at Rehoboth, September fourth, and they with Elkanah Ingalls, (a young preacher in Elder Hicks's church, without

And the same may be said concerning ministerial tyranny.   An instance of it was before given, in the selling of their ministerial lands in Rehoboth, and obtaining an act to incorporate the committees who should be annually chosen in each parish, to manage their funds of money, so that the interest thereof might support their ministers.   The Congregational name was not in the original grant of those lands, though the produce of them is now claimed under that name.   And since the foregoing account was written, a

his church's consent) with other private persons, laid on hands to ordain Winchester over this new gathered society.   And next day he baptized nine, and four more on September ninth; next day came and preached at Raynham, as he had done before, and endeavored to alienate people from our church.

"Note.   Mr. Winchester has since made a full and satisfying confession about his conduct before marriage, and also has retracted his joining in mixed communion at Rehoboth, for which the majority of his church rejected his preaching, and he with a minor part met by themselves; for which the others sent the following censure :—

"'We, the church of Christ, who were formerly under the pastoral care of our brother, Elhanan Winchester, being met together, were all agreed that brother Elhanan Winchester has broken covenant, for which we admonish you to repentance in the name of our Lord Jesus Christ.

SIMEON BOWEN,   } In behalf of
JOSEPH ALLYN, JR. } the Church.

Rehoboth, October 22, 1772.'

"Elder Winchester sent a notification to them to come to the council, dated December 18.   They sent an answer, dated the 21st, wherein they give some reasons for their not coming; but as to their charge they say :—'As to breach of covenant, charged in the admonition, there is a cloud of witnesses that heard him solemnly covenant and promise before God, angels and men, to walk in the open communion, to administer ordinances, to break the bread to all Congregational brethren as well as others; and that their different sentiments about baptism, were no more to him than their different complexion or stature, or the color of their clothes; with which he also invited the Congregational brethren into the church; and promised in the above named manner, that he would sooner die than break the covenant thus confirmed; therefore no man ought to disannul or add thereto.   Gal. 3, 15.

JOSEPH ALLYN, 2d., in behalf, &c.' "

Mr. Backus wrote in his Diary :—"October 22, [1771.]   Elhanan Winchester came to visit me, and gave me account that he was born in September 1751; that he experienced a change in the spring, 1770; was (as he believes) called to preach the beginning of the next October, was baptized and joined with Ebenezer Lyon's church in Canterbury last winter; began to preach at Rehoboth last spring, but Mr. Samuel Peck preached violently against him on June 2, which caused great uneasiness, and in about a month his treatment produced a separation, and a new society was gathered, over which Winchester was ordained on September 4, since which he has baptized thirty persons, and has two more in his church who are not baptized. He appears to be a man of good sense, and to have many just notions about religion, though in others inexperienced and rash."

After Mr. Winchester had renounced free communion, and joined the Baptist church in Bellingham, a council was called by that church with a view to setting him apart as an evangelist.   But his extravagance had now taken a new turn; he had adopted the principles of ultra-Calvinism, maintaining that ministers had no "right to call or

"Narrative" has been published, "by James Ellis, A. M., attorney-at-law." He is a son of the minister before named ; and his narrative confirms what I had before written, if it is carefully examined. He says, "The inhabitants of the precinct, at a lawful meeting, called for that purpose, unanimously concurred with the church in the choice of Mr. Ellis." This was on November 10, 1784. Page 11. But he did not accept of that call, and wanted more money. Therefore at another meeting, December 27, 1784,

invite sinners, as sinners, now to come to Christ." The council therefore declined to take the proposed action.

In October, 1780, Mr. Winchester was engaged to preach to the Baptist church in Philadelphia, six months or longer. The following extract from an address of that church to sister churches in America, as quoted in Manning and Brown University, pp. 333, 334, will describe his course there.

"Popular applause, the idol which too many worship, was soon discovered to be an object zealously sought for and courted by Mr. Winchester. To accomplish this, persons were every week hastily admitted to baptism, upon the slightest examination; though we really believe that among the number are several sincere Christians, who, during this season of trial, have not been ashamed openly to discountenance his errors. Various innovations, contrary to our established discipline, were introduced through his means. The church undertook a reform. In some respects success attended us; in others an obstinate adherence marked his character.

"The principal foundation of the greatest uneasiness we shall now proceed to consider. Early in the winter it was whispered to a few, that Mr. Winchester, notwithstanding his artful endeavors to conceal the same in his public discourses, held the doctrine of a final restoration of bad men and angels from hell; that the whole of Adam's progeny, yea, the devils themselves, at certain different periods, would be delivered from their torment and made completely happy; in other words, he peremptorily denied the endless duration or perpetuity of future punishment. The method taken by him at first to propagate this wicked tenet, was by creeping into houses and leading captive persons of weak capacities, wherein he met with too much encouragement. Alarmed at this authenticated report, he was at times privately conversed with on the subject by several of the members. He did not presume to contradict it fully, and yet his confession was by no means satisfactory. Upon these occasions he would frequently intimate his intention of going away, provided the smallest division took place on his account; while at the same juncture, as opportunity served, he failed not to use arguments in order to gain proselytes."

In March, 1781, nearly one half of the church, including the older and more substantial members almost without exception, protested against the continuance of Mr. Winchester's ministry with them. An intense excitement ensued. The original church took possession of the meeting-house, which the other party attempted to wrest from them by violence. The question was tested by law, and Winchester and his party defeated.

President Manning wrote to Dr. Rippon :—"The apostasy of Mr. Winchester has been for a lamentation amongst us. Self-exaltation was the rock on which he split, though he had from the first, been remarkable for instability of character." See Manning and Brown University, p. 327. He afterwards preached widely and published largely in defence of Universalism, both in England and America. Mr. Backus replied to his arguments in a treatise entitled, "The doctrine of Universal Salvation, examined and refuted;" published in Providence in 1782.—Ed.

they offered him a hundred pounds a year, and then he accepted their call ; though this sum was voted by but little more than twenty men, and nearly three hundred men were taxed to pay it. Our author says, " Every person within the precinct was taxed, and the collector ordered to gather the moneys without favor or partiality or the least discrimination." Page 63. Yet some of them belonged to Mr. Snow's church, some to Mr. Peck's, and many to Baptist churches ; and a large majority never had any concern with Mr. Ellis as their minister. Yet his son says of the party who chose his father, " Though they begun a good work, yet, being destitute of the grace of perseverance, they failed in its final completion, and brought difficulties to themselves and all concerned." Page 16. But can any man believe that it was a good work, for the minority to essay to force the majority to support a minister whom they never chose ; or that grace was ever given to enable any to persevere in such a way? As these people found that they could not do it, and called back the bills from the collectors in the spring of 1790, Mr. Ellis sued the whole precinct for his salary in the fall after, but the action was continued to March. And as the leaders of the precinct were not willing always to lie under this yoke, they called a meeting, February 7, 1791, when it was voted, " That the precinct do not agree that the Rev. John Ellis shall officiate as minister in said precinct at the expense of said precinct." And his son says, " Thus they flattered themselves they had discharged their minister, and boasted much of their novel and short method of dismission." Page 23. Though the whole community of the Massachusetts had dismissed their Governor nearly four years before, and all America have still the right to leave their highest rulers out of office at appointed times. But God says of Mystery Babylon, The woman which thou sawest, is the great city which reigneth over the kings of the earth. Rev. xvii. 5, 18. And how evident is it, that the ministers who are supported by law in our country belong to that great city? For the most of them were very active in procuring the revolt of America from the government of Great Britain, while they have never allowed the people here the same liberty concerning their religious teachers, as they have concerning their governors and legislators. And how can our legislature give ministers a power that they never had themselves? Can men be any longer blinded about these affairs? If Mr. Ellis would have given up his claim upon that precinct for the future, his past salary would have been paid, and all the trouble of shutting him out of their meeting-house, and the expense of courts upon these matters, would have been prevented. But in October, 1794, their fund of money, as well as a salary for seven years, was given to Ellis's party by our supreme judicial court, with vast costs of courts against his opponents. His son says, "A very full and candid hearing (continuing for two days and a half) was given both by judges and jurors. All records, from the first settling of the town of Rehoboth, were brought into view, the facts fully stated, and the law candidly considered." Page 49. And he says, " Respecting the fund, it appears by the records, that in the year of our Lord, 1640, the old colony of Plymouth granted to the people of Rehoboth certain lands for the purpose of supporting public teachers of the gospel." Page 55. Very true ; and for seventeen years after, all the arts of ministers, and of other colonies, could not bring Plymouth legislature to interfere with the law of Christ, who says, They which preach the gospel, should live of the gospel. I Cor. ix. 14. But in 1658, Governor Bradford, and other fathers of the colony, being dead, their children yielded to the other colonies, in introducing the use of the sword to support religious ministers. And four Quakers were hanged directly after at Boston, whose blood hath brought a lasting reproach upon New England ; though it has been ignorance or wickedness, in all men who have not exempted Plymouth colony from that reproach. And how could lands which were given to support preachers of the gospel, be taken away to support men who will not trust the Lord Jesus Christ and his influence for their temporal living? For though Abraham was an eminent servant of God, yet his children were a generation of vipers when Christ came in the flesh. Matt. iii. 7. And God says of such, They hatch cockatrice' eggs, and weave the spider's web ; he that eateth of their eggs dieth, and that which is crushed breaketh out into a viper. Is. lix. 5. And how is this word now verified in this and other countries? For justice can often be had in civil causes, while it is denied in religious affairs. In the year 1760, they sold six hundred and seventy-four acres of ministerial land in Rehoboth for more than four thousand dollars ; but half of that money, which belonged to the first parish, with seven hundred pounds more for Ellis's salary, with great costs of court, has been taken from the majority of the inhabitants, and given to a small party therein. And because two men placed themselves upon the stairs of the pulpit, to prevent Mr. Ellis from crowding into it, on the day when the first Baptist minister preached therein, his son says, " They were adjudged guilty of a breach of the peace, and sentenced to pay costs of prosecution, amounting to ninety-five pounds, fifteen shillings and eleven pence ; a high price for a seat upon the stairs in a decayed meeting-house." Page 32. Yes ; and if a Baptist justice of the peace had not bound Mr. Ellis to his good behavior until the next March, we have no reason to think that Baptist ministers could peaceably have preached in said house all that time.[1] And his son now says of them, " This conduct has unwillingly obliged many, even of the charitable, to fear that they were not men of piety, or common honesty." Page 68. Which gives a plain view of what many call piety and charity in our days.

But the people who invited Baptist ministers to preach there, soon observed that they preached another kind of doctrine, as well as in another manner from that of their former ministers; and a visible change was wrought in many thereby, and the Baptists who used to go to other meetings gathered to this. Also since Mr. Peck's death, his church is dissolved, and many of his society have come here. A number of souls were hopefully converted, and old believers were quickened, and they sent for ministers to baptize them at sundry times, until these, with some who were members of Baptist churches before, having called in advice, formed a Baptist church there, November 27, 1794. And Mr. John Pierce Jones, of Providence, having preached to them through the winter, was ordained their pastor, March 18, 1795. They have since built themselves a convenient meeting-house, in sight of that which was taken from them, at the distance of more than a quarter of a mile. Their worship therein is to be governed by the church, and harmony appears among them. And the majority of the inhabitants of the towns of Rehoboth, Taunton, and some other towns, are now exempted from the taxing power of the Congregational denomination. And it is hoped that this freedom will prevail through the country, so that all men who are willing to obey the laws of Christ may no longer be oppressed by any who do not love him above all the things of time.

The Baptist church of Taunton was first gathered in Norton. Mr. William Carpenter was ordained the pastor of a Separate church there, September 7, 1748. He was born in Rehoboth in 1710, and his labors in this church were successful, until he and the majority of the church, became Baptists, and he was installed in that order, April 1, 1761. Some of the members of that church, especially they who lived in Easton, had run into the most delusive notions that could be conceived of; even so as to forsake their lawful wives and husbands, and to take others; and they got so far as to declare themselves to be perfect and immortal, or that the resurrection was past already, as some did in the apostolic age. II Tim. ii. 18.[1] But Elder Carpenter, and a majority of the church, rejected those abominations, and he continued faithful unto his death, which happened August 23, 1768. The most of his church then lived in the east part of Norton, towards Taunton, where a Baptist meeting had been long kept. Mr. Jeremiah Basset lived there, who was a member of Elder Round's church in Rehoboth, and obtained liberty from thence to hold worship on the Lord's days at his house, as early as 1774; and he improved his gifts there, and their society increased, until they built a good meeting-house, upon the great road from Taunton to Boston, in 1767, and in April, 1769, the Baptist church of Norton united with the society in Taunton, and have held their worship in that house ever since. Their second pastor was William Nelson,[2] A. M., who was born in Middleborough, July 18, 1741, bap-

---

[1] Shadrach Ireland, hereafter mentioned, was connected with them.—B.
See p. 111—Ed.   [2] Son-in-law of Mr. Backus.—Ed.

tized in June, 1761, educated in Rhode Island College, and ordained the pastor of this church, November 12, 1772. A great harvest of souls was granted among that people in 1780, which increased their church to near eighty members. But as Mr. Nelson was not of a strong constitution, a sudden cold, after preaching at a funeral, seized his lungs in such a manner, that he was not able to preach for some years; and he removed down to the sea in Dartmouth, in 1786, where he has recovered his strength so far as to be able to preach occasionally. His brother Ebenezer Nelson, was ordained a colleague with him, November 10, 1790.

A Separate church was formed in Attleborough, and Mr. Nathaniel Shepard was ordained their pastor, January 20, 1748; and he was well esteemed until his death, April 4, 1752.[1] Afterwards the Baptist principles gradually prevailed among them, until they constituted a Baptist church there in 1769, and Mr. Job Seamans was ordained their pastor, December 15, 1773. He was born in Swansea, May 13, 1748, and went to Nova Scotia with Elder Nathan Mason in 1763, and was converted and began to preach there. But upon a visit to his native place, he went and preached in Attleborough, which was so agreeable to this church, that they prevailed with him to remove and become their pastor; and a great blessing was granted on his labors in the winter before the American war; and a greater in the glorious year 1780, which increased his church to eighty-one members. Mr. Seamans was also very successful in laboring in many other places. But his people grew very slack about his support, and the insurrection in 1786 produced unhappy effects in his society, so that he asked a dismission from them, which the church granted in November, 1787, though with reluctance; and he removed the next summer and settled at New London, in New Hampshire, where (in its place) we shall have a good account of him. This church in Attleborough sought for other helps, and Mr. Abner Lewis removed there in 1789, and ministered to them until 1794, when he removed back to Freetown; and though they have had other preachers since, yet they have no settled pastor. Their meeting-house is upon the great road to Providence, thirty-two miles from Boston. Six miles south of them is the Second Baptist church in Attleborough. A Separate church was formed there, and Mr. Elihu Daggett was ordained their pastor, July 3, 1765. He was born in that town, August 6, 1710; and he was beloved by his people, until he was taken away by death, August 29, 1769. He was baptized, and so were a number of his church, which increased to forty-three members; but a part of them were only sprinkled in infancy. Mr. Elisha Carpenter was ordained their pastor, June 17, 1778. He also was born in Attleborough, August 17,

---

[1] An "Account of the Experiences and Dying Testimony of Mr. Nathaniel Shepherd," written by Mr. Backus, was published as an appendix to his treatise on "An Internal Call to Preach the Gospel."—Ed.

1745, and was a Baptist before the church came into the Baptist order in 1781, iu which they now appear to be well established.[1]

The town of Dighton lies north from Swansea, and east from Rehoboth, and a powerful work began in those towns in the fall of 1771, and a large number were baptized there soon after. Mr. Enoch Goff was one of them, who was born in Dighton, November 3, 1740, converted in 1765, baptized in 1771, and began to preach the next summer. And as his preaching was powerful upon many, a Baptist church was formed in the west part of Dighton, and he was ordained their pastor, December 2, 1772. And though his advantages as to human learning were not great, yet spiritual teaching has made him a very useful and acceptable minister, at home and abroad; and his church and congregation have become very large. Mr. David Seamans was raised up in this church, and was ordained a colleague with Mr. Goff, January 4, 1781, who was a useful minister at Freetown afterwards. Mr. Isaac Case was also raised up in this church, and labored to good purpose in various parts of the land, until he went into the District of Maine, where we shall hear more of him hereafter.

Freetown, which is on the east side of the river, against Dighton and Swansea, was so abusively treated by a Presbyterian minister above seventy years ago,[2] that a number of the people turned to the Quakers, and many others disregarded any religious worship for a long time after. But it pleased God to pour out his Spirit upon the east part of the town in 1773, when many were hopefully converted, and joined the Second Baptist church in Middleborough. The next year they obtained preaching among themselves, and they built them a house for worship, and formed a church there, September 13, 1775, being regularly dismissed from the church they had joined in Middleborough, and Mr. Abner Lewis was ordained their pastor, June 26, 1776. He was born in Middleborough, March 16, 1745, joined the First Baptist church there in 1765, began to preach in 1770, and had preached in Freetown two years before he was ordained; and such a blessing was granted among them afterwards as increased their church to a hundred and twenty-eight members in 1780. But the public difficulties in the country, with the unhappy temper of some of the members of the church, caused Mr. Lewis to ask a dismission from them, which he obtained in August, 1784; and he has travelled and labored in various places since, and has supplied the church in Harwich for more than a year past. The behavior of some in this church has caused a number to

---

[1] The history of this church presents the rare example of excessive tendency to rigorous discipline. The pastor was excluded and the ruling elder deposed, both, it would seem, on very slight grounds. Two members were excluded for not saying "Amen" at the close of the preacher's prayer. The church was speedily rent with dissension, and, early in the present century, it disappears.—ED.

[2] See p. 500.—ED.

ask and receive dismissions from it to other churches, while some have died, and others removed away, until they have become very small. The west part of Freetown enjoyed but little of the blessings which were granted round them, until the glorious year 1780, when a happy revival took place there, and a Baptist church was formed in 1781, and Mr. David Seamans was installed their pastor, August 13, 1783. He was a good preacher, and an exemplary walker. He was drowned, by falling out of a canoe in the night, June 7, 1786, as he was returning from visiting one of the sick of his flock. After this mournful providence, they obtained occasional supplies, from time to time, until Mr. Philip Hathaway was installed their pastor, June 13, 1792. He had been ordained in Middleborough, September 30, 1790. They have built a good house for public worship since he was settled, and things appear to be encouraging among them.

New Bedford was once the east part of Dartmouth, and a Baptist church was formed there, October 7, 1774 ; and Mr. Zaccheus Tobey preached to them for many years, until he was ordained there in 1792. The first minister in Dartmouth was a Baptist, but the Quakers have been a great majority in the town for many years, until they censured and excluded one of their chief ministers, in 1778, for appearing openly in favor of the Americans, while at war with Great Britain. This caused a division in their society, and gave their children liberty to go to hear the preaching of other ministers, which was denied them before, notwithstanding their great name for liberty of conscience. Baptist ministers from Rehoboth and Swansea frequently preached in Tiverton and Dartmouth, and such a blessing was granted upon their labors in 1780, that many went and joined those churches, until a Baptist church was formed in Dartmouth, June 2, 1781, and Mr. Daniel Hicks was installed their pastor, the 10th of October following. He is a son of Elder John Hicks, of Rehoboth, where he was born, November 30, 1755, and was ordained there, July 12, 1780. Another revival was granted in Dartmouth in 1784, which added thirty members to this church by the close of the next year. In 1787, a great blessing was given upon the north part of New Bedford, and a meeting was set up there, and many were baptized among them, who chose to join as a branch of Dartmouth church. Mr. Tucker Tabor was raised up to preach there, who, with a number of his brethren, afterwards removed into the State of New York, though others have continued this meeting ever since. A revival of religion in Dartmouth, in 1788, caused the addition of about forty members to the original church. A cold and trying time followed for several years, but a fresh revival began in January, 1794, which spread in Dartmouth, Freetown, New Bedford, and Rochester ; and Mr. John Lawrence was ordained a colleague with Elder Hicks, the 23d of October following. He was born in Freetown, August 30, 1761, and he preaches chiefly in the east part of that town.   A Baptist meeting-house was built in the west part of Rochester in 1793, and such a blessing was now granted there that about forty persons were baptized, who also joined as a branch of Dartmouth church ; and their addition in this revival in all their branches was a hundred and fifty members.

The Baptist church in Raynham sprang from the great revival of religion which began in these parts in 1779, and it was formed in the year 1780, and increased to above fifty members the next year.   But some of them were drawn away with corrupt principles, and others removed into distant parts of the country, so that their number is now small, though these few appear to be steadfast in the faith.

The first Baptist church in the county of Barnstable is in Harwich.   The ministers of that county generally opposed the great work which was in our land, in and after 1741 ; but Mr. Elisha Paine, who was born in Eastham, went and preached there, and also at Harwich, in 1744, with great success.   A separation from the opposing ministers was the consequence ; and Mr. Joshua Nickerson was ordained the pastor of a Separate church there, February 23, 1749.   Some of them were fined for separating, and distress was made upon many for ministerial taxes ; but this served to increase their number, until another church was formed in the west part of the town, and Mr. Richard Chase was ordained their pastor, December 11, 1751.   These churches held to free communion with all Christians, whether they were sprinkled in infancy, or baptized by immersion ; but as Mr. Chase was thus baptized in 1753, believers' baptism prevailed among them so much, that many gave up mixed communion, and a Baptist church was formed there, and Mr. Chase was installed their pastor, September 29, 1757.[1]   And their principles prevailed so much, that Mr. Nickerson left his people, and went and settled at Tamworth, in New Hampshire.   Mr. Chase ministered to his church for twenty years, and then the lust of intemperance had prevailed so upon him, that he was deposed from his office, by the advice of a council, in January, 1777, and he remained out of fellowship until he died in January, 1794, above eighty years old.   And though his fall into sin was very shocking to many, yet the faithfulness of the Baptists in deposing him raised the credit of their profession ; and a fresh revival of religion among them caused their principles to prevail, so that the south parish in Harwich received a Baptist minister to preach in their meeting-house, and a Baptist church was gathered there, and a minister ordained in 1781.   But they were not in fellowship with the other church, and their minister proved himself to be a deceitful man, and finally went away and left them, and their church was dissolved.   And in No-

---

[1]This church is now the Baptist church in West Harwich.   Mr. Backus baptized Mr. Chase when they were both Separatists.   He also preached Mr. Chase's Installation Sermon, his text being Mal. ii. 6.—ED.

vember, 1792, a minor part of the inhabitants of that parish settled a Congregational minister there, and about two years after, they taxed all the Baptists to him, and in January, 1795, they appeared fierce for collecting it, though advice from a distance restrained them therefrom. A happy revival of religion was again granted among the Baptists in Harwich in the spring of 1793, which might occasion this fresh attempt of their adversaries to hold them in bondage as Pharaoh did. And in December, 1795, they set out in a cruel manner to collect said tax, and hauled a number to jail, and seized the estates of others without mercy.

A few people in Barnstable withdrew from their parish worship, and set up a meeting by themselves in 1748; but they were fined therefor, and two women were set in the stocks for not paying it. Yet their cause prevailed, and a church was formed there, and Mr. Nathanael Ewer was ordained their pastor, May 10, 1750, and he continued with them for more than ten years, and then went and settled at Newmarket, in New Hampshire; and the Baptist principles gained ground in Barnstable, until they formed a church there, June 20, 1771; and it increased gradually for ten years, in which time the most of them were exempted from taxes to Congregational ministers, as they had given in certificates to that party. But as a powerful work began among them in 1781, and a minister was raised up to preach among them, and he was ordained their pastor, December 4, 1788, the ruling party resolved to try what they could do towards holding them in bondage, as we have before related.[1] Mr. Enoch Eldridge, who is their pastor, was born in Harwich, and he has preached a part of his time to the Baptist church in Harwich, ever since he began in the work of the ministry, until 1794. A fresh revival of religion was granted in those two churches in the beginning of 1793, and Mr. Shubael Lovel, a young physician, was converted in Barnstable in March, and he began to preach

---

[1] "Timothy Phinney, a church member, collector of taxes for Mr. Mellen, minister of the first parish in Barnstable, took away two young cattle from Ichabod and Lemuel Lombard, worth about twelve dollars, and sold them for two pounds, fourteen shillings. The man who bought the cattle returned them to the original owners upon their paying said taxes and costs, which were about two pounds, two shillings.

"Mr. Enoch Eldridge has preached to that church ever since April, 1785; and he and Mr. Lombard judge that in that time they have taken from that society in taxes, not less than a hundred and fifty dollars. Samuel Scudder, of the Baptist society there, was taken and imprisoned for a tax. After he was confined in prison he paid it and came out; and he paid his two next taxes to Phinney. David Hallet of said church was, on January 5, 1791, called upon by Phinney to pay two taxes to Mr. Mellen, and rather than go to jail he paid them. The Baptist church in Barnstable were generally exempted from taxes until they got a minister ordained, December 4, 1788; since which, by parish vote, they have taxed all the brethren of the church [who live] in the first parish in Barnstable, but afterwards released two poor men." Backus's Manuscripts. See pp. 351, 352.—ED.

there in January, 1794, and he was ordained as an itinerant minister, April 29, 1795. Baptist meetings have been held for some years in Sandwich, Welfleet, and Provincetown, in that county, though Baptist churches have not yet been formed among them.

Duke's county includes Martha's Vineyard and some adjacent islands, on which are the largest number of Indians that remain any where in this part of America. Peter Folger was a schoolmaster among them, when Mr. Mayhew sailed for England in 1657, and he became a Baptist, and joined Mr. Clarke's church in Newport about 1675 ; and he promoted the Baptist principles among the Indians, who formed a Baptist church among them about 1694, which continues to this day ; though Silas Paul, their last pastor, died August 24, 1787. Mr. Folger removed to Nantucket, and was much esteemed among the early planters there ; and a daughter of his was mother to the late famous Dr. Benjamin Franklin.[1] Baptist ministers had preached among the English on the Vineyard at times ever since 1753 ; and after some were remarkably turned from darkness to light, without preaching, in the spring of 1780, they called over several Baptist ministers to preach and baptize there, until a church of fifty members was constituted there the 20th of December following.[2] Major Peter Norton, the

---

[1]See Vol. I, pp. 346, 347. Massachusetts Historical Collections, Vol. III, p. 160.
[2]See p. 269.—B.

Mr. Backus first visited Martha's Vineyard in March, 1753. He remained two weeks, preaching in different parts of the island. His next visit was occasioned by his receiving a copy of the following letter :—

"To the Rev. Messrs. E. Hinds, I. Backus, and others, whose business it is to send forth laborers, under Christ, into his vineyard, We, inhabiting at and near Holmes's Hole, on the island of Martha's Vineyard, humbly pray you to take our case, as to a preached gospel, into your serious consideration. We, living five, six, and some of us seven or eight miles from the places of public worship, and most of us, consisting of sixty or more families, seem to be solicitous for the attendance on the First-day Baptist preachers, and if any church is ever gathered here, we think it will be of that sect. The Rev. Mr. Lewis, who has preached here several times, and has refreshed us very much, can inform you more particularly in this affair; and whom we greatly value. Now we hope that some one or other of you will visit and preach to us, and endeavor to gather a church here, as soon as possible. In the mean time, we are your poor, destitute servants.

"ELISHA WEST, [and thirteen others.]
" Tisbury, May 7, 1772."

Mr. Backus reached the island August 14, and labored there till August 25, and much interest attended his preaching. Concerning his visit there in 1780, Mr. Backus writes in his Diary as follows :—

" Wednesday, December 20. We had a pleasant passage over to Martha's Vineyard, and I preached in the evening at Jonathan Manter's, where Elder Lewis and brother Samuel Parker met us. A glorious work of God has lately taken place here, which began in the following manner, viz. :—David Butler, his cousin, Rebecca Butler, and Abigail Pease, on the east side of Holmes's Hole, and Ebenezer

high sheriff of the county, was a father in that church, and it increased to about eighty members.   But the late plundering of vessels by the British ships has caused a large part of that society to remove to the new lands up Kennebeck River.

Daggett's wife, on the west side, were brought under soul concern a year ago, the latter by the loss of a son, another by means of a transient preacher; and after great distress of soul they were converted in April and May; and they were instrumental in awakening many others.   And the last of June, D. Butler came over and was baptized by Elder Lewis, who went to the island in July, and baptized Peter Norton, Esq., high sheriff of the county, and seven more.   He went over again in August, and a third time in October.   Elder Hunt went there in November; and such a blessing was granted upon their labors that they sent a request to each of us to come over at this time to assist in forming a church among them; therefore,

"Thursday, December 21, we met at Thomas Butler's, in Edgartown.   I preached from Isa. 61. 4, and a copy of our articles of faith and covenant was considered of, and the nature of such transactions explained; after which sixteen men and thirty-four women freely and solemnly signed covenant together, to whom two men and four women were joined the 24th, who had all been baptized before."—ED.

30

CHAPTER XXXVIII.

OF THE BAPTIST CHURCH IN HAVERHILL.—ROWLEY, DANVERS AND AMESBURY.—CHELMSFORD.—NEWTON. — CAMBRIDGE, WOBURN AND WESTON. — LEICESTER. — STURBRIDGE. — CHARLTON. — SUTTON AND NORTHBRIDGE.—PETERSHAM AND HARDWICK.—ROYALSTONE.—DELUSIONS AT HARVARD.—AND A BAPTIST CHURCH.—ASHBURNHAM.—TEMPLETON.—GRAFTON, UPTON, DOUGLASS, DUDLEY, AND OTHERS.

Before the revival of religion which took place in 1764, there was no Baptist church in any part of our country northward of Boston, except one that is since dissolved. The ministers on both sides of Merrimack River were combined together against the former reformation in our land ; and though a few people in Haverhill were subjects of that work, and set up a meeting in separation from those ministers, yet it did not continue long. But a minister of the west parish in Haverhill offended his people so much, as to cause controversies in councils, and in publications to the world, which were followed with a forcible shutting of him out of their meetinghouse, and then a dismission from his office there. And the people saw so much partiality in other ministers towards him, that they would not be directed by them in calling another minister ; therefore they had been destitute for some years, before Mr. Hezekiah Smith came and preached there in 1764, and then gathered a church in the heart of the town in May, 1765, as is related in this volume, pages 137, 138, 141—146. Their church increased to a hundred and fifty members before the war ; and when that broke out, Mr. Smith engaged very heartily in the cause of his country, and was a chaplain in our army through the most distressing part of the war, only he was at home with his people in the winters. A fresh revival of religion began among them in 1778, which caused the addition of fifty-four members in three years ; since which, many have been dismissed to other churches, and others have been added to this. Mr. Edmund Pilsbury, pastor of the church in Northwood, was a member of this church. Asa Messer, A. M., a member of this society, was educated in the college at

Providence, in which he is an esteemed tutor, as well as a preacher of the everlasting gospel.

A branch of Haverhill church was at the west part of Rowley, where a meeting was held for several years, until a Baptist church was formed there in 1785, and Mr. William Ewing became their minister. He was born in Scotland in 1728, and after he came to America and became a Baptist, he preached in various parts of the country, till he was ordained an itinerant preacher at Sturbridge, September 27, 1768. Afterwards he labored a while at South Brimfield, and then at Halifax in Vermont, from whence he removed to Shutesbury, before he came to Rowley, where he had some success; but in about four years, this church dismissed him from them, and he removed to Weston, and now preaches but little anywhere. In 1789 this church called Elder Abishai Crossman, from Chelmsford, and in three years their church increased from forty-four to ninety-nine members. Yet in 1793 he was dismissed, and removed into New Hampshire, and this church is at present destitute of a pastor. A number of people from Danvers had joined the church in Rowley; but they were dismissed and formed a Baptist church in Danvers, July 16, 1793, and Mr. Thomas Green removed from Cambridge, and became their minister, of whom more will be said when we come to Cambridge church. A Baptist meeting has been held for many years at Amesbury, in Essex county, and Mr. Moses Chace is their minister; but they have considered themselves as a branch of the Baptist church at Brentwood in New Hampshire.

The first Baptist church in the county of Middlesex was formed at Chelmsford, in October, 1771, and Mr. Elisha Rich was ordained their pastor, October 5, 1774. He had preached to them for a year and a half before, and he labored among them until the beginning of 1778; but then some of the members appeared to be so much against him, that he requested and obtained a dismission, and removed into Vermont, and he is now a pastor of a church there in the town of Pittsford. Mr. Samuel Fletcher removed to Chelmsford directly after, and preached there for some years, and then went and settled at Salem, in New Hampshire, where he was pastor of a Baptist church until his death last March. Mr. Abishai Crossman, of Northbridge, was called to Chelmsford, and was ordained the pastor of this church, September 24, 1783, and in four years it increased from eighty-seven to a hundred and thirteen members; yet he was dismissed and went to Rowley in 1789, as before related. Mr. John Peckens, who was born in Middleborough, and ordained in Vermont, removed to Chelmsford and became their minister in 1792.

The Baptist church in Newton sprang partly from members who formerly joined the Second Baptist church in Boston, and partly from the Separate churches of Brookline and Newton. A Separate church was formed in Brookline, and Mr. Jonathan Hide was ordained their pastor,

January 17, 1751 ; and he ministered to them until a Baptist church was formed in Newton, with which he met in his old age. A Separate church was also formed in Newton, and Mr. Nathan Ward was ordained their pastor, January 17, 1753. But different sentiments about the support of the ministry, and about the improvement of gifts in the church, caused them to call a council, in April, 1758, after which Mr. Ward was dismissed, and he has been a minister in the town of Plymouth, in New Hampshire, for thirty years past. Some of the old brethren died, and others removed into distant parts of our country, and things were in a broken posture in Newton for many years. But a shower of heavenly blessings was granted there, and a Baptist church was formed by them, July 5, 1780, which increased to seventy members in fourteen months. And Mr. Caleb Blood, who was born in Charlton, August 18, 1754, and ordained at Marlow in October, 1777, was settled as their pastor in 1781, and his ministry appeared to be very useful among them for near seven years. But then the times became so difficult, that the society thought they could not support him and his family ; and he had an earnest call to Shaftsbury, in the State of Vermont, therefore he was dismissed to Shaftsbury, where he is still useful. But a fresh revival was granted at Newton, and Mr. Joseph Grafton was called to preach there, and he was ordained their pastor, June 18, 1788. He was born in Newport, June 9, 1757, and had preached in various places, for several years, before he came to Newton, where a fresh revival was granted in 1794. He has published a piece upon baptism, and a funeral sermon.

There was a Baptist church in Cambridge in 1751, and they had a minister who was educated at New Haven College ; but he was drawn away by a parish minister in Cambridge, and left his church, and others of them fell in with Shadrach Ireland, so that this church was dissolved. Yet there were a few names in Cambridge who had not defiled their garments ; and in the glorious year 1780 a number more were converted, and a new Baptist church was formed there in 1781, and Mr. Thomas Green was ordained their pastor, November 26, 1783. He is grandson to the first Baptist minister of Leicester, and was born at Worcester, January 3, 1761 ; and this church increased under his ministry to fifty-six members. Their house for worship is near the borders of Lexington and Woburn, and members of this society in each of these towns were forced to pay taxes to Congregational ministers, until they had sued the money out of the hands of their oppressors, first in Cambridge, then in Lexington, and lastly in Woburn ; and the Baptists never recovered half so much money in either of these towns, as had been unjustly taken from them ; and as soon as the Congregational party found that they could not hold the money, they collected no more taxes for any ministers from the Baptists. And not long after their last cases in court were decided in favor of the Baptists, their minister left them, in April, 1793, and removed to Danvers, as was before mentioned. Yet such a revival was granted among them soon after, especially in Woburn, as caused the addition of thirty-seven members to this church in two years, and a new meeting-house was built in Woburn. Mr. John Peak labored among them more than a year, and Mr. Lovel succeeded him last fall. And in 1795 the first parish in Cambridge procured an act of our legislature, to empower them to sell some ministerial lands in the town, and to secure all the moneys obtained thereby, for the support of Congregational ministers in that parish. A Baptist church was formed in Weston, July 14, 1789, in which were nineteen members the next year; but they have not increased since. A Baptist meeting has been upheld for many years in Framingham, where no church is yet formed.[1]

The Baptist church at Leicester, in the county of Worcester, was constituted September 28, 1738, under the charge of Elder Thomas Green, who was ordained a year before, a colleague with Elder Marsh, of Sutton; but they now became two churches by mutual consent. Elder Green went from Malden, and was an early planter at Leicester, and became a very useful physician, and acquired such an estate, that he was the main support of his society in temporals as well as spirituals all his days. He travelled much in the country as a physician, and preached frequently, and baptized many, until he was called away by death, August 20, 1773, aged seventy-three. Benjamin Foster, D. D., who was educated at Yale College, was ordained his successor, October 23, 1776, and the church increased under his ministry, from thirty to seventy-six members, in five years. But as he inclined to devote himself entirely to study, and to the ministry of the word, the people, who had not been used to support their minister, neglected him so much, that he requested a dismission from that church, which they at length granted, though reluctantly, in 1782, and he went and preached at Danvers, his native place, above two years. And in January, 1785, he was called to the first church in Newport, where he labored with success for more than two years, and then went to New York, and is now the pastor of the First Baptist church in that city. Mr. Isaac Beals was the next pastor of the Baptist church in Leicester, where he was ordained December 1, 1784, and they prospered under his ministry for two years; but then an insurrection took place in that part of the country,[2] which greatly affected that church and society, and after many endeavors to settle matters among them, without so good an effect as to unite them all again, he was dismissed in 1789, and went and settled at Clarendon, in Vermont, where he is now a useful minister. Mr. Nathan Dana, from Newton, was soon after called to preach at Leicester; and he was ordained at Newton as an itinerant minister, November 20, 1793, and now ministers to this people.

[1] See p. 98, note.—ED.   [2] See p. 330.—ED.

A Separate church was formed in Sturbridge, and Mr. John Blunt was ordained their pastor, September 28, 1748 ; and they became numerous, before the Baptist principles were embraced among them in June, 1749, and before the end of that year above sixty members, including all the officers of the church, were baptized. Some account of their sufferings was given in pages 94—96. But some Separate ministers in Connecticut made such terrible representations of its being a wicked thing for any to be rebaptized, that Mr. Blunt retracted his being dipped,[1] and he left his people, and went into our army, where he was slain near Lake George, September 8, 1755. And though the main body of the church persevered in their profession, yet they passed through many trying scenes, and did not obtain a settled minister for many years. Mr. William Ewing preached there for some time, and was ordained there, September 27, 1768, as an itinerant minister ; and he went from thence to South Brimfield, and since to other places, as was before observed. Mr. Jordan Dodge, from Canterbury, was called to preach at Sturbridge, and he was ordained their pastor, October 27, 1784, and they prospered under his ministry for several years ; but in the close of 1788, such difficulties arose that he asked and obtained a dismission, and went and settled in the State of New York, where he was found to be a deceitful man, and was rejected by the Baptist churches in those parts. However, the school of afflictions which this church has been in, with the spiritual teachings that have been granted to them, has brought them to considerable fruitfulness in Christian knowledge and conduct, in which it is hoped they will grow and increase unto the end. A fresh revival was lately granted among them under the preaching of brother Zenas L. Leonard, who is likely to become their pastor.

The Baptist church in Charlton, was first formed in Spencer, in 1762,[2] and Mr. Nathanael Green was ordained their pastor, October 12, 1763. Their meeting was afterwards held in the west part of Leicester, until it was removed into Charlton in 1773, where it continues. And though it was a low time with them for several years, yet a glorious work began among them in 1779, which caused the addition of a hundred and nine members in three years. The wonders of divine grace in this land at that time when the war raged on every hand, and had greatly corrupted the morals of the people, and public credit was fallen to the ground, was evidently a great cause of saving America from destruction. This work was then powerful in Virginia, as well as in other parts of our lands. Elder

---

[1]Mr. Backus, led by his own experience to sympathize with Mr. Blunt in his difficulties, paid him a visit. He says that Mr. Blunt was led to return to his former practise, not "by seeing any Scripture light for infant baptism;" but by the apparent effects of the Baptist movement, "some running into errors, and making a discussion among the saints, and the like."—ED.

[2]July thirteenth.—ED.

Green was continued a faithful pastor and an exemplary walker, until he fell asleep in Jesus, March 21, 1791, in the seventieth year of his age.[1] And the church soon after called Mr. David Rathbun to preach to them, and he was ordained their pastor, September 25, 1793. He was born in Stonington, May 29, 1763, and his father, uncle, and one of his brothers, are all now pastors of Baptist churches.

A Baptist church was constituted in Sutton, September 16, 1735, and Mr. Benjamin Marsh was ordained their pastor, September 28, 1737, colleague with Mr. Green. Mr. Marsh was esteemed a godly man, of an exemplary life, though not of large gifts, until his death, January 4, 1775, aged ninety. But the church was then small, and it is since dissolved. There had been a great revival of religion in the Congregational society in Sutton, in the year 1741, and a Separate church was formed among them, and Mr. Ezekiel Cole was ordained their pastor, January 31, 1751. But they were broken and scattered afterwards, and a Baptist church was gathered there, April 27, 1765, and Mr. Jeremiah Barstow was installed their pastor, May 26, 1768. But a difference in sentiment about the doctrines of grace caused his dismission from them, by the advice of a council,[2] Oc-

---

[1] Mr. Green was arrested for ministers' rates, and taken to Worcester to be imprisoned. By the advice of Colonel Chandler, who is mentioned on page 65, " he paid the fine and was released, after having been in custody six hours. The constable gave him the following receipt.

" 'Leicester, February 13, 1769.

This day I made distraint upon Mr. Nathanael Green's body, of Leicester, for his rate which he was rated in the year 1767, and received of said Nathanael Green, seventeen shillings, nine pence, one farthing, so much being in full for his province rate; and also of said Nathanael Green, three shillings, nine pence, one farthing, being in full for his town and county rates for the year 1767: I say, received by me,   BENJAMIN BOND, Constable for the year 1767.'

"Mr. Green brought an action against the assessors for damages. The inferior court gave judgment in his favor, and allowed him forty shillings and costs of suit. The assessors appealed to the superior court, and the case was again decided in Green's favor. He was allowed all the money he had expended in the law and lawful costs." Rev. S. Hall's Collection of papers.—ED.

[2] A part of the church refused to concur with the council, and to them Mr. Barstow preached for a time, supporting himself by teaching school. A second council recognized them as the original church, and him as their pastor.

"In 1748, Mr. Barstow was imprisoned in Worcester jail for speaking to a clergyman in the pulpit, and for exhorting the people after he was turned out of the meeting-house. This offence was committed in Thompson. He was confined one month and was then dismissed by the court. The crime alleged was, asking the minister for liberty to tell his experience; but the king's attorney said he had broken no law.

"He, with others, was seized by a constable, February 12, 1750, and was confined ten or twelve days in Worcester jail, when his father paid the rate and took him out.

"Mr. Barstow attended a Congregational ordination in Brookfield, and after the

tober 1, 1772 ; and he removed to Thompson, in Connecticut, and never took the charge of any other church, though he preached occasionally, until he died suddenly, by a fall from his horse, June 4, 1795.   Mr. Elisha Ransom preached to this church for some years, and was ordained there as an itinerant, November 11, 1778 ; but he went the next year to Woodstock, in Vermont.   This church in Sutton remained without a pastor, until such a division arose therein, that they were left out of the Warren Association in 1786.   But the majority of them obtained a comfortable settlement again, and Mr. Ebenezer Lamson removed there from Ashford, and was their minister from 1788, until April, 1794, when they discovered that he had fallen into the opinion of universal salvation, and rejected him.   The other part of this church embraced the opinion of mixed communion, and at length joined the Groton Conference ; but both churches were favored with a happy revival of religion in 1792, and are now in comfortable circumstances.   Two of the brethren of the first church in Sutton, Samuel Waters and Samuel King, have been called to improve their gifts in preaching the gospel, though they are not ordained.   Mr. William Batcheller, a member of the church in Northbridge, who lives in the east part of Sutton, has preached in those parts for several years, until a fresh revival was granted there, a church was formed, and he was ordained their pastor, October 10, 1792.   The Baptist church in Northbridge was constituted, August 31, 1780, and Mr. John Cooper was ordained therein, October 11, 1792, when there was a happy time among them.

A Baptist church was formed in Petersham in 1768,[1] and Mr. Samuel Dennis preached to them for a number of years, before he was ordained their pastor in October, 1778.   He was so well esteemed in the town, that he was chosen a member of our legislature in the time of the war ; but worldly affairs did not turn him aside from faithfulness in the church, until he rested from his labors in April, 1783.   His church persevered in their profession, though their meeting is removed into the bounds of Hardwick, where it is still continued.

Royalstone lies upon the north borders of our State, adjoining to Rich-

---

services were over, he, while sitting on his horse, gave notice that Mr. Blunt would preach that evening in the house of James Walker, in Brookfield, when the people fell upon him, in the presence of fourteen clergymen, with their horse whips, some whipping him with the lashes and others striking him on the head with their whips clubbed, with as much apparent good will as if they intended to take the life of this profaner of their ordination festival.   It was supposed that they gave him, at least one hundred blows, as the exercise continued about half an hour.   He exhorted while they whipped and attempted to drag him from his horse.   No effort was made to quell the mob, though officers of the peace were present." Rev. S. Hall's Collection of papers.—Ed.

[1] A copy of the letter of this church to the Warren Association, in 1769, in Mr. Hall's Collection of papers, gives its date, June 19, 1767.—Ed.

mond, in New Hampshire. Mr. Whitman Jacobs had been pastor of the Baptist church at Thompson, in Connecticut, more than twenty years, before a part of them removed and settled in Royalstone, formed a church there, and he was installed their pastor, December 13, 1770. Their number was twenty-nine the next year; and they had a revival in 1774, and another in 1779, and their church increased to eighty-nine. But such controversies arose in their church about discipline, and about some political affairs, that their minister was dismissed in 1786, and he is now at Guilford, in Vermont. In 1789, Mr. Moses Kenny was settled as the pastor of Royalstone, and they had a large increase of members for several years after.[1]

Harvard is a place where the goodness of God and the folly of man have been remarkably discovered. A powerful work of grace was wrought in that town, in the time of the great revival of religion through this land; but amazing delusions appeared there afterwards. For Shadrach Ireland, of Charlestown, near Boston, after acting as a teacher for some years, professed to have experienced such a change, both in body and mind, that he was become perfect and immortal, and a number more with him, in the spring of 1753. And he set himself up as the head of the church, and assumed God's prerogatives in such a blasphemous manner, that he was in danger of being punished by authority; upon which he absconded, and his followers said he was gone out of this wicked country. But he was concealed in Harvard, where a large house was built for him, in part of which another family lived, and scarcely any men knew that he was there but his followers, who resorted to him for his blessing, from various and distant parts of the country, and brought him a plenty of provisions. Ireland forbade them to marry, or to lodge with each other, if they were married, and he had left a wife and children in Charlestown; yet he took another woman, and lodged with her in Harvard all his remaining days. And when he was suddenly seized with death, he said, " I am going, but don't bury me; for the time is short; God is coming to take the church." Therefore he was put into a large box filled up with lime, and laid in the cellar, where it continued from September, 1778, to July, 1779, when the body scented so much that it was carried out in the night and buried in a corn-field. This account I have from under the hand of one of his followers, who has since been delivered from that delusion. But in the spring of 1780, another company appeared above Albany, with a woman at their head, with great signs and lying wonders, and such uncommon motions of their bodies, that they were called *Shakers*. They removed from place to place, until they fixed their headquarters at the house where Ireland died, in August, 1781; and they carried on at so high a rate there, that a mo-

[1] A branch of this church was formed in Warwick, May 12, 1773.—ED.

tion was made in our legislature to have them punished by authority, which motion was negatived by the majority of a single vote, as we were well informed. But the fear of a mob caused the removal of their leaders from Harvard in 1782, and they came to Norton, and then to Rehoboth in the fall of that year. And they prevailed with many of their society to sell their estates, in order to build a ship to carry the church to the New Jerusalem, as they said. And a large vessel was built in Rehoboth ; but it was sent a voyage to the West Indies, from whence a rich cargo was brought, and the vessel and cargo were sold, and a few men cheated the rest out of their estates, and their community is dissolved in these parts. Some of them remain in the county of Albany.

But a more happy scene now opens upon Harvard. A young physician was converted there, June 18, 1775, the day after the bloody battle at Charlestown ; and while the war raged through the country, he was engaged in real religion, and began to preach the gospel the next winter.[2] He was born at Westford, November 13, 1752, and studied physic with Dr. Green, of Leicester, and then settled in Harvard. And having called Elder Rich from Chelmsford, Isaiah Parker, Stephen Gates, Tarbel Willard, William Willard, Joseph Stone, Josiah Willard and eight women were baptized, and they were formed into a church, June 27, 1776, and Dr. Parker was ordained their pastor, June 10, 1778. But two years after, they were remarkably oppressed, in a time when it might have been least expected. For the constitution of the Massachusetts government was published March 2, 1780, when the compilers of it said to the people, " Your delegates did not conceive themselves to be vested with power to set up one denomination of Christians above another ; for religion must at all times be a matter between God and individuals." This they said because Protestants were not set above Papists in our legislature ; but in each town, one denomination has been set up above all the rest to this day, which they then acknowledged they had no right to do. And one member of the Baptist church in Harvard was imprisoned at Worcester three months, another five, and one of their society six months, between the publication of the constitution, and its taking place in October, for taxes to a Congregational minister, who was settled in the name of the king of Great Britain. These three men kept exact accounts of all their expenses while in prison, with all that was given them there ; and their accounts were examined the next year by two judicious men, who have given it from under their hands, that they expended a hundred and three dollars and a third, more than all that they received there. And no recompense has ever been made therefor by their oppressors. And can any man who believes that God governs the world, think it strange that the powers of Britain have been suffered to rob the Americans of their property, when

[1]See pp. 297, 298.—Ed.   [2]See p. 199.—Ed.

robberies for religious ministers under British commissions have been openly approved of in our country? May we not say with Jacob, O my soul, come not thou into their secret ; unto their assembly, mine honor, be not thou united ! This church in Harvard was soon after attacked by the spirit of delusion, so that they said in a letter to the Warren Association, September 8, 1783 :—

For twelve months we had but two persons added, and several left us, and joined the Shakers. We excommunicated eight persons in that time. A form of godliness appeared on one hand, and a false power on the other, and the church in such a low state, that we feared at times that our candle- stick would be removed out of its place. We saw the enemy coming in like a flood, and that except the Spirit of the Lord should lift up a stand- ard against him, we were a ruined people. Therefore we appointed a day of fasting and prayer, that God would pour out his Spirit among us, and work wonders under the name of his holy child Jesus ; and we have reason to think that the Lord gave us a spirit of grace and supplication, and, for his own name sake, was pleased to answer us in mercy. The fast was on September 4, 1782, when there was a remarkable display of God's power and grace, in convincing sinners of their lost state, the hardness of their hearts and blindness of their minds, with their pride of life and rejecting the gospel of Jesus Christ ; and then giving them to behold the Lamb of God that taketh away the sin of the world ; the free salvation of the gos- pel, and causing them to rejoice therein ; so that forty-nine persons were baptized among us from September 22 to November 24, and fifty-eight per- sons have been baptized among us since the work began ; and we have often sat under Christ's shadow with great delight, and his fruit was sweet to our taste. Our present number is a hundred and ten.

They have enjoyed many blessings since.

The Baptist church in Ashburnham was constituted in February, 1779, and they have gone through scenes of prosperity and adversity ; have en- dured oppression from others, and many trying things among themselves. In 1787, such a revival was granted among them, as increased their church in one year from thirty-seven to sixty-one members. But they have never had an ordained pastor, nor any great alterations since. Several gifted brethren among them assist in carrying on their worship, and they get help at times from other churches.[1]

[1] In June, 1778, Isaiah Parker, of Harvard, preached in Ashburnham, and bap- tized sixteen persons. For several years the members of the Baptist church in this town were taxed for the support of the Congregational minister, and the taxes col- lected by force. We extract the following from a sketch of their history :—

"February 26, 1781. About three weeks after the rate was made, the collectors went about from house to house amongst our brethren, seizing their effects, espec- ially their pewter, leaving some families not a platter to use. One family had a cow taken away ; another poor family their grain. Now the grain never was posted nor exposed to public sale, but was applied to the use of the robber and the minister that it was robbed for. The number that were distressed were seven. Our breth- ren made no resistance, but used the most striking arguments to convince our op-

The Baptist church in Templeton was formed August 21, 1782, and Mr. John Sellon was ordained their pastor, November 19, 1783. He was born in England in 1727, and lived a while at Boston after he came to America. He ministered to this church about two years, and then was dismissed ; and he has preached since in various places, and is now living in Petersham. This church has had many ministers to labor with them, and a happy revival of religion has been granted there in two years past, though they have not obtained another settled pastor. The Baptists are so much esteemed in that town, that two members of their church have lately been representatives in our legislature.

A Baptist church was formed in Grafton in 1767, and they prospered for some years, and had thirty-nine members in 1780.[1] Above three years after, Mr. Elkanah Ingalls, of Rehoboth, went and lived there, and was their minister for about four years ; and then it was discovered that he, with the majority of the church, had fallen into the opinion of universal salvation, and they were left out of the Warren Association in 1788, and he removed back to Rehoboth, and is become a common drunkard.[2] But a minor part of the church continued in their former faith, and set up their meeting in Upton, and Mr. Simeon Snow was ordained in their community in June, 1791.[3] They hold worship steadily there, though, their number being small, they have joined as a branch to Bellingham church. A Baptist church was once formed in Douglas, and Adam Streeter was ordained their pastor, November 24, 1774 ; but he fell into the opinion of universal

pressors of the unlawfulness of their conduct. It seemed as though our oppressors endeavored to take things that would distress us most, or, at least, such things as are most difficult to be replaced at this day, perhaps thinking that would induce us to redeem them. .... Yet they took joyfully the spoiling of their goods, and rejoiced that they were counted worthy to suffer for the cause of Christ." Backus's Manuscripts.—ED.

[1]This church was organized with only four members, Joseph Whipple, Jacob Whipple, Ebenezer Wheeler and Robert Leathe. They were all dismissed from Elder Green's church in Leicester.—ED.

[2]Elkanah Ingalls is mentioned on pages 441, 442, as having assisted, irregularly, in the ordination of Elhanan Winchester. He was a member of Elder John Hicks's church, in Rehoboth. Like Winchester, he adopted open communion views, and by this and other means, gave much trouble to the church. At last a council was called which declared him guilty of breaking various gospel rules and addressed to him a severe admonition.—ED.

[3]According to the following memorandum, found in Rev. S. Hall's Collection of papers, a Baptist church had been formed in Upton as early as 1753.

"Property was taken from the following persons in Upton for minister's rates : In 1753, two cows from Benjamin Palmer, Jr.; in 1751, a cow, and one in 1752, and one in 1753, from Jonah Pease ; in 1751 and 1752, a cow each year from William Barker. In March, 1753, Abraham Bloss, pastor of the Baptist church in Upton, was carried to jail for a tax to the minister, and was confined forty days. In 1751, Robert Wooks was imprisoned six days for the same cause."—ED.

salvation, and was deposed from his office in 1781, and the church is since dissolved, though a Baptist meeting is often held there still. Streeter preached up his new opinions in various parts of the country for several years, and is since dead. A Baptist church was formed in Dudley in 1775, and Elder Obed Warren was raised up among them, who afterwards removed into the State of New York; but as many removed away, their church is small if it is not dissolved.[1] Baptist meetings have been held in Brookfield, Shrewsbury, and Holden, where churches are not yet formed.

[1] A Baptist church was formed in Dudley as early as 1744, as appears from the town records. The church which Mr. Backus mentions was formed May 5, 1775, with eight members. Still another Baptist church was formed here in 1798, which "existed long enough to illustrate the sad consequences of dissension and then ceased to be." Discourse on the fiftieth anniversary of the Baptist church in Webster, Rev. C. W. Reding, pp. 5, 6, 7; Semi-Centennial Discourse of the Worcester Baptist Association, pp. 5, 6, 8.

A complete list of the Baptist churches in Worcester county previous to 1795, should probably include one in that part of Mendon called Mill River. This church sent a request to "the church of Christ in Middleborough" that Elder Backus and other delegates be appointed to a council to be held October 11, 1758, "publicly to devote and set apart" Samuel Hovey as pastor of "the church of Christ in Mill River." On page 79, note, it is stated that Samuel Hovey was ordained pastor of a Separate church in Mendon in 1749, and that he afterwards became a Baptist.—ED.

CHAPTER XXXIX.

An Account of South Brimfield.—West Springfield.—Ashfield.—Montague and Leverett.—Wilbraham.—New Salem.—Shutesbury.—Others in Hampshire.—First in Cheshire.—Second and Third.—Pittsfield.—Hancock.—Washington and Sandisfield.—Other Churches in Berkshire.—The Work illustrated in a particular Instance.

The first Baptist church in the county of Hampshire was formed in Brimfield, November 4, 1736, and Mr. Ebenezer Moulton was ordained their pastor, November 4, 1741. His father and a majority of the church opposed the work that was then going on in the land, while he and a minor part were alive in it; and they had much controversy about it for seven years, and then about fifteen of them told their experiences to each others' satisfaction, and signed new articles and a covenant; and Mr. Moulton took them as his church, and would not allow any others to commune with them, without coming in at this door. The majority complained of this as unreasonable, but acted nothing as a body against them. And many from other towns joined with them, in this new form, from time to time; and Elder Moulton was often called to other places to preach and baptize, in and after the year 1749. Yea, he was called above eighty miles that year, and baptized ten at Bridgewater, and three in Raynham. But as his people had been trained up with prejudices against hireling ministers, they did very little for the support of their own minister; therefore he took to merchandizing, when there were scarcely any merchants in that part of the country; and he seemed to prosper for a number of years, and was a leader in building them a new meeting-house. But towards the close of the war, which ended in 1763, money was plenty, and merchants were multiplied; and Mr. Moulton found himself involved in debt, and his creditors ready to devour him, and he fled to Nova Scotia, where he preached in several places. Hereupon the church looked out for another minister, and at length obtained Mr. James Mellen, who was ordained their pastor, September 11, 1765. He was of Framingham, but had joined the First Baptist church in Middleborough; and he was a faithful and successful pastor, until he finished his course in a joyful manner, August 5, 1769. After his death many of the old members, who had been excluded from church for twenty years, came up and claimed a right therein ; upon which they sent to other elders and churches for advice, and when they had heard the case, their advice was for each of them to endeavor to satisfy the others about the reality of their religion, and so to covenant together anew. And this advice was taken and followed with good effects. After this they called Mr. Elijah Codding, another member of the First Baptist church in Middleborough, and he was ordained their pastor, November 11, 1773. And though it was a low time with them at South Brimfield for some years, yet such a heavenly shower was granted in 1779, as increased their members from twenty-three to two hundred and thirty-six in four years, and their minister still remains with them. And in those times Mr. Moulton obtained letters of license from his creditors to come home, and he was esteemed among his old people, until he died there in 1783.[1]

A Baptist church was formed in West Springfield, and Edward Upham, A. M., was ordained their pastor, October 15, 1740. He was born at Malden, March 26, 1709, and educated in the college at Cambridge, where he took his first degree in 1734. After the death of Mr. John Callender, he was prevailed with to move to Newport, in 1749, and he ministered to the first church there, only visiting his old people once or twice a year, until he removed back to them in April, 1771. Though in the mean time some of the wealthiest Baptists had been drawn into the incorporation of a new parish there, and to settle a minister, who was to sprinkle or dip people as they chose, and all were to commune together. And when Mr. Upham came back and set up worship at his usual place, taxes to the government were laid upon him, and he could not obtain the liberty that all settled ministers have, without suing for it in two or three courts. And many broils, and great bitterness of spirit has been among them ever since. Mr. Upham has been so infirm that he has not been able to preach for some years past, and the people are in very broken circumstances.[1]

The town of Ashfield was planted in 1751, and a Baptist church was formed there, July 10, 1761, and Mr. Ebenezer Smith was ordained their pastor the 20th of August following. An account of their sufferings was given in pages 148—153. In 1770 they had thirty-two members, and they increased from time to time, until the glorious blessings of the year 1780 raised their number to ninety-four. But the uncommon difficulties about money, after the war, caused a contention between the minister and the majority of the church about his support, which produced an open division in 1785. They called a council in December, 1786, who justified the minister, and condemned the majority of the church, and in September, 1788, he prevailed with the Warren Association to leave them out of their num-

---

[1]See pp. 31, 278, 279.—Ed.   [1]See pp. 33, 34; Vol. I, pp. 512—516.—Ed.

ber. But a powerful work began among them at that time, and they increased to a hundred and thirteen members in less than two years, having ordained his brother as their pastor. But as there have been some very unhappy actions in both parties, they have need of considering the warning which was given to the churches of Galatia, which is, If ye bite and devour one another, take heed that ye be not consumed one of another. Gal. v. 15.

A Baptist church was formed at Montague, July 1, 1765. An account of their sufferings is in pages 163—165. Mr. Simeon Coombs, from the Third Baptist church in Middleborough, removed there, and was ordained in that church, November 10, 1791. The majority of their society then lived in Leverett, and they now bear that name. Mr. Coombs ministered to them about three years, and then was dismissed, and removed to Wardsborough, in Vermont.

The First Baptist church in Wilbraham was constituted in 1768, and Mr. Seth Clark was ordained their pastor, June 13, 1770. He was born in Northampton in April, 1723, and experienced a change of heart in the glorious work there in 1735, under the ministry of President Edwards. This church had thirty-nine members in 1773, after which our national controversies and a bloody war engaged the minds of men in general, until it pleased God to pour out his Spirit in such a manner in 1778, as increased this church to a hundred and sixty-one members in four years, beside those who had died, been dismissed or excluded. After peace was restored to our land, the minds of people were amazingly carried away with earthly vanities, and the love of many waxed cold about religion. Yet this church enjoyed many blessings, and they wrote to our Association in 1792, and said, "Through the goodness of God, we are visited with the down-pouring of his Spirit in a most marvellous manner, not only in almost all parts of this town, and in each denomination, but also in the adjoining towns. Our present number is two hundred and thirty-five." They wrote again in 1794, that they had dismissed thirty-four, who were formed into a second Baptist church in Wilbraham, while two hundred and twenty-eight members remained in the first church. These blessings will appear the more wonderful, if we consider that the insurrection[1] in 1787 was in these parts.

The Baptist church in New Salem was formed in January, and Mr. Samuel Bigelow was ordained their pastor, May 21, 1772. He was born at Watertown in 1738, and new born in 1763. A gradual increase was granted to this church, until they had thirty-eight members in 1785. But controversies about discipline in the church were followed by a bloody contest in the State, which made rending work among this people. The army which marched up against the insurgents in the winter of 1787, took their

[1]See p. 330.—ED.

course through Wilbraham to Springfield, where a few were slain, from whence they went to Hadley, and then turned through New Salem to Petersham. Mr. Bigelow wrote to a friend on August 31, 1787, and said:—

Church travel and ordinances have ceased here, ever since the people arose in arms against government; though at present we are better united as to public worship. There is in general a good agreement between me and the body of the people about worship. I have said but little about the family quarrel that has been in this Commonwealth the year past; but what I have said has been to condemn both sides. I think the political fathers have provoked their children to wrath, and by oppression wise men have been mad, and the children have been unruly and rebellious.

And it was a low time among them for three years. But he wrote to the same friend, February 12, 1790, and said:—

This part of Zion has scarce ever been without a few drops of the rain of righteousness; but about six weeks ago, the Lord began to rain such a shower as has not fallen in these parts before. It is chiefly on the youth, from ten to twenty years old. The people in general are bowed before it. A goodly number are hopefully gathered in, and some from almost every family. There is also some shaking among the dry bones in Shutesbury.

Mr. Bigelow had been dismissed from his pastoral relation to this church before, by the advice of a council: and he preached in various places afterwards, until he gathered a church in Belchertown, and is at present their minister. They obtained several ministers to preach in New Salem, until Mr. Josiah Orcutt was ordained their pastor, October 30, 1794, and continues with them.

When the late war began, the Congregational minister of Shutesbury openly appeared to favor the British claims over America; therefore the people shut him out of their meeting-house, and he afterwards removed from the town. Yet after the war he sued the town for his salary, and our courts compelled the town to pay it, which caused ministerial tyranny to appear so odious, that no minister of that order has been received in the town since. Mr. William Ewing was called to preach there for several years, and in 1779, he was elected a delegate to the convention which formed the Massachusetts constitution of government, and he earnestly opposed the continuance of the Congregational establishment therein, as other Baptist members also did, though the majority prevailed against them. A happy revival of religion was granted in Shutesbury in 1780, when a Baptist church was formed there, and Ewing ministered to the town until 1785, when he went to Rowley. Mr. Joseph Smellage was called from South Brimfield to preach at Shutesbury directly after, and he was ordained the pastor of this church in October, 1786, and they have enjoyed many blessings since, and he is continued with them to this time.

The Association Minutes give the number of members in the churches of Leyden, Chesterfield, and Coleraine; but a more full account of them, which I had an encouragement of, has not arrived. Mr. Adam Hamilton, who came from Britain, had lived some years in Westfield before a revival of religion was granted there, and a Baptist church was formed in 1784, and he was ordained their pastor in November, 1785. He was much esteemed as a preacher of the gospel, and labored much at home and abroad ; and when the Danbury Association was formed, he had a chief lead therein for two or three years. But he then removed to New York, and was minister to a church there in 1793 ; after which he came back to Westfield, but fell into some scandals, which caused him to cease from preaching. Another Baptist church was formed in part of Westfield, in 1785, which part is since incorporated by the name of Russell, and Mr. Ebenezer Stow is their pastor. The other churches in the county of Hampshire, with the date of their constitution and their present state, are given in the foregoing list, from printed minutes and the best information I could gain. I am favored with a more particular account of some of the following churches.

COUNTY OF BERKSHIRE.

The lands near the head of Hoosac River, which runs into the Hudson at Stillwater, were purchased by some men in Providence and Coventry in 1766, and a number of men removed there the next year. They first called the place New Providence ; but the place was afterward a part of the town of Adams, having Lanesborough on the south of it, until part of several towns was incorporated by the name of Cheshire in 1793. The first inhabitants soon set up public worship among them, and being joined by others from various parts of the country, they formed a Baptist church there, August 29, 1769. Elder Peter Worden paid them a visit in the fall after ; and, as many of them had been his people before, he, at their earnest request, removed there in March, 1770. He was born June 6, 1728, and ordained at Warwick, May 21, 1751, and, after many labors in those parts, now removed to this place, and has been, to a large extent, a leader among the churches which form the Shaftsbury Association. An uncommon death in the beginning of 1772, with a sermon at the funeral, was the means of beginning a revival of religion among this people ; and in the fall after, the work came on more powerfully, and prevailed through the winter. As the church gave a written account of this work, the most material part of it is here inserted. They say :—

The children of God began to be more manifestly quickened, and more earnestly engaged than they before had been. Love and unity daily increased, and concern of mind began to be powerful on the minds of the unregenerate ; and not long after, some began to give hopeful evidences that they had passed from death unto life. The first of our young converts that made a public declaration of what God had done for them, were received into the church and baptized on November 15, 1773. Soon after this, distress of soul, and awakenings on the consciences of sinners, became more general, so that it was manifest by their uncommon attention and solemnity in public meetings, and their earnest inquiries and lamentable complaints in their private conversation, that the Spirit of God was operating on many of them ; and in the course of the ensuing winter and spring, we had reason to hope that near forty were savingly brought home to God, by a living union to Jesus Christ. Our number of members has increased to about eighty. And although upon the most close inquiry, there appears to be a great variety of circumstances in the subjects of the late work, yet in several things there appeared a general agreement. A clear conviction of sin, of the universal depravity of human nature, the reasonable requirements of God's holy law, his just declaration of vengeance against sin, and the total shutting up of all the sources of their natural hope, which is ever seeking some legal qualification to prepare for God's mercy ; and then a discovery of the all sufficient righteousness of the Son of God, as Mediator between God and man, a sensible union to God, love to holiness, hatred of sin, union to the children of God, and pity and benevolence to all mankind ; in these and in other things of like nature, there appeared a very general agreement. The means of awakening people among us have been various, as, the preaching of the word, prayer, exhortation, religious conversation, occurrences of divine providence, and the like ; but the public relations of experiences of those who have been wrought upon, have been as frequent a means as any. The most of the subjects of this work were in the vigor of youth, from fifteen to twenty-five years ; though we have reason to think that some who were advanced in age, and some little children, have been made the happy partakers of the salvation of God. This church does not receive any as members, but such as give satisfying evidences that they are born of God, neither have they table-communion with any but those who profess and practice believers' baptism. They make no bar of communion, whether persons come under hands or not. They hold to a general right in the brethren to improve their gifts, and yet believe that the church ought to exercise government therein, so that the church may be edified by the gifts of the brotherhood. We believe the entire depravity of human nature, and that the justification of a sinner before God is alone in the righteousness of Christ. This was publicly read and acknowledged by the church as a true relation.

PETER WORDEN, Elder,
JONATHAN RICHARDSON, ⎫
STEPHEN CARPENTER, ⎬ Deacons.
SAMUEL LOW, ⎭

January 15, 1774.

Another powerful work began among this people in 1779, which increased the church to a hundred and thirty-three members in 1782. A great blessing was again granted in 1788, which caused the addition of eighty members to this church in a year. A like favor was given again in 1791, so that the next year they had a hundred and ninety-four members. But many have been dismissed to other churches, while some have died, and some have been excluded, so that their present number is not so large.

Elder Nathan Mason and his people, who went to Nova Scotia in 1763, enjoyed many spiritual blessings there, and Mr. Job Seamans was converted, and began to preach among them ; but not finding the lands in that country, nor the government of it, to answer their expectations, they removed back, and settled in Lanesborough, a few miles from Elder Worden, where a church was established in 1771 ; and the work which came on in 1770 was powerful in both churches, and caused such a friendship between them as gradually removed the separation that had been handed down from their fathers, about laying on of hands upon every member. His church increased to a hundred and fifty members in 1784, and enjoyed many blessings afterwards. But when Elder Mason joined with Elder Leland in 1791, a few of the church parted from him, and retain their old constitution, as was before mentioned. Elder John Leland was born in the county of Worcester, and was baptized and began to preach there in 1774. In the fall of 1776, he set off with his wife, whom he had newly married, and removed into Virginia, and settled in the county of Orange ; and he travelled and preached abundantly in those parts, and in fourteen years he baptized six hundred and seven persons, and chiefly in the years 1780 and 1788, in which years religion was greatly revived in Virginia. He was very helpful in obtaining the law, in 1786, which abolished all taxes and compulsion in Virginia for the support of any religious ministers. He published a pamphlet called the Virginia Chronicle, in which was the address of the Baptists to President Washington, and his answer, which we have referred to under 1789. He has also published several other things ; and he returned with his family to New England in 1791, and settled in Cheshire, in that part which once was Lanesborough, and Elder Mason is in the church with him, which is now large.[1]

[1]John Leland was born in Grafton, May 14, 1754. He united with the Baptist church in Bellingham. He had rare natural powers of eloquence and a wonderfully ready wit, but was eccentric, and sometimes unstable and unsound. While he was settled in Cheshire the farmers around him made a mammoth cheese, weighing thirteen hundred pounds, and sent it by him as a present to President Jefferson. Mr. Leland made the journey a grand preaching tour of four months, in which he preached seventy-four times, tarrying wherever an interest was aroused and a prospect opened of doing good. Curiosity to see the mammoth cheese, and to hear the "mammoth priest," drew together immense congregations.

In his later years, Mr. Leland labored efficiently in Massachusetts in the cause of religious freedom, which he had done so much to secure in Virginia. A characteristic speech on this subject, which he delivered to the legislature of Massachusetts in 1811, may be found in Benedict's History, Vol. II, pp. 482—486.

In 1810, Mr. Leland wrote, "The number of persons that I have baptized is now eleven hundred and sixty-three."

As indicating his views and the character of his preaching, we subjoin an extract from his brief manuscript autobiography, now in the possession of the Backus Historical Society :—" At the close of the year 1806, I got amazingly distressed on account of my preaching, fearing that my barrenness in the ministry was owing to improper addresses. The Methodists were exceedingly zealous and successful, and

Mr. Valentine Rathbun was born at Stonington, in December, 1723, and after he, with many of his friends, removed to Pittsfield, they formed a Baptist church there in 1772, and he was ordained their pastor, and they became a large church in 1780. But many of them had now become corrupt in their opinions, and imagined that great and new things were at hand, with a more glorious dispensation than had before been known. And in April that year a man came into the place, and informed them that a company of Christians appeared above Albany, who had greater light and power than any had enjoyed before in latter ages; and many went up and joined to them, among whom were Mr. Rathbun, of Pittsfield, and Mr. Samuel Johnson, a Presbyterian minister in New Lebanon, west of Pittsfield, in the State of New York; and most of the inhabitants of that town received them, as well as a large part of Elder Rathbun's church. Though in about three months he left them, and published a discourse against their abominations, dated December 5, 1780, which was so well received, that it passed five editions in a year, and was read much in all parts of the country. His brother, Daniel Rathbun, continued with them about four years, and then he came out from them, and published a more full account of their delusions than any before had done. But though those Shakers are now reduced to a small number, and their power to deceive others seems to be gone, yet many who had joined with them have turned off to other delusions, instead of coming into the way of truth. But a few names in Pittsfield are steadfast in their profession.[1]

The place now called Hancock, upon the New York line, was first called Jericho, into which a number of Baptists moved in 1768, and following years, it being a wilderness before; and they met for worship with a num-

the addresses of their ministers were general and undaunted. I visited them; I conversed with them; they were all for heaven, and assured they were in the way; but their zeal and confidence appeared to me like the mighty wind and fire in Elijah's vision, and I could not discover that any with whom I conversed had any knowledge of themselves, of the law of God, or of the way of pardon. The Gillite mode of addressing sinners seemed a little different from the New Testament mode. The Hopkinsian method appeared as if it took all the wisdom of God to devise a way for an honorable pretense to damn men. Dr. Fuller only cast another bundle of straw on the fire. So that the great query that has agitated my mind for more than thirty years,—" How is a congregation of sinners to be addressed?" at the time which I am now treating of, fell with such distress upon my mind that I could hardly contain myself. But in the midst of my difficulties, I had a meeting at a schoolhouse. In the time of service, my soul got into the *trade winds*, and, without consulting Gill, Wesley, Hopkins, or Fuller, without comparing our translation with the Septuagint, Chaldee, or the king of Spain's Bible, I addressed the scholars and young people in a way that I never can without God helps me. The Spirit of the Lord fell upon them. Very soon after this, five of them came forward and confessed Christ." —ED.

[1] See p. 297.—ED.

ber of brethren who lived over said line, until they chose to be a society by themselves, where Steventon church now is. Therefore in June, 1772, fifteen persons in Hancock joined in covenant as a church of Christ, and Elder Clarke Rogers became their minister, though I have not obtained the date of his ordination. He went from West Greenwich, in the State of Rhode Island, from which State a large number of people went, who planted that northern wilderness. In the fall and winter after this church was formed, a powerful work came on among them. They say :—

There seemed to be a remarkable out-pouring of God's Spirit on the people, and the saints were much engaged in his cause, while the word, like arrows, pierced the hearts of sinners, who were crying out under the guilt of sin ; and when some obtained deliverance, they were expressing the joy of their hearts, visiting their neighbors, warning them to flee from the wrath to come, and to lay hold on the hope of eternal life. Old and young were bowing to the sceptre of King Jesus, and with one united voice saying, Blessed is he that cometh in the name of the Lord ; hosanna in the highest. There were open conferences held once a fortnight, to hear the declarations of any who desired to join the church ; and there was not a conference for many months, but that some were added to our number. Twenty were baptized in one day, and fifteen more in about a fortnight. Our number increased in one year from fifteen to one hundred and eleven, and other churches were gathered round us, and some were given up to them for conveniency, and some few were disciplined and have gone off from us, so that our present number is ninety-six.

This account was signed August 13, 1774, by Clark Rogers, elder, David Vaughan, Caleb Carr, William Douglass, Jesse Southwick and Ichabod Southwick. But in the most trying time of the war, when General Burgoyne sent out part of his army towards Bennington in 1777, and Captain Douglass collected his company together, ready to march against them next morning, some of his men went off to the enemy in the night, and appeared with them in battle the next day, when such a victory was gained as greatly revived the hearts of the Americans, and Burgoyne and his army were captivated soon after. This defection of some of the Baptists in Hancock, caused a division in the church, and another was formed and continued many years ; but they are lately united again, and one young man who then went to the enemy, has not only manifested repentance, but also such ministerial gifts, that he is ordained the pastor of a large Baptist church near the place where Burgoyne was taken. How marvellous are the works of God !

A Baptist church was formed in Washington in November, 1777, and Mr. John Nichols is their pastor, who was ordained in 1784. Another church was constituted in Sandisfield in August, 1779, and Elder Joshua Morse became their pastor. He was born in an uncultivated part of Rhode Island colony, where he never went to any religious meeting until he was sixteen years old ; but in hearing the clear preaching of the gospel soon after, he not only became acquainted with experimental religion, but an exhorter of others to regard it, until he commenced a public preacher, and he was ordained the pastor of a church in New London, in Connecticut, May 17, 1750.   It was in that part of the town which is now set off by the name of Montville.   The Stonington Association met there in 1773, the year after they were first formed.   Mr. Morse was much esteemed as a clear preacher of the gospel, with uncommon solemnity, and with much success. But in the time of the war, his people were much exposed to the enemy, and many of them removed away, until their minister, by the advice of a council, removed also and settled at Sandisfield, where his public ministrations, and private conversation, were edifying and beneficial, and he preached occasionally elsewhere, until he died in a joyful manner, in June, 1795, in the seventieth year of his age.   The other Baptist church in that town I have not received a history of,[1] nor of Great Barrington and Williamstown.

[1]The following is from an account of the Second Baptist church in Sandisfield, which was sent to Mr. Backus by a committee of the church in 1801 :—

"In the year 1784, not far from the month of June, Daniel Fowler, Timothy Judd, and Amos Spring, living in a place since called Bethlehem, and Isaac Walker, in the east part of Tyringham, being remote from any meeting, agreed to set up one at Timothy Judd's, to sing and pray and read sermons.   These, with their families, were of the Presbyterian denomination; and agreed that no other denomination should ever come among them, to assist in carrying on their worship.   Thus they continued about three years and a half.   About the month of November, 1787, a stranger stopped in the neighborhood, who was of the Baptist denomination, and attended those meetings.   Notice was given that this man sometimes spoke in public. A council was held whether they should let this man speak with them.   The result was, ' He might speak *once*.'   There seemed to be such a blessing that followed his improvement, that they desired him to improve with them again, which he did. From this, in a most wonderful manner, the Lord began to work like himself.   Displays of redeeming grace were conspicuous.   Dagon fell before God's holy ark. The wilderness began to bud and blossom like the fields of Paradise, and on them that sat in the valley of the shadow of death, the sun of righteousness beamed the effulgence of his glory.   This continued through the winter following.   This work spread into the adjacent vicinities, and awakened much opposition, some saying that it was the work of the devil; others said, ' Can he that hath a devil open the eyes of the blind?'   However, in April following, Elder Seth Clark, Joseph Dunham, and Ezekiel Wright, from Wilbraham, were sent for, and on the 25th of said month, nineteen were baptized, and a church was then constituted and fellowshipped by Elder Clark, with the delegates, it being called the Second Baptist church in Sandisfield, because it was constituted in that town, and the most of the members belonged to it. Still a general opposition on every hand continued; but the Lord added to the church, and carried on his glorious work with a continued increase for about two years, which brought us to the number of forty.   In March, 1790, the church agreed to set apart Brother Benjamin Baldwin to the work of the ministry, which was performed on the 9th of June following, by ordination."

The sketch goes on to describe the acts of oppression to which the church was subjected, by being taxed for the support of Presbyterian ministers, and to build a

Bullocksgrant is a tract of land which was granted to some men from Rehoboth, which lies between Cheshire and Hawley, but it is not yet incorporated as a town. A number of people from Middleborough, Taunton, and Berkeley, have also removed there, and a number of them joined to the first church in Cheshire. But a powerful work came on among them, and a Baptist church was formed, and Mr Nathan Haskins was ordained their pastor, January 28, 1789. He went from Berkeley in the county of Bristol, and many blessings have been granted under his ministry since. A Baptist church was formed in West Stockbridge, January 29, 1781, and Mr. Elnathan Wilcox was installed as their pastor ; but they were afterwards broken and scattered. Yet a Baptist church was gathered in Stockbridge and West Stockbridge in 1790, and Samuel Whelpley, A. M. was ordained their pastor. He was graduated by the college at Providence in 1790, and still continues with that people. I have not obtained a particular history of the other Baptist churches in that county.

But a particular account of the change which was wrought in one person, may give a more clear idea of the nature of the work that was going on in those parts. A poor woman who was brought up in the wilderness, in such a manner as not to have learned to read, gave the following relation of her experiences, in the time of the revival at Hancock in the fall and winter of 1772, 1773. She said :—

I lived in Little Hoosac, and I heard of a wonderful work of God in Jericho, how many were converted, which caused me to reflect on my past life, which terrified me much. One night I dreamed that the devil was come for me ; I thought he came in a flash of fire, which struck me down to hell, into great torment ; then I lamented my condition, how I had neglected my salvation, and now my day was over. Thus I awoke in great surprise, and told my husband, who told me not to regard it, for dreams were nothing. But my guilty conscience terrified me so that I could have no rest, day nor night ; my sins appeared very heinous, until I thought I could not live long under such horror. I went one day to meeting at Jericho, and thought I would never return till I had found some relief, for I could not live so ; and I went and heard the number of fifteen tell the dealings of God with them ; and they would tell my heart, only they had found

Presbyterian meeting-house. At first they gave certificates, or escaped distraint or imprisonment by payment of taxes, but at last they said, " ' Be it known to thee, O king, (or civil power in religion,) that we will not serve thy gods, nor worship the image which the civil court at Boston has set up, believing that our God is able to deliver us from the fiery furnace.' Able attorneys were employed, and the Presbyterians found that their town meetings had not been conducted in a legal manner. They revoked their own doings, and assessed finally only their own denomination."

In 1798, the two Baptist churches in Sandisfield were blessed with a revival, and about sixty were added to each church. In the two succeeding years, the Second church received about twenty each year. In 1801, their number was a hundred and seventy-five.—Ed.

deliverance, and I had not, which made me think there was no mercy for me : I was an undone creature, and my sins appeared more heinous than before.   There was a lecture in the evening, and I went to hear it, and the minister preached very powerfully, and instead of yielding me any relief, it added to my torment.   I thought I had one more sermon to account with God for, unless I obtained pardon through Jesus Christ, which I thought was not for me, I had been such a great sinner.   My load was so heavy that I thought I could not bear up under it.   I called my sister out of meeting, and told her that I felt so that it seemed as though I could not live.   She gave me but little answer, and meeting being over, I went to a house to lodge, and the people were talking of religion, but I was no company for them.   I felt like a lonesome monument of God's displeasure. I got but a little sleep that night.   Next morning I set out to go home, and these words were ushered into my mind, Turn, O sinner, why will you die? But I thought that I had done all that I could, and there was no mercy for me ; then these thoughts came into my mind, You have not given up your heart to God ; and I found my whole heart to be a sink of sin, and that I had been at enmity against a just and holy God all my life long, and that God was angry with the wicked every day ; and I saw myself to be such a creature that I wondered that he would suffer me to walk on his footstool. I wondered that the earth did not open and swallow me up ; as I passed along I was afraid that every tree would fall on me and dash me to pieces, and I would run to get clear of one, and the fear of another would take me.   Still these words would follow me, Turn, O sinner, why will you die? At length I was brought to view the justice of God, and that I was a rebel justly condemned, and had been provoking God to anger all my life long, and was now about to receive the just reward of my deeds, and could only plead guilty before God, on which consideration I was brought to yield myself into his hands, with this repeated cry, Mercy, Lord, mercy, if possible ; though I could see no way that God could be just and shew mercy to such a wretch as I was.   While I was, as it were, sinking with these melancholy thoughts, those words were ushered into my mind in a remarkable manner, " Ye believe in God, believe also in me."   These words gave me some glimpse of hope.   The heft of my burden seemed to be taken away, and I felt calm and peaceable, but I could not tell what it might be. I thought that if I was converted I should see Christ, and I would go out in the evening, and look on the firmament, expecting to see Christ ; but then these words were ushered into my mind, "Peace to all the children of God, and peace to thy soul."   Then I went in and got the Bible, for my husband to try to learn me to read, and I could spell a little : and as I tried to read I thought the Lord assisted me in reading ; and I said, Husband, it seems to me that the Lord assists me in reading, I never could read so before.   I had no sooner spoken than my soul was filled with divine love, yea, more than full. I thought there was enough for all the world to swim away unto the blissful shores of eternal day.   My tongue broke out in raptures of praise, crying, Glory, glory to God in the highest ! for he hath redeemed my soul from the horrible pit !   I thought I wanted to tell all the world of the fullness there was in Christ.

CHAPTER XL.

A CONCISE VIEW OF THE DISTRICT OF MAINE.—ACCOUNTS OF BAPTIST
CHURCHES IN THE COUNTY OF YORK.—COUNTY OF CUMBERLAND.—
CONTROVERSIES ABOUT LAND IN THE COUNTY OF LINCOLN.—OF THE
FIRST BAPTIST CHURCHES THEREIN.—OF THEIR GREAT INCREASE SINCE
1790.—OF THEIR FAITH AND ORDER, AND OPPRESSION FROM OTHERS.
—OF THE COUNTIES OF HANCOCK AND WASHINGTON, WITH A REVIEW
OF LINCOLN.

The kings of England claimed a power of giving the lands of the heathen
in America to their subjects; and in 1639 a grant was made to Sir Ferdinando Gorges, of all the lands between Piscataqua and Sagadahoc, and a
hundred and twenty miles into the country, under the name of The Province of Maine. But this grant, and all others of the like nature, were
imitations of the Pope of Rome, who received his power from the old dragon. And the inspired apostle says, I beheld another beast coming up out
of the earth, and he had two horns like a lamb, and he spake like a dragon,
and he exerciseth all the power of the first beast. Rev. xiii. 2, 11, 12.
The same power had before granted the charter of the Massachusetts,
which extended three miles north of every part of Merrimack River, which
they construed so as to reach a line from the head of the river to Casco
Bay. And though New Hampshire was taken from them in 1680, yet they
exercised a power beyond it afterwards. In 1681, a number of men came
from Kittery to Boston, and joined the Baptist church there, one of whom
was William Screven, to whom they gave an approbation to preach the gospel, January 11, 1682. But he was persecuted for preaching in those parts,
by ministers and rulers. Yet Elder Hull and others were sent from Boston, by the request of those people, to organize a church among them.[1]
And a church was constituted in Kittery, September 25, 1682, consisting
of William Screven, elder, Humphrey Churchwood, deacon, Robert Wil-

[1] See Vol. I, pp. 400—405.

liams, John Morgandy, Richard Cutts, Timothy Davis, Leonard Drown, William Adams, Humphrey Azell, George Litten, and a number of sisters. Elder Screven and others were repeatedly carried to courts, where sentences were passed against them, of fines and imprisonment, until they removed from such persecutors ; and Screven went to South Carolina, and became the pastor of the Baptist church in Charleston, from whence he wrote to Mr. Ellis Callender, of Boston, June 2, 1707. He wrote again to him, August 6, 1708, and said, " I rejoice that you are inclined to, and employed in the blessed work of the Lord, for the support of his cause and the comfort of his saints, left of that poor languishing church with you." Colonel Thomas Screven, a leading man amongst the Baptists now in Charleston, sprang from him. Leonard Drown removed to Boston, and his son was deacon in the Baptist church there for many years, and his posterity remain in these parts ever since, one of whom is a Fellow of our college at Providence.[1] But we hear no more of any Baptist church in those parts for above eighty years after.

There was a revival of religion in Berwick about the time that there was through a great part of the country, and after Mr. Hezekiah Smith was settled at Haverhill, he was sent for to Berwick, in 1767, and baptized a considerable number ; and he went again the next year and assisted in forming a Baptist church there, June 28, 1768. Mr. Joshua Emery was their teacher, though he was not ordained ; and they gave in certificates of their society according to law, and yet were taxed to parish ministers, and spoiling of goods or imprisonment was fiercely pursued for some years, for the collection of those taxes, until some trials in courts put a stop thereto.[2] A division took place in this church and society a few years after, and Mr. Emery preached to one part, and Mr. William Hooper was ordained pastor of the other, August 14, 1776, in which office he has continued ever since. He was born at Berwick, February 28, 1747, but he resides at Madbury, where is a branch of this church, and he preaches part of his time at each place. Sanford is above Berwick, where a Baptist church was formed, and Mr. Pelatiah Tingley, who went from Attleborough, was ordained there, October 22, 1772. But he afterwards removed to Waterborough, where he is pastor of a church that is not in full fellowship with most of our Baptist churches ; though another church was formed in that town in their fellowship, and Mr. Henry Smith was ordained their pastor in 1794. A Baptist church was formed at Wells, in 1780, and Mr. Nathaniel Lord, of Berwick, was ordained their pastor. Dr. Moses Hemmenway lives in that town, whose writings have been before mentioned. A Baptist church was formed in Coxhall, October 29, 1782, and Mr. Simon Lock was ordained their pastor, December 18, 1783. Mr. Tozer Lord, an older brother to Nathaniel, was ordained in a church at Lebanon, above Berwick, in

[1] Solomon Drown, M. D.—Ed.   [2] See p. 165.

1776 ; but that church is dissolved, and he now is minister of a church in Shapleigh. Another church was formed in that town in 1785, and Mr. Nehemiah Davis is their pastor. Mr. Zebadiah Richardson was minister of the church at Sanford in 1788, who is now pastor of a church in Frye-burg, on the west borders of the county of York. There was a powerful work in Francisburg in 1788, from whence above twenty persons joined to Sanford church. A Baptist church was formed in Cornish in 1792.

The first Baptist church in the county of Cumberland was formed at Gorham, by assistance from Haverhill, June 20, 1768. Mr. Smith, of Haverhill, had been sent for, and baptized some persons there the fall before. An account of their sufferings is in pages 179—181. It is said that a majority of them have since embraced the opinion of general redemption, and yet hold to the final perseverance of the saints ; and they are not in fellowship with most of our churches. A Baptist church was formed in New Gloucester in May, 1782, and they tried various ways to get clear of oppression from the Congregational party, and to support their own wor-ship, until they applied to our legislature, and obtained an incorporation of a Baptist society, invested with all the powers and privileges of other par-ishes. But in about four years many of them found this to be such a bond-age, that they renounced the scheme, and formed a new Baptist church in October, 1794, and they joined the Bowdoinham Association in August, 1795. A number of people in Harpswell had experienced a happy change in former times, and a fresh revival.began among them in 1783, which led on to the forming of a Baptist church there, January 20, 1785. Mr. James Potter had labored with success among them, and on October 6, 1785, he was ordained there as a travelling minister ; and Mr. Samuel Woodward, who was raised up among them, was ordained their pastor in October, 1792. In the mean time such a rain of righteousness was granted in those parts, as caused the wilderness to become a fruitful field ; and three churches were formed in one year. Those of Hebron and Buckfield were formed in Au-gust, and that of Paris in November, 1791 ; and Mr. James Hooper, brother to William, was ordained at Paris, June 25, 1795. Mr. Samuel Flagg, who went from Boston, is preaching at Hebron. Mr. Abraham Cummings, who was educated in the college at Providence, where he took his first degree in 1776, preached for some years in the Congregational way, until he was convinced that believers' baptism was the way that Christ in-stituted, and was baptized in March, 1783 ; and in the spring of 1787 he removed into the county of Cumberland, and preached so much in the par-ish of Freeport, that they gave him a good farm, but he could not be or-dained as a parish minister because he could not sprinkle infants. He has travelled and preached in many of our new plantations, but a number of persons were baptized in North Yarmouth in the fall of 1795, who purpose to form a church there, and to call him to be their minister. He lately published a discourse upon baptism. The late revival was powerful in Livermore, and a Baptist church was formed there, August 7, 1793. Two brethren, Elisha Williams and Otis Robinson, are preachers among them, though not ordained. The first of them is a son of Dr. Williams, of East Hartford, and was educated at Yale College; but the spiritual teaching which he has received in that wilderness, he prefers above all human learning. The other went from Attleborough. A Baptist church was formed at Sudbury, Canada, August 30, 1795.

The great collection of the waters of the rivers Kennebeck and Andro-scroggin, with the rivers that fall into them, were called Sagadahoc. A number of men came from England, and began a plantation there in 1607, thirteen years before our fathers began at Plymouth, but they went back again the next year. But the colony of Plymouth obtained a grant from England of a tract of land of fifteen miles wide on each side of Kennebeck River, where they carried on a trade with the Indians from 1630 to 1661, when they sold the same to four men. Though in the mean time, after the parliament of England had prevailed against the king who made those grants of American lands, particular men obtained deeds of a great part of them from Indian sachems, until an agent for the Massachusetts bought the whole of Gorges's grant of his heirs in 1676, and then those lands were claimed by this government. And the charter of 1691 gave them all the lands from thence to Nova Scotia, and this government has been often granting lands since to particular men unto this time. So that a great part of the same lands have been claimed by grants from the crown, by deeds from the Indians, and by grants from the legislature of the Massachusetts. Unspeakable troubles and costs of courts have been caused by these opposite claims, and when these controversies will all be settled no man can tell. A gentleman who was born in Berwick, but now lives in Boston, and is attorney-general for this State, published a history of the District of Maine in 1795, which gives much light into these affairs. Yet he appears to be not so clear in religious matters. For he says, "There never was any thing like persecution in the District of Maine, nor was there much pains taken, in the settlement of it, to establish a regular support for the clergy; the want of this was a great injury to the people, for experience fully advocates the point, that without a regular fixed mode of establishing teachers of piety, religion and morality, a country can never be made virtuous and happy." And yet he afterwards says, " In the present state of our governments in America, and in the enlightened age in which we live, religious opinions, however strongly they may be expressed, or however forcibly they may be urged, can do us no hurt."[1] But all ought to know, that reviling and lying, as well as spoiling of goods and imprisonment for matters of conscience, are persecution in the sight of God.

[1] Sullivan's History, pp. 79, 232.

Matt. v. 10, 11 ; Heb. x. 42—34. And has there been nothing like these in the District of Maine? And if religious opinions can do no hurt in our governments, how can teachers of piety, religion and morality do any good therein? For these virtues are plainly described in the word of God, which says, If any have children or nephews, let them learn first to shew piety at home, and to require their parents. I Tim. v. 4. Pure religion, and undefiled, before God and the Father, is this, To visit the fatherless and widows in their affliction, and to keep himself unspotted from the world. James i. 27. Therefore all things whatsoever ye would that men should do to you, do ye even so to them ; for this is the law and the prophets. Matt. vii. 12. This is God's description of piety, religion and morality ; but all men who support religious worship by force, violate these rules, more or less. The nation of Israel was the only visible church in the world which God empowered to use the sword in religious affairs ; all adulterers, idolaters and blasphemers were to die without mercy. And when Christ by his death had abolished all hereditary distinctions among mankind, and built his church of those who were born again among all nations, the power of his gospel dashed the great Roman empire to pieces, without any help from the sword of the magistrate. But Mystery Babylon was built, by confounding nature and grace, church and world together. And when the fathers of the Massachusetts fled from her tyranny to America, they formed a government in imitation of the church of Israel, and they made a law to put all adulterers to death, the year after they first came to Boston. And they had plain Scripture for it, if the church of Christ is in the same covenant that God made with Abraham ; for by that covenant all adulterers were to be put to death, and all bastards were excluded from the church. Levit. xx. 10 ; Deut. xxiii. 2. But the circumcision of the heart is essentially necessary, to give any person a right in the church of Christ. Therefore an inspired apostle says. Beware of dogs, beware of evil workers, beware of the concision. For we are the circumcision, who worship God in the spirit, and rejoice in Christ Jesus, and have no confidence in the flesh. Phil. iii. 2, 3. All men who trust in any arm of flesh, are cursed with blindness, so as not to see when good cometh ; but they who trust in the Lord, and make him their hope, are like trees planted by a river, whose leaf shall be green, and they shall not cease from yielding fruit. Jer. xvii. 5—8. And all mankind are in one or the other of these two classes.

There was but little appearance of religion in the county of Lincoln, until God poured his Spirit upon them within a few years past. Mr. James Potter was born there in 1734, and was awakened to some sense of sin when he was about ten years old ; and convictions followed him from time to time, until a clear deliverance was granted him, October 3, 1781. And he says :—

Now I began to see the base views I formerly had of the Lord Jesus Christ, and of the plan of salvation ; for when I had a discovery of actual sins, and of the danger I was exposed to thereby, I would repent and reform, and think what a glorious Saviour Christ was, and that some time or other he would save me from hell, and take me to glory, with a desire to be happy, but no desire to be holy. But, glory be to God! he now gave me another view of salvation. Now I saw his law to be holy, and loved it, though I and all my conduct were condemned by it. Now I saw that God's justice did not strike against me as his creature, but as a sinner ; and that Christ died not only to save from punishment, but from sin itself. I saw that Christ's office was not only to make men happy, but also to make them holy, and the plan now looked beautiful to me, and I had no desire to have the least tittle of it altered, but all my cry was to be conformed to this glorious plan.[1]

It was then a very cold and stupid season all round him ; but the views which were then given him of the glory of the gospel, and of the worth of immortal souls, with the call of God to him to hold up the light which was given him to others, caused him to leave the management of his farm to his family, and to go from house to house, in his own town and to neighboring places, to hold forth light to all he could converse with, about the great concerns of the soul and eternity. And in the spring of 1782, he says, " The work began to break out wonderfully. Some were in great distress, and others praising God, and inviting others to come away to Jesus Christ." And a number of them were brought to hold believers' baptism, before they had ever seen a Baptist minister. Mr. Job Macomber was then preaching at New Gloucester, and, hearing of the work in the county of Lincoln, he went there in December, 1782, and preached in several places with great satisfaction ; and in January, 1783, he wrote a letter to Middleborough about it, which was read to Mr. Isaac Case, which had such an effect upon his mind, that he was ordained for the purpose in September, 1783, and went directly into those parts, and preached with success in Harpswell, and then with greater power at Thomaston, where he first arrived in February, 1784. Mr. Macomber also removed to Bowdoinham, in the fall of 1783, at the request of the people. And in the spring Mr. Lock was sent for from Coxhall, and a Baptist church was formed in Bowdoinham, May 24, and another at Thomaston, May 27, 1784. And Mr. Macomber was ordained the pastor of the first of these churches, August 18, 1784, while Mr. Case was settled as the pastor of the other, having been ordained before. Macomber was son to a Congregational deacon in Middleborough, but joined the First Baptist church there in 1772, began to preach in 1774, and labored in various parts of the country, until he settled where he now is. Case was born in Rehoboth, February 25, 1761, met with a change in December, 1779, began to preach in July, 1780, and was an early member of the Baptist church of Dighton, where he was ordained

[1]See pp. 281—283.

September 10, 1783, and went directly into those parts, where he is still useful.[1] As there was a great field for labor, and Mr. Elisha Snow, of Thomaston, was called into the work, their elders and brethren met at Harpswell, June 11, 1788, and ordained him as an itinerant minister. On the 29th of the same month, a Baptist church was formed in Vassalborough, and another at Bowdoin in the fall after, where Mr. Potter lived, and he became their pastor. Mr. Humphrey Purinton is also a useful preacher in that church. And a Baptist church was formed at Ballston, January 3, 1789. The churches of Bowdoinham, Thomaston, and Harpswell, began their Association in 1787, which had become six churches in August, 1790, and three hundred and seventeen members.

[1] The following extracts are from letters of Mr. Case, the former to James Lovell, of Barnstable, the latter to Mr. Backus :—

"Thomaston, June 22, 1784.

" DEAR AND BELOVED BROTHER IN CHRIST :—I readily embrace this opportunity to write to you, to inform you of the gracious dealings of God with me of late, and not me only, but many others in these parts. I came from Rehoboth last September, and have been in these eastern parts ever since; and I desire to bless the Lord for directing me to this part of his vineyard. I think I have seen more of the power and glory of our God, since I have been in these parts, than ever I saw before; poor, shelterless souls fleeing to Christ for shelter, and praising the Lord for free grace through the merits of Christ's righteousness, [which] which runs down our streets like a mighty stream. The eyes of the blind are opened, and the ears of the deaf are unstopped. .... I have had occasion to baptize eighty-two persons since I came to this town. .... The brethren here have embodied themselves into a church in the Baptist order. I trust the Lord hath done this for his glory. . . . . ."

"Thomaston, June 23, 1785.

" HONORED AND VERY DEAR SIR :—I would inform you that the dear Redeemer reigns in these parts. God hath done great things for this town in particular. It hath been a very stupid, barren wilderness in time past; but, thanks be to the God of love, he hath done great things for us, and caused the wilderness to bud and blossom as the rose. The work of the Lord begun here about the 18th of February, 1784, and went on very powerfully, and held so for about three months, and I believe there were sixty or seventy savingly brought home to God, and the chief of them were baptized; and the 27th of May, there were fifty unitedly and understandingly embodied into a church, and forty-six added since, several out of other towns. .... There are twenty-four in the church now that seem well established and united in the faith of the gospel, and we expect a number more will join next Saturday. We have spent this day in fasting and prayer to God. I trust it was not time spent in vain. .... There is a church embodied in Harpswell, in Cumberland county. There were twenty embodied together the 20th of January, 1785, and fourteen have joined since, so that there are thirty-four that seem well united. There are several more that stand ready to join when I visit them again. .... I hear the Lord is at work in a powerful manner up Kennebeck River, and to the head of Sheepscot River, and at Deer Island. I was there in May. Several were under deep concern, and several brought to rejoice in Christ Jesus. Surely God hath done, and is still doing, great things for these parts. . . . . ."—ED.

32

These new churches in a wilderness had the powers of the world against them, and also many under the Baptist name, who gathered some churches who held to doctrines which they could not have fellowship with, while they had many difficulties among themselves. Yet God was pleased to grant a fresh revival among them. The Second Baptist church in Bowdoin was constituted, August 17, 1791, and Mr. William Stinson was ordained their pastor, July 5, 1792. Another church was formed in Sidney, June 20, 1791, and Mr. Asa Wilbur was ordained their pastor, November 13, 1793. Mr. Lemuel Jackson, a member of that church, was ordained as a travelling minister the same day. The first of them was born in Bridgewater, the other in Middleborough, in the county of Plymouth. Mr. Potter was very successful in Lewiston, from the beginning of his public labors, and many joined his church from thence, until they obtained a regular dismission, and a church of twenty-two members was formed in Lewiston, March 3, 1792. And on August 3, 1793, thirteen of their members were dismissed, and formed a church in Greene. They also dismissed fourteen more, who formed the Third church in Bowdoin, February 13, 1794, at which time they had fifty-nine members left. And they say, " It appears that Elder James Potter, and Elder William Stinson, were the instruments that the Lord blessed in the awakening the greatest part of these, who appear to have been brought out of nature's darkness into the glorious liberty of the gospel." A Baptist church was formed at Readfield, May 11, 1792, and Elder Case removed and became their pastor, leaving the church in Thomaston under the care of Elder Snow. And on July 27, 1792, a church was formed in Stirling, now called Fayette, and Elder Eliphalet Smith became their pastor. He was converted at Stratham in 1764, and was ordained the pastor of a Congregational church in Deerfield, in New Hampshire, in January, 1770, though he and the majority of his church became Baptists in June following.[1] But in some years after, he removed into the county of Lincoln, and now became the pastor of this church. A Baptist church was formed on Muscongus Island, near Bristol, in 1792, and Mr. Andrew Fuller, who went from Middleborough, was ordained therein, October 30, 1793. Another church was formed at Cushing in 1792, and Mr. Ephraim Hall was ordained their pastor, October 24, 1793. A Baptist church was formed at Nobleborough, July 25, 1793, another at New Sandwich, January 9, 1794, and a third at Barretstown in December following. As many of the Baptists have removed from Martha's Vineyard to Sandy River, a high branch of the Kennebeck, they have called their town New Vineyard, and they formed a Baptist church there, August 8, 1795. Another was formed at Clinton the 5th of September after. Their elder, Mephibosheth Cain, was ordained at Clinton, January

[1]See p. 169.

12, and Nehemiah Gould and Job Chadwick at Vassalborough, January 15, 1796.

Thus, in less than twelve years, twenty-six Baptist churches have been formed in two counties, in which are fifteen ordained ministers, and about a thousand members. And in August, 1795, their Association gave a declaration of their faith, wherein they say :—

We believe that the Scriptures of the Old and New Testaments are the word of God ; we believe there is but one living and true God ; we believe the important doctrines of three equal persons in the Godhead, eternal and personal election, original sin, particular redemption, free justification by the imputed righteousness of Christ, efficacious grace in regeneration, the final perseverance of real believers, the resurrection of the dead, the future judgment, the eternal happiness of the righteous, and everlasting misery of the impenitent. We believe that baptism and the Lord's Supper are ordinances of Christ, to be continued until his second coming, and the former is requisite to the latter ; that is to say, that those are to be admitted into the communion of the church, and so to partake of its ordinances, who, upon profession of their faith, have been baptized by immersion in the name of the Father, of the Son, and of the Holy Ghost.

Now in all these articles they agree with the most eminent fathers of New England, except in sprinkling infants upon the faith of their parents and calling it baptism, for which there is not a word in all the Holy Scriptures. But as a son of Gideon by his concubine, slew seventy of his lawful children, so one error of our fathers has prevailed against all their good principles and conduct. And all men who are now contending for the faith which was once delivered to the saints, are daily exposed to reviling and lying, spoiling of goods and imprisonment, from those who support their worship by force. We are well informed, that more than a hundred dollars have been taken from people of the Baptist sentiments in Topsham for a Pædobaptist minister in the town, by blending civil and ministerial taxes together ; and the like is done in many other parts of the country. Thus men would hold their religion by the same power by which they hold their worldly estates ; though they daily deny their neighbors the liberty about their souls which all enjoy about their bodies and estates. For no man is compelled to pay a farthing to any physician, unless he is pleased to employ him. And God says of false teachers, They have healed the hurt of the daughter of my people slightly, saying, Peace, peace, when there is no peace. They have rejected the word of the Lord, and what wisdom is in them ? Jer. vi. 14 ; viii. 9—11. And who can tell how many such teachers there are in our day ? Neither is any man obliged to employ or support lawyers, if he will live without them. But many who handle the law of God, shut up the kingdom of heaven against men, and neither go in themselves, nor suffer others to go into it. And yet, four States in New England deny the liberty to all men therein about their souls and eternity, which they allow them concerning their bodies and temporal estates.   And when will men open their eyes, and renounce this iniquity?

A revival of religion began on an island in Penobscot Bay, in the county of Hancock, now incorporated by the name of Islesborough, in the fall of 1790, and a Baptist church was formed there, May 27, 1791, and Mr. Thomas Eames was ordained their pastor, June 19, 1794.   He and a number of his people went from Marshfield in the county of Plymouth.   There is also a Baptist church at Eppin in this county, and Mr. Joshua Young is their pastor, who was ordained at Ballston, April 8, 1795.   We have also heard of some Baptists in Gouldsburg, and Canaan, in this county, as well as of some in the county of Washington, but have not any such accounts of them as may be of service to the public.   When the work of God was powerful in the county of Lincoln in 1784, one of the subjects of it observed, that the ministers who were settled and supported by law were not made use of therein, even when they preached good doctrine, which caused a serious inquiry in his mind, why it should be so.   And having obtained a satisfying answer, he wrote the same to a friend, saying, " The voice of the general conduct of true ministers to sinners is, We pray you, in Christ's stead, be ye reconciled to God that your souls may live : but the voice of others, to the church and the world is, We pray you, in Christ's stead, be ye reconciled together that we may live."   And the help of all the power of the ruling party in our government has not settled but thirteen of this last sort of teachers, in all the counties of Lincoln, Hancock and Washington, wherein are near sixty incorporated towns, and many other plantations.

CHAPTER XLI.

The first civil government upon earth, since the rise of antichrist, which
gave equal liberty of conscience, was begun in Providence; and there was
also the first Baptist church in America. Mr. Roger Williams was born
in Wales, in 1599, was educated at Oxford University,[1] and was introduced
into the ministry in the church of England for some years, before he came
over to America, and landed at Boston in February, 1631. When he came
there, he could not agree with the ruling party, in their use of the sword
in religious affairs, nor in their receiving the grant of American lands from
the kings of England. This caused his going to Plymouth, where he
preached above two years, and then he was called and ordained at Salem;
but the controversy arose so high between him and the teachers and rulers
of Massachusetts, that they passed a sentence of banishment against him
in October, 1635, and in January, 1636, they attempted to seize him and
send him back to England, but he fled to Rehoboth, and from thence to
Providence, where he obtained a grant of lands from the Narragansett Indians.[2] And he says, " I was sorely tossed for fourteen weeks, in a bitter
winter season, not knowing what bread or bed did mean."[3] Yet he was so

[1]See a different account in Vol. I, p. 40, note.—ED.
[2]Winthrop's Journal, pp. 91, 92. [Vol. I, pp. 175, 176.]
[3]Massachusetts Historical Collections Vol. I, p. 276.

far from seeking any revenge upon those who banished him, that, at the hazard of his life, he went into Narragansett, and prevented the Indians there from joining with the Pequods, who were for driving all the English out of the country, when Boston was not seven years old. And any man who will read the books referred to in the margin, may see that Williams was a chief instrument of saving all the English then in New England, from ruin; though ministerial influence was so great in the Massachusetts as to exclude him from liberty of coming into their government all his days. But the very year after Williams died in peace, the Massachusetts charter was taken away, and the king of England claimed all their lands, and his governor and council made laws, and imposed taxes upon them, without any house of representatives, and introduced the taxes upon commerce, which finally brought on the late war. Mr. Williams, having obtained a deed of the lands in Providence, gave twelve men an equal right therein with himself, and he drew a covenant of such a government in the town in civil affairs, as excluded them from governing in religious matters. And because Joshua Verin refused to allow liberty of conscience to his wife, he was excluded from the privilege of voting in the town, until he granted that liberty. Upon this Verin removed to Barbadoes, and left his estate in Providence.[1] As Williams and a number of his friends were convinced that professing believers were the only gospel subjects of baptism, they formed a Baptist church in Providence, in March, 1639, when one of them baptized him, and then he baptized the rest.[2] But the unruly passions of some among them, with other things, caused such scruples in Williams's mind, in about four months, that he refrained from administering or partaking of special ordinances in any church ever after, as long as he lived, though he would preach the gospel, and join in social worship with such as agreed with him, all his days. The reasons of this conduct may be seen in our first volume, pp. 118, 119. He went to England in 1643, and published an account of the Indians, of their language, and of his labors to instruct them concerning Christianity, which the Historical Society at Boston have lately reprinted. He procured a charter for his colony the next year, and went to England again to defend it in 1651, where he stayed until 1654, when he returned, and was elected their chief ruler for near three years; and all his life after was spent in seeking the good of his country, until he died in the spring of 1683.

Mr. Thomas Olney, who had been a member of the Congregational church in Salem, but left them, and came to Providence in 1638, was the next pastor of this Baptist church, and was also useful in civil offices, until his death in 1682. But a division arose in this church in 1652, about lay-

---

[1] In Winthrop's Journal he is called Urdin, p. 167. [Vol. I, p. 283.] But it is Verin in Providence Records.

[2] Winthrop, p. 174. [Vol. I, p. 293.]

ing on of hands upon every member of the church after baptism.[1] Ten years before, the Baptists in England had adopted the opinion, that every man who had a gift given him to preach the gospel, had also a right to baptize, even before he was ordained in any church; which opinion was held by some men of note in Providence for eighty years after. Mr. William Wickenden was a chief leader in that part of the church in Providence who held to the laying on of hands upon each member, which they supposed to be intended in the sixth chapter of the Hebrews; and he was an esteemed minister therein, until he died, February 23, 1669. Gregory Dexter was President of this colony in 1653, and he was very useful in government, and a father in this church, and lived to be ninety-one years old. Pardon Tillinghast was " a leading man among the Baptists in Providence," in 1672 ;[2] and he was much esteemed as a minister among them, until his death, in 1718. He gave the lot upon which their first meeting-house was built. Chad Brown was an early member of this church, and he is said to have been a teacher among them. And his son John Brown was a minister in this church, as well as a useful man in the State. And his son James Brown was a pastor of this church for many years, and died October 28, 1732, aged sixty-six. His son James had four sons, three of whom have been at great expense towards the college in Providence, and towards the Baptist meeting-house there, as well as the support of worship in that society.[3] Joseph Jencks came over from England, about the time that Charles the Second came to the throne, and settled in Providence, and was a useful man in his day; and his son Joseph was a magistrate, Deputy Governor, and then chief Governor of this colony; as well as a leading member in this church, and lived to be above ninety. His brother Ebenezer Jencks was ordained a pastor of this church in 1719, and continued so until his death, August 14, 1726, aged fifty-seven. His son Daniel Jencks, and grandson John Jencks, were both members of this church, and were employed in several offices in the government, and also gave very liberally towards the college, and for the support of the Baptist cause in Providence. Deacon Samuel Winsor was ordained a pastor of this church in 1733, and continued in that office until he died, November 17, 1758, aged seventy-one. His son Samuel Winsor was ordained his successor, and continued with this church until after President Manning came to Providence, and then, in 1771, he, with a number more of the church, went and formed another church in Johnston, where he yet is minister. Mr. Thomas Burlingham was also ordained in this church in 1733; but he preached the latter part of his time in Cranston, where he died January 7,

---

[1]See Vol. I, p. 405; Vol. II, p. 22; Manning and Brown University, pp. 149, 153; Hague's Historical Discourse, p. 103.—Ed.

[2]Williams's Dispute with the Quakers, p. 208.

[3]See Manning and Brown University, pp. 143—176.—Ed.

1770, aged eighty-two. After Elder Winsor and his brethren had formed their church in Johnston,[1] this church in Providence sent a committee to treat with them about their right in their old meeting-house, and they agreed to take two hundred dollars, which was given them accordingly. This summary has been collected from the best light that could be obtained, for no regular records have been found in this church before the year 1770.

James Manning, D. D., was born at Elizabethtown, in New Jersey, October 22, 1738; was early changed by grace, and joined the Baptist church in the town where he was born. His education, and his service in the college, have been described before, but we shall speak more of him as a minister of the gospel. He was called to that work, and was ordained as an itinerant minister, by the church where he was baptized; and he removed to Warren in the summer of 1764, and a Baptist church was formed there the 15th of October following, and he became their pastor. But when the college was removed to Providence, in the spring of 1770, he went with it, and was frequently invited to preach in the Baptist church there, until Elder Winsor, and a part of the church, drew off in the summer of 1771, and formed another church in Johnston, and then Elder Manning was chosen to preach and administer ordinances to this church in Providence; and he continued so to do, until he resigned that office in the spring of 1786, although he ministered to them occasionally afterwards as long as he lived. And though his powers of mind and human accomplishments were very great, yet he used great plainness of speech, and was as easily understood by common people, as almost any preacher in the land. And few men ever prized the special influence of the Spirit of God in preaching, more than he did. He was at the Philadelphia Association in October, 1774, where he met with Mr. Daniel Fristoe, from Virginia, whom he heard afterwards, with such clearness, life, and power, though not a man of liberal education, as fired his soul with fresh zeal and courage in preaching salvation to perishing souls; and Mr. Manning labored with such faithfulness and success, after his return to Providence, that he baptized a hundred and ten persons by September, 1775; and a large number more joined Mr. Snow's church, even notwithstanding the confusions of war which then broke out in our land. And when Governor Cooke was chosen member of the college corporation, and some scrupled whether he could properly be denominated a Baptist, because he was a member of a Congregational church, he informed them that he was ever a Baptist in principle, and was baptized by immersion, and should have joined the Baptist church in Providence, if such doctrine

---

[1]Elder Winsor was a rigid Six Principle Baptist, and was opposed to singing in public worship. He, and a party with him, withdrew because the church fellowshipped President Manning, who did not sympathize with him in these views. See Hague's Historical Discourse, pp. 105, 106; Manning and Brown University, pp. 178, 179.—ED.

had been preached therein then as there was now. President Manning made it his constant practice, to charge his scholars, when they left the college, not to imagine that they were qualified to preach the gospel, until they were satisfied that they were taught of God. At the Commencement in September, 1789, he said :—

Should the Christian ministry, with any of you, become an object, reflect on the absurdity of intruding into it while strangers to experimental religion. See that you yourselves have been taught of God, before you attempt to teach godliness to others. To place in the professional chairs of our universities the most illiterate of mankind, would be an absurdity far less glaring, than to call an unconverted man to exercise the ministerial function. This is to expose our holy religion to the scoffs of infidels, and furnish to their hands the most deadly weapons. I omit to insist on the account such must render in the great, tremendous day.

And his constant behavior was agreeable to his teaching ; and he united dignity and condescension, authority and mildness, in such a manner as to be feared and loved by the generality of his scholars. He married a daughter of John Sites, an alderman of Elizabethtown, and a useful member of the Baptist church there ; and she met with a happy change, and joined the Baptist church in Providence, in January, 1775, of which she is still an agreeable member. She has no children. Dr. Manning died in a fit of the apoplexy, July 29, 1791, when he, undoubtedly, entered into eternal rest.[1]

The opinion of laying on of hands upon every member in the church, had long made a separation among the Baptist churches in this land ; but soon after Dr. Manning came to Providence, he prevailed with this church to admit other Baptists to occasional communion with them, though they would receive none as members until after his death. But on August 4, 1791, the church had a full meeting, and this point was distinctly considered, and a clear vote was gained to admit members who did not hold that doctrine. At the same meeting the church concluded to have another pastor ordained therein, namely, Jonathan Maxcy, A. M. He was born in

[1]The life of President Manning was one of eminent service, alike to the college over which he presided with marked ability for the first twenty-six years of its existence, securing to it a character from the beginning from which its subsequent honorable history has largely sprung,—to the First Baptist church in Providence, of which he was the pastor for years, and which by his discipline was brought to far greater purity of doctrine and practice, and was largely increased in numbers,—to the Baptist denomination, with which he identified himself in all its interests,—and to the whole country, which is to no small extent indebted to him for the blessing of religious liberty. No one deserves a more extended notice than he, in a history of early New England Baptists. It is well, however, that the need of an extended notice here is obviated by the frequent mention of his services in previous pages, and by the full and valuable memoir, entitled " Manning and Brown University," from the pen of R. A. Guild, the University Librarian.—ED.

Attleborough, September 2, 1768, educated in the college at Providence, where he took his first degree in 1787, and was a tutor in the college, until he met with a change in October, 1789, and joined to this church, in which he began to preach in April, 1790, and was ordained their pastor, September 8, 1791.   Mr. John Pitman, who was born in Boston, and had been a minister some years at Freehold, in New Jersey, removed to Providence, and he and his wife were now the first members who were received into this church, without holding to the laying on of hands upon every member. He has frequently preached the gospel in various places ever since, without taking the pastoral charge of any particular church.   Thomas Ustick, A. M., took his first degree in the college at Providence in 1771, was ordained in this church as an itinerant minister, July 29, 1777, preached a while at Ashford, from whence he removed to Grafton in May, 1779, and then to Philadelphia in June, 1782, where he has been pastor of the Baptist church in that city ever since.   A powerful work of grace came on in Providence in the beginning of 1790, which caused the addition of above fifty members to this church in about two years.   September 6, 1792, Mr. Maxcy was chosen President of the college, *pro tempore*, and he has been continued in that office ever since.   He resigned his pastoral office in this church two days after he was first elected President, and they immediately called Mr. Stephen Gano to be their minister for six months, and he has been so ever since.   He was ordained before in the State of New York.   Mr. John Gano, his father, was a minister in the city of New York before the late war, but he is now in Kentucky; and he has been the most extensive traveller to preach the gospel, of any man now living in America.   Forty-six members have been added to this church in Providence, since Mr. Stephen Gano came there.   He drew the circular letter for the Warren Association in 1795.

The corporation of the college at Providence consists of twelve Fellows, and thirty-six Trustees.   The Fellows, as a learned faculty, have the power of conferring the degrees, but in other affairs the college is governed by the concurrence of both branches.   The President is always to be a Baptist, and so are seven more of the Fellows, while the other four may be chosen out of any of the other denominations.   Twenty-two of the Trustees are also to be Baptists, five of them are to be Episcopalians, five Quakers, and four Congregationalists.   The Chancellor is chosen out of the Trustees, and the Secretary out of the Fellows.   No religious test is ever to be required of any of the corporation, nor of the scholars who are graduated therein; though great care is to be taken as to the morals of the college.   Their first funds were collected by Mr. Morgan Edwards, in England and Ireland, and by Mr. Hezekiah Smith in South Carolina and Georgia; to which additions have been since made from various quarters, but all by personal generosity.   These moneys were chiefly lent to Rhode

Island government, though some have been put into a national bank; but the interest thereof, with the income from the students, who are near eighty, is scantily sufficient to support the officers of the college.[1] The building and repairing of the college edifice, the President's house, with the purchase of the lands about them, and also the college library and apparatus, were all done by personal benefactlous, aud chiefly in the town of Providence. And so was the Baptist meeting-house, bell and clock, with the lot on which it stands, all which cost about seven thousand pounds.[2] They first met in said house, May 28, 1775. How false then are the pretences of many, that religion and learning would fail from among us if they were not upheld by the power of the magistrate! It is readily granted that there has been much religion and knowledge among those who have gone on in that way; but the light and power of the gospel is directly against all deceit or violence. And God says of his church, In this mountain shall the Lord of hosts make unto all people a feast of fat things, a feast of wines on the lees; of fat things full of marrow, of wines on the lees well refined. And he will destroy in this mountain the face of the covering cast over all people, and the vail that is spread over all nations. Isaiah xxv. 6, 7. A covering and appearance of religion have been kept up by the power of the magistrate, which the feast of the gospel, in the church of Christ, will destroy.

Ever since the reformation in Germany, many have cast the reproach of all the evils which have appeared among the Baptists upon that denomination in general; which is as unjust as it would be for others to charge all the evils that ever were in national churches, upon all men who hold to infant baptism. But abusive treatment on either side is exceedingly apt to beget prejudices in the mind against good principles and conduct, which are held by their opposites. And as Calvinism was held by those who banished the first planters of Providence and of Rhode Island colony, and who greatly abused those people all their days, many of their children have imagined that the true liberty of moral agents could not be secured upon that plan of doctrine. Though it is abundantly evident, that Mr. Williams, who procured the first charter, and Mr. Clarke, who procured the second, for this colony of liberty, held to that plan of doctrine as firmly as any men in

[1] In 1795, they had given degrees to three hundred and eighty scholars who were educated in this college.

[2] The Baptist meeting-house in Providence, built "for the public worship of Almighty God, and also for holding Commencements in," with steeple, "bell and clock," was justly the pride of early New England Baptists. In beauty, size, and costliness, it far surpassed any other Baptist meeting-house in the colonies. It was eighty feet square; while Dr. Stillman, in Boston, was preaching in a house fifty-seven by fifty-three. A representation of it was engraved for the Massachusetts Magazine, and for Rippon's Register, and, as Dr. Rippon wrote, created astonishment among English Baptists. See Manning and Brown University, pp. 225—230, 440; History of Brown University, pp. 248—253.—ED.

their day. And how can any man enjoy comfort and liberty in his soul, in the midst of the confusions of the world, without believing that men nor devils can never deceive their faithful God, nor defeat any of his designs? That he never makes use of any positive influence to move men to sin, or to hinder their coming to Christ, I as firmly believe as I believe he is just and good; but the lusts of men are so powerful, and the wiles of the devil are so many, that no man can overcome them of himself; though the Spirit of God makes every true believer a conqueror over them all. But as a separation among the Baptists in the last century, was followed with a departure from these sentiments, and their churches have not been in fellowship with most of the Baptist churches lately gathered in this land, I shall say but little about them, more than to mention where they are, and who have been their ministers. Mr. Samuel Fisk was ordained the pastor of a Baptist church in Scituate, and continued with them to old age ; but I have not obtained the date of his ordination, nor of his death, though he was one of their Association in 1729.[1] Elder Reuben Hopkins was their last minister, who died in January, 1792. Elder Peter Place was in their church in Smithfield in 1731, where now is Elder John Winsor. Elder Edward Mitchel was in their church in Gloster for many years, and he died, October 22, 1795, aged ninety-eight. Elder William Bowen was a colleague with him, and now succeeds him. Elder Cooke was in their church in Cumberland, where now is Elder Ballou. I suppose the rest of the churches in their connection in that county have had but one minister, and their names, with the number of their members, are given before, taken from Asplund's Register for 1794.

A few people in Gloster met with a change about the time of the separations in Connecticut, and Thomas Knowlton from thence was at the Separate ordination in Plainfield, September 11, 1746. A Baptist church was afterwards formed in Gloster, and he was their minister for a number of years. After his death, they had other preachers, until Mr. Joseph Winsor (brother to Samuel) was ordained their pastor, October 31, 1763 ; and they prospered for a number of years under his ministry, and had seventy-nine members when they joined the Warren Association, in 1782, and had some increase afterwards. But, as many have removed into other parts of the country, and their pastor is so aged as not to be able to preach, their number is much reduced, as I am informed, though I have not their present number. A Baptist church was formed in North Providence, and Mr. Ezekiel Angell was ordained their pastor, June 20, 1765 ; and he continued so until his death, September 27, 1782, aged sixty. Mr. Rufus Tefft, who was born March 14, 1752, was ordained their second pastor, June 16, 1784. There were but nineteen members in this church when their former pastor died, but a great revival began in the fall of 1791, and prevailed much in the east part of Smithfield, as well as in this town, and

[1] See Vol. I, p. 521.

their number last June, when I was there, was a hundred and seventy. Many of these had been brought up in a careless neglect of all religion; but we hope that their future life may be as becometh the gospel. Mr. John Hammond was baptized in 1780, began to gather a church in the town of Foster, in February, 1789, in which he was ordained in June, 1791, and they increased to about ninety members in three years. There was a second Baptist church in Cumberland above thirty years ago, but they were much broken and scattered for some years; though there have been revivals since, and especially within a few years past. A Baptist church was formed in Cranston, and Mr. Elisha Greene was ordained their pastor, July 30, 1764. He was born in Warwick, August 5, 1698, baptized in 1717, began to preach in 1741, and, after a useful life, died in Gloster, October 29, 1780. This church is now very small. There is another meeting-house in Cranston, upon the great road to Warwick, where Mr. Pitman often preaches, and a number of members from thence have joined the Baptist church in Providence.

COUNTY OF NEWPORT.

Mr. John Clarke, a physician from London, was one of the first planters of Rhode Island, and the pastor of the second Baptist church in America, which was formed at Newport in 1644. His brother, Joseph Clarke was a member of it, and often a ruler in the State, and adorned his profession for above forty years after the church was constituted; and his posterity are numerous and respectable unto this day. Samuel Hubbard was born in England in 1610, came over to Salem in 1633, joined to the Congregational church in Watertown in 1635, but went up to Windsor, and helped to begin the colony of Connecticut the same year. But as he and his wife embraced the Baptist principles, they removed to Newport, and joined with this church in 1648; and he lived there above forty years after, and preserved many writings which have been very serviceable in our history. He left no son, but he had three daughters, who were married to Joseph Clarke, junior, Robert Burdick, and Andrew Langworthy, whose posterity are respectable to this day, especially among the Baptists in Hopkinton. In 1651 Mr. Coddington obtained a commission from the ruling powers in England, to be governor of Rhode Island, without the consent of the people, when he had the deeds of their lands in his hands. Therefore Mr. John Clarke went to England, with Mr. Roger Williams, and got that commission disannulled; and he was agent for his colony in that country, until he procured their second charter in 1663. Mr. Hubbard wrote a letter to him, the spring after he went to England, and Clarke wrote him an answer, October 11, 1652, and said:—

There can be nothing in the present evil world, so far as I am acquainted with my own heart as it stands to Godward, that is more pleasing and delightful to it, than the manifestation of the enlargement of the kingdom of his dear Son, and that many obedient servants are added to the Lord, whom God the Father has resolved to exalt above every name that is named, not only in this present world, but in that which is to come ; and that they who are so added, being living members of that body which by a spirit of life is joined unto that living Lord who is head over all, may increase with all the increase of God, is the earnest desire and prayer of my soul. But I must tell you, that as the promise of the glorious coming of our Lord doth quicken and freshen in my heart, so doth that prophecy follow in my mind, When the Son of man cometh, shall he find faith on the earth?

He returned to Newport in 1664, and was a faithful pastor of this church, being also useful in the State, until he died in a happy frame, April 20, 1676. When Mr. Clarke sailed for England in 1651, he left the care of this church with Joseph Tory, and Obadiah Holmes, and they were useful teachers therein all their days. Holmes succeeded Clarke as pastor of the church, until he died, October 15, 1682. Mr. Richard Dingley succeeded him ; but in 1694, he left them and went to South Carolina. In 1710 Mr. William Peckom was ordained their pastor, and continued so until he died in 1734. He was esteemed as a pious man, but his gifts were small ; and Mr. John Comer was ordained a colleague with him, May 19, 1726. He was born in Boston, August 1, 1704, met with a happy change in November, 1721, and after obtaining a good share of human learning, he began to preach the gospel at Swansea in May, 1724, and went to Newport in the fall of 1725, and preached in this church four years, in which time it increased from seventeen members to fifty-two. Yet two powerful men in the church prevailed with the majority to vote him a dismission in 1729, and he went and preached two years in the Second church in Newport with considerable success, and then removed and gathered the First Baptist church in Rehoboth, where he died, as we before noted. Mr. John Callender, who was born in Boston, and was educated at the college in Cambridge, was the next pastor of this church, where he was ordained, October 13, 1731, colleague with Elder Peckom. He was a man of superior powers, and published a Century Sermon in 1738, and a Funeral Sermon for Mr. Clap, the first Congregational minister in Newport, in 1745, with some other things. He also collected many papers, which have been serviceable in our history. But he was taken away by death, January 26, 1748, in the forty-second year of his age. Mr. Edward Upham, of Springfield, at the request of this church, removed to Newport in 1749, and ministered to them until April, 1771, when he returned back to Springfield, as we before related. Mr. Erasmus Kelly, who was born in Pennsylvania, July 24, 1748, educated at the college in Philadelphia, and began to preach in those parts, was called to Newport, and was ordained a pastor of this church, October 9, 1771. And the church and society increased under his ministry, until the enemy came to Newport, and he removed to Warren,

where they followed him, and burnt the house and goods where he resided,
May 25, 1778. He then removed to Connecticut, and from thence to Pennsylvania. But upon the return of peace, he came again to Newport, and
ministered to this church, until he was taken away by death, November 7,
1784, before he had been with them a year in this last turn. Mr. Josias
Lyndon was of this society, and did much for the support of worship therein. He was governor of the colony in 1760, and was very serviceable in
the State all his days. He died of the small pox, March 30, 1778, aged
seventy-four, leaving much of his estate to this church. The calamities of
the war scattered this church, and others were taken away by death, so
that only three male members remained at Newport, and but twenty-seven,
male and female, remained anywhere, when Dr. Benjamin Foster came
there in January, 1785, and above twenty were added to this church that
year, and many to their society, a number of whom attended no worship
before. In September, 1786, this church was received into the Warren
Association, when they had sixty-nine members. But in 1788 some of them
raised opposition against their minister, and he had an earnest call to New
York ; therefore he was dismissed from this church, and has been pastor of
the First Baptist church in that city ever since. After various trials, this
church obtained Mr. Michael Eddy, who was ordained in Swansea, in 1785,
but removed to Newport in January, 1790, and he is now their pastor, and
they have prospered under his ministry.

The doctrine of laying on of hands upon every member, came into the
First church in Newport in 1652, and the Second church was formed about
1656. Mr. William Vaughan was their first pastor, and continued so un-
til his death in August, 1677. Mr. Thomas Baker succeeded him for a
time, and then he removed and began a society in North Kingstown. Mr.
John Harden was their third pastor, who died in the year 1700. Mr.
James Clarke was the next, who was ordained in 1701, and continued with
them until he died, December 1, 1736, aged eighty-seven. Mr. Daniel
Wightman was ordained a colleague with him in 1704. He was born in
Narragansett, January 2, 1668, and died in Newport, August 31, 1750.
They were well esteemed among their brethren, as faithful ministers, and
exemplary walkers ; and in January, 1729, when Elder Clarke was not
able to preach, through the infirmities of age, Mr. Comer was received to
preach one half of the Lord's days with Elder Wightman, and continued
to do so for two years. Their church increased to a hundred and forty-
two members, being the largest church then in their colony. They had
built the first meeting-house in the colony, in 1707. On June 21, 1729,
they had the largest Association of Baptist ministers and churches that
ever had been seen in America. The elders present were, James Clarke, Daniel Wightman, and John Comer, of Newport, Jonathan Sprague and James
Brown, of Providence, Nicholas Eyers, of New York, Valentine Wight-

man, of Groton, Philip Tabor, of Dartmouth, Stephen Gorton, of New London, and Daniel Everett, of South Kingstown. Beside whom, the elders, Peter Place, of Smithfield, Samuel Fisk, of Scituate, Joseph Mason, of Swansea, Manassah Martin, of Warwick, and Richard Sweet, of North Kingstown, were in their connection of churches ; and Mr. Comer says, "Each of these holds to general redemption. Three other churches hold to the doctrine of free grace. One in Newport, formerly my flock ; one at Swansea, Mr. Ephraim Wheaton ; one at Boston, Mr. Elisha Callender." And these, with one at Newport, and one at Westerly, who kept the seventh day, were all the Baptist churches then in' New England. Comer gave his ideas of election in these words, saying, "If God does not choose us, we shall never be moved to choose him. It is from his choice of us that we are led to choose him. I Pet. ii. 9 ; II Thess. ii. 13. They are chosen to obedience, and not for obedience. I Pet. i. 2. We are chosen not in time upon works, but before time exclusive. Eph. i. 4. All is rich, sovereign, free and pure grace in God through Christ."[1] But as some would not hear him preach that doctrine there, he removed to Rehoboth, and Elder Nicholas Eyers came to Newport in October, 1731, and was a pastor of this church until his death, February 13, 1759. He was born in England, August 22, 1691, educated in the city of Bristol, came over to New York about 1711, was baptized and ordained there in 1724, but his church broke up in 1730, and he had great influence among these churches as long as he lived, and he left many manuscripts, some of which have been serviceable in our history. His son, Dr. Thomas Eyres, was educated at Yale College, and was one of the first Fellows of our college. Mr. Gardner Thurston was born in Newport, November 21, 1721, met with a change and joined this church in 1741, and was ordained their pastor, April 29, 1759. The doctrines of grace gradually gained ground in this church, and singing in public worship was introduced into it in 1765, and many blessings have been granted among them since. Dr. William Rogers, one of the first class in our college, was called to preach in this church, and he went to Philadelphia in 1771, where he has been useful ever since. Elder Burroughs, of Tiverton, and Elder Jones, of Rehoboth, sprang also from this church. Their pastor continued with them through all the calamities of the war, and is still useful to old age.

The Third Baptist church in Newport was formed in the following manner :—Stephen Mumford came over from London in 1664,[2] and brought the opinion with him, that the whole of the ten commandments, as they were delivered from Mount Sinai, were moral and immutable ; and that it

---

[1]Comer's Diary.

[2]In Vol. I, p. 324, this date is given as "in the beginning of 1665." The discrepancy may be accounted for by supposing that, in the present instance, Backus neglected to reduce the date to new style.—ED.

was the antichristian power, which thought to change times and laws, that changed the Sabbath from the seventh to the first day of the week. Several members of the First church in Newport embraced this sentiment, and yet continued with the church for some years, until two men and their wives who had so done, turned back to the keeping of the first day again. But they who believed that this practice came from antichrist, were much concerned about it, and wrote to their friends in England for advice thereon. An answer was returned from London, and another from Mr. Edward Stennett, of Abington, March 6, 1670, who said :—

My dear friends, as for those that have drawn back from the Sabbath to profaneness, after light and establishment therein, yourselves must not take pleasure in them, but must withdraw yourselves from them, as sinful and disorderly persons ; and if the church will hold communion with those apostates from the truth, you ought then to desire to be fairly dismissed from the church, which if the church refuse, you ought to withdraw yourselves, and not be partakers of other men's sins, but keep yourselves pure, but with all humility, meekness, and brokenness of heart.

This brought on warm debates on both sides, and finally a separation took place, in December, 1671, when William Hiscox, Samuel Hubbard, Stephen Mumford, Roger Baster, and three sisters, joined in covenant as a distinct church. Mr. Hubbard wrote to their brethren in London, October 3, 1672, and said, " Dear brethren, pray for us, a poor, weak band in a wilderness, beset round with opposites, from the common adversary, and from Quakers, generals and profane persons, and most of all from such as have been our familiar acquaintance : but our battles are only in words, praised be God."[1] Mr. Hiscox was pastor of this church until he died,

---

[1] If the following things are considered, it may prevent divisions among Christians upon this article. That God is Lord of all our time is a moral and immutable truth, but the sanctification of a particular day was never known to man without a positive precept. It does not appear that Israel knew anything about the Sabbath of the seventh day, until after they came into the wilderness, when it was said to them, To-morrow is the rest of the holy Sabbath unto the Lord. And he afterwards said, It is a sign between me and the children of Israel for.ever; for in six days the Lord made heaven and earth, and on the seventh day he rested, and was refreshed. Ex. xvi. 23; xxxi. 17. And every man in Israel who broke the Sabbath, was to be stoned to death. Numb. xv. 35. But when Christ came, he said to the Jews, The Son of Man is Lord even of the Sabbath day. Matt. xii. 8. And after his ascension to heaven, an inspired apostle said, He also hath ceased from his own works, as God did from his. Heb. iv. 10. Christ our passover was sacrificed for us on the sixth day of the week, and the next day was the Sabbath, and fifty days from thence was the first day of the week, when the Holy Ghost was given, and three thousand souls were converted, as the first fruits of the death of Christ. Levit. xxiii. 5, 15, 16; Acts ii. 1—41. And how often is the first day of the week spoken of under the gospel ! Matt. xxviii. 1—7; Mark xv. 2; Luke xxiv. 1; John xx. 1, 19, 26; Acts xx. 7. And as contributions to the saints are sacrifices to God, he commands them to be provided on the first day of the week. I Cor. xvi. 1, 2; Phil. iv. 18; Heb. xiii. 16. And the glory of the ministration which was written and engraven in stones, is

33

May 24, 1704, aged sixty-six.   Mr. William Gibson, who came from London, was their second pastor, until he died, March 12, 1717, aged seventy-nine.   Mr. Joseph Crandal had been a colleague with him for two years, and he continued in that office until he was taken away by death, September 13, 1737.   Mr. John Maxon was their next pastor, from 1754 unto March 2, 1778, when he died.   Mr. Ebenezer David, from Philadelphia, was converted while in the college at Providence, where he took his first degree in 1772, and he was called to preach the gospel the next year by this church with their brethren at Hopkinton ; and he was a chaplain in the American army, much esteemed, until he died in Pennsylvania, March 19, 1778.   Thomas Ward was an early member of this church, whose son Richard was governor of the colony in 1741, 1742 ; and his son Samuel was governor in 1762 and 1765, and a member of Congress in 1774 and 1775, until he died at Philadelphia, March 26, 1776, aged fifty-two.   All of these were members of this church.   Mr. William Bliss was called to preach the gospel by this church before the American war, and he continued with them through the war, and preached frequently on the island when the British forces were there, from whom he suffered much.   He was ordained as an evangelist, December 11, 1779, and was installed as pastor of this church, December 24, 1780.   And he is so well esteemed by the Congregational ministers in Newport, as to be frequently called to supply their pulpits when they go journeys into the country.

There have been a number of Baptists in Newport for many years, who did not agree fully with either of the old churches in some things, but chose to meet by themselves, and to call elders from abroad to minister occasionally to them, until they formed another church in the town.   They carried the liberty for every brother to improve his gifts in public worship, beyond what the other churches did ; and though a motion was lately made to have two of their most gifted brethren ordained, yet the matter was deferred for further consideration.   However, we are well informed, that a greater harmony has lately appeared among all denominations in Newport, than was heretofore known among them.

Elder Philip Tabor was pastor of the Baptist church in Tiverton and Dartmouth, before he was imprisoned at Bristol for not favoring ministerial tyranny.   Both of these towns were under the Massachusetts government until 1741 ; and because the majority of the inhabitants would not receive and support Congregational ministers, a salary for such was put into their State tax, and they were to draw it out of the State treasury.   But their assessors being informed of it, left that part of the tax on those two towns out of their assessment.   Tabor was one of them, and he, with three

done away under the New Testament. II Cor. iii. 6—8.   But the Lord's day is ever to be regarded.   Rev. i. 10.   Though he who does not regard it to the Lord, does not regard it at all.   Rom. xiv. 6.

asseesors more, were seized on May 25, 1723, and were imprisoned at
Bristol until an agent went over to London, and procured their release by
an order from the king and council.[1] He lived within the bounds of Dartmouth, but their meeting was held in the east part of Tiverton, where he
ministered to this Baptist church, until he died in November, 1752. Mr.
David Round was born in Rehoboth, in January, 1706, and was ordained
the next pastor of this church about 1755, and ministered to them for many
years, and is now living among them, and esteemed as a pious man. But
as his gifts were small, the church called Mr. Peleg Burroughs, from the
Second church in Newport, to preach to them in May, 1775, and he was
ordained their pastor, April 13, 1780. A happy rain of righteousness was
then granted among them, which caused the addition of about a hundred
members in two years. Elder Burroughs was born in Newport, June 5,
1748, converted in 1766, and began to preach in 1774 ; and he is still continued with this church. That revival of religion caused the gathering of
a Baptist church in the south borders of Freetown, February 15, 1781,
and Mr. Amos Burris, from Groton, in Connecticut, was installed their
pastor, May 22, 1783. But in October, 1784, he removed into the State
of Vermont, and they removed their meeting into the north borders of Tiverton, where it now is ;[2] and two men were raised up to preach among
them, who were unitedly ordained as their pastors, May 19, 1795, namely,
James Boomer and Job Borden. The latter is blind, as to natural sight,
but he has such spiritual light as to be esteemed a clear preacher of the
gospel. A Baptist church was formed in New Shoreham, on Block Island,
and Mr. Thomas Dodge was ordained their pastor in 1784.

COUNTY OF BRISTOL.

Though the charter of Rhode Island colony, which Mr Clarke obtained
in 1663, plainly included the lands which now are in the towns of Bristol,
Barrington and Warren, as well as two more towns which are in the county of Newport and one in the county of Providence, yet the Massachusetts
held them until the year 1741 ; since that time, the three towns first named,
form the county of Bristol, in this State. Warren was a part of the town
of Swansea, and a number of the members of the first church there were
formed into a church in Warren, October 15, 1764, and Dr. Manning was
their minister until he removed to Providence in 1770, as we before observed. After some time, this church obtained Mr. Charles Thompson to
preach to them, and he was ordained their pastor, July 3, 1771. He was
born at Amwell, in New Jersey, April 14, 1748, was one of the first gradu-

[1]See Vol. I, pp. 500—506.
[2]For several years this church held meetings in Fall River, till, in 1825, its meetings in Tiverton were discontinued, and the church became the First Baptist church
in Fall River. Manuscript Sketch of the Church, by Rev. A. Bronson.—ED.

ates in our college at Warren, in 1769 ; and such a blessing was granted on his ministry there as to increase the church from fifty to eighty-three members in four years.   But when the war came on, it had many pernicious effects ; and the enemy came up to Warren and burnt their meeting-house and their house for the ministry, May 25, 1778, and carried Mr. Thompson away as a prisoner, and confined him in a guard-ship at Newport.   After his deliverance was obtained, he went up into Connecticut and preached in several places, and then was called and settled at Swansea in 1779, as was before related.   The burnings and destructions which were made by the British forces at Warren prevented their erecting another house for worship for many years ; neither could they unite in settling another pastor until lately.   Mr. Luther Baker was raised up among them, and he was ordained their minister, October 17, 1793, and it is hoped that he may be useful to them for many years to come.

COUNTY OF WASHINGTON.

As there is no settled minister who holds to infant baptism, in any part of this State west of Newport and Providence, it may be proper to inquire into the reasons of it.   A leading cause of it appears to be the sufferings of many of their fathers from Pædobaptists.   After Samuel Gorton and his friends had purchased the lands in Warwick of Indian Sachems, they were seized and carried to Boston by an armed force, in the fall of 1643, and were confined in those parts all winter, and then were banished upon pain of death, not only out of the Massachusetts colony, but also from their own lands.   And Captain Edward Johnson, who was one of the officers that carried them away, published the views they had in these proceedings, in a history which was printed in London in 1654.   He represents it as the command of Christ to them, that they should subdue all his enemies in this country, as Israel did the heathen in Canaan.   And he says :—

Fail not in prosecution of the work, for our [your] Lord Christ hath furnished you with able pilots, to steer the helm in a godly, peaceable, civil government [also] ; then see that you make choice of such as are sound, both in profession and confession, men fearing God and hating bribes ; whose commission is not [only] limited with the commands of the second table, but they are to look to the rules of the first table also.   And let them be sure to put on Joshua's resolution and courage, never to make a league with any of these seven sectaries.   1. The *Gortonists*, who deny the humanity of Christ, and most blasphemously and proudly profess themselves to be personally Christ.   2. The *Papists*, who with (almost) equal blasphemy and pride, prefer their own merits and works of supererogation as equal with Christ's invaluable death and sufferings.   3. The *Familists*, who depend upon rare revelations, and forsake the sure revealed word of Christ.   4. *Seekers*, who deny the churches and ordinances of Christ.   5. *Antinomians*, who deny the moral law to be the rule of Christ.   6. *Anabaptists*, who deny civil government to be proved of Christ.   7. The *Pre-*

lacy, who will have their own injunctions submitted unto in the church [churches] of Christ.[1]

But Gorton and some of his friends went over to England, and procured an order from thence, for them to enjoy the lands which they had purchased. And as he actually held, that what we read about the coming, death and resurrection of Christ, is to be understood mystically, and not literally, he taught his followers in that way, and fixed lasting prejudices in their minds against all church government, as well as against tyranny under religious pretences. And many of their posterity neglect public worship even to our times.[2] The sufferings of the Quakers also, who came to America after Johnson's History was published, filled many with great dislike to the ruling denomination in the Massachusetts. To which we may add, that no communities who held to infant baptism, ever prevailed much without the sword of the magistrate to uphold them, or oppression to drive them together. Neither have Baptist churches prospered much without the power of the Spirit of God among them.

The first Baptist church in the county of Washington was in North Kingstown. Elder Baker went from Newport, and began a meeting there towards the close of the last century, as Mr. Comer informs us; and a paper of their own, dates the beginning of their church about 1710. Mr. Richard Sweet was their pastor for many years, and lived till after 1740. Mr. David Sprague was ordained a colleague with him about 1739. The great awakenings in other parts of the country, in and after 1741, affected a number of people in these parts, which caused various controversies. The laying on of hands upon every member had been carried so far, as not to allow their members to hear any others pray or preach. And when Mr. Bound, of Boston, met Elder Wightman, of Groton, at Warwick, in 1743, the elders with whom he was connected opposed his acting in the ordination; and Mr. John Callender, of Newport, wrote an unfavorable account of it to England, and also of the work then going on in the land, and said, "I have seen no cause to alter the opinion I early entertained of Mr. Whitefield, that he was a second George Fox." But all experience since has evidenced his great mistake. For the plan of doctrine which Whitefield held forth was directly opposite to that which Fox taught, and he ever appeared against the idea of raising any new sect in the world, and exerted all his powers to revive pure religion, according to the Holy Scriptures, among all sorts of people wherever he came, and left the government of churches to others. But Mr. Wesley and his followers have been exceed-

[1] Johnson's History, p. 8.
[2] A sensible man in Cranston, by particular request, took an account of all the inhabitants of that town in 1774, and he found thirty-eight families who attended no religious meeting at all, nor their fathers before them. These sprang from the first planters of Warwick.

ingly zealous for the doctrines which Fox held, and to raise a new sect under another name. The work which began in the year 1740, naturally caused opposition to arise in all who were settled down in formality, of every denomination. And the general meeting of the Baptist churches at Newport, September 11, 1749, sent an address to their brethren, in which they said :—

We have endeavored to promote and maintain general peace and unity among the brotherhood, and have not been altogether unsuccessful ; and we heartily desire that the fruits and effects of our endeavors may diffuse and spread themselves abroad in other places, and throughout the churches. And though we should have been glad to have had the company and assistance of more of our ministers and brethren, to carry on and encourage the great work of our Redeemer's kingdom ; yet we who are assembled in our General Meeting, according to our general character, do take courage in the Lord to consider by what means the general interest and peace of the churches might be promoted, and grieve at any measures or steps that were or had been taken, by which the same were lessened and impaired. This gave us occasion to consider the sad dissensions and divisions which seem to be carrying on in several churches ; more especially at South Kingstown, North Kingstown, Warwick, Greenwich, &c.

This was signed by Daniel Wightman, Philip Tabor, Nicholas Eyers, Samuel Winsor, Job Mason, and Stephen Gorton, elders, with seven brethren. Elder Sprague had been much engaged in preaching up the doctrines which had promoted the late revival of religion in this country, and he assisted in ordaining Mr. Samuel Drown, as pastor of a Baptist church lately formed in Coventry, October 11, 1749, where he met with several Separate ministers from Connecticut, and invited them to come and preach among his people, which they did with great effects. And on April 4, 1750, Sprague acted with Mr. Paine, in ordaining Mr. Stephen Babcock as pastor of a Baptist church in Westerly. And upon these things, above seventy members of this church, male and female, signed a paper in May, 1750, to shut him out of their meeting-house, and he went and gathered a church in Exeter. Mr. James Wightman was afterwards ordained a pastor of this church, and remained so until his death in the spring of 1791. Mr. Nathan Hill was ordained a colleague with him in 1781, and still continues in that office. And for some years past they have received men to preach in their meeting-house, who have held forth the doctrine that was shut out of it in 1750. A church was formed in connection with them in Richmond, and Mr. John Pendleton was ordained their pastor in June, 1771 ; and Mr. Henry Joslin succeeds him therein.

Hopkinton was once the north part of Westerly, where some of Mr. Clarke's church lived, before the separation on account of the Sabbath took place in 1671. Mr. John Crandal was one of them, who was imprisoned with Clarke and Holmes at Boston, in 1651. He was called over to New London, and baptized some men there in 1674, for which the minister of the town threatened him with a prosecution the next court ; and "old Mrs. Rogers was laid under admonition for maintaining that children had no right to baptism." In 1678, Mr. Hubbard wrote to a friend in Jamaica, and said, "Our number here is twenty, at Westerly seven, and at New London ten." On December 7, 1681, he wrote to England, that two Indians came to Newport that week from Nantucket, who were Baptists, and one of them a preacher, with "a letter of recommendation from one Peter Folger, a member of our old church ;" that is, of Mr. Clarke's church. This preacher was going over to Soconet to preach to the Indians there, of which Captain Church had given them notice. Thomas West and his wife, and another English woman, and two Indians, of Martha's Vineyard, had joined this church at Newport before ; and on January 28, 1682, Hubbard wrote to Providence, and said, "There is a brother here, of Martha's Vineyard, one Isaac Takkamme, an Indian, who brings word that all are well there ; brother West and his wife, and sister Rogers, and our brother David Okes, an Indian, and that they stand fast in the faith." Isaac Decamy was afterwards pastor of a Baptist church among the Indians there, who might be the same person.[1] In 1708, the brethren at Westerly were amicably dismissed, and formed a church there. I have not obtained an exact account of their ministers since, though I find. by Mr. Comer, that Mr. Joseph Maxon was their pastor in 1729, and Mr. Thomas Hiscox was a preacher among them ; and he was a minister there to old age. Mr. Joshua Clarke was a minister at Hopkinton for many years, and died in June, 1792. And by a letter from Rhode Island, September 11, 1795, we are informed as follows :—

The church at Hopkinton at present consists of four hundred and sixty-two members, under the care of the Reverend John Burdick, who was ordained an evangelist, June 6, 1774, and installed pastor of the church, September 3, 1793. At the same time and place, Henry Clarke, (son of the late Elder Joshua Clarke,) was ordained an evangelist. Also Asa Coon was ordained an evangelist the same day. Three churches have been set off from this church at Hopkinton in fellowship in fifteen years. One at Bristol, in Connecticut, constituted in September, 1780, formerly under the care of the Reverend John Davis, deceased, of about seventy members. A second church at Petersburgh, in New York State, of ninety-two members, under the care of the Reverend William Coon. A third at New London, Great Neck, of forty-two members, under the care of the Reverend Davis Rogers. Elder Clarke has lately moved to Brookfield, at the Unodille, in the State of New York, where are about twenty members who meet stately on the Sabbath for divine worship, and it is expected that they will soon form into a church.

Mr. David Sprague was born at Hingham, in the Massachusetts, and was converted at Scituate, in this State, where he joined to the Baptist church under the care of Elder Fisk. As he was a man of superior gifts,

[1] See Vol. I, pp. 346, 347.

he was invited to preach among them ; but a sense of the greatness of the
work made him afraid to attempt it, until a passage of Scripture was opened
with peculiar clearness to his mind, and then he came forward and delivered
a sermon.   This was very agreeable to his minister, and to the people ; but
when he preached his second discourse, they observed more the tenor of
his teaching, and said to him, "If you go on in this way, you will be as bad
an *electioner* as any of the Presbyterians."   This account I received from
his own mouth ; and he informed me that their opposition turned him back
into their general way of preaching, for a number of years.   And his coming forward in preaching as he was first taught, caused his being shut out
of the church where he was first ordained, and another was formed at Exeter, in the fall of 1750.   But as they had before made so much of external baptism and laying on of hands, they now went over to the other extreme, and received one or more to the ordinance of the Supper without
any water baptism.   The powerful effects of the preaching of Separate
ministers from Connecticut, had a great influence to cause this turn in their
minds ; and an acquaintance with lively Baptist ministers, also removed
the prejudices against the Baptists, from the minds of many in Connecticut,
and many were soon baptized, and it seemed as though all their Separate
churches would become Baptists.   But this raised such opposition to what
they called *rebaptizing*, in the mind of the pastor of the Separate church in
Canterbury, where the separation began, that he, with others, prevailed
with seven or eight teachers to retract their baptism by immersion.   And
a council of them censured the pastor of the First Separate church in Middleborough, because he refused to follow that example.   But this censure
caused the meeting of the delegates of twenty-seven churches at Exeter,
May 23, 1753, who condemned the censuring of each other on either side.[1]
Though the divisions and controversies that have appeared where believers'
baptism has been introduced have been held up as a strong argument
against it from age to age.   In 1653, Mr. Henry Dunstar, president of the
college at Cambridge, gave up infant baptism, and preached against it in
the pulpit there.   But Mr. Jonathan Mitchel, pastor of their church, went
to talk with him upon it, after which he said :—

I had a strange experience ; I found hurrying and pressing suggestions
against pædobaptism, and injected scruples and thoughts whether the other
way might not be right, and infant baptism an invention of men, and
whether I might with good conscience baptize children, and the like.   And
these thoughts were darted in with some impression, and left a strange confusion and sickliness upon my spirit.   Yet, methought, it was not hard to
discern that they were from the *evil one*.   1. Because they were rather injected, hurrying suggestions, than any deliberate thoughts, or bringing any
light with them.   2. Because they were *unseasonable*, interrupting me in
my study for the Sabbath, and putting my spirit into [a] confusion, so as I

[1]See pp. 112, 113.

had much ado to do aught in my sermon. It was not now a time to study that matter ; but when in the former part of the week I had given myself to that study, the more I studied it, the more clear and rational light I saw for pædobaptism ; but now these suggestions hurried me into scruples. But they made me cry out to God for his help, and he did afterward calm and clear up my spirit. I thought the end of them was—First. To shew me the corruption of my mind ; how apt that was to take in error, even as my heart is to take in lust. Secondly. To make me walk in fear, and to take hold on Jesus Christ to keep me in the truth ; and it was a check to my former self-confidence, and it made me fearful to go needlessly to Mr. Dunstar ; for, methought, I found a venom and poison in his insinuations and discourses against pædobaptism. Thirdly. That I might be mindful of the aptness in others to be soon shaken in mind, and that I might warn others thereof, and might know how to speak to them from experience. And indeed my former experience of irreligious injections, was some help to me to discover the nature of these. I resolved also on Mr. Hooker's principle, that I would have an argument able to remove a mountain, before I would recede from, or appear against a truth or practice received among the faithful.[1]

Dr. Cotton Mather published this account in 1697, and Mr. John Cleaveland, of Ipswich, inserted it in the introduction to a large pamphlet on infant baptism, which he published at Salem, 1784. Mr. Cleaveland was expelled out of New Haven college in 1744, for meeting for worship on the Lord's day in a house separate from the parish meeting-house in Canterbury, with the First Congregational church in that town, who had refused to receive a teacher whom the world would have forced upon them. But our Lord says, Many that are first shall be last, and the last shall be first. Matt. xix. 30. And so it has been in our land. Those Separate churches began in Canterbury, from whence they spread through all our country ; but there is not one of them now left in the Massachusetts, and but few in Connecticut, while Canterbury still refuses to give up infant sprinkling. The church in Exeter prospered under the ministry of Elder Sprague for about ten years, and then he gave up communion in the ordinance of the Supper with all who were only sprinkled in infancy, which caused his dismission from this church. He then went and preached a while at New London, and another season on Block Island, which is called New Shoreham ; after which he returned to Exeter, where he died in 1777. His son, Solomon Sprague, was early changed by grace, and he was ordained a pastor of this church June 1, 1769. He was a good physician, as well as a faithful and successful minister of the gospel, until he fell asleep in February, 1794, aged sixty-five. Mr. Joseph Case was a useful preacher in this church, until he removed into the State of New York, in 1791. This church have experienced greater blessings since they gave

[1]Mitchel's Life, pp. 69, 70. [Magnalia, Vol. II, p. 79.]—B.
See also, Vol. I, p. 228.—Ed.

up mixed communion than they ever did before. Mr. John Tillinghast has been a main elder among them lately.

Mr. Stephen Babcock was one of the first members of a Congregational church that was formed in Westerly, May 5, 1742.[1] But in a few years after he saw such opposition in his minister and others, against what he believed to be the power of godliness, that he withdrew and set up a meeting at his own house, and a church was gathered there, and he was ordained their pastor, April 4, 1750; in whose ordination Elder David Sprague and Elder Solomon Paine united, it being the first instance of the two denominations uniting in such an action among these churches. Elder Babcock was zealous for such a union all his days, while others renounced it. He died after the war began in 1775. His son, Oliver Babcock, was his successor in that office until he died, February 13, 1784. His cousin, Elkanah Babcock, was their next minister, until the majority of the church rejected him because of his turning off into corrupt principles. In the mean time another church was gathered in Westerly, about the year 1770, and Mr. Isaiah Wilcox was ordained their pastor, who was very zealous for the communion of the two denominations together, and they were a large church when he died in March, 1793. In the fall of 1750, such a church was formed in South Kingstown, and Mr. James Rodgers was ordained their pastor, and he continued so about twenty years; but he had entangled himself so much in the affairs of this life, and was involved so deeply in debt, that he went off into the State of New York, and his church was divided and dissolved. A number of them, who still hold to mixed communion, have lately had a revival among them, to whom others have joined, and they are of the Groton Conference. But in the work which began in 1778, a number gave up mixed communion, and formed a church there, and Mr. Benjamin Weight was ordained their pastor, in August, 1781, in which office he is yet continued. Another church arose out of the ruins of the former about 1774, who since meet in Richmond, and Mr. Benjamin Barber was ordained their pastor in 1793. In another part of Richmond a new church was formed, and Mr. Charles Boss was ordained their pastor in June, 1781, and he was well esteemed in his office until his death in 1789. These three churches do not hold to mixed communion. But when the church in Exeter gave up that practice, Deacon Philip Jenkins drew off from them, and gathered a church in that way, July 21, 1764, and he was ordained their pastor the 6th of September following, and is still continued with them. Their meeting is in North Kingstown. And in the glorious year 1780, religion was revived in the south part of that town, and a new church was gathered, and Mr. William Northup was ordained their pastor in 1782, and they are now a large church. An Indian Baptist church was formed in Charlestown, in this county, above thirty years ago, of which

[1]Prince's Christian History, Vol. I, pp. 207, 210.

James Symonds was pastor, and then Samuel Niles; and they had many valuable Christians therein;[1] but most of them are since dead, and the church is dissolved. The chief of the Indians who are living have removed into the State of New York.

COUNTY OF KENT.

The first Baptist church in this county was in Warwick, and Mr. Manasseh Martin was their minister, before 1730. In a letter from Governor Jencks, in February that year, he says, "I have often heard, that Elder Martin denied that Christ received any part of the human nature of the Virgin Mary, in whose womb he was conceived, and by whom he was born into the world." He held Jesus to be the only begotten Son of God, but held his humanity in a mystical way, which caused much uneasiness among his brethren, excepting Elder Everet, who appeared to be of his mind. Mr. Charles Holden succeeded Martin, and was pastor of this church for many years; and Mr. Abraham Lippet was ordained therein in October, 1782; but in 1794 he removed into the State of New York, and Mr. Samuel Littlefield was ordained in his place at Warwick. The church in East Greenwich was formed, and Mr. Daniel Fisk was ordained their pastor in June, 1743. He was son to Elder Fisk, of Scituate; and he ministered to this church about four years, and then was dismissed and went and preached in various places, until he died with the small-pox in Swansea in 1764. Mr. John Gorton was born in Cranston, April 22, 1723, and was ordained a pastor of this church, September 6, 1753; and he was an acceptable minister among them until his death in 1793. And Mr. Manchester, of Coventry, now ministers also to this church. Mr. Timothy Greene was formerly the pastor of a Baptist church in Coventry, wherein Mr. Thomas Manchester was ordained, September 12, 1782. A church was formed in the west part of Warwick, in connection with these, and Mr. David Corpe was ordained their minister in 1791. A Baptist church had been formed in the same place about fifty years ago, and Mr. Benjamin Pierce was ordained their pastor, and they came into fellowship with Exeter church and others in 1750. And they increased so much, that Mr. Peter Werden was ordained a colleague with him, May 21, 1751. And he labored there until April, 1757, when he removed up to Coventry, by the consent of the church. After Mr. Pierce's death, Mr. Budlong was their minister for a while, and then his church was dissolved, and many of them removed into other parts of the country. There was a powerful work in Coventry in 1748, and a Baptist church was formed there, and Mr. Samuel Drown was ordained their pastor, October 11, 1749. But in a few years he gave up his Baptist principles, and went and settled at Portsmouth, in New Hampshire, where

[1]In 1784, Niles's church had about fifty members.

he practiced infant baptism the remainder of his days.   He died three January 17, 1770.   After Elder Werden removed to Coventry, he minis- tered to the church there for twelve years, in which time many were hope- fully converted, and Christians were built up in the ways of God, and then, as a large part of his people had removed, he also went and settled where he now is in Berkshire.   The west part of Coventry, and of the towns adjacent, had very little of the appearance of religion among them, until God was pleased to pour out his Spirit upon them in the beginning of 1773.   Mr. Caleb Nichols was greatly blessed in his labors there after- wards.   He was born in West Greenwich in March, 1743, met with a change in 1767, and began to preach among this people in 1773, and a church was formed, and he was ordained their pastor in June, 1774.   When the war came on, it produced many evil effects ; yet in May, 1779, such a revival of religion was granted in these parts, that he baptized above sixty in two months, and his church increased to three hundred members in five years.   But in the great shakings and confusion which took place in 1786, this church was scattered, and many removed into other parts of the land, and Elder Nichols was dismissed in the spring of 1788, and went and set- tled at Pownal, in Vermont, where he is still useful.   Mr. Nathaniel Price was raised up to preach to this church, and he now holds meetings with some of them at the house where Elder Werden formerly preached, and Mr. John Benson preaches where Nichols did, though neither of them is ordained.   A Baptist church was formed in West Greenwich in 1773, and Mr. Elisha Greene was ordained their pastor, September 21, 1775, and re- mains so still.

A few general remarks shall close this chapter.   The multiplicity of sects in this State, has often been advanced as an argument against the re- ligious liberty which was granted therein ; but there are now about as many sects in the town of Boston, as there are in the whole State of Rhode Island.   There are some in Boston who pray for souls in purgatory, while others boldly preach up the fire of hell as that which will finally purge away all sin, without the prayers of any in this world.   And these things are carried the highest in Boston and Philadelphia, of any part of America. A party spirit, and bribery in election of rulers, were formerly laid as a great reproach on the colony of Rhode Island ; but our land is full of these evils now, and they have been carried as high as any where in the town of Boston.   Our land has also been filled, in the year past, with publications against our highest rulers, because a man was sent to England, and made a treaty with the rulers there, which gives them more power here than they had before.   But in the year 1786 two ministers came over with commis- sions from the bishops in England, and they have made other bishops in most of the United States, to whom moneys and lands are given by gov- ernments ; yet most men are silent about these things, or else commend them as evidences of candor and catholicism in our land. Whereas the bishops, and their ministry in England, who have been supported by law, have had more influence in their late wars against liberty in America and France, than all other men in their nation. But as the government of Rhode Island never granted any lands to religious ministers, nor supported any by tax, all the power of the church of England has raised no more than four of their societies in the whole State, and one of them is now nearly dissolved if not quite.[1] Governor Jencks was a leader in making the law in 1716, to exclude all suing for ministers' salaries from their courts, though he was in earnest to have the ministers of Christ supported voluntarily.[2] But a custom was introduced into their government in 1770, of incorporating societies to collect and manage funds of money for the support of religious ministers; and the hope of obtaining such a fund in Mr. Snow's congregation in Providence, was an evident motive for the ordination there in 1793, which shut him out of a house that he had as just a right in, as any minister has to any house for worship in our land. And the four ministers from the Massachusetts, who acted in that affair, are far from allowing the people in their own government a power to dismiss their minister without his own consent, or else the advice of a council whom he had a voice in calling. And according to the word of God, the only ministers who are to be followed, hold forth Christ in their conversation, the same yesterday, to-day, and forever, and are willing in all things to live honestly. Heb. xiii. 7, 8, 18. But how can any man live honestly, who eats the bread of others for nought? II Thess. iii. 7—10. And how can a people live honestly, if they require their minister to go a warfare at his own charges? I Cor. ix. 7—14. Each of which iniquities has long prevailed under the mask of religion, beyond what they could possibly have done in any other way.

[1]Bishop Seabury. who claimed a power there, died in March, 1796, since the first part of this book was printed.

[2]See p. 22; Vol. I, p. 482.

CHAPTER XLII.

STATE OF CONNECTICUT.—COUNTY OF NEW LONDON.

A CONCISE VIEW OF THE GOVERNMENT OF CONNECTICUT.—OF THE BAP-
TIST CHURCHES IN GROTON.—NEW LONDON.—STONINGTON.—LYME.—
COLCHESTER, BOZRAH AND PRESTON.—THOMPSON.—ASHFORD.—WOOD-
STOCK.—HAMPTON AND KILLINGLY.—PLAINFIELD AND MANSFIELD.—
FARMINGTON.—SUFFIELD.—ENFIELD AND OTHERS.—WALLINGFORD.—
STRATFIELD.—STAMFORD, &c.—COUNTY OF LITCHFIELD.—OF MIDDLE-
SEX.—TOLLAND.

Connecticut has ever had the privilege of choosing her own rulers, and
of making her own laws, as well as Rhode Island; and ministerial influence was much more mild there at first, than it has been in our days. John
Haines was the governor of Massachusetts Bay in 1635, and pronounced
the sentence of banishment against Roger Williams; but he and Mr.
Thomas Hooker went up to Connecticut soon after. And when Williams
was at his house at Hartford, Haines said to him, "I must now confess to
you, that the most wise God hath provided and cut out this part of his
world for a refuge and a receptacle for all sorts of consciences. I am now
under a cloud, and my brother Hooker, with the Bay, as you have been.
We have removed from them thus far, and yet they are not satisfied."[1]
No, nor ever could be satisfied in that way. For in 1708, a governor who
had been a minister, and came from the Massachusetts, obtained an act to
set up ministers above all their churches. And in 1742, their ministers
procured a law to punish every man who should preach the gospel in any
parish, without the consent of the parish minister. And as Mr. John
Owen, pastor of the first parish in Groton, ventured to preach against such
proceedings, he was complained of to the legislature at Hartford, in May,
1743, and an act was passed to bring him before them the next October.
A resolve was also passed, that no persons of the Presbyterian or Congregational denominations should have the benefit of the Act of Toleration,

[1] Massachusetts Historical Collections, Vol. I, p. 280.

granted to dissenters from their establishment, and that no courts below the legislature should have power to admit any to that privilege. Owen avoided being taken in October, when a law was made against the preaching of any itinerant minister who might come from any other government. And as a complaint was entered against Dr. Benjamin Pomeroy, of Hebron, for preaching against their laws, both he and Owen were ordered to be brought before them the next May. And in May, 1744, both of them were brought before the Assembly at Hartford, and were compelled to make a confession for said preaching, to pay costs of prosecution, and Pomeroy was bound to his good behavior. And in the December following, the ministers of Windham county ordained a minister for the first parish in Canterbury, against the vote of the church there ; which began the separation in our country, from such ministers and their churches. And how can any men be justly blamed for separating from those who claimed a power above the churches of Christ ?

The first Baptist church in Connecticut was formed in Groton about 1705. Elder Valentine Wightman came from North Kingstown, and settled in Groton, and was the first pastor of this church. They suffered for a while from the ruling party ; but in the glorious year 1741, he and Mr. Owen were agreed in the work which was then going on in the land, and they enjoyed liberty until Elder Wightman was taken away by death, June 9, 1747, aged sixty-six. He introduced singing in public worship into his church, and published a pamphlet to defend it. And being called to preach in Lyme, Mr. Bulkley, of Colchester, came and held a dispute with him upon baptism and the support of gospel ministers, June 7, 1727, of which Bulkley published an account, and Wightman answered it.[1] After his death the church called Elder Daniel Fisk to be their minister, and he continued with them seven years ; but they were then so much divided, that many of them gave a new declaration of their experiences, and signed new articles of faith and a covenant, June 28, 1754, and elected Mr. Timothy Wightman to be their pastor, and he was ordained as such, May 20, 1756, and continues so still. He is a son of their first pastor, and was born November 20, 1719. His brother, John Wightman, was ordained as an evangelist by this church, June 15, 1774, and travelled and preached in various parts of the country.[2] A daughter of their first pastor married a Mr. Rathbun, who has two sons and two grandsons, who are ordained Baptist ministers. Elder Timothy Wightman's son, Jesse, is also a Baptist minister at Springfield. A dispute arose in this church in September, 1765, about the nature of spiritual teaching and the improvement of gifts, upon

[1]See Vol. I, pp. 519, 520.
[2]Mr. Wightman was a shining example of uniform piety and benevolence, until death put an end to his useful life, which he ended in the most joyful manner at Farmington.

which a division ensued, and another church was formed, in which Mr. Silas Burris was ordained; and they held to mixed communion, and the Groton Conference was named from thence. But a revival of religion was granted in the mother church in 1774, which caused the addition of thirty members to it in about a year; and another church was formed in the north part of Groton, May 25, 1775, and Mr. Rufus Allen was ordained their pastor, and they had thirty-six members in 1784. But their pastor died not long after, since which their church is dissolved. Though the First Baptist church in Groton had seventy-eight members in 1787, and they increased to one hundred and fifty-eight in two years, and to one hundred and eighty-two in 1794, beside all that have died, have been dismissed or excluded.

The second Baptist church in Connecticut was formed at New London, and Mr. Stephen Gorton was ordained their pastor, November 28, 1726. He was a man of considerable gifts, and was minister there for many years; but he fell into some scandalous conduct, and his church was finally dissolved. It was in that part of the town where the church now is which keeps the seventh day as the Sabbath, of which we have spoken before. In January, 1744, Elder Timothy Peckom baptized some persons in the heart of the town, and some more at Saybrook, for which he was put in prison; and a church was gathered a year or two after, of the two denominations together; and Mr. Noah Hammond was ordained in this church in July, 1754, who afterwards was pastor of a church on Long Island, where he died in October, 1774. Elder Lester was also of this church, who is now at Saybrook. Another church was formed, and Mr. Joshua Morse was ordained their pastor, May 17, 1750, who in the time of the late war removed to Sandisfield, and Mr. Reuben Palmer is minister in that place, which now is called Montville. Mr. Zadoc Darrow was an early teacher in the first of these churches, of which he has been pastor many years. He was born in December, 1728, and his church gave up mixed communion in 1790, and there was such a revival among them in 1794 as caused the addition of ninety-one members in one year. John Rogers began a sect in this town in 1677, upon the following principles. As to language and dress they held with the Quakers, but they held the external use of baptism and the Supper as the Baptists do. But they held that the establishing the first day of the week as the Sabbath was idolatry, and they took much pains to pull it down, by testifying against it, and interrupting others in their keeping it. They were also earnestly set against supporting ministers by law; and they suffered much for their opposition to these two practices; and they were singular in refusing to employ any physicians in sickness, or midwives for women in travail, holding that they were to be healed or delivered by the prayer of faith. But as a few of them were left to put an end to their own lives, and rulers have been so wise of late

34

as to avoid their former severities towards them, their society is nearly dissolved, and many of their children are very useful men in various parts of the country.[1]   Three brethren of one family are deacons in three Baptist churches.

The work of the Spirit of God in our land in 1741, was very powerful in Stonington, where there were three Congregational societies, with ministers in each of them. Two of those ministers favored the work as long as their churches were increased thereby ; but a new piece of cloth, if put into an old garment, makes the rent worse, and new wine will burst old bottles, as our Lord observes to those who were building upon their own doings and traditions. Luke v. 31—38.   Such opposition appeared against the late work, and Elder Wightman was so clear in it, that a number of people were baptized and formed a church in Stonington, and Mr. Wait Palmer was ordained their pastor in September, 1743.   And after the separation began at Canterbury, it spread into Stonington, and a church was formed there, and Mr. Matthew Smith was ordained their pastor, December 10, 1746 ; and he continued with them until the spring of 1749, and then left them and removed out of the town.   And many embraced believers' baptism and went and joined to Elder Babcock's church in Westerly ; and when Mr. Paine had determined to use all his influence to stop the prevalence of the Baptist principles in their Separate churches, he and Babcock joined in writing letters to all their churches ; and delegates from forty churches met at the house of Mr. Simon Brown, of Stonington, May 29, 1754, and spent three days in hearing the controversies between the two parties.   Mr. Solomon Paine took much pains to prove, that it was a bad temper and conduct in the Baptists that caused the breach between him and them.   But his brother, Elisha Paine, a man of much more knowledge and experience, gave it as his mind, that the difficulty sprang from the nature of opposite principles.   For sprinkling of infants upon the faith of their parents, and burying of believers upon the profession of their own faith, are opposite principles.   And Mr. Elisha Paine said, "Dear brother, if you can reconcile the above principles, in the essential parts thereof, you will remove all the grounds of bars and disputes ; but if there be an essential difference in the above articles, and consequently in the practice on them, then there is an Achan in the camp : and no marvel that Israel hath, in all reformations, been troubled therewith."[2]   Infant baptism is built upon the covenant of circumcision, which made a great difference between Jews by nature, and all other men ; but in the Christian church the apostle Peter could not countenance that distinction without dissimulation.   Gal. ii. 11—16.   And for stealing of holy things, and dissembling about them, Achan was destroyed in the valley of Achor.   Joshua vii. 11—26.   And God says of his church, I will allure her, and bring her into the wilderness,

---

[1]See pp. 11, 12; Vol. I, pp. 376—384, 388.—ED.   [2]See p. 114.

and speak comfortably unto her; and I will give her her vineyards from thence, and the valley of Achor for a door of hope, and she shall sing there as in the days of her youth, and as in the day when she came out of the land of Egypt. And I will have mercy upon her that had not obtained mercy; and I will say to them which were not my people, Thou art my people; and they shall say, Thou art my God. Hosea ii. 14, 15, 23. This he says to his church under the gospel. I Peter ii. 10; Rom. ix. 25. The Holy Scriptures are our rule, and not the best of men upon earth; yet love to men as Christians was then set up by many as the rule of communion, instead of the written word; and their inward feelings were also made a rule of discipline, until some were censured for not concurring therewith. Upon this they renounced mixed communion, and gathered a Second Baptist church in Stonington, and Mr. Simeon Brown was ordained their pastor in March, 1765. And a parish minister in Stonington said two years after, "Not less than two-thirds of the congregation, formerly under my care, have withdrawn from my ministry, and formed themselves into Baptist and Separate churches."[1] And in January, 1769, Mr. Eleazar Brown was ordained in the First Baptist church in that town, which is four miles north of the other. He was born in Stonington, in June, 1728, and was a faithful and successful minister, until he died in peace, July 11, 1795. Such a blessing was granted there in 1792, as caused the addition of fifty-six members to this church; and in 1793, Mr. Peleg Randal was ordained a colleague pastor in this church, in which he yet continues. And on October 22, 1794, they ordained Mr. Abel Brown as an evangelist, to go and labor in the State of New York. Elder Wait Palmer is yet living, but has not preached much for many years. Elder Simeon Brown was born in Stonington, January 31, 1723, and his usefulness is still granted, and in the revival of 1792, seventy-six members were added to his church. The Third Baptist church in Stonington was constituted down at the harbor, April 22, 1775, and Mr. Valentine Wightman Rathbun was ordained their pastor in May, 1787. He was born May 13, 1761. Mr. John Rathbun, his father, was ordained there as an evangelist, March 15, 1781, and is settled in Ashford. A fourth church was formed in Stonington, and Mr. Samuel Northup, from Narragansett, was ordained their pastor in 1793, in connection with the Groton Conference.

A Separate church was formed at Lyme, and Mr. Ebenezer Mack was ordained their pastor, January 12, 1749. He and many of the church became Baptists afterwards, and he continued with them until he was dismissed, in September, 1768, and he removed to Marlow, in New Hampshire. And Mr. Jason Lee was ordained the pastor of this church, and has had great success therein, being connected with the Groton Conference. There had been a Baptist church in the east part of Lyme before this, but they were broken and dissolved. There was also a Baptist church

[1] Preface to Fish's Nine Sermons, p. 3.

formed in the north part of that town, and Mr. Christopher Minor was their minister for some years, who is now at Enfield.

A Baptist church was formed in Colchester, in 1743, and Mr. Zebulon Waterman was their minister for a number of years.   After him Mr. Ichabod Allen ministered to them for a longer time, and he is still living among them ; but he has been rather unsteady both in his principles and conduct, which served to scatter the flock.   But in May, 1784, a new gathering and union took place among them, and Mr. Abel Palmer became their pastor, under whose ministry they have enjoyed many blessings.   Their house for worship is near the borders of Montville.   Another Baptist church had been formed in Colchester, in 1783, near the borders of Lebanon, and Mr. Christopher Palmer, father to Abel, was ordained their pastor.   They came from Stonington.   Many blessings have been granted upon these churches, and upon people who have sprung from them, many of whom have settled in the wilderness, upon the head branches of the Mohawk and Susquehanna rivers, in the State of New York, where a new Association was formed in 1795, of thirteen churches, and more than five hundred members, which churches have been all formed in five years, as Mr. Abel Palmer says, who was at said Association.   Those people went mainly from New England, and a large part of them out of the Stonington Association.   There has been a mixed communion church in Norwich, in that part which is now Bozrah, for several years, and Mr. Peter Rogers was their minister, who is now at Hampton, but I know not how their state now is.   The mixed- communion church of Preston, have many of their members in Canterbury, and meetings are often held in both places.

COUNTY OF WINDHAM.

As the great reformation in our land was opposed by the ruling party in Thompson, then a part of Killingly, a separation took place there, and a Baptist church was formed in 1750, and Mr. Whitman Jacobs was ordained their pastor.   They held the laying on of hands upon every member as a term of communion, and an Association was formed upon those principles, which increased to about eight churches in 1763 ; but in two years after, the most of them gave up that bar of communion, of whom Mr. Jacobs was one, and a council was called at Thompson in February, 1767, which could not unite the church ; and as a number of them removed soon after to Royalstone, their minister removed there also in 1769.   The brethren in Thompson, after many labors, covenanted together anew in September, and Mr. John Martin was ordained their pastor, November 3, 1773.   He went from Rehoboth, and is still useful among them.

Mr. Thomas Dennison was baptized by Elder Wightman, of Groton, in the summer of 1743, and he gathered a small church at Ashford, where he was ordained in November following.   Elder Moulton assisted in his ordination, who derived his succession from Mr. John Callender, and he from his uncle Elisha Callender, in whose ordination three Congregational ministers of Boston assisted. And this line of succession is much valued by some, while all who consistently hold the Congregational principles, adopted by the fathers of the Massachusetts, hold that the power of ordination is in each church. This church in Ashford broke up in a year or two, and Mr. Dennison turned back to infant baptism, and he assisted in the ordinations of the first Separate ministers in Mansfield, Canterbury, Plainfield, and Norwich; and was installed himself as pastor of a church in that part of Norwich which is now Franklin, all in the year 1746. But in a few years he left that people, and preached occasionally in various parts of the country, without being settled over any other flock, until he died in Brooklyn, near Canterbury, October 24, 1787. A new Baptist church was formed in Ashford in 1774, and Mr. Ustick preached to them for a year or two, and then went to Grafton, and Mr. Ebenezer Lamson was ordained their pastor, June 10, 1778. But he removed to Sutton in April, 1783, as was before observed; and after several years, they obtained Mr. Dyer Stark for their minister, who has had considerable success among them. The Second Baptist church in Ashford was formed in the glorious year 1780. Mr. John Rathbun had removed from Stonington, into the north part of Ashford before; and after this church was formed, he was ordained at Stonington, March 15, 1781, and has been the pastor of this church ever since. He was born June 26, 1729. In a revival of religion in the east part of Ashford, a third church was formed, and Mr. Daniel Bolton was ordained therein, June 27, 1792. He went from Bridgewater. Part of this church live in Pomfret. About three years after, Mr. Bolton gathered another church near the adjoining corners of Ashford, Union and Woodstock, and settled as their minister.

The first Baptist church in Woodstock was gathered in the following manner. Biel Ledoyt was a chief leader in mirth and vanity among young people there, before he heard a Baptist minister preach a sermon in the town, in December, 1763, which was a means of fixing conviction of sin in his conscience, and in the March following, his soul was brought into gospel liberty; but as soon as his change was heard of abroad, four of his old companions came one evening, to try if they could not draw him back to his former ways again. He readily retired with them to a place where they could be by themselves, and he laid open to them the way of sin and death, and the way of life and peace, in such a manner that two of them went home with a deep sense of sin upon their minds, which terminated happily, and religious meetings were frequent among young people, until a large number were hopefully converted. For some time after this work began, they attended the parish meetings for worship, as they had done before; but such opposition was raised against the work by the Congregational party, as convinced these young believers that they could not be edified among them ; and upon searching the Scriptures, they were convinced that believers' baptism was the way that Christ had instituted, and many obeyed him therein, and a Baptist church was formed in Woodstock in 1766, and Mr. Ledoyt was ordained their pastor, May, 26, 1768, and they had forty-eight members in 1773.[1]   And though it was a dark time with

[1] " On December 9th, 1763, it pleased the Lord to begin his mighty work in Woodstock ; and was pleased to take hold of my heart on that day, who was the first person (so far as I know) that was convicted, and who had been noted for vanity.   I soon saw myself an undone sinner, condemned by God's law, and an heart-enemy to God and to all that was good, unable to help myself, and no way open to escape his wrath.   All hopes of escaping his wrath were almost gone, when God convinced me of his sovereignty and justice, and on the 12th day of March following, caused me to fall into his hands and revealed his Son to me and in me.   I then saw a world lying in wickedness, and the necessity of men being made new creatures fell with weight upon my mind, and I felt myself disposed to speak to them about it; which was surprising to them who heard me, the rather because it came from such a noted sinner.   The unexpected and surprising news soon flew abroad, upon which some of my companions came to see me one evening, to see if they could not laugh me out of that notion which I was possessed of, as some of them soon confessed.   I soon began to talk with them about death and the need of being prepared for it, and when they heard, they stood like men amazed.   I spent the evening with them, and, at the desire of one of them, I prayed with them, and while I was praying, one of them was pricked in the heart and cried out 'What shall we do?' and one of them was hardly able to go home, and these two were hopefully converted soon after. But they desired that a meeting might be appointed at a school-house, which I gladly complied with.   When I came to the house I was astonished, for, though it was a dark, cloudy night in March, people flocked from all parts of the society, until the house was full.   The people were chiefly youths, that met, and there was no one to carry on the meeting but myself and the other two young men.   We prayed and sang and read a sermon, and I exhorted.   Those two young men were convinced, but were not as yet converted.   They manifested their distress of soul, saying that they were going to hell, and warned others not to go to that place of torment.   That was a night much to be remembered, for I believe that there were forty persons struck under conviction, and those persons that were convicted became loud preachers to those that were around them, both by their countenances and talk.   Meetings were now attended two or three times a week.   Convictions increased greatly. Parents were surprised to see their giddy children distressed for their souls.   Some old professors, who had thought themselves Christians, now began to see that their building was upon the sand, and cried 'God be merciful to us sinners!' and at the first there were hardly any that dared to say a word against the work.   Frolicking, which had been much practised, came to a stop.   The Bible, and other good books, that had never been regarded, were now much in use.   Our groves rang with the bitter outcries of the distressed youth.   God was soon merciful to some of them, and delivered them from their distresses, and their sorrow was turned into joy, and their mouths filled with praise to their Redeemer, and they were then calling upon all to praise the Lord with them, and they recommended him to others, and this increased their distress.

" And this stirred up all the Christians in the society.   Those who had been sleep-

them through most of the war, yet on September 8, 1780, they said in a letter to the Warren Association :—

After a long day of desertion and heavy trials, our God has returned to us. By means of the uncommon darkness in May last, the Lord was

ing, with the foolish virgins, bagan to lament their backslidings, and with joy, own the work to be of the Lord, and endeavored to be workers together with him; and those who were no more than professors, and intended to remain where they were, then were stirred up to oppose the work, and sought to use means to stop the progress of it. But all in vain. First, they met with them, and sought to regulate them, striving to keep them from exhorting each other. Then they began to talk much of errors, cautioned against spending too much time in meetings, and being out too late at night, and of being too much distressed, &c. But when they found they could not obtain their end in this way, they withdrew from our meetings, and fell to accusing, crying 'Error and delusion;' neighboring ministers were called in, and a fast proclaimed; and instead of being workers together with the Lord, they fell to reading about false spirits, and Satan's transforming himself into an angel of light, against false ministers, Separatists and separations, Baptists and Baptist preachers; intimating that the work was from Satan, and such ministers, the instruments of it, were the servants of Satan; and for no other reason, as I conceive, but that they were instruments in turning many from sin to God. Such preaching was much admired by the church in general, but it grieved the hearts of the tender lambs. They labored for a reformation, but all in vain, and they soon saw the need of a separation; and in the fall ensuing, they separated and met together as a society, and improved the gifts which God had given them, and it was attended with a blessing. Saints were comforted and sinners converted. The saints read the Scriptures to know their duty, and soon found they were not baptized, and a considerable number were baptized by immersion, and the number increased. We met as a society for more than a year, and then we thought that there were enough agreed to embody into a church; and in February, 1766, we embodied, to the number of fifteen, and had the ordinance of the Supper administered, and God's blessing attended it. There were some additions soon made. We made several attempts to obtain an elder but were disappointed. Some gifted brethren among us were very helpful, and brotherly love continued. It was apparent to all who had eyes to see, that God's work went on amongst us. But, with lamentation may we speak it, many that were awakened, turned off to their old courses again; but all that were members of the church, remained steadfast. We were greatly favored with several gifted elders, who were very helpful to us in our infancy; and in about three years after the work began, it pleased the Lord to call me forth publicly to preach his word, and, I trust, I was so enabled to do it, that it was satisfactory to the church. I preached among them constantly for several months, and then the church gave me a call to be their pastor, and I was ordained May 26, 1768; and in the June following, several members were added to us by baptism, and God blessed us together." Extract from a letter of Mr. Ledoyt to Mr. Backus.

Mr. Backus relates that during this revival, some persons waylaid Mr. Ledoyt, "to mob him as he came to meeting, but he happened to come in another road. Next time they waylaid that, and he came the former road. The third time they waylaid both roads, and providence so ordered that he came on foot across the fields, and thus was three times preserved from violence and abuse, by an unseen hand." Rev. S. Hall's Collection of papers.—ED.

pleased to awaken some souls among us, and from that time the work of God has been going on gloriously in the west part of this town, where a goodly number are hopefully converted, and peace and love abound in the church, and we have had twenty-eight added to us, and there is a prospect of the spreading of the good work in other parts of this town and towns around us. Yet we are much affected with the long confinement of our brethren in Worcester goal,[1] and cannot but remember them in bonds as being bound with them; nor can we expect to fare better ourselves very long, notwithstanding our endeavoring to answer the unjust law of the ruling party, by giving certificates to the members of our society, which have been carried to the parish clerk; yet a considerable number of them are rated to the standing ministry, and soon expect to be distressed on that account.[2] Our oppressors are deaf to all reasoning upon the subject, and are determined to prosecute their design, let the consequence be what it may. These things, brethren, are peculiarly mortifying to us, especially when we consider that we have freely fought and bled by their sides in defence of liberty. It appears to us, that if ever there was a time, since tyranny had existence in America, that we were called upon to exert ourselves to obtain what is our own, it is now. Should we let slip this golden season, we fear our chains will be so fast rivetted that we shall not be able to shake them off. We feel but little heart to hold the sword against a British invader in defence of liberty, while our countrymen are endeavoring to deprive us of liberty of conscience. Oh, brethren! if we must be deprived of this, who would desire to live and possess the rest?

Their church increased the next year to a hundred and forty members. But in 1787 a member of a Congregational church obtained a meeting of this Baptist church, to hear a complaint which he had against one of their members, without taking the steps prescribed by our Lord in Matthew xviii; and it divided, and raised such a fire of contention in this church, as caused the dismission of their pastor, at his request, in March, 1790, and he went into New Hampshire, where he is still useful. Another revival was granted in this church in 1792, and Mr. Samuel Webster was ordained there the 28th of June, who is now at Monson. A second Baptist church was then formed in Woodstock, and Mr. Amos Wells was ordained their pastor, August 9, 1792, and the Stonington Association met there in October, 1795, when it was a good time with them.

Mr. Ledoyt was called to preach in the south part of Pomfret, and a happy number were hopefully converted there, where were also several old believers; and they embraced the Baptist principles, and formed a church there, January 18, and Mr. William Grow was ordained their pastor, June 19, 1776, and they prospered under his ministry for several years. But in June, 1783, he confessed that he had fallen into the sin of adultery, and resigned his office, and afterwards removed into Vermont. Though this was very shocking, yet the church persevered in their profession, and obtained

[1] Three men of Harvard Society, before spoken of.
[2] Several of them were strained upon for such taxes.

occasional supplies from time to time, until they called and settled Mr. Peter Rogers as their pastor in 1794, who had before been a minister in Bozrah. The place where this church meets, with a part of Windham, were lately incorporated into a town by the name of Hampton. A Baptist church was formed in Killingly, May 22, 1776, and Mr. George Robinson was ordained their pastor the 13th of November following, and they increased to sixty-one members in five years. But there arose such difficulties in the church, about the time of the close of the war, that they called a council, and then dismissed and recommended their minister, and he removed to Bridgewater in June, 1784, where he is still useful. They have passed through many changes in Killingly since, without obtaining so happy a settlement as were to be wished.

The separation in Plainfield prevailed so far, that the general scheme of taxing all to Congregational ministers was given up, and a minister was settled in their town meeting-house in 1784, who is supported by subscription and a public fund, and the Separate meeting was dissolved. But in the summer of 1792, a remarkable awakening took place in the east part of the town, and in Stirling, under the ministry of Mr. Nathanael Cole; and a Baptist church was formed there, October 16, 1792, and he was installed their pastor the 5th of December after, having been ordained at Swansea before; and in two years this church increased to eighty-seven members. I have not obtained any distinct account of the present Baptist church in Mansfield, only what Mr. Asplund has given in his Register.

COUNTY OF HARTFORD.

The First Baptist church in the county of Hartford was first constituted in Wallingford. A number of people in that town became Baptists about 1731, and joined the Baptist church in New London, but usually met for worship at Wallingford, until they obtained a dismission, formed a church there, and ordained Mr. John Merriman as their pastor, in 1739. He was born in Wallingford, October 15, 1695; and as he was a hearty friend to the great work which came on in our land two years after he was ordained, he obtained Dr. Bellamy, and then Mr. Robbins, to preach in his society, as they were clear preachers of the gospel. But Mr. Robbins was most cruelly persecuted by his brethren in the ministry, for preaching among the Baptists against their advice, as we have before shown.[1] In the year 1750, the body of this church removed to the south part of Farmington, where they still remain. Mr. Merriman continued their faithful pastor as long as he was able to labor with them, and he died there in 1784. Afterwards they obtained various helps, until they came into the state that is before described, from the Minutes of the Danbury Association for 1795. Bristol

[1]See pp. 42, 43, 81—85.

is not far from them, where is the church which keeps the seventh day as the Sabbath.

Suffield, on the west side of Connecticut River, had a powerful work in 1735, and a greater work six years after ; and when the separations came on, two Separate churches were formed in the town, and each had an ordained minister. Mr. Israel Holly was one of them, who published several things in favor of their Separate churches, and then against the Baptists, after which he turned back, and became a parish minister. But Mr. John Hastings, son to their other Separate minister, was called to preach the gospel, and embraced believers' baptism ; and just as the war-was coming on in our land, such a blessing was granted upon his labors, that a Baptist church was formed, and he was ordained their pastor in 1775, and it increased to above two hundred members in about a year. He has been very useful, at home and abroad, ever since.

Enfield, on the east side of the river against Suffield, had also two Separate churches, in one of which the Baptist principles were early adopted. Mr. Joseph Meacham was their minister, and they joined the Warren Association in 1769, when they had thirty members ; but they afterwards declined from their profession, and their minister fell in with the Shakers, and is since dead. The church was broken and scattered for a number of years ; but we hear of a late gathering among them, and that they have obtained Mr. Christopher Minor as their pastor. He came from Lyme, and was minister to the Baptist church in East Hartford for a number of years, who now have Mr. Stephen Shepard as their minister. A Baptist church was formed in the city of Hartford in 1789, which increased to fifty-three members in two years, and greater blessings are hoped for. A Separate meeting was set up at Windsor, as early as 1747, and Daniel Marshall went from thence in 1754, and labored with great success in the southern States, and began the first Baptist church in Georgia in 1772. His brother, Eliakim Marshall, was frequently a representative for Windsor in Connecticut legislature, before his cousin, Abraham Marshall, came there from Georgia, and baptized him, and he was pastor of a Baptist church there for four or five years, before he died there in June, 1791. But I know not how things have been in that church since. There has been a Baptist meeting in Wethersfield for many years, but perhaps not a church formed. The other Baptist churches in this county appear in the foregoing list.

COUNTY OF NEW HAVEN.

After the Baptist church of Wallingford was removed from thence, their parish minister died, and a division took place in the town, and the Consociation of the county assisted in forming another church, and ordaining a second minister, because the majority had got a minister from Cambridge, whom they judged to be an Arminian. And as the corporation of Yale

College were very zealous against admitting any into it but strict Calvinists, long controversies were carried on in the government about it. And in February, 1783, the controversy was introduced into the public papers at Hartford, and it was pursued therein until June. And to shew how injurious the rulers of the college had been to its true interests, it was said :—

Mr. Collins, late of Newport, offered eight volumes to the library of Yale College. Being a Baptist, four of the volumes were in defence of this system. The offer of the books was accompanied with an intimation, that if the eight volumes were received with a good grace, the whole library of the said Mr. Collins, (who was a bachelor,) consisting of seven or eight hundred volumes, would probably be given to the college. But the condition of giving the eight volumes was not complied with. This condition was, that they should be placed in the library so that the students might see them, and, if they chose, read them.

The writer who gave this information styled himself Parnassus, to whom an answer was given by one who says :—

Parnassus finds fault that they did not accept of the Anabaptist books upon a shameful condition, which, if they had done it, would have been a ground of objection, that they had introduced erroneous books, and have given up the government of the college.

Thus it appears, that the corporation of the college were afraid to have any of their scholars read any books against infant baptism, lest it should weaken their plan of orthodoxy ; while men who wanted to pull down Calvinism, made use of this action as a means to do it, though they were far from favoring the Baptists. A change in the government of the college took place soon after, and the minister who had caused a separation at Wallingford removed and settled in New Haven, and two Baptist churches have since been formed at Wallingford. And through all the country the new Baptist churches have evidently sprung from the spiritual work therein, while the towns where that work was rejected remain in their old formality.

COUNTY OF FAIRFIELD.

Mr. John Sherwood was born in 1706, converted in 1741, and he with others separated from the parish worship in Stratfield, because a minister was settled there who did not appear to them to be a gospel preacher. In October, 1751, Elder Joshua Morse baptized him and a number more, and a Baptist church was then formed there, and on December 15, 1757, Mr. Sherwood was ordained their pastor, by the assistance of Elder Morse and Elder Timothy Wightman.[1] He ministered to that church about ten years,

---

[1]Mr. Sherwood was taxed for the support of Presbyterian worship, and the first year after his settlement, "a new tea-kettle" was taken by the collectors; the second year, "a brass kettle containing half a barrel, and a pewter basin containing half a gallon, and another containing three pints, with about six plates and two platters." Similar distress was made upon the members of his church.—ED.

and then his health failed, and Mr. Benjamin Coles was called from Long Island to preach to them, in the spring of 1768, and he labored with them until the fall of 1774, when he was called into New Jersey. Mr. Sherwood was then weak in body, but steadfast and comfortable in his mind ; and how long he lived afterwards I know not. But the church called Mr. Seth Higby from Middletown, and he was ordained their pastor, and he continued so until 1793, and then he removed to a church in the State of New York, and Elder Stephen Royce, from New Hampshire, became their pastor.

The Baptist church in Stamford was formed in the following manner :— Dr. Joseph Bellamy published a piece in 1768, to prove that a credible profession of saving grace was necessary, in every person who came to the Lord's Supper, or who was active in baptism. But Dr. Moses Mather, of Stamford, published a discourse in April, 1769, wherein he owned that the covenant of circumcision with Abraham was not the covenant of grace, in the strict sense of the word, but held it to be a covenant wherein parents and their children were constituted members of the visible church of God, and that they ought to come to the Lord's Supper as a converting ordinance, if they were not converted before. Mr. Ebenezer Farris, of Stamford, had newly joined the first church in that town ; but these things gave such a turn to his mind as caused him to search the Scriptures afresh, whereby he was fully convinced that baptism and the Holy Supper were instituted only for professing believers ; and he was baptized by Mr. John Gano, of New York, in April, 1770, as others were afterwards, until they obtained a regular dismission, and also assistance from the church in New York, and formed a Baptist church at Stamford, November 6, 1773, of twenty-one members. By a like dismission and assistance, a Baptist church was formed three days before on the borders of Greenwich, called Kingstreet ; and Mr. Asplund mistakes in dating the beginning of that church in 1747. Mr. Farris was afterwards ordained the pastor of the church in Stamford, and also published a defence of believers' baptism. Mr. Ebenezer White, of Danbury, was a hearty friend to the revival of religion in our land ; and when he read Sandeman's letters, he manifested an approbation of his ideas concerning the finished atonement of Christ, and so did a majority of his church ; but a minor part went and entered a complaint against Mr. White to their Association, upon which he and a large majority of his church, on June 28, 1763, renounced the power that was claimed over the churches on the Saybrook Platform. But the ministers of that county were so unwilling to part with that power, that they met at Danbury, against the consent of Mr. White and the majority of his church, and rejected them as men who had separated from the ecclesiastical constitution of their government. This was on March 27, 1764. Sandeman came into our country the next October, and gathered churches in several places ; but when he came to Danbury, Mr. White could not agree with him in many things, though a number joined with him there, and also at New Haven, and Mr. Sandeman died at Danbury, April 2, 1771, aged fifty-three. But in the ensuing war, most of his followers held with Britain, and a number of them went off to Nova Scotia, and their societies are generally dissolved. In 1770, Mr. David Judson, minister at Newtown, renounced the Saybrook Platform, and published his mind against it, while the majority of the ministers exerted all their influence against him ; and two Baptist churches have since been gathered in Danbury, and one in Newtown. Ridgefield is also in this county.

COUNTY OF LITCHFIELD.

There was more of a reformation in this county, in and after 1741, than in many parts of the country. Dr. Bellamy was a very active instrument of that reformation, and his writings afterwards upon the nature of religion, and also upon qualifications necessary for communion in the Christian church, scattered much light in our land ; and several other ministers in the county of Litchfield have been clear preachers of the gospel, and successful in their labors, who now rest therefrom, and others have been introduced in their stead, who are men of another spirit. And since the late war, nine Baptist churches have been formed in this county, and seven of them in six years. But as new towns have been constituted, and old names have been altered, while some meetings have also been removed, a little explanation is necessary. The Baptist church in Litchfield was the first in Watertown, and Roxbury was once called South Britain, while the names of the other seven remain as they were. Some of their ministers have removed from place to place. Elder Elisha Ransom was at Watertown in 1790, who before and since has been at Woodstock, in Vermont. Elder Stephen Shepard was at Torrington in 1790, who is now at East Hartford. Elder Isaac Roots was at Warren in 1790, and at the second in Watertown in 1793, but at no church in that Association in 1795. Elder Nathaniel Norton was at Danbury in 1790, and at Wallingford in 1791, but out of that Association since. In new churches, and in changes of sentiments, men are often more unsteady than when they obtain more clear establishment. Though travelling ministers, if they are wise and faithful, have done much good in every age ; while deceitful teachers, whether supported by law, or travelling through the world, have done infinite evils to mankind.

COUNTY OF MIDDLESEX.

There were some Baptists in Saybrook as early as 1729, who then complied with the certificate law, to exempt them from taxes to established ministers, as Dr. Stiles informed me. In January, 1744, Elder Timothy Peckom visited them, and baptized some persons on a Lord's day, when the water of a brook was raised for the purpose. For these things he and a number more were imprisoned at New London, one of whom was a woman with a child at her breast. Mr. Elnathan Wilcox was a minister in the church there for a number of years before 1770, but in 1780 he was settled at Stockbridge. Elder Lester, from New London, was settled at Saybrook afterwards, and remains there. But in 1788, a number drew off and formed another church, and ordained Mr. William Hill as their pastor, and they are connected with the Groton Conference. The other Baptist churches in this county belong to the Stonington Association, and their state has been given from their Minutes. Abraham Doolittle, of Middletown, went to the Separate meeting there for some years, to hear Mr. Ebenezer Frothingham preach, who was first ordained at Wethersfield, October 28, 1747, but removed his meeting to Middletown a few years after. But as Mr. Doolittle embraced the Baptist sentiments, Frothingham openly and frequently prayed and preached against them, and then published a bitter pamphlet upon the subject; therefore Doolittle and his friends withdrew and set up a meeting by themselves in 1769, and Mr. Seth Higby, who married his daughter, began to preach there, who went afterwards to Stratfield, as was before related. Doolittle is a member of a Baptist church in Wallingford. But about the year 1781, Mr. Frothingham was rejected by his church, and they ordained Mr. Stephen Parsons in his stead, who was well esteemed in his place, until he was constrained to give up infant baptism, and was baptized, with about fifteen of his church, in the close of the summer of 1795; so that a Baptist church is like to be settled there soon.

COUNTY OF TOLLAND.

A Baptist church was formed in Tolland, and Mr. Shubael Stearns was ordained therein, March 20, 1751, by the assistance of the elders Wait Palmer and Joshua Morse. But in July, 1754, Stearns baptized Mr. Noah Alden, of Stratford, and he set off the next month, with others, to go into our southern governments. And Stearns wrote to Alden, from Hampshire county, in Virginia, June 13, 1755, and informed him that some of their company were then settled in North Carolina, who said to him in a letter, "that there was no established meeting within a hundred miles of them, and that the people were so eager to hear, that they often came forty miles each way, when they could have an opportunity to hear a sermon." He went himself and gathered a Baptist church on Sandy Creek, Orange county, North Carolina. When I was in Virginia in 1789, I saw a record of the beginning of their Associations, and was informed that Daniel Marshall baptized Samuel Harris, who had been a member of their legislature, and a judge of court in Virginia. Their first Association met in January, 1760, and they met again in July that year, when the list of their churches stood thus, including both meetings. Sandy Creek, Elder Shubael Stearns; Deep River, Nathaniel Powel, a brother; Abbot's-Creek, Elder Daniel Marshall; Little River, Joseph Breed, a brother; Neuse River, Ezekiel Hunter; Black River, John Newton; Dan River, Pittsylvania county, Elder Samuel Harris; Lunenburg county, William Murphey. The two last are in Virginia, the rest are in North Carolina. Elder Stearns wrote again to Elder Alden, from Sandy Creek, October 16, 1765, and said, " The Lord carries on his work gloriously in sundry places in this province, and in Virginia, and South Carolina." And he labored in those parts as long as he lived; but Marshall went and gathered the first Baptist church in Georgia, whereof his son, Abraham Marshall, is pastor. And it appears by the Minutes of their Association in 1792, that they had fifty-six churches, and three thousand seven hundred and ninety-six members in the State of Georgia. How wonderful are these events! They who were left of the church in Tolland, joined with others in Stafford, and ordained Mr. Alden as their pastor, June 5, 1755, and he labored with them ten years, and then such disorders had crept into the church, that he was dismissed by the advice of a council, as was before observed. They have passed through various changes since, and their present state is given above. A Separate church was formed in Somers about 1751, and Mr. Joseph Marshall was ordained their pastor, who soon became a Baptist, and then turned back to infant baptism, and he was installed at Canterbury, successor to Mr. Paine; but after a few years he was dismissed, and has preached about the country ever since, without taking the charge of any other flock. But we are informed that a Baptist church was constituted in Somers in 1790, and that Mr. Seth Parsons is since ordained their pastor. Mr. Lillebridge, the pastor of the Baptist church in Willington, came from the State of Rhode Island, and is esteemed in his place. But I have no further accounts of that church, nor of the other Baptists in the county of Tolland, that appear to be serviceable to the public, than what are already given.

CHAPTER XLIII.

All the lands between Merrimack and Piscataqua rivers, and sixty miles
into the country, were granted to Captain John Mason, in 1629, under the
name of New Hampshire. But the Massachusetts charter extended three
miles north of Merrimack River, and Mason, with his heirs or assigns,
claimed all the rest of those lands; and this was the cause why New
Hampshire was not included in the second charter to the Massachusetts, in
1691, as Georges's grant was, which this government had purchased of his
heirs. None of the lands within this grant, nor from thence to Connecticut River, were ever the free property of the people, so as to be granted by
their representatives, before the late American war; and quit-rents were
reserved upon the lands which were granted by their governors, until the
American revolution put an end to them. Dr. Belknap has given a clear
view of these things, in his elegant History of New Hampshire. And as
the governors and counsellors of that government were appointed by the
crown, the Congregational denomination were never exalted so high above
all others there, as they have been in Massachusetts and Connecticut; and
since the revolution, if the majority of any town elect a Baptist teacher for
their minister, he may have the privilege of the lands therein which were
granted for the ministry, and also may be supported by tax if he will.
And the Baptists increased so much in the year 1780, that a minister of
Rowley published a letter against them, in a Boston paper of February 8,
1781, in which he said:—

Alas, the consequence of the prevalence of this sect! They cause divisions everywhere. In the State of New Hampshire, where there are

35

many new towns, infant settlements, if this sect gets footing among them, they hinder, and are like to hinder, their settling and supporting learned, pious and orthodox ministers ; and so the poor inhabitants of those towns must live, who knows how long? without the ministry of the gospel, and gospel ordinances.

As if the gospel and gospel ordinances, were confined to the Congregational party. Yea, he said to the Baptists :—

You have had two grand conventions (the second of them upon adjournment) within a few months past, at a town in the State of New Hampshire, to serve and promote this cause ; at which conventions, these illiterate and unskilful preachers, and delegates from your little churches around, were members. And one thing I heard of as a part of your business at said convention, was, to consult what measures you should take to make void in part our new constitution of government ; that part of it which respects the public worship of God.

But all the pretence he could have for this representation, was because the Warren Association met in September, 1780, at Royalstone, which adjoins New Hampshire, and after it was over, the church there agreed to call a council the next month, for advice upon some difficulties among themselves, and not upon the concerns of the government. Though as three men of the Harvard society had been imprisoned at Worcester, and others were daily exposed to the same sufferings, for taxes to Congregational ministers, the Warren Association drew up a testimony against such oppression, in their said meeting, and printed many copies of it, which were sent into all parts of the government, and were signed by many hundreds of men, of various denominations. And is it a crime for any men who are oppressed, to expose the iniquity of their oppressors, and openly to testify against the same?

The first Baptist church that was formed in New Hampshire, was at Newton, northward of Haverhill, in 1755. In June that year, Mr. Walter Powers was ordained their pastor, and they increased under his ministry for some years ; but then different sentiments about church discipline, with unhappy tempers in controversies, caused such difficulties, that a council of four churches was called, May 18, 1761, and held four days, without being able to reconcile pastor and people.[1] And he was afterwards dismissed and removed away, and is since dead ; but his son is a useful minister at Gilmanton. This church at Newton labored through many difficulties, until

---

[1]Mr. Backus has preserved full minutes of this council, of which he was Moderator. Many accusations were made on both sides, and both pastor and people were censured, the former with most severity. He afterwards presented a confession, but the church were not satisfied with it, and excluded him. He went to Middleborough and submitted his confession to Mr. Backus and his church, and they judged it sufficient. It may be inferred from the next sentence of the paragraph above, that the church afterwards restored him.—ED.

a Baptist church was formed in Haverhill, in 1765, and then many of the members joined there, and this church was dissolved. But the main body of the inhabitants of Newton, have lately come so much into the Baptist sentiments, that they prevailed with Mr. John Peak, who had been preaching at Cambridge and Woburn, to remove there in the fall of 1795, and a Baptist church was formed here in February, 1796. He was born at Walpole, in this State, September 26, 1761, was ordained at Windsor, in Vermont, and has been a successful preacher in various parts of the country.

The revival of religion in 1764, spread into several towns in New Hampshire, and the doctrine of believers' baptism followed it, until Mr. Smith, of Haverhill, was sent for, and he baptized thirty-eight persons in a week, in June, 1770. Fourteen of them were the Congregational minister and majority of his church in Deerfield, who were settled as a Baptist church the same month. Mr. Eliphalet Smith was their pastor, who is now at Fayette, in the county of Lincoln, before spoken of. A Baptist church was formed at Stratham, July 18, 1770, of fourteen members, and another at Brentwood of thirteen members, May 2, 1771, and one of sixteen members was constituted at Nottingham the next day ; and these churches unitedly called Mr. Samuel Shepard to receive ordination, and he was ordained at Stratham, September 25, 1771, when Dr. Stillman preached the sermon, Mr. Smith, of Haverhill, gave the charge, and Dr. Manning, of Providence, the right hand of fellowship. Mr. Shepard was born at Salisbury, near Newbury, in 1739, was early changed by grace, and was a useful physician, before he was baptized in June, and began to preach in July, 1770. These three churches have united as one, and others have joined with them from other places, so that they had one hundred and sixty-one members in 1785 ; and though they did not increase for five years after, yet such a blessing was then granted that they had three hundred and ninety-seven members in 1792, and five hundred and twenty-six in 1793. And one hundred and twenty-one were dismissed the next year, though they have a large number now. Mr. Joshua Smith was of this church, who labored much in various places, with considerable success, until he died with a consumption in February, 1795. Elder Samuel Currier was also of this church, who is now ordained at Wentworth. Elder Shepard has travelled and labored much in our new towns, especially in 1780.[1] And he has since published several books in defence of our sentiments.

A Baptist church was formed at Salem, in this county, in 1780, and Mr. Samuel Fletcher was ordained their pastor, December 6, 1781. He was born in the county of Middlesex, in August, 1747, born again in 1767, and began to preach in 1777. He was called to preach at Chelmsford in the spring of 1778, and preached there the main of the time for two years, and his labors were also very successful in several other places, which appeared

[1]See p. 280.

to be the cause of his meeting with uncommon abuse in one place. For being called to Pepperell, in company with Dr. Parker, of Harvard, they met by the side of a river, for the conveniency of baptizing, within an inclosed field; but while Mr. Fletcher was preaching, a large mob broke into the field, and interrupted him in his sermon, while a dog was carried and plunged in the river, in evident contempt of our mode of baptism. The chief officers of the town were leaders of the mob; therefore a gentleman invited these ministers to go and hold their meeting at his house, near another river, and they did so, and Fletcher went through with his sermon, after which two dogs more were dipped in that river, and one young man also dipped his companion, in a most scornful manner, and some officers of the town advised said ministers to depart immediately out of town for their own safety. But they privately agreed with their friends to disperse, and they met at another place of water, and baptized six persons near night, though further abuse was offered them afterwards.[1]   Elder Fletcher continued a faithful pastor of this church, until he was taken away by death in March, 1795, when his corpse was carried to the Congregational meeting house in Salem, where a Baptist minister preached a funeral sermon for him, and then several Congregational ministers were his pall bearers, with others of his own denomination.

The Baptist church in Northwood was also formed in 1780, and Mr. Edmund Pillsbury was ordained their pastor, who had been a member of Haverhill church. They had forty-four members in 1785, but had no increase for five years after, and then such a blessing was granted that seventy members were added in two years, and they appear to be in harmony. But after two churches were formed, in two parts of Canterbury in this county, in 1779 and 1780, some corrupt teachers drew away a number of them, and those churches, as well as one in Chichester, are not among our associated churches, if they are not entirely scattered and dissolved. For although parishes that are formed and supported by the civil magistrate, will continue as long as that power can uphold them, yet churches that are formed by the laws of Christ, are removed out of their places if they leave their first love, and refuse to repent. Rev. ii. 1—5. Which is a solemn warning to all mankind.

COUNTY OF STRAFFORD.

The Baptist church in Gilmanton was formed in 1772, and Mr. Walter Powers was ordained their pastor about four years after. In 1789 they had thirty members, in 1792 they had forty-four, and in three years they increased to seventy-six. The church in Meredith was formed in 1780, when forty-three persons were baptized in one day by Elder Shepard. Mr. Nicholas Folsom was ordained their pastor in 1782, who went from Brent-

[1] See pp. 220—222.

wood, and continues in that office. Their Association began in 1789. The church in Sanbornton was also formed in 1780, and Mr. John Crocket was ordained their pastor September 3, 1794. The church in Sandwich was formed in 1793, and Mr. Jacob Jewel is their pastor. Madbury contains a part of Berwick church, and we have no late account of any other Baptist church in this county.

COUNTY OF HILLSBOROUGH.

A Baptist church was formed at Weare, and they joined with the Warren Association in 1768, when Mr. Pelatiah Tingley was their messenger. In 1770, they had sixteen members, but such unhappy controversies arose among them, that they sent no more to the Association, and they were left out of it in 1774. But they were revived again in 1783, and Mr. Amos Wood, who graduated at Rhode Island College in 1786, was ordained their pastor, and has continued so ever since. The town of Hopkinton is not far from Weare, and such a work took place there, under the preaching of Mr. Smith, of Haverhill, and others, that they had seventeen baptized persons among them in 1769, and they joined as a branch of Haverhill church, until they were dismissed and formed a church in Hopkinton, in May, 1771. But false teachers and corrupt principles prevailed so much among them afterwards, as to dissolve their church. Though Elder Seamans, in a letter to a friend, in 1794, gave the following account of a revival among them :—

Soon after I came into this wilderness I found that the Baptist interest was much smaller than I expected. In Hopkinton, there had been a Baptist church, but not one stone of that building was left upon another. I preached some there, and baptized three persons ; and after a conference or two with them, they came into church state, adopted our articles of faith, and I administered the communion to them, which they had not had for a number of years. The reformation began there in the summer of 1792, and now there is a church there, with its two branches in Bow and Goffstown, of one hundred and thirteen members ; a very respectable body of Christians.

This was their state in 1794, and they have since obtained Elder Elisha Andrews to be their pastor. There had been some Baptists in Temple for seventeen years, even from the beginning of that plantation, until they formed a church there, August 21, 1782, of twenty-two members. Another had been formed the April before in Perryston, now Sutton, and Mr. Samuel Ambrose was ordained their pastor in September after. The church in Mason, formed in 1786, obtained Mr. William Elliott for their minister, but we are informed that he labors part of his time at Hollis, where a Baptist church was formed in 1791.

We have a more particular account of two other churches in this county. The first is at New London, where Elder Seamans removed from Attleborough in 1788. As he was the first minister of the town, they gave him the lands which were granted for the ministry therein, and also supported him by a tax. A Baptist church was formed there in 1788, and he settled as their pastor, but they had very little increase for four years ; and he had many fears that he took a wrong step in removing from Attleborough, although he then thought he had good reasons for it. These fears were very distressing to his mind, until a blessing was granted upon his ministry in 1792, which appeared the most visible in and after August in that year. In a letter to a friend,[1] of January 29, 1793, he said :—

This town consists of about fifty families, and I hope that between forty and fifty souls have been translated out of darkness into God's marvellous light, in this town, besides a number in Sutton and Fisherfield, who congregate with us. Fifteen have been baptized, and joined to the church, and I expect that a number more will come forward in a short time. Indeed I know not of one of them but what is likely to submit to gospel order, nor one person in the town who stands in any considerable opposition. We have lectures or conferences almost every day or evening in the week. Our very children meet together to converse and pray with each other ; and I believe I may safely say, that our young people were never a quarter so much engaged in frolicking, as they now are in the great concerns of the soul and eternity. Some things in this work have exceeded any thing I ever saw before. Their convictions have usually been very clear and powerful, so that industrious men and women have had neither inclination nor strength to follow their business as usual. And they freely acknowledge the justice and sovereignty of God. They also have desires beyond what I have ever before known, for the universal outpouring of the Holy Spirit.

And in another letter, December 1, 1794, directed to another friend, he said :—

The work began here in 1792 ; our church then consisted of eighteen members, and now we have one hundred and fifteen, all except three or four within five miles of our meeting-house. Some of all ages from seventy down to eight years old have joined to the church. I think we have thirty-seven men with their wives in the church.

The town of Salisbury, upon the great road from Boston to Dartmouth College, is not far from him ; and a number of men in that town were of the Baptist sentiments, and built a good meeting house there, when there was hardly a baptized person among them. Elder Seamans was called to preach among them in 1792, and he says in said letter :—

A number wanted to have a Baptist church constituted, as they intended to have a Baptist minister. But I told them that there must be something done amongst them which man could not do, before a Baptist church could be gathered there. And this work the Lord begun about the same time as at Hopkinton, and now there is a flourishing church there of one hundred and twenty-five members, with a fine preacher.

[1]Mr. Backus himself.—ED.

Mr. Elias Smith, who came from Connecticut, and preached in many places, and was ordained as a travelling minister, is settled as their pastor.

COUNTY OF CHESHIRE.

A Baptist church was formed in Richmond, and Mr. Matturean Ballou was ordained their pastor, September 27, 1770, being the first minister of any denomination in the town.   They joined to the Warren Association in 1771, when they informed the Association, that a number of the inhabitants were unwilling to allow their minister the privileges of the first minister of the town, and that neighboring towns would not regard the certificates which they gave to some of their society who lived therein.[1]   Their church had then twenty-nine members, and they increased to seventy-nine in three years ; and then they were in a low condition for six years after, until the revival in 1780 caused the addition of forty-four in three years more.   In the mean time a division took place among them, and another church was formed, in which Mr. Artemas Aldrich was ordained.   And they were in broken circumstances, until another revival began in 1790, which caused the addition of one hundred and six members in about two years, and their two ministers were dismissed, and the two churches united, with Mr. Isaac Kenney for their pastor.   In 1794 they were dismissed to the Leyden Association.

Many of the inhabitants of Westmoreland went from the first Baptist society in Middleborough, and they formed a Baptist church there in 1771,

---

[1]The following is an extract from their letter :—

"We request some special advice on several occasions, for we are young in such cases, for we meet with great opposition in our province, and the main point of their objection is, they say our settlement is not according to law, so that they threaten to pay no regard to our certificates given to our brethren living in other towns.   Another particular is, it is so ordered in our charter by the king's grant, that one whole share of land shall be given to the church of England, one whole share to the incorporated society to propagate the gospel in foreign parts, and one whole share to the first settled minister of the gospel in said town.   These are the express words in the charter of our town.   Our elder being the first, we think it belongs to him, but being opposed by the inhabitants of the town of other denominations, we ask your advice, what we had best do.   Further, there are a number of brethren in the town of Rindge, in our province, who are embodied in church state, with government and articles of faith agreeable to ours, and are under our care to assist them in administering the ordinances of the gospel.   These brethren have suffered much by the inhabitants of their town, who have taken away their cattle and sold them at the post for their minister's rates, and they are threatened still to be used in like manner.   They require us to make request for them, what they had best do."

It appears from this extract that a Baptist church had been organized in Rindge as early as 1771, though it is not noticed by Backus.   In relation to the church in Richmond, see a letter of James Manning to Hezekiah Smith, in Manning and Brown University, p. 186.—ED.

and Mr. Ebenezer Bayley was ordained their pastor, November 30, 1773. But after some years a division took place among them, and another church was formed, in which Mr. Nathaniel Wilbore preached, though he is not ordained. Another church was formed in Marlow in 1777, and Mr. Eleazar Beckwith was ordained their pastor, and so continues. He and many of his people went from Lyme, in Connecticut. Mr. Caleb Blood was ordained therein in October, 1777, who is now at Shaftsbury. When this church joined to the Woodstock Association in 1786, they had one hundred and eighteen members, and in 1790 they had one hundred and eighty-four. A Baptist church was formed at Croyden in 1778, and in 1790 they joined with Newport, and settled Elder Biel Ledoyt as their pastor, who went from Woodstock in Connecticut. And a revival of religion began among them in June, 1793, by means of an alarming providence. For the eldest son of Mr. Seamans, a lovely youth, came to assist in raising the frame of a meeting-house at Newport, but he fell from the top of it, and died soon. The affliction was exceeding great to his parents, and very alarming to others, which the Spirit of God made use of for their good. And on September 16, 1793, Mr. Ledoyt said in a letter to a friend :—

It hath been a long, dark, and cloudy night with me, and the people here ; but glory to our God, the cloud is dispersing fast. His work is begun among us ; Newport and Croyden are greatly blessed. There have been forty souls hopefully converted in a few weeks among us. I have baptized twenty-nine in four weeks. The work appears still going on. I cannot be idle, it is out of my power to answer all the calls I have at this time ; but I endeavor to do all I can. Being favored with health, and the spirit of preaching, I ascend the mountains easy. There is a prospect of a glorious reformation in these parts. O may it spread far and wide ! God hath remembered my family also for good ; my three eldest daughters, I hope, are converted ; the oldest, seventeen years, and the youngest, ten years old, are baptized. O bless the Lord with me, and let us exalt his name together. I never more sensibly needed wisdom than at present. You will not cease to pray for me. O, dear brother, be strong in the Lord, and in the power of his might.

I must leave the rest of the churches in this county, as they appear in the foregoing list.

COUNTY OF GRAFTON.

The first Baptist church in this county, was formed at Lebanon, in June, 1771, and Mr. Jedidiah Hubbard was ordained therein in 1784. But so many of them removed to other places, that in 1790 they concluded that the church was dissolved. Elder Hebbard has since been pastor of the church in Cornish. A Baptist church was formed in Canaan in 1783, wherein Elder Baldwin was ordained, and he ministered to them until he removed to Boston in 1790. Many of the inhabitants of Grafton went from Rehoboth and Swansea, and they formed a Baptist church there in

1785, and Mr. Oliver Williams was ordained their pastor, and continued so until he died in a joyful manner, August 15, 1790, aged thirty-nine. He went from the State of Rhode Island, and probably was one of the posterity of Mr. Roger Williams, the founder of that State. The church in Rumney was formed in 1780, and Mr. Cotton Hains was ordained their pastor in August that year. The church in Holderness was formed the same year, and Mr. Jeremiah Ward is their pastor. The rest of the Baptist churches in this county appear in the foregoing list, of which I have not received so full accounts as I expected. But I have some things of a more extensive nature, concerning this part of the country, which may be beneficial to the public.

Dr. Eleazar Wheelock was settled in the ministry, in the west part of Lebanon, in Connecticut, and was acquainted with experimental religion before Mr. Whitefield came into our country; and he was an active and successful laborer in the reformation that followed, until the work was much abated, and then he turned his attention to the instruction of the Indians, in order to spread the gospel among them; which led on to the forming of Dartmouth College, which was established in Hanover, in this county, to which he removed in the summer of 1770. Some revival of religion was granted in this wilderness soon after, and things looked encouraging until war broke out in our land, which tried the hearts of all. And as a quantity of money for this college had been collected in England and Scotland, which was put into a fund in London, from whence the interest was to be drawn annually, some imagined that Dr. Wheelock was biased in favor of Britain in the war, which occasioned the following actions:—He lived so remote from the seat of their government, that proclamations for fasts and thanksgivings sometimes failed of reaching him until the days appointed were past; and as Connecticut government had appointed November 16, 1775, for their annual thanksgiving, of which he had received an account, he and his people kept that day. But in the week following he received a proclamation from the authority of his own government, which appointed another day a fortnight after the other; and he was willing that all who had not kept the former day should keep the latter, while he could not in conscience keep two thanksgivings in that season, only to obey the commandments of men. Yet because he refused to do it, he was threatened to be prosecuted by authority, therefore he preached a sermon on said day, from John xviii. 36, and published it to the world, under the title of Liberty of Conscience; or, No King but Christ in his Church. He observed that rulers have only power to propose the keeping of such days, and to protect all in their worship from being injured by others, while the consent of the people to keep the day, is the only thing that can make it binding upon them to do it. And he says:—

When civil power encroaches an inch upon Christ's prerogative, a sanctified and enlightened conscience can never be compelled to a compliance; and if they are of the truth, and hear Christ's voice, no instruments of cruelty will avail any thing in this attempt. .... The least yielding in this case is dangerous, and a direct and leading step to a flood of persecution, however remote it may seem at present.[1]

Yea, and supporting religious teachers by compulsion has been a greater source of persecution, than a compelling of people to keep days of fasting or thanksgiving ever was. Of this Mr. Eden Burroughs, pastor of the church in Hanover, became so sensible that he gave up the practice. He had been a minister in Connecticut, and he was so much affected with a view of the corruption of their churches, that he published a discourse in 1784, from those words, Why call ye me Lord, Lord, and do not the things which I say? And he plainly shews that the conduct of men, be it in obedience to the laws of Christ, or in conformity to the world, is the language which speaks the loudest in all rational minds, and much more to the Son of God. And he says :—

If the confidence of professing Christians one towards another is not founded upon a mutual apprehension that each other is governed by a sacred regard to what Christ has said and enjoined in his word, there is no Christian confidence, and consequently no Christian charity amongst them. .... And it is absolutely impossible for professing Christians to have this mutual confidence towards each other, while they see that they are so commonly disposed to bite and devour one another, by seeking to get the advantage of each other, in their commerce and dealings; or to slander, backbite, and reproach one another; or to be unfaithful in fulfilling their promises and engagements to each other; or to be insensible of the wants and distresses of each other.

Again he says :—

There is nothing that can have such a tendency to prejudice the minds and harden the hearts of men against the truth, as, on the one hand to hold it up to view as being of the most sacred and weighty importance, and on the other hand to trifle with it in our daily practice. And this one observation is sufficient to account for that flood of deism and infidelity that so awfully threatens to deluge the land. It is in vain for professing Christians to call upon mankind to believe that which it is evident, by their daily practice, they do not believe themselves. .... Those corporations who call themselves churches of Christ, whilst they refuse to put the laws of his kingdom into execution, and will suffer them to be trampled under foot, are more awfully guilty of the blood of souls than every other set of men under heaven.[2]

These things caused many controversies among their churches, as well as moved many to withdraw from them. And we are informed that Elder Seamans has found it to be such a bondage to be supported by tax and compulsion, that he has already renounced that practice.

[1]Wheelock's Sermon, p. 26.   [2]Burroughs on the Laws of Christ, pp. 14, 67, 68.

A foundation doctrine of Christianity was also openly struck against in this part of our country, even the atonement of Christ. For a minister of Newport published three sermons in 1786, to prove that all the sufferings of Christ were from wicked men and devils, and that God never inflicted any punishment at all upon him for the sins of men; but that the whole of the atonement of Christ was his good teaching and good example in life and death. His first argument for this opinion is this :—" Nothing could merit favor for sinners, which was not in itself agreeable to the divine mind." And having proved that God has no pleasure in the death of sinners, he says, " Reason forbids the conclusion, that he should have any pleasure in the sufferings of his dutiful and well beloved Son."[1] But we ought to know, that the favor and love of God never could be purchased; for it was his love that caused him to give his Son to suffer the curse of the law, that God might be just, and the justifier of him who believeth in Jesus. Where is boasting then? It is excluded. By what law? of works? Nay, but by the law of faith. Rom. iii. 24—27. And if men deny that God could have any pleasure in the death of his Son, yet he says, It pleased the Lord to bruise him, he hath put him to grief: when thou shalt make his soul an offering for sin, he shall see his seed, he shall prolong his days, and the pleasure of the Lord shall prosper in his hand. He shall see of the travail of his soul and shall be satisfied : by his knowledge shall my righteous servant justify many, for he shall bear their iniquities. Is. liii. 10, 11. Christ loved us, and hath given himself for us, an offering and a sacrifice to God for a sweet smelling savor. Eph. v. 2. Wherefore he is able to save them to the uttermost that come unto God by him, seeing he ever liveth to make intercession for them. Heb. vii. 25. Yet this author, in his second argument, says, " If this great work could not be finished until divine justice had its free and natural course, in such a sense, as that his sufferings are to be considered as sin punished ; the consequence is unavoidable, that he in a *very short season* endured the same quantity of misery which would have borne sinners down to eternity. A thought which exceeds all rules of computation, and departs from all principles of just reasoning." As if the Son of God could not do more in a short time, than sinful men can ever do. Man was first drawn into rebellion against God, by setting up reason above revelation ; and the world is still held in bondage by the same means. Yet our author says, " Let no one be alarmed, if we positively deny, that he suffered any of that divine wrath which sinners justly deserve ; for there can no such contradictory idea exist, that a being should be *angry* with an object with which he is at the same time *well pleased*."[2] But how weak is this reasoning ! For a parent cannot correct a child as he ought, if he is angry with the child ; neither can a judge give

---

[1]Remele on Atonement, p. 19.   [2]Ibid, pp. 21, 33.

sentence against a debtor, or a criminal, if he feels angry with them. And when a surety freely engages to pay the debt of another, justice as clearly exacts the debt of him as of the debtor, while the discharge of the debtor is as great a mercy as it would have been if the creditor had forgiven him without a surety. And when a sinner is convinced of the greatness of his debt, and God frankly forgives him all, the sinner will love him much. Luke vii. 41, 42, 47. For the love of Christ constraineth us, because we thus judge, that if one died for all, then were all dead ; and that he died for all, that they which live should not henceforth live unto themselves, but unto him who died for them, and rose again. .... Therefore if any man be in Christ, he is a new creature ; old things are past away, behold, all things are become new. II Cor. v. 14—17. Fear and love are the great principles of all voluntary actions, and they were divided by the fall ; but Christ took on him flesh and blood, of the seed of Abraham, that through death he might destroy him that had the power of death, that is, the devil ; and deliver them who through fear of death were all their life-time subject to bondage. Heb. ii. 14—15. And herein the promise of God to Abraham was accomplished, who said, My covenant shall be in your flesh for an everlasting covenant. Gen. xvii. 13. For Christ was given for a covenant of the people, and for a light of the Gentiles. Is. xlii. 6.

CHAPTER XLIV.

STATE OF VERMONT.—COUNTY OF BENNINGTON.

A GENERAL VIEW OF THE PLANTING OF VERMONT.—OF SHAFTSBURY CHURCHES.—POWNAL AND OTHERS.—WOODSTOCK AND BRIDGEWATER. A VIEW OF OPPRESSION IN VERMONT.—AND OF FASTING FOR STRIFE AND DEBATE IN THE MASSACHUSETTS.—THE MINORITY ARE USING FORCE WITH THE MAJORITY ABOUT RELIGIOUS WORSHIP.

The royal prophet says, Surely the wrath of man shall praise thee; the remainder of wrath shalt thou restrain. And this truth shines with great clearness in our day, and as clearly in Vermont, as in any part of our country. All the lands therein were once claimed by the government of New Hampshire, and Bennington was named from Benning Wentworth, the Governor, who granted the town. He also granted a large number of other towns on the west side of Connecticut River, and made much money thereby, until some politicians of New York obtained an act of the king in council, in 1764, to annex all those lands to their government. Many of those who had purchased lands of Wentworth, had made large improvements thereon; and to have all their property taken away deceitfully, or to buy it again of men whose government they disliked, raised a high degree of resentment against them; and the controversy was pursued for ten years, which produced a hardy set of men, who did great exploits in the American war, in the time of which they formed themselves into a distinct government, and they are now owned as one of our United States.[1] The folly of many in Connecticut and the Massachusetts, who ran into debt at the close of the wars in 1763 and 1783, caused the planting of the wilderness in New Hampshire and Vermont, beyond what human wisdom could possibly have done. The Massachusetts had made some beginnings at Northfield before the war which began in 1675, and we are well informed that there was not one English family settled above Number Four, about

[1] Belknap's History of New Hampshire, Vol. II, pp. 314—316, 455.

fifty miles from Northfield, until the peace in 1763. In all that time the French and English were contending with each other about lands which neither of them had any right to, and were employing the savages in their quarrels, until the French gave up their claim to this continent. And then Britain engaged in the cruel design of enslaving her own subjects, and forced them to renounce their power, and the French assisted them in obtaining their liberty, and thereby learned how to assert their own rights; upon which Britain has deluged their land with blood, to prevent the prevalence of light and liberty in Europe. Popery is abolished in France, much more than it is in England, and this has raised the cry of many teachers and lawyers against them, representing them as bloody infidels! But we ever should remember, that hypocrites were much more fierce for the crucifixion of our Lord Jesus Christ than heathen infidels were; and they are ever so against true religion and liberty. And can men be blinded by them any longer? For God sent such a drought and scarcity into Canada in 1795, as compelled them to have recourse to Vermont and New Hampshire for food for man and beast, where they had a plenty of both. Yea, England herself now wants food from America, where they have cruelly oppressed the inhabitants heretofore.

The first Baptist church in Vermont was formed in Shaftsbury in 1768. Mr. Bliss Willoughby, who was ordained pastor of a Separate church at Newent, in Norwich, in 1753, and went to England as an agent for their churches in 1756, and preached for Dr. Gifford, in London, became a Baptist after the year 1764, and was a leader among this people, where his son Ebenezer has also been a teacher, though neither of them have been pastors of this church. On August 4, 1774, the church wrote that they had thirty-nine members, twenty-one of whom were males. But how things were among them for six years after, we know not. A second church was formed in 1780, and a third in 1781, the last of them upon the principles of the old Baptists, who held laying on of hands upon every member as a term of communion. And the Association which was begun there in 1781, and has united a large number of other churches, yet has not united all these in the town where it begun. But to promote union among them, many of the brethren sent an earnest request to Mr. Caleb Blood, of Newton, and he removed there in the beginning of 1788, when a fourth church was formed, which had one hundred and twenty-four members the next year, and one hundred and sixty in 1795. Mr. Blood is so much esteemed in their government, that he was called to preach their Election Sermon, October 11, 1792, which was published by their authority. One passage therein says:—

A wise magistrate will set a constant guard over the words of his mouth; that with a becoming moderation, he may express his resentment of injuries done him, and have all his language such as shall tend to prevent others from an uncivil, profane way of treating their fellow citizens. A magistrate who is rough and profane in his language, is a monstrous character. He is not civil himself, and we cannot expect but that the practice, at least, will do hurt in the community. He is not the gentleman; for any person of sense knows that a rough, profane way of treating mankind, better fits the character of a clown than a gentleman. Can I suppose myself in danger of giving offence? No; I cannot think that so respectable a body as I am now called to address, will think me too severe in censuring so great an evil; especially seeing it so much prevails in our land at the present day.[1]

After the settlement of Pownal, the people lived for some time in a very careless way, neglecting public worship, and indulging themselves in all kinds of vanity and iniquity, until they were visited with distressing sickness, in March, 1773, which alarmed their consciences, and they set up the worship of God among them, and the Spirit of God fixed conviction in many minds, and about two hundred often attended their meetings. A church was formed in April, which increased to forty-nine members in fifteen months. This is a summary of the account which the church gave in July, 1774. How things were among them for ten years after, we know not; but in the spring of 1788, Elder Caleb Nichols removed there, having been dismissed from the church in Coventry, and this church joined the Shaftsbury Association in 1793, when they had seventy-two members; and such a blessing was granted there, that they increased to one hundred and sixty-five in two years. I must leave the other churches in this county as they appear in the foregoing list.

COUNTY OF WINDSOR.

As people removed very fast into this county towards the close of the war, several Baptist ministers were sent to preach among them from year to year. In May, 1779, our elders Seamans and Ledoyt visited those parts, and labored in various places to good purpose. And Mr. Elisha Ransom, who was ordained at Sutton, November 11, 1778, as a travelling minister, removed up to Woodstock, where a Baptist church was formed in July, 1780, and he became their minister. He came as one of their messengers, and joined the Warren Association in September following, when they had twenty-eight members. And in three years they increased to eighty members, when, in February, 1783, they joined with three other churches in forming the Woodstock Association, to which a fifth church joined that year, and opened a correspondence with the Warren Association, which has continued ever since. In three years the Association increased to fourteen churches, and four hundred and ninety-six members. These churches were those of Woodstock, Canaan, Croyden, Sutton, Wendel, Lebanon, Royalton, second in Woodstock, Claremont, Temple, Windsor, Westminster,

[1] Blood's Sermon, pp. 32, 33.

Westmoreland and Marlow. Mr. Joel Butler was ordained in Woodstock, January 5, 1785, and ministered to their second church for some time, and then he labored in several places in the Massachusetts, from whence he removed into the State of New York. As the members of this church were chiefly dismissed from the first, they have since re-united in one again. Mr. William Grow, mentioned above, removed from Pomfret, in Connecticut, to Bridgewater, in Vermont, and recovered his credit so far, by a penitent and good behavior, that he was settled as the pastor of a church gathered in Woodstock and Bridgewater, and for two or three years they appeared to prosper ; but then new difficulties arose, and he was dismissed. I find that Mr. John Peckens, who went from Middleborough, and who had been ordained at Claremont, was at Woodstock in 1786, who is now at Chelmsford. Mr. Joseph Call, was also an ordained elder there in 1789, who was at Cambridge in 1793. This work has spread into Canada, where a Baptist church was formed at Coldwell's Manor, which joined the Woodstock Association in 1794. And Elder Jedidiah Hebbard says, " I have been four journeys into those parts, and have seen much of the power and grace of God there."

Mr. Ransom has not only been a successful preacher of the gospel, but also has earnestly contended for Christian liberty, against the ministerial tyranny which has been carried into that wilderness, from the States of Connecticut and the Massachusetts. And on March 23, 1795, he said in a letter :—

A brother living in Hartford, in Vermont, belonging to Elder Drew's church, has suffered much about rates from another denomination. He was first carried to goal, and then came out by paying the money, and prosecuted them in vain, for he was beat three times. I cannot ascertain the costs, for his last trial was the last day of February past ; but it is supposed that his costs will be above fifty pounds. Five petitions were carried into the Vermont Assembly last fall, with more than two hundred signers, against the certificate law, and I went to speak for them ; and after my averment that the certificate law was contrary to the rights of man, of conscience, the first, third, fourth, and seventh articles of our constitution, and to itself, for it took away our rights, and then offered to sell them back to us for a certificate, some stretched their mouths ; and though no man contradicted me in one argument, yet they would shut their eyes, and say they could not see it so. I had many great friends in the house, but not a majority. They sent out a committee who altered the law much for the better, if any law could be good of that kind, which was, that every man might assert his own sentiments to the town clerk, and that should answer ; but because it would still be a bad law, and I would not thank them for it, and none of our friends would acknowledge it as a favor, it fell back to where it was before. Only we have this to comfort us, The Lord reigneth, and their power is limited, and we shall have no more affliction than is needful for us. Duty is ours, the event is the Lord's.

As I failed of obtaining more accounts of their churches, and of their sufferings in Vermont, which were expected, I shall close this chapter with some late things in the Massachusetts, the mother of all the persecutions in New England.

God said to the church of Israel, Behold ye fast for strife and debate, and to smite with the fist of wickedness. .... Wilt thou call this a fast, an acceptable day to the Lord? Is not this the fast that I have chosen? to loose the bands of wickedness, and to undo the heavy burdens, and to let the oppressed go free, and that ye break every yoke? Isaiah lviii. 4— 6. And is not this language applicable to our country? For dissenters from the established worship in New England were several times relieved from cruel oppression, by special acts of the British court. But when our first Congress was called at Philadelphia, in the fall of 1774, and they were like to be our highest power of government for the future, the Warren Association sent an agent there to try if some security for our religious rights could not be obtained, while we united with our countrymen in defence of the civil rights of America. And a conference was granted by the delegates in Congress from the Massachusetts, to whom the Baptist agent declared, that we wanted no more religious liberty in the country, than they had long enjoyed in Boston; and this appeared so reasonable to the gentlemen who were present, that said delegates promised to use their influence to obtain such liberty through all the country. Yet a report was spread in New England, before the Baptist agent got home, that he had been to Philadelphia on purpose to try to break the union of the colonies in the defence of their civil rights. Therefore he soon met the committee of the Warren Association at Boston, and presented an address to the Massachusetts Provincial Congress upon it, and they returned an answer in which they said:—

The establishment of civil and religious liberty, to each denomination in the province, is the sincere wish of this congress. But being by no means vested with powers of civil government, whereby they can redress the grievances of any person whatever, they therefore recommend to the Baptist churches, that when a General Assembly shall be convened in this colony, they lay the real grievances of said churches before the same, when and where their petition will most certainly meet with all that attention due to the memorial of a denomination of Christians so well disposed to the public weal of their country.[1]

Here they denied that they were vested with powers of civil government, while they assumed the whole power of government in the Massachusetts; and as a General Assembly was called in July, 1775, the Warren Association presented a memorial to them in September, which they slipped away out of sight, without granting any relief at all to the Baptists. And when the convention was called, which formed our new constitution, the first

---

[1] See pp. 200—204.—Ed.

draft that was made by their committee, was wholly partial for one denomination. They met and chose the committee to make the draft in September, and then adjourned to October 28, 1779. A general fast was appointed upon the occasion on November 4 ; and though the Third Article was new drawn, with some appearance of favor to dissenters from their worship, yet as they expected opposition to it from the Baptists, two men, who were members of Congress in 1774, accused them of sending an agent then to Philadelphia to break the union of the colonies, and evidently carried the vote for the Third Article by inflaming the convention against them. And was not this a fasting for strife and debate, and smiting with the fist of wickedness? For the same men knew that they had promised to exert all their influence to obtain all the liberty that the Baptists asked for ; but they have never fulfilled their promise to this day, although they have been in high offices in our government. And for any men to violate their promise, is to exalt themselves above the eternal God, who never failed of fulfilling any one promise, nor ever can. Yet all men in this government, who support one denomination by tax and compulsion, violate the promise in the constitution, which says, " Every denomination of Christians demeaning themselves peaceably, and as good subjects of the commonwealth, shall be equally under the protection of the law ; and no subordination of any one sect or denomination to another, shall ever be established by law."

But as this has restrained our legislature from making any certificate law to exempt the dissenters from the Congregational denomination from taxes to their worship, and they have put the whole power into the hands of the majority of voters in each town or parish, this iniquity has no covering left among us. For ministers are supported by worldly men, who act without any sort of religious qualification, and therefore there is no religion in their doings. And they now violate the most essential rule of all civil government, which is, that the majority of every civil community is the body politic, and that the minority is not the body. Therefore Mr. Ellis was never elected as pastor of the first parish in Rehoboth,[1] from which many thousands of dollars have been taken for him ; neither was Mr. Nathan Underwood ever elected the pastor of the second parish in Harwich, by the body of the parish, who have been all taxed to him. But Mr. Ellis's great success appears to have emboldened Mr. Underwood, and his collector seized six men who were Baptists, on the first day of December, 1795, and carried them as far as Yarmouth, where one of them was taken so ill, being old and infirm before, that he saw no way to save his life but to pay the tax and costs, which he did, and the other five were carried to

---

[1] Just before this work was finished at the press, news came from Rehoboth, that a number who had been zealous for Mr. Ellis have turned against him, so that he is gone off, not likely to return to be their minister any more.—B.
See pp. 354, 355, 442–445.—ED.

the prison at Barnstable, where they also paid the money, rather than to lie in a cold prison all winter. And these things moved many to pay said tax, rather than to be distrained upon. Though as all did not do it, their collector went with aid to the house of one of the Baptists, when he was not at home, January 8, 1796, and seized a cow for a tax to said minister ; but his wife and daughter came out and took hold of the cow, and his wife promised to pay the money, if her husband would not do it, and they let the cow go, and she went to Mr. Underwood the next day, and paid the tax and costs, and took his receipt therefor. Yet four days after, the woman and two daughters, one of whom was not there when the cow was taken, were seized and carried before authority, and fined seven dollars for talking to the collector and his aid, and taking hold of the cow while they had her in possession, so that they let her go. These things we have had very distinct accounts of, and if there is the least mistake therein, let them point it out in welcome. Another instance in the county of Plymouth is similar to these in one respect, though not in others. The minister of a parish, lately incorporated, was never chosen by the majority of the inhabitants therein, nor by many who are taxed to him, one of whom was lately seized to be carried to prison, but he paid the money, and others are threatened with the like treatment. Before this distress was made for the salary of said minister, he got several Baptist ministers to preach in his pulpit, and seems to be in earnest to draw them into compulsive measures also. Yet the line of his parish was extended eight or nine miles from his meeting, in order to take in two valuable lots of ministerial lands, which lie near a Baptist meeting, where a Baptist minister is settled. These are a few of the evils which have come from the practice of confounding the church and world together, about the government of the church, and the support of religious ministers. Whereas if the civil government would protect all its subjects impartially, without supporting any ministers by tax and compulsion, all true believers would lead a quiet and peaceable life in all godliness and honesty, and the power of other men to oppress them on religious accounts would be taken away.

CHAPTER XLV.

OBSERVATIONS ON THE FOREGOING HISTORY.

Antichrist described, and also the Church of Christ.—The Old and New Testaments, believed and obeyed by the Children of God, are his Two Witnesses.—A being anointed with the Spirit of Christ, is essential to Christianity.—Evidence that this Spirit hath lately increased the Baptist Churches.—The evil of confounding Church and World together.—The Glory of having them distinct.—All Men should act by the Golden Rule.—The Gates of Hell cannot prevail against such.—For they stand on the Sea of Glass mingled with Fire.—How the Two Witnesses are slain.—And how they shall rise again.—Mystery Babylon described.—And the Nature of Heresy.—Men are known by their Fruits.

How clearly has the word of God been fulfilled! For he says, That day shall not come except there come a falling away first, and that man of sin be revealed, the son of perdition: who opposeth and exalteth himself above all that is called God, or that is worshipped; so that he, as God, sitteth in the temple of God, shewing himself that he is God. And now ye know what withholdeth, that he might be revealed in his time. For the mystery of iniquity doth already work; only he who now letteth will let, until he be taken out of the way: and then shall that Wicked be revealed, whom the Lord shall consume with the spirit of his mouth, and shall destroy with the brightness of his coming: even him, whose coming is after the working of Satan, with all power, and signs, and lying wonders, and with all deceivableness of unrighteousness in them that perish; because they received not the love of the truth that they might be saved. And for this cause God shall send them strong delusion that they should believe a lie; that they all might be damned who believed not the truth, but had pleasure in unrighteousness. But we are bound to give thanks alway to God for you, brethren, beloved of the Lord, because God hath from the beginning chosen you to salvation, through sanctification of the Spirit, and belief of the truth : whereunto he called you by our gospel, to the obtaining of the glory of our Lord Jesus Christ. II Thess. ii. 3—14. Here all men are described as in two parties. So our Lord says, Every one that doeth evil hateth the light, neither cometh to the light, lest his deeds should be reproved. But he that doeth truth cometh to the light, that his deeds may be made manifest that they are wrought in God. John iii. 20, 21. It is impossible for God to violate his promise, or his oath, or to entice any into sin. Heb. vi. 13—18. James i. 13, 14. But all men are guilty of these evils, more or less, who are not born again. And when Constantine removed the seat of his empire from Rome, and then divided it at his death, the way was made for the bishop of Rome to exalt himself above God in his church, and above all the kings of Europe, who gave their power unto him. And forbidding to marry, and commanding to abstain from meats, was held in that church for many centuries before Luther's reformation. I Tim. iv. 1, 2, 3. Yet an external succession of baptisms, and of ministerial power, through all those abominations, is now held fast in our land, as we have before proved. Yea, and the doctrines of original sin, particular election, efficacious grace in conversion, justification wholly by faith in the perfect righteousness of Christ, and the final perseverance of his saints, are denied by multitudes in Europe and America. And are they not left to a strong delusion to believe a lie? For all the holy priesthood that God has under heaven are, *elect* according to the foreknowledge of God the Father, through sanctification of the Spirit, unto obedience, and sprinkling of the blood of Jesus Christ. I Pet. i. 2. ii. 5, 9. Yet ministers and parents still imagine, that they can make children holy members of the church before they can choose for themselves, and holy ministers by an external succession of ordinations. And a minister before named[1] says, " When you re-baptize those in adult years, which we have baptized in their infancy, you and they jointly renounce that Father, Son, and Holy Ghost, whom we adore and worship as the only living and true God, and on whom we depend for all our salvation."[2] So some Jewish teachers said, Except ye be circumcised, after the manner of Moses, ye cannot be saved. But the Holy Ghost, in the church at Jerusalem, said, Why tempt ye God, to put a yoke upon the neck of the disciples, which neither our fathers nor we were able to bear? Acts xv. 1, 10. The Sinai covenant yoked believers and unbelievers together. And another minister says, " Some who are not inwardly sanctified, are yet so far in covenant, that they are rightful members of the visible church, as all but the Ana-

[1]See p. 315.—ED.
[2]Dr. Huntington, the author of this, died in 1795, when it appeared that he had embraced the doctrine of universal salvation.

baptists must grant." And again he says, "It is certain that the rule of admission is such, that some, yea, many unsanctified persons may be, and are regularly admitted. All the congregation of Israel were admitted or recognized as members of the visible church by God himself at Mount Sinai; yet who will say that one in ten of them were saints in heart? The children of believers are reputed saints, and as such, have a right of admission; yet we are not sure that the greater part of them are inwardly sanctified from the womb, or even afterwards."[1] Yea, we are so far from seeing any evidence of inward sanctification in most of the children of professors, that they generally evidence the contrary in their lives as much as other men. And when the church of Israel were entering upon the promised land, Moses said, The Lord hath not given you an heart to perceive, and eyes to see, and ears to hear unto this day. Deut. xxix. 4. So far was he from giving them any idea that all their national church were inwardly sanctified. But a little before the Babylonian captivity, it was said, Behold, the days come, saith the Lord, that I will make a *new covenant* with the house of Israel, and with the house of Judah; *not according* to the covenant that I made with their fathers in the day that I took them by the hand, to bring them out of the land of Egypt (which my covenant they brake, although I was an husband unto them, saith the Lord;) but this shall be the covenant that I will make with the house of Israel, After those days, saith the Lord, I will put my law in their inward parts, and write it in their hearts, and will be their God, and they shall be my people: and they shall teach no more every man his neighbor, and every man his brother, saying, Know ye the Lord: for they shall all know me, from the least of them unto the greatest of them, saith the Lord; for I will forgive their iniquity, and I will remember their sin no more. Jer. xxxi. 31—34. And this is the covenant upon which the gospel church is built. Heb. viii. 8—12. And it is as distinct from the covenant of circumcision with the nation of Israel, as Sarah was from Hagar, or Zion from Sinai; yea, as distinct as Jerusalem which is above, and is free, being the mother of all the children of God, is from Jerusalem below, which is in bondage with her children. Gal. iv. 22—26. And language cannot make a clearer distinction, than is here made, between the national covenant with Israel, and the covenant of grace with the church of Christ.

When the Jews returned from Babylon, and began to build the temple, their enemies sent false accusations against them to the court of Persia, and procured an order from thence to force them to cease from that work. But after another king came to the throne, two prophets were raised up, to reprove the Jews for their negligence, and to encourage them to finish the house of God. Ezra iv. 11—24. v. 1, 2. And because the old men wept to see how much inferior this house was, to the glorious temple which

---

[1]Hemmenway on the Church, pp. 29, 49.

was built by Solomon, one prophet said to them, I am with you, saith the
Lord of hosts; according to the word that I covenanted with you when ye
came out of Egypt, so my Spirit remaineth among you; fear ye not. For
thus saith the Lord of hosts, Yet once, it is a little while, and I will shake
the heavens and the earth, and the sea, and the dry land; and I will shake
all nations, and the Desire of all Nations shall come, and I will fill this
house with glory, saith the Lord of Hosts. Hag. ii. 4—7. And after the
Son of God came and taught in that house, as no man ever did before, and
then offered himself a sacrifice to God for the sins of his people, and arose
and ascended to Heaven, and gave the Holy Ghost from thence, to enable
his ministers to preach the gospel to Jews and Gentiles, an inspired apostle
said, Yet once more, signifieth the removing of those things that are shaken,
as of things that are made, that those things which cannot be shaken may
remain. Wherefore, we receiving a kingdom which cannot be moved, let
us have grace, whereby we may serve God acceptably, with reverence and
godly fear; for our God is a consuming fire. Heb. xii. 27—29. The
other prophet had a candlestick all of gold, set before him, with mediums
to convey oil into it for light; and upon his inquiry what was meant thereby, the answer was, This is the word of the Lord unto Zerubbabel, saying,
Not by might, nor by power, but by my Spirit, saith the Lord of hosts.
Who art thou, O great mountain? Before Zerubbabel thou shalt become
a plain, and he shall bring forth the headstone thereof, with shoutings,
crying, *Grace, grace* unto it! Zech. iv. 1—7. And when they obeyed
this call of God, their enemies wrote again to the court of Persia against
them, but a decree in their favor was procured thereby, and all was plain
before them. Ezra v. 7—17; vi. 1—16. The golden candlestick represented the church of God, and the two olive trees were his precepts and
promises, whereby he poured the oil of his grace into his church, to hold
up light to the world, who hated it because it tormented their consciences.
Before the coming of Christ there was but one candlestick, with two olive
trees to pour oil into it; but when Christ came he broke down the middle
wall of partition between Jews and Gentiles, and built his church upon the
foundation of the apostles and prophets, for an habitation of God through
the Spirit. Eph. ii. 14—22. And when antichrist arose, God said, I will
give power unto my two witnesses, and they shall prophecy a thousand two
hundred and threescore days, clothed in sackcloth. These are the two
olive trees, and the two candlesticks standing before the God of the earth.
And it is to be observed, that the church is in the wilderness, and the beast
continues all the time that these witnesses prophecy in sackcloth. Rev.
xi. 3, 4; xii. 6; xiii. 5. The two Testaments, believed and obeyed by
the children of God, appear to be the two witnesses.

And a being anointed by the Spirit of Christ, is essential to the name
Christian. For the disciples were not called by this name, until after the

Gentiles were received into the church without circumcision. Acts xi. 26. And it is said, If ye be reproached for the name of Christ, happy are ye; for the *Spirit* of glory, and of God resteth upon you; on their part he is evil spoken of, but on your part he is glorified. But let none of you suffer as a murderer, or as a thief, or as an evil doer, or as a busy body in other men's matters. Yet if any man suffer as a *Christian*, let him not be ashamed; but let him glorify God on this behalf. I Peter iv. 14—16. Ye are not in the flesh, but in the *Spirit*, if so be that the *Spirit* of God dwell in you. Now if any man have not the *Spirit* of Christ, he is none of his. Rom. viii. 9. Again, it is said, Hereby we know that he abideth in us, by the *Spirit* which he hath given us. I John iii. 24. And Jesus said, If a man love me, he will keep my words, and my Father will love him, and we will come unto him, and make our abode with him. John xiv. 23. Whosoever transgresseth, and abideth not in the doctrine of Christ, hath not God; he that abideth in the doctrine of Christ, he hath both the Father and the Son. If there come any unto you, and bring not this doctrine, receive him not into your house, neither bid him God-speed; for he that biddeth him God-speed is partaker of his evil deeds. II John 9—11. And how clearly do these things shew, that no person can be a Christian without a change of heart by the Spirit of Christ! Yea, and that receiving and supporting true ministers, and refusing to receive false teachers, is ever a matter between God and individuals, as much as faith in Christ is for eternal salvation! And no men can have any more right to support religious teachers by the sword, than they have power to pull down the Son of God from his throne in heaven. For he says, All they that take the sword, shall perish with the sword. Matt. xxvi. 52. My kingdom is not of this world; if my kingdom were of this world, then would my servants fight, that I should not be delivered to the Jews; but now is my kingdom not from hence. John xviii. 36. How then will any men dare to support religious ministers by the sword of the magistrate? For his power is to punish none but those who work ill to their neighbors; and it is a matter of conscience with Christians to be subject to such rulers, who are not a terror to good works, but to the evil. Rom. xiii. 1—10. But the royal prophet says of wicked rulers, They break in pieces thy people, O Lord, and afflict thine heritage. They slay the widow and stranger, and murder the fatherless. Yet they say, The Lord shall not see, neither shall the God of Jacob regard it. Psalm xciv. 5—7, 20. Shall the throne of iniquity have fellowship with thee, which frameth mischief by a law? .... The Lord at thy right hand shall strike through kings in the day of his wrath. He shall judge among the heathen, he shall fill the places with the dead bodies, he shall wound the heads over many countries. Psalm cx. 5, 6. And how awfully is he now doing it! Rev. xix. 11—21.

And is it not evident that the late increase of Baptist churches has been caused by the influence of the Spirit of God? For before he poured out his Spirit in the county of Hampshire, in and after 1734, there were but six Baptist churches in all New England, except in Rhode Island government, wherein are now two hundred and eighty-five churches. And in these four States, where ministers have been supported by law, all the power of such ministers and rulers has been against the Baptist churches; and they have found so much difficulty in supporting their own ministers, and in guarding against oppression from others, that some societies have obtained incorporations by the laws of men. But our Associations have published testimonies against all such incorporations, as they implicitly deny that the laws and Spirit of Christ are sufficient to govern his church, and to support his ministers. And while they act all the affairs of their Associations openly, before all men who have a mind to hear them, and then publish their conclusions to the world, how can they hope for any earthly advantage thereby? If heavenly influence has not increased their churches, what cause can be assigned therefor? All true believers in Christ are born again, not of blood, nor of the will of the flesh, nor of the will of man, but of God. John i. 12, 13. Natural descent, the power of our own wills, and of the wills of other men, are all excluded from this affair. And where the opposite principles have crept into Baptist churches, their welfare has been obstructed thereby, and many such churches have been dissolved. Yet the word and Spirit of God have reformed old churches, and raised many new ones in all parts of America. There was one Baptist church in Virginia, and a few in the Carolinas seventy years ago; but they were dark and feeble societies until some spiritual preachers were sent among them, in and after 1753. The elders, Benjamin Miller, Isaac Stelle, Peter Peterson Vanhorne, and John Gano, went from New Jersey and Pennsylvania, and labored in those parts to good purpose. And Elder Shubael Stearns, Daniel Marshall, and others, went from Connecticut, and spent their lives in those parts, as was before observed; and how great has been the increase of the Baptist churches in those southern States! And though vast pains have been taken, by men who have supported their worship by force, to make the people believe that the Baptists were enemies to good government, yet how are they now confounded in those attempts! For it now appears that government and liberty are united in their plan of conduct, which tends to bring all wars to an end. And in a prophecy concerning that glorious event, it is said, All people will walk every one in the name of his god, and we will walk in the name of the Lord our God forever and ever. Micah iv. 5. All men who love any creature above the Creator are idolaters.

But our Lord says, If ye keep my commandments, ye shall abide in my love; even as I have kept my Father's commandments, and abide in his love. .... If ye were of the world, the world would love his own; but because ye are not of the world, but I have chosen you out of the world, therefore the world hateth you. John xv. 10, 19. How then will any men dare to confound the church and world together in religious affairs? For as long as natural birth could bring the children of Israel into the church, and into the priesthood, God said to them, The man that committeth adultery with another man's wife, even he that committeth adultery with his neighbor's wife, the adulterer and the adulteress shall surely be put to death. Levit. xx. 10. And he now says to all the world, Ye adulterers and adulteresses, know ye not that the friendship of the world is enmity with God? Whosoever therefore will be a friend of the world, is the enemy of God. .... There is one lawgiver, who is able to save, and to destroy; who art thou that judgest another? James iv. 4, 12. Yet men in general have assumed the power of lawgivers and judges for the church of Christ, and of bringing children into it before they could choose for themselves; and they have invented a multitude of other names and denominations of men, besides the righteous and the wicked, the church and the world. Though the word of revelation says, Whosoever is born of God, doth not commit sin; for his seed remaineth in him; and he cannot sin, because he is born of God. In this the children of God are manifest, and the children of the devil: whosoever doeth not righteousness, is not of God, neither he that loveth not his brother. For this is the message that ye have heard from the beginning, that we should love one another. Not as Cain, who was of that wicked one, and slew his brother: and wherefore slew he him? Because his own works were evil, and his brother's righteous. I John iii. 9—12. Woe unto them; for they have gone in the way of Cain, and ran greedily after the error of Balaam for reward, and perished in the gainsaying of Core. Jude 11. Because the worship of Abel, by faith in the blood of Christ, was accepted of God, and the worship of Cain without such faith was not accepted, he was filled with envy against his brother. But the Lord said unto Cain, If thou doest well, shalt thou not be accepted? and if thou doest not well, sin lieth at the door. And unto thee shall be his desire, and thou shalt rule over him. Gen. iv. 4—7. True believers have ever been the best subjects of civil government; but men have discovered enmity against them in every age, because of the light of holiness which God hath caused to shine in their lives, to expose the hypocrisy and wickedness of others. But every man is guilty of adultery, who hath not been made dead to the works of the law, in order to be married to Jesus Christ. Rom. vii. 1—6. For every true Christian hath been presented as a chaste virgin to him. II Cor. xi. 2. But after God had consecrated Moses as the lawgiver to his church, and Aaron and his lawful posterity to be the only priests therein, to offer sacrifices for iniquity, until Jesus came and offered himself without spot to God for sinners, Korah gathered a large company against them, saying, Ye take too much upon you, seeing all the congregation are holy every one of them, and the Lord is among them; wherefore then lift you up yourselves above the congregation of the Lord? But for this they perished most terribly. Numb. xvi. 1—3, 32, 33. This gives a plain view of the way of Cain, the error of Balaam, and the gain-saying of Core, which evils many have charged upon believers, because they have held to salvation by faith in the perfect righteousness of Christ, and to have his church governed by his laws, which admit none into it without a credible profession of the new birth. Thus men have called evil good, and good evil; have put darkness for light, and light for darkness, bitter for sweet, and sweet for bitter. Is. v. 20.

But an inspired apostle says, We have received not the spirit of the world, but the Spirit which is of God, that we might know the things that are freely given to us of God. Which things also we speak, not in the words which man's wisdom teacheth, but which the Holy Ghost teacheth; comparing spiritual things with spiritual. I Cor. ii. 12, 13. And let us now attend to this rule. For God says, Thy Maker is thine husband (the Lord of hosts is his name;) and thy Redeemer, the Holy One of Israel, the God of the whole earth shall he be called. .... And all thy children shall be taught of the Lord, and great shall be the peace of thy children. Is. liv. 5, 13. And Jesus says, No man can come to me, except the Father which hath sent me, draw him; and I will raise him up at the last day. It is written in the prophets, And they shall be all taught of God. Every man therefore that hath heard, and hath learned of the Father, cometh unto me. John vi. 44, 45. The *children* of the church of Christ, are *men*, who have been taught of God, and have learned of the Father, so as to come to the Son. So Paul says, Jerusalem which is above, is free, which is the mother of us all. Gal. iv. 26. And John says, I saw the holy city, Jerusalem, coming down from God out of heaven, prepared as a bride adorned for her husband. Rev. xxi. 2. And Jesus says, Give not that which is holy unto the dogs, neither cast ye your pearls before swine, lest they trample them under their feet, and turn again and rend you. .... The kingdom of heaven is like unto a merchantman, seeking goodly pearls; who when he had found one pearl of great price, he went and sold all that he had, and bought it. Matt. vii. 6; xiii. 45, 46. So likewise, whosoever he be of you, that forsaketh not all that he hath, he cannot be my disciple. Luke xiv. 33. Except a man be born again, he cannot see the kingdom of God. John iii. 3. Every several gate was of one pearl. Blessed are they that do his commandments, that they may have right to the tree of life, and may enter in through the gates into the city. For without are dogs, and sorcerers, and whoremongers, and adulterers, and whosoever loveth and maketh a lie. I Jesus have sent mine angel to testify unto you these things in the churches. I am the root and the offspring of David, and the bright and morning star. And the Spirit and the bride say, Come; and let him that heareth, say Come; and let him that is athirst, come; and whosoever will, let him take the water of life freely. Rev. xxi. 21; xxii. 14—17. And how clearly do these things shew, that the government of the church of Christ is as distinct from all worldly governments, as heaven is from earth! Yea, and that no one has any true right in his church, until he comes to Christ by faith which worketh by love that is as free as water! For God says, In the last days it shall come to pass, that the mountain of the house of the Lord shall be established in the top of the mountains, and it shall be exalted above the hills, and people shall *flow* unto it. And many nations shall come and say, Come and let us go up to the mountain of the Lord, and to the house of the God of Jacob, and he will teach us of his ways, and we will walk in his paths; for the law shall go forth of Zion, and the word of the Lord from Jerusalem. And he shall judge among many people, and rebuke strong nations afar off, and they shall beat their swords into ploughshares, and their spears into pruning-hooks; nation shall not lift up sword against nation, neither shall they learn war any more. Micah iv. 1—3. Now all men may know, that this prophecy has never yet been fulfilled; but it will as surely be accomplished, as any prophecy ever was in this world. How earnest then should all be to hear and obey the revealed will of God!

And no man can obey him without denying himself, and taking up his cross, and following the example of Christ. And the apostle Paul says to the ministers of Christ, I have not shunned to declare unto you all the counsel of God. Take heed therefore unto yourselves, and to all the flock, over the which the Holy Ghost hath made you overseers, to feed the church of God, which he hath purchased with his own blood. For I know this, that after my departing shall grievous wolves enter in among you, not sparing the flock. Also of yourselves shall men arise, speaking perverse things, to draw away disciples after them. Therefore watch, and remember that by the space of three years, I ceased not to warn every one night and day with tears. And now, brethren, I commend you to God, and to the word of his grace, which is able to build you up, and to give you an inheritance among all them which are sanctified. I have coveted no man's silver, or gold, or apparel. Yea, you yourselves know, that these hands have ministered unto my necessities, and to them that were with me. I have shewed you all things, how that so laboring ye ought to support the weak; and to remember the words of the Lord Jesus, how he said, It is more blessed to give than to receive. Acts xx. 27—35. And how has this prophecy been fulfilled in every age since it was published! And how few believe that God, and the word of his grace, is able to build up his church, and to guard against grievous wolves, and against perverse schismatics, without the laws of men enforced by the sword! Yea, how much has the sword promoted both of these evils! And how little do we believe, that it is more blessed to give than to receive! It is blessed to re-

ceive, when we receive in a right manner; but all things below perish in
the using, while all that is given for the benefit of the bodies or souls of
others, is laying up treasure in heaven, which will turn to praise, honor
and glory at the appearing of Jesus Christ. And though Paul had written
to the church of Corinth, upon their duty to support the preachers of the
gospel, yet as deceitful teachers had tried to destroy his character, pretending that he acted from selfish motives, he refused to receive any support
from them, until he could come and have those accusations tried before that
church, in the mouth of two or three witnesses, according to the law of
Christ. But as his refusal to receive any thing of them, as he did of other
churches, might seem to be a dishonor to the church of Corinth, he said,
Forgive me this wrong. II Cor. xi. 12; xii. 13; xiii. 1—4. And this
shews that a particular church of Christ is the highest judicature that he
has established upon earth, to carry his laws into execution in his name.
And the people also are to act towards their ministers as they can answer
it to God in the last day. For he says, The laborer is worthy of his reward. I Tim. v. 18. Let him that is taught in the word, communicate
unto him that teacheth in all good things. Be not deceived: God is not
mocked; for whatsoever a man soweth, that shall he also reap. For he
that soweth to the flesh, shall of the flesh reap corruption; but he that
soweth to the Spirit, shall of the Spirit reap life everlasting. And let us
not be weary in well doing; for in due season we shall reap, if we faint
not. Gal. vi. 6—9. Thus ministers and people are required to act towards each other, as they can answer the same to God, who only can bless
or curse them in time and eternity. And Christ says to his ministers, He
that heareth you, heareth me; and he that despiseth you, despiseth me;
and he that despiseth me, despiseth him that sent me. Luke x. 16. And
how solemn are these considerations! Yea, and how safe are all true believers in Christ!

For he says, Upon this Rock I will build my church; and the gates of
hell shall not prevail against it. Matt. xvi. 18. And though many have
made strange work of this saying, and others have paid no regard to it,
yet many ancient passages may serve to explain its vast importance. For
it is said of God's people of old, When he slew them, then they sought
him; and they returned and inquired early after God. And they remembered that God was their Rock, and the high God their Redeemer. Nevertheless they did flatter him with their mouth, and they *lied* unto him with
their tongues; for their *heart* was not right with him, neither were they
steadfast in his covenant. Psalm lxxviii. 34—37. Wherefore hear the
word of the Lord, ye scornful men that rule this people which is in Jerusalem. Because ye have said, We have made a covenant with death, and
with hell are we at agreement; when the overflowing scourge shall pass
through, it shall not come unto us; for we have made *lies* our refuge, and

under falsehood have we hid ourselves ; therefore thus saith the Lord God, Behold, I lay in Zion for a foundation, a stone, a tried stone, a precious corner-stone, a sure foundation ; he that believeth shall not make haste. Judgment also will I lay to the line, and righteousness to the plummet, and the hail shall sweep away the refuge of *lies*, and the waters shall overflow the hiding place ; and your covenant with death shall be disannulled, and your agreement with hell shall not stand. Isaiah xxviii 14—18 And this prophecy is applied to them who followed after the law of righteousness, but sought it not by faith in Christ, but as it were by the works of the law. They had a zeal of God, but not according to knowledge. For they being ignorant of God's righteousness, and going about to establish their own righteousness, have not submitted themselves unto the righteousness of God. For Christ is the end of the law for righteousness to every one that believeth. And whosever believeth on him, shall not be ashamed. Rom. ix. 31—33 ; x. 1—4. He that believeth on him shall not be confounded. I Peter ii. 6. From whence we may learn, that all men who trust in their own doings, instead of the perfect righteousness of Christ, are in covenant with death, and at agreement with hell. And earthly monarchy has generally been the darling of such men. Therefore God says to them, Thou wentest to the king with *ointment*, and didst increase thy perfumes, and didst send thy messengers afar off, and didst debase thyself even unto hell. Thou art wearied in the greatness of thy way, yet saidst thou not, There is no hope ; thou hast found the life of thine hand, therefore thou wast not grieved. Isaiah lvii. 9, 10. David, and his race of kings, were *anointed* of the Lord to their office, as eminent types of Christ. And the rage of hypocrites and infidels, against the Lord, and against his *anointed*, was against his *Christ*. Psalm ii. 2 ; Acts iv. 26. And every child of God has the *anointing* of his Spirit abiding in him, which effectually teacheth the soul to abide in Christ. I John ii. 27. But the calling any ruler, since the death of Christ, The Lord's *anointed*, and the setting up any earthly heads to the church, is a practice which came from hell, from the bottomless pit ; and this is the beast who causeth God's witnesses to prophesy in mourning, and at length kills them. Rev. xi. 7 ; xiii. 1, 2, 12 ; xvii. 8.

And the saints have a gradual victory over him. For John says, I saw as it were a sea of glass, mingled with fire ; and them that had gotten the victory over the beast, and over his image, and over his mark, and over the number of his name, stand on the sea of glass, having the harps of God. And they sing the song of Moses, the servant of God, and the song of the Lamb, saying, Great and marvellous are thy works, Lord God Almighty ; just and true are thy ways, thou King of saints. Who shall not fear thee, O Lord, and glorify thy name? for thou only art holy ; for all nations shall come and worship before thee, for thy judgments are made manifest. Rev. xv. 2—4. The sea of glass, mingled with fire, is the word of God, enforced upon the souls of men by his Holy Spirit. For one apostle says, Where the Spirit of the Lord is, there is liberty. But we all with open face, beholding as in a *glass* the glory of the Lord, are changed into the same image, from glory to glory, even as by the Spirit of the Lord. II Cor. iii. 17, 18. And another says, Lay apart all filthiness, and superfluity of naughtiness, and receive with meekness the ingrafted word, which is able to save your souls. But be ye doers of the word, and not hearers only, deceiving your own selves. For if any be a hearer of the word, and not a doer, he is like unto a man beholding his natural face in a *glass;* for he beholdeth himself, and goeth his way, and straightway forgetteth what manner of man he was. But whoso looketh into the perfect law of liberty, and continueth therein, he being not a forgetful hearer, but a doer of the word, this man shall be blessed in his deed. James i. 21—25. And when a prophet met with most cruel treatment, he said, I will not make mention of him, nor speak any more in his name. But his word was in mine heart as a burning *fire* shut up in my bones, and I was weary with forbearing, and I could not stay. And God says, The prophet that hath a dream, let him tell a dream ; and he that hath my word, let him speak my word faithfully ; what is the chaff to the wheat? saith the Lord. Is not my word like as a *fire?* saith the Lord, and like a hammer that breaketh the rock in pieces? Jer. xx. 9 ; xxiii. 28, 29. Therefore they who stand upon the sea of glass mingled with fire, are they who hear and obey the revealed will of God. Moses was the lawgiver to the church of Israel, and the Lamb is so to the church of God among all nations. And Moses verily was faithful in all his house as a servant, for a testimony of those things which were to be spoken after ; but Christ as a Son over his own house ; whose house are we, if we hold fast the confidence, and the rejoicing of the hope firm unto the end. .... Now faith is the substance of things hoped for, the evidence of things not seen. Heb. iii. 5, 6 ; xi. 1. And how clearly do these passages prove, that true believers in Christ are the only persons of whom his house or church is composed ! For no others can hold fast the confidence, and the rejoicing of hope of salvation in Jesus Christ. The beast appears to be the church of Rome, over many nations ; his image, all national churches ; his mark, all supporting of worship by tax and compulsion, and the number of his name, includes all the schemes of men to hold the church in bondage, so that she might not be governed wholly by the laws of Christ.

And this may lead us to consider, what is intended by the killing and resurrection of the two witnesses. If they be the two parts of the Holy Scriptures, believed and obeyed by the children of God, then their death is the triumphing of the world over them. And the prophecy says, When they shall have finished their testimony, the beast that ascendeth out of the bottomless pit shall make war against them, and shall overcome them, and kill them. And their dead bodies shall lie in the street of the great city, which spiritually is called Sodom and Egypt, where also our Lord was crucified. And they of the people, and kindreds, and tongues, and nations, shall see their dead bodies three days and an half, and shall not suffer their dead bodies to be put in graves. And they that dwell upon the earth shall rejoice over them, and make merry, and shall send gifts one to another; because these two prophets tormented them that dwelt on the earth. Rev. xi. 7—10. Our Lord was crucified by hypocrites, and infidels; and he declared those hypocrites to be worse than the old Sodomites. Matt. xi. 23, 24; Luke x. 12. And God said in prophecy, Sodom thy sister hath not done, she nor her daughters, as thou hast done, thou and thy daughters. Behold, this was the iniquity of Sodom, pride, fulness of bread, and abundance of idleness was in her and in her daughters, neither did she strengthen the hand of the poor and needy. And they were haughty, and committed abomination before me; therefore I took them away as I saw good. Neither hath Samaria committed half thy sins; but thou hast multiplied thine abominations more than they. .... Nevertheless, I will remember my covenant with thee in the days of thy youth, and I will establish unto thee an everlasting covenant. Then thou shalt remember thy ways, and be ashamed, when thou shalt receive thy sisters, thine elder and thy younger; and I will give them unto thee for daughters, but not by thy covenant. Ezek. xvi. 48—51, 60, 61. According to which prophecy, the church of Christ was erected in Jerusalem, and she received the Samaritans, and then the Gentiles into the church as daughters, but not by the covenant of circumcision, which the Jews were in after the Samaritans were separated from them. But this *proverb*, this high *figure* which God delivered to Jerusalem, is now held up as a *literal prophecy*, that all the old Sodomites will finally be saved from hell.[1] Though God said to Jerusalem, Thy father was an Amorite, and thy mother a Hittite. Ezek. xvi. 3. Which could not be literally true, because Abraham and Sarah sprang from Shem, and the Amorites and Hittites from Ham. But it is said of false teachers under the gospel, As Jannes and Jambres withstood Moses, so do these also resist the truth; men of corrupt minds, reprobate concerning the faith. II Tim. iii. 8. Jannes and Jambres were magicians of Egypt, who hardened the heart of Pharaoh against the call of God, to let Israel go and serve him according to his own institutions. And Sodom was never more set against purity, nor Egypt against liberty, than the world now is against the purity and liberty of the gospel. For truth is fallen in the street, and equity cannot enter. Isaiah lix. 14. The nations of the world will not suffer *a form* of godliness to be buried from among them; but how are they set against the power thereof! For as the body without the

[1] Winchester's Dialogues, pp. 197—200.

spirit is dead, so faith without works is dead also. James ii. 26. Thou hast a name that thou livest, and art dead. Rev. iii. 1. Whereas an inspired apostle said, The law of the spirit of life in Christ Jesus, hath made me free from the law of sin and death. Rom. viii. 2. We having the same spirit of faith, according as it is written, I believed, and therefore have I spoken ; we also believe, and therefore speak. .... For our light affliction, which is but for a moment, worketh for us a far more exceeding and eternal weight of glory ; while we look not at the things which are seen, but at the things which are not seen ; for the things which are seen, are temporal ; but the things which are not seen are eternal. II Cor. iv. 13—18. But how is this life of faith now killed by a deceitful world !

Though the prophecy says, After three days and a half, the Spirit of life from God entered into them ; and they stood upon their feet, and great fear fell upon them which saw them. And they heard a great voice from heaven, saying unto them, Come up hither. And they ascended up to heaven in a cloud, and their enemies beheld them. And the same hour was there a great earthquake, and the tenth part of the city fell, and in the earthquake were slain of men seven thousand ; and the remnant were affrighted, and gave glory to the God of heaven. The second woe is past, and behold, the third woe cometh quickly. And the seventh angel sounded, and there were great voices in heaven, saying, The kingdoms of this world are become the kingdoms of our Lord, and of his Christ, and he shall reign forever and ever. Rev. xi. 11—15. And we are to observe, that when the seventh angel shall begin to sound his trumpet, the mystery of God shall be finished, as he hath declared by all his prophets. Rev. x. 7. So that the resurrection of the two witnesses, in the eleventh chapter, and the resurrection of the souls of the faithful, in the twentieth chapter, appear to be the same glorious event, given under different views. For our Lord said to John, Write the things which thou hast seen, and the things which are, and the things which shall be hereafter. Rev. i. 19. When Christ was born of a virgin, in the true church of God, the nation of Israel was part of the Roman empire, which had seven heads, and ten horns ; and Herod sought to slay the child Jesus, as soon as he was born, and Pilate crucified him, after which he was caught up unto God, and to his throne, where he will rule all nations with a rod of iron, and dash them in pieces like a potter's vessel. Rev. xii. 1—5 ; Luke i. 32, 33 ; Matt. ii. 3—16 ; xxvii. 24 ; Acts ii. 23, 24 ; iv. 25—28 ; Psalm ii. 1—9. And these things John *had seen.* He had seen the crucifying of Christ by the rulers of the Roman empire, urged on to do it by false teachers among the Jews ; for God had before said, The ancient and honorable, he is the head ; and the prophet that teacheth lies, he is the tail. Isaiah ix. 15. And deceitful teachers have ever been the meanest and worst of all men upon earth, and they were the tail of the dragon in the Roman empire. But no men who have supposed that this twelfth chapter speaks of another child who should be born after the apostolic age, could ever give any rational account of him. Many have supposed it was Constantine, the first emperor who owned the Christian name ; but he divided the empire, and prepared the way for the advancement of the man of sin, as we have before proved. And after the ascension of Christ to heaven, it was said, Now is come salvation and strength, and the kingdom of our God, and the power of his Christ ; for the accuser of our brethren is cast down, which accused them before our God day and night. And they overcame him by the blood of the Lamb, and by the word of their testimony ; and they loved not their lives unto the death. Rev. xii. 10, 11. In this way the power of the devil was destroyed in the old Roman empire. And when Satan shall be bound, so as not to deceive the nations any more, the prophecy says, I saw thrones, and they sat upon them, and judgment was given unto them ; and I saw the souls of them that were beheaded for the witness of Jesus, and for the word of God, and which had not worshipped the beast, neither his image, neither had received his mark upon their foreheads, or in their hands ; and they lived and reigned with Christ a thousand years. But the rest of the dead lived not again until the thousand years were finished. ˙ This is the first resurrection. Rev. xx. 4, 5. And is not this the same resurrection which is spoken of in the eleventh chapter? For the kingdoms of this world will become the kingdoms of our Lord, and of his Christ, according to each of these prophecies. And Daniel says, The saints of the Most High shall take the kingdom, and possess the kingdom forever, even forever and ever. Dan. vii. 18. And the raising of the souls of the old martyrs, appears to mean the same as the coming of John in the spirit and power of Elijah. Mal. iv. 5, 6 ; Luke i. 17. Neither have we any more reason to think, that the bodies of all the saints will be raised, before their reign with Christ a thousand years, than the Jews had to expect that Elijah would personally come down from heaven, before the Messiah appeared among them. And as all men are dead in trespasses and sins, until they are made alive to God, through Jesus Christ our Lord, and yet they have ever assumed the place of lawgivers and judges for the church of Christ, I believe that that when God says, The rest of the dead lived not again until the thousand years were finished, he means that they shall not have the power of government over the church, as they have ever had since the rise of antichrist. For as Christ is the only Husband of his church, how much like Sodom are all men who assume any power of government over her in religious affairs, so as to hinder her from obeying him as a chaste virgin ! There were some ministers of the devil, who transformed themselves as the ministers of righteousness, in the apostolic age, whose end was according to their works. II Cor. xi. 2—15. And we may well conclude that there are many such in our day ; and how pernicious is their influence among all people who receive them! And supporting such with the sword, is using of it to uphold the kingdom of the devil. Nevertheless, the foundation of God standeth sure, having this seal, The Lord knoweth them that are his. And let every one that nameth the name of Christ, depart from iniquity.

We readily grant, that no prophecy of Scripture was ever clearly understood by men, until the event explained it. The disciples of Christ knew not the Scriptures that he was to rise again from the dead, until he appeared to them, and explained the prophecies concerning it. Luke xxiv. 25—27; John xx. 9. And how long was it before they were clearly convinced that circumcision was abolished? And it is most evident that all national churches have sprung from an abuse of the covenant of circumcision. That covenant gave Israel a right to seize upon the lands of the heathen in Canaan, and to buy others for servants; and all the plantations that have been made in America, under the name of Christianity, have been made by those who imagined that Christians had a right to deal thus with all heathens. But as our Lord hath expressly excluded slavery, and the use of the sword of the magistrate from the government of his church, we may know that all these things belong to Mystery Babylon. Literal Babylon had her name from Babel, where they said, Let us build us a city and a tower whose top may reach unto heaven, and let us make us a name, lest we be scattered abroad upon the face of all the earth. Gen. xi. 4. And is not the pursuit of all men naturally, to get to heaven by their own doings, and to make themselves a name upon the earth? Babel signifies *confusion*; and an inspired apostle says, Where envying and strife is, there is *confusion*, and every evil work. But the wisdom that is from above, is first pure, then peaceable, gentle, and easy to be entreated, full of mercy and good fruits, without partiality and without hypocrisy. James iii. 16, 17. And no men have this wisdom, but they who are born again by the Spirit of God. And to such another apostle says, We have not followed cunningly devised fables, when we made known unto you the power and coming of our Lord Jesus Christ, but were eye-witnesses of his majesty. For he received from God the Father, honor and glory, when there came such a voice to him from the excellent glory, This is my beloved Son, in whom I am well pleased. And this voice which came from heaven we heard, when we were with him in the holy mount. We have also a more sure word of prophecy, whereunto ye do well that ye take heed, as unto a light that shineth in a dark place, until the day dawn, and the day-star arise in your hearts; knowing this first, that no prophecy of the Scripture is of any private interpretation. For the prophecy came not in old time by the will of man; but holy men of God spoke as they were moved by the Holy Ghost. But there were false prophets also among the people, even as there shall be false teachers among you, who privily shall bring in damnable heresies, even denying the Lord that bought them, and bring upon themselves swift destruction. And many shall follow their pernicious ways, by reason of whom the way of truth shall be evil spoken of. And through covetousness, shall they with feigned words make merchandise of you ; whose judgment now of a long time lingereth not, and their damnation slumbereth not. II Peter i. 16—21 ; ii. 1—3. And how clearly are our times here described! For the fleets and armies which have filled the world with confusion and slavery, have been raised and upheld by national churches ; and their vast funds of money, which are daily bought and sold by deceitful men to enrich themselves, have been kept in credit- by the labors of the faithful. Thus, God says, shall they make merchandise of you. And if it had not been for this wicked conduct our national debt might all have been paid off before now. But instead of it the debt is daily increasing, and many have tried all their arts to draw America into another war with foreign nations. Though when the church of Christ shall be wholly governed by his laws, above all the powers of the world, nation shall not lift up sword against nation, neither shall they learn war any more. Isaiah ii. 1—4.

But, instead of such a blessing, more blood has been shed in latter ages, by the nations who have borne the name of Christianity, than by all other nations in the world ; and this is now loudly proclaimed in Europe and America, as a strong argument against divine revelation. Whereas, we have just seen that damnable heresies will cause the way of truth to be evil spoken of. The light of revelation has ever enlarged the capacities of men, beyond any other means in the world ; but they who have not received the word into an honest and good heart, have been hardened afterwards like a rock, or have been as sharp as thorns, to tear away the property, or to destroy the lives of others. Luke viii. 4—15. But that which beareth thorns and briers is rejected, and is nigh unto cursing, whose end is to be burned. Heb. vi. 8. Yet many teachers now bring this last passage, to prove that the true children of God may fall away and perish forever ; while others are holding up hell as a purging fire, which will finally purge away all sin from every child of Adam : as if the sufferings of a creature could purge away sin, instead of the blood of Christ applied by the Spirit of God. Thus they crucify to themselves the Son of God afresh, and put him to an open shame. His person was crucified between two thieves, and his cause is crucified between opposite teachers and professors. But our Lord says, Enter ye in at the strait gate ; for wide is the gate, and broad is the way, that leadeth to destruction, and many there be who go in thereat ; because strait is the gate, and narrow is the way, which leadeth unto life, and few there be that find it. Matt. vii. 13, 14. Though the world is full of men who deny this, and who bring in damnable *heresies*. And they have perverted this word so much, as often to turn it against all those who have withdrawn from worldly churches, while others have applied the word to doctrines rather than practice. But if we take our ideas from the word of God, and not from the traditions of men, we may find that heresy means *rebellion* against God in his church. For when the Jews accused Paul of sedition, and being a leader of a new sect, he denied the charge, and said, After the way which they call heresy, so worship I the God of my fathers, believing all things which are written in the law and the prophets. Acts xxiv. 5, 14. They accused him of rebellion against government, and of being the leader of a new sect, who preferred Jesus of Nazareth above Moses, the great lawgiver to Israel. This last charge he owns, and so was a firm believer in revelation, while they rejected the counsel of God against themselves. And each heretic is subverted, and sinneth, being condemned of himself. Titus iii. 10, 11. For our Lord says, All things whatsoever ye would that men should do to you, do ye even so to them; for this is the law and the prophets. And each professor who breaks this law of equity, and will not repent, is to be rejected by the church. And when such men form other communities, with other laws than the laws of Christ, it is a way which tries the hearts of all. Therefore the voice of inspiration says, If any man seem to be contentious, we have no such custom, neither the churches of God. Now in this that I declare unto you, I praise you not, that you come together not for the better, but for the worse. For first of all, when ye come together in the church, I hear that there be divisions among you, and I partly believe it. For there must also be heresies among you, that they which are approved may be made manifest among you. I Cor. xi. 16—19. Hatred, variance, emulations, wrath, strife, seditions and heresies, are all works of the flesh. Gal. v. 20. Now in all these passages, heresy appears to mean rebellion against God in his church. And another apostle says of them who loved the world above God, They went out from us; but they were not of us; for if they had been of us, they would no doubt have continued with us; but they went out, that they might be made manifest, that they were not all of us. And this is the spirit of antichrist. I John ii. 15—19. All religious communities wherein the love of the world prevails above the love of God, are chargeable with damnable heresies.

In monarchical governments the power is in a few hands, but in America all power of government is derived from the people, who have a fair opportunity to know teachers by their fruits. And where is the man who cannot distinguish thorns and brambles from trees which bear good fruit? Luke vi. 44, 45. Our Lord here plainly refers us to a parable concerning the first man who set himself up as king of the church of Israel, when God was their only king. All the good trees refused any such power over other trees, but the bramble said, If in truth ye anoint me king over you, then come and put your trust in my shadow; and if not, let fire come out of the bramble, and devour the cedars of Lebanon. Judges ix. 8—15. The tongue setteth on fire the course of nature, and it is set on fire of hell.

James iii. 6.   And such men would destroy the best characters in the land, if they would not yield to their darling schemes.   But no man should ever be elected into office, who has not been found to be a good tree by his fruits in private stations ; and all teachers should be avoided, as wolves in sheep's clothing, who tear away the property of any unjustly.   And it is impossible for any community to be clear of this evil, where religious teachers are supported by force.   For as the church of Israel were never allowed to do it, when they came into that practice, God said, Her princes within her are roaring lions, her judges are evening wolves, they gnaw not the bones till the morrow.   Her prophets are light and treacherous persons, her priests have polluted the sanctuary, they have done violence to the law.   Zeph. iii. 3, 4.   And all the natural lions and wolves in the world, never destroyed so many men, as national churches have done in our day.   Again it was said of Israel, The heads thereof judge for reward, and the priests thereof teach for hire, and the prophets thereof divine for money ; yet will they lean upon the Lord, and say, Is not the Lord among us ? none evil can come upon us.   But for these iniquities their nation was ruined, and the mountain of the house of God will be exalted above all earthly powers, when wars shall come to an end.   Micah iii. 11, 12 ; iv. 1—5.   Is not the Lord among us ? none evil can come upon us, was the language which brought ruin upon Jerusalem, and such confidence in negatives will ruin all people who build thereon.   For reason as well as Scripture discovers, that the more light men have, the greater is their guilt and misery if they sin against it.   But when the knowledge of the Lord shall cover the earth as the waters cover the sea, the wolf shall dwell with the lamb, and they shall not hurt nor destroy in all his holy mountain.   Isaiah xi. 6—9. And this is life eternal, that they might know thee the only true God, and Jesus Christ whom thou hast sent.   John xvii. 3.   This is the only way of peace and eternal happiness.

———

END OF VOLUME II,

INDEX.

303, 487, 104, 105. Oppressed in Virginia; II, 333, 495.
BAPTIST CHURCHES, lists of; II, 306, 391.
BARNSTABLE, Baptist church in; II, 270, 351, 451. Baptists oppressed in; II, 351, 451. Letter to the Congregational Committee; II, 352.
BAXTER, George, brings the charter of R. I.; I, 279.
BAXTER, Josiah, forgery concerning; I. 323.
BEALS, Isaac, pastor in Leicester; II, 458.
BELCHERTOWN, Baptist church in; II, 470.
BELLINGHAM, Baptist church in; II, 277, 424.
BERNARD, Richard, author of "The Separatists' Schism"; I, 1. Extracts from his work; I, 2.
BERWICK, Baptists oppressed in; II, 165. Baptist church formed; II, 480.
BIGELOW, Samuel, pastor in New Salem; II, 469. Letters of; II, 470.
BISHOP, George, Account of his "New England Judged"; I, 374.
BLOOD, Caleb, pastor in Newton; II, 457. In Shaftsbury, Vt.; II, 546. Election Sermon of; II, 546.
BLUNT, John, Baptist minister in Sturbridge, returns to Pædobaptism; II, 459.
BOUND, James, a Baptist in Danvers; II, 30.
BOSTON, settlement of; I, 33. 1st church in; I, 33. Brattle St. church; I, 461.
BOSTON, 1st Baptist church in; I, 288 289. Its discipline; I, 387. Letter of; I, 389. Meeting-house nailed up; 390. Writes to London for minister; I, 407. Reply to; I, 407, 466. John Emblen, pastor; I, 419. Letter to London for aid; I, 489.
BOSTON, 2d Baptist church formed; II, 53, 421.
BOUND, Ephraim, pastor 2d Baptist church, Boston; II, 422.
BOWDOIN, Me., Baptist churches in; II, 485, 486.
BRADFORD, William, Governor, opposes religious oppression; I, 432, 434.
BRAINARD, David, expelled from Yale College; II, 44.
BRAINTREE, Mr. Wheelwright in; I, 64.
BREWSTER, William, letter to the Council for Virginia; I, 24. Comes to America; I, 24. Ruling elder at Plymouth; I, 30.
BRIDGES, Robert, arrests Clarke, Holmes, and Crandal; I, 178.
BRIDGEWATER, Baptists oppressed in; II, 229. Baptist church in; II, 270, 430.

BRIGGS, Joel, II, 425.
BRIMFIELD, Baptist church in; II, 31, 278, 467. Baptists in, misrepresented; II, 143. Revival in; II, 278.
BRISCOE, Nathaniel, writes against supporting ministers by compulsion; I, 80.
BROWN, John and Samuel, banished from Massachusetts colony; I, 32.
BROWN UNIVERSITY. See R. I. College.
BUET, Hugh, the first man banished from Massachusetts on pain of death, for heresy; I, 95.
BULKLEY, Mr., disputes with Wightman; I, 519; II, 516.
BULLOCKSGRANT, Baptist church in; II, 477.
BUNKER HILL, battle of; II, 193, 205.
BURDICK, Robert, of R. I. imprisoned by Mass.; I, 269.
BURDICK, Ruth, letter of to Samuel Hubbard; I, 330.
BURGOYNE, Gen., surrender of; II, 212.
BUTLER, Bishop, on religious declension; II, 37.
BUTTERFIELD, Joseph, pastor in Marshfield; II, 431.
BYLES, Mather, becomes an Episcopalian; II, 13.

CALLENDER, Elisha, education of; I, 420, 483. Ordained by aid of Congregationalists; I, 421, II, 419. Secures Hollis's gifts to Cambridge College; I, 485, II, 419. Refusal to appoint him overseer of Cambridge College; I 495. Baptizes in Springfield; I, 513. Death of; II, 32, 419.
CALLENDER, Ellis, pastor 1st Bap. church, Boston; I, 420, II, 419.
CALLENDER, John, extracts from his Century Sermon; I, 357, 370, II, 285. Account of Century Sermon; II, 31, 498. Settled in Newport; II, 29, 498. Death of; II, 287.
CAMBRIDGE, Bap. church; II, 277, 328. 2d church; II, 457.
CAMBRIDGE College; I, 81, 446, II, 330, 346.
CANTERBURY Archbishop of, commission to; I, 49.
CARPENTER, Wm., minister in Norton; II, 134.
CARVER, Bap. church in; II, 431.
CATHOLICISM, work entitled; I, 535, II, 171.
CASE, Isaac, preacher in Maine; II, 484, 486. Letters from; II, 485.
CHAMBERLAIN, Peter, letter from; I, 379. Reply to; I, 379. 2d letter of; I, 388.
CHANDLER, Thos. B. "Appeal to the Public"; II, 188.

B

CORRIGENDA.

The reader is requested to note the following errors : —

Vol. I, page 96, 3d line from bottom, read " On page 86."

Note 1, page 139, should have been referred to the 2d line from the bottom of the preceding page.

Page 303, 2d line from bottom, for " 1741 " read " 1641."

Page 325, 8th line from bottom, for " Baxter " read " Baster."

Page 373, 3d line from bottom, for " peaceably " read " peaceable."

On note 2, page 473, — " Mr. Backus seems to have misapprehended the force of the above Article, &c.," — the following criticism of one who has examined the work in sheets, is evidently just. — " Does he not mean that the provision of the Article requiring the major part of the elders to concur, which elders were *ex-officio* members of the synod, and not such by appointment of the churches, was 'an innovation then made'? It was not enough that the *majority* of a council should concur; the ministers must be counted separately, and the major part of them must concur. Was not this feature an innovation?"

Vol. II, page 68, the note should be marked " ED."

Pages 173, 175, page heading, for " BOSTON " read " BOLTON."

Other errors may be detected by the reader. — ED.